THE
BEATLES
BOOK

THE
BEATLES
BOOK

HUNTER DAVIES

With Spencer Leigh, Keith Badman and David Bedford

EBURY
PRESS

1 3 5 7 9 10 8 6 4 2

Ebury Press, an imprint of Ebury Publishing
20 Vauxhall Bridge Road
London SW1V 2SA

Ebury Press is part of the Penguin Random House group of companies
whose addresses can be found at global.penguinrandomhouse.com

First published by Ebury Press in 2016

www.penguin.co.uk

A CIP catalogue record for this book is available from the British Library

ISBN 9780091958619

Printed and bound in India by Replika Press Pvt. Ltd

Penguin Random House is committed to a sustainable future for our business, our readers
and our planet. This book is made from Forest Stewardship Council® certified paper.

Contents

Introduction

This is going to be my last Beatles book. I know, the world will weep.

Actually, I haven't done all that many. I did the authorised biography in 1968 and after that came a 44-year gap, during which I did 40 odd books on 40 odd different sorts of topics, till in 2012 I did *The Lennon Letters* followed by *The Beatles Lyrics* in 2014. Just three Beatles books in a long-legged lifetime of writing – or four if you count the book I did about The Quarrymen in 2001.

So, I do genuinely bow before the massive knowledge and material that so many Beatles experts all around the world have, resulting in so many excellent publications since 1968. I estimate there must be at least 2,000 books about The Beatles out there, for I have at least 1,000 on my shelves, but I know I have missed loads, some of them erudite academic ones, or self-published amateur books in foreign languages I can't read.

I forget Beatles facts all the time, easy stuff like now, was it in 1957 or 1956 that John and Paul first met? How could I ever get that wrong, but I did in the first edition of my biog in 1968. On page 21 it states, 'on June 15, 1956' a school friend of Paul took him to Woolton Parish Fete to meet John. I didn't get the month right, let alone the year. (As every foo-el now knows, the correct date is 6 July 1957.)

My excuse at the time was that none of the four Beatles was sure of the date themselves, so I had relied on their consensus. I was more worried at the time about getting the dates of their Hamburg trips correct, with the right clubs in the right order, for each of them had a totally different memory – one thought they did five trips, another three, and

John couldn't remember how many or the names of the clubs. In fact I got the Hamburg dates and places right, by going over there and retracing their steps, meeting people like Astrid Kirchherr.

It is remarkable today how all over the world there are Beatles Brains who always seem to get it right, who know every fact, every figure, every detail of the lives of the Fab Four – and yet they never met them. They never heard or saw them play live, far less met their mums and dads, brothers and sister.

All I can claim, in place of reams of facts at my fingertips, is memories. I was fortunate to follow them around for 18 months between 1966–1968, managing to interview people now long gone, such as Aunt Mimi, Alfred Lennon (John's father), Paul's dad Jim and even Ringo's real dad who had separated from Ringo's mother when Ringo was about three. I tracked him down to Crewe where he was working as a window cleaner. Didn't get a lot out of him. But I did meet him, oh yes.

I also had the privilege of being in the studio when The Beatles were writing and recording. I only wish I had made more notes – or best of all, used a tape recorder. I have 30 little red notebooks in which I wrote down everything, but now I can't read my own handwriting.

While not writing regularly about The Beatles, I have been a faithful and constant fan these last 50 years, playing their music all the time. I am also a mad, passionate, dopey collector of Beatles memorabilia. I accumulated stuff about them at the time, back in the sixties, while I was doing the biog, and have kept it up ever since. I must have about a thousand mags and newspapers from back then, plus programmes and leaflets, souvenirs and assorted tat, all about The Beatles. And I am still at it, collecting. None of this is particularly valuable. My best stuff, letters from them, plus originals of The Beatles' lyrics, have long since been handed over to the British Library. Where it will stay together, for ever.

I show my cheapo, mass produced Beatles mags and souvenirs to friends who come to the house, if they happen to be Beatles fans, and let them admire my hundreds of Beatles badges and bubble gum cards. I am sure many wonder why on earth anyone would want to collect this stuff.

It was showing them to Andrew Goodfellow of Ebury Books, who is the publisher of the current, updated edition of my biog in the UK, which started off this project. He said I should do an encyclopaedia, use all this material I have gathered over all these decades. I said, you are confusing me with a Beatles expert. 'This could be your legacy,' he added. I think the word 'legacy' meant that after this, I can pack it in, dunwriting. No chance of doing that, while I have the breath to cool my porridge. But Beatleswise, maybe.

I pointed out, though, that there have been several so called encyclopaedias of The Beatles in the past, many of them potboilers and patchy, usually written by one Beatles fanatic, with lots of blind spots. There have, admittedly, also been some heavily researched biographies, often so dense you get lost in the prose, confused by the details. Then there have been countless rather more esoteric and specialist studies, about one small part of their life, revealing things and people and connections we didn't know existed.

So the idea of a proper, comprehensive *Beatles Book*, aimed at the general public as well as the fans, began to appeal to me – but it would have to be a joint effort. I couldn't do it on my own.

I wanted it to combine the best research and recent scholarship, making it invaluable for all those interested in Beatley things all over the world. I wanted to make it logical, easy to use. Most of all, I wanted it so you found yourself reading on, to find out more, a book that would be both offbeat and mainstream, with views and opinions, fun and amusing as well as informative. Simple aims, huh?

With me on the journey have been three of today's best-known Beatles experts and researchers, who between them have written loads of books featuring the lads from Liverpool, but also many about popular culture generally. Really, *they* have done all the hard work – painstaking research and great attention to detail. I have done the easy stuff, like the Songs, and given the book a shape, plus writing odd bits here and there and the introductions to each section. I had all the fun. They did the slog.

Please note well that *The Beatles Book* is only really about The Beatles – by which we mean the group known as The Beatles, who first called themselves that in 1960 and had split up by 1970, going their separate ways. Their post-Beatles careers, as solo artists, which have proved more productive than many people expected, do not really concern us here.

The basic format is very simple – four separate major sections, with items listed alphabetically, thus making it convenient to look up specific people and places, cross-refer or just happily browse. Each of the separate sections has its own introduction, explaining what it is we think we are doing. The four main sections are:

1. **People:** All those people connected with The Beatles and their lives, who had some sort of importance and influence, including succinct but detailed biogs of each of the Fab Four.
2. **Places:** Locations connected with The Beatles, where they lived, visited, played live – either in

huge arenas or tiny dance halls (and, of course, a rooftop right at the end) – and generally spots on the globe that are somehow significant, to them or to Beatley people today.

3. **Broadcast and Cinema:** The Beatles worked hard to reach their audience, and not just by performing live or releasing vinyl. They also connected to the world via the airwaves, the small screen and mega films, all of which can be found here, split into three subsections – *Radio, TV, Movies.*

4. **Songs:** The inspiration, background, recording details and releases of every song The Beatles ever composed and recorded – when they were The Beatles.

While each of us has been mainly responsible for one section, we have worked together, having meetings, reading each other's stuff, rubbishing each other's dopier opinions.

Along the way, we have jointly collected odd facts and information, cuttings, titbits and quotes, which you will come across scattered throughout the book.

At the end, after a short Appendix, there is an extensive Beatles Chronology, listing key dates in their lives and Beatles career, including, where possible, the set-lists from their gigs.

One unique feature of *The Beatles Book* is a *Ratings* system. This is common when considering hotels, restaurants, films, when some reviewer gives stars or marks, based usually on his or her own prejudices. Putting our joint and awfully knowledgeable heads and hearts together, we decided to rate everything to do with The Beatles, from their Songs to the People in their lives.

Each rating, given out of ten and indicated by a number of mop tops at the end of the entries, represents how important or influential or meaningful we consider the song, the place, the person

or the gig was in the history, pattern or content of their lives and creations. A lot of this will be controversial, as most people have their own favourites, their own likes and dislikes, but we hope it will serve as a rough guide, enabling you to see at a glance what we believe is the *Best* about The Beatles.

And we fondly hope, of course, that *The Beatles Book* will be the Best Beatles Book Ever, worthy of all the Top Ratings…

Hunter Davies
London, 2016

My three co-writers are:

Spencer Leigh is the author of 25 books, most of them connected with The Beatles or popular music. He wrote music obituaries for the *Independent* and for 30 years has had his own music programme on BBC Radio Merseyside. He has written Section One, *Beatles People.*

David Bedford is the author of two books about the beginnings and history of The Beatles in Liverpool. He is currently Chairman of the Governors at Dovedale Juniors, the Liverpool school attended by John Lennon and George Harrison. He has compiled Section Three, *Beatles Places.*

Keith Badman is an author, journalist and film and video archives researcher. He has written or contributed to ten books about popular music, including four on The Beatles, and been a columnist for *Record Collector* magazine for 20 years. He assisted with the archive film and video research on The Beatles *Anthology* series. He is responsible for Section Four, *Beatles Broadcast and Cinema*, and is also our expert on all their live performances and set-lists.

SECTION ONE
Beatles People

Introduction

Is it true, as John sang, that we never lose affection for people and things that went before? In the main, yes, unless of course they were horrible to us, or the things in question were something nasty we would like to forget, or the people and things proved to be so insignificant in our later lives that we have long forgotten them.

We all go through life trailing clouds of people behind us, our family and friends, most of whom do stay with us in our mind and thoughts, even if they are long gone, or if we hardly see them any more.

With The Beatles, there are just so many 'Beatles People', or people claiming to be Beatles People, giving interviews about how they sat next to them at school, chauffeured them around, once made some clothes for them, or cut their hair.

This is the norm with people who become famous. The famous person soon forgets the people they once sat beside, but when the famous person becomes famous, the other person remembers everything from the past; in fact it gets clearer and brighter. It's not that people along the way make it up. It's just that they get it out of proportion – it has become big in their life, if not in the Famous Person's life.

There are loads of people in The Beatles' lives who believe they helped along the way – gave them a push, gave them publicity, gave them their name, their hairstyle, made their boots, taught

them stuff, supplied drugs, suggested words and phrases and chords for their songs, always knew they would make it, tra la la.

Thank goodness then for Spencer Leigh, who has built up the best files and recordings of musicians, friends and people in the lives of The Beatles, having interviewed so many of them. He is responsible for this section, so well done Spencer, but the matter of the ratings did lead to some heated discussions. He seems to have interviewed almost every popular musician and composer from the sixties, in the UK and US, and is more aware than most of us of the possible influences they might have had on the career of The Beatles.

And yet how do we really know that someone, or some group, or some style, some tune, was a real influence as opposed to something they just happened to like at one time? Perhaps they would have developed and grown and written what they wrote anyway? It was in all their heads. Just waiting to come out.

So the criteria for rating Beatles People is highly subjective – trying to decide what impact they had on The Beatles, on their work, their lives, their reputations. Value judgements can never, of course, be scientific.

The Beatles themselves would doubtless have different opinions about some of the people supposedly in their lives – and would probably argue among themselves or rubbish some of those we have listed. Perhaps they would even have no memory or knowledge of them. But, we bashed on, persevered. Our aim is to make clear the ones we consider were important in some way, as opposed to those who were simply folks who passed in the night.

The range of people takes in the obvious, like Brian Epstein and George Martin, but also left-field candidates such as journalists, reviewers, critics, club managers, PRs, musicians, actors, promoters, TV presenters. Some might not have been friends, perhaps never even spoke to them, or met them, but at some stage, somehow, they contributed a small footnote to the Beatles saga.

The range of the ratings goes from no rating at all – listed because the person was in some way fairly interesting – up to ten out of ten. Only four individuals achieved that. Guess which ones.

Yes, it is in this section that you will find potted biogs of each of the Fab Four. The people who had most influence on them were, of course, themselves . . .

ALEX, MAGIC – SEE MARDAS, YANNI ALEXIS

ASHER, JANE [B. 1946]

Jane Asher was among the most attractive and talented young actress of the sixties, although she did not have the opportunities to show her range until later decades, when she became a West End regular, often playing the lead in revivals of Sir Alan Ayckbourn's bitter-sweet tales of contemporary life. When she was starring in *House & Garden* at the National Theatre (2000), she was appearing in two plays in different auditoriums at the same time.

Jane Asher was born in Willesden, north-west London on 5 April 1946. Her father Richard was an eminent neurosurgeon and his wife Margaret a professor at the Guildhall School of Music, who had taught George Martin to play the oboe. They had three children: Peter (b. 1944), Jane (b. 1946) and Clare (b. 1948). Jane was educated at an exclusive girls' school in west London, acting in school plays and making occasional film appearances. Her first role was in *Mandy* (1952) and as a teenager she was in *The Greengage Summer* (1961) and *The Prince and the Pauper* (1962). She also appeared in the highly successful science-fiction film *The Quatermass Xperiment* (1955), although its horror seems mild today. When Jane was 14, she was the youngest actress to play Wendy in the annual West End production of *Peter Pan*.

The confident, well-spoken Jane was regarded as a typical teenager for the purposes of BBC TV's *Juke Box Jury* and she became one of their most astute panellists. In April 1963, she accepted an interview assignment with The Beatles from the *Radio Times*. They knew her from *Juke Box Jury* and appearances in the TV series *The Adventures of Robin Hood* (theme song from Dick James).

Paul asked her on a date and before long he was staying with the Ashers in their five-storey house at 57 Wimpole Street. Paul had the top floor and he and John and wrote several songs on the premises. Paul was not intimidated by living in such a cultured household; indeed, he relished meeting the family and enjoyed their company.

When Paul moved into his own house in St John's Wood, Jane was tidying his possessions and discarded a notebook containing lyrics – potential Beatles songs lost for ever. Pete Shotton revealed this in his memoir, causing Paul to explain that the lyrics dated from the fifties and nothing significant was lost.

Jane rarely toured with The Beatles, preferring to continue her own career. She was among Michael Caine's conquests as the philandering *Alfie* (1966). The following year Jane appeared in a touring version of *Romeo and Juliet* with the Bristol Old Vic in America, and Paul flew over to celebrate her twenty-first birthday. The relationship however could be stormy, with Paul writing 'You Won't See Me' and 'I'm Looking Through You' following arguments. The best song to emerge from their association was 'Here, There and Everywhere'.

Most Beatles songs were love songs, and it is difficult to say precisely which songs relate to this relationship but in all probability there is also 'All My Loving', 'And I Love Her', 'Things We Said Today', 'Every Little Thing', 'What You're Doing', 'The Night Before', 'Tell Me What You See', 'Another Girl' and 'Wait' – thereby covering both the best and the most humdrum songs in The Beatles' canon. Admittedly, some of them would fit any girlfriend and are not Jane-specific.

Her brother Peter, of Peter and Gordon, had success with Paul's songs – see separate entry.

Paul and Jane were engaged on Christmas Day 1967 but it was not to last. Jane went with The Beatles to see Maharishi Yogi in India in February 1968 but she and Paul were to split up in July. Uncharacteristically, she announced their break-up on a TV chat show, Simon Dee's *Dee Time* (20 July

1968). The exact circumstances aren't fully known as Jane and Paul had an understanding never to discuss their break-up and indeed, Jane has dodged all questions about their relationship. She became the only key figure in The Beatles' story not to have told her tale. That she has never chosen to make money from The Beatles is commendable, but it frustrates Beatles historians as that final piece of the puzzle is missing.

Jane enjoyed her greatest film role when starring as the bathhouse attendant who seduces a teenager in *Deep End* (1970), written and directed by Jerzy Skolimowski. The score is by Cat Stevens but the film is partly a cult classic because of Jane Asher's nudity. She also appeared in *Henry VIII and his Six Wives* (1973) and in the TV series *Brideshead Revisited* (1981).

In 1971 Jane met and later married the political cartoonist Gerald Scarfe. Jane spent several years raising their three children but she took occasional film roles and developed a passion for creating lavish party cakes. She wrote several cookbooks, has a cake shop in Cale Street, Chelsea, and fared remarkably well as an orchestral conductor in the reality TV series *Maestro* (2008). The fact that she looked much younger than her age was used to comic effect in the TV series *The Old Boys*.

Bringing culture and sophistication to The Beatles and an inspiration for several songs.

ASHER, PETER – SEE PETER AND GORDON

ASHLEY, APRIL [B. 1935]

George Jamieson was born in Liverpool in 1935 and, working as a merchant seaman, he was unsure of his sexuality. He had a sex change operation in Morocco in 1960, thus emerging as April Ashley. George/April was a media sensation as the first known person in the UK to change sex, and because of her stunning looks, she was able to work as a model. The Beatles were fascinated when they met her at the Ad Lib club in London and their subsequent comments show they were enlightened for the time. Paul described how he enjoyed her company but turned down an opportunity 'to come and feed the ducks in St James' Park'. April Ashley, like The Beatles, received an MBE but April's was for supporting transgender equality.

'I quite like her. Him. It. That.' John Lennon

ASPINALL, NEIL [1941–2008]

Neil Aspinall would have made the perfect diplomat. Who else was a trusted friend of John, Paul, George, Ringo *and* Pete? He began as The Beatles' road manager but he ended up managing Apple and increasing their personal fortunes by millions. He has a major claim to be that Fifth Beatle but to outsiders, he was simply 'Who?'

Neil Stanley Aspinall's parents came from Liverpool but his mother moved to Prestatyn during the war for his birth in October 1941. When eleven, he was in the same class as Paul McCartney at the Liverpool Institute. Known as 'Nell' since childhood, he was a better student than any of them and left in July 1959 to train as an accountant. Nell became a lodger in Pete Best's family home and helped with the opening of the Casbah. In July 1961 he became The Beatles' full-time road manager.

Nell's affair with Pete's mother Mona led to their son Roag being born in July 1962, but – however unlikely this may sound – this did not destroy his relationship with Pete. That friendship *was* tested in August 1962, when Pete was sacked by Brian Epstein. Pete discussed the issue with Nell and was surprised that he was prepared to take the band to Chester, 'as they haven't sacked me'. When he asked Lennon about Pete's sacking, John replied, 'It's nothing to do with you. You're only the driver.'

As Beatlemania took hold, Nell and the band were joined by Mal Evans, another Liverpool friend. These six became The Beatles' inner circle, as others such as Tony Barrow and Peter Brown were employed by Brian Epstein. Mal and Nell's duties sometimes included testing out the girls who would visit The Beatles in their hotel rooms.

When Nell travelled with The Beatles on their first trip to America in 1964, he stood in for George for camera rehearsals on *The Ed Sullivan Show*. He attended recording sessions and occasionally got roped in, being part of the choir on 'Yellow Submarine' and playing harmonica on 'Being for the Benefit of Mr Kite!'.

Once The Beatles established Apple, Neil became an administrator and had a desk job from then on, exhibiting management skills even in the chaotic first two years. The company became impossible to control because of the ever-changing whims of the individual Beatles. In 1969 Allen Klein attempted to sort out the mess and stop the company haemorrhaging money. Lennon told Klein, 'Do what you need to do, but don't touch Neil and Mal.'

After Klein himself was dismissed in 1973, Neil slowly but surely resolved the litigation and disarray that Klein had left behind. By then the four owners of the company were failing to agree, but Neil managed to make The Beatles more money than they had ever known. He was wary of overexposure and he disliked anniversary products as that highlighted how old they were – The Beatles were still, in his view, a contemporary group.

Neil's speciality was the protection of The Beatles' trademark and copyright. He secured as many photographs as he could, as this would then give them control over how they were presented. He was admired by other music executives, although many filmmakers and publishers found it exasperating to deal with Apple.

In the early 1990s Neil was the executive producer for the *Anthology* project, which involved a series of TV documentaries, a coffee-table book and three double CDs. The *1* album in 2000 was his concept and sold 27 million copies worldwide.

In August 1968 Neil had married Suzy Ornstein, daughter of Bud Ornstein, the chief executive at United Artists Pictures. The couple ran Standby Films, which released *Hendrix: Band of Gypsies* in 1999. At the time of his death in 2008, he was completing a book of drawings as he was a talented artist. It was hoped that he would write his memoirs, but whatever secrets they had were safe with him.

A loyal and trustworthy confidant, whose administrative skills ensured that The Beatles remained the world's biggest group.

BACH, BARBARA [B. 1947]

Barbara Goldbach was born in New York City in 1947, the daughter of an Austrian father and Irish mother. She became a model at sixteen, working as Barbara Bach. When she married the industrialist Augusto Gregorini, she moved to Rome and they had two children – Francesca (b. 1968) and Gianni (b. 1973). She was a Bond girl in *The Spy Who Loved Me* (1977). After her marriage broke up, she had a relationship with cameraman Roberto Quezada. She met Ringo Starr on the set of *Caveman*, with real life proving much more passionate than anything on the screen. They were married in London on 27 April 1981. They had a tumultuous marriage at first, with both of them attending rehab in 1988, but they have become much more settled with the years.

Isn't it gratifying to know that Ringo married a Bond girl?

BARBER, ADRIAN – SEE BIG THREE, THE

BARDOT, BRIGITTE [B. 1934]

The French actress was the ultimate sex kitten of the fifties, wearing underwear, a towel or nothing at all. Her films were highly scandalous at the time, but seem rather mild today. She mesmerised The Beatles, especially John Lennon, who had her poster on his bedroom ceiling and persuaded his girlfriend Cynthia Powell to dye and fashion her hair like her. George Harrison compared his first wife Pattie Boyd to Bardot; Bob Dylan mentioned her in song ('I Shall Be Free') and Andy Warhol's silkscreens of her fetch millions.

Brigitte Bardot was born in Paris on 28 September 1934. Her pouting child-woman image on the cover of *Elle* intrigued the film director Roger Vadim, and they were married from 1952 to 1957. He directed her in *Et Dieu … Créa La Femme (And God Created Woman)*, which made Bardot an international star. Her subsequent films included *Les Bijoutiers Du Clair De Lune (The Night Heaven Fell)* (1958) and *La Vérité (The Truth)* (1960).

There had been talk of The Beatles and Bardot working together on a film in 1964 but it came to naught. Lennon and Bardot met at the May Fair Hotel in 1968 but John recalled, 'I was on acid and she was on her way out.'

Bardot cut the original version of 'Je T'Aime … Moi Non Plus' with Serge Gainsbourg, but her husband, the industrialist Gunter Sachs, thought it was several steps too far and it was not released at the time. She retired from films and used her fame to campaign for animal rights. She was fined in 2008 for inciting racial hatred when she criticised French immigration policy.

The best story about Bardot relates to a BBC reporter who asked her what she wanted from life. She replied, ''appiness' to which the reporter said, 'A penis?'

But 10 in their dreams.

BARROW, TONY [B. 1936–2016]

Anthony Frederick James Barrow was born in Crosby, a northern suburb of Liverpool, on 11 May 1936. He was educated at the local private school, Merchant Taylors', and studied English, History and French at Durham University, although he dropped out after two years. When only 17, he was writing a weekly record review column for the Saturday edition of the *Liverpool Echo* under the pseudonym of Disker. With the help of his girlfriend Corinne Griffin, whom he married in 1961, he published the first charts based on sales in Liverpool. He promoted some dances around Crosby.

Although he kept writing for the *Echo*, Tony moved to London to work for the Decca record group, mostly writing LP liner notes or adjusting the original American notes for UK publication. Despite being a small cog in Decca's wheel, his name, nevertheless, was on numerous Decca EPs and LPs.

In November 1961 Brian Epstein wrote to Disker in the hope that he could provide valuable local publicity for The Beatles, who up to that point had been ignored by the editorial pages of the newspaper. Brian was surprised to receive a reply from London and he visited Tony at the Decca offices. Tony said he would be happy to write about The Beatles in his column once they had a record released and he would see if Decca's production team would audition them. Appreciating that Epstein was an important North West retailer, The Beatles were auditioned on New Year's Day 1962.

The audition was unsuccessful, but Brian was impressed by Tony Barrow's professionalism and asked him to write the press release for their first EMI single, 'Love Me Do'. Tony agreed, but he could not put his own name to it as he worked for Decca. His friend Tony Calder, who was to establish Immediate Records, had formed his own PR company and so Barrow prepared the press release under Calder's name. It was a well-written, five-page introduction to the band.

When Brian asked Tony Barrow to leave Decca and join him full-time for double his salary, Tony knew he would be taking a step into the unknown. Soon he was touring with The Beatles worldwide and promoting other NEMS acts including Cilla Black, Billy J. Kramer and Gerry and The Pacemakers. This time, under the name of Frederick James, he wrote a pictorial history of the Cavern.

In time, Brian Sommerville and Derek Taylor were brought in to help with The Beatles while Tony concentrated on other artists. However, he was there for the more significant events: the meeting with Elvis Presley in 1965; the mayhem in Manila; and the fallout from John's remark about The Beatles being bigger than Jesus. In 1966 he attended their final concert at Candlestick Park and, at Paul's request, recorded the performance, albeit on a cheap, hand-held machine. Tony wrote the liner notes for the first three Beatles albums and in 1967 he wrote the strip cartoon for the *Magical Mystery Tour* booklet.

Tony left The Beatles to establish his own PR company, Tony Barrow International, the 'International' being a typical Barrow flourish. He managed Lyn Paul of The New Seekers and Helen Shapiro, as well as handling publicity for Cilla Black and Wings. He wrote regularly for *The Beatles Book Monthly* (a quasi-official UK magazine that enjoyed unique access to The Beatles and presented new photographs every month) and his memoir, *John, Paul, George, Ringo & Me* (2005), lived up to his journalistic adage, 'Rework your catalogue'. Barrow retired to Morecambe in 1980 as he felt that the constant socialising was affecting his health, but he still undertook special projects such as working on the Cannes MIDEM festivals and writing for *The Stage*. Barrow never cared for intellectualising The Beatles' music, saying that rock music was never intended to be taken too seriously.

The Beatles needed good and effective publicity and Tony Barrow was the best. He coined the phrase, 'the Fab Four'.

BEACH BOYS, THE

The similarities and the differences between The Beach Boys and The Beatles are worthy of a book in their own right. In terms of creativity, The Beach Boys were the biggest rivals to The Beatles and each was intent on seeing what the other was doing.

Many British beat groups were formed in the face of family opposition – Aunt Mimi was certainly not alone – but there was more active encouragement in the US. Murry and Audree Wilson supported their three sons – Brian (b. 1942), Dennis (1944–1983) and Carl (1946–1998) – when they formed a beat group. Murry, who was a factory worker, wrote songs in his spare time and 'Two Step Side Step' was recorded by Bonnie Lou and Alma Cogan. He was impressed when his nephew Mike Love (b. 1941) started harmonising on doo-wop songs with his sons. With the addition of Brian's classmate Al Jardine (b. 1942) they became The Beach Boys in December 1961. Intriguingly, Murry told Brian that Dennis wasn't a good enough drummer and suggested they look for somebody else.

Many of their influences were the same as The Beatles' – Chuck Berry, The Everly Brothers, Leiber and Stoller songs and early Phil Spector productions – but while The Beatles favoured black R&B, The Beach Boys loved surf instrumentals (few of which were heard in the UK) and novelty records ('Alley-Oop', 'Monster Mash'). Being based in southern California, The Beach Boys sang about surfing, girls on the beach and hot rod racing. Few records are more exquisite than 'Surfer Girl', but accepting the status quo The Beach Boys sang 'Be True To Your School'. Brian Wilson's tastes dominated the musical side of the group – he loved the middle of the road harmonies of The Hi-Los and The Four Freshmen, and he brought that to rock 'n' roll. Their harmonies were less harsh than their east coast rivals, The Four Seasons.

After recording for smaller labels, The Beach Boys joined Capitol in 1962 and had their first US Top 10 record with 'Surfin' USA', Chuck Berry's 'Sweet Little Sixteen' with a new lyric. They made a major impact on the US charts during 1963 but they did not appear on *The Ed Sullivan Show*, probably because their manager and father Murry was too confrontational. Murry was deeply jealous of his son Brian, who could so easily write songs that were much better than his.

In 1964 Capitol spent promotional money on The Beatles and they became a phenomenon, but The Beach Boys made some stunning records including the immaculate 'Don't Worry Baby', only a B-side but an indication that Brian was a major creative force. What other beat musician

could warm up by playing George Gershwin's 'Rhapsody in Blue'?

When The Beatles released *Rubber Soul* in 1965, Brian Wilson was determined he would not be left behind. While the other Beach Boys were touring, he wrote and recorded *Pet Sounds*, asking them to add their vocals when they returned. The result was an extraordinarily inventive album. Lennon and McCartney attended a preview in London and fell deep into conversation afterwards. The album, and the single 'God Only Knows', fared better in the UK than in the US; McCartney has often called 'God Only Knows' his favourite song.

Mike Love felt *Pet Sounds* was a mistake and that the band should stick with songs about California girls. To some extent his criticism was justified, as the back-to-basics *Party!* album was a bigger seller and included the ultra-catchy 'Barbara Ann'.

Back on the cutting edge, The Beach Boys released the stunning 'Good Vibrations', a US and UK No. 1, but Brian Wilson was finding the pressure too great and an adventurous album, *Smile*, was abandoned. Rather like the fiasco with the *Get Back* sessions, a makeshift LP, *Smiley Smile*, was salvaged. Paul McCartney munched his way onto their track 'Vegetables'.

Although naturally combative, Mike Love joined The Beatles in Rishikesh and The Beach Boys and Maharishi toured together in the US, not a beneficial decision for either party. The Beatles recorded 'Back In The USSR' to show they could emulate The Beach Boys' sound with a sense of humour and a nod to Chuck Berry as well. Both groups had associations with Charles Manson: Manson resided with Dennis Wilson for a while and they did record his song, 'Never Learn Not To Love', while Manson used The Beatles' 'Helter Skelter' as a source of secret messages.

When Dennis Wilson died in 1983, Ringo briefly toured with The Beach Boys. They became a touring oldies act. Brian Wilson returned to performing in 1995, working with a remarkable band on stage and occasionally joining The Beach Boys.

When Brian Wilson was stunningly original, John and Paul had to better it, and vice versa, until Brian cracked.

BERNSTEIN, SID [1918–2013]

Sid Bernstein never knew his parents, having been adopted shortly after birth by Israel and Ida Bernstein, New York immigrants from Kiev. Israel was a tailor and although the couple spoke Yiddish, the young boy learnt English. An early memory was discovering Cushman's Bakery when he was seven and it developed into a life-long passion for food. During the war, he served in Europe and shot at enemy aircraft, but he was always relieved that he never, to his knowledge, killed anyone. After the war, Sid managed a Latin ballroom in Brooklyn.

Sid worked for the agents Shaw Artists and General Artists Corporation (GAC), and was responsible for placing some major acts into Carnegie Hall. He presented Miles Davis for a week at the Apollo in Harlem, and organised rock 'n' roll at the Brooklyn and New York Paramounts with the disc jockey Alan Freed. He defied the tough negotiator, Allen Klein, by refusing to give his artist Sam Cooke top billing.

In 1961 Sid ran the Newport Jazz Festival. Although it had been a success in earlier years, the residents of Rhode Island were tiring of this invasion of privacy. Sid retaliated by adding two performers that the residents would definitely want to see – Bob Hope and Judy Garland – and gave them free tickets.

Sid studied politics at the New School in Greenwich Village. A lecturer instructed the class to read

British newspapers to see how UK politics were reported. Around September 1963 Sid became intrigued by references to The Beatles, who were taking the country by storm. He'd not heard their records, but instinct told him to do something.

As GAC showed no interest in the band, Sid contacted Brian Epstein on his own behalf. He offered to present them at the highly prestigious Carnegie Hall. He recalled, 'It worked in my favour that The Beatles were unknown in America. Carnegie had a policy of no rock bands, but they didn't know who The Beatles were when I booked it.'

In January 1964 The Beatles exploded in America, topping the charts with 'I Want to Hold Your Hand'. The concerts were sold out before they even landed. 'Carnegie had never seen a gathering like it,' Sid recalled, 'and they told me never to come back again. I had to use other venues for a few years after that.' Sid wanted to capitalise immediately on The Beatles' success. He told Brian that they should book Madison Square Garden but Brian thought it better to leave the crowds waiting.

Then Sid had a better idea. He offered Epstein Shea Stadium for a mammoth concert in 1965. No pop stars had ever played such a huge venue, but Sid was so confident that he offered Brian $10 for every empty seat. The event sold out and Sid said, 'You couldn't hear the music, but you could hear the roar of the crowd in the Bronx, and Shea Stadium is in Queens. It was so new that I underestimated my expenses. On a gate of $304,000, I made a profit of $6,500. Brian Epstein was very upset when he heard that and wanted to give me a gift. I said, "Brian, your gift was in giving me the boys."' Lennon later told Sid that Shea was 'the top of the mountain'.

A year later The Beatles made a second appearance at Shea. It was at the height of the controversy following John's comments about being bigger than Jesus. Sid ignored the furore, arguing, 'The religious fervour was much greater down south. New York is a liberal city.' By then, Bernstein was managing The Young Rascals, later The Rascals. Bernstein flashed their names on the scoreboard at Shea Stadium, and the publicity led to a record contract and a succession of US hit singles.

Although Sid never presented The Beatles at Madison Square Garden, he did promote several British rock concerts there including The Animals, the Rolling Stones and The Moody Blues. He introduced the Bay City Rollers to America and, because he was now a better negotiator, he made more money from the Rollers than The Beatles.

Sid married the actress and singer Geraldine Gale in 1963. She was in the Broadway production of *The Sound of Music* and Sid loved telling friends, 'I married a nun.' They had six children, who helped their dad with his later productions.

After The Beatles broke up, Sid made a few attempts to get them back together. Huge fees were bandied about, but Sid regarded it as self-publicity as he knew that the bids would never be accepted. He saw John Lennon in New York from time to time, often recommending restaurants, and once having Lennon as his guest at a Jimmy Cliff concert he was promoting at Carnegie Hall.

Sid was marvellous company, a huge man who knew as much about ice cream as he did about The Beatles. He was a persuasive speaker, smiling broadly and speaking slowly in a low, sincere voice. He published his autobiography *Not Just The Beatles* ... (2000), which was later revised and reissued as *It's Sid Bernstein Calling* ... (2001).

Sid presented The Beatles at Shea Stadium, the start of arena rock.

BERRY, CHUCK [B. 1926]

Chuck Berry was the most influential rock 'n' roll songwriter, writing about teenage preoccupations with wit and accuracy, although he was well past his adolescence when he started recording. His guitar playing was a seminal influence on the British beat musicians of the sixties, and, indeed on almost everyone who has picked up a guitar since.

Charles Edward Anderson Berry was born in St Louis, Missouri on 18 October 1926 and he learnt to play guitar as a teenager. He spent three years in prison for armed robbery and car theft, and in the early fifties formed a bar band with Johnnie Johnson (piano) and Ebby Hardy (drums). He was strongly influenced by Nat King Cole, liking Cole's precise diction.

In 1955 his favourite artist, the blues singer Muddy Waters, recommended him to Chess Records in Chicago and Leonard Chess suggested that he rework his composition about a cow, 'Ida Mae', into a rock 'n' roll car chase, hence 'Maybellene'. The single became a US hit but Chuck was annoyed that Alan Freed's name had been added to the songwriting credits in exchange for airplay. Chuck wouldn't allow that to happen again, although Johnnie Johnson claimed in 2000 that he deserved credits for some of his arrangements. The case was dismissed as the judge ruled that too much time had elapsed.

Whatever, a succession of great singles followed 'Maybellene', including 'Roll Over Beethoven', 'School Day', 'Rock And Roll Music', 'Sweet Little Sixteen' and the song with the best-known guitar riff of all time, 'Johnny B. Goode'. Chuck Berry was the first rock artist to perform at a jazz festival – the Newport Jazz Festival in 1958 – where the audience was bemused as he went into his duck-walk. Surprisingly in view of his influence, he only had one UK Top 20 hit in the fifties, 'Sweet Little Sixteen', which peaked at No. 16.

In 1961 Berry was incarcerated for the second time – on this occasion for his relationship with a 14-year-old girl – serving 20 months. On asking the guards for an atlas, they assumed he was planning an escape, but he was writing 'The Promised Land'. When he was released, he cut another batch of great songs including 'Nadine', 'No Particular Place To Go' and 'You Never Can Tell'. A similar offence today would ruin a performer's career but it didn't impinge on Berry's, who now found a new audience in the UK.

Both The Beatles and the Rolling Stones acknowledged their debt to Chuck Berry – The Beatles offered 'Roll Over Beethoven' and 'Rock And Roll Music' and recorded on tape seven more at different times: 'Carol', 'I've Got To Find My Baby', 'I'm Talking About You', 'Johnny B. Goode', 'Memphis Tennessee', 'Sweet Little Sixteen' and 'Too Much Monkey Business'. The Stones' first single was 'Come On' and they recorded 'Around And Around', 'You Can't Catch Me', 'I'm Talking About You' (retitled 'Talkin' 'Bout You'), 'Carol' and 'Bye Bye Johnny'. When Keith Richards assembled an all-star band in St Louis for his sixtieth birthday, the result being the concert film *Hail! Hail! Rock 'n' Roll*, he had so much trouble with Chuck that he said he would never complain about Mick again.

The Beach Boys' first US Top 10 hit 'Surfin' USA' was based on Chuck Berry's 'Sweet Little Sixteen', and Brian Wilson shared his songwriting credit with Chuck. John and Paul also wrote compositions owing something to Chuck: 'Back In The USSR' (Paul), 'The Ballad Of John And Yoko' (John) and 'Get Back' (Paul), the last even named using one of Chuck's characters, Jo Jo (Gunne). 'Come Together' was too close for comfort, although John maintained that his refer-

ence to 'You Can't Catch Me' was a tribute. John came to an agreement with publisher Morris Levy, but it was no hardship – he had to include two Chuck Berry songs on his next album, *Rock 'N' Roll*, one being 'You Can't Catch Me' and the other, 'Sweet Little Sixteen'.

Although the British beat groups constantly acknowledged their debt to Chuck Berry, his songwriting slowed down, but there was an occasional classic such as 'Tulane' (1969). Then, against all the odds, Chuck had a UK No. 1 in 1972 with the innuendo-laden 'My Ding-A-Ling', part of its success coming from the ridiculous opposition mounted by Mrs Mary Whitehouse. Okay, Chuck was selling out but it was a great live number and its lyrics are totally in keeping with the sex-obsessed Berry.

In the same year, Chuck jammed with John and Yoko on *The Mike Douglas Show*, where they performed 'Memphis Tennessee' and 'Johnny B. Goode'. 'Jamming' is the operative word because by now Chuck had a total disregard for his audiences. He would perform with pick-up bands and refuse to rehearse. The only instruction was that he was going to play 'Chuck Berry songs'. As some shows were shambolic, it is hardly surprising that he insisted on being paid in cash before each gig. Chuck would perform his stipulated 60 minutes or whatever and if the promoter wanted an encore, then he had better have some readies in the wings. Known for parsimony, Chuck Berry was jailed for tax evasion in 1979, only days after he had played at the White House.

Chuck wrote *The Autobiography* (1987). It is very well written but although Chuck may think he is presenting himself in a good light, he comes across as money and sex obsessed, and the sympathies lie with his long-suffering wife Themetta. Worse was to come as he was arrested for installing video cameras in the ladies' toilets at his amusement complex, Berry Park. Berry settled out of court with the complainants but he maintained that he had merely installed the cameras to catch a thief.

Chuck was still playing in his eighties, but forgetting the lyrics and sometimes the tune, and the constant talk of a new album had worn thin after 30 years.

John Lennon said, 'If you tried to give rock 'n' roll another name, you might call it "Chuck Berry".' Right on.

BEST, MONA [1924–1988]

On 3 January 1924 Thomas Shaw, an army major in India, and his Irish wife, Mary Shelverton, had their fourth child, Alice Mona, who was born in Delhi. When she was 17 she was dating a marine engineer, Donald Scanland, and they had a son, Randolph Peter, born in Madras on 24 November 1941. No record of their marriage can be found. Donald was lost at sea and declared dead.

Mona was working for the Red Cross when she met an army lieutenant stationed in India, Johnny Best. They married at St Thomas Cathedral, Bombay, on 7 March 1944, with Johnny treating Pete as his own. Johnny and Mona then had their own son, Rory, born on 29 January 1945. When the war was over, the family sailed on a troopship to the UK and arrived in Liverpool on Christmas Day 1945. They stayed with Johnny's father at Ellerslie, a large house in West Derby, but after some family friction they eventually settled with

TURNING POINTS

Six men who changed our perception of rock music without really knowing it.

RECORD REVIEWS. In 1963 **William Mann** in *The Times* wrote his review about The Beatles Aeolian cadences. It was the first time that a serious publication had taken rock seriously. Nowadays, the latest rock releases are reviewed as a matter of course by all quality newspapers.

FASHION. In 1963 **Dougie Millings** produced The Beatles first stage suits and many more of their clothes besides. The connection between fashion and rock was being forged, with the result that the leading fashion designers wanted to work with rock stars.

FILMS. In 1964 **Richard Lester** directed *A Hard Day's Night*. Up until then, most rock films were little more than a visual jukebox with a flimsy storyline. Once this film was taken seriously, the artistic quality of rock films dramatically improved.

ACCEPTED BY SOCIETY. In 1965 **Harold Wilson** gave The Beatles their MBEs for their contribution to Britain's exports; now it was okay for adults to like them too.

ALBUM PACKAGING. In 1967 **Peter Blake** designed the sleeve for *Sgt Pepper's Lonely Hearts Club Band*. After that, album covers were considered an art form in their own right. In addition, *Sgt Pepper* was among the first albums to print the lyrics.

POP BIOGRAPHY. In 1968 **Hunter Davies** wrote the first authorised biography of a rock group. At the time there were few rock books. Hunter's opened the floodgates for books about The Beatles and rock in general.

Mona's parents at 17 Queenscourt Road, nearby. Johnny Best Sr. was a boxing promoter who managed the Liverpool Stadium. Johnny Best Jr. was a boxer who joined his father in the management of the business. When Johnny Best Sr. died in 1956, Johnny Jr. took over and his brother Bill organised the wrestling bouts.

In 1954 Mona (or Mo as she was called) is said to have pawned the family's jewellery and put the money on Lester Piggott's horse Never Say Die, which won at 33-1. This enabled them in 1957 to move into a large Victorian house, 8 Haymans Green, West Derby. This extraordinary family story has many loose ends: if someone has a large win like that, wouldn't they gamble again and again? Why did she do it and what would have happened had she lost? Why wait three years to purchase the house?

The house had 15 large rooms and an extensive complex of cellars, but by 1959 things were going wrong. Johnny Best is shown on the electoral role for Queenscourt Road and he had to relinquish the Stadium, citing financial difficulties. Mo took in some boarders, one of them being an accountancy student called Neil Aspinall.

Mo had noticed that a large house opposite, Lowlands, had opened a coffee bar and beat club and she decided to do the same. With help from her sons and Neil Aspinall, the Casbah was ready for business in September 1959. The Quarrymen played on the opening night but they fell out with her over whether they should share their earnings with an indisposed member, Ken Brown. It was none of Mo's business but it was typical of her to butt in.

Mo soon made it up with The Beatles and once Pete had joined she promoted gigs with them not only at the Casbah but also at St John's Hall, Tuebrook and the Knotty Ash Village Hall. She also found other bookings for The Beatles, but she was treating the group as though Pete were the leader. Once Brian Epstein took over the band's management, he had to contend with many calls from Mo asking what he was doing for Pete. She never accepted that her son was sacked because his drumming was below par. She felt he was sacked because he was too good-looking and the others were jealous.

But Mo had other things on her mind. Pete was soon to find that his mother was having an affair with his best friend, Neil. Their son Vincent Rogue (known as 'Roag') was born on 21 July 1962. Although Johnny was no longer with Mo, his name is shown as the father on the birth certificate.

Even though Neil remained The Beatles' road manager, he was still close enough to the Bests to be allowed to store the band's equipment in Haymans Green. She still saw him after he had moved to London and allowed John Lennon, of all people, to borrow her father's medals for the cover of *Sgt Pepper*.

Mona Best died on 9 September 1998. The death notice from the family in the *Liverpool Echo* said, 'United we stand, divided we fall.'

Starting the Casbah club and encouraging The Beatles were crucial to the development of the band, but in the end she couldn't see past her own son.

BEST, PETE [B. 1941]

The phrase 'doing a Pete Best' is commonplace in rock music. It refers to the sacking of a band member, and the most notorious example is the removal of Pete Best from The Beatles on 16 August 1962. Whatever views you may hold on why he had to go, there is no doubt the dismissal was handled abysmally by Brian Epstein and the other Beatles.

The drummer was not born Pete Best, but Randolph Peter Scanland in Madras, India on 24 November 1941, the son of Donald Scanland and Mona Best (née Shaw). After Donald was lost at sea, Mona married a British soldier, Johnny Best, and they came to England in 1945.

Pete went to the grammar school Liverpool Collegiate, a school famed for its support of rugby union. Pete was a good player and became a strong advocate for the game. He was a decent student, passing O-levels, studying A-levels and planning to go to teacher training college.

In 1959 Pete's mother opened the Casbah in the basement of their large home in Haymans Green, West Derby. He sometimes played there with his own group, The Blackjacks (coincidently the same name as an early incarnation of The Quarrymen) and was an adequate drummer.

In August 1960 The Beatles had the offer to play in Hamburg but they had no drummer. They needed a musician with no regular job, and despite what is said about unemployment in Liverpool there were not many suitable drummers around. Pete Best was waiting to go to college and, although The Beatles gave him an audition at the Jacaranda, he already had the job because there was nobody else. He had a useful additional asset – O-level German – so he could converse, albeit shakily, with the people they met.

Best soon found that the cramped quarters behind a cinema were not for him and he became the boyfriend of a local girl, whose lover was in prison. More and more in Hamburg, he steered his own course, turning up to play but residing elsewhere. His drumming was loud and powerful, emphasising the four beats in the bar, but he played similarly on everything. He made no effort to become more versatile or flexible.

At first that didn't matter. Back in Liverpool in 1961, the new stomping Beatles were the flavour of the day, amassing a huge local following. The girls loved Pete's looks; he was exceptionally handsome with a winning, shy grin. Bob Wooler, writing in *Mersey Beat*, compared him to the actor Jeff Chandler and said that he was 'mean, moody and magnificent'. He wasn't any of them but, in this business, image is everything. The Beatles gave him a solo spot: sometimes he would sing 'The Peppermint Twist' and demonstrate the dance while Paul played drums.

It is said that the other Beatles were jealous of the girls screaming for Pete, but that is unlikely as they all did very well with female company. However, when The Beatles appeared on the radio show *Teenagers' Turn*, Jim McCartney remonstrated with Pete as he felt he had been milking the screams.

Pete's drumming can be heard on The Beatles' unsuccessful audition for Decca Records on New Year's Day 1962 and on various tracks with Tony Sheridan, including 'My Bonnie'. Tony was outspoken in his criticism of Pete, saying that he wasn't putting enough effort into his playing. Instead of Pete accepting that the remarks had some validity, he chose to fight, with the after-hours bust-up in Hamburg apparently lasting two hours with no obvious victor.

In June 1962 Pete Best was exceptionally bad when The Beatles recorded 'Love Me Do', his drumming resembling the banging of bin-lids. It is no surprise that George Martin wanted to replace him with a session player. The Beatles did not want to sack him personally and they told Brian that it was his role. Once they had lined up Ringo Starr as his replacement, Brian called Pete to his office on 16 August 1962. Pete thought it was a meeting about The Beatles' future bookings, but he was told that The Beatles didn't want him in the group any more.

Pete maintained that he was not told why he was sacked, but that is untrue. Brian told him that he was not good enough but Pete didn't believe it, thinking that there must be another reason. However, the diligent research in Mark Lewisohn's *Tune In* reveals that this was undoubtedly the main reason. Of course he was the silent Beatle, but what did that matter? A group with two John Lennons would have been intolerable.

Brian Epstein had hoped that he could place Pete with The Merseybeats, a curious decision as they already had a drummer, but Pete didn't want to have anything more to do with him. He chose Joe Flannery who managed his brother's group, Lee Curtis and The All-Stars. They secured a contract with, irony of ironies, Decca Records, but Curtis was out of time, too late for Elvis and too early for Tom Jones. Still, largely due

to Pete's appeal and many multiple submissions, they came runner-up to The Beatles in the *Mersey Beat*'s annual popularity poll. Pete only saw The Beatles twice after the sacking but no one spoke. Ringo, who played no part in the sacking, made a derogatory remark about him in *Playboy*, falsely suggesting that he took drugs (which was something he denied) and the magazine made an out of court settlement.

After Lee Curtis, Pete formed The Pete Best Combo with Wayne Bickerton and Tony Waddington. They made some decent, but dated, singles of rock 'n' roll songs. Bickerton and Waddington went on to become a formidable songwriting and production partnership, with hits for The Rubettes and Mac and Katie Kissoon.

WHO WAS THE FIFTH BEATLE?

Calling someone a 'Fifth Beatle' is a great hook for the media and public alike and it has been applied to numerous people over the years. The most obvious candidate is Pete Best, who was a Beatle for two years from 1960; no one can take that away from him. Another possibility is Stuart Sutcliffe but he, as well as his fellow Beatles, knew he was a far better artist than musician.

While Ringo was having his tonsils removed in 1964, his drum seat was occupied by Jimmie Nicol, who demonstrated that being a Beatle, even for a few days, can affect the rest of your life. Then there's the organist Billy Preston, who lent his talents to 'Get Back' and is the only person to be named alongside The Beatles on one of their Parlophone singles. And from their Hamburg days, how about Tony Sheridan, who played alongside The Beatles on 'My Bonnie'?

The Fifth Beatle could, of course, be someone behind the scenes, the best candidates being manager Brian Epstein and record producer George Martin. Certainly what The Beatles did would have been different without them, but that doesn't make them Beatles.

Maybe the Fifth Beatle is not a person at all, but the city of Liverpool? The fact that they all came from there gave them an identity they wouldn't have had if each had come from a different place. The city, with its network of venues, helped to establish and shape The Beatles as a group. Long after they had left Liverpool, they still spoke with Scouse accents.

When Ringo Starr was in Liverpool for the European Capital of Culture celebration in 2008, a local journalist asked him who was the Fifth Beatle. Who or what would be Ringo's choice? 'No one,' he simply said. 'There was no Fifth Beatle. There was just the four of us.'

As The Beatles' career climbed into the stratosphere, Pete worked at a local bakery and, depressed, attempted suicide. When he had resolved his problems, he took a job in the civil service and became the north west's champion of Restart, which gave redundant workers the chance of tackling new careers. Imagine going along there for advice and being told 'Pete Best will see you'. His background helped him in understanding their problems.

In the late 1980s, Pete Best started appearing at local Mersey Beat events and he formed The Pete Best Band, tellingly with his brother Roag as a second drummer. This made it hard for an audience to judge his personal ability. They toured around the world and made several albums. The Best brothers opened the Casbah, now a national heritage site, to the public and all tours are conducted by a member of the family.

Roag's daughter, Leanne, has become a well-known actress, as a member of the National Theatre's company and often appearing in TV dramas.

Pete was featured on 12 tracks on the first *Anthology* album in 1995 and the worldwide sales have ensured that he did very well financially. He married one of his fans, Kathy, in 1963 and they have two daughters and four grandchildren. Unlike the other four Beatles, Pete stayed with the same partner so 'doing a Pete Best' worked out okay for him.

He was more a journeyman than an actual Beatle, but he was the first Beatle to draw screams.

BICKNELL, ALF [1928–2004]

'The qualities of a chauffeur are to be a good driver, to be discreet, to be honest and not to get carried away with the people in the back of your car,' said Alf Bicknell, chauffeur to The Beatles during their key years. 'The important thing is just to do your job. Whatever goes on around you is private business that has nothing to do with you. It can be summed up in one word, loyalty.'

Alfred George Bicknell was born in Haslemere, Surrey in 1928 and became an accomplished driver. In the fifties he was working as a chauffeur, often for foreign embassies, and he had a partnership in a private hire firm, working for show business personalities such as James Stewart.

In October 1964, following a recommendation to Brian Epstein, Alf became The Beatles' chauffeur, ferrying them to and from concert dates. He had to ensure quick and clean getaways, although he did once run over a policeman's foot. 'When they came off stage, they were wrecked,' he recalled, 'and I would have the towels ready for them in the car. I would make sure the ciggies were there, the door would slam and away we would go.' On one occasion, Lennon threw Alf's chauffeur's hat out of the window with the phrase, 'You're one of us now.'

Alf Bicknell took them to the set for their second film, *Help!* (1965) and attended the sessions for their albums *Rubber Soul* and *Revolver,* where he would arrange the delivery of food. Bicknell was proud of his appearance on their 1966 single, 'Yellow Submarine'. 'I did some sound effects and sang in the chorus. You can hear the anchor going down just before a voice says, "Full steam ahead, Mr Bo'sun." That was me with an old tin bath and a piece of chain.'

Alf was one of the privileged few at their meeting with Elvis Presley at his Bel-Air home in August 1965. 'It impressed me to see how many people he had working for him. With The Beatles, there was only Mal Evans, Neil Aspinall and me and I used to drive them around on my own.

Elvis's workers felt that they were stars themselves but I never felt that.'

Alf lived in a flat about a mile from John's Weybridge mansion so he was often recruited for individual jobs, taking John out for the evening. He advised The Beatles on the cars they should drive. In August 1966 Alf left their employment and started working with captains of industry including Sir Robert, later Lord, McAlpine, and he spent some years at Tilbury Construction. His most treasured possessions had been five tapes of The Beatles rehearsing 'If I Fell' and reading from the Bible in comic voices, and he sold them privately after they had failed to reach their reserve at Sotheby's.

His autobiography *Baby, You Can Drive My Car,* written with Beatles expert Garry Marsh, and with a foreword from George Harrison, was unsatisfactory. It was written in the form of a diary (although Bicknell had not kept one) and he sounded more like a 12-year-old schoolgirl than a dignified chauffeur. The authors fell out, leading to legal action, and the material was reworked into a book and video package in 1995.

Alf Bicknell, looking like one of The Dubliners, became a favourite at Beatles conventions, but, whenever he spoke, he was always respectful and never gave any salacious details of what he must have witnessed with the band. He always described the Fab Four as real gents; he was one himself.

Chauffeur, so good.

BIG THREE, THE

The famed power trios of the sixties were The Jimi Hendrix Experience and Cream, but The Big Three from Liverpool were there first. 'What do you need

a rhythm guitarist for?' said Johnny Hutchinson (b. 1940). 'All he does is stand around looking pretty. There were only three of us but we made more noise than other group on Merseyside.'

The origins of The Big Three start with a merchant navy seaman from Hull, Adrian Barber, who heard Brian Casser singing in a Liverpool coffee bar. He introduced himself and soon they had formed Cass and The Cassanovas with Johnny Gustafson, bass (1942–2014) and Johnny 'Hutch' Hutchinson. They were resident on Sunday afternoons at the Cassanova Club in Dale Street and also at the Jacaranda. They were the first rock 'n' roll band to appear regularly in the city centre. They invited Johnny and the Moondogs, an early incarnation of The Beatles, to one session. They were thinking of becoming The Beatles and Brian 'Cass' told them that the name was too short. Why not Long John and the Silver Beatles? Hutch introduced John to a song by The Olympics, 'Well (Baby Please Don't Go)'. John Lennon sat in with them on 'Ramrod' by Duane Eddy.

Cass and The Cassanovas played on the Liverpool Stadium extravaganza in May 1960, topped by Gene Vincent, and then took part in the audition for Larry Parnes at the Wyvern Club. Hutch, looking bored, stood in as The Beatles' drummer. The Cassanovas were booked to accompany Parnes' artists on short Scottish tours, namely, Duffy Power, Dickie Pride and, in August 1960, Johnny Gentle. Parnes had thoughts of making the good-looking Johnny 'Gus' a solo star, but blew his chance by trying to jump into his bed.

Hutch, a good vocalist in his own right, felt that Cass was holding the group back and they disbanded and immediately re-formed, without Cass, as a power trio named for the summit featuring Roosevelt, Stalin and Churchill – The Big Three. Their sound was intensified by Adrian Barber's home-made 'coffin' amps, which impressed Paul so much that he commissioned one for himself.

The Big Three sounded (and behaved) rougher and tougher than any other group on Merseyside. 'There was more violence in the attack of our instruments,' says Gus, 'and our drumming was loud and raucous.' Hutch used to hold the sticks the wrong way round to create a more forceful sound. They became the group's group on Merseyside and had a strong male following. There were fights on stage and fights with the audience.

Brian Casser formed Casey Jones and The Engineers, who briefly had Tom McGuinness and Eric Clapton in their line-up, and then became minor stars in Germany, landing Top Ten hits as Casey Jones and The Governors. Brian Epstein, having signed The Beatles and Gerry and The Pacemakers, was keen to add The Big Three to his books. They agreed as it would mean more work and he sent them to the Star-Club in Hamburg. The contract stipulated four musicians and so they recruited Brian Griffiths 'Griff' (b. 1943) from The Seniors. They partied with booze and pills, but they learnt how to improvise and how to play for hours at a time. Says Gus, 'I was reduced to being a physical wreck after four days but it was enjoyable to be a physical wreck.' They became close friends with Tony Sheridan while Adrian Barber, a technical whiz, in August 1962 became the stage manager at the Star-Club. He subsequently moved to America and produced the Allman Brothers Band.

Returning as a trio from Hamburg, they went straight to Decca's recording studio and put down 'Some Other Guy', the archetypal Merseybeat record. It was produced by Noel Walker, a Liverpool jazz musician who had landed a job at the label with no producing experience.

It has been said that Johnny Hutch was considered as a replacement for Pete Best in The Beatles, but this is unlikely as he was disruptive and would have come to blows with Lennon. However, he did play drums for The Beatles for the few days until Ringo was available.

'Some Other Guy' was a minor hit, but Epstein wanted them to perform like pop puppets. They recorded the teen pop of 'By the Way' (written by Mitch Murray) and 'I'm With You' (written by Tony Hiller). The B-sides, 'Peanut Butter' and their own 'Cavern Stomp', were more representative of their stage performances. Walker recorded the live EP *The Big Three At The Cavern*, which is fiery and noisy and features an excellent song of their own, 'Don't Start Running Away'. On a live album with various artists recorded at the Cavern, Bob Wooler introduced them as 'the boys with the Benzedrine beat'.

The group disbanded over the division of earnings and Hutch formed a new Big Three for Kennedy Street Enterprises, working with Faron and Paddy Chambers from Faron's Flamingos, but it soon fell apart and Hutch moved into the building trade. Gus became a session musician and in later years worked with Roxy Music. He wrote 'Dear John' for Status Quo and was on the original album of *Jesus Christ Superstar*. In 1973 he and Griff asked Nigel Olsson to join them for an album as The Big Three, called *Resurrection*. Griff worked in a timber yard and later moved to Calgary, although he still played guitar from to time to time. Gus died in 2014 after a long illness but he was able to appear in a documentary being made by Griff about the band.

After a 50-year absence from the drum kit, property developer Johnny Hutch is set to play at the Liverpool Beatles Convention in 2016 and a DVD about the band will be released in 2017.

A Big 3. How The Beatles might have sounded without Brian Epstein.

BLACK, CILLA [1943–2015]

Paul McCartney has referred to Cilla Black as 'the scruff from Scottie Road', an indication of the working class subdivisions in Liverpool. She was born Priscilla Maria Veronica White on 27 March 1943 in the roughest, toughest area of the city, a mile from the city centre and also where Frankie Vaughan came from. Her father was a docker and her mother had a stall on Paddy's market. When Cilla was 13, she dyed her hair red and it remained that way.

Cilla was an office worker who was soon going to the Cavern, often on duty in the cloakroom. She was amused that American books often describe her as 'the hat-check girl'; as she said, 'Who wore a hat to go to the Cavern?' Her friends encouraged her to sing. With her strident voice, she was billed as 'Swinging Cilla' and would sing with Kingsize Taylor, Rory Storm, The Big Three and Gerry and The Pacemakers, indeed at any opportunity she could find. She regularly sang 'Boys' and 'Fever' and she was encouraged by her boyfriend Bobby Willis, who became her husband and, after Brian Epstein, her manager.

By accident, the *Mersey Beat* newspaper printed her name as Cilla Black and her stage name was born. John Lennon asked Brian Epstein to audition her. On the first occasion Brian was not impressed, but then he heard her sing a jazzy 'Bye Bye Blackbird' with The Mastersounds at the Blue Angel and appreciated her talent. George Martin was similarly convinced and Paul McCartney's 'Love of the Loved' was her first single and a minor hit. Brian heard Dionne Warwick's 'Anyone Who Had a Heart ' in the States and gave it to George Martin. Although he wanted to record it with Shirley Bassey, Brian convinced him to try Cilla and her version went to No. 1.

As a result, songwriters Burt Bacharach and Hal David gave her a song inspired by the Michael Caine film *Alfie*. The film of the session reveals that she had to endure Bacharach's endless takes. Eventually Burt said, 'I think we got it this time, George,' to which George added drolly, 'I think we had it on take two, Burt.'

Cilla had a second No. 1 with 'You're My World' and Paul wrote the jazz-waltz 'It's For You' for her. She challenged The Righteous Brothers with 'You've Lost That Lovin' Feelin'' and reached No. 2. She became a stage favourite, starring for months at the London Palladium, but Brian Epstein could not persuade Gracie Fields to let Cilla take the lead in a biographical film of her life.

In 1965 Cilla was the first person to cover 'Yesterday' and although only a B-side, it became one of her most requested songs. In 1968 Paul wrote 'Step Inside Love' as a theme for her TV series. She recorded another song by a Liverpool writer, Stan Kelly's 'Liverpool Lullaby', but her favourite local songwriter was perhaps Bobby Willis, as she recorded many of his songs.

In the eighties Cilla presented two hugely successful shows for London Weekend Television, *Surprise, Surprise* and *Blind Date*. In both she made great play of her Scouse accent, coining popular catchphrases, and became a major family entertainer. Although she still toured from time to time, most of her stage performances were in pantomime. After the death of her husband Bobby, she was managed by her son Robert. In 2014 Cilla's credibility received an unexpected boost through a surprisingly good TV series simply called *Cilla*, with Sheridan Smith in the title role.

Cilla died in her holiday home on the Costa del Sol on 2 August 2015 or as the *Metro* put it, 'Ta-Ra Chuck'. There was an enormous showing of public affection for her, including the televising of her funeral. Cilla was only 72 but maybe reaching that age took her by surprise. 'I count myself lucky to have survived childhood. Scottie

Road was a dual carriageway back then and there was no such thing as a zebra crossing.'

Cilla consolidated the feeling that there must be something in the water in Liverpool and gave us a lorra, lorra laughs.

BLAKE, PETER [B. 1932]

What is the world's best-known album cover? There are surely only two contenders: *Sgt Pepper's Lonely Hearts Club Band* and Pink Floyd's *Dark Side Of The Moon*. Peter Blake would have been one of the foremost British artists of the sixties in any event, but his design for *Sgt Pepper* meant that he became a household name. He did not need to compromise himself at all – the packaging covers many of his interests as well as perfectly capturing the retro yet progressive character of the music.

Peter Blake was born in Dartford, Kent in 1932. From his early years he was intrigued by painting, by graphic design and by the importance of found objects. He did his National Service in the RAF and then studied at the Royal College of Art, leaving with a first class diploma. He developed a love for blending popular culture with art, incorporating wrestlers, strippers, circus performers and musicians in his work. In 1961 he won the first prize in the junior section at the John Moores Exhibition with *Self Portrait With Badges*, in which he was holding a copy of *Elvis Monthly*. He married fellow artist Jann Haworth, and taught at the Royal College of Art from 1964–76. He founded the Brotherhood of Ruralists with Jann and did several Pre-Raphaelite styled paintings before separating from her in 1979 and returning to chronicling urban culture. He married another artist, Chrissy Wilson, in 1987.

Peter Blake liked to paint images of singers in primary colours and his subjects include Bo Diddley, LaVern Baker and Elvis Presley, all artists he admired. He included US teen idols Fabian, Frankie Avalon, Ricky Nelson, Bobby Rydell and Elvis in *Got A Girl* (1961) and his painting of The Beatles in 1962 was used on the cover of George Melly's study of the sixties, *Revolt Into Style*.

Paul McCartney had the concept for the *Sgt Pepper* cover and Peter and Jann worked on the montage and inserts, resulting in the most lavish packaging for any LP to date. It led to a host of extravagant LP covers. Over the years there have been numerous tributes to Blake's cover, not least from Blake himself, who did one for Liverpool becoming European Capital of Culture in 2008 and another for his eightieth birthday in 2012. The only sleeve he has publicly disliked was for the Mothers of Invention's *We're Only In It for The Money,* which he thought was cruel.

For *Sgt Pepper*, Blake admitted that he was inspired by James Ensor's painting *Christ's Entry into Brussels* (1889) but that he never saw Adrian Henri's *The Entry of Christ into Liverpool* (1964).

He designed both the picture sleeve and the poster for Band Aid/Live Aid in 1984–5 and the poster for Live 8 in 2005. His many album sleeves include Roger McGough's *Summer with Monika* (1967), Pentangle's *Sweet Child* (1968), The Who's *Face Dances* (1981), Paul Weller's *Stanley Road* (1995) and Oasis's *Stop the Clocks* (2006).

He became Sir Peter Blake in 2002 and there have been numerous exhibitions of his work. Although his style has a simplicity that appeals to a mass audience, there have been several essays on his complexity.

Sgt Pepper sleeve was an event in itself, but it was Paul's idea.

BONZO DOG DOO-DAH BAND, THE

So many of the key British musicians of the sixties came out of art school – John Lennon, Ray Davies and Pete Townshend among them – and it's easy to understand why: art schools were creative places with little discipline and lacking the formality of a college of music (plus you could get your posters done for free). The art colleges encouraged unconventional behaviour, a textbook example being The Bonzo Dog Band, originally The Bonzo Dog Doo-Dah Band, who evolved in the canteen at the Royal College of Art in 1965 and were originally a somewhat unlikely pub band. They had a fluid line-up but the mainstays included Vivian Stanshall (1943–1995), Neil Innes (b. 1944) and 'Legs' Larry Smith (b. 1944). Their hilarious stage props were constructed by saxophonist Roger Ruskin Spear (b. 1943) and were inspired by another British eccentric, Professor Bruce Lacey. The Bonzos described their music themselves as 'Art with a capital F'.

The Bonzo Dog Band had many diverse influences, but at their core they celebrated the music of the thirties with trad jazz and rock overtones. Their debut album, *Gorilla* (1967), is a masterpiece of English eccentricity and inventiveness including 'Cool Britannia' (a title purloined by Tony Blair's government), 'The Equestrian Statue' (written about a statue outside St George's Hall, Liverpool) and a comic way of introducing a band, 'The Intro and the Outro'. Their parody of a *True Crime* magazine, 'Death Cab For Cutie', was performed with a stripper in Raymond's Revuebar for *Magical Mystery Tour*. They had a residency on the ATV show *Do Not Adjust Your Set,* with the comic actors who would become Monty Python's Flying Circus.

When the Bonzos were making their second album, *The Doughnut in Granny's Greenhouse*, Viv told Paul that they were having difficulty in making singles. Paul offered to produce them and he selected Neil Innes's quirky 'I'm The Urban Spaceman', which he produced under the pseudonym, Apollo C. Vermouth. Surprisingly, the line 'I'm the urban spaceman, baby, I got speed' avoided a BBC ban.

Although 'Urban Spaceman' was a chart single and the Bonzos performed memorable concerts with Scaffold, the band never had a united front about what to do next and their albums *Tadpoles* and *Keynsham*, both 1969, lacked consistency. The band split up but they did return for *Let's Make Up and Be Friendly* (1972). Viv and Neil joined Scaffold (John Gorman, Roger McGough, Mike McGear) and the guitarist Andy Roberts from Liverpool Scene for a highly entertaining group called Grimms, although the line-up was not as rigid as that.

Viv Stanshall put his rich tones to financial use by voicing commercials and was the narrator in Mike Oldfield's *Tubular Bells*. He released what many think is his best work, *Sir Henry at Rawlinson End*, in 1978.

'Legs' Larry Smith, originally drummer with the Bonzos, and a comic dancer in his own right, became a close friend of George Harrison. He designed the cover of George's album *Gone Troppo* (1982) and George wrote 'His Name Is Legs' about him. See *The Rutles* entry for more on Neil Innes.

Around 2006, the Bonzos reformed for a series of concerts and an album, *Pour L'Amour Des Chiens*, with guest vocalists replacing Viv Stanshall. Most of the Bonzos are still active and working in different combinations, and Neil Innes has now devised a Bonzos plus Rutles stage show.

Their witty 'Death Cab For Cutie' is one of the highlights of *Magical Mystery Tour*.

BOYD, PATTIE [B. 1944]

The eldest daughter of a fighter pilot, Patricia Anne Boyd was born in Taunton, Somerset, on 17 March 1944 and the family lived in Nairobi from 1948 to 1953. Her parents divorced, and on leaving school she worked in a hairdressing salon. She had blonde hair, blue eyes and was beautiful with a winning smile. A client who worked for a fashion magazine asked her if she would like to be a model. An early assignment was a series of commercials for Smith's crisps, directed by Richard Lester. He invited her to appear in two short scenes in *A Hard Day's Night*, where she met George Harrison. His chat-up line was, 'Will you marry me? If you won't marry me, will you have dinner with me tonight?'

Pattie continued as a model and was photographed by David Bailey and Terence Donovan. In 1965 they moved into George's bungalow in Esher and were married at Epsom Register Office on 21 January 1966 with Paul McCartney and Brian Epstein as joint best men. They had their honeymoon in Barbados.

Pattie shared George's love of eastern mysticism and encouraged all four Beatles to meet Maharishi Mahesh Yogi in London in August 1967. She went with them to Rishikesh in February 1968. In 1970, she and George moved to Friar Park in Henley-on-Thames.

When George took Pattie to see Cream at the Saville Theatre, she met Eric Clapton. He became besotted by her, and lived with her sister Paula (b.1951) for a while. Paula left when she heard 'Layla' and realised that Eric really wanted Pattie. When Pattie did leave George for Eric, George said, 'I'd rather she was with him than with some dope.' Pattie had a short affair with Ronnie Wood in 1973 but we don't know where George stood on that. She remained friendly with George and they were not divorced until 1977.

Pattie had a torrid time with Eric, trying to cope with his heroin addiction and then heavy drinking. She married Eric in Tucson, Arizona on March 1979. They lived together for five years and were divorced in 1986. Pattie became a professional photographer and opened an agency for older models, Deja Vu.

Pattie Boyd is one of the most celebrated women in rock. George Harrison wrote 'Something' about her, and Eric presented 'Layla' and then 'Wonderful Tonight', which was used for the title of Pattie's autobiography in 2007. Not to be outdone, Pattie's sister Jenny (b.1947) is the subject of Donovan's delightful 'Jennifer Juniper'.

But it's a 10 from George.

BRAMWELL, TONY [B. 1946]

When a schoolboy, Tony Bramwell delivered meat for a local butcher, calling on the Harrison household in Speke where he and George would discuss rock 'n' roll. George was impressed that he had won a competition to meet Buddy Holly in Liverpool. Then on 27 December 1960 he met George on a bus ride and offered to carry his guitar so that he could get into the Litherland Town Hall for free. He became a devoted fan and Brian Epstein employed him as an office boy. He often went on the road with The Beatles and he became increasingly useful to the NEMS organisation. He became the stage manager at the Saville Theatre, Shaftesbury Avenue, for Brian Epstein, and when he joined Apple he became involved in promotional films for their singles.

Possibly it was his Beatles connection, who knows, but Tony Bramwell became one of the UK's leading bachelors, dating three Miss Worlds, Christine Keeler and the actress Julie Ege, among others. He subsequently married and settled down. He had many industry jobs and established the late Eva Cassidy in the UK. He wrote a highly colourful memoir, *Magical Mystery Tours* (2005).

A Beatles gofer, but not as crucial to The Beatles as he makes out. He'd settle for no less than 7 or 8.

BROWN, KEN [1940–2010]

Ken Brown was born in Enfield, Middlesex in 1940, and his family moved to Liverpool when he was nine months old. He was raised in the Norris Green area and worked for a tools supplier. He bought an electric guitar, a Hofner Senator, and in 1959 became part of the Les Stewart Quartet with George Harrison. They were offered a Saturday night residency at the new Casbah club. Unfortunately, a disagreement meant that Les and drummer Geoff Skinner left the band, leaving Ken and George to fulfil the booking. The Quarrymen were not doing anything and so George contacted John and Paul. They regrouped as The Quarrymen although they never regarded Ken as a member.

The Quarrymen were paid £3 a night (15 shillings each). In January 1960 Ken had injured his leg and didn't want to play, so Mona Best put him on the door collecting admission. At the end of the evening she paid him the same money, whereas John, Paul and George thought they should have had £1 each. Mona was in the wrong: she had hired the group for £3 – how they split the proceeds was up to them. Paul said he would never play the Casbah again.

Ken Brown's time with The Quarrymen was over but he did once lend John Lennon £5 that was never returned (something of a recurring theme in Lennon's early life.) In later years, Ken ran a

snooker club in Essex and had a little studio of his own, making private recordings for his friends. He wrote his memoirs but they were never published. In June 2010 his brother expected to see him at a wedding but he didn't arrive. He suffered from emphysema and had died alone at his home up to five days earlier.

Would John and Paul been reunited with George without him?

BROWN, PETER [B. 1937]

Peter Brown was born and raised in Bebington on the Wirral, Cheshire, and after attending grammar school served in the RAF. He trained for management at Lewis's store in Liverpool and ran their record department effectively. He met Brian Epstein at a party in September 1958 and they became close friends. Both were gay but Brown says that their friendship was based around common interests and not sexual. For example, they were smart dressers who enjoyed the theatre. At first Brown could not see the attraction of The Beatles and he loathed the dark, dank and sweaty Cavern. When Brian obtained an EMI recording contract for The Beatles, he relinquished the management of NEMS record store in Liverpool's Whitechapel and handed it to Peter. Although as was Brian's way, he was reluctant to let Peter have full control.

In 1965 Brown went to London with NEMS Enterprises and became intensely involved in arranging The Beatles' personal and business affairs, working in a similar but senior capacity to Alistair Taylor. He had a red telephone on his desk that any Beatle could ring in an emergency. Following Brian's death, he did his best to steady The Beatles and became an executive of their company, Apple Corps. He was best man when John married Yoko in Gibraltar and is mentioned in 'The Ballad of John and Yoko'.

The Beatles had told Allen Klein that he could not sack Peter Brown, but Peter resigned on the day the group announced their break-up (31 December 1970). He then became an executive for the Robert Stigwood Organisation, helping to establish The Bee Gees as disco superstars. In 1983 he wrote *The Love You Make: An Insider's Story of The Beatles*, an unsympathetic and gloomy account of The Beatles years, and many Beatles associates felt that he had not respected their friendship. Brian Epstein's mother was horrified by the revelations about Brian's sexuality. Peter formed a PR company and moved to New York, going on to become chairman and CEO of PR firm BLJ. He is an American citizen living in Manhattan.

The Beatles relied on him and trusted him for many years, and then he wrote that book.

CALDWELL, LOUISE – SEE HARRISON, LOUISE

CALDWELL, VI – SEE STORM, RORY AND THE HURRICANES

CASEY, HOWIE [B. 1937]

Howard Casey was born in Huyton, Liverpool in 1937, and as a teenager became intrigued by the saxophone he heard on jazz records by Stan Kenton and Lester Young. Awaiting conscription, he realised that if he signed up for a third year, he could join a military band. He was demobbed in 1958 and knew he wanted to play rock 'n' roll. He played in local clubs as part of The Rhythm Rockers and then formed Derry and The Seniors with lead singer Derry Wilkie doing his best to emulate Little Richard. They played on the Gene Vincent show at the Liverpool Stadium in May 1960.

Later that month, Allan Williams arranged an audition for backing musicians with the London impresario Larry Parnes, at which The Silver Beatles also performed. Parnes offered Derry and The Seniors a Blackpool summer season but then changed his mind. Howie, who was tough and defiant, ordered Allan to find them alternative employment. He took them to London and by chance met Bruno Koschmider in the 2i's coffee bar. Koschmider offered them a residency at the Kaiserkeller in Hamburg. They went down well but the accommodation was terrible – Howie slept with a Union Jack for a bedsheet.

Howie was horrified when he heard that Williams was sending over The Beatles as they would 'ruin it for everyone' because of their inexperience. However, when they played the Indra, he realised that they had greatly improved since the Parnes audition. When Derry and The Seniors finished in October 1960, they looked for work elsewhere, mostly in strip clubs, but it ended with Casey pawning his saxophone to return home.

The group returned to Liverpool to open Allan Williams's new club, the Top Ten, but it burned down in the first week. Howie added vocalist Freddie Fowell (later Freddie Starr) to the line-up, now called Wailin' Howie Casey and The Seniors, and they had some success at the Twist at the Top club in Ilford, recording an album for the Fontana label, the first LP by a Merseybeat group. A single, 'Double Twist', was played so frantically that anyone twisting to it was prone to injury.

The group disbanded in June 1962 and Casey became part of Kingsize Taylor and The

Dominoes. As The Shakers, they recorded a chart album in Germany and back in the UK, they accompanied Chuck Berry on tour. Howie was a versatile musician, able to play tenor, baritone and soprano sax, and after the group disbanded in 1964, he took on session work. He worked with T Rex and The Who, but his most noted contributions are with Wings in the mid-1970s. He was strongly featured in *Band On the Run* and played a solo on 'Bluebird'. More recently, Howie has had his own rock 'n' roll band and worked with Elvis impersonator Liberty Mounten, and Roy Young. His wife, Sheila, was one of The McKinleys, who toured with The Beatles, and prior to her death in 2012 they often worked together.

The Merseybeat scene would have been less colourful without him and his professionalism was a spur to The Beatles' own improvement.

CASSER, BRIAN – SEE BIG THREE, THE

CLAPTON, ERIC [B.1945]

In the mid-1960s, there was a fierce debate as to whether white men could play and sing the blues. The advent and the popularity of Eric Clapton, Van Morrison, Joe Cocker and Chris Farlowe demonstrated that they certainly could.

Eric Patrick Clapton was born in Ripley, Surrey, on 30 March 1945, the consequence of a quick liaison between his 15-year-old mother and a Canadian serviceman. He was raised by his grandparents, who gave him a guitar for his fourteenth birthday. Trying to match his favourite blues guitarists note for note became an obsession. Although he went to the Kingston School of Art, he lacked commitment and was asked to leave.

In 1963 Eric became a 'Rooster', with future Manfred Mann bass player Tom McGuinness. He and Tom then briefly joined Casey Jones and The Engineers with the Liverpool vocalist Brian Casser (of Cass and The Cassanovas). When Eric jammed at the Crawdaddy club in Richmond, the promoter Giorgio Gomelsky introduced him as 'Slowhand'.

In October 1963 Eric joined a commercial R&B band, The Yardbirds, and played on their hit single 'For Your Love'. The Yardbirds supported The Beatles for Christmas shows at Hammersmith Odeon, but Eric was uneasy with screaming fans and wanted to play in a serious blues band. He was replaced by Jeff Beck and went on to join John Mayall's Bluesbreakers. The slogan 'Eric Clapton is God' became a favourite with graffiti writers.

In 1966 he formed the most influential of all rock trios, Cream, with Jack Bruce on bass and Ginger Baker on drums. This band was a powder keg as the musicians, high on alcohol and drugs, perpetually argued among themselves and with others. Around this time Eric became close friends with George Harrison. George wrote 'Here Comes the Sun' in Eric's garden and together they wrote Cream's hit single 'Badge', so-called because Eric was reading George's handwriting upside down and said, 'What's this "Badge"?'. George had written 'Bridge', indicating the song's middle section.

The Beatles were having their own share of arguments and Eric reluctantly played on 'While My Guitar Gently Weeps'. Although Eric did not make solo records for Apple, he played on sessions for Billy Preston, Doris Troy and Jackie Lomax as well as George Harrison's album *All Things Must Pass*. John and Yoko used Eric in the Plastic Ono Band. He played on 'Cold Turkey' as well as making live appearances in Toronto and London.

After another fractious supergroup, Blind Faith, with Ginger, Steve Winwood and Ric Grech, Eric toured in Delaney & Bonnie and Friends, also with

George. It was after the gig at Liverpool Empire that Eric told George that he loved his wife, Pattie. Following some drug-fuelled sessions in Miami, Clapton formed Derek and The Dominos, whose line-up included another outstanding guitarist, Duane Allman, and they went on to make the famed double album *Layla And Other Assorted Love Songs*, the title song being written for Pattie. As if it was the most natural thing in the world, George asked Eric to play lead guitar on *The Concert for Bangla Desh*. Considering that there have been so many stage and film biographies of The Beatles, it is surprising that no Hollywood producer has picked up on the George, Eric and Pattie love triangle.

Eric Clapton's heroin addiction was costly and his finances were chaotic. Pete Townshend of The Who staged Eric Clapton's Rainbow concert, possibly the only concert to raise money for someone's addiction (although to be fair that wasn't the intention) and it did restart his interest in playing. He went into rehab, which freed him from drugs, but he became an alcoholic. Eventually with considerable willpower, he managed to shake himself free of his addictions.

In 1974 Eric made the classic album *461 Ocean Boulevard*, and had an international hit with Bob Marley's 'I Shot the Sheriff'. In 1978 he appeared with The Band in their final concert filmed as *The Last Waltz* by Martin Scorsese. In 1991 George and Eric toured Japan.

Eric Clapton is revered as the best guitarist in the world, although purists wish he would visit his blues roots more often. His most acclaimed song 'Tears In Heaven' was written after the accidental death of his son Conor.

More if you're George Harrison, less if you're Paul.

CLEAVE, MAUREEN [B. 1935]

Maureen Cleave, the daughter of an army major, had been born in Mussoorie, India in 1935 and the family moved to Northern Ireland when she was four. Her father returned to India, and when his wife and daughter sailed to join him in 1940 their ship was torpedoed and they had to be rescued. Maureen spent most of her childhood in

---

JOHN LENNON'S MORE OUTRAGEOUS COMMENTS

(What did you think of the Hunter Davies book?) 'It was bullshit. Really bullshit. There was nothing about the orgies and the shit that happened on tour.'

'I must have had a thousand trips. I used to just eat it all the time.'

'If there is such a thing as a genius, I am one.'

'I'm not going to record with another egomaniac.'

'If you put me with B.B. King, I would feel silly.'

'Yoko's bottom thing is as important as *Sgt Pepper*.'

'Our tours were like *Satyricon*.'

Ireland and studied at St Anne's College, Oxford. In 1959 she was appointed a features writer for the *London Evening Standard* and although past her teens, she had a regular column, *Disc Date*.

Cleave was one of the first journalists in London to notice The Beatles and her piece for the newspaper on 2 February 1963, 'Why The Beatles Create All That Frenzy', was an astute analysis on their popularity. In her opinion, the looks were the deciding factor.

Maureen Cleave, dubbed Maureen Cleavage by *Private Eye*, befriended The Beatles, who would tease her constantly. She could take their ribbing and greatly enjoyed their company. However, she never introduced them to her boyfriend, later husband. He was well over six feet and, according to her, The Beatles felt uncomfortable with tall people. She came to know the band and their associates very well and was particularly friendly with John and Cynthia. She offered suggestions for the lyrics of 'A Hard Day's Night' and 'Help!'

Tony Barrow considered her 'an outstanding features writer' and she was trusted to write about The Beatles. She could probe their innermost thoughts and she compared George Harrison's comment about children being corrupted by society with William Wordsworth's *Intimations of Immortality*. When it came to discussing religion, she did not get far with Paul, whom she described as a 'flabby agnostic'.

In 1966 Maureen could see how shallow and empty life had become for John Lennon, what ridiculous things he was buying and how adrift he was in his Weybridge mansion. He said that, 'Sex is the only physical exercise I bother with' and although it is obvious that John was addicted, she did not mention drugs during her feature, part of a series for the *London Evening Standard* under the title, 'How Does a Beatle Live?'

John had been reading a book, *The Passport Plot*, which prompted his remarks. 'Christianity will go, it will vanish and shrink. I needn't argue about that. I'm right and I will be proved right. We're more popular than Jesus now; I don't know which will go first, rock 'n' roll or Christianity.' This was hard-hitting stuff for a pop interview in 1966 but a shrewd comment on the decline in Christian beliefs. The *Guardian* picked on his comments but, to most readers, it was just John sounding off again. However, when the comments were reprinted in the American magazine *Datebook* in July 1966, shortly before their US tour, they created a furore, especially in the Bible Belt. It led to burnings of Beatles memorabilia and The Beatles never toured again. John later said that the interview did him a favour. 'If it hadn't happened, I might still be up there with all the other performing fleas.'

In 2009 Maureen Cleave wrote a feature for the *Daily Mail*: 'Did I Break Up The Beatles?' The rule in journalism is that if you have a question in the title, the answer is invariably no.

John might have said his 'bigger than Jesus' to any one of 20 journalists.

COX, MAUREEN – SEE STARKEY, MAUREEN

CUTLER, IVOR [1923–2006]

The Beatles had a fondness for eccentric humourists such as Spike Milligan, Max Wall, Viv Stanshall, Stanley Unwin and Ivor Cutler, who lived in their own worlds. It's often hard to distinguish between authentic behaviour and attention-seeking devices, but if Cutler was artifice he maintained it for the whole of his career.

Isadore Cutler was born the son of Jewish immigrants in Glasgow in 1923 and he was victimised by schoolchildren for not being a real Scot. He became an eccentric teacher, encouraging children to parody popular songs, and through this he found his voice and creativity as a performer. In 1961 he recorded the LP *who tore your trousers?* for Decca – yes, they turned down The Beatles and accepted Ivor Cutler – with sleeve notes from Tony Barrow.

Paul McCartney heard Ivor Cutler on the radio and wanted to know more about his harmonium playing. After they met, Paul cast him as the bus conductor, Buster Bloodvessel, in *Magical Mystery Tour*. His album *Ludo* (1967) was produced by George Martin, and he could count John Peel, Billy Connolly and later Billy Bragg among many admirers. His albums included *Dandruff* (1974) and *Jammy Smears* (1976) and his best-known story was *Gruts For Tea*, told as always in his precise, clipped delivery. He performed until he was 80, living in a small flat in London with an indoor washing-line on which he would hang his paintings to dry.

If only the conversations between John and Ivor Cutler had been filmed during the making of *Magical Mystery Tour*.

DAKOTAS, THE – SEE KRAMER, BILLY J., WITH THE DAKOTAS

DAVIES, HUNTER [B. 1936]

Edward Hunter Davies was born on 7 January 1936 to Scottish parents in Johnstone, Renfrewshire. The family moved to Carlisle when Hunter was 11, and he went to Carlisle Grammar School then Durham University. He joined the *Sunday Times* in 1960, going on to become becoming editor of the *Atticus* column, chief feature writer and editor of its colour magazine. His first book, a novel about contemporary youth, *Here We Go Round The Mulberry Bush*, was published in 1965.

In 1967 his wife Margaret Forster achieved international success when her book *Georgy Girl* was filmed, with a title song from The Seekers. The film of *Here We Go Round The Mulberry Bush* followed, with an exceptional soundtrack from Traffic and The Spencer Davis Group. Hunter had hoped for a theme song from Paul McCartney and although that did not materialise, Hunter floated the concept of an authorised biography. This was a highly original idea as very few rock books had been published. Paul helped Hunter make contact with Brian Epstein and following approval, Hunter set about his research. He had unparalleled access to The Beatles and their families and was the only outsider to have observed Lennon and McCartney writing their songs, notably 'With a Little Help from My Friends'. The chapter on their music is intriguing; you can sense that Hunter was bursting to contribute to the creative process but knew he was there as an observer.

The Beatles (1968) was the first rock biography to become an instant international bestseller: it has remained in print and Hunter has updated it from time to time. The book does have its faults – Hunter didn't do many interviews outside The Beatles' inner circle – but it is a remarkable piece of work and candid for an authorised biography. At John's request, Hunter dropped an unkind reference John had made to his mother Julia's partner and Hunter was also asked to keep Aunt Mimi happy. In 1971, Lennon hypocritically dismissed the book as 'bullshit' in *Rolling Stone*.

In 1972 Hunter wrote *The Glory Game*, a highly acclaimed biography of his football team Tottenham Hotspur. Among many other books,

ENOUGH!

A disgruntled reader wrote to *Life* magazine in November 1968, after they had serialised Hunter Davies's biography of The Beatles.

'Sirs:

Only about a month ago I was congratulating you on (in my opinion) the year's best issue, but since then we have had the Sept. 16 issue with six pages on John Lennon and Yoko, the Oct. 14 issue with pages of The Beatles and the horrible promise of more to come!

Please, please, no more of The Beatles for a good year – we have had enough, *more than enough*...

S. F. Burden
Chichester, England

Hunter has also written the autobiographies of Paul Gascoigne and Wayne Rooney. In addition he has produced several books about his beloved Lake District, including a biography of the fell walker Alfred Wainwright.

Hunter Davies has been a chronicler of family life and of collecting – probably no author has covered such a wide range of subjects. He has returned to The Beatles from time to time, notably for *The Quarrymen* (2001) and *The John Lennon Letters* (2012). His chapter on the Casbah in his book *Behind the Scenes at the Museum of Baked Beans* (2010) is truly comic writing about The Beatles. In 2014 he published *The Beatles Lyrics*, containing over a hundred original handwritten manuscripts of The Beatles' songs.

Hunter was awarded the OBE for his services to literature in 2014. In terms of rock literature alone, he opened the floodgates for books on The Beatles and indeed, rock music overall.

A man who was both building monuments and jotting down notes.

DAVIS, ROD [B. 1941]

Rodney Verso Davis was born in Liverpool in 1941 and his father worked at Tate & Lyle, the sugar refinery. He was a good student and had an interest in folk songs, getting by on the banjo, guitar and ukulele. He was attracted to skiffle music and was happy to join The Quarrymen. He recalls, 'You can learn to busk quickly when there are only three or four chords. It did things for my image as before that I was the studious Rod Davis with his spectacles.'

Rod played with them until 1958 but says he never really left. He drifted away to do other things (notably becoming head boy) while Paul McCartney was fulfilling his function. His mother thought John Lennon was a bad influence, always referring to him as 'that Lennon'.

Rod was the only Quarryman dedicated to studying and he read foreign languages at Trinity College, Cambridge, on a scholarship. In 1961, he made 'Rag Day Jazz Band Ball' as part of The Trad Grads for Decca, the band including the 1500 metre Olympic gold medallist, Herb Elliot. Rod met John Lennon in a Liverpool street and John asked him to play drums for The Beatles in

Hamburg, but his mother forbade him to associate with 'that Lennon ' again.

Rod had a variety of teaching jobs and for several years, he organised foreign trips for a London company, Minitrek Expeditions. He met his first wife, Vivien, while leading an expedition to Turkey, and they had two children. He met his second wife, Janet, in 1985 and they became keen windsurfers.

He continued to sing in folk clubs and played in a country/rock band, The Armadillos, and also in The Bluegrass Ramblers for a time. Rod is a born organiser and the one who really put The Quarrymen back together again. He has performed and recorded with Tony Sheridan. He sometimes sings with his sister Rosie, and his younger brother Bernie, who is noted in Liverpool folk clubs for playing the saw, complete with comic bandages. Bernie occasionally fills on double bass for The Quarrymen.

Outside of the three Beatles, the most musically gifted of The Quarrymen.

DELANEY, PADDY [1931–2009]

First impressions count and during the Cavern's heyday in the sixties, the first person you would see was the 'gentle giant', Paddy Delaney, standing in the doorway. Born in Liverpool in 1931, Patrick Joseph Delaney had come to the Cavern as its doorman in 1959, and after clearing out the rough element he kept it trouble-free during the historic Merseybeat years.

When Ray McFall took over the Cavern in October 1959, he found there was an uncontained unruly element. To resolve its problems he hired Delaney, a former guardsman working at a Liverpool dance hall, the Locarno. At first he received one pound a night at the Cavern, but it quickly increased to one pound and ten shillings. 'I had read about the trouble with Teddy Boys in the *Liverpool Echo*,' recalled Paddy, 'and I knew I had to sort it out. I did get a broken jaw because someone came at me from behind, but I put five of them in hospital that night. My main rule was that when people were banned, they were banned for life. Too many clubs let them back after a week or so and the trouble started again. I told Ray McFall that I could clean the place up, but it would take three months and I'd need more men. That's the story and I never looked back. I was at the Cavern until it was demolished in 1973.'

Paddy did his job effectively: he knew how to deal with disputes and how to escort troublemakers off the premises peacefully. He never liked being called a bouncer. 'Never call me that,' he said. 'I always thought that people were human beings and they were paying good money to see the show and also paying my wages. Nowadays a fella who's never had a dinner suit on before thinks it's a licence to belt anyone who says a word out of place.'

Paddy Delaney's hero was Al Jolson and he would perform or mime his songs in Liverpool pubs. He even sang 'Mammy' at the Cavern, jumping on stage while the groups were packing up their equipment at the end of the night. George Harrison particularly appreciated hearing these songs.

Paddy had a large family to support and he spent the daytime delivering the *Mersey Beat* newspaper and undertaking odd jobs. He managed The Nomads and secured them a record contract with Decca, where they became The Mojos and had a Top 10 hit with 'Everything's Al'Right'.

Delaney had a succession of jobs – notably, patrolling Liverpool's parks – and he supported his wife Margaret, a local councillor. He advised the architect David Backhouse on his plans to rebuild the Cavern, and the new premises opened in 1984. The Cavern's original entrance is now marked with a life-size photograph of Paddy standing in the doorway. 'That's the story of my life,' he would muse, 'I've spent my whole life standing in a doorway.'

Paddy watched them all go in and watched them all go out.

DONOVAN [B. 1946]

Donovan Leitch was born in Glasgow in 1946 and was discovered as a young bohemian in Cornwall. In February 1965, the ITV programme *Ready Steady Go!* promoted Donovan as 'Britain's Bob Dylan'. Like Dylan, he wore a corduroy cap and denim jacket and played a guitar with a harmonica on a rack. On his guitar he had written 'This machine kills', an amended version of Woody Guthrie's 'This machine kills fascists'. He had Top 10 success with 'Catch The Wind' and 'Colours', plus a successful EP that featured Buffy Sainte-Marie's 'Universal Soldier', and the album *What's Bin Did And What's Bin Hid*. His socialising with Bob Dylan was filmed for the documentary *Don't Look Back*, where it is seen to be more friendship than rivalry.

Donovan's songs were more whimsical than Dylan's and he came into his own during the flower power era. He helped Paul McCartney with 'Yellow Submarine' although he admitted anyone could have written 'sky of blue, sea of green'.

He had further hits 'Sunshine Superman' and 'Mellow Yellow' and went with The Beatles to study with the Maharishi in India. He wrote 'Jennifer Juniper' about Pattie Boyd's sister and George Harrison added a verse to his vibrato-laden 'Hurdy Gurdy Man'. Donovan did not record this for the single but has since included Harrison's contribution in concert.

In 1968 Paul added backing vocals and tambourine to Donovan's hit single 'Atlantis' and also used Donovan's songs on his production, *Postcard,* for Mary Hopkin. He and Donovan played guitars on the track 'Voyage Of The Moon'. There was a session in which Paul and Donovan swapped songs but this has not been officially released.

In 1969 Donovan recorded 'Goo Goo Barabajagal' with the Jeff Beck Group, but he was too firmly entrenched with the hippie movement to remain in fashion, a similar fate as befell John Sebastian in the States. Everything changed when he toured with the Happy Mondays in 1991 and he became a popular touring attraction. Go to one of his concerts and you will think you are back in 1967.

A good friend of The Beatles, but more of a journeyman than an influence.

DUNBAR, JOHN – SEE FAITHFULL, MARIANNE

DYLAN, BOB [B.1941]

George Harrison introduced the *Concert for Bangla Desh* (1971) by saying, 'I'd like to bring on a friend of us all, Mr Bob Dylan.' Bit of a clue to how much they admired him. It wasn't just his music. His lyrics encouraged The Beatles, and John in particular, to realise they could use more imaginative words, instead of the prototype pop tune 'I-feel-blue' lyric.

The Beatles first met Bob Dylan in a New York hotel suite in 1964, when he congratulated them for sneaking a drugs reference into 'I Want To

Hold Your Hand'. He had thought they were singing 'I get high', instead of 'I can't hide'. Dylan passed a huge spliff around and Ringo, not knowing the etiquette, thought it was all for him. Lennon wore a peaked hat similar to that on the cover of *Bob Dylan* (1962), but Lennon and Dylan were wary of each other – perhaps because they had too much in common: awkward, arrogant, opinionated, prepared to offend and writing surreal poetry and lyrics.

Although Dylan based 'Fourth Time Around' on the melody of 'Norwegian Wood', Lennon was flattered rather than offended; later Lennon's 'Working Class Hero' was 'Masters Of War' revisited. Dylan and Lennon are equally stoned in the documentary film *Eat the Document,* filmed in 1966. In 'Yer Blues', Lennon says that he is as suicidal as 'Dylan's Mr Jones', a nod to 'Ballad of A Thin Man', but a deliberate misreading of the lyric, as Mr Jones is more out of place than suicidal.

The Beatles saw Bob Dylan and The Band at the Isle of Wight Festival in 1969 but Lennon was disappointed, telling the *Daily Express,* 'Everyone was expecting a Godot, a Jesus to appear.' In 1970 Lennon screamed, 'I don't believe in Zimmerman [Dylan's family name]' on the track 'God' from *John Lennon/Plastic Ono Band.* George Harrison did believe in Zimmerman, writing with him on *All Things Must Pass* and playing together in The Traveling Wilburys. Ringo was the only Beatle to join The Band for *The Last Waltz.*

In the sixties, Lennon wanted to write anthems for rallies like Dylan, little knowing that many Beatles songs would suit this role, but he realised his ambition with 'Give Peace a Chance', which includes a reference to 'Bobby Dylan'.

One of only two contemporary musicians on the *Sgt Pepper* cover: the other one, Dion, was Peter Blake's choice.

EASTMAN, LINDA – SEE MCCARTNEY, LINDA

ECKHORN, PETER [1939–1978]

The club Die Hippodrom, on the Reeperbahn, hadn't been used for some time, but it had been a circus involving donkeys and horses. By removing the stables and undergoing some conversions, the club could be made to seat 400 customers. Horst Fascher persuaded its 21-year-old owner Peter Eckhorn to turn it into a beat club. Eckhorn gave it an English name, Top Ten Club.

When Peter Eckhorn poached Tony Sheridan from Bruno Koschmider's Kaiserkeller, you might think that Eckhorn was taking his life into his hands, but he was supported by his family and, as his minders were tougher than Koschmider's, he did not fear retaliation. The Beatles held Sheridan in high regard and they would often visit the Top Ten during their breaks from the Kaiserkeller. It wasn't long before they were breaking their contract by performing on stage with Sheridan.

The Beatles played in their own right at the Top Ten in 1961, but Eckhorn was not able to consolidate his club's success because of the opening of the Star-Club. He told his story in the film *Damals In Hamburg* (1967). When Peter Eckhorn died in 1978, his widow presented live acts for a while but the club became a disco in 1980. Since then, it has had several makeovers including one as an Irish pub.

A brief impact on The Beatles, but he did get them back to Hamburg.

EDELMANN, HEINZ [1934–2009]

With its startling innovations, the 1968 feature-length, animated film *Yellow Submarine* took cartoon work to a new level, and its stylistic achievements were largely due to art director Heinz Edelmann.

Heinz was born in Czechoslovakia in 1934, and from 1953-58 he studied and then worked at Düsseldorf Academy of Fine Arts, with a keen interest in printmaking. In 1958, he became a freelance graphic designer. By the time he was 30, he was among the most promising designers in Europe. He did innovative work for the avant-garde German magazine *Twen,* including drawings on the horrors of war.

To appeal to younger American fans, in 1965 ABC TV commissioned a series of short cartoon films about The Beatles for Saturday morning viewing. They were undemanding and simplistic, but very popular, although The Beatles disliked being portrayed 'like the bloody Flintstones'. By 1967, the creative team needed a new challenge, particularly as The Beatles themselves had moved on with *Sgt Pepper.*

The producer Al Brodax, and director George Dunning, planned something more substantial than a longer version of the existing series. They developed a story from The Beatles' hit single 'Yellow Submarine', and having seen *Twen* they asked Heinz for designs. He submitted two-dimensional pictures of each Beatle and was appointed art director. Unquestionably, Edelmann was an inspired choice. He was a quiet, considerate man, who was quick to praise and eager to work hard. He would not go to the pub with the production team, saying he was too busy. He claimed to have survived on four hours' sleep every second night for over a year while making *Yellow Submarine.*

Inspired by the newspaper cartoon Flook, Edelmann created the Boob, who is used to such effect in the 'Nowhere Man' sequence. Many of his illustrations shaped the plot, which was written, among others, by Erich Segal and Roger McGough. The animation director Bob Balser recalled, 'When we were running out of money, Heinz said, "I have an idea, we can fill the screen with numbers and it will be very cheap." He was full of ideas. Heinz invented the Blue Meanies and that gave us a logical battle against Pepperland. It is the same story as *Star Wars* really, you've got The Beatles instead of the Jedi Knights, and the force is music.'

Being the first full-length feature cartoon made in the UK since *Animal Farm* (1954), *Yellow Submarine* opened to high expectations from public and critics alike. Although it appealed to children, it was also a commentary on the sixties and even though Heinz had no personal experience of hallucinogenic drugs, it depicted a psychedelic landscape. Markedly different from Disney, *Yellow Submarine* showed what could be done with animation and it led to feature-length cartoons from other studios, including *Fritz the Cat* (1972). Both Terry Gilliam (*Monty Python's Flying Circus*) and Alan Aldridge (*The Butterfly Ball*) drew inspiration from Heinz's work.

Heinz hoped that its success would lead to further work on feature films, but such projects did not materialise. He was to make commercials, off and on, throughout his life. Moving to Stuttgart, Heinz became a professor at the Stuttgart Academy of Fine Arts. He would tell his students that graphic designers were not paid adequately, but it was better than digging ditches.

Heinz's short film *Der phantastische Film,* used to introduce horror movies on German TV, is in the same mould as *Yellow Submarine* and can be seen on YouTube.

Despite exhibitions in Europe, the US and Japan, Heinz was said to be bored that *Yellow Submarine* had become the cornerstone of his reputation. If that is so, he disguised it very well when he came to Liverpool in 1999 for the launch of a 33 cent US stamp depicting the film, which had also been restored. He compared himself to the Ancient Mariner with an albatross round his neck, chuckling, 'Who likes to think that he did his best work when he was only 33?'

Heinz Edelmann gave The Beatles' catalogue a new dimension with his brilliantly imaginative work for *Yellow Submarine*.

ELLIS, ROYSTON [B.1941]

The author and beat poet Royston Ellis was born in Pinner in 1941. Supremely intelligent and free-spirited, he left school at 16 and determined to make it as a poet. Just as Allen Ginsberg read poetry to jazz music, Royston instituted 'rock-etry' around the Soho coffee bars, reading poetry to rock 'n' roll. His first book was *Jiving to Gyp* (1959), quickly followed by *Rave* (1960). He was sometimes accompanied by Cliff Richard's Drifters, and wrote about touring with the band in *Driftin' with Cliff* (1959). When he came to Liverpool, he performed at the Jacaranda coffee bar and was accompanied by The Beatles, lodging with John and Stu in Gambier Terrace. He showed them how to get high by using the Benzedrine inhalers in Vicks, their first contact with drugs.

That much is fact. Some of his claims, however, need to be taken with several pinches of salt. Royston has said that he made The Beatles a chicken pie, but he burned it – so he was the man on 'a flaming pie'; when they were called The Beetles, it was Royston who suggested that they became The Beatles; Paul was impressed with his books and said he would like to be a paperback writer (cue for song); and Royston introduced John to Pam, a girl who liked chewing polythene (cue for another song).

In 1961 Royston published the first account of UK rock 'n' roll, *The Big Beat Scene,* a valuable social study today. One chapter is devoted to an up-and-coming group, The Blanks, based on his time with The Beatles. In 1961 he read his poetry at the Mermaid Theatre in London, accompanied by Jimmy Page.

In 1963 Royston moved to Las Palmas and wrote several books while there. Then he moved to the Caribbean, writing the *Bondmaster* historical novels under the pseudonym of Richard Tresillian. When his home was destroyed by Hurricane David in 1979, he moved to Sri Lanka, from where he now writes travel books.

Though after a few minutes with Royston, you'll wonder if it should be 10.

EMERICK, GEOFF [B. 1946]

Geoff Emerick was a recording engineer who was born in London in 1946. He started training at EMI when only 15 and on his second day at work, under the tutelage of Norman Smith, he assisted on the first EMI session by John, Paul, George and Ringo. He worked with numerous other artists including Manfred Mann ('Pretty Flamingo'), The Hollies and Judy Garland.

He was at The Beatles' sessions with Norman Smith up to April 1966, at which point he took over as recording engineer and proved up to the challenge, with 'Tomorrow Never Knows', 'Strawberry Fields Forever' and 'Being For The Benefit Of Mr Kite!' calling for innovative thinking and experimentation. Emerick won Grammys for his work on *Sgt Pepper* and *Abbey Road*, but he did leave The Beatles for a time in 1968 as he tired of their squabbling. He helped to build The Beatles' own studio at Apple.

During the 1970s/80s he worked with Badfinger (including 'Without You'), Robin Trower, Elvis Costello and Art Garfunkel, as well as recording the EMI audition tapes for Kate Bush. He worked on several of McCartney's albums, winning another Grammy for *Band on the Run* (1973). Paul was best man at Emerick's wedding in 1979. He worked with the out-takes and unreleased cuts that became the three volume *Anthology* series.

In 2003 Geoff received a special Grammy (his fourth) for his technical work, and in 2006 he wrote a memoir, *Here, There and Everywhere*.

A superb technician who brought The Beatles' recordings to life.

EPSTEIN, BRIAN [1934–1967]

Brian's grandfather, Isaac Epstein, a penniless Polish immigrant, settled in Liverpool in 1901 and by sheer tenacity established a local business selling furniture, eventually calling it I. Epstein & Sons. One of the sons, Harry, married Malka ('Queenie') Hyman from Leeds and they had two sons, Brian Samuel (born 19 September 1934) and Clive John (born 1936). Largely on account of his shyness and Jewishness, Brian was bullied at school, including his public school (Wrekin), and left at 16 to enter the family business. He was equally uncomfortable with National Service and was robbed following a homosexual liaison. In 1956 he briefly studied at RADA, but he realised that his acting skills could be put to better use selling furniture.

Epstein persuaded his father to move into the city centre and to stock gramophone records. Two branches of NEMS (North End Music Stores) were opened, one in Whitechapel (he managed the records; Clive the electrical goods) and one mainly selling records in Great Charlotte Street (managed by Peter Brown). Although his interests lay in light classical music and show tunes, he proved to be a brilliant salesman, predicting, for example, that 'Johnny Remember Me' would fly to No. 1 and that the Everly Brothers had made a mistake with 'Muskrat'. Hence, his shops had copies of John Leyton's single when others in the locality had none; and he didn't have boxes of 'Muskrat' gathering dust.

Epstein determined to stock at least one copy of every record issued in the UK, making NEMS the most dependable store in Liverpool. Local beat groups were keen to cover obscure releases by American R&B artists. As NEMS had booths in which potential purchasers could hear the records, the musicians – including The Beatles – would go in, scribble down the words and chords, then say, 'Naw, don't want it.'

In 1961 a local art student, Bill Harry, persuaded Epstein to stock copies of his *Mersey Beat* newspaper. Epstein was soon contributing record reviews, all of which were available at NEMS (of course). He had read of The Beatles and his curiosity was aroused when a customer, Raymond Jones, asked for a copy of their German single 'My Bonnie'.

Accompanied by his assistant Alistair Taylor, Brian went to see The Beatles at a lunchtime session at the Cavern on 9 November 1961. As a debonair businessman, the sweaty club was not to his liking but he was transfixed by the group. When George Harrison asked, 'And what brings Mr Epstein here?', Brian realised that it wasn't just to ask about 'My Bonnie'. Much to the annoyance of his parents (they had suffered his short-lived passions), he said that he was going to manage the band through a new company, NEMS Enterprises. Others had tried to manage The Beatles

Engagements - week commencing 23.6.62

Saturday 23rd June - MEMORIAL HALL, NORTHWICH
You are required to play two spots 9.0 -
9.30 p.m. and 10.15 - 11.0 p.m. This
booking is for Lewis Buckley Entertainments
Limited and in that respect is an important
one as we would like to be offered some
return bookings as a result of this
engagement. Programme, continuity, suits,
white shirts, ties etc. all essential.

Sunday 24th June   - CASBAH CLUB (See Neil)

Monday 25th June   - Midday CAVERN CLUB (as usual)
PLAZA BALLROOM, ST. HELENS
Neil will call for you between 6.30 and
6.45 p.m. in order to arrive at St.Helens
not later than 7.20 p.m. This is our
first engagement for the "Whetstone
Circuit" who control 16 venues in the
Northwest.   There was some difficulty
in obtaining your fee for this booking
and the Directors of the Company concerned
are watching these four Monday bookings
most carefully and have assured me that
if successful they will be pleased to use
the group at other venues on their circuit.
For this first night, at least, programme,
continuity (as always) suits, white shirts
ties etc. One hour spot.

Wednesday 27th June- Midday CAVERN CLUB (as usual)
CAVERN CLUB (as usual)

Thursday 28th June - MAJESTIC BALLROOM, BIRKENHEAD.
Neil will call for you between 6.45 and
7.0 in order to arrive at The Majestic
not later than 7.30 p.m. Comments as
above for the St. Helen's booking apply
again here except that this is our first
booking for Top Rank who control, of
course, venues all over the country and
if successful this engagement (which is
also a season of three Thursdays) could
prove both now and when we have a disc
in the charts of great importance.
One hour spot.

Cont...../

Brian Epstein's personal, typewritten notes to the boys in 1962, given to Hunter Davies by Brian himself. These show how organised Brian was, despite his difficulties in getting money for one of the bookings at the Plaza Ballroom, St Helens. He instructs them to wear suits, white shirts – and to not be late.

before and even though he had no experience, they appreciated that Brian had the vision to take them forward; it wasn't his aim to make £10 profit on a dance.

The first management contract was for five years and gave NEMS Enterprises 10 per cent of their income up to £1,500 and 15 per cent above that. This was later changed to 25 per cent, which was not as severe as some commentators have suggested as Epstein was acting as both manager and agent. He put up their fees, expanded their catchment area and promoted some of the bigger concerts and dances himself.

In return The Beatles, or as he called them 'The Boys', had to behave themselves on stage: they should wear suits, not leathers; they must stop swearing and smoking; and they must always arrive in good time. By and large The Beatles, even John Lennon, accepted this while another Liverpool band, The Big Three, were continuously rebellious and unpleasant. 'Come on, Eppy,' teased Big Three Johnny Hutchinson, 'give me a fiver and I'll let you feel me arse.'

As an important record retailer, Epstein could ask Decca for an audition and although it was not successful, he had a copy of the tape to play elsewhere. Eventually he secured them a contract with Parlophone, and in August 1962 he sacked Pete Best, telling him that his drumming was not good enough. The new line-up recorded 'Love Me Do', but the story of Epstein purchasing 10,000 copies to push it into the charts is fiction: one, the listings were an amalgam of the chart positions of many different stores; and two, there were far easier and cheaper ways of fiddling the charts.

From the start BE (as he was often called) had told people that The Beatles were going to be bigger than Elvis. Did he believe that or was it management hype? Probably hype, as why else would he have bothered with the other acts? As

it is, NEMS Enterprises soon had a chart-busting roster with The Beatles, Gerry and The Pacemakers, Cilla Black, The Fourmost and Billy J. Kramer with The Dakotas. NEMS Enterprises had to move to London and Brian had manic years in which he was arranging personal appearances, record dates, TV and films for his artists (or 'artistes' as he called them.). A key advantage of having such a stable of talent was that it enabled him to devise complete touring packages and create Christmas specials. Unlike the money-grabbing managers of the day, Epstein took the concerns of his artists and his fans seriously.

In 1964 Brian Epstein took The Beatles to America and many commentators have criticised him for practically giving away the rights for official merchandise. Such comment is easy with hindsight but no one, not even Elvis, had been as big as this and Epstein was operating in new territory. When he realised his mistake, he had difficulty in telling The Beatles in case they wanted to replace him.

When Epstein appeared on *Desert Island Discs* in November 1964, he said that 'All My Loving' was his favourite Lennon and McCartney composition, thus revealing his taste for more middle of the road pop. Always the businessman, however (he couldn't stop himself), he also included their latest release, 'She's A Woman'. His 1964 autobiography, *A Cellarful of Noise*, was ghosted by Derek Taylor, who fabricated girlfriends and didn't reveal his addiction to gambling and rent boys. Even if he had wanted to, he could not tell the truth – homosexuality was still illegal. It is possible that he had a liaison with John Lennon when they went on holiday to Spain, but John Lennon often said things to shock people. While in Spain, Epstein loved the theatricality of bullfighting and did consider managing English bullfighter Henry Higgins.

Once NEMS Enterprises was in London, he expanded his empire (Bob Wooler called him 'The Nemperor') by taking on many other UK acts including Cliff Bennett, Sounds Incorporated, The Silkie and The Moody Blues.

When in 1965 the individual Beatles received MBEs for their services to exports, Epstein felt that he had been excluded because he was Jewish. Cilla Black liked to joke that the award stood for Mr Brian Epstein.

In 1965 Brian Epstein secured the Saville Theatre in London's West End and the following year he was putting on plays. These were not successful but the Sunday rock concerts were an instant winner with performances from Chuck Berry, Cream and Jimi Hendrix.

The Beatles had stopped live performances and so were less dependent on him, but he had visions of making Cilla Back an international star (a possibility) and Billy J. Kramer a film actor (no chance). Epstein himself had some thoughts on being a TV presenter, but his appearance as a guest host on the US variety show *Hullaballo* was wooden.

Brian Epstein was found dead in bed at his Belgravia home on Bank Holiday Monday, 27 August 1967. He had probably died two days earlier. Conspiracy theories abound, but the coroner ruled his death was an accidental overdose. His father had died recently and it seems unlikely that he would put his mother through another ordeal.

John Lennon told *Rolling Stone*, 'The Beatles were over when Brian died. It was just me and a backing group and Paul and a backing group. I knew we were in trouble then. I thought we've fucking had it.' Paul said, 'If anyone was the Fifth Beatle, it was Brian.'

Brain Epstein had died when he was only 33, although he seemed older, and as he left almost £500,000, it suggests he was rather better at business than some allow. Allen Klein rescued The Beatles when they were going into free fall and although he renegotiated their record contracts, he soon discovered that managing such a free-spirited group was not easy.

Brian Epstein is buried in the Jewish cemetery in Long Lane, Aintree, and the Neptune Theatre in Liverpool has been renamed the Epstein Theatre in his honour. 'I can't see Brian approving of that,' says his former employee, Tony Barrow. 'He wouldn't have settled for anything smaller than the Liverpool Empire.'

Manager of The Beatles from 1962-67. Sure, he made mistakes but he was a vastly positive influence in The Beatles' lives and career.

THE DEATH OF BRIAN EPSTEIN

Disc, September 1967

Ringo: 'It was lucky, in a funny way, that we got the news when we were in Bangor with the Maharishi. We asked him what to do and he told us we mustn't let it get us down. If we got really brought down about it Brian would know this because he would be able to feel our feelings in his spiritual state and depression is not good for anybody.'

John: 'He was due to come up to Bangor, it's a drag he never made it. It's a loss of genius but other geniuses' bodies have died and the world still gains from their spirits. Would The Beatles be where they are today if it weren't for Epstein? Not the same as we know it, no. But the question doesn't apply because we met him and what happened happened. We all knew what we wanted to get over and he helped us and we helped him.'

EVANS, MAL [1935–1976]

Malcolm Frederick Evans was a telephone engineer from the Mossley Hill suburb of Liverpool. He was married with a baby son, but when he was working around the city centre he could go to the Cavern at lunchtime. He was a diehard Elvis Presley fan, but was immediately impressed by The Beatles and soon requesting Elvis songs such as 'I Forgot To Remember To Forget'.

The Beatles would play with his name, sometimes calling him 'Malcontent'. He was six feet three inches tall, burly and muscular and George said to him, 'Mal, you're big and ugly so why don't you get a job as a bouncer? That way you get paid and can go into the band room and meet the bands.' So in 1962 Mal Evans started deputising for Paddy Delaney at the Cavern (one pound and ten shillings a night) or working on special shows for Brian Epstein (two pounds a night.). He was reliable and able to pacify potential troublemakers. Everybody loved Mal, and The Beatles would joke that he always had *Elvis Monthly* in his pocket.

As The Beatles became nationally known, Brian Epstein asked Mal to give up his job and assist Neil Aspinall as road manager. His wife Lily had some misgivings about this as he had rock-solid employment, but he went with The Beatles. His adventures appeared in *The Beatles Book Monthly*, although the articles were ghosted by Tony Barrow as part of that well-oiled publicity machine. In 1965 Mal went with The Beatles' party to meet Elvis Presley and he was the most impressed.

As Mal was musical, he found himself contributing to The Beatles' records – a bit of Hammond organ on 'You Won't See Me', a tambourine on 'Dear Prudence', a trumpet on 'Helter Skelter' and an anvil on 'Maxwell's Silver Hammer'. He sang backing vocals on 'Yellow Submarine' and 'You Know My Name (Look Up the Number)'. Indeed, there are enough tracks to issue *Mal Evans' Greatest Hits.* He appeared on screen in *Help!*, *Magical Mystery Tour* and *Let It Be*. His diaries suggest that he was writing songs with Lennon and McCartney but this is fantasy.

In 1968 Mal became an executive at Apple Records and he discovered the Iveys, who became Badfinger. Following his time with The Beatles, he had acquired a love for LSD and he showed Badfinger how to party. He was less successful when it came to producing records and they soon looked elsewhere.

He resigned from Apple as he didn't care for Allen Klein, and settled in America. Or rather he didn't. Having been at the centre of the musical universe for many years, he felt restless and uneasy and couldn't hold down a regular job. He left his wife and took up with a young mother and her daughter in Los Angeles. He had hopes for a new group he had discovered, Natural Gas. On 5 January 1976, he was depressed, taking drugs and waving around an air rifle. His girlfriend Fran Hughes called the police, who misread the situation and shot him dead. Fran sent the bill for cleaning the blood off the carpet to Apple, who balked at paying it. Mal's ashes were sent to the UK but got lost in the mail.

His memoir, *Living The Beatles Legend*, written with John Hoernle, remains unpublished but Mal's sister sometimes appeared at Beatles events.

Nowadays rock stars are surrounded by minders, but The Beatles could rely on Mal. He got the gear from A to B and a lot more besides.

EVERETT, KENNY [1944–1995]

The staid BBC disc jockeys of the early 1960s were in total contrast to their wild and wacky counterparts in America. The DJ who changed all that was Kenny Everett, but he was so unique that he owed little to the Americans. In addition to his zaniness and highly engaging, over-the-top personality, Kenny Everett was technically adept and could create his jingles and sound effects without outside help.

Kenny Everett was born Maurice Cole in Liverpool in 1944, and while working in a bakery he spent his evenings with tape machines, merging records together and adding comic vocals. In December 1964 he joined a pirate ship, making offshore broadcasts from Radio London. His highly irreverent style was much appreciated but he was always prone to going too far. His first clash was in mocking Radio London's sponsored religious programme *The World Tomorrow*, run by Garner Ted Armstrong. He was sacked.

In 1967 Kenny Everett was part of the new intake of DJs for BBC Radio 1 and he had several scoops with The Beatles surrounding the release of *Sgt Pepper* and 'All You Need Is Love'. The Beatles enjoyed his company so much that he produced their Christmas flexidiscs for 1968 and 1969.

In 1970 Kenny was sacked by the BBC, after suggesting that the Transport Minister's wife had bribed her driving examiner. He later joined commercial station Capital Radio, and was the first to champion Queen's 'Bohemian Rhapsody'.

From the late 1970s, Everett was a television star, first for ITV and then the BBC. He created characters such as Captain Kremmen, Sid Snot and Cupid Stunt and made catchphrases out of 'naughty bits' and 'all in the best possible taste'. He often dressed in drag with a beard and was reprimanded by Penelope Keith on a live show for inhaling helium and speaking in a funny voice.

As with Spike Milligan, Kenny Everett had long bursts of manic energy and also suffered from depression. He was gay and in 1993 he announced that he had AIDS, saying, 'We all have death hang-

ing over us. It's just that I'll get there a bit sooner than most.' Kenny Everett died in 1995.

Kenny had the same approach to authority as The Beatles and if told not to do something, he did it.

FAITHFULL, MARIANNE [B. 1946]

What artist in the sixties had a better stage name than Marianne Faithfull? And it was her real name too. What's more, everything about her was unusual. Her father, Glynn Faithfull, was a psychologist and university lecturer who engaged in intelligence work during the war, and her mother Eva had been a Weimar cabaret dancer in Berlin in the twenties and thirties. She was Austro-Hungarian and was related to Baron von Sacher-Masoch, who gave his name to masochism. She referred to herself as Baroness Erisso.

Marianne went to convent school, where she was spotted by Andrew Loog Oldham, manager of the Rolling Stones, who described her as 'an angel with big tits'. She sang Jagger and Richards' dreamy 'As Tears Go By', which led to a run of successful singles including 'Come And Stay with Me' and 'This Little Bird'.

In 1965 Paul McCartney attended the session for her cover of 'Yesterday', arranged by Mike Leander, but it was Matt Monro's version that made the Top 10. Paul apparently wrote a song, 'Etcetera', for Marianne but she had no memory of this.

Faithfull married art dealer John Dunbar in 1965, and their son Nicholas was born later that year. The two Johns (Dunbar and Lennon) would take LSD together, and in 1966 Dunbar invited Lennon to an exhibition of Yoko Ono's work. We all know what happened next. When John and Marianne Dunbar split, she became Mick Jagger's girlfriend. She made the tabloids, anonymously, as the naked girl wrapped in a rug when the police raided the home of Keith Richards in February 1967.

Mick and Marianne can be seen together in the studio for The Beatles' 'All You Need Is Love', and they went with The Beatles to Bangor to see the Maharishi. She became a heavy drugs user and wrote 'Sister Morphine' with Mick and Keith. In the seventies she was seriously addicted but, nevertheless, made the stunning album *Broken English* (1979), which included her version of 'Working Class Hero' and managed to free herself from her addiction. Her concerts today, half spoken, half sung in a deep voice far removed from that of 1965, recall the German cabarets of her mother's day. She is an acquired taste, to be sure, and in an infamous feature the journalist Lynn Barber was certainly not hooked.

But 4 if this were a Stones encyclopaedia.

FASCHER, HORST [B.1936]

Horst Fascher is a small, well-built, cheerful man with a silver stud in his ear. At Beatles conventions, he seems like your favourite uncle, but make no mistake, Horst Fascher is the toughest of all The Beatles' associates. The three Fascher brothers, Horst, Fredi and Uwe, were menacing guys who had trouble with the authorities, dishing out their own form of justice in the back alleys of St Pauli. Mess with them at your peril.

Horst had been a successful flyweight boxer, representing both Hamburg and West Germany. However, his career took a dive in 1958 when a foolish sailor saw him on the Reeperbahn and referred to his lack of height by calling him 'a pipsqueak'. Fascher punched him hard and he fell to the ground, hitting his head on the kerb and dying. Fascher was found guilty of manslaugh-

ter and was given a year's imprisonment. The Hamburg Boxing Academy withdrew his licence to box.

In the St Pauli clubs the waiters doubled as bouncers, and upon release Fascher found employment at the Lachende Vagabund, but wanted to work in a music club. He was mesmerised by both Tony Sheridan and The Beatles at the Kaiserkeller. Horst moved to the Kaiserkeller but he also spoke to the young Peter Eckhorn and persuaded him to turn one of his family's venues into a beat club, giving it an English name, Top Ten Club.

In mid-January 1962, Horst Fascher came to Liverpool with the British rock 'n' roll singer Roy Young, but was now working for Manfred Weissleder, who was opening the Star-Club and wanted The Beatles.

The Beatles were restless at the Star-Club, knowing that they were riding a wave and desperate to consolidate their success in the UK. On New Year's Eve 1962 they gave their final appearance there, which was captured on tape. Horst Fascher joins The Beatles for 'Hallelujah I Love Her' and his brother Fredi, then a waiter/bouncer at the club, sings 'Be-Bop-A-Lula'. Horst Fascher says, 'The day I have never forgotten is New Year's Eve 1962 and it was The Beatles' last time in Hamburg. I was the singer and The Beatles backed me, even John Lennon said, "Thank you, Horst" so he was satisfied about it.'

Spencer Lloyd Mason, manager of The Mojos and other Liverpool bands, recalled, 'I would ask Horst for the money for the three or four bands who were working there and once he said to me, "Come back Monday." I said, "No, I want the money now. The boys have to eat." "Come back Monday," he yelled. The third time I asked him, he put me up against the wall and I got the message: "Okay, I'll come back Monday".'

Mark Peters of The Silhouettes ran into trouble the first night he played at the Star-Club. 'Horst

Fascher gave me a bunch of flowers, and I threw them back because I thought that he was insinuating that I was a poof. It was hard to calm him down because he wanted to kill me. In Germany, giving flowers is one of the biggest compliments he could have paid me.'

Many of Horst's friends from the boxing academy worked with him in the Hamburg beat clubs, but there were tensions between the venues. The Top Ten and the Star-Club decided to settle their differences by a late-night fight, each club choosing their best fighter. Horst chose himself for the Star-Club and he knocked his hapless opponent senseless. Horst was arrested over this, and several other incidents, but there was always difficulty in finding witnesses who would testify. Horst was eventually jailed. When he came out, Horst was barred from the St Pauli clubs, so he suggested to Tony Sheridan that he accompany him to Vietnam where Tony would entertain the troops.

Late in life, Horst Fascher married Alison Ruffley, the daughter of another Liverpool singer who played in Hamburg, Bill Ruffley, known as 'Faron'. They named their son Rory after Rory Storm. In 1992, the two-year-old boy was sleeping in a folding wall bed, which returned to its vertical position and suffocated him.

Two years later, Horst and his Hungarian girlfriend had a baby daughter, Marie-Sophie, but she was born with a heart defect. After talking with Paul McCartney, Horst brought the baby to the Great Ormond Street Hospital for treatment. Although she survived the surgery, she died a fortnight later. Paul settled the bills, an indication of his high regard for Horst Fascher.

Although not a club owner at the time, Horst Fascher has a significant role as it is through him that The Beatles came to play in the Top Ten and the Star-Club.

GARRY, LEN [B. 1942]

Len Garry was born in Liverpool in 1942 and his father was a printer for the *Liverpool Echo*. He attended the Liverpool Institute and was in the same class as Paul McCartney and Ivan Vaughan. Ivan introduced Len to John Lennon in 1955, and he joined The Quarrymen at the end of 1956. He would have preferred being the lead singer, but he had to be content with plucking the tea-chest bass. Tall and gangly, Len is easily recognisable on that famous photograph of The Quarrymen at the St Peter's garden fete, Woolton, in July 1957. 'I did do some backing vocals,' he says, 'but usually there was only one microphone – and John had that.'

Len's stay in The Quarrymen was curtailed as he contracted tubercular meningitis. He attributes this to the appalling sanitation at the Cavern, and he could be right. Len was in hospital for seven months; his days as a Quarryman were over; and he was only 16.

After going to night school to catch up, Len was articled to a firm of architects, and then worked as an architect's assistant for Birkenhead Council. His wife Sue was a nurse and he followed her into a Pentecostal sect. They were told that pop groups were evil, and as a result they destroyed Len's photos of The Quarrymen.

In the seventies, they moved south and settled in Exeter with their family of four children. They emigrated to New Zealand in 1987 but soon returned to Liverpool where Len worked in a day care centre and sometimes sang to his charges.

Len became an important part of the re-formed Quarrymen in 1997, sharing the lead vocals with Rod Davis and playing guitar. He has a rock 'n' roll feeling in his voice and could easily have played with a hit-making Liverpool band in the sixties.

A journeyman Quarryman whose talents could have been better employed within the group.

GENTLE, JOHNNY [B. 1936]

That birth year may surprise you. Johnny Gentle was no teen idol – his teenage years being well behind him – when he met rock 'n' roll impresario Larry Parnes. Larry made the 22-year-old a teenager again.

John Askew was a ship's carpenter from Litherland who sang in local talent shows and social clubs as Ricky Damone, the name a combination of Ricky Nelson and Vic Damone. In 1958 he read how Parnes had signed another Liverpool singer, Billy Fury, so he sent Parnes his photograph with a note indicating that he too could write songs. As he was handsome with a winsome smile, Parnes invited him to London. He played him a Marty Wilde record and told him to sing along. 'Very good,' said Parnes. 'You are now Johnny Gentle and earning fifteen pounds a week.'

The Gentle name was chosen because Parnes wanted him to sing dreamy beat-ballads and set the girls swooning. His first singles were 'Wendy' and 'Milk From The Coconut'. He appeared on the teenage TV shows *Cool for Cats* and *Boy Meets Girls,* and got to know Eddie Cochran, who was impressed that he had made his own guitar.

Following an audition in Liverpool, Parnes asked The Beatles to back Johnny on a short Scottish tour in May 1960. The tour was uneventful but Johnny did inform Parnes of their potential. While in Inverness, he showed John Lennon his composition, 'I've Just Fallen For Someone', and said he couldn't think of a middle section. Lennon supplied a few lines, admittedly based around Barrett Strong's 'Money', but it worked.

In the summer, Johnny Gentle had a residency in *Idols on Parade* in Blackpool, where he was backed by another Liverpool band, Cass and The Cassanovas. Then it was all over: Parnes dropped him. He had made four singles, had four chances as it were, and none had made the charts.

In 1962 Adam Faith recorded 'I've Just Fallen For Someone' for his second Parlophone album, effectively the first Lennon composition on record, albeit uncredited. Later in the year, and just before 'Love Me Do', Johnny Gentle recorded his own version for Parlophone. In 1964 Johnny replaced Gordon Mills in The Viscounts. After touring for some years, he started his own joinery business in Bromley and settled down to a family life. Occasionally he appears at Beatles conventions.

The Beatles discovered that life could be a dreary slog even if you had made a couple of records.

GERRY AND THE PACEMAKERS

When the comedian Stan Boardman made his debut at the Cavern in 2008, he described the Germans bombing Liverpool in 1942, adding, 'And what did Mr and Mrs Marsden do? They named their son Gerry.'

Frederick and Mary Marsden lived in the Dingle area of Liverpool and had two sons, Freddie (1940–2006) and Gerry (b.1942). Frederick played the ukulele in a local pub on Saturday nights, and in 1956 Gerry and Freddie started playing skiffle music and then rock 'n' roll. Freddie, who graduated from playing a Quality Street tin to a full drum kit, recalled, 'We called ourselves the Mars Bars and we wrote for permission to use their name. We never thought of sponsorship. They wrote back and told us to stop using the name.'

The group became Gerry and The Pacemakers after their pianist, Arthur McMahon, heard a sports commentator refer to an athlete as a pacemaker. A number of fledgling Liverpool groups supported the American rock 'n' roll star Gene Vincent at Liverpool Stadium in May 1960 – Gerry and The Pacemakers, championed by Bob

Wooler, were chosen but The Beatles, much to their chagrin, were not considered good enough.

The show's organiser, Allan Williams, arranged for Liverpool groups to play in Hamburg, but Gerry and The Pacemakers were reluctant to go at first because of their day jobs, Gerry being a railway porter. They developed a popular act and played the hits of the day. If it made the charts on Friday, it could be in their repertoire on Saturday. They eventually went to Hamburg in 1961 to play the Top Ten Club, and Gerry Marsden was mesmerised by Tony Sheridan. 'I watched him as much as I could and he influenced me in the way he could play rhythm guitar and drive the band like mad.'

Gerry was also traumatised by another event. 'John Lennon and I went down the Herbertstrasse and the windows were full of young ladies who couldn't afford many clothes. John said, "Let's go in," and this German geezer said, "Ya vol, vot?" I said, "Can we come in please?" and he said, "Eighty Deutschemarks." John had twenty and so did I, and we asked if forty was any good. He shouted at us and we left. Next week, same house, knock, knock, knock, same big man. I said, "Here's the money" and he said, "Danke schoen." He came back with the biggest woman I have ever seen. I looked at John and he looked at me and we jumped up and ran out of the door. I said, "What a waste of time, John. Eighty Deutschemarks and we got nothing." He said, "I did. I got the shock of me bloody life."'

On one memorable night in 1961, The Beatles and Gerry and The Pacemakers (by now Gerry, Freddie, guitarist Les Chadwick (b. 1943) and saxophonist/keyboard player Les Maguire (b. 1941)) combined forces as The Beatmakers with no rehearsals for a night at Litherland Town Hall.

The Beatles and Gerry and The Pacemakers were the regular groups at the Cavern's lunchtime sessions, as well as numerous evening appearances.

Gerry says, 'The Cavern was always special, it was always like a party when we played there. They would shout out for songs and we would wear jeans and sweaters until Brian Epstein made us wear suits. It was a dirty, horrible cellar that stank of sweat and Dettol, but it had a great atmosphere.'

In May 1962, after returning from Hamburg, the group was signed by Brian Epstein. George Martin wanted The Beatles to record a Tin Pan Alley song by Mitch Murray, 'How Do You Do It?'. The Beatles thought it a jaunty, inconsequential pop song but did, reluctantly, commit it to tape. Brian Epstein told George Martin that he had another group who could perform the song to perfection – Gerry and The Pacemakers. He was right – Gerry's delivery owed something to both Tommy Steele and Bobby Vee, and the chirpy song made No. 1 in April 1963. Many fans preferred the B-side, a Beatley ballad, 'Away From You', which Gerry had written for his girlfriend Pauline Behan while he was in Hamburg. They wed in 1965, the delay caused by Brian Epstein, who thought Gerry would lose his female following if he were married. Brian was angry when Les Maguire ignored his warnings and married his German girlfriend.

Gerry and The Pacemakers had a second No. 1 with Mitch Murray's innuendo-ridden 'I Like It'. Gerry had seen Tony Sheridan singing 'You'll Never Walk Alone' from *Carousel* as the big ballad in his act, and wanting to better Paul McCartney, who was singing 'Over The Rainbow', they had started performing the song around the Merseyside clubs. George Martin liked the idea of this being their single and he added strings. As a result, Gerry and The Pacemakers became the first act to reach No. 1 with their first three singles. Gerry supported Everton Football Club, but changed his allegiance once the Kop started chanting 'You'll Never Walk Alone', loving both its sentiment and its long notes. It has become the anthem for Liverpool FC.

Gerry himself wrote their fourth single, 'I'm The One', but it was not quite strong enough to knock 'Needles and Pins' by The Searchers from the top. Freddie thought they would have had a fourth No. 1 if they had instead released 'Pretend' as a single, from their LP *How Do You Like It?*, as that was such a popular part of their stage show.

Their fifth Top 10 single was with a group composition, 'Don't Let The Sun Catch You Crying', although they had to concede part of the royalties to Ray Charles's publishers as he had recorded a song with the same title. It was the group's first US hit, reaching No. 4, and was subsequently recorded by José Feliciano.

Because The Beatles movie *A Hard Day's Night* had been such a success, Tony Warren, the creator of *Coronation Street*, was asked to write a film for Gerry and The Pacemakers. It was set in Liverpool and Warren called it *Ferry Cross the Mersey*. The title gave Gerry his most poignant composition, used by Mersey Ferries to this day. Ignore the plot, ignore the silliness, the film is a wonderful documentary about the Liverpool of 1964, much of which has been replaced.

When Gerry had been at the Cavern, he had enjoyed hearing the record that the DJ Bob Wooler played as people were leaving – Bobby Darin's 'I'll Be There'. The group recorded it as a single, and in 1965 it became their final Top 20 hit. By now, The Beatles were experimenting with *Rubber Soul*, and more sophisticated sounds were coming in: it's doubtful if they even gave a second thought to what Gerry was doing. Similarly, the psychedelia of 1966 held no interest for Gerry and he was far too down to earth to follow The Beatles and visit the Maharishi.

In 1967 Gerry Marsden was offered a starring role replacing Joe Brown in the West End musi-

cal *Charlie Girl*. In accepting the work, he made The Pacemakers redundant and created ill feeling. They thought of having a replacement singer, but in the end Les Maguire and Les Chadwick bought a garage and Freddie joined the GPO. Gerry Marsden made a single to promote the show with the Liverpool actor Derek Nimmo, and although he released several further records, none of them made the charts. He became a children's favourite via regular appearances with the glove puppet Sooty.

Gerry returned to rock 'n' roll with a new look Pacemakers in 1973. An audience of 13,000 came to Madison Square Garden to see him on a show with Herman's Hermits, Wayne Fontana and The Searchers.

In 1985 Gerry wanted to make a charity single for the disaster fund following the fire at Bradford Football Club. He asked a host of celebrities to join him for a new version of 'You'll Never Walk Alone'. Released under the name of The Crowd, it became a No. 1 record.

A few weeks after the Hillsborough disaster in 1989, Gerry Marsden led the community singing at the local derby between Liverpool and Everton. He revived 'Ferry Cross The Mersey' with fellow Liverpudlians Paul McCartney, Holly Johnson and The Christians for the appeal. It was another No. 1. Paul also wrote the sleeve notes for Gerry's 1985 album *The Lennon/McCartney Songbook*.

Despite health setbacks, Gerry has a tough working schedule, both with The Pacemakers and undertaking a huge number of social events. He was awarded the MBE in 2003 and did much to help Liverpool win its bid to become the European Capital of Culture in 2008.

In 1961/62, Gerry and his Pacemakers were the biggest threat to The Beatles' supremacy in the Liverpool beat venues.

GOOD, JACK [B. 1931]

In 1956, the BBC employed Jack Good, a young Oxford graduate in English philology and president of the university's drama society, for eighteen pounds a week. The Corporation wanted him to create programmes for the new teenage audience. They had picked the right man, although his rebellious ideas did not go down well with the status quo. He thought that rock 'n' roll singers should not mime but perform live among teenage dancers and he came up with *Six-Five Special*, which started in February 1957 and became a phenomenal success. Good recognised that a show featuring the likes of Tommy Steele would attract teenage viewers, but despaired when the BBC insisted on sober features about classical music, army recruitment and hill-walking. He was fired after using the programme's name for a rock 'n' roll touring show, without seeking permission.

Good moved to ITV and created *Oh Boy!*, a fast-moving, barnstorming music show with around 15 songs in half an hour. Cliff Richard and Marty Wilde became stars and Good featured many of Larry Parnes' artists, including Billy Fury, Dickie Pride and Johnny Gentle, as well as visiting US stars – Johnny Cash, Brenda Lee, Ronnie Hawkins and Conway Twitty. Good was disappointed when Cliff released 'Living Doll' and became a family entertainer, despairing, 'I had spent hours making this guy mean, moody and magnificent and he threw it away with one bloody song.' Few of the programmes have been preserved, but they are fondly remembered as there was nothing else like them.

Good wrote a highly engaging and opinionated weekly column for *Disc*, and produced Billy Fury ('Wondrous Place', *The Sound of Fury* album, 1960), The Vernons Girls and Jet Harris. There was a High Court argument over who was Lord Rockingham: was it the arranger Harry Robinson or Jack Good who formed the band? In the end, Robinson could take the band on the road and Good held the rights for records and television, but Good simply put his energies into a new band, The Firing Squad.

Marty Wilde hosted his next series, *Boy Meets Girls*, which included several performances from visiting Americans Eddie Cochran and Gene Vincent. Inspired by staging *Richard III* at Oxford University, Good dressed Vincent in black leather for an iconic rock 'n' roll image. Good's third ITV show, *Wham!*, was an anticlimax and a sign that he was losing interest. He moved to the States, working mostly as an actor, but he returned to make the TV special *Around The Beatles* in 1964, which featured his latest discovery, P.J. Proby. Good produced his first hit records, 'Hold Me' and 'Together'.

Good shook up American teenage television with *Shindig!*, a live music show with Leon Russell, Glen Campbell and James Burton in the back-up band. This time he discovered Sonny and Cher and The Righteous Brothers. A special edition of *Shindig!* was made in London with The Beatles and screened on American television in October 1964. Good played a hotel clerk in the Elvis Presley film *Clambake* (1967) and the following year his rock 'n' roll *Othello*, called *Catch My Soul*, was staged in Los Angeles with Jerry Lee Lewis playing Iago. It came to the West End with himself as Othello.

Rather disappointingly, Jack Good revived *Oh Boy!* for ITV in the late 1970s. Rock 'n' roll was by then light-hearted cabaret, although the programme made Shakin' Stevens a star. Good devised the hit West End musicals *Elvis* and *Good Rockin' Tonite!*, which told his life story. In 2003 he unveiled a statue of Billy Fury in Liverpool, but his main interest was in painting religious murals. He said, 'I'm always glad that I was the first rock 'n' roll producer, as if I'd been the second I might not have made a name for myself.'

Rock 'n' roll TV would not have been the same without him.

GORMAN, JOHN – SEE SCAFFOLD

GRETTY, JIM [1913–1992]

James Constantine Gretty, to give him his full name, was born in 1913 and expected to be working until retirement in the Blood Transfusion Service. He loved country and western music and would dress as a cowboy and sing with his guitar in local variety shows. Quite possibly, he was the first guitarist that John Lennon saw. John was to call him 'Grim Jetty'.

In 1956 Frank Hessy asked Jim if he would demonstrate the guitar to potential purchasers at his music centre. Initially, this was at weekends but it soon became a full-time job. He also gave out-of-hours instructions to would-be guitarists. Everybody wanted to learn his so-called 'jazz chord'.

Most musicians moved on from Jim Gretty, but he got many Merseybeat musicians started. He promoted the occasional show, the most notable being at the Albany, Maghull, in 1961 where The Beatles played on a variety bill topped by Ken Dodd.

Nearly all the Merseybeat guitarists spoke fondly of Jim Gretty as his enthusiasm got them started.

GRIFFITHS, BRIAN – SEE BIG THREE, THE

GRIFFITHS, ERIC [1940–2005]

John Lennon's Quarrymen would not have existed without Eric Griffiths' staunch support and he remained a Quarryman for five months.

Eric Griffiths was born in Denbigh in 1940 and his father, a fighter pilot, was killed in action a few months later. After the war, his mother, who worked for the Employment Exchange, moved to Bootle with Eric and his sister Joan. When Eric was ten the family had a further move to Woolton, and on Griffiths' first day in Quarry Bank High School he met two rebellious pupils, John Lennon and Pete Shotton. They grew up with an interest in girls, clothes and cigarettes, and, come 1956, the skiffle music of Lonnie Donegan. 'We both went to a guitar teacher in Hunts Cross,' Griffiths recalled, 'but the idea of trying to play the guitar properly and not being able to get a tune out of it for some time was pretty boring. John's mother retuned our guitar strings and showed us her banjo chords and we played in that manner until Paul McCartney joined. We were more interested in playing than learning.'

When the 15-year-old guitarist George Harrison joined the group in 1958, Griffiths was asked to switch to bass, but he could not afford a new instrument. Griffiths became an officer cadet in the Merchant Navy. In 1963 he heard The Beatles' 'Please Please Me' while in the Persian Gulf, but he never basked in reflected glory.

Eric found his niche when he joined the prison service in 1967 and became the head of planning and promotion for detention centres in Scotland. In 1985 Griffith bought a launderette and developed a chain of dry-cleaners around Edinburgh.

In 1997 Griffiths was reunited with Pete Shotton, Len Garry, Colin Hanton and Rod Davis and they re-formed as The Quarrymen. Griffiths had a crumpled face but he retained his mop of thick brown hair. He was too taciturn to be much of a stage performer but he was always courteous with fans. Asked if they sounded like they did in 1957, he responded, 'Yes, we were pretty awful back then, much the same as tonight.' He died in Edinburgh in 2005.

He encouraged John to keep The Quarrymen going.

GUITAR, JOHNNY – SEE STORM, RORY AND THE HURRICANES

GUSTAFSON, JOHNNY – SEE BIG THREE, THE

HAMILTON, RICHARD [1922–2011]

The contrast between the covers of *Sgt Pepper* (1967) and *The Beatles* (1968) could hardly be greater, and many purchasers would have been surprised to know that the white sleeve had been designed by a leading British artist, Richard Hamilton.

In 1956 Hamilton exhibited a collage, *Just what is it that makes today's homes so different, so appealing?*, which became the first well-known painting of the British branch of the Pop Art movement.

Like Peter Blake, Richard Hamilton found great pleasure in everyday objects and when he curated an exhibition at the Royal Academy in 1978 he placed ironing boards and easy chairs in the gallery rooms alongside the paintings.

When the Rolling Stones were convicted of drug offences, he created a collage that appealed to Paul McCartney and led to him being invited to design the packaging for the follow-up to *Sgt Pepper*. Hamilton suggested the simplest of titles, *The Beatles*, and a white sleeve with an embossed name and a serial number so that, for the first time, each album that was purchased would be individual. Hamilton also created a poster of photographs covering their career.

Richard Hamilton realised the potential of computers and digital printers for art and he replaced such terminology as 'oil on canvas' with 'Epson inkjet on Hewlett-Packard'. In his eighties he returned to painting the female nude, and he had one such painting on his easel when he collapsed and died aged nearly 90: what a way to go.

Sometimes the simplest ideas are the best.

HANTON, COLIN [B. 1938]

Colin Hanton was born in Bootle, a northern suburb of Liverpool, in 1938 and when he left school he became an apprentice upholsterer. This became his life's work and one major commission was to fit the seating for 60,000 passenger seats on buses.

As Colin was known to have bought a set of drums from Hessy's, he was invited to join The Quarrymen. He gave them a steady beat, nothing fancy, but they got by and he can be heard on the private recording they made in 1958 of 'That'll Be The Day' and 'In Spite Of All The Danger'. It was included on The Beatles' *Anthology* in 1995 and Colin, a very modest man, was amazed to find his music in 13 million homes.

He met his fellow Quarrymen at the fiftieth anniversary party for the Cavern in January 1997 and as a result, he has toured the world with the re-formed group.

Colin kept the beat in The Quarrymen.

HARRISON, GEORGE [1943–2001]

George Harrison was born at home in Wavertree, Liverpool, on 25 February 1943, the fourth child of Harold and Louise. Like John Lennon, he attended Dovedale Road School, but they didn't know each other. In 1949 the family moved to Speke, and in 1954 George passed the 11-plus, enabling him to go to the Liverpool Institute. He did little academic work and annoyed the authorities by misinterpreting the dress code, looking very cool with his quiff and drainpipe trousers. He passed O-level Art and became an electrician's apprentice at Blacklers department store.

Encouraged by his mother, George practised the guitar, mostly by listening to records, and discovered he had a good ear for music. With his brother Peter (b. 1940) and some friends, George performed as The Rebels at the British Legion Club in Speke. Another 'Inny' boy, Paul McCartney, invited George to see The Quarrymen in February 1958, and despite George's youth, John allowed him into the group. His proficiency can be heard on 'In Spite Of All The Danger', a private recording made a few months later.

George, who had no intention of sticking to a routine job, went with The Beatles to Germany in August 1960, his understanding parents raising no objections. Their repertoire had to expand rapidly to cope with playing up to six hours a night, enabling George to include Carl Perkins songs at every opportunity. Unlike John and Paul, he sang in a deadpan Scouse accent and some German girls screamed for the young boy. He added an important third part harmony, which would make The Beatles sound very distinctive, but perhaps because of his age, perhaps because of his personality, he was very much in the shadow of John and Paul. In November 1960 the German authorities deported George for being underage.

At The Beatles' recording session for Parlophone on 11 September 1962, George Martin said, 'Let me know if there's anything you don't like', to which Harrison replied, 'Well, for a start, I don't like your tie.'

Everybody had their favourite Beatle and George was well represented, especially as he took the lead vocals on two of their early tracks, 'Do You Want To Know A Secret' and 'Roll Over Beethoven', which was often their opening number. Bill Harry encouraged George to write his own songs, which led to 'Don't Bother Me' on *With The Beatles* (1963). He only had one or two songs per album, but they were good ones including 'If I Needed Someone' (also a hit single for The Hollies), 'Taxman' (showing his obsession with money) and 'Only A Northern Song' (suggesting he was not happy with the publishing arrangements). Intriguingly, John and/or Paul were often missing from the sessions for George's songs: when George published his book of lyrics, *I Me Mine* (1980), he hardly mentioned them in the text.

During 1963 George Harrison became known as 'the quiet one', and while he was certainly quieter than the garrulous John and Paul, he could hold his own when talking guitars. In 1964 George acquired a Rickenbacker electric 12-string guitar and played it on the album *A Hard Day's Night*. As his style was copied by Roger McGuinn, it could be argued that George Harrison was the instigator of that chiming folk-rock sound. He played a classical guitar on 'And I Love Her', and introduced the wah-wah pedal to The Beatles (and possibly the world) on 'I Need You'.

In February 1964 Harrison's influenza nearly led to him missing *The Ed Sullivan Show* but he recovered just in time. While making *A Hard Day's Night* in March 1964, George met and then dated the model Pattie Boyd. They married on 21 January 1966 but had no children.

It was all smoking in them days. George has a fag, or similar, in San Franciso in August 1967, when he mingled with the hippies in Haight Ashbury. © Bettmann / Contributor

After the final concert of their 1966 American tour, on August 29 at Candlestick Park, San Francisco, George got on the plane and said, 'That's it, I'm not a Beatle any more.' That was impulsive but telling; The Beatles never played another concert.

George first visited India in September 1966, and he became interested in Indian music, eastern religion and transcendental meditation. He persuaded the other Beatles to join him and Pattie at a seminar hosted by Maharishi Mahesh Yogi in Bangor, Wales, in August 1967. Although the other Beatles would fall out with the Maharishi, George stayed loyal. He wrote a song about the experience, 'Not Guilty', which was recorded by The Beatles but not released until *Anthology 3* (1996). That was often the way with George; Lennon and McCartney dominated the albums and singles with their compositions and George had to fight hard for his songs.

In 1965 George brought the sitar to popular music by playing it on 'Norwegian Wood' and he wrote his own composition, 'Love You To' (1966), a love song for Pattie, which featured sitar and tabla. At the time, many purchasers thought that George's 'Within You, Without You' was the weakest track on *Sgt Pepper*, but now it is regarded as one of the best. Harrison took instruction on playing the sitar from a master player, Ravi Shankar.

George was a very effective producer for The Beatles' Apple label, producing Jackie Lomax's' 'Sour Milk Sea' (which he also wrote), the Radha Krishna Temple's 'Hare Krishna Mantra' and Billy Preston's 'That's The Way God Planned It'. He brought to a Beatles session Billy Preston, whose organ playing is featured on 'Get Back'. George and Eric Clapton wrote 'Badge', a hit single for Cream. He wrote 'Here Comes The Sun' in Eric's garden after leaving a tedious business meeting at Apple.

Harrison wrote the Eastern score for the film *Wonderwall*, which starred Jane Birkin, and released an album called *Electronic Sound* (1969). He enjoyed this aspect of Apple so much that in 1974 he set up his own label, Dark Horse, and produced the band Splinter.

The origins of several of George's songs come from elsewhere. Part of the line, 'While my guitar gently weeps' can be found in the Chinese text *I Ching*; the lyric of 'Savoy Truffle' comes from a box of chocolates; and James Taylor recorded a love song called 'Something In The Way She Moves' for Apple some months before The Beatles' 'Something'. However, the purloining of 'He's So Fine' by The Chiffons for the melody of 'My Sweet Lord', a No. 1 solo single in 1971, was a step too far. Harrison commented on the judge's decision in 'This Song' (1976), made with his friend Eric Idle.

For all that, his triple album *All Things Must Pass* (1970) was a remarkable work, beautifully produced by Phil Spector and revealing how restricted he had been in The Beatles. He supported humanitarian causes and his *Concert For Bangla Desh* (1971) brought together Bob Dylan, Eric Clapton, Billy Preston, Leon Russell, Ringo Starr and himself.

In 1970 George bought Friar Park in Henley-on-Thames for £140,000 and from this moment on, he was regarded as a recluse. However, as Friar Park was a 120-room mansion with large grounds, it is easy to appreciate that George was otherwise occupied. He became an expert gardener and his other pastimes were motor racing and the films of George Formby. He recorded Formby's songs in private sessions with his neighbour, Joe Brown.

In a very amicable arrangement, Pattie moved over to his best friend Eric Clapton. Pattie and George were divorced in 1977 and she married Eric in 1979. George, who was known to play the field, had a close relationship with Ringo's wife Maureen, but in 1978 he married Mexican

Olivia Arias, the same year that their son Dhani was born.

George did spectacular work for the British film industry when he established HandMade films in 1979, and over ten years he produced such classics as *Monty Python's Life of Brian* (1979), *Time Bandits* (1981), *The Long Good Friday* (1981), *Mona Lisa* (1986) and *Withnail and I* (1987). It ended in tears when he had to sue his business partner, and he then sold the company.

In 1988 George was part of supergroup The Traveling Wilburys, with Bob Dylan, Jeff Lynne, Tom Petty and Roy Orbison. Following the death of Orbison, the second album was an anticlimax. In 1991/92, George toured with Eric Clapton, and in 1992 he gave a concert at the Royal Albert Hall to promote the UK Natural Law Party.

In 1997 George was treated for cancer and lost part of a lung. Two years later he was attacked by a schizophrenic from Liverpool, who stabbed him ten times; George was saved by his wife, who knocked out the assailant with a table lamp. The cancer returned and George Harrison died in Los Angeles on 29 November 2001. His ashes were immersed in the Ganges in accordance with his Hindu beliefs.

George Harrison once said, 'My biggest break was joining The Beatles. My second biggest break was getting out of them.'

INTERESTING GEORGE FACTS

George's personal Christmas card one year had him scowling at the camera.

George said he liked the British confectionery jelly babies, but in the US they took this to mean 'jelly beans', a hard coated confectionery, so they were pelted with little missiles.

HARRISON, HARRY [1909–1978] AND LOUISE [1911–1970]

George Harrison's father, Harold Hargreaves Harrison, was born in Liverpool in 1909. His father died when he was six and he left school aged 14. He sold mangles for a while, and then joined the merchant navy as a steward on the White Star line. He met Louise French, the daughter of a Liverpool lamplighter, who worked for a Liverpool greengrocer and they were married in 1930. They had four children: Louise, Harry, Peter and George.

After leaving the sea, Harry became a bus conductor for Liverpool Corporation and was promoted to driver. He became a union official and the management could see he had a flair for working out timetables.

Harry ran the events at the Corporation's social club. In 1959 he booked The Quarrymen for their Christmas party. He and his wife Louise adored ballroom dancing and their love for old standards rubbed off on George, as well as the urge to drive. Harry once turned up at the Institute to hit a schoolmaster who had hit George.

Louise Harrison had many penfriends from around the world and so it was no hardship for her to respond to fans once George was famous. Hundreds of fans received personal letters from her and she and Harry were sympathetic towards anyone who knocked on the door. George bought them a new home in Warrington in 1965 but Louise was diagnosed with a brain tumour in 1969 and died the following year. Around the same time, Harry was in hospital with ulcers and George's frustrations came out in his song 'Deep Blue'. His father, who had retired early, died from emphysema in 1978.

Excellent and supportive parents.

HARRISON, LOUISE [B. 1931]

George Harrison's sister Louise was born on 16 August 1931 and was almost 12 years older than him. She went to grammar school and then studied child psychology in Newcastle. In 1954 she married Gordon Caldwell, a mining engineer from Scotland. When they emigrated to Canada in 1956, George waved them off from the Liverpool landing stage. They had two children, George (b. 1957) and Leslie (b. 1959). George wanted to see them and visit North America, the opportunity came in September 1963 when he had some earnings from The Beatles and some holiday time. The Caldwell family was living in Benton, Illinois and he travelled there with his brother Peter (b. 1940). They camped in the Shawnee National Park and George played Hank Williams songs with a local band, The Four Vests. He was impressed by Kenny Welch's Rickenbacker and purchased one for himself. Louise was to remark that as nobody had heard of The Beatles, in George's words, this was the only time a Beatle was in America as 'a normal human being'.

In February 1964 Louise came to New York for The Beatles' appearance on *The Ed Sullivan Show* and nursed George as he recovered from a virus. She often spoke about George on radio, and a compilation album from those interviews, *All About The Beatles*, was released in the US in 1965. She says, 'George may well have had me in mind when he wrote "Cheer Down". I was forever on the go and he was always telling me to simmer down.'

Louise and Gordon divorced in 1982 and she settled in Florida, occasionally appearing at Beatles conventions. In 1999 her home in Benton was converted into A Hard Day's Nite boarding house.

An early supporter of The Beatles in America.

HARRY, BILL [B. 1938]

The editor of the *Mersey Beat* newspaper, Bill Harry was born in Liverpool on 17 September 1938. His father was killed during the war and he was raised in poverty in a house with no electricity. He had a traumatic childhood, being bullied and at one stage severely beaten by his classmates. Undeterred, he won a scholarship to the Liverpool Junior School of Art and started a school newspaper. He started a science-fiction fanzine when only 13, and often corresponded with the author Michael Moorcock.

When Bill was 16, he studied typography at the Liverpool College of Art and was soon putting his knowledge to practical use by starting a newspaper about local events, *Jazz,* and then a newsletter for Frank Hessy's instrument store, Frank Comments. He was very industrious, running the college's film society in his spare time and securing a diploma in design. He became friendly with Stuart Sutcliffe and, through him, John Lennon. With another art student, Rod Murray, they drank in Ye Cracke and planned to change the world. There is a plaque to commemorate The Dissenters, as they were called, in the pub.

Outside of paid ads, the *Liverpool Echo* ignored beat music, so Bill believed that there was an opening for a newspaper devoted to local performers. With a fifty-pound loan from a civil servant, Jim Anderson, he started the fortnightly *Mersey Beat.* There had been a column called *Mersey Beat* in the *Liverpool Echo,* but it related to jazz. Soon Bill was applying the term to beat music.

The first issue of *Mersey Beat* sold out. Brian Epstein, who stocked it in NEMS, was impressed and he was writing record reviews from the third issue. Another regular columnist was the Cavern's DJ, Bob Wooler. Bill had created something unique, as this was the first UK city with a what's on beat guide; others would soon follow. There was a Liverpool rival in *Combo,* but then the city had 300 groups, rather more than any other.

Bill's wife Virginia left her job at Woolworth's to join him at his attic office in Renshaw Street, Liverpool. He gave the Cavern's doorman, Paddy Delaney, a daytime job of delivering copies to newsagents.

Bill Harry loved The Beatles so much that other group members referred to the newspaper as *Mersey Beatle.* John Lennon gave him stories, poems and drawings, which sometimes appeared under the pseudonym of Beatcomber. One famed contribution was Lennon's fantasy on how The Beatles got their name.

Bill Harry arranged for Brian Epstein to see The Beatles at the Cavern in November 1961. Brian was always supportive of the newspaper and gave Bill the scoop when The Beatles secured their recording contract, not that the *Liverpool Echo* would have shown much interest.

As The Beatles became famous, Brian Epstein bought the newspaper and had plans to launch it on a national basis under the name *Music Echo.* Bill would be retained as editor, but he resigned when Brian appointed two columnists without his approval. Brian's idea came to fruition as *Disc and Music Echo* in 1964.

Bill Harry went into public relations and his many clients have included The Kinks, The Hollies, Pink Floyd, David Bowie and Jethro Tull. He worked for producer Mickie Most at RAK for several years, establishing Hot Chocolate, Suzi Quatro and Kim Wilde. He wrote a book about the seventies band Arrows, but let's forget about that.

In the eighties Bill Harry edited *Tracks,* a monthly music magazine for Boots, and then *Idols,* which covered many of his passions. He still

writes prodigiously about The Beatles and was an associate producer for the documentary film *The City That Rocked the World.*

The *Mersey Beat* newspaper established a community spirit for the Liverpool beat groups and their fans.

HESSY, FRANK [1910–1983]

The Hesselbergs were a Russian family who sought refuge in Liverpool at the start of the twentieth century. The family, shortening their name to Hessy, opened a music shop in Manchester Street, Liverpool, in 1923, at first selling records but soon concentrating on musical instruments.

In 1956, Francis Hesselberg (Frank Hessy) decided to branch out on his own. He was intrigued by the huge teenage interest in skiffle and rock 'n' roll and opened his own store in the city centre in Whitechapel. Everything was available on easy terms, and he took a risk with hire purchase arrangements, as it was relatively easy to provide false details and walk away with an instrument. The shop moved round the corner to Stanley Street in 1960 and remained there until its closure in 1995. It was only 50 yards from Brian Epstein's NEMS store.

Hessy was a short, stout man with an excitable personality, who was good with both staff and customers. He retired to Tel Aviv and he died there in 1983, aged 74.

Owned the most important music store and several of The Beatles' instruments and amplifiers were purchased there.

HOPKIN, MARY [B. 1950]

Mary Hopkin was born in Pontardawe, Glamorganshire, Wales, in 1950 and was bilingual, recording several folk songs for the Welsh label Cambrian, and appearing on regional TV. In 1968 she took part in the ITV talent show *Opportunity Knocks*, and the studio audience placed her first. So did Swinging Sixties model Twiggy, who phoned Paul McCartney and said she would be ideal for The Beatles' new Apple label.

Paul McCartney had heard a husband and wife duo, Gene and Francesca (Rankin) perform Gene's 'Those Were The Days', an English lyric to a Russian folk song, in a London nightclub and he thought the song perfect for Mary's first Apple single. The arrangement brought out the difference between the reflective verses and the upbeat choruses. It went to the top of the charts, deposing The Beatles' own 'Hey Jude'.

Mary had further hits with 'Goodbye' (written by Paul), 'Temma Harbour', 'Knock Knock Who's There?' (the UK's Eurovision entry in 1970) and 'Think About Your Children'. Her Top 10 album *Postcard* (1969) included some of the first songs by Apple writers Gallagher and Lyle. Mary Hopkin was reluctant to tour under her own name, but she has worked as part of Oasis (with Peter Skellern and Julian Lloyd Webber) and Sundance (with Mike Hurst from The Springfields). Mike recalls, 'We toured the UK with Dr Hook and the band, and the road crew were fancying her like mad. It was very hot when we did our soundcheck at Newcastle and Mary fainted. One of the roadies shouted, "Let me through, I was a medic in 'Nam." He went up to her, ripped open her blouse and went "Cor!"'

Mary added backing vocals to several Ralph McTell albums as well as joining Iggy Pop on David Bowie's *Low* (1977), which included the hit single 'Sound and Vision'. Bowie's album was co-produced by Mary's then-husband Tony Visconti. Mary's daughters run a studio and Mary had made the occasional record. She worked on George Martin's production of *Under Milk Wood* (1988).

Mary's first hit single showed that the Apple label was not solely for The Beatles.

HUTCHINSON, JOHNNY – SEE BIG THREE, THE

INNES, NEIL – SEE BONZO DOG DOO-DAH BAND, THE AND RUTLES, THE

JACOBS, DAVID [1926–2013]

Everything about broadcaster David Jacobs was polished and immaculate: the mellifluous voice, the smartly cut single-colour blazers with brass buttons, the sharply creased trousers, the military stance. He was the perfect frontman for BBC broadcasts.

David Jacobs was born into a Jewish family in Streatham Hill, London, in 1926. His father was a successful fruit importer in Covent Garden and the Jacobs had both a chauffeur and a maid. However, the family's fortunes changed during the war: his father became bankrupt, and his mother Jeanette took in dressmaking to make ends meet. David started broadcasting in Ceylon (now Sri Lanka) during his service with the Royal Navy.

David joined the BBC Overseas Service in 1947 and became a newsreader, although he was still prone to practical jokes. From 1953–58 he was an actor on the hugely popular radio serial *Journey Into Space*, but his real strength lay in presenting records. He hosted *Forces Favourites* and *House-wives' Choice*, introducing both Bill Haley and Elvis Presley to the British public. Being 'D.J. the DJ' was not for him: he reflected, 'I have never thought of myself as a disc jockey as it seems to me a marginally derogatory term, perhaps because it is American. A lot of people found American cars unattractive and I am a bit that way about the American disc jockey.'

Jacobs attempted to interest the Corporation in his TV concept *Hit or Miss,* where a panel would discuss the latest record releases. The BBC thought that watching people listening to records had little appeal and rejected the idea. Meanwhile, a similar idea, *Juke Box Jury,* found success in America. It was imported to the UK in 1958 and Jacobs was invited to become the host. 'I saw myself as the chairman of a television panel game but our game was talking about gramophone records,' said Jacobs. 'What the panel said was not to be taken too seriously. Sometimes I thought the panel was completely wrong and I would say so, but I never thought that my ability to spot hits was anything special. After all, the recording managers had done that before me.' On one occasion, he thought that The Beatles had made a mistake by releasing 'Strawberry Fields Forever'.

In his own quiet way, David Jacobs was so influential that Brian Epstein sought him out in 1962 for advice on how to promote The Beatles nationwide, even offering him a percentage of the group's profits. Jacobs said, 'I've never done anything like that and I couldn't possibly present them on a BBC programme because it would be totally wrong.'

Jacobs played himself in the films *The Golden Disc* (1958) and *It's Trad, Dad!* (1962), and presented the radio chart show *Pick of the Pops* (1957–61). In 1963 a special edition of *Juke Box Jury* with The Beatles at the Liverpool Empire reached an audience of 24 million. Some of The Beatles, Brian Epstein and Jane Asher were individual panel members on other editions of *Juke Box Jury.*

Jacobs was one of four regular presenters on *Top of the Pops*, but sometimes he gave the impression that he was not too fond of the hits and would rather be at home playing his Vic Damone collection. A new wave of presenters came up through the pirate radio stations and with the advent of Radio 1 in 1967, the four-way domination of Jacobs, Alan Freeman, Pete Murray and Jimmy Savile was over. Around this time, Jacobs stood in for an ailing Freddie Grisewood on the serious topical debate show *Any Questions?*, and when Grisewood retired a few months later, Jacobs was the natural successor.

Despite his cool exterior, Jacobs had a traumatic personal life. His marriage fell apart in 1969, and his son Jeremy was killed in a road accident in Israel whilst doing charity work. In 1975, he married his long-standing girlfriend Caroline Munro, and they went on holiday to Spain with Richard Marsh, then chairman of British Rail, and his wife, also called Caroline. While there, they were rammed from the back on a mountain road. Both Carolines were killed, but only four weeks after the tragedy Jacobs returned to *Any Questions?*, with Marsh as a guest. Both parties regarded it as therapeutic, and as further therapy Jacobs wrote a book about his marriage, *Caroline* (1978), which was surprisingly candid.

In 1975, Jacobs was voted Radio Personality of the Year, and in 1984 he received a Sony award for his outstanding contribution to radio. He has presented numerous programmes for Radio 2 including *Melodies for You* (12 years) and *The David Jacobs Collection*, which took him into his seventh decade as a BBC presenter. He was a founder member of Capital Radio and presented travel programmes for Sky.

Jacobs was made a Deputy Lieutenant for Greater London in 1983, and he undertook charity work for the Stars Organisation for Spastics, the RSPCA and many other organisations. He was a natural chairman.

David Jacobs was an influential BBC DJ, who fortunately was impressed 'by the thump coming down the railway line from Liverpool.'

JAMES, DICK [1920–1986]

History has not been kind to Dick James. His duplicitous arrangements for Elton John and Bernie Taupin's songs were exposed in a High Court action. Undoubtedly, he was feathering his own nest when he promoted The Beatles' original songs, but he also played a major role in making them world famous. Paul McCartney has since questioned the ethics and the naivety of signing with one of George Martin's friends, but it is unlikely that the business practices would have been much different elsewhere and the outcome might not have been as successful.

James was born Isaac Vapnick, the son of a butcher, in Spitalfields, London, on 12 December 1920. He left school aged 14, and by the time he was 17 he was singing at Cricklewood Palais, often performing Al Jolson medleys. He married Frances Aarons in 1943, and went on to change his name to Richard ('Dick') Leon James.

After serving in the Royal Army Medical Corps, James made records with the bands of the day – Geraldo, Cyril Stapleton, Stanley Black – as well as recording with The Stargazers. His most unusual record is 'The Petite Waltz (La Petite Valse)' from 1950, a duet with Anne Shelton and featuring Anton Karas on zither. He was one of several artists to cover 'Nature Boy', but what chance did anyone have against Nat King Cole? He released 84 singles, 44 of them for Parlophone, a far greater total than The Beatles.

Dick James preferred Tin Pan Alley to trudging up and down the country in variety packages. He might do two months of variety in a year, and otherwise he would be working for the music publisher Sydney Bron, aiming to interest fellow performers and bandleaders in Bron's catalogue. His tenacity paid off in 1955 when 'Ev'rywhere' topped the sheet music charts. In that same year he recorded the theme for *The Adventures of Robin Hood*, starring Richard Greene.

At first the TV series was shown in the London region and the station was bombarded for details about the theme song: who was the singer and was it on record? The arrangement was expanded by Ron Goodwin and included a children's choir, led by Dick's eight-year-old son Stephen. A coach picked them up from school and they were paid in chocolate and lemonade. With rockin' Robin in the Top 20, Dick James revealed that he had given his son a pair of football boots for his efforts. Dick followed it with another Top 20 hit, 'The Garden of Eden', although Frankie Vaughan's version outsold him.

Dick James hosted a community series, *Sing Song Time*, on Radio Luxembourg. Its popularity led to several *Sing Song Time* releases for Parlophone. He was tempted out of retirement for a party medley, 'Sing A Song of Beatles' in

1964. 'Very good indeed, a lot of fun,' said Paul McCartney, diplomatically.

The Beatles' first Parlophone single, 'Love Me Do' was published by EMI's in-house company Ardmore & Beechwood, but Brian Epstein was disappointed by their lack of promotion. George Martin recommended Dick, who at the time only had 60 songs in his company Dick James Music, several by Martin himself. So, on the old pals network, Dick James acquired the world's most lucrative publishing catalogue, setting up a separate company, Northern Songs. Although The Beatles were his prime concern, Dick James published songs by Gerry and The Pacemakers, The Hollies, The Troggs and Roger Cook and Roger Greenaway.

In 1965 Dick persuaded Brian Epstein to float Northern Songs on the stock exchange. The move was a financial triumph, but John and Paul felt that they were no longer working for themselves but for thousands of shareholders and the relationship between Dick James and The Beatles became strained. After Brian Epstein's death, Dick was concerned that The Beatles might break up, which could dramatically affect the share price. In 1969, and much to the annoyance of Lennon and McCartney, he secretly sold his shares in Northern Songs to his former agent, Sir Lew Grade, at ATV. He had not told Lennon and McCartney because he did not trust Allen Klein, who might have launched a countermove.

Dick developed new interests with Elton John and the record company DJM, and had management roles with the Music Publishers Association and the Performing Right Society. He received an Ivor Novello award for his services to entertainment. Following heart surgery in 1981, he stepped down as managing director of DJM. In 1985 the courts awarded Elton John and Bernie

Taupin increased royalties, but the copyright of their songs remained with DJM, enabling both sides to claim victory. The proceedings contributed to James's frailty, and following a massive heart attack he died on 1 February 1986 at the age of 65. In his will he left £6.9m.

Music publishers are often depicted as bad guys, but The Beatles needed a publisher and nobody could have been more encouraging or worked harder to promote them than Dick James. From an ethical standpoint, he took more than he should but hey, that's show business.

JANOV, DR ARTHUR [B. 1924]

The Los Angeles psychologist and psychiatrist Dr Arthur Janov explained his concept of primal therapy in a book, *The Primal Scream* (1970). The highly impressionable John and Yoko were intrigued by the idea that their neuroses were probably caused by childhood traumas (rather than by copious drug-taking!). They underwent primal therapy under the personal supervision of Dr Janov and although the treatment only lasted four months, it led to the harrowing songs of *John Lennon/Plastic Ono Band* and *Yoko Ono/Plastic Ono Band*. It is a shame that we don't have Aunt Mimi's views on these songs, as certainly Ringo had a far more traumatic childhood than John. At the time of his therapy, John gave his infamous interview to *Rolling Stone*, by far the most extraordinary comments ever given by a celebrity about his past career. Primal therapy has had a rocky ride since the seventies but it has been praised by the actor James Earl Jones, the pianist Roger Williams and the eighties rock duo, Tears For Fears. The actress Dyan Cannon set aside a special room for screaming in her Hollywood home. Janov's most recent book is *Life Before Birth: The Hidden Script that Rules Our Lives* (2011).

John had screamed on 'Twist And Shout', and now he did it with a purpose.

JONES, RAYMOND [B 1941]

In 1961, a youth called Raymond Jones went into the NEMS record store in Whitechapel, Liverpool, and ordered 'My Bonnie' by The Beatles. Or did he? The order is said to have sparked Epstein's interest in the band, but over the years Raymond Jones never appeared at Beatles conventions. Was there such a person? Apparently not, according to the promoter Sam Leach, who said that 'Raymond Jones' was a false name, used by someone ordering the single because Epstein had antipathy towards him. Then again, Alistair Taylor appeared at Beatles conventions stating that he was 'Raymond Jones'. All nonsense.

Yes, there was a real Raymond Jones, a keen follower of The Beatles, and he spent his adult years running a printing works in Ormskirk. His children now run the business and he has retired to Spain. He tells us, 'A friend told me that The Beatles had made a record so I went to NEMS to get it. Brian Epstein asked me about them and I said, "They are the most fantastic group you will ever hear."'

To add to the confusion, there was a Raymond Jones in the Manchester group, The Dakotas. But he is someone else again.

So yes, the Nowhere Man exists.

KAEMPFERT, BERT [1923–1980]

A very good question for a music quiz is: 'Who is the only musician who has worked with Elvis Presley, The Beatles and Frank Sinatra?' The answer is the German bandleader Bert Kaempfert.

Bert Kaempfert, known as 'Fips' to his friends, was born in Hamburg on 16 October 1923. A graduate of the Hamburg School of Music, he mostly played piano and he could get by on clarinet, saxophone and accordion. He played in Hans Busch's orchestra, but was conscripted during the war and served in the navy. He was captured and spent some time in a POW camp in Denmark, where he formed a band with fellow captives. Upon release, he returned to Germany and often played for US army officers. Although American big band music had been forbidden by the Nazis, he was drawn towards Glenn Miller and the Dorseys.

Living in Hamburg with his wife and two daughters, he discovered Freddy Quinn and Ivo Robi, who scored an international hit with 'Morgen' in 1959. He made his own orchestral records and had some international success with 'Mitternachts-Blues' ('Midnight Blues') in 1958 and then topped the US charts in 1961 with 'Wunderland bei Nacht' ('Wonderland by Night)'. He updated a German folk song 'Muss I Denn', which became 'Wooden Heart', a million-selling single that Elvis Presley performed with a puppet show in *GI Blues*.

Following a recommendation in May 1961 from a protégé, Tommy Kent, Kaempfert signed Tony Sheridan and The Beatles to Der Bert Kaempfert Produktion with a view to recording for Polydor. He produced 'My Bonnie' as well as 'Ain't She Sweet' with John Lennon's lead vocal. When Brian Epstein wanted to secure a UK record contract for The Beatles he found that they were under contract to Kaempfert, but Kaempfert was amenable to releasing them. He made several more records with Sheridan.

Kaempfert released two or three albums a year of easy listening (or Schlager) instrumental music. He had several notable compositions including 'A Swingin' Safari', 'Danke Schoen' (Wayne Newton) and 'L-O-V-E' (Nat King Cole). His 'Moon Over Naples' was given an English lyric and transformed into 'Spanish Eyes', which meant that a Neapolitan tune by a German writer became a song about a Mexican girl sung by an Italian-American crooner, Al Martino.

In 1966 Kaempfert wrote the music for the James Garner film *A Man Could Get Killed*. The main theme was played to the American producer, Jimmy Bowen, under the title 'Beddy Bye'. Bowen thought it was of interest. 'Get me some lyrics for this,' he said, 'and I'll give it to Sinatra. But don't call it "Beddy Bye".' The result was 'Strangers in the Night', one of Frank's biggest records, although he never cared for it, largely because Dean Martin told him he was singing abut 'two fags'.

Although his music was cheesy listening, Kaempfert filled the concert halls of the world including the Royal Albert Hall. He died in 1980 in Majorca.

Kaempfert produced 'My Bonnie' but waived his rights to future recordings.

KAUFMAN, MURRAY [1922–1982]

Murray Kaufman, better known as 'Murray the K', was born into a family of Jewish entertainers in New York in 1922. His mother was a vaudeville pianist who would write 'Splish Splash' with Bobby Darin. Murray's military service was in organising shows for the troops during the war. He became a highly effective song plugger, and in the fifties started broadcasting on 1010 WINS, taking over the 7–11pm slot after the payola scandal that wrecked Alan Freed's career. He presented and produced rock 'n' roll package shows at the Brooklyn Fox and the Brooklyn Paramount as Alan Freed had done.

Murray the K became a hysterical broadcaster who often spoke in his own dialect, Meusurray, where every word had an extra letter attached. This became wearing for his workmates as he was Murray the K all day, every day.

Rather than send a news reporter to The Beatles' first press conference at New York's Kennedy Airport in February 1964, WINS told Murray to go along. He stood out and monopolised the event. He was close enough to Paul to confirm that his hair was real. If Paul had reciprocated, he would have pulled off Murray's wig. Murray was soon calling himself the Fifth Beatle, a phrase that resounds to this day.

Using his friendship with The Ronettes, he got inside The Beatles' suite at the Plaza Hotel and was soon creating mayhem. He clung to The Beatles, but Brian Epstein was wary about throwing him out as this could rebound badly on them. In terms of publicity, Murray the K did The Beatles a lot of good. He also saw them socially, taking John, Paul and Ringo to the Playboy Club after *The Ed Sullivan Show* and then travelling with them on the train to Washington. He broadcast from the set of *A Hard Day's Night* and introduced the show at Shea Stadium in 1965, though Ed Sullivan introduced The Beatles.

WINS went all news in 1965, but Murray pioneered FM rock with the idea of grouping records with themes. He promoted 'attitude music', his term for Bob Dylan and Janis Ian. His nationwide TV show *It's What Happening, Baby* (1965–70) was the first to make extensive use of pop videos. Bill Murray played a parody of him in the spoof documentary *All You Need Is Cash*.

Everybody says that Murray was a lovable if irritating guy, which could explain why he had six wives.

Murray the K would settle for nothing less than 10 but we say 2.

KELLY, FREDA [B. 1945]

Freda (actually, Frieda) Kelly was born in Dublin on 14 July 1945. Her mother died when she was young and her father's second wife lived in Liverpool, where they settled when Freda was 13. On leaving school, she learnt shorthand typing and did secretarial work for Princes Foods, close to the Cavern. From 1961 she became a Cavern regular, and especially enjoyed seeing The Beatles at lunchtime sessions as they were not so crowded. A girl who worked for a travel agency, Bobbie Brown, started The Beatles' fan club and Freda took it over when Bobbie got engaged and the novelty had worn off. Freda was very thorough, joining other fan clubs to see what members would get for their money. She was dismayed that some of them gave printed signatures: this would not happen with The Beatles, she decided.

In 1963 she was working as a shorthand typist for NEMS Enterprises and running the fan club from her home address. Her father complained to Brian Epstein about the sacks of mail being delivered to his house and a PO box was set up. She would badger The Beatles for autographs and they became very fond of her, knowing that she was someone they could trust.

Brian Epstein wanted Freda to move to London with NEMS Enterprises, but her father would not allow it. Epstein let her stay in Liverpool running the northern side of the fan club and replying personally to requests from fans. She would visit

The Beatles' families and help them with their mail. Ringo's mother, Elsie, thought that Freda was so considerate that she asked Brian Epstein to give her a rise – and he did.

In 1967 Freda was a passenger on the *Magical Mystery Tour*, and the following year she married Brian from the Liverpool band The Cryin' Shames. They had a son and a daughter, and when Freda left The Beatles' organisation in 1972 to bring up her family George Harrison sent her a note. 'You were there at the beginning and you were there at the end.'

Freda and Brian's marriage didn't last and she had to cope with the death of her son. In more recent times she has been working as a secretary for a legal firm. Her memories of The Beatles are very positive and she told her story in *Good Ol' Freda*, a delightful feature-length documentary in 2013. To this day, she describes working for The Beatles as the greatest job of all.

Dealing with your fans is very important and Freda Kelly was the perfect fan club secretary.

KENT, TOMMY [B. 1942]

Born Guntram Kühbeck, Tommy Kent was a teenage rock 'n' roll singer who was discovered by Bert Kaempfert. In 1959 he had success with a cover version of Robin Luke's 'Susie Darlin'', but his major success was 'Alle Nächte', a huge hit in Germany, Switzerland and Austria. In 1961, the 'Schlager' star was in Hamburg to record, and on the night before the session he was on the Reeperbahn, where by chance he heard Tony Sheridan and The Beatles in the Top Ten Club. He was so impressed that he told Kaempfert about them. They went the next night and Tommy performed 'Be-Bop-A-Lula' and 'Kansas City' with The Beatles.

Kaempfert was to sign Sheridan and The Beatles, and Tommy himself had hits until the mid-1960s. He appeared in several German feature films, but he left the business to study architecture. He always painted and his work has been exhibited around the world. He lived and worked in a 500-year-old inn in the Bavarian Alps.

A chance meeting leads to The Beatles' German recording contract.

KIRCHHERR, ASTRID [B. 1938]

Throughout their years of performing, The Beatles were blessed with exceptional good fortune as they rarely worked with anyone who did not enhance their career. They met the photographer Astrid Kirchherr on their first trip to Hamburg in 1960, and she took outstanding black-and-white images of the band, both individually and collectively. Looking at the first photographs today, it is hard to credit that The Beatles were completely unknown. What's more, she is also an integral part of their story.

Astrid Kirchherr was born in Hamburg in 1938, where her father was a salesman for Ford Motors. Astrid was evacuated during the war while her father delivered supplies to troops. As a teenager, she studied fashion design at the Meisterschule für Mode, Textil, Graphik und Werbung, until a tutor, Reinhard Wolf, who was taken with her photography, asked her to switch courses. After graduation, she worked as his assistant.

Inspired by the 'Exis' (existentialists) on the Left Bank in Paris, Astrid and her friends, including fellow students Klaus Voormann and Jürgen Vollmer, copied their stark appearance. Astrid played down the intellectual aspect of this, saying, 'We knew of Sartre and we dressed like the French existentialists. Our philosophy then, and remember we were only little kids, was more in following their looks than their thoughts. We were going around looking moody. We wanted to be different and we wanted to look cool.'

Klaus was dating Astrid and living in her family home. One night in 1960, he stormed out of the house following an argument. Walking down Grosse Freiheit, he heard live rock 'n' roll music coming from basement club the Kaiserkeller, and wanted to investigate. He was apprehensive because he looked like a student, but he was entranced by the music. He took Astrid and Jürgen the following night, and they discovered that both John and Stuart were at the Liverpool College of Art.

Astrid invited them to a nearby fairground, but she did not want to photograph them on the rides. She wanted them among the trucks and heavy machinery. One photograph captures them as five working musicians with their instruments. Following Astrid's lead, they all started wearing black leather.

Soon Astrid Kirchherr was in a relationship with Stu and when John's girlfriend, Cynthia, visited him in Hamburg, she stayed at Astrid's house. Astrid recalled, 'They were all a knockout but my little Stuart blew my mind. It was fantastic to look at him and see all that beauty. Did you ever see eyes as lovely as that? When Stuart became my boyfriend, he didn't feel right in Klaus's company but after Klaus told him how happy he was that I was happy, they became very close friends.'

Several students in Hamburg, including Klaus and Jürgen, had the now-familiar Beatles hairstyle; longish, flattened and brushed forward with a fringe. Stu asked Astrid for a similar look and the others followed.

Stuart continued his studies in Hamburg and he impressed Eduardo Paolozzi, a British artist who was working as a guest lecturer. Stu returned to Liverpool in February 1961 to introduce Astrid to his family, but his mother refused to have her in the house – at the time a normal reaction towards anyone who was German.

Stuart had been suffering headaches, probably relating to a gang beating in Liverpool, and, in April 1960, when he was only 21, he died in Astrid's arms on the way to a Hamburg hospital. Two days later she told The Beatles what had happened when they returned to open the Star-Club. Later that year, she was commissioned to take photographs that would publicise their first Parlophone single, 'Love Me Do'. Her style was copied by Robert Freeman for the cover of their album *With The Beatles* (1963).

In 1964, Astrid took photographs of The Beatles filming *A Hard Day's Night* for the German magazine *Stern*, and she and Max Scheler arranged a photograph of over 200 local beat musicians outside St George's Hall, Liverpool. However, Astrid lost confidence in her work and did little professionally after 1967. She took the cover portrait for George Harrison's album *Wonderwall Music*.

In 1967 Astrid married another Liverpool musician, the drummer Gibson Kemp, who worked with Klaus and Paddy Chambers in the group Paddy, Klaus and Gibson. They were divorced in 1974 and Astrid had another brief marriage, but she often worked for Gibson in his English restaurant in Hamburg.

Disinterested, Astrid had not chased copyright fees when her pictures were reproduced and her friend, Ulf Kruger, resolved the matter. As a result she had several exhibitions of her work and published two books, *Liverpool Days* (1994) and *Hamburg Days* (1999). She was a consultant for the film *Backbeat* in 1994, in which Sheryl Lee played her.

Astrid said, 'The most important thing I gave them was my friendship.' The most important thing she gave Beatles fans were those early photographs. 'They trusted me,' she says. 'There is no fear of being photographed.'

KLEIN, ALLEN [1931–2009]

Many clever but unscrupulous individuals have become involved in rock management, but no one has been smarter, tougher or more divisive than Allen Klein. He played to his image, of course, and enjoyed John Belushi's parody as Ron Decline in The Rutles' film *All You Need Is Cash*, but he certainly wasn't a man to cross. 'Artists fuck groupies and I fuck the groups,' sounds like Ron Decline, but was said by Klein himself.

Quite appropriately, Allen Klein's father was a butcher. He had come from Hungary to America but he couldn't cope with Allen and his two older sisters after his wife died. He sent the three children to the Hebrew Orphanage in Newark, and Allen didn't see his father again until 1941 when he was introduced to his stepmother. He lived with his grandparents in Newark, and after school served two years in the military. While doing menial jobs, he attended evening classes and became an accountant in 1956.

Klein joined the Harry Fox Agency, which specialised in collecting royalties for artists and publishing companies. He quickly grasped how the industry worked and how many artists were cheated, especially the young rock 'n' roll stars. With a loan from his father-in-law, he started his own company, ABKCO (Allen and Betty Klein), and helped Buddy Knox and Jimmy Bowen collect royalties from Roulette Records, a label owned by the notorious Morris Levy. These were dangerous waters, but Klein's skill enabled him to perform similarly successful audits for Bobby Darin, Bobby

Vinton, and Steve Lawrence and Eydie Gormé. Klein would take 25 per cent as his finder's fee.

To his credit, Klein did love music and he truly appreciated the exceptional talent of Sam Cooke. When he became his manager, he re-negotiated Cooke's contract with RCA, securing over $100,000 of unpaid royalties. Inspired by Bob Dylan's ability to write about civil rights, Cooke wrote 'A Change Is Gonna Come' but was unsure about moving into the political arena. Klein assured him that it was the right thing to do, but Cooke didn't live to see its success as a key song of the sixties.

In March 1964 Allen Klein made arrangements for promoting British acts in the US, striking deals with Dave Clark for The Dave Clark Five and Mickie Most for The Animals and Herman's Hermits. He took over the Philadelphia label Cameo-Parkway Records, and released singles by The Kinks, The Ivy League and Pete Best.

In August 1965, Klein joined Andrew Loog Oldham in the management of the Rolling Stones, but with ruthless efficiency, he was soon to oust him and become their sole manager. He negotiated a new deal with Decca Records, but somehow the £1m advance found its way to Klein's bank account rather than theirs.

At first Mick Jagger was pleased with Klein, and he introduced him to John Lennon and Yoko Ono when they were making *Rock And Roll Circus* in December 1968. Lennon told Klein that Apple would be bankrupt within six months unless someone would take charge. Klein went to work, sacking staff, abandoning projects and saving The Beatles from total embarrassment. However, he was not able to manage the whole group, as Paul McCartney wanted to be represented by Lee and John Eastman. Even so, he secured The Beatles a much more lucrative deal on their catalogue, especially in the US.

For a short period, Klein was the manager of the two biggest groups in the world, The Beatles and the Rolling Stones. The Stones realised their mistake and Mick Jagger confronted Klein in a hotel lobby, demanding his money. The stalemate was settled in May 1972 when Klein kept the rights to their past recordings. However, the Stones had still ended up much wealthier and become tax exiles.

Like Jagger, Lennon was taken in at first, telling *Playboy,* 'Allen's really beautiful. He handles everything and I can trust him.' Undoubtedly his very presence increased the tensions in The Beatles. It was not just John, George and Ringo v Paul, as they all had misgivings at various times. 'Beware Of Darkness' (George Harrison) and 'Steel And Glass' (John Lennon) are about Klein. Pete Townshend of The Who also had dealings with Klein, and wrote 'Who Are You' about him.

On 31 December 1970, Paul took legal action to dissolve The Beatles, primarily to be rid of Klein. He had made them £9m richer during his 18-month tenure, as well as increased future royalty payments, but it cost them £4m to lose him. Ungrateful bastards, thought Klein, who wanted to get even. When George Harrison was sued for plagiarism over 'My Sweet Lord', Klein bought the publishing for the song in question, 'He's So Fine', so he could sue Harrison himself. The judge, aware of Klein's character, did find in Klein's favour but in a brilliant judgment decreed that Harrison was to purchase 'He's So Fine' from Klein at the amount he had paid.

As a separate matter, George Harrison was disappointed that Klein held onto the charity funds from the *Concert for Bangla Desh* and it was later discovered that he had been selling promotional copes of the album to dealers and pocketing the money. Klein was jailed for tax evasion in 1979. Klein's son, Jody, started to handle ABKCO and although his father returned to the business, he developed Alzheimer's disease and died in 2009.

Sorting out The Beatles' finances came at a heavy price and they must have longed for Brian Epstein.

KOSCHMIDER, BRUNO [1926–2000]

The club owners that The Beatles met in Hamburg were very different from the ones in Liverpool. If they told you to 'Mach Schau!', you did precisely that, and smartish

Bruno Koschmider was born in Danzig (now Gdańsk) on 30 April 1926. He was a circus acrobat who had been crippled following a fall from a trapeze, although he claimed it was a war injury. In 1950 he opened a small strip club on Grosse Freiheit in Hamburg called the Indra. It was a bar with tables around a raised stage. The stage was higher than might be expected in order that patrons could get a better view.

Koschmider acquired further properties in the area: a bigger club, the Kaiserkeller; a sex cinema, Bambi Kino; and a coffee shop, Heaven And Hell. The Kaiserkeller opened in October 1959 and could hold 700. It was designed for sailors, with nautical decor and seating in rowing boats, which limited intimacy in the club itself.

Koschmider realised that the visiting sailors might want more than endless striptease. If he supplied music, then patrons might visit the club for longer and therefore drink more. He put a jukebox in the Kaiserkeller and found that American rock 'n' roll music was very popular. For live music, he hired an Indonesian group based in Holland.

Enter Liverpool entrepreneur Allan Williams, who heard their limp rock 'n' roll and told Koschmider that he could provide good Liverpool bands. Allan Williams remembers, 'One of the waiters took me in to meet Herr Koschmider and while I was doing my sales pitch for the Liverpool groups, somebody shouted, "There's a fight!" and I could see these fellers scrapping on the marble floor. Herr Koschmider got out a truncheon and beat them to a pulp. That's the type of man he was.'

Although Koschmider was intrigued by The Beatles' name, as 'Peedles' was German slang for penis, no bookings were made. Instead, Koschmider signed Tony Sheridan and The Jets on his next visit to London. Meeting by chance in London, Koschmider took Howie Casey and The Seniors from Allan Williams and then offered the Indra to The Beatles. The living quarters were behind the cinema screen in the Bambi Kino. An elderly neighbour complained about the loud music at the Indra and the authorities told Koschmider to stop rocking and start stripping. He closed the club in October 1960 and moved The Beatles to the Kaiserkeller.

Koschmider had a winning formula at the Kaiserkeller, and now he was presenting two groups per night for non-stop entertainment. The Seniors were about to finish and Koschmider combined The Beatles with another Liverpool act, Rory Storm and The Hurricanes. The poster is intriguing as it features Rory Storm and The Hurricanes prominently, with The Beatles as an afterthought.

When Bruno Koschmider booked his acts, he issued the following instructions: 'While on stage, the musicians are not allowed to eat or smoke. Their dress should be clean. Good appearance and behaviour of language is required. Conversation with the public by use of the microphone is not desired.' But this was not all he wanted. He wanted the musicians to give a show. He hated musicians standing still and he would shout, 'Mach Schau! Mach Schau! (Make show! Make show!)' You could do anything you liked – standing on the piano, jumping into the audience – but you had to have some action. If the music could be heard on the street, so much the better – passers-by would be drawn in to buy beer. One night The Hurricanes and The Beatles conspired to break the stage, and succeeded with heavy stomping.

Koschmider was furious when The Beatles started performing with Sheridan at the Top Ten Club and gave them a month's notice. He informed the German authorities that George Harrison was under 18 and so was not allowed to frequent a nightclub after 10pm, let alone play in one. On 21 November 1960, George Harrison was deported and, oddly considering this was child protection legislation, he had to find his own way home by train and ferry.

On 29 November 1960, Paul McCartney and Pete Best returned to the Bambi Kino to pack their belongings. The cinema was closed and lighting turned off at the mains, so they lit condoms for light in the windowless room. They packed their clothes and left. Within minutes, Koschmider had informed the police that The Beatles had attempted arson. Paul and Pete were arrested and thrown into a cell, then sent home.

Bruno Koschmider had had enough of rock after his problems with The Beatles and Rory Storm, and returned to strippers. The Kaiserkeller became the Colibri, although it is now back to being the Kaiserkeller with the occasional tribute show. But Koschmider never got the breaks and he became little more than a tramp wandering around St Pauli, sometimes working as a club doorman. He died a pauper in 2000.

Would The Beatles have Mach Schau'd without him?

KRAMER, BILLY J. [B. 1943], WITH THE DAKOTAS

Early in 1963, the merging of the Liverpool vocalist Billy J. Kramer with the Manchester group The Dakotas was among Brian Epstein's most inspired moves. It led to a succession of hit records, including three UK No. 1s.

William Howard Ashton was born in the Liverpool suburb of Bootle on 19 August 1943. While training as an engineer for British Railways, in his spare time he was the lead vocalist with a local band, The Coasters. They performed covers of Jerry Lee Lewis, Ricky Nelson and Cliff Richard hits, and when they needed a name for their frontman they rang a telephone operator to ask, 'Which one sounds the best?' She replied, 'Billy Kramer,' and so they became Billy Kramer and The Coasters, until John Lennon thought it would sound even better as Billy J.

Their manager, 59-year-old Ted Knibbs, secured them club bookings on Merseyside, but Brian Epstein had the vision to see further. If they turned professional, he would manage them. In the end, The Coasters stayed with their day jobs and Brian put Billy with The Dakotas. The group consisted of Mike Maxfield (lead guitar), Robin MacDonald (rhythm guitar), Ray Jones (bass) and Tony Mansfield, really Tony Bookbinder, the brother of Elkie Brooks, on drums. They could read music and usually backed the singer Pete Maclaine.

Billy went with The Dakotas to Hamburg to establish their act. 'We'd had "Do You Want To Know A Secret" on a tape from John Lennon,' he says. 'We did it every night at the Star-Club and we came back to England and did a test for EMI. Two weeks later, Brian Epstein told me that we had passed the test and I said, "Let's find a good song 'cause that's not strong enough."' Epstein told him that EMI were happy with the test recording, which was being released. Billy realised that it was going to be successful when he appeared on a North West TV programme, *Scene at 6.30*. The TV producer, Johnnie Hamp, asked him to pull 'secret' files out of a cabinet – a nod to the Profumo affair that was to bring down the government – and by the time Billy returned home, there were fans on his doorstep.

'Do You Want To Know A Secret' was a fine performance of a fine song, written when Lennon and McCartney were emulating the Brill Building sound. George Harrison took the lead vocal on The Beatles' own version, but they never officially recorded Billy's B-side, another fine Lennon and McCartney song, 'I'll Be On My Way'.

Helped by Billy's pop idol looks, 'Do You Want To Know A Secret' topped the *NME* charts, and Billy had a direct line to John and Paul. He recalls, 'When we were in Bournemouth, John gave me "Bad To Me" and "I Call Your Name". We couldn't get "Bad To Me" together at first, largely because our producer George Martin wanted me to sing it in E. When we switched to D, I got it in a few takes. I wanted "I Call Your Name" as the A-side as it was a bopper, but George Martin said, "It sounds too Beatleish and you're Billy J. Kramer."' You can measure the strength of The Beatles' songwriting through what they gave away – 'Bad To Me' went to No. 1.

When Billy pulled a drunken John Lennon away from Cavern DJ Bob Wooler at Paul Mc-Cartney's twenty-first party, Lennon snarled, 'You're finished, Kramer. You're nothing without us.' He later apologised for the remark.

'I'll Keep You Satisfied', a well-crafted Lennon and McCartney song, should have been another No. 1, but Kramer, always a nervous performer, went to pieces on the live TV show *Sunday Night at the London Palladium*.

The music publishers, Aberbach, had given Billy a new song, 'Little Children', which had been co-written by the American writer Mort Shuman, now based in the UK. Brian Epstein was opposed to it, perhaps because he wasn't making the decision, but Billy persevered and when released it sold 78,000 copies on the first day and then went to the top.

The Dakotas, usually Mike Maxfield, Robin MacDonald and later Mick Green from The Pirates (who replaced Ray Jones), wrote songs for Billy, and they had their own Top 20 hit with Mike's instrumental 'The Cruel Sea', released in the US as 'The Cruel Surf'. Their second single, 'Magic Carpet', written by George Martin, was less successful and their solo career fizzled out.

Billy returned to a Lennon and McCartney composition with 'From a Window'. It made No. 10, and he comments, 'I think "From a Window" was the best of all the Lennon and McCartney songs I recorded. Paul offered me "Yesterday" and I said, "Paul, all my records have been nicey-nicey. I want a real headbanger."' Billy recorded Lennon and McCartney's 'I'm In Love', but the presence of John Lennon in the control room, commenting like a reality TV judge, inhibited him and instead the song became a hit for The Fourmost.

As Billy had had US Top 10 singles with 'Bad To Me' and 'Little Children', they toured the US and an ecstatic crowd in California can be heard on the 1965 EP, *Billy J. Plays the States*.

With Mick Green borrowing his father's mandolin, the group covered 'Trains And Boats And Planes', not knowing that Burt Bacharach was releasing his own version as a single, but both recordings made the charts.

Kramer can be seen as a continuation of the 'pretty boy' singers like Frankie Avalon, Fabian and Bobby Rydell, who lost their footing with the British Invasion.

By 1966, chart success had dried up and Billy acknowledges this as his own fault. He was drinking heavily and he had put on weight. He says, 'Brian Epstein used to lecture me but that only made me worse. I went to see Liverpool FC one night and Ian St John introduced me to a girl who said, "Billy, you used to be a nice-looking guy. What have you been doing with yourself?" I walked out and I didn't drink for five years.'

Billy J. Kramer has been based in America for many years and he tours with Joey Molland (Badfinger) and Terry Sylvester (Escorts, Hollies) in a British Invasion show. His voice has both deepened and strengthened, making his hits sound really distinctive. His 2013 album *I Won the Fight* includes his self-penned tribute to Brian Epstein.

An excellent outlet for Lennon and McCartney's more commercial leftovers.

LEACH, SAM [B. 1936]

As a Liverpool entrepreneur and promoter, Sam Leach exhibited unbounded enthusiasm and plenty of ideas, but his organisational flaws prevented him from making the big league. He would announce events before they had been properly planned, and a letter from George Harrison to a fan tells how Sam had ten bands booked for the following weekend and nowhere to put them. Right from the start, when Sam was conducting business from a telephone booth, he would call his one-man set-up The Leach Organisation.

Sam began presenting rock 'n' roll shows on Merseyside as early as 1958, usually with local bands but occasionally with national names such as Emile Ford and The Checkmates. He saw The Beatles at Hambleton Hall early in 1961 and was soon working with them at the Cassanova Club. In the depths of the Cold War, he described them as the boys with the Atom Beat. In March 1961, he started presenting shows at the Iron Door, close to the Cavern, including all-nighters with The Beatles. He did consider managing them but a badly organised gig in Aldershot put paid to that.

Under the name of *Operation Big Beat*, Sam presented beat shows at the Tower Ballroom, New Brighton. Brian Epstein spoke at his wedding in June 1962 but that didn't stop him gazumping Sam to book Little Richard for the Tower. Possibly the agent Don Arden sensed there would be less hassle in getting money from Epstein. Sam's precarious finances depended on each individual show doing well.

Sam and his bouncer Terry McCann also considered managing Cilla Black but again Brian Epstein took control. Later, McCann became the inspiration for Dennis Waterman's character in the TV series *Minder*.

Sam Leach started a chain of hairdressers and occasionally promoted concerts. To give him credit, he staged the memorial service and concert for John Lennon outside St George's Hall, Liverpool, less than a week after Lennon's death, a remarkable achievement for anyone and especially for Sam. Sam has spoken at many Beatles festivals and written his memoir, *The Rocking City*, and even though he has been dogged by ill health in recent years, he makes time for the fans.

A firm believer in local talent, which included The Beatles.

LEITCH, DONOVAN – SEE DONOVAN

LENNON, ALFRED [1912–1976]

The official story of the Lennons emanates from Aunt Mimi, that is from the Stanleys, and as a result the Lennon side of John's family has been maligned. Alf Lennon was not the wastrel that some might think and had many good qualities. The first book to appreciate that there might have been an imbalance was Albert Goldman's *The Lives of John Lennon* (1988), which described Alf as 'a brave merchant seaman', but few readers took any notice of what Goldman had to say about anything

Alf Lennon's father, also called John Lennon, was born in Dublin and raised in Liverpool. John and his wife Polly had six children including Alfred, also known as 'Freddie', who was born in 1912, with the youngest, Charles, born in 1918. When John died in 1921, the family had little money and it was common practice for children without a father to be raised at an orphanage, in this case the Bluecoat Orphanage, with only short holidays at home. Both Alf and his sister Edith attended the orphanage, where they received a decent education. Alf met Julia Stanley in Sefton Park in 1929, when he was 16 and she 15.

Alf became a merchant seaman and he saw Julia when he returned home, dating her over many years. Her family did not approve and none of them attended their wedding at Mount Pleasant Register Office in Liverpool on 3 December 1938. Straight after the wedding Alf sailed to the West Indies on a three-month tour.

The Stanleys notwithstanding, everybody liked Alf. He was a small, good-looking man (five feet three inches), always singing and whistling. He was the life of any party and loved amending the words of current hits, later one of John Lennon's pastimes. He could sing Italian arias. The Stanleys thought he lacked stability, a quality shared with Julia.

Alf was at sea when John was born in October 1940. While in New York he missed a ship leaving for Britain and was jailed on Ellis Island for drunkenness. There are many stories of him being disciplined and possibly he exaggerated them. In 1944 he was jailed for a month for stealing provisions and was flogged. In 1946 he was arrested in Buenos Aires as a possible murder suspect. It appears that the police were looking for a man called Alennon, and thought 'A. Lennon' might be the one.

While Alf was away, Julia was seeing other men and she gave a birth to a girl in 1945 after an affair with a Welsh soldier, Taffy Williams. Julia then lived with Bobby Dykins, and John was raised by her sister Mimi. In 1946 Alf asked if he could take John to Blackpool. His intention was to start a new life with him in New Zealand but Julia demanded his return.

When Alf saw The Beatles on TV, he realised that it was his son, but he and John did not make contact until 1964. The *Daily Express* found him working as a porter in a London hotel. For a time he was managed by Tony Cartwright (road manager for Tom Jones) and together they wrote his Pye single 'That's My Life (My Love and My Home)', now a Beatles curio. John did not approve of the 45, but he did have Alf and his 19-year-old wife Pauline Jones as house guests, although John soon fell out with them. They had two sons, David and Robin.

Alf died from lung cancer in Brighton on 1 April 1976 and though John offered to pay for the funeral, Pauline refused the money. Alf had begun working on his autobiography and Pauline completed the text as *Daddy, Come Home*, which was published in 1990, the title a reference to John's song 'Mother'.

John hardly saw him but he certainly had his genes.

LENNON, UNCLE CHARLIE [1918–2002]

For many years before his death, John Lennon's Uncle Charlie would attend Beatles conventions and tell everyone that the story of his brother, Alf, was completely wrong and that he was a decent guy. He became a great local favourite, known to everyone as 'Uncle Charlie'. His visits to the shops around Sefton Park would coincide with the timetable for the Magical Mystery Tour bus, so that the guide could say, 'Oh look, there's Uncle Charlie!' The bus would stop and Charlie would pose for photographs and maybe sing a snatch of his own song 'Ships of the Mersey'. He was full of pride for his nephew, and would say, 'He changed the world, didn't he? A Lennon changed the world.'

Charlie witnessed the tensions between the Lennons and the Stanleys, which came to a head when Alf received a letter in 1945 telling him that Julia was having an affair with a gunner, Taffy Williams. Alfred jumped ship to return home and Julia claimed her pregnancy was a result of being raped. Charlie went to see the soldier and discovered that they had been having an affair, condoned by Julia's father. 'They called it quits,' said Charlie, 'but Alfred had no intention of divorcing her. He worshipped her and he even offered to bring up the child as his own.'

After seven years in the Royal Artillery, Charlie returned to civilian life in 1946. His mother died in 1948 and as his brothers wanted to sell the house, he moved to Warwickshire and qualified as a chef. He lost touch with the young John Lennon until 1963. 'People would say to me, "There is someone who looks like you in The Beatles." I said, "There can't be anyone who looks like me," but sure enough it was John.' He contacted Alf and they went to a Beatles Christmas show at Finsbury Park Empire.

Alf wanted to contact his son but John slammed the door in his face. 'He had been painted as the black sheep of the family,' said Charlie, still angry about the event 40 years later. 'Mimi, whom I call the Wicked Witch of Woolton, had poisoned his mind about the Lennons. I wrote John a stinking letter telling him that he shouldn't believe all he had been told. There was another side to the story. He was reconciled with his father and he invited me round to the house. He said, "Charlie, you're just like me, you've got two left feet in your mouth."' Charlie continued to work in restaurants and would tell people, 'John is the working class hero, but I am the working class Lennon.'

Everybody's Uncle Charlie.

LENNON, CYNTHIA [1939–2015]

Every relationship is different and nobody really knows what goes on behind closed doors, but if you had ever met Cynthia Lennon at a Beatles convention you would have wondered why John ever left her. She seems to have been, and probably was, the perfect rock-star wife.

Her parents, Charles and Lilian Powell, were Liverpudlians but like many expectant mothers, she was evacuated to Blackpool when the war started. Her daughter Cynthia was born there on 10 September 1939. She was raised with her two elder brothers in Hoylake on the Wirral, but by 1956 her father had died and they had left home. She started at the Liverpool College of Art in September 1957 and was engaged to a local window cleaner. She got to know John Lennon in the lettering class and although John was taken with her beauty, he mocked her Wirral (that is, posh) accent and her neatness – being in a lettering class was not John Lennon's idea of fun.

John and Cyn, as he called her, soon became a couple, but on his terms. He slapped her when she danced (and only danced) with somebody else, but he was persistently unfaithful. He wanted her to look like his favourite actress, Brigitte Bardot, so she changed her hairstyle, went on a diet and wore tight sweaters. He could be affectionate, creating an eight-page Christmas card-cum-love letter in 1959.

The ever-possessive Mimi had no time for Cynthia, possibly regarding her as another distraction in his wayward life, and Lilian thought John was a waste of space. John would write to Cynthia from Hamburg and she would transcribe lyrics of new American records and send them to him. She and Dot Rhode, Paul's girlfriend, went to Hamburg to see The Beatles in 1961, a mixed blessing for all parties, although Cynthia did become friendly with Astrid Kirchherr.

Ignoring contraceptives, Cynthia became pregnant with their son Julian in 1962 and even the feckless John felt that he had to do the right thing. They were married in the Mount Pleasant Register Office in Liverpool on 23 August 1962, conveniently timed for when Lilian was in Canada to visit relations. Brian Epstein allowed them to stay at his flat at 36 Falkner Street. As many fans dreamed of marrying their music heroes, Brian was mindful that The Beatles might lose their popularity if John's marriage became public knowledge and for the first part of 1963 at least, this was kept secret. When The Beatles appeared on *The Ed Sullivan Show* in February 1964, a caption telling the fans that John was married was shown on screen.

For most of the time, John behaved as though he were single. When The Beatles had time off in 1963, John chose to go to Spain with Brian Epstein rather than be with his wife. Although John never said any of the songs were about Cynthia, he did write 'Norwegian Wood' about an affair he was having.

In July 1964 John and Cynthia moved into Kenwood, their house in Weybridge, which, with improvements, cost £60,000. When John was at home, he was more like a big kid. She hated his drug-taking and when she did agree to an LSD trip, she saw him transformed into an animal with razor-sharp teeth. She was happier when John found the Maharishi and she thought Transcendental Meditation was beneficial for him.

In 1968 Cynthia went for a two-week holiday in Greece with friends, including 'Magic' Alex Madras, at John's suggestion; but he had an ulterior motive. She returned home to find Yoko Ono in her dressing gown. She was comforted by Alex and when John wanted a divorce, he said it was because of her adultery. Cynthia would only agree if it was because of his relationship with Yoko, and they were divorced in November. She came to accept that Yoko was good for him as she herself had never been a part of his creative life.

In 1970 Cynthia married Roberto Bassanini, the son of an Italian hotel owner, but the relationship was short-lived. She then opened a restaurant in Ruthin, North Wales, and Julian went to school there. Her third marriage, in 1976, was to an engineer from Lancashire, John Twist. In 1978 Cynthia published her autobiography *A Twist Of Lennon*, which contained her own illustrations. The settlement with John was not generous; however she did enjoy success as a designer. Some of her ceramics can be seen above the entrances in Liverpool's Cavern Walks. Many tourists miss this, as they are not attributed to her.

Cynthia and John Twist divorced in 1983, and she then had a long relationship with a chauffeur from Liverpool, Jim Christie, living with him in Penrith and then the Isle of Man and Normandy. She spoke at Beatles conventions and recorded a single, 'Those Were The Days', in 1995. She married her fourth husband, nightclub owner Noel Charles, in 2002 and they moved to Majorca. Cynthia was widowed in 2013.

She wrote a new biography of her first husband, *John* (2005), admitting for the first time that he had physically abused her. In 2006, she and Yoko met publicly for the opening of *Love* from Cirque du Soleil in Las Vegas. In 2009 she and Julian opened an exhibition of their artefacts at The Beatles Story in Liverpool.

Cynthia Lennon died on 1 April 2015. Her ventures into design, owning restaurants, singing and writing were not always successful and it seemed that no matter what she did or whom she married, she would always be John Lennon's wife.

An object lesson in how to be a rock star's wife.

LENNON, JOHN [1940–1980]

Despite the widespread belief that German bombs were dropping on Liverpool on 9 October 1940, John Winston Lennon was born during a respite from the air raids at Oxford Street Maternity Hospital, Liverpool. His parents, Alf and Julia, split up in 1942 and because Julia was feckless, her family thought that John should be raised by her sister, Mimi, and her husband, George, who had a dairy business in the middle class suburb of Woolton. In 1945 they moved into a large semi-detached house at 251 Menlove Avenue, which is now a National Trust property.

John attended Dovedale Road School until 1952 but although he didn't show much aptitude for learning, he passed the 11-plus and moved to Quarry Bank High School. Again, he lacked application and rebelled against the teachers and the curriculum. He told *Rolling Stone* in 1971, 'When I was about 12, I used to think I must be a genius but nobody's noticed.' He only took an interest in art, and he preferred reading books to doing homework. His *Daily Howl* notebooks mocked staff and fellow pupils and foreshadowed his books of poetry and prose. He had an unhealthy obsession with the disabled and he would ridicule them in his work.

Hard as it is to believe, the unruly boy sang in the church choir at St Peter's and, inspired by the emergence of Lonnie Donegan in 1956, he formed a skiffle group mostly from fellow pupils, The Quarrymen, who performed at the church's summer fete in July 1957. There he met Paul McCartney, and once Paul had joined the group moved defiantly away from skiffle and into rock 'n' roll. John and Paul wrote songs together but they would rarely be performed on stage before 1962.

John Lennon failed his O-levels in 1957 but his headmaster, William Pobjoy, managed to secure him a place at the Liverpool College of Art. There, John would only be one of many bohemians, but he still antagonised the teachers. By now he was dressing as a Teddy boy, and spending his allowance on alcohol and girls.

Although John saw little of his mother in his early years, he got to know her in his teens. She could play the banjo and when he bought his first guitar, she taught him banjo chords, which effectively meant he was using four strings. She was killed in a road accident on the dual carriageway outside Mimi's Menlove Avenue house in 1958. In the aftermath of the tragedy, John became resentful and argumentative, but he bonded with Paul who had lost his mother two years earlier.

In 1960 The Beatles, through Allan Williams, secured a residency in Hamburg's red light district, which transformed their music and their style. They learned to play lengthy sets and how to handle aggressive audiences. In a world of sex, drugs (pep pills) and rock 'n' roll, Lennon became a supreme stage performer, the focal point of the group, and he was a good rhythm guitarist. They returned to Liverpool in December 1960, totally unrecognisable from four months earlier, and they

Lennon.

25/11	Comments		GJB.
29/11	Talk	D. 29/11 /	1 H.D.
29/11	Talk after warning	D. 2.12.55 /	2RSS
2/12	Nuisance.		(JMW)
6/12	Fighting in the classroom	D 7/12/55 /	2RSS
6.12	Shortening work	D 8/12/55 /forms	2 RLB
	c/f	c	/

9.1.	misconduct	D. 17/1.56	RAR
16/1	Noise during lesson		1RSS.
16/1	Chewing.		1H.J.
16/1.	Silliness.	D 18/1/56	1H.D.
23.1	Talk	D. 24/1/56/	RAR
23.1	No import.		K14.
9.2	Impudent answer to question	D. 9.2.16	R.L.J.
6.2	Late for lesson		1RLB
10/2	Nuisance.	D 13/2/56 /	1 JMW)
13.2	Misconduct	D. 16/2/56 /	R.L.J.
13.2	Talk after warning	D 17/2/ /	2RSB
13.2	No H.W.		K14.
	Late 31/1 8/2	D 21/2/	1ERO

PLEASE TURN ON

John's detention notes from Quarry Bank High School, 1955-56, showing what a naughty boy he had been – talking after a warning, fighting, being a nuisance, chewing, silliness… Surprising he wasn't expelled at once!

took the city, especially the Cavern, by storm. Brian Epstein became their manager.

John's best friend at art college, Stuart Sutcliffe, had left the group to study in Hamburg and when The Beatles returned in April 1962, they learnt that he had died, another tragedy that affected John badly. John married another art student, Cynthia Powell, in August 1962, after she fell pregnant with his child. That same month Ringo Starr replaced Pete Best in The Beatles, and the world-changing line-up of John, Paul, George and Ringo was born, as it happens in the order that they joined the group and also in order of import-ance. It was John's group, no doubt about that.

Lennon could easily have been his defiant self in 1963 and destroyed whatever The Beatles were doing, but even he had the sense to see that he should hold himself in check and do as he was told. Often his only rebellion was to loosen his tie. As a result, The Beatles were incredibly product-ive in 1963-64, having hit single after hit single, recording four albums, making a film and under-taking extensive tours. Lennon later said that he hated being paraded like a circus animal and the concept of disabled children being brought to see them at gigs appalled him: what could he, a mere Beatle, do for them? The strain of having to be persistently polite was getting to him.

He transformed the whole concept of press conferences with his witty one-liners, and the other Beatles followed his lead. In November 1963, he was seen as an endearing scamp when he stepped out of line at the *Royal Variety Perform-ance* to tell those in the expensive seats to 'rattle your jewellery'. He was clearly uncomfortable at a Foyles literary luncheon for the launch of his book of comic prose, poetry and drawings, *In His Own Write* (1964), but he wrote a second one, *A Spaniard in the Works* (1965). The influence of Edward Lear and *The Goon Show* is strong, but the work is unmistak-

ably Lennon. It could be argued that the books are among the top-selling poetry books of all time.

Both John and Paul had a sound knowledge of the popular music of the day, be it standards, pop, rock 'n' roll, country or R&B. They often wrote by playing a song they loved and then changing the chords and the lyrics, so that Bobby Parker's 'Watch Your Step', say, became 'I Feel Fine'. Their results were often startlingly original and their lyrics quirky and streetwise. It is frequently said that McCartney reined in Lennon's excesses, while Lennon discouraged McCartney's sentimentality. This is partly true as they had their own comfort zones, but 'Goodnight' sounds like a McCartney song and 'Let Me Roll It' pure Lennon.

However, whereas Paul has always been reluc-tant to reveal his true self in songs, John was doing just that from an early stage and 'Help!', 'I'm A Loser' and 'Nowhere Man' reveal the cracks in Beatlemania. John admired the way Bob Dylan put both political ideas and surreal images into his songs and this fuelled John's songwriting. He wanted to emulate the songs crowds chanted at rallies. The fact that he had already written songs that would suit that purpose escaped him, and the first song to deliberately have that quality was 1967's 'All You Need Is Love'.

John was smoking marijuana during 1964–65 and then came LSD. John went into his 'fat Elvis' period – eating, drinking and spending to excess, while living reclusively in his stockbroker belt mansion in Surrey. Not too reclusive though as he would travel in his psychedelic-coloured Rolls-Royce, which fetched $2.2m at auction in 1985.

In March 1966, in a frank profile by Maureen Cleave in the London *Evening Standard*, he said that The Beatles 'were more popular than Jesus now'. There was little reaction to this remark in the UK but there was furore across the Bible Belt in America. Radio stations banned their records and memorabilia was burned. Brian Epstein forced Lennon to apologise – that in itself being a first – and the 1966 summer tour was their last.

No songwriter ever admits that their work has been influenced by drug-taking, but how else would John have come up with 'Tomorrow Never Knows' in 1966, a record that gave the Chemical Brothers their whole career? John viewed his childhood through a psychedelic prism in 'Strawberry Fields Forever' and no record before or since 'A Day in the Life' has so captured the terrifying feeling of a mind spinning out of control. Coming at the end of the brightly coloured *Sgt Pepper*, it suggested that drugs were not the answer.

John, who was always keen to replace one passion with another, took up Transcendental Meditation as practised by Maharishi Mahesh Yogi, but was disappointed to discover that his spiritual teacher was as human as he was. By April 1968 John was not only back on LSD but taking heroin and cocaine as well. In 1968 he was convicted, but only for possession of marijuana, and so could count himself lucky that it wasn't a more serious charge.

On 9 November 1966, John attended a preview of an exhibition of Yoko Ono's work at the Indica gallery in London. The precise date of this preview is uncertain. Numerous sources suggest it was 9 November, but as the brochure indicates the exhibition opened on 8 Novemter, the preview may well have been on 7 November. Whatever the date, John was charmed by its surrealism, but their relationship didn't blossom until May 1968. The avant-garde sounds that they recorded on their first night together were released as *Unfinished Music No. 1: Two Virgins*, with the front and back sleeves showing them completely naked. The front cover was reproduced on the cover of *Private Eye* with John saying, 'I tell you officer, it won't stand up in court.' That and the companion album, *Unfinished Music No. 2: Life With The Lions*, sold poorly, the first Beatle

product to have no following. Even less appealing were the avant-garde films that he made with Yoko.

Unusually for the time, John and Yoko were openly living together and Yoko attended the sessions for the so-called *White Album*, and it was this, not her nationality, which alienated her from the other Beatles. John was divorced from Cynthia on 8 November 1968 and he married Yoko in Gibraltar on 20 March 1969, writing about it in 'The Ballad Of John And Yoko', this time likening his unpopularity to Christ's crucifixion. On 22 April 1969, he changed his name to John Ono Lennon. From now on, he was to see little of his and Cynthia's son, Julian. In so doing, John was duplicating the behaviour of his own father.

John and Yoko formed their own group, the Plastic Ono Band, and the hit singles 'Give Peace A Chance' (recorded during a bed-in at a Montreal hotel) and 'Happy Christmas, War Is Over' continued the love and peace theme of 'All You Need Is Love'. John's withdrawal from heroin was harrowingly captured in the brilliant 'Cold Turkey', but it wasn't for everyone. On 25 November 1969, Lennon returned his MBE in protest 'against Britain's involvement in the Nigeria–Biafra thing, against our support of America in Vietnam, and against "Cold Turkey" slipping down the charts.' He was earnest but he had not lost his sense of humour.

John often changed his appearance and now he chose round, National Health-styled spectacles (he had poor eyesight and hated contact lenses), grew shoulder-length hair and wore white suits.

His later tracks with The Beatles include the anguished 'I Want You (She's So Heavy)', the frivolous 'Mean Mr Mustard' and the sentimental 'Julia', written for both his mother and Yoko. In 'Revolution', he cannot decide whether to be counted in or out for violent demonstration. He supported Irish nationalism and it is possible that he funded the IRA.

The end of 'John Beatle' came with the release of the 1970 album *John Lennon/Plastic Ono Band* and the no-holds-barred *Rolling Stone* interview the following year. John had screamed before, notably in 'Twist and Shout', but never like this. He faced his childhood traumas in 'Mother', and in the stark 'God' he sang, 'I don't believe in Beatles'. He sniped at McCartney in 'How Do You Sleep', and the dream was over.

In parallel with all this, several of his lithographs were seized from the London Arts Gallery on the grounds that they were 'erotic and indecent'. The defence lawyers compared Lennon's work to Picasso, which was over-egging it, but they won the day and the lithographs were returned.

In September 1971, John moved to New York, first to Greenwich Village and then to the Dakota building close to Central Park. Fearing

JOHN ON JOHN

'I never lie awake thinking about show business. Show business people are like a little bunch of red nosed people who live together. We know some in that club, but we don't belong to it.' Talking to *Melody Maker*, 3 September 1961

'I want no more from being a record star. I'd like to see us making better and better films. I'm not craving any more gold discs even though they are a nice boost. That's all over. I just want to be an all round spastic, LP winner. I mean nothing nasty, honest I don't think I'd know a spastic from a Polaroid lens. When I use the word spastic in general conversation, I don't mean it literally. I feel terrible sympathy for these people – and we've had quite a lot of them on our travels.' Talking to *Melody Maker*, 10 April 1965 (Note journalist Ray Coleman's – later the paper's editor – comment during the interview: 'Lennon is currently playing a game all his own. He makes outrageous, seemingly irrelevant statements like that one, and then adds the words, "LP winner!" It's a send-up of *MM*'s Mailbag writers, renowned for advancing deep theoretical arguments about what's folk and what isn't and what's R&B and what isn't. John finds it hilarious.')

'Even if we were more successful in America, we'd never leave Britain. I don't like anywhere but Britain. We've been to 12 countries and I never want to go abroad again. Not even for my holidays. There's just something missing about abroad. Not that I mind foreigners. I just prefer them to be here, that's all.' Talking to Virginia Ironside, *Daily Mail*, November 1964

'Most people in Britain think I am somebody who won the pools. Won the pools and married a Hawaiian dancer. Whereas in the States we're treated like artists. Which we are! Or anywhere else for that matter. But here [in the UK] it's like the lad who knew Paul, got a lucky break, won the pools and married the actress.' Talking to *Melody Maker*, 2 October 1971

'Society is under the delusion that art is something you have extra, like crème de menthe. But societies don't exist with no artists. Art is a function of society. If you don't have artists you don't have society. We're not some kind of decadent strip show that appears on the side. We're as important as prime ministers and policemen. So "Power to the People" isn't expected to make a revolution. It's for the people to sing like the Christians sing hymns.' Talking to *Melody Maker*, 2 October 1971

his political radicalism, the US authorities used his drugs conviction to deny him residential status – in other words, if he left the country, he couldn't return. After a legal battle, his Green Card was approved in 1976 and at the time of his death he was considering a world tour.

Although he wrote his most famous song, 'Imagine' during the 70s, John's work during the decade was otherwise patchy and what should have been a brilliant album, *Rock 'n' Roll*, produced by Phil Spector and released in 1975, was a disappointment. John hated the sound of his voice and so had been drawn to Spector and his echo-enhanced productions.

John mellowed with the years, raising Sean, his son with Yoko who was born in October 1975, while Yoko resolved their business affairs. On 8 December 1980 John was assassinated, shortly after the release of their album *Double Fantasy*. It is possible that his return to public life pressed his killer into action. John's body was cremated at Hartsdale Crematorium, New York, two days later. Judging by the sorrowful gatherings everywhere, a major world figure had died.

There have been numerous memoirs and biographies about him, the most infamous being Albert Goldman's *The Lives of John Lennon* (1988), which took the worst possible slant on every event in his life and left some fans maintaining he had been assassinated twice. In reality, this mean-spirited book was not far from the truth. There have been biographical films and plays, notably Bob Eaton's 1981 *Lennon*, which originally starred Mark McGann. In 2002 Liverpool Airport was renamed the Liverpool John Lennon Airport and its advertising slogan, 'Above us only sky', indicated that there is a John Lennon line for everything.

Quite aside from his enormous talent, John Lennon is endlessly fascinating because he was a mass of contradictions. His main legacy is, and always will be, his remarkable songs, even though

they were often personal and self-indulgent. Yes, John Lennon was a narcissist but we love him for it.

Imagine no John Lennon.

LENNON, JULIA [1914–1958]

Many of John's characteristics can be found in his mother Julia, who was born in Liverpool on 12 March 1914, one of five daughters of George and Annie Stanley. She was a slim, pretty and short-sighted child, not a good student and one who developed an unconventional sense of humour. She could sing and her grandfather, William Stanley, taught her to play the banjo.

In August 1929, the 16-year-old Alf Lennon met 15-year-old Julia in Sefton Park. Julia worked as a cinema usherette, her perfect job as she loved the films of the day. They liked dancing, and Alf's brother Charlie referred to Alf and his redheaded girlfriend as 'Fred and Ginger'. In 1938 Julia married Alf, despite parental opposition, and their only child, John, was born in 1940.

While Alf was away at sea, Julia had a brief affair with a Welsh soldier, Taffy Williams, and their child, Victoria Elizabeth (born 19 June 1945), was adopted. Alf and Julia stopped living together after this but they never divorced. Julia moved in with Bobby Dykins, a porter at the Adelphi Hotel, and they had two daughters, Julia (born 5 March 1947) and Jackie (26 October 1949).

John was raised by Julia's sister Mimi, and for a long time did not realise that his mother was nearby. They became close when he was in his teens. Julia was far more tolerant of his bad behaviour than Mimi, and supported The Quarrymen. At first John learnt her banjo chords, and played them on four strings of his guitar. Paul said, 'Julia was lively and heaps of fun and way ahead of her time. Not too many blokes had mothers as progressive as she was.'

On 15 July 1958 Julia came to see Mimi, possibly even to hear the private recording that The Quarrymen had made. On leaving Mimi, Julia crossed the carriageway and, emerging from the hedge in the middle of the road, she was knocked down and killed by off-duty policeman Eric Clague. She disliked wearing her spectacles and possibly she didn't see the car coming, but in any event the driver was an unaccompanied learner.

The accident devastated John and he shared a bond with Paul as they had lost their mothers early. His ambivalent feelings about her are in two very different songs – 'Julia' and 'Mother'.

Encouraging her son's talent and supporting The Quarrymen.

LENNON, JULIAN [B. 1963]

Whether he likes it or not, and quite often he doesn't, Julian Lennon is the best-known offspring of a rock star, although he, naturally, wants to be assessed on his own talent and freed to an extent from the association. In the 2014 documentary film *Through The Picture Window* he frequently says, 'I'm not talking about my father.' According to him, the worst thing in the world is to have John Lennon for your dad. Of course he's wrong – he's got a tremendous advantage as he has his father's genes for a start.

John Charles Julian Lennon was born in Sefton General Hospital, Liverpool, on 8 April 1963, the only child of John and Cynthia Lennon. His godfather was Brian Epstein. Julian has been hurt by some of his father's uncaring comments about him, such as saying that his birth was the result of a drunken coupling.

A painting of his school friend Lucy O'Donnell, in the sky with diamonds, inspired one of the songs on *Sgt Pepper*. John wrote the lullaby 'Goodnight' for him. After the Lennons broke up, Paul visited Cyn and Julian and was inspired to write 'Hey Jude', the original title being 'Hey Jules'.

In an echo of his own father's behaviour, John had little contact with Julian when he and Yoko moved to New York. However, the couple's assistant, May Pang, then encouraged John to make contact. John bought him a drum kit and the 11-year-old played with his dad on 'Ya Ya', the final track of the 1974 album *Walls and Bridges*.

Julian had international success with *Valotte* (1984), which included two hit singles, the title track and 'Too Late For Goodbyes', with videos directed by Sam Peckinpah. He followed it with *The Secret Value of Daydreaming* (1986), and performed songs for the West End stage projects *Time* (for Dave Clark) and *The Hunting of the Snark* (for Mike Batt). He sang 'Ruby Tuesday' in the TV series *The Wonder Years* and 'When I'm Sixty-Four' for an insurance commercial. In 1991 his album *Help Yourself* contained Julian's best known single, 'Saltwater', but he left the business, appreciating the dangers of a rock 'n' roll lifestyle, to pursue interests in cooking, sailing and sculpting. There was talk of him joining 'The Threatles' for Live Aid and *Anthology*, but nothing came of it and it appears to be simply press speculation.

He returned with *Photograph Smile* in 1998, and emerged himself in film, in particular making a feature-length documentary, *Whale Dreamers*, about whales in Australia. In 2009, he made a charity single for Lucy O'Donnell when she died from lupus. In that same year he launched his White Feather Foundation, a charity for the well-being of the planet. His father had said that when he died, he would convey a message to him in the form of a white feature, so to Julian, a white feather symbolises peace. He has published a book of his Lennon memorabilia and been seen at several Beatles-related events.

However, there is an element of 'methinks, thou dost protest too much' about his self-pitying remarks. If he really wanted to get away from the shadow of his father, why does he turn on the echo and sound so much like him?

Far too young to have any effect on The Beatles as a working group, but he did inspire three songs.

LENNON, YOKO ONO – SEE YOKO ONO

LESTER, RICHARD [B. 1932]

The Beatles were so hot and so celebrated at the start of 1964 that even a simple, straightforward pop film would have been a major success. The fact that it was the astonishing *A Hard Day's Night* is further testimony to the remarkable talent that surrounded The Beatles during the so-called Swinging Sixties. In this case, the director Richard Lester. *A Hard Day's Night* was true to The Beatles, true to the social changes that were taking place, and true to the very notion of cinema itself.

Richard Lester was a childhood prodigy. He was born in Philadelphia in 1932, went to university when he was 15 and graduated in clinical psychology four years later. Having obtained his degree, he chose to work with CBS Television and soon found he was directing programmes, thereby putting his training to good use. Rather rashly, he made a live western that went off air when the horse chewed the microphone.

In 1954 Dick came to Europe and toured around, happy to play the piano in a restaurant in exchange for a meal. He settled in England in May 1955 and with his experience in US television, he was able to work for new commercial station Associated Rediffusion. He brought the radio humour of The Goons to TV with *The Idiot Weekly, A Show Called Fred* and *Son of Fred*. When Peter Sellers bought a new 16mm camera he asked Dick to film them in a field, resulting in the famed comedy short *The Running Jumping & Standing Still Film* (1960). It has been shown constantly since that time and cost £70 to make.

The main source of Dick's income came from making commercials, which he regarded as invaluable work as he could experiment with lenses and various techniques. He directed a pop musical, *It's Trad, Dad!*, featuring Helen Shapiro and Craig Douglas in a mundane storyline that gave them the opportunity to visit recording studios and clubs to see the artists at work. Dick later commented, 'It was a three-week pop quickie. It makes *A Hard Day's Night* seem like the work of Jean-Paul Sartre.' If you want to know what popular music was like just before The Beatles, watch this film.

It's Trad, Dad! has cultural importance, being the only film covering all the popular jazz acts in the UK. Plus, Dick's wacky filming of The Temperance Seven gave a taste of things to come; and like *It's Trad, Dad!*, *A Hard Day's Night* was about youths who were constantly hassled by adults.

The United Artists producer Walter Shenson thought Dick would be right for a quirky British comedy about the space race, *The Mouse on the Moon*, with Margaret Rutherford and Bernard Cribbins. That worked well, so Shenson offered him a film with The Beatles. Dick met Brian Epstein and was pleased that he was no Colonel Parker, who was stifling Elvis Presley's film appearances. Dick knew the playwright Alun Owen and asked him to spend time with The Beatles and write a script.

A Hard Day's Night, shot documentary style in black and white, was perfect, showing The Beatles on tour and how hard it was for them to escape their fans. The cast included some fine British character actors – Richard Vernon, Wilfrid Brambell, Norman Rossington and Victor Spinetti. John and Paul wrote classic songs that were filmed like today's pop videos, with Dick using what he had learnt from the *Running Jumping* film. *A Hard Day's Night* was a commercial and critical success, a very hard trick to pull off with a pop film, making other performers realise they could make films with some artistic validity.

Staying with United Artists, Dick made a film from Ann Jellicoe's stage play *The Knack…And How To Get It,* staring Rita Tushingham (also from Liverpool), Ray Brooks, Michael Crawford and Donal Donnelly. Dick said that *A Hard Day's Night* was about four people who could communicate with each other without speaking, while *The Knack* was about four people who spoke endlessly but couldn't communicate with each other.

His second film with The Beatles, *Help!,* was a huge success but lacked the grittiness of the first. It was made in colour, on location, with a screenplay by Charles Wood that was more pantomime than reality. Still, the songs were fine and the actors, Leo McKern, Eleanor Bron, Victor Spinetti and Roy Kinnear, did their best. John Lennon remarked that The Beatles were guest stars in their own film, and the band were reluctant to make a third feature for United Artists.

In 1966 Dick made the musical *A Funny Thing Happened On The Way To The Forum* staring Zero Mostel and Phil Silvers, with a witty score from Stephen Sondheim. Oddly, both Ringo Starr and Phil Silvers had the same problem; they would twitch if the camera was on them for too long. Dick was often praised for his flashy cutting techniques, but sometimes he was just hiding the twitches.

Dick always considered content to be more important than form, and did not object when so much of his style was picked up by The Monkees. Francis Ford Coppola's first film, *You're a Big Boy Now* (1966), is almost an homage to Richard Lester.

Dick's first major misjudgement was with *How I Won the War,* again written by Charles Wood, with Michael Crawford, Michael Hordern and John Lennon, appearing with a short haircut and wearing National Health spectacles. The audience at the time did not know what to make of it – why were these soldiers making a cricket pitch when they were supposed to be fighting a war? – and as irony doesn't sell, the film died at the box office. Although it was muddled, it was intended to be an anti-Vietnam film, and today it can stand alongside *M*A*S*H* and *Oh! What A Lovely War.*

Dick made his first American film, *Petulia* (1968), with Julie Christie, George C. Scott, Richard Chamberlain and the Grateful Dead. It was very negative about America and failed to find an audience, but many consider it his best work.

Worse was to come. He returned to United Artists to both produce and direct a film of Spike Milligan's surreal stage play *The Bed Sitting Room.* Despite a remarkable cast, including Sir Ralph Richardson as 'the bed sitting room', this film totally failed to find an audience, although looking at it today, it is a remarkably brave work about how life could continue after a nuclear war. Despite his huge successes, Richard Lester had become unbankable.

For over a year Dick tried to get funding for the filming of one of George MacDonald Fraser's books about Flashman, the bully in *Tom Brown's Schooldays* The project was highly commercial, but nobody wanted to trust him with a film. He did not make another film until his light-hearted remake of *The Three Musketeers* in 1973 with a script by Fraser. Very cleverly he shot enough for two films at once and *The Four Musketeers* was released the following year. The cast included Michael York, Oliver Reed and Charlton Heston, and Spike Milligan thanked Dick for the scene in which he went to bed with Raquel Welch.

Dick hit the big time with an out-and-out thriller, *Juggernaut* (1974), in which Richard Harris has to choose between cutting the red or blue wire – his choice will either kill the ocean liner's passengers or save them. In retrospect, it would have been good to have made the film with two endings, so that audiences would not know what they would be seeing. He was then able to make his Flashman film, *Royal Flash* (1975), with Malcolm McDowell.

Robin And Marian (1976) was another success, and then in 1981 he hit the motherlode with a $25m film, *Superman II*, featuring Christopher Reeve and Gene Hackman. He followed this two years later with *Superman III*, starring Reeve and Richard Pryor. In that film, when Clark Kent meets an old flame we hear The Beatles' 'Roll Over Beethoven' on the soundtrack, a clear allusion to Dick's past.

Richard Lester's work can be seen as very varied. He was someone who was always running and jumping and not standing still. He worked in several genres, and as a result his work has been underrated.

One reason that The Beatles' legacy endures is because of the brilliance of *A Hard Day's Night*.

LEWISOHN, MARK [B. 1958]

Mark Lewisohn was born in Kingsbury, north London, in 1958. He attended the Pinner Grammar School before working in administrative roles for the BBC and the trade publication *Music Week*.

He soon appreciated the benefits of archives and accurate research, and his prime area of study has been The Beatles. He wrote regularly for *The Beatles Book Monthly* and his first book, *The Beatles Live!* (1986), was a finely chronicled history of all The Beatles' known performances (many of them revealed for the first time). This was followed by *The Complete Beatles Recording Sessions* (1988), which looked at all The Beatles' tapes at Abbey Road. Mark has often been employed by Paul McCartney, EMI and Apple Corps to research and annotate back catalogue releases, notably the *Anthology* series of double CDs.

There have been other Beatles books, but the prime achievement will be Lewisohn's three-volume history *All These Years*, of which *Volume 1 – Tune In* was published by Little, Brown in 2013, the expanded edition covering 1,700 pages. The volumes will go up to the break-up of The Beatles, and are unlikely to be completed until 2030 by which time most of the participants will be dead, although they will come to life in his text.

As well as his interest in The Beatles, Mark wrote the extraordinary *Radio Times Guide to TV Comedy* (1998), which has become an invaluable reference source online and makes the reader wonder how one man could have watched and then annotated so much television. He also wrote *Funny, Peculiar: The True Story Of Benny Hill* (2002), again beautifully researched but not easy to read because the subject is, well, funny, peculiar.

Many major figures have biographers devoted to their work, including Peter Guralnick (Elvis Presley), Johnny Rogan (The Byrds), Greil Marcus and Michael Gray (Bob Dylan) and Clinton Heylin (Bruce Springsteen), but no performer has been better served than Mark Lewisohn's subjects. In his diligent research, little is left to speculation, and he has built up a comprehensive archive that no doubt will benefit future researchers.

George Harrison once corrected Mark by saying The Beatles had only played Shea Stadium once, but Mark was right; they had played there twice.

Mark has helped to keep The Beatles' story alive for this and future generations.

LINDSAY-HOGG, MICHAEL [B. 1940]

Michael Lindsay-Hogg was born in New York City in 1940, and into the British aristocracy – or was he? His father was Sir Edward Lindsay-Hogg, and his mother the American actress Geraldine Fitzgerald, who appeared with Laurence Olivier in *Wuthering Heights*. However, he always nursed suspicions that his father was the family friend, Orson Welles, to whom he bears a physical resemblance.

Michael came into The Beatles' world as director of ITV's *Ready Steady Go!*, and went on to direct the promotional films for 'Paperback Writer', 'Rain', 'Hey Jude' and 'Revolution'.

Michael directed the shambolic Rolling Stones film *Rock And Roll Circus*, which featured John and Yoko, where it seemed that the participants had overindulged in herbal refreshments. That should have set alarm bells ringing about filming a documentary on The Beatles recording a new album, but nonetheless Michael accepted the commission and the band were filmed all through January 1969 for *Let It Be*. He told *Rolling Stone*, 'Every day there was a different one to hate.' Much in the same way as *Rock And Roll Circus* is regarded, the *Let It Be* film is now seen as a telling documentary about the price of fame.

Having seemingly a passion for fraught relationships, Michael went on to direct Simon and Garfunkel's *The Concert In Central Park* (1982). He has had success in other areas, notably directing the Broadway play *Whose Life Is It Anyway?*

(1979), co-directing the TV drama series *Brideshead Revisited* (1981), and both writing and directing the film *The Object of Beauty* (1991), starring John Malkovich. He also directed Paul McCartney's video for 'London Town' (1978).

His former wife, Lucy Davies, became the second wife of Lord Snowdon.

He told it like it was and we have a clear picture of what went wrong for The Beatles.

LITTLE RICHARD [B. 1932]

Which song did The Beatles perform on stage more times than any other? Well, we haven't got all the set-lists but it's a fair bet that it is 'Long Tall Sally'. It was in their repertoire at the start and it was in their repertoire at the end. Paul sings it to this day, with Little Richard himself having acknowledged that McCartney does a brilliant version, and he is often scathing about white singers covering his songs.

The rock 'n' roll explosion started with 'Rock Around The Clock', but Bill Haley was nobody's idea of a teenage revolutionary and was soon sidelined by Elvis Presley. Little Richard, with his six-inch pompadour, mascara, pencil-thin moustache and baggy trousers, was seen screaming his way through cameo appearances in *The Girl Can't Help It* (1956) and *Don't Knock the Rock* (1957), yelling his head off and playing the piano standing up. Even so, there was still an element of standard showbiz about him – after a wild explosion of rock 'n' roll, he would bow to the audience as though he had been playing a Chopin minuet.

Little Richard was born Richard Wayne Penniman in Macon, Georgia, on 5 December 1932, although for a long time he claimed to have been born on Christmas Day 1935. He cut blues and gospel tracks in his youth, but came to fame when he recorded for the Specialty label in 1955. With 'Long Tall Sally', 'Tutti Frutti, 'Ready Teddy' and 'Good Golly Miss Molly', Little Richard created the new language of rock 'n' roll. The songs were nonsensical, as daft as nursery rhymes, but that was the point. They were free-spirited and exciting and led to outlandish vocal performances. No wonder teenagers rioted as he sang about exactly that in 'Rip It Up'.

We can now see that Little Richard was preposterously camp, but nobody thought in such terms at the time. He claimed to have had a bisexual lifestyle and there are numerous stories about his backstage excesses. He became known as the 'Georgia Peach', although the Georgia Screech would have been as appropriate. Both John and Paul were turned on to Little Richard by 'Long Tall Sally'' and they found Paul could mimic his voice perfectly.

During a bumpy plane trip to Australia in October 1957, Little Richard swore that if he got out alive he would dedicate himself to God. True to his word, he threw his rings off the Sydney Harbour Bridge and became a minister. Specialty signed up Larry Williams, a bad boy of rock in a way that the Stones could only dream of, who sounded like Little Richard on 'Bad Boy', 'Slow Down' and 'Dizzy Miss Lizzy'. Another rival singer, and another bad boy, was Esquerita, sometimes known as S.Q. Reeder.

During 1962, Little Richard intended to perform gospel music on a UK tour with Sam Cooke, but as soon as he saw the ecstatic reception for Cooke he didn't want to be upstaged and was rocking wildly. He appeared with The Beatles and many other Liverpool groups at the Tower Ballroom on 12 October 1962, and cursed both The Swinging Blue Jeans and The Merseybeats for doing his songs. It is said (by Little Richard, it has to be noted) that Brian Epstein offered him a 50 per cent management deal on The Beatles. Still, Brian Epstein did book him to top the bill at the Liverpool Empire on 28 October 1962, but the show was intended as a showcase for The Beatles' first single.

Little Richard returned to the UK in 1963 with the best rock 'n' roll package ever seen in the UK – The Everly Brothers, Little Richard, Bo Diddley and the Rolling Stones. When Richard returned to America, he recorded for Vee-Jay and his wild version of 'Whole Lotta Shakin' Goin' On' opens with a rap about the rockin' craze over in England.

Jimi Hendrix was part of Little Richard's US road band and featured on some recordings, notably the utterly soulful 'I Don't Know What You've Got (But It's Got Me)', which indicates that Richard could have gone in other directions. Richard went on to sack Jimi, for upstaging him with colourful shirts.

There are many songs that have been written in Little Richard's style including 'I'm Down' (The Beatles) and 'Travelin' Band' (Creedence Clearwater Revival). Early tracks by Joe Tex and Otis Redding were very much in a Little Richard vein and Michael Jackson acknowledged his influence.

Little Richard recorded for Reprise in the early 1970s, and Slade had a hit with one of his little-known recordings, 'Get Down With It'. In 1986 the British producer Stuart Colman made an album with him, *Lifetime Friend*, recalling, 'I will never record a finer black voice than Little Richard's. To see him work in the studio was spine-tingling. He psyches himself into singing and it's rather like watching a weightlifter. Before they pull up the barbells, they are hollering and beating their chests and getting the adrenalin pumping. Richard is like that and he'll suddenly say, "I'm ready now."'

Following some unsuccessful surgery, Little Richard was confined to a wheelchair, but he did perform at the White House for President Obama in 2011, and his voice was still in amazing condition.

His 1984 authorised biography, *The Life And Times Of Little Richard* by Chas 'Dr Rock' White, remains the funniest and most entertaining of all rock biographies, although Richard's anecdotes are often fictional. Chas contends that 'Little Richard makes Pavarotti sound like a squeaking mouse.'

Like the sci-fi film, he came from outer space.

LOMAX, JACKIE [1944–2013]

Although Jackie Lomax had a full and fascinating musical career, he was one of Liverpool's unluck-iest musicians, possibly the nearest of the nearly men. With a little more publicity, his singles with The Undertakers could have sold much better and his George Harrison-produced album for The Beatles' Apple label, *Is This What You Want?* (1969), should have been a bestseller. Music fans cite 1968's 'Sour Milk Sea' as a Top 10 single that never was, so why didn't they buy it?

John Richard Lomax was born in Wallasey in 1944, and was a founder member of Dee and The Dynamites in 1960. The following year he joined The Undertakers, who admired his passionate voice with its punchy falsetto. He recalled, 'There were five of us instead of the usual four and having Brian Jones on sax was tremendous. We looked for obscure songs by the artists that we liked and I would give out the wrong names on stage to guard against other acts looking for the same songs.' Lomax married his childhood sweetheart Dionne Armitage when he was 18, and they were known around Liverpool as 'the golden couple'.

Although more forceful on stage than their records suggest, The Undertakers, who also featured Chris Huston, Geoff Nugent and Bugs Pemberton, did make some excellent singles includ-

ing their cover versions of 'Stupidity' (Solomon Burke), 'Everybody Loves A Lover' (Shirelles) and 'Just A Little Bit' (Rosco Gordon), their solitary chart entry. However, their best-known record was the 1963 hard-hitting dance number '(Do The) Mashed Potatoes', but as Jackie admitted in 2004, 'I was just shouting, and I didn't even know how to dance the mashed potato.'

After the band split up, Jackie went to New York with Huston and Pemberton and formed The Lomax Alliance. Their single, 'See The People', didn't sell but they did play support gigs at Brian Epstein's Saville Theatre.

In 1968 The Beatles invited Jackie to join their new label, Apple. George Harrison wrote and produced 'Sour Milk Sea', a mystical song about the age of the world. 'I thought it would be a hit,' said Lomax, 'but Apple released four singles on the same day and other labels would have complained if the BBC had played them all. Also, how could I compete against "Hey Jude" and "Those Were The Days"?'

The LP *Is This What You Want* followed, featuring 'Sour Milk Sea' and 11 of Lomax's own compositions. The musicians included Paul Mc-Cartney and Eric Clapton but the album suffered the same fate as ones by Doris Troy, James Taylor and Billy Preston: namely, Apple was in turmoil, partly because The Beatles were disintegrating. Among Lomax's unissued tracks was the punchy 'Goin' Back To Liverpool' with Billy Preston.

Back in America, Lomax recorded several solo albums, working with members of The Band and Allen Toussaint among others. He released *The Ballad of Liverpool Slim* (2001), which included his tribute to George Harrison, 'Friend-A-Mine'. Lomax often played at Beatles conventions and had regular bookings at the Cavern. He would listen to young bands taking up the songs from the sixties and his criticism was invariably the same, 'They're playing the songs too fast. They should listen to our records.'

After living in America for many years, Lomax returned to his first wife Dee in 2013. Although he was having medical treatment, he was so happy to be back where he felt he belonged. He was listening to his forthcoming album, *Against All Odds*, as he died in September.

A frontman and guitarist much admired by The Beatles, especially George Harrison.

LOVE, MIKE – SEE BEACH BOYS, THE

LOWE, JOHN DUFF [B. 1942]

John Duff Lowe, always known as 'Duff', was born in the West Derby area of Liverpool in 1942. He met Paul McCartney at the Liverpool Institute, and was invited to join The Quarrymen in January 1958 at gigs where a piano was to hand. This enabled them to perform Jerry Lee Lewis and Little Richard hits with more authenticity. Fortunately, as Paul had a piano in the living room they could practise at his house, although Jim McCartney stressed that they must play quietly and not disturb the neighbours.

Duff played on the private recording of 'That'll Be The Day' and 'In Spite Of All The Danger', which ended up in his possession. Amidst much publicity, he sold it to Paul McCartney for an undisclosed sum in 1981.

Duff raised a family in Bristol and dealt in stocks and shares. In the eighties he was part of the reformed Four Pennies and more recently he rejoined The Quarrymen.

Only 1, but he did play on The Quarrymen's first recording.

LYNCH, KENNY [B. 1938]

Born into a West Indian family in 1938, Kenny Lynch was raised in Stepney, London, and first appeared on stage with his sister Gladys, who under the name Maxine Daniels went on to perform as a singer in West End jazz clubs and became a recording artist in her own right. He worked with several dance bands but most of the time he was selling goods out of a suitcase on Oxford Street.

Kenny's first single, 'Mountain Of Love', made the charts in 1960 and he had his first Top 20 entry with 'Up On The Roof' in 1962. Like The Beatles, he was a supporting act on Helen Shapiro's tour in February 1963, and according to Kenny he heard her turn down 'Misery', as the song was not right for her. He offered to record it himself and his record was released on the same day as The Beatles' first album, also including 'Misery'. Kenny Lynch was therefore the first artist to cover a Lennon and McCartney composition. John Lennon had reservations about the guitar solo, saying he could have done better himself. Kenny had a Top 10 hit a few months later with 'You Can Never Stop Me Loving You'.

Kenny became a hit songwriter in his own right, often working with the American composer Mort Shuman. They wrote 'Sha-La-La-La-Lee', which reached No. 3 for The Small Faces, and 'Love's Just A Broken Heart' for Cilla Black. Kenny often worked as a comedy duo with his golf partner Jimmy Tarbuck, and he appeared in several comedy series including the highly controversial *Curry and Chips*, with Spike Milligan and Eric Sykes. In 1973 he was among the celebrities on the cover of *Band on the Run*. He was awarded an MBE and continues to perform, be it comedy, pop or jazz.

The first person to cover a Beatles song.

THE FIRST 20 LENNON/MCCARTNEY COVERS

1. 'Misery' by Kenny Lynch (March 1963)
2. 'I Saw Her Standing There' by Duffy Power (April 1963)
3. 'From Me To You' by The Typhoons (April 1963)
4. 'Do You Want To Know A Secret' by Billy J. Kramer with The Dakotas (April 1963)
5. 'I'll Be On My Way' by Billy J. Kramer with The Dakotas (April 1963)
6. 'Tu Perds Ton Temps (Please Please Me)' by Petula Clark (May 1963)
7. 'There's A Place' by The Kestrels (May 1963)
8. 'Please Please Me' by The Kestrels (May 1963)
9. 'Susie (Please Please Me)' by Die Team-Beats (June 1963)
10. 'From Me To You' by Del Shannon (June 1963)
11. 'Bad To Me' by Billy J. Kramer with The Dakotas (July 1963)
12. 'I Call Your Name' by Billy J. Kramer with The Dakotas (July 1963)
13. 'Tip Of My Tongue' by Tommy Quickly (August 1963)
14. 'Bad To Me' by Mike Redway (August 1963)
15. 'Liverpool Pops' by Russ Conway (August 1963) included 'From Me To You', 'Please Please Me', 'Thank You Girl' and 'Do You Want To Know A Secret'
16. 'Ich Komm Nicht Los Von Dir' (From Me To You)' by Gina Dobra (August 1963)
17. 'Hello Little Girl' by The Fourmost (August 1963)
18. 'She Loves You' by The Typhoons (September 1963)
19. 'Hello Little Girl' by The Typhoons (September 1963)
20. 'Love Of The Loved' by Cilla Black (September 1963)

McCARTNEY, JIM [1902–1976]

James McCartney was born 7 July 1902, the fifth child of Joe and Florrie McCartney, in the Everton district of Liverpool. Joe worked in a tobacco factory and played the tuba in the brass band. Although Jim had damaged his hearing by falling off a wall, he learnt to play the piano, bought from Isaac Epstein's store, and could entertain at family singsongs. He was always interested in the theatre and would sell programmes at the Theatre Royal in Everton.

When he was 14, he started work at the Cotton Exchange in the centre of Liverpool. He formed a dance band, at first called The Masked Melody Makers (and performing in black harlequin masks) but soon renamed Jim Mac's Jazz Band. They sometimes performed for silent movies. Their repertoire included 'Chicago' and 'After You've Gone', and Jim wrote a catchy instrumental, 'Eloise'. In 1974 Paul McCartney recorded this tune as 'Walking In The Park With Eloise' by The Country Hams, actually top Nashville session men.

Jim had known ward sister Mary Mohin for some time, but as he was approaching 40, it looked as though he would remain a bachelor.

They started dating during the war – their first date was in a shelter during a German bombing raid – and they married in April 1941. Their children, Paul and Mike, were born in 1942 and 1944 respectively. The Cotton Exchange was closed during the war and Jim worked in a munitions factory, plus some night duty as a fireman.

After Mike's birth, Mary did not want to return to hospital work and became a district midwife. This meant the family could be moved to different areas by Liverpool Council, but her employer provided the houses. They spent some years in Speke, and in 1955 moved to 20 Forthlin Road, Allerton.

After Mary's death in 1956, Jim brought up the two boys on his weekly salary of £8. If you visit the Forthlin Road house, now a National Trust property (the smallest in the UK), you will see that the living room carpet is comprised of off-cuts. They couldn't afford the luxury of a lounge carpet. The McCartney family was very close-knit, and two of Jim's sisters, Milly and Jin, helped to raise the boys.

Jim McCartney encouraged an interest in music, and told the boys to do crosswords as it would increase their word power. His key phrase, 'D I N' (Do it now), has been adopted by Paul and is practised to this day. He supported Paul's involvement with The Beatles and stressed the importance of groups acting together, once telling Pete Best off for milking the screams.

As a result of The Beatles' success, Jim McCartney retired in 1964 and Paul bought him a house in Heswall on the Wirral, which Paul still owns. After the London premiere of *A Hard Day's Night*, Paul gave him a painting of a horse. Jim wondered why, and it turned out to be a racehorse that Paul had bought for him, Drake's Drum.

In November 1964 it was Jim's turn to surprise Paul as he remarried, this time 28-year-old Angie

Williams, who had a five-year-old daughter, Ruth. Around 1968 Jim developed arthritis, which became increasingly serious.

In the seventies Jim had a close friend, Monty Lister, who presented BBC Radio Merseyside's *Tune Tonic*. Monty would visit him and he had a special armchair with hollowed arms that acted as a hearing aid. He told Monty, 'You don't play many of The Beatles' records on your show.' 'Well, I like them but they're not my favourite group,' said Monty. 'They're not mine either,' said Jim, smiling.

Jim McCartney died on 18 March 1976. His final words were, 'I'll be with Mary soon.' Paul named his son, James, in memory of his father.

Paul inherited his musical genes and his work ethic.

McCARTNEY, LINDA [1941–1998]

Shortly after he married Linda Eastman, Paul McCartney said, somewhat ungallantly, 'We had both sown our wild oats and got it out of our systems.' During their marriage from 1969–98, they were hardly apart, the only major separation being Paul when was jailed in Tokyo in 1980.

Linda Louise Eastman was born on 24 September 1941 in Scarsdale, New York, the second child of Lee and Louise Eastman. Despite widespread beliefs to the contrary, the family was not linked to Eastman Kodak in any way, but it was wealthy and well connected. Lee Eastman, who had been born Leopold Vail Epstein (a nice coincidence) in 1910, was the head of a legal practice with many celebrity clients, including playwright Tennessee Williams and modern artist Willem de Kooning. Louise came from a family who owned department stores and on the birth of their first child, John, they took the surname Eastman.

In 1946 the songwriter Jack Lawrence wanted Lee Eastman's advice on a copyright matter. He said he would not charge for his services if Jack wrote a song for his daughter. The delightful 'Linda' was a hit for both Buddy Clark and Matt Dennis and it was given a rock 'n' roll workout by Jan and Dean in 1963. The song has also been covered for the UK market by Dick James (another coincidence).

Linda was educated at Scarsdale High School and the Sarah Lawrence College: yet another coincidence as Yoko Ono moved to Scarsdale in 1953 and attended Sarah Lawrence. Linda spent the summers in their family home at Cape Cod where they entertained such famous guests as Hoagy Carmichael and William Boyd (*Hopalong Cassidy*). She grew up with a love of rock 'n' roll and doo-wop and would go to Alan Freed's shows at the Paramount to see Chuck Berry and Bobby Darin.

On 1 March 1962 Linda's mother was killed in a plane crash. She was devastated and a few months later, on 18 June, she rushed into a marriage with geophysicist Mel See; she was pregnant and their daughter, Heather, was born on New Year's Eve. Mel wanted to work in Africa but Linda thought it would wreck their marriage. They were incompatible anyway and divorced in 1965, with Linda reverting to the name Eastman. Mel was on good terms with Paul and Linda when she died in 1998 and the tragic event might have triggered his suicide in 2000.

After her divorce, Linda studied photography at the University of Arizona. Because of the state's glorious brightness, she thought it was a wonderful place for this. She then took a job as an editorial assistant for *Town & Country* magazine in New York.

In 1966 Linda was invited to a photocall for the Rolling Stones on a boat in the harbour in New York. She was a willowy girl with long, blonde hair and the band invited her to take some exclusive shots. The results were stunning, enabling her to photograph the rock acts appearing at Fillmore East. Outside of Paul McCartney and The Beatles, her photographs of Jimi Hendrix are her most renowned. Because of her financial standing, she was able to tell magazines and newspapers, 'Give me a credit and pay for the film and I'll do it.' Her work was published in *Life* and *Mademoiselle*, and was collected in the book *Sixties: Portrait of an Era* (1992).

After meeting Paul socially at the Bag O'Nails in London in 1966, she received an invitation to the press launch for *Sgt Pepper*. John had been her favourite Beatle but, 'I found the fascination fading fast and it was Paul I liked.' Paul was getting over his romance with Jane Asher, and within five months they were living together, initially with no thought of marriage. In December 1968 they had a family holiday, along with Linda's daughter Heather, joining Hunter Davies and his family in the Algrave, Portugal.

Paul and Linda were married at Marylebone Town Hall on 12 March 1969. This proved to be controversial; fans wondered why was Paul marrying an American divorcee instead of an English rose, and believed – rather unfairly – that Yoko and Linda were responsible for breaking up The Beatles. The animosity between The Beatles was accentuated when Paul wanted the group to be represented by his father-in-law and brother-in-law, Lee and John Eastman. That would have been as unworkable as Allen Klein.

Paul adopted Heather and they had three children together, Mary (b. 1969), Stella (b. 1971) and James (b. 1977). Mary made her first public appearance peering out of Paul's jacket on the back of his first solo album, *McCartney* (1970). The album included two songs for Linda, 'The

Lovely Linda' and 'Maybe I'm Amazed'. Many of the compositions on *Ram* (1971) were attributed to Paul and Linda McCartney.

Linda had played piano at school but not touched the instrument for some years. Paul offered to coach her and she became part of Wings, playing keyboards and adding background harmonies. Many suggested that she was incapable, but she played with him until 1980, firstly at fairly small shows but building up to Wembley Stadium. She contributed to *Band on the Run* (1973) and *Venus and Mars* (1975), and the single, 'Mull Of Kintyre', which sold two million copies in the UK alone.

In 1979 Linda released her first solo song in the UK, 'Seaside Woman', which was issued under the name of Suzy and The Red Stripes and became the soundtrack for a short, animated film. (The song was originally written and recorded in 1972 and a remixed version of that came out in the US in 1977.) An album of her compositions with a few covers, *Wild Prairie*, was issued shortly after her death.

Linda McCartney became a vegetarian in the early 1970s with Paul following suit. She created her own range of frozen foods, presenting vegetarian food that looked like meat. Her *Home Cooking* (1989) became the world's biggest-selling vegetarian cookbook and several publications followed. She became a prominent animal rights campaigner, demanding the ethical treatment of animals. In view of their shared interests, Paul and Linda were close friends with the TV comedy writer Carla Lane, and Linda made a cameo appearance in her BBC series *Bread* (1988).

Linda was uncomfortable on stage, preferring to take photos rather than play music. Her photographs became more and more acclaimed with the years, and once museums and galleries realised that rock music was a way to attract audiences, she had several exhibitions of her work.

Linda contracted breast cancer in 1995 and died on the McCartneys' ranch close to Tucson, Arizona, on 17 April 1998, although the family at first said she had died in Santa Barbara, California, to maintain privacy. There were several tribute concerts and events for her and the Linda McCartney Centre was established at the Royal Liverpool Hospital.

Linda supported Paul at the very time he needed it.

McCARTNEY, MARY [1909-1956]

Mary Patricia Mohin was born in Fazakerley in the suburbs of Liverpool on 29 September 1909. Her mother, also called Mary, died giving birth four years later. Her father Owen was a coal merchant and when he remarried Mary did not like her stepmother and so was raised by relatives. Mary trained as a nurse at Alder Hey Hospital, and became a ward sister at Walton Hospital when she was 24. For a time she was staying with Jim McCartney's sister, Jin, and gradually this led to the blossoming of a romance with Jim. He was a Protestant and she a Catholic and they married in a Catholic chapel, St Swithin's in Gillmoss, Liverpool, in April 1941: he was 38 and she was 31. Mary wanted any children to be raised as Catholic and Jim did not object.

After the birth of their children, Mary returned to nursing as a district midwife, working where Liverpool Council sent her. They lived in Speke for a while and moved to 20 Forthlin Road, Allerton, in 1955. Wearing a navy blue uniform, she would ride her bicycle to her patients. Paul recalls her whistling her favourite tunes as she did the housework. She did not want Paul to have a Scouse accent and sent him for elocution lessons.

Mary suffered breast pains, but she did not see a doctor until the cancer was advanced and nothing could be done. She died on 31 October 1956, leaving Jim to raise their two children on his own and without Mary's salary. Once Paul started gigging, there are many stories of Jim sending messages, telling Paul at what time to put on the oven and where to buy the chops.

Paul has made direct reference to his mother in song, notably 'Lady Madonna' and 'Let It Be' with its reference to 'Mother Mary'. Paul named his first daughter, Mary, after her.

Mary died a fortnight after Paul's first appearance with The Quarrymen.

McCARTNEY, MIKE [B. 1944] – SEE ALSO SCAFFOLD

Peter Michael McCartney, the younger brother of Paul, was born in Liverpool on 7 January 1944. Mike was old enough to be Paul's regular playmate but young enough to be intimidated by him. In one noted incident, Paul swung Mike round by his ankles and he was hit in the face by a concrete post. They did occasionally harmonise on Everly Brothers songs, notably at Butlin's Filey holiday camp in August 1957. This relationship of being at one moment close friends, and the next stand-offish, continued into adulthood.

Like Paul, Mike went to the Liverpool Institute and on leaving school, he trained as a ladies' hairdresser. He became interested in photography and took many early photographs of The Beatles. When he went to an audience-participation 'Happening' at the Everyman in Liverpool, he tried to interest the organisers into booking The Beatles but they looked down on rock 'n' roll and declined. Despite this refusal,

however, connections had been made and as a result Mike went on to become part of the satirical group, Scaffold, with Roger McGough and John Gorman.

When Paul gave Mike a Nikon camera in 1967, he spontaneously burst into a little song, 'Thank U Very Much', which he developed into a single for Scaffold. It became a Top 10 hit, and to this day Mike McCartney has never revealed who or what the 'Aintree Iron' was. Scaffold were always adding new verses on stage. Mike, Roger and John also had many alternative verses for 'Lily The Pink', which became a UK No. 1 in 1968.

Also in 1968, Mike (who in 1963 had adopted the stage name 'Mike McGear' – although he no longer uses it) and Roger made the poetry and music LP *McGough & McGear*, produced by Paul and featuring Jimi Hendrix. Mike's album, *Woman* (1972), had a picture of his mother as a nurse on the front cover. Paul also produced Mike's 1974 LP *McGear*. Mike wrote children's books and over the years his photographs have appeared in numerous publications. *Mike McCartney's Live8 Coolpix* was published in 2006, and several of his early photographs are on display at his childhood home, 20 Forthlin Road. He toured with his one-man show, *Sex, Drugs and Rock and Roll...I Wish* in 2014.

Mike married Angela Fishwick in 1968 and they had three daughters, divorcing in 1979. He married Rowena Home at St Barnabas Church in Penny Lane in 1982 and they have had three sons. Mike is a keen supporter of the arts on Merseyside. If you meet him, Mike is always pleasant but he does strike most people as an oddball, often answering questions with non sequiturs. Still, he does have the unenviable role of being the brother of the most famous man alive.

In interviews, Mike rarely refers to his brother by name, but often talks about 'our kid'. There will be confusing conversations if he ever talks to Noel Gallagher.

His early photographs of Beatle life are to be treasured.

McCARTNEY, PAUL [B. 1942]

James Paul McCartney was the first child of Jim and Mary McCartney, born on 18 June 1942 in Liverpool's Walton Hospital. Mary was a midwife and the family had several addresses before settling in 1955 at 20 Forthlin Road, Allerton, now a National Trust property. Paul attended the Stockton Wood and Joseph Williams primary schools before passing the 11-plus examination and entering a grammar school, Liverpool Institute. He befriended a younger pupil, George Harrison, as they had a shared interest in guitars and the new rock 'n' roll music. McCartney lost his mother through cancer in 1956 and this became a shared experience with John Lennon, whom he first met at St Peter's church fete in Woolton in 1957.

A former local jazz musician, Jim McCartney had encouraged Paul to be musical. He practised on the living room piano and although his dad had bought him a trumpet, he traded it for a Framus Zenith acoustic guitar because he wanted to sing and play at the same time. He was left-handed, so reversed the strings and played it the other way round, having seen the country singer Slim Whitman play that way. He wrote his first song, 'I Lost My Little Girl', and several others on that guitar. His father encouraged his sons, Paul and Mike, to do crosswords to increase their word power.

Paul gave John the words to Eddie Cochran's 'Twenty Flight Rock' and showed him how to play the correct chords on a guitar. As a result, Paul joined The Quarrymen and by August 1960 there were four of them – John, Paul, George and

Stuart Sutcliffe – and they recruited Pete Best for a residency in Hamburg. Their time at the Indra and the Kaiserkeller transformed their performance and repertoire, but Paul and Pete were deported on a trumped-up charge of setting fire to their lodgings.

Oddly, Paul's instrumental abilities were not fully used in the early years, but he took over the bass when Stuart Sutcliffe left in 1961. He was never a florid player but he knew the right notes. He plays a Hofner violin bass and much of his technique has been developed from American soul records. He has played lead guitar on several Beatles records including a blistering solo on 'Taxman'. He is on piano for 'The Long And Winding Road' (The Beatles' most successful single in the US) and 'Let It Be'.

When Brian Epstein signed The Beatles to a management contract early in 1962, he found that Paul had the greatest appetite for success. Paul was the natural PR man within the group. He was effortlessly charming and could woo the media, which still holds good although his tantrums are well documented. The baby-faced singer was seen as 'the cute Beatle'.

Paul could match John's voice on the rockers, especially Little Richard numbers. Richard himself has praised Paul's 'Long Tall Sally', a song that was always in their repertoire and was copied by Paul when he wrote 'I'm Down'. Even this pales when compared to Paul's all-out shrieking on 'Helter Skelter', a record that foreshadowed heavy metal.

Paul often included standards in The Beatles' set-list, including 'Falling In Love Again', 'Over The Rainbow' and 'Till There Was You'. Paul could write in a variety of styles and excelled in middle-of-the road balladry with songs such as 'All My Loving', 'And I Love Her' and the most recorded song in musical history, 'Yesterday'. He could be exceptionally inventive and both 'Eleanor Rigby',

Paul and Linda at their wedding in 1967. Looking on are Martha (the dog) and Heather, Linda's daughter by a previous relationship. © Mirrorpix

recorded with a string quartet, and 'Penny Lane' were unlike anything that had ever been recorded before. Even 'Yellow Submarine' was wholly original and inspired a feature-length animated film.

In 1963 Paul started dating the actress Jane Asher and lived for a time at her family home in London's Wimpole Street. He wrote 'Here, There And Everywhere' for her, but since their break-up five years later, he has rarely talked about their relationship.

Paul bought a house in St John's Wood, close to EMI's Abbey Road studio and to the city centre, so that he could keep up with what was happening. Asher introduced him to the theatre and he went to classical concerts and assimilated the work of avant-garde composers, notably Karlheinz Stockhausen.

As a result, McCartney was always full of ideas, not just musical, and the concept for *Sgt Pepper* came from him. The album included 'She's Leaving Home', which looked at a family falling apart from both sides, something that Lennon would never have done. You could argue that the album both celebrated and mocked King's Road fashions. McCartney wanted to ensure that The Beatles did not break up after Brian Epstein died, and suggested the TV film *Magical Mystery Tour,* which was pointless, plotless and poorly received, although the music was good.

In 1967, Paul composed his first film soundtrack, *The Family Way,* and wrote for Chris Barber's Jazz Band and the Black Dyke Mills Brass Band.

Paul started dating the rock photographer Linda Eastman in 1968, and they were married the following year. Linda already had a daughter, Heather, and with Paul she had three more children, Mary (b. 1969), Stella (b. 1971) and James (b. 1977). Linda steered Paul towards supporting animal rights and being a vegetarian. A contributory factor in the break-up of The Beatles was

over their management: Paul was wary about Allen Klein but the other Beatles did not favour the Eastman family taking control. The Eastmans encouraged Paul to invest in something he knew about – music publishing. He acquired Buddy Holly's song catalogue in 1971 and now has 25,000 copyrights under his MPL (McCartney Productions Ltd.) stewardship.

The divisions within the group became all too public. Paul believed that they should return to live performance but John and George objected. Paul favoured an orchestral suite on *Abbey Road* while John thought it pretentious. At the same time, John hated the silliness of 'Maxwell's Silver Hammer'. In the film of *Let It Be,* George was fed up with Paul's criticisms, but during *Abbey Road* he stuck in a couple of great songs when John and Paul weren't paying attention.

John was persuaded to hold back from announcing his departure from The Beatles, but he had been outmanoeuvred by Paul, who announced the break-up, in John's opinion as part of the publicity for his first solo album, *McCartney* (1970). Paul was soon on the road with Wings, a band featuring his wife Linda, Denny Laine and a revolving door of musicians. They had major hit records, including a James Bond theme, 'Live And Let Die' (1973), produced by George Martin, and 'Mull Of Kintyre' (1977), which became the first single to sell two million copies in the UK. He was, however, arrested for growing cannabis on his Scottish farm. In 1980 he was jailed in Tokyo for possessing drugs.

The only album that stands alongside the best of The Beatles is *Band On The Run* (1973). His own attempt at writing a feature film, *Give My Regards to Broad Street* (1984), suffered from a feeble script and unconvincing acting.

Although he did not often see John in the seventies, they did watch *Saturday Night Live* together in New York and toyed with the idea of going to the studio and offering to play live.

Paul developed another role as the patriarch of the large McCartney clan, who are given tickets for his shows and private parties. His love of pub singalongs was revealed in the TV documentary *James Paul McCartney* (1973). His wife Linda died of cancer in 1998, and he married the model Heather Mills in 2002. They had a child, Beatrice

Milly, the following year. He supported Heather's campaign for the abolition of landmines, but they were incompatible and divorced acrimoniously in 2008. Paul married the American businesswoman Nancy Shevell in 2011.

Paul is the Beatle who retained roots to his home city. When he saw the Liverpool Institute building was dilapidated, he determined to do something about it and established the *Fame*-like

'PAUL IS DEAD'

On 9 November 1966, Paul McCartney had a minor injury in a road accident. A Beatles fan in America started looking for clues that he had been killed, with the whole thing having been hushed up and Paul replaced by a *doppelgänger*. No one knows who started this rumour but the first public Paul-bearer was Russ Gibb on the Detroit station WKNR, talking to the student Tom Zarski in 1969. It followed rumours that Bob Dylan had been killed in a motorcycle accident, but this was far more fun as there were so many clues. Paul issued a rebuttal that no one wanted to believe. Here is some of the 'evidence' for the most ghoulish myth in pop history:

1. John appears to mumble 'I buried Paul' at the end of 'Strawberry Fields Forever'. Paul said he was actually saying 'cranberry sauce'.

2. On the front cover of *Sgt Pepper*, The Beatles are standing in front of a grave. Three Beatles are carrying gold instruments but Paul has a black one. The hyacinths are arranged as a white guitar but you can read it as 'Paul?'

3. Inside the cover, Paul is wearing an armband saying 'OPD', said to stand for 'Officially Pronounced Dead'. No, it's the Ottawa Police Department.

4. Paul was not facing the camera on the back of *Sgt Pepper*. The real reason? He wasn't there as he was going to see Jane Asher and the taller Mal Evans stood in for him.

5. On the cover of the *Magical Mystery Tour* EP, Paul wears a hippo mask and has a hole in his chest.

6. If you turn the back cover of the *Magical Mystery Tour* EP by 90 degrees clockwise, the white figures spell out 'R.I.P'.

7. If you play part of 'Revolution 9' backwards, it sounds like 'Turn me on, dead man.'

8. On the *Abbey Road* sleeve, Paul was out of step with his bandmates – how unusual. Paul was barefoot, like a corpse, John in his white suit was the minister, George the gravedigger and Ringo the funeral director.

9. A car number plate on the cover of *Abbey Road* is 281F and Paul would have been 28 IF he had lived. He was in fact 27 when *Abbey Road* was released.

10. 'Drive My Car' was what Paul was doing when he was killed; 'I'm Only Sleeping' refers to his death;' 'Nowhere Man' was Billy Campbell, the person said to have replaced him; 'Dr Robert' was the surgeon attending to McCartney; but 'Yesterday' has gone and The Beatles will get away with it if only they 'Act Naturally'. Although if they had wanted to get away with it, why did they plant these clues?

Liverpool Institute For Performing Arts (LIPA) in 1996. It has been an astonishing success, with demand for places so high that only four per cent of applications can be accepted.

McCartney has mostly written his own songs, but has worked with Eric Stewart and Elvis Costello among others. One reason why the songs have not reached the brilliance of Lennon and McCartney's oeuvre is because those two were so exceptionally good at commenting on each other's work, thus making it stronger. Paul does, however, realise the benefit of criticism, and much to his credit he finds time for one-on-one songwriting seminars at LIPA each year. Maybe he should ask the students to comment on his new compositions.

But he is nothing if not adventurous. He moved into classical music with the *Liverpool Oratorio* (1991), choral music with *A Garland For Linda* (2000) and ballet with *Ocean's Kingdom* (2011). He wrote a book of poetry, *Blackbird Singing* (2001) and a children's book, *High In The Clouds* (2005). In 1991 there was an exhibition of his paintings at the prestigious Walker Art Gallery in Liverpool.

Paul still records regularly, but his album of standards, *Kisses on the Bottom* (2012), showed that his voice was faltering; but then he was 70. He doesn't want to stop touring as playing a huge stadium in America can net $2m. In 2009 he opened the new Citi Field in Queens, New York, which replaced Shea Stadium, the venue for The Beatles' greatest triumph.

At first Paul was reluctant to include Beatles songs in his stage shows, but gradually he has come to realise this is what audiences want. As a result, his concerts today are about 70 per cent Beatles. Starting with Live Aid in 1985, he has been happy to close major musical events all over the world with a Beatles singalong, including Live

8 (2005), the Diamond Jubilee Concert (2012) and the Summer Olympics (2012).

Paul received an honorary degree from the Royal College of Music in 1995, and two years later he was knighted for his services to music. Although he cannot read music, he has said, 'I am like the primitive cave artists who drew without training.'

Paul has often said that his favourite song is The Beach Boys' 'God Only Knows' (1966) because it goes to 'very unusual places'. The same can be said of the best of his own music.

Again and again Paul has made the whole world sing and, if he didn't dye his hair, he'd be a Silver Beatle once again.

McFALL, RAY [1926–2015]

The Cavern is the most famous club in the world and yet, in its prime, it was run by two notably unhip people, its owner Ray McFall and its DJ Bob Wooler. They wore suits and ties and looked squarer than square, but knew exactly what they were doing and how to make it work.

Andrew Raymond McFall was born in Garston, south Liverpool, on 14 November 1926, and although he didn't qualify as an accountant, he was an experienced employee of an accountancy firm. In the fifties he helped with the running of a jazz club at the Temple restaurant in Dale Street. One of his firm's clients was Alan Sytner, who owned and managed another jazz club, the Cavern. When Sytner's lavish lifestyle led to financial difficulties, Ray McFall bought the premises for £2,750 and left his job for a new career as a club manager.

McFall realised that rock 'n' roll was the way to success. Live beat music was making its mark in the suburbs and the Cavern became its first city venue. McFall introduced all-night sessions, lunchtime breaks for office workers, and even Saturday afternoon dances for the under-16s. He promoted 'Riverboat Shuffles' on the *Royal Iris* and he and Brian Epstein jointly sponsored two concerts with Little Richard and The Beatles at the Liverpool Empire in October 1962.

Everything worked well, but McFall had strict rules. He hated crudity on stage and especially loathed the outlandish vocalist Freddie Starr. He favoured punctuality and tidiness, and although at first he thought The Beatles slovenly he knew that they would be the backbone of his success. Once, The Beatles indulged him by allowing him to sing two standards with them.

The Beatles appeared over 270 times for McFall at the Cavern, but McFall was always sympathetic to Brian Epstein's needs and would allow them to change dates if something significant was in the offing. Possibly McFall was too tolerant because although the Cavern had helped to make The Beatles stars, the club's fortunes faded after they left the city.

In February 1964 McFall travelled with The Beatles to New York, where he received one indignity after another. That was typical of The Beatles; they often ignored people who had passed their usefulness.

McFall became the owner of the *Mersey Beat* newspaper in June 1961 but he didn't use it to further his own interests. He failed to see the tourist potential of the Cavern, and invested in a recording studio that unfortunately didn't make commercial records. Additionally, times were changing and the Cavern was handicapped by not being licensed, but as McFall said, 'You never know why Joe Public stays away.'

The Cavern went into liquidation in February 1966 and as McFall had failed to make it a limited company, he was declared bankrupt. He moved to London and undertook clerical work for an accountancy firm until he retired in 1993. He had a very happy family life with his wife, Shirley, and six children. He died in Merstham, Surrey on 8 January 2015.

The Cavern holds some painful memories, but Ray McFall should have been proud of the way he promoted The Beatles between 1961-63.

McGOUGH, ROGER – SEE SCAFFOLD

McGEAR, MIKE – SEE McCARTNEY, MIKE AND SCAFFOLD

MAHARISHI MAHESH YOGI
[1917–2008]

'The philosophy of life is this: Life is not a struggle, life is not a tension,' said Maharishi Mahesh Yogi to his followers. 'Life is bliss.' How that resonated with The Beatles in 1967. Here was an approach to help them cope with the pressures and demands that were placed upon them. For a short period of time, less than a year, The Beatles were highly influenced by the Maharishi and there has been much debate about him ever since. Was he a sage or was he a charlatan? Just who was His Divine Grace, Maharishi Mahesh Yogi?

Mahesh Prasad Varma was born in Jabalpur, central India, on 12 January 1917. The son of a tax official, in 1942 he graduated from the University of Allahabad with a degree in physics. Whilst in college, he studied Sanskrit under Swami Brahmananda Saraswati, a Hindu leader known as Guru Dev ('divine teacher'). Following his death in 1953, Varma retreated into the

Himalayas for meditation and reflection. When he emerged in 1955, he devoted himself to spreading his master's form of meditation, which was derived from Advaita Vedanta. He adopted the name Maharishi, which means 'great sage', and rebranded the philosophy as 'Transcendental Meditation', which calmed the spirit and would, he hoped, bring peace to the world. Before he had met the Maharishi, John had written 'All You Need Is Love', while 'Across The Universe' pays thanks to Guru Dev.

In 1959 the Maharishi established the International Meditation Society and with bases in London and San Francisco, he recruited followers. He set up his headquarters in Switzerland (moving to Amsterdam in 1990), and at its height he had two million devotees including 90,000 in the UK. They paid a subscription or tithed part of their earnings, and as a result the movement became rich, with the Maharishi running his own helicopter.

In February 1967, George Harrison's wife Pattie became intrigued after attending a lecture on TM at Caxton Hall, London. She told George, who was developing his own interest in Indian culture. On 24 August 1967, The Beatles heard the Maharishi speak at the Hilton Hotel in Park Lane. One of the most divisive figures in popular music, Mike Love of The Beach Boys, commented, 'Hearing him speak was the most profound experience I'd ever felt and the practice of meditating was so simple, yet so powerful. If everyone did it, it would be an entirely different world out there – relaxed and peaceful.'

The Maharishi invited The Beatles to a course on TM that weekend at University College, Bangor. The train journey, with The Beatles appropriately attired, turned the event into a media circus. The Maharishi told them, 'You have created a magic air through your names. You have now got to use

that magic influence on the generation who look up to you.'

On Sunday 27 August, Brian Epstein died, probably as the result of an accidental overdose. The Maharishi comforted The Beatles and told them to think positively. This led to a bizarre media interview, which did not accord with public thinking on the tragedy.

In February 1968, the Maharishi invited The Beatles to spend three months at his ashram in Rishikesh, about 150 miles from Delhi. The Beatles wanted to explore their spiritual growth, but the press was more questioning. The Maharishi had a tendency to laugh merrily so he became 'The Giggling Guru' and *Private Eye* referred to him as 'Veririchi Lotsamoney Yogi Bear'. Ringo's uncle had advised him to be careful, saying 'He's after your money, lad' and Ringo spoke for the common man when he described the compound as being 'like Butlin's' and left early. The Beatles were lampooned for subscribing to what was held to be nonsense.

Daily meditation helped The Beatles, particularly John Lennon who came off drugs completely. The songwriting Beatles became prolific and some compositions relate to what they were being taught – Paul McCartney's 'Mother Nature's Son' for instance.

The actress Mia Farrow was on the compound, recovering from the break-up of her marriage to Frank Sinatra, and accompanied by her sister Prudence. It is possible that the Maharishi made advances to Prudence, but whatever the circumstances, both John and George told him that they were returning home. 'Why?' he asked. John, having an opportunity to rework an old joke, said, 'If you're so fucking cosmic, then you'll know.' John mocked the guru in song, calling him 'Sexy Sadie'. If anything, it could be argued that the visit to India created disharmony rather than harmony in the band, but there were many other factors at work including John Lennon's love for the Japanese artist Yoko Ono, who could be seen as another spiritual leader for him.

The Beatles never liked people capitalising on their fame and rejected the idea of appearing in a film or touring with the Maharishi. He did tour the US with The Beach Boys, which didn't help either party. The Maharishi maintained his celebrity following in the seventies with Shirley MacLaine and Kurt Vonnegut. He established TM centres round the world, with several in the UK and US and founded a university in Fairfield, Iowa.

In later years, the Maharishi developed an interest in yogic flying that led to a political offshoot, the Natural Law Party. George Harrison and Ringo Starr both appeared at a concert for the party just before the general election in 1992 and Paul McCartney reunited his friendship with the Maharishi on a visit to the Netherlands. George Harrison, who practised meditation until his death in 2001, commented, 'The Maharishi was fantastic and I admire him for being able, in spite of the ridicule, to keep on going.' The Maharishi died in Vlodrop, Netherlands, on 5 February 2008.

The spiritual leader for the Summer of Love, but was his influence on The Beatles positive or negative?

MANN, WILLIAM [1924–1989]

William Mann, born in Madras in 1924, was a Cambridge graduate appointed the chief music critic of *The Times* in 1960, a post he held for 22 years. He had a progressive outlook and stunned his readers in 1963 by stating that Lennon and McCartney were, 'the greatest songwriters since

Schubert', referring to their Aoelian cadences in 'Not A Second Time', and even likening their work to Mahler. John Lennon dismissed this as 'bullshit', and although The Beatles never acknowledged his contribution, it heralded a wider acceptance of their work and led to serious papers discussing rock music.

In 1966, William Mann made two appearances on *Juke Box Jury*, where he lucidly talked about chord progressions, thereby surprising the other panellists. He wrote a stunning review of *Sgt Pepper*, but was also quick to point out that The Monkees were releasing songs that were no more than The Beatles' first two albums crossed with *The Oxford Book of Nursery Rhymes*.

The Times they are a-changin'.

MARDAS, YANNI ALEXIS [B. 1942]

Alexis Mardas, renamed 'Magic Alex' by John Lennon, was born in Athens in 1942, the son of a Greek military officer. He came to England on a student visa and worked illegally as a TV repairman. He created a light sculpture for John Dunbar at the Indica gallery in London and this led to a psychedelic light box for the Rolling Stones that they used on stage. It being the hippie sixties, The Beatles were impressed by his ideas, including one to attach paint to an electronic current to make it glow and so dispense with light bulbs.

The Beatles offered to fund his company Fiftyshapes, but once they had set up Apple, Magic Alex became the head of Apple Electronics. To celebrate his new role, he gave The Beatles badges that bleeped and flashed at random and he devised an electronic apple that would tremble with light and music. They were probably fun if you had ingested an industrial quantity of LSD.

He told The Beatles that he would devise a signal that would prevent fans from taping their records from radio and would also build a 72-track recording studio for them.

When The Beatles went to Rishikesh to see the Maharishi, they missed his company and wild ideas and sent for him. Alex thought that Maharishi Yogi was fleecing them and was also making sexual advances to female guests, which led to The Beatles leaving the compound.

The Beatles asked for his help when they wanted to buy a Greek island but they soon tired of the idea and sold their property.

Alex lived, platonically, with Jenny Boyd, Pattie's sister, and they went on holiday with Donovan and Cynthia Lennon. When they returned to the Lennons' house, they found John and Yoko together.

When The Beatles were to be filmed making the *Let It Be* album, they wanted to use the new Apple studio. They were disappointed by the progress and others were brought in to complete a conventional studio. When Allen Klein was asked to resolve Apple's problems, Alex quickly resigned.

In recent years, Alex has been selling items that were given to him by John Lennon, including a Vox guitar that fetched over $250,000.

A magical mystery bore.

MARSDEN, GERRY – SEE GERRY AND THE PACEMAKERS

MARTIN, GEORGE [1926–2016]

As well as being the world's most respected and best-known record producer, Sir George Martin redefined the role, turning it into a collaboration between him and his artists. His work with The Beatles changed popular music for ever but he was charmingly modest, saying in 1974, 'Whatever I did shouldn't be stressed too much. I was merely the bloke who interpreted their ideas.'

George Henry Martin was born on 3 January 1926 in Holloway, north London, the son of a carpenter. He was an adept pianist, and when he was 16 he ran a local dance band, The Four Tune Tellers, with his sister Irene as a vocalist. He served in the Fleet Air Arm during the war and retained the bearing of a military man. His marriage to Sheena Chisholm in 1948 led to the children, Alexis and Gregory.

After graduating from the Guildhall School of Music, George was appointed assistant recording manager for EMI's Parlophone label. He became label manager in 1955 and, following an affair with his secretary, Judy Lockhart-Smith, he divorced Sheena and married Judy in 1966. They had two children, Lucy and Giles, the latter now a noted record producer himself.

George made some brilliant comedy albums, notably *The Best Of Sellers* and *Songs For Swingin' Sellers* with Peter Sellers (both 1959), and the West End successes *At The Drop Of A Hat* (1959) and *Beyond The Fringe* (1961). His hit singles included Peter Sellers and Sophia Loren's 'Goodness Gracious Me', Bernard Cribbins' 'Right Said Fred' and Charlie Drake's 'My Boomerang Won't Come Back'. He experimented with sound on 1962's 'Time Beat', released under the fictitious name of Ray Cathode, and encouraged Rolf Harris to bring Aboriginal instruments into the studio. He made skiffle hits with The Vipers and rock 'n' roll ones with Jim Dale and The King Brothers. He had his first No. 1 with The Temperance Seven's 'You're Driving Me Crazy' in 1961. All of this can be viewed as invaluable training for working with The Beatles.

The first composition that Dick James published under Dick James Music in 1961 was George's 'Double Scotch', recorded by their good friend Ron Goodwin. George produced many albums with Goodwin including his soundtrack for *633 Squadron* (1964).

When George first met Brian Epstein in February 1962, he was unimpressed by the performances he was played – 'Hello Little Girl' and 'Till There Was You'. A few months later he was told to change that decision, as EMI's in-house publishing company, Ardmore & Beechwood, was keen to have Lennon and McCartney on board. As a result The Beatles won a contract with Parlophone.

In June 1962 George wanted to replace Pete Best with a session drummer, the final straw that led to his sacking. George tried to interest them in a Tin Pan Alley novelty by Mitch Murray, 'How Do You Do It', but he accepted 'Love Me Do' for the first single. His hunch about Mitch's song was right as he produced a version for Gerry and The Pacemakers that went to the top.

George Martin was exceptionally busy in 1963, as the minor label Parlophone became the key player in EMI's portfolio. From April 1963 to April 1964, George Martin's productions were at No. 1 for 40 weeks: The Beatles, Gerry, Billy J. Kramer and Cilla Black. His small team included his engineer Norman 'Hurricane' Smith and his tape operator George Emerick.

Following Cilla Black's success with 'Anyone Who Had A Heart', Burt Bacharach played piano and wrote the arrangement for 'Alfie', which was produced by George. The film of the event shows Bacharach insisting on take after take, finally nailing it on the twenty-seventh. 'I think we had it on take two, Burt,' says Martin laconically.

George Martin quickly realised that The Beatles were exceptional. 'The "yeah, yeah, yeah" in "She Loves You" was a curious singing chord. It was a major sixth with George Harrison doing the sixth and the other two the third and the fifth. It was the way Glenn Miller wrote for the saxophone.' He chose the best musicians to supplement The Beatles' sound, notably recruiting David Mason to play piccolo trumpet on 'Penny Lane'. Martin himself played an electric piano (which was speeded up) on 'In My Life'.

Lennon and McCartney's songs could be performed in any number of ways. George produced Ella Fitzgerald's 'Can't Buy Me Love' (1964) and, following a suggestion from the actor John Junkin, he encouraged Peter Sellers to reinterpret Lennon and McCartney's lyrics. The crowning glory is 'A Hard Day's Night', delivered as though he were Laurence Olivier playing Richard III.

In 1966, 'Strawberry Fields Forever' was seen by George as a modern-day Debussy. They recorded the song in two different arrangements in different keys and tempos. John asked George to merge them. By changing the speed on the recorders, George combined the versions, culminating in what we hear.

As late as 1968, George was still only using four-tracks for the *White Album*, and yet he would experiment with different speeds, repeated loops and backward tapes. At times it was done for novelty effects like on 'Yellow Submarine', while on other occasions it was used to create something unnerving, as on 'Tomorrow Never Knows'.

George had nearly left EMI at the start of 1962, as he believed he should be sharing in the royalties of successful records he produced. Even in 1965 he was only earning £3,000 a year, a reasonable salary but minuscule compared to the millions of pounds his records were generating. Unable to convince EMI to be more generous, he established a team of independent producers,

AIR (Associated Independent Recordings), with himself, John Burgess, Ron Richards and Peter Sullivan. It was a gamble. EMI could have decided, out of spite, not to use them. However, they still wanted Martin to produce The Beatles, and this time they would have to pay. Even so, the royalty rate that George Martin negotiated was only 0.2 per cent.

George wrote the incidental music for the films *A Hard Day's Night*, *Ferry Cross the Mersey* and *Yellow Submarine*, as well as the theme for David Frost's television interviews and 'Theme One' for the opening of BBC Radio One in 1967.

His defining moment came in 1967. 'It's very difficult for me to be impartial but I do think *Sgt Pepper* is the best thing they ever did. I suppose it was a producer's dream. I was able to do everything that I ever wanted and the boys were similarly anxious to make it far-out for its time. I did wonder if we'd gone too far, if people would think it pretentious, but fortunately they accepted it.'

The Beatles returned from India in 1968 with many new songs. Martin tried to persuade them to make one great single album but they insisted on a double album of 30 tracks, some of which he regarded as substandard. He subsequently discovered an ulterior motive – in order to negotiate a new contract, The Beatles were fulfilling their quota on the existing one.

In January 1969, to honour a film contract, The Beatles allowed the cameras to capture them creating an album, which became *Let It Be*. This was to be totally honest and John told George that there were to be, 'no echoes, no overdubs and none of your jiggery-pokery'. George approved of the aims but the collapse of friendships within the group created tension. George was annoyed when John surreptitiously gave the tapes to Phil Spector, and thought that the credit on the resulting album should have read, 'Produced by George Martin, over produced by Phil Spector.' Not one to take an insult lying down, Spector said they were not in the same league. 'He's an arranger, that's all.'

When The Beatles split up in 1970, both Lennon and Harrison preferred Spector for their solo recordings. McCartney recorded by himself, but returned to George Martin in 1973 for *Live And Let Die*. George then produced *Tug Of War* (1982), which included the No. 1 single 'Ebony And Ivory' with Stevie Wonder, and *Pipes Of Peace* (1983).

George's hearing had been damaged from working with The Beatles and he knew he would not receive further commissions if this were widely known. He grew his hair to cover his ears to conceal a hearing aid and accepted short-term work. His most durable relationship was with the soft-rock group America, and he produced their US hits 'Tin Man' (1974) and 'Sister Golden Hair' (1975). Among his many one-off projects were Tommy Steele's musical autobiography *My Life, My Song* (1974), Jeff Beck's album *Blow By Blow* (1975), Jimmy Webb's *El Mirage* (1977) and Gary Brooker's *No More Fear Of Flying* (1979).

In 1974 Martin conducted symphony orchestras in concerts entitled *Beatles to Bond and Bach*. The high spot was when he merged The Beatles' 'I Feel Fine' with Tchaikovsky's Piano Concerto No. 1.

The one project to be viewed with suspicion is the film *Sgt Pepper's Lonely Hearts Club Band* (1978), with The Bee Gees and Peter Frampton. George said he produced the soundtrack on the dubious grounds that the movie would otherwise have been worse. A few tracks, 'Got To Get You Into My Life' by Earth, Wind and Fire and 'Get Back' by Billy Preston, were fine.

He wrote his autobiography, *All You Need Is Ears*, in 1979 and a further volume, *Playback –*

The Autobiography of George Martin in 2002. The award-winning TV special *The Making of Sgt Pepper* (1992) led to a book of the same name. George was an engaging host on the BBC series about the appeal of music, *The Rhythm of Life* (1997/98), and if he had not had trouble with his hearing he might have had a new role presenting documentaries.

The first AIR Studios opened in Oxford Street in October 1970, the first client being Cilla Black. The studios were used round the clock and the takeover of AIR studios by Chrysalis meant that George became a board member of several related companies. A new AIR studio in a converted church in Hampstead was opened in 1992. Another highly successful AIR studio in the tropical paradise of Montserrat was devastated by a hurricane, and George arranged fundraising concerts to help the local population.

George's later productions were multi-artist affairs. In 1988 he recorded *Under Milk Wood* with Anthony Hopkins reprising Richard Burton's role, and a new score from George. In 1994, he worked with the harmonica player Larry Adler on *The Glory of Gershwin*, with several guest performers.

In 1996 George Martin became the first record producer to be knighted. His farewell to the industry, the album *In My Life*, recorded in 1997, featured celebrity performances of Beatles numbers, including Sean Connery narrating the title song. Martin's final production was Elton John's homage to Princess Diana, 'Candle In The Wind 1997', the biggest-selling record of all time. In his later years he organised *Party at the Palace* in 2002, which included Brian May playing the national anthem from the roof of Buckingham Palace, and undertook fundraising for charities.

No other producer could have been more attuned to The Beatles' needs and he loved a challenge, always encouraging them to be innovative. He said, 'The genius was theirs, no doubt about that.' But we know better.

MILES, BARRY [B. 1943]

Barry Miles, born in Cirencester in 1943, grew up obsessed with the Beat Generation and its key figures – Jack Kerouac, Allen Ginsberg and William Burroughs. Working at Better Books in Charing Cross Road, he was well placed to organise his own events in London including a reading by Ginsberg, which was to lead to the *International Poetry Incarnation* event at the Royal Albert Hall. Miles opened the Indica gallery, which was also a bookshop, and founded the counterculture's newspaper *International Times*. Mocking *Playboy* with its Playmates, Miles featured Frank Zappa sitting nude on the toilet.

Both McCartney and Lennon would visit the Indica. McCartney enjoyed Miles's hash brownies and was introduced to avant-garde music. John met Yoko there in 1966. In April 1967, Miles organised the *14-Hour Technicolour Dream* at Alexandra Palace, ostensibly a fundraiser for *International Times*. It featured live performances from Pink Floyd, Soft Machine and Yoko Ono, plus some previously unheard psychedelic sounds from The Beatles.

In 1969 Miles became the manager of Apple's spoken word subsidiary, Zapple, but the position was short-lived as Allen Klein closed down non-profitable operations.

Miles has written numerous books about rock music and beat poetry, at first just using his surname for the *In His Own Words* series. In 1998 he co-wrote Paul McCartney's official biography *Many Years From Now*, and he has written biographies of Bob Dylan, David Bowie, Frank Zappa,

Charles Bukowski and many key figures of the counterculture. He drew on his own interviews and research and his left-wing views are apparent in all his writings.

Meeting Barry Miles was a Milestone for John and Paul.

MILLINGS, DOUGIE [1913–2001]

There is an amusing scene in *A Hard Day's Night* in which The Beatles are being fitted for new suits. As they can't keep still, the tailor has a difficult job taking measurements. That put-upon man was no actor; he was The Beatles' tailor, Dougie Millings, himself.

Tailor to the stars, Douglas Arnold Millings was born in Manchester in 1913. He worked as a cutter on Regent Street in London and sang with a dance band at the Astoria. During the war, he was a motorcycle messenger for the army, but was invalided out when he broke his back in an accident. Eventually he recovered and returned to tailoring.

Dougie Millings opened his own shop at 63 Old Compton Street in 1958. His first show-business client was the impresario Tito Burns, who wanted stage clothes for Cliff Richard, and then Larry Parnes wanted suits for his stable of stars including Tommy Steele and Marty Wilde. A stream of well-known names followed. Billy Fury looked magnificent in his Millings gold and silver lamé suits and Wee Willie Harris had his name on the back of his Millings frock coat. Dougie made plaid jackets for Bill Haley and his Comets, and sharp suits for Phil and Don Everly and French rock 'n' roll star Johnny Hallyday. Dougie was so trusted that Sammy Davis simply told him to go to a drawer and take out as much money as he needed.

There are conflicting stories as to how The Beatles came by their collarless jackets, but Millings was adamant that he had created them as a variant on the jackets for ship's stewards. Millings was to make all their clothes, often several copies of each as they would be needed for stunt doubles in films or were ripped by fans. 'There was regular repair work,' says his son Gordon, who worked in his father's business. 'A suit could go to the dry-cleaners and come back missing a pocket because a fan had taken it as a souvenir. There is a scene in *A Hard Day's Night* where Ringo is using a hand drier and it rips the sleeve off his jacket. We had a special sleeve fitted with Velcro to make that work. Ringo had to have his suit covered in red paint in *Help!* and after every take, we rushed to put it into a washing machine before the paint dried.'

Douglas Millings & Son moved to new Soho premises in Great Pulteney Street, with John Lennon remarking affectionately, 'He keeps moving with all the profit he makes.'

The firm also made suits for the rest of the NEMS artists, as well as the yellow and red trousers for the Stones, the hunting jackets for The Kinks and mod-style clothes for The Who. They also made hard-wearing suits for Steve McQueen's acting sequences in *Bullitt* (1968).

Dougie Millings supplied the suits for the Beatles waxworks in Madame Tussauds, and his suits can now be seen in museums around the world. Gordon continues the family business to this day and you can purchase a Beatles suit for yourself. He has spoken at Beatles conventions across the globe and is proud to display his father's designs.

Suits you, sir.

MIMI, AUNT – SEE ENTRY FOR SMITH, MIMI

MONTEZ, CHRIS [B. 1943]

Ezekiel Christopher Montanez was raised by Mexican parents in Los Angeles, and started by singing Spanish-language songs and dancing polkas with his family. He loved rock 'n' roll when it started and was amazed that a Mexican boy, Ritchie Valens, could make it big. He said, 'Elvis may have been the king of rock 'n' roll but Ritchie Valens was the king on my block.' Chris wanted to sing ballads like 'Donna'.

Chris knew Jim Lee, who produced hit records for Kathy Young. Jim had written an uptempo song, very much in the vein of 'La Bamba', called 'Let's Dance' and he wanted Chris to try it. The result was one of the most infectious singles of all time. It soared up the US charts and Chris found himself on tour with Sam Cooke 'who taught me how to sing to the ladies'. His second hit, 'Some Kinda Fun', was in the same vein as 'Let's Dance', but he could handle more romantic material.

When Chris and Tommy Roe came to the UK for a nationwide tour, they were supported by The Beatles. Although Chris was a dynamic performer, he found it hard to cling to his spot at the top of the bill and he soon gave way to The Beatles. George Harrison would disparagingly refer to Chris as 'the little Mexican'. This increased the tensions on tour and Tommy Roe had to break up a fight between Chris and John Lennon, although they all made up in the end. The Beatles greatly admired Chris's jacket with a round collar and a belt and ordered identical ones.

In 1965 Chris met Herb Alpert who suggested he should sing soft, lilting romantic songs for his A&M label. Chris scored with 'Call Me' and 'The More I See You'. He did well, but Herb Alpert decided to keep 'This Guy's In Love With You' for himself.

Chris is proud of his Mexican heritage and has recorded albums of Spanish songs. He has kept himself extremely fit and he is a sensation when he tours the UK on oldies shows.

The Beatles loved his sound – and his jacket.

MURRAY, MITCH [B. 1940]

The songwriter Mitch Murray was born Lionel Michael Stitcher in Hove in 1940. His first success was with the novelty song 'My Brother' for Terry Scott in 1962 and he wrote B-sides for Mark Wynter and Shirley Bassey. In 1962 the music publisher Dick James passed his song 'How Do You Do It?' to George Martin, who asked The Beatles to record it. They thought the song was too lightweight and their recording, which was not released until 1995, lacked enthusiasm. George Martin released their own song, 'Please Please Me', instead and Mitch's composition became a No. 1 for Gerry and The Pacemakers. John Lennon told Mitch, 'If you get Gerry's follow-up, I'll give you a thump', but Gerry went with Mitch's 'I Like It' instead of John's 'Hello Little Girl'; it was another No. 1, which Mitch says was worth a thump, although he didn't get one.

Mitch wrote 'You Were Made For Me' for the Searchers but it went to Freddie and The Dreamers. With Freddie, he wrote their US No. 1, 'I'm Telling You Now'.

Many of Murray's subsequent hits were written with Peter Callander, including 'Even The Bad Times Are Good' (Tremeloes), 'The Ballad Of Bonnie And Clyde' (Georgie Fame), 'Hitchin' A Ride' (Vanity Fare) and 'I Did What I Did For Maria' (Tony Christie). They produced Tony Christie's 'Is This The Way to Amarillo?' and Mitch had his own success with 'Down Came The Rain' as Mr Murray.

When they formed their own label, Bus Stop, they had huge hits with TV talent show winners Paper Lace, having a UK No. 1 with 'Billy Don't Be A Hero' and a US No. 1 with 'The Night Chicago Died'.

With the privatisation of British Telecom, Mitch starred in his comedy programme, *The Telefun Show*, which could only be heard over the phone. He became an authority on humorous speechmaking. Although no longer writing songs, he formed SODS, the Society of Distinguished Songwriters. Sting has said that he started writing songs as a 12-year-old after reading Mitch's book, *How to Write a Hit Song*.

Mitch was married to the actress Grazina Frame and they have two daughters, Gina and Mazz, who are part of the band Woman.

The Beatles didn't care how he did it.

MURRAY, ROD [B. 1937]

Rod Murray was born in Liverpool in 1937 but he was moved to Blackpool during the war and didn't go to school until he was eight. He was educated by Christian Brothers at St Edward's in Sandfield Park, but lost more time through contracting TB by drinking unpasteurised milk when he was in the country. Nevertheless, he was accepted for the Liverpool College of Art in 1956. He soon befriended Stuart Sutcliffe and after being evicted from Percy Street for burning furniture, they moved into Gambier Terrace, Flat 3, Hillary Mansions (with two female students from the art school). They were soon joined by John Lennon.

Rod, Stuart, John and Bill Harry would drink at the art school pub, Ye Cracke, and they became known as 'The Dissenters' for their plans to change the world. There is a plaque in the pub today. Rod

was to marry one of their female friends and fellow student, Margaret Morris, known as Diz.

In the summer of 1959, Rod and Stu took Stu's painting to the Walker Art Gallery for the John Moores Exhibition. The large painting was in two parts but they preferred to go to Ye Cracke rather than deliver the second section. John Lennon had told Stu and Rod that whoever came up with a bass guitar could join the band. Rod was making his own guitar (and still has it), while Stuart used part of the money from selling his painting as a deposit on a guitar. Stu became a Beatle and Rod didn't. Rod, Stu and John were involved in the art school pantomime, *Cinderella*.

After graduation, Rod returned for a teaching certificate and taught there from 1972 to 1989. He specialised in light projectors, 3D images and holograms.

When John Lennon left the art college, he owed Rod £15 for back rent. He told him, 'You can have my stuff,' referring to the writings and drawings he had left behind. Rod later sold them at auction.

Being with such original thinkers as Rod was certainly a spur for John Lennon.

MURRAY THE K – SEE KAUFMAN, MURRAY

NILSSON, HARRY [1941–1994]

'In 1941 a happy father had a son and by 1944, the father walks right out the door.' In '1941' Nilsson told the story of his early life, and in the final verse he realises that he has exhibited exactly the same behaviour as his father following the birth of his own son.

Harry Edward Nilsson III was born in Brooklyn in 1941 and in the early 1960s he was developing computer systems for a bank. He was earning good money but he longed to be a professional songwriter and session singer. In 1964 he sang all the voices in the Foto-Fi Four's 'Stand Up And Holler', a 45 to celebrate The Beatles coming to America.

In 1967 The Beatles' press officer Derek Taylor was very impressed by 'You Can't Do That' on Nilsson's album *Pandemonium Shadow Show*. Instead of singing the Lennon and McCartney song straight, he incorporated snippets from their other songs to make an ingenious tribute. All four Beatles shared Taylor's view, and they referred to Nilsson as their 'favourite group'. His second album, *Aerial Ballet* (1968), included 'Everybody's Talkin'', which appeared on the soundtrack for *Midnight Cowboy* and soon everybody was talkin' about Nilsson. The Beatles wanted Nilsson on Apple but he was contracted to RCA. He did, however, write 'The Puppy Song' for Mary Hopkin and supplied all the background vocals on Ringo's hits 'You're Sixteen' and 'Only You'.

As with The Beatles, Nilsson never stayed with any genre for long. His hit album *Schmillson* (1971) touched many bases, and included his outstanding cover of Badfinger's Apple recording 'Without You', which was a transatlantic No. 1. Both George and Ringo played on the follow-up, *Son Of Schmillson* (1972), and he started the fashion for rock stars recording standards with *A Little Touch Of Schmillson In The Night* (1973), where he is smoking a large spliff on the cover.

John Lennon shared his passion for boozy, druggy nights, and in 1974 they ruined the Smothers Brothers performance in an LA club. John produced Nilsson's rock 'n' roll album *Pussy Cats* (1974), but encouraged him to sing hoarsely and

his voice never recovered. After Lennon's death, Nilsson campaigned for the banning of handguns.

Nilsson enjoyed being a good-time friend of The Beatles and he never had any inclination to tour. His ill-disciplined life is a cautionary tale for any singer. One of his final songs had the couplet, 'There's no more Oyster Bar, There's no more Ringo Starr.'

His studio wizardry impressed The Beatles but all too often he indulged their bad habits.

OLDHAM, ANDREW LOOG [B. 1944]
– SEE ENTRY FOR ROLLING STONES

ONO, YOKO [B. 1933]

In 1596 the ruthless samurai warrior Hideoshi installed his three-year-old child as the Emperor of Japan and Yoko Ono identified with him, believing he had been reincarnated in her. She would say, 'It means I would take over the world one day.' Was she joking or was she really that full of self-importance? More than anyone else in The Beatles' story, the jury is still out on Yoko Ono.

Yoko Ono was born into the Yasuda banking dynasty. Her mother Isoko wanted to marry concert pianist Eisuke Ono, but her parents would only allow the match if he joined their banking fraternity. Eisuke agreed and turned out to be very good at his job. The marriage went ahead and their daughter Yoko, the name meaning 'ocean child', was born on 18 February 1933. Because her father was managing a branch in America, she spent her early years in both Tokyo and San Francisco and knew something of both cultures.

In 1940, Emperor Hirohito of Japan sided with Germany and Italy and Yoko's family, fearing an imminent war between Japan and the USA, returned to Tokyo. Eisuke worked in Hanoi and when that fell to the Allies, he was placed in a concentration camp in Saigon.

In March 1945 the US began firebombing Tokyo and over 80,000 citizens were killed. Isoko took her three children into the country, but they were not welcome among the peasants, who hated their privilege. In August the Americans ended the war swiftly and mercilessly by exploding atomic bombs over Hiroshima and Nagasaki. Yoko recalled returning to Tokyo. 'It was a big field of nothing, but I knew I could survive anything.'

After the war, Eusike was deemed a war criminal as the financiers were said to have helped the military leaders. For a couple of years he was unemployable but once America wanted to rebuild Japan, he worked for the Bank of Tokyo. Yoko continued her schooling in Japan, but gave up studying philosophy at Gakushuin University to move with the family to the affluent Scarsdale suburb of New York. She attended the Sarah Lawrence College from 1953–56. Although she studied music, her preference for avant-garde sounds meant that she stopped attending lectures and did not complete the course.

Yoko met a Japanese musician, Toshi Ichiyanagi, who was studying at Juilliard. He was determined to become a concert pianist and Yoko wanted to marry him. In a rerun of their own marriage, her parents would only agree if he became a banker. Yoko stubbornly argued against this and married him anyway in New York in 1956, falling out of contact with her parents.

The newlyweds were drawn to the progressive art group in New York known as Fluxus. A key member was John Cage, who became a founder member of The Velvet Underground. Yoko was keen on mixed-media events and her first art exhib-

ition, in 1960, included *Painting To Be Stepped On*, a scrap of canvas on which visitors would walk. In 1961 the couple separated and Yoko began spending a lot of time with gallery owner George Maciunas. Maciunas was soon to flee to Germany to escape his creditors.

With her brother Keisuke about to get married, Yoko repaired her relationship with her parents and went to live in one of the family's apartments in Tokyo. Toshi was enjoying some success in Japan but her parents remained unimpressed. In 1962 Yoko took an overdose of sleeping pills and was admitted to hospital.

A musician and arts promoter from New York, Tony Cox, had developed such a fascination with Yoko that he had gone to visit her in Tokyo. When he arrived, she was in hospital and he did his best to revive her spirits. Toshi and Yoko were divorced in 1962 and Yoko married Tony the following year. Their daughter Kyoko was born in Tokyo on 8 August 1963.

Inspired by Allen Ginsberg and others from the Beat Generation, Yoko and Tony Cox organised 'Happenings', that is, artistic events that would involve the audiences, often in unexpected ways. The best known is *Cut Piece* (1964), in which Yoko sat on a chair and invited the audience to cut her clothing from her body. Tony also invited the audience to wrap Yoko in bandages and volunteers climbed inside large white bags. Some considered this pretentious nonsense but many in the artistic community took it seriously.

Yoko and Tony Cox made films for the art circuit. The most notorious is *Film No. 4: Bottoms*, in which Yoko filmed 365 bare bottoms, one for every day of the year – a film that has been praised by many modern galleries while others still think it is a bum idea.

On the evening of 7 November 1966 John Lennon attended the preview of Yoko's art exhibition at the Indica gallery in London (there is some confusion as to the actual date; some sources suggest it was 9 November, but as the opening party was on 8 November, the preview showing on the previous day is most likely correct) and was amused with the idea of hammering imaginary nails into the wall. According to Yoko, she knew very little of popular music and didn't appreciate his standing, although this barely seems credible.

In 1968, while their partners were away, John and Yoko made some avant-garde recordings, which were released as *Unfinished Music No. 1: Two Virgins*. They were shown fully naked on both the back and front of the album sleeve, a controversial move that suggested that whatever they did, they were never going to be boring. John, who never grasped the intended seriousness of the American avant-garde, declared, 'I've finally found someone as barmy as me.'

Many diehard Beatles fans were horrified, as it appeared that Yoko was breaking up the band. In truth, they were already on a collision course. The articles in the press were hateful, a mixture of racism, sexism and contempt for the unknown. The comedian Bob Monkhouse appeared on ITV's *The Golden Shot* and got laughs by saying that 'Yoko Ono' was Japanese for 'scumbag'. Few appreciated 'Revolution 9' on the *White Album*.

In October 1968, shortly before the release of *Two Virgins*, John and Yoko's flat in Montagu Square was raided for drugs, with John insisting that the drugs had been planted. The arrest possibly caused Yoko to have a miscarriage. When their divorces came through, the pair married in Gibraltar in March 1969.

By now, they were seen every day in the papers, usually dressing in white, and treating their lives as performance art. In that sense, the Lennons were a forerunner for TV reality shows such as *Big Brother*. They had bed-ins for peace, planted acorns in Coventry for peace appeared on bill-boards for peace and made records for peace. They formed the Plastic Ono Band, and that same key message was there in their first single, 'Give Peace a Chance' (1969), and in their seasonal hit 'Happy Xmas (War Is Over)' (1971). John was coming off heroin in 'Cold Turkey', but surprisingly 'The Ballad Of John And Yoko' was released as a Beatles single. The band appeared at a music festival in Toronto, but John had no intention of going on the road. Many of their ideas come from Yoko's earlier work and her poems about 'imagine' inspired his famous song.

Right from the start, John was saying that Yoko's contributions were as valid as his own, but it is only in more recent times that her shrieking and yelling have found some recognition. Among her champions have been Harry Nilsson and Elvis Costello. Her albums include *Yoko Ono/Plastic Ono Band* (1970), *Fly* (1971) and *Approximately Infinite Universe* (1973). Yoko's 1971 'Open Your Box' was banned for obscenity by the BBC but later became an unexpected clubbing favourite. Primal Scream and the B-52s have clearly been influenced by Yoko Ono.

Yoko Ono had won custody of her daughter, Kyoko, but Tony Cox had visiting rights. He became alarmed that the young child was being exposed to drug-taking and kidnapped her in 1971. Yoko did not know where they had gone but she never feared for her safety. Tony and his new wife brought Kyoko up in a Christian cult and she finally contacted her mother in 1994. She was married with children, thus making Yoko a grandmother.

John and Yoko settled in America but in 1972 they lived apart at Yoko's suggestion. John went to Los Angeles with May Pang and was reunited with Yoko in 1974. John always called her 'Mother', and after several miscarriages they had a son, Sean, born on John's birthday in 1975. John became a 'house husband', leaving Yoko to handle their business affairs – she had some of those banking genes.

They returned to music with *Double Fantasy* (1980), and the world forgets that half the tracks on this multimillion-selling album were by Yoko. They were returning home from mixing a new track, 'Walking On Thin Ice', when John was shot in the lobby of their Dakota apartment on 8 December 1980.

Yoko has since been the keeper of his legacy. She has supervised releases of new albums and DVDs and approved film scripts. She has accepted honorary degrees, opened an airport, donated his childhood home to the National Trust and arranged sculptures in his honour, notably in Iceland. After 9/11, she took a hoarding in Times Square for six months, which simply said, 'Imagine all the people living life in peace'.

Yoko has performed in concert from time to time, in later years, working with her son Sean. Several of her albums were collected in *Ono Box* (1992) and her most recent work is *Take Me To The Land Of Hell* (2013). She has been accused of bad taste, for example displaying John's blood-stained spectacles on the cover of her 1981 *Season Of Glass* album, and exhibiting his bloody clothes for an art exhibition in 2009.

There has been a thawing in Yoko's personality. She no longer seems as cold as she was and every-body loves the elfin lady with her black and white image, even if her music is an acquired taste. She is still working and says, 'Every day I want to do something to let my heart dance.'

If John was self-indulgent before Yoko, there was no stopping him once she came into the picture.

ORTON, JOE [1933–1967]

Imagine The Beatles as political activists, dressed as women, committing murder and going to jail. Possibly not? Joe Orton could, however, and he submitted his screenplay, *Up Against It*, to them in 1967.

Joe Orton was born into a working class family in Leicester in 1933, graduating from RADA when he was 20. While he was there he befriended another student, Kenneth Halliwell, who was seven years older, and they lived together. They both thought that they should be writers and wrote eight raunchy novels in ten years, some singly and some together. In 1962 they were jailed for six months apiece for defacing library books, usually with obscene language and photographs. Kenneth attempted suicide while inside, but Joe became ever more the prankster, Joe Ought'nt, in fact.

In 1963 Joe had his first radio play accepted, *Ruffian On The Stair*, and then his play, *Entertaining Mr Sloane*, made the West End, partly due to Terence Rattigan's financial backing. The controversy over this sex-filled play was fuelled by letters in the *Daily Telegraph* from an Edna Welthorpe, actually Orton himself. In 1966 he added necrophilia and corrupt police to the mix, for *Loot*. His diaries reveal that Halliwell was jealous of his success and Orton was taking his pleasure from rough trade in public lavatories. He compiled *The Orton Gazetteer of Convivial Conveniences*, though not for publication.

In 1967 he completed another frenzied play, *What The Butler Saw*, where the doctors are madder than their patients. He was the hottest playwright of the day and his camp, sex-obsessed, gratuitously offensive style was described as 'Ortonesque'. The United Artists producer Walter Shenson asked Orton if he would like to write a screenplay for The Beatles. He had not written a screenplay before but came up with the wild, outlandish *Up Against It*, in which the four Beatles assassinate a female Prime Minister. This initiates a guerrilla war between the sexes.

Orton submitted the script on 29 March and it was returned on 4 April with no explanation why. Orton, in his diaries, blamed Brian Epstein. 'An amateur and a fool. He isn't equipped to judge the quality.' The film producer Oscar Lewenstein liked it, and suggested that Orton should meet Richard Lester. This was arranged for 9 August 1967. A chauffeur called to collect Orton but discovered mayhem. Kenneth Halliwell had beaten Joe Orton to death with a hammer, and then taken an overdose of sleeping pills to kill himself. Orton was cremated to the sounds of 'A Day In The Life'. Both Charles Wood and Roger McGough tried to salvage Orton's script, but got nowhere. It could only have been revised satisfactorily by Orton himself.

Up Against It was a starting point and who can say how it might have developed. It might have been thought that The Beatles would reject such a ridiculous script out of hand, but then they did make *Magical Mystery Tour* in 1968 and Ringo appeared in Frank Zappa's *200 Motels* and recorded 'Men's Room, LA' with Kinky Friedman. Anything was possible in Beatleworld.

A biopic, *Prick Up Your Ears*, was successful in 1978, but a production of *Up Against It* with music from Todd Rundgren was staged with only limited success in New York in 1989.

Kicked into touch.

OWEN, ALUN [1925-1994]

In 1961, when Lionel Bart wanted to write a musical around the Liverpool folk song 'Maggie May',

the playwright Alun Owen told him, 'You've got to learn a whole new language. The Liverpool dialect is part-Irish, part-Welsh and part-catarrh.' Bart moved to Liverpool to soak up the atmosphere and their West End musical, *Maggie May*, starring Rachel Roberts and then Georgia Brown as Maggie, opened in September 1964.

Alun Owen was born in 1925 to Welsh-speaking parents, his father being a merchant seaman. Alun was married in 1942 to Mary O'Keefe, when he was only 16. They were married until his death in 1994 and had two sons. Shortly after the wedding Alun did wartime service as a Bevin boy down the mines. He then worked as an actor and trained with the actor/manager Sir Donald Wolfit, while his wife Mary worked as a stage designer. He wrote his first play, *Progress To The Park* (1958) by ad-libbing Scouse dialogue into a tape recorder. It was staged by Joan Littlewood's Theatre Workshop.

His gritty *No Trams To Lime Street* (1959) was an unvarnished look at three sailors and their girls in Liverpool. It made television history as the first 'kitchen sink' drama, although many in the city thought it shamed the area. Several more dramas followed and Alun Owen is now regarded a pioneering writer of TV drama.

Richard Lester had used Alun Owen as a stooge for his television work with The Goons, and was impressed by his powerful film script for *The Criminal* (1960) starring Stanley Baker. In 1963 he thought Alun would be ideal for *A Hard Day's Night* and so Alun accompanied The Beatles on various dates in November to get a feel for the mayhem around them. In the film, he emphasised their moptop images: the witty John, the cute Paul, the quiet George and the amiable Ringo.

The film had immense *joie de vivre* but was almost plotless, and deliberately so. For a pop film, it made a serious point: The Beatles' fame had not brought great freedom but had imprisoned them.

Such was the cleverness of Alun's script that the lines appeared to be improvised although The Beatles were, in the most part, reciting his work. He was paid £1,200 and the script was nominated for an Oscar but lost out to *Father Goose*. Still, The Beatles' score wasn't even nominated.

Richard Lester wanted Alun for the second film, but as The Beatles thought they had been treated one-dimensionally, they told Epstein to insist on a different writer. Alun wrote numerous TV plays – eight in 1967 alone – but strangely did not work on any more films.

Many famous Beatle witticisms were written by Alun Owen.

PANG, MAY [B. 1950]

If a writer for a soap opera suggested that a boss's wife might encourage the secretary to sleep with the boss, it might be dismissed as far-fetched. Welcome to the mad world of John Lennon and Yoko Ono where nothing is real, nothing to get hung about.

May Pang was born to Chinese immigrant parents in Manhattan in 1950. She was a good student but quickly tired of further studies. She failed an interview as a receptionist for a Japanese bicycle company in New York, but noting that Apple Records had an office in the same building, she asked for a job. She couldn't type but she was diligent, with the right personality, and was soon working for Allen Klein, the high-powered accountant sorting out The Beatles' affairs. 'He's had a bad press,' she maintains. 'There was something of the gangster about him, sure, but he wasn't a total gangster like some of the record moguls. He genuinely loved the music and he renegotiated The Beatles' contracts with EMI.'

She started working for John and Yoko in 1970, and was an assistant on their avant-garde (and in one instant derrière-garde) films. She was John's girlfriend from 1973–75, the period known as his 'lost weekend'. She wrote her memoir, *Loving John* (1983), and published a book of photographs, *Instamatic Karma* (2008). May married the record producer Tony Visconti in 1989, but they divorced in 2000. She exhibits many of her photographs of John Lennon and has a range of feng shui jewellery.

Though clearly a higher rating for John himself.

PAOLOZZI, EDUARDO [1924–2005]

Eduardo Paolozzi was born of Italian descent in Leith, Edinburgh in 1924. Although only 16, he was interned during the war, and while there he learnt that his father and grandfather had been drowned when a ship taking them to Canada had been sunk by the Germans. He studied at the Slade School of Fine Art from 1944 to 1947 and established himself as a sculptor in Paris.

In 1947 he created *I was a Rich Man's Plaything*, in which the word 'Pop!' appears from the barrel of a gun pointing at the plaything herself. This was the first time that pop and art were associated, although he never attached the pop art movement to himself and said he was a surrealist.

In the early sixties, he was teaching in Hamburg and his presence encouraged Stuart Sutcliffe to enrol there. Stuart found him very instructive and Eduardo was to praise his work after his early death.

During the sixties, his sculptures often considered the relationships between man and machine. He created the mosaics for Tottenham Court Road tube station (1982) and his work has been included in the artwork for Paul's albums *Red Rose*

Speedway (1973) and *Off The Ground* (1993). He was knighted in 1989.

One of the reasons Stuart Sutcliffe stayed in Hamburg.

PARNES, LARRY [1929–1989]

In the mid-1950s, Laurence Maurice Parnes was in the family clothing business in Romford when he met the publicist John Kennedy, who had discovered Tommy Hicks and renamed him Tommy Steele. Larry became his partner, offering his business acumen, and soon Tommy was topping the charts with 'Singing The Blues' (1956). When the two entrepreneurs fell out, Parnes became his sole manager and started renaming new young male singers – Reg Smith (Marty Wilde), John Askew (Johnny Gentle), Roy Taylor (Vince Eager) and Ronnie Wycherley (Billy Fury). It is said that Parnes named them because that is what he thought they would be like in bed. 'He may have done,' says Vince (not so) Eager, 'but he certainly never found out with me.' How Larry and his friend Russ Conway must have laughed when they renamed Richard Kneller Dickie Pride. Among Larry's boyfriends was the American singer Johnnie Ray.

The TV director Jack Good used many of Larry's artists on *6.5 Special, Oh Boy!* and *Boy Meets Girls*, which was hosted by Marty Wilde. Larry brought the American rock 'n' rollers Gene Vincent and Eddie Cochran to Britain, and they showed a whole generation of youngsters how it should be done. Larry came to Liverpool and heard The Beatles audition as a backing group for Billy Fury. He decided instead to use them for a short Scottish tour with Johnny Gentle. Johnny told Larry how good they were but Larry didn't pick up on this.

Brian Epstein spoke to Larry in Liverpool, asking him for advice. In several ways, Brian copied Larry. He had the same concept of a stable of male performers; he gave the performers house rules for how they should behave and sacked them if they fell out of line (Larry with Tony Sheridan and Dickie Pride, Brian with The Big Three), and he liked the idea of promoting his own package shows (*Larry Parnes Presents, NEMS Enterprises Presents*).

However, he didn't copy Larry's parsimony. Joe Brown once reclaimed a taxi fare and asked Larry for five shillings and sixpence. 'The taxi fare was five shillings,' said Larry. 'What's the sixpence for?' 'The tip,' said Joe. 'Sixpence!' exploded Larry. 'Threepence was quite enough.' Larry threatened to sue the BBC after Paul McCartney joked about his meanness on *Desert Island Discs* in 1982 and an out of court settlement was reached.

Brian didn't want to acquire the same reputation as Parnes, who was parodied on record ('So Little Time', Peter Sellers), in literature (*Absolute Beginners*, Colin MacInnes) and in the theatre and cinema (*Expresso Bongo*). Larry could never take a joke against himself because as far as he was concerned, he was behaving normally.

In November 1962 Larry wrote to Brian about booking The Beatles for a nationwide tour. He added, 'I believed I auditioned these boys a couple of years ago.' The correspondence went back and forth but Parnes would not go beyond £140 and Brian wouldn't accept less than £200.

They did not fall out over this and Brian would occasionally confide in Larry, once telling him that The Beatles were going to leave him. Larry said, 'I can never see the boys leaving you. You are depressed over nothing.'

The sixties groups knocked Larry's artists off the charts. Larry moved into West End theatre with *Charlie Girl*, where Joe Brown was eventually replaced by Gerry Marsden, and the first UK production of *Chicago*. He managed the ice skater John Curry and, always saving money, argued with him over the size of skating surfaces on stage. Parnes retired after a severe bout of meningitis and died in 1989. Although he never wrote his autobiography, he did have the title, *The Popfather*.

A role model for Eppy, both for what to do and what not to do.

PETER AND GORDON

Peter Asher (b. 1944) and Gordon Waller (1945-2009) were the children of doctors who met at Westminster School. They had a love of rock 'n' roll music and they would harmonise at social occasions with their acoustic guitars. Peter left to study philosophy at London University, but Waller was still at school when they secured late-night engagements at the Pickwick Club, owned by Harry Secombe. Gordon would climb over the school gates every evening and, returning on one occasion, he put a spike through his foot, causing permanent damage.

Secombe recommended them to the recording manager Norman Newell, who signed them to EMI's Columbia label. His initial thought was to release the folk song '500 Miles', but he did not know of the ace up their sleeve, that is, the direct line to Paul McCartney.

Peter was living at home in Wimpole Street, and so was his actress sister Jane – with their red hair they were the carrots of Wimpole Street. Jane was seeing Paul McCartney and Peter liked his song, 'A World Without Love'. Paul had no plans to use it with The Beatles as John Lennon mocked its opening line, 'Please lock me away' and so

Peter and Gordon recorded it, double-tracking their voices for a fuller sound, with Paul writing a bridge at the last minute. They were wooden but likeable performers, simply playing and singing their songs, with harmonies that lacked the razor sharpness of The Everly Brothers.

Ironically, the single knocked The Beatles' 'Can't Buy Me Love' from No. 1, and it repeated its success in America. The noted songwriter Doc Pomus was to describe 'A World Without Love' as his favourite Lennon and McCartney composition: possibly it is the one that is closest to the classic Brill Building songs of the early sixties.

Paul wrote their melodic follow-up, 'Nobody I Know', which again did well, but his third song, 'I Don't Want To See You Again', was weaker, although it still made the US Top 20. Befriending the American hitmaker and songwriter Del Shannon, Peter and Gordon were given the superbly catchy 'I Go To Pieces', a fine record on which Waller played 12-string guitar. Inexplicably, it failed to make the UK charts but it did reach the US Top 10.

The duo returned to the UK Top 10 with a revival of Buddy Holly's romantic 'True Love Ways' and a full-blooded treatment of Phil Spector's 'To Know Her Is To Love Her', on which each voice was recorded four times. A cover of Barbara Lewis's 'Baby I'm Yours' made the UK Top 20, and, highlighting their international appeal, they recorded in French, German and Italian.

Paul McCartney wondered if his songs were strong enough to sell without his name and offered them 'Woman', which listed the fictitious Bernard Webb as its writer. This was muddled thinking as there had been several songs that hadn't sold despite 'Lennon and McCartney' on the label. In any event, it was hardly a Webb of deceit as it was soon revealed that it was McCartney's song. The single made the UK Top 30 and

US Top 20; McCartney did himself a disservice, as it was a fine song.

In 1966 Mike Leander wrote and produced the novelty 'Lady Godiva', which was censured by the Mayor of Coventry, who should have had better things to do. Really, it was a cynical attempt to exploit the American interest in British eccentricity and was following the US success of Herman's Hermits with music hall material. In the same vein, Peter and Gordon recorded the ultra-silly 'Knight in Rusty Armour' and the quaint 'Sunday for Tea'. They sang the happy-go-lucky theme for the Michael Winner film about Swinging London, *The Jokers*, starring Michael Crawford and Oliver Reed.

Their first LP, *Peter and Gordon*, had been a big seller in 1964 and they released a further five albums in the UK. They recorded additional albums specifically for the US market, including *Peter and Gordon Sing and Play the Hits of Nashville, Tennessee* (1966), *In London for Tea* (1967) and *Hot Cold and Custard* (1968).

With a strong wit, Waller was more charismatic than the duo's bland image would imply. From time to time, his wild partying made the news and he had a succession of girlfriends including Jenny

Dunbar (whose brother John married Marianne Faithfull and was to start the Indica Bookshop with Peter Asher and Barry Miles) and American songwriter Sharon Sheeley (the former girlfriend of Eddie Cochran).

Feeling cheated by their management, the duo stopped performing in 1968 with Asher working for The Beatles' Apple label and discovering, and then managing, James Taylor. He produced many artists including Linda Ronstadt and Carole King. Gordon began his solo career with the magnificent 'Rosecrans Boulevard', written by Jimmy Webb, but it failed to chart. Calling a solo album *...And Gordon* was simply ridiculous.

Gordon played Pharaoh as a pastiche Elvis Presley in the musical *Joseph and the Amazing Technicolor Dreamcoat*, in both the West End and on tour. Moving out of the record business, he became a landscape gardener. He did solo shows from time to time and as the years went by, he appeared at Beatles festivals in America.

Always a heavy drinker, Waller had lost his looks by the time Peter and Gordon re-formed in 2005 for a benefit concert for Mike Smith of the Dave Clark Five. They performed 'I Want Love'

THE BEATLES AND THE DUKE OF EDINBURGH

In October 1964, the Duke of Edinburgh was reported as saying that The Beatles were 'on the wane'. Naturally The Beatles were asked for their reactions, which were quoted in *Melody Maker*.

'I bet the Duke's book hasn't sold so many as John's book.' – Paul
'That bloke's getting no money for his playing fields from me.' – John
'Tell him I'm withdrawing from his award scheme.' – George
'You can't keep it up for ever, whether you are John Lennon or the Duke of Edinburgh.' – Ringo

Then Brian Epstein received a telegram from the Duke of Edinburgh that explained that the Duke had said The Beatles 'were away' not 'on the wane'.

So that was all right.

at a showcase for Elton John's songwriting, and in 2009 they appeared at the Surf Ballroom in Clear Lake for the fiftieth anniversary of Buddy Holly's death. Since Gordon's death in Connecticut in 2009, Peter has made some affable solo appearances at Beatles festivals, but Gordon was the lead singer and had the stronger voice.

Peter is currently managing and producing The Webb Sisters, who sing behind Leonard Cohen.

Well-performed versions of Lennon and McCartney songs.

POOLE, BRIAN [B. 1941]

After seeing Buddy Holly and The Crickets on their UK tour in March 1958, Brian Poole and his friends formed The Tremolos, who subsequently became Brian Poole and The Tremeloes. Brian purchased spectacles like Buddy's and his optician offered to run their fan club. Another client of the optician was Mike Smith, a young A&R man at Decca. Mike gave them an audition and also tested The Beatles. Mike's boss, Dick Rowe, told him he could only have one beat group and it was twist and out for The Beatles. On any other day of the week, choosing The Tremeloes would have been an excellent decision. They had hits in their own right and accompanied other acts in the studio including Tommy Steele, The Vernons Girls, Delbert McClinton and Jimmy Savile.

Alan Blakley of The Tremeloes had bought The Isley Brothers record 'Twist and Shout' in 1962 and they were performing it on stage. The Beatles included the song on their first LP, but Brian Poole and The Tremeloes released it as a single, making the Top 10. 'We did it entirely differently from The Beatles,' says Brian. 'It was more like a Buddy Holly treatment but it was also fast and furious like a punk band.'

The group hit No. 1 with a cover of The Contours track 'Do You Love Me', and it was Roy Orbison who suggested they should cover 'Candy Man'. Buddy's producer, Norman Petty, wrote and played piano on 'Someone, Someone'.

In 1965 Brian Poole went solo but his ballads were not hits, while The Tremeloes had a succession of radio-friendly successes including 'Here Comes My Baby', 'Even The Bad Times Are Good' and the No. 1, 'Silence Is Golden'.

Brian Poole returned to the family business of butchering, but he still sang from to time and in more recent years has appeared on sixties tours. His daughters, Shelly and Karen, have had hits as Alisha's Attic and Shelly is now part of Red Sky July.

What would have happened if The Beatles had been better than Brian Poole at the Decca audition?

POWELL, CYNTHIA – SEE LENNON, CYNTHIA

PRESLEY, ELVIS [1935–1977]

Elvis Presley's music was a formative influence on The Beatles and they performed many of his songs, including 'I Forgot To Remember To Forget', 'I'm Gonna Sit Right Down And Cry (Over You)' and 'That's All Right (Mama)'. In Hamburg, Paul would attempt the German lyrics of 'Wooden Heart' and Stu Sutcliffe would sing 'Love Me Tender', which won the heart of Astrid Kirchherr.

By 1963 Elvis was making lightweight, instantly forgettable films and The Beatles criticised him on *Juke Box Jury*, saying he had 'gone down the nick'. This criticism can't have travelled to America, as a few weeks later Ed Sullivan read out a goodwill message from Elvis and his manager, Colonel Tom Parker.

On their 1965 US tour, a meeting with Elvis was brokered by Chris Hutchins of the *NME* and on 27 August they went to his west coast home in Bel Air. It is unthinkable today, but neither side wanted press coverage, TV footage or even private photographs. They arrived at 11pm and were intrigued to find Elvis fiddling with a remote control for the television as they had not seen one before.

Elvis said, 'If you're just gonna stare at me, I'm going to bed.' His entourage brought out guitars and they had a jam session (again unrecorded) in which they sang Cilla Black's 'You're My World' and Paul showed Elvis the bass chords for 'I Feel Fine'. Epstein and the Colonel discussed business (undoubtedly, Brian wanted to present Elvis in the UK). By all accounts, Ringo Starr had the most fun of the evening by playing pool with the Memphis Mafia.

The Beatles stayed for four hours and there was no return visit. Indeed, Elvis became disappointed in The Beatles, telling President Nixon that their admissions of drug-taking were a damaging influence on American youth.

In his Vegas years, Elvis sang 'Yesterday' and 'Something' and occasionally merged 'Get Back' with his own 'Little Sister'.

The superficiality of their meeting perhaps illustrates that you should never meet your heroes. Tony Barrow insists that the fault was all Elvis's and that he was 'a boring old fart'.

'Before Elvis, there was nothing.' John Lennon

PRESTON, BILLY [1946–2006]

There was only one musician with whom The Beatles shared their billing on a record and that was Billy Preston. The Rolling Stones, Elton John, Little Richard and Sam Cooke hired Billy Preston to play keyboards, and Ray Charles even said, 'This man is gonna take my place.' Billy was a flamboyant but modest man, regarding his talent as a gift from the Lord, proclaiming 'Music is the voice of God.'

William Everett Preston was born in Houston in September 1946, but the family moved to Los Angeles where his mother became the organist for the Victory Baptist Church. Billy was playing piano from the age of three, and by age ten he was being featured on television shows. In 1956 he played organ for the gospel singer Mahalia Jackson, and a film producer was so impressed that he cast him as the young W.C. Handy in *St Louis Blues*. In 1962 Preston came to the UK as an organist with Little Richard.

Little Richard played in Europe and he and Billy met The Beatles at the Star-Club. Sam Cooke signed Billy to his record label, and his first album, *16 Year Old Soul*, was released in 1963. Billy played in the house band for Jack Good's TV show, *Shindig!* When Ray Charles appeared, Billy Preston took his place at rehearsals and performed 'Georgia On My Mind'. Ray was so impressed that he asked him to join his orchestra. Billy was featured on Ray's album *Crying Time*, and played on the title track and 'Let's Go Get Stoned'. In 1967 Preston's UK single 'Billy's Bag' became a party favourite, being praised by Stevie Wonder and featured on several TV programmes.

In 1969 The Beatles were in London, being filmed about the making of an album. They resented each other's company and the sessions were going poorly. George Harrison invited Billy along, rightly surmising that the situation would change as they all respected him. With Billy playing a Fender Rhodes electric piano, The Beatles recorded 'Get Back' and were so impressed that the single was billed as 'The Beatles with Billy Preston'. Billy took part in their last-ever performance on the Apple rooftop in Saville Row. John Lennon wanted him to join The Beatles permanently and he played on several tracks on *Abbey Road,* including 'Something'.

Billy recorded for Apple with George Harrison producing. The title song from his first album, *That's The Way God Planned It* (1969), was a Top 20 hit. The second album, *Encouraging Words* (1970), included the first recorded version of 'My Sweet Lord', with Billy performing with the Edwin Hawkins Singers. Billy worked with John, George and Ringo on their solo projects as well as being an integral part of the charity event, *The Concert For Bangla Desh.*

Billy signed with the A&M label and he composed and produced *I Wrote A Simple Song* (1971), with George Harrison on lead guitar and arranged by Quincy Jones. His instrumental, 'Outa-Space', on which he played clavinet, was a US No. 2.

While Preston was writing *Music Is My Life* (1972), he asked a friend, Bruce Fisher, to help him complete 'Will It Go Round In Circles'. That track topped the US charts and Fisher gave up his job in a mailroom. In keeping with the fashions of the time, Preston sported an enormous Afro and played an electric keyboard on a strap round his neck. The instrument had limited sounds and made him look like a novelty act.

The next album *Everybody Likes Some Kind Of Music* (1973) included another hit single, 'Space Race', a tune Preston had written while coming to terms with synthesisers. The fourth A&M album, *The Kids And Me* (1974), included another US No. 1, the funky 'Nothing From Nothing', which

was played on a barroom piano for singalong appeal. Preston released his composition 'You Are So Beautiful' as a B-side, but Joe Cocker was quick to spot the ballad's potential and it became a US Top 10 hit.

Billy is featured on scores of albums including Merry Clayton's *Gimme Shelter* (1970), Aretha Franklin's *Live At Fillmore West* (1971), Delaney & Bonnie's *Together* (1972) and Eric Clapton's *No Reason To Cry* (1976), plus some stoned ramblings with Cheech & Chong. He continued to work with Harrison and played with Splinter on their albums for Harrison's Dark Horse Records. Throughout all this, he made further solo albums for A&M, but by now the hits had ceased.

Starting with *Sticky Fingers* (1971) and *Exile On Main Street* (1972), Billy became a favourite with the Rolling Stones. He toured with them in 1975 and would have continued but for a dispute over fees. In 1978 he appeared in the risible film *Sgt Pepper's Lonely Hearts Club Band,* performing 'Get Back' on top of a church steeple, but it was marginally better than being involved in *Blues Brothers 2000.*

In 1979 Stevie Wonder's former wife Syreeta joined him for a romantic duet, 'With You I'm Born Again', on the soundtrack of the basketball film *Fast Break.* Their record was an international hit, almost topping the UK chart and leading to the Tamla Motown album, *Billy Preston & Syreeta* (1981). He recorded three solo albums for Tamla Motown, before moving to the HI-NRG label Megatone.

Billy's career lost its momentum in the 1980s as he became addicted to cocaine and alcohol. In 1991, he was arrested after a 16-year-old boy claimed that Preston had shown him pornography and committed obscene acts with him. He was also accused of assault with a deadly weapon. Preston's sentence was a mixture of rehab, house arrest and then probation. In 1997 he broke his parole by testing positive for cocaine and was given a three-year sentence. While inside, other crimes came to light. With a team of people he had been staging car crashes, burglaries and fires for insurance purposes. He received a further year in jail.

Preston's problems did not affect his talent. He played on the Luther Vandross album *The Night I Fell In Love* (1985) and joined Ringo Starr's All-Starr Band for an album and a tour in 1989. He was back with Ray Charles for *My World* in 1992, and was featured on the Bonnie Raitt and Elton John duet 'Love Letters' the following year. He made it up with the Stones and joined them for *Bridges To Babylon* (1997) as well as having steady employment as the MD for the US TV series *Nightlife*, starring the comedian David Brenner. In 2002, he performed with great success on *The Concert For George* at the Royal Albert Hall, but he was suffering from hypertension and kidney failure.

He returned to his Hammond organ for Eric Clapton's roots album *Me And Mr Johnson* (2004) and worked with Steve Winwood and the Funk Brothers in Europe. He appeared in the film *The Derby Stallion* (2005), and his final recordings were for Ringo Starr and for a Beatles tribute album of his own. He died in 2006, a full life to say the least.

In 1969 The Beatles were in freefall and he brought some temporary respite.

ROE, TOMMY [B. 1942]

Atlanta-born Tommy Roe had an international hit in 1962 with 'Sheila', very much a cousin of Buddy Holly's 'Peggy Sue', and he also scored with the poignant saga of 'The Folk Singer'. In 1963 he toured the UK with Chris Montez and The Beatles, who were enjoying their first successes. Tommy went on to have further US hits with 'Sweet Pea' and 'Hooray for Hazel'. By 1969, the hits had dried up – or so everybody thought, until he topped the charts in both Britain and America with the ultimate bubblegum success, 'Dizzy'.

Tommy recalls, 'I am very proud to be a part of the history of The Beatles and my memories of our tour are all great. They were getting hot in England and it was tough following them. I was so impressed that I started doing their songs and tried to get them a deal in the States. My record company turned them down and I think now that they should have seen them. Once The Beatles started getting publicity in America, they were bound to happen. I was so influenced by what I heard in this country that I wrote "Everybody" on the way home. I tried to get that same sound. We recorded it in Muscle Shoals and it was a big record for me.'

The Beatles had 'Sheila' in their set in 1962.

ROLLING STONES

The only group of the sixties that seriously challenged The Beatles' supremacy was another British band, the archetypal bad boys, the Rolling Stones. The innumerable 'Beatles v Stones' features suggested that they were bitter rivals, but they were all good friends.

The Rolling Stones emerged from the blues scene in London, led by Alexis Korner and Cyril Davies. The famous five – vocalist Mick Jagger (b. 1943), guitarist Keith Richards (b. 1943), guitarist Brian Jones (1942–1969), bassist Bill Wyman (b. 1936) and drums Charlie Watts (b.

1941) played their first gig together on 12 July 1962 at the Marquee jazz club in Oxford Street, London. Unlike most groups including The Beatles, the Stones favoured a twin lead guitar approach as opposed to lead and rhythm. They did vary this, however, and the Brian Jones slide guitar solos are among the highlights of their early records.

The band took their name from the Muddy Waters song 'Rollin' Stone', and were much more into hardcore blues than The Beatles, who at the time might not even have heard Robert Johnson. There was however much common ground; they both loved black rock 'n' roll (Chuck Berry, Larry Williams) and R&B (Arthur Alexander, Barrett Strong).

Brian Epstein employed a young publicist, Andrew Loog Oldham, to work on The Beatles' first records. When he saw the scruffy, unkempt and long-haired Rolling Stones, he had found the perfect marketing opportunity. He could promote them as the anti-Beatles, as by comparison the Liverpool lads were decent and homely, and did as they were told. The press was soon full of shock, horror stories. 'Would you let your daughter marry a Stone?' The claim that the band never took baths particularly rankled Bill Wyman, who kept himself immaculately clean.

The publicity benefited both groups as teenagers were constantly asked, 'Are you a Stones fan or a Beatles fan?' Surely there was no reason why you couldn't like both and just hate Freddie and The Dreamers.

Early in 1963 club owner Giorgio Gomelsky had arranged for The Beatles to see the Rolling Stones at the Crawdaddy. As he suspected, they were both impressed and they became friendly. Indeed, George Harrison came back to Liverpool and told his friends that he had seen a group that was 'almost as good as The Roadrunners' (Liver-

pool's R&B group), and when he met Dick Rowe at a 'Battle of the Bands' competition at the Philharmonic Hall in Liverpool, he told him about the Stones. Rowe, keen not to make a second mistake, rushed to see for himself, and signed them to Decca. John and Paul wrote their second single, 'I Wanna Be Your Man'. In December 1964, they took Howlin' Wolf's 'Little Red Rooster' to No. 1, a remarkable achievement as it was the first time a blues song had ever reached the top.

Andrew Oldham told them that they had to write their own songs and the first Jagger/Richards composition, 'As Tears Go By', became a hit for Marianne Faithfull. Soon they were writing a succession of No. 1 singles, including 'The Last Time', '(I Can't Get No) Satisfaction' and 'Get Off of My Cloud'. In 1966, Mick and Keith wrote all 15 songs on their album *Aftermath*, and a No. 1 for Chris Farlowe, 'Out Of Time'

In 1965 Oldham's misguided sleeve note for *The Rolling Stones, Now!* was criticised in the House of Commons, which led to a reprint by Decca. The offending passage reads: 'This is THE STONES' new disc within. Cast deep in your pockets for loot to buy this disc of groovies and fancy words. If you don't have bread, see that blind man knock him on the head, steal his wallet and lo and behold you have the loot, if you put in the boot, good, another one sold!'

The year 1967 was not vintage for the Stones. Keith Richards had his home raided – possibly George Harrison had left swiftly before the police came charging in – and both Mick and Keith were jailed, leading to the famed *Times* leader, 'Who Breaks A Butterfly On A Wheel?' John and Paul showed support by adding backing vocals to their single, 'We Love You'. In 1968 John and Yoko joined with the Stones in their *Rock and Roll Circus*, which was not screened at the time because the band were not happy with their performance;

Brian Jones, in particular, hardly knew what he was doing.

In June 1969 Jones left. Once the leader, he had lost interest having been sidelined by Mick and Keith. Less than a month later, he was found dead in his swimming pool and conspiracy theories abound. The Stones, like The Beatles, were in disarray but Mick and Keith were more determined than John and Paul to stay together and they continued with Mick Taylor. The free Hyde Park concert became a tribute to Brian and was an enormous success, with the band performing to a live audience of 250,000.

From that moment, the Stones revelled in huge concerts with their jumpin' jack flash Mick Jagger becoming rock's leading frontman, his athleticism perhaps helped by the fact that his father was a PE teacher. Their killer singles included 'Honky Tonk Women', 'Brown Sugar' and 'Tumbling Dice'. They made mistakes, the most serious being to let Hell's Angels act as security for their Altamont concert outside of San Francisco. This disastrous event, which resulted in death and serious injuries, is seen as the end of the sixties' dream, as it were. The Stones made a bizarre film for Jean-Luc Godard, *One Plus One*, around their recording of 'Sympathy For The Devil' and Mick Jagger's acting ability was found wanting in *Ned Kelly* and *Performance*, although the latter is now a camp classic.

Despite having a horrendous time with their second manager Allen Klein (something they did before The Beatles), the Rolling Stones were rich enough to become tax exiles, leading to the album *Exile On Main St* (1972). Keith Richards recovered from drug addiction and has become, against the odds, one of the most loved characters in rock. Johnny Depp created Jack Sparrow around him for *Pirates of the Caribbean*. Bill Wyman left the Stones and formed his Rhythm Kings with Albert Lee, Georgie Fame and various guest musicians.

In 1995 even the main UK TV news bulletins were reporting the Blur v Oasis 'chart race' as they both released singles on the same day. It was said to emulate the Stones v Beatles chart races, although they had never had one. Both Brian Epstein and Andrew Oldham were too astute for that, making arrangements never to release singles at the same time.

The Rolling Stones – now Mick, Keef, Charlie and Ronnie Wood from The Faces –have become the hottest ticket in rock 'n' roll, even with Mick Jagger in his seventies, and they were filmed very successfully by Martin Scorsese for 2008's *Shine A Light*.

As Tom Wolfe wrote in 1965, 'The Beatles want to hold your hand but the Rolling Stones want to burn down your town.'

ROSS, ERWIN [1926–2010]

Erwin Ross was a German motor mechanic who became a POW after being posted to Italy during the war. He was moved to Egypt and found special favour as he could paint street signs and portraits of the wives of the officers. When he returned to East Germany he painted the Soviet leadership; his portrait of Stalin was in every store, although there was little food.

Labouring on the docks in Hamburg, Erwin found work as a graphic designer at the Tabu club on Grosse Freiheit, where he met the electrician Manfred Weissleder. He painted posters for Bruno Koschmider for beat nights at the Kaiserkeller and created the mural of the Manhattan skyline for the Star-Club. The Beatles asked him for a motif for their drums and he devised the logo with the long T. He charged them 30 DM, which they tried to get Weissleder to pay, but he refused.

Most of the time, Ross painted voluptuous nudes and he became known as the 'Rubens of St Pauli'. His spreadeagled legs image can still be seen above the entrance to the Ritze. He died in 2010 after being hit by an ambulance.

But he had The Beatles down to a T.

ROWE, DICK [1921–1986]

Although his catchphrase was, 'I know nothing about music but...', Dick Rowe was the A&R manager at Decca Records in the fifties. He persuaded the jazz singer Lita Roza to record a children's novelty, '(How Much Is That) Doggie in the Window', which went to No. 1. He had hits with Jimmy Young, David Whitfield (his 'My Son John' was a favourite of Julia Lennon's) and the rock 'n' rollers Tommy Steele and Terry Dene.

Rowe spotted the potential of Billy Fury and wanted to produce him, but Fury's manager Larry Parnes wanted Jack Good to do that. As Decca's management had not supported Rowe over this, he took an A&R post with a new UK label, Top Rank. His first signing, in January 1959, was Tony Sheridan but the wayward singer/guitarist was dropped before he made a record. Rowe had chart success with The Brook Brothers and Craig Douglas.

When Top Rank was sold to EMI in July 1960, Rowe returned to Decca. He gave his assistant, Mike Smith, the task of choosing between The Beatles and Brian Poole and The Tremeloes. Smith, and hence Rowe, went with the Trems. It is unlikely that Rowe told Brian Epstein that guitar groups were on the way out as he was still signing them. Also, in 1962, he placed another act from Liverpool under contract, The Vernons Girls.

While judging a beat contest in Liverpool in 1963, George Harrison told him of the Rolling Stones and he immediately sought them out and gave them a contract. Over the next few years, he signed The Zombies, Them, The Moody Blues, Tom Jones and Engelbert Humperdinck, not to mention his continuing success with Billy Fury. He also managed Decca's large orchestral catalogue. He died from complications from diabetes in 1986.

Dick Rowe's track record is impressive, but he will be forever known as 'the man who turned down The Beatles'.

RUTLES, THE

After Neil Innes left The Bonzo Dog Band (see separate entry) and Grimms, he made a solo album, *How Sweet To Be An Idiot* (1973), and wrote music for various Monty Python projects. He worked on sketches for Eric Idle's TV series, *Rutland Weekend Television* (1975/76), among them The Rutles, a group described as 'the prefab four', who looked suspiciously like The Beatles. Innes played the Lennon role, Ron Nasty.

The sketches were so successful that it led to the feature-length film for Warner Brothers, *All You Need Is Cash*, which is easily the most devoted and funny pastiche of The Beatles and their story. Eric Idle wrote the script and Neil Innes the songs, which remind you of The Beatles but are original (and funny) in their own right. 'Ouch!', for example, was their take on 'Help!' The songs covered all phases of The Beatles', sorry, Rutles' career and included 'I Must Be In Love', 'Doubleback Alley', 'Cheese And Onions' and 'Let's Be Natural'. Amazingly, Neil signed over half his royalties to Lennon and McCartney, a one-sided agreement. With pleasing irony, Neil was subsequently to sue

Noel Gallagher for basing part of the Oasis hit single 'Whatever' on his song 'How Sweet To Be An Idiot'.

The parody has led to Innes often appearing at Beatles conventions and doing stage shows, albeit without Eric Idle, as The Rutles. Fans have taken them so much to heart that there are even tribute bands to The Rutles. The Rutles released a second album, *Archaeology*, in 1996.

Innes himself is known for the TV series *The Innes Book of Records*, and the children's cartoon series *The Raggy Dolls*. A documentary film about his life, *The Seventh Python*, was released in 2008. When performing at Beatles conventions Neil's brilliant opening line is 'I've suffered for my music. Now it's your turn', which receives a round of applause in its own right.

The Rutles parodied what The Beatles had done.

SAVILE, JIMMY [1926–2011]

Although Jimmy Savile has posthumously been exposed as one of Britain's most prolific sex offenders, in the sixties he was one of the leading DJs and TV presenters, playing his part in The Beatles' story.

James Wilson Vincent Savile was born in Leeds on 31 October 1926, although he didn't disclose his age during his lifetime, pretending he was much younger. During the war, he worked in a coalmine as a Bevin boy. Always fit, he was a professional wrestler and a champion cyclist, and later ran over 100 marathons. He claimed to be the UK's first DJ but there were plenty before him.

Savile ran dance halls in Leeds and Manchester and he twice booked The Beatles to appear. His eccentric, flamboyant personality made him ideal for radio, starting on Radio Luxembourg in 1958,

and television, starting with the *Young At Heart* series for Tyne Tees in 1960. He fronted Decca's *Teen and Twenty Disc Club* for Radio Luxembourg and enrolled Elvis as a member.

On New Year's Day 1964, he presented the first edition of BBC TV's *Top of the Pops*, and throughout the sixties he was a regular host. Savile introduced 'Please Please Me' with the words, 'Well, here it is, the big new record from Liverpool's Beatles. I sure hope that it pleases somebody, as it sure isn't me.' He quickly changed his tune and became a fervent supporter. He hosted The Beatles' Christmas show at the Hammersmith Odeon in 1964/65 and took part in a comedy sketch with them, playing the Abominable Snowman. He heard Paul say that the next single would not be a love song and would be about Ringo reading a paperback.

Savile was regularly asked to front advertising campaigns – notably 'This is the age of the train' for British Railways and 'Clunk click every trip' for seatbelts. He was soon developing catchphrases of his own, such as 'Now then, now then', 'Goodness gracious' and 'How's about that then?' He spoke with a much-imitated yodel and always had a cigar to hand. As the years went by, he was known for his shell suit, bling and platinum blond hair. He travelled the country in his caravan for the radio series *Savile's Travels*. He was devoted to his mother, 'the Duchess', and never married. Everybody thought he was odd but few realised his real motives.

In 1975 he hosted the peak-time TV series *Jim'll Fix It*, which ran for nearly 20 years. He would invite children onto the programme and make their fantasies come true. He did unpaid voluntary work for hospitals and was constantly making appeals for charity. He raised over £40m for good causes and was knighted in 1990.

Jimmy Savile died on 29 October 2011 and

was buried in Scarborough with the grave at an angle so that he could look out to sea. There had been rumours and mutterings about his behaviour during his lifetime, but an ITV documentary in 2012 showed that something very nasty had been going on. Since then, there have been hundreds of allegations of child sex abuse, rape and sexual contact with corpses. The police described him as a predatory sex offender. The complaints ranged from 1955 to 2009, with victims as young as eight years old.

If it hadn't been Jimmy Savile, it would have been another compère.

SCAFFOLD – SEE ALSO, MCCARTNEY, MIKE

In the early 1960s, teacher Roger McGough and post office engineer John Gorman, both born in 1937, were involved in Happenings at Hope Hall, an arts cinema and basement club in Liverpool. Happenings were spontaneous events designed to involve the audience, following what was taking place in New York and San Francisco but imbued with Liverpool wit. With Mike McCartney and a few others, they became The Liverpool One Fat Lady All Electric Show, a theatre group with bookings for Allan Williams in the Blue Angel. Roger, John and Mike became Scaffold, taking their name from a French film, *Ascenseur pour l'echafaud (Lift To The Scaffold)*. As The Beatles were becoming known, Mike asserted his independence by becoming Mike McGear.

Scaffold became popular on the late-night ABC TV series *Gazette*. McGough also had a parallel career as a poet, wittily chronicling modern life and being published with Adrian Henri and Brian Patten as *The Mersey Sound*, a volume in the Penguin Modern Poets series that sold a remark-able 250,000 copies. McGough's wordplay could also be appreciated in many of Scaffold's sketches such as 'Dear Diary'. 'Poem For National LSD Week' was simply four words, 'Mind, how you go'. You might think that Roger and John Lennon would have been great mates but they were wary of each other, perhaps because they had too much in common.

Scaffold was signed by NEMS but Brian Epstein failed to appreciate how such eccentric singles as '2 Day's Monday' and 'Goodbat Nightman' could be marketed. Switching to Noel Gay, they had a Top 10 single with 'Thank U Very Much' in 1967 and followed it with the Christmas No. 1, 'Lily The Pink', an updated rugby song, in 1968. They toured with The Hollies and Manfred Mann but Roger was uneasy. 'I knew half the audience could sing better than me.' When Erich Segal submitted a script for *Yellow Submarine* that was full of New York Jewish humour, McGough adapted it for The Beatles, also creating the Sea of Monsters.

Scaffold wrote and performed the theme for the TV series *The Liver Birds*, but were criticised heavily by the former Prime Minister Harold Wilson for their satirical title song featured on the BBC documentary *Yesterday's Men*. They went bust in 1973, but had another Top 10 single in 1974 when Paul McCartney produced their folky singalong of Dominic Behan's 'Liverpool Lou'. Scaffold have had occasional reunions over the years, including a cultural visit to Shanghai in 2010 with the Royal Liverpool Philharmonic Orchestra.

All three Scaffold members believe that they created the groundwork for Monty Python's Flying Circus. None of the Pythons have ever acknowledged this but Scaffold could be right.

The Beatles enjoyed their blend of comedy and music.

SELLERS, PETER [1925–1980]

The individual Beatles were huge fans of Peter Sellers, for his 1959 comedy albums produced by George Martin – *The Best of Sellers* and *Songs For Swingin' Sellers* – and his role as a Goon alongside Spike Milligan and Harry Secombe. Although he often wasted his talents, he was a brilliant comic actor and his many films included *I'm All Right Jack* (1959), *Never Let Go* with Adam Faith (1960), *Only Two Can Play* (1962), *The Pink Panther* (1963) with several sequels, and the Cold War satire, *Dr Strangelove* (1963).

Peter starred opposite Sophia Loren in *The Millionairess* (1960), but spent much of his time trying to seduce her. One of his suggestions was an album together, *Peter and Sophia*, which included the hit singles 'Goodness Gracious Me!' and 'Bangers And Mash'.

In 1965 Sellers, appearing on Granada's *The Music Of Lennon and McCartney*, made up and dressed like Laurence Olivier as Richard III and recited an innuendo-drenched 'A Hard Day's Night'. On the B-side of his hit single, he played a vicar requesting funds in 'Help!' We now know that he recorded many out-takes including a brilliant 'She Loves You' as two Irish navvies. Surely there is enough for a CD.

Sellers was married to Britt Ekland from 1964 to 1968, but their romance was marred by ill health and he always claimed to have died on the operating table. There are mixed feelings about *What's New Pussycat?* with Peter O'Toole and Woody Allen (1965) and *After the Fox* (1966), where he joined The Hollies to record the title song.

Ringo Starr played Sellers' adopted heir in the Apple production *The Magic Christian* (1969), a product very much of the hippie era and written by Terry Southern. Ringo and Peter sang 'Octopus's Garden' together on *Frost on Saturday* in December 1969.

Peter Sellers is seen with his back to camera on George's *Dark Horse* (1974) album. He is listed as 'not appearing' on George's *Extra Texture* (1975). Sadly he introduced George to the accountant and lawyer Dennis O'Brien, who misused his trust. Peter Sellers won an Oscar as the trance-like Chance in *Being There* (1979), released shortly before his death.

For all that oddball humour and love of funny voices.

SHAPIRO, HELEN [B.1946]

Helen Shapiro was born in Bethnal Green, London, on 28 September 1946 and studied singing at Maurice Burman's singing academy. Norrie Paramor's assistant at EMI, John Schroeder, heard the pupils and was impressed by the 14-year-old Helen. When John played Norrie a tape, he was astonished by her deep voice and was sure he was listening to a male singer. Her debut single was 'Don't Treat Me Like A Child', released in 1961, which Helen jokingly calls 'the first protest song'. It was a hit and later that year her second single, the ballad 'You Don't Know', went to No. 1.

Like Norrie Paramor, the media was fascinated by Helen's voice, but Helen says, 'That never bothered me. Ever since I was a kid, I was called 'Foghorn'. I was used to it. The main thing is whether you've got talent and actually, it's handy to have something distinctive. Whether they like it or not, people recognise my voice.'

The pop paper *Disc* described 'Walkin' Back To Happiness' as a 'cute bouncy ballad with thumpy backing of rhythm and girl group directed by Norrie Paramor. This one should please her fans all right.' But not Helen Shapiro herself. 'I was brought up on blues and jazz and I thought 'Walkin' Back to Happiness" was corny – all that "woop-bah-oh-yea-yeah". I still don't like the song but everyone goes mad for it so I've been proved wrong.'

The single was promoted by a 15-minute *Look at Life* cinema feature that showed Helen making the record, but although it went to the top, Helen's records never took off in America: 'I blame Capitol for that. They released "You Don't Know" and then they immediately released "Walkin' Back To Happiness". By the time The Beatles had opened the way for British artists, I'd stopped having hits.'

Helen was unlucky. She was the first to record 'It's My Party' when she went to Nashville, but somebody passed the song to Lesley Gore. Norrie Paramor turned down an early Lennon and Mc-Cartney song, 'Misery', which went to Kenny Lynch instead. (Helen maintains that all the books that say she herself turned the song down are wrong.)

When Helen starred in a nationwide tour in 1963, The Beatles were the supporting act. She was younger than they were, but she was the old and they were the new. Helen recalls, 'I had heard "Love Me Do" before I met them and straightaway I thought, "Yes, it's good, gutsy, bluesy music and they're bringing it back." I was pleased that I was going on tour with them and we got on like a house on fire. They were very raw because, although they'd done a fair bit, it had been in clubs and ballrooms rather than theatres and concert halls. I watched them adapt themselves and polish up their act, not too much polish though – I was glad that they kept some rawness. As the tour went on, they released "Please Please Me" and I could see how they were developing a following of their own.'

Helen Shapiro was rarely comfortable as a pop singer, and in 1962 she recorded a hit EP, *A Teenager Sings the Blues*. Following an appearance on a Duke Ellington tribute concert in 1984, she started making concert appearances and records with Humphrey Lyttelton and his Band. Humph commented, 'I always thought her voice was marvellous. It is a unique voice, especially when it was coming out of a 14-year-old. We didn't care much for the songs, but we all knew the voice was tremendous.'

These days Helen is part of Jews For Jesus and she only performs in churches. She has managed to adapt 'Walkin' Back To Happiness' to her new situation.

The Beatles gained experience and confidence from being on their first national tour with Helen Shapiro.

SHENSON, WALTER [1919–2000]

When Walter Shenson died in 2000, the newspaper headlines read 'Beatles Producer Dies'. The media often singles out a Beatles connection, but here it was appropriate as *A Hard Day's Night* and *Help!* were his most commercially successful productions.

Walter Shenson was born in San Francisco in 1919 and wrote and produced several promotional shorts in Hollywood, occasionally making a B-movie like *Inner Sanctum* (1948) and *Korea Patrol* (1951). In 1955 Columbia asked him to go to Europe to arrange the publicity for their films, and he liked London so much he settled there. In 1959 he produced a farcical film about the Cold War, *The Mouse That Roared*, starring Peter Sellers. This did very well and led to *A Matter of WHO* (1961) with Terry-Thomas, and *The Mouse on the Moon* (1963) with Margaret Rutherford.

Shenson took a hands-on interest in the Beatles film *A Hard Day's Night*, attending the filming on most days. When his wife Geraldine asked him if they could act, he replied, 'I don't know but you can't take your eyes off them.' Shenson was prepared to negotiate 25 per cent of the net income for The Beatles, but Brian Epstein settled for 7 per cent. The film was so successful that the production costs of $600,000 were recouped in one day.

After the success of *A Hard Day's Night*, it was easy to obtain a bigger budget for *Help!*, although bigger did not mean better. Shenson's other productions include *30 Is A Dangerous Age, Cynthia* (1967) with Dudley Moore, *A Talent For Loving* (1969) with Richard Widmark and Topol, and the children's favourite, *Digby – The Biggest Dog In The World* (1973) with Jim Dale and Spike Milligan. He both produced and directed the US military comedy *Welcome to the Club* (1971) with Brian Foley, but he was not up to the job and the actors lacked conviction.

Anyone who helped to make *A Hard's Day Night* deserves credit.

SHERIDAN, TONY (1940–2013)

Tony Sheridan was one of the angry brigade. He argued with everyone and he thought every promoter was ripping him off. He played for himself rather than his audiences, and so in almost every performance Beatles fans could experience both a talent that should have made it and the rage and resentment that ensured he didn't. Whenever he came close to success, he would wreck his chances, usually deliberately.

Born Anthony Esmond Sheridan McGinnity in Norwich on 21 May 1940, Tony was a bright schoolboy who sang with his mother in Gilbert and Sullivan productions. He said, 'It was very good training to be in *The Mikado* when you're eleven, but I got so frustrated doing all this shit

that as soon as I heard Lonnie Donegan, I wanted a guitar – and freedom.'

After Sheridan's group The Saints won £15 in a talent contest, he decided that he might be good enough for London. By day Sheridan shifted beer crates in a brewery; by night he played the 2i's and other coffee bars. He worked in Vince Eager and The Vagabonds and Vince Taylor and The Playboys, who recorded for Parlophone in 1958. The bass player Licorice Locking recalls, 'We did "Right Behind You Baby" on the first take. I was expecting just one 12-bar solo from Tony Sheridan but he took two and the second one was awe-inspiring. It lifted the track off the ground.' The TV producer Jack Good signed Sheridan for ITV's *Oh Boy!* and he toured with Eddie Cochran early in 1960, carefully studying how he played the guitar.

In May 1960, a strip-club owner from Hamburg, Bruno Koschmider, came looking for a British rock group for his club the Kaiserkeller. When Tony Sheridan went there as part of The Jets, he found that the wild and crazy lifestyle suited him fine. The wilder he became, the more the audiences responded, but Sheridan's philosophy wasn't for everyone. 'If you play "Blue Suede Shoes" two thousand times, you have got to find ways to do it differently – you put in sevenths and ninths and elevenths. That is what Hamburg can do for you – you become something else, but I believe that the only way to play is spontaneously.'

The Jets moved to the Top Ten Club and the chief waiter, Horst Fascher, became a close friend. 'The first British group I saw was Tony Sheridan and The Jets and it was such a surprise to see rock 'n' roll live on stage. There was sweat all over him, he looked like he had just come out of the swimming baths. We liked him very much.'

Both John Lennon and Gerry Marsden copied Sheridan's defiant stage stance – facing the audience straight on, legs apart, guitar high on the chest. Sheridan often performed a rock arrangement of 'You'll Never Walk Alone' from *Carousel*. He said, 'I would play it two or three times a night, and Gerry copied my version. He even sounded like me, so it's me that Liverpool Football Club should be thanking.'

The first session by Sheridan and The Beatles (appearing as The Beat Brothers) for Polydor took place in June 1961 and the producer, Bert Kaempfert, wanted rocked-up folk songs. Sheridan said, 'We had about fifteen whiskys the night before and we had agreed on "My Bonnie" and "When The Saints Go Marching In". We went to bed at 5am and got up at 8am to be taken to the studio to make the record. We took some uppers and the guitar solo was all right. I didn't feel too good about making the German charts. I would rather it had been with a good song.'

Sheridan continued to record for Polydor and had German Top 10 singles with 'Let's Slop' and 'Skinny Minnie'. Polydor released an album *Let's Do the Madison, Twist, Locomotion, Slop, Hully Gully, Monkey* but Sheridan broke his contract by recording for Philips as Dan Sherry. In 1963 he was arrested for inciting a riot but released with a caution.

In 1967 Sheridan and his manager Horst Fascher went to Vietnam to entertain US troops. Often he was playing with just his guitar for accompaniment, and as a result he became self-sufficient, a competent one-man troubadour. Sheridan returned to Germany in 1969. His gallantry was recognised by the US Army as he was made an honorary captain.

In 1975 Tony Sheridan's old associate, Paul Murphy, found the finance for Sheridan to record a concert of new material with the Royal Liverpool Philharmonic Orchestra. It went well, but afterwards Sheridan's disgraceful behaviour meant

that a BBC special was dropped and the album was never released. He had better luck in 1978 when an album, *Worlds Apart*, was recorded with Elvis Presley's former musicians.

Sheridan was dogged by his link to The Beatles and most of his later bookings were concentrated on Beatles-based events, where he sometimes performed with his son Tony Sheridan Jr. In 2002, Sheridan recorded an album of new material, *Vagabond*, produced by the Hamburg musician and historian Ulf Kruger. Sheridan found happiness with his third wife, Anna Sievers, and settled in a farmhouse in the north of Germany. He was devastated when she died of cancer in 2011.

Without Sheridan, The Beatles might have been a covers band. He taught them to add your own personality to every song.

SHOTTON, PETE [B. 1941]

John Lennon's best friend, Pete Shotton, was born in Liverpool in 1941 and his father worked as a planner at Tate & Lyle, the sugar refinery. He met John Winston Lennon at Sunday school when he was six years old and started calling him Winnie, much to his irritation. They attended Quarry Bank High School (sort of) and hung out in the same gang, but there was a problem when John wanted a skiffle group; Pete had no musical ability. John thought Pete couldn't go wrong with a washboard, which continued for the best part of a year. It was Pete who called them The Quarrymen. 'I said the name without even thinking about it. The original kids who were in the band were at Quarry, we lived in Woolton with the quarry, and maybe there was a subconscious thing about quarry being stone and stone being rock.'

In January 1958, John realised that washboards were so 1957 and dismissed Pete by breaking it over his head, which suggests John could have sacked Pete Best himself if he'd wished.

Although a rebel at school, Pete joined the Liverpool Police College and graduated when he was 19. However, he didn't care for life on the beat and soon resigned. He helped to run a cafe in Smithdown Road, Liverpool, for some years. Although John didn't officially dedicate *In His Own Write* (1964) to him, the opening cartoon is of Pete communing with some birds.

John set Pete up in business, and he and his wife Beth ran a supermarket in Hayling Island, near the Isle of Wight. They sometimes visited The Beatles for what must have seemed fantasy weekends, by comparison. Pete maintains that John wrote, 'I do appreciate you being around' as a thank you in 'Help!'

In 1968 Pete moved to Apple and made arrangements for the opening of their boutique, commissioning the striking mural on the outside wall of 94 Baker Street. However, the boutique was a disaster and they gave the clothes away. Pete wrote his memoir, *John Lennon: In My Life*, in 1983.

After a successful fish and chip business, Pete and a business partner expanded the concept into Fatty Arbuckle's American Diner. During the eighties, the business grew rapidly, by securing more premises or franchising the concept. Pete joined The Quarrymen in 1997, again playing washboard, but he was mainly there to tell anecdotes about life with Lennon. He did tearfully sing 'Imagine' in the church hall in Woolton. He left the band when he sold Fatty Arbuckle's for around £10m and became a tax exile, mostly living in Dublin.

A great chum to all The Beatles, John Lennon especially.

SINATRA, FRANK [1915–1998]

What was the first single released on the Apple label? 'Hey Jude'? Not quite, although it was on the Apple label with Parlophone catalogue number R 5722. Apple label's second release, Apple 2, was Mary Hopkin's 'Those Were The Days'. Surprisingly, Apple 1 was a privately pressed, strictly limited 45 by Frank Sinatra. Read on…

Frank Sinatra was born in Hoboken, New Jersey, on 12 December 1915 and came to prominence with Tommy Dorsey's dance band in the forties, before going solo. He had a string of major successes including 'I'll Never Smile Again' (1940), 'All Or Nothing At All' (1943), 'You'll Never Walk Alone' (1945), 'Young at Heart' (1954), 'Love And Marriage' (1955), 'Chicago' (1957), 'All The Way' (1957) and 'High Hopes' (1959). By the time The Beatles had started recording, he was mostly working in Vegas and associated with Dean Martin, Sammy Davis Jr, British actor Peter Lawford and comic Joey Bishop as the Rat Pack. His singing style was copied and updated with immense success by Bobby Darin.

McCartney had dreams of writing for Sinatra and during his Cavern days he had written 'Suicide' with him in mind. He did submit it but nothing happened. Frank might have thought that it was a send-up. After all, who would record a song called 'Suicide'?

Ringo liked to surprise his wife Maureen on her birthday. In 1968, he asked Peter Brown to persuade Frank Sinatra to record something for her. Sammy Cahn rewrote 'The Lady Is A Tramp' and 'But Beautiful' and Frank sang the new words. A single was pressed as Apple 1 and given to Maureen as a present. It is not known how many copies were pressed. It is a shame that it has not appeared on a compilation, as it is witty and engaging, even acknowledging that Maureen had once been out with Paul.

Frank did record 'Yesterday' in 1969 and he twice recorded 'Something', saying that it was his favourite love song, although initially he thought John and Paul, rather than George, had written it. Although he appears to have genuinely liked the song, he did add 'Stick around, Jack', an indication that his mind was not quite on the job.

If Frank had his way. But there is an easy listening component to The Beatles' work, so probably 2.

SMITH, MIKE [1935–2011]

Michael Robert Smith was born in Barking, Essex, in 1935 and his father, a brass band enthusiast, encouraged him to learn trombone, although he had little interest in the instrument. After school, Mike took a clerical job until conscription, when he became an electrician for the RAF. After National Service, he joined the BBC as a recording engineer. Two workmates moved to Decca's classical division and told him of their trips to Vienna, Paris and Milan. Mike joined Decca but 'to my irritation, I never got further than the studios in West Hampstead.'

Mike had been hired by A&R head, Frank Lee, and assisted Lee on sessions for Mantovani, Edmundo Ros, Vera Lynn and Winfred Atwell. Frank Lee would often fall asleep, allowing Mike to take over. When Smith made a spoof radio tribute about him for an office party, Lee was so impressed by his technical ability that he upgraded him to a producer, raising his salary to £11 a week. The first artist he produced was the Irish singer Bridie Gallagher. When Dick Rowe rejoined Decca as A&R manager, he worked closely with him, assisting on such records as Billy Fury's 'Halfway To Paradise'.

Following Brian Epstein's request, he arranged an audition for The Beatles. 'Somebody had to show some interest in The Beatles,' said Mike, 'because Brian Epstein's shop, NEMS, was an important account for our sales people. I went to the Cavern and I should have trusted my instincts as they were wonderful on stage. We arranged for them to come to London on New Year's Day 1962 and they weren't very good. I think that we got to them too early, but it was just as well as I couldn't have worked with them the way that George Martin did. I would have got too involved in their bad side and not enough in their good.'

Dick Rowe asked Mike to choose between The Beatles and Brian Poole and The Tremeloes. Mike picked the Trems, which at the time seemed a good decision. The group had many hit records, but it meant that Smith had turned down The Beatles. 'I did meet them subsequently,' he said, 'and they gave me a two-finger salute but that's par for the course.' While at Decca, Mike also produced hits for The Applejacks and Dave Berry.

When Brian Poole split with The Tremeloes, Mike moved with them to CBS and a long succession of mostly happy-go-lucky hit singles followed including 'Here Comes My Baby' and 'Even The Bad Times Are Good'. The Tremeloes topped the charts by covering a Four Seasons B-side, 'Silence Is Golden', in 1967, but when they were unenthusiastic about releasing 'Yellow River' as a single, he recorded it with the song's writer, Jeff Christie. Recorded under the name Christie, the single made No. 1 in 1970.

Mike often worked with Georgie Fame including an album of standards, *Georgie Does His Thing With Strings* (1969) and an album of duets with Alan Price, *Fame & Price/Price & Fame/Together* (1971), which included the hit single 'Rosetta'. In 1967, Mike produced Georgie Fame's No. 1, 'The Ballad Of Bonnie And Clyde'.

When Love Affair were signed to CBS, they made 'Everlasting Love' with the producer Muff

Winwood, but their playing was not thought strong enough and the lead vocalist, Steve Ellis, remade the song with Mike Smith. The fact that Love Affair's hit single featured session men was a media scandal in 1968. Mike also recorded Marmalade's cover of 'Ob-La-Di, Ob-La-Da', another No. 1. He later worked for GTO Records and in a record-pressing factory, and occasionally spoke at Beatles conventions. Mile was delightful company and self-deprecating about his achievements.

Turning down The Beatles did them a favour.

SMITH, MIMI [1906–1991]

You could argue that the Merseybeat phenomenon was a matriarch as there were three powerful women behind the scenes in their different ways – Ma Storm (Rory Storm's mother), Mona Best (Pete's mother) and John Lennon's Aunt Mimi.

Mary Elizabeth Stanley was born on 24 April 1906, the first of five sisters who survived to adulthood and regarded as the most responsible. She worked as a nurse in a convalescent home and was engaged to marry a doctor but when that fell through, she dated the milkman, George Toogood Smith, who made the daily deliveries to the home. They were married in September 1939 but George, although 36, was soon fighting in the war. Like many servicemen, he became old before his time, traumatised by what he had seen.

She regarded her younger sister Julia's husband, Alf, as a ne'er-do-well and after he had left, she became concerned for their son John's welfare because Julia was living with another man. Perhaps she desperately wanted a child of her own but whatever the circumstances, John Lennon came to live with her and George. John always called her Mimi, but this was a family that thrived on pet names. The dairy was close to where they lived at 251 Menlove Avenue, Woolton, a three-bedroom semi on a busy dual carriageway.

There has been much criticism of Mimi's upbringing of John Lennon, almost as though she was some sort of monster, but this wasn't true at all. She, like many parents of the time, had strict Victorian values and such a mischievous child as John Lennon needed discipline. George was more benign and John got on very well with him.

Mimi found it difficult to get John to settle down to schoolwork but she did instil in him a love of reading. She read many books herself but she had no time for romantic slush, telling John, 'If I read a book, I want to be wiser afterwards.' She was house-proud, insisting that John's friends came in through the back door.

George Smith died after a sudden heart attack in June 1955 and Mimi took in university students as lodgers to make ends meet. It is now known that she had a relationship with a biochemistry student, Michael Fishwick. John almost certainly did not know of this, but if he had he surely would have said, 'Good on you, Mimi.'

Mimi bought John his first guitar and Julia showed him banjo chords. They both attended The Quarrymen's performance at the Woolton garden fete in July 1957 but Mimi regarded this as yet another distraction. She told him, 'A guitar's all right, John, but you'll never make a living out of it.'

Considering John's innate intelligence, his school record was a disgrace. However, by badgering his headmaster into action, Mimi had managed to place John in the Liverpool College of Art. Once there, he was soon to find lodgings and escape from Mimi's restrictions, although he frequently returned home. Mimi was always interested in what he was doing and despite her snobbishness, she went to see The Beatles at a lunchtime session

ON AUNT MIMI...

Aunt Mimi, who brought up John, was always incensed if anyone suggested that she was less than middle class. One day a reporter visited her at her house in Woolton. The reporter looked around and exclaimed, 'My, my, John has really done you proud, hasn't he.'

'If anyone did well by me,' replied the incensed Mimi, 'it was my husband.'

Aunt Mimi watched The Beatles in the US on *The Ed Sullivan Show*, and later being interviewed on other programmes, and was always furious.

'They were described as street corner boys. They were nothing of the sort. And times without number people have said they come from the slums of Liverpool. But their homes were certainly *not* slums.' Mimi to *Record Mirror* in March 1971

John was about eight or nine when he came into Aunt Mimi's kitchen and informed her solemnly, 'I've just seen God.'

'Well, what was he doing?' Aunt Mimi asked.

'Oh, just sitting by the fire'.

'Oh' Aunt Mimi said, nodding thoughtfully, 'I expect he was feeling a bit chilly.'

---

at the Cavern. Freddie Marsden, the drummer with Gerry and The Pacemakers, told her that John would certainly make a living out of his guitar.

When The Beatles became successful, John bought Mimi a bungalow in Poole, Dorset, and she stayed there for the remainder of her life. John gave her his MBE, which she kept on top of the television. In 1969 John asked someone to collect it and she was horrified to find that it was being returned to the Queen as a protest. We don't know what she thought of John's 'Working Class Hero' but it is easy to guess. Nevertheless, she didn't fall out with John and he constantly rang her from America and regarded her with great affection. When she died on 6 December 1991, both Yoko and Cynthia attended her funeral. Paul, George and Ringo sent flowers.

No musical input although she did buy John his first guitar.

SMITH, NORMAN 'HURRICANE' [1923–2008]

It is the recording engineer who states the song and number of take before a recording starts, and the voice on The Beatles' recordings up to April 1966 belongs to Norman Smith.

Norman Smith was born in Edmonton, north London, in 1923 and was in the RAF during the later stages of the war. After trying to make a living as a jazz singer and pianist, he saw an ad in *The Times* in 1959 for apprentice engineers at EMI but with an age limit of 28. He lied, told them they did not know how to produce Cliff Richard, and somehow got the job. In 1960 he became a fully-fledged recording engineer at Abbey Road, and often worked alongside George Martin. He was involved with The Beatles' recordings up to and including *Rubber Soul*, as well as those by The Swinging Blue Jeans, Billy J. Kramer, Cliff Bennett and Freddie and The Dreamers.

In June 1965 when The Beatles were short of a song for the *Help!* album, Smith played them one of his own, 'Don't Let It Die'. Dick James offered to buy the song outright but George Martin told him to ask for more. However, the next time they came to the studio, Paul told him they had forgotten to record a song for Ringo and they cut 'Act Naturally' instead.

Although Smith left The Beatles before they went psychedelic, he helped define British psych with his albums for Pink Floyd, and played drums on their track, 'Remember A Day'. He produced the 1968 concept album, *S.F. Sorrow*, by Pretty Things, and worked with Barclay James Harvest.

In 1971 Smith had his own UK Top 10 hit as the long-haired, moustachioed Hurricane Smith, the name coming from a 1952 film, with 'Don't Let It Die'. The follow-up, 'Oh Babe, What Would You Say', about his shy days at ballrooms in his youth, was a Top 10 single in both Britain and America. Even though Smith did not retain his momentum as a solo star, he did play many dates on the northern cabaret circuit.

He left the business to breed horses and to run a medical equipment business. He released a new album, *From Me To You*, in 2004 and his memoir, *John Lennon Called Me Normal*, was launched at a Beatles fest in New Jersey in 2007.

Not so much a hurricane as unhurried and unflappable, and perfect for recording The Beatles.

SOMMERVILLE, BRIAN [1932–1994]

On leaving school, Brian Sommerville enlisted in the Royal Navy where he rose to Lieutenant Commander. He retained an air of military authority in civilian life, working as a film publicist for Theo Cowan and then a show business correspond-

ent for the *Daily Express*. In November 1963, he befriended Brian Epstein who invited him to become publicity manager for The Beatles. Unlike Tony Barrow and Derek Taylor, he was ill-suited to the role as he did not appreciate The Beatles' humour (they called him 'old baldie', which admittedly was not very funny) or their lateness, and he showed contempt for journalists. Tony Barrow felt that he was destroying the goodwill he had created.

When Sommerville reprimanded George Harrison for being late, George threw a jug of orange juice over him, to which Sommerville responded by boxing his ears. When The Beatles arrived in New York in February 1964, he lost his rag at a press conference, yelling at journalists to be quiet.

Although Sommerville had ability, Epstein realised he had made the wrong appointment and criticised Sommerville for lavish expenses. This became the reason for his dismissal. Sommerville placed an ad in *The Times*, 'Ex-Beatles Publicity Manager looking for a job'. Having learnt from his mistakes, he did fine work for The Kinks, The Who and Manfred Mann. He left the industry to become a stipendiary magistrate.

A brief and uncomfortable time as The Beatles' publicist, which only highlights how good Tony Barrow and Derek Taylor were in their own very different ways.

SPECTOR, PHIL [B. 1939]

The world's best-known record producers are Phil Spector and George Martin, and they could hardly be more different. Spector dismissed Martin as 'a technician', and his own approach could be compared to Orson Welles in the cinema. He saw himself as an auteur, choosing the songs, arrangements and singers and regarding his production as the most important feature. Whereas George Martin strove to be invisible, Phil Spector wanted everybody to know that it was a Phil Spector production.

Harvey Philip Spector was born in the Bronx on Boxing Day 1939. His father Ben was an ironworker who committed suicide when Phil was nine years old. His mother, Bertha, made dresses and pampered her son. Phil grew up short and skinny, asthmatic and diabetic. He was musical and could play guitar, piano and drums.

In 1958 he was touched by the inscription on his father's grave, 'To know him was to love him' and he wrote a slow, deliberate ballad, 'To Know Him Is To Love Him', which he recorded with two friends as The Teddy Bears for a mere $40. It was released on Dore and, rather like an Internet sensation, it topped the US charts for three weeks. The song became a rock 'n' roll standard and was performed by The Beatles when they auditioned for Decca Records on New Year's Day 1962.

It looked as though lightning wouldn't strike twice but then Spector produced hits for The Paris Sisters ('I Love How You Love Me'), Ray Peterson and Curtis Lee. Jerry Leiber and Mike Stoller gave him production advice and he co-wrote 'First Taste Of Love' and 'Spanish Harlem' for Ben E. King. When he heard Vikki Carr sing 'He's A Rebel' for Liberty, he realised that the song was a potential million seller. Much to Liberty's annoyance, Spector rushed out his own version by The Crystals and had the hit.

Spector became famous for records with girl groups, notably The Crystals ('Da Doo Ron Ron', 'Then He Kissed Me') and The Ronettes ('Be My Baby', 'Baby I Love You'), and said that he was creating 'little symphonies for the kids'. Known as the Wall of Sound and sometimes compared to Wagner, Spector's productions employed leading session musicians, often twice as many as usual,

with arrangements written by Jack Nitzsche. Very often he would use Darlene Love as the lead singer although her name was rarely on the label.

In 1963 he made the seasonal album to end all seasonal albums, *A Christmas Gift for You*, but it had the misfortune to be released on 22 November, the day President Kennedy was assassinated. Nobody was in the mood for Spector's good cheer and the album didn't sell, although it is now a perennial classic.

Spector visited the UK to promote his records, arguing with Joe Meek, whom he thought was stealing his ideas, and appearing on *Juke Box Jury*. He returned to America on the same flight as The Beatles in February 1964. They got on well together and were delighted when he brought The Ronettes to their hotel.

Although 'You've Lost That Lovin' Feelin'' (1964) was a remarkably atmospheric, millionselling record from The Righteous Brothers, his arrogance alienated many US disc jockeys. They refused to play Ike and Tina Turner's 'River Deep – Mountain High', despite its obvious brilliance. For a while he stopped making records and went on to play a drug dealer in the 1969 film *Easy Rider*.

In 1968 Phil married Ronnie Bennett, the lead singer of The Ronettes, who believed she could change his antisocial behaviour. He locked her up for weeks at a time and when she went out, she had to have a life-size model of him in the passenger seat. They divorced in 1974 and he would forward alimony cheques with 'Fuck you' written on the back.

In January 1969 The Beatles had been recorded at Twickenham Film Studios 'warts and all', where nothing would be added to the tapes. Glyn Johns produced a mix of a potential album, but they realised how below standard they had been. Allen Klein told Lennon that Phil Spector was doing very little and perhaps he could salvage the tapes. Lennon gave them to Spector who added his usual touches, but McCartney was not informed. He was horrified when he heard The Mike Sammes Singers on 'The Long And Winding Road', but the public loved it. As a single it topped the US charts. The *Let It Be* film has been off the market for years, but the release of *Let It Be…Naked* (2004) gave the public an opportunity to hear the tracks before Spector; critical opinion was divided.

After that, Spector worked on George's triple album *All Things Must Pass*, which included his No. 1, 'My Sweet Lord'. The starkness of *John Lennon/Plastic Ono Band* was wholly unlike anything that Spector had done before or since, but he brilliantly created the mood that John wanted, perhaps because he was just as psychologically damaged. He produced several of his hit singles including 'Imagine' and 'Happy Xmas (War Is Over)'.

John wanted Phil to give him the full Wall of Sound treatment on *Rock 'n' Roll* (1975), but John was left to complete the project after they fell out. Spector was becoming paranoid and waving guns around the studio. Leonard Cohen, John Prine and The Ramones all worked with Spector and just about lived to tell the tale.

In 2003 Spector killed a Hollywood actress, Lana Clarkson, in his mansion. His bizarre court appearances in grotesque wigs cannot have helped his case. He is now in prison.

Probably did The Beatles more harm than good, but was crucial to John and George's early solo records.

SPINETTI, VICTOR [1929–2012]

Paul McCartney called Victor Spinetti 'the man who makes clouds disappear', and his friendly manner and penchant for comedy gave the impression of a man who was satisfied with the lighter side of life. Nevertheless, he was a versatile actor, although he never reached the heights of his fellow Welshmen, Richard Burton and Anthony Hopkins.

During the twenties, many Italians came to Wales and worked in the mines, one being Spinetti's grandfather, Giorgio. His son, Giuseppe, known as Joe, married a 16-year-old local girl, Lily Watson, and their first child, Vittorio Giorgio Andrea Spinetti, was born in Cwm, Ebbw Vale on 2 September 1929. They lived over their fish and chip shop, the Marine Supper Bar. Although Joe was integrated into the community, he was interned in the Isle of Man during the war.

In 1947 the teenage Spinetti was attacked by a gang, who hit him with a brick, leaving him deaf in his left ear. He was still eligible for National Service, but he was discharged after suffering from pleural effusion. While in hospital, a crush on a fellow patient made him realise he was gay. Spinetti studied at the Cardiff College of Music and Drama and met a fellow actor, Graham Curnow, who became his partner until Curnow's death in 1997. As well as acting, Spinetti developed a witty cabaret act that he later performed in London clubs, which included miming to Danny Kaye's records. One of Spinetti's four brothers, Henry, who was not born until 1951, became a noted rock drummer, working with Eric Clapton and Katie Melua.

Vic was part of the chorus in the West End production of *South Pacific* (1954), but had a significant role in *Expresso Bongo* (1958), a satire on popular music starring Paul Scofield and written by Wolf Mankowitz. Mankowitz recommended him to Joan Littlewood for his next play, *Make Me an Offer*.

Joan Littlewood ran the Theatre Workshop at the Theatre Royal, Stratford East, and her energetic and highly distinctive productions often transferred to the West End and Broadway. Victor went to New York with her production of Brendan Behan's play, *The Hostage*. He played an IRA officer and Littlewood told him that he had to bully everyone, both on and off stage.

Littlewood cast him as the MC in a savage attack on British officers in the First World War, *Oh! What a Lovely War* (1963), and had him improvise the gibberish he had heard from drill sergeants. Spinetti won a Tony when the production transferred to Broadway.

When The Beatles saw *Oh! What a Lovely War*, they told director Richard Lester that he would be ideal for their first film, *A Hard Day's Night* (1964). Lester cleverly cast The Beatles alongside stalwart British actors, and Spinetti played a neurotic TV director. Spinetti commented, 'I had worked with Joan Littlewood for six years and I was used to people improvising. They didn't keep to the script in *A Hard Day's Night* and there were many out-takes which haven't been seen. I walked round the set in my furry sweater and I said, "I'm the director and you're late for rehearsals." John Lennon said, not in the script, "You're not a director. You're Victor Spinetti playing the part of a director." I said, "I am a director, I have an award in my office." John responded, "Office? You haven't even got a dressing room."'

The results were less spontaneous in *Help!* (1965), in which Spinetti played Professor Foot. George Harrison particularly enjoyed Spinetti's company, telling him, 'If you're not in our films, my mum won't come to see them.' 'George Harrison told me that I had an incredible karma,' said Spinetti, 'I said, "Thanks" and went away to look it up.'

Spinetti had his greatest West End success in the first London production of *The Odd Couple* (1966), which ran for two years. He perfected an American accent as the house-proud Felix, who had to cope with the shambolic Oscar, played by Jack Klugman.

As Spinetti was committed to the West End, he could not accept the role of courier in The Beatles TV film, *Magical Mystery Tour* (1967). Instead, he had a cameo as a drill sergeant, effectively reprising his role from *Oh! What a Lovely War*. Victor is the only outsider to appear in their three films, and additionally, he can be heard on a Christmas record for their fan club and seen as an out-of-work actor in Paul McCartney's video for 'London Town' (1978).

While starring in *The Odd Couple*, a young girl came to his dressing room and suggested that he stage John Lennon's books, *In His Own Write* (1964) and *A Spaniard in the Works* (1965). Spinetti saw Lord Olivier at the newly formed National Theatre, who said, 'Dear boy, come and direct it for us.' Spinetti recalled, 'John said, "Let's go somewhere warm." I thought he meant another room, but we ended up in Africa.' The result, called *In His Own Write*, was staged at the Old Vic in June 1968, and mixed Lennon's surrealistic poetry with childhood reminiscences. When Spinetti introduced Lennon to Olivier, Oliver said, 'If this is made into a film, the National Theatre will own 60 per cent of the film rights.' Lennon responded, 'Don't you have people that you pay to talk about these kind of things to the people that I pay to talk about these kind of things?'

The tempestuous media-driven couple, Richard Burton and Elizabeth Taylor, brought their relationship to the screen in Shakespeare's *The Taming of the Shrew*, directed by Franco Zeffirelli and made in Rome in 1966. Spinetti excelled in a conniving role and was also with Burton and Taylor in *Under Milk Wood* (1972).

Vic has said that an actor has to learn the 3 R's – redundancy, rejection and resting – and his solution was to take anything that was going. In the seventies he appeared as a comic Mexican who stole Jaffa Cakes in a TV commercial, which prompted the catchphrase, 'That's orangey!'. He directed the Dutch production of *Hair* in 1971, acted in sex comedies for Paul Raymond and was featured in many TV sitcoms. In 2003, he appeared in the London Palladium's high-tech production of *Chitty Chitty Bang Bang*.

He wrote prose and poems and published *Watchers Along the Mall* (1963) as well as his autobiography, *Up Front...*(2006). He was a brilliant raconteur and Ned Sherrin directed his one-man show, *A Very Private Diary*, which he often performed. He loved appearing at Beatles conventions, telling everyone that John Lennon wrote nothing more important than 'All You Need Is Love'. He died from prostate cancer in 2012.

An inspirational figure to The Beatles when they were filming.

STANLEY, JULIA – SEE LENNON, JULIA

STANSHALL, VIV – SEE BONZO DOG DOO-DAH BAND, THE

STARKEY, MAUREEN [1946–1994]

The least known of The Beatles' wives is Maureen Starkey, but she never wanted to be a public figure or to give interviews. She was born Mary Cox in Liverpool on 4 August 1946, the daughter of a merchant seaman and a sugar packer at Tate & Lyle. She failed her 11-plus but her parents found enough money to send her to a convent school. She left at 15 and, calling herself Maureen, she

trained as a hairdresser, spending her evenings with friends at the Cavern. She briefly dated Paul but was soon attached to Ringo. They referred to themselves as Richy and Michy.

Maureen was a keen follower of The Beatles, but as they became famous she found that some girls, overcome with jealousy, would come into the salon to argue with her. She left the job in September 1963 and moved to London to be with Ringo. They were married on 11 February 1965 at Caxton Hall Register Office. They had three children, Zak (b. 1965), Jason (b. 1967) and daughter Lee (b. 1970). She and Ringo were uncomfortable when The Beatles travelled to Rishikesh to study with the Maharishi in 1968, Maureen disliking the insects and Ringo the food, and they came home early.

For one of her birthdays, Adam Faith had recorded a special song for her but this was topped in 1968 when Frank Sinatra was persuaded to record new, Mo-centric, lyrics to 'The Lady Is A Tramp' and 'But Beautiful'. Mo often went on holiday with Cynthia and Pattie as Beatles wives and she is part of the backing choir on 'The Continuing Story of Bungalow Bill'.

It was a difficult marriage. Ringo was unable to resist temptation and he became a heavy drinker. Once she sought solace with George Harrison, and George's wife Pattie caught them together. John, who was hardly in a position to take a moral stance, called it 'virtual incest'.

In 1973 they bought John's home, Tittenhurst Park, near Ascot, but they divorced in 1975 with Ringo's affair with the American model Nancy Lee Andrews cited as grounds. Maureen became depressed and, attempting suicide, she rode a motorcycle into a brick wall.

In 1976 she befriended Isaac Tigrett, a founder of the Hard Rock Cafe, and they married in 1989, having one daughter. He collected memorabilia and referred to her, jokingly, as the 'ultimate collectible'. Maureen died from leukaemia on 30 December 1994 with both her husbands and all her children at her bedside. Paul McCartney dedicated a song to her, 'Little Willow', in 1997.

A friendly face in the inner circle.

STARR, RINGO [B. 1940]

In January 2008 Ringo Starr returned to Liverpool for the opening ceremony of the city's year as European Capital of Culture. Everything went fine, and a few days later he was talking to Jonathan Ross on BBC TV. Asked whether there was anything about Liverpool he missed, he answered, 'No.' He then went on to say that earlier in the week he'd felt he had to tell the audience that it was all so exciting he was 'That close to coming back'. If this was joking, it went disastrously wrong. Ringo's head was lopped off the topiary of The Beatles, and one caller after another on local radio phone-ins called him a disgrace. Just as the city was back on the rise, Ringo had made a remark as controversial as John's comparison with Jesus. What was interesting was that Ringo lacked the media skill to correct it: he seemed bewildered by the furore.

We don't know whether it was misguided banter or whether Ringo was exposing his true feelings, but the safe money is on the latter. Unlike the other Beatles, Ringo's childhood had included lengthy hospital stays and his education had suffered. What he had known of the city had been no fun at all and although the media assumed that John had a hard childhood (because John said so), Ringo had much more to complain about, but he was a decent bloke who didn't let it bother him.

Richard (or 'Richy', as he signed postcards from Hamburg to his grandmother) Starkey was born 7 July 1940 at 9 Madryn Street, a terraced house in the Dingle, home of his parents, Richard and Elsie. In 1944 they moved a few hundred yards to the even smaller 10 Admiral Grove in an effort to reduce costs. His parents separated and soon divorced. Elsie took cleaning jobs to supplement her weekly allowance of one pound ten shillings (£1.50). Richy attended St Silas Church of England School, where another sickly classmate was Ronnie Wycherley who became Billy Fury.

When he was six, Richy contracted appendicitis but an operation went wrong and he developed peritonitis, falling into a coma that lasted three days. His recovery at the Royal Liverpool Children's Hospital, Myrtle Street, took a year. When he returned home in May 1948, his mother allowed him to remain in the house, causing him to miss more lessons. He was eight years old and could hardly read or write. Dubbed Lazarus by the neighbourhood children, when he did attend school, the other, more educated classmates mocked him and he played truant in the park. A kindly neighbour gave him extra tuition but then, in 1953, he caught tuberculosis and was admitted to a sanatorium where he remained for two years. The hospital staff encouraged physical activity and Richy realised he had a natural flair for drumming.

In April 1954, his mother married Harry Graves, a Londoner who had moved to Liverpool after his first marriage. When Richy returned home in late 1955, he was through with school. He preferred to stay home, playing along to Harry's big band records by tapping on biscuit tins. He failed the physical examination for British Railways but in mid-1956, Graves found him a job as an apprentice machinist at Henry Hunt & Son, which made climbing frames for schools. He met the guitarists Eddie Myles and Roy Trafford and they formed

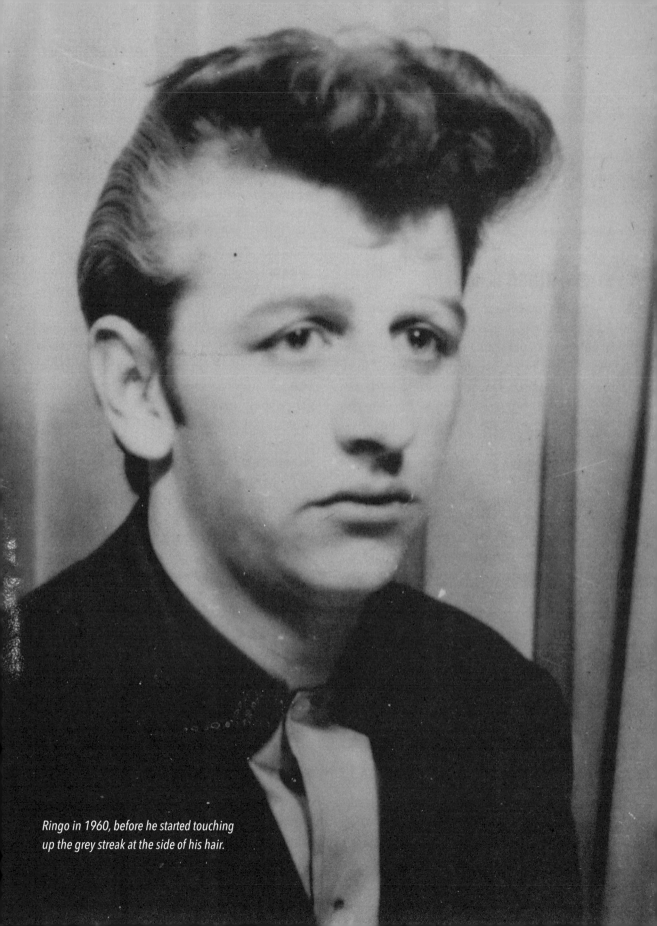

Ringo in 1960, before he started touching up the grey streak at the side of his hair.

a band, Eddie Clayton Skiffle Group, with Richy running a thimble across a washboard for percussion. In 1957 Richy received a second-hand and makeshift drum kit for Christmas. Richy lived in a tough area and he dressed as a Teddy boy with a splendid quiff, admittedly with a streak of grey.

In November 1959 Richy joined Rory Storm and The Hurricanes and Rory gave him the appellation 'Ringo Starr' because of his rings and because his drum solo could be billed as 'Starr Time'. They were a rock 'n' roll band with a sense of showmanship, and in May 1960 they were offered a three-month residency at Butlin's Holiday Camp in Pwllheli at £100 a week for the five of them. With the prospect of good money and easy women, Ringo left his apprenticeship – and his fiancée – to play there. This was followed by bookings on American Air Force bases in France and then a residency at the Kaiserkeller in Hamburg in October 1960. They played alongside The Beatles and Ringo occasionally sat in with them. Ringo continued with Rory Storm but in January 1962, he returned to Hamburg to play drums for Tony Sheridan.

Richy wrote to the Chamber of Commerce in Houston about emigrating to America, but he was put off by the bureaucracy. He chose Houston because Tony Sheridan had introduced him to the music of the blues performer, Lightnin' Hopkins, who came from Texas.

In August 1962 Starr replaced Pete Best in The Beatles and began his career with them at Port Sunlight on the Wirral. He recorded 'Love Me Do' with them on 4 September, but when they were recalled a week later a second recording of the song was made with the session man Andy White on drums and Ringo on tambourine. Ringo felt that they were 'doing a Pete Best on me', but it was simply George Martin being cautious, wondering if he could make a better record. (He couldn't.) The other Beatles didn't want to lose him; he played well, right on the beat, and was friendly with all of them, especially George. 'He was a bricklayer like me,' says ELO's Bev Bevan of his style. Ringo was not flamboyant like Buddy Rich or Keith Moon, but he was ideal for the role and one of his idiosyncrasies came through being a left-hander playing a right-hand kit.

The fans loved his solo spot when he would sing 'Boys', shaking his head to the beat. His so-called 'Ringoisms' – 'It's been a hard day's night' and 'Tomorrow never knows' – found their way into songs. His deadpan delivery of one-liners was used to good effect in *A Hard Day's Night* and there is a touching scene where he is walking sadly by the river. His success in the film led to a more central role in *Help!*.

In the States, Ringo was often seen as the favourite Beatle and there were novelty records like 'We Love You Ringo' and 'Ringo For President'. It was world news when Ringo contracted tonsillitis in June 1964 and was taken to hospital. He was replaced for five days by the session drummer Jimmie Nicol.

On 11 February 1965 he married Maureen Cox, a hairdresser from Liverpool he had known for three years. Brian Epstein was best man and Frank Sinatra forwarded a song and personal greeting for their wedding. They had three children – Zak (b 1965), Jason (b. 1967) and Lee (b. 1970). They were divorced in 1975 because Ringo, in common with the other Beatles, rarely said no to temptation.

As The Beatles became more inventive, he found himself with time on his hands, playing cards as he waited for the sessions to start. John and Paul sometimes wrote songs for him including 'I Wanna Be Your Man' (1963), the UK No. 1 'Yellow Submarine' (1966) and 'With A Little Help From My Friends' (1967). Every Beatle album could have been improved musically by giving Ringo's song to John or Paul, but Ringo's contributions added to the overall personality and unity of the band.

They gave up touring in August 1966, with Ringo commenting that four years of Beatlemania were enough for anyone. He was a keen photographer and he picked up editing skills while making *Magical Mystery Tour*. In 1972 he shot and directed the Marc Bolan documentary, *Born To Boogie*.

Ringo left The Beatles in India after ten days as he didn't like the food, but he did write a mawkish country song while he was there, 'Don't Pass Me By', which appeared on the *White Album*. He sang with Cilla Black on her TV series, *Cilla* (1968). In the final years of The Beatles, he found John aggressive and Paul overbearing, and utterly fed up he left them for a holiday in Sardinia, from where he returned with a new song, 'Octopus's Garden', a feeble companion to 'Yellow Submarine'.

When The Beatles split up, Starr released two albums in quick succession; one of standards, *Sentimental Journey*, and one of country songs with top Nashville musicians, *Beaucoups of Blues*. At the time of writing, he has released 17 solo albums – remarkable for a limited singer – as well as several live ones.

Ringo often wrote with George Harrison and the hit singles included 'It Don't Come Easy', 'Back Off Boogaloo' and 'Photograph'. He revived 'You're Sixteen' and 'Only You (And You Alone)'. John Lennon wrote 'I'm The Greatest' and 'Nobody Told Me' (which he didn't record) for him.

Ringo has worked with The Beach Boys and has recorded with such mavericks as Frank Zappa and Kinky Friedman. He has starred in several films including *The Magic Christian* (1969) and *That'll Be The Day* (1973). In 1980 he met the Bond girl

Barbara Bach on the set of the lamentable *Caveman*, and they were married the following year.

From 1984–86, Ringo was the narrator for the children's cartoon *Thomas the Tank Engine*, which gave him a new career. In 1988 he and Barbara attended a detox clinic in Tucson, Arizona, and the following year he formed the first All-Starr Band, a brilliant concept in which he invited other well-known musicians to join him and perform their best-known songs. From time to time, he has played with his son Zak, who is best known for his work with The Who and Oasis.

Ringo Starr appears on Rich Lists with a value of around £150m. He owns houses in Los Angeles and Monte Carlo and there has been much debate in recent times as to whether to save his Dingle birthplace. At a council meeting in Liverpool, it was said to be of 'no historical significance'. It's no wonder that Ringo has mixed feelings about Liverpool. There is a grumpy side to Ringo, borne out in his decision to stop signing autographs. Fair enough, but why not drop the peace sign instead: it is even more irritating than McCartney's thumbs-up.

Ringo's solid drumming helped to make The Beatles' records, and a more flamboyant drummer would have ruined them. He was perfect for the role and had a lovable personality too.

STORM, RORY [1938–1972] AND THE HURRICANES

When talking about Rory Storm, Cavern DJ Bob Wooler used to say, 'Vanity, vanity, all is vanity.' The writer of Ecclesiastes had summarised Rory Storm's excesses: he was a flawed but immensely entertaining character who brought personality and showmanship to the Merseybeat scene.

Rory Storm started life as Alan Caldwell, born at home in the Broadgreen area of Liverpool on 7 January 1938, although few people knew that date. He told his fellow musicians that he had been born in 1940, and switched the month to July so that he could celebrate his birthday while playing holiday camps and enjoy the sexual benefits that would bring.

The change of name came gradually. First of all, he and his friend, Johnny Byrne, played skiffle music together as The Texans, then it was The Ravin' Texans, Al Storm and The Hurricanes, Jett Storm and The Hurricanes, and finally Rory Storm and The Hurricanes. But it didn't stop there – on lead guitar Charles O'Brien became Ty Brien; on rhythm guitar Johnny Byrne was Johnny Guitar; on bass Wally Eymond turned into Lu Walters; and on drums Richy Starkey appeared as Ringo Starr. Ringo had his own spot, *Starrtime!,* in which he would sing either 'Alley-Oop' or 'Boys', although he could never outshine Rory with his shocking pink and gold lamé suits. As Ringo sang, Rory would comb his huge blond quiff with a large, golden comb.

Scarcely able as he was to complete a sentence without stuttering, it seems odd that Alan Caldwell should name himself after a musician he had seen at Butlin's holiday camp, R-R-R-Rory Blackwell, but once on stage he became Rory Storm and the stutter disappeared. There was no trace when he narrated 'All American Boy' (with local references) at the Jive Hive in Crosby in March 1960, part of a complete concert that was discovered and released on CD some 52 years later.

Rory Storm lived with his parents, Ernie and Vi, and sister Iris (b. 1944), at 54 Broadgreen Road. Vi called herself Mrs Storm and the house became known as 'Hurricaneville'. Mrs Storm would gladly welcome beat group members after a gig.

Alan/Rory was exceptionally fit, running for Pembroke Harriers and winning championships.

He loved football, rarely missing a Liverpool game, and he organised the Merseybeat XI, for which he insisted on taking the penalties. Sam Leach, furious about that Storm monopoly, once ran in front of Rory and kicked the ball, missing the net. Rory was so mad that he chased him round the field.

Rory Storm and The Hurricanes alternated with The Beatles at the Kaiserkeller in Hamburg in 1960 and at Rory's suggestion, they destroyed the rickety stage by jumping on it. It gave way during Rory's performance and he ran out of the club for fear of retribution.

While in Hamburg, their agent Allan Williams thought it a good idea to make a private recording of Lu Walters, backed by John, Paul, George and Ringo on 15 October 1960 for 'Summertime', the first time the famed line-up had recorded together. None of the copies have ever surfaced and it is the ultimate record collector's dream.

No one would claim that Rory Storm and The Hurricanes were great musically and as Cilla Black remarked, 'They could only play in one key and it certainly wasn't mine.' Bernard Jewry, who became Shane Fenton and married Iris Caldwell in 1964, commented, 'His group was a bit like the Stones were later on. Listen to them in concert and it's totally exciting. Everybody's moving around and it's incredible. Listen to the tape afterward, and there's a fair amount out of tune but it still doesn't detract from the magic that was there on the night.'

If all the votes had been allowed, Rory Storm and The Hurricanes would have won the *Mersey Beat* popularity poll in January 1962. However the editor, Bill Harry, was suspicious about 40 entries all in the same handwriting and in green ink – all, naturally, from Rory himself – and so The Beatles were declared winners. Not to be outshone, later that year Rory decided to leap from the balcony at the 15 December *Poll-Winners Concert* at the Majestic Ballroom, Birkenhead. The official photographer Graham Spencer was laughing so much that he missed the picture.

In August 1962 Rory Storm and The Hurricanes were playing a summer season at Butlin's holiday camp in Skegness when The Beatles poached their drummer. When Ringo became famous, he sent Rory £500 as he and the band would have to declare all their earnings for tax purposes. After Ringo, Rory had Gibson Kemp on drums but he went to The Dominoes, prompting Rory's remark, 'I make 'em and they take 'em.'

Outside of the Jive Hive recording, there is little of Rory Storm and The Hurricanes on record. They appeared on Oriole's two-LP set *This Is Mersey Beat* in 1963, and Rory's version of Bo Diddley's 'I Can Tell' is particularly good. Brian Epstein produced a Trini Lopez-styled arrangement of 'America' from *West Side Story*, which wasn't right for Rory. Rory didn't mind: he preferred to stay in the North West, regarding himself as the King of Liverpool, and it was fitting that he should play on the last night of the original Cavern in 1966. However, even though musically not much remains of Rory Storm, there is a valuable historical archive of life in a beat group through Johnny Guitar's diaries.

Rory worked as a DJ in holiday centres in Europe and at the Silver Blades Ice Rink in Liverpool. He was proud of his American car and was happy with his girlfriend. His father died in 1972 and a few weeks later, on 28 September, both he and his mother died on the same night. Nobody knows what happened but the likelihood is that Rory accidentally killed himself by mixing sleeping pills with Scotch, following which his mother, so upset with losing both her son and her husband in the same year, took her own life.

Whatever happened, it was a tragedy and who can say what would have happened had Rory

lived. Soon Glam Rock was in full swing: Shane Fenton had reinvented himself as Alvin Stardust and another old rocker, Paul Raven, had become Gary Glitter. It could have happened for Rory Storm and as Iris says, 'You've only got to look at Rod Stewart with a microphone stand to see Rory, but Rory was good-looking with it.'

The Golden Boy's life would make a fabulous film.

SULLIVAN, ED [1901–1974]

It was a different world. Today's TV shows are as much about the presenter as the performer. Ed Sullivan was so formal, so stiff, that he would stand no chance of presenting a national show today. Yet *The Ed Sullivan Show* was, far and away, the most popular of all TV variety shows, having an audience of over 73m US viewers for The Beatles' first appearance in February 1964.

Of Irish extraction, Edward Vincent Sullivan was born in Harlem on 28 September 1901 and began his working life as a boxer. He was soon writing about sport for the *New York Evening Mail*, and in an unlikely move, he became a gossip columnist and theatre critic for the *New York Daily News*. The syndicated columns under his name (though not necessarily written by him) appeared throughout the time that *The Ed Sullivan Show* was on air.

In 1948 he was the host of a new variety show, *Toast of the Town*, which had the good fortune to feature the new comedy duo Dean Martin and Jerry Lewis. Hollywood stars had been reluctant to appear on TV, fearing that if viewers could see them at home, they wouldn't go to the cinema. Ed said, 'Nonsense, it will gain publicity for your movies,' and as a result James Stewart and John Wayne appeared, to great acclaim.

From 1955, the programme was recast as *The Ed Sullivan Show*. It was a variety show featuring singers, comedians, ventriloquists, jugglers, circus acts and usually some culture – a snatch of opera or a scene from a Broadway play. Ed even had Albert Schweitzer playing the organ, but his most frequent guest was a puppet mouse, Topo Gigio. The whole family would watch the show, everyone knowing that if a particular act didn't excite them, the next could light their fire.

When Ed was in his fifties, he wanted to associate himself with the new rock 'n' roll music, and after a rival host Steve Allen had stolen a lead on him, he presented Elvis Presley, but with a gimmick. Elvis would only be shown from the waist up as his gyrations might upset viewers. This was a masterstroke. Sullivan got 60 million viewers and at the end he added, somewhat paradoxically, 'Let's have a big hand for a very nice person.' He had given Elvis Presley America's seal of approval

Ed Sullivan was not a natural performer. Like Buster Keaton, he was a Great Stone Face, speaking with his chin on his chest, as though he had no neck, and with a funny way of laughing. His strange pronunciation and his botched introductions were a gift for impressionists but Ed didn't mind, even having them on the show. He appeared as himself in the film *Bye Bye Birdie* (1963).

Ed Sullivan was keen to promote European talent and Edith Piaf, Marcel Marceau, Johnny Hallyday, Cliff Richard and Matt Monro all appeared before The Beatles. On 31 October 1963, Ed Sullivan and his wife Sylvia happened to be at London Airport (now Heathrow) when The Beatles returned from Sweden. He heard the fans screaming and thought he would investigate. He was soon negotiating with Brian Epstein and whereas he would pay normally $7,500 for a major act, he signed The Beatles to perform two live shows on February 9 and 16

with a third appearance recorded for February 23 for $10,000 overall.

After President Kennedy was assassinated on 22 November, Ed Sullivan featured The Singing Nun, and her record of 'Dominique' became an unlikely US No. 1, but perhaps it reflected the mood of the country. That all changed when The Beatles shot to the top with the exuberant and life-affirming 'I Want To Hold Your Hand' and made their first barnstorming appearance on *The Ed Sullivan Show*.

Ed was a benign host who didn't criticise his guests on air, no matter what he thought of them. Contrast this with Dean Martin who made his distaste for the Rolling Stones apparent when he introduced them. However, Sullivan was uncomfortable with rock groups and did have backstage arguments with the Stones and The Doors. He loved The Beatles though, calling himself 'Uncle Beatle', and had them appearing on the show six times, along with some promotional films. He introduced The Beatles at Shea Stadium in 1965 and his production company filmed this 'rilly big shew'. Most of all, he favoured The Dave Clark Five and Herman's Hermits, having each group on the show around 20 times.

Ed Sullivan lived with his family in the Delmonico Hotel and broadcast his programme from CBS's Studio 50 in Manhattan. The audience capacity was 728 but over 50,000 fans had applied for tickets for The Beatles in 1964. The premises were renamed The Ed Sullivan Theatre with *Late Night with David Letterman* coming from there.

The Ed Sullivan Show ran for over a thousand episodes, finishing in June 1971. Ed developed Alzheimer's disease and died from cancer on 13 October 1974. Over 3,000 mourners attended his funeral in New York.

As more and more viewers acquired their own TVs, family viewing diminished and variety shows disappeared from the networks. However, reality TV has found a way to recast variety shows in a contemporary setting.

Mister Ed was an important TV innovator introducing main-stream American audiences to rock 'n' roll, Elvis, Motown, and, most of all, The Beatles and the British Invasion.

SUTCLIFFE, STUART [1940–1962]

Stuart Fergusson Victor Sutcliffe was born in Edinburgh on 23 June 1940. His father, Charles, a Protestant, was an engineer in the merchant navy, while his mother Millie's Catholic family hoped she would become a nun. They were disowned by both families and probably did not marry. The family moved to Roby near Liverpool in 1943, as his father was involved with wartime work inspecting aircraft engines. After the war, Charles became a ship's engineer and would often be away for several months. Stuart had two younger sisters, Joyce (b. 1942) and Pauline (b. 1944).

From 1946–50, Stuart attended Park View Primary School in Huyton and then went to Prescot Grammar School. He was seen as very bright and his mother, a teacher, was delighted when he decorated her classroom with paintings. She was convinced he would be a genius, but Stu found this praise stifling. When he was only 16 he entered the Liverpool College of Art. He sang in a church choir, and at different times dabbled with the family piano, a bugle and a Spanish guitar, which he owned.

Stuart impressed the teachers at the art college, especially Arthur Ballard. He supplemented his grant by emptying dustbins during the holidays. In 1957 he appeared on a live Granada TV documentary, *Youth Wants to Know*, which looked at the relationship between surreal humour and surreal art and featured Spike Milligan.

He became close friends with Rod Murray, Bill Harry and John Lennon and they would drink, when they had the money, at a nearby pub, Ye Cracke. Stuart would have made a brilliant forger. He would paint his girlfriends in the style of Matisse or Cézanne, and painted Bill Harry in the style of Van Gogh in exchange for a jacket. A small, slender boy, he cultivated his dark, moody look after seeing Zbigniew Cybulski in the Polish film, *Ashes and Diamonds (Popiol I Diament)* (1958).

Stuart and Rod Murray often roomed together, finding bedsits and studio space in the once grand but now dilapidated houses of Liverpool 8. They sometimes did a moonlight flit to avoid paying rent arrears. Stu was painting all the time, sometimes all night, and he passed his intermediate exams with honours in 1958.

Art students were encouraged to submit paintings to the biannual John Moores Exhibition at the Walker Art Gallery, although few were accepted. In 1959 Stuart had painted a large abstract in two parts called, unadventurously, *Summer Painting*, and he and Rod carried the first part to the gallery. Having a drink in Ye Cracke was more attractive than delivering the second part, but the painting was nevertheless accepted for the exhibition and bought for £65 by the philanthropist John Moores himself, as a present for his son.

The Quarrymen, such as they were, only consisted of John, Paul and George. John suggested that if either Stu or Rod had a bass guitar, they could join the band. Rod set about making his own (which he has to this day) while Stu used his windfall to place a deposit on a bass guitar at Frank Hessy's music store. The group became the Silver Beatles (or Beetles) so Stu was now the fourth Beatle and it appears, though impossible to prove, that he had renamed the band. When it was later shortened to Beatals, John amended that to Beatles, with a shared love for puns.

Early in 1960, Rod and Stu moved into Flat 3, Hillary Mansions, in Gambier Terrace, sharing the three pounds ten shillings weekly rent with fellow art students, Diz (Margaret Morris, a dizzy blonde) and Ducky (Margaret Duxbury). Following an audition for the impresario Larry Parnes, the Silver Beatles accompanied Johnny Gentle on a week of Scottish dates. The band gave themselves fictitious names and Sutcliffe became Stu de Stael, a nod to a favourite painter, Nicholas de Stael.

Stu Sutcliffe's ability has been held in question, but those who heard him say that he was competent. Playing bass can be very hard on the fingers and possibly as an artist Stuart was not prepared to put in the practice. The famous shot of Stu with his back to the audience has fuelled the myth that his playing embarrassed him.

In July 1960, the *People*, a scurrilous Sunday newspaper, wrote an exposé about their flat in Gambier Terrace calling it 'The Beatnik Horror', but it was no worse than other student pads at the time or indeed, now. Stuart graduated with a National Diploma in Design.

Stuart went with The Beatles to Hamburg in August 1960 when they played the Indra and the Kaiserkeller. They befriended the German students Astrid Kirchherr, Klaus Voormann and Jürgen Vollmer, and Stuart was soon to replace Klaus as Astrid's boyfriend. Astrid loved Stu's solo spot when he would serenade her with Elvis Presley's 'Love Me Tender'. Stuart moved into Astrid's family home and although they were engaged in November 1960, they were in no hurry to marry. They were the same size and Stuart often wore her leather jacket.

Stuart played some shows with The Beatles in 1961 and was involved in a brawl at Lathom Hall, Litherland, where he was kicked in the head. He may have fractured his skull against a wall but he did not go to a doctor.

Stuart intended to study as an art teacher at the Liverpool College of Art, but the college would not have him back as they held him responsible for equipment that The Beatles had borrowed but not returned. Instead, he enrolled as a post-grad student at the Hamburg college, Staatliche Hochschule für bildende Küntse, in June 1961 and left The Beatles. He passed his bass to Paul McCartney and it later went to Klaus Voormann. Under the guidance and encouragement of Eduardo Paolozzi, his art became more abstract and is now regarded as Abstract Expressionism.

Stuart had horrific headaches and became sensitive to light. The doctors could not determine what was wrong. The headaches undoubtedly influenced the passion and intensity of his paintings. He died on 10 April 1962. The official cause of death was a cerebral haemorrhage and the underlying cause was probably the fight some 15 months earlier. Because his father was working on a ship bound for South America, he did not hear of the death for three weeks. Stuart's body was brought back to Liverpool for burial.

Stuart Sutcliffe was only 21 when he died, but he left a large body of work and numerous lengthy letters have been made public. They reveal what a considerate, loving person he was and how deeply in love he was with Astrid. He had ideas for the way The Beatles should be presented, including their collarless jackets.

Starting with the retrospective at the Walker Art Gallery in 1964, there have been several exhibitions. His sister Pauline has done much to keep his name alive but the conclusions in her books are sometimes fanciful. Stuart is often portrayed in films and plays of The Beatles' early years, notably *Backbeat* (1994), which concentrated on the friendship between Astrid, Stu and John. The Beatles thought so highly of him that his photograph is included on the cover of *Sgt Pepper*.

Many art critics have said that he would have been recognised without The Beatles. However, the connection with the Fab Four does enhance his standing and considering the many links that there have been since then between art colleges and rock musicians, it is worth nothing that Stuart Sutcliffe was the first.

'Stu was more than just the bass player – he was like the art director.' George Harrison

SWINGING BLUE JEANS, THE

In October 1961, Bob Wooler, the DJ at the Cavern club in Liverpool, compiled a list of the most popular rock groups on Merseyside. The Beatles were at No. 1, but The Swinging Blue Genes (as they were known then) were omitted from his ratings. Wooler wrote, 'They are beyond comparison. They are in a class of their own.' Another time, he referred to them as the Swinging Blue Geniuses.

Bob didn't include them in his Top 10, because, unlike The Beatles and Gerry and The Pacemakers, they did not play rock music. That transformation wouldn't happen for another year. They weren't a jazz band either, but a hybrid of skiffle, traditional jazz, pop and rock with George Formby thrown in for good measure. 'We had the rhythm section of a trad jazz band with the double bass, the drums and driving banjo,' says Ralph Ellis. 'The front line of a normal trad jazz band would be clarinet, trombone and trumpet, but we had three guitars, and Ray Ennis and I used to play harmony on our guitars. That was the sound we had – a trad jazz rhythm section with a rock 'n' roll front line.'

Initially formed as The Blue Genes Skiffle Group in 1957, the band had a wide repertoire and in July 1959, they appeared on the BBC Light Programme performing 'Guitar Boogie' and 'Steamline Train'. They were doing well enough to have their own van, decorated on the outside by the cartoonist Bill Tidy. They were constantly recording themselves, and over 80 songs by The Blue Genes were taped.

In 1961, as the Swinging Blue Genes, they had a weekly residency at the Cavern but on 21 March, they were unhappy when the club's second owner, Ray McFall, booked The Beatles as their guests. Ray McFall recalls, 'Three of the Blue Genes tackled me in Mathew Street and they were most upset. As far as they were concerned, The Beatles didn't have musical talent and unlike them, they weren't clean, fresh and well-organised.'

In September 1962 and at the recommendation of Paul McCartney, they became the latest Liverpool group to visit Hamburg. Paul must have known the likely reception. The audience at the Star-Club wanted beat music and booed them off. The group realised that they would have to change overnight, and they did with the help of The Undertakers. The group returned to Liverpool with a new rock 'n' roll sound and a new name, the Swinging Blue Jeans. John Lennon told them to drop the banjo – bye bye Paul Moss – and they now had the standard beat group line-up with Ray Ennis (b.1940) (vocals, rhythm guitar), Ralph Ellis (b.1942) (lead guitar), Les Braid (1937–2005) (bass) and Norman Kuhlke (b.1942) (drums).

They signed with HMV and the release of Chan Romero's 'Hippy Hippy Shake' coincided with The Beatles' appearance on BBC TV's *Juke Box Jury* in December 1963. They noted its potential, but were irked that the Blue Jeans were plundering their repertoire. Maybe, but it was a great record – two minutes of high energy in which Ray's rough-edged vocal with its celebrated ooo's is matched by Ralph's much-copied guitar solo.

The Blue Jeans performed the song in *Z Cars* and appeared on the first edition of *Top of the Pops*. On their second appearance, the record, to which they were miming, was played at the wrong speed.

'Hippy Hippy Shake' climbed to No. 2 and they secured sponsorship from the Liverpool jeans company, Lybro. Because of some Swedish dates, they turned down *The Ed Sullivan Show*, but the single did make the US Top 30. They had further UK hits with 'Good Golly Miss Molly' and 'You're No Good'.

In July 1964, the group completed their first album, *Blue Jeans A'Swinging*, which included rock 'n' roll standards, country songs, two compositions from The Shadows, and originals (both from the group and their publicist, John Chilton). Another album, *Live at the Cascade Club, Köln*, was released in Germany, but sadly, there are no recordings of their UK tour with Chuck Berry. The Blue Jeans weren't authentic enough for the rock 'n' roll audiences and, in one show, Ray had to dodge a flying Christmas pudding.

Just when it looked as though the Blue Jeans were losing their impact, they made their finest record, 'Don't Make Me Over', written by Burt Bacharach and Hal David. The dramatic single deserved a higher placing than No. 31, but it was the title track for a Canadian LP.

By February 1966, Ralph Ellis had left to sell insurance, very successfully as it happens, but he retained his passion for guitars. Terry Sylvester from another Liverpool band, The Escorts, was a very capable replacement. They often disagreed with producer Wally Ridley and when they recorded their own single, the psychedelic 'Keep Me Warm ('Til The Sun Shines)', EMI refused to release it.

In 2014 Ray is still on the road, exhorting audiences to dance the hippy hippy shake. He has sung it over 5,000 times and he's not finished yet.

A very competent Liverpool band who set performance standards high.

TAYLOR, ALISTAIR [1935–2004]

James Alistair Taylor was born in Runcorn, Lancashire in 1935 and had a succession of jobs on leaving school. He worked for John Lewis in London, but after lifting a bulky package, he was in plaster for eight months. While living in Battersea, he met Lesley Gillibrand and they were married in 1959. He returned to Liverpool to work as a personal assistant to Brian Epstein. Taylor went with Epstein to see The Beatles at the Cavern on 9 November 1961, and was as impressed as his boss. He wanted to continue with Epstein but his wife's asthma was aggravated by living in Liverpool, so he went to London to work for Pye Records. Meanwhile, The Beatles were making their mark and when Epstein told Taylor he too was moving to London, he asked him to be general manager of NEMS Enterprises at £1,000 pa.

Taylor enjoyed working with The Beatles and all the other artists in NEMS Enterprises, but he was puritanical when it came to their habits. 'I had seen what drugs had done to a lot of the jazz musicians I loved,' he said, 'so I was never keen when The Beatles were indulging themselves. John Lennon spent months trying to persuade me to go on an LSD trip, but I wasn't even tempted.'

At Taylor's instigation, NEMS signed the folk group, the Silkie. Their single, 'You've Got to Hide Your Love Away', was a US Top 10 success. Epstein thought Taylor would be a good tour manager for his supergroup, Cream. 'I took Cream on their first trip to America. It was the most amazing week I have ever spent because they hated each other's guts and would spark one another off. Although I'd seen friction in The

Beatles, I'd never witnessed a direct row between John and Paul, so this was mind-blowing.' Brian Epstein died in 1967 and Taylor was convinced it was accidental as they had just been planning a UK tour for the Four Tops.

The Beatles established Apple in 1968 with Taylor as general manager. Paul McCartney had him photographed as a one-man band for an advertising campaign to encourage audition tapes. Largely because any crazy scheme was financed, Apple ran into difficulties. When Allen Klein came from America to sort things out, he sacked Taylor and several others.

Taylor did not remain in the business and he and Lesley managed a tearoom in Derbyshire. He did factory and hotel work and he would joke, 'I started at the top and worked my way down.' He contributed to a biography of The Beatles by another NEMS employee, Peter Brown, but was horrified by the scurrilous results, *The Love You Make* (1983). He determined to set the record straight although his own book, *Yesterday – The Beatles Remembered* (Sidgwick and Jackson, 1988) was written as a series of letters to an imaginary fan, Michelle, and was irritating to read. Taylor became a favourite speaker at Beatle conventions and his stage show, *From Cavern to Rooftop*, was the first Beatle-related event to be staged in the Paul McCartney Auditorium at LIPA.

Meticulous, reliable and loyal, Alistair Taylor was The Beatles' Mr Fix-It.

TAYLOR, DEREK [1932–1997]

Nobody disliked Derek Taylor. He was the perfect press officer, knowing instinctively how to promote his clients and how to enhance what they were doing. When John and Yoko were in danger of becoming a laughing-stock, he found a way to turn it round without compromising their integrity.

Derek Wyn Taylor, the middle name revealing his Welsh origins, was born in Liverpool on 7 May 1932 but was raised in West Kirby on the Wirral. He went to grammar school, did National Service and then worked for regional newspapers, joining the *Liverpool Daily Post & Echo* in 1952. He became a theatre critic for the *Daily Express* and reviewed The Beatles' appearance at Manchester Odeon in May 1963, calling them 'fresh, cheeky, sharp, young entertainers'. He ghosted a weekly newspaper column for George Harrison and they became close friends.

Brian Epstein invited him to be his personal assistant and he ghosted Brian's autobiography, *A Cellarful Of Noise*, which was more a public relations exercise than an accurate account. Taylor became a press officer for NEMS, accompanying The Beatles to Australia and America in 1964. However, he fell out with Brian when he mistakenly took his limousine on the final night of the tour and was sacked for insolence.

Derek took a job with the *Daily Mirror* but soon resigned and moved to Los Angeles where he set up his own public relations company. He worked with The Byrds, The Beach Boys, The Grateful Dead and, surprisingly, Mae West. He was a party animal, befriending his clients and consuming vast amounts of alcohol and LSD, although this did not impair his ability to do the job. Having become a mixture of hippie and English gentleman, he was part of the organising committee for the Monterey festival in California, which starred Jimi Hendrix and Otis Redding.

In 1968 Derek became the publicist for The Beatles and helped them establish Apple Records. As it turned out, he ended up presiding over their break-up and was too good-natured to stop the excessive spending at Apple.

In 1970 he became the head of public relations at Warner Brothers Records and produced albums for George Melly, notably *Nuts* (1972), in which he tried to make the veteran jazz singer and drinking companion a music star. He had greater success with Nilsson, another heavy drinker. Derek wrote a memoir, *As Time Goes By* (1973), which was followed by *Fifty Years Adrift – In An Open Necked Shirt* (1984) and *It Was Twenty Years Ago Today* (1987). He helped George Harrison with his book of lyrics, *I Me Mine* (1980).

Derek married a Liverpool girl, Joan Doughty, in 1958 and they had six children. Despite his immense charm and gentle wit, his behaviour through drink and drugs got out of hand and she gave him an ultimatum – sober up or leave. He went into rehab and never relapsed.

He returned to working with The Beatles for the *Anthology* project and was one of the few insiders interviewed for that series. He was working on the book of the project when he died in Sudbury, Suffolk on 8 September 1997.

The perfect PR man – and I'll drink to that.

TREMELOES, THE – SEE POOLE, BRIAN

VAUGHAN, IVAN [1942–1994]

Ivan Vaughan's family lived in Vale Road, round the corner from Aunt Mimi and although he was two years younger than John, they became firm friends. He shared some of John's eccentricities, at one stage painting his own name in large letters across the front of his house. They both loved *The Goon Show* and mimicked the characters.

Although both Ivan and John had attended Dovedale Primary School, Ivan's mother decided that John Lennon would be too disruptive a friend if he joined him at Quarry Bank and so Ivan attended Liverpool Institute. He found himself in the same class as Paul McCartney – they had been born on the same day.

Ivan had been an initial member of The Quarrymen, painting his tea-chest bass with the slogan, 'Jive with Ive, the ace on the bass'. His place was taken by Len Garry but he maintained his friendship with the group and invited Paul to see them at St Peter's summer fete. Paul had recently lost his mother and Ivan thought that this would cheer him up. Ivan introduced Paul to John Lennon and the rest is hysteria.

Ivan was a good student, graduating from University College London, and becoming a teacher, specialising in educational psychology. He and his wife Jan often visited The Beatles and Jan helped Paul with the French lyrics in 'Michelle'. When The Beatles were launching Apple, there were plans to establish an Apple school with Ivan and Jan in charge, but nothing came of this.

During the seventies, Ivan contracted Parkinson's disease and he chronicled how it affected him. In 1984, a BBC TV documentary, *Ivan*, was presented by Jonathan Miller. The book, *Ivan: Living with Parkinson's Disease* was published in 1986 and he died in 1994. His death inspired Paul to write some poems.

Who knows? John and Paul might never have met without Ivan but don't make too much of this. Both John and Paul lived in the same area: both would have been in beat groups; and their meeting was inevitable.

VINCENT, GENE [1935–1971]

Rock 'n' roll introduced a new type of personality to the world – artists who were dangerous both to themselves and to others. The role model was

PAPERBACK WRITERS

There must be at least 2,000 Beatles books out there by now – with more appearing all the time. Now you have this book, there is really no need for any other, of course, but here are some personal recommendations, easy to find, not too specialist, which have come out over the decades and should interest those Beatles fans starting up their own Beatles library.

1. *The True Story of The Beatles* **by Billy Shepherd, Beat Publications, 1964**

This was the first Beatles book to appear, yet it's still quite cheap, if you can find it. Little more than an extended fan club magazine, badly written and with awful drawings, in large print aimed at small minds, but now wonderful to read. Ah, such innocence.

2. *Love Me Do* **by Michael Braun, Penguin Books, 1964**

First good bit of writing about The Beatles, done by an American journalist. Rather limited, as it's mainly slice of life stuff, picked up on tour, but fascinating.

3. *A Cellarful of Noise* **by Brian Epstein, Souvenir Press, 1964**

Brian's life story, in fact written by Derek Taylor, and not very well written at that, but this was how Brian wanted to present himself to the world, back in 1964.

4. *The Beatles* **by Hunter Davies, Heinemann, 1968**

The first proper, and only authorised, biography, endlessly updated since, still a primary source, especially the fly-on-the-wall accounts of them making their music. Top marks, of course.

5. *Lennon Remembers* **by Jann Wenner, Rolling Stone interviews, 1971**

This was the first, and best, of John shooting his mouth off. Some good stuff on the background to his songs.

6. *A Twist of Lennon* **by Cynthia Lennon, Star Books, 1978**

An early confessional book, by someone who was there, but pleasant and harmless, compared to the flamed-up scandals that have come out since by people who were hardly there at all.

ABOVE: John aged 8, with his mother Julia in 1949. John gave me this photo himself.
© Mark and Colleen Hayward / Contributor

RIGHT: John aged 6, outside Mendips, the house where he lived with his Aunt Mimi.
© Gems / Contributor

LEFT: Ringo aged 10 with his mother Elsie. He's looking rather musical, or appearing to be, even at that age.

BOTTOM LEFT: Paul aged 9, looking ever so toothy and winsome.

BOTTOM RIGHT: Paul at primary school in 1953, aged about 10. He's on the back row at the far right. © Tracks Ltd

OPPOSITE: George in 1957, aged about 14 and looking like a real musician. © Michael Ochs Archives / Stringer

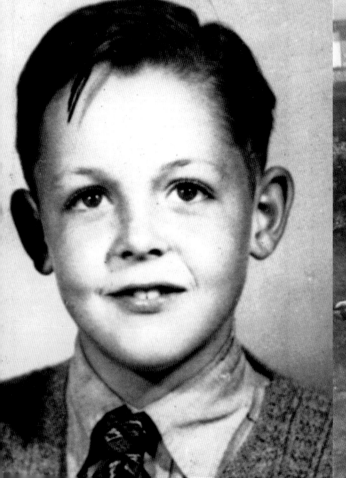

TOP: 22 June 1957. The Quarrymen on the back of a truck in Roseberry Street, Liverpool. Colin Hanton on drums, Eric Griffiths with the guitar, John at the microphone, Pete Shotton on washboard, Len Garry and Rod Davis at the back.
© Charles Roberts

ABOVE: The first stage at St Peter's Church Hall in Woolton, 1957.

LEFT: Paul and John on stage at the Casbah Coffee Club in West Derby, 1959, where the band performed many times. © Sam Leach

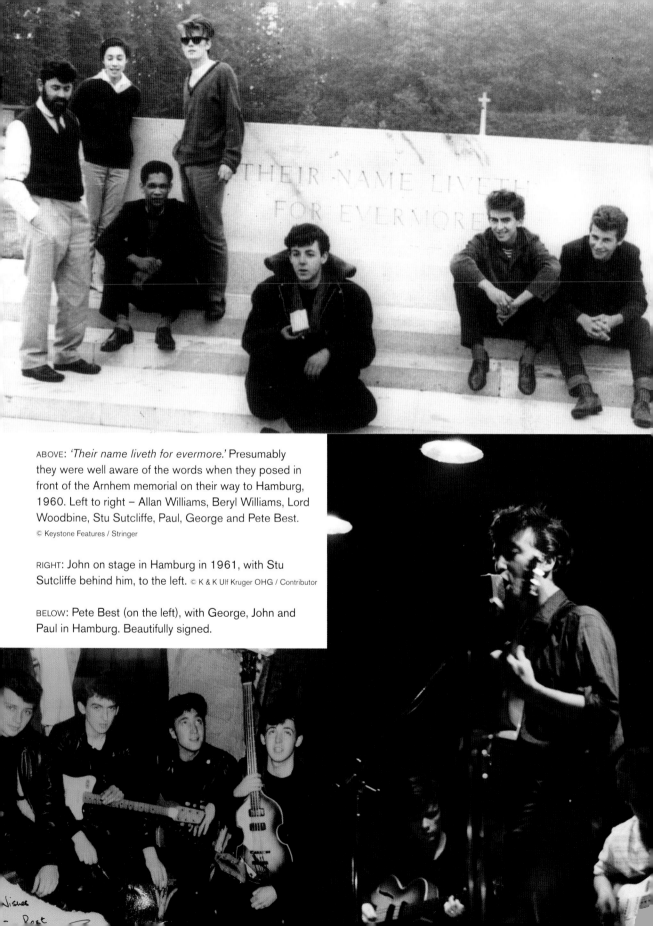

ABOVE: *'Their name liveth for evermore.'* Presumably they were well aware of the words when they posed in front of the Arnhem memorial on their way to Hamburg, 1960. Left to right – Allan Williams, Beryl Williams, Lord Woodbine, Stu Sutcliffe, Paul, George and Pete Best.
© Keystone Features / Stringer

RIGHT: John on stage in Hamburg in 1961, with Stu Sutcliffe behind him, to the left. © K & K Ulf Kruger OHG / Contributor

BELOW: Pete Best (on the left), with George, John and Paul in Hamburg. Beautifully signed.

ABOVE: The Beatles in Hamburg, with Tony Sheridan singing. © Ellen Piel - K & K / Contributor

BELOW LEFT: George, Paul and John in cowboy boots, on a roof in Hamburg.
One of the Hamburg snaps given to me by John.

BELOW RIGHT: Passport photo of John, with his hair brushed forward – not his
usual Teddy boy look of that time.

LEFT: Another happy snap from Hamburg. Paul on the lav, with bowler hat and newspaper.

BELOW LEFT: John being silly, out in the street in his underpants, perhaps carrying the very same newspaper.

BELOW: Astrid Kirchherr and Stu Sutcliffe, who got engaged in Hamburg. Stu died there in April 1962 after a brain haemorrhage, aged just 21.

ABOVE: 'My Bonnie.' The Beatles make a proper record at last – but only as the backing group to Tony Sheridan.

BELOW: Gene Vincent in the centre, with John, George and Pete Best, at the Star-Club in Hamburg, 1962.

7. *Revolution in the Head* by Ian MacDonald, Fourth Estate when first published 1994

Perhaps the best book on their music, if a bit intense, academic. Invaluable for any musicologist.

8. *A Hard Day's Write* by Steve Turner, Little, Brown when first published 1994

Also about the music, but more fun, easier to read.

9. *The Complete Beatles Chronicle* by Mark Lewisohn, Chancellor Press, 1996

Lewisohn is one of today's living, walking, breathing Beatles brains, who seems to know everything and has forgotten nothing. Details almost every day of The Beatles lives from 1957–1970. Invaluable reference.

10. *Paul McCartney – Many Years From Now* by Barry Miles, Secker and Warburg, 1997

Written with Paul's help, so that's a plus. There's a little too much self-justifying about Paul's contributions, but it does give an interesting insight into his relationship with, and feelings about, John. Very good on the background to Linda and how she came into Paul's life.

11. *The Beatles Anthology*, Cassell & Co, 2000

A massive book, in size and content, with The Beatles' story from the mouths of The Beatles themselves, told in the way they want to present it – so there are not too many warts. The words and stories are mostly well known, and well loved, by Beatles fans, having appeared elsewhere, but a great many of the illustrations have rarely been seen before. A beautiful looking publication, but not all that easy to use.

12. *The Beatles: All These Years, Volume 1 –Tune In*, Little Brown, 2013

The first volume of Mark Lewisohn's masterwork, which promises to take us through every step, every day, of their Beatley lives.

Gene Vincent. Both Jerry Lee Lewis and Chuck Berry caused some scary moments but neither had the manic personality and the self-destructiveness of Gene Vincent. Did his detractors make enough allowances for the pain he suffered and the fact that he had endured two major accidents?

Vincent Eugene Craddock was born into a poor family in Norfolk, Virginia, on 11 February 1935. He played with toy soldiers, and from an early age longed to own guns and knives. His lack of education made him suspicious; he felt that anyone who was helping him was bleeding him dry. He joined the navy in 1952 but his wish to see active service in Korea didn't materialise.

In July 1955, Gene rode his Triumph motor-cycle to visit a girlfriend, but a woman in a Chrysler ran a red light, smashing into Gene's bike and crushing his left leg. The police claimed the accident was Gene's fault and it was settled out of court, largely because Gene had signed papers while under medication. He was not given compensation but he did receive medical pay from the navy of $136 a month, which kept him in cigarettes. For the rest of his life, Gene was incensed about the way he had been treated.

The doctors wanted to amputate Gene's leg, but when his mother visited him he made her promise not to sign the papers as he was under 21. Gene was so keen to get back into action that he ignored medical advice, and as a result he remained in constant pain. He felt that the doctors had got it wrong and he would talk to anyone and everyone about suing them for $1m.

One consolation was that he began writing songs in hospital. 'Be-Bop-A-Lula' was inspired by the comic strip, 'Little Lulu' and he co-wrote it with another patient, Donald Graves. He won a radio talent contest by singing 'Heartbreak Hotel' and a radio DJ, Sheriff Tex Davis, whose title was as phony as Colonel Parker's, offered to manage him. Davis secured a contract with Capitol, a major label desperate for a rock 'n' roll star. With an echo chamber switched to the max, Gene recorded 'Be-Bop-A-Lula' with the Blue Caps. With a little chicanery, Sheriff Tex bought Donald Graves's share for $25.

It was an extraordinary recording debut. 'Be-Bop-A-Lula' begins with Gene's protracted 'Wel-l-l-l-l-l-l', which became his vinyl signature as surely as a painter signs his pictures. In two minutes, we have the essential Gene Vincent: his strange pronunciation, his breathless delivery, his high-pitched dexterity and above all, a tremendous presence that gives the record a neurotic edge. The record is so intense as he is desperate to tell you about this girl with an implausible name. Even seeing her walking round the store drives him berserk. The utterly bizarre B-side, 'Woman Love', was banned by the BBC for being too suggestive. 'Let's face it,' said a spokesman, contradicting himself, 'it's suggestive and you can't understand what he's saying anyway.' It was the first record that Paul McCartney bought.

Capitol called him 'The Screaming End' and described 'Be-Bop-A-Lula' as a 'novelty record'. Gene received national exposure on *The Perry Como Show* and the single climbed to No. 7, but Sheriff Tex told him that you only made records for publicity purposes: there was no money in them. Bad leg or not, Gene was soon touring and he slept with one woman after another, his marriage quickly over. He fired the Blue Caps a hundred times, and once when he lost a card game he threw a bottle of whisky through a TV screen.

He befriended Eddie Cochran on the set of *The Girl Can't Help It* and they toured Australia for a short while. Gene's second marriage was to a divorcee, Darlene Hicks, and he dedicated 'Wear My Ring' to her and held her hand on stage. They had a daughter, Melody Jean, in April 1959.

By the standards of rock 'n' roll performers, Gene Vincent recorded prolifically for Capitol, making several albums as well as singles. He had a flexible voice and could handle both wild rockers and tender ballads with ease – his 1957 B-side, 'Important Words', is exquisite. However, he never built upon the success of 'Be-Bop-A-Lula'. In the US, the follow-up, 'Race With The Devil', mysteriously stopped at No. 96 and then 'Bluejean Bop', 'Crazy Legs' and 'Say Mama' found no takers at all.

For a start, Gene had alienated himself from many American DJs. Also, Capitol Records was a legitimate company that refused to deal in payola (plays for pay), hence they had few hit records. Elvis Presley had gone into the army, Little Richard had found religion and Chuck Berry a prison cell. Rock 'n' roll was turning saccharine; artists like Bobby Rydell, Frankie Avalon and Fabian were clean-cut, good-looking and no trouble. Gene Vincent was thuggish, drunk and vulgar.

Paul McCartney gives a good indication of what Gene was like on the road: 'I got to know Gene in Hamburg when he was at the Star-Club. He was the star and we were the supporting group. Gene had been a marine and he was forever offering to knock me out. Marines can do that sort of thing: they touch your two pressure points. I'd say, "Sod off", but he'd say, "Go on, Paul, you'll only be out for a minute." I always resisted that. I didn't fancy being unconscious, thank you very much.'

1958 was a disastrous year for Gene Vincent and his Blue Caps. One of them crashed a car, two were arrested, and another was beaten up by a Canadian Mountie. Gene was arrested for wrecking a motel room, being drunk around minors and performing a lewd show: pure punk.

Gene owed $60,000 to the IRS and when he didn't pay, they took possession of his home in Dallas. He didn't believe in lawyers so didn't contest the assessment. It was typical Gene Vincent behaviour – he accepted whatever happened to him but he always complained about it. Gene and Darlene moved in with friends. It was a stormy relationship but that applies to all Gene's relationships – a subsequent wife was nicknamed 'Rocky' because of her constant black eyes.

Gene got so fed up with the Blue Caps that he left them without pay and facing a $500 hotel bill. The Blue Caps reported him to the Musicians' Union and he lost his card. But that's the way he was: Gene was always arguing with someone – managers, wives, friends, musicians. He never got along with anyone for long. You couldn't joke with him as he might turn on you. Drinking heavily and racked with pain, Gene was washed up by the end of 1959.

The British promoter Larry Parnes held out a lifeline, inviting Gene to the UK in December 1959. TV producer Jack Good thought he would accentuate Gene's image as a dagger boy, insisting on him wearing black leathers and a medallion and requiring him to walk up steps with his bad leg. When Vincent negotiated them rather well, Good shouted, 'Limp, you bugger, limp!'.

Gene persuaded Eddie Cochran to join him for a nationwide tour and Eddie discovered what a monster he was, threatening tour members with knives and accusing complete strangers of sleeping with his wife. The tour was an immense success and British rockers on the bill (Billy Fury, Joe Brown) learnt a lot by watching them. Both John and George caught the tour in Liverpool. After the final show in Bristol, there was a car accident in which Eddie was killed and Gene received further injuries.

Parnes insisted that Gene should return to fulfil further commitments and he topped a beat show at Liverpool Stadium on 3 May 1960. His nationwide tour ended abruptly when in Nottingham he read out a telegram stating that his daughter

Melody had died. She hadn't; Gene had said that to escape from his contract.

When he returned to Europe, it was for the no-nonsense promoter Don Arden, but he booked Gene into the Star-Club, Hamburg, where he indulged his love for guns and knives. He was the first star that The Beatles had seen at close quarters and they realised that fame was not all it was cracked up to be. There is a photograph of Gene with The Beatles and both John and Pete are threatening him with knives. As for Gene, he looks out of it.

Both John and Paul sang 'Be-Bop-A-Lula' from time to time and both 'My Bonnie' and 'Ain't She Sweet', which they recorded in Hamburg, had been album tracks for Gene. Paul loved Gene's wistful, low-key arrangement of 'Over The Rainbow', which became a showstopper for The Beatles at the Cavern.

For the rest of the sixties, Gene spent most of his working life in the UK and on the Continent, often performing erratically with back-up bands. He made a fine comeback album, *I'm Back and I'm Proud*, for John Peel's Dandelion label in 1970 but he died, broke and alcoholic, from a bleeding ulcer on 12 October 1971. He was 36 years old and looked 60.

Object lessons in how to do it and how not to do it.

VOLLMER, JÜRGEN [B. 1939]

Jürgen Vollmer was an artist and friend of Astrid Kirchherr and Klaus Voormann. He went with them to the Kaiserkeller to see The Beatles in 1960 and was similarly entranced. He had started as an assistant photographer, and borrowing a camera he photographed The Beatles when they moved to the Top Ten. Some of the photos appeared in *Mersey Beat*. Jürgen recalled, 'I was attracted to

them because they were so menacing looking, but that was just the act. They looked like rockers, but inside they were artists.'

His photograph of John in a Hamburg doorway was used on the cover of John's album *Rock 'N' Roll* (1975). 'I wanted John to stand in the doorway totally in focus and I wanted Paul, Stuart and George to pass by out of focus. I wanted his shoes in the picture because they looked new and strange to me. Johnny is really looking cool, isn't he? He has that "I can take on anybody" look.' John said in his introduction to a book of Jürgen's photographs, *Rock 'N' Roll Times*, that he was, 'the first photographer to capture the beauty and the spirit of The Beatles.'

During 1961 Jürgen moved to the Left Bank of Paris, where he was visited by John and Paul and gave them the same combed-forward hairstyle as his own.

Jürgen became a celebrity photographer in Hollywood and found that both Sylvester Stallone and Barbra Streisand would only be photographed from one side. 'It was fun,' he said, 'but nothing has compared to The Beatles.' Asked if he had any regrets, he replied, 'Yes, I wish I had taken more pictures.'

He had the look and he had the camera.

VOORMANN, KLAUS [B. 1938]

It is hard to imagine anyone more friendly or pleasant than the multi-talented Klaus Voormann, who has become a great favourite at Beatles conventions.

Born the son of a doctor in Berlin in 1938, Klaus Voormann suffered from dyslexia as a child. His family recognised his artistic leanings and he graduated in graphic design in Hamburg. He remained in Hamburg, living in the family home of his girlfriend Astrid Kirchherr. He loved rock 'n' roll and wanted to design album sleeves. After an argument with Astrid one evening, he went walking around St Pauli and was enticed by the music he heard coming from the Kaiserkeller.

As an arts student, he was wary about going inside. 'I was scared because Rockers were all over the place and they might want to fight. Rory Storm was playing with Ringo on drums and they were very good, but then Stuart came on with his dark glasses and I remember thinking, "Is he blind?" [Laughs] The whole band appeared and Paul was greeting the people in German – he had learnt a little at school – and immediately there was a spontaneous friendship. George could speak a bit of German too. They started playing and they were amazing, just like those American records.'

Klaus reported back to Astrid and their friend Jürgen Vollmer and they all went the following night. Hoping to impress The Beatles, Klaus took them a sleeve he had drawn for the single 'Walk – Don't Run'. Soon they were close friends, but Stuart Sutcliffe became Astrid's boyfriend and Klaus had to find new lodgings; this was all very good-natured.

Once Stu had left the band, Paul played Stu's bass but he preferred a left-handed instrument. The bass player in Tony Sheridan's group had a violin-shaped Hofner bass guitar and Paul ordered a left-handed model in Hamburg. Klaus Voormann remembers, 'Stuart needed money for paint and canvasses and so he wanted to sell his guitar and he asked me to buy it. I gave him 200 DM. I was always a musician at heart but I had never played the bass.'

During the Merseybeat boom, Klaus teamed up with two Liverpool musicians, Paddy Chambers (Faron's Flamingos, Big Three) and Gibson Kemp (Dominoes) to form the trio, Paddy, Klaus & Gibson. They were managed by Tony Stratton-Smith, recorded three singles for Pye and had a residency at one of London's swinging clubs, the Pickwick. In 1965 they switched management to Brian Epstein but soon disbanded. Klaus became a bass player for Manfred Mann replacing, of all people, Jack Bruce. He can be heard on all their hit singles with lead vocalist Mike d'Abo including 'Fox On The Run' and their No. 1, 'The Mighty Quinn'.

Klaus maintained his friendship with The Beatles and won a Grammy for his sleeve design for *Revolver* (1966). In 1965 he married the *Coronation Street* actress Christine Hargreaves, and George Harrison was so entranced by the harmonium in their house that he started composing 'Within You Without You'.

When Paul left The Beatles, the *Daily Mirror* ran a front page story stating that Klaus Voormann would be his replacement. This was nonsense but he did play on records by John ('Cold Turkey', 'Instant Karma'), George ('My Sweet Lord') and Ringo ('It Don't Come Easy', 'Back Off Booga-loo'). He appeared on stage with the Plastic Ono Band and on *The Concert for Bangla Desh*. He created the lithographs for the album *Ringo* (1973). Klaus moved to Los Angeles and played on albums by Carly Simon, Billy Preston and Nilsson.

In 1979 Klaus returned to Germany and discovered Trio, who had a UK No. 2 with 'Da Da Da' (1982), produced by Klaus. In 1995 he worked again with The Beatles, designing the collages for their *Anthology* collections. He returned to art and often drew scenes from St Pauli in the early 1960s. In 2009, he unpacked his bass and made a CD and DVD, *A Sideman's Journey*, with some famous friends, Paul McCartney ('I'm In Love Again'), Dr John and The Manfreds.

Instant karma.

WALLEY, NIGEL [B. 1941]

Christopher Nigel Walley, rechristened 'Wallogs' by John, was the son of a senior police officer. He lived close to John but went to Bluecoat Grammar School rather than Quarry Bank. Nevertheless, John was keen to have him in The Quarrymen and he joined on tea-chest bass. Dragging a splintery old crate around was no fun, and instead he became their manager – effectively, The Beatles' first manager. He had a business card printed and put details in the small ads. As an apprentice golf professional at the Lee Park Golf Club, he was able to obtain a booking there. Alan Sytner saw them and booked them for the Cavern in August 1957.

In July 1958 Nigel escorted Julia Lennon to the bus stop, and as he walked away he heard the noise of her being hit by a car. Maybe if he had spoken to her for another 30 seconds it would have made a difference, but he was blameless. He continued to find them gigs but Paul objected to him having an equal cut and thought he should only have 10 per cent. The family moved to New Brighton at the end of 1958 and the following year, Nigel became the UK's youngest golf pro at a club in Kent. There was a now a vacancy for The Beatles' manager…

Nigel put some organisation into The Quarrymen's first bookings.

WALTERS, LU – SEE STORM, RORY AND THE HURRICANES

WEISSLEDER, MANFRED [1928–1980]

In mid-January 1962, Horst Fascher came to Liverpool with the rock 'n' roll singer Roy Young to seek out talent for a Hamburg beat club, but Horst wasn't acting for Peter Eckhorn at the Top Ten. He was now working for Manfred Weissleder, who was opening the Star-Club at the Stern-Kino premises on Grosse Freiheit 39, and in particular Weissleder wanted The Beatles.

Tall, blond and powerful, Manfred Weissleder had been born in Dortmund on 29 January 1928 and moved to St Pauli in the mid-1950s as an electrician. He worked at the Tabu nightclub and, apart from diving, he saved his money, lived on dry bread and was soon able to produce his own porno movies. His 3D erotic films proved very popular and he was able to buy a Mercedes.

Weissleder showed erotic films at the Paradieshof, which backed onto the Stern-Kino premises in Grosse Freiheit. The Stern-Kino had started as a dance hall for the poorer people of Hamburg, then became a cinema and a restaurant. Its owner felt that Manfred's sex films were disturbing his regular clientele and told him he would have to move. Manfred made him an offer he couldn't refuse and came to own the Stern-Kino.

The premises were too big for a sex club, which needs intimacy, so Manfred opened it as a nightclub with live music. Horst Fascher encouraged him to go for British rock 'n' roll. Because the twist was popular, Weissleder considered calling it The Twist Club, but went with the English translation of 'Stern' and made it the Star-Club.

Weissleder was prepared to pay the 500 DM per Beatle per week that Brian Epstein demanded. To sweeten the pill, Fascher offered Epstein a 'special arrangement' fee of 600 DM. Manfred was annoyed when The Beatles asked for overtime. He told them, 'Okay, you can have 200 DM for overtime this week, but you're going to play until you fall off the stage.'

There had been posters all over Hamburg advertising the opening of the Star-Club on 13 April

1962. By the standards of the area, this was a plush venue – and a big one, accommodating 1,000 patrons. As well as Liverpool talent, Weissleder wanted the biggest names in rock. Ray Charles demanded 20,000 DM and Weissleder bought a gold-painted piano for his performance. The Star-Club was the only one of the four Hamburg clubs to charge admission, but even increasing the entry fee from 2 DM to 20 DM meant Ray Charles was a loss-leader. You did however have to pay to see the films in the cinema above and at least one Mersey-beat musician was captured on celluloid.

There was a danger that young musicians could be fleeced of their earnings, but no one messed with groups from the Star-Club. Manfred Weissleder gave all the musicians Star-Club pins, which ensured that anyone who bothered them might get a visit from the Fascher brothers (Fredi Fascher, headbutting a speciality). When Gene Vincent described his trouble with a taxi driver, the heavies sought out the taxi and turned it upside down. Weissleder was as tough as anyone, well capable of dishing out the punishment himself.

In 1963, Manfred Weissleder tried without success to get The Beatles back to play the Star-Club, and if not the Star-Club then an event he could promote. There was a snag. During their last visit to the venue, Father Mackels accused The Beatles of urinating on the pulpit at St Joseph's Church on Grosse Freiheit, but they had left Germany before charges could be pressed. Weissleder knew that this could prevent The Beatles appearing in Hamburg again. The public prosecutor dropped the charges in 1965; Father Mackels was no longer sure of his story.

Although Weissleder booked British and American acts for his club, he knew he should foster local talent. It made economic sense as his expenses would be reduced and he could build up local followings. The young German boys wanted to be like The Beatles. The Rattles won his first competition in 1963. They became German chart regulars and had an international success with 'The Witch' in 1970.

Weissleder's Star-Club label released nearly 100 singles and 40 albums in its five years of existence. He realised the importance of marketing with Star-Club stickers, mugs and T-shirts. Copying *Mersey Beat*, he started *Star-Club News*. Weissleder franchised the Star-Club brand to clubs in other German cities, but this was unsuccessful.

The torrid, explosive album, *Live at the Star-Club, Hamburg*, recorded by Jerry Lee Lewis with The Nashville Teens in April 1964, is a contender for the most exciting live album of all time. It is utter mayhem, brilliantly captured and typical of the uninhibited life on St Pauli. The Searchers also recorded a live album at the Star-Club but it is tame by comparison.

The guests at the Star-Club were often exceptional and Jimi Hendrix played there for three days in March 1967. The venue closed on New Year's Eve 1969 with Hardin and York the final performers. It became a sex theatre, Salambo. Weissleder died in 1980 but Horst Fascher continued with several projects in the Star-Club name. Many British performers took part in his new Star-Club in 1980, albeit at a different location, but the club did not have the same impact and did not last.

The Beatles had developed their sound by the time the Star-Club opened, but this club was much bigger than the previous ones.

WHITE, ANDY [1930–2015]

Pete Best was sacked from The Beatles and Ringo Starr stepped in. He recorded 'Love Me Do' with

The Beatles at EMI on 4 September 1962. George Martin felt it could be improved and invited them back a week later. When they arrived, Ringo found another drummer, Andy White, in his place. Feeling it was love me don't, Ringo reluctantly stayed and banged a tambourine. Apart from that, the two recordings were similar and the original single of 'Love Me Do' was Ringo's version. He commented, 'Andy White didn't do anything that I couldn't do.'

TOP TEN BEATLES NOVELTY SONGS

1. 'Beatle Crazy' by Bill Clifton (1963) The US bluegrass performer visited the UK and was surprised by what he saw. 'Beatle Crazy' was good training in novelty songwriting for composer Geoff Stephens, who later wrote 'Winchester Cathedral'.

2. 'All I Want For Christmas Is A Beatle' by Dora Bryan (1963) The West End musical star took this novelty into the Top 20.

3. 'We Love The Beatles' by The Vernons Girls (1963) The Liverpool girls had revved up their Scouse accents for 'Funny All Over', but this time out they missed the charts.

4. 'A Beatle I Want To Be' by Sonny Curtis (1964) Sonny Curtis was touring the UK with The Crickets, saw what was going on and cut one of the first US Beatle novelties. He made the album *Beatle Hits – Flamenco Guitar Style*, also in 1964, and covered several Beatle songs with The Crickets: he was a fan. The fact that The Crickets loved The Beatles so much suggests that Buddy Holly would have felt the same way.

5. 'Like Ringo' by Dick Lord (1964) *Bonanza* actor Lorne Greene topped the US singles charts with his western drama 'Ringo', where the title was said to be coincidental, but it prompted this spoof from Dick Lord, who was a scriptwriter for Bobby Darin.

6. 'A Letter To The Beatles' by The Four Preps (1964) What do you do in 1964 if you had been a chart act on Capitol? You join the party. The record was on the US charts for three weeks, reaching No. 85. The Preps maintained that Brian Epstein ordered the record to be withdrawn as it was disrespectful to The Beatles. Actually, it is not disrespectful to The Beatles, but disrespectful to the marketing of The Beatles, so Eppy may well have taken umbrage.

7. 'We Love You Beatles' by the Carefrees (1964) Composer Charles Strouse wrote 'Born Too Late' for the Poni-Tails, and the music for numerous Broadway musicals including *Annie*. In his parody musical about Elvis joining the army, *Bye Bye Birdie*, Birdie's fans sang, 'We Love You Birdie'. It was easy to parody the parody to praise the Fab Four.

8. 'Stamp Out The Beatles' by The Hi-Riders (1964) A Beatles novelty for the folk who don't like The Beatles … why would they buy it?

9. 'The Beatle Bounce' by Bobby Comstock (1964) Bobby Comstock recorded 'Let's Stomp', which the Mersey groups loved, but as for his concept of turning Beatlemania into a dance like the twist – well, he should have known better.

10. 'Ringo For President' by Rolf Harris (1964) Now disgraced Harris performed 'Tie Me Kangaroo Down Sport' with The Beatles for the BBC in 1963, and that is one Beatle performance that will never be reissued. And what was the thinking here? Ringo could never have been President, he was not born in the US.

Andy White was a Scottish drummer who had been born in London but raised in Glasgow. He'd had an injury to his left ear and commented, 'I've managed to bumble along as I don't really know what perfect hearing is.' He learnt the drums by listening to the jazz greats Gene Krupa and Louie Bellson. He played in bands around Glasgow and then secured a job with Vic Lewis and his Orchestra. As luck would have it, Paul McCartney heard him in 1957 as Lewis supported Bill Haley and his Comets at the Liverpool Odeon.

Andy played in the house bands for the TV shows *Boy Meets Girls* and *Drumbeat* and also played on Billy Fury's rockabilly album, *The Sound of Fury* (1960), produced by Jack Good. In total contrast, he toured with Marlene Dietrich.

In 1962 he married Lyn Cornell, a solo singer who had been with the Liverpool group, The Vernons Girls, and he was playing nightly in the adventurous West End musical *Stop the World – I Want to Get Off*, starring Anthony Newley. He had returned from a belated honeymoon when he got the call to go to Abbey Road. Years later all four Beatles heard Andy again when he backed Tiny Tim at the Royal Albert Hall.

Andy White played with the BBC Orchestra in Glasgow but after losing his job following some BBC cuts, he moved to New Jersey and gave drumming instruction. Asked what he thought of Ringo he said, 'Oh I thought Ringo was very good once he'd settled in.'

The Beatles' history would have been the same without him as there is little difference between the *Love Me Dos*.

WILLIAMS, ALLAN [B. 1930]

Allan Williams called himself 'the man who gave The Beatles away', but why let truth get in the way of a good story. He was known for exaggerating his adventures, but no one objected as this was part of his engaging personality. The Beatles would have never got to Hamburg without his embellishments.

Allan Williams was born into a Welsh family in Bootle in 1930. The following year his mother died giving birth to twins, who also died. It was some years before he learnt that the person he called his mother was actually his stepmother. His father was a joiner, who promoted concerts in his spare time. Allan became a plumber and he met his wife Beryl in an operatic society. There was some family opposition by both parties to their marriage as Beryl was half-Chinese.

Keen to follow the London trend for coffee bars, Allan opened the Jacaranda in Liverpool in September 1958. John Lennon and Stuart Sutcliffe were students at the nearby College of Art and Allan asked them to paint the toilets and provide a mural in the basement, which had been a coal cellar. The mural is there to this day – it is unlikely either Stuart or John were involved.

When Eddie Cochran and Gene Vincent played the Liverpool Empire for a week in March 1960, Allan and the impresario Larry Parnes agreed a one-off concert at Liverpool Stadium in May. After Eddie was killed in a road crash, Allan added local groups to the line-up: Gerry and The Pacemakers, Rory Storm and The Hurricanes, Cass and The Cassanovas (later The Big Three), but not The Beatles. Allan did not consider them good enough.

The concert went well and Larry asked Allan to organise an audition for potential backing groups for his artists. As a result, The Beatles went to Scotland for a week with another Liverpudlian, Johnny Gentle. Allan found them a drummer, 26-year-old Tommy Moore, but Tommy hated John's sarcasm and on returning to Liverpool he stuck with his job at Garston Bottle Works. Paul McCartney, needing cash, asked Allan to loan him £15. 'He gave me an IOU,' said Williams, 'but he never paid me back. I'm glad he didn't as I sold the note for £500.'

Allan had a share in the Cabaret Artists Social Club, the first strip joint in Liverpool, and when a Manchester stripper called Janice demanded live music, The Beatles were recruited to accompany her for a week, easily the nadir of their career. When he sold the club, he and his partner, a calypso singer called Lord Woodbine (Harold Phillips), went to Amsterdam and then Hamburg to assess their club life.

In the Indra, Allan heard a German band singing 'Tutti Frutti' and he told the club's owner, Bruno Koschmider, with typical hyperbole that he could supply Liverpool bands who would be better and more authentic. Nothing came of it at the time, but a few weeks later Allan took Howie Casey and The Seniors to the 2i's coffee bar in London and found Koschmider there, looking for 'The Peetles'. Whatever the truth of the matter, the first Liverpool group to play in Hamburg were Howie Casey and The Seniors with their vocalists Derry Wilkie and Freddie Fowell (later Freddie Starr). Koschmider was delighted and wanted more. Most of the Liverpool bands had day jobs but not The Beatles. Allan told Koschmider he would send them, and Howie, incensed, sent Allan a letter telling him not to send 'that bum group, The Beatles'.

The Beatles did well but fell out with Koschmider when they wanted to move to the Top Ten. Koschmider had George deported for being underage and Paul and Pete arrested for starting a fire.

In August 1960 Williams opened the Wyvern Club, later the Blue Angel nightclub, but he had no intention of using beat groups. They would play at the Top Ten Club (the name borrowed from Hamburg), which he opened in December 1960. He employed a railway clerk, Bob Wooler, as his stage manager and the opening night with Howie Casey and The Seniors was a success. The club burned down within a week and he maintains, 'History would have been altered if the Top Ten had not caught fire. The Cavern was only doing jazz at the time and there wasn't a venue in the centre doing rock 'n' roll.'

The new-look Beatles played Litherland Town Hall on 27 December 1960 and stunned the audience. Allan fell out with them over commission on their subsequent Hamburg appearances. He maintained that he was entitled to his 10 per cent, and they disagreed. When Brian Epstein wanted to manage them, he sought Allan's advice. He told him, 'I wouldn't touch them with a fucking bargepole.'

Allan had success with the Blue Angel, even introducing bullfighting with a real bull given to him by friends from the abattoir. His scheme to turn Spain into another Blackpool by manufacturing sticks of rock fell foul of the authorities, and, by all accounts, he ended up on street corners, going, 'Psst, wanna buy some rock?'

The Blue Angel became a late-night haunt for Merseybeat musicians, and Williams promoted a beat festival at the Stanley Stadium in 1963, possibly the first open-air rock concert in the UK. However, he knew he had wasted his big chance. He watched The Beatles on the *Royal Variety Performance* in November 1963 and he said, 'That's when I knew I'd blown it. I threw a cushion at the TV – I wish I'd had a brick.'

In 1975 Williams wrote his autobiography, *The Man Who Gave The Beatles Away*, with the *Daily Mirror* journalist, Bill Marshall. When he told Bill that he could not remember any more anecdotes, Bill invented some for his approval. They appeared in the book and years later, Allan was telling the stories as his own. A short while later, Allan asked

Paul McCartney to sign a copy of his book, and Paul said, 'I've got to be careful here. Whatever I write is going to be quoted on the paperback.' He wrote, 'To Allan, Some parts of this book are partially true, Paul McCartney.'

A Liverpool singer, Kingsize Taylor, made some private recordings of The Beatles at the Star-Club in Hamburg. In 1977 Allan decided to exploit these commercially but he was double-crossed and even though the album was released, amidst much court action, neither he nor Taylor saw any money from it.

After a series of personal appearances to promote his book, Allan, in partnership with Wooler, organised the first Beatles convention in 1977. It promised an appearance by a Beatle. The tension mounted as the audience wondered which one it would be. It was Tommy Moore, and to make matters worse, Tommy could remember very little about his short time with The Beatles.

It was only when Allan Williams relinquished the control of Beatles festivals that they made an impact, but he became a popular guest. He spent 20 years travelling to conventions around the world. When he and Wooler stayed at the same hotel in Paris as the former President Nixon and his aides, they ran up the larger bar bill.

In later years, Allan made his living selling antiques and manning stalls at flea markets, but the provenance of some of his stock was questionable. Some black leather trousers, allegedly worn by Paul McCartney, were offered for sale by a London auction house with a certificate of authenticity from Allan Williams. They belonged to Faron of Faron's Flamingos, a musician some inches shorter than McCartney.

Allan's wife tired of his duplicity and drunkenness, but they never divorced. Allan got together with Bob Wooler's former wife, Beryl – he would refer to them as Beryl 1 and Beryl 2 – and he was devastated when Bob Wooler and then Beryl 2 died within a year.

In 2002 a biographical play, *The Man Who Gave The Beatles Away*, written and directed by Ronan Wilmot, was premiered in Dublin. A second volume of Allan's memoirs, *The Fool on the Hill*, this time with *Liverpool Daily Post* journalist, Lew Baxter, was launched at the Beatles festival in Liverpool in August 2003. Over the years, Williams had been vituperative about his relationship with The Beatles, but, somehow, he has become a changed man – and he has now sobered up. He told audiences, 'I am a millionaire. I am a millionaire of memories and no one can take that from me.'

Buy him a pint and hear a good story.

WILLIAMS, LARRY [1935–1980]

Larry Williams was born in New Orleans in 1935 and worked as a pianist for Lloyd Price in the mid-1950s. He seized his opportunity when Little Richard retired in 1957 by writing and recording several rock 'n' roll songs for Specialty in the same vein, his songs often displaying a good sense of humour. The Beatles were to record 'Dizzy Miss Lizzy', 'Bad Boy' and 'Slow Down' and as a solo artist John Lennon added 'Bony Moronie'. The Rolling Stones, Roy Young, Cliff Bennett and Kingsize Taylor all recorded 'She Said Yeah'. In the mid-1960s, Williams recorded and toured very successfully with Johnny 'Guitar' Watson, but he was making his money from pimping and pushing drugs. He was murdered in 1980 and still nobody knows what really happened. (Well, at least one person does but he's not talking.)

Derivative of Little Richard but The Beatles loved his records in their own right.

WILSON, BRIAN – SEE BEACH BOYS, THE

WILSON, HAROLD [1916–1995]

Although a Yorkshireman, Harold Wilson was the Labour MP for Lancashire constituencies Ormskirk and then Huyton. He was Prime Minister from 1964 to 1970 and from 1974 to 1976. The Beatles met him in March 1964 at the Dorchester Hotel in Park Lane, London, when he gave them awards as the Show Business Personalities of 1963 for the Variety Club of Great Britain. John Lennon thanked him for the 'purple hearts'.

On the eve of the General Election in October 1964, Brian Epstein sent him a telegram, 'Hope your group is as much a success.' Although Wilson looked older than his years, he was the first politician to appeal to younger voters. This could be why The Beatles were awarded MBEs for their services to industry (not for music) in May 1965. If so, the politician Tony Benn saw through it, writing in his diary, 'No doubt Harold did this to be popular,' and concluding that it was 'an appalling mistake'. George referred to Wilson by name in his song, 'Taxman' (1966).

Unknowingly perhaps, Harold Wilson encouraged a wider acceptance of The Beatles by his generation.

WOOD, CHARLES [B. 1932]

Although *Help!* had a deliberately frivolous script, it was written by one of the UK's most serious playwrights, Charles Wood. He had had a lifetime of theatre, as his parents, John Wood and Mae Harris, were actors in various travelling repertory companies. He was born in St Peter Port, Guernsey, raised in Chesterfield and worked with his parents in a theatre in Kidderminster when he left school.

He served five years in the army, becoming a corporal, and the tensions of military life appear throughout his work, including the West End trilogy *Cockade* (1963) and *How I Won the War* (1967), which featured John Lennon in its cast. His most feted, and also most controversial, work was the TV play about the Falklands war, *Tumbledown* (1988), with Colin Firth.

Charles wrote the screenplay for Richard Lester's film, *The Knack … And How To Get It* (1965), which led to him being offered The Beatles' second film, *Help!* Again working with Lester, he adapted Spike Milligan's *The Bed Sitting Room* for the cinema.

His many films include *The Charge of the Light Brigade* (1968), *An Awfully Big Adventure* (1995), which was set in the Liverpool Playhouse of the fifties, and *Iris* (2001) about the senility of the novelist Iris Murdoch. His television work includes the TV series *Wagner* with Richard Burton (1983) and *My Family and Other Animals* (1987). He wrote episodes of *Sharpe* with Sean Bean, again looking at that favourite theme of an officer coming through the ranks but frowned upon by other officers because he was not a gentleman.

Wrote the screenplay for *Help!*, but given his reputation he could have written something more substantial for The Beatles.

WOOLER BOB [1926–2002]

'Like The Shadows, I am a man of mystery,' said the Cavern DJ, Bob Wooler, and certainly he was reluctant to talk about his private life. The books that have him born as Robert Wooler in 1932 are wrong. That was what Bob would have you believe. He was born Frederick James Wooler in Liverpool on 19 January 1926. He had been much older than the young musicians he had been promoting and he never wanted them to know his true age. He was brilliantly witty and would circumvent questions with his aphorisms, known to all Merseybeat musicians as 'Woolerisms'.

Bob's father died, an alcoholic, in 1930 and he feared that he would go the same way. He was raised by his mother and said of his childhood, 'School taught me the traditional three r's, and Mother taught me the other three r's – respect and the difference between right and wrong. I had an enquiring mind, but having a lot of whys does not necessarily make one wise.'

Bob was a clerk on the docks railway at Garston, but he quipped that it was not his station in life. He became interested in skiffle and rock 'n' roll, arranging appearances for The Kingstrums, Carole Crane and, in 1960, Gerry and The Pacemakers. He became, 'by accident, the only rock 'n' roll DJ on Merseyside.' A local impresario, Allan Williams, persuaded Wooler to leave his job and become a full-time DJ at his new club, the Top Ten, but it was destroyed by fire a week later.

The fledgling Beatles had been deported from Hamburg and were looking for work in Liverpool. Bob arranged a booking for £6 at Litherland Town Hall on 27 December 1960 and the promoter Brian Kelly billed them as 'Direct from Hamburg'. The bookings poured in for The Beatles and Bob introduced them all over Liverpool, starting with a few bars from 'Piltdown Rides Again' by The Piltdown Men to get attention.

The Cavern's owner, Ray McFall, was so impressed with Bob that he offered him a permanent position. Bob booked the bands for the Cavern and wrote the innovative ads that would appear in the *Liverpool Echo*.

Bob wrote a column for the *Mersey Beat* newspaper called 'The Roving I'. He gave the perform-

ers appellations – Faron was 'the panda-footed prince of prance' (surely a misprint for 'panther' but Faron stuck with the panda), Rory Storm 'Mr Showmanship' and Gerry Marsden 'Mr Personality'. He named several of the groups, including his discoveries the Merseybeats. In October 1961 he published his Top 10 groups on Merseyside with The Beatles at No. 1. Bob Wooler, who also listed the 300 beat groups on Merseyside, was prophetic when it came to The Beatles, calling them 'the stuff that screams are made of'.

The Beatles sought his advice when Brian Epstein of NEMS record store approached them for management. He attended the first meeting in December 1961 where John Lennon introduced him to Epstein as 'my dad'. (Lennon was obviously not fooled by Bob's supposed age.)

Many of the groups were impressed by the records Bob was playing during changeovers at the Cavern. Paul McCartney borrowed Chan Romero's 'Hippy Hippy Shake' for The Beatles, and it was then copied by The Swinging Blue Jeans; Gerry Marsden was entranced by his goodnight record 'I'll Be There' by Bobby Darin. John Lennon, in Bob's words, went 'from rage to riches' and the Cavern was 'the best of cellars'.

Wooler introduced the Radio Luxembourg series *Sunday Night at the Cavern*, as well as a live LP featuring Dave Berry, Beryl Marsden and Heinz and an EP, *The Big Three at the Cavern*. Always pushing the boundaries, he introduces The Big Three as 'the boys with the Benzedrine beat'. Bob compèred beat nights at other venues, notably with Jerry Lee Lewis and the Rolling Stones at the Tower Ballroom. He was featured on the Merseybeat edition of ITV's *Thank Your Lucky Stars*, but he turned down a job with NEMS Enterprises, preferring to remain in Liverpool than work for 'The Nemperor' in London. Most of all, he wanted to be a lyricist like Lorenz Hart but he only had two songs recorded – 'I Know', written with George Martin, for Billy J. Kramer with The Dakotas and 'Sidetracked' for Phil Brady and The Ranchers.

More than anything, Bob was reluctant to talk about the events at Paul McCartney's twenty-first birthday party on 18 June 1963. Bob apparently made insinuations about John's holiday with Brian Epstein in Spain. Lennon punched him, which put him in hospital and led to a modest, out of court settlement. Bob would dismiss what he read in Beatles books. 'All rubbish,' he would say. 'Only myself, John Lennon and Brian Epstein know what actually happened that night.'

Bob spoke very clearly with no trace of a Scouse accent, and he would have been an ideal DJ for the opening of the BBC's new Radio 1 station in 1967 but he showed up drunk for the audition. Also in 1967, he married Epstein's former secretary, Beryl Adams, although it only lasted three years. Gay magazines were found after his death but there are no known partners.

Bob became a DJ at the Silver Blades Ice Rink and then took work as a bingo caller, mainly to clear back taxes. He promoted Liverpool's first Beatles Convention in 1977 and his subsequent appearances at this annual event with Allan Williams were hilarious, as they would settle old scores in public. They did some joint business as W&W Promotions, and without a phone or an office they would conduct their business from a booth in the post office.

Bob Wooler became sad and disillusioned, alone in his flat and surrounded by his files. One medical condition followed another and he said, 'Ken Dodd says you have to be a comedian to live in Liverpool, so why am I so miserable?'

He was horrified by the way some Merseybeat figures would enhance stories to make themselves more important. He renamed Mathew Street as 'Mythew Street' and said, 'People take liberties with things and they think, "No one will remember, I can say what the hell I like." Well, I've got news for them all. This is my o-bitch-uary. I am coming back to haunt them. I am the ghost of Merseybeat Past.' Bob Wooler died of kidney failure on 8 February 2002. A few weeks later Allan Williams stood up in The Grapes pub, opposite the Cavern, called for attention and said, 'I have here the ultimate Beatles souvenir, Bob Wooler's ashes, what am I bid?' How Bob would have laughed.

All the Merseybeat musicians went to Bob for advice and encouragement and Bob knew how to build up excitement for The Beatles.

YOUNG, ROY [B. 1934]

At a TV audition in 1958, Roy Young pounded the piano and screamed 'Long Tall Sally' and the producer Jack Good yelled, 'You're in! You're in!' As a result, the former merchant seaman became a regular on the Saturday teatime rock 'n' roll shows *Oh Boy!* and *Drumbeat*. He was an immediate success but he found it difficult to make hit singles as record-buyers preferred the originals of 'I Go Ape and 'She Said Yeah'. He was a competent writer, writing the B-side 'Big Fat Mama' as a tribute to his mum. He coached Adam Faith and did a good job as 'What Do You Want' went to No. 1.

Roy befriended The Beatles when he went to Hamburg for a residency at the Top Ten Club. He played piano and organ in The Beat Brothers with Tony Sheridan and Ringo Starr. In 1962 he moved to the Star-Club and when Little Richard saw him, he said, 'You sound great, man, you sound like me.'

Young often worked with The Beatles on stage, and in May 1962 he and The Beatles recorded

'Sweet Georgia Brown' and 'Swanee River', and he claims that Brian Epstein invited him to join the band.

In the mid-1960s, Roy was playing keyboards for Cliff Bennett and The Rebel Rousers and can be heard on their hit single 'Got To Get You Into My Life', produced by Paul McCartney. He formed the Roy Young Band in the early 1970s but he was always available for one-off projects, such as touring with Chuck Berry or making *Low* with David Bowie. When Paul wanted Roy to give Linda some piano lessons, he had to say no because he was working in America.

Roy cut a Joe Cocker-styled 'Nowhere Man' for the *Lennon/Bermuda* project in 2013. His friend and occasional working partner Howie Casey says, 'Roy was a great singer, still is. He can still sing Little Richard's song in F and G and even Little Richard can't do that.'

The Beatles loved his energetic performances and choice of material.

The Beatles arrive at Los Angeles airport in 1965 on their second US tour
© Bill Ray / Contributor

SECTION TWO
Beatles Songs

Introduction

In the end, as in the beginning, it is the songs that matter, and it is the songs that will remain, long after the people and places and performances have faded in our minds or disappeared from the planet.

The songs have been taken apart over the years, so we now know which instruments were used, what notes were hit, what the lyrics really really meant, but as for where they came from, why they picked those notes and words instead of other words and notes, well, it's the creative process, innit. Who knows where it all comes from?

Most of the times they didn't know themselves – only that while working on each song they knew instinctively what was not working. They also knew what had been in their head. The problem and challenge then was to get it out, get it down, with a little help from their friends. Either their fellow creative friends, which usually meant John trying it out on Paul and Paul trying it on John, or their techno friends, the boys with the knobs, behind the glass panels, some of whom could actually read and write music and so could make intelligent guesses when John went 'la la la', 'bing bang, woosh woosh', and suggest instruments and effects and arrangements in order to achieve the sounds and images in their minds.

Where did it all come from, their musical ability? In the case of Paul, the most naturally music-ally talented of the four, from whom melodies endlessly flowed, he clearly inherited a gift from his father Jim. Jim had his own little jazz band at

one time, but he never did it full-time, working instead as a cotton salesman. He could play the trumpet, till his teeth went, and the piano, skills that Paul picked up without ever being taught or going to lessons – his dad told him if he played the piano he would always be invited to parties.

The McCartney family seemed to have musical parties all the time when Paul was growing up, big family gatherings in which different people took turns to entertain the rest. Very common among working-class families of the pre-war era. There was always someone able to knock out a tune on the fiddle or the piano.

The influence of old-style music hall numbers can be seen and heard in many of Paul's songs, once he had moved on through the rock 'n' roll stages – affectionate parodies of styles he had grown up with.

John also had music in the family, but not to the same extent. John's father Fred had a good voice, so everyone said, especially him, but all he ever seems to have done is entertain his shipboard friends, or himself. He never performed in public, in front of a proper audience. John's mother Julia was at a similar level – could sing for her own amusement and pleasure and strum on the banjo, but was not a performer.

George had even less music in his family. His father did learn the guitar for a while, but doesn't seem to have played it while George was growing up.

Liverpool, in British and especially Liverpool folklore, is said to be a naturally musical place, often attributed to its strong Welsh and Irish influence, two nations with a renowned musical tradition. So did that help? Who knows? Would growing up in Hamburg have made them write different sorts of songs? We can never tell.

When the skiffle mania hit the UK at the end of the fifties, encouraging young lads – for they were mostly male – who up to then had had no apparent musical ability to pick up home-made instruments and have a go, there were suddenly scores of groups on Merseyside, springing up like mushrooms overnight, far more proportionally than in any other region.

Humour, that's another element in the Scouse make-up, hence all the well-known comedians who have come from the Liverpool area. The Beatles, once they got going, definitely tried to amuse the audiences, not just in their press conferences but in their words and music.

With hindsight, you can list and tick off things that surely influenced most major creative artists, saying yes, it must have come from there, this element was due to her, oh that's obviously a pinch from howsyourfather.

What is harder to explain is how and why The Beatles developed. When they first began, they were hardly different from hundreds of other groups. And when their first records appeared, no one could really have predicted their future. Yet throughout their creative life they continued to change and develop and progress. In the sixties, when we rushed to buy each new album, we knew it would be different from what had gone before, a new experience for us and for them.

The Beatles have left behind for our delight almost two hundred songs, most of which will be hummed as long as there are people left with enough breath in their body to manage to hum a tune. What were catchy pop songs of the day have been transformed into classics.

Many of them are now seen by the present generation as traditional songs, like nursery rhymes or folk tunes, the sort that have been here for ever, with no one knowing or bothered to wonder about who actually wrote them.

The songs considered here are the ones composed and played by them as Beatles. They did produce some excellent songs in their later, individual careers, several just as memorable as their Beatles years, and they also wrote good songs for other artists to record, but we are restricting ourselves to the songs they wrote and sang as Beatles, till 1970 when The Beatles, as we knew and loved them, were no more.

The ratings and comments are purely personal – even more so than the ratings given for People, Places, TV, Movies and Radio. This is my section, so it was stuff I liked, then what we all thought was important, was significant in some way, was a new development or just a monster hit. But basically they are opinions. Feel free to scream.

They are arranged strictly alphabetically. If there was a definite or indefinite article at the beginning of a title – i.e. 'The' or 'A' – we have stuck to that. So if you want to look up 'A Day In The Life', don't look under 'D'. On the cover of *Sgt Pepper* it was clearly 'A Day In The Life', so who are we to argue.

The 185 Beatles songs considered here were written, recorded and released by The Beatles between 1962–1970.

They do not include songs recorded by them but written by other people (as on many of their early albums); songs written by them but recorded by other groups; songs they wrote and recorded later after The Beatles finished; bootleg songs; songs that were given their first airing later, such as on *Anthology*. We had to draw the line somewhere. Anyway, this is called *The Beatles Book*.

Under the heading 'Composers' we have also had to simplify, take short cuts. All Beatles songs were stated to be composed by Lennon/McCartney (apart, of course, those by George and, eh, Ringo), so that should technically make it very simple to state who the composers were. But we knew, especially as the years went on, that lots of them were not strictly joint compositions, and instead mainly the work of just one of them, with perhaps the other helping out. As a rough guide, whoever was the lead singer generally indicated who had been the original creator.

If it was indeed basically a joint composition then under 'Composers' we have put 'John and Paul', meaning John and Paul did it together; 'Mainly John' or 'Mainly Paul' indicates one had the major input; 'John' or 'Paul' named on their own means it was almost all their own work, though of course there might have been the odd line or chord contributed by others.

'Vocal' is another area that cannot always be pinned down exactly, as they did so much double-tracking, adding voices to their own, bringing in others. Lead vocal would usually mean the main singer, who was driving the song along, carrying the melody and words. But of course there could be two lead vocalists, as in 'A Day In The Life', with two songs put together, when they take turns. So we have stuck simply to 'vocal', which in essence means the lead vocalist. 'Harmony vocal' covers all the fancy stuff, like duets with one counterpointing, or in a higher or different key, complementing the melody being sung by the lead vocalist. 'Backing vocal' covers a voice that is more in the background, usually repeating the same stuff or going 'la la la'.

The dates listed under 'Released' refer to the first time the track was issued in the UK or US, either as a single or album track. 'Charts' means the highest position the single reached in the main/official UK or US charts during the period 1962–1970. Songs released/re-released after 1970 (such as 'Back In The USSR' in 1976) are not included. Once again, this is *The Beatles Book*, and focuses on the years the band was in existence. It was almost always the A-side that was most popular, but for the sake of our 'Charts' ratings, the B-side (and for tracks on an EP see 'Magical Mystery Tour') is accorded the same lofty status – which can make some of the B-sides appear more successful than they were. (Though in the US charts, for a while they rated the A- and B-sides separately – have a look at 'Love Me Do'/'P.S. I Love You' as an example.)

Right: one, two, three – let's go …

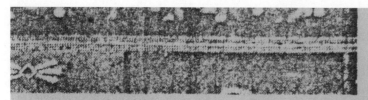

Y.M.C.A. where they gave an excellent concert. Standing is Miss Sylvia Thomas, the accompanist. — Photo by ...waite.

ENTAIL BAN

...o be closed ...is summer

...e work started on Wirral ... Valley Drainage Scheme ...has now been completed, ...be done in linking up and

... the coming months will ...inconvenience to members ...the closure to vehicles of

News from Wirral Churches

'ROCK' NIGHT IS THURSDAY

Cass and his Cassanovas, a rhythm group making a name for themselves in Neston, will be missing from the Thursday "rock" nights in the Institute for the next few weeks. They are going on tour with Billy Fury, one of the top teenage idols of the day.

In their place the teenagers—and older—of Neston and district will be able to dance to the music of the Silver Beetles. This new five-piece group has made a terrific impact on Merseyside, pulling in capacity houses wherever they appear.

North western promoter Mr. Les Dodd, of Paramount Enterprises, has satisfied a long felt need of the district by providing an evening of "rock and jazz" for the teenagers' enjoyment.

Levett, the bridegroom Miss Sandra Bell, a friends, Miss Grace Le Miss Grace Panter, w full length gowns of ap nylon chiffon and carrie of miniature pale pink pink roses and lilies-of-th

At the service, condu Mr. Charles Stokes, M best man was Mr. Norm ards, and the ushers w Tom Farrell, the hurdler, Mr. Stuart Dalgl Mr. David Glascott.

In a marquee in the gr the bride's home, her mo ceived the 100 guests. dressed in a petrel b gown and a floral hat. her was the bridegroom' who favoured a sky b sheath dress with a flora

The couple are spendi honeymoon in the Chan and to travel the bride blue floral patterned dre lace hat trimmed with rose.

Twelve tre caught fir

Twelve small trees a square yards of bushes fire off Limbo Lane, Tuesday evening. Hesw Brigade extinguished th

From Hunter Davies' archives. A copy of the first mention of them in any newspaper, given to Hunter by John in 1967. John had kept it for seven years. Shows how proud he had been at the time.

A DAY IN THE LIFE

Composers: John and Paul
Performers: John - vocal, guitar, piano; Paul - vocal, piano, bass guitar; George -congas; Ringo - drums, maracas. Plus 13 violins, 4 violas, 3 trumpets, 3 trombones, 2 double basses, 2 clarinets, 2 bassoons, 2 flutes, 2 French horns, 1 harp, 1 oboe, 1 tuba, 1 timpani
Recorded: 19, 21 January and 3, 10 February 1967, Abbey Road
Released: LP *Sgt Pepper* 1 June 1967 (UK), 2 June 1967 (US)

The final song on the *Sgt Pepper* album, 'A Day In The Life' is widely considered The Beatles' greatest ever song, the best produced, most inventive, most moving, often described as their masterpiece or pop music's version of T.S. Eliot's *The Waste Land*.

And yet it came out of two little scraps of songs, which were not connected, not related, leaving them, and George Martin, with the task of somehow fitting them together musically. In the first recording sessions, an arbitrary gap of 24 bars was left vacant, as they had not yet worked out how to join the two pieces. Mal Evans, their roadie, counted out the bars, and his voice can be heard on the finished recording.

John's contribution was the major part, writing the beginning and the end, about reading the news today, oh boy. Paul filled the sandwich in the middle, how he woke up, got out bed. Both of them, at some stage, later claimed to have first suggested the idea of an orchestral crescendo to fill the gap.

It began, as it often did, with John lying around at home, fairly aimless, reading the day's newspapers, scribbling notes, tinkling on the piano, then picking up on two stories. One was about the death of someone they knew vaguely – Tara Browne, an Irish socialite around town and member of the Guinness family, whose inquest was reported in

the *Daily Mail* on 17 January 1967. He had been driving his sports car and smashed into a parked vehicle, killing himself – possibly drugs had been involved. He was not in fact in the House of Lords but was the son of a lord. 'Tara didn't blow his mind out, but it was in my mind when I was writing that verse,' so John told me when I was writing *The Beatles*, the 1968 biography.

In the same paper was a small story, really just a filler, about there being four thousand potholes in Blackburn, Lancashire – which raises the question: who counted them? It amused John to imagine how big the holes would be, what sort of space they would take up. He had been looking for something to rhyme with 'rather small', and Terry Doran, his friend from the motor trade, suggested 'Albert Hall'.

The unfinished song that Paul came into the session with was even smaller: a memory of his school days, back in the fifties, about him getting up, combing his hair, running for the bus. Just nine lines, getting nowhere, with no narrative or development – and of course no connection with the lyrics John had written.

The references to drugs – with John singing, 'I'd love to turn you on,' and Paul having a smoke and going into a dream – resulted in the BBC banning the song.

The music has been endlessly analysed, the sliding crescendos that filled the 24-bar gap taken to pieces and the instruments identified. For the final recording the musicians – almost a complete orchestra – wore formal evening dress, with the addition of some novelty noses. The recording was captured by seven hand-held cameras. At the finale, those listening in the studio burst into applause.

The final final conclusion was a single note played at the same time on several pianos, by John, Paul, Mal, Ringo and George Martin. It was the longest track they had recorded so far, lasting 5 minutes 3 seconds.

Altogether, it took 34 hours to record. (The whole of their first LP had taken only one day.) They knew at the time, as so much thought and love and attention had gone into its creation, that 'A Day In The Life' was a big event. Which it has remained.

A handwritten manuscript of the song was first sold at auction in 1992, when it was said to have come from the estate of Mal Evans, for the record sum of $100,000. In 2010 it was resold at Sotheby's in New York for $1.2 million, which remains the highest price paid for a Beatles lyric. The phrase 'A Day In The Life' never actually appears in the lyrics.

Arguably the most cataclysmic, orgasmic, crashing, vibrating, shuddering, juddering, shattering, echoing end in the whole of popular music. Little wonder it gets played at many funerals all over the world.

A HARD DAY'S NIGHT

Composer: John
Performers: John - vocal, rhythm guitar; Paul - vocal, bass guitar; George - lead guitar; Ringo - drums, bongos
Recorded: 16 April 1964, Abbey Road
Released: LP *A Hard Day's Night* 10 July 1964 (UK), 26 June 1964 (US)
Charts: UK No. 1 released 10 July 1964, with B-side 'Things We Said Today'; US No. 1 released 13 July 1964, with B-side 'I Should Have Known Better'

The title song of the album, and title of their first film, was only agreed upon at the last moment. Until then the working titles had included 'Beatlemania', 'Let's Go' and 'On The Move'.

The usual explanation for the unusual title, handed down over the decades, is that it was a Ringo malapropism. 'It just came out,' he said in 1964, on the film's release. 'We went to do a job and we worked all day and night and I came out, thinking it was day, and I said, "It's been a hard day." I saw that it was still dark, and so I altered it to, "A hard day's night."'

However, John had used the same phrase in a little story called 'Sad Michael', which featured in Lennon's book *In His Own Write*, published in March 1964, so presumably written at least six months earlier. And in 1963 Eartha Kitt had released a single on Columbia, 'I Had A Hard Day Last Night'.

Anyway, once it was agreed, John went off and wrote the song, knowing it was to be the title of the film and the album, and he wanted to be the lead singer.

'A Hard Day's Night' has probably the most recognisable opening chord in all of The Beatles' music, possibly in all of popular music – a strident, crashing, magnificent, explosive opening of a chord. How many songs can be instantly identified by just one note? It seems a shame, and somehow dehumanising, to call it by the technical term that most musicologists have given it – G eleventh, suspended fourth.

The words are very simple, with a lot of repetition – work hard, bring the money home, and you will get marital bliss.

Maureen Cleave of the *London Evening Standard* happened to be interviewing John on the day they were about to record the song and went with him to Abbey Road in a taxi.

In the cab, John showed her the words of the song, written down on an old birthday card given to his son Julian – recently one year old – that had an illustration of a little boy on a toy train.

'I said to him that I thought one line of the song was rather feeble. It originally said, "But when I get home to you, I find my tiredness is through, then I feel all right." Seizing my pen, John immediately changed the second line of it and came up with the slightly suggestive "I find the things that you do, will make me feel all right." The recording was finished in just three hours.'

The lyrics of 'A Hard Day's Night' received a clever backhanded compliment when in 1965 Peter Sellers made a record, produced by George Martin, in which he recited all the words as if he was Laurence Olivier declaiming Shakespeare. Which was very convincing.

Not great lyrics, but a great opening chord and the title of their well-loved first film.

ACROSS THE UNIVERSE

Composer: John
Performers: John - vocal, rhythm guitar, lead guitar; Paul - backing vocal, piano; George - backing vocal, sitar, tambura; Ringo - maracas; George Martin - Hammond organ; Lizzie Bravo and Gayleen Pease - backing vocal
Recorded: 4, 8 February 1968 and 1 April 1970, Abbey Road
Released: 12 December 1969 (UK and US) on World Wildlife Fund charity LP *No One's Gonna Change Our World*; later on LP *Let It Be* 8 May 1970 (UK), 18 May 1970 (US)

They have gone down in Beatles history as the backing vocalists, but who were Lizzie Bravo and Gayleen Pease? 'Apple Scruffs', as they were affectionately known, female fans who hung around Abbey Road or Paul's house. It was on a Sunday that they were recording 'Across the Universe', hard to suddenly call up any proper singers, so they opened the Abbey Road doors and asked for volunteers. In stepped Lizzie and Gayleen and for two hours they had to sing 'Nothing's gonna change my world'. Lizzie was a 16-year-old from Brazil, given a trip to London by her parents as

a birthday present, who then stayed on to hang around the Fabs. Today she is a grandmother, singer and writer back in Brazil.

John was very pleased with the words and music of this song, which had come to him in a dream-like state while at home in Kenwood and just poured out of him – very much as he said in the lyrics. 'Words are flying out like endless rain into a paper cup'. But he was never quite pleased with the actual recording, feeling his voice and playing were not quite right, which is why he gave it to a charity record. And he never liked what Phil Spector did to it on *Let It Be*. Some musicologists have said the music is listless and the words pretentious and must have been influenced by drugs. But it is meant to be a semi-conscious stream of words and music.

One of John's most poetic songs.

ALL I'VE GOT TO DO

Composer: John
Performers: John - vocal, rhythm guitar; Paul - backing vocal, bass; George - backing vocal, lead guitar; Ringo - drums
Recorded: 11 September 1963, Abbey Road
Released: LP *With The Beatles* 22 November 1963 (UK), LP *Meet The Beatles!* 20 January 1964 (US)

A John song, i.e. written entirely by John, which was unusual at this period in their early recording career, when most of their numbers were bashed out together – at home, in hotel rooms, or on the road. In his head, in his imagination, John was trying to sound like Smokey Robinson and The Miracles, so he sings sweetly with nice melodies.

Music rather derivative and words a bit corny.

ALL MY LOVING

Composer: Paul
Performers: Paul – vocal, bass guitar; John – backing vocal, guitar; George – backing vocal, guitar; Ringo – drums
Recorded: 30 July 1963, Abbey Road
Released: LP *With The Beatles* 22 November 1963 (UK), LP *Meet The Beatles!* 20 January 1964 (US)
Charts: US No. 45 (Canadian import, with B-side 'This Boy')

A love song written by Paul – one of the best they had produced so far. The words are fairly conventional, sending all his love to someone who is away, promising he will always be true, rhyming 'kissing' with 'missing', 'you' and 'true', but it sounds sincere. It's the tune that really makes it, the first four bars being especially haunting. So it's strange that, according to Paul himself, it all began with the words and not the tune. 'It was the first song I ever wrote where I had the words before the music.' They first came to him while shaving, so he once said, later saying he then jotted the words down while on the tour bus, writing them as a poem. Normally with Paul, the tune came first; with John, he often had the words before the tune.

The girl Paul was missing was his new girlfriend Jane Asher, a 17-year-old actress from a middleclass, professional family (father doctor, mother music professor). He had first met her a few months earlier, in April 1963, at a BBC radio recording at the Albert Hall. By the end of the year he had moved into her family home as a lodger at 57 Wimpole Street, London. She became the inspiration for several of his songs, which were often written at Wimpole Street. The day of the release of their LP *With The Beatles*, 22 November 1963, was the day that President Kennedy was assassinated.

One of Paul's best love songs – and the first song they

performed in February 1964 on *The Ed Sullivan Show*, watched by 73 million Americans.

ALL TOGETHER NOW

Composer: Mainly Paul
Performers: Paul – vocal, acoustic guitar, bass; John – backing vocal, acoustic guitar, ukulele, harmonica; George – backing vocal; Ringo – drums
Recorded: 12 May 1967 Abbey Road
Released: LP *Yellow Submarine* 17 January 1969 (UK), 13 January 1969 (US)

Apart from the above instruments, most of the sound was done manually – in other words, there is a hell of a lot of clapping. Written as a simple singalong children's song, in the style of a nursery rhyme or skipping song, for their cartoon film *Yellow Submarine*. John thought it might even get sung on the football terraces. No chance. Football fans do have standards.

As easy to sing as ABC – and just as boring.

ALL YOU NEED IS LOVE

Composer: John
Performers: John – vocal, harpsichord, banjo; Paul – vocal, bass; George – vocal, violin, guitar; Ringo – drums; George Martin – piano (plus 13-part orchestra and assorted friends joining in the chorus)
Recorded: 14 June 1967, Olympic Sound Studios; 19 and 23–25 June 1967, Abbey Road
Released: single 7 July 1967 (UK), 17 July 1967 (US), with B-side 'Baby, You're A Rich Man'
Charts: UK No. 1, US No. 1

In June 1967 The Beatles were asked to contribute a song to the first ever live global television link-up, *Our World* – and John rushed off and wrote this. He knew it had to be simple words with a simple message, to be understood and enjoyed worldwide – and it still is. The tune remains seen and sung as an anthem, not just for the peace and love generation, but for all times, for all crowds, everywhere. The music is fun, with snatches of 'La Marseillaise', 'Greensleeves' and 'In The Mood' thrown in – thus amusing French, British and US audiences – but the lyrics are a bit more complicated than they first appear. 'There's nothing you can't do that can't be done.' Oh really? What exactly did John mean by that? But the message is still pretty clear.

Still a worldwide anthem - and part of the English language.

AND I LOVE HER

Composer: Paul
Performers: Paul - vocal, bass; John - acoustic rhythm guitar; George – acoustic lead guitar; Ringo – bongos, claves
Recorded: 25-27 February 1964, Abbey Road
Released: LP *A Hard Day's Night* 10 July 1964 (UK), 26 June 1964 (US)
Charts: US No. 12 single 20 July 1964, with B-side 'If I Fell'

It starts on a conjunction, 'and', which Paul thought was pretty cool. It was, for the times, but it's the beauty of the melody, the tender lyrics, plus Paul's sweet voice that does it, making it one of his best love songs. Even John praised it, saying it was Paul's first 'Yesterday'.

It was written while Paul was living with Jane Asher, and undoubtedly he had her in mind, as their romance was still going strong, but he has later said it was not about any particular girl. There are echoes of Peggy Lee's 'Till There Was You', especially the way Paul sings it. The two

guitars used were both acoustic, the first time on a Beatles number.

'And I Love Her' and 'All My Loving' (both Paul) were in many ways the first of The Beatles' classics – in the sense that almost at once, and ever since, there have been endless cover versions by other artists.

A beautiful ballad.

AND YOUR BIRD CAN SING

Composer: John
Performers: John - vocal, rhythm guitar; Paul - harmony vocal, bass; George - lead guitar, harmony vocal; Ringo - drums, tambourine
Recorded: 20, 26 April 1966, Abbey Road
Released: LP *Revolver* 5 August 1966 (UK), LP *Yesterday And Today* 20 June 1966 (US)

One of the few Beatles songs that began life with a different title – in this case 'You Don't Get Me'. Both titles do appear as lines in the song, but 'You Don't Get Me' is perhaps the more apt, as the lyrics are about someone not being understood or appreciated. Is this supposed to be Paul not getting John, or perhaps even Paul getting above himself, now that he had gone all arty, showing off that he has seen the seven wonders? Or just lack of communication generally? The chosen title makes the meaning more elliptical. What bird? Birds are supposed to sing anyway. Or was it a bird meaning a girl? It was an early attempt by John at semi-stream of consciousness lyrics.

It took two 12-hour sessions in the recording studio to get it right, but John was still not satisfied that he'd got it, whatever *it* was in his head.

Don't worry about the words - feel the mood.

ANOTHER GIRL

Composer: Paul
Performers: Paul – vocal, bass, lead guitar; John – vocal, acoustic rhythm guitar; George – harmony vocal, electric rhythm guitar; Ringo – drums
Recorded: 15–16 February 1965, Abbey Road
Released: LP *Help!* 6 August 1965 (UK), 13 August 1965 (US)

Paul wrote this on holiday in Tunisia. On the surface he is rather cruelly telling someone – Jane, so we all presumed – that he has got another girl; an unusual topic for a pop song of the times. When they were about boy-girl-love, which they mainly were, they were usually about moon and June and the wonders of love, or sometimes the miseries, but not often about one partner deliberately chucking the other. Paul does make it pretty clear – and it turned out to be true. But the tone of the tune, and the words, veer between wistful and jaunty.

Stark sentiments, rockabilly beat.

ANY TIME AT ALL

Composer: John
Performers: John – vocal, acoustic rhythm guitar; Paul – harmony vocal, bass, piano; George – lead guitar; Ringo – drums
Recorded: 2 June 1964, Abbey Road
Released: LP *A Hard Day's Night* 10 July 1964 (UK), 20 July 1964 (US)

John later admitted that with 'Any Time At All' he had been pinching stuff from himself – which surely is allowed – by recycling some of the chords and harmonies he had used earlier in 'It Won't Be Long'. Even if he did, the song bursts with energy, fitting perfectly into *A Hard Day's Night*.

Great drumming from Ringo.

ASK ME WHY

Composer: Mainly John
Performers: John – vocal, rhythm guitar; Paul – backing vocal, bass; George – lead guitar; Ringo – drums
Recorded: 6 June and 26 November 1962, Abbey Road
Released: single 11 January 1963 (UK), 25 February 1963 (US), with A-side 'Please Please Me'
Charts: UK No. 2

A very early song, one of the three own compositions they played to George Martin at their first recording session with him. (George preferred 'Love Me Do' for their debut.) Simple, corny words – how he loves her, there is a bit of crying, but he will never be blue again – but the tune rips along with some clever, complicated chords with jazz overtones.

Great to dance to.

BABY'S IN BLACK

Composers: John and Paul
Performers: John – vocal, acoustic rhythm guitar; Paul – vocal, bass; George – lead guitar; Ringo – drums
Recorded: 11 August 1964, Abbey Road
Released: LP *Beatles For Sale* 4 December 1964 (UK), LP *Beatles '65* 15 December 1964 (US)

Knocked out together in a hotel bedroom, just as they used to in their very early days, probably as a bit of a lark, thinking of nursery rhythms such as 'Oh Dear, What Can The Matter Be', which gave them their first line 'Oh dear, what can I do?'. But then it gets dark. Complicated theme, with some clumsy lyrics – his baby is in black, and he is feeling blue.

Bit of a dirge.

BABY, YOU'RE A RICH MAN

Composers: John and Paul
Performers: John – vocal, keyboard; Paul – harmony vocal, bass, piano; George – harmony vocal, guitar; Ringo – tambourine, maracas (plus Eddie Kramer – vibraphone)
Recorded: 11 May 1967, Olympic Sound Studios
Released: single 7 July 1967 (UK), 17 July 1967 (US), with A-side 'All You Need Is Love'
Charts: UK No. 1, US No. 34 as an individual track (No. 1 as B-side of 'All You Need Is Love')

Composed by John and Paul, but not together. Like 'A Day In The Life', it was originally two separate songs, with neither properly finished, which then got shoved together in the studio. 'The beautiful people' part of the lyrics, which begins the song, was written by John and appears to be mocking the Californian hippies – but they loved the song, so it could have been a double bluff. The 'rich man' part, contributed by Paul, was supposedly a dig at Brian Epstein, who had made a lot of money out of The Beatles. But then so had they.

Good marks for experimentation – but a bit of a mess.

BACK IN THE USSR

Composer: Paul
Performers: Paul – vocal, acoustic guitar; John – backing vocal, lead guitar, bass, drums; George – backing vocal, bass, drums (no Ringo – he had quit during the first session, for a few days)
Recorded: 22–23 August 1968, Abbey Road
Released: LP *The Beatles* 22 November 1968 (UK), 25 November 1968 (US)

A good joke, in words and lyrics, to ape a very American-type rocker. Instead of being back in the USA, which is what Chuck Berry had sung about in 1959, it's back in the USSR; a twist that might be hard to get for future generations, unless the USSR comes back into being. Paul at his wittiest and also loudest, building up a good wall of sound, and excitement, with jet engines in the background and Beach Boys-style falsettos. Not many Russians would have heard the record at the time – The Beatles were not officially approved by the communist government and their records were hard to obtain. Paul sings that, 'man, I had a dreadful flight'. Will that mean that, unlike John, he will never get an airport named after him?

Great fun, great sound.

BECAUSE

Composer: John
Performers: John – vocal, lead guitar; Paul – vocal, bass; George – vocal, Moog synthesiser; George Martin – electric spinet
Recorded: 1,4, 5 August 1969, Abbey Road
Released: LP *Abbey Road* 26 September 1969 (UK), 1 October 1969 (US)

The inspiration for the tune, so John told us later, began with Yoko playing a Beethoven sonata on the piano and John telling her to now play the chords backwards. Did he really? Or was that a joke, thought up later? Well Yoko did play the piano and it sounds the sort of thing John might well have said.

The visual image it still conjures up, and trying to work it out, can rather distract from the pleasure of simply sitting down and listening to this excellent piece of music making. The lyrics are sparse, just six lines, and of course awfully meaningful in a druggie way. 'Because the world is round it turns me on.' But the harmonies are beautifully done, complex yet complete. George

Harrison always said it was his favourite tune on the whole *Abbey Road* album.

Stunning harmonies.

BEING FOR THE BENEFIT OF MR KITE!

Composer: John
Performers: John – vocal, Hammond organ; Paul – guitar; George – harmonica; Ringo – drums, tambourine, harmonica; George Martin – harmonium; Mal Evans and Neil Aspinall – harmonicas (plus loads of sound effects)
Recorded: 17, 20 February and 28, 29, 31 March 1967, Abbey Road
Released: LP *Sgt Pepper* 1 June 1967 (UK), 2 June 1967 (US)

The lyrics are what are known as 'found' lyrics, meaning they were just lying there, waiting to be picked up and put to music – though in this case they were lying on an old Victorian circus poster that John had bought. He took almost everything, word for word, from the poster – changing only odd bits to fit in, or because he wasn't sure how to pronounce them. On the poster, the horse was called Zanthus, but it got changed to Henry. The original venue for the concert, as on the poster, was Rochdale. That became Bishopsgate – presumably because he was able to rhyme it with 'don't be late'.

The music must have set George Martin a right headache when they started off, with John demanding a fairground production, where he could smell the sawdust. And that's what they produced, a swirling, twirling, organ grinding, kaleidoscope of noises. In sticking to the names and some archaic Victorian phrases, John also set himself some tongue twisters, but he enunciates everything perfectly clearly.

Wonderful fun.

BIRTHDAY

Composer: Paul
Performers: Paul – vocal, piano; John – vocal, lead guitar; George – 6-string bass; Ringo – drums, tambourine; Pattie Harrison, Yoko Ono – backing vocal
Recorded: 18 September 1968 Abbey Road
Released: LP *The Beatles* 22 November 1968 (UK), 25 November 1968 (US)

Let's do a song celebrating someone's birthday, said Paul, so they did, and this was the result. Not much else to say really, except they knocked it off quickly, making up the words as they went along, and appear to have enjoyed themselves. So that's all right, then. For them anyway. Not much fun for us, though, listening to it again today.

John thought it was garbage.

BLACKBIRD

Composer: Paul
Performer: Paul – vocal, acoustic guitar
Recorded: 11 June 1968, Abbey Road
Released: LP *The Beatles* 22 November 1968 (UK), 25 November 1968 (US)

Written and played by Paul, done on his own in the studio, recorded and finished off with a blackbird singing, taken from the Abbey Road sound archives – all in six hours. A perfect piece, a spontaneous act of creation that came to him from, well, who knows where. He has said later that he was thinking of the struggles for freedom of black American slaves, who were once known as blackbirds, but this could be with the use of hindsight. Anyway it is clearly about more than a blackbird singing; it's about people generally, wanting to be free. Paul called his 2002 book of poems *Blackbird Singing*, which suggests he was quite proud of the lyrics.

Paul's playing has also been much admired. Folk singer Richard Digance has written that 'Blackbird' was one of his party pieces. 'If there are any guitarists reading this who have tried "Blackbird" and don't know how to do it, I'll let you in on the secret. It's impossible to play with conventional tuning and Paul McCartney tunes his guitar in a different way. You drop the two E-strings down a tone to D and use the second and fourth strings and suddenly "Blackbird" takes shape. It's a well-structured song, but if you don't know that, you won't be able to play it.'

A little masterpiece.

BLUE JAY WAY

Composer: George
Performers: George – vocal, Hammond organ; Paul – backing vocal, bass; John – backing vocal; Ringo – drums, tambourine
Recorded: 6, 7 September and 6 October 1967, Abbey Road
Released: EP *Magical Mystery Tour* 8 December 1967 (UK), LP *Magical Mystery Tour* 27 November 1967 (US)
Charts: UK No. 2

George was sitting in Los Angeles, waiting for his friend Derek Taylor – a friend of all the band. Derek was lost in fog and traffic, so George amused himself by sitting at a Hammond organ – and finished the song in just two hours, writing down the words based on what was actually happening. Some have tried to read more into the words than is there – saying that 'don't be long' should really be 'don't belong', i.e. opt out, and

that 'lost their way' refers not just to Derek but a whole generation. The music is a bit of a drone, and doesn't get very far, but it is haunting.

A bit foggy.

CAN'T BUY ME LOVE

Composer: Paul
Performers: Paul – vocal, bass; John – acoustic rhythm guitar; George – lead guitar; Ringo – drums
Recorded: 29 January 1964, EMI Pathé Marconi, Paris, then 25 February and 10 March 1964 Abbey Road
Released: single 20 March 1964 (UK), 16 March 1964 (US), with B-side 'You Can't Do That'
Charts: UK No. 1, US No.1

Written by Paul on a piano in a hotel room in Paris, just after they had heard that 'I Want To Hold Your Hand' had become No. 1 in the US. And then sung by him, in a Paris recording studio, then back in London. A change from composing together, eyeball-to-eyeball, as they had mostly done till then. The song was also unusual in that Paul does all the singing, with no backing or harmony vocals from the others.

A monster hit, all round the world, so exciting and energetic, so no need to worry too much about the simplistic lyrics. Money can't buy me love? Gee, we never thought of that.

Global hit.

CARRY THAT WEIGHT

Composer: Paul
Performers: Paul – vocal, piano, rhythm guitar; George – vocal, lead guitar; John – vocal; Ringo – drums, vocal (plus 12 violins)

Recorded: 2–4, 30, 31 July and 15 August 1969, Abbey Road
Released: LP *Abbey Road* 26 September 1969 (UK)
1 October (US)

This was part of the long medley of short pieces that made up the second half of the second side of *Abbey Road*. They were unfinished, hardly worked on, half realised scraps that got melded together, running into each other, with the odd reprise, to fill up the end of the album. The 'weight' that Paul was finding hard to carry was presumably the weight of Apple, all the money rows and arguments with John. Perhaps he was also suffering from the weight of being The Beatles, after seven years of recording. *Abbey Road* was the last album they recorded (though *Let It Be* was released later) It's interesting to wonder if they had carried on, as chums and colleagues, and if they had made more albums, whether they would have worked harder and longer on these unfinished songs.

Nice idea, shame it was never finished.

COME TOGETHER

Composer: John
Performers: John – vocal, lead guitar; Paul – harmony vocal, bass, electric piano; George – guitar; Ringo – drums, maracas
Recorded: 21–23, 25, 29, 20 July 1969, Abbey Road
Released: LP *Abbey Road* 26 September 1969 (UK) 1 October 1969 (US)
Charts: UK No. 4, US No. 1, released 31 October 1969 (UK), 6 October 1969 (US), with double A-side 'Something' (US charts stopped listing B-sides/double A-sides separately in November 1969)

It began as a campaign song, to help Timothy Leary, who had used that phrase when he was going to run as Governor of California, then later John knocked it into shape in the studio, making it the first track on *Abbey Road*. 'Knocking into shape' meant mucking around with it, adding names and lists and gobbledygook generally. John later got into legal trouble for having lifted a couple of lines about 'old flat top' from Chuck Berry's 'You Can't Catch Me', but this was resolved when John agreed to record some Chuck Berry numbers on his later *Rock 'N' Roll* album.

The basic message of 'Come Together' was 'you got to be free,' which was taken up by all the hippies and similar of the time, especially in America. It has a good, insistent, pounding beat, not quite a marching song, or a shouting-out-loud song, more of a druggie mumbling song, which is why they all loved it so much.

Right on, man.

CRY BABY CRY

Composer: John
Performers: John – vocal, acoustic guitar, piano, organ; Paul – bass; George – lead guitar; Ringo – drums, tambourine; George Martin – harmonium
Recorded: 15, 16, 18 July 1968, Abbey Road
Released: LP *The Beatles* 22 November 1968 (UK), 25 November 1968 (US)

John took the title from a TV advert he had been watching – for years he did little else during the day but sit and stare, with the TV on in the background – which had the line 'cry baby cry, make your mother buy'. It was just a scrap of an idea and a rhythm that he then worked on when they were in India, at Rishikesh. The finished lyrics, with references to nursery rhymes, and the atmospheric music, make it a rather haunting and disturbing song.

Unsettling.

DAY TRIPPER

Composer: John
Performers: John – vocal, lead guitar; Paul – vocal, bass; George – lead guitar; Ringo – drums, tambourine
Recorded: 16 October 1965, Abbey Road
Released: single 3 December 1965 (UK), 6 December 1965 (US), with double A-side 'We Can Work It Out'
Charts: UK No. 1, US No. 5 as an individual track (No. 1 as double A-side of 'We Can Work It Out')

It was mainly John's song, as he had come up with the lyrics and the basic guitar rhythm, and wanted it to be the A-side of the forthcoming single, but Paul preferred the other side, 'We Can Work It Out'. So they decided each would be an A-side – a splitting of hairs, hard to believe that such things mattered, but it meant the record company could boast it was the first ever double A-side single.

The lyrics are clearly drug-related, as even then we all knew what taking a trip meant. John was mocking those hippies who turn up and turn on at weekends, then go back to their boring day jobs – day trippers. The girl in question was originally a prick teaser, but became a 'big teaser', in order not to annoy or upset the nation's sensitivities. (Though they did use the word 'prick ' in some stage performances.) It begins with one of the longest and most recognisable guitar riffs, before you hear Paul singing 'Got a good reason'.

Lots of reasons.

DEAR PRUDENCE

Composer: John
Performers: John – vocal, guitar; Paul – backing vocal, drums, piano; George – backing vocal, lead guitar
Recorded: 28–30 August 1968, Trident Studios
Released: LP *The Beatles* 22 November 1968 (UK), 25 November 1968 (US)

John wrote this song in India, while with the Maharishi, worried that one of the other residents, Prudence Farrow, sister of Mia, was getting a bit too carried away with all the meditating, perhaps even going a bit potty, so he wanted her to relax, come out and play. It's a gentle, soothing, lyrical song, sung beautifully by John, showing that he could do the soft stuff. No Ringo (he hadn't yet returned after quitting on 22 August), so Paul dusted the skins.

Donovan, who was with them in India, has claimed he was involved with two songs in particular. 'I showed John Lennon the finger-styled guitar playing that I had learned from the folk scene: it comes from the Carter Family and it is called clawhammer. When anybody learns a new style, they write differently and he wrote "Julia" and "Dear Prudence" from this. My influence is obvious on "Dear Prudence". Paul would not sit down and learn it like a good boy but would peer over our shoulders and pick up little bits as shown in "Blackbird". He was like a sponge and absorbed things by listening.'

Beautiful song.

DIG A PONY

Composer: John
Performers: John – vocal, lead guitar; Paul – harmony vocal, bass; George – lead guitar; Ringo – drums
Recorded: 22, 24, 28, 30 January 1969, Apple Studios
Released: LP *Let It Be* 8 May 1970 (UK), 18 May 1970 (US)

The reason for the long delay between the recording and the release was because of all the faffing around, bad temper and arguments that became a feature of the *Let It Be* sessions. 'Dig A Pony', and in fact most of the words, don't mean nothing, just words and sounds, made up as they went along, which John admitted was garbage, except for one line addressed to Yoko, 'all I want is you'. The song was one of those they performed live on the rooftop at the Apple office in Savile Row on 30 January 1969; though not quite always in tune with the music, it is clear they are enjoying themselves – and for once, in tune with each other.

More fun to watch than listen to.

DIG IT

Composer: John and Paul
Performers: John – vocal; Paul – piano; George – lead guitar; Ringo – drums; Billy Preston – Hammond organ
Recorded: 24, 26 January 1969, Apple Studios
Released: LP *Let It Be* 8 May 1970 (UK), 18 May 1970 (US)

Hardly a composition, as such, more of an improvised jam session, with random words shouted out, ranging from 'CIA', still with us, to 'Matt Busby', now gone, but once the manager of Manchester United (a football club).

Mercifully short – just 50 seconds.

DO YOU WANT TO KNOW A SECRET

Composer: John
Performers: George – vocal, lead guitar; John – backing vocal, rhythm guitar; Paul – backing vocal, bass; Ringo – drums
Recorded: 11 February 1963, Abbey Road
Released: LP *Please Please Me* 22 March 1963 (UK), LP *Introducing … The Beatles* originally scheduled 22 July 1963, actual 10 January 1964 (US)
Charts: US No. 2 released 23 March 1964, with B-side 'Thank You Girl'

John wrote it and then gave it to George, saying that it suited George's voice. 'It only had three notes,' said John, 'and he wasn't the best singer in the world.' The sort of jocular but snide remark that deeply hurt George.

The catch line came from a song from Walt Disney's *Snow White* – 'wanna know a secret' – that John's mother used to sing. Billy J. Kramer with The Dakotas did it as a single – the first cover version of a Beatles song to become a hit – but it was always a rather thin, tinkly song with poor lyrics, recorded in a hurry. George makes a slight mistake by singing, 'I've known a secret for the week or two,' instead of 'a week or two'. But no one noticed.

There wasn't one.

DOCTOR ROBERT

Composer: John
Performers: John – vocal, rhythm guitar, harmonium; Paul – harmony vocal, bass; George – lead guitar, maracas; Ringo – drums
Recorded: 17, 19 April 1966, Abbey Road
Released: LP *Revolver* 5 August 1966 (UK), LP *Yesterday And Today* 20 June 1966 (US)

Unusual for a pop song to be about a doctor, and one who supplied drugs. He has been identified by some as a well-known New York doctor of the day – but John also said it was about himself, as he supplied drugs to the others. Others have suggested the Robert could have referred to Robert Dylan. Neat harmonies, coming down the scales.

Novelty but nice.

REVOLVER

Reviews of songs on *Revolver*, *New Musical Express*, 29 July 1966 by Allen Evans

'Yellow Submarine': 'Straightforward tune which should become a nursery or college or public house singalong classic like "Green Grow The Rushes" or "Ilkley Moor". It should be a household favourite soon. Words are crazy, like in John's poetry.'

'Dr Robert': 'John Lennon's tribute to the medical profession about a doctor who does well for everyone. Straightforward beat song.'

DON'T BOTHER ME

Composer: George
Performers: George – lead guitar, vocal; John – rhythm guitar, tambourine; Paul – bass, claves; Ringo – drums, bongos
Recorded: 11, 12 September 1963, Abbey Road
Released: LP *With The Beatles* 22 November 1963 (UK), LP *Meet The Beatles!* 20 January 1964 (US)

George's first song, with his own words and music, written while he was feeling a bit poorly at the Palace Court Hotel in Bournemouth, where they were doing six performances at the local Gaumont Cinema. It was in the hotel that Robert Freeman took the black and white photograph for the album cover of *With The Beatles,* with half their faces in shadow.

Most fans at the time probably did not spot it was a George composition, assuming it was another Lennon/McCartney number, though PR Tony Barrow made it clear on the sleeve notes. '… the disc debut of George Harrison as a composer. It is a fairly fast number with a haunting theme tune. Behind George's double-tracked voice the rest of the fabulous foursome create some unusual instrumental effects. Paul beats out a lean, hollow-boned rhythm from the claves, John uses a tambourine and Ringo hits out at a loose-skinned Arabian bongo (don't ask me where he picked that up!) to pound out the on-beat percussive drive.'

As for the lyrics, they are very George – suggesting, even at this early stage in their career, that he was becoming fed up with being a Beatle, though he half turns it into a love song about a girl who has left him. But mainly the theme is don't bother me, which according to *Mersey Beat* editor Bill Harry was a phrase he often used to Bill Harry, when he was bothering him.

George later rubbished the song, telling me in 1967 that it was, 'a fairly crappy song – I forgot about it completely once it was on the album.' He didn't get round to writing another for two years – but he had proved to himself that he could do it. So well done George.

George's debut.

DON'T LET ME DOWN

Composer: John
Performers: John – vocal, rhythm guitar; Paul – harmony vocal, bass; George – lead guitar; Ringo – drums; Billy Preston – electric piano.
Recorded: 22, 24, 27–30 January, 1969, Apple Studios
Released: single 11 April 1969 (UK), 5 May 1969 (US), with A-side 'Get Back'
Charts: UK No. 1, US No. 35 as an individual track (No. 1 as B-side of 'Get Back')

John could appear at times tough, aloof, arrogant, detached, yet he was just as needy as most of us, worried that people might let him down, as his parents did all those years ago. In this case he is worried about Yoko, whom he was about to marry. Would she in some way let him down, when he loves her so much, would it be a love that lasts for ever, a love that has no past? Strong, sincere, heartfelt emotions and he sings it with feeling, no nonsense, no tricks, no electronic wizardry, except perhaps a trace of echo on John's voice.

This is John.

DON'T PASS ME BY

Composer: Ringo
Performers: Ringo – vocal, drums, sleigh bells, piano; Paul – piano, bass; Jack Fallon – violin
Recorded: 5, 6 June and 12, 22 July 1968, Abbey Road
Released: LP *The Beatles* 22 November 1968 (UK) 25 November 1968 (US)

Ringo made it at last, with his first composition on a Beatles album. He had been trying to persuade them to record it since he had written the song some four years earlier, but they always seemed to have a reason why not to include it – the main one being, presumably, they thought it was pretty rubbish. But now with a double white album to fill, they finally agreed. The words are pretty dire – 'you were in a car crash and you lost your hair' – but worth listening to for Ringo's Liverpool accent on the word 'hair'. The music is in fact pretty catchy – sort of country and western, bluegrass, fairground barrel organ – and trundles merrily along with a very nice bit of fiddling from Jack Fallon.

Hello Ringo.

DRIVE MY CAR

Composer: Mainly Paul
Performers: Paul – vocal, piano, lead guitar; John – vocal; George – harmony vocal, bass; Ringo – drums, cowbell, tambourine
Recorded: 13 October 1965 Abbey Road
Released: LP *Rubber Soul* 3 December 1966 (UK), LP *Yesterday And Today* 20 June 1966 (US)

Cracking start to the *Rubber Soul* album, driving off with lots of energy and speed and beep beeps. Don't worry too much about what it all means. It could be sexual, wanting to drive some girl who is besotted by fame, or be driven by her, nudge nudge, but then it turns out she is in the driving seat, having sport with him, the little minx. And in the end she hasn't got a car anyway. All nice fun, which goes at a lick.

Good sport.

EIGHT DAYS A WEEK

Composers: Paul and John
Performers: John – vocal, acoustic guitar; Paul – vocal, bass; George – vocal, lead guitar; Ringo – drums
Recorded: 6, 18 October 1964, Abbey Road
Released: LP *Beatles For Sale* 4 December 1964 (UK), single 15 February 1965 (US), with B-side 'I Don't Want To Spoil The Party'
Charts: US No. 1

On the way to John's house for a writing session, Paul's driver came out with the remark. 'Busy? I've been working eight days a week.' Paul had never heard the phrase before, which is surprising, and told John. Together they knocked out a jolly song. Got to No. 1 in the States.

Jolly, upbeat refrain.

ELEANOR RIGBY

Composer: Paul
Performers: Paul – vocal; John – harmony vocal; George – harmony vocal (plus four violins, two violas, two cellos)
Recorded: 28, 29 April and 6 June 1966, Abbey Road
Released: LP *Revolver* 5 August 1966 (UK), 8 August 1966 (US)
Charts: UK No. 1 released 5 August 1966, US No. 11 as an individual track (No. 2 with double A-side 'Yellow Submarine', released 8 August 1966)

One of the most analysed, enjoyed and admired of all The Beatles' songs. Novelist Antonia Byatt said it has 'the minimalist perfection of a Beckett story.' Yet who knows where it all came from? There was no Eleanor Rigby – despite a grave with the same name being found in Liverpool many years later. Paul's original name was Daisy Hawkins, but he changed her surname to Rigby, after a shop in Bristol, and Eleanor after the actress Eleanor Bron. The tune and the image of a woman sweeping up the rice in a church where a wedding had been just appeared in Paul's head, without knowing who she was or why she was there, and he only had one verse when he arrived at John's house. Other people who were there added bits – such as Pete Shotton, John's old school friend, who claims he suggested that the two people in the song, the other being Father McKenzie (originally Father McCartney) should somehow come together at the end.

The lyrics form a narrative, about a named person, which was most unusual, and contain one of the best images in all popular music – 'wearing the face that she keeps in a jar by the door'. Paul sings it beautifully, practically on his own, apart from a string octet.

Perfect ten.

EVERYBODY'S GOT SOMETHING TO HIDE EXCEPT ME AND MY MONKEY

Composer: John
Performers: John – vocal, guitar; Paul – backing vocal, bass; George – backing vocal, lead guitar; Ringo – drums
Recorded: 27 June and 1, 23 July 1968, Abbey Road
Released: LP *The Beatles* 22 November 1968 (UK), 25 November 1968 (US)

A loud, shouty 'Come On, Come On' rocker with the longest title of any Beatles song. What does it all mean? Whatever you want it to, or the opposite, for your inside is out, the outside is in. The monkey, so it would appear, was Yoko, as people were not being kind to her and only she and John knew what was going in the world. Or monkey could have been a drugs reference. Having got the title, John then resorted to making up the words, loudly.

Come on, come on, don't think about the words.

EVERY LITTLE THING

Composer: Paul
Performers: John – vocal, acoustic rhythm guitar; Paul – harmony vocal, bass, piano; George – lead guitar; Ringo – drums
Recorded: 29, 30 September 1964, Abbey Road
Released: LP *Beatles For Sale* 4 December 1964 (UK), *Beatles VI* 14 June 1965 (US)

Usually, whoever is the lead singer gives a clue to who wrote it. In this case John is the lead singer but the original creator was Paul, writing it while still living with and loving Jane, though Paul and John then worked on it and shaped it together. It is very emotional, very loving, if a bit soppy, though today we might not praise a woman for doing everything for the man.

Heartfelt, but a bit of a dirge.

FIXING A HOLE

Composer: Paul
Performers: Paul – vocal, lead guitar; John – backing vocal; George – harpsichord; Ringo – drums
Recorded: 9 February 1967, Regent Sound Studio, 21 February 1967, Abbey Road
Released: LP *Sgt Pepper* 1 June 1967 (UK), 2 June 1967 (US)

Was it a real hole or a metaphorical one? Any road up, the metaphors are well done, well worked out, and can apply to the tired mind being fixed up with a spot of pot or to fixing a dodgy roof where the rain lets in – or just painting a dreary room in a colourful way to cheer yourself up. All very clever. As is the idea of a wandering mind – which of course could be heard as 'wondering', which applies just as well.

Record producer Stuart Colman is a big fan. 'I love "Fixing A Hole" because of the bass and the harpsichord lines which open it up. The juice between one instrument and another can only happen in a situation like that. If you cut and pasted it on an Apple Mac you wouldn't get anything like that. There is magic that will always be in that record. It has lost none of that charm.'

Clever stuff.

FLYING

Composers: George, Paul, John and Ringo
Performers: John – vocal, organ, mellotron; Paul – vocal, bass; George – vocal, guitar; Ringo – vocal, drums, maracas
Recorded: 8, 28 September 1967, Abbey Road

Released: EP *Magical Mystery Tour* 8 December 1967 (UK), LP *Magical Mystery Tour* 27 November 1967 (US)
Charts: UK No. 2

Not a song, as strictly speaking a song has to have lyrics, more than just la la la, but an instrumental number intended for the soundtrack of *Magical Mystery Tour* to give the impression of being up in the clouds, flying along, gently wafting us all away, away. Quite hypnotic, in small doses. You could be having a massage in a very upmarket spa. The only Beatles composition credited equally to all four of The Beatles. Saved them arguing about the royalties.

Sleepy times.

FOR NO ONE

Composer: Paul
Performers: Paul – vocal, bass, clavichord; Ringo – drums; Alan Civil – horn
Recorded: 9, 16, 19 May 1966, Abbey Road
Released: LP *Revolver* 5 August 1966 (UK), 8 August 1966 (US)

Classic Paul, beautifully sung and played, with the help of a haunting horn, and meticulously worked out words. He wrote it while with Jane on holiday in Switzerland, but it clearly suggests they were having words, if not downright arguments. The original working title, 'Why Did It Die', gives away the reality and sadness of what was happening between them – or between any couple when things are going wrong. Interesting that it is written in the third person – with Paul perhaps wanting to distance himself from whatever had been the problem.

Perfect Paul.

FOR YOU BLUE

Composer: George
Performers: George – vocal, acoustic guitar; Paul – piano; John – slide guitar; Ringo – drums
Recorded: 25 January 1969, Apple Studios; 8 January 1970, Olympic Sound Studios
Released: LP *Let It Be* 8 May 1970 (UK), 18 May 1970 (US)
Charts: US No. 1 released 11 May 1970, with A-side 'The Long And Winding Road' (US charts stopped listing B-sides separately in November 1969)

In the manuscript version, George titled it 'For You Blues', but then the final 's' got lost, perhaps to create an internal rhythm, or because it didn't quite turn out a blues number, more of a honky-tonk bar number, which was what he wanted it to sound like, a thrown-off, one-take (although the vocals were re-recorded in January 1970) amusement by some amateur musicians. It is surprisingly upbeat and jolly and simple for George, but there is little development in the words, apart from saying how sweet and lovely his girl is – which we all presumed to mean Pattie.

Simple, catchy.

FROM ME TO YOU

Composers: John and Paul
Performers: John – vocal, rhythm guitar, harmonica; Paul – vocal, bass; George – lead guitar, harmony vocal; Ringo – drums
Recorded: 5 March 1963, Abbey Road
Released: single 11 April 1963 (UK), 27 May 1963 (US), with B-side 'Thank You Girl'
Charts: UK No. 1, US No. 41 as individual track when re-released on 30 January 1964, with A-side 'Please Please Me' (and No. 3 as B-side of 'Please Please Me')

Written in February 1963, while on their first national tour, with Helen Shapiro, a truly joint composition, the inspiration being the letters page of the *New Musical Express*, which was called 'From You To Us'. One of their early No. 1 successes, which stayed at the top for many weeks. It confirmed in the public and record buying minds that yes, this new group did have something different, and possibly, maybe, they might be here to stay, well for some time. Again, John delights us with his harmonica.

Confirmation they could be fab.

GET BACK

Composer: Paul
Performers: Paul – vocal, bass; John – harmony vocal, lead guitar; George – rhythm guitar; Ringo – drums; Billy Preston – electric piano
Recorded: 23, 24, 27–30 January 1969, Apple Studios
Released: single 11 April 1969 (UK), 5 May 1969 (US), with B-side 'Don't Let Me Down'
Charts: UK No. 1, US No. 1

Simple rocking song, started by Paul and then helped out by John, which belts along nicely, but the words have led to complicated interpretations. Was Paul staring at Yoko as he sang it in the studio, fed up with her presence? Or did it all begin with various anti-immigration speeches, such as one by Enoch Powell, which had been in the news? In the end, the lyrics are fairly nonsensical, about Jo Jo, a man who thought he was a loner, and Sweet Loretta who thought she was a woman. Exciting foot-tapping stuff though, a big hit all round the world, just like the old days.

Got back to where they belonged.

HOW THE SONGS WERE WRITTEN

If only John and Paul had carried paper and pen with them all the time, how many more songs were there fluttering around their brains that never got pinned down? At vital, creative moments, they were so often searching for any old scrap of paper on which to jot down their latest gems or germs of ideas before they disappeared – backs of envelopes, old birthday cards, flyers, hotel notepaper, airline notepaper, bills and backs of letters. Fortunately, they managed to find a suitable scrap when it came to writing down a first manuscript version of the following.

A HARD DAY'S NIGHT

Written by John on the back of a birthday card given to Julian, his son, on his first birthday. It shows a little boy driving a little toy steam engine. The card was given to the journalist Maureen Cleave, who had suggested that he re-write one of the lines as it was a bit limp. The manuscript is now in the Manuscript Room of the British Library in London.

I'M ONLY SLEEPING

John scribbled the lyrics on the nearest scrap he could find – which was a bill from the Post Office in April 1966 telling him he owed them twelve pounds and three shillings. He gave it to Pete Shotton, his best friend and PA, to pay it – and Pete found it many years later, crumpled up in the pocket of an old suit.

WHAT YOU'RE DOING

Many songs in their early years were written down while on tour, in the back of the van, in coaches going around the UK and later on planes, while touring the globe. This one was written by Paul on hotel notepaper while staying at the Lafayette Motor Inn in Atlantic City in December 1964.

FOOL ON THE HILL

Notepaper from The Hotel Negresco in Nice was the lucky recipient of Paul's first attempts at the words of 'Fool On The Hill' in 1967

BECAUSE

Paul used the back of a legal letter from Eastman and Eastman that concerned more rows relating to Apple and Allen Klein – writing down the words of 'Because'. Because it was handy.

STRAWBERRY FIELDS FOREVER

John used some airline notepaper while on a Lufthansa flight in January 1967 to scribble the first few verses of 'Strawberry Fields Forever' – though in this early version there is no reference to Strawberry Fields (or Field).

IT'S GETTING BETTER

Paul used a flyer for a rave being held at the Roundhouse in London in 1967 to scribble down some of the words.

GOOD DAY SUNSHINE

John had been sent a fan letter from an American fan – and had left the envelope lying round. It proved handy when Paul wanted to write down the words for 'Good Day Sunshine', which came to him in 1966 one sunny day, while sitting around at John's house, waiting for John to get up and start work.

HERE, THERE AND EVERYWHERE

Brian Epstein had sent his boys a lengthy typewritten list of their engagements for 1966. Paul turned it over and jotted down the words of 'Here, There And Everywhere'. Perhaps the title and theme was inspired by all the places they were about to travel across the globe?

I'M DOWN

Paul was stuck for paper, while sitting around in Brian's office, and so used the back of a typed letter from a US radio station to Wendy Hanson, on 3 June 1965. He only scribbled the first four lines of the lyrics – but enough to pin them down.

YOU'VE GOT TO HIDE YOUR LOVE AWAY

John was in his Rolls-Royce, being driven by his chauffeur Anthony, in August 1965, when he needed desperately to write down the words in his head. The only paper Anthony could find was his own diary. He handed it to John opened on a blank page, which happened to be the W page.

BLUE JAY WAY

George also, when stuck, used anything handy; in this case, while in LA waiting for his friend Derek Taylor to arrive, he picked up a piece of headed notepaper belonging to 'Robert Fitzpatrick, President'. And wrote the words, relating how he was stuck waiting in LA.

WHILE MY GUITAR GENTLY WEEPS

This time George used some NEMS Enterprises headed notepaper when a sudden creation came to him.

LONG LONG LONG

George wrote this in a diary, taking a full page for 11–14 August 1968, which is how we know when it was written.

OCTOPUS'S GARDEN

Ringo didn't write many of The Beatles' songs – in fact only two, though he is also credited as the co-author of 'Flying' – and he too had the same problem of finding paper when the muse struck. 'Octopus's Garden' was scribbled by him in 1969 on a sheet of promotional notepaper for the film *The Magic Christian*, in which he was starring with Peter Sellers.

GETTING BETTER

Composers: Paul plus John
Performers: Paul - vocal, bass; John - backing vocal, lead guitar; George - backing vocal, guitar, tambura; Ringo - drums; George Martin - piano
Recorded: 9, 10, 21, 23 March 1967, Abbey Road
Released: LP *Sgt Pepper* 1 June 1967 (UK), 2 June 1967 (US)

The title and first four bars came to Paul one spring day, walking on Primrose Hill with Martha his dog (and Hunter Davies, his faithful biographer). It was a day in which the weather was getting better but he was also thinking of the phrase Jimmie Nicol used to say, when asked how he was getting on, replacing an ill Ringo during part of their Australian tour in June 1964. John would mock him for making the same boring reply. Turned into a good song, after John got working on it – adding the lines about being cruel to his woman – with Paul at his house and then round the corner at Abbey Road.

Gets better the more you listen to it.

GIRL

Composer: John
Performers: John - vocal, acoustic guitar; Paul - backing vocal, bass; George - lead acoustic guitar; Ringo - drums
Recorded: 11 November 1965, Abbey Road
Released: LP *Rubber Soul* 3 December 1965 (UK), 6 December 1965 (US)

Paul gave us his sexy French voice for 'Michelle' – this is John's Euro reply with German and Greek overtones in the background, with hints of marching music and throbbing bouzoukis, plus some heavy intakes of breath. He has a bit of trouble on the word 'girl', forcing it into three syllables, just to keep the rhythm going. The lyrics are rich, deep and emotional, more complicated and more religious – about pain and pleasure – than they first appear. John was imagining a dream girl, whom he later felt must have been Yoko, long before he met her.

Rich and complex.

GLASS ONION

Composer: John
Performers: John - vocal, acoustic guitar; Paul - bass, piano, recorder; George - lead guitar; Ringo - drums (plus string octet)
Recorded: 11-13, 16 September and 10 October 1968, Abbey Road
Released: LP *The Beatles* 22 November 1968 (UK), 25 November 1968 (US)

The Beatles' songs had been endlessly over-analysed by 1968, with experts telling John and Paul what they really, really meant. This time John deliberately trotted out nonsense, any old words and phrases and images that came into his head, just to see what the critics would make of it – and to amuse himself. It is self-regarding, in the sense that other Beatles song titles are dragged in, such as 'Strawberry Fields Forever' and 'I Am The Walrus', but that's part of the amusement. Or lack of new ideas. The noise, made by the music, as opposed to the words, makes a bit more sense, all atmosphere and discordance, to fit the mixed-up mood.

Doesn't get anywhere.

One of the millions of Beatles souvenirs from the Sixties – a paper napkin, supposedly signed by each of them. Still worth treasuring.

GOLDEN SLUMBERS

Composer: Paul
Performers: Paul – vocal, piano, rhythm guitar; John – vocal chorus; George – lead guitar, bass, chorus; Ringo – drums, chorus (plus mini orchestra)
Recorded: 2–4, 30, 31 July and 15 August 1969, Abbey Road
Released: LP *Abbey Road* 26 September 1969 (UK), 1 October (US)

This was another part of the long medley of short pieces that made up much of the second side of *Abbey Road* – running into 'Carry That Weight'. Paul pinched almost all the words, and the idea, from the traditional children's lullaby of the same name, originally based on a 1603 poem by Thomas Dekker. (Not of course to be confused with Decca.). Paul did make up his first line, 'Once there was a way to get back homewards.'

Sweet but a bit soppy.

GOOD DAY SUNSHINE

Composer: Paul
Performers: Paul – vocal, piano, bass; John – harmony vocal, guitar; George – harmony vocal; Ringo – drums; George Martin – piano
Recorded: 8, 9 June 1966, Abbey Road
Released: LP *Revolver* 5 August 1966 (UK), 8 August 1966 (US)

Simple song, written by Paul at John's house, looking around on a lovely day, with very simple words – he is in love, she's loving me, I feel good, good sunshine. What could be better? The music is much subtler and richer, managing to make you feel the day and the sunshine breaking out, with clever crescendos, plus hints of American folksy music and also old-time music hall rhythms.

Infectious piece of music making.

GOOD MORNING GOOD MORNING

Composer: John
Performers: John – vocal, rhythm guitar; Paul – backing vocal, lead guitar; George – backing vocal, guitar; Ringo – drums (plus saxophones, trombones and French horn)
Recorded: 8, 16 February and 13, 28, 29 March 1967, Abbey Road
Released: LP *Sgt Pepper* 1 June 1967 (UK) 2 June 1967 (US)

Similar title and subject matter to 'Good Day Sunshine', but this time written by John a year later. He got the idea while lolling around watching TV, as he so often did, with his mind apparently miles away, when 'Good morning, good morning,' was belted out in a TV commercial for Kellogg's Corn Flakes. He played with the words and the rhythm later, polishing it into shape in the studio, with the help of lots of animal noises, which start off with a cock crowing. The final animal sounds are supposedly in a sort of order – each one followed by a predator or attacker, like a dog coming after a bird, but you would have to be really bored to work it all out.

Morning fun.

GOOD NIGHT

Composer: John
Performers: Ringo – vocal; George Martin – celesta; Mike Sammes Singers – vocal (plus mini orchestra)
Recorded: 28 June and 2, 22 July 1968, Abbey Road
Released: LP *The Beatles* 22 November 1968 (UK), 25 November 1968 (US)

The third Beatles song with a similar sort of title, which appears here alphabetically and chronologically in the correct order – as night does follow morning. It sounds as if it could be a Paul song, at his soppiest, but was in fact written by John, a lullaby for his five-year-old son Julian. It was given to Ringo to sing, supposedly to give him a chance to shine, but presumably the others realised it was too schmaltzy to be associated with. Of course it could all have been an ironic pastiche.

Sentimental soppiness.

GOT TO GET YOU INTO MY LIFE

Composer: Paul
Performers: Paul – vocal, bass; John – rhythm guitar; George – lead guitar; Ringo – drums; George Martin – organ (plus three trumpets and two tenor saxes)
Recorded: 7, 8, 11 April, 18 May and 17 June 1966, Abbey Road
Released: LP *Revolver* 5 August 1966 (UK), 8 August 1966 (US)

A big brassy, urgent, fast-moving number that fairly belts along, with Paul getting a bit too high-pitched at times. The words and sentiments make you think it is about a girl – 'say we'll be together every day' – whom he can't do without, she was meant to be near him, and as such it is quite a touching love song. But Paul admitted to his biographer Barry Miles in 1997 that is actually an ode to pot. 'I took a ride,' is a fairly strong clue. Shock. Horror.

A belter, but don't tell the vicar.

HAPPINESS IS A WARM GUN

Composer: John
Performers: John – vocal, lead guitar; Paul – backing vocal, bass; George – backing vocal, lead guitar; Ringo – drums, tambourine
Recorded: 23–25 September 1968, Abbey Road
Released: LP *The Beatles* 22 November 1968 (UK), 25 November 1968 (US)

The title, one of their most emotive, came from a headline in a copy of an American rifle magazine lying around the Abbey Road studio – but it was not exactly original, being a parody of 'Happiness Is A Warm Puppy', the phrase used in 1962 by Charles Schulz in his *Peanuts* strip and book title. The name of the song doesn't really have much to do with the rest of the lyrics, serving merely as a sort of chorus. In fact the lyrics seem to be an assemblage of several different scraps, with odd phrases and references thrown in, for little apparent reason. John just liked the sound of them.

There are some sexual undertones, probably aimed at Yoko, his loveheart – 'I feel my finger on your trigger' – and some druggie references – 'I need a fix'. While the words might have been pretty well chucked together, the music was endlessly worked on, requiring 70 takes. It does have some interesting and clever changes of tone and pace and voices, irregular beats and rhythms, making it one of John's more subtle creations.

Complex and clever.

HELLO, GOODBYE

Composer: Paul
Performers: Paul – vocal, piano, bass, bongos; John – backing vocal, lead guitar, organ; George – backing vocal, lead guitar; Ringo – drums, tambourine. Plus two violas.

Recorded: 2, 19, 20, 25 October and 2 November 1967, Abbey Road
Released: single 24 November 1967 (UK), 27 November 1967 (US), with B-side 'I Am The Walrus'
Charts: UK No. 1, US No.1

John was a bit upset that his 'Walrus' song got relegated to the B-side, but you see the reasoning. 'Hello, Goodbye' was much simpler, easier to understand and commercial – and it duly stayed at No. 1 in the UK charts for many weeks, the longest since 'She Loves You' back in 1963. Having thought of the clever title, Paul then asked people around to shout out the opposites of other words and phrases – such as 'stop' and 'go', 'yes' and 'no'. 'High' followed by 'low' is even smarter than he probably intended – as it can sound like 'Hi' followed by 'Lo', which also makes sense. Sort of. Anyway, according to Paul later, it is all about duality. The final 'Aloha' chorus, based on a Hawaiian greeting, was used in the *Magical Mystery Tour* film.

Clever, infectious singalong.

HELP!

Composer: John
Performers: John – vocal, acoustic guitar; Paul – backing vocal, bass; George – lead guitar, backing vocal; Ringo – drums, tambourine
Recorded: 13 April 1965, Abbey Road
Released: single 23 July 1965 (UK), 19 July 1965 (US), with B-side 'I'm Down'
Charts: UK No.1, U No. 1

Despite being well into the shooting of *Help!*, they still hadn't thought of the title for the film – but when it was decided, John rushed off and wrote 'Help!'. It must have been in his mind for it is very personal, his own cry for help. But we didn't realise it at the time. The music bounces along, with John shouting it out rather than going all slow, moaning and melancholy. The anguish is fairly disguised, so you think at first it is another love song, pining for some girl. He is in fact pining for real help, feeling down, insecure, his life has changed, help me, help me. It contains some quite complicated sentences, not normally found in pop songs in 1965, such as 'my independence seems to vanish in the haze.' Peter Sellers did a good version of it – as a vicar.

John giving himself away.

HELTER SKELTER

Composer: Paul
Performers: Paul – vocal, lead guitar; John – backing vocal, lead guitar; George – backing vocal, rhythm guitar; Ringo – drums; Mal Evans – trumpet
Recorded: 18 July and 9, 10 September, 1968, Abbey Road
Released: LP *The Beatles* 22 November 1968 (UK), 25 November 1968 (US)

Composers and singers, like most of us, like to try different things, different formats, just to see if we can do it, which is really why Paul got it into his head to do a loud, shouty, chaotic, clashing, screaming, heavy metal type number. He had read that The Who had made their rawest and dirtiest record ever, 'I Can See For Miles', so decided he would have a go. The result is pretty loud and, well, shouty. There are those who find it exciting and sexy and others to whom it gives a headache, such as the music critic Ian MacDonald (*Revolution In The Head*), who described it as 'clumsy' and 'embarrassing'.

The image of a helter-skelter – a fast and furious fairground spiral ride – is known to most British people, but the American murderer Charles Manson took it to be an exhortation to kill. But then he could see hidden and violent meanings in many of The Beatles' lyrics.

Head banging.

HERE COMES THE SUN

Composer: George
Performer: George - vocal, acoustic guitar; Paul - backing vocal, bass; Ringo - drums (plus violas, cellos, double bass, piccolos, flutes, clarinet)
Recorded: 7, 8, 16 July and 6, 11, 15 August 1969, Abbey Road
Released: LP *Abbey Road* 26 September 1969 (UK), 1 October 1969 (US)

George got fed up with yet more boring Apple meetings and went into Eric Clapton's garden to cheer himself up, telling himself spring was coming, these awful things can't go on for ever, here comes the sun. Not many words, but a pretty, sweet, cheerful song. John had got involved in a car crash in Scotland with Yoko, and so missed the recording sessions.

One of George's prettiest songs.

HERE, THERE AND EVERYWHERE

Composer: Paul
Performers: Paul - vocal, acoustic guitar, bass; John - backing vocal; George - backing vocal, lead guitar; Ringo - drums
Recorded: 14, 16, 17 June 1966, Abbey Road
Released: LP *Revolver* 5 August 1966 (UK), 8 August 1966 (US)

Honestly, some people are never happy. Like a handful of others, Ian MacDonald (*Revolution In The Head*) took against this song, dismissing it as 'chintzy and cloying'. Fortunately the vast majority of Beatles fans love it, as did Paul himself. You have to listen carefully to the words, or see them written down, to realise how cleverly they are crafted, each verse beginning with one of the three adverbs from his title – 'Here' then 'There', then 'Everywhere'. And the music is simple yet cunning, the harmonies subtle, the playing delicate. Many think it is Paul's masterpiece, better even than 'Yesterday'. He wrote it down at John's house, one summer's day, waiting for John to wake up and work. They polished it off together, John helping out with some of the lyrics. But the magic had already happened.

A pearl of a song.

HER MAJESTY

Composer: Paul
Performer: Paul - vocal, acoustic guitar
Recorded: 2 July 1969, Abbey Road
Released: LP *Abbey Road* 26 September 1969 (UK), 1 October 1969 (US)

This was really a joke, a little squib, a throwaway that Paul taped one afternoon in Abbey Road before the others had arrived, not really intending to use it; but almost as an afterthought it was tacked on after the long medley at the end of *Abbey Road*. Where it works well. An *amuse-bouche* – but coming at the end rather than a taster at the beginning. It's only 23 seconds long, the shortest Beatles song, and in it Paul says Her Majesty does not have a lot to say but she's a pretty nice girl and one day he wants to make her his. Affectionate teasing that did him no harm – for in 1997 it was arise Sir Paul.

An amusing squib.

THE BEATLES BOOK

HEY BULLDOG

Composer: John
Performers: John – vocal, lead guitar, piano; Paul – vocal harmony, bass; George – guitar; Ringo – drums, tambourine
Recorded: 11 February 1968, Abbey Road
Released: LP *Yellow Submarine* 17 January 1969 (UK), 13 January 1969 (US)

There was no bulldog – the nearest being a reference to a bullfrog, but someone started barking so it turned into a bulldog. And there is no message, in fact no real meaning, but there are a couple of good lines. 'What makes you think you're something special when you smile?' Could John have aimed that at Paul? They were not exactly getting on at the time. 'Some kind of happiness is measured out in miles.' Also sounds good, if not really clear. In the studio that day, for the first time, John's new love-heart Yoko was there throughout. A watershed in his life, if not in his music, though it has a great beat.

Some good lines in search of a song.

HEY JUDE

Composer: Paul
Performers: Paul – vocal, bass, piano; John – backing vocal, acoustic guitar; George – backing vocal, lead guitar; Ringo – backing vocal, drums (plus mini orchestra)
Recorded: 29, 30 July 1968, Abbey Road; 31 July and 1 August 1968, Trident Studios
Released: single 30 August 1968 (UK), 26 August 1968 (US), with B-side 'Revolution'
Charts: UK No. 1, US No. 1

A song for Julian, John's five-year-old son, whom Paul was going down to visit after John had left Cynthia for Yoko. It was a song to cheer the lad up, give him something to feel optimistic about, instead of carrying the world on his shoulders – but it became more general, to cheer us all up, make us all feel better, and 'Hey Jules' got changed into 'Hey Jude'. John thought it might even refer to him, to go off and be happy with Yoko. Now it's become a sort of national anthem round the world at mass gatherings, from football games to political rallies as well as pop concerts. At over seven minutes, it is a marathon of a song, but not everyone keeps on la la-ing to the very end.

Classic singalong.

HOLD ME TIGHT

Composer: Mainly Paul
Performers: Paul – vocal, bass; John – backing vocal, rhythm guitar; George – backing vocal, lead guitar; Ringo – drums
Recorded: 12 September 1963 Abbey Road
Released: LP *With The Beatles* 22 November 1963 (UK), LP *Meet The Beatles!* 20 January 1964 (US)

Paul always called this a 'work song', meaning a bit of a trudge, getting through the day, getting through the gig, with nothing memorable – either in it or in its creation, not that he could remember anyway. Written early, probably during 1961 at Forthlin Road, he was influenced by several girl groups of the time, such as The Shirelles. The Beatles did have a go at recording it on 11 February 1963 for their first album *Please Please Me*, but couldn't get it right, so had another go later, and decided to include that version on their second album *With The Beatles*. Trite words, simple tune, not very good singing, lots of hand clapping – but heh, this is how they began, this is what The Beatles were turning out in their early years, simple songs to dance to, with no one knowing where it would all lead.

Interesting historically.

200

HONEY PIE

Composer: Paul

Performers: Paul - vocal, lead guitar, piano; John - lead guitar; George - 6-string bass; Ringo - drums (plus six saxophones, two clarinets)

Recorded: 1, 2, 4 October 1968, Trident Studios

Released: LP *The Beatles* 22 November 1968 (UK), 25 November 1968 (US)

One of Paul's best pastiche pieces, taking us back to, well, to things he heard his father enjoying and playing when he was young, but also to music halls, early Hollywood and flapper ballrooms, which he can only have imagined in his head. The words are witty, well worked out, all in period, about a working girl, north of England way, who makes it big time in the USA.

The song, and the arrangement, might well have been influenced by The Temperance Seven, a humorous, British band of the late 1950s who played 1920s style jazz music. Their 1961 record 'You're Driving Me Crazy' was a big success, produced by George Martin – his first No. 1, well before The Beatles.

What fun.

I AM THE WALRUS

Composer: John

Performers: John - vocal, electric piano; Paul - backing vocal, bass; George - backing vocal, lead guitar; Ringo - drums (plus eight violins, four cellos, three horns, one clarinet, and Mike Sammes Singers)

NURSERY RHYMES AND THE BEATLES

The first songs that we hear are nursery rhymes – simple tunes with simple words, ideal for teaching children how to sing together. Paul McCartney's first composition, 'I Lost My Little Girl', resembles a re-write of the nursery rhyme that starts, 'There was a little girl,' and The Beatles' first single was with that old standby, 'My bonnie lies over the ocean'.

While making *Magical Mystery Tour*, John Lennon delivered his take on nursery rhymes, 'I Am The Walrus'. The Beatles also played around with children's rhymes in 'Christmas Time (Is Here Again)' on their 1967 fan club giveaway.

'Cry Baby Cry' doesn't even hide its origins with a reference to 'The queen was in the parlour'. The inspiration for 'Piggies' was the rhyme for counting toes that begins, 'This little piggy went to market.'

'All Together Now' is typical of the counting songs we learnt as children, although there is the adult reference, 'Can I take my friend to bed?' 'Golden Slumbers' is taken almost word for word from an old lullaby used for first piano lessons.

Paul grabbed 'See how they run' from 'Three Blind Mice' for 'Lady Madonna'. On his first solo album, John Lennon wrote new words for 'Three Blind Mice', making it 'My Mummy's Dead', although his mother had died when he was 17, not when he was a child. The album also included a reference to 'Remember, remember the fifth of November'.

In his solo career, Paul McCartney sang the original verse of 'Mary Had A Little Lamb' and then added new ones. He wrote his own nursery rhymes with 'The Frog Chorus' (1984) and 'Tropic Island Hum' (2004).

And what will happen 100 years from today? Many of The Beatles' songs, such as 'Yellow Submarine' and 'Ob-La-Di, Ob-La-Da', will surely have been added to the lexicon of nursery rhymes.

Recorded: 5, 6, 27, 29 September 1967, Abbey Road
Released: single 24 November 1967 (UK), 27 November 1967 (US), with A-side 'Hello, Goodbye' (simultaneous US release on LP *Magical Mystery Tour*)
Charts: UK No. 1 as single (and No. 2 as *Magical Mystery Tour* EP), US No. 56 as an individual track (No. 1 as B-side of 'Hello, Goodbye')

Written by John, naturally, an amalgam of at least three bits of songs, a mixture of total nonsense lyrics, made-up words and heartfelt rants, plus eerie, disjointed rhythms and rich musical arrangements. It confused most fans on first listening to it in 1967 – now it seems to have a logic of its own, everything fitting together perfectly. We now know it was not meant to make sense, so just let it swirl over you. But of course the thoughts and words in John's mind did come from somewhere. The Eggman was supposedly Eric Burdon of The Animals, who was reputed to enjoy breaking eggs over naked girls before sexual congress. Eric Burdon was interviewed in 2002 by Spencer Leigh for his BBC Radio Merseyside programme and asked about this story. 'There was a wild party one night,' explained Burdon, 'and John Lennon said to me "Go for it Eggman!"' But why was he called that? 'Use your imagination …'. Of course Eric may not actually have been the source of inspiration. It might just as easily have been the more prosaic encounter The Beatles enjoyed with Newquay egg deliveryman Ted O'Dell. Have a look at the *Magical Mystery Tour* entry in the *Movies* section and then decide.

The Walrus itself comes from Lewis Carroll, clearly an influence all the way through the lyrics. There are also half remembered playground chants from his childhood, such as 'yellow matter custard'. There is a reference to Hare Krishna, which could have been a dig at the ever-so-spiritual George – or himself. And all the way through John is crying. It is a hugely rich and complicated piece of work, with so much to enjoy in the words, and in George Martin's orchestration, which has its own musical echoes and associations. It has even survived being mangled by Russell Brand at the opening of the Olympics in London in 2012.

A masterpiece of nonsense.

I CALL YOUR NAME

Composer: John
Performers: John – vocal, rhythm guitar; Paul – bass; George – lead guitar; Ringo – drums
Recorded: 1 March 1964, Abbey Road
Released: EP *Long Tall Sally* 19 June 1964 (UK), LP *The Beatles' Second Album*, 10 April 1964 (US)

One of John's earliest known songs, written back in his Quarrymen days, which could mean the late 1950s, when he was just learning to play the guitar. A period piece then, to which he added a Jamaican ska beat, but he was clearly never happy with it. It was given to Billy J. Kramer to record in 1963, then dragged out for The Beatles' EP *Long Tall Sally* in June 1964. It never appeared on a Beatles album – except in the US. The lyrics are quite interesting, though, an early example of John soul-searching, unable to sleep, crying out someone's name in the night. Ringo performed this song – vocal and drums – with Jeff Lynne for the Lennon tribute concert in Liverpool in 1990.

Faded period piece.

I DON'T WANT TO SPOIL THE PARTY

Composer: Mainly John
Performers: John – vocal, rhythm guitar; Paul – harmony vocal, bass; George – lead guitar, vocal; Ringo – drums, tambourine

Recorded: 29 September 1964, Abbey Road
Released: LP *Beatles For Sale* 4 December 1964 (UK), single
15 February 1965 (US), with A-side 'Eight Days A Week'
Charts: US No. 39 as an individual track (No. 1 as B-side of
'Eight Days A Week')

A vaguely country and western number, which at one time Ringo was going to sing, just to give his country and western vocal cords an airing, but John, aided by Paul and George, sang it themselves; a trifle dolefully.

Falls flat – just like the title.

I FEEL FINE

Composers: John plus Paul
Performers: John – lead guitar, vocal; Paul – bass, harmony vocal; George – lead guitar, harmony vocal; Ringo – drums
Recorded: 18 October 1964, Abbey Road
Released: single 27 November 1964 (UK), 23 November 1964 (US), with B-side 'She's A Woman'
Charts: UK No. 1, US No. 1

Original inspiration came from John, who also claimed credit for the early use of feedback – before The Who did it. It has some interesting riffs and musical tricks, all very catchy. And popular – No. 1 in the UK and also in the US. Effervescent and uplifting – just like its title.

Early fave with all the fans.

IF I FELL

Composer: John
Performers: John – vocal, acoustic guitar; Paul – vocal, bass; George – lead guitar; Ringo – drums
Recorded: 27 February 1964, Abbey Road

Released: LP *A Hard Day's Night* 10 July 1964 (UK), 26 June 1964 (US)
Charts: US No. 53 as an individual track (No. 12 as B-side of 'And I Love Her', released 20 July 1964)

John's first proper love ballad, a sincere and beautiful song, sung from the heart, with no self-mocking voices or larking around. He later admitted the theme was semi-autobiographical, about an affair he was having, but of course he had to disguise the details as he was still, apparently, happily married to Cynthia. The lyrics are rich and subtle as is the music.

John's beautiful ballad.

IF I NEEDED SOMEONE

Composer: George
Performers: George – double-track vocal, lead guitar; John – harmony vocal, rhythm guitar; Paul – harmony vocal, bass; Ringo – drums, tambourine
Recorded: 16, 18 October,1965 Abbey Road
Released: LP *Rubber Soul* 3 December 1965 (UK), LP *Yesterday And Today* 20 June 1966 (US)

One of George's love songs to Pattie, and his second composition on the *Rubber Soul* album. It has often been dismissed as monotonous, being pretty much, well, on one note. George himself said it was really just an exercise. 'It's like a million other songs written on the D chord.' But it has a certain simplistic charm, avoiding anything too clever, or overtly Indian.

Just avoids being monotonous.

I'LL BE BACK

Composer: John
Performers: John – vocal, rhythm guitar; Paul – harmony vocal, acoustic guitar; George – lead guitar; Ringo – drums
Recorded: 1 June 1964, Abbey Road
Released: LP *A Hard Day's Night* 10 July 1964 (UK), LP *Beatles '65* 15 December 1964 (US)

Another of John's cries from the heart, should he leave her or not, but again all a bit complicated, disguising whatever was going on in his life, and in his mind. Good swinging beat, though, supposedly influenced by Del Shannon's big 1961 hit 'Runaway'.

Great chords.

I'LL CRY INSTEAD

Composer: John
Performers: John – vocal, rhythm guitar; Paul – bass; George – lead guitar; Ringo – drums.
Recorded: 1 June 1964, Abbey Road
Released: LP *A Hard Day's Night* 10 July 1964 (UK), 26 June 1964 (US)
Charts: US No. 25 released 20 July 1964, with B-side 'I'm Happy Just To Dance With You'

Again, John is crying – but also vowing to get his own back, breaking girls' hearts all over the world. It is an early indication of his cruel streak, but it's such a jaunty little song, from a jaunty interlude in the film, that you just hum along, not getting too bothered about what it all might mean.

Don't worry about John being nasty.

I'LL FOLLOW THE SUN

Composer: Paul
Performers: Paul – vocal, lead guitar; John – harmony vocal, acoustic guitar; George – lead guitar; Ringo – percussion
Recorded: 18 October 1964, Abbey Road
Released: LP *Beatles for Sale* 4 December 1964 (UK), LP *Beatles '65* 15 December 1964 (US)

An early song written by Paul, possibly in 1959, sitting in the front room at Forthlin Road, Liverpool, where there was not generally a lot of sun. But in his mind there was, so it is an optimistic number, though with a rather cruel underlying theme – that one day he's gonna leave that girl and follow the sun. But very nicely sung and played.

An old sweet song.

I'LL GET YOU

Composers: Paul and John
Performers: John – vocal, rhythm guitar; Paul – vocal, bass; George – lead guitar, harmony vocal; Ringo – drums
Recorded: 1 July 1963, Abbey Road
Released: single 23 August 1963 (UK), 16 September 1963 (US), with A-side 'She Loves You'
Charts: UK No.1, US No. 1

Done together at John's home Mendips – which Aunt Mimi did not usually allow – it was written quickly and was soon eclipsed by the song they wrote a day or two or later, 'She Loves You', which became the A-side and the much more successful song on the single. But perhaps 'I'll Get You' – about getting the girl in the end – inspired 'She Loves You' – when he has got the girl's love – suggesting themes and chords for the follow-up. Fairly corny words, but a good pop song of its time. The repeated use of the word 'imagine' is interesting, knowing what we do about a John song to come.

Not an A but a good B-side.

I ME MINE

Composer: George
Performers: George - vocal harmony, lead guitar; Paul - harmony vocal, bass; Ringo - drums (plus 18 violins, 4 violas, 4 cellos, 1 harp, 3 trumpets, 3 trombones)
Recorded: 3 January and 1 April 1970, Abbey Road
Released: LP *Let It Be* 8 May 1970 (UK), 18 May (US)

The Beatles were disintegrating when George wrote this – and John did not even bother to turn up for the recording – and George himself appears to have been cracking up as well, bothered by his own ego, the mysteries of Hinduism and probably too many nasty drugs. It is lightened slightly by the background hint of a waltz tune, but it is all rather a swirling mess and confusion, the music and the words, though not to George, who used the song's title for his own book about his own music.

Bit of a dirge.

I NEED YOU

Composer: George
Performers: George - double-tracked vocal, lead guitar; John - harmony vocal, acoustic rhythm guitar; Paul - harmony vocal, bass; Ringo - drums, cowbell
Recorded: 15, 16 February 1965, Abbey Road
Released: LP *Help!* 6 August 1965 (UK), 13 August 1965 (US)

Another love song, reputedly for Pattie, whom George first met while filming *A Hard Day's Night*. George's first contribution to a Beatles album after almost two years, and two albums, and it is not normally reckoned as one his best – though in fact it is just as good as many of their early, simple, basic love songs. George himself missed it out in his *I Me Mine* book, but that might have been because he couldn't find a copy of his original song … or perhaps he just forgot to include it.

Haunting.

I'M A LOSER

Composer: John
Performers: John - vocal, rhythm guitar, harmonica; Paul - bass, harmony vocal; George - lead guitar; Ringo - drums, tambourine

AND THE WINNER IS – GEORGE!

On 22 May 1971 in the *Record Mirror* George topped all three polls
Best Single – George's 'My Sweet Lord' No 1, with 'The Wonder Of You' by Elvis No. 3, 'Brown Sugar' by the Rolling Stones No. 8 and 'Another Day' by Paul McCartney No. 9
Best Album – George's *All Things Must Pass* at No. 1, *Elvis Country* No. 2, *Bridge Over Troubled Water*, Simon and Garfunkel, No. 4, *Let It Be*, The Beatles, No. 8
Best Songwriter – George Harrison No. 1, Neil Diamond No. 2, Paul McCartney No. 3, Paul Simon No. 4, Elton John/ Bernie Taupin No. 5

Recorded: 14 August 1964, Abbey Road
Released: LP *Beatles For Sale* 4 December 1964 (UK),
LP *Beatles '65* 15 December 1964 (US)

How could John Lennon be a loser? In 1964, had they not conquered the US, having already knocked them out in the UK and most other countries? Yes, but John had still lost the girl and felt he might even be a loser in life, and not what he appeared to be. It was about the first time that John had been self-reflecting and autobiographical in his songs, giving us a hint of how he really saw himself, which of course came out more strongly much later on. So a song that on the surface was a Dylan-inspired folksy style tune, turned out to be quite a watershed in John's development

Sign of things to come.

PAUL ON *BEATLES FOR SALE*

The Beatles did not always explain the background to their songs, not in the very early years, but in December 1964 *Disc* magazine managed to get Paul to go through all their songs on their fourth album, just as it came out.

NO REPLY: John sings this one, and I do the vocal harmony. We tried to give it different moods, starting off quietly with a sort of vaguely bossa nova tempo, building up to a straight beat crescendo in the middle, and then tailing off quietly again.

I'M A LOSER: I reckon the best way to describe this one is a folk song gone pop. John and I both sing, but John does most of it. He also plays some nice harmonicas, too.

BABY'S IN BLACK: I better explain what John and I meant by this title hadn't I? The story is about a girl who's wearing black because the bloke she loves has gone away for ever. The feller singing the song fancies her, too, but he's getting nowhere. We wrote it originally in a waltz style, but it finished as a mixture of waltz and beat.

I'LL FOLLOW THE SUN: John and I wrote this one some while ago, but we changed the middle eight bars before we actually recorded it. John and I sing it, and Ringo played the top of a packing case instead of his drums this time. Just for a change, you know!

EIGHT DAYS A WEEK: I got the title for this one while I was being driven over to visit John. The chauffeur was talking away to me, saying how hard his boss worked the staff – so hard they seems to do eight days a week. We've altered the plot a bit for the song, of course. The bloke loves the girl for eight days a week. John and I do the singing.

EVERY LITTLE THING: John and I got this one written in Atlantic City during our last tour of the States. John does the guitar riff for this one, and George is on acoustic. Ringo bashes some timpani drums for the big noise you'll hear.

I DON'T WANT TO SPOIL THE PARTY: We went after a real Country and Western flavour when we wrote this one. John and I do the singing in that style, and George takes a real country solo on his guitar.

WHAT YOU'RE DOING: We wrote this one in Atlantic City, like 'Every Little Thing'. It's not that Atlantic City is particularly inspiring, it's just that we happened to have a day off the tour there. Ringo does a nice bit of drumming decoration in the introduction. I double-track on the vocal as well as playing some piano.

I'M DOWN

Composer: Paul
Performers: Paul - vocal, bass; John - backing vocal, rhythm guitar; George - backing vocal, lead guitar; Ringo - drums, bongos
Recorded: 14 June 1965, Abbey Road
Released: single 23 July 1965 (UK), 19 July 1965 (US), with A-side 'Help!'
Charts: UK No. 1, US No. 1

Is this Paul taking the piss, his reply to John's cry for 'Help!', or to show that he too was not always all smiles and joy and thumbs up? Possibly, for there is a hint of pastiche in the arrangement and Paul's exaggerated voice. On the surface, though, it is simply a Little Richard, shouting and screaming rocker, so no need to worry about who or what it was really aimed at.

Little Paul, doing his Little Richard act.

I'M HAPPY JUST TO DANCE WITH YOU

Composers: John and Paul
Performers: George - vocal, lead guitar; Paul - backing vocal, bass; John - backing vocal, rhythm guitar; Ringo - drums
Recorded: 1 March 1964, Abbey Road
Released: LP *A Hard Day's Night* 10 July 1964 (UK), 26 June 1964 (US)
Charts: US No. 95 as an individual track (No. 25 as B-side of 'I'll Cry Instead', released 20 July 1964)

Originated mainly by John, but with Paul's help, it was created for George, trying not to over-extend what they believed, rather unkindly, was George's limited vocal range, and to give him a chance to have his own bit of spotlight in the *Hard Day's Night* film. George sings it rather turgidly, at times

not sounding terribly happy, but it is a great tune, the sort that gets into your skull and will not leave you alone.

Hypnotic – without any nasty drugs or funny sound effects.

I'M LOOKING THROUGH YOU

Composer: Paul
Performers: Paul - vocal, rhythm guitar, lead guitar; John - harmony vocal, rhythm guitar; George - guitar; Ringo - drums, tambourine, Hammond organ
Recorded: 24 October and 6, 10, 11 November 1965, Abbey Road.
Released: LP *Rubber Soul* 3 December 1965 (UK), 6 December 1965 (US)

Paul and John in their lyrics often used the notion of 'looking' and 'seeing' both literally and metaphorically – what you can actually, physically see as well as understanding someone or something. Paul is looking at Jane – for it was clearly inspired by her, after some row – and seeing not the physical Jane but someone who has changed, who has gone, because love has disappeared overnight. A sad, rather bitter but haunting song, neatly constructed and worked out with some clever harmonies. Steve Earle, the American singer-songwriter, has raved about the chords. 'It has every inversion of a key in one song – it's amazing.'

One of Paul's classics.

I'M ONLY SLEEPING

Composer: John
Performers: John - vocal, rhythm guitar; Paul - harmony vocal, bass; George - lead guitar, harmony vocal; Ringo - drums
Recorded: 27, 29 April and 5, 6 May 1966, Abbey Road

Released: LP *Revolver* 5 August 1966 (UK), LP *Yesterday And Today* 20 June 1966 (US)

John did a lot of sleeping during his years at Kenwood when he was still married to Cynthia, trying to forget, or to lose himself, or just let the drugs float over him. So this is an example of a lyric that came straight out of what he was actually doing. It is also of course mocking the rest of the crazy world for running about at such speed. The lyrics are excellent, without being deliberately obscure – 'floating upstream' is what do you in a dream, as of course in real life the currents would make you float the other way. It doesn't necessarily refer to drugs. The music is some of the most subtle so far, with Indian overtones, mystical sounds and dream-like changes of speed.

A classic John song.

I'M SO TIRED

Composer: John
Performers: John – vocal, lead guitar, organ; Paul – harmony vocal, bass, electric piano; George – lead guitar; Ringo – drums
Recorded: 8 October 1968, Abbey Road
Released: LP *The Beatles* 22 November 1968 (UK), 25 November 1968 (US)

With all that sleeping, how could John still be so tired? Because he was in India and desperately missing Yoko. Another song telling us exactly what he was doing when he was writing the song. The music ebbs and flows, which is clever, just how sleep goes, when you are searching for it. Sir Walter Raleigh, usually blamed for introducing tobacco to England, gets a name check – and then called a stupid git. Not very polite.

Self-indulgent, but original.

IN MY LIFE

Composer: Mainly John
Performers: John – vocal, rhythm guitar; Paul – harmony vocal, bass; George – harmony vocal, lead guitar; Ringo – drums, tambourine; George Martin – electric piano
Recorded: 18, 22 October 1965, Abbey Road
Released: LP *Rubber Soul* 3 December 1965 (UK), 6 December 1965 (US)

John and Paul had been thinking vaguely of some sort of concept album, long before *Sgt Pepper* floated into their minds, based on their childhoods in Liverpool, the places, the people, their memories. Strange in a way, when they were so young, and had hardly been away from Liverpool for long – but of course they had. They had seen the world by then, and the world had seen them. John's first attempt at the lyrics contains references to Penny Lane, which emerged later in another song. It also includes references to bus rides and tram sheds, but he cut out all the specific places in the final version, turning it into a wistful but optimistic meditation on memory and times past generally. Good lyrics, even if some of the lines are possibly derivative. John thought it was his first major piece of work – though Paul later claimed he wrote part of it, one of the few occasions on which they differed about who-wrote-what.

It is possible that John nicked some of the words from a poem by Charles Lamb (1775–1834) called 'The Old Familiar Faces', as Steve Turner pointed out in his book *A Hard Day's Write*. It has these lines: 'I have had playmates, I have had companions/All, all are gone, the old familiar faces/How some have died, and some have left me.' The poem appears in *Palgrave's Golden Treasury of English Songs and Lyrics* – the sort of book Aunt Mimi would have had in the house and children in the forties and fifties learned at school.

Great, moody song.

I SAW HER STANDING THERE

Composers: Paul plus John

Performers: Paul - vocal, bass; John - backing vocal, rhythm guitar; George - lead guitar; Ringo - drums

Recorded: 11 February 1963, Abbey Road

Released: LP *Please Please Me* 22 March 1963 (UK), LP *Introducing … The Beatles* originally scheduled 22 July 1963, actual 10 January 1964 (US)

Charts: US No. 14 as an individual track (No. 1 as B-side of 'I Want To Hold Your Hand', released 26 December 1963)

Paul wrote it, but they worked on it together, head-to-head in Forthlin Road, creating one of their best, rawest most energetic early rock numbers, quickly seen in the UK and the US as the pure, original, distinctive Beatles sound. How could anyone not want to dance to it, the perfect way to open their first ever album. But it was doing it live on stage or on TV – as on *The Ed Sullivan Show* – that caused the most excitement and fun and screams. There have been several suggestions about the identity of the 17-year-old girl that Paul saw standing there, but he has denied it was based on any one girl. No matter. Just get dancing.

Fab.

I SHOULD HAVE KNOWN BETTER

Composer: John

Performers: John - vocal, rhythm guitar, harmonica; Paul - bass; George - lead guitar; Ringo - drums

Recorded: 25, 26 February 1964, Abbey Road

Released: LP *A Hard Day's Night* 10 July 1964 (UK), 26 June 1964 (US)

Charts: US No. 53 as an individual track (No. 1 as B-side of 'A Hard Day's Night', released 13 July 1964)

Considered pretty good by The Beatles at the time, good enough to kick off the *Hard Day's* *Night* film, coming right after the title track, but has since been seen by many as something of a pot boiler, not much to it really, but it is a cheerful, charming little song. The title makes it sound moany, but it's an upbeat, if simple, love song.

Perfectly okay.

IT WON'T BE LONG

Composer: John

Performers: John - double-tracked vocal, rhythm guitar; Paul - backing vocal, bass; George - backing vocal, lead guitar; Ringo - drums

Recorded: 30 July 1963, Abbey Road

Released: LP *With The Beatles* 22 November 1963 (UK), LP *Meet The Beatles!* 20 January 1964 (US)

Originally written as a single, mainly by John, as a follow-up to 'She Loves You', but they realised it was not quite strong or upbeat enough, so it became the first track on the their new album *With The Beatles*. The words are rather mournful, with John sitting there alone crying, now someone has left him – some have suggested they were really not about a girlfriend but his dead mother. There is a neat pun on the title – with 'it won't be long' turning into 'till I belong to you'.

Crafty.

IT'S ALL TOO MUCH

Composer: George

Performers: George - vocal, lead guitar, Hammond organ; Paul - harmony vocal, bass; John - harmony vocal, lead guitar; Ringo - drums, tambourine (plus four trumpets, one clarinet)

Recorded: 25, 31 May and 2 June 1967, De Lane Lea Studios

Released: LP Y*ellow Submarine* 17 January 1969 (UK),
13 January 1969 (US)

A monotonous, childlike, possibly drug-induced,
dirge, dressed up with psychedelic effects, but
signifying very little. Would they have allowed
George to indulge himself if he had suggested
such nonsense three years earlier? Probably not.
On the other hand, done in 1964, it would have
been awfully avant-garde

Yes a bit too much.

IT'S ONLY LOVE

Composer: John
Performers: John - vocal, rhythm guitar; Paul - bass;
George - lead guitar; Ringo - drums
Recorded: 15 June 1965, Abbey Road
Released: LP *Help!* 6 August 1965 (UK), LP *Rubber Soul*
6 December 1965 (US)

It's only another song about love, which later
John rubbished, saying he felt ashamed of the
lyrics, which are pretty banal, but then falling in
love can be banal. It has happened loads of times
before. John does sing it nicely though.

Another love song.

I'VE GOT A FEELING

Composers: Paul and John
Performers: Paul vocal, bass; John - vocal, rhythm guitar;
George - backing vocal, lead guitar; Ringo - drums; Billy
Preston - electric guitar
Recorded: 24, 27, 28, 30 January 1969, Apple Studios
Released: LP *Let It Be* 8 May 1 969 (UK) 18 May 1970
(US)

A joint collaboration, like the old days of their
partnership – but not quite head-to-head as in
Forthlin Road, just two songs, written separately
by each of them but never finished, then brought
in and joined up. Paul's bit is about his feeling of
love, presumably for Linda, while John is giving us
bits as if from his diary, about the hard year he was
having, presumably about all the Apple rows that
were driving them apart. Got blasted out on the
Apple roof, forgetting for a moment their tribu-
lations down below.

Two good little songs for the price of one.

I'VE JUST SEEN A FACE

Composer: Paul
Performers: Paul - vocal, acoustic guitar; John - acoustic
guitar; George - lead guitar; Ringo - drums, maracas
Recorded: 14 June 1965, Abbey Road
Released: LP *Help!* 6 August 1965 (UK), LP *Rubber Soul*
6 December 1965 (US)

Another of Paul's love songs, inspired by Jane,
with whom he was still living in Wimpole Street.
Paul composed the tune on the piano, before he
had all the words, and it does have a sort of tinkly,
jangly, piano-exercise feeling, going up and down
the scales, so you feel like going 'da da da' along
with it, knowing what must be coming, while
jiving of course.

Good little mover.

I WANNA BE YOUR MAN

Composers: Paul plus John
Performers: Paul - backing vocal, bass; John - backing
vocal, rhythm guitar; George - lead guitar; Ringo - vocal,
drums; George Martin - Hammond organ

Recorded: 11, 12, 30 September and 3, 23 October 1963, Abbey Road
Released: LP *With The Beatles* 22 November 1963 (UK), LP *Meet The Beatles!* 20 January 1964 (US)

One of their early, poptastic, fantastic early hits, and yet at the time they didn't reckon it was all that exceptional – in fact they gave it away to the Rolling Stones. They had gone along to chat to the Stones – roughly a year behind them in their development – who were in a London club. The Stones said they were hard up for a new song so John and Paul said what about this one. It was half finished at the time, but there and then they knocked it into shape and handed it over. The Stones were well impressed.

It got the Stones to No. 12 in the UK charts and inspired them to try writing their own songs. If The Beatles could do it, why couldn't they? Originally Paul had had Ringo in mind to sing it, which he does when it was included on their second album *With The Beatles*, another sign that they feared it was not top notch. But it is, it is, becoming one of their best-loved, best-known signature numbers.

Top of the range.

I WANT TO HOLD YOUR HAND

Composers: John and Paul
Performers: John – vocal, rhythm guitar; Paul – vocal, bass; George – harmony vocal, lead guitar; Ringo – drums
Recorded: 17 October 1963, Abbey Road
Released: single 29 November 1963 (UK), with B-side 'This Boy'; 26 December 1963 (US), with B-side 'I Saw Her Standing There'
Charts: UK No. 1, US No. 1

When Capitol Records in the US finally got round to The Beatles, their LP *Meet The Beatles!*, issued in early January 1964, announced on the sleeve: 'England's Phenomenal Pop Combo – You've read about them in *Time*, *Newsweek*, *The New York Times*. Here's the big beat sound of that fantastic, phenomenal foursome.'

The single version had already got to No. 1 in the UK in time for Christmas, but it had been delayed in the US and it didn't appear till 26 December – on a single, then the LP. It zoomed to No.1. The Beatles' first big hit in the States.

It is said by some to have helped lift the national gloom after the assassination of President Kennedy (22 November 1963). But its success was due to its explosive impact on American youth, generating a feeling of intense excitement, which had gone missing in much of US pop music since the early days of rock, becoming bubblegum and bland, sung by nice boys with crew cuts.

Paul and John had written the song together, head-to-head, on a piano at Jane's house, competing to outdo each other in words and riffs, shouts and yells.

The Beatles were in Paris when they heard the news from America. Brian Epstein had always said he didn't want them to go on a US tour until they achieved a hit single there. Now they had. The rest is, well, pop music history.

Did they only want to hold a girl's hand? That was left to your own fertile mind to decide. Sexual intercourse did not of course begin till The Beatles' first LP – according to Philip Larkin – so obviously, for all teenagers of the time, hand holding was quite exciting enough.

In a handwritten version of the lyrics done for me in 1967 and now on show at the British Library, Paul wrote, 'let me hold your thing'. How rude. And yet nobody noticed it till 2014.

10/10 – for its place in pop history.

I WANT TO TELL YOU

Composer: George
Performers: George – vocal, lead guitar; Paul – harmony vocal, bass, piano; John – harmony vocal, tambourine; Ringo – drums, maracas
Recorded: 2, 3 June 1966, Abbey Road
Released: LP *Revolver* 5 August 1966 (UK), 8 August 1966 (US)

George had three of his own compositions on the *Revolver* album (along with 'Taxman' and 'Love You To') and this one probably has the best lyrics. It describes the avalanche of thoughts that come into our head, about the problems of communication, and those words that just seem to slip away. George was into Indian music and mysticism by this time, but there are in fact no Indian instruments. It just feels like that. A significant song on George's path to becoming, for a while, the leader of the other Beatles.

Good for George.

I WANT YOU (SHE'S SO HEAVY)

Composer: John
Performers: John – vocal, lead guitar; Paul – harmony vocal, bass; George – harmony vocal, lead guitar; Ringo – drums, congas; Billy Preston – Hammond organ

Recorded: 22 February 1969, Trident Studios; 18, 20 April and 8, 11 August 1969, Abbey Road
Released: LP *Abbey Road* 26 September 1969 (UK), 1 October 1969 (US)

No proper lyrics, not really, just that he wants her, wants her so bad, endlessly repeated – but that was John's point, to create a song with minimalist lyrics. And the person he wants is Yoko. The fact he says, 'She's so heavy' – the song's subtitle, put in brackets, a complicated and confusing device – does not today sound very flattering. But back in the sixties, ah blessed times, 'heavy' could mean almost anything you liked, from quite good to excellent, even fab. The Beatles, as a band, are playing as a band, working so well together – and it was a track much admired by other bands of the time.

But not quite fab.

I WILL

Composer: Paul
Performers: Paul – vocal, acoustic guitar; Lennon – percussion; Ringo – cymbals, bongos, maracas
Recorded: 16, 17 September 1968, Abbey Road
Released: LP *The Beatles* 22 November 1968 (UK), 25 November 1968 (US)

One of those simple songs, with simple I-love-you words and a simple, artless arrangement that in fact took Paul ages in the studio to get right – 67 takes in all, just to make it sound natural. Which it does. Paul first wrote the tune in India, creating some words later, by which time he had met Linda, who he was hoping would say, 'I will'.

Sweet and lovely.

JULIA

Composer: John
Performer: John – vocal, acoustic guitar
Recorded: 13 October 1968, Abbey Road
Released: LP *The Beatles* 22 November 1968 (UK), 25 November 1968 (US)

Julia was John's mother, though she did not bring him up; that was left to his Aunt Mimi, for reasons still being argued about. Was Julia selfish or cruel to allow her son to be dumped on her sister? Was it all Mimi's doing, grasping to take him in?

Julia was just coming back into John's life, aged 15, when she was killed. John's blind rages can be put down to the loss of a mother, whom he never really had, yet who haunted him emotionally for the rest of his life. The mention of 'ocean child' in the lyrics refers to Yoko (in Japanese 'Yoko' means 'child of the ocean') whom John now saw as a replacement for his lost mother. John did later take to referring to Yoko as 'Mother'.

A moving, touching, heartbreaking song, played and sung beautifully by John, all on his own.

John's most haunting song.

LADY MADONNA

Composer: Paul
Performers: Paul – vocal, bass, piano; John – backing vocal, lead guitar; George – backing vocal, lead guitar; Ringo – drums (plus Ronnie Scott and three other saxophones)
Recorded: 3, 6 February 1968, Abbey Road
Released: single 15 March 1968 (UK), 18 March 1968 (US), with B-side 'The Inner Light'
Charts: UK No. 1, US No. 4

THE BEATLES – SOLO
The Beatles had plenty of practice for their solo careers as they all made Beatle records without the other three, or with just minimal Beatle involvement.

Paul McCartney	John Lennon	George Harrison	Ringo Starr
Yesterday	Julia	Love You To	Goodnight
Eleanor Rigby		Within You Without You	
Blackbird		The Inner Light	
Wild Honey Pie			
Why Don't We Do It In The Road			
Mother Nature's Son			
Her Majesty			

THE BEATLES at EMI Wednesday 6th June 1962

Suggested opening medley:

1)	Besame Mucho	Paul McCartney
2)	Will you Love Me Tomorrow	John Lennon
3)	Open (your Lovin' Arms)	George Harrison

Individual numbers:

PAUL McCARTNEY - P.S. I Love You   )
                   Love Me Do   )   ORIGINAL
                   Like Dreamers Do   )   COMPOSITIONS
                   Love of the Loved   )
                   Pinwheel Twist   )
                   If you've gotta make a Fool of
                                        Somebody

                   'Til There Was You
                   Over The Rainbow
                   Your Feets too big
                   Hey! Baby
                   Dream Baby
                   September in the Rain
                   Honeymoon Song

JOHN LENNON   - Ask Me Why   )   ORIGINAL
                   Hullo Little Girl   )   COMPOSITIONS
                   Baby It's You
                   Please Mister Postman
                   To Know her is to Love her
                   You Don't Understand
                   Memphis Tennessee
                   Show of Rhythm'n'Blues
                   Shimmy Like My Sister Kate
                   Lonesome Tears in my Eyes

                                              Cont.../

GEORGE HARRISON - A Picture of You
                   Sheik of Araby
                   What a Crazy World we Live In
                   Three Cool Cats
                   Dream
                   Take Good Care of my Baby
                   Glad All Over

THE BEATLES   - John Lennon   Rhythm

                   Paul McCartney   Bass

                   George Harrison Lead

                   Pete Best   Drums

More historic stuff: the set list which Brian Epstein presented to George Martin for their first test at EMI in 1962. Note the original compositions they were offering, that Pete Best was still with them and Brian's nice monogram at the top of the page.

This is Paul's hymn to motherhood, done earlier in the year, which came out as a single, but it is not directly related to his own mother – though it might well have been in his mind for Paul, like John, lost his mother as a teenager. It is more in praise of mothers generally. Paul's mother was Irish Catholic, so the Lady Madonna reference links it to his mother, but he has also said the title was sparked off by a photo in *National Geographic* with the caption 'Mountain Madonna'. The music has a period, honky-tonk, jazzy feeling – hence hiring Ronnie Scott and some other jazzmen to join in.

It was suggested that The Beatles had been influenced by Humphrey Lyttelton's 'Bad Penny Blues', but Humph himself poo-pooed the idea. 'A number of idiots came up to me and said, "They've borrowed the introduction to 'Bad Penny Blues'. What are you going to do?" They wanted me to sue them but I told them not to be so stupid. You can't copyright a rhythm and the rhythm was all they'd used. Anyway, we'd borrowed it from Dan Burley. It was absolutely stupid and I've never had any sympathy with the notion of, "Here are some guys, they're worth a fortune, let's try and get some of it by suing them." In fact, I was very complimented. Although, none of The Beatles cared for traditional jazz, they all knew and liked "Bad Penny Blues" because it was a bluesy, skiffley thing, rather than a trad exercise.'

All that jazz.

LET IT BE

Composer: Paul
Performers: Paul - vocal, piano, maracas; John - bass; George - backing vocal, lead guitar; Ringo - drums; Billy Preston - organ, electric piano (plus two trumpets, two trombones, tenor sax, cellos)

Recorded: 25, 26, 31 January 1969, Apple Studios; 30 April 1969 and 4 January 1970, Abbey Road
Released: single 6 March 1970 (UK), 11 March 1970 (US), with B-side 'You Know My Name (Look Up The Number)'
Charts: UK No. 2, US No. 1

It was so hard for them in late 1968 and 1969 to let it be, when there was endless squabbling over Apple, personal rows between John, Paul and George, and Ringo getting increasingly fed up. One night, after ceaseless tossing, Paul woke up from a dream in which his mother Mary told him just let things be. Cue for another song. John, in the studio, when they were recording it, mocked the piety and religiosity.

It was released as a single in March 1970, before the *Let It Be* album itself came out, and has been treated since almost like a religious experience, with its choral setting, references to Mother Mary and hours of darkness. Bob Geldof asked Paul to sing it at the of the 1985 Live Aid open-air charity concert in London. After that, when Paul was performing the song in public, which was pretty often, audiences often lit candles – or at least held up their mobile phones, this being the modern age – as if in an act of worship. Which of course it is. At the feet of Paul.

Sentimental but sincere.

LITTLE CHILD

Composers: Paul and John
Performers: John - vocal, rhythm guitar, harmonica; Paul - vocal, bass, piano; George - lead guitar; Ringo - drums
Recorded: 11, 12 September and 3 October 1963, Abbey Road
Released: LP *With The Beatles* 22 November 1963 (UK), LP *Meet The Beatles!* 20 January 1964 (US)

The words wouldn't make it today in a pop song – asking a little child to come on come on, dance with him, as he is so sad and lonely. The lyrics were considered innocent at the time, guilty today, but it's a pot boiler of a song, one of the album fillers from their early years. Originally Ringo was going to sing it, but John took it over. Also did the harmonica, very nicely.

Little song.

LONG LONG LONG

Composer: George
Performers: George – vocal, acoustic guitar; Paul – backing vocal, organ, bass; Ringo – drums (plus pianist)
Recorded: 7–9 October 1968, Abbey Road
Released: LP *The Beatles* 22 November 1968 (UK), 25 November 1968 (US)

This is George's love song – not to Pattie or any girl but to God, so he later revealed. Soppy idea, and some fairly soppy words about how he loves him, he needs him, oh please, but the music is much more interesting and original and atmospheric.

Too long long long.

LOVE ME DO

Composers: John and Paul
Performers: Paul – vocal, bass; John – vocal, rhythm guitar, harmonica; George – rhythm guitar, backing vocal; Ringo – drums on version one; Andy White – drums on version two
Recorded: 6 June and 4, 11 September 1962, Abbey Road

Released: single 5 October 1962 (UK), 27 April 1964 (US), with B-side 'P.S. I Love You'
Charts: UK No. 17, US No. 1

More research has been done on this record, at least its convoluted recording history and changing line-up, than almost any other Beatles song, certainly from their early years. Was it at an audition when they first played it to producer George Martin in June 1962, hoping desperately to get a record deal? That's what they themselves considered at the time. But Mark Lewisohn, the leading Beatle expert of our times, has documented that behind the scenes EMI had already agreed to take them. So it was not an audition as such – just a performance of a selection of their stage songs, out of which George Martin eventually agreed that 'Love Me Do' would be their first single.

Paul wrote the main theme early on, aged about 15 or 16, and played it at Forthlin Road to John, who added a middle section. Best to forget the words, which are pretty trite, but then that's what most people, including John and Paul, expected of pop song lyrics of the time. The harmonica, as played by John, was fairly unusual, though not unique, but it did give it a raw, new sort of sound. George Martin was not thrilled by poor old Ringo's drumming, which was why on a later recording he brought in a session drummer, Andy White – and both versions were in fact released. Real fans can tell the difference.

Only ever got to No. 17 in any of the UK charts, but all the same – ground-breaking stuff, for The Beatles and for pop music, as we now know and love it.

Has to be top marks – because look what happened afterwards.

JOHN ON BEATLES SONGS

John was asked by *Record Mirror* in October 1971 for his memories of many of their songs – though he was not always totally reliable on his own contributions.

LOVE ME DO: Paul wrote the main structure of this when he was about 16, or even earlier. I think I had something to do with the middle.

P. S I LOVE YOU: Paul. But I think we helped him a bit. It was meant to be a Shirelles kind of song.

PLEASE PLEASE ME: I wrote all of this one – I was trying to do a Roy Orbison.

FROM ME TO YOU: Paul and me – we wrote this one together in a van.

THANK YOU GIRL: Paul and me – this was just a silly song we knocked off.

SHE LOVES YOU: Both of us – we wrote it together on tour.

MISERY: Both of us – this was mainly mine, though, I think.

DO YOU WANT TO KNOW A SECRET: Me – I wrote this for George

I CALL YOUR NAME: Me – I started it when I was about 15 and finished the middle eight years later, around 'Help!' or 'Hard Day's Night' time.

I'LL BE ON MY WAY: Paul – this was early Paul.

IT WON'T BE LONG: Me – I wrote this on the second album. It was the song with the so-called Aeolian cadences, the same as in a Mahler symphony, at the end. I don't know what the hell it was all about.

ALL MY LOVING: Paul – this was one of his first biggies.

LITTLE CHILD: Both of us – this was a knock-off between Paul and me for Ringo.

HOLD ME TIGHT: Both of us, but mainly Paul.

I WANNA BE YOUR MAN: Both of us, but mainly Paul. I helped him finish it.

CAN'T BUY ME LOVE: Me and Paul – but mainly Paul.

AND I LOVE HER: Both of us – the first half was Paul's and the middle eight is mine.

I'LL BE BACK: Me – a nice tune, though the middle is a bit tatty.

I FEEL FINE: Me – this was the first time feedback was used on a record – it's right at the beginning.

SHE'S A WOMAN: Paul – though I helped with the middle, I think.

NO REPLY: Me – I remember Dick James coming to me after I did this one and saying, 'You're getting much better now – that was a complete story.' Apparently, before that he thought my songs tended to, sort of, wander off.

I'LL FOLLOW THE SUN: Paul – a nice one – one of his early compositions.

EIGHT DAYS A WEEK: Both of us. I think when we wrote this we were trying to write the title song for *Help!* because there was at one time an idea of calling the film *Eight Arms To Hold You* or something. I THINK that's the story, I'm not sure.

JOHN ON BEATLES SONGS continued

IT'S ONLY LOVE: Me – that's the one song I really hate of mine. Terrible lyric.

YESTERDAY: Paul – wow, that was a good 'un.

DAY TRIPPER: Me – but I think Paul helped me out with the verse.

WE CAN WORK IT OUT: Paul, but the middle was mine.

NORWEGIAN WOOD: Me – but Paul helped on the lyric.

MICHELLE: I wrote the middle with him.

WHAT GOES ON: Me – a very early song of mine. Ringo and Paul wrote a new middle eight together when we recorded it.

IN MY LIFE: Me – I think I was trying to write about Penny Lane when I wrote it.

RUN FOR YOUR LIFE: Me – another one I never liked.

PAPERBACK WRITER: Paul. I think I may have helped with some of the lyrics. Yes, I did. But it was mainly Paul's tune.

ELEANOR RIGBY: Both of us. I wrote a good lot of the lyrics, about 70 per cent. Ray Charles did a great version of this. Fantastic.

HERE, THERE AND EVERYWHERE: Paul – this was a great one of his.

YELLOW SUBMARINE: Both of us. Paul wrote the catchy chorus. I helped with the other blunderbuss bit.

SHE SAID SHE SAID: Me – I wrote it after meeting Peter Fonda who said he knew what it was like to be dead.

GOOD DAY SUNSHINE: Paul – but I think I may have helped him with some of the lyric.

AND YOUR BIRD CAN SING: Me – another horror.

DR. ROBERT: Me – I think Paul helped me with the middle.

GOT TO GET YOU INTO MY LIFE: Paul – but I think George and I helped him with some of the lyrics. I'm not sure.

TOMORROW NEVER KNOWS: Me – this was my first psychedelic song.

PENNY LANE: Paul – I helped him with the lyric.

WITH A LITTLE HELP FROM MY FRIENDS: Paul. It was Paul's idea. I think I helped with some of the words. In fact I did, because Hunter Davies was there when we did it and mentioned it in the book. 'What do you see when you turn out the light, I can't tell you but I know it's mine,' that was mine.

LUCY IN THE SKY WITH DIAMONDS: Me – and once again folks, this was Julian's title. It was nothing to do with LSD. I think Paul helped me with the last verse.

GETTING BETTER: Paul – I think I helped with some of the words in the middle.

JOHN ON BEATLES SONGS continued

SHE'S LEAVIING HOME: Both of us. Paul had the basic theme. But all those lines like, 'We sacrificed most of our lives; we gave her everything money could buy;.. never a thought for ourselves,' those were the things Mimi used to say. It was easy to write.

BEING FOR THE BENEFIT OF MR. KITE!: Me – I got some of the words off an old circus poster. I have it in the billiard room. The story that 'Henry the Horse' meant heroin was rubbish.

WHEN I'M SIXTY-FOUR: Paul. I think I helped Paul with some of the words, like 'Vera, Chuck and Dave,' and 'Doing the garden, digging the weeds'.

GOOD MORNING GOOD MORNING: Me – a bit of a gobbledygook one – but nice words.

A DAY IN THE LIFE: Both of us. I wrote the bit up to 'woke up fell out of bed,' and I think Paul wrote, 'I'd love to turn you on'. I got the idea from a news item in the *Daily Mail* about four thousand holes in Blackburn.

BABY, YOU'RE A RICH MAN: Both of us. In fact, we just stuck two songs together for this one – same as 'A Day In The Life'

I AM THE WALRUS: Me – I like that one. That was the time when I was putting Hare Krishna and all that down. I hadn't taken it up then.

MAGICAL MYSTERY TOUR: Paul – I helped with some of the lyric.

HEY JUDE: Paul – that's his best song. It started off as a song about my son, Julian, because Paul was going to see him. Then he turned it into 'Hey Jude'. I always thought it was about me and Yoko but he said it was about him and Julian.

REVOLUTION: Me – I should never have put that in about Chairman Mao. I was just finishing off in the studio when I did that.

BACK IN THE USSR: Paul – maybe I helped a bit, but I don't think so.

HAPPINESS IS A WARM GUN: Me. That's another one I like. They all said it was about drugs but it was more about rock and roll than drugs. It's a sort of history of rock and roll. The title came from an American gun magazine. I don't know why people said it was about the needle in heroin. I've only seen somebody do something with a needle once and I don't like it at all.

ROCKY RACCOON: Paul – I might have helped with some of the words. I'm not sure.

WHY DON'T WE DO IT IN THE ROAD: Paul – one of his best.

JULIA: Me – Yoko helped me with this one.

BIRTHDAY: Both of us – we wrote it in the studio.

EVERYBODY'S GOT SOMETHING TO HIDE: Me – Fats Domino did a great version of this one.

SEXY SADIE: Me – that was about the Maharishi.

BECAUSE: Me – this is a terrible arrangement. A bit like Beethoven's Fifth backwards.

ACROSS THE UNIVERSE: Me – one of my best songs. Not one of the best recordings, but I like the lyrics.

LOVE YOU TO

Composer: George
Performers: George – vocal, acoustic guitar; Paul – harmony vocal; Ringo – tambourine (plus various Indian musicians on sitar, tambura, etc.)
Recorded: 11, 13 April 1966, Abbey Road
Released: LP *Revolver* 5 August 1966 (UK), 8 August 1966 (US)

George's first proper Indian song – written for Indian instruments, extensively used in the recording session when he hired the North London Asian Circle musicians. The sound they made was a revelation at the time, to the ears of normal pop pickers, but we quickly got used to it, captivated by the mystical, magical quality. The words, though, were hardly way out – wanting to make love to someone. The track is one of the few Beatles songs in which the words of the title do not appear in the lyrics.

The start of something new.

LOVELY RITA

Composer: Paul
Performers: Paul – vocal, piano, bass; John – backing vocal, rhythm guitar; George – backing vocal, guitar; Ringo – drums; George Martin – piano
Recorded: 23, 24 February and 7, 21 March 1967, Abbey Road
Released: LP *Sgt Pepper* 1 June 1967 (UK), 2 June 1967 (US)

There was no specific person who Paul had in mind – though one meter maid later did step forward to identify herself – it was just the whole notion of female parking attendants, something new in the UK in 1967, which intrigued Paul when he heard that the American term was meter maids. The

notion of a fair maid and puns on the word meter – i.e. meet her – amused his fertile brain. Don't say that Beatles tunes did not reflect life around them. The music itself reflects life gone past, with its jaunty, honky-tonk music-hall rhythm and all four of them trying their hand, and mouths, at paper and combs, just to add to the silly noises.

Uplifting, upbeat.

LUCY IN THE SKY WITH DIAMONDS

Composer: John
Performers: John – vocal, lead guitar; Paul – harmony vocal, organ, bass; George – harmony vocal, lead guitar, tambura; Ringo – drums, maracas
Recorded: 1-2 March 1967, Abbey Road
Released: LP *Sgt Pepper* 1 June 1967 (UK), 2 June 1967 (US)

Most people by now accept that the main initials of the title, L.S.D., do *not* stand for that nasty drug. It was pure happenstance – and yet how neatly that theory fitted with the song itself, with its druggy overtones, psychedelic babbling, dream-like sequences and some nonsense, if interesting, words. Lucy was in fact a little girl at school with Julian, John's son, and Julian was doing a drawing that he said was about Lucy, and oh, that blue bit is the sky and that's a diamond. All very obvious, really, to a four-year-old.

And yet Spencer Leigh has recently come up with the theory that the LSD reference might well have been deliberate after all. 'No one has picked up that Jimi Hendrix wrote and recorded a song about "Laughing Sam's Dice" at precisely the same time. To me this takes the LSD coincidence too far. My guess is that Hendrix and Lennon at some London club thought it would be fun to have LSD in the titles of their songs …'

SGT PEPPER

Reviews of songs on *Sgt Pepper*, *New Musical Express*, 2 May 1967 by Allen Evans

LUCY IN THE SKY WITH DIAMONDS: 'A fantasy song, sung by John in a high pitched voice, with distorted long way off sound. Song is about a girl and pier, with its electric lights. Slow, insistent beat.'

WITHIN YOU WITHOUT YOU: 'This side starts and ends with tapping noises, then there's a weird Indian tune up of strings. George sings softly in English but it is hard to make out the words because they merge with the sitar music so closely they are often drowned by it. At the end, the audience comes in, laughing a bit.'

TOMORROW NEVER KNOWS: 'John's vocal, telling you to relax and float down stream. But how can you relax with the electronic outer space noises, often sounding like seagulls? John's voice is weirdly fractured and given a faraway sound. Only Ringo's rock steady drumming is natural.'

Whatever, the words and images are fascinating, literary lunacy, and the music full of changes of key and rhythm, counter harmonies and melodies.

Still hypnotic, after all these years.

MAGICAL MYSTERY TOUR

Composer: Paul
Performers: Paul – vocal, bass, piano; John – harmony vocal, rhythm guitar; George – backing vocal, lead guitar; Ringo – drums, tambourine; Mal Evans and Neil Aspinall – cowbells, maracas, tambourine (plus four trumpets)
Recorded: 25–27 April and 3 May 1967, Abbey Road
Released: EP *Magical Mystery Tour* 8 December 1967 (UK), LP *Magical Mystery Tour* 27 November 1967 (US)
Charts: UK No. 2

Right, said Paul, just sing out any words and phrases that you can think of. Not of course *any* words, but stuff that might be shouted out by someone wanting people to roll up and go on a coach ride, such as 'Invitation', 'Reservation', 'Satisfaction Guaranteed'. Mal Evans had been sent round the London bus stations to pick up any posters that might be advertising such trips, so they could lift actual phrases, but with no luck, so they had to think of words on the hoof, sitting in the studio, listening to the music tape they had already laid down. A *Magical Mystery Tour* was Paul's idea for a TV special and also an EP and LP, thinking back to the Mystery Tour coach rides that had been a feature of his childhood in the fifties, and also about Ken Kesey and some hippies in California who went around in a psychedelically painted old bus. They needed an opening chorus, to set the scene, so it didn't really need a lot of words. You could say this lack of detail and proper preparation was one of the reasons why the whole TV show was rather slammed by the critics when broadcast. Now, to all true Beatles fans, it is a little gem, and also to TV historians, fascinated by this early example of hand-held, impromptu film-making.

Not really a song, just a roll up, roll up.

MARTHA MY DEAR

Composer: Paul
Performers: Paul - vocal, piano, lead guitar, bass guitar, drums, most things really (plus a mini orchestra to help out)
Recorded: 4, 5 October 1968, Trident Studios
Released: LP *The Beatles* 22 November 1968 (UK), 25 November 1968 (US)

Eleanor Rigby did not exist, Lovely Rita was imagined, Sexy Sadie was not a woman – but Martha, oh yes, she did exist. And she was a dog, Paul's Old English sheepdog. But of course, when the words came to be finalised, the sentiments expanded and so could refer to the end of an affair with a human female, such as, er, Jane? It is a sweet song, with a jaunty rhythm, almost like a set of musical exercises, well enunciated and sung by Paul, with the help of a small brass band and a string ensemble. Apart from that, he did everything on his own – no other Beatle took part.

Don't forget me – how could we?

MAXWELL'S SILVER HAMMER

Composer: Paul
Performers: Paul - vocal, piano, guitars; George - backing vocal, lead guitar; Ringo - backing vocal, drums; George Martin - organ
Recorded: 9-11 July and 6 August 1969, Abbey Road
Released: LP *Abbey Road* 26 September 1969 (UK), 1 October 1969 (US)

Ian MacDonald, the greatly admired musicologist, who died in 2003, gave this song a right hammering in his book *Revolution In The Head*, calling it, among others things, 'ghastly' and 'sniggering nonsense'. He considered it the worst example of Paul's lack of taste as a Beatle, a piece of pure indulgence and egotism, and only wishes John (who always hated the song) could have been in the studio, which he wasn't, to have knocked some sense into Paul's head, and into his composition.

The narrative is fairly ghastly – about someone called Maxwell who goes round killing people – but it is all a metaphor, about how just when things seem to be going well in life, down on your head comes a hammer – metaphorically, of course. Paul worked so hard on it, to get it right as he imagined it, and the words are witty and well enunciated, and he clearly had fun getting his tongue round 'pataphysical'. The music is jaunty, a music hall pastiche. It's just a song, for goodness sake, nothing to get worked up about, if hardly a classic.

Mal Evans is excellent on the anvil.

MEAN MR MUSTARD

Composer: John
Performers: John - vocal, lead guitar, maracas; Paul - harmony vocal, bass, harmonium, piano; George - lead guitar; Ringo - drums, bongos; George Martin - organ
Recorded: 24, 25, 29 July 1969, Abbey Road
Released: LP *Abbey Road* 26 September 1969 (UK), 1 October 1969 (US)

Mr Mustard didn't exist either, just one of John's schoolboy jokes about a dirty old man he had read about in a newspaper. The name is reminiscent of a character from Cluedo or Happy Families. It's only one minute long, so more of a scrap than a song, sandwiched between 'Sun King' and 'Polythene Pam' in the long medley towards the end of the second side of *Abbey Road*.

An amusing squib.

MICHELLE

Composer: Paul
Performers: Paul - vocal, acoustic guitar, lead guitar; John - backing vocal; George - backing vocal; Ringo - drums.
Recorded: 3 November 1965, Abbey Road
Released: LP *Rubber Soul* 3 December 1965 (UK), 6 December 1965 (US)

Another non-existent female, chosen because Paul wanted something sounding French. Pretending to be French, playing a French song, used to be one of his party pieces back in Liverpool in 1959 at art student gatherings, hoping to impress girls. Six years later, he worked it up to include it on *Rubber Soul*, getting the wife of one of their old Liverpool friends, Ivan Vaughan, to suggest a rhyme in French for 'Michelle'. She suggested 'Ma Belle'. Paul does sing quite a few lines in French, unusual for a pop song. John suggested the repetition of 'I love you, I love you' as a middle eight, having been listening to Nina Simone singing 'I Put A Spell on You'.

Paul plays and sings the whole song almost as a solo – John and George being restricted to backing harmonies. Paul probably tried to take over the drums from Ringo as well. Never quite as popular as 'Yesterday', his other 'solo', but still loved by folkies and guitarists on London Underground stations.

Pas mal.

MISERY

Composer: John and Paul
Performers: John - vocal, rhythm guitar; Paul - vocal, bass; George - lead guitar; Ringo - drums; George Martin - piano
Recorded: 11, 20 February 1963, Abbey Road
Released: LP *Please Please Me* 22 March 1963,

LP *Introducing … The Beatles* originally scheduled 22 July 1963, actual 10 January 1964 (US)

One of eight self-composed numbers on their first LP. It was mainly the work of John, as the subject matter might indicate, convinced the world was treating him bad. Paul, later on, might have made it less of a dirge more of a parody. John, with Paul's help, wrote it during their first tour, with Helen Shapiro in mind, in early 1963, hoping she might record it, but she never did. So that was miserable. Helen Shapiro has no memory of being offered the song, but it was covered by Kenny Lynch, who was also on that tour – the first cover version to be recorded of any Beatles song.

The title says it all.

MOTHER NATURE'S SON

Composer: Paul
Performers: Paul - vocal, acoustic guitar, drums (plus brass section)
Recorded: 9, 20 August 1968, Abbey Road
Released: LP *The Beatles* 22 November 1968 (UK), 25 November 1968 (US)

Back to nature, sitting by a mountain stream, poor country boy, tra la, the sort of fantasies and images of which urbanites are awfully fond. Having thought of it – supposedly inspired by a talk from the Maharishi on man and nature – Paul rather ran out of ideas, as the lyrics are only ten short lines, but the tinkly tune is attractive and the arrangement clever.

Nice and healthy.

NO REPLY

Composer: John
Performers: John – vocal, acoustic guitar; Paul – harmony vocal, bass; George – acoustic guitar; Ringo – drums; George Martin – piano
Recorded: 30 September 1964, Abbey Road
Released: LP *Beatles For Sale* 4 December 1964 (UK), LP *Beatles '65* 15 December 1964 (US)

Their first narrative song – in that it tells a story, or at least describes a situation, as opposed to 'I love you … you love me'. It was written by John, about watching a girl's house, seeing a shadow, then she comes out – with another man and he nearly died. Not quite an original storyline, as an American group called The Rays had produced a record called 'Silhouettes' in 1957 that had a similar tale. A bit bleak and heavy, but an interesting departure.

Storyville.

NORWEGIAN WOOD (THIS BIRD HAS FLOWN)

Composers: John plus Paul
Performers: John – vocal, acoustic rhythm guitar; Paul – harmony vocal, bass; George – sitar; Ringo – tambourine, maracas, cymbal
Recorded: 12, 21 October 1965, Abbey Road
Released: LP *Rubber Soul* 3 December 1965 (UK), 6 December 1965 (US)

Another song telling a story, which by 1965 they were now frequently doing, but the narrative conceals as much as it reveals, probably so that John's wife Cynthia did not suspect that John had been having an affair. Paul, interviewed just before the LP's release, said there were going to be some jokes in *Rubber Soul*. Presumably the joke at the end of 'Norwegian Wood' is that the person having the affair sleeps in the bath and burns the Norwegian wood. Stripped pinewood walls, which lots of people had, were very popular in the sixties. Nice melody, with the sitar giving an Indian undercurrent.

Hello to the sitar.

NOT A SECOND TIME

Composer: John
Performers: John – vocal, acoustic guitar; Paul – bass; George – acoustic guitar; Ringo – drums; George Martin – piano
Recorded: 11 September 1963, Abbey Road
Released: LP *With The Beatles* 22 November 1963 (UK), LP *Meet The Beatles!* 20 January 1964 (US)

One of those early Beatles numbers – written by John – which few seem to remember now, far less sing, but at the time it caused quite a stir because a strange thing happened. William Mann, the classical music critic of *The Times*, decided to give it his intellectual treatment, analysing every note and praising, among other things, its 'Aeolian cadences'. You what? said John, and most Beatles fans, but it marked the beginning of The Beatles receiving serious musical attention. All the same, it is a pretty feeble song, all about John being hurt by some girl, who has made him cry.

Thanks to Mr Mann.

NOWHERE MAN

Composer: John
Performers: John – vocal, acoustic rhythm guitar; Paul – harmony vocal, bass; George – harmony vocal, lead guitar; Ringo – drums

Recorded: 21, 22 October 1965, Abbey Road
Released: LP *Rubber Soul* 3 December 1965 (UK), single
21 February 1966 (US), with B-side 'What Goes On'
Charts: US No. 3

One of John's songs, like 'I'm Only Sleeping', where he is looking at himself looking at himself. Which of course we all do. That was presumably his second thought, realising he could make a song out of it, on a theme most of us would identify with. He had had a sleepless night, struggling to come up with a new song for the *Rubber Soul* album, and then thought of himself as a nowhere man, sitting in his nowhere land, getting nowhere. Cue for a song. In this case, he did see it all through, working on the music and lyrics, with a little help from Paul, developing the original idea – moving on from being nowhere, to seeing nobody, having no point of view, seeing only what he wants to see, then adding in the generalised observation – 'isn't he a bit like me and you?'

Everyman John.

OB-LA-DI, OB-LA-DA

Composer: Paul
Performers: Paul - vocal, bass; John - backing vocal, piano; George - backing vocal, acoustic guitar; Ringo - drums, bongos (plus three saxophones)
Recorded: 3-5, 8, 9, 11, 15 July 1968, Abbey Road
Released: LP *The Beatles* 22 November 1968 (UK), 25 November 1968 (US)

The music critics have been rather against this song, dismissing it as trite, if very commercial, and John thought it a bit twee, but it's a joke, an amusement, a pastiche, not meant to be taken seriously. The title comes from a Nigerian phrase meaning 'life goes on', which a club musician

friend of Paul called Jimmy Scott always used to say. (Paul has said he later gave him a cheque, for borrowing his expression.) Paul gave it a Jamaican ska beat and a West Indian setting; at least that's where Molly and Desmond Jones appear to be living, apart, of course, from inside Paul's head.

Ah ha ha. Fun.

OCTOPUS'S GARDEN

Composer: Ringo
Performers: Ringo - vocal, drums, percussion; George - backing vocal, lead guitar, synthesiser; Paul - backing vocal, bass, piano; John - guitar
Recorded: 26, 29 April and 17, 18 July 1969, Abbey Road
Released: LP *Abbey Road* 16 September 1969 (UK), 1 October 1969 (US)

Ringo had left The Beatles for a while, fed up with being ignored, or with Paul showing him how to play the drums, and went off for a holiday on Peter Sellers's yacht; they had met when Ringo co-starred with Sellers in the film *The Magic Christian*. The captain of the ship told him about the octopuses underneath the ship, and their habits, such as making a garden with stones, which fascinated Ringo. He wrote a song about it, not quite as catchy as that other maritime classic 'Yellow Submarine', but it made a good Ringo number for the *Abbey Road* LP, saving them the trouble of writing one for him, when he eventually returned and was warmly welcomed back into The Beatles' fold. George helped him finish it off, convinced it was a deeper, more cosmic song than it might appear on the surface.

Ringo's second and final Beatles song.

OH! DARLING

Composer: Paul
Performers: Paul – vocal, bass, guitar; John – backing vocal, piano; George – backing vocal, guitar; Ringo – drums
Recorded: 20, 24 April, 17, 18, 22, 23 July and 11 August 1969, Abbey Road
Released: LP *Abbey Road* 26 September 1969 (UK), 1 October 1969 (US)

Paul, for some reason, decided to treat us to his Little Richard voice, which he had often used back in his live stage performances. A mistake, really. The lyrics are poor – darling, don't leave me – and the singing a strain.

10cc had a hit in 1972 with a song called 'Donna' that appeared to be based on 'Oh! Darling'. 'Paul McCartney has said to me a few times, 'Where are my royalties for "Donna"?' Eric Stewart, a member of 10cc, told Spencer Leigh. 'I tell him he can afford it. The song didn't come from him actually. In the fifties there was another screaming song just like that, but I can't remember the title of it. We both got the idea from that.'

Oh dear.

OLD BROWN SHOE

Composer: George
Performers: George – vocal, guitars, organ; Paul – backing vocal, piano, bass; John – backing vocal; Ringo – drums
Recorded: 25 February and 16, 18 April 1969, Abbey Road
Released: single 30 May 1969 (UK), 4 June 1969 (USA), with A-side 'The Ballad Of John And Yoko'.
Charts: UK No 1, US No. 8

The 'old brown shoe', out of which he is stepping in the first verse, and which is only mentioned once, would appear to be a metaphor for this old earthly, boring, materialistic life. Or it could have simply been a reference to wanting Mal Evans to go and get him a new pair of shoes. That first verse, with the first line about wanting a love that's right, 'but right is only half of what's wrong,' is about the best of the lyrics, as the rest of the verses verge on the banal. But the basic meaning, according to George later, was really about 'the duality of things – yes no, up down, right wrong.' Of course it was.

Old rope.

ONE AFTER 909

Composer: John
Performers: John – vocal, lead guitar; Paul – vocal, bass; George – rhythm guitar; Ringo – drums; Billy Preston – electric piano
Recorded: 28–30 January 1969, Apple Studios
Released: LP *Let it Be* 8 May 1970 (UK), 18 May 1970 (US)

A down-memory-lane composition, written by John when he first met Paul, back in 1957, a clear copy of the sort of skiffle/rockabilly/train ride blues that everyone was playing or listening to at the time. The girl in the song says she is travelling on the 'one after 909'. Why didn't she give the exact time? Or was something else happening at nine minutes past nine? Who knows now, if they ever did.

It first got recorded on 5 March 1963, but never used, then dragged out again in 1969 to fill up the *Let It Be* album. Hardly worth it really, but of historic interest as it is the oldest known Lennon/McCartney composition.

For nostalgia lovers only.

ONLY A NORTHERN SONG

Composer: George
Performers: George – vocal, organ; Paul – bass, trumpet;
John – piano; Ringo – drums
Recorded: 13, 14 February and 20 April 1967, Abbey Road
Released: LP *Yellow Submarine* 17 January 1969 (UK),
13 January 1969 (US)

This is a V-sign song, bugger you, I don't care, having a go at Northern Songs, the publishing company that George hated for having them under contract and taking all their money, so he maintained. It was during George's anti-Beatles phase, fed up with them and the whole damn business. He was probably surprised that the suits ever allowed it to be recorded – originally for the *Sgt Pepper* album, but not used, for obvious reasons, then it was tagged on to the soundtrack for the *Yellow Submarine* cartoon film. It is a rubbish song, with rubbish lyrics, so George is clearly saying, but what you do expect, it's only a Northern Song.

Cheeky.

PAPERBACK WRITER

Composer: Paul
Performers: Paul – vocal, bass; John – backing vocal, rhythm guitar; George – backing vocal, lead guitar; Ringo – drums, tambourine
Recorded: 13, 14 April 1966, Abbey Road
Released: single 10 June 1966 (UK), 30 May 1966 (US), with B-side 'Rain'
Charts: UK No. 1, US No. 1

One of Paul's wittier lyrics – in the manuscript form it was written out as a letter, beginning 'Dear Sir/or Madam', from an aspiring author asking

to be published, using all the clichés aspiring authors do use – how it will make millions, how he can make it longer or shorter. They had a lot of fun recording it by the sound of things (John and George sing the words 'Frère Jacques' from the French nursery rhyme in the background, for goodness sake – now that's fun), doing exaggerated harmonies and falsettos, with Paul trying out the possibilities of his new Rickenbacker bass guitar. Paul had come across some paperback authors, but it seems that it was the sound of the two words 'paperback writer', playing with the ways to sing the two words, that sparked him off.

Bestseller – in that it made No. 1 in UK and US.

PENNY LANE

Composer: Paul plus John
Performers: Paul – vocal, piano, bass, harmonium; John – backing vocal, piano, guitar, congas; George – backing vocal, guitar; Ringo – drums, hand bell; George Martin – piano (plus mini brass band)
Recorded: 29, 30 December 1966 and 4-6, 9, 10, 17 January 1967, Abbey Road
Released: single 17 February 1967 (UK), 13 February 1967 (US), with double A-side 'Strawberry Fields Forever'
Charts: UK No. 2, US No. 1

Were the two sides of this single the cleverest, simplest, richest, most original smartest single The Beatles ever made? Or any group ever made? The easy appeal, singalong tune and happy sunny-side-up glow of 'Penny Lane' on one side with the awesome, disturbing 'Strawberry Fields' on the other. What a combination.

Penny Lane, as a place mentioned in a lyric, had appeared in a verse by John before ('In My Life') but was never used in the final version of the song. Penny Lane had been a feature in both of their lives, a Liverpool landmark, known by all, but Paul got a tune out of it, then with John's help, using real places and people, such as the barber's shop and the fireman, turned it into a universal story, as if from a children's picture book, or a toy town play, where everything is gay and lovely, bright and cheerful, where we can all march along happily into the future. The lyrics are witty, refusing the temptation to moralise or push any message. There is one rude reference to amuse Liverpool teenage boys – 'fish and finger pie' was what they hoped for from teenage girls – but otherwise it is ever so innocent, making everyone want to sing aloud and march in step to the jolly brass band, all blowing our own trumpets.

Winsome winner.

PIGGIES

Composer: George
Performers: George – vocal, guitar; Paul – bass; Ringo – tambourine (plus John on tape loops, four violins, two violas, two cellos, one harpsichord)
Recorded: 19, 20 September and 10 October 1968, Abbey Road
Released: LP *The Beatles* 22 November 1968 (UK), 25 November 1968 (US)

Another song disliked by Ian MacDonald (*Revolution In The Head*), who described it as 'an embarrassing blot on [George's] discography,' which is a bit unfair. Despite its jaunty tune, it contains some of the hardest-hitting social comments in all The Beatles' lyrics, lashing out at capitalist pigs, living piggy lives, with their piggy wives. He says they need a 'damn good whacking', a line suggested by George's mum when he was stuck for a rhyme for 'backing' and 'lacking' – and which

Charles Manson and his gang took literally in 1969 in California, seeing it as an incitement to murder.

A bit of a rant, but heartfelt.

PLEASE PLEASE ME

Composer: John
Performers: John – vocal, rhythm guitar, harmonica; Paul – vocal, bass guitar; George – harmony vocal, lead guitar; Ringo – drums
Recorded: 26 November 1962, Abbey Road
Released: Single 11 January 1963 (UK), 25 February 1963 (US), with B-side 'Ask Me Why'
Charts: UK No. 2, US No. 3 (when re-released 30 January 1964, with B-side 'From Me To You')

Just as important as 'Love Me Do' in the Beatles song saga, for this was the one that first got them to No. 1 in the *NME* charts (the *Record Retailer* chart was regarded as the 'main chart at the time; the single reached No. 2) and made the British record industry sit up and the fans start yelling – yet at the time they were still on a provincial tour, as a supporting group to Helen Shapiro. That all changed when 'Please Please Me' broke through. John wrote it in his bedroom at Menlove Avenue, and could remember the pink eiderdown on his bed. The lyrics rather bothered the Americans, some suspecting there could be a hint of fellatio in the title; what a thought, wash your mouths out, as if anyone in the UK had ever heard of such a thing. Capitol – owned by EMI – refused to release it in the US, so the Chicago label Vee-Jay brought it out first in February 1963 and then again with a new B-side in January 1964, reaching No. 3 in the US charts.

Worth top marks in the Beatles canon.

POLYTHENE PAM

Composer: John
Performers: John – vocal, acoustic guitar; Paul – vocal, bass, lead guitar; George – lead guitar, backing vocal; Ringo – drums, cowbells
Recorded: 25, 28, 30 July 1969, Abbey Road
Released: LP *Abbey Road* 26 September 1969 (UK), 1 October 1969 (US)

One of the scraps of half finished songs bunged into the long medley towards the end of *Abbey Road* just to, well get rid of them really. They knew this was the end, the last album, they would make together as The Beatles (though not the last to be released). They knew they would never be arsed to work together again, or get round to finishing off all their leftover bits into a proper song, so might as well unload them now, have done with it, bye bye Beatles.

Various girls have been said to have been the originator of 'Polythene Pam' – a girl who dressed up in plastic or polythene in order to please please – but it doesn't really matter now, it's only a last Beatles song, though it does have a good strong, driving refrain, making you wish they had stuck together, stuck it out.

Half marks for a half song.

P.S. I LOVE YOU

Composer: Paul
Performers: Paul – vocal, bass; John – backing vocal, acoustic rhythm guitar; George – lead guitar, backing vocal; Ringo – maracas; Andy White – drums
Recorded: 11 September 1962, Abbey Road
Released: single 5 October 1962 (UK), 27 April 1964 (US), with A-side 'Love Me Do'
Charts: UK No. 17, US No. 10 as an individual track (No. 1 as B-side of 'Love Me Do')

The notion of a pop song as a letter was not entirely original, and Paul later used the format in 'Paperback Writer' and, less obviously, in 'When I'm 64', but the P.S. idea was unusual. And cute. At the time, most people thought it was inspired by Paul writing from Hamburg to his girlfriend at the time, Dot Rhone, but he has since denied it was about her. The Beatles, surprisingly, did not create all that many new songs in Hamburg – too busy pumped up with pills working eight days a week – so this song is an interesting footnote in their composing history. It became the B-side of their first ever record, so another fascinating fact, but it also earns extra points for just being there, on the other side, a totally unknown group back in the dark ages, c 1962, being allowed to have their songs on *both* sides of their debut record. Note also Andy White was in there drumming, while dear Ringo twiddled his thumbs, or similar.

Historic stuff.

RAIN

Composers: John plus Paul
Performers: John – vocal, rhythm guitar; Paul – bass, backing vocal; George – lead guitar, backing vocal; Ringo – drums, tambourine
Recorded: 14 April 1966, Abbey Road
Released: single 10 June 1966 (UK), 30 May 1966 (US), with A-side 'Paperback Writer'
Charts: UK No. 1, US No. 23 as an individual track (No. 1 as B-side of 'Paperback Writer')

One of those Beatles songs that never makes it when well-known persons go on the BBC Radio 4 show *Desert Island Discs*, or even in most ordinary folks top 100 fave Beatles tunes. Yet over the years it has consistently had lots of fans among the musicologists – perhaps because of the use of backward tapes – who consider it fantastic. Others are not quite as impressed by all the psychedelic clap trap, sorry, interesting metaphors on the nature of rain and whether it is just a state of mind. Discuss.

Wet, wet wet. (Unless of course you are in the 'Fantastic' camp, like Spencer Leigh, when naturally you will be giving it a big 10.)

REVOLUTION

Composer: John
Performers: John – vocal, lead guitar; Paul – bass, Hammond organ; George – lead guitar; Ringo – drums; Nicky Hopkins – electric piano
Recorded: 10–12 July 1968, Abbey Road
Released: single 30 August 1968 (UK), 26 August 1968 (US), with A-side 'Hey Jude'
Charts: UK No. 1, US No. 12 as an individual track (No. 1 as B-side of 'Hey Jude')

Students, and student types, were revolting in 1968, in France, the UK and US, taking to the streets, protesting about the Vietnam War, among other issues, and John felt a kinship with them all, whatever they were protesting about, supporting lots of groups with money and messages. But he was not, in fact, in favour of direct, physical, violent action. In this first released (though not first recorded) and faster version of 'Revolution', which went out on a single as the B-side to 'Hey Jude', when it came to destruction, he said 'count me out'. He also made it clear he felt everything was going to be all right – which upset many of the die-hard revolutionaries.

Worthy, upbeat try.

REVOLUTION 1

Composer: John
Performers: John – vocal, lead guitar; Paul – backing vocal, piano; Hammond organ, bass; George – backing vocal, lead guitar; Ringo – drums (plus six brass)
Recorded: 30, 31 May and 4, 21 June 1968, Abbey Road,
Released: LP *The Beatles* 22 November 1968 (UK), 25 November 1968 (US)

'Revolution 1' was another version of 'Revolution', recorded earlier but put out later, on *The Beatles* album (*White Album*). John had always been in two minds about what he really felt about violent action, and in 'Revolution 1' he rather prevaricated by saying his position was now both out/in, which was a bit hard to sing, or at least to make out exactly what he was saying. This version had otherwise exactly the same words, but was more slowed down than the one released as the B-side of 'Hey Jude'.

Slightly more turgid.

REVOLUTION 9

Creator: John, plus a little help from his friend Yoko
Performers: Assorted sounds
Recorded: 30 May and 6, 10, 11, 20, 21 June 1968, Abbey Road
Released: LP *The Beatles* 22 November 1968 (UK), 25 November 1968 (US)

This was a musical collage, bunging in lots of sounds, backward tapes, awfully avant-garde, done by John with Yoko's help, with no lyrics, as such, though you can hear a voice going on about 'Number Nine, Number Nine', which was a tape they found lying around announcing the question number from an examination for Royal Academy of Music students.

Self-indulgence.

ROCKY RACCOON

Composer: Paul
Performers: Paul - vocal, acoustic guitar; John - backing vocal, harmonica, tambourine, bass; George - backing vocal; Ringo - drums; George Martin - piano
Recorded: 15 August 1968, Abbey Road
Released: LP *The Beatles* 22 November 1968 (UK), 25 November 1968 (US)

Began as a knockabout jam session when they were in India, led by Paul with John and Donovan joining in, pretending to play a type of western, barrel organ song, perhaps the sort they had heard during cowboy films at Saturday morning matinees as kids. Paul worked pretty hard on the lyrics, creating a proper narrative about a young boy called Rocky whose girl has gone off with another guy. Doesn't make total sense, but is quite amusing – checking into the rival's room, but only finding a Gideon Bible, words that Paul clearly found good fun to sing. Intellectual analysts have found no hidden meanings anywhere in the lyrics – so far.

Harmless fun.

RUN FOR YOUR LIFE

Composer: John
Performers: John - vocal, acoustic guitar, lead guitar; Paul - harmony vocal, bass; George - harmony vocal, guitar; Ringo - drums, tambourine
Recorded: 12 October 1965, Abbey Road
Released: LP *Rubber Soul* 3 December 1965 (UK), 6 December 1965 (US)

John never liked this song, saying he had done it in a hurry for the *Rubber Soul* album, and pinched one of the lines – about wanting his girl dead if he saw her with another man – from the Elvis song 'Baby Let's Play House'. The lyrics are a bit violent, admitting he is wicked and jealous and might kill his girl. Not very peace and love. But the song has good pace and sounds jaunty and cheerful, despite the awful things he is actually saying.

Dance, don't ponder.

SAVOY TRUFFLE

Composer: George
Performers: George - vocal, lead guitar; Paul - bass; Ringo - drums, tambourine; Chris Morgan - organ, electric piano. Plus six saxophones.
Recorded: 3, 5 October 1968, Trident Studios; 11, 14 October 1968, Abbey Road
Released: LP *The Beatles* 22 November 1968 (UK), 25 November 1968 (US)

By this stage in their career, The Beatles could almost get away with anything, writing song lyrics about any old stuff that came into their heads, or nothing at all. George had done it, telling us how bad his song was when mocking Northern Songs. Now he took the lyrics for a song from the list of chocolates in a box of Mackintosh's Good News. The excuse was that he was warning his friend Eric Clapton, who had a very sweet tooth, about the dangers of things like Savoy truffle, creme tangerine and montelimart – all nice evocative names but, come on, song lyrics are meant to be lyrical.

Tooth-rotting lyrics.

SEXY SADIE

Composer: John
Performers: John - vocal, acoustic guitar, electric rhythm guitar; Paul - backing vocal, bass, piano; George - lead guitar, backing vocal; Ringo - drums, tambourine

Recorded: 19, 24 July and 13, 21 August 1968, Abbey Road
Released: LP The Beatles 22 November 1968 (UK), 25 November 1968 (US)

The only Beatles song in which the words 'sex' or 'sexy' appear – though you can usually find sex under the surface, if you look hard enough. In the early songs, there was a lot of *Love* – but that was nice boy-girl love. In later songs, *Love* was still up there, but was more about love of Peace, the World, Life, rather than sexual activity. So it is good to see it being sung about – except it isn't. 'Sexy Sadie' isn't about sex or a girl, but about the Maharishi, who, according to John, the world was waiting for, but he made a fool of everybody. For libel reasons, he couldn't in the song lyrics repeat the rumour – never substantiated – that the Maharishi was sex-mad, so he took his name out and turned him into a girl. The music also seems to be disguising itself, stopping and starting, hiding its true motives.

Interesting tease.

SGT PEPPER'S LONELY HEARTS CLUB BAND

Composer: Paul
Performers: Paul – vocal, bass, lead guitar; John – harmony vocal; George – guitar, harmony vocal; Ringo – drums (plus four French horns)
Recorded: 1, 2 February and 3, 6 March 1967, Abbey Road
Released: LP *Sgt Pepper* 1 June 1967 (UK), 2 June 1967 (US)

It was mainly Paul's idea, planning an album round a theme, about a supposedly old-fashioned Edwardian band having a show.

Like the 'Magical Mystery Tour' song, though with a bit more thought put into it, this is an introductory number, to start the album off, set the scene, so the lyrics introduce us to the band, guarantee to raise a smile, tell us we are all a lovely audience, in fact the band would like to take us home for tea. With fanfares from the brass band, we are then led into the first number by Billy Shears, who turns out to be Ringo. Is he supposed to be Billy Shears? The name Billy Shears never gets mentioned again. Later in the album, there is a reprise of the 'Sgt Pepper' tune – which they recorded on 1 April – to wrap up the album. It has slightly different words, thanking us for listening, and hoping we enjoyed the show. Which we all did, oh yes we did. Super fun.

The start – and end – of a great concept.

SHE CAME IN THROUGH THE BATHROOM WINDOW

Composer: Paul
Performers: Paul – vocal, bass, lead guitar; John – vocal, guitar; George – backing vocal, lead guitar; Ringo – drums, tambourine
Recorded: 22 January 1969, Apple Studios; 25, 28, 30 July 1969, Abbey Road
Released: LP *Abbey Road* 26 September 1969 (UK), 1 October 1969 (US)

This was another part of the long medley towards the end of *Abbey Road* – and about the best of the bunch. It has a good melody, though the lyrics are confusing, sounding as if bits got shoved in from other songs, other places, such as a dancer who worked 15 clubs a day, and someone else who is quitting the police department. The girl who came in through the bathroom window was real enough – one of the so-called 'Apple scruffs' who had broken into Paul's house.

Confusing scrap.

SHE LOVES YOU

Composers: John and Paul
Performers: John - vocal, rhythm guitar; Paul - vocal, bass;
George - harmony vocal, lead guitar; Ringo - drums
Recorded: 1 July 1963, Abbey Road
Released: single 23 August 1963 (UK), 16 September
1963 (US), with B-side 'I'll Get You'
Charts: UK No. 1, US No. 1

After 'Love Me Do', which was addressed to the second person singular, and 'P.S. I Love You', which was in the first person, this is a song in the *third person*. Don't say The Beatles did not ring the grammatical changes. So many of their early songs were about boy-girl teenage love, as you might expect, being teenagers, which was what the market wanted. The idea of a third person in love came to Paul while on tour, sitting in their hotel in Newcastle after a performance at the Majestic Ballroom on 26 June 1963. Five days later, they were belting it out at Abbey Road for their fourth single.

It was the most enormous success, becoming their biggest-selling record, and it set the seal on Beatlemania, which was now beginning to sweep the UK. Pictures of them were soon everywhere, shaking their moptop hair, jumping up and down, watched by screaming girls. And in all our ears was the sound of them singing, or more like yelling 'YEAH YEAH YEAH, YEAH YEAH YEAH'. Not exactly original words for a popular song (Are they words? And should the spelling be 'Yeh' anyway?) It was how they sang them that caught the national attention. In many ways The Beatles had made a feature of being British, not aping the Americans, or putting on a mid-Atlantic accent, as many popular UK singers had been doing, such as Cliff Richard. 'Yeah Yeah' until then had been considered American usage by most British adults. In fact Paul McCartney's father ticked him off, saying he

liked the song, but couldn't they sing 'Yes Yes Yes'? He thought that would be much nicer.

Yeh Yeh Yeh!

SHE SAID SHE SAID

Composer: John
Performers: John - vocal, rhythm guitar, Hammond organ;
George - backing vocal, lead guitar; Ringo - drums
Recorded: 21 June 1966, Abbey Road
Released: LP *Revolver* 5 August 1966 (UK), 8 August 1966
(US)

John pinched the first line from something the actor Peter Fonda had said to him at some drunken, druggie party. Fonda had told John he knew what it was like to be dead – thanks to a shooting accident as a child when his heart stopped beating. It greatly appealed to John's often twisted mind. The music as well as the lyrics is rich, complicated, unexpected and dramatic; it is considered by many to be the best track on *Revolver* – an album that many still think of as their best. Paul wasn't there at the main recording session. Bit of a mystery. He and John appeared to have had words over something, so George helped John to knock it into shape, with assistance from George Martin, and of course Ringo, and they created the song and the sound on their own. Quite an achievement.

A top song on a top album.

SHE'S A WOMAN

Composer: Paul
Performers: Paul - vocal, bass, piano; John - rhythm guitar;
George - lead guitar; Ringo - drums

Recorded: 8 October 1964, Abbey Road
Released: single 27 November 1964 (UK), 23 November 1964 (US), with A-side 'I Feel Fine'
Charts: UK No. 1, US No. 4 as an individual track (No. 1 as B-side of 'I Feel Fine')

Just five weeks earlier Dylan had given them their first pot to smoke. Surprising it took them so long. Dylan was amazed they had never used marijuana before as he had assumed they had from listening to 'I Want To Hold Your Hand', with what he thought was a line that said 'I get high'. So in 'She's A Woman' they shoved in the phrase 'turn me on', showing they were well in the groove, man. It's the first reference to drugs in any Beatles song, contextually. Musically, it's a shouty, screamy, rocker of a song, with Paul doing his Little Richard voice.

Interesting.

SHE'S LEAVING HOME

Composer: Paul
Performers: Paul – vocal; John – backing vocal (plus small string orchestra)
Recorded: 17, 20 March 1967, Abbey Road
Released: LP *Sgt Pepper* 1 June 1967 (UK), 2 June 1967 (US)

Paul took inspiration from a human interest story in the *Daily Mail*, about a middle-class girl who suddenly leaves home, much to the surprise of her parents. 'I cannot imagine why she should run away,' so her father was quoted, 'she has everything here.'

Paul turned this situation into a proper song, with proper lyrics, proper narrative, imagining she was off to meet a man from the motor trade. (In real life she had gone to meet a croupier.) The Greek chorus in the background of the wailing parents, as sung by Paul and John, saying they never thought of themselves, struggled hard, is especially poignant. A most unusual idea, in any lyric or poem, to give us both sides of the same story. The string orchestra does pull on the heartstrings – but without being syrupy. One of the gems of *Sgt Pepper* – and one of Paul's best-loved songs.

Classic.

SOMETHING

Composer: George
Performers: George, vocal, lead guitar; Paul – backing vocal, bass; John – guitar; Ringo – drums; Billy Preston – Hammond organ (plus mini string orchestra)
Recorded: 25 February, 16 April, 2 May, 11, 16 July and 15 August 1969, Abbey Road; 5 May 1969, Olympic Sound Studios
Released: LP *Abbey Road* 26 September 1969 (UK), 1 October 1969 (US)
Charts: UK No. 4, US No. 1, released 31 October 1969 (UK), 6 October 1969 (US), with double A-side 'Come Together' (US charts stopped listing B-sides/double A-sides separately in November 1969)

George took the first line – 'Something in the way she moves' – from a song by James Taylor, who happened to be working in Abbey Road at the same time. George had trouble finishing the lyrics, not sure what it was that attracted him to the woman in the song. John suggested he should just sing nonsense, that she attracted him like a cabbage, till he got it right. (In the end she attracts him 'like no other lover.') Then in the studio, George had numerous different attempts at recording it, spread over several months, before he was happy. Despite this complicated birth, it turned out to be George's finest.

It's a love song, again supposedly with Pattie in mind, but it transcends the particular and stands as a love song for all time. After 'Yesterday' it has become the most recorded of any Beatles song. Sinatra sang it a lot, describing it as 'the greatest love song of the last 50 years.' Rather insultingly, though presumably not deliberately, Sinatra described it as a Lennon/McCartney composition. Both Paul and John agreed it was probably the best song on the *Abbey Road* album.

Top marks for George's top Beatles tune.

STRAWBERRY FIELDS FOREVER

Composer: John
Performers: John - vocal, acoustic guitar; Paul - bass, mellotron; George - electric slide guitar; Ringo - drums (plus trumpets, tambourines, cellos, maracas)
Recorded: 24, 28, 29 November and 8, 9, 15, 21 December 1966, Abbey Road
Released: single 17 February 1967 (UK), 13 February 1967 (US), with double A-side 'Penny Lane'
Charts: UK No. 2, US No. 8 as an individual track (No. 1 as double A-side with 'Penny Lane')

Strawberry Field, without an 's', was a Salvation Army home where John used to play when young. They had been thinking of an album based on their Liverpool childhood, but this was actually written in Spain, when John was filming *How I Won The War*. As a child, he would often think he was in a trance, in a dream – not uncommon in childhood, as Wordsworth has told us – but John managed to make both the words and music have a hallucinatory feeling. It completely puzzled most people when they first heard it, considering it pretty weird and far out, but it is now seen as one of John's best ever songs. It was at one stage going to be on the *Sgt Pepper* album, but came out as a single – and for various didn't make it to No. 1 in the UK (where Engelbert Humperdinck, ugh, stayed top). It was the first time since 'Please Please Me' in January 1963 that a Beatles single had not reached the No. 1 spot. It is now seen as possibly their most original composition, marking a vital stage and progression in their development. The day after the recording of the song was complete, at John's suggestion George Martin joined together two versions they had made of the track, the first more simple, the second with all that intense, layered sound, to produce the song we all now know. And love.

Breakthrough.

GETTING THE HUMP

Beatle fans would have liked Engelbert Humperdinck to have said, 'Don't release me,' as their run of UK No. 1s was halted when Engelbert soared to the top with 'Release Me' and 'Penny Lane'/'Strawberry Fields Forever', a contender for the best single ever released, stalled at No. 2. But don't expect any misgivings from Engelbert Humperdinck. He says, 'I don't feel bad about it at all and, indeed, I feel proud that I kept The Beatles from being No. 1. To be in front of them in the charts was totally amazing, and I do think that my record is as good as theirs.'

There were some other unlikely winners during the Beatle years. The top-selling record of 1965 was Ken Dodd's 'Tears' and the biggest-selling album of 1967 was not *Sgt Pepper* but the soundtrack for *The Sound Of Music*.

SUN KING

Composer: John
Performers: John - vocal, lead guitar, maracas; Paul - harmony vocal, bass; George - lead guitar; Ringo - drums; George Martin - organ
Recorded: 24, 25, 29 July 1969, Abbey Road
Released: LP *Abbey Road* 26 September 1969 (UK), 1 October 1969 (US)

Another of those half songs bunged in on the second side of *Abbey Road*, which runs straight into 'Mean Mr Mustard'. Supposedly John was thinking of Nancy Mitford's biog of Louis XIV, *The Sun King*, and was trying for a Mediterranean feel to the music and words – throwing in three lines of random European phrases at the end. Actually more like a quarter song, as he only managed seven lines of lyrics all together.

Euro scrap.

TAXMAN

Composer: George
Performers: George - vocal, lead guitar; Paul - backing vocal, bass, lead guitar; John - backing vocal; Ringo - drums
Recorded: 20-22 April and 16 May 1966, Abbey Road
Released: LP *Revolver* 5 August 1966 (UK), 8 August 1966 (US)

This is George with a bee in his bonnet, but unlike some later songs when he is moaning on, such as 'Only A Northern Song', he has actually thought it out, worked on it, and has some good rhythms, effects and lyrics and some witty lines. Tax at the top rate at the time was 95 per cent, hence his fury. Mr Heath and Mr Wilson (former British Prime Ministers) get a name check – the first time living persons were mentioned in a Beatles song. They had not met Heath but Wilson was a local

Liverpool MP and had been PM in 1965 when they were awarded their MBEs.

'Taxman' kicks off *Revolver* – one of three original compositions by George on the LP. They were being awfully kind to him.

Unusual topic, but heartfelt.

TELL ME WHAT YOU SEE

Composer: Paul
Performers: Paul - vocal, electric piano, guiro; John - harmony vocal, rhythm guitar; George - lead guitar; Ringo - drums
Recorded: 18 February 1965, Abbey Road
Released: LP *Help!* 6 August 1965 (UK), LP *Beatles VI* 14 June 1965 (US)

Another of Paul's songs playing on the word 'see', meaning physically seeing someone and also understanding them. Contains some religious overtones, remembered from their Sunday School days, about putting 'your trust in me'. A simple tune, simple words, presumably addressed to Jane, but there is no story, no narrative.

Sweet nothings.

TELL ME WHY

Composer: John
Performers: John - vocal, rhythm guitar; Paul - harmony vocal, bass; George - harmony vocal, lead guitar; Ringo - drums
Recorded: 27 February 1964, Abbey Road
Released: LP *A Hard Day's Night* 10 July 1964 (UK), 26 June 1964 (US)

Written quickly by John for the film. The words are fairly plaintive – asking her why she lied, why she cried – but the mood and music are upbeat, which of course suited the sequence in the film.

Upbeat beat, downbeat words.

THANK YOU GIRL

Composers: John and Paul
Performers: John – vocal, rhythm guitar, harmonica; Paul – harmony vocal, bass; George – lead guitar; Ringo – drums
Recorded: 5, 13 March 1963, Abbey Road
Released: single 11 April 1963 (UK), 27 May 1963 (US), with A-side 'From Me To You'
Charts: UK No. 1, US No. 35 as individual track when re-released on 23 March 1964 as B-side of 'Do You Want To Know A Secret' (and No. 2 as the B-side of 'Do You Want To Know A Secret')

Another early song, quickly written and recorded on the run, head-to-head, while they were rushing round the UK on tour. Can be seen as a 'Thank You' to all the girls who were currently being kind to them, in every way, er, and buying their records.

Thanks, pet.

THE BALLAD OF JOHN AND YOKO

Composer: John
Performers: John – vocal, lead guitar; Paul – harmony vocal, bass, drums.
Recorded: 14 April 1969, Abbey Road
Released: single 30 May 1969 (UK), 4 June 1969 (US), with B-side 'Old Brown Shoe'
Charts: UK No. 1, US No. 8

Now we come to eight song titles beginning with the word 'The', which can be confusing when looking them up, as in many cases you don't real-ise that the title should start with a The. So take time to find them.

John was trying to find himself in the lyrics – an early example of autobiographical content in a pop song, most unusual at the time. He tells us exactly what he and Yoko had been up to – getting married, the bed-in, etc. – and also what was in his head, such as his fear that 'they' wanted to crucify him. When high on various drugs, John did some-times imagine he was Jesus Christ. The crucify reference and its clear connotation did not please some American stations who banned it. Again though, despite the theme, the beat is jaunty.

John's slice of autobiography.

THE CONTINUING STORY OF BUNGALOW BILL

Composer: John
Performers: John – vocal, acoustic guitar, organ; Paul – backing vocal, bass; George – backing vocal, acoustic guitar; Ringo – drums; Yoko Ono, plus others, backing vocal.
Recorded: 8 October 1968, Abbey Road
Released: LP *The Beatles* 22 November 1968 (UK), 25 November 1968 (US)

John was amused, or horrified, by a young all-American guy, one of those who was meditat-ing with them at Rishikesh, who went off on a tiger hunt – with his mum – then came back to meditate. So the story is not a made-up satire, as it might appear, though it does have jokey, mock-ing sound effects and girly chorus from, among others, the one and only Yoko (who also sings, 'Not when he looked so fierce,' the first female solo line in a Beatles song). The title harks back to Saturday morning children's films from the fifties.

Singalong.

THE END

Composer: Paul
Performers: Paul – vocal, bass, piano, lead guitar; John – backing vocal, lead guitar; George – backing vocal, lead guitar; Ringo – drums (plus mini orchestra)
Recorded: 23 July and 5, 7, 8, 15, 18 August 1969, Abbey Road
Released: LP *Abbey Road* 26 September 1969 (UK), 1 October 1969 (US)

Can't omit the 'The' from the title with this one, as it was Theeeee End, the concluding melody at the end of *Abbey Road* – and the end of their career as Beatles, as they knew *Abbey Road* would be the last album they would make together. (Actually in the end 'Her Majesty' was shoved on as the very very last track on *Abbey Road*.) Not many words but a chance for the three guitarists and Ringo to give us a little solo, thus going out with a flourish. And also a message – telling us that the love we take is equal to the love we make. Which Frank Zappa thought was 'the dumbest lyric ever'.

A squib, but good marks to mark its meaning.

THE FOOL ON THE HILL

Composer: Paul
Performers: Paul – vocal, piano, acoustic guitar, recorder; John – harmonica; George – acoustic guitar, harmonica; Ringo – drums (plus two flutes)
Recorded: 25–27 September and 20 October 1967, Abbey Road
Released: EP *Magical Mystery Tour* 8 December 1967 (UK), LP *Magical Mystery Tour* 27 November 1967 (US)
Charts: UK No. 2

Did Paul's inspiration come from seeing a man one morning on Primrose Hill, who just seemed to disappear, or was it based on the notion of a Maharishi guru figure? Except he hadn't met the Maharishi at the time he wrote the song. Anyway, it's about an idiot savant figure, an apparent foolish person who is in fact pretty wise, a notion that has appeared in literature down the centuries. Paul worked hard on the lyrics and the music has a wonderful ethereal quality, complete with flutes, which suggests a world spinning round. He recorded a demo of the song, all on his own, on 6 September 1967.

Charming.

THE INNER LIGHT

Composer: George
Performers: George – vocal; John – backing vocal; Paul – backing vocal (plus eight Indian musicians)
Recorded: 12 January 1968, EMI Recording Studio, Bombay; 6, 8 February 1968, Abbey Road
Released: single 15 March 1968 (UK), 18 March 1968 (US), with A-side 'Lady Madonna',
Charts: UK No. 1, US No. 96 as an individual track (No. 4 as B-side of 'Lady Madonna'

One of George's finer Indian-inspired compositions, though he took most of the words and ideas for the lyrics from an existing text, sent to him by a Sanskrit scholar at Cambridge. As the B-side of 'Lady Madonna' it became George's first song to make it onto a Beatles single.

Inner George.

THE LONG AND WINDING ROAD

Composer: Paul
Performers: Paul – vocal, piano; John – bass; George – guitar; Ringo – drums (plus mini orchestra and female chorus)

Recorded: 26, 31 January 1969, Apple Studios; 1 April 1970, Abbey Road
Released: LP *Let It Be*, 8 May 1970 (UK), 18 May 1970 (US)
Charts: US No. 1 released 11 May 1970, with B-side 'For You Blue'

Another of Paul's metaphor songs – in that you can take it to be about a real road, and Beatles fans have identified it as a road in Scotland near where Paul had his Scottish retreat – or an abstract road, a journey, that takes you to true love; in this case it must be Paul's love for Linda. Any road up, it is a beautiful song, beautifully sung by Paul, but over the years its history gets written about as much as the song itself. It was recorded quickly at the height of all the *Let It Be* troubles and disagreements, with John later bringing in Phil Spector who added all the lush, mushy orchestral arrangements that upset Paul.

Stormy road.

THE NIGHT BEFORE

Composer: Paul
Performers: Paul - vocal, bass, lead guitar; John - harmony vocal, electric piano; George - harmony vocal, guitar; Ringo - drums
Recorded: 17 February 1965, Abbey Road
Released: LP *Help!* 6 August 1965 (UK),13 August 1965 (US)

A slightly sad love song. Is Paul saying goodbye to Jane? One of those middling songs the critics have had little to say about, not seeing much to praise, or much to attack, except to say it is slightly reminiscent of 'She's A Woman'. As so often with Paul, the music is upbeat, jaunty, covering over and diverting us from the disquiet that the words are clearly expressing. It's the sort of song that courting couples could pick as 'our song', knowing it will never get hammered to death.

Tender is the night.

THE WORD

Composer: John plus Paul
Performers: John - vocal, rhythm guitar; Paul - vocal, bass; George - vocal, lead guitar; Ringo –drums, maracas; George Martin - harmonium
Recorded: 10 November 1965, Abbey Road
Released: LP *Rubber Soul* 3 December 1965 (UK), 6 December 1965 (US)

And the word is love – not lovey-dovey, boy fancies girl, girl fancies boy, but love as in peace and love, love as in the Good Book, back in the beginning, quite an unusual topic for a pop song in 1965. The Beatles were trying out new stuff by then, not just dope – John and Paul did smoke a few joints after finishing the song, with Paul writing down the words complete with psychedelic drawings – but new rhythms and harmonies. Paul said later that they had really been trying to write a song all on one note. Good job they never managed it. The manuscript was later given to John Cage, the avant-garde American composer, and now safely resides in the library at Northwestern University in the States.

Peace and love anthem for the hippies.

THERE'S A PLACE

Composers: Mainly John
Performers: John - vocal, harmonica, rhythm guitar; Paul - vocal, bass; George - backing vocal, lead guitar; Ringo - drums

Recorded: 11 February 1963, Abbey Road
Released: LP *Please Please Me* 22 March 1963 (UK), LP *Introducing … The Beatles* originally scheduled 22 July 1963, actual 10 January 1964 (US)
Charts: US No. 74 as an individual track (No. 2 as B-side of 'Twist And Shout', released 2 March 1964)

John originally tried to claim it as one of his creations, that was his memory, but Paul later remembered they did it together at Forthlin Road, after Paul had played Bernstein's 'Somewhere (There's A Place For Us)' from *West Side Story*. But the concept sounds very John, and unusual for their early pop songs, in that the 'place' is a not a physical place – it is all in his mind, a theme that John explored later in 'Strawberry Fields', 'In My Life' and 'I'm Only Sleeping'. The music, so John maintained, was his attempt at creating a Motown feeling.

Hints of mind games to come.

THINGS WE SAID TODAY

Composer: Paul
Performers: Paul – vocal, bass; John – acoustic rhythm guitar, piano; George – lead guitar; Ringo – drums, tambourine
Recorded: 2 June 1964, Abbey Road
Released: LP *A Hard Day's Night* 10 July 1964 (UK), LP *Something New* 20 July 1964 (US)
Charts: UK No. 1 released 10 July 1964, with A-side 'A Hard Day's Night'

A hard driving, rocking tune that speeds along, taking you with it, typical of many of their songs of the period, but Paul's lyrics are not quite as bouncy as the music. He wrote it in the Caribbean, while on holiday with Jane, along with Ringo and Maureen, and he is already hinting at problems to come, realising that both he and Jane have careers that might well pull them apart. He manages to

think ahead and at the same time look back, as if remembering what is happening to them now, which is pretty wise and mature, for a 21-year-old.

Classic, perfect Paul.

THINK FOR YOURSELF

Composer: George
Performers: George – vocal, lead guitar; John – harmony vocal, electric piano; Paul – harmony vocal, bass; Ringo – drums, maracas, tambourine
Recorded: 8 November 1965, Abbey Road
Released: LP *Rubber Soul* 3 December 1965 (UK), 6 December 1965 (US)

George being sad and bitter, telling some girl who has caused him grief to go off, do her own thing, think for herself, because he won't be there any more. Surely it can't have been Pattie, because that relationship appeared to be going great, at the time he composed the song? Or was he worrying about what could happen? (And of course it did.) Or is it a more general observation, that we should all think for ourselves? A tune that doesn't actually get very far, though it has neat harmonies, with some sharp lines and original thoughts. One of George's two contributions to *Rubber Soul* (the other being 'If I Needed Someone'), both of which hold up against the greater polish of John and Paul.

George, thinking for himself.

THIS BOY

Composer: John
Performers: John – vocal, acoustic guitar; Paul – vocal, bass; George – vocal, lead guitar; Ringo – drums

Recorded: 17 October 1963, Abbey Road
Released: single 29 November 1963 (UK), with A-side 'I Want To Hold Your Hand'; LP *Meet The Beatles!* 20 January 1964 (US)
Charts: UK No. 1

A bit of a plod, with few words, all of them limp, enlivened by some three-part close harmony by John, Paul and George getting their moptops up close and personal. John knocked it out in a hotel bedroom while on tour and dismissed it later as merely 'a sound and a harmony'. Well, what else do songs do?

Very fifties.

TICKET TO RIDE

Composers: John and Paul
Performers: John - vocal, rhythm guitar; Paul - harmony vocal, bass, lead guitar; George - harmony vocal, rhythm guitar; Ringo - drums, tambourine
Recorded: 15 February 1965, Abbey Road
Released: single 9 April 1965 (UK), 19 April 1965 (US), with B-side 'Yes It Is'
Charts: UK No.1, US No. 1

One of their early classics, which went to No. 1 in the UK and the US and was also loved by the critics, for its rich, inventive, electric guitars and also the rich lyrics, just waiting there to be analysed. Was the ride a reference to a druggie experience, such as LSD, that they had recently taken for the first time, or sexual, or just a ride on something, like a ferry across to Ryde on the Isle of Wight, where Paul had in fact been? John wrote most of it, with a lot of help from Paul, and together they managed to eliminate any weak lines. At 3 minutes 12 seconds it was their longest track so far. Usually their songs had run for around two

and a half minutes. Now considered to have been their first psychedelic record.

Rich pickings.

TOMORROW NEVER KNOWS

Composer: John
Performers: John - vocal, organ; Paul - bass; George - guitar, sitar, tamboura; Ringo - drums; George Martin - piano
Recorded: 6, 7, 22 April 1966, Abbey Road
Released: LP *Revolver* 5 August 1966 (UK), 8 August 1966 (US)

This was the wonderful, shattering, swaying climax to the marvellous *Revolver* album – and it was also their most truly psychedelic so far. Highly imaginative and mystical, both in music and lyrics, influencing a whole generation – and not all of them stoned hippies. It brought Indian music and instruments, and Indian spiritual concepts, to the ears and minds of millions who would otherwise never have experienced them. John took some of the references from the *Tibetan Book Of The Dead*, though its basic message is very simple – love is all. The title does not appear in the song – John took it from one of Ringo's spontaneous remarks. 'Turn off your mind', which is in the first line, might have been a better title. It's a song you hear in your mind, long after the needle has stopped.

A revolution in itself.

TWO OF US

Composer: Paul
Performers: Paul - vocal, acoustic guitar; John - vocal, acoustic guitar; George - lead guitar

Recorded: 24, 25, 31 January 1969, Apple Studios
Released: LP *Let It Be* 8 May 1970 (UK) 18 May 1970 (US)

John, for some reason, later tried to take some of the credit for this song – though it was not the sort of song he normally liked. More like a Wings song, which he often mocked. Perhaps it was because he enjoyed singing it so much, in close harmony with Paul, as seen in the film of *Let It Be*, reminding him of their good old days on stage. It makes you think the 'two of us' might in fact be the *two of them* – but it is clear Paul wrote it with Linda in mind.

Good road song.

WAIT

Composers: John and Paul
Performers: John – vocal, rhythm guitar; Paul – vocal, bass; George – guitar; Ringo – drums, maracas
Recorded: 17 June and 11 November 1965, Abbey Road
Released: LP *Rubber Soul* 3 December 1965 (UK), 6 December 1965 (US)

Originally recorded for *Help!*, but never made it, which could be a clue as to its worth. Repetitious words and thoughts – wait, I'm coming – which would suggest that the words began with Paul thinking of Jane. John and Paul worked it up and sing it neatly together, with Ringo on drums driving it along when it looks like flagging.

Pot boiler.

WE CAN WORK IT OUT

Composers: Paul with John
Performers: Paul – vocal, bass; John – harmony vocal, acoustic rhythm guitar, harmonica; George – harmony vocal; Ringo – drums, tambourine
Recorded: 20, 29 October 1965, Abbey Road
Released: single 3 December 1965 (UK), 6 December 1965 (US), with double A-side 'Day Tripper'
Charts: UK No. 1, US No. 1

Another song originating during Paul's relationship with Jane. She declared she was going off to Bristol on an acting job, with Paul wanting her to stay, trying to be positive. John provided the middle eight, which is tougher, more cynical, in words and music, declaring there is no time for all this messing about. The fusing together of the two was a hint of what was to come, with other songs being built up out of separate parts. It became a joint composition, but reflects the work of different hands, different attitudes. 'Try to see it my way' sounds like Paul at the time. As if he were saying, 'I am in the right, so there.'

The different hands are reflected in the irregular beat and the changes of pace. The waltzy background and fairground noise suggests we are all on one of life's roundabouts.

Worked so well.

WHAT GOES ON

Composer: John plus Paul and Ringo
Performers: Ringo – vocal, drums; John – harmony vocal, rhythm guitar; Paul – harmony vocal, bass; George – lead guitar
Recorded: 4 November 1965 Abbey Road
Released: LP *Rubber Soul* 3 December 1965 (UK), single 21 February 1966 (US), with A-side 'Nowhere Man'
Charts: US No. 81 as an individual track (No. 3 as B-side of 'Nowhere Man')

An early number by John, which was played to George Martin back in 1963 as a possible follow-up to 'Please Please Me', but George didn't fancy it. Two years later, with The Beatles now calling the shots for The Beatles, it was dug out again to give Ringo a solo on the *Rubber Soul* album. It got polished up in the studio with Paul's help – and also Ringo's. Hence his first credit on a Beatles composition. Ringo sings it like, well, Ringo, giving away his Scouse origins.

Treat him kind.

WHAT YOU'RE DOING

Composers: Paul plus John
Performers: Paul – vocal, bass; John – harmony vocal, acoustic rhythm guitar; George – harmony vocal, lead guitar; Ringo – drums; George Martin – piano
Recorded: 29, 30 September and 26 October 1964, Abbey Road
Released: LP *Beatles For Sale* 4 December 1964 (UK), LP *Beatles VI* 14 June 1965 (US)

Simple love song, or at least a love-going-wrong love song, so presumably Paul was having problems with Jane when he wrote it, but it is rather tossed off, three chords, poor lyrics. He is feeling blue and lonely, she's got him crying. Oh please.

What was Paul doing?

WHEN I GET HOME

Composer: John
Performers: John – vocal, rhythm guitar; Paul – harmony vocal, bass; George – harmony vocal, lead guitar; Ringo – drums
Recorded: 2 June 1964, Abbey Road
Released: LP *A Hard Day's Night* 10 July 1964 (UK), LP *Something New* 20 July 1964 (US)

An upbeat, rousing, even arousing – come on, come on – song by John. Whether he was rushing home for the pleasure of Cynthia, his wife, or from, or to, some other home, where he had no business to be, is not made clear; but Cynthia should have had her suspicions. Some clichéd phrases – loving her 'till the cows come home' – and some non-words – 'whoa-ho, whoa-ho' – but the spirit and speed carries it along. It was finished off during the last recording session for the *Hard Day's Night* album – presumably with some happiness and relief.

Good rocker.

WHEN I'M SIXTY-FOUR

Composer: Paul
Performers: Paul – vocal, piano, bass; John – backing vocal, guitar; George – backing vocal; Ringo – drums, chimes (plus three clarinets)
Recorded: 6, 8, 20, 21 December 1966, Abbey Road
Released: LP *Sgt Pepper* 1 June 1967 (UK), 2 June 1967 (US)

Something for all the kiddies – and the grown-ups, for everyone really. That was one of the many pleasurable things about every new Beatles LP – there was always such a mixture. (Though sticking to the same groove for a whole album, like Dylan, is not necessarily bad – just different.)

After the unsettling complexities of 'Within You Without You', the next track on *Sgt Pepper*, right on cue, brought something to make the oldies tap their feet and smile. Paul's father had celebrated his sixty-fourth birthday on 7 July 1966, so it was a nice belated present, although Paul had written the song, but not all the words, some years earlier. He used to play it on stage, in gaps when the amps went down, and on 3 August 1963, during their final ever show there, he played it at the Cavern when the lights went off.

It is the sort of pastiche of a pre-war music-hall song, with appropriate tune and period postcard phrases, that greatly amused his dad. But it is witty as well as wise, able to imagine the fears of the old, even though Paul himself could only have been a teenager when he first wrote it. And of course at that stage in life, someone aged 64 was incredibly old.

In many ways, when I am 65 would have been more resonant, as 65 was normally the retirement age. Not much special, really, about being 64 – but perhaps Paul found it easier to find rhymes for 'four' than for 'five'.

When Ringo turned 64 in 2004, Paul sang him the song down the telephone.

Period fun.

WHILE MY GUITAR GENTLY WEEPS

Composer: George
Performers: George – vocal, acoustic guitar, Hammond organ; Paul – backing vocal, piano, organ, bass; John – lead guitar; Ringo – drums, tambourine; Eric Clapton – lead guitar
Recorded: 25 July, 16 August and 3, 5, 6 September 1968, Abbey Road
Released: LP *The Beatles* 22 November 1968 (UK), 25 November 1968 (US)

Another song that Ian MacDonald (*Revolution In The Head*) didn't like very much, calling it plodding and dull grandiosity, yet musically it is so rich, so interesting. George worked so hard, with many, many takes to get it right, believing that John and Paul were not taking it seriously enough. Finally he brought in Eric Clapton to create the effect of what does sound like a guitar gently weeping.

There is a lot of Indian influence, though in fact the origins go back to when George was visiting his parents in Liverpool, reading a book of Chinese philosophy, then deciding to pick out a phrase at random – which happened to be 'gently weeps' – to see if he could make a song out of it. The lyrics contain some of George's best lines, 'the love there that's sleeping', and also some of his clumsiest, 'I look at the floor and I see it needs sweeping', but today it is generally seen as one of George's finest, most haunting, most recognisable compositions.

Gently becomes a classic.

WHY DON'T WE DO IT IN THE ROAD

Composer: Paul
Performers: Paul – vocal, acoustic guitar, lead guitar, piano, bass; Ringo – drums
Recorded: 9, 10 October 1968, Abbey Road
Released: LP *The Beatles*, 22 November 1968 (UK), 25 November 1968 (US)

Paul's little bit of self-indulgence, done all on his own – just with Ringo on drums – possibly as a reaction to John leaving him out of 'Revolution 9'. While in India, Paul had observed some monkeys copulating in the road, not at all fussed. Paul wondered why humans did not do that. He should have left it at that. Not bothered trying to get a song out of it. Clearly a strain to play – and to listen to – though several heavy metal bands have made a decent fist of doing cover versions. At least it's short, with few words.

Why did he do it...

WILD HONEY PIE

Composer: Paul
Performer: Paul – vocal, acoustic guitar, drums
Recorded: 20 August 1968, Abbey Road
Released: LP *The Beatles* 22 November 1968 (UK), 25 November 1968 (US)

Another example of Paul being self-indulgent – or self-reflecting. Or perhaps they were struggling to fulfil the contract they had agreed to create 30 or more new songs for the double album. A short, instrumental work, under one minute long, with no lyrics apart from the title. No connection with 'Honey Pie', which is a proper song, and which comes later on the same album.

Short, quite sweet.

WITH A LITTLE HELP FROM MY FRIENDS

Composer: John and Paul
Performers: Ringo – vocal; Paul – backing vocal, piano, bass; John – backing vocal; George – lead guitar; George Martin – Hammond organ
Recorded: 29, 30 March 1967, Abbey Road
Released: LP *Sgt Pepper* 1 June 1967 (UK), 2 June 1967 (US)

A Ringo song, composed because they were in a hurry to finish the *Sgt Pepper* album and a Ringo song was due, a self-imposed tradition. Written jointly by Paul and John, bashed out in Paul's house, with a lot of mucking around, then taken round, still in various bits, to Abbey Road, handed over to Ringo, like a waiter delivering a meal. Here you are Ringo, they said, this is for you, your latest song. Ringo did it justice, despite having to cope with a few bum rhymes, singing his little heart out. Some people, though, consider that

Joe Cocker did it even better when he recorded it.

Was there a hidden double meaning? A little help from your friendly drug dealer? Perish the thought. No, the intentions were pure, druggie wise. Possible explanations came later. But 'What do you feel when you turn out the light' was possibly not so pure – more like teenage sniggering.

Ringo at his Ringo-est.

WITHIN YOU WITHOUT YOU

Composer: George
Performers: George – vocal, sitar, acoustic guitar, tambura (plus Indian musicians and mini string orchestra)
Recorded: 15, 22 March and 3 April 1967, Abbey Road
Released: LP *Sgt Pepper* 1 June 1967 (UK), 2 June 1967 (US)

People at the time, when the album first came out, were rather shocked and hurt on George's behalf when this obviously sincere, carefully carved, aphoristic Indian-influenced, portentous, if rather dirge-like, number finished with the clear sound of – the others laughing. How cruel. But it was actually George's idea, the laughs. Sending himself up. Yet at the same time, he meant it all. He was deep into his Indian phase, in music and philosophy, and this was his best attempt so far to express what he felt. The title line was lifted from a Buddhist book, but it is still George's song, his creation, and now doesn't seem at all strange or weird. It is one of the signature sounds from *Sgt Pepper*. In fact some think it is the best on the album. Back in 1967 'world music' was viewed suspiciously, a fear of the unknown, unless it was a novelty song. Now the world for world music has grown enormously.

George recorded the song with the help of some Indian and classical musicians, without any of the other Beatles being present. (Like Paul and 'Yesterday'.)

George on top Indian form.

YELLOW SUBMARINE

Composer: Paul
Performers: Ringo – vocal, drums; Paul – backing vocal, bass; John – backing vocal, acoustic guitar; George – backing vocal, tambourine; Mal Evans – bass drums. Plus backing vocal and noises from others in the studio
Recorded: 26 May and 1 June 1966, Abbey Road
Released: LP *Revolver* 5 August 1966 (UK) 8 August 1966 (US)
Charts: UK No. 1 released 5 August 1966, US No. 2 released 8 August 1966, with double A-side 'Eleanor Rigby'

This song must have been almost as fun to record as it is to listen to now, all these years later, yet it took them 12 hours to add on all the bells, whistles, shouts, echos, hooters, chains and assorted nautical effects. John blew through a straw into a bowl of water to get the sound of bubbles. Paul wrote it very quickly, while living at Jane's, having decided to write a children's song for Ringo to sing, using short words and amusing images that would appeal to youngsters, such as living in a yellow submarine – and of course it also appealed to druggies. In 1968, it was used as the title tune in the animated film *Yellow Submarine*.

Today it has a global appeal to football fans and crowds everywhere – who put their own words to it, some of them not repeatable, having taken it over as is if it is a traditional children's song, hundreds of years old, mostly unaware who wrote it. In a way, that is the definition of a classic – something believed to have always been with us.

Impossible not to like.

YER BLUES

Composers: John
Performers: John – vocal, lead guitar; Paul – bass; George – lead guitar; Ringo – drums
Recorded: 13, 14, 20 August 1968, Abbey Road
Released: LP The Beatles 22 November 1968 (UK), 26 November 1968 (US)

A blues song, written by John, yet blue is not quite the word – more like pitch black, as John appears to be suicidal, wanting to die. He wrote it in India – so much for meditation calming the soul – missing Yoko, which was why he felt so lonely, hating everything, even his rock 'n' roll. There is a hint of mocking himself, but mostly he is dead serious, and dead miserable. Blues, of course, were often about people in despair – even when in real life they were not. 'Yer Blues' does have its stout fans, who among other things admire the amount of echo on John's voice.

Misery memoir.

LUCIUS IN THE SKY WITH DIAMONDS

Politician Derek Enright gained a Classics degree at Oxford and worked as a schoolteacher until he became the MEP for Leeds and later MP for Hemsworth. In 1993, during a debate on educational reform, he said that he had translated Beatle songs into Latin to encourage his students. He then sang 'Yellow Submarine' in Latin but he was ordered to sit down as he was breaking the rule of the House.

YES IT IS

Composer: John

Performers: John – vocal, acoustic rhythm guitar; Paul – harmony vocal, bass; George – lead guitar, harmony vocal; Ringo – drums

Recorded: 16 February 1965, Abbey Road

Released: single 9 April 1965 (UK), 19 April 1965 (US), with A-side 'Ticket To Ride'

Charts: UK No. 1 US No. 46 as an individual track (No. 1 as B-side of 'Ticket To Ride')

John never properly explained this song, except to say it began as an attempt to rework 'This Boy', which he had recorded 18 months earlier. In the lyrics, he is thinking back to a lost love who wore red. Could it have been his late mother, Julia? But then it gets complicated, going on about his pride, then lapses into clichéd rhymes – feeling blue, it's true. Bit of a puzzle, and another song that is a bit of a moan.

Not really.

YESTERDAY

Composer: Paul

Performers: Paul – vocal, acoustic guitar (plus string quartet)

Recorded: 14, 17 June 1965, Abbey Road

Released: LP *Help!* 6 August 1965 (UK), single 13 September 1965 (US), with B-side 'Act Naturally' (not composed by The Beatles)

Charts: US No. 1

Now the stuff of pop music legend, and legendary cover versions, 'Yesterday' came into Paul's head, just like that, so he has recalled, as if by magic. He woke up one morning with the whole tune in his head, so formed and perfect, he imagined at first that someone else had written it. Which in a way they had – his subconscious. He played it to several people, checking they did not recognise

it, and they all said it was wonderful. He had no words for some time, except silly words and a title, 'Scrambled Eggs'. It was on holiday with Jane in Portugal some months later that he eventually wrote the real words.

The lyrics are short, with no story, no narrative, no clue as to why she had to go and why a shadow is hanging over him – but that is in a way its strength. You can imagine for yourself what went wrong. In the studio, Ringo and the others said they couldn't see how they could add to Paul simply playing the song on his own – which he did. George Martin suggested a string quartet to back it up, which Paul was not keen on at first, worrying it would be either schmaltzy or pretentious. It was George Martin's first major contribution to a Beatles song – and the first Beatles song that was a 'solo', with only one Beatle performing. They did not want it to come out as a Beatles single in the UK – as none of the others were performing on it – so in the UK it appeared on the album *Help!* but it came out later as a single in the US. Three years later it had already been recorded by over 100 other artists. Today it is reckoned to have been professionally recorded around 3,000 times, making it the most recorded popular song ever. Has it been loved to death? Some people of taste, the self-elected arbiters, consider it has. But it will live on, for ever, so deserves top marks.

Has to be.

SOME OBSERVATIONS ON 'YESTERDAY'

As told to Spencer Leigh on his BBC Radio Merseyside programme *On The Beat*

Willie Nelson: 'They wrote great songs. "Yesterday" is my favourite, one of my favourite all-time songs and not just a favourite Beatle song. It is a great piece of literature.'

But can it be a great song when you don't find out what happened yesterday?

Willie Nelson: 'That's what makes it a great song. In a way, the songwriter is telling you everything. He tells you that his troubles are here to stay. [Laughs] Period. End of story.'

Tim Rice: '"Yesterday" is a great song and it is not just because it is a great tune, it is a staggering lyric. The concept of "How I long for yesterday," is a brilliant line. It is so simple and yet it has such brilliant words. The reason why all those Beatle classics are classics are because of the lyrics. "Do You Want To Know A Secret" is a simple, direct lyric that people can relate to. "She Loves You" is not a song that people can identify with because it is one step away: it is a bloke singing about somebody else's situation, so that song is not covered as much as "Yesterday" or "Here, There And Everywhere". I'm generalising as there are many songs that were only meant to work for them, but it is the lyrics time and time again that determine whether a song is a song for everybody or a song just for the band who did it.'

Rick Wakeman: 'I've looked at a lot of The Beatles' songs and tried to be analytical and see if there is a pattern as to why they work. There are great wide sweeps of melody. There are never more than two or three ideas in any song, whereas Yes used to throw in hundreds of ideas. Just occasionally you come across someone who can write classics, songs that can be sung by anyone from 9 to 90. Much as I enjoyed all the stuff I did with Yes, there isn't a Yes song that could be sung by that age range. That talent is rare. To write something like "Yesterday" is something very special.'

YOU CAN'T DO THAT

Composer: John
Performers: John – vocal, lead guitar; Paul – backing vocal, bass; George – backing vocal, rhythm guitar; Ringo – drums
Recorded: 25 February 1964, Abbey Road
Released: single 20 March 1964 (UK), 16 March 1964 (US), with A-side 'Can't Buy Me Love'
Charts: UK No. 1, US No. 48 as an individual track (No. 1 as B-side of 'Can't Buy Me Love')

One of the early examples of each side of a single being composed, more or less, individually, instead of head-to-head. Paul did the A-side, 'Can't Buy Me Love', so John replied with 'You Can't Do That', indicating he was still the leader of the gang. The lyrics are very John, hinting at what he will do if he catches her with another man. He doesn't actually say what the threat is, except she will be left 'flat'. Does he mean disappointed, broke, or literally flattened? Sounds nasty anyway.

Paul was in a sense a conservative, with a small c, liking the status quo, willing to work things out, wanting to please, though of course he could have private rages. John saw himself as revolutionary, wanting to do what was forbidden, even if it were cruel.

But John did.

YOU KNOW MY NAME (LOOK UP THE NUMBER)

Composer: John

Performers: John – vocal, guitar, maracas; Paul – vocal, piano, bass; George – backing vocal, guitar, vibes; Ringo – drums, vocal; Brian Jones – alto sax

Recorded: 17 May, 7, 8 June 1967 and 30 April 1969, Abbey Road

Released: single 6 March 1970 (UK), 11 March 1970 (US), with A-side 'Let It Be'

Charts: UK No. 2, US No. 1 (US charts stopped listing B-sides separately in November 1969)

Possibly John's most prosaic inspiration – the London telephone book. He was waiting at Paul's house one day and saw it lying on the piano. On the front was the exhortation, 'You have their name, look up the number.' John himself was notoriously bad at phone numbers, not even knowing his own, so the subject matter was a bit of a joke, even before he turned it into a song. After a fashion. There were no lyrics, as such, just the title plus some other random phrases shouted out in the studio. But it amused John. Presumably he thought he was being ironic.

Weak joke.

YOU LIKE ME TOO MUCH

Composer: George

Performers: George – double-tracked vocal, lead guitar; John – acoustic guitar, electric piano; Paul – bass, piano; Ringo – drums, tambourine

Recorded: 17 February 1965, Abbey Road

Released: LP *Help!* 6 August 1965 (UK) LP *Beatles VI* 14 June 1965 (US)

George doesn't mention this song when describing his songwriting in his *I Me Mine* book.

Perhaps he had forgotten it, or couldn't remember anything to say about it. It is not typical of most of his songs, especially the later ones, being jolly and upbeat, simple and repetitive, and of course there is nothing basically wrong with all that. It's a love song and though she has left him, he feels she will be back that night and it will all turn out right in the end, because they like each other too much. Which alas did not happen, when eventually his wife Pattie left him for Eric Clapton.

Poignant George.

YOU NEVER GIVE ME YOUR MONEY

Composer: Paul

Performers: Paul – vocal, piano, bass, guitars; John – backing vocal, guitar; George – backing vocal, guitars; Ringo – drums, tambourine

Recorded: 6 May 1969, Olympic Sound Studios 1, 11, 15, 30, 31 July and 5 August 1969, Abbey Road

Released: LP *Abbey Road* 26 September 1969 (UK), 1 October 1969 (US)

This starts off the long medley on the second side of *Abbey Road* – but in itself it is a medley, three of Paul's part songs, in different styles, strung together, but not really connected. One bit is about a college student with no money, another a sweet dream – presumably about Linda. The first bit, the title bit, refers to the money problems around Apple and Allen Klein, which is the most haunting, sticking to the back of your mind, whether you want it to or not. It could have been a really good song, on its own, but getting three for the price of one is still a bargain.

Late gift from Paul.

YOU'RE GOING TO LOSE THAT GIRL

Composer: John
Performers: John – vocal, acoustic rhythm guitar; Paul – backing vocal, bass, piano; George – backing vocal, lead guitar; Ringo – drums, bongos
Recorded: 19 February 1965, Abbey Road
Released: LP *Help!* 6 August, 1965 (UK), 13 August 1965 (US)

John is threatening to take away a girl, if his friend does not treat her right – and that's about it really, story-wise. But the music is built up with some mock choral harmony and nice falsettos. Hard to sing, unless you have the voice, or the right studio equipment. One of the songs from *Help!* that still stands up today. John actually sings it as 'gonna' lose that girl, in the American fashion, but on UK labels it is spelled grammatically correctly, and we should think so too.

On the subject of grammar, why did they write 'I Wanna Be Your Man' and yet 'I Want To Hold Your Hand', each written around the same time? Discuss among yourselves.

Still with us.

YOUR MOTHER SHOULD KNOW

Composer: Paul
Performers: Paul – vocal, piano, bass; John – backing vocal, organ; George – backing vocal, guitar; Ringo – drums, tambourine
Recorded: 22, 23 August 1967, Chappell Studios, and 16, 19 September 1967 Abbey Road
Released: EP *Magical Mystery Tour* 8 December 1967 (UK), LP *Magical Mystery Tour* 27 November 1967 (US)
Charts: UK No. 2

Didn't they look smart in their white suits in the *Magical Mystery Tour* film descending the stairs

with all the dancers – and clearly enjoying themselves as they sang 'Your Mother Should Know'. Paul wrote it as a nostalgic show song, a showstopper, harking back to the pre-war, Busby Berkeley film tunes his mother – everyone's mother at the time – would have still been humming in the fifties. He wrote it at home in Cavendish Avenue, playing it on a harmonium, trying it out on his Liverpool aunties. '"Your Mother Should Know" has the feel of the Grafton Rooms,' so George Melly told Spencer Leigh. 'That was a Liverpool dance hall from my youth. It's brilliantly captured that feeling of dressing up and ballroom dancing to Mrs Wilf Hamer.'

Still a showstopper.

YOU'VE GOT TO HIDE YOUR LOVE AWAY

Composer: John
Performers: John – vocal, acoustic rhythm guitar; Paul – acoustic rhythm guitar; George – acoustic lead guitar; Ringo – tambourine, maracas; Johnnie Scott – flute
Recorded: 18 February 1965, Abbey Road
Released: LP *Help!* 6 August 1965 (UK), 13 August 1965 (US)

John doing a Dylan-type folksy number, about a love that got away, leaving him two feet small – a clumsy and not exactly romantic metaphor. There have been those who have suggested it was not some girlfriend of John's that he had lost, but instead it was about Brian Epstein's homosexuality, which under the laws at the time Brian had to keep quiet, or risk prosecution. The flute was an unusual addition – the first time an instrument had been added that none of The Beatles could play.

Wistful.

YOU WON'T SEE ME

Composer: Paul
Performers: Paul – vocal, bass, piano; John – backing vocal; George – backing vocal, lead guitar; Ringo – drums, tambourine; Mal Evans – Hammond organ
Recorded: 11 November 1965, Abbey Road
Released: LP *Rubber Soul* 3 December 1965 (UK), 6 December 1965 (US)

Another Paul song, indicating his fraught relationship with his girlfriend Jane who had gone off on an acting job. It was completed hurriedly, and would have gained by more work on the words and music, but it all rings true and heartfelt and Paul sings it beautifully. The title can be taken two ways – literally and metaphorically. Mal Evans, on the Hammond organ, only actually played one note, held throughout the last verse, but he did it jolly well.

Haunting.

FURTHER COMMENTS ON BEATLES SONGS BY GEORGE MELLY, AS TOLD TO SPENCER LEIGH

'I'm bored very quickly by Indian music on account of what appears to be its monotony. I know that it isn't monotonous. I know that if I understood it, I would find it marvellous. The thing about drugs is that they make everything less boring and more significant, so that The Beatles were able to listen to Indian music for hours at a time without ever looking at their watches and it seeped into their own music. It went with the incense and the bells and the pot and the LSD and the kaftans, all the sixties images which now seem extremely tiresome and dated, but, in the case of The Beatles, their genius was strong enough to give continuous validity to their music of the period.

There was a certain moment in The Beatles' development when they took LSD and it utterly changed their music and their imagery. Now, you can say that LSD was a very bad thing, and certainly it was for some people. There are some who "blew their minds" and became casualties, but, treated as a help towards art, in The Beatles' case and in some other cases, it changed their visual approach to life. I only took LSD once, I didn't like it much, but I did hallucinate.

Here were four creative figures who previously had to rely on the world as seen by everybody else. Okay, a joint blurs things a bit, but it doesn't do much. After LSD in which the wallpaper fills up with kissing mouths and sofas become hippopotamuses, a stream of consciousness was released which went into the songs. I would say that "A Day In The Life" was their richest drug-created invention. It's partially about drugs of course, but it's doomy, a bad trip, whereas "Eleanor Rigby" is beautiful and cheerful and pretty. "A Day In The Life" also emphasises the bad side of drugs, the despair and the doom that can come out of them, but it is a considerable work of art and it would not have been created without LSD. Whether art is justified by this way of living, I don't know. I'd give it the benefit of the doubt because, without it, we wouldn't have had their best song.

Strawberry Field was a reform home for girls, but John was attracted to the title because the idea of Strawberry Fields is a very trippy idea, glowing and glimmering in the sun. The Beatles' hallucinatory songs were unlike anything that had been done before, both as tunes and images, and I'm glad they're there.'

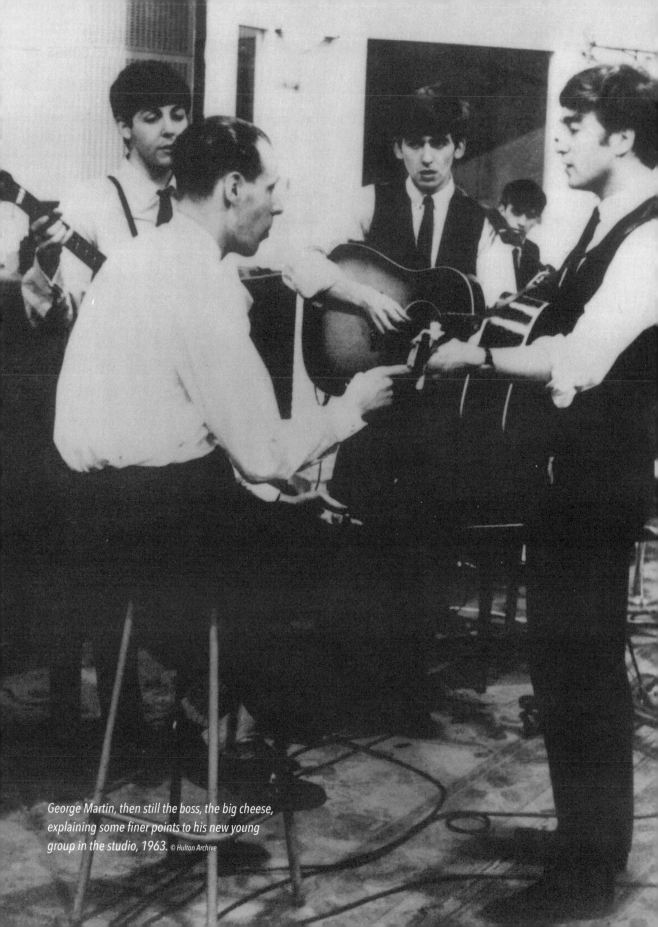

George Martin, then still the boss, the big cheese,
explaining some finer points to his new young
group in the studio, 1963. © Hulton Archive

THE BEATLES LPs

In chronological order, the LPs as they were recorded (which is not always the same as the order of their release). There were no bad or even mediocre Beatles LPs; they were all fab, with something in each of them for everybody, and each one was a massive event for all Beatles fans, eagerly awaited. We all knew each new album would be moving The Beatles on, with new ideas, new instruments, new influences. One of the joys of the original LPs was getting to know the exact order, so you knew precisely what was coming next when the last chord sounded, the first hint of the next track echoing forward in your head while there was still silence. Later compilations, and the early US versions, ruined that simple pleasure.

Giving each LP a rating is therefore harder than doing it for a single, but come on, it has to be done, this silly, subjective self-imposed task.

1. PLEASE PLEASE ME

Mostly recorded: 11 February 1963
Released: 22 March 1963 (UK), *Introducing … The Beatles* originally scheduled 22 July 1963, actual 10 January 1964 (US)
Tracks: Side 1 – I Saw Her Standing There, Misery, Anna (Go To Him)*, Chains*, Boys*, Ask Me Why, Please Please Me; Side 2 – Love Me Do, P.S. I Love You, Baby It's You*, Do You Want to Know A Secret, A Taste Of Honey*, There's A Place, Twist And Shout*
*Not composed by The Beatles

The full title on the album, if you look again at the original 1963 UK album sleeve, is not just *Please Please Me* but there is a subtitle that reads 'With Love Me Do and 12 Other Songs'. This gives away the situation at the time – EMI were cashing in on a group who had not yet had a No. 1, but had enjoyed success on tour and suddenly found a following with their first two singles – 'Love Me Do'/'P.S. I love You' and 'Please Please Me'/'Ask Me Why'.

This is what often happened at the time, with a group who might just be a passing fad, or had a film out. There was a mad rush to get them into the studio and record an album as quickly as possible. And goodness, was it done quickly. A whole album tied up in one day, 11 February 1963.

Of the fourteen tracks that appeared on the album, they had already got four tracks in the can from their first two singles, so only ten of them were done in the studio that day. (In fact they recorded eleven songs in the session, but it was decided to hold back one of them, 'Hold Me Tight') Eight out of the fourteen were original Beatles creations, while six were the work of others.

George Martin, who produced, had thought of recording the whole album at a live concert at the Cavern club, but decided to bring them into the studio and bash out the stuff they had done umpteen times before in their stage show. He recorded on two tracks, doing three sessions of three hours each at Abbey Road. One track was mainly instrumental and the other vocals, the idea being that they can be better balanced when put together. The next day, they went out on the road again. That again was typical of the times.

The day of the recording was cold and miserable in London, and John had a nasty cold that meant keeping himself going with cigarettes and cough sweets. That very same day, not far from Abbey Road, the American poet Sylvia Plath committed suicide.

It was two weeks later that the single of 'Please Please Me' got to No. 1 in the *NME* charts. The LP itself also reached the top spot in the UK LP charts – but in the US, Capitol Records, EMI's American affiliate company, did not fancy their chances and so the album came out later, with a different title, *Introducing ... The Beatles*, on the little-known Vee-Jay label, and with a slightly different track listing (the tracks 'Ask Me Why' and 'Please Please Me' were originally dropped, then reinstated to replace 'Love Me Do' and 'P.S. I Love You', for legal reasons).

On the UK sleeve notes, written by their PR Tony Barrow, it describes how The Beatles have 'their own built-in tunesmiths team of John Lennon and Paul McCartney,' who had 'already tucked away enough self-penned numbers' to keep them going until 1975.

The eight original Beatles compositions were credited on the album to McCartney–Lennon, not Lennon–McCartney, which is how it later became.

At one time the album was going to be called *Off The Beatles Track*, which was quite a good pun, and Paul had roughed out a design for it. George Martin's first idea for the cover photo was also a pun – he wanted The Beatles to be shot outside the insect house at London Zoo. The Beatles were still at that stage when a large number of the population were still saying, 'what, the Beetles, you mean like the insects?'

In the end a cover photo was taken by the well-known theatrical photographer Angus McBean

on the staircase at EMI headquarters in Manchester Square, London. They look very young, very posed, very amateurish.

On all the tracks George plays lead guitar, John rhythm guitar and Ringo drums. The cost of the recording session was £400.

The album did manage to convey a sense of a live as opposed to a studio recording, capturing their enthusiasm and roughness. Norman Smith, George Martin's sound technician, positioned the microphones slightly away from their instruments in order to give the atmosphere of a public performance.

John later said that this first album did capture something of their real sound, from their Hamburg and Liverpool days, before they became 'the clever Beatles'.

The first of the non-Beatles compositions on the album – all of them already recorded by other artists – was 'Anna (Go To Him)', one of John's favourites, written by Arthur Alexander. 'Chains' was by Gerry Goffin and Carole King, a song that had been recorded by a group called The Cookies. 'Boys' was by Luther Dixon and Wes Farrell and had been a hit for The Shirelles. 'Baby It's You', words by Mack David and Barney Williams and music by Burt Bacharach, was another hit recorded by The Shirelles. 'A Taste Of Honey', by Bobby Scott and Ric Marlow, had been created for the Broadway production of the play by Shelagh Delaney, later a film. It was a bit soppy and sentimental, but it was thought it would appeal to an older audience as opposed to teenage rock 'n' roll fans. John dismissed it as 'A Waste Of Money'. 'Twist And Shout', by Phil Medley and Bert Russell, had already been a success for The Isley Brothers. It made an explosive, exciting screamer of a final track.

High marks for coming out and existing, but low marks for all those cover copies.

2. WITH THE BEATLES

Recorded: 18 July–23 October 1963
Released: 22 November 1963 (UK), *Meet The Beatles!*
20 January 1964 (US)
Tracks: Side 1 – It Won't Be Long, All I've Got To Do, All My Loving, Don't Bother Me, Little Child, Till There Was You*, Please Mr Postman*; Side 2 – Roll Over Beethoven*, Hold Me Tight, You Really Got A Hold On Me*, I Wanna Be Your Man, Devil In Her Heart*, Not A Second Time, Money*
*Not composed by The Beatles

By the time they started recording their second album, four months after the release of their first, they were in a froth and lather of touring, making TV and radio appearances, which meant they were now composing many of their songs while on tour, in hotel bedrooms or on the coach, rather than in their homes. It also meant they had to record the new album in bits and pieces, fitting it into seven sessions over three months. The total hours in the studio was around 30, roughly double that of the first. Again eight of the tracks were originals while six were covers. Seven of the originals were composed by Lennon/McCartney, now the credit order on the LP, and one was by George, 'Don't Bother Me', his first song on a Beatles album.

The six covers were again versions of American records, which were part of their usual stage show. 'Till There Was You', by Meredith Wilson, had first been recorded in 1957, and later by Peggy Lee. Sung by Paul, it sounds very like the sort of sentimental wholesome ballad he might have composed at the time. 'Please Mr Postman', credited on the record to Frank Holland, though there were four others who helped write it, had been a success for the girl group The Marvelettes. 'Roll Over Beethoven' was a Chuck Berry number and a rock 'n' roll classic. 'You've Really Got A Hold On Me' had been a huge hit for The Miracles with Smokey Robinson as the lead singer. 'Devil In Her Heart', by Richard Drapkin, was hardly known in the UK till The Beatles' version. 'Money (That's

What I Want)', by Berry Gordy and Janie Bradford, had been played a lot by The Beatles since their Hamburg days and was one of those they had recorded for the failed Decca audition.

For the cover, they went for something a bit artier than their first LP. They had long admired the half light/half dark portraits that Astrid Kirchherr had done in Hamburg, but she had not photographed all of The Beatles in that same style. Robert Freeman was commissioned to do a similar shot of all four of them, which was done while they were on tour in Bournemouth. It led to him becoming for a while their official cover photographer.

With The Beatles had advance orders of half a million, and then soon sold another half million, making it only the second album to sell a million copies in the UK. The first had been the soundtrack to the 1958 film *South Pacific*.

The mixture of tracks was on the same lines as *Please Please Me*, with love songs mixed up with rock 'n' roll, Beatles originals plus American covers. Paul's version of 'Till There Was You' was reminiscent of a 'Taste Of Honey' on that first album while John belted out 'Money (That's What I Want)' in his best 'Twist And Shout' shouting. Ringo took the lead vocal on 'I Wanna Be Your Man', as he had done with 'Boys' on the first LP, which became a pattern for the future, giving Ringo a Ringo type song to sing. On tour, the audiences always gave an extra cheer when it was Ringo's turn to be the main singer.

The finest new song on the album was probably Paul's 'All My Loving' and also popular at the time was 'I Wanna Be Your Man' – with Ringo singing and John playing the Hammond organ in the background. The sound quality was a bit better than the first album, now they had mastered the art of double-tracking.

The US version, *Meet The Beatles!*, which came out in January 1964, had only 12 tracks, six either side. Four of the American cover songs from the UK album were dropped, with 'I Want To Hold Your Hand' and 'I Saw Her Standing There' added.

It was The Beatles' first record from Capitol. On the front cover, which featured the same Robert Freeman photo, it announced: 'The First Album by England's Phenomenal Pop Combo'. On the sleeve notes, it explained that, 'The Beatles all hail from Liverpool, a seaport city which, because its sailing men bring in the latest hit singles from America, is the hippest pop music spot in England. They wear "pudding basin" haircuts that date back to ancient England, and suits with collarless jackets which they have made the new rage.'

It described how they had enjoyed huge success in England. 'In Carlisle, frantic schoolgirls battled police for four hours in a do-or-die effort to gain admission to a sold-out show.' That wasn't all. They had done a *Royal Variety Performance* in London and were about to do three *Ed Sullivan* shows in New York. Plus: 'They are shortly to film in England a feature length United Artists movie for worldwide release.' So it was all go, for the phenomenal Plantagenets.

Again it has to lose marks for not being all Beatley creations.

3. A HARD DAY'S NIGHT

Recorded: 29 January–2 June 1964
Released: 10 July 1964 (UK), 26 June 1964 (US)
Tracks: Side 1 – A Hard Day's Night, I Should Have Known Better, If I Fell, I'm Happy Just To Dance With You, And I Love Her, Tell Me Why, Can't Buy Me Love; Side 2 – Any Time At All, I'll Cry Instead, Things We Said Today, When I Get Home, You Can't Do That, I'll Be Back.

At last, an all-Beatles album – starting with that best-known Beatles chord ever. All the songs were Beatles compositions, which means Lennon and McCartney wrote them all. Alas George did

not make it. In fact Paul hardly made it either as John, the leader and onlie begetter of the group, was at his bossiest best, and at his most creative and productive, and he was responsible wholly or mainly for ten out of the 13 tracks on the LP. The first seven (Side 1) were from the film, with the others written to complete the album. ('I'll Cry Instead' was written for the film, but cut out at the last moment.)

It was thought at the time that the film was being made to sell their music, which often happened when passing pop stars were shoved into a quickie film in order to push their records, but the film itself was a massive hit, seen as fresh and funny and inventive.

The songs, despite several being written at the last minute for the film, are all of a high quality. The lyrics were still basically boy-girl love songs, and why not, as they were all still so young, nobbut boys. But more thought had been taken with the words and the feelings, and the harmonies were more complex than on the earlier two albums. Paul was becoming more personal in his lyrics, as in 'And I Love Her', which was clearly about girlfriend Jane Asher; and John a bit darker in 'I'll Cry Instead' – hints of feelings to come.

In America, the *A Hard Day's Night* album, produced by United Artists Records, came out two weeks before the UK, but it only featured the seven soundtrack songs from the film, plus 'I'll Cry Instead'. The others were orchestral versions of Beatles songs arranged by George Martin. On 20 July 1964, Capitol then released an LP called *Something New*, their third Beatles album, which included several of the songs from the UK *A Hard Day's Night* (and repeated some tracks from the US version).

A big nine, for being all their own work, and a total break-through for being part of the first Beatle film, a double joy for all true believers.

A HARD DAY'S NIGHT FILM LOCATIONS

Most indoor scenes in *A Hard Day's Night* were filmed at Twickenham Film Studios, while for the outdoor action many London locations were used, all shot within a short space of time in the spring of 1964. These include: running down Boston Place alongside and then inside Marylebone Station; Paddington Station (plus Minehead, Crowcombe and Taunton Stations in Somerset, and Newton Abbott in Devon); dancing in Les Ambassadeurs; the ultimate destination in the film at the Scala Theatre; running down the fire escape staircase at the Hammersmith Odeon; running around to 'Can't Buy Me Love' and the helicopter pad in Thornbury Playing Fields in Isleworth; the final scenes of the film with the helicopter at Gatwick Airport South; Ringo walking about on his own in Lancaster Road; Ringo then wanders down the Thames towpath in Kew; the Turks Head pub in Twickenham was where Ringo walked in and started causing trouble; on Edgehill Road at 1 Lakeside, Ringo gallantly places his raincoat over a puddle for a woman before she disappears down the hole; the police station was actually St John's Secondary School at 83 Clarendon Road; the four Beatles ran into a dead-end street at Heathfield Street near Portland Road; and by the demolished church of St Luke's in St Luke's Road we see The Beatles running past the church several times.

4. BEATLES FOR SALE

Recorded: 11 August–26 October 1964
Released: 4 December 1964 (UK), *Beatles '65* 15 December 1964 (US)
Tracks: Side 1 – No Reply, I'm A Loser, Baby's In Black, Rock And Roll Music*, I'll Follow The Sun, Mr Moonlight*, Kansas City/Hey-Hey-Hey-Hey!*; Side 2 – Eight Days A Week, Words of Love*, Honey Don't*, Every Little Thing, I Don't Want To Spoil The Party, What You're Doing, Everybody's Trying to Be My Baby*
*Not composed by The Beatles

A backward step in some senses, in that only eight out of the 14 tracks are by The Beatles, with the other six covers of American rock or country music. The main reason was that it was all a rush job, trying to cram two new LPs into a year while touring the world and attending hundreds of other engagements. No wonder they look a bit knackered on the cover – the photo by Robert Freeman had to be fitted in in a hurry in Hyde Park, near the Albert Memorial.

There was no song with the title 'Beatles For Sale', another of Ringo's remarks, but choosing it for the album title summed up how they were beginning to feel at the time – like a product.

The sleeve notes were by their friend and PR Derek Taylor, rather than Tony Barrow, and he also sounds a bit jaded, not managing many words about the content, basically just spinning it out. The sleeve though did have one novelty – it had a gatefold for the first time – i.e. you opened it up, to get out the vinyl.

The six cover versions included two by Carl Perkins – 'Honey Don't' and 'Everybody's Trying To Be My Baby', which was sung by George. 'Rock And Roll Music' was a Chuck Berry classic, first recorded by him in 1957. 'Words Of Love' was by Buddy Holly. 'Mr Moonlight' was written by Roy Lee Johnson and 'Kansas City' by Jerry Leiber and Mike Stoller. Once again the cover versions were all American, most of them already considered greats. Interesting that they were not doing cover versions of any British hits, for example by the Rolling Stones. Were they thinking of the US market, or not wanting to give any exposure to any British rivals? More likely they chose

American artists because they had always been influenced by them in their growing-up years, and loved playing their songs on stage.

Their eight original songs – none by George – again showed a progression, with John becoming even darker with 'I Don't Want To Spoil The Party' and 'I'm A Loser', while Paul kept us all pensive but cheerful with 'I'll Follow The Sun'.

In the US, eight of the tracks from *Beatles For Sale* appeared on Capitol's *Beatles '65*, while the others were used on *Beatles VI* issued in June 1965.

Because of the copies.

5. HELP!

Recorded: 15–19 February, 13 April, 10 May and 14, 15, 17 June 1965
Released: 6 August 1965 (UK), 13 August 1965 (US)
Tracks: Side 1 – Help!, The Night Before, You've Got To Hide Your Love Away, I Need You, Another Girl, You're Going To Lose That Girl, Ticket To Ride; Side 2 – Act Naturally*, It's Only Love, You Like Me Too Much, Tell Me What You See, I've Just Seen A Face, Yesterday, Dizzy Miss Lizzy*
*Not composed by The Beatles

The first side on the UK album were the songs from the soundtrack of the film while on side two they came from elsewhere. Ten of the songs were by John and Paul while two were by George, 'I Need You' and 'You Like Me Too Much' – his first appearance on a Beatles album since their second LP.

There were also two cover versions, following the pattern of the album for their first film. The 'Ringo song' was 'Act Naturally', a well-known country and western number written by Voni Morrison and Johnny Russell. It fitted in with the film, in which Ringo did a lot of acting. The other cover was the well-loved rocker, 'Dizzy

Miss Lizzy' written by Larry Williams. It was first recorded in 1958, had been covered by other artists since, and had made regular appearances in The Beatles' live shows.

Two other songs by John and Paul were recorded and intended for the film but were not used. 'If You've Got Trouble' was initially meant for Ringo, but he preferred 'Act Naturally'. With the other one, 'That Means A Lot', The Beatles were not satisfied with their performance. It was given to P.J. Proby who did it as a single and it made No. 24 on the *NME* charts.

All the soundtrack songs were written blind, in that they were written without The Beatles having read the script or done the film. Dick Lester then dropped them in where he thought suitable. Except for John's 'Help!' – that was written at the last moment, once the title had been chosen.

The album cover, for the first time, had no sleeve notes. Derek Taylor had probably gone for a lie-down, after exhausting himself knocking out 600 words for the previous album cover. But what the cover included, which was new, was the addition of two or three words under the song titles, telling us, for example, who was playing electric piano – John on 'The Night Before' and Paul on 'Tell Me What You See'. In the past, George Martin had usually added any of the keyboard bits, anonymously, and not been credited. Were The Beatles showing off that they could do all that stuff?

Under the title of 'Yesterday', after crediting Paul as the singer and guitarist, it says 'and string quartet'. Flutes were listed as being used in 'You've Got To Hide Your Love Away'. It was on this album that extra instruments began to appear – and got themselves a name check. Normal pop song conventions and beat group line-ups were gradually being eroded. And in the lyrics of the

---

HELP! FILM LOCATIONS

After the success of *A Hard Day's Night*, The Beatles had more of a scripted film as a follow-up, which took them beyond the streets and studios of London. Once again the majority of the indoor locations were filmed at Twickenham Film Studios. Outside of the capital, they also filmed with tanks at Knighton Down near Larkhill on Salisbury Plain; appeared on the ski slopes of Obertauern in Austria; and enjoyed the sunshine on the beaches of Nassau and in the surroundings of New Providence Island in the Bahamas. Back in London, they filmed the front doors of their magical house at 5, 7, 9 and 11 Ailsa Avenue; the letterbox at 1 South Western Road; a grocer's shop at 42 Winchester Road; the jeweller's shop at 13a–14a New Bond Street; an Indian restaurant at 4–6 Blandford Street; Asprey jewellers at 165–169, New Bond Street; walking down Post-Office Alley to Strand-on-the-Green and the City Barge pub, with tigers in the cellar; and a palace at Cliveden House in Taplow, near Maidenhead in Berkshire.

---

title song, real, raw feelings were being exposed. And of course with Paul singing 'Yesterday' all on his own, with none of the other Beatles, that was another first, Beatlewise.

Four-track recording was being used and John was making greater use of acoustic guitar instead of his famous Rickenbacker, though that was not pointed out on the cover.

The cover photo, again by Robert Freeman, was jolly clever. It had each of the four Beatles standing making semaphore signals with their arms. Handy having a group with just four members and an album title with just one, four-letter word – a trick that would not have been possible with any other of their album titles. Most people, having worked out the joke, assumed it did spell out in semaphore the word HELP. Robert Freeman tried that and decided that visually it looked better when they signalled other letters – hence their arms ended up sending the message NUJV. Which stood for New Underpants Just Vanished. Or was it Not Under John's Vest?

In the US version of *Help!* they stuck to the same four images, but slightly rearranged the order, so that Paul is standing on the right with his left arm pointing straight at, wait for it, the word Capitol. Cunning, huh. The Americans in fact spread the contents around – some tracks appeared on the album called *Help!* and others on *Beatles VI*, *Yesterday And Today* and two tracks, 'It's Only Love' and 'I've Just Seen A Face', popped up on the US version of *Rubber Soul*.

Despite dragging in some cover versions, the album broke new ground.

6. RUBBER SOUL

Recorded: 12 October–11 November 1965
Released: 3 December 1965 (UK), 6 December 1965 (US)
Tracks: Side 1 - Drive My Car, Norwegian Wood (This Bird Has Flown), You Won't See Me, Nowhere Man, Think For Yourself, The Word, Michelle; Side 2 - What Goes On, Girl, I'm Looking Through You, In My Life, Wait, If I Needed Someone, Run For Your Life

Was this it? Is this still it? The greatest album they ever produced? Many still think so.

Firstly, it was all theirs, all 14 songs written by The Beatles. There were 12 new songs from John and Paul, though on one of them, 'What Goes

On', Ringo was given a third of the credit, his first appearance as composer on a Beatles track. Plus there were two from George, 'Think For Yourself' and 'If I Needed Someone'.

Secondly it was done at remarkable speed, taking just four weeks in October–November 1965, despite still rushing round the world on tour and having a deadline to complete, as Brian and EMI and the suits desperately wanted a second album out by Christmas.

Most of all, it was the contents that done it – the songs and sounds and instruments, subject matters and emotions and lyrics were all a giant leap forward compared with what had gone before. Till then, they had mostly been a beat group, playing and creating beat music. Now they were artistes. They had taken over the studio, and themselves, making the music they wanted to make.

The new instrument was of course the sitar, which George played on 'Norwegian Wood,' though the more overt Indian influence on their music was still to be revealed. The new subject matter took them on from soppy love songs and into narratives, stories with beginnings and sorts of ends, with dialogue, different formats, using a foreign language, pretending to write a letter, pastiches. There were of course some love songs, but they concerned troubled love, such as Paul's 'I'm Looking Through You', and personal anguish, as in John's 'Nowhere Man'.

The word that 'The Word' was about was love, but not the lovey-dovey sort, more the grand philosophical quasi-religious love as in love and peace, man.

The album was also seen as their first druggy-influenced record, but not overtly or heavily psychedelic. But some drug-induced references were clear, as was the cover image.

The album also marked the beginning of a major shift in the dynamics of the group. John, who had always been the leader, from now on was beginning to be less dominant – either due to too many drugs, the collapse of his marriage or just boredom. Paul began to take more control of their direction and group decisions, though on this album, John was still the major creator of their songs – seven came from his inspiration while Paul contributed five.

There was some 'funny stuff' on the record, as Paul had predicted in an interview a few months previously, mentioning 'Norwegian Wood'. The album title itself is a complicated joke. It's a pun first of all – on rubber sole, har har. The 'soul' can refer to the spiritual soul or soul as in soul music. It was Paul's idea, sparked off by a comment on Mick Jagger and the Rolling Stones by an African-American blues singer – he had dismissed them as being merely 'plastic soul'.

In the US, some of the goodies on the UK album were again spread around – with four tracks appearing on *Yesterday And Today* while two songs were imported onto the US *Rubber Soul* from the UK's *Help!*.

The cover photo, taken again by Robert Freeman, is also a tease. The four of them, dressed in arty, fifties Paris, Left Bank, black polo necks, got snapped at John's house at Weybridge. When Freeman showed them the results, he projected the slides on to some cardboard, the size of the record sleeve, but the cardboard fell over, making the results look distended, as if the photo had been taken in a distorting mirror. They all immediately liked the elongating effect. It was as if their souls were being stretched – along with their music.

The name 'Beatles' does not appear on the cover, which was most unusual, indicating either their conceit, believing that everyone would know who the group were, or a sign of their growing control, for surely no record sales executive would agree to their top group being nameless.

The cover artwork for the two words 'Rubber Soul', up in the top left corner, was by Charles Front, although he was not credited on the sleeve. It fits the feeling of the photograph, as if the lettering had also been pushed and extended. (His daughter is the actress Rebecca Front.) It was only in 2007 that he realised he still had the original artwork lying in a drawer in his attic, where it had been for 42 years. It got sold at Bonhams in London in 2008 for £9,500. In 1965, he had been paid 26 guineas for his efforts.

9.5/10, top of the LPs – so far – for consistent quality and innovation.

7. REVOLVER

Recorded: 6 April–21 June 1966
Released: 5 August 1966 (UK), 8 August 1966 (US)
Tracks: Side 1 - Taxman, Eleanor Rigby, I'm Only Sleeping, Love You To, Here There And Everywhere, Yellow Submarine, She Said She Said; Side 2 - Good Day Sunshine, And Your Bird Can Sing, For No One, Doctor Robert, I Want To Tell You, Got To Get You Into My Life, Tomorrow Never Knows

Another breakthrough, another milestone, what a roll they were on. Apart from all the fab new content, *Revolver* was the first album they created that was totally studio based – creating songs that they had not, did not, could not, perform in public. Nor did they want to. It coincided with them giving up touring for good. All that noise, my dears, all those people, most of them screaming.

The album came out on 5 August 1966 when they were on their final tour – giving their last ever scheduled public performance on 29 August, 1966 at Candlestick Park in San Francisco. (Their last scheduled live UK performance had been on 1 May, at a *New Musical Express* event at Wembley.)

They spent the longest time so far on an album – starting recording the tracks on 6 April and finishing on 21 June (with final mixing on 22 June), clocking up a total of 300 hours of studio time. They were now in charge of themselves, taking their own time, doing it their own way.

Again, all the tracks were new self-composed songs. This time George contributed three, his best total so far – 'Taxman', 'Love You To' and 'I Want To Tell You'. The range of subject matter included a taxman and a doctor. The latter was the one who had introduced them to LSD, which was why John later said that while *Rubber Soul* was the 'pot album' *Revolver* was the 'acid album'. He could have been showing off a bit, sounding cool and hip and in the groove tra la. They never recorded while high, how could they, it is bloody hard and long work, but at home, some of their inspiration, and confusions, did arise from having a few puffs.

The biggest new influence was Indian music rather than West Indian ganja, thanks to George turning them on to his new instruments and new spiritual awakening.

Paul contributed most songs – six, one more than John. Three of them being among the finest that Paul had ever written – 'Eleanor Rigby', 'Here, There And Everywhere' and 'For No One'. John's were no less excellent, especially 'I'm Only Sleeping'.

The Indian music, the clever technical tricks, the psychedelic influences, perhaps did surprise if not confuse some fans but as ever, there was an overall balance, with the inclusion of an old-fashioned children's singalong for Ringo, 'Yellow Submarine'. (Though some did detect druggie influences in it)

The Beatles wanted the whole album to have no gaps or pauses between the tracks (how avant-garde was that, eh?) but EMI said no way, or reactions to that effect.

In the US most of the tracks appeared on their *Revolver* album, released on 8 August, but three of the tracks – all John's – came out earlier, in June 1966, on the *Yesterday And Today* LP ('I'm Only Sleeping', 'And Your Bird Can Sing', 'Doctor Robert').

Robert Freeman was not this time responsible for the cover image – instead they got an old friend from Hamburg, the artist and musician Klaus Voormann, to do a suitably arty, psychedelic montage-cum drawing, with lots of cut-out images of them emerging from their hair. Very groovy, very dreamy. His fee was a measly £50, but it did go on to win him awards for best cover.

The album was at one time going to be called *Abracadabra*, till they discovered the title had already been used. (There is no copyright in song titles, or book titles, but no one wants to be suspected of copying or causing confusion.) Other possibilities included *Four Sides Of The Eternal Triangle*, *Magic Circles*, *After Geography*, till they all agreed on *Revolver*. It was another pun, but pretty straightforward this time. It did not refer to a gun but something that revolves, in this case a record on the turntable. In this modern age, despite the resurgence of vinyl, there must presumably be some people today who don't realise that music used to come from a piece of round, thin vinyl that revolved and produced music, once a needle had been applied to the grooves. Marvellous, when you think about it.

Another triumph of creation, innovation and technique.

8. SGT PEPPER'S LONELY HEARTS CLUB BAND

Recorded: 6 December 1966-21 April 1967
Released: 1 June 1967 (UK), 2 June 1967 (US)
Tracks: Sgt Pepper's Lonely Hearts Club Band, With a Little Help From My Friends, Lucy In The Sky With Diamonds, Getting Better, Fixing A Hole, She's Leaving Home, Being For The Benefit Of Mr Kite!; Side 2: Within You Without You, When I'm Sixty-Four, Lovely Rita, Good Morning Good Morning, Sgt Pepper's Lonely Hearts Club Band (reprise), A Day In The Life.

Was this the greatest album the world has ever seen? Don't just feel the quality, look at the length and breadth and depth of the millions of words written about it ever since. And that's just the cover.

So, this was it, the first album since they had finished touring, with nothing else in their lives to worry about, no deadlines, no time limits, no expenses spared, no constraints on their whims, they could clear the decks and concentrate on, well, whatever it was they decided to concentrate on. They might well have disappeared up their own fantasies, got carried away by their own clevernesses, totally indulged themselves. But they didn't, which is amazing in itself. It might have taken a long time – three months – and cost £25,000, as opposed to one day and £400 for their first album – but actually it shows. The work and effort they put into every aspect of its production is very clear. They were totally disciplined; not a track is poor, not a note is wasted.

In the early months of 1967, I used to feel sorry for George Martin and his crew sitting up in the gallery at Abbey Road, twiddling their thumbs instead of their techno knobs, having to wait while the young masters down below sorted themselves out. In just five years, the tables had been turned; the boys were now in charge of the men. Meanwhile down on the studio floor they were not messing around. Sometimes they spent ten hours, just to get a backing track to their satisfaction when I could see no difference between the first attempt and the one hundredth. You could argue it was self-indulgent of them to arrive in the studio without all their ideas worked out, as they had done in the past, but with no longer playing or working together elsewhere, the studio was not only a recording place, but a creative place.

Although Paul was clearly the boss by now, keeping the others at it, pushing them on, there were still four of them, not all easily pushed around. That's one of the advantages a four-man group has over a solo performer – they can keep each other in check. George was in many ways the real leader now, at least musically, leading them into Indian sounds and instruments, while Paul was more the dynamo, the most focused on the matter in hand, which was the album.

It was his idea, his concept, of an Edwardian band meeting together to give a concert. It was also a way of getting away from being The Beatles, which John and George were beginning to get fed up with anyway, so why not pretend to be another group, another band.

There are different versions of where the title came from – but from my memory, talking to Paul at the time, it started through a mishearing by Mal Evans, their roadie, on a plane. When asked to pass the salt and pepper he thought someone had said 'Sergeant Pepper'. Longer, omnibus titles were in fashion at the time, whether for shops, such as I Was Lord Kitchener's Valet, or pop groups such as The Incredible String Band.

The notion of keeping in character and performing a show all linked together was quickly forgotten when they got down to it. Only the first two tracks are really linked – with Billy Shears being introduced at the end of the first song, who turns out to be Ringo singing 'With A Little Help From My Friends'. There is a slight afterthought towards the end of the second side, with the reprise of the *Sgt Pepper* theme tune, but then we are into the major masterpiece on the record, 'A Day In The Life,' when again all thoughts of Sgt Pepper giving a continuous band show are forgotten.

There were no love songs of the type on their early albums, no 'I love you' or 'please love me', unless you count 'She's Leaving Home'. That's more like social commentary, though we are led to believe she has gone off with her lover in the motor trade, and it could be said that 'Lovely Rita' has a love element, with someone clearly lusting after a meter maid.

There are several tracks that do reflect the main theme, about a show put on by a period band, such as 'Being For The Benefit Of Mr Kite!', which John wrote, and Paul's 'When I'm Sixty-Four', which have circus and music-hall overtones, pastiches of what old-fashioned songs might have sounded like. But George's wonderful 'Within You Without You' makes no pretence at being anything like the sort of tune an Edwardian brass band might have played.

One thing they did keep up during the whole record was having no proper breaks or pauses between tracks – every song almost segues into the next.

They also put some jokey sound effects into the grooves, right on the last day of recording. At the end, when the record just goes round and there is no more music, there is a noise only dogs can hear – a high-pitched 15 khz whistle. Also, in the middle circle there's some mixed up, back-to-front chatter overheard in the studio. That was, of course, pure self-indulgence, to amuse themselves.

For once, the US version was the same as the UK one, same tracks, same order. The Beatles had long grown fed up with Capitol mucking around with compilation albums, changing the order, changing the content.

The cover design, and the whole album package, was Paul's idea, though of course various artists, such as Peter Blake and his wife Jann Haworth, and the photographer Michael Cooper, had to implement his initial ideas and make them work.

The figures on the cover are meant to represent their heroes, though Elvis is not there, as they decided he was the King and beyond parody or acclaim. Hitler was on the list at one time, so not all were their heroes, and so was Jesus, but they were persuaded at the last moment not to include either. Most of the figures are cardboard cut-outs, plus waxworks, a statue and a stuffed doll that says 'Welcome the Rolling Stones'. Many did think they were deadly rivals, and fans were split in their loyalties, but they were chums in real life. The four Beatles appear as waxworks and also stand at the front, in the flesh, dressed as if in the Sgt Pepper band. Not every image has been identified, as one or two cut-outs are not clear, but around 60 have been named.

It is noticeable that among their heroes there are only four who are musical – Bob Dylan, singers Bobby Breen and Dion, plus the composer Stockhausen – yet there are nine writers – Lewis Carroll, Edgar Allan Poe, Dylan Thomas, Aldous Huxley, Terry Southern, Stephen Crane, William Burroughs, H.G. Wells and George Bernard Shaw. It is an indication that their personal influences were as much literary as musical.

The cover has a gatefold, in that you opened it like a book, and found two pockets inside, one for the record itself and the other containing a sheet of goodies – cardboard cut-outs of a moustache, military stripes, badges, a postcard and a picture of the band with the band name that you could fold and stand up. So, lots of fun for boys and girls.

And then, oh joy, they also gave us the exact words of all the songs, printed on the back of the cover. It had been so hard for the previous six years, as Bob Dylan had found out (see entry for 'She's A Woman'), to be totally sure of every word, every syllable. Now there were no more arguments.

Yes, many put *Revolver* at the top, but has there been a more influential album than *Sgt Pepper*? So a big 10/10.

9. THE BEATLES (DOUBLE ALBUM)

Recorded: 30 May–14 October 1968
Released: 22 November 1968 (UK), 25 November 1968 (US)
Tracks: Record One Side 1 – Back In The USSR, Dear Prudence, Glass Onion, Ob-La-Di Ob-La-Da, Wild Honey Pie, The Continuing Story Of Bungalow Bill, While My Guitar Gently Weeps, Happiness Is A Warm Gun; Side 2 – Martha My Dear, I'm So Tired, Blackbird, Piggies, Rocky Raccoon, Don't Pass Me By, Why Don't We Do It In The Road, I Will, Julia
Record Two Side 1 – Birthday, Yer Blues, Mother Nature's Son, Everybody's Got Something To Hide Except Me And My Monkey, Sexy Sadie, Helter Skelter, Long Long Long; Side 2 – Revolution 1, Honey Pie, Savoy Truffle, Cry Baby Cry, Revolution 9, Good Night

This was their ninth LP to come out, chronologically speaking (though before it they had also been working on songs for two films) and it was a beezer, a double helping, a monster mash. And different in so many ways from the arty, farty, elaborate, multicoloured, multilayered *Sgt Pepper*.

Like political parties, especially when things have failed, they like to turn to a totally different sort of leader with a different sort of face. There was no need of course, as *Sgt Pepper* was so successful, but as ever, The Beatles did not want to repeat or be seen to repeat previous formats. So it was out with all that clutter on the cover and no more long or fancy titles.

They did at one time contemplate calling it *A Doll's House*, till they discovered someone else had the same title. So they went for something dead simple – *The Beatles*. Too simple, really, because no one ever called it that, nor do they now. People did not walk into a record shop and say, 'Can I have *The Beatles* please.' It was always 'The Beatles White Album', or 'The Beatles Double Album', or 'The Beatles Double White Album'. So in the end the title was just as much of a mouthful.

The reason for the double album – two records with 30 songs in all – was that while away in India meditating and stuff during February–April 1968, cut off from modern studios and nasty influences like drugs, they had experienced an outflowing of inspiration. Not all the songs they brought back or thought of while out there ended up on the *White Album* – okay, that's what we will call it – but many did.

George contributed four songs, one on each side – 'While My Guitar Gently Weeps', 'Piggies', 'Long Long Long' and 'Savoy Truffle'. And Ringo, tarran tarran, got to make his debut as a composer with 'Don't Pass Me By'.

With so many songs, there was something for everyone as the range of styles and subject matter was so extensive – far-out Indian, psychedelic, country and western, noisy rock, lyrical ballads, love songs.

It was the first album to be produced by their own recording company, Apple, and it came out in the US exactly as they wanted it this time. So sucks to Capitol.

The cover, while appearing so simple, did have a designer – Richard Hamilton. You do need one, even when the front and back were all white. But it wasn't quite. On the front cover were the words The BEATLES – note upper case for BEATLES – easy to miss, as it was small and discreet and in white, and appeared to have been randomly embossed towards the middle of the cover. In the lower right was a number, suggesting it was a limited edition, a collector's item. The number 0000001 was grabbed by John. I wonder where it is today? In 2008, number

0000005 was sold for £19,000. They stopped the numbering of each one in 1969, by which time the highest known number was 3,116,706. If you don't have a number, it means you have a later copy.

Inside, there was loads going on. There was a gatefold, as in *Sgt Pepper*, with a record in either side, plus a large poster. On one side of it were the words of all the lyrics, hurrah again for that, and on the other side were lots of photographs of our heroes. Some were taken from their private archives, such as John as a teenager. There was one of Ringo dancing with Elizabeth Taylor, snaps of other people from their lives, such as Neil Aspinall, Mal Evans, Brian Epstein, some covers of the Beatles fan mag *The Beatles Book Monthly*, plus a naked John with Yoko in bed.

Inside the gatefold, on the right-hand side, there were four moody black and white shots of each of The Beatles, taken by John Kelly. (He is credited, with Hamilton and some others, but in print so small on the poster you need your best specs.)

Despite the cleverness and amusement of the cover, and so many excellent songs, which are still considered among their very best and most loved – 'Happiness Is A Warm Gun', 'Martha My Dear', 'Blackbird', 'Julia', 'I Will', 'Helter Skelter', 'Dear Prudence', 'Back In The USSR' – behind the scenes during the making of the album there was the beginning of turmoil and conflict, which we, the fans, were not yet aware of.

Apple affairs and problems were taking up time. Paul was being bossy, annoying George. Ringo got fed up and walked out during the first day recording 'Back In The USSR' – then returned during the session for 'While My Guitar Gently Weeps'. Their long-time sound engineer Geoff Emerick gave up and left. John, now that Yoko had come into his life, and also George, with all his new passions, had both lost interest in continuing to be a Beatle. They had ceased to be each other's best friends and the atmosphere during much of the studio work was becoming pretty much fragile or fraught. But really, as far as the tracks on the album went, it didn't show. There were some mixed reviews for it, saying it was patchy or had little of importance to say about the world's real problems, but it was a massive and rich and wonderful musical offering, without taking them in any amazingly new or surprising directions (apart from 'Revolution 9', which was a bit of a cul de sac), for all Beatles fans to treasure.

Double helping of delights, though nothing really ground-breaking.

10. YELLOW SUBMARINE

Recorded: 26 May 1966–23 October 1968
Released: 17 January 1969 (UK), 13 January 1969 (US)
Tracks: Side 1 - Yellow Submarine, Only A Northern Song, All Together Now, Hey Bulldog, It's All Too Much, All You Need Is Love; Side 2 - orchestral arrangements from the film score by George Martin

A bit of a cheat, this album based on the film, almost a con, because Beatles fan who rushed to buy it found only four new Beatles songs – 'Only A Northern Song', 'All Together Now', 'Hey Bulldog' and 'It's All Too Much'. The other two songs that appeared on the first side had been heard and released already – 'Yellow Submarine' was a single in August 1966, and appeared on *Revolver*, while 'All You Need Is Love' had been seen and heard on TV and as a single in July 1967.

The second side need not concern us here as the instrumentals are not even based on Beatles songs, but slushy, mushy orchestral background music scored by George Martin and recorded on 22 and 23 October 1968.

The Beatles were under contract to do a third film for United Artists and had put it off, until the idea of an animated film came up, for which they would not have to appear or do much work. So to fulfil their commitments, they used up a few old songs, recorded and not yet released, in fact might never have been released except for the film.

The film itself came out in July 1968 but the album of the film did not appear till the following January. It was put back six months for various reasons, mostly because *The Beatles*, the double album, was still at No. 1 on the LP charts, so why compete against yourselves.

Even the sleeve notes are a disgrace – Derek Taylor, their normally clever and fluent and literate PR guy, could not be arsed to write anything worth reading – telling us merely that he was called Derek, that he loved The Beatles dearly, and that he was paid too much to be free to write anything interesting. After that, the back of the sleeve is filled up with notes about an entirely different album, *The Beatles*. And even that was a reprint – of a review written by Tony Palmer in the *Observer*.

As for the four new songs, they were clearly from the bottom drawer, and probably should have stayed there. 'Only A Northern Song', George's dig at Northern Songs, is funny – if only because he had the cheek to do it and got away with it. But, the film itself was well-loved, and still is today

Being generous.

11. ABBEY ROAD

Recorded: 22 February–19 August 1969
Released: 26 September 1969 (UK), 1 October 1969 (US)
Tracks: Side 1 - Come Together, Something, Maxwell's Silver Hammer, Oh! Darling, Octopus's Garden, I Want You (She's

So Heavy); Side 2 – Here Comes The Sun, Because, You Never Give Me Your Money, Sun King, Mean Mr Mustard, Polythene Pam, She Came In Through The Bathroom Window, Golden Slumbers, Carry That Weight, The End, Her Majesty

This was the last album they ever did together as Beatles – though it came out second last because *Let It Be* got delayed. They knew when they were doing it that was it, the game was up, they were going their separate ways, which is why the last track listed on the cover is 'The End' – though in fact it wasn't. Paul shoved in his tribute to the Queen at the very end, as his little joke, just when you think it is all over.

Considering it was *The End*, and considering on the second side they threw in lots of half finished, half realised songs, segued together, commonly known as the medley, and considering John and Paul were hardly talking, with John not even being present for some of Paul's songs, such as 'Maxwell's Silver Hammer', which he really hated – well, the quality is surprisingly good. By chucking in scraps of songs, on which they don't dawdle, moving on to the next so quickly, we in fact got more than normal for our money. 'You Never Give Me Your Money' and 'She Came In Through The Bathroom Window', however brief, give us enough for the melodies to linger long in the mind.

There are some tracks with downbeat, pessimistic messages and observations, such as 'Maxwell's Silver Hammer' and 'Carry That Weight', but they are not drudges, not depressing to listen to.

George has two songs on *Abbey Road* – perhaps the finest two he ever wrote with The Beatles – 'Something' and 'Here Comes The Sun', each of which has been endlessly covered by other groups and singers. Ringo contributed his second song to a Beatles album, 'Octopus's Garden', which is a pretty good Ringo song, possibly the best song Ringo ever wrote for a Beatles album. (At least the second best, definitely...)

The first reaction to the album by some critics at the time was not favourable, feeling that that we have been short-changed, they are foisting second-rate ideas upon us, but today *Abbey Road* often features at the top of Beatles all-time best albums lists.

The cover brings the progression of their cover designs, which they had taken control of – or at least influenced – since *With The Beatles* when they suggested those half shadow portraits, to a sort of ultimate conclusion. Who would have imagined just six years previously that they would ever get away with a cover that not only didn't include their name, but didn't include the title of the album either.

Paul sketched out his idea for the cover, the four of them walking across a pedestrian crossing near the Abbey Road Studios. Photographer Iain Macmillan, on the morning of 8 August 1969 at around 11.30, had just 15 minutes to get up on his step ladder and snap them while a policeman held back the traffic. He took just six shots – and his fifth was chosen.

They are walking across the crossing, left to right, led by John, obviously – had he not been their leader from the beginning? – followed by Ringo, Paul and George. George is in jeans and denim shirt, the others are in smart but casual suits made by Tommy Nutter. Paul is in bare feet, and out of step with the other three, which led many to suspect he was dead. He carries a cigarette in his right hand, which was deleted in some of the US posters for the album.

To the left-hand side, parked half on the pavement, is a white VW Beetle car, with the number plate LMW 281F, owned by someone who lived nearby. It later became famous in its own right, being shown in museums in Germany. On the right-hand-side pavement they are being watched by a vaguely interested middle-aged passer-by. He was Paul Cole (1911–2008) a US tourist, unaware he had been photographed until he saw the album cover months later. While conspiracy theorists were convinced that Paul being out of step proved his demise, no one suggested that the connections with Germany, through the car, and with America, through the passer-by, might also have been deliberate plants – a farewell to countries that played big parts in their careers.

In the cover photograph, there are no markings in the gutter, as there are today, at pedestrian crossings. Perhaps because of this difference between then and now, there have been reports, untrue, repeated in many reference books and April Fool's stories, that the crossing site has been moved a few yards. In 2010, the crossing was declared a listed site – which did sound at first like a joke – but it was given Grade II Listed Status, being of national, historical importance, so it can not ever be removed. And I should think not. It is now a mega pilgrimage site for Beatles fans from all over the world to take snaps and selfies of themselves. In its simplicity and ordinariness, and the very fact of it being such an, er, pedestrian image, it makes the cover of *Abbey Road* perhaps even better known and parodied today than the elaborately engineered and crowded *Sgt Pepper* montage.

A rich, but fun farewell.

12. LET IT BE

Recorded: February 1968, January, April 1969 and January 1970
Released: 8 May 1970 (UK), 18 May 1970 (US)
Tracks: Side 1 – Two Of Us, Dig A Pony, Across The Universe, I Me Mine, Dig It, Let It Be, Maggie Mae*; Side 2 – I've Got A Feeling, One After 909, The Long And Winding Road, For You Blue, Get Back

The story of *Let It Be,* the film, is long and messy and complicated, annoying and frustrating, as you know now, having read this book thoroughly.

It began as a nice upbeat idea, suggested by Paul, to film the group performing live and real for a TV documentary, as opposed to acting someone else's script, or following someone else's directions, which would bring them all together, chums once again, show the fans the inside workings of their creative genius and engaging personalities, but Oh God, did it all go wrong. Instead of healing the wounds it just opened them all up. By the time it hit the cinemas and the record stores it was all over, for ever, The Beatles had ceased to exist.

The delay was about 18 months, from them going into the Twickenham film studios in January 1969, where they had a few laughs, but also bitched and bickered. They then decided they were not happy with what they had done, with the film and also the tapes, and neither appeared till May 1970.

About the best, most unusual, most amusing thing to come out of it all was their rooftop performance on 30 January 1969, by which time they had moved from Twickenham into their own Apple Studios in Savile Row. They went up on the roof to be filmed for the documentary, playing to the sky, mostly, plus other rooftops, then hundreds of onlookers who gathered down below to witness this mad event. It turned out to be their last ever performance together. Looking at it, then and now, they did seem to be having so much fun, amused by themselves and their reactions. So sad it was the end.

The LP, which is what concerns us here, did not contain all that many unexpected delights for the fans. 'Let It Be', the song itself, had already come out as a single as had 'Get Back'. They had also reverted to earlier ways of filling up an album by including a song written by someone else, in this case Mr or Mrs Traditional, who is generally accepted as being the author of 'Maggie Mae'. According to Liverpool folk legend, she was a prostitute who, after entertaining a sailor back from a long trip, then robbed him of all his money. It was a popular song with skiffle groups, such as The Beatles back in the fifties. Paul's contributions were good and interesting, particularly 'The Long And Winding Road', while John's 'Across The Universe' is probably the best track on the LP, but it had been recorded a long time previously and had already appeared on a charity album. By the time the LP was released, they had not only split but gone off to do different things on their own. Paul produced his first solo album, *McCartney*, released a few weeks before the *Let It Be* album.

It turned out that the *Let It Be* album had been finally knocked into shape by Phil Spector, brought in to rescue all the tapes that had been lying around for months. Paul was totally appalled by the way Spector had remixed his 'The Long And Winding Road,' adding strings and other lush arrangements.

The cover photo by Ethan Russell shows each of them, equal size, in a block of four. George is the only one giving a big cheesy grin – an ironic choice by him, one presumes, as he was the most pissed off by what had recently been happing.

On the back of the album cover came a brief, four-line explanation of what Spector had done, which must surely be the most pretentious, sick-making and ungrammatical of any sleeve notes on any Beatles album. Perhaps any album ever. What a way to end.

'This is a new phase BEATLES album … essential to the content of the film, LET IT BE was

that they performed live for many of the tracks; in comes the warmth and freshness of a live performance; as reproduced for disc by Phil Spector.'

The LP came out first of all in a black box, which was a novelty, if very expensive, as there was so much packaging plus a glossy, 160-page booklet. If you look at the book carefully you'll see it is called *The Beatles Get Back* – which was originally going to be the title of the project. Inside it, the publishing year is given as 1969. So all the books had been lying in storage for at least six months, perhaps a year, gathering dust.

It is mainly photos, with some bits of phoney dialogue and chat taken from the studio recordings, plus a long quotation from the *Confessions of St Augustine*, originally written in Latin around 400 AD. Please, spare us.

The best bit in the book, as in the film, is the shots from the rooftop session – a valuable record of an unusual event.

The booklet was not sold on its own. An unpackaged, simpler, standard version of the album, sans book, came out later in the year. The original complete box-set is now a valuable collector's item – in good condition. Not many are, as the packaging and the book's pages easily came to pieces. But you can now buy reproduction cardboard 'trays', which hold the book and the record, so no need to panic. A snip at $30. While an intact original box-set can be up to $1,000. A piece of Beatles packaging history, if not a masterwork of Beatles music making.

Okay, make it 6 for the perfect box-set.

THE BEATLES EPs

Extended Players, or EPs, were the same size as normal single records, played at 45 rpm, but had more on them, normally two tracks on either side as opposed to one. They usually came in a better quality, better-designed sleeve, on cardboard rather than paper, which was how most singles were packaged. The Beatles produced 12 EPs but only one of them contained a song not already released ('I Call Your Name' on the EP *Long Tall Sally*).

The only EP of interest and importance is therefore *Magical Mystery Tour*, which deserves to be included with The Beatles' 12 LPs. It was a double EP, giving us six tracks in all, a mini album

MAGICAL MYSTERY TOUR

Recorded: 25 April–7 November 1967
Released: EP *Magical Mystery Tour* 8 December 1967 (UK), LP *Magical Mystery Tour* 27 November 1967 (US)
Tracks: Record One Side 1 – Magical Mystery Tour, Your Mother Should Know; Side 2 – I Am The Walrus
Record Two Side 1 – The Fool On The Hill, Flying; Side 2 – Blue Jay Way

This was a double EP, with two records, featuring six of the tracks from the TV film of the same name. They hadn't got enough for an album.

In the US, where the concept of EPs was not as popular, Capitol bumped it up into a full-length LP by adding five previous songs: 'Hello, Goodbye', 'Strawberry Fields Forever', 'Penny Lane', 'Baby, You're A Rich Man' and 'All You Need is Love'. (This LP version did not come out in the UK till 1976.)

It was once again Paul's idea, dreamt up on a plane home from the US. The intention was to create their own hour-long TV film, in which they all go off on a coach and have some magical and mysterious adventures. They had finished *Sgt Pepper* and were looking for a new and amusing project, well Paul was. And he did most of it, directing, producing and script writing … correction, there was no script, not in the conventional sense. So much was made up as they went along.

It got hammered, most critics putting the boot in, pleased to have a chance to cut The Beatles down to size for being self-indulgent, after five years of constant media adoration. But the *Magical Mystery Tour* record itself, the double EP, was very popular and sold well.

Of the six tracks, all from the soundtrack, one was not a song but an instrumental number, 'Flying', created by the four of them. So Starkey got a composing credit. The 'Magical Mystery Tour' song that starts off the EP was an example of their over-confident, slipshod approach to the making of the film – even in the studio they did not have enough lyrics and had to ask Mal Evans and others to suggest suitable words and phrases.

But 'I Am The Walrus' is, of course, a true and proper Beatles classic – and John's only contribution to the EP. George's 'Blue Jay Way' is also there, along with Paul's 'Fool On The Hill' and his clever pastiche 'Your Mother Should Know'.

The EP had a gatefold, with a record in each pocket, front and back. In the middle came a 28-page booklet. The whole package was modest but clever and inventive. The small format booklet, edited by Tony Barrow, with editorial consultants Neil Aspinall and Mal Evans (their roadies), contained photos and scenes from the film, the lyrics of all the five songs, and a cartoon strip with 36 parts. It told the plot of the film, as it if were a children's story.

On the inside of the back gatefold are listed all the songs. After 'I Am The Walrus' the next line reads '"No, you're not!" said Little Nicola'. The unsuspecting might well have thought this was the title of another song, but 'Walrus', with all its psychedelic effects and echoes and assorted instruments, takes up the whole of the side.

Little Nicola was a four-year-old girl on the coach who does say that to John – but you don't hear her on the record. She was called Nicola Hale, and her grandmother was one of the coach passengers. (Nikki, as she became, was last heard of in the US, working as a drugs counsellor.) There is quite a bit of chattering at the end of 'Walrus', though it does not include Nicola. They used a live feed from a BBC Radio production of *King Lear* going out on 29 September 1967. The lines are hard to make out but it appears to include, 'I know thee well: a serviceable villain.' Gosh, what fun they all had.

A high rating for what was only a mini album, but it did have the Walrus.

MAGICAL MYSTERY TOUR FILM LOCATIONS

From the freedom of *A Hard Day's Night* to the scripting of *Help!*, The Beatles' third film, created by themselves, was a mixture of the two styles. They made a lot of it up as they went along, creating some great scenes, though overall it never seemed to quite work the way they wanted. They began the tour at Allsop Place in London on 11 September 1967 initially with only Paul, until John, George and Ringo climbed aboard in Virginia Water near to their homes. They also filmed Ringo buying his tickets in a newsagent's shop at 90 High Street, West Malling in Maidstone; Ringo and Aunt Jessie walked up Acanthus Road in Battersea and boarded the bus at Lavender Hill; the striptease scene was shot at the Raymond Revuebar, 11 Walker's Court in London. For seven days in September 1967, the whole crew descended on West Malling Air Station in Maidstone, Kent. The airfield had a strange collection of concrete obelisks at obscure angles that had acted as protection for planes during the war. These were used to great effect in the filming of 'I Am The Walrus'. In the movie, the great chase scene was filmed on the main runway of the airport and parts of the perimeter road. The inside of the hangars were used for the grand finale of 'Your Mother Should Know', and Major McCartney was filmed inside one of the nearby huts. On the road, the journey took in towns such as Basingstoke in Hampshire; and in the West Country, Teignmouth, Plymouth, Widecombe, Liskeard, and Bodmin in Devon, and Newquay in Cornwall, though not much of the footage was used. The only foreign trip was to Nice in France to film the sequence for 'Fool On The Hill'.

SECTION THREE
Beatles Places

Introduction

There are places we'll remember all our lives, though some have changed, some for ever – but do places make us, mar us, or mark us?

One of the joys of The Beatles, when they first arrived in our lives, was that they were clearly from Liverpool. You heard it when they spoke, and when they sang. They did not perform in a mid-Atlantic accent as so many of the fifties and sixties British singers did. Their humour and slang was very Liverpool and when, eventually, they began to write lyrics that were not following the normal pop song format of boy and girl, feeling blue, they started to use material from their own lives. They sang about their own feelings and thoughts, and we learnt about some of the places in Liverpool that mattered to them when growing up. They gave namechecks to places like Penny Lane and Strawberry Field, which no one outside of Liverpool had ever heard of.

At one time they had thought of an album about their childhood, songs that reflected whence they had come. In the first manuscript version of 'In My Life' John lists places he remembered on a bus ride from his house into town, such as the docks, the tram sheds, an old cinema, Penny Lane. The verses naming these specific places were dropped – though Penny Lane later reappeared, as a song on its own.

So there is no doubt that they thought that places from their past mattered to them – but how much did they matter? If, say, they had all grown up and met in Hampstead or Hamburg, in Tokyo or Toronto, would they still have created music? And would it have been any

better? Different, presumably, based on different sorts of experiences and memories, producing different lyrics and topics, but if you consider John and Paul and George to be natural musical geniuses, which of course we do, sitting here, slogging away on this book, then surely you have to believe they would have succeeded anywhere. You could argue that where they came from might well have made no essential difference to the quality of their music. We all grow up somewhere, after all. But of course it mattered. And we can pinpoint places that did affect their lives and music in some way.

Firstly there are the places where they lived, where they spent their childhood and youth, which means loads of locations in Liverpool, from their family homes to their schools.

Then there are the places where they performed – in Liverpool, in London, on tour, around the world. Now, of course The Beatles did not spring out of nowhere, man, fully formed as *The Beatles*. No, The Beatles, as a group called *The Beatles*, can be recognised, traced and tracked from 1960 onwards, and that is our main subject matter in this book. But as most people know, their first, early, hesitant performances were as a skiffle group known as The Quarrymen, named after the school John attended, Quarry Bank High School.

The Quarrymen years were certainly vital in their development, but unfortunately we don't have proper records of when and where they performed, as so many of the gigs went unrecorded. This makes it impossible to list everywhere the Fab Four ever played. The members of The Quarrymen, the ones who did not go on to become Beatles – Rod Davis, Eric Griffiths Len Garry, Colin Hanton and Pete Shotton – have remembered first playing in other people's homes, or for parties in various houses, for no fee of course, as early as 1956, but they could never remember or agree on exact dates.

Their first performance for which details do exist was at the Empire Theatre in Liverpool in June 1957, when they auditioned for a Carroll Levis discovery show. They did not win.

After that, John and Paul and George went on to conquer the known world with Ringo, while the other original members of the group went on to become ordinary people in the ordinary world.

So the Live Performances included here, ranging from small clubs to mega stadiums, are those, in the main, that involved The Beatles. Where specific pre-Beatles Quarrymen gigs can be identified and verified, we've added those as well. By 'we', we mean Keith Badman, who is the expert in this field, pulling their many many shows into some sort of coherent order.

Then there are the grown-up places, the homes they eventually lived in, offices they used, together with locations that will for ever be associated with them but are not buildings as such, more abstract concepts, such as the crossing on Abbey Road. All such places that played a significant role in the Beatles story are included in this section.

We have not given ratings to every location or performance – most theatres and cinemas are much the same, and as for their endless, gruelling tours, when they often played two shows a night without having any idea where on earth they were, it is not possible now to assess how well they performed. The big, important venues though, those that in some way hosted a noteworthy event, or an interesting, unusual, ground-breaking show, all of those have been rated. And of course they stayed in hundreds of hotels, which we have not bothered to list, unless in some way it figured highly in their saga, if it happened to be the scene of a Happening, such as a bed-in.

David Bedford, who has done the bulk of this section, still lives in Liverpool, and Liverpool figures most in his listings, naturally enough, but it took Liverpool a while to realise what they had spawned. For a few years after The Beatles first left the city and moved to London, Liverpool rather turned its back on them, as if they had been disowned, allowing places associated with them to be knocked down, such as the original Cavern club. Now it has all changed. The boasting is everywhere. Liverpool makes millions every year from fans from all over the world coming to gape and enjoy the Beatles trails.

What is more interesting is how in hundreds of places around the world where mostly they just passed through, on one-night stands, they still remember The Beatles. A whole book has been written, for example, about The Beatles in Bournemouth, based on the fact that they stayed and played there on nine occasions. Even places they never visited or played in haven't escaped the attention of authors – you can read about The Beatles in relation to Cuba and Portugal, for instance, though as a group they never set foot in either country.

Whenever there is a Beatles anniversary, and we seem to get them at least once every year, local papers all over the world dig out old photographs of when The Beatles passed through or, even better, performed in their town.

The Beatles played only twice in my home town of Carlisle, but the *Cumberland News* always delights its readers with the old snaps – which very often encourages people to dig out

THE BEATLES IN CARLISLE (FROM THE FACTORY MAGAZINE OF CARR'S BISCUIT WORKS, CARLISLE 1963)

B-day in Carlisle was 21 November 1963 (for those squares who don't know the meaning of B-day it means Beatle Day). Every seat in the Lonsdale Cinema was taken. All entrances were guarded. There was no chance of anyone getting on to the stage, which was a pity!

As the time for The Beatles' appearance neared, fans began to get restless, me too. The curtains were slowly drawn and there they were, the fabulous four, The Beatles! Many girls made a rush for the stage. I would have gone myself but it meant jumping off the balcony, so I didn't bother; anyway the girls were sent back to their seats. Of course, by this time the screaming had begun and I added my little bit to the noise. The stage was littered with jelly babies. My friends and I had jelly babies too but ours would never have reached the stage so we ate them. The screaming was deafening. My friend and I were screaming for Paul McCartney (he's the greatest). My other friend was nearly in tears over Ringo Starr. Many girls were standing in the aisles stomping. Boys complain about girls screaming, but one boy, who was sitting near me, was dancing and shouting.

In between songs Paul was trying to quieten us down but it just made us worse. George Harrison was hit in the eye by an apple core (wish I'd been that apple core). Ringo Starr was really getting with it on his drums. Man, could he go! John Lennon looked rather tired but is very nice.

I've not mentioned any of the songs they sang, because, I never heard any. I'm told they sang 'She Loves You', 'Boys', 'Money' and eight others.

As they finished their act everyone went wild. The curtains closed and they were gone. In the middle of the National Anthem some fan started to scream.

As I left the cinema I bought a large photo of my heroes. We went to a local Youth Centre until 10.15 then returned to the cinema to catch a glimpse of The Beatles as they left. On the way we met two men from the show who gave us their autographs. One of them told us from which entrance The Beatles were leaving. At about 10.35 they left in a Post Office van. Screaming fans tried to catch it but the driver was too quick for them. As I walked home, busloads of cheering fans passed me. I was lucky; a man who works at the cinema got their autographs for me. All I want now is to meet them personally.

Here's Hoping!

stuff they thought they had forgotten. Not long ago someone found a scratchy old tape recording he had managed to make while in the audience at their 1963 concert in the local cinema, which up until the previous year had been known as the Lonsdale. Radio Cumbria proudly broadcast bits of it as a world exclusive. I listened to it, a bit bemused. I could make out so little because of all the screaming.

While doing some research on a different topic, I came across an account – reproduced here – by a 16-year-old girl, Elizabeth Obington, who worked in the local biscuit factory, Carr's of Carlisle. She had been at the Beatles concert in Carlisle on 21 November 1963, and contributed the article to the factory magazine of Carr's biscuit works, the *Topper Off*. It's unusual in this early period to have a first person, amateur article, written by a fan, describing a Beatles concert. It contains some nice period details.

There are places that The Beatles remembered – but there are far more places around the globe that still remember The Beatles. And always will.

Only performances between 10 May 1960 (Wyvern Club, Liverpool) and 30 January 1969 (Apple HQ rooftop, London) are listed in this section. In the transition from Quarrymen to Beatles during 1960 the group appeared under a number of names – The Beatals in March, The Silver Beats on one occasion in May, and with little consistency until they departed for Hamburg in August as The Beatles, they could be found performing as The Silver Beetles, The Silver Beats or The Beetles. However, from that August, they were most definitely *The Beatles*.

Accordingly, for the sake of consistency throughout this book, we have settled on using *The Silver Beatles* during this period of flux. As with a clock that has stopped, we will be correct at least some of the time.

The entries are separated into three regions: UNITED KINGDOM and REPUBLIC OF IRELAND, UNITED STATES OF AMERICA and REST OF THE WORLD, to make it easier to search. Within these regions, locations are listed alphabetically by country, city and place name.

Within the UK, locations are listed under *Liverpool* or *London* according to their postcodes. Locations with 'L' postcodes fall under the heading of Liverpool. Please note the Liverpool section also includes locations on the Wirral peninsula – such as Birkenhead, Ellesmere Port, Heswall, Hoylake, Irby, Neston Wallasey – as these were included within the L postcode during the time of The Beatles.

Other locations in the general Merseyside area – such as Frodsham, Runcorn, Southport – are listed separately.

Similarly, locations with the following Inner London postcodes fall under the London heading: N, NW, SW, SE, W, WC, E, EC. Areas in Greater London – such as Borehamwood, Croydon, Esher, Romford and Twickenham – have individual entries.

UNITED KINGDOM (England, Scotland, Wales, Northern Ireland) and REPUBLIC OF IRELAND

In a few short years, The Beatles managed to cover most of the UK, starting in 1960 when they spent two weeks travelling around the highlands of Scotland. Thereafter they embarked on national tours of across the UK followed by Europe, the USA, and then, well, here, there and everywhere.

ENGLAND

ALDERSHOT

Palais Ballroom, Queens Road

One of the most infamous performances by The Beatles took place here on 9 December 1961. Due to an advertising mix-up between the band's promoter and the local newspaper, the *Aldershot News*, only 18 people turned up for the gig. Promoted by Sam Leach, it was intended to be a Liverpool v London, 'Battle of the Bands' contest, between The Beatles and the top local one, Ivor Jay and The Jaywalkers. This was in a town 37 miles from London and the home of the British Army.

After the performance, John, Paul, George and Pete's brief southern jaunt continued with a show in Soho at The Blue Gardena Club.

The Beatles' first concert in the south of England. A pity it was such a disaster.

ASCOT

Gables, London Road, Sunningdale

Derek Taylor, who became The Beatles' press officer in 1964, lived here from 1968 to 1977.

BATH

The Pavilion, North Parade Road

The Beatles made their only appearance here on 10 June 1963.

BEDFORD

Corn Exchange, St Paul's Square

The Beatles stepped in for the advertised Joe Brown here on 13 December 1962.

Granada Cinema, 5-9 St Peters Street

The Beatles made their first appearance here on 6 February 1963 as part of the Helen Shapiro tour. They returned on 12 March 1963 with the Chris Montez/Tommy Roe tour, minus a sick John.

With John officially 'still suffering from a heavy cold', Paul and George had to rearrange the songs to share the vocal parts between them. However, his non-appearance was down to another matter. Fed up with the concerts The Beatles were performing in and feeling homesick, he had walked out and decided to return, albeit briefly, to his home town of Liverpool. 'One night, on my way home from the Cavern,' the club's resident doorman and bouncer, Paddy Delaney recalled, 'I walked into the Blue Angel [and] as I walked in, I saw John's back at the bar. He was sitting on a stool and I knew immediately it was him because he was wearing a light-blue mohair jacket. He never wore anything else. The thing was he was supposed to be in Bedford on The Beatles' first, big tour of the country. He told me, "It's like a cemetery, and I'd had enough so I decided to come back to Liverpool." He insisted we drink whisky after whisky and we didn't leave the club until twenty past four in the morning.' John would rejoin the tour on 15 March 1963 for their two performances at the Colston Hall, Bristol.

BIRMINGHAM

Alpha Television Studios, Aston

On 18 August 1963, on their 300-mile journey from North Wales to Torquay in Devon, The Beatles stopped off here to tape an appearance on *Lucky Stars (Summer Spin)*.

Hippodrome Theatre, Hurst Street

The Beatles made two visits here in 1963, on 10 March as part of the Chris Montez/Tommy Roe tour and 10 November on their autumn tour.

For their March appearance, due to their increasing popularity The Beatles were placed at the top of the bill. The comedian Les Dawson's dresser, Harry Brown, was working at the venue

when The Beatles asked him to nip out and fetch them four lots of fish and chips, which cost him a pound. They said they would pay him later, but they never did. One of the police helmets worn by the group in some of the pictures taken at the venue had been borrowed from the future Welsh singing sensation, Tom Jones, who was then a police constable.

Maney Hall, Sutton Coldfield

On a trip to the Midlands, The Beatles made two appearances on 1 February 1963 in towns just outside of Birmingham. Their first was here in Sutton Coldfield, where they performed in this hall, also known as St Peter's Church Hall, on Maney Hill Road, before making the short trip to Tamworth.

Odeon Cinema, New Street

The Beatles appeared here on 11 October 1964 and again on 9 December 1965, where a crowd of 2,439 saw each of the two shows on that day.

Ritz Ballroom, York Road, Kings Heath

The Beatles were originally scheduled to play here on 11 January 1963, but heavy blizzards made the roads impassable, preventing them making the journey to Kings Heath. The concert was rescheduled for 15 February, which worked well for the promoter. By the time The Beatles performed here, they had a single in the top three of the charts. Following the show a fan, Yvonne, picked up her coat from the cloakroom and bumped into Paul, who was coming out of the toilets. After giving her his autograph, she followed him into the bar, where he called her over to meet the rest of the group, who subsequently gave her their signatures too. She then took up Paul's kind offer of giving her a lift back into town in their van, where, so she said, she sat on his lap and shared a kiss. He then handed her his address and asked her to write, before dropping her and a friend off at a bus stop.

Town Hall, Congreve Street

The Beatles appeared here during the Roy Orbison tour, on 4 June 1963. George returned here with husband and wife musical act Delaney & Bonnie on 3 December 1969, when he performed two shows.

BLACKBURN

King George's Hall, Northgate

The concluding date on the 1963 Roy Orbison tour saw The Beatles make their only appearance in this Lancashire town on 9 June in front of 4,500 fans for each of the two shows. Tickets cost from five shillings and sixpence to ten shillings and sixpence. Teddy bears and boxes of jelly babies were thrown onto the stage. One boy had to courage to scream 'Up The Rolling Stones!' and was promptly hit on the head with an umbrella by a girl sitting next to him. At the end of their second show, with the fans surging towards the stage, John, Paul and George unclipped their guitars and ran for it, leaving Ringo behind, stuck behind his drums and with no alternative but to kick them over and sprint for cover. Backstage in their dressing room, John told a reporter from the *Telegraph*, 'They were the best crowds we have had yet. I could have played for another hour.'

BLACKPOOL

ABC Theatre, Church Street

This cinema in, the popular Lancashire seaside resort, played host to The Beatles during their Sunday evening summer seaside tour of 1963. They appeared here on 7 July, 14 July, 11 August and 25 August and 8 September (final Sunday of the tour). The compère for these shows was the future *Carry On* film comedian, Jack Douglas.

A three-and-a-half-minute, colour 8mm film of The Beatles' 25 August performance, and clowning around backstage, was taken by Chas McDevitt of The Chas McDevitt Skiffle Group, which was one of the support acts that night. The movie was put up for auction by Ewbank's Auctioneers of Woking, Surrey in February 2015.

The Beatles also performed here for two live TV broadcasts of the ITV show *Blackpool Night Out*, on 19 July 1964 and 1 August 1965.

37 Ivy Avenue

Towards the end of May 1946, John's father Alf was staying over at Mimi's house when, without telling anyone, he took John out and disappeared to this nearby seaside resort. John remained away from Liverpool for a few weeks, staying with Alf's friend's parents, Mr and Mrs Hall.

On 22 June 1946, John's mother Julia and her partner Bobby Dykins turned up at the Hall's house to take John back to Liverpool. Alf again suggested to Julia that they should give the marriage another go but she said no. Alf then asked John to choose between him and his mother. After initially deciding to stay with his father, John then ran after his mother as she walked out of the room, calling, 'Mummy don't go, Daddy come home!' He wouldn't see his father again for around 20 years, when he was famous.

Pivotal moment in John's life when he chose to return to Liverpool.

Opera House, Church Street

Before heading to Sweden on 28 July, The Beatles appeared at the Opera House, Church Street, on 26 July 1964, and returned here a few weeks later for a second appearance on 16 August. Also on the bill for that second visit were The Kinks and an exciting, new R&B group, The High Numbers, who would shortly rename themselves The Who. 'We were bottom of the bill, and The Beatles were top of the bill,' Who bass player John Entwistle recalled. 'They couldn't understand why we were setting up this huge amount of equipment for ourselves. When our stuff was taken off, they brought out The Beatles' stuff and it was about half the size, and they were using the theatre's PA system, which was diabolical. The little microphones looked like electric shavers. We couldn't understand why they put themselves through such rubbish!'

Queen's Theatre, Bank Hey Street

The Beatles' first appearance here, on 21 July 1963 during their Sunday evening summer seaside tour, went without incident, but, when they returned two Sundays later on 4 August, there was pandemonium. There were so many fans outside they had to enter the theatre in a most unusual way. They had arrived at 5pm to find the audiences for *both* shows had already started to gather outside, as John humorously recalled. 'We might have got through the massed ranks of fans if we had been inside a tank or if we had been mounted on elephants, but any other way was impossible. In the end we were smuggled round to some doorway, near the back of the venue, this took us into a builder's yard. We got on a ladder and climbed up that, onto some scaffolding, climbed higher and found ourselves on the roof. Then our guide led us along near the front edge of the roof and when the fans below spotted us, they cheered so loud, you could hear them on Wigan pier. Then we were led to a skylight. We went through that into a loft, from the loft to the flies of the theatre, and down yards

n' yards of iron ladder to the stage. We were in, but all evening we were worrying about how were going to get out. In the end, we decided to hang around and wait 'til most of the crowd had gone. That meant four Beatles sitting in the dressing room 'til one in the morning, having a huge supper of fish and chips and Cokes.'

BOREHAMWOOD

ATV Elstree Studios, Eldon Avenue

At these studios, in the north-west of London near Watford, Lew Grade's ATV stars Morecambe and Wise had one of the top shows in the country, and on 2 December 1963 The Beatles were the special guests. What followed was partly scripted and partly ad-libbed, including Eric Morecambe turning to Ringo and calling, 'Hello Bongo!'

Bring me sunshine with The Beatles.

BOURNEMOUTH

Gaumont Cinema, Westover Road

The Regent Cinema, as it was originally called, opened in 1929, the second 'super-cinema' in the UK. It became the Gaumont in 1949. The cinema was taken over by the Odeon chain in 1986.

From 19–24 August 1963, The Beatles performed in a six-night residency here by the seaside on the south coast of England, playing two shows each night. They twice made the 220-mile round trip to London to visit Abbey Road during the day.

One night, in their hotel room, George recorded a demo of his future *With The Beatles* album track 'Don't Bother Me', on John's reel-to-reel tape machine. The first of the 21 August shows was recorded by the cinema's chief technician. On 10 December 1998 it was sold by Christie's auction house in London for £25,300 to a private collector. The reel-to-reel tape, which was put up for the sale by the technician's daughter, included The Beatles' jokey repartee with the audience, and John's humorous introduction to 'She Loves You', which had yet to be released. 'Here's a new song for us,' he said, 'released on Friday. Buy your copy, please.'

The Beatles returned to the venue twice the following year, on 2 August – where they were supported by The Kinks, Mike Berry and Adrienne Poster (then known as Posta) – and 30 October.

Palace Court Hotel, Westover Road

In a spare hour in the group's busy schedule, at noon on 22 August, during their six-day residency at the Gaumont in August 1963, The Beatles were photographed in half-shadow by Robert Freeman in one of this hotel's corridors. The result, among other uses, famously graced the cover of their November 1963 album, *With The Beatles*, one of the most memorable, and imitated, album covers of all time. It was Freeman's suggestion that the image should be in b&w. Since he was the last to join, Ringo was placed in the bottom-right corner. He had to kneel on a stool to be comfortable in the right position for the shoot. 'It was very un-studio-like,' Paul recalled. 'The corridor was very dark, and there was a window at the end and by using this heavy source of natural light, he got that photo … People think he must have worked for ever and ever in great technical detail to get that shot. But it was just an hour. He sat down, took a couple of rolls, and he had it.'

One of the most iconic of images of The Beatles photographed here.

Winter Gardens Theatre, Exeter Road

Fans at this venue watched a regular Beatles concert on 16 November 1963, part of the band's autumn tour. However, as the new phenomenon of Beatlemania was spreading across America, news crews from US networks NBC and ABC filmed a portion of the performance, and the crowd, for transmission in the States during November and December 1963.

Since the original audio of 'She Loves You' from the concert was marred by the screaming fans, for the benefit of the US viewers the original studio recording was dubbed on top for the broadcasts.

Journalist Edwin Newman's four-minute report on The Beatles, during the 18 November 1963 edition of the flagship NBC evening news programme *The Huntley-Brinkley Report*, became the very first time that many US TV viewers had a chance to sample Beatlemania and see footage of the group in action. This came several weeks before their appearance, also by way of film, on the 3 January 1964 edition of *The Jack Paar Show* and, importantly, almost three months before their famed debut on *The Ed Sullivan Show*.

An important engagement for the band, due to the presence of the American TV cameras.

BRADFORD

Gaumont Cinema, New Victoria Street

The Beatles' first nationwide tour, with two shows per night, began in this Yorkshire town on 2 February 1963 where, having been top dogs in Liverpool, they were now bottom of the six-act bill, headlined by 16-year-old singer, Helen Shapiro, who had just released her new single 'Queen For Today'. 'The first thing I remember about this tour,' Shapiro recalled, 'was being introduced to The Beatles at the start. Paul, who was always the spokesman and diplomat, introduced me, one by one, to the rest of the group. They were funny fellows with the funny hair. I had heard of them, of course and heard "Love Me Do". I loved it! I also remember certain incidents, like Paul practising his autograph loads of times on a photograph and coming in to show me and asking what I thought of them. George was always talking about being rich and wanting to make loads of money.'

Despite it being the opening night of their first major tour, John later mentioned he had never enjoyed it. 'The music was dead before we even went out on that theatre tour of Britain,' he said. 'We were feeling shit because we had to reduce an hour or two hours playing … to twenty minutes and go on and repeat the same twenty minutes every night. The Beatles died then as musicians. That's why we never improved as musicians. We killed ourselves to make it and that was the end of it. George and I are more inclined to say that.'

Irish comedian Dave Allen was compère for the tour.

On 21 December 1963 The Beatles performed a preview of their Christmas show here (see entry for Astoria, Finsbury Park).

The Beatles returned to the venue once more, on 9 October 1964 for the opening night of their only British tour that year. Their fee for two shows each evening was £850.

The opening night of the group's first nationwide tour. A true landmark gig.

BRIGHTON
Hippodrome Theatre, Middle Street

The first of The Beatles' three appearances at this south coast resort was on 2 June 1963 during the Roy Orbison tour. Prior to the shows, the group's press officer, Tony Barrow introduced The Beatles to Mary Cochram. She would soon become known as Anne Collingham, the joint national head secretary of The Official Beatles Fan Club at 13 Monmouth Street, London. Because the organisation, and the group's business, had grown so much by this point, Barrow effectively closed operations in Liverpool and moved everything down to London.

Their second appearance came just over a year later on 12 July 1964. One of their support acts was the six-piece, jazz-influenced band, The Shubdubs, whose drummer Jimmie Nicol had temporarily performed with The Beatles during part of their June 1964 tour after Ringo had been taken ill with tonsillitis. Speaking in 1987, he recalled talking with them backstage. 'We talked,' he said, 'but the wind had changed since we last saw each other … They were pleasant.'

Their final performance here was a few months later on 25 October.

BRISTOL
Colston Hall, Colston Street

This was the only venue The Beatles played in Bristol, a city in the south-west of England. They appeared here on three occasions. The first appearance was on 15 March 1963 on the Chris Montez/ Tommy Roe tour. John rejoined the group this night, after missing the three previous concerts due to 'illness'. The Beatles also performed here on 15 November 1963 during their autumn tour, and on 10 November 1964.

The 1964 concert was the closing night of The Beatles' only British tour of that year. It will be remembered for the practical jokers who managed to climb up to the ceiling of the venue and tip a bag of flour over the band while they performed. With brilliant timing, it happened just as they hit the final chord of their quietest number, 'If I Fell'. With flour covering everything, the group fell about laughing. Ringo had to turn his tom-tom drum upside down and bang it to clear the powder from it. Bent double with laughter, Paul leaned forward, grabbed the microphone and explained, 'It's the last night of the tour, you see.'

The theatre's manager, Ken Crowley, however, wasn't impressed, saying to reporters at the time, 'The thing that worries me is that, somehow our security measures were dodged. And even more worrying is the fact that the joker risked his life. One false step on to a part of that slender ceiling and he'd have plunged 50 foot to the stage, probably injuring one of The Beatles as well as himself.' It was later revealed that in fact there were four culprits behind the joke; three young men and a policeman's daughter.

BUXTON

Pavilion Gardens Ballroom, St John's Road

This is situated in the rural town of Buxton, Derbyshire. The Beatles made two appearances here on 6 April and 19 October 1963. There was a terrible accident before the first concert when a scrum broke out between overexcited fans, causing one young girl to lose an eye.

CAMBRIDGE

Lady Mitchell Hall, Sidgwick Avenue

On 2 March 1969, John and Yoko performed in an experimental style here before a small audience of 500 students. The performance, the first concert appearance for a Beatle outside of the group, was recorded and included on the album *Unfinished Music No 2: Life With The Lions*, released that May.

Regal Cinema, St Andrews Street

This cinema was the location of two performances by The Beatles, the first on 19 March 1963 during the Chris Montez/Tommy Roe tour and the second on 26 November of the same year as part of their autumn tour.

An audience of over 4,000 saw the November show. People lined the street outside the cinema from about 10.30am and the group had to be smuggled down Downing Street by police escort. The Beatles were protected from their riotous fans by members of Shelford Rugby Club, who stood guard in front of the stage. Before the performance, The Beatles were interviewed in their dressing room for local television.

CARLISLE

ABC Cinema, Warwick Road

The first appearance by The Beatles at this venue, formerly known as the Lonsdale, in the far northwest of England occurred on 8 February 1963 during the Helen Shapiro tour. The cinema's big screen had to be pushed back so they could play. As a result of John mentioning in a newspaper report that George had eaten his jelly babies, fans pelted the band with the sweets and the group had to ask them to stop. Calum Scott-Buccleuch, the then 25-year-old stagehand and son of the cinema's manager, recalled they got hit with a vengeance. 'It just rained jelly babies,' he said. One of his jobs was to clear them up. 'They filled a two-foot high box,' he remembered.

After the shows, the group, along with Shapiro and Kenny Lynch, travelled a few hundred yards through Carlisle city centre to Carlisle Golf Club's annual dinner-dance and began tucking into the buffet. However, Bill Berry, the chairman of the establishment, wasn't having any of it. When he caught sight of the 'four rather scruffy young chaps' he decided that their behaviour – and dress – simply wasn't acceptable for the four-star Crown and Mitre Hotel. So he approached them, had a quiet word, and the four leather-jacket-clad Beatles, as well as their tour mates, had to quietly slip away.

The Beatles obviously hadn't upset too many people the first time round in Carlisle because they returned to the same venue for a second and final time on 21 November 1963 during their autumn tour, playing in front of 2,000 fans. John Wilson, 25, of Denton Holme, was among the audience and recorded the show on his trusted, reel-to-reel tape recorder.

Unlike in February, this time The Beatles were top of the bill and in the ascendancy. They had to be smuggled into the venue by the back door surrounded by policemen with their dogs, and posed for pictures in a lift. Between performances, police dogs and handlers were on patrol to keep the crowds from invading the building. The Beatles left Carlisle for the last time the following morning, en route to Stockton-on-Tees for a show at the Globe Cinema. It was a momentous time for them, and the rest of the world. Their second Parlophone album, *With The Beatles*, was about to be released and, one day later, President John F. Kennedy was assassinated in Dallas, Texas.

CAVERSHAM

Fox and Hounds Pub, Gosbrook Road

On 23 and 24 April 1960. John and Paul had travelled south to visit Paul's cousin Bett and her husband Mike at their pub, where Lennon and McCartney performed as The Nerk Twins.

Valuable lessons for Lennon and McCartney in show business and how to play to an audience.

CHATHAM

Invicta Ballroom, High Street

On 12 January 1963 The Beatles made the 170-mile journey to Kent to play their only gig here, the furthest south they had performed to date. This is their last known performance with a 'RINGO STARR' logo on Ringo's bass drum skin. Backstage each of the group signed a b&w promotional Parlophone postcard for one of their fans, Vivian. Besides xxx from each, Ringo added, 'To Viv Love and Luck' above his name.

CHELTENHAM

Odeon Cinema, Winchcombe Street

The day after returning from Sweden, The Beatles started their autumn tour at this cinema on 1 November 1963. It was their fourth British tour of the year. The following day's *Daily Mirror* carried a report of the concert with the headline 'Beatlemania! It's happening everywhere, even in sedate Cheltenham'. This is thought by some to be the first use of the word in print, although the press reports of their 13 October 1963 appearance on *Val Parnell's Sunday Night At The London Palladium* is the more likely origin. Unable to leave their rooms for fears of their safety, to ease their boredom the group amused themselves by playing with Scalextric, the 1:32 scale, slot car racing game.

CHERTSEY

JP Fallon, 8 Guildford Street

When John decided he wanted to change the colour of his Rolls-Royce, he took it to this coachworks

CHECK THE ATTIC

Everything Beatles-related has a value, so throw nothing out.

At the top end, in June 1985 John Lennon's psychedelic Rolls-Royce was sold at auction by Sotheby's for a whopping £1,768,000, and his white piano was bought by George Michael for £1,500,000 in 2000. An original manuscript of any of their songs, written in their own fair hands, can fetch huge sums – 'A Day In The Life' and 'All You Need Is Love' each sold for $1 million while others have reached £250,000. Handwritten letters can be worth anything up to £100,000 (depending on content of course, and especially if pre-1963), and posters, programmes and autographs are also coveted. The highest amount of money paid for an autograph was in 2013, when an unnamed buyer bought a signed *Sgt Pepper* album for $290,500.

If you think you have something of unusual interest, most auction houses would value it for you, or sell it. In the UK, Tracks Ltd is the world's leading dealer in Beatles material (tracks.co.uk) or Bonhams auctioneers (bonhams.com).

company, who painted it in the famous psychedelic design, returning it to John on 25 May 1967.

CHESTER

Riverpark Ballroom, Union Street

The first of four appearances here in the Roman town of Chester on Thursday 16 August 1962 was unremarkable on the schedule, but was one of the performances that Pete Best had agreed to play after he was dismissed. He didn't show and was replaced by Johnny Hutchinson. Their second appearance was on 23 August 1962, the evening of the wedding of John Lennon and Cynthia Powell in Liverpool. How romantic. The Beatles also performed here on 30 August and 13 September of that year.

Royalty Theatre, City Road

The second venue in Chester The Beatles played saw them make just the one appearance at this theatre, on 15 May 1963.

At the venue, a ten-year-old fan, Gail, was able to fleetingly encounter The Beatles backstage through her father knowing the theatre's manager,

Mr Critchly. Gail and her best friend Judy were ushered into a small, dark, exceedingly cramped area that led to the dressing rooms. Unsure what Ringo and George looked like, she spent minutes preparing for the meeting by gazing at the *Please Please Me* album cover. She soon noticed them, doing some very playful things with some of the other female fans gathered there. Paul appeared briefly. He signed their autograph books and then went off to use a payphone attached to a wall alongside the stairs. He was in conversation for a while, and regularly pumped thruppeny-bits into the slot. Gail watched him for ages and decided that once he came off the phone, she was going to ask him if he knew where John was. Sure enough, when he put down the receiver, she went up to him and asked, 'Do you know where John is, please?' He answered that he was probably in the dressing room, and offered to take her autograph books to get them signed. She handed them over and thanked him.

Minutes passed and Paul hadn't reappeared, so she decided to go in pursuit of John herself, and both girls began trudging through the venue's bleak corridors, and past the various dressing rooms, until they came to a stop outside The Beatles' one. The door was ajar, and Paul was standing in the gap, leaning against the doorframe. On the other side, through the small gap between the door and its hinges, Gail watched as John, wearing his thick-framed glasses, sat eating a bag of crisps. He was talking to someone. Paul seemed not to notice the girl was there, until John suddenly turned and met her gaze with one of his legendary stares. Gail felt intimidated. It was at this point that Paul, trying to dissipate the potentially difficult situation, chirped up, in his bright and breezy voice, 'Oh, there you are girls,' as though he had been expecting them all along. Probably just to usher them away without any fuss, clearly having forgotten he had done so already, he signed one of Gail's autograph books twice. The two girls duly complied and left. They never did speak to John. Once dressed, The Beatles visited a restaurant opposite the Royalty Theatre, and during the course of their late-night meal signed a paper napkin for a fan. Paul added the dedication 'To Pat, lots of love'.

COVENTRY

Coventry Theatre, Hales Street

During 1963, The Beatles made two appearances here, on 24 February during the Helen Shapiro tour and 17 November as part of the autumn tour.

Matrix Hall, Fletchamstead Highway

After spending two weeks in Hamburg at the Star-Club, and a day recording at EMI House in London, The Beatles made a 100-mile journey to the Midlands on 17 November 1962 to play here, where they were billed as 'Hit Recorders of "Love Me Do" Direct from their German Tour'. In the 1970 movie *Let It Be*, Paul and John talk about this night, although Paul is mistaken in thinking

it took place at Leicester's De Montfort Hall. During the conversation Paul describes the gig as 'the worst first night ever'.

St Michael's Cathedral

On 15 June 1968, John and Yoko visited Coventry Cathedral to plant acorns as part of their attempt to promote world peace. The original acorns were immediately stolen by Beatles fans, so replacements were sent by John and Yoko and planted again.

Another opportunity for John and Yoko to do something for peace.

CREWE

Majestic Ballroom, High Street

John, Paul, George and Pete appeared here on 13 August 1962, but when The Beatles returned a week later they had their new drummer Ringo Starr behind them. The Majestic Theatre was a Top Rank venue, and they called it 'The Biggest Rock Since Blackpool Rock', an allusion to the bars of rock confectionery you could purchase at the seaside.

CROYDON

ABC Cinema, London Road, Broad Green

After recording for the BBC Radio show *On The Scene*, the Fab Four made the short journey to Croydon, where they continued the Chris Montez/Tommy Roe tour here, playing two shows on 21 March 1963.

Fairfield Hall, Park Lane

The fourth of Brian Epstein's *Mersey Beat Showcase* concerts took place in the ballroom here on

The Beatles showing their rather respectable, restrained mop tops, on the cover of the tour programme for their concert in Croydon, September 1963.

25 April 1963. It was arranged back in January, and fearing the show might not attract enough fans, promoter John Smith had arranged for the singer/actor John Leyton to headline the concert. However, on the day of the show Leyton became ill and was forced to cancel his appearance, leaving The Beatles to replace him at the top of the bill. Ringo's kit went missing before the gig and he was forced to borrow the one belonging to The Dakotas. Black and white photographs of the event, taken with his Rollei camera, were captured by 15-year-old Andy Wright, a Woodcote Secondary School pupil. Andy's father was a steward at the venue. After the show, Andy went backstage to meet The Beatles. With film being so expensive then, he was only able to take 12 pictures on the night.

The Beatles returned to the venue on 7 September of the same year, for the final night of the John Smith-promoted mini-tour.

George also made an appearance here backing Delaney & Bonnie on 7 December 1969.

DARWEN

Co-operative Hall, School Street

Organised by the Baptist Youth Club and promoted as 'The Greatest Teenage Dance', The Beatles' only appearance in this town on the edge of Blackburn, Lancashire was on 25 January 1963. John and Ringo were driven to the venue by their roadies in a van, while Paul and George had made their own way in McCartney's first car, a 4-door, Ford Consul Classic, in Goodwood Green. Paul suffered a bout of stage fright during the gig. 'I had a lead solo in one of the songs,' he recalled, 'and I totally froze when my moment came. I played the crappiest solo ever! I said, "That's it! I'm never going to play lead guitar again!"' 'When they were ready to go,' bouncer David Yates remembered, 'Paul asked me which was the best way to get to Southport. I said, "Down the main road," and asked if they'd give me a lift, as I was going that way as well. They were happy to oblige and they chatted away as we drove towards Blackburn. Paul dropped off me at the corner of Birch Hall Estate and they disappeared down the road.'

DONCASTER

Co-operative Ballroom, St Sepulchre Gate

A trip of almost 90 miles across the Pennines to Yorkshire saw The Beatles appear here on 8 August 1962.

Gaumont Cinema, Hall Gate

The Beatles appeared at this Yorkshire cinema on three occasions.

The first was on 5 February 1963, the second date of the Helen Shapiro tour, three days after the opening night. During their one-night stay in Doncaster, the group took up residence at the Punch Hotel. Mick Longworth, 15, whose father owned the place, cancelled his paper round that morning to meet the group and ended up serving John morning tea in his bed. In the hotel register, each Beatle gave a Liverpool address and, under the nationality section, John scribbled 'White Man' while Paul scrawled 'Green'.

The Beatles performed here for a second time, on 22 March 1963 during the Chris Montez/ Tommy Roe tour.

Their final appearance at the Gaumont was on 10 December 1963 as part of the band's autumn tour. Prior to this show, in their dressing room at the venue the group gave an interview to the Australian reporter Dibbs Mather for overseas distribution by the BBC's Transcription Service. Excerpts of which, including John reciting his poem 'Neville Club', and announcing his intention to publish a book of his writings, were featured in both the 61st edition of *Dateline London* and the 453rd of *Calling Australia* and were available to any radio stations that paid the Corporation's annual subscriptions.

St James' Street Baths

On 19 February 1963 The Beatles were at the Cavern in Liverpool. After the gig they drove through the night to London, to appear on the BBC Light Programme radio show *Parade of The Pops* at the Playhouse Theatre, on 20 February (see entry in the *Radio* section). They then travelled 160 miles north to Yorkshire to perform on the same day at this public swimming pool, which was floored over during winter to create a dance floor and concert venue.

DUDLEY

Plaza Ballroom, Old Hill

On the date EMI released the single 'Please Please Me', the 100-mile trip from Liverpool to Old Hill near Dudley in Staffordshire on 11 January 1963 was hazardous due to bad weather, but the band made it in time. However, the weather worsened and the coldest night in the area for many years halted their onward journey to Birmingham, meaning they missed their concert there.

The band returned to the venue on 5 July 1963. Also on the bill on that date were Denny Laine and The Diplomats, whose titular lead singer was a future member of The Moody Blues and McCartney's post-Beatles band, Wings.

ELSTEAD

Brookfield, Cutmill Lane, Elstead

Ringo purchased this Surrey house on the River Wey, about ten miles from Guildford, in Novem-ber 1968 from actor Peter Sellers. He was only there until 5 December 1969 when he sold it on to another famous name, Stephen Stills.

One of Ringo's homes in and around London.

EPSOM

Epsom Register Office, Ashley House

On 21 January 1966, George Harrison married Pattie Boyd here, accompanied by two best men, Brian Epstein and Paul McCartney.

ESHER

Kinfauns, Claremont Estate

Kinfauns, a single-storey house situated at 16 Claremont Drive on a private estate (similar to where John and Ringo lived at the time) in Surrey owned by the National Trust, was home to George Harrison and Pattie Boyd from 1965 to 1969. George decided to make it unique by having it painted in vivid psychedelic colours. Hunter Davies visited Kinfauns many times. 'You enter the estate through a gateway from the main road, then pass into what looks like the wooded gardens of a stately home. The name of his house, Kinfauns, is not even on his house or in his garden. The bungalow has two wings to it, which enclose a rectangular courtyard at the back. In this he has a heated swimming pool. He has no Beatle Gold Discs or souvenirs in sight.' The Beatles recorded some demos here in May 1968 for the *White Album*. On the day Paul and Linda married, 12 March 1969, Sergeant Norman Pilcher of the Drugs Squad, who had previously arrested John and Yoko, arrived at the house.

George's first marital home for his first marriage.

EXETER

ABC Cinema, London Inn Square

The Beatles made their first appearance here on 28 March 1963 as part of the Chris Montez/Tommy Roe tour, having made the near 200-mile journey to Devon in the south-west of England after being in Northampton the night before.

Before the shows, The Beatles popped into a record store opposite the cinema to check whether the shop was stocking their newly released first album, *Please Please Me*. A fan noticed them and grabbed a paper bag for the group to sign.

The Beatles returned to the venue on two other occasions, once as part of their autumn tour that same year, on 14 November, and again on 28 October 1964.

Following their 1964 appearance at the venue, the group spoke to *Playboy* journalist and New York radio host Jean Shepherd. The interview took place in a Torquay hotel room, and was first published in the February 1965 edition of the American adult magazine. Although very little was said about their music, it was most revealing about The Beatles' views on sex, race, religion, politics and their former drummer Pete Best.

FLEETWOOD

Marine Hall, The Esplanade

John spent holidays as a boy in this small fishing town north of Blackpool, about 60 miles from Liverpool. The Beatles made a solitary appearance in the ballroom here on 25 August 1962, just a week after Ringo had made his debut with the group.

FRODSHAM

Mersey View Pleasure Grounds, Overton Hill

Overlooking the town of Frodsham in Cheshire, Mersey View was a popular vantage point looking over the whole area. At the ballroom there The Beatles made a solitary appearance on 20 April 1963, supported by Bill Gorman and his orchestra. Tickets cost six shillings and sixpence.

GLOUCESTER

Regal Cinema, St Aldate Street

As The Beatles continued to zigzag across the country during the Chris Montez/Tommy Roe tour, they left Peterborough and travelled 135 miles to Gloucester where they appeared on 18 March 1963.

GREAT YARMOUTH

ABC Cinema, Regent Road

Starting their ten-week Sunday evening run playing popular English seaside resorts, The Beatles made their first appearance here on 30 June 1963, returning on the tour four weeks later on 28 July.

Sandwiched between their two shows on 30 June, The Beatles were interviewed in their dressing room by Gianni Bisiach, a director, writer and reporter for the Italian television station RAI. The b&w footage, which lasted a little under two minutes, was broadcast in the country six months later on 23 December 1963. Although dubbed into Italian for the transmission, the original audio has survived and has since been overdubbed onto the footage.

GUILDFORD

Odeon Cinema, Upper High Street

The county town of Surrey played host to top-of-the-bill The Beatles on 21 June 1963, where they played two shows at this cinema as part of the John Smith-presented *Jimmy Crawford Package Show*. Ticket prices ranged from six shillings and sixpence to ten shillings and sixpence. A long queue of fans, stretching up Jenner Road and into Sydenham Road behind the Odeon, had built up before the shows. A reporter for the *Guildford and Godalming Times* said in his review of the concert, 'The Beatles did their best to sing above the deafening screams of the audience ... I recognised their hit numbers but most of the words were inaudible.' After the concerts, fans stood outside the venue, banging on the lavatory windows, hoping that the group would hear them and come outside to sign autographs. They didn't.

HANLEY, STOKE-ON-TRENT

Gaumont Cinema, Piccadilly

The final night of the Helen Shapiro tour was here in the central county of Staffordshire, about halfway between Liverpool and Birmingham, on 3 March 1963.

Derek Adams, a junior journalist on the Stoke-on-Trent *Evening Sentinel*, encountered the band that night. 'Helen Shapiro was billed as the star of the show,' he recalled for the *Derby Evening Telegraph*. 'The Beatles were the third act down on the official programme ... I watched both houses from the wings adjoining the stage and recall The Beatles larking around [backstage] and pushing each other before they actually appeared before the screaming hordes that had solidly packed the venue.

'When they finished their act, they were all bathed in perspiration and both John and Paul dunked their heads beneath the dressing room's cold water tap... Ringo actually chucked a glass of water through the open dressing room window to the delight of the screamers.' Following the second show, Adams was just about to leave the venue when John said to him, 'Hey Wack, where can we get some fish and chips at this time of night and without the fans leering and screaming

at us?' Adams knew of a fish and chip shop in the area known as Etruria, near Hanley, where you could sit at tables in the back of the shop. It was arranged that The Beatles followed his car in their Transit van and they ate together.

He shared a fish and chip supper with the group and was treated to the sight of John making chip sandwiches, Paul pouring tomato sauce over everything he ate, George drinking his hot tea direct from a saucer, Ringo mistakenly shaking sugar on his chips instead of salt and the occasional chip being rescued from someone's cup of tea. When the bill arrived, there was much arguing among The Beatles about who should foot the bill. Ringo eventually coughed up. They said their goodbyes and The Beatles drove off in their van to 6 Adventure Place, Hanley, where they were booked to stay that night.

The Beatles returned to the Gaumont just over two months later, on 19 May, during the Roy Orbison tour. Tickets ranged in price between five shillings and sixpence and ten shillings and sixpence.

HARROGATE

Royal Hall, Ripon Road

The Beatles' only performance in the scenic North Yorkshire spa town of Harrogate was on 8 March 1963. They arrived for the gig in an old yellow van and even helped to offload their instruments themselves. Ringo broke the tip off one of his 11A Joe Morello Ludwig USA, 14-inch drumsticks during the show.

HENLEY-ON-THAMES

Friar Park

George moved into the vast Friar Park estate in early 1970. The mansion and grounds was owned

THE BEATLES BOOK

by Sir Frank Crisp until his death in 1919, and later passed on to Roman Catholic nuns belonging to the Salesians of Don Bosco order. The nuns ran a local school in Henley, the Sacred Heart School, but by the late 1960s Friar Park had fallen into disrepair and was due to be torn down. In early 1972, Harrison installed a 16-track tape-based recording studio in a guest suite, known as FPSHOT (Friar Park Studio, Henley-on-Thames), which at one stage was superior to the one at EMI's Abbey Road Studios. By 1974, the facility had become the recording headquarters for his company, Dark Horse Records.

On 30 December 1999, an intruder broke into Friar Park, stabbing George several times and leaving him seriously injured.

George's home that belonged to the eccentric Frankie Crisp.

HOUNSLOW
Brydor Cars Limited, Hanworth Road

In 1965, with one of his best friends from Liverpool, Terry Doran, Brian Epstein set up a new business, Brydor Cars Limited, with a motor workshop nearby at 65 High Street. Through this business, The Beatles and their friends made several purchases of motor vehicles here.

Meeting the man from the motor trade.

HUDDERSFIELD
ABC Cinema, Market Street

Between performances in Lincoln and Sunderland, The Beatles made their only appearance in this West Yorkshire market town on 29 November 1963 during their autumn tour. In between their

two sets, the group were visited by Gorden Kaye, who later became famous for his character René Artois in the highly popular, 1980s/early 1990s BBC Television sitcom 'Allo, 'Allo. At the time of The Beatles' visit, he represented the Huddersfield Tape Recording Society, and had requested an interview with each of the group for their monthly *Music Box* programme, which aired on several local hospital radio stations. Kaye also got the group to read aloud several record requests and found time to ask them questions. 'What have you got ambitions in, George?' 'Umm, to join the Navy,' he replied. 'I want to join the Navy and be a lieutenant commander on HMS *Queen Victoria*.'

HULL
ABC Cinema, Ferensway

The first of two appearances at this cinema in the far east of Yorkshire was on 24 November 1963 during their autumn tour. They returned almost a year later, on 16 October 1964, playing two shows for a fee of £850.

Majestic Ballroom, Holderness Road/Clarence Street, Witham

With 'Love Me Do' recently released, The Beatles made the 130-mile trip across the country for their first appearance in this East Yorkshire town on 20 October 1962. They returned to the venue almost four months later, on 13 February 1963. Their fee for this 1963 show was £100. Following the show, the group was introduced to a young fan, Pat, who had been taken backstage by Leon Riley, a local singer who had compèred the show. The Fab Four happily signed for her (in black ink) a copy of 'Love Me Do' and (in blue ink) a Parlophone Records publicity card. On 4 June 2010, the items sold for over £7,000 at a Christie's auction in London.

IPSWICH

Gaumont Cinema, St Helen's Street

After spending the previous day at the Playhouse Theatre in London recording for BBC radio, they then made the 80-mile journey eastwards to Suffolk, where they made their only appearance at this cinema during the Roy Orbison tour on 22 May 1963. Approximately 1,500 fans saw each of the two shows, with tickets priced from five shillings and sixpence to ten shillings and sixpence.

The Beatles returned to this venue once more, on 31 October 1964 as part of their long UK autumn tour.

LEEDS

Odeon Cinema, The Headrow

Between visits to Birmingham and Glasgow, The Beatles made the first of three appearances here in this Yorkshire city on 5 June 1963 as part of the Roy Orbison tour.

The band's second appearance at the venue was during their autumn tour that same year, on 3 November. Recorded by Bernard Weaver, this was one of two concerts that were taped for use as evidence in a court case, on 10 December 1963, involving promoters and the PRS – the Performing Rights Society. The PRS was demanding more money for the pop music presented in concerts; the promoters disagreed, insisting that with the fans screaming throughout each show, they weren't listening to the artists perform anyway.

The Beatles' final appearance here was on 22 October 1964 as part of their long autumn tour of the UK.

Queens Hall, Sovereign Street

On 28 June 1963 The Beatles made their only appearance here, playing two shows in front of a 3,200 crowd, on the same bill as the jazz clarinettist Acker Bilk. During the band's first performance, one of the stewards helping to control the crowd was bitten on his upper arm by a female fan.

LEICESTER

De Montfort Hall, Granville Road

The final night of the 1963 tour with Tommy Roe and Chris Montez saw The Beatles perform for the first time at De Montfort Hall in Leicester on 31 March 1963. They made two further appearances here, on 1 December of the same year during their autumn tour and 10 October 1964.

Tickets for the two shows on 1 December 1963 went on sale one Sunday morning in October at the Leicester Corporation offices in Charles Street. Approximately 3,000 fans began queuing on Saturday evening, while hundreds of others had been there since Friday night. The first sign of trouble began at 9.30 on the Sunday morning when the box office doors opened for business. Sixty local police officers tried to create a human barrier as the tidal wave of Beatles fans swept forward. Desperate not to miss out on tickets, the mass of fans bulldozed ahead, causing injury and damage to the much-loved Beatles items many were clutching. First to secure their tickets were Wyggeston schoolgirls Susan Williams and Rosalyn Oaskley, but at a cost. The Fab Four records they had been carrying shattered in the melee. Fifty girls needed attention; some required hospital treatment for crushed ribs. The shopfront of the nearby Halfords store also fell victim to the onslaught, with a ten-foot-high pane of glass shattering. Thankfully, no one was injured. By midday, all 4,500 tickets had gone.

Important and notable for two very different reasons.

LEIGH

Casino Ballroom, Lord Street

This Lancashire town played host to The Beatles on 25 February 1963 at a sell-out NEMS Enterprises *Showdance*. The group was advertised in some papers as 'Stars of TV, BBC and Parlophone Records'.

LINCOLN

ABC Cinema, Saltergate

The Beatles' only appearance in Lincoln was here on 28 November 1963 during their autumn tour.

LIVERPOOL AND THE WIRRAL

Abbey Cinema, Wavertree

The 'Abbey' was referred to in John's original lyrics to 'In My Life'. It was the old Abbey Cinema on the roundabout at the top of Church Road and Wavertree High Street. It was a favourite meeting place for John and his friends, who spent many hours there watching Saturday morning matinee westerns from the balcony, while flicking objects down on to the girls below and generally making a nuisance of themselves. The Abbey Cinema eventually became a supermarket, ironically owned by a chain of stores called 'Lennons'.

What a scamp that Lennon was.

10 Admiral Grove, Dingle

Elsie Starkey moved herself and her son to this address in 1945, when Richy was nearly five, and they lived there until Beatlemania overtook their lives in 1963. Richy was only three when his parents divorced, and Elsie could not afford the rent on Ringo's Dingle birthplace, 9 Madryn Street, so she exchanged houses with the residents of 10 Admiral Grove, who needed more

room. It was a simple two-up, two-down terraced house, with no bathroom or inside toilet. Bathing required bringing in the old tin bath, placing it in front of the fire and filling it with hot water. The toilet was in a small brick outhouse at the bottom of the concrete backyard. Richy practised with his first group, The Eddie Clayton Skiffle Group, in the living room here. Ringo's twenty-first birthday party was held here on 7 July 1961, attended by many entertainers such as Cilla Black and Gerry and The Pacemakers. Somehow they managed to squeeze up to 80 people into the house. Once The Beatles had become famous, Ringo's parents were inundated with fan mail, and occasionally fans would turn up at the house and steal parts of the door or scribble on the walls. Eventually, Ringo bought Elsie and stepfather Harry a house in Woolton, which was much more private.

Ringo's childhood was spent here.

11 Admiral Grove, Dingle

This house, adjacent to Ringo's home at number 10, belonged to Eddie Myles, Ringo's good friend with whom he formed the Eddie Clayton Skiffle Group.

Eddie Myles was Ringo's first musical collaborator.

37 Aigburth Drive, Aigburth

Stuart Sutcliffe's family lived in Ullet Road, on the other side of Sefton Park, before moving across the park to Aigburth Drive. The home is near the gates of Sefton Park by the lake, and is now called the Lakeside Hotel.

Stuart's family home though he was in Hamburg most of the time.

Aintree Institute, Longmoor Lane, Walton

The Beatles first appeared here on 7 January 1961 and made 30 further appearances at this venue, with the last on 27 January 1962. Aintree Institute was a popular jive club. It was demolished in 2007.

One of the most important venues for Liverpool bands, including The Beatles.

Albany Cinema, Maghull

Just outside Aintree is the small town of Maghull. On 15 October 1961 The Beatles made their only appearance here in a Sunday afternoon *Star Matinee* charity event for the local branch of the St John Ambulance Brigade. Headlining the 16-act bill was the popular Liverpudlian comedian, Ken Dodd. The building has been replaced by a supermarket.

9 Albert Grove, Wavertree

This residence, owned by George Harrison's maternal grandparents John and Louise French, is the next road over from George's Arnold Grove home. George visited John and Louise many times when his parents were at work.

Albert Marrion's Photo Studio, 268 Wallasey Village, Wallasey

After Brian Epstein became The Beatles' manager, he set up a photo shoot at Albert Marrion's studio on the Penny Lane roundabout. Unfortunately, there was a mix-up and so the session took place at his other studio here in Wallasey. It is now a pizza shop.

Brian's first promotional photos of The Beatles.

Alexandra Hall, Coronation Road/College Road, Crosby

In the heart of Crosby sat Alexandra Hall, which hosted many bands in its day. The Beatles only appeared here once, on 19 January 1961. It has since been demolished.

Allerton Cemetery, Allerton

John's mother, Julia Lennon, was buried here at 10am on Monday 21 July 1958 in the Church of England section 38, grave No. 805.

Julia's death shaped the rest of John's life and music.

Allerton Golf Course, Allerton

John often sat in the brick shelter on the golf course with his girlfriend Thelma Pickles while waiting for Mimi to leave the house. Once the coast was clear, they would sneak into 'Mendips'. Paul remembers how he and John played a few rounds of golf there. The golf course was a convenient short cut between John and Paul's houses, a trail they often took. Paul recalls walking from John's house across the golf course in the dark nights, singing to himself with his guitar strapped over his back.

Allerton Synagogue, Allerton

Situated on the corner of Mather Avenue and Yew Tree Road, this synagogue, built in the fifties and replaced in 2005, played host to The Beatles in December 1961. The building was just a short walk from Paul's home at Forthlin Road.

27 Anfield Road, Anfield

This was the home of Isaac and Dinah Epstein, Brian's grandparents. Brian often visited the home. It is now Epstein's Guest House, a bed and breakfast.

An important family home for Brian to visit.

Anglican Cathedral, St James' Mount

John Duff Lowe, occasional pianist with The Quarrymen, failed his audition for the Liverpool Cathedral Choir along with his friend Paul McCartney. He later retook it and passed but Paul didn't bother. The Royal Liverpool Philharmonic Orchestra performed Paul's *Liverpool Oratorio* here on 28 June 1991, and Paul invited the choirmaster who had turned him down to attend.

Apollo Roller Rink, 195 Pasture Road, Moreton

The Beatles made one appearance here on 26 March 1962 at one of Tony Booth's famous *Rock and Twist Nights*. It is currently the Apollo Dance Club.

12 Ardwick Road, Speke

The McCartney family moved here from Western Avenue in Speke, in 1950 when Mary resigned her job as a district nurse. The house was very close to George Harrison's home in Upton Green, which enabled them to visit each other and learn guitar together.

Paul and George formed their friendship at each other's homes in Speke.

12 Arnold Grove, Wavertree

George Harrison was born here at the family home on 25 February 1943. Arnold Grove is a small cul-de-sac off the High Street near the Picton Clock and Abbey Cinema. The Harrisons moved into this residence after their wedding in 1930. It is a two-up, two-down terraced property, with a yard and alley to the rear. As with most of the housing of this type, there was no indoor bathroom or toilet. Instead, they used an outhouse in the backyard. George was bathed in the kitchen sink as a baby and then progressed to a tin tub, brought in from the yard and placed in front of the fire.

George's birthplace in Wavertree.

Bioletti's Barber Shop, Penny Lane

'Penny Lane, there is a barber showing photographs.' Right on the corner of the roundabout by Church Road is a hairdresser's shop called 'Tony Slavin'. The original barber's was called 'Bioletti's', on the same site. This is where Paul, George and John received haircuts.

One of the most important focal points of the song 'Penny Lane'.

Blacklers Store, Great Charlotte Street

George served a brief apprenticeship as an electrician here. Blacklers was eventually replaced by a Wetherspoons pub.

George had a job here while he raised the money for more guitars.

Blair Hall, Walton Road, Walton

In 1961 The Beatles played five times at this venue above the Co-op, with their first appearance on 5 February followed by 16, 23, 29 and 30 July.

They played for a fee of £12 and asked to be bumped up to £15, but promoter Bob Wooler didn't think they were worth it. He didn't book them there again. The building has since been demolished.

1 Blomfield Road, Springwood

Julia Lennon had separated from Alf and had set up home with her new partner, John Dykins. When

John's half-sister Julia was two, the family moved to this residence on the Springwood Estate. John and Julia reunited in his teenage years and spent a lot of time re-establishing their relationship. John was a frequent visitor and when he and Mimi had a row, he would stay at Julia's house. Julia would join in The Quarrymen's rehearsals in the house, which often took place in the bathroom.

Julia Lennon was an inspiration to John and taught him to play here, while also letting The Quarrymen rehearse at her home.

Blue Angel, Seel Street

Formerly known as the Wyvern Club (see entry), this was the Silver Beatles manager Allan Williams' second club, situated at the top of Seel Street.

From around 1962 and onwards, it was frequented by many of the Merseybeat bands, including The Beatles for a while, once they were allowed back in. Having been barred after a falling-out over commission Williams felt he was due for some of their Hamburg appearances, The Beatles' re-entry was facilitated by Brian Epstein, by then their manager, who had persuaded the band to apologise to Williams.

It was also at this club on 12 August 1962 that Ringo was introduced to Brian Epstein and was offered the position as Pete Best's replacement as drummer with The Beatles.

Great meeting place for the local musicians.

British Legion Club, Dam Wood Road, Speke

George Harrison formed a group called The Rebels, which included his brother Peter and friends Arthur Kelly and Alan Williams, and they played their one and only gig here. The headlining

act never turned up and The Rebels covered for them, playing the only two songs they knew. It didn't matter to the audience, who were gracious in their applause.

George's debut with his first group, The Rebels.

54 Broad Green Road, Old Swan

Paul was a regular visitor here during his courtship with Iris Caldwell, as was George Harrison before him. Iris's brother was Alan Caldwell, better known as Rory Storm, and this address became known as 'Stormsville'. Paul and John met at the house occasionally to write and play songs.

Important meeting place for musicians and friends.

92 Broadway Avenue, Wallasey

In the second half of 1942, when Paul was still an infant, the McCartneys moved to this address on the Wirral from Sunbury Road, but only stayed a few months. The area suffered bomb damage during the war and the family moved back to Liverpool.

Cabaret Artists Social Club, Toxteth

Allan Williams booked The Silver Beatles at his and Lord Woodbine's strip club at 174a Upper Parliament Street, most likely around the first week or so of June 1960. It was an old cotton merchant's house, with big white pillars and black railings. Williams had auditioned a well-proportioned stripper named Janice from Manchester, who demanded live music, unlike the other strippers who performed to records. Williams agreed because he knew she would be good for business, and so he convinced the lads to play there, even though they were against the idea. They backed Janice on a stage that was seven feet square, and in return they received 50p a man per night for a week. As they were again drummer-less, Paul played drums that week.

The Beatles backing a stripper. Priceless.

Casbah Coffee Club, West Derby

Much has been written about the Cavern and its place in Beatles history. While the Cavern was entertaining jazz fans, the Casbah became the place to be. For the book, *The Beatles – The True Beginnings*, there is a quote from Paul McCartney: 'I think it's a good idea to let people know about the Casbah. They know about the Cavern, they know about some of those things, but the Casbah was the place where all that started. We helped paint it and stuff. We looked upon it as our personal club.' The club was the brainchild of Mona Best, mother of Beatles drummer Pete Best, and opened on 29 August 1959 with the re-formed Quarrymen as resident group. John, Paul, George and Ken Brown launched one of Liverpool's first rock 'n' roll clubs and played host to many of the biggest groups and performers on the emerging music scene that became known as Merseybeat. To get the club ready to open, John, Paul and George helped to paint it, which included a huge ceiling hand-painted by John Lennon, a rainbow ceiling painted by Paul, with George assisting the stars on the ceiling in the coffee bar.

When The Beatles returned from Hamburg at the end of 1960, with their future looking bleak, they were given the opportunity to play at the Casbah, a welcome home concert on 17 December, and overnight became the greatest rock 'n' roll group in Liverpool.

'My mother billed us as "The Fabulous Beatles From Germany",' Pete Best recalled, 'so everyone was waiting to see who the fabulous Beatles

were. Down the stairs came, John, Paul, George and, in behind them, was me. It was, "Hang on a minute, they're not The Beatles. They are The Quarrymen, who used to play here. And that's Pete from The Blackjacks. [Note: This was the name of Pete's former group formed in autumn 1959 – totally different from Lennon's Blackjacks who pre-dated The Quarrymen] What's going on?" [But] the minute we started playing, that was it. The whole atmosphere changed. The place was going wild and it was never the same.' With Sutcliffe still in Hamburg, suffering from a cold, Chas Newby, the former rhythm guitarist with Pete's The Blackjacks, stood in on bass.

The band used the club as a launch pad, eventually playing at the venue 37 times in total, and were soon playing at the Cavern and heading back to Hamburg. On 10 December 1961, The Beatles, consisting of John, Paul, George and Pete, signed their management contract with Brian Epstein at the Casbah. An amended version was signed shortly after at NEMS. As The Beatles became more successful, Mona struggled to continue running the club and on 24 June 1962 The Beatles closed the club after less than three years. Within a few weeks, Mona's son Pete had been replaced by Ringo Starr and the club was forgotten for many years. It has now reopened as a tourist attraction and retains most of its original features, including those hand-painted ceilings.

If any club in Liverpool is the birthplace of The Beatles, then it is the Casbah Coffee Club. It offered a historic homecoming and was the first place they played outside Hamburg as The Beatles.

Cassanova Club, Dale Street

Named after Liverpool band Cass and The Cassanovas, and located in the Temple building on

Dale Street. The Beatles appeared here at an afternoon session on the day of the club's launch. The Beatles had a regular following at the Cavern and owner Ray McFall considered them his exclusive band. McFall told The Beatles they couldn't play at both his club and the Dale Street Cassanova. Sam Leach had promoted the Cassanova concert so he had a bit of a problem. Allegedly, The Beatles turned up because someone had let off stink bombs in the Cavern and it was forced to close for the afternoon. They never officially appeared again at this location.

Cassanova Club, London Road

The new Cassanova Club opened above Sampson & Barlow's Restaurant. The Beatles first performed here on 11 February 1961 and went on to make 6 further appearances, the last on 12 March of that year.

An 8mm silent, 30-second colour film clip of The Beatles performing at the 14 February Valentine's Day Dance was uncovered in 1996. Regarded as the earliest known film of the group and pre-dating Granada Television's footage of the group live at the Cavern by over 18 months, it sold for £15,000 ($22,000) at an auction on 18 September that year. Shot by the then owner's father, it had been expected to sell for at least six times that figure. Its sale was no doubt hindered by its free-to-air screenings on the ITN news bulletins throughout the day on 15 May 1996.

The Cavern, Mathew Street

The most iconic club in popular music, sometimes also called the 'Birthplace of The Beatles', was once an air-raid shelter during the Second World War and began life as a jazz venue on 16 January 1957 after Alan Sytner had returned from a trip to Paris. While in the French capital he had visited an atmospheric cellar jazz club called Le Caveau de la Huchette, and decided he wanted a similar one of his own. Back in Liverpool, together with his friend Keith Hemmings, he found the basement of an old warehouse in Mathew Street and rented it. Although Hemmings left after just a few months, Sytner turned the Cavern into Liverpool's first live music venue and one of the best jazz clubs in Britain, with a membership of 25,000. When Sytner left for London in 1958, he sold it to Ray McFall, who continued the club's traditions, though by the end of the 1950s the popularity of jazz was tailing off. It was Lonnie Donegan who started the skiffle craze that slowly crept into the Cavern, including a performance by The Quarrymen. The first advertised beat music session was on 25 May 1960, featuring Rory Storm and The Hurricanes with a certain Ringo Starr on drums, and it wasn't long before that music became the dominant sound in the Cavern.

The Beatles made their debut on 9 February 1961 at lunchtime, with their first evening performance on 21 March 1961. Between then and their last performance on 3 August 1963, they made nearly three hundred appearances. Alan Sytner tried to claim that without the Cavern, there would have been no Beatles. John, however, disagreed. 'The Cavern didn't make The Beatles; The Beatles made the Cavern.'

'We used to have marvellous raves down at the Cavern,' Paul recalled. 'We had to keep ourselves laughing. We used to come on with the maddest gear on. I had shredded newspaper sticking out of the bottom of my trouser leg. John wore a cellophane bag around his shoes, and we came on wearing collars and ties and nothing else above the waist, things like that. Another time at the Cavern, we had a rave on a song called "Mama Don't Allow". We all took solos on everything, whether we could play it or not. Banjo, harmonica, trumpet, Jew's harp ... The condensation on the walls of the club dripped water in the amps and they used to fuse, so we had to have community singing on songs like "Ma, She's Making Eyes At Me". The fans all used to sing with us.' 'We'd even have our tea and sandwiches and cigarettes onstage … and tell a few jokes,' George remembered. 'We used to do a Tiller Gills routine like The Shadows, only all kicking in line.' 'It was a very sweaty place,' said Pete Best, looking back, 'but we loved it.'

Those people who visited the Cavern also remembered it well. Being a basement, it was dark and damp. It had previously been used for storing fruit and vegetables, with the rotting smell of decaying food still ingrained in the walls. There were only the stone steps in and out, which would undoubtedly fail today's health and safety laws. To improve visibility, the owners painted the walls white, giving rise to 'Cavern dandruff', where the paint would flake off on to patrons' clothes. With so many people crammed into a small place, sweat and condensation would pour off the walls. Add this smell to the cigarette smoke and a lack of ventilation and an unpleasant picture starts to emerge. One of the most memorable aromas, and not a pleasant one, came from the gents' toilets, which were constantly flooded. If you were sensible, you stood on the plank of wood provided, to stop your feet getting too wet. Conscious of all the smells, the Cavern counteracted them with strong pine disinfectant. It's fortunate that the music was so good, because with no alcohol on sale to dull the senses, there was no sane reason to go there. Sadly, in 1973 British Rail decided that they needed a new ventilation shaft for the underground rail system in Liverpool, and obtained a compulsory purchase order. This meant that the Cavern and the abandoned warehouses were all demolished, in spite of protests from Beatles fans. Frustratingly, the ventilation shaft was never

constructed and the demolition was pointless. After John was murdered in 1980, some local business people decided that it was a good time to bring back the Cavern, together with a new shopping mall, Cavern Walks. The revamped Cavern Club, using 15,000 of the original bricks, opened in 1984. The club is deeper underground with 30 steps now (18 originally), and occupies about 50 per cent of the original site. On the evening of 19 December 1999, Sir Paul McCartney was back, performing in a show broadcast around the world on the Internet.

The Beatles made the Cavern, as John said, and made it the most famous club in the world, giving them the platform to become the greatest pop group.

The exact number of Beatles appearances at the Cavern is disputed, with 292 perhaps the most accurate tally. What's certain is they performed here, on a stage just 18 inches off the floor, more than at any other venue. Over the course of almost two and a half years, there were many important and memorable Beatles performances at the Cavern; too many to list them all here. Some, however, demand specific mention because of a relevant quote or pivotal moment in the history of the Fab Four. Here, then, are those standout dates.

9 February 1961

Their debut, a lunchtime gig. 'My mother, Mona got us our first dates there,' drummer Pete Best recalled. 'She phoned the boss, Ray McFall, and we tried out … The shops were closed and we played a packer. The result, a long list of bookings.' However, first impressions went against them with McFall. 'I didn't like what I saw because they were so scruffy. But I was knocked out by what I heard. The fans were going wild, even the bouncers came in from the door to take in a bit of the entertainment.'

For their debut, The Beatles were paid £6 between them, £1 each and £1 for their driver, and trainee accountant, Neil Aspinall.

How historic. The Beatles' debut at the world's most famous club.

5 August 1961

An all-night session. 'The bill was half jazz, half rock,' Pete Best recalled. 'The band room was about six foot by six, with half-a-dozen groups all trying to change. Kenny Ball was hemmed in one corner and occasionally struggled free and let rip on his trumpet.'

9 November 1961

A lunchtime gig, attended by the local NEMS record-store owner Brian Epstein.

His arrival was even announced by the DJ Bob Wooler. 'I saw The Beatles at a midday session and I liked them enormously,' Brian remembered. 'I immediately liked the sound I heard. I decided I should at least talk to them and find out, for my own satisfaction, what it was that made them tick. So I pushed my way through to the front [of the crowd] and got within speaking distance, allowing for all the noise that was going on. I heard their sound before I met them. I actually think that's important because I think it should always be remembered that, in fact, people hear their sound and like this sound before they meet them ... I immediately liked what I heard and I thought it was something that an awful lot of people would like. They were fresh, honest and had, what I thought, a sort of presence and star quality, whatever that is.'

Brian's assistant at NEMS, Alistair Taylor, accompanied him. 'Brian and I looked out of place in white shirts and dark business suits,' he recalled. 'The Beatles were playing "A Taste Of Honey". We were particularly impressed that they [also] included [an] original song. At the end of their performance, Paul announced they'd like to close with a song he and John had written, "Hello Little Girl"... They were bloody awful, and yet they were incredible! They were scruffy, loud, not good musicians but their soul hit you in the chest. Later, after their set, we had a very brief meeting with them in the band room. Brian said to them, "Can you come to the shop and talk? We might be able to talk management." They were quite interested and Brian and I went off to lunch [at the restaurant, Peacocks] afterwards, but it was kind of "Panicksville!" You know, "What does managing a group mean? Could we do it?"'

Still unsure about what he was about to get involved in, shortly afterwards Brian played a copy of 'My Bonnie' to his parents, Harry and Malka (Queenie) and told them, 'Forget about the singer, just listen to the backing group. They are four boys and I'd like to manage them,' adding it would be a 'part-time occupation, taking up just two weekday afternoons of my time and certainly wouldn't interfere with business.' Determined to press ahead with his plan, his first meeting with The Beatles and Taylor took place at NEMS at 4.30 on the afternoon of 3 December 1961. Exactly one week later it was decided that Brian would be the group's manager. Their first contract, for a five-year period, was formally signed at NEMS on 24 January 1962 with Taylor as witness, although Brian himself didn't actually sign it. When later asked why, Brian replied. 'Well, if they ever want to tear it up, they can hold me but I can't hold them.'

A landmark Beatles gig when Brian Epstein watched the band and experienced their magic in person for the very first time.

13 December 1961

Mike Smith, A&R assistant at Decca Records, was among the sell-out crowd that night. 'Someone at Decca had to show interest in The Beatles because Brian ran NEMS, which was an important account for the sales people. I thought The Beatles were absolutely wonderful on stage.' Impressed by what he saw, he invited the group for an audition down in London. It took place on 1 January 1962, at the label's studios in Broadhurst Gardens.

Another landmark show, when they were watched by Mike Smith of Decca Records.

5 February 1962

With Pete Best unwell (he returned for the next performance, on 7 February), Ringo was on drums at this lunchtime session as well as at the group's evening gig at Southport's Kingsway Club. 'One day, Pete Best went sick,' Ringo recalled. 'A car came for me, and the driver asked if I would play drums for The Beatles at a lunchtime session down at the Cavern. What a laugh it turned out to be. We all knew the same numbers, but they did them differently. I didn't fit in at all at first.'

5 April 1962

The group played the first half in their black, leather outfits and then changed into their smart, tailor-made Beno Dorn suits and ties for the second half.

7 April 1962

With George unwell, and the group set to travel to Germany for their third Hamburg residency in just

a few days' time, manager Brian Epstein decided to prevent him from performing at the Cavern on this evening, plus the earlier Casbah engagement and the one there the following afternoon. Keeping him healthy for the group's seven-week residency at the Star-Club in Hamburg was uppermost in his mind.

19 August 1962

Evening show and Ringo's first gig at the club as an official member of The Beatles. 'When Ringo sat in for Pete Best,' former manager Allan Williams recalled, 'some of the fans let their loyalties run away with them. One of the kids took a swing at George and blacked his eye.'

Another landmark concert when Ringo performed for the first time at the Cavern as a member of The Beatles.

22 August 1962

Less than a week after Pete Best had been sacked from the group, and just three days after Ringo had officially debuted there with the band, Granada Television filmed a part of The Beatles' performance for inclusion in their regional news show, *Know The North*. (For more details see relevant entry in *TV* section).

Notable for being the only film of the band live at the club.

7 October 1962

Sometime in the region of this date, possibly out of interest in hearing how they sounded as a live act, the group recorded a tape of themselves rehearsing in the club. The tracks featured 'I Saw Her Standing There', 'The One After 909' (two takes) and 'Catswalk' (two takes of the McCartney-penned instrumental). Almost five years later, on

20 July 1967, at the Chappell Recording Studios, 52 Maddox Street, London, The Chris Barber Band recorded an over-the-top arrangement of it, with a chorus of ad-libs and catcalls. Paul and girlfriend Jane Asher were among those taking part. It's believed he also played organ on the recording. Retitled 'Catcall', it was released as a single in the UK by Marmalade Records on 20 October 1967, with McCartney given a composer credit. Then, on 24 January 1969 at Apple's headquarters at 3 Savile Row, London, the song was briefly resurrected by The Beatles during rehearsals for their *Get Back/Let It Be* project. (For more details see entry in *Movies* section.)

20 January 1963

First night as band's roadie for Cavern regular-cum-bouncer and a keen rock 'n' roll fan, Mal Evans.

3 August 1963

The Beatles' final appearance at the Cavern. Tickets went on sale at 1.30pm, 21 July, and sold out within 30 minutes.

Inside and out, the place was absolutely packed. 'The crowds outside the club were going mad,' doorman Paddy Delaney remembered. 'By the time John had got through the cordon of girls, his mohair jacket had lost a sleeve. I grabbed it to stop the girls getting away with a souvenir. John immediately stitched the sleeve back on.' Despite the hysteria, it was still a less than satisfactory end to the group's historic residency. Tony Crane and Billy Kinsley of The Merseybeats, also performing that night, recall sitting in the dressing room with The Beatles prior to the gig and they all had long faces. Crane remembered John kept saying, 'We shouldn't have done this, we shouldn't have come back to do this. It'll all go wrong.' And unfortunately it did.

Due to the claustrophobic heat inside the venue, two members of another group on the bill, Faron's Flamingos, collapsed. Then just one number into The Beatles' set a power cut silenced their instruments, plunging the club into temporary darkness. Whilst waiting for the electricity to return, John and Paul burst into an impromptu, albeit brief version of 'When I'm Sixty-Four', a track they wouldn't release for another four years. The Beatles all voiced their concerns about the night, particularly John, who said later, 'We couldn't say it at the time but we really didn't like going back to Liverpool. Being local heroes made us nervous … We felt embarrassed in our suits and being very clean. We were worried that friends might think we had sold out, which, in a way, we had.'

'The Beatles were paid £300, which was quite a bit of money then,' said Bob Wooler. 'We never made any money out of it because Brian restricted the audience to 500 and, as the admission price was ten shillings, this meant just £250 on the door. All the staff had to be paid, and the other groups on the bill too.' To appease Wooler, Epstein foolishly promised him that The Beatles would return, but they never did. They had now outgrown their old stamping ground. (Paul, however, did make two further trips there: the first, on 25 October 1968, was a non-performing visit with his then girlfriend Linda Eastman, with him even posing for a picture on the Cavern stage behind the group Curiosity Shop's drum; the second was his 14 December 1999 performance at the 'new' Cavern club.)

The Beatles' rather forgettable farewell to the Cavern.

27 Cedar Grove, Maghull

In December 1944, Alf Lennon took young John to Maghull (ten miles north of Liverpool) to stay with John's Uncle Sydney, Auntie Madge and cousin Joyce. John's mother Julia was pregnant at the time – following a brief affair with a Welsh soldier – and unable to look after her four-year-old son (see Elmswood Nursing Home entry). They left after about three weeks but returned in the new year for what would be – in John's case – long enough for Madge to consider the possibility of enrolling John into a local school and for her and Sydney to become legal guardians. However, some three months later Alf took his son John back to Liverpool.

John could have grown up in Maghull, and never met Paul, George or Ringo.

Clarendon Furnishing, The Quadrant, Hoylake

On his return from National Service in 1954, Brian Epstein took up the role of running this new venture of his father's. The business was profitable within a year.

Civic Hall, Civic Way and Whitby Road, Ellesmere Port

Ellesmere Port, an industrial town on the Wirral more famous for its oil refinery, hosted The Beatles on behalf of the Wolverham Welfare Association Dance on 14 January 1963. The show was attended by 700 people, and afterwards a few fans were invited backstage to meet the group. They walked into The Beatles' dressing room and were greeted with the sight of the four friendly musicians larking about and writing messages on the mirrors.

The Colony Club, Toxteth

Situated at 80 Berkley Street, this was run by the famous Lord Woodbine (Harold Phillips). The Beatles made a couple of appearances here in 1960. They liked the club and often hung out when they had nothing to do. It has since been demolished.

57 Copperfield Street, Dingle

Alfred Lennon was born here in 1912. The Victorian terraced houses in the area have since been replaced by new housing. Many of the streets were named after Charles Dickens' characters.

Birthplace of John's father.

Dairy Cottage, Woolton

This small house at 120a Allerton Road was attached to the dairy farm owned by George Smith, Mimi's husband. At Mimi's invitation, Julia Lennon lived here for a short time with John while Alfred was away on his voyages. Harriet, Mimi's sister, also lived at the house with her husband Norman, and became guardians to Julia and Jackie, John's half-sisters.

One of many homes that young John lived in.

Dairy Farm, Woolton

The dairy farm was owned by Mimi's husband George Smith and his family. George made daily trips on his horse-drawn cart around the village, delivering the milk straight from the churn. Occasionally, John delivered milk with his Uncle George and looked after the horse, including cleaning the stables.

Down on George's farm.

David Lewis Theatre, Great George Street

The one-month-old Beatles Fan Club hired this hall on 17 October 1961 for their first official event. The Beatles performed but had no PA equipment and were forced to improvise. The David Lewis Theatre has been demolished.

147 Dinas Lane, Huyton

The home of Paul's Auntie Jin. She was close to Paul and Mike and took an active role in raising the boys after their mum had died. This home was also where Cavern DJ Bob Wooler had the infamous fight with John Lennon at Paul's twenty-first birthday party on 18 June 1963, with John putting Wooler in hospital.

Important haven for the young Paul and scene of his infamous twenty-first birthday party.

Dingle Vale Secondary Modern School, Dingle

Ringo attended Dingle Vale Secondary Modern School (which later moved site and became Shorefields Comprehensive for a while, before undergoing subsequent name changes) in 1951 at the age of 11, though he contracted tuberculosis and missed his last two years of school. While recuperating at a children's hospital on the Wirral he became interested in playing the drums and never looked back. With Ringo's financial support, the school created 'Starr Fields' with a community centre and playing fields for the local children.

Ringo was hardly ever there.

69 Dovedale Road, Mossley Hill

The home of John Lennon's school friend Mike Hill, where John had his rock 'n' roll epiphany. John and Mike, together with their friends Pete Shotton and Don Beattie, would regularly listen to rock 'n' roll records together. It was Little Richard's 'Long Tall Sally' that struck a chord with the young Lennon. 'This boy at school, Mike Hill, had been to Holland and said he had a record by someone who was better than Elvis', recalled Lennon. 'When I heard it, it was so great I couldn't speak.'

Turning John on to rock 'n' roll was a pivotal moment.

Dovedale Road School, Mossley Hill

Both John Lennon and George Harrison attended the infant and junior schools. George and John were in different years and it is unlikely they met. John's friend Ivan Vaughan only attended the junior school. John was enrolled here on 6 May 1946 with his address noted as '251 Menlove Avenue'. Mimi took John to and from school on the bus to begin with, but he very soon started to catch the bus on his own. Aged 11, John started to work on a series of comic books with the title *Sport, Speed and Illustrated*. He added a postscript 'Edited and illustrated by JW Lennon'. It contained pictures of film stars and football players, which he pasted in among cartoons, poems and short stories he composed. George was enrolled in Dovedale School in April 1948.

The school that John enjoyed and where he flourished.

Elmswood Nursing Home, Mossley Hill

Julia Lennon became pregnant after an affair with a Welsh soldier, Taffy Williams, and on 19 June 1945 gave birth here to a girl, whom she named Victoria Elizabeth Lennon. That would be the only influence she would ever have on her daughter's life. Arranged by Mimi, Victoria was adopted by a Norwegian-born seaman and his wife who lived in Crosby. John never met Victoria despite searching for her for years. She had been renamed Ingrid Pederson, and was tracked down by a journalist a few years after John had been killed.

Birthplace of John's half-sister Victoria whom he never met.

43 Elswick Street, Dingle

This was the home of Ian James, a school friend of Paul McCartney. It was Ian's guitar that Paul first played before he purchased his own. They attended the Liverpool Institute together, and Ian helped Paul to learn various chords and songs. The Rex guitar was kept by Ian and auctioned in July 2006 with a provenance from Paul.

Ian helped to teach Paul to play guitar, which helped him when he met John.

Embassy Club, Borough Road, Wallasey

The Beatles appeared here in July 1960. The club is now a bingo hall.

Empire Theatre, Lime Street

Liverpool's largest theatre is the Empire and it was the venue for the big acts of the fifties and sixties. Paul saw skiffle king Lonnie Donegan here when he was 14 and queued for his autograph; George found out where Donegan was staying and obtained his autograph as well. The Quarrymen's first recorded engagement was here on 9 June 1957 at a Carroll Levis audition, though they didn't make it through. In 1958, John, Paul and George entered another Carroll Levis competition as Johnny and The Moondogs, coming in third. That same competition saw Rory Storm and The Hurricanes, featuring their new drummer Richard Starkey, placed second behind Kingsize Taylor and The Dominoes.

The Beatles appeared at the Empire several times over the years, the first on Sunday 28 October 1962 when they were on the bill with Little Richard and Craig Douglas, for whom they also acted as backing band.

On 24 March 1963, in the week their debut album *Please Please Me* was released, The Beatles made a triumphant homecoming here during the Chris Montez/Tommy Roe tour. It was their first performance in the city since their night-time show at the Cavern on 19 February. As it was in their home town, Montez kindly let The Beatles close this show. However, his generosity soon backfired, because the management decided that they should close for the remainder of the tour. McCartney later remarked, 'It was embarrassing as hell for him. I mean, what could you say to him? Sorry, Chris? But he took it well.'

They played at the Empire three further times that same year, first during the Roy Orbison tour, on 26 May 1963. The second occasion, on 7 December, was a special performance for The Beatles Northern Area Fan Club, incorporating a recording of *Juke Box Jury* in the theatre at 2pm, followed by an afternoon concert taped by the BBC. Both shows were broadcast that evening, *Juke Box Jury* at 6.05pm and the concert, under the title *It's The Beatles!*, at 8.10pm. This second broadcast was watched by an estimated 23 million people. (For more details, see relevant entries in *TV* section.)

Finally for 1963, on 22 December The Beatles performed a preview of their Christmas show here (see entry for Astoria, Finsbury Park).

In 1964 the band played here only once, on 8 November, their first concert in their home city in almost 11 months.

The Beatles' last ever Liverpool concert took place at the Empire on 5 December 1965. The demand for tickets was huge, with over 40,000 applications for the 2,550 available for each of the two shows on this date. John had handed out many to his family. Pattie Boyd and George's parents were in attendance. During the second show, Paul took to the drums during one of the support acts, The Koobas' rendition of 'Dizzy Miss Lizzy'. That afternoon, two fans were seen

A very early snap of George, John and Paul in 1961, outside Paul's council house in Forthlin Road, Liverpool. © KEYSTONE USA/REX/Shutterstock

outside the venue handing out leaflets for their 'Save the Cavern Club' campaign. Paul saw them and brought them in to explain. The teenage girls told him the club had fallen on hard times and the city council was demanding that the club's owner, Ray McFall, should have new toilets and plumbing fitted, but he didn't have the required finances. The Beatles lent their support to the club in a press conference before their shows, but offered no money. The following day the group spent the day resting in Liverpool, visiting family and friends.

One of the most important venues in Liverpool for the various incarnations of The Beatles.

Empress Pub, Dingle

This pub on High Park Road at the top of Admiral Grove, where Ringo lived, was commemorated in March 1970 when just before The Beatles officially split, Ringo released his first solo album *Sentimental Journey*, the cover of which featured a photo of the pub, with Ringo and his family superimposed into the picture.

A sentimental journey to the top of Admiral Grove.

36 Falkner Street, Liverpool

The ground floor flat was rented by Brian Epstein in the early sixties, primarily for his secret homosexual liaisons away from his family. After John Lennon and Cynthia Powell married, Epstein invited the newly-weds to live here. It was in this flat that John wrote 'Do You Want To Know A Secret'.

John and Cynthia's first home.

20 Forthlin Road, Allerton

In 1955, the McCartney family made their move from the working-class council estate in Speke to this more suburban location. Sadly, on 31 October 1956 Mary died as a result of breast cancer. With Jim left to bring up his boys, Paul and Mike both lost themselves in their creative hobbies. For Paul, music was his escape and way of dealing with his grief. Forthlin Road proved to be the inspirational location for many early Lennon and McCartney collaborations. The family's fortunes had changed after The Beatles struck it big, and in 1964 Paul moved his dad to Heswall on the Wirral, to the new home, 'Rembrandt'. The property at 20 Forthlin Road is now a National Trust house and open to visitors.

Of all of the McCartney homes, this is where Paul became a Beatle.

Gambier Terrace, Liverpool

Gambier Terrace, with its Georgian façade, is in the shadow of the Anglican Cathedral. Stuart and John shared Flat 3, Hillary Mansions, with Rod Murray. The Beatles also rehearsed in the flat many times.

An important meeting place for the early Beatles.

93 Garmoyle Road, Wavertree

It was while John Lennon was at art college that he met Cynthia Powell. Cynthia took a flat here and John virtually moved in. It was also at this location that Julian was conceived. When confronted with the news, John said to Cynthia, 'There's only one thing for it Cyn, we will have to get married.'

Not the best news John had ever heard.

Gaumont Cinema, Allerton

The Quarrymen made a couple of unrecorded appearances here.

Grafton Rooms/Ballroom, West Derby Road

The Grafton Rooms was one of the biggest dance halls in Liverpool. The Quarrymen entered skiffle contests here in the late 1950s, including one in April 1957. The Beatles appeared at this venue four times in 1962–63. The first was on 3 August 1962 where they topped the bill, ahead of fellow Liverpool bands, Gerry and The Pacemakers and The Big Three.

They returned to the venue on 10 January 1963 in a show covered by Vincent Mulchrone of the *Daily Mail* and Maureen Cleave of the *Evening Standard*, who wrote, 'John Lennon has an upper lip which is brutal in a devastating way. George Harrison is handsome, whimsical and untidy. Paul McCartney has a round baby face while Ringo Starr is ugly but cute. Their physical appearance inspires frenzy. They look beat-up and depraved in the nicest possible way.' Cleave would later loom large in John's 1966 'Beatles Bigger Than Jesus' controversy.

The band's third appearance at the Grafton Rooms was on 12 June 1963 in a fundraising gig for the charity The National Society for the Prevention of Cruelty to Children (NSPCC). They received no fee for their performance. The event was staged by the Oxford student Jeffrey Archer, who later became a novelist, Conservative party politician and a disgraced peer.

Their final show here was on 2 August 1963.

Graham Spencer Studios, Childwall

In 1963, just a few hundred yards from Epstein's house on Queens Drive, sat Graham Spencer's photo studio. Epstein engaged Spencer for a photo session with his stable of stars.

The Grapes Pub, Mathew Street, Liverpool

Situated just down from the Cavern on Mathew Street, The Grapes was a popular place for The Beatles to get a drink, and there is still a photo in the back room that was taken of the four – John, Paul, George and Pete – in the snug. It was established in the late seventeenth century in what was then Pluckingtons Alley. The stables have gone but some of the Victorian wallpaper and original wooden beams are still there. In the sixties it stood alone as the only place to get a proper drink in Mathew Street. Nowadays, it is surrounded by themed pubs and clubs and can be lost in a modern street of neon lights, but still manages to retain its authentic feel.

Where the musicians, including The Beatles, would meet for a proper drink before playing the Cavern.

Greenbank Drive Synagogue, Wavertree

This was the synagogue the Epstein family regularly attended. Attached to it was the Max Morris Hall, which hosted performances by most of the big bands in Liverpool during the summer of 1961, including The Beatles before Epstein became their manager. Brian Epstein's funeral was held here on 29 August 1967, from where his body was carried to the Jewish Cemetery in Long Lane, Aintree. The synagogue closed in January 2008.

Grosvenor Ballroom, Grosvenor Street, Liscard, Wallasey

The group first performed here as The Silver Beatles on 4 June 1960. The line-up was John, Paul, George, Stuart and drummer Tommy Moore. When they appeared here again on 11 June, Tommy failed to turn up, leaving them without a drummer. When John jokingly asked if there was a drummer in the house, an imposing rocker named

'Ronnie' jumped up on the stage and began hitting the drums with reckless abandon. No one had the courage to kick him off the stage and the group members went blank when he asked at the end of the gig if he could join them. This date is, also, potentially hugely important for another reason.

For when the band had a drummer called Ronnie 'The Ted'.

The group played at The Grosvenor on 14 occasions, from 4 June 1960–15 September 1961, with the violence at the venue eventually persuading them to stop appearing.

Notable dates in this run of gigs:

11 June 1960

Historic night for the group when, according to the British beat poet, Royston Ellis, they officially changed their name to The Beatles.

For the important night in the group's history when, as told by a poet, they performed as The Beatles for the very first time.

18 June 1960

Paul's eighteenth birthday. With the group still in need of a permanent drummer, behind the kit tonight was 16-year-old Jackie Lomax. A friend of the band and future member of the Liverpool combo, The Undertakers, he travelled with The Beatles to Shea Stadium in 1966 before signing to Apple Records in early 1968.

2 July 1961

Featuring a cameo appearance by the singer, Johnny Gentle (see Alloa entry, Scotland).

Haig Dance Club, Haig Avenue, Moreton

The Quarrymen appeared at the Haig Dance Club four times, the first time in November 1957. It has since been replaced by houses.

Hambleton Hall, St David's Road, Huyton

The Beatles appeared at this venue in the Page Moss neighbourhood of Huyton 15 times, from 25 January 1961–13 January 1962. 'In those days you could see The Beatles for half-a-crown,' Pete Best recalled. '"The Sensational Beatles" they called us. But you would pay a tanner more if you came in after 8pm. We used to play there once a week and the crowd's favourite was "Hully Gully". This used to go down well, in fact, perhaps too well. For some strange reason, it usually started a fight, but we just used to play on.' The hall has since been demolished.

8 Haymans Green, West Derby

(See Casbah Coffee Club)

Heath Hey, Gateacre

When Beatlemania became too much for Elsie and Harry Graves, Ringo moved his mother and step-father to a bungalow in Woolton.

Ringo looking after his mum and stepfather.

Henry Hunt & Son, Dingle

Registered at 21a Maud Street, just off North Hill Street in the Dingle, this manufacturer of gymnastic apparatus was Richy Starkey's place of employment. It was a five-minute walk from his home at Admiral Grove. The building has since been demolished. The main buildings were on Windsor Street, taking up the addresses at numbers 85, 87, 89, 91 and 93. It was a good apprenticeship and the place where Richy and his next-door neighbour Eddie Myles formed the Eddie Clayton Skiffle Group. These buildings were demolished years ago.

Where Ringo's first group was formed.

Hessy's Music Centre, Stanley Street

The Beatles and most other Merseybeat bands bought their musical gear at Hessy's. Jim Gretty came up with the idea of giving free guitar lessons with every purchase. John's Aunt Mimi bought him his first decent guitar here for £17. Ringo also purchased a new drum kit here in 1958. It was also from Hessy's that Stuart bought his bass guitar with the proceeds from his painting.

The most important music store in Liverpool.

Heswall Jazz Club, at Barnston Women's Institute, Barnston Road

The Beatles played here, in what looks like a village hall, near Heswall, on three occasions in 1962, on 24 March, 30 June and 25 September. For their March appearance, to accommodate the upmarket venue, the band wore their smart, tailor-made Beno Dorn suits on stage for the first time. For the June gig, the band was billed as 'The Fabulous Beatles, Parlophone Recording Artistes'.

Holyoake Hall, Smithdown Road, Wavertree

Holyoake Hall is opposite the tram sheds on Smithdown Road and about 200 yards from Penny Lane. The Quarrymen played here regularly in 1958. The Beatles played twice, on 15 and 22 July 1961.

Hulme Hall, Bolton Road, Port Sunlight

The band played here in the Wirral's Port Sunlight on four occasions in 1962, on 7 July, 18 August, 6 October and 27 October, hired by The Horticultural Society, the Golf Club and Recreations Associations among others. The gig on 18 August is notable for Ringo's first appearance with The Beatles, marking the official beginning of John, Paul, George and Ringo. Hulme Hall was the location where on 27 October 1962 Monty Lister, representing hospital Radio Clatterbridge, carried out the first radio interview with the Fab Four.

Another landmark gig when the Fab Four officially performed as the recognisable line-up we all know and love for the very first time.

The Institute, Hinderton Road, Neston

The Silver Beatles appeared at this venue on the Wirral six times, on consecutive Thursdays commencing on 2 June 1960. The Institute is now a civic hall. The *Birkenhead News and Advertiser* (Heswall and Neston edition) covered the event, mentioning that the group had been 'pulling in capacity houses on Merseyside'. The reporter attributed their names as John Lennon, Paul Ramon, Carl Harrison, Stuart De Stael and Thomas Moore. These were the pseudonyms they used for their Scottish tour. The report also referred to the band as 'The Beatles', the first time the group's name had appeared as such in print.

Iron Door, Temple Street

This club was opened on 9 April 1960 by Geoff Hogarth and Harry Ormesher. The Silver Beatles made one appearance at the Iron Door, at lunchtime on 15 May 1960. The venue then changed its name to the Liverpool Jazz Society in December 1960 and, although jazz bands still appeared regularly, they began promoting beat music. The Beatles made five appearances here in March 1961. In September 1961, the name had briefly changed once more, this time to the Storyville Jazz Club, and The Beatles made two appearances in March 1962. The Beatles also appeared at the club on 1 August 1961, at a private party organised by the then managers, Clem Dalton and Brian 'Jess' James. By the end of the 1962, the club was back to the Iron Door once more.

One of the best, yet little praised, clubs in Liverpool.

Irby Village Hall, Thingwall Road

The Beatles made one appearance at this hall on the Wirral, on 7 September 1962 at a youth club gig in front of 80 teenagers for £35. Also known as the Mary Newton School of Dance, the hall has retained the original stage, and also the bar where they were served their drinks. After their appearance, the band packed up and left but guitarist George Harrison forgot a suitcase. It was later found by Ernie Irlam, whose son David had been in one of the other bands appearing that night. Ernie had contacted Brian Epstein at the time about the suitcase, and Epstein said someone would collect it, but no one ever arrived and the suitcase was put in an attic and forgotten. Local author Ray O'Brien advised on the historical significance of the suitcase and helped arrange its sale. The case is made of compressed cardboard with plastic trim, and has George Harrison's initials on its sides. A small note on it says: 'Mr George Harrison c/o Beatles Party'. It was full of odds and ends such as spare guitar strings and bits of electrical wire. The case was sold in 2006 for just under £2,500. Regarding the event in 1962, Ray O'Brien commented, 'The organisers didn't raise the £35 on the night and

held a sale, a bit like a modern car boot sale, on the bowling green opposite the village hall to get the extra money. Brian Epstein came round in his Rolls-Royce to pick up the rest of the cash.'

Jacaranda Club, Slater Street

This former watch repair shop was opened as a coffee bar in 1958 by Allan Williams, with a basement club that would become best known for being the first venue to book the group that would become The Beatles. With John and Stuart attending the nearby Liverpool Art College, and Paul and George being students at the Liverpool Institute adjacent to the college, the four of them would hang around the 'Jac' looking for a free cup of coffee or toast, and badgering Williams to find them work.

Instead of offering a gig, Williams put them to work redecorating the venue, with Lennon and Sutcliffe painting the ladies' toilets. Stuart was also commissioned to paint a mural in the basement, which he did with his flatmate and fellow art student Rod Murray. Sadly these were destroyed years later after dampness caused the plaster to fall off, with only a fragment surviving. The group would also rehearse at the club.

During 1960 Williams eventually did ask them to perform on Monday nights when the normal house group, The Royal Caribbean Steel Band, had a night off. Their payment for each gig was beans on toast and Pepsi-Cola.

It was on 30 May 1960, when the band were performing at the club during their Monday night slot, that they met and backed the teenage London rock 'n' roll beat poet Royston Ellis during one of his 'Rocketry' (rock 'n' roll poetry) performances. Sensing they worked well together, Ellis suggested taking them to London to back him on various stage and television shows and asked John what he called the band. 'The Silver Beetles,' Lennon replied. Ellis, England's answer to the USA's Allen Ginsberg, suggested that since they both liked beat music, he was a beat poet, and they were going to play for him, why not call themselves 'The Beatles'. A little under two weeks later, on 11 June 1960, they did.

The group never ended up travelling to London with Ellis, but invited him instead to Hamburg to appear on stage with them as their so-called 'poetical compère' during their stint at the Indra Club, due to start on 17 August 1960. He declined the offer but remained friends with the band, especially John. Lennon would often say The Beatles' name was given to them by a 'man on a flaming pie', a jovial reference to the evening Ellis cooked a frozen chicken and mushroom pie for them in their flat at Gambier Terrace and managed to burn it. Incidentally, The Beatles/Ellis connection gave rise to the group's first major musical press reference. On 9 July 1960 *Record Mirror* reported that Ellis was, 'thinking of bringing a Liverpool group called The Beetles to London to back him on his poetry readings.' There was a follow-up in the next issue, 16 July 1960, in which Ellis said, 'For some time I have been searching for a group to use regularly and I feel that The Beetles fit the bill.'

With no bookings and no drummer, this is where Allan Williams got the band together, giving them somewhere to play.

Jewish Cemetery, Aintree

After his funeral service on 29 August 1967, Brian Epstein's body was taken to the Jewish Cemetery at Long Lane, Aintree. He was buried in grave H12, Section A. Brian's parents and brother are also buried here.

Quiet resting place for The Beatles' manager.

38 Kensington, Liverpool

This small recording studio was tucked inside a Victorian terraced house and is where The Quarrymen made their first and only demo record. It was a disc that eventually became one of the most historic recordings in popular music. John, Paul, George, Colin Hanton and John Duff Lowe paid seventeen shillings and sixpence (87.5 pence) and cut a two-sided disc made of shellac. They couldn't afford to pay for a tape and so the recording was made straight to disc. The five-piece ensemble recorded Buddy Holly's 'That'll Be The Day' and 'In Spite Of All The Danger', an original McCartney–Harrison tune. It was seen as Paul's song with George providing the guitar solo. Percy Phillips owned the studio, which was on the ground floor. His clients waited in the front parlour and recorded in the back room. The studio consisted of two tape recorders, a microphone hanging from the ceiling, a piano and disc-cutter, which produced these shellac records. Colin Hanton, drummer with The Quarrymen, recalled how excited they were. 'He gave us the disc and off we went. It was a big thing. How many people had records like popular crooner, Matt Monro? So we had a record too, and could listen to ourselves. It was a momentous day for us. I can still remember it so clearly.' A plaque was unveiled at the property in 2005, with Quarrymen Colin Hanton and John Duff Lowe present at the ceremony.

Not quite Liverpool's Abbey Road, just the back room of a small house.

Knotty Ash Village Hall, East Prescot Road

Mona Best booked The Beatles for some of their seven appearances at this local hall, the first being on 15 September 1961, through to 17 November. Promoter Sam Leach also booked The Beatles plus Rory Storm and The Hurricanes for a St Patrick's Night Gala on 17 March 1962 to celebrate his engagement.

Lathom Hall, Lathom Avenue, Seaforth

This one-time cinema became famous for a gig by The Silver Beats.

The group's first performance at this venue was on 14 May 1960, although they were neither advertised nor scheduled to appear. They had originally turned up at the Cassanova Club in London Road. However, Cliff Roberts and The Rockers were double booked for both venues that night, so Roberts suggested they take his band's place at Lathom Hall. They did so, performing for the one and only time as The Silver Beats.

Liverpool promoter Brian Kelly, known as 'Beekay', ran a number of Liverpool venues including Lathom Hall, the Aintree Institute, Alexandra Hall and the Litherland Town Hall. He was suitably impressed with what he saw at this impromptu gig and hired the band to appear again the following week, on 21 May – this time advertised as The Silver Beats. This was to be their first serious engagement.

However, four days later, London-based promoter, Larry Parnes called, offering them a tour of Scotland as the backing band for another Liverpudlian singer, Johnny Gentle. They accepted, but failed to inform Kelly, who had already advertised their performance and had to face many disgruntled fans on the night when they didn't show up. As a result, they would not receive any more bookings from Kelly for several months, eight in fact, until the Cavern DJ Bob Wooler convinced him to change his mind. They went on to return as The Beatles on ten further occasions in 1961, between 7 January and 25 February. At one performance Stuart was jumped by a gang of thugs. When Pete and John were

told about the incident, they quickly ran to Stu's rescue, finding him with his face covered in blood. John broke a finger in the fight.

One of the most important venues for the early Silver Beats and The Beatles.

Lewis's Department Store, Ranelagh Street

Paul and John routinely visited Lewis's on Saturday mornings to go through the record department's selection for the week, buying discs with saved pocket money when they could. Peter Brown, who later became Brian Epstein's personal assistant, had previously run the Lewis's record department. Paul also worked here for a short time as a second man on one of their delivery vans. The Beatles made an appearance on the top floor at the Lewis's staff *Young Idea Dance* on 28 November 1962 in the 527 Club.

Good record store and funny little staff club.

Litherland Town Hall, Hatton Hill Road

After The Beatles had returned from Hamburg in late 1960, they had no immediate gigs lined up. Bob Wooler bumped into Pete and John in Liverpool's Jacaranda and they told Wooler of their adventures in Germany. Bob arranged with Brian Kelly to give them 30 minutes at the Litherland Town Hall concert, between The Del Renas and The Searchers. On 27 December 1960, the venue saw the birth of a phenomenon later known as Beatlemania. John, Paul, George, Pete Best and Chas Newby (rhythm guitarist with Pete Best's former band The Blackjacks, who was standing in on bass for Stuart Sutcliffe, who remained laid low with a cold in Hamburg) were sensational.

ABOVE: The Beatles were second on a 12-act bill for a Little Richard concert at the Tower Ballroom, New Brighton, on 12 October 1962. John, being a fan, asked Little Richard for his autograph on the show's programme, which he did, also adding his address in California. He invited John to pop in if he was ever in the USA, something which, at the time, John could never imagine happening. This programme is another treasure given to me by John.

RIGHT: George's parents, George and Louise Harrison, in 1963. They were keen fans of The Beatles and took it upon themselves to help with fan mail and presents. © Manchester Daily Express / Contributor

ABOVE: Ringo with his mother Elsie and his stepfather Harry Graves, in 1963. His real father, Richard Starkey, had departed when Ringo was 3. He never gave interviews or traded on Ringo's fame. In 1967, I tracked him down to Crewe, where he was working as a window cleaner. © Max Scheler - K & K / Contributor

BELOW: Dick James (left), The Beatles' music publisher, with the band as they sign their music contract in 1963. © Terry O'Neill / Contributor

LEFT: The Beatles in the studio with George Martin, their producer.

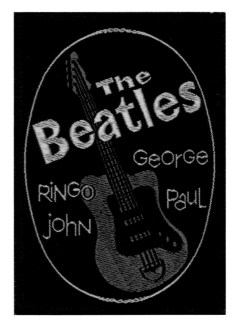

BELOW: The Beatles in Abbey Road Studios, 1963.

OPPOSITE: The Beatles at the Cavern in 1963. Paul is to the left and John is at the microphone. © Michael Ward / Contributor

BELOW: The Beatles performing after being made *New Musical Express* poll winners, 1963. © V&A Images / Contributor

RIGHT: Flyer for an early Beatles concert at the Odeon Cinema, Leeds.

BOTTOM: The Beatles at the Alpha Studios in Birmingham, December 1963, recording for the show *Thank Your Lucky Stars*.

© Mark and Colleen Hayward / Contributor

ABOVE LEFT: The Beatles recording *Ready Steady Go!* in 1963 with Helen Shapiro (fourth from the left), who had been the real star until then. Also Keith Fordyce (second from the left), Dusty Springfield (third from the right) and Eden Kome (far right). © David Redfern / Staff

ABOVE RIGHT: The Beatles on *The Morecambe and Wise Show*, December 1963. © ITV/REX/Shutterstock

BELOW: Recording for Granada TV's *People and Places*. © ITV/REX/Shutterstock

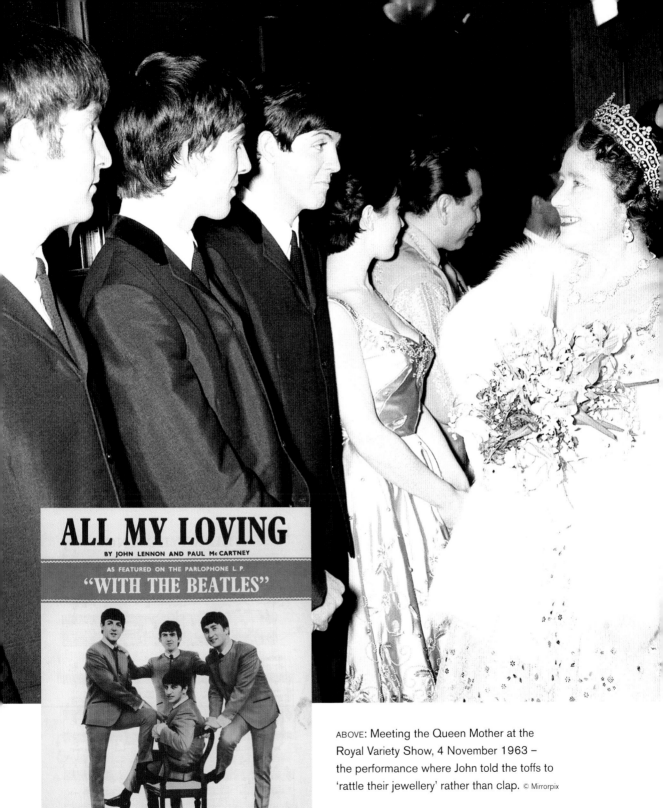

ABOVE: Meeting the Queen Mother at the Royal Variety Show, 4 November 1963 – the performance where John told the toffs to 'rattle their jewellery' rather than clap. © Mirrorpix

LEFT: Sheet music for 'All My Loving', which featured on their second LP, *With The Beatles*.

LEFT: Jimmy Nicol, who stood in for Ringo on drums when he was ill for several concerts in 1963.

RIGHT: Neil Aspinall (right) with George. Neil was originally one of The Beatles' two roadies, later a boss at Apple.
© Mirrorpix

BELOW: An unbelievably awful chocolate-box colour photo of The Beatles in 1963 – but the Americans loved it, and them, when they first hit the USA in 1964.

The compère for the evening was the Cavern club DJ Bob Wooler. 'It was the Christmas crowd,' he recalled, 'and the curtains were closed. We primed each other as to exactly what we were going to do and I announced, "Here they are, direct from Hamburg, the sensational Beatles!" As the curtain swept open, Paul burst into "Long Tall Sally".' 'It was funny,' George admitted, 'we'd spent so much time in Germany, nobody [in Liverpool] knew us. We were billed as "Direct From Hamburg" and naturally, everybody thought we were German. One girl came up to me and said, "Aye, don't you speak good English."' 'It was the evening that we really came out of our shell and let go,' John revealed. 'We discovered that we were quite famous. This was when we began to think for the first time that we were good.'

Another landmark concert in Beatles history. As the birth of Beatlemania, this venue should be celebrated.

In total The Beatles played this venue, situated in Hatton Hill and now a health centre, on 20 occasions, from that first night on 27 December 1960 to 9 November 1961. In addition to their debut, one other performance stands out in particular. On the 19 October, halfway through the night, The Beatles joined forces with fellow Mersey band Gerry and The Pacemakers. Calling themselves The Beatmakers, John played piano, Paul rhythm guitar, George lead guitar, Gerry Marsden vocals/lead guitar, with Pacemaker Les Maguire on sax and Les Chadwick bass, while Pete Best shared drumming duties with Pacemaker Freddie Marsden. Karl Terry, of Karl Terry and The Cruisers, also on the bill, joined them for some singing. 'The Litherland Town Hall was the scene of many of The Beatles' triumphs,' Pete Best remembered. 'As the curtains opened,

The Beatmakers exploded onto an astonished crowd with a sound bigger than [the 1961 film] The Guns Of Navarone. The cause was actually The Beatles and The Pacemakers together. Freddie Marsden had his drums on stage and I had mine. We went to town on numbers like "What'd I Say".'

Liverpool College of Art, Hope Street

Also known as the Art College. Stuart Sutcliffe left Prescot Grammar School in 1956 with five O-levels and was admitted to the Art College at 16. Since the Liverpool Institute was next door, Paul and George often joined John and Stu in the canteen for lunch. Stu arranged for them to rehearse here and booked them for many Saturday night dances. In return, the college bought PA equipment, which the group liberally borrowed for their gigs. John enrolled at the Art College in the autumn of 1957, turning up in tight jeans and a long black jacket. He put his normal trousers over the top to fool Mimi, and then took them off at the bus stop. John met his first wife Cynthia Powell here in lettering class. John produced a pantomime at the Art College in December 1959, where he appeared as an ugly sister in their version of Cinderella. John also met Bill Harry here, who created Mersey Beat newspaper.

Where John found refuge after school, and met Stuart Sutcliffe, Cynthia and Bill Harry, as well as practising with Paul and George.

Liverpool Institute High School, Mount Street

The Liverpool Institute was a grammar school adjacent to the Art College. It opened on 15 September 1837 (it had previously been the Mechanics Institute). In 1890, one half of the facility became the Art College. The motto of the school was 'Non nobis solum sed toti mundo nati', which translates from Latin as, 'Not for ourselves alone but for the whole world were we born'. How appropriate for a band who would leave Liverpool and conquer the world. Paul and George attended, as did Ivan Vaughan, Len Garry, Tony Bramwell and Neil Aspinall. Paul was taught by one of John's uncles, Alfred 'Cissy' Smith. He also won a music prize here in 1959. Paul befriended Quarryman Len Garry, who was also at the Institute. Len remembers morning assembly and practising their 'counterpoint harmonies' during hymns, especially when singing 'Onward Christian Soldiers'. With corporal punishment common in most schools, it is no surprise that Paul, like his friends, was caned regularly by the 'sadistic' headmaster, affectionately known as 'The Baz' – meaning 'bastard'.

On his last day of school, Paul performed 'Long Tall Sally' and 'Tutti Frutti' on the desks as his parting shot. George Harrison had passed his 11-plus exam at Dovedale School and progressed to the Institute the year after Paul. He was delighted to have won his place, but he soon regretted it. A constant rebel against conformity, George rarely wore his uniform correctly, and let his hair grow long. He was terrorised, as were many lads, by teacher Frank Boot, who slippered the boys when they stepped out of line. On his last day, George gave his gym shoe to Boot as he said that he had used it on him more than he had used it himself. George left school without any qualifications as he spent many days sagging off school (playing truant) by visiting local cinemas.

In 1996, Paul, with the help of local business people, transformed the old school building, earmarked for demolition, into the Liverpool Institute for Performing Arts, known as LIPA.

Paul actively supports the 'fame' school, and rarely misses graduation day.

Where Paul and George became friends and George learned guitar.

Liverpool Jazz Society, Temple Street

(see Iron Door)

Liverpool Stadium, St Paul's Square

Still a popular venue for bands in the seventies, in its heyday Pete Best's family had promoted many high-profile boxing matches at this city centre stadium. Pete's dad John, and grandfather Johnny Best Sr., were regular compères at the bouts. Although it never resounded to the rock 'n' roll of The Beatles, this was a great venue. It was here that Allan Williams co-promoted an Eddie Cochran and Gene Vincent concert with Larry Parnes. However, shortly before the Liverpool event, the two rockers were travelling through Wiltshire when their taxi was involved in a fatal crash that took Cochran's life. Vincent, though injured, agreed to perform at the Liverpool show on 3 May 1960. Without Cochran, Williams bolstered the concert by placing Gerry and The Pacemakers, Rory Storm and The Hurricanes (with Ringo on the drums) and Derry and The Seniors on the bill among others. John, Paul, George and Stuart wanted to enlist Williams' help in getting them bookings, though Williams admitted that he didn't even realise they had a group.

This appearance by Gene Vincent at this venue showed John, Paul, George and Stuart that they needed to perform.

Liverpool Town Hall, High Street

The City of Liverpool held a civic reception here for The Beatles on 10 July 1964. There they looked over the balcony to view the surrounding streets filled with adoring fans: estimated to be approximately two hundred thousand people. In the downstairs foyer is a brass plaque bearing the names of John, Paul, George and Ringo, acknowledging their award of the Freedom of the City.

Liverpool residents came out in their thousands to welcome home The Beatles.

Locarno, West Derby Road

Standing next to The Grafton Rooms, this is where The Quarrymen performed in skiffle contests in the late 1950s. The Beatles made their first appearance here at a special Valentine's Day dance on 14 February 1963.

Just before the group finished the show, Ringo told his then girlfriend Maureen Cox to go outside and sit in the car and wait for him so no one would see her. As she recalled for Beatles biographer Hunter Davies, she was sitting in the car when this girl came up. 'She must have followed me. She said, "Are you going out with Ringo?" I said, "No, oh no, not me. He's just a friend of my brother's." "Liar," she said, "I just saw you talking to him."' Having forgotten to wind the window up, before Maureen could do anything the girl pushed her hand through the window and scratched Maureen down her face. 'She started screaming and shouting some very select language at me. I thought this is it. I'm going to get stabbed. I just got the window up in time, if I hadn't she would have opened the door and killed me.'

Lowlands, West Derby

Lowlands was a community hall in Haymans Green, located on the same road as the Casbah, and featured the Pillar Club, which is reckoned to be the first rock 'n' roll club in Liverpool. The Les Stewart Quartet, which featured Ken Brown, George Harrison, Les Stewart on guitar and Geoff Skinner on drums, played several times at Lowlands. They were then approached to open the Casbah Club by Mona Best.

Gave George somewhere to play, and became the springboard for re-forming The Quarrymen to open the Casbah Club.

174 Macketts Lane, Woolton

The Harrison family moved from Upton Green in Speke to this address in Hunts Cross (on the edge of Woolton) in 1962. Fans camped outside the house and fan mail was delivered in sacks. The Harrisons were extremely nice to these uninvited visitors, but eventually they placed a screen on the front window to give them some privacy. George moved the family in 1965 to Appleton, near Warrington, Cheshire, to a bungalow set in three acres – far cry from Arnold Grove where George was born. A few industrious fans still found the house and received the usual courtesy and welcome from George's parents.

George's parents spent hours replying to fan mail here.

9 Madryn Street, Dingle

Richard Starkey was born at this address on 7 July 1940 in the front bedroom. This working-class house was typical of thousands of similar homes built in Victorian Liverpool at the end of the nineteenth century. The houses were larger than Admiral Grove where Ringo grew up, but still had no bathroom or toilet inside the house. Occupants used the outhouse at the bottom of the concrete yard behind the house. After his parents split up, little Richard's grandparents, who lived at 59 Madryn Street, spent a lot of time babysitting the toddler. He was soon nicknamed 'Richy' to distinguish him from his father, after whom he was named. The house became too big and too expensive for Elsie Starkey to manage, so she arranged to swap houses with a family in nearby Admiral Grove. They moved there when Richy was nearly five years old.

Birthplace of Richard Starkey, aka Ringo.

21 Madryn Street, Dingle

Home of Ringo's paternal aunt Nancy Starkey, while he was growing up in Madryn Street and Admiral Grove.

59 Madryn Street, Dingle

Home of John and Annie Starkey, Ringo's paternal grandparents, and where Ringo's father moved to when he left the family home of 9 Madryn Street.

Where Ringo visited his grandparents.

Majestic Ballroom, Conway Street, Birkenhead

Opened in 1962 by The Rank Organisation. The Beatles made the first of 17 appearances here on 28 June 1962. Their final appearance was on 10 April 1963. The Majestic was also the venue where Pete Best made his debut with Lee Curtis and The All Stars after being sacked from The Beatles. They passed each other but didn't speak.

Massey & Coggins, Wavertree

Situated in Bridge Road in Wavertree. Paul landed a job winding coils here, although the job didn't last long and Paul decided music was a better option. The business is no longer in existence.

The job that Paul had to do but gave up quickly.

The Melody Inn, Grove Road, Wallasey

The Beatles appeared here in 1961. The club burned down in 1969.

251 Menlove Avenue 'Mendips', Woolton

Set within a still picturesque and attractive suburb of Liverpool, the naming of the house 'Mendips' (after a range of hills in the south of England) was a typical middle-class affectation that Mimi was quick to adopt. How Mendips was acquired has been a mystery for years but has finally been explained by John's half-sister Julia Baird. George and Mimi Smith rented a house behind Mendips in Vale Road. They witnessed the previous tenants preparing to leave and stored their furniture at the bottom of the garden by the fence that separated the two homes. The day the tenants vacated Mendips, Mimi and George lifted their furniture over the fence and moved in. Essentially they were squatters. With long-term possession being important under English England, this forced the owner to sell the property to them. The house had three bedrooms, a bathroom and inside toilet. John's bedroom, above the front porch, was small and his bed sat under the window. His room was invariably untidy and Mimi was eventually banned from entering. His walls boasted posters of Elvis Presley and Brigitte Bardot, and he had his books. Uncle George installed a speaker by taking an extension lead up the stairs from the radio in the morning room downstairs. This private retreat was where John spent hours reading and thinking. He wrote poetry and most nights sang himself to sleep. Sally, his dog, curled up at the foot of his bed to sleep and kept his feet warm. When Paul rehearsed with John, they were usually found in the enclosed porch by the front door. Mimi didn't like the noise of the guitars, and the room offered respite for her and great acoustics for John and Paul.

The morning room – between the entrance hall and the kitchen – was John's favourite hangout when he had friends over. As with most homes in Liverpool, the front room was out of bounds to all but the most important of visitors. It was the showroom and not for general use. John was seen by Paul and George as the posh kid in the middle-class area with the expensive house and furniture, and all the books on the shelves. Mendips was sold in October 1965 for £6,000, after John had bought Mimi a house in Poole, Dorset in August of that year. Mendips was later bought by Yoko Ono and given to the National Trust, so that Beatles fans could visit and see what the house would have looked like when John was growing up there.

The home where John lived from the age of five with his Aunt Mimi and Uncle George.

Merseyside Civil Service Club, Lower Castle Street

This downstairs club was host to The Beatles on five occasions in 1961, the first on 7 February and then on four consecutive Tuesdays from 7 November.

Moreton Co-operative Hall, Hoylake Road, Moreton

The Beatles appeared here in 1961. The room was on the first floor and was their only appearance.

The Morgue, Broadgreen

A club that was set up and run by Rory Storm, established in the basement of a house in Oak Vale Drive and now demolished. The Quarrymen made a couple of appearances here, including when it opened on 13 March 1958. The Morgue closed soon after on 22 April because of unsafe conditions.

Mosspits Lane Primary School, Wavertree

John's first school was Mosspits Lane Primary School where he was enrolled in November 1945.

After some incidents at school, and coinciding with Mimi taking over guardianship of John, he was moved from Mosspits to Dovedale Road Primary School in May 1946.

Not the best start to John's education.

Mossway Hall, Moss Way

The Beatles' only appearance in the Croxteth area of Liverpool took place here on St Patrick's Day, 17 March 1961. The venue has since been demolished. The gig didn't earn them any wages, but they could drink as much Guinness as they could manage, which was seen as an acceptable payment for their night's work.

64 Mount Pleasant, Liverpool

This once grand Georgian terrace, the second-oldest domestic building in Liverpool, contained the Register Office where John and Cynthia Lennon were married on 23 August 1962. Paul McCartney, George Harrison and Brian Epstein attended as well as Cynthia's brother Tony and his wife Margery. The persistent noise of a pneumatic drill disrupted the ceremony and provided comedic fodder for those in attendance. Cynthia recalled the event in her book *A Twist of Lennon*. 'None of us heard a word of the service; we couldn't even hear ourselves think.' When the registrar asked for the groom to step forward, George Harrison stepped up as a cheap laugh. 'The registrar saw nothing funny in either the drilling or George's joke', she recalled, 'so we all struggled to keep our faces straight.'

Scene of 'scandal' that Brian was keen to keep quiet.

Napier & Son, Knowsley

As part of the war effort, Jim McCartney's job at the cotton broker was put on hold. He went to work in the Napier aircraft factory during the day and as a fire-watcher at night. The factory was located on the East Lancashire Road in Knowsley and, classed as part of the Royal Air Force, they made aircraft engines.

NEMS, Whitechapel

The main office of NEMS (North End Music Stores) was opposite Button Street, near the bottom of Mathew Street. Located at 12–14 Whitechapel, next to Thorntons, the shop was opened in 1959 by actor and singer Anthony Newley. The record department of NEMS was in the basement and was considered to be the biggest and best in Liverpool. The Beatles would spend hours there listening to the latest records, and occasionally buying them. Epstein's offices were on the first floor, which is where he held his meetings with The Beatles. When Epstein later set up NEMS Enterprises to manage The Beatles' affairs, he took up the entire top floor. The Beatles made a guest appearance at the NEMS store to sign copies of their 1963 single 'Please Please Me'. They also gave a brief acoustic performance.

NEMS also had stores at 44 Allerton Road, near Penny Lane; 90 County Road, Walton; 2 Marian Square, Netherton; 37 St Mary's Road, Garston; 25 High Street, Runcorn; 6 Central Way, Maghull and the original NEMS store at 62–72 Walton Road.

Brian's empire was built here and so enabled him to become The Beatles' manager.

New Clubmoor Hall, Norris Green

Paul McCartney probably made his official, paid debut with The Quarrymen here on 18 October 1957. It was a booking arranged by Nigel Walley via promoter Charlie McBain. It is famous because Paul tried a lead guitar solo on 'Guitar Boogie', which he fluffed. Part way through John stopped the song and told the audience, 'He's our new boy – he'll be all right given time.' The audience laughed and John rescued Paul from awkward embarrassment. The first photograph of Paul with The Quarrymen was taken this night, with Paul and John the only two wearing suit jackets. The club closed in 2014.

Paul's debut in a small hall in the north of Liverpool; this was the start.

9 Newcastle Road, Wavertree

After his birth at Oxford Street Maternity Hospital, John was brought back to Newcastle Road and lived here for the majority of his first five years. Julia's father worked for the Liverpool Salvage Company and was often away from home, as was her husband Alf Lennon. When Alf returned from sea, this was where he and Julia set up home. They briefly shared the house with Julia's parents, who initially blessed their marriage. However, when Alf went AWOL in New York, there was no money coming home. After their marriage failed, Julia initially lived here with her partner John Dykins, before they left to set up home in a small, one-bedroom flat in Gateacre. Newcastle Road is just a couple of hundred yards from the Penny Lane roundabout, within the area referred to locally as 'Penny Lane'.

John's first home.

Odd Spot Club, Bold Street

The Beatles made two appearances here in 1962, on 29 March and 11 August. The club was where Ringo Starr was invited by George to meet up with them, before John, Paul and George took Ringo to meet Brian and arrange for Ringo to replace Pete Best.

Odeon Cinema, London Road, Liverpool

The Beatles played two shows here as part of their autumn tour in the evening of 7 December 1963 after having taped two BBC specials, *Juke Box Jury* and *It's The Beatles!*, at the Empire Theatre earlier in the day (see Empire Theatre entry). This cinema also premiered their debut motion picture *A Hard Day's Night* in the north of England, with a charity gala screening on 10 July 1964. John often ditched art college to take in a movie at the Odeon Cinema with girlfriend Thelma Pickles, who most likely paid for his ticket. The cinema closed in 2009.

A hard day's day and night at this cinema make it a hit.

Oxford Street Maternity Hospital

John Winston Lennon was born here on 9 October 1940 in a room on the second floor. The blond-haired child weighed seven-and-a-half pounds. The notice of his birth in the *Liverpool Echo* read: 'LENNON – October 9, in hospital to JULIA (nee Stanley), wife of ALFRED LENNON, Merchant Navy (at sea), a son – 9 Newcastle Road'. A plaque has been placed on the hospital wall commemorating this event. Mimi told biographer Hunter Davies about John being born in the middle of a heavy bombing raid. There had been a raid the night before – on 8 October – but the next one wasn't until 10 October, with not many more over the next couple of weeks. This large building has been converted into apartments, called 'Lennon Studios'.

Birthplace of John Winston Lennon, though not during an air raid.

Pavilion Theatre, Lodge Lane, Toxteth

Known locally as the 'Pivvy', this venue has seen many famous music hall and variety acts in its time, and even a young Julia Lennon appeared there in a dance troupe. Before settling on the name The Quarrymen, John Lennon and a couple of his friends, and future Quarrymen, performed here as The Blackjacks, appearing in a skiffle contest in the spring of 1957. The judges ensured that they didn't even finish their rendition of 'Maggie Mae'. They made a couple of appearances at the Pavilion as The Quarrymen in skiffle contests during 1957. The Beatles played here on the evening of 2 April 1962 when they appeared with the Royal Waterford Showband from Ireland. In an Epstein-signed agreement on 5 February 1962, The Beatles agreed to be paid £20 for the night.

Peel Hall, Dingle

The Eddie Clayton Skiffle Group, with Ringo on the drums, made its debut here as did another Dingle lad, Gerry Marsden, with his skiffle group. Gerry later formed Gerry and The Pacemakers, and was also managed by Brian Epstein. Peel Hall, on the corner of Peel Street and Park Road, was the local Orange Lodge (Protestant Order) Hall where Ringo was a member of the accordion band. He remembers playing a tin drum during one Orange Day parade when the 'Lodge' marched around the area, something they still do to this day.

Ringo's debut.

Penny Lane

Penny Lane, one of the most famous roads in the world, actually doesn't have a lot to do with the song 'Penny Lane'. Most of the song is based on the roundabout at the top, officially shown as

Smithdown Place on a map, but known locally as the 'Penny Lane' roundabout. The roundabout is at the centre of what then became known as the 'Penny Lane' area. All three – the road, the roundabout and the area – are significant in the story of The Beatles and the song. The roundabout is like the hub of the wheel where the suburbs of Wavertree, Mossley Hill and Allerton converge and so it became a popular meeting point. Much has changed over the last century, when once it was mainly surrounded by fields, including Allerton Road Farm, going away from the roundabout. Penny Lane was also the terminus for the trams, and then buses, from the city centre. The local City Council hadn't even extended the trams beyond Penny Lane by 1926, though this followed shortly after when the line was extended up to Woolton along Menlove Avenue, running by Mimi's house, Mendips. The song 'Penny Lane' is about John, Paul and George's childhood – literally in their ears and in their eyes. The area was the centre of The Beatles' lives from a very young age. John lived his first few years in Newcastle Road, just off the Penny Lane roundabout and within the Penny Lane area. This is where he was pushed in his pram and later walked around with his mum when she was shopping there. Aunt Mimi enrolled John into Dovedale School, and he jumped off the bus with her at the Penny Lane roundabout, and waited here for the return trip to Mendips. The bus that John rode to the Liverpool Art College passed through Penny Lane roundabout every day. George's house at 12 Arnold Grove was at the top of Church Road, which leads off Penny Lane roundabout. George walked down Church Road, across the roundabout and down Penny Lane on his way to and from Dovedale School. When the Harrisons moved to Speke from Arnold Grove, George caught the bus to Penny Lane on weekdays, to attend Dovedale School. When Paul

attended the Liverpool Institute from the age of 11, he passed through Penny Lane roundabout every day on his journeys to and from school. The Quarrymen frequently travelled to and from their gigs by bus, and they often took refuge in the Penny Lane shelter in the middle of the roundabout where they waited to change buses. The barbershop, Bioletti's, was where they got their hair cut. At the end of the same block is the bank where the banker kept his motorcar – probably the only person who could afford to run one. On the opposite corner to the barbershop is St Barnabas' Church, where Paul was in the choir. This roundabout and area is at the centre of The Beatles' childhood, and one of the first places Beatles fans want to visit on a trip to Liverpool.

The centre of the young Beatles' lives beneath the blue suburban skies.

9 Percy Street, Liverpool

Stuart Sutcliffe moved into a flat here with his friend Rod Murray. It was just round the corner from the Liverpool College of Art, where Stu practised Elvis Presley songs on a guitar purchased by his father. Stuart's sister Pauline remembers her brother reminisced when he and John Lennon tape-recorded Gene Vincent and Elvis songs. The Quarrymen occasionally rehearsed at Stuart's flat, with Rod Murray joining in on the washboard. They were evicted in 1959 when their landlady, Mrs Plant, entered the flat and found various rules had been broken. She especially didn't like it when she discovered one of her chairs was being used for firewood.

Where Stuart was invited to join the group.

Philharmonic Hall, Hope Street

Buddy Holly and The Crickets appeared here on 20 March 1958. Nigel Walley recalls that he and John made it a point to see their idol. It was Buddy Holly who made it cool to wear glasses, which gave John the confidence to wear his in public occasionally. Epstein also frequented the Philharmonic Hall and indulged his love of classical music by reserving the finest seats to listen to the world-famous orchestra. On 10 May 1963, George Harrison helped judge a 'beat group' competition here with Dick Rowe – the Decca man who was famously responsible for turning down The Beatles. It was here that George told him that if he didn't want to make the same mistake twice, he should sign the Rolling Stones. Rowe immediately headed south for London to snap them up.

Yes, Buddy Holly and The Crickets played here. That'll be the day.

Pillar Club

(see Lowlands)

Prescot Cables Social Club, Prescot

The Quarrymen appeared here in 1959. They were one of many music groups who were booked at this social club.

Quarry Bank High School, Allerton

The school, on Harthill Road, was opened in 1922. It was constructed with stone from the local quarry from which it takes its name. It was here that John Lennon attended school from the age of 11. He rode his bicycle there with Pete Shotton every weekday along Menlove Avenue and around the edge of Calderstones Park. On entering Quarry Bank High School, boys were divided into 'houses' named after the area of Liverpool in which they lived. John, Pete Shotton, Eric Griffiths and Rod Davis were all placed in 'Woolton'. John must have eventually held a few good memories of Quarry Bank as he asked Mimi for his school tie, which he took with him everywhere, even while in New York. He wore the tie for his thirty-ninth and Sean's fourth joint birthday party on 9 October 1979, and slept with a picture of the school above his bed. Lennon and Pete Shotton were often in school detention. After they'd been late too many times, headmaster Mr Pobjoy sent them home on suspension. They decided that they shouldn't tell their families so instead they visited Julia, who found it hilarious. For the next few days John met Pete and left for school at the normal time. The two then cycled to Julia's house where they served out their suspension.

John's friend Geoff Lee suggested John should start a skiffle group. John enlisted Pete Shotton, Eric Griffiths and Bill Smith, before Rod Davis was quickly added. The Quarrymen, the group that became The Beatles, had been founded.

Where The Quarrymen were formed.

197 Queens Drive, Childwall

When Harry Epstein married Malka Hyman in 1933, her parents gave them this house as their wedding present. Because of the anti-Semitism that was sweeping across Europe in the 1930s, many Jews had anglicised their names. Malka, whose name means 'Queen' in Hebrew, decided that she would now be called 'Queenie'. Epstein held meetings here with The Beatles about their bookings and his plans for the group. The Epstein family also held a cocktail party for Paul's twenty-first birthday.

Brian Epstein's home.

17 Queenscourt Road, West Derby

This was the home of Pete Best's family for a while. Mona Best wanted a bigger house and moved her family to 8 Haymans Green, which became the home of the Casbah Club.

Home to the Best family.

Reece's, Clayton Square

After John and Cynthia Lennon's wedding on 23 August 1962, the party ran down Mount Pleasant in the pouring rain to this cafe for a wedding breakfast, courtesy of Brian Epstein. Reece's wasn't a licensed premises, so the toast was made with water.

Rembrandt, Baskervyle Road, Heswall

Paul McCartney persuaded his father Jim to retire in 1964 to this house, on the Wirral, overlooking the Dee Estuary and Wales. Jim was 62 and had been working since he was 14 and was more than happy to accept. Paul purchased the house for £8,750 and spent another £8,000 in furnishings and decorations, installing a central heating system. Jim had two part-time gardeners and he looked after the vines in a heated greenhouse, and studied ornithology while watching birds in the garden. While visiting towards the end of 1966, Paul and Mike invited Guinness heir Tara Browne to stay with them. (Tara was killed in a car crash in December of that year, and was referred to in the song 'A Day In The Life' on the *Sgt Pepper* album.) The three of them smoked 'grass' and then jumped on their motorbikes. Paul took one bend too fast and parted company with the motorbike, smashing his face. They returned to Rembrandt and rounded up the family doctor to put a few stitches in Paul's lip. (Paul's chipped tooth can be seen in the 'Paperback Writer' video). Jim met and quickly married 34-year-old Angela Williamson in November 1964.

She brought her five-year-old daughter Ruth into the marriage, and they lived here for many years.

Paul providing a retirement home for his father as a thank you for all he had done for him.

81a Renshaw Street, Liverpool

It was in this small office that Bill Harry and his girlfriend (and later his wife) Virginia started the first Liverpool music paper, *Mersey Beat*. The publication, which launched its first edition on 6 July 1961, was essential for anyone interested in the local music scene. John Lennon and Brian Epstein were regular contributors and the paper religiously followed The Beatles' progress.

Bill Harry's Mersey Beat was essential reading and gave support to The Beatles.

Rialto Ballroom, Toxteth

On the corner of Berkley Street and Upper Parliament Street. The Quarrymen played in a couple of skiffle contests at this popular ballroom and dance hall. On 6 September 1962, during a Sam Leach promotion featuring The Beatles, Epstein was worried about the threat of violence at this inner-city venue. Leach promised them bodyguards, but Epstein wasn't satisfied, and he asked them to pull out, but John and Paul sided with Leach. Epstein felt humiliated, and he decided he had to break The Beatles' loyalty to Leach, eventually squeezing him out financially. The Beatles played here for a second and final time on 11 October of the same year. The original Rialto was burned down in the Toxteth riots of 1981.

Riversdale Technical College, Aigburth

Ringo was employed by British Railways and was seconded to this college on Riversdale Road to

SEX AND THE BEATLES

'That's why most musicians are on stage, to get a little extra. I'd say that was the incentive for any performer. In the very early days when we were playing dance halls, there was a certain type that would be available at the end of the night. Most kids would go home with their boyfriend or whatever, but there was always a small group that just went for the performer. They didn't care whether it was a comedian or a man who ate glass. Actually the people who work for rock groups get most action. They audition the groupies. They say, "If you want to see Elvis Presley, you'll have to see me first."' John quoted in the *Daily Express*, 27 April 1975, taken from a radio interview in the US with Tom Snyder

complete his formal education before taking up a messenger job with British Railways. The college has since been demolished.

3 Roach Avenue, Knowsley

The McCartneys moved from Broadway Avenue, Wallasey, in 1943 to this small, prefabricated home on the Knowsley Estate on the outskirts of Liverpool. These homes came in kit form and were made of recycled aluminium and scrap metal from the wartime salvage. Thousands of these temporary houses were erected in the 1940s, since so many homes had been destroyed in the war. They were built to last about ten years, though some have lasted for decades and are only now being demolished.

4 Rodney Street, Liverpool

The Harley Street of Liverpool is the office of several private doctors. It was here in a private nursing home that Brian Samuel Epstein was born on 19 September 1934.

Birthplace of Brian Epstein.

Rosebery Street, Toxteth

This was the site of one of the first proper gigs for The Quarrymen, when they played from the back of a lorry at a street party on Saturday 22 June 1957. The gig was arranged through Colin

Hanton's friend Charles Roberts. Julia Baird remembers them calling themselves Johnny and the Rainbows because they sported different-coloured shirts. It was also here that John's poor eyesight meant he was staring hard to see who was standing in front of him. This glare was misunderstood for aggression. Word went round that the lads in the crowd were going to 'get Lennon'. As soon as they had finished playing, the boys dived into their friend's house and called the police, who escorted them to safety.

First photographs of John and his group.

(M.V.) *Royal Iris*, River Mersey

The famous Mersey Ferry hosted many four-hour dance cruises on the Mersey, starting at The Pier Head. These 'Riverboat Shuffles' were originally jazz cruises, with rock 'n' roll and Merseybeat bands joining a little later. The Beatles made their first appearance on the *Royal Iris* on 25 August 1961 (second on the bill to jazz clarinettist Acker Bilk). The Beatles would go on to make three further cruises in 1962, on 6 July, 10 August and 28 September.

Ferry 'cross the Mersey.

Royal Liverpool Children's Hospital, Myrtle Street

Just before his seventh birthday, Richard Starkey was rushed here by ambulance with stomach pains. It was soon discovered that he had appendicitis, which then developed into peritonitis, leaving him in a coma. The hospital was located close to the fruit shop in Myrtle Street where Elsie Starkey, Ringo's mum, worked for a short time.

Royal Liverpool Children's Hospital, Telegraph Road

When diagnosed with tuberculosis (TB) in his early teens, Ringo was sent across the River Mersey to this hospital on the Wirral, with its dedicated wing for those young people suffering with TB. It was here that young Ringo developed his fascination with the drums when participating in music lessons.

This is where Ringo decided to become a drummer.

Rushworth's Music House, Whitechapel

Situated on the corner of Whitechapel and Richmond Street, this store was once the biggest musical instrument suppliers in Liverpool, supplying guitars to many Merseybeat bands including The Beatles. They managed to import John and George's special Gibson guitars from America. Chairman James Rushworth presented John and George with the guitars before they set off on tour. Rushworth's was the place that Jim McCartney had brought a young Paul McCartney.

Became the important musical instrument store for The Beatles.

11 Scargreen Avenue, Fazakerley

This was Jim McCartney's family home in Fazakerley, where he lived with his parents Joe and Florrie McCartney. This is where he met Mary Mohin, his future wife. She had been staying temporarily with Jim's sister Jin and her husband. An air raid forced them to spend the night cuddled together in the shelter. Mary was 31 and Jim was 39 when they married.

97 School Lane, Woolton

After Julia Lennon was killed, John Dykins moved from their home at 1 Blomfield Road to this address, where his daughters would visit. He also invited John to pop in whenever he wanted and gave him a spare key. John would often bring Paul and listen to records on 'Twitchy's' record player.

17 Sedberg Grove, Huyton

When Stuart's family first moved from Edinburgh, they set up home here. Stuart's sister Pauline was born at this address in 1944.

Stuart Sutcliffe comes to Liverpool.

Sefton General Hospital, Wavertree

Sefton General Hospital on Smithdown Road was the main hospital for the south end of the city. The site has now been replaced by an ASDA supermarket (part of the Wal-Mart group), with new homes built on the rest of the property. During its heyday, many Beatle-related events took place at the hospital. Rod Davis of The Quarrymen was born here on 7 November 1941; George Smith, Mimi's husband and John Lennon's uncle, was rushed to here from Mendips and died on 5 June 1955; this was where Julia Lennon was taken after she was hit by an off-duty policeman on Menlove Avenue on 15 July 1958 – she was pronounced dead on arrival; Julia's partner, John 'Bobby' Dykins, also died here, in 1966 after a road accident on Penny Lane; Len Garry was rushed here by ambulance, unconscious, in 1958 and spent seven months in the hospital with tubercular meningitis, ending his career with The Quarrymen; Stuart Sutcliffe visited the hospital after returning from Hamburg in 1961 and saw a neurosurgeon who didn't detect anything wrong with him after examining the X-rays – not long after his visit, Stuart died; Cynthia Lennon gave birth to Julian on Monday 8 April 1963 at 7.45am with John exclaiming on seeing his son, 'Who's going to be a famous little rocker like his dad, then?' They arranged a private room for Cynthia, but it was surrounded by glass windows. Many faces appeared at the glass, looking at the new Liverpool celebrity, John Lennon. It was Cynthia's first taste of what it would be like living in the public eye. The main hospital building has been demolished.

A mixture of sadness and joy.

Sir Thomas White Gardens, Everton

After a short stay at the prefabricated bungalow on Roach Avenue, Knowsley, the McCartneys moved here in 1944. This was the first home that came with Mary's new job as a district nurse and midwife. Soon after, the family moved to Western Avenue in Speke. This estate of high-rise flats has since been demolished.

Another one of the McCartney homes.

Speke Airport, Speke

As a boy, John Lennon rode his bike to the airport to watch the planes take off and land. John 'Bobby' Dykins, Julia Lennon's partner, worked as the manager at the airport's restaurant and secured John a job there. This is no longer Liverpool's airport since the site has moved a short distance to the edge of Speke. It is now called Liverpool John Lennon Airport. The old terminal building is now a hotel, which has won several design awards. On Friday 10 July 1964, The Beatles returned to a triumphant crowd at Speke Airport where they gave a press conference. That was followed by a drive through the streets of Liverpool flanked by cheering fans to their civic reception at the Liverpool Town Hall. George Harrison recalled an incident at the airport when The Beatles' plane aborted a take-off. As they were taking off again, the emergency door flew off. He was a white-knuckled passenger and hated flying. This incident did nothing to help.

Get Back home to Liverpool boys.

St Aloysius Church, Huyton

The Quarrymen appeared at the church's Youth Club in September 1957.

43 St Anne's Road, Huyton

Stuart's family moved to this address in 1950.

St Barnabas Church Hall, Penny Lane

St Barnabas Church Hall was a popular dance venue where John and his friends would meet. Now called Dovedale Towers, the dance hall was affectionately known locally as 'Barnys'. Quarrymen drummer Colin Hanton remembers it well. 'Barnys was a great place, and if you didn't have a tie on you didn't get in. There was a dress code – very different from today. You had to get past the doormen – I think the police ran it – and if you couldn't dance, you just stood against the wall. There was no alcohol served, just cold drinks. We usually went to the pub beforehand. John's mum Julia came to see us here at the Vespa Scooter Club Dance – she was the only one at the side of

PRESS CONFERENCE GEMS

The Beatles were known for their quick wit when replying to questions at press conferences – some of course seemed much funnier at the time than they do now, years later in cold print. But they do have a period charm.

'Ringo, why do you wear all those rings on your fingers?'
'Because I can't get them through my nose.'

'Which is the biggest threat to your career? The H bomb or dandruff?'
'The H Bomb. We've already got dandruff.'

'I don't suppose I think much about the future. I don't really give a damn. Though now we've made it, it would be a pity to get bombed.' John

'The French have not made up their minds about The Beatles. What do you think of them?'
'Oh we like The Beatles.' John

'Why do you not sing "ooooh" in "I Want to Hold Your Hand"?'
'We'd washed our hair that day and left all the oooos in the shampoooo.'

'We've discovered a new kind word for Ringo – drummer.'

'As you can't read music, how do you remember the notes of your songs?'
'We buy copies of our records '

'What are you going to do with your gold discs?'
'We're keeping them to pawn when we're old and poor.'

'Who has the longest fringe?'
'We once took out a tape measure,' replied Paul, 'but George was last in the queue and he cheated by growing some more while we were measuring the others. Actually, I won – the others say it's because I have the biggest head.'

'George is wearing a wig borrowed from a slightly larger head than his. He borrowed it from John. It must be the only wig in the world with dandruff.'

'When Ringo joined The Beatles he even had a ring through his nose, but it had to be removed. He kept catching his drumsticks in it.'

'Have you any plans to meet the Johnson girls?' [daughters of then US President Lyndon Johnson]
'We didn't know they were on the show.' John

'Why do you think you are so popular all of a sudden?'
'I don't know. It could just be the weather.' John

the stage clapping. We were pretty rubbish but we enjoyed it.'

One of the few occasions Julia watched her son perform.

St Barnabas Church, Penny Lane

Opposite the 'shelter in the middle of the round-about' of Penny Lane is St Barnabas Church, which opened in February 1914. The 'Penny Lane' video of the single includes an aerial shot of the roundabout from the top of the church tower. It was at St Barnabas that Paul remembered singing in the choir. Brian Johnson, who joined the St Barnabas Church choir back in1953 and is still a member, believes that Paul sang occasionally, but there are no records to prove that he was a long-term member of the choir. Paul returned to the church on 29 May 1982, when he was best man at his brother Mike's wedding.

Paul's training in the choir stalls at Penny Lane.

St Charles Catholic Church, Aigburth

It was at St Charles Church on Aigburth Road that Paul's maternal grandparents, Owen Mohin and Mary Teresa Danher, were married. Owen came to Liverpool from Ireland, via Glasgow.

St Edward's College, West Derby

The Beatles made a Sunday evening appearance here at a dance, sometime around October 1961. St Edward's is still one of the leading schools in Liverpool.

St Gabriel's Church, Huyton

Stuart's family attended this church in Huyton Quarry, where nine-year-old Stuart joined the choir. Stuart was the head chorister and sang at three services every Sunday, at weddings and other special occasions. He was also confirmed here into the Church of England. Stuart died in Hamburg, aged 21, on 10 April 1962 and his funeral service was held at St Gabriel's.

Stuart's singing education.

St George's Hall, Lime Street

This neoclassical building dominates its surroundings. Designed by Harvey Lonsdale Elmes, it was built to hold Liverpool's musical events in a grand ballroom that had an ornate mosaic floor. In a bid to recreate the Chelsea Ball, Allan Williams rented St George's Hall for a party. He arranged for Stuart and John to create a few floats for the ball with some help from Paul and George. They created a magnificent guitar-shaped float, which was destroyed at the end of the evening. In 1980 on the plateau in front of St George's Hall, an estimated 25,000 people congregated after the death of John Lennon. Fans also gathered here after the announcement that George had died in 2001.

St John's Hall, Snaefell Avenue, Tuebrook

This church hall hosted the first of 11 shows by The Beatles on 17 February 1961, running through to 8 September of the same year. The shows were often promoted by Mona Best's 'Casbah Promotions'. In their performance on 17 August, in the style of a solo singer, Paul ditched his bass guitar for the night and performed his vocals unburdened by any instrument. The Big Three's bassist, Johnny Gustafson, filled in for him.

St John's Hall, Oriel Road, Bootle

The Beatles made five appearances at this venue, opposite Bootle Town Hall, the first on 6 January

1961 and the last on 30 July 1962. The dances were run by promoter Dave Forshaw, who operated from this location as the Blue Penguin Club, which had a membership and therefore could be licensed. As a club they were also allowed to hold dances on Sundays.

St Luke's Hall, Crosby

The Quarrymen appeared here once in November 1957, at the Youth Club opposite the church. Ringo also appeared here with The Eddie Clayton Skiffle Group. It was a popular venue for the Liverpool bands.

St Paul's Presbyterian Church Hall, Youth Club, North Road, Birkenhead

The Beatles made two appearances here, on 10 February and 10 March 1962. The building has since been demolished. A short film of The Beatles' first appearance here was recently unearthed, and can be seen on the *Pete Best Of The Beatles* DVD. It was one of the earliest known films of the group and the only time they were filmed wearing their leather suits.

St Peter's Church, Woolton

St Peter's Church is famous as the site where John Lennon met Paul McCartney. Paul had been invited by a mutual friend of his and John's, classmate Ivan Vaughan, to watch The Quarrymen play at the church summer fete. The date was 6 July 1957. The rest is history…

This auspicious meeting is not, however, the church's only Beatles link. Lennon attended Sunday School from the age of eight. Most of the original Quarrymen attended St Peter's – Rod Davis, Pete Shotton, Ivan Vaughan and Nigel Walley. Eric Griffiths married in the church in 1963. John sang in the church choir with friends Pete Shotton, Nigel Walley and Dave Ashton.

They only did it for the half-a-crown payment. John spent most of the time inventing words and his own 'harmonies' to the hymns. The boys attended rehearsal one evening during the week, singing at two services on Sundays, and also for funerals and weddings, for which they were paid extra. John and Pete had the distinction of being thrown out of the choir for continually being disruptive and giggling.

Following his own free will, according to his Aunt Mimi, John was confirmed at the age of 15 into the Church of England at St Peter's. His confirmation was for materialistic reasons, Lennon later said, thinking he'd better do something in case he 'didn't make it'. Lennon was also a member, for a short time, of a Boy Scout group that met here.

John Lennon's Uncle George, husband of Mimi, is buried in St Peter's graveyard. When John Lennon saw the gravestone, he discovered that his Uncle George Smith's middle name was 'Toogood' and that his ancestors were the Toogoods from Woolton. He was so proud that he showed the grave to all his friends. It was too good to be true. If John had showed Paul this family memorial, could he not also have seen the Eleanor Rigby gravestone, which is located at St Peter's? Paul later admitted to author Barry Miles that he must have seen the gravestone in his youth because The Quarrymen played at the Youth Club quite often. Therefore, it could have been hidden in his subconscious, unlocked years later by a series of completely unconnected events.

Eleanor Rigby, who died on 10 October 1939, aged 44, lived in Pit Place, just off Quarry Street in Woolton. In 1990, McCartney donated an accounts register from Liverpool's City Hospital to charity – revealing that an E. Rigby worked there.

The document has been signed by her, suggesting she was a scullery maid. Not far from Eleanor Rigby's grave is a headstone with the name of

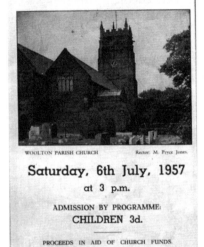

GARDEN FETE
ST. PETER'S CHURCH FIELD

WOOLTON PARISH CHURCH   Rector: M. Pryce Jones.

Saturday, 6th July, 1957
at 3 p.m.

ADMISSION BY PROGRAMME:

CHILDREN 3d.

PROCEEDS IN AID OF CHURCH FUNDS.

Historic stuff – the programme for the church fete in 1957 when John met Paul for the first time.

PROGRAMME

STALLS — **SIDESHOWS** — **ICE CREAM** — **LEMONADE**

Teas and Refreshments in large Marquee situated behind the hut.

2-00 p.m. PROCESSION leaves Church Road, via Allerton Road, Kings Drive, Hunt's Cross Avenue; returning to the Church Field.
Led by the Band of the Cheshire Yeomanry.
Street Collection by the Youth Club during the procession.

3-00 p.m. CROWNING OF THE ROSE QUEEN (Miss Sally Wright) by Mrs. THELWALL JONES.

3-10 p.m. FANCY DRESS PARADE.
Class 1. Under 7 years.
Class 2. 7 to 12 years.
Class 3. Over 12 years.
Entrants to report to Miss P. Fuller at the Church Hall before the procession.

3-30 p.m. to 5-00 p.m. MUSICAL SELECTIONS by the Band of the Cheshire (Earl of Chester) Yeomanry. Bandmaster: H. Abraham.
(By permission of Lt.-Col. G. C. V. Churton, M.C., M.B.E.).

4-15 p.m. THE QUARRY MEN SKIFFLE GROUP.

5-15 p.m. DISPLAY by the City of Liverpool Police Dogs. By kind permission of the Chief Constable and Watch Committee.

5-45 p.m. THE QUARRY MEN SKIFFLE GROUP.

8-0 p.m.   GRAND DANCE in the CHURCH HALL

GEORGE EDWARDS BAND also The Quarry Men Skiffle Group

TICKETS 2/-

REFRESHMENTS AT MODERATE PRICES.

McKenzie – the last name of the priest in the song. Did Paul come across that as well? Years later another McKenzie, Tom McKenzie, entered the world of The Beatles. Tom worked for two years as a compère, PA transporter and host at many Beatles gigs around Liverpool. The musicians referred to him as 'Father' McKenzie and there is a plaque dedicated to his memory in Cavern Walks. Father McKenzie once reported that during a conversation with The Beatles, he had told them how, during the war, he would darn his socks in order to keep awake while on air raid watch. So are these pure coincidences or subliminal influences?

Thank you Ivan Vaughan for bringing Paul to meet John.

St Peter's Church Hall, Woolton

It was here that Ivan Vaughan brought his school friend Paul McCartney to meet his childhood friend John Lennon. After Paul played 'Twenty Flight Rock' and 'Long Tall Sally' to John on Lennon's own guitar – and played it upside down – John decided that Paul should join his group.

The most important audition in Beatles history.

St Silas Church, Dingle

St Silas Church, situated on the corner of Admiral Street and High Park Street, was built in 1864. As a boy, Alf Lennon with his sister and brothers was christened here and then sent to Sunday School. Ringo's parents were married at the church in 1936 and Richy was christened here in July 1940 and attended Sunday School from the age of four. He was also a member of the church choir. The church suffered bomb damage during October 1940 – when Richy was three months old – and was closed until December 1942. It was

finally closed in 1952 and demolished in 1954. Years later Ringo made a generous donation to the church of 'St Philemon with St Silas' – after the two parishes were combined – towards a minibus for the older members. St Silas was the church affiliated with Peel Hall Orange Lodge, and was where they would hold their services.

St Silas School, Dingle

Ringo's primary school was St Silas School on High Park Street – just 200 yards from the top of Admiral Grove. Ringo was five when he started here in 1945, though his schooling was disrupted by illness. St Silas was erected in 1870. It was a red Victorian building, one of the National Schools erected by the Church of England to teach children reading, writing, arithmetic and religion. A fellow classmate of his was Ronnie Wycherley, who later achieved fame as Billy Fury. He had many hit records and it was for the chance to back Billy Fury that The Silver Beatles auditioned at the Wyvern Club. Having missed a whole school year through illness, Richy fell behind. He was considered almost illiterate and was taught with the children in the year below. This wasn't enough and his mum asked her neighbour's daughter, Marie Maguire, to come in a couple of times a week to help with his reading and writing.

Was great when he was there, but Ringo missed a lot of school.

Stanley Abattoir, Prescot Road

Not a person as one Beatles fan thought, but a place. The Quarrymen appeared at this meat slaughterhouse in 1957, at the social club, and made such a cacophonous noise that they were never invited back.

One of the strangest venues, and probably best forgotten.

Starline Club, Toxteth

The Starline Club was a former cinema that stood behind the pub on the corner of Windsor Street and Upper Warwick Street. It was a popular rehearsal hall for The Beatles back in 1961, but it has since been demolished.

Stevedores & Docker's Club, Anfield

One of the undated appearances by The Quarrymen was here, accompanied on piano by John Duff Lowe.

Stockton Wood Primary School, Speke

Built on the new Speke Estate, Stockton Wood Primary School was opened in 1940. It was just a short walk from the McCartneys' home on Western Avenue, and Paul was enrolled there. However, once the number of pupils reached the 1,500 mark, he and many others were moved to Joseph Williams School in Netherley. The old school was finally demolished in 2005 with a new school building erected on the site of the original playing fields.

Paul was a good schoolboy.

Storyville Jazz Club, Temple Street

(see Iron Door)

Strawberry Field, Woolton

Strawberry Field (not Fields) was a Salvation Army children's home in Beaconsfield Road off Menlove Avenue. Much has been written about this place made famous in the song. The earliest reference to Strawberry Field dates to 1870. Originally it was a field where strawberries were grown. A wealthy ship-owner, George Warren, purchased the land and built the house. Later, Alexander C. Mitchell, another shipping magnate, owned the property

until his death in 1927. His widow sold the estate to the Salvation Army in 1934. The charity was able to purchase the mansion and convert it to a home for approximately forty homeless girls from the poorest slums of Liverpool, most of whom were orphans, using a legacy from Mary Fowler, a Liverpool woman. On 7 July 1936, the house and grounds were opened by Commissioner Bates in the presence of General Evangeline Booth, who was the fourth General of the Salvation Army, and daughter of William Booth, the founder.

It was the fourth home of its kind opened in England by the Salvation Army. In the mid-1950s, boys under five years of age were taken into the Strawberry Field home. Later, older boys were admitted. Thinking about Strawberry Field, Lennon recalled, 'I used to go to garden parties as a kid with my friends Nigel and Pete. We would go there and hang out and find empty lemonade bottles and get a penny back on them. We always had fun at Strawberry Field.'

Lennon commented that he felt he had something in common with the children there; his dad had left him and his mum had given him away, so he too was without his parents. The Vale Road entrance to Strawberry Field had a high wall, which to John was the real Strawberry Field – not the famous red gates on Beaconsfield Road. Once they scaled the wall, John and his friends played for hours in the grounds. Much to Mimi's displeasure, John played with the children from the home. Mimi didn't want her little boy playing 'with the commoners'. John enjoyed gathering conkers from the large horse chestnut trees on the grounds.

The only time John and his friends visited the big house at Strawberry Field was when they attended the annual summer fete. They later admitted to stealing items from the stalls. Bill Parr remembers that the unmarried mothers who lived in the small cottage in the grounds sent signals to boys. If the coast was clear to come over the wall, the girls hung out a piece of washing on the line. If it was blue, it was the signal to stay away. If not, they were made welcome. They were known locally by the lads as the 'naughty girls'. The early 1970s saw the demolition of the original house and the erection of the Salvation Army's first purpose-built home for children. Major Ida Cawthorne was at Strawberry Field in 1973 and she recalled, 'We had a large amount of ground so we sold some of the land in order to fund the building of a modern house for the children. The site of the old house was turned into a play area with slides and swings. The adults were a bit sorry to see the house go, but the children were thrilled with the new building.'

In 1979, the Beatles connection was renewed when new accommodation for staff and older boys and girls was named Lennon Court following a donation from John. John had promised his son Sean that one day he would take him to Strawberry Field, but his death meant he was unable to do so. However, John's widow Yoko Ono did not let his promise go unfulfilled. In 1984, almost fifty years after General Evangeline Booth's motorcade stopped off at Strawberry Field for its opening, a three-car cavalcade brought Yoko and Sean to John's childhood haunt. The pair made two visits that day. During the first visit, the children were not present as they were at school, though hordes of reporters and camera crews were. At the end of the visit, Yoko asked the officer in charge, Captain David Botting, if she and Sean might return privately that evening. This time there was no press, but the children were home from school. Yoko signed autographs for them and looked at their homework and drawings, while Sean played games with the children. Before leaving, Yoko told the kids, 'John loved this place. He was just an ordinary Liverpool lad.'

The children's charity called 'Merseycats', formed by Merseybeat musicians from the sixties, has been supporting Strawberry Field for many years, including paying for the construction of a new playground, which was opened in 2000 to mark what would have been John's sixtieth birthday. In January 2005, the Salvation Army announced the closure of Strawberry Field, an action that was initially condemned. However, the nature of modern childcare has changed dramatically and there were only three children in residence with some 25 coming in on weekends for respite care. Social Services and the Salvation Army acknowledged that the place for children should be within a loving family, and so they placed all the children within foster families. Discussions are ongoing at present as to the long-term future use of the site, a process that Beatles fans want to be involved in. On 31 May 2005, Strawberry Field closed its doors as a children's home for good. The Salvation Army still owns the site.

Strawberry Field where everything is real.

10 Sunbury Road, Anfield

Jim and Mary McCartney moved to this address after they exchanged wedding vows in April 1941. It was here in June 1942 that a newborn James Paul McCartney was brought home from the nearby Walton hospital.

Paul's first home.

Technical College Hall, Borough Road, Birkenhead

The Beatles made three consecutive Friday night appearances here from 9 February 1962. It is located on Borough Road, one of the main thoroughfares leading out of Birkenhead. On one occasion, Epstein remembered calling for each of The Beatles to pick them up for the concert, and Paul informed him that he was not ready. They could not wait for him, making that the only time a group member refused to play or missed a concert. The college was demolished in 2005.

86 The Northern Road, Crosby

When Julia Lennon gave birth to a baby girl at Elmswood Nursing Home, she was adopted, had her name changed to Ingrid Pederson, and came to live here with her adoptive parents.

Sadness for Julia Lennon, Victoria and for John, but thankfully Ingrid had a happy home.

2 Third Avenue, Fazakerley

Paul's mother, Mary Mohin, was born here on 29 September 1909. Mary's mother died in childbirth when Mary was only four years old. Her father Owen remarried soon after, but Mary didn't get on with her new stepmother, and lived with an aunt.

Thistle Cafe, Banks Road, West Kirby

This 1 February 1962 appearance, in Macdonna Hall, above the cafe, was The Beatles' first gig under Brian Epstein's management, arranged through promoter Sam Leach. Panic had set in when Epstein found out that John Lennon had laryngitis. Epstein was ready to cancel the gig, billed as 'The Grand Opening of The Beatles Club', but Leach insisted the show must go on. At Leach's recommendation, Epstein picked up Rory Storm, who stood in for John at this concert. And so, Epstein's first line-up as Beatles manager was Paul, George, Pete and Rory Storm. The fee was £18, of which Epstein received 10 per cent, which just about covered his petrol and expenses.

Coinciding with their recent change in style (leather jackets were out, matching suits were in) and new management, the group introduced a new repertoire for this performance, one that would feature over their next set of concerts.

Tower Ballroom, New Brighton, Wallasey

One of the biggest concerts The Beatles ever did in the UK was at this New Brighton venue, situated on the other side of the River Mersey to Liverpool. *Operation Big Beat*, the brainchild of promoter Sam Leach, brought together the best groups on Merseyside and showcased the incredible talent in the area. With an estimated crowd of over 4,000, there was nowhere like it in the area. The first *Operation Big Beat* was on 10 November 1961, the band's first appearance here. Recalling their early performances at the Tower Ballroom, Paul commented, 'When we played outside Liverpool, as often as not we would hire a couple of coaches and take an audience with us. On any of those dates … we had to work hard to please our audience, but sometimes we couldn't do it. We either went down a treat, or very badly.'

The Beatles played here 27 times, including an Epstein-organised, 12-act extravaganza on 12 October 1962, headlined by one of The Beatles' rock 'n' roll heroes, Little Richard. 'When I first saw The Beatles,' Richard admitted, 'I didn't think they'd make it. Brian Epstein booked me to play with them and Paul would sit down and look at me. He'd say, "Oh, Richard, you're my idol. Just let me touch you." He wanted to learn my little holler, so we sat at the piano going, "Oooooo," until he got it.'

The band's final appearance here was on 14 June 1963, the penultimate date of the *Mersey Beat Showcase* concerts.

With the biggest UK audience in their formative years, and so close to home, the Tower Ballroom was the place to be seen.

'Treetops', Glenrose Road, Gateacre

This was the house where Brian Epstein's parents Harry and 'Queenie' moved to in the sixties. After Brian's death, The Beatles returned from a trip to Bangor to visit Queenie at home to offer their condolences. She asked them not to come to the funeral because she felt their presence would draw a large crowd and wouldn't be appropriate. They respected her wishes and mourned in silence.

18 Trinity Road, Hoylake

This was Cynthia Powell's family home. Because her marriage to John was kept secret, Cynthia took Julian to her mother's. Once the press found out where she was living, a throng of journalists and photographers camped outside the home, desperate for a story and photo of Mrs Lennon and her baby.

John's future wife lived here.

53 Ullet Road, Wavertree

The Sutcliffe family moved to this address on the edge of Sefton Park. It was here that Stuart returned having been beaten up after the gig at Lathom Hall. His face was smothered in blood with extensive bruising on his forehead. His mum remembers Stuart coming home and practically collapsing in his bed. When she went to wake him in the morning, the pillow was covered in blood. Stuart refused to see a doctor. It was only on his return from Hamburg after he had been suffering with headaches that he was convinced to get medical help. This is also where Astrid stayed on her first visit to Liverpool, but Astrid and Stuart were not allowed to sleep together. Soon after they moved to stay with Allan Williams and his wife.

25 Upton Green, Speke

The Harrisons moved here from Arnold Grove in January 1950. In contrast to the two-up, two-down terraced house of Arnold Grove, Upton Green was not only new, but also much bigger. George had a 20-minute walk from Upton Green to the bus stop, which was close to Paul's house on Western Avenue, and they became friends, riding on the same bus to school. George's mum was always keen to encourage her son's musical talent. George and Paul often played Lonnie Donegan songs together in the house, and later John and Paul would regularly call round to practise. George remembered that the first time he heard 'Love Me Do' on Radio Luxembourg, he was in his bedroom at Upton Green. He described it as the best buzz of all time.

This is where George obsessed over his guitar playing and perfected his skill.

84 Vale Road 'Vega', Woolton

The home of Ivan Vaughan, the friend of John Lennon who would go down in Beatles history as the one who introduced his new school friend Paul McCartney to his childhood friend John Lennon at St Peter's Church on 6 July 1957.

John's first friend in Woolton lived here; without him we wouldn't have The Beatles.

Victoria Hall, off Village Road, Higher Bebington

The Beatles played in this small Wirral town on 4 August 1962. A plaque on this village hall commemorates the occasion.

Walker Art Gallery, William Brown Street

Stuart Sutcliffe's work entitled *Summer Painting* was selected for the John Moores Liverpool Exhibition in 1959. It was the only student piece accepted. Moores, a Littlewoods Pools millionaire, bought Stu's painting for £65. It was with this money that Stuart made a down payment on an electric bass guitar and joined his friend John Lennon's group. This painting was in fact one portion. The other half never made it down from Stuart's Percy Street flat and rotted outside the back door for months. Two years after his death, the gallery held an exhibition of Stuart's work. In 1984, local Beatles historians Ron Jones and Mike Evans curated a similar show called *The Art of The Beatles*, which was opened by Cynthia Lennon.

The art exhibition where Stuart sold his painting and enabled him to join the group and name them Beatals.

Walton Hospital, Rice Lane

This hospital was originally built in 1868 as a workhouse. James Paul McCartney was born there on 18 June 1942. His mother was given a private ward because she was a nurse at the hospital. Paul had a difficult delivery and he was born with white asphyxia, which is a lack of oxygen, and had to be resuscitated. Paul's brother Mike was also born here on 7 January 1944.

Birthplace of James Paul McCartney.

Wavertree Town Hall, High Street

The Quarrymen appeared at this venue, located near George Harrison's home at Arnold Grove, several times during 1957 and 1958, though no record was kept of the dates. It was also where George's birth was registered. There is still the motto above the door, which reads 'Sub umbra floresco', which translates to 'I flourish in the shade'. The motto is quite appropriate for George Harrison, the Beatle who flourished in the shade of John Lennon and Paul McCartney to become a great songwriter in

his own right. This former Town Hall is now a pub with function rooms for hire.

Wellington Pub, Garston

This was one of the places where Ringo's mum Elsie worked to make ends meet.

72 Western Avenue, Speke

The McCartney family moved to this two-bedroom house on Western Avenue when Paul was four, and lived here from 1947 to 1950. They had to move to Ardwick Road when Mary resigned as a midwife.

The first McCartney home in Speke.

White Star Pub, Rainford Gardens

The Beatles sometimes visited this pub after appearing at the Cavern. The White Star was named after the famous shipping line, for which both George's father Harry and John's father Alf worked as stewards.

Wilson Hall, Garston

Paul made his debut appearance with The Quarrymen here, apart from a few unrecorded performances at St Peter's Church. George Harrison was invited to watch a Quarrymen gig here on 7 December 1957, and afterwards George auditioned for John and was invited to join the band. Ringo had also appeared at the venue with the Eddie Clayton Skiffle Group. The building is now a carpet warehouse.

George passed the audition.

Winter Gardens, Garston

The Quarrymen appeared here once in June 1957 at this Co-operative Society hall, tucked away in the back streets of Garston.

Woolton Cinema, Woolton

Situated in Mason Street in Woolton Village, this cinema became the regular haunt of Lennon and his Quarrymen gang. They named it the 'Bug House' and feasted on westerns and Jerry Lewis comedies on Saturday mornings. 'The Picture House', as it was originally known, is a one-screen cinema yards round the corner from St Peter's Church. The cinema opened on Boxing Day 1927 and survived World War II and the multiplex invasion of the eighties and nineties.

Woolton Quarry, Woolton

At the heart of Woolton just behind where John, Ivan, Nigel and Pete lived was this quarry, which was part of the reason for the name for their new skiffle group – The Quarrymen. There was a public footpath through the quarry from Church Road, which Colin, Rod and Eric used to cross from the other side for the village when going to John or Pete's house for rehearsals. The quarry was active until about 1950. On the top of the quarry is St Peter's Church, and the field where The Quarrymen played and were watched by a teenage Paul McCartney, who toyed with the idea of joining them.

The quarry at the heart of The Quarrymen's Woolton.

Woolton Village Club, Woolton

The Quarrymen played here on Saturday 24 January 1959. This was the last known booking for them and the group effectively disbanded after this gig. Woolton was the birth and now appeared to be the death of The Quarrymen.

Could have been the end.

Wyvern Club, Seel Street

The date 10 May 1960 marks the birth of The Silver Beatles, when they performed under that name for the first time, at an audition here in front of the London-based music promoter Larry Parnes. He had travelled to Liverpool to try out groups to back singer Billy Fury on a tour of northern England and Scotland. Also auditioning were several other Liverpool acts, such as Cass and The Cassanovas, Cliff Roberts and The Rockers, Derry and The Seniors and Gerry and The Pacemakers. Fury himself was present at the auditions, during which John asked him for his signature. Although they weren't successful in securing the top booking, and despite The Silver Beatles' drummer Tommy Moore showing up late, forcing Johnny Hutchinson of Cass and The Cassanovas to sit in with them until Moore arrived, Parnes still liked what he saw and called eight days later offering the group the chance to go on their first ever tour – a seven-date trip of Scotland, backing singer Johnny Gentle (see Alloa entry).

A typical set-list for this period, prior to their Scottish dates with Johnny Gentle, would usually feature a selection from the following: Johnny B. Goode, Gone Gone Gone, Ain't She Sweet, Hallelujah, I Love Her So, Carol, Sweet Little Sixteen, Milk Cow Blues, Move It On Over, Your True Love, Blue Suede Shoes, Honey Don't, Lend Me Your Comb, Dance In The Street, Up A Lazy River, Somebody Like Me, Home, Winston's Walk (Lennon/McCartney), Catswalk (McCartney-composed instrumental, later retitled 'Cat Call' – see Cavern entry for 7 October 1962), Roc-A-Chicka, Be Bop A Lula, What'd I Say, Down The Line, I Don't Care (If The Sun Don't Shine), Whole Lotta Shakin' Goin' on.

The Wyvern Club was later renamed the Blue Angel after the Roy Orbison hit (or possibly the Marlene Dietrich film).

The start they needed, which led to their first tour and soon after it, Hamburg.

Ye Cracke, Rice Street,

John and Cynthia often met at this pub, near the Liverpool Art College, for drinks. John and Stu also met here with friends Bill Harry and Rod Murray to discuss art and were known as 'The Dissenters'. A plaque has now been erected to commemorate the meetings.

A meeting of minds.

YMCA, Birkenhead Road, Hoylake

Located near Cynthia Powell's home. The group's only appearance here was on 24 February 1962. It was a bad night for them and they were booed off stage. The building has since been demolished.

YMCA, Whetstone Lane, Birkenhead

The Beatles performed here once, on 8 September 1962, going on later the same evening to play the Majestic Ballroom, also in Birkenhead.

Zodiac Club, Duke Street

This coffee house was a popular venue for local bands, including The Beatles. The club also played host to an impromptu jam session that included The Beatles, The Big Three, Rory Storm and The Hurricanes and Gerry and The Pacemakers. It has since been demolished.

LONDON

The Beatles were born in Liverpool, grew up in Hamburg but matured in London under the watchful eye of George Martin at Abbey Road Studios. London gave The Beatles a recording studio, access to radio, television, film and the press, plus a nightlife amongst the artists and national celebrities of the sixties.

33 Abbey Road

It was at the New London Synagogue on 17 October 1967 that the memorial service for Brian Epstein was held, so close to the studios where his boys had made their records. The four Beatles and everyone connected with The Beatles were in attendance.

Abbey Road Crossing

Is there a more famous pedestrian crossing in the world? Four men walking across a street doesn't sound the most inspirational idea ever, and yet it remains an iconic image to this day. John, Paul, George and Ringo stepped out at 11.35am on 8 August 1969 and were photographed doing so, as seen for ever on the *Abbey Road* cover. It was certainly easier than their first idea, which was to call the album *Everest* and photograph themselves on the world's tallest mountain. Photographer Iain MacMillan only took six shots in a ten-minute session, choosing the best for the cover image. MacMillan then drove along Abbey Road to photograph the road sign at the junction with Alexandra Road. London tour guide Richard Porter estimates that about one hundred and fifty thousand fans recreate this scene every year.

If you go to London you have to walk on the famous crossing.

Abbey Road Studios, 3 Abbey Road

Opened on 12 November 1931, Abbey Road Studios will forever be associated with some of the greatest names in music, from the classical music of Bach to singer Paul Robeson, Cliff Richard and The Shadows and, of course, The Beatles. Their

PRODUCERS FOR HIRE

John Lennon and Paul McCartney, just the one track but it was a US Top 10 hit.

'You've Got To Hide Your Love Away' by the Silkie (1965). Paul on rhythm guitar too.

John Lennon

Yoko Ono/Plastic Ono Band (1969), with Yoko Ono

The Pope Smokes Dope by David Peel and the Lower East Side (1972)

Elephant's Memory by Elephant's Memory (1972)

Approximately Infinite Universe, double album by Yoko Ono (1973). Including John and Mick Jagger on guitars.

Pussy Cats by Nilsson (1974)

Paul McCartney

'From Head To Toe' by The Escorts (1966)

'Got To Get You Into My Life' by Cliff Bennett and the Rebel Rousers (1966)

As Apollo C. Vermouth, 'I'm The Urban Spaceman' by The Bonzo Dog Doo-Dah Band (1968)

'Those Were The Days' by Mary Hopkin (1968)

'Thingumybob' (Lennon/McCartney composition) and 'Yellow Submarine' by The Black Dyke Mills Band (1968)

McGough & McGear by Roger McGough and Mike McGear (1968). The musicians include Jimi Hendrix and Graham Nash.

'Goodbye' by Mary Hopkin (1969)

'That's The Way God Planned It' by Billy Preston (1969)

Post Card by Mary Hopkin (1969)

'Come And Get It' by Badfinger (1969), a McCartney song

'Thumbin' A Ride' by Jackie Lomax (1969)

'Rosetta' by Fourmost (1969). Dave Lovelady deliberately played some bad piano on this session so that Macca would say, 'Here, I'll do it.'

'Liverpool Lou' by Scaffold (1974)

'Let's Love' by Peggy Lee (1974), a McCartney song

McGear by Mike McGear (1974)

Holly Days by Denny Laine (1977)

Three tracks on *Stop And Smell The Roses* by Ringo Starr (1981)

'Rockestra Theme' by Duane Eddy (1987)

'My Old Friend' by Carl Perkins (1996)

Wild Prairie by Linda McCartney (1998)

George Harrison

'Hare Krishna Mantra' by Hare Krishna Temple (1969)

That's The Way God Planned It by Billy Preston (1969)

Is This What You Want by Jackie Lomax (1969), includes Harrison song 'Sour Milk Sea'

Encouraging Words by Billy Preston (1970), includes original version of Harrison song 'My Sweet Lord'

Raga by Ravi Shankar (1971). Includes Ravi Shankar and Yehudi Menuhin working together.

Four tracks on *Straight Up* by Badfinger (1971), including hit 'Day After Day'

The Concert For Bangla Desh (1971)

'Try Some, Buy Some' by Ronnie Spector (1971)

'Sweet Music' by Lon and Derrek Van Eaton (1972)

'Down And Out' by Ringo Starr (1973)

As Hari Georgeson: *The Place I Love* by Splinter (1974)

As George 'Onothimagen' Harrison: 'Lumberjack Song' by Monty Python's Flying Circus (1975)

Ringo Starr

Executive producer, *Son Of Dracula* by Nilsson (1974)

first visit was on 6 June 1962, with the line-up John, Paul, George and Pete Best, for their first recording session with George Martin. Although The Beatles thought it had gone well, George Martin and his producer Ron Richards decided that Pete's drumming wasn't good enough for the record and told Brian that he would be using a session drummer in the next session. These remarks began the process for ending Pete Best's time with The Beatles. The Beatles returned to the studio on 4 September with Ringo Starr, but his drumming still wasn't enough to satisfy Martin. Another session was arranged for the following week, with Andy White, a popular session drummer, sitting in with John, Paul and George as they made their first record. The Beatles' very last session at Abbey Road was in January 1970 when they recorded 'I, Me, Mine'.

The Beatles were musicians and it was here that they made some of their greatest records.

Ad Lib, 7 Leicester Square

John was the first of The Beatles to venture to this new club, opened in 1964, which quickly became the place to be seen. Ringo soon started visiting and even proposed to Maureen Cox here. John, Cynthia, George and Pattie ended up here after they were given LSD without their knowledge at a dinner party. John and George hallucinated in the lift as it took them to the club on the top floor.

Less Said, Done.

Advision Recording Studio, 83 New Bond Street

John and Paul produced the single 'Lullaby' for the Apple band Grapefruit at this recording studio.

Aeolian Hall, 135-137 New Bond Street

This building, dating back to 1876, was leased by the BBC for their radio programmes. Starting on 24 May 1963, The Beatles recorded seven sessions here, the last being on 25 November 1964.

23 Albermarle Street

The Beatles' accountants, Bryce Hanmer, Isherwood & Company, were based here and handled everything for NEMS, Brian and The Beatles.

Allsop Place

The bus for the *Magical Mystery Tour* set off from here to begin their fun-filled journey.

Roll up roll up for the mystery tour.

Les Ambassadeurs, 5 Hamilton Place

As well as being used as one of the locations in *A Hard Day's Night*, The Beatles were interviewed in the walled garden of this exclusive club by Ed Sullivan on 17 April 1964. Ringo, John and Paul, plus their respective partners, attended a party here to celebrate the film *The Magic Christian*, in which Ringo had appeared.

American Embassy, 24–31 Grosvenor Square

On 15 May 1969, John arrived at the US Embassy to apply for a visa. However, he was unsuccessful, due to his conviction for marijuana possession the previous year.

John would, however, spend plenty of time in the US.

Anello & Davide, 96 Charing Cross Road

The world-famous Cuban heel 'Beatle boots' were created and sold at their premises here.

Annabel's, 44 Berkeley Square

Named after owner Mark Birley's wife, this was one of the most fashionable nightclubs in London and one of George's favourite hangouts.

Apple Boutique, 94 Baker Street

With tax of 95 per cent, The Beatles were advised to invest their money or see it go to the government. With Apple established, this boutique was their first venture. A group of designers from Holland, known as 'The Fool' – which should have given them a clue – offered every hippy accessory you could think of. George's sister-in-law, Jenny Boyd and Pete Shotton, John's best friend from Quarry Bank High School, were among the staff. The Fool also painted a mural on the side of the shop, though after protests it was removed. Only John and George attended the opening of the store on 7 December 1967. It was a disaster, and closed after only 8 months, with all of the stock given away. Above the shop, Apple Music Publishing was established, with a group called Grapefruit the first band to be signed to Apple Music Publishing, headed by Terry Doran. They soon moved premises to Wigmore Street.

Nice idea, but a retail disaster.

Apple Electronics, 34 Boston Place

John Alexis Mardas, known by The Beatles as 'Magic Alex', set up this research laboratory. Not a single one of his inventions ever made it to market, despite substantial investment by The Beatles.

The Apple money 'magically' disappeared.

Apple Headquarters, 3 Savile Row

The Beatles purchased this Mayfair building in 1968 to be the headquarters for their new company, Apple. The address of the Apple offices became well known, and a group of fans, known as the 'Apple Scruffs', would gather here religiously to see their favourite group. George Harrison recorded their story in his song 'Apple Scruffs', which appeared on his first solo album *All Things Must Pass*.

The Apple building was the location where, on 22 April 1969, John and Yoko chose to reaffirm their commitment to each other following their marriage, and when, in front of a commissioner for oaths, John officially changed his name to John Ono Lennon, finally ridding himself of his middle name 'Winston' that had dogged him all of his life.

The building is probably more famous for its staging of the famous rooftop concert on 30 January 1969, filmed for the concluding scene in the group's *Get Back/Let It Be* movie project. The Beatles chose this location for their performance, having rejected the chance to play in Tunisia, the Sahara Desert, at the Pyramids or on a cruise ship. (For much more information on this, see Day Nineteen: 30 January 1969 – Apple Headquarters (rooftop) in the *Let It Be* entry of *Movies* section.)

In May 2016, it was announced that a document from November 1980, relating to the sale of the building was to go under the hammer. It is one of the last documents signed by John Lennon, and likely to be the last thing signed by all four members of the band.

Classic, legendary, momentous, the core of Apple and where The Beatles bid farewell with their final 'live' appearance. Pity only a lucky few were able to see it.

Apple Tailoring (Civil and Theatrical), 161 King's Road

Although the Apple Boutique is better known, the boys also established another clothes shop on the premises of the former Dandie Fashions, run jointly by Apple and the executives of Dandie. The basement became a hairdressing salon and the new Beatles barber, Leslie Cavendish, operated from here. However, it came as no surprise that this Apple venture also failed not long after the first boutique had closed.

The Beatles were stitched up again.

Ashcroft & Daw, Charing Cross Road

While attending the Royal Academy of Dramatic Art (RADA) in 1956, Brian Epstein had a temporary job in this record store.

Asprey (Jewellers), 167 New Bond Street

One of the important scenes in The Beatles' film *Help!* is when Ringo enters this store, where one of the jewellers attempts to remove the ring from Ringo's finger with various implements without success.

Ringo running rings round the baddies.

Astoria Cinema, Finsbury Park

One of London's greatest rock venues, this former cinema at 232–236 Seven Sisters Road played host to The Beatles in 1963, 1964 and 1965. The building later became a boxing venue, and is now a Pentecostal church.

In 1963 The Beatles performed their Christmas show here. Seen by an estimated one hundred thousand people, the concerts were conceived and presented by manager, Brian Epstein, and directed by Peter Yolland, and comprised 30 shows in total between 24 December and 11 January (see Chronology for dates and number of shows). In order, the other acts on the bill were the singing comedy group The Barron Knights (featuring Duke D'Mond), singer Tommy Quickly, pop groups The Fourmost, Billy J. Kramer with The Dakotas, singer Cilla Black, and the Australian singer, TV and radio star, Rolf Harris. The Beatles naturally closed each show, with a performance of approximately 25 minutes. Sandwiched in between the support acts, to bring a pantomime feel to proceedings, The Beatles took to the stage to perform a number of light-hearted, but actually under-rehearsed, seasonal comedy sketches. The Beatles would host a second Christmas show one year later at the Hammersmith Odeon (see entry).

The Beatles returned to the Astoria on 1 November 1964 and played their last scheduled London concert here on 11 December 1965, just six days after their final appearance in Liverpool. A crowd of 3,040 saw each of the two shows that evening. During the second concert, just as they were about to come on stage, the lights dimmed and, with the start of 'Day Tripper' being played over the speakers, the compère, Jerry Stevens walked out and said, 'Ladies and gentlemen … The Beatles.' With the audience now screaming hysterically, the curtains pulled back to reveal … The Moody Blues, who were standing there, centre stage, laughing and holding John, Paul and George's guitars. But within moments, the also chuckling Beatles rushed on, took back their instruments and launched into 'I Feel Fine'.

A fantastic venue, especially at Christmas where the shows were an overwhelming success.

Bag O'Nails, 9 Kingly Street

This Soho club was opened in 1966 by the Gunnell brothers, and became the most popular hangout for the country's pop stars. All of The Beatles visited here, though none more so than Paul, and it was here that he first set eyes on American photographer Linda Eastman, later to become his wife. Situated close to Carnaby Street, the club was open seven nights a week, and also, for The Beatles who often recorded long into the night, the only place they could go after they had finished in the studio.

Maybe Paul was amazed.

BBC Lime Grove Studios, Shepherd's Bush

The Beatles' first BBC television appearance was on *The 625 Show* on 16 April 1963, recorded here three days earlier. They also filmed here on 7 July 1964 for a segment in *Top Of The Pops*. John returned here on 23 March 1964 for the live TV show *Tonight*, and again on 18 June 1965, plus two further appearances with Yoko.

The ultimate BBC show to appear on.

BBC Maida Vale Studios, Delaware Road

The Beatles visited these famous radio studios twice in 1963 to record for their *Pop Goes The Beatles* radio series.

BBC Paris Studio, 12 Lower Regent Street

Between 1962 and 1964 The Beatles made numerous recordings here for BBC Radio, including their own *Pop Goes The Beatles*. Recordings from these sessions have been released by the BBC and mainly include covers of songs that The Beatles played but didn't record for EMI. The BBC quit this studio in the nineties.

Paris in London gave us a glimpse of the rock 'n' roll group, The Beatles.

BBC Piccadilly Studios, 196 Piccadilly

The Beatles recorded the first of their five sessions at these radio studios on 21 March 1963. Their last BBC radio appearance was recorded here on 26 May 1965.

Radio was as important as television and the BBC made the most of The Beatles.

BBC Television Centre, White City

In studio 2 of the home of BBC television, The Beatles mimed to 'Paperback Writer' and 'Rain' for an edition of *Top of the Pops* on 16 June 1966. The film, sadly, has been lost. The Plastic Ono Band also recorded an edition of *Top of the Pops* on 11 February 1970. In addition, Paul, Ringo and John made individual appearances here on television programmes during the sixties. It is now closed.

30 Bedford Square

Publisher Jonathan Cape had offices here. John arrived for a private launch party for his first book, *In His Own Write*, which was published the following day, 23 March 1964.

14 Berkeley Street

Allan Williams, The Beatles' first manager, owned a club in Liverpool called the Blue Angel, and London had one too at this address. It was one of many clubs The Beatles liked to hang out in after the pubs were closed.

Blue Gardenia Club, St Anne's Court, Soho

Hot-foot from their disastrous show in Aldershot, where only 18 people turned up to see The Beatles perform, the group appeared at the Blue Gardenia Club in London's Soho district in the early hours of 9/10 December. Run by their old friend Brian Casser, the former front man of Cass and The Cassanovas, there were regular rock 'n' roll nights at the club, which became 'All-Nighters' after midnight, with local musicians meeting and jamming on stage (keyboard player and R&B/jazz singer Georgie Fame being the most famous one on this occasion). Legend has it George chose not to participate in the group's impromptu set, but those present at the gig assure us that in fact the opposite is true. Terry McCann, who was there with promoter Sam Leach, acting as his minder, remembers the occasion well. 'George was the only one who got up and jammed that night, because he was a talented guitarist who could play with anyone.'

The Beatles stayed until about 3am and then, with their friend Terry at the wheel, headed back to Liverpool. Unfortunately their journey home was blighted when the van they were travelling in ran out of petrol. McCann managed to refuel it by spending his last £5, which he had kept hidden. As he recalled, 'They never knew I had it, otherwise I wouldn't have had it! They would always be borrowing your last anything, ciggies, two bob, whatever.' They arrived back in Liverpool around midday on 10 December and later that evening performed in the City at Hambleton Hall in Huyton.

Bowater House Cinema, Knightsbridge

On 8 July 1968, *Yellow Submarine* was previewed in this small cinema. John couldn't attend, so the other Beatles turned up with a cardboard cut-out of John's character from the film.

Brad's Club, Duke of York Street

Not long after they met on the set of *A Hard Day's Night* in March 1964, George brought Pattie Boyd here for their first date.

Broadcasting House, Portland Place

The home of the BBC since 1932. As well as many interviews, they performed at two sessions here on 16 March 1963 and 14 July 1964.

165 Broadhurst Gardens, West Hampstead

Home to Decca Recording Studios, Brian Epstein was true to his word and managed to arrange a recording audition for The Beatles on 1 January 1962, which, although they felt it had gone well, was to prove unsuccessful.

Only 3 for Decca for turning The Beatles down, but 10 because they wouldn't have worked with George Martin if they had passed the audition.

Broadwick Street Toilets

Not the greatest sounding place in the world, but these toilets were the film location for John's appearance on the comedy show, *Not Only … But Also*, featuring Peter Cook and Dudley Moore. John appeared here with them on 27 November 1966, being seen wearing his now-famous round glasses, which he had worn during filming for *How I Won The War*.

14-16 Bruton Place, Mayfair

Within the club known as Le Prince was a discotheque called Revolution, which was frequented by all four Beatles at different occasions, including George who went to see his wife Pattie in a fashion show.

Buckingham Palace

The Beatles arrived at the royal residence on 26 October 1965 to receive their MBEs – making them Members of the British Empire. There followed many protests from prior recipients who complained that the award, usually for heroes in a time of war, should not be given to pop stars. Some returned their medals in protest, just as John would later do, saying in his letter, 'Your Majesty, I am returning my MBE as a protest against Britain's involvement in the Nigeria–Biafra thing, against our support of America in Vietnam and against "Cold Turkey" slipping down the charts. With love. John Lennon of Bag.'

By Royal arrangement, though Mr Brian Epstein never got the award he deserved.

7 Bury Place, Bloomsbury

George helped the International Society for Krishna Consciousness to purchase this building in September 1969.

Café Royal, 68 Regent Street

The Beatles visited this London restaurant at the invitation of their music publisher, Dick James, after a successful year. John and Yoko also popped in here for an appearance on *The Eamonn Andrews Show* on 3 April 1969.

Carnaby Street

The famous centre for 'Swinging London' in the sixties, The Beatles, like many of their counterparts, were frequent visitors here, making it the place to be seen to buy the latest fashions. However, when everyone realised that this was where the great and the good were hanging out, the musicians couldn't visit any more for fear of being mobbed.

7 Cavendish Avenue, St John's Wood

Paul purchased this property in April 1965, though didn't move in until August 1966. Unlike the other Beatles who had moved out of London, Paul's house was only 5 minutes from Abbey Road. Hunter Davies visited Paul many times here, and described it in his Beatles biography. 'He took a large, detached, three-storey house in St John's Wood. He didn't do much knocking about, compared with John and Ringo. The garden became a jungle, completely overgrown,

MAD DAY OUT LOCATIONS

In 1968, The Beatles were in need of some new publicity photographs so, instead of posing in a studio yet again, Paul contacted photographer Don McCullin and set up, on 28 July, what became known as 'The Mad Day Out' with The Beatles. They were photographed at Thomson House at 200 Gray's Inn Road, the headquarters of *The Times* and the *Sunday Times*. After Thomson House they headed for the Mercury Theatre at 2 Ladbroke Road where they were filmed with a parrot. Highgate Cemetery is one of London's more famous cemeteries, housing the tomb of Karl Marx, where The Beatles had originally intended being photographed, but they never made it that far. Running through the cemetery is Swain's Lane, and the Fab Four were shot outside houses numbers 59 and 79 with Paul wearing a Liverpool FC rosette, even though he supports Everton FC. As afternoon became evening, they arrived near the Old Street underground railway station around 6pm. In the middle of the nearby roundabout was a traffic island, with an unusual concrete sculpture. Around 100 photos were taken with The Beatles in various poses, backed by the GPO Building at 207–209 Old Street. The next port of call was St Pancras Old Church and Gardens where they were photographed on a grassy knoll, a monument, a drinking fountain, grass near the grave of Sir John Sloane, St Pancras Coroner's Court and the flowerbed by the hospital buildings. Moving around the gardens, they stopped at a bench in front of a monument, before reaching the arched church doorway. Having attracted a crowd, McCullin photographed The Beatles with the fans by the railings, pictures that were used on the famous 'red' and 'blue' albums. Their penultimate destination was the eighteenth-century houses at Wapping Pier Head where The Beatles became more daring. One of the most famous images from the day has John in his black undershirt and Paul topless, then John 'played dead' while the others looked on before the final shots here with John lying on the ground, leaning on his arm with the other three standing behind him. The final location was Paul's home at 7 Cavendish Avenue. At the bottom of Paul's garden was a sunhouse, where they were joined by McCartney's dog Martha to capture the last photos as the sun set on their day's work.

inhabited only by the prowling Martha. He got the idea of building a magical house in it, a sort of pagoda on a raised platform with an open glass roof onto the skies. The house is guarded by a high brick wall and large double black gates, which are controlled from the house. You speak into a microphone, someone inside answers and, if you say the right thing, the doors swing open. The ground floor contains the kitchen, which is very large and well appointed, a large haughty dining room which looks completely unused, and his living room at the back, which is the most used of any Beatle room. This is where The Beatles and Mal Evans and Neil Aspinall and others congregate before recording sessions and, in fact, most times they are in London. It has an unpretentious lived-in feeling. On the top floor is his work room, where he and John do most of their hard slog together when they need some more songs to fill up an album.'

Paul set down roots finally in London.

Caxton Hall, Westminster

On 11 February 1965, Ringo married his Liverpool-born girlfriend Maureen Cox at the register office here on Caxton Street, with John, George and Brian in attendance. Paul was on holiday.

24 Chapel Street, Belgravia

At the end of 1964, Brian Epstein purchased this house and lived here until his premature death in August 1967. He had used the house for the press party to celebrate the release of *Sgt Pepper* in May 1967 but just three months later, at the age of only 32, The Beatles' manager was dead.

Brian should have spent many more happy years here.

Chappell Recording Studios, 52 Maddox Street

The Beatles attended recording sessions here on 22 and 23 August 1967, where they recorded 'Your Mother Should Know'. Paul returned here in August 1968 to produce the hit single 'I'm The Urban Space Man' by the Bonzo Dog Doo-Dah Band under the pseudonym Apollo C. Vermouth.

Another of the recording studios The Beatles used in London.

132 Charing Cross Road, Westminster

The office of music publisher Dick James was here, on the first floor of Shaldon Mansions, with Dick James Music and Northern Songs registered at this address. Brian and The Beatles signed away the rights for 'Ask Me Why' and 'Please Please Me'. James moved to 71–75 Oxford Street in 1964.

It's only a Northern song.

Chelsea Manor Buildings Hall of Remembrance, Flood Street

Before filming the TV show *Around The Beatles*, the Fab Four rehearsed in this old parish hall on 18 and 25 April 1964.

Chelsea Manor Studios, 1–11 Flood Street

Photographer Michael Cooper established this studio in 1966. On 30 March 1967 he welcomed The Beatles here, where for the past few weeks Peter Blake had created his elaborate collage of nominated individuals for them to stand in front of – and so the *Sgt Pepper's Lonely Hearts Club Band* album cover was born.

Creating the most iconic and imitated album cover ever.

Chelsea Old Town Hall, King's Road

On 3 July 1969, Ringo Starr launched 'Give Peace a Chance' by the Plastic Ono Band. John and Yoko should have been there but they were still in hospital, with John having crashed their car in Scotland. Ringo obligingly stepped in, even though it wasn't a Beatles release.

All we are saying is where was John?

Chiswick House

The promotional films for 'Paperback Writer' and 'Rain' were shot here in May 1966.

Cine Tele Sound (CTS) Studios, Kensington Gardens Square

This audio specialist was visited by The Beatles during May 1965 for some post-production work on the movie *Help!*, and again in January 1966 when additional sound recording was required for their film *The Beatles At Shea Stadium*.

Cinecentre, Panton Street

On 12 January 1969, the film *Wonderwall*, for which George composed the music, was premiered here.

Claridge's, Brook Street

One of the most prestigious hotels in London, it was the scene of a crucial meeting in the business life of The Beatles, when in the spring of 1969 the future of The Beatles' management was decided. Paul was represented by his future father-in-law Lee Eastman, while Allen Klein appeared on behalf of the other three Beatles. Klein won the argument and began working on restructuring Apple immediately.

Paul versus John, George and Ringo – epic fight.

26–27 Conduit Street, Westminster

At Flat 8 lived one of Brian Epstein's most trusted friends from their time in Liverpool, Peter Brown. He worked as assistant to Brian at NEMS and was one of the most important people in The Beatles' inner circle.

Connaught Hotel, Carlos Place, Mayfair

On 19 February 1965, chairman of EMI Sir Joseph Lockwood held a party here in honour of The Beatles' outstanding success.

Crazy Elephant, 57–58 Jermyn Street

A regular Beatles haunt, in November 1964 this restaurant was where John and George met up with a couple of the members of their favourite Motown group, The Miracles. The restaurant then became a nightclub known as Dolly's, which The Beatles also visited on numerous occasions.

Crockford's, Carlton House Terrace

This popular gambling club was a frequent destination for Brian Epstein who loved to gamble. He even managed to drag John along one night in 1967.

Dance News, 76 Southwark Street

One of the first promotional interviews The Beatles did after 'Love Me Do' was released was at this weekly music paper, on 9 October 1962.

Devonshire Arms Pub, 7 Duke Street

Just round the corner from EMI House, this Marylebone pub was popular with The Beatles and was also where they first met Tony Barrow, recently appointed as the group's press officer.

Tony Barrow was an invaluable ally in promoting The Beatles.

Disc and Melody Maker, 161–166 Fleet Street

On their return from Hamburg on 16 November 1962, The Beatles visited the offices of the popular music paper *Disc* to give an interview about their recent trip. They made further visits here in 1963 and 1964 to *Melody Maker*, which had relocated to this building in 1962.

Donmar Rehearsal Theatre, 41 Earlham Street

Before appearing on Val Parnell's *Sunday Night At The London Palladium* in October 1963, The Beatles used this venue to run through their songs and prepare for what would be an important television appearance.

Dorchester, Park Lane

Another of London's smart hotels, this Mayfair establishment was host to The Beatles on several occasions. The first was for the Variety Club's annual awards ceremony on 19 March 1964, where they collected the 1963 award for 'Show-business Personalities of the Year', presented by future Prime Minister Harold Wilson, who would later award them their MBEs. John returned the following month for the Foyles Literary Lunch following the success of his recently published book, *In His Own Write*. He was expected to give a speech to the assembled dignitaries, but nobody told him, so he was unprepared and simply said, 'Thanks, it has been a pleasure.' It also didn't help that John was still nursing a hangover from the night before.

Dougie Millings and Son, 63 Old Compton Street

One of the most popular bespoke tailors in London, this Soho showroom was a regular haunt of The Beatles. They were photographed here by Dezo Hoffmann on 2 July 1963 during his photo shoot for *A Day In The Life Of The Beatles*.

Drum City, 114 Shaftesbury Avenue

This music store was where Ringo Starr purchased his famous Ludwig drum kit.

You can't beat it.

18–19 Eaton Row, Belgravia

Tara Browne, friend of The Beatles and heir to the Guinness fortune, lived at this address. Paul had his first encounter with LSD with Browne here. Browne, of course, is forever linked with The Beatles' 'A Day In The Life'.

He blew his mind out in a car.

EMI House, Manchester Square

The headquarters of EMI, this building was frequently visited by The Beatles and was the location for the cover photo, by Angus McBean, for their first album, *Please Please Me*. They later recreated the photo, intended for the *Let It Be* album, but it wasn't used. However, both EMI balcony shots did feature as the covers for the compilations known as the *Red* and *Blue* albums. EMI moved out of here in 1994.

At a lunchtime award ceremony here on 5 April 1963, attended by the press and EMI record executives, the group was presented with their first silver disc, for 250,000 sales of the single 'Please Please Me'. They also performed a short set and posed for photos with producer George Martin. While in London that day, the group also made their first visit to the Mayfair offices of their accounting firm Bryce Hanmer, Isherwood & Company.

For the building. For EMI the company, a big R8.

13 Emperor's Gate, Flat 3, South Kensington

John, using the pseudonym 'Hadley', moved into this flat in November 1963 with Cynthia and his young son Julian. The drawback was that the flat was up six flights of stairs – hardly ideal with a baby and shopping, while trying desperately to evade the fans. When it became too much, John moved his family out to Weybridge. In Flat 2 lived photographer Robert Freeman and his wife Sunny, with whom John had a secret affair.

Not the greatest place for the Lennons to live.

Empire Ballroom, 5–6 Leicester Square

The Beatles received two Carl Alan awards from Prince Philip, the Duke of Edinburgh, at a ceremony here on 23 March 1964.

Empire Pool, Wembley

The biggest audience The Beatles had played to date was here at the Empire Pool and Sports Arena (now Wembley Arena) on 21 April 1963 at the *New Musical Express 1962–63 Annual Poll-Winners' All-Star Concert*. The Beatles were second on the bill. Topping the 15-act line-up was Cliff Richard and The Shadows. Although the Fab Four had not actually won any awards that year, the organisers decided that in recognition of their two recent number one singles, 'Please Please Me' and 'From Me To You', they should be the penultimate act, performing to over ten thousand people. Years later in an interview for the *Daily Mirror* about his history of pre-gig nerves Paul said, 'When The Beatles did Wembley for the first time, I felt sick. I thought, "I've got to give this up."' This 1963 event was not filmed; however, the next three were with The Beatles returning as winners in 1964, 1965 and 1966. (For more details, see relevant entry in *TV* Section.)

The biggest venue The Beatles had played in the UK.

New Musical Express 1963–64 Annual Poll-Winners' All-Star Concert, 26 April 1964.

Backstage, just prior to their performance, John and Ringo were interviewed by the Aloha-based, WGH Radio DJ, 'Lean Gene' Loving. Sitting among the crowd that night was the future BBC DJ and *Old Grey Whistle Test* presenter 'Whispering' Bob Harris. The awards were presented by *The Saint* star Roger Moore, with The Beatles winning World Vocal Group, British Vocal Group and Best British Disc of the Year for 'She Loves You'.

New Musical Express 1964–65 Annual Poll-Winners' All-Star Concert, 11 April 1965.

The awards were presented by singer Tony Bennett, with The Beatles winning World Vocal Group, British Vocal Group and John receiving the runner-up award to Cliff Richard for British Vocal Personality.

New Musical Express 1965–66 Annual Poll-Winners' All-Star Concert, 1 May 1966.

Although The Beatles would perform on the rooftop of Apple HQ on 30 January 1969 this was actually their very last scheduled live appearance in Britain. And it was not filmed. Even though ABC TV was once again recording the event, Brian Epstein failed to reach an agreement with them over terms, so their cameras were turned off while The Beatles – as well as the Rolling Stones – performed. However the group was recorded receiving their awards from *Cheyenne* star, US actor Clint Walker, picking up once again World Vocal Group and British Vocal Group with John this time also winning British Vocal Personality.

To escape their adoring fans, the group arrived at the rear of the building in a van, dressed as four chefs, with white hats and aprons and with trays of goodies in their hands. Once inside the venue, they sprinted across the kitchen but Ringo tripped, sent his tray of cakes everywhere and caused a pile up with the other three Beatles. Midway through the Rolling Stones' set, the group, instruments in hand, assembled at the foot of the stairs that led directly to the stage. Maurice Kinn, owner of *NME*, told them they were 25 minutes early, but John was uninterested, insisting they were going on now. Kinn told him they couldn't. 'Didn't you hear me the first time?' the Beatle shouted. 'We're going on now or we're not going on at all!' In a rapidly convened discussion with Brian Epstein, Kinn outlined his dilemma. He'd promised the Rolling Stones, in writing, that The Beatles should not follow them immediately onto the stage. He had arranged for the awards presentation to come between the two bands and explained to Epstein that if his group did not come on at the arranged time, he would be left with no option but to send the MC, Jimmy Savile, on to the stage to explain to the 10,000 crowd that The Beatles were in the stadium but they weren't going to perform. He explained very clearly what the consequences would be – a riot. 'Wembley would be destroyed,' Kinn informed him, 'and Wembley and the *NME* would both sue [Epstein].' Brian immediately conveyed this to Lennon and he exploded. 'He gave me abuse like you've never heard before in all your life,' Kinn remembered. 'You could hear him all over the backstage area. He said, "We'll never play for you again!" But he knew he had no choice.' Fifteen minutes later, The Beatles went on stage, collected their awards and played the show. When their 20-minute set ended, they raced off stage with their *NME* awards in hand, ran down the ramps towards the limo, which was already revving up, and literally threw the awards to their assistants (Neil and Mal) who seemed to be waiting there for exactly that purpose. The car

hurriedly pulled away from the venue with the doors still flapping. It was a most unfitting end to The Beatles' last scheduled performance in Britain.

Notable for being The Beatles' last scheduled UK appearance.

234 Euston Road

One of the most famous pictures of The Beatles was taken in the rubble of the old Orange Tree pub in the spring of 1963 and used on the cover of their *Twist And Shout* EP. Photographer Fiona Adams also photographed them in front of 222 Euston Road, and at the junction of Gower Street and Euston Road.

Another of those memorable record sleeves.

Euston Station

The main railway station that Brian and The Beatles used on their trips to London from Liverpool, one of the platforms here became a mad scene on 25 August 1967 when The Beatles boarded a train to visit the Maharishi in Bangor, North Wales. In the ensuing chaos the train left without Cynthia, leaving her in tears.

Did John even notice Cynthia was missing?

Farringdon Studio, 23 West Smithfield

After photographer Robert Whitaker had held a session with The Beatles at Abbey Road, he was enlisted by NEMS to schedule a session here, which was carried out in October 1964. Pictures from the shoot appeared on the cover of the US album *Beatles '65* and in the UK on the *The Beatles Million Sellers* EP that came out in December 1965.

The Flamingo Club, 31 Wardour Street

This popular club was frequented by all four of The Beatles.

Fleetway House, 22 Farrington Street

Between 1963 and 1966, the Fab Four made several visits to the photographic studio housed here, for photographer Bill Francis.

Fordie House, Flat 14, 82-87 Sloane Street

Neil Aspinall lived here between 1967 and 1968. For some of this time, Mal Evans shared the flat with Neil. It is thought that Paul wrote some of the title song for *Sgt Pepper* in this flat.

Gaumont State Cinema, High Road, Kilburn

The largest picture house in Europe when it opened in 1937, this Grade 2 listed Art Deco building was host to The Beatles on 9 April 1963 and for two shows on 23 October 1964.

Granada Cinema, Barking Road, East Ham

Five days after completing the Helen Shapiro tour, The Beatles performed here on 9 March 1963. This was not only the opening night of a new tour with American singers Chris Montez and Tommy Roe (two shows per night), it was also the very first time the band had performed in London. Unfortunately for the two headliners, The Beatles proved to be the act the audiences most wanted to see, and from Liverpool onwards, 24 March, they took over top billing, closing the shows.

The Beatles returned to the venue on 9 November 1963 during their autumn tour. Among the audience that night was the screenwriter Alun Owen, who had been following the group for the past three days, observing their characters and lifestyle for the script of their first, as yet untitled, feature film. It would later become *A Hard Day's Night*.

Granada Cinema, Mitcham Road, Tooting

During the Roy Orbison tour, The Beatles played here twice on 1 June 1963 to a capacity audience of around three thousand people.

Granada Cinema, Hoe Street, Walthamstow

The Granada Cinema, a grand 1930s building with a 'Moorish' design, was host to The Beatles on two occasions, the first being 24 May 1963 where they played two houses during the Roy Orbison tour. A privately taped audio of highlights of one of the shows survives. They returned on 24 October 1964 where they also played twice.

Granada Cinema, Powis Street, Woolwich

The Beatles played two houses here on 3 June 1963 during the Roy Orbison tour, the only time they appeared at this cinema.

Granville Theatre, Fulham Broadway

This ITV studio on Fulham Broadway was host to The Beatles on 2 October 1964 to rehearse for a special British edition of *Shindig!*, the American pop show. They returned the following day to record their performance, transmitted on 7 October 1964.

57 Green Street, Mayfair

After initially staying at the Royal Court Hotel, then moving on to the President Hotel, The Beatles left hotel life behind in September 1963 and moved to this apartment. They only stayed here a short time, with Paul first to move out followed shortly after by John by the end of November. Eventually, George and Ringo completed the exodus.

Grosvenor House Hotel, Park Lane

One of the exclusive hotels in London, where Brian Epstein stayed in 1963 until he found a flat at

Whaddon House. The Beatles performed a charity concert here on 2 December 1963 in aid of cerebral palsy sufferers. Earlier that day the group recorded an appearance for ATV's *The Morecambe And Show*. (For more details see entry in *TV* section.)

Guildford Street, Bloomsbury

One of the most-used photographs of The Beatles was taken in Guildford Street by Dezo Hoffmann as they walked towards Russell Square. It appears on the cover of the *On Air – Live At The BBC Volume 2* album.

Hammersmith Odeon, Queen Caroline Street

The Beatles became regulars here from 24 December 1964 for 20 days, through to 16 January 1965, performing in *Another Beatles Christmas Show*. With music, comedy, pantomime sketches and a host of special guests, this Christmas show pretty much replicated the formula of the previous one at the Finsbury Park Astoria. The Beatles' comedy skit saw them dressed as Antarctic explorers searching for the Abominable Snowman. They hated appearing in such things and vowed never to appear in such an event again. They didn't. Joining them on the bill that year were the groups and singers Freddie and The Dreamers, Sounds Incorporated, Elkie Brooks, The Yardbirds, Michael Haslam, The Mike Cotton Sound and Ray Fell. The compère throughout the run was the now shamed BBC television and radio presenter, Jimmy Savile. The Fab Four unsurprisingly closed each show.

One of the greatest venues in London.

The Beatles returned to Hammersmith on 10 December 1965, the third last date on what proved to be their final UK tour. They played two houses, with 3,487 fans at each. On the day of the concerts the *New Musical Express* paper announced the results of its annual Readers Poll, with The Beatles winning World Vocal Group and British Vocal Group, while John was voted British Vocal Personality. (For more details, see 'Empire Pool, Wembley' entry in this section and *NME Poll-Winners All-Star Concert* entry for 1 May 1966 in *TV* section.)

Monumental due to the fact the group performed in the knowledge they had, once more, been voted best British Group and best World Group by the readers of the UK's biggest-selling music paper.

Hanover Banqueting Rooms, 6 Hanover Street

John and George, on behalf of The Beatles, hosted a private party here for the secretaries and friends of the Official Beatles Fan Club on 17 December 1967.

Hanover Gate Mansions, Flat 5, Park Road

Yoko moved to this Regent's Park address with her husband Tony Cox at the beginning of 1967. John soon became a regular visitor as their relationship blossomed, and when they married Yoko gave her address as '25, Hanover Gate Mansions, London W1.'

Heathrow Airport (at the time known at London Airport)

If there is one location in London synonymous with Beatlemania, it is Heathrow, one of the busiest airports in the world. Probably one of the most significant occasions was 31 October 1963, when on their return from the tour in Sweden they were mobbed by screaming fans, witnessed by US television show host Ed Sullivan.

How important was this meeting in getting The Beatles to America?

The Beatles as Eskimos for their show at the Hammersmith Odeon in 1964. Why Eskimos? Well it was their Christmas show…

© Terry O'Neill / Contributor

Heroes of Alma Pub, 11 Alma Square

This little pub was just a short distance from Abbey Road studios and so The Beatles, as well as the staff, were regular visitors.

9 Hertford Street, Mayfair

Walter Shenson, the American-born producer of *A Hard Day's Night* and *Help!*, had offices here. Shenson invited The Beatles to a meeting to discuss the plot of the film that would become *Help!*. John and Paul attended on behalf of the band. Shenson lived nearby at 11 Hyde Park Gardens.

They knew where to go when they needed *Help!*

38 Hertford Street, Mayfair

The London offices of Radio Luxembourg, essential listening for British would-be musicians in the fifties and sixties.

Radio Luxembourg brought American music to The Beatles and their friends when they were growing up.

HMV, 363–367 Oxford Street

After the rejection of a contract by Decca Records, in a desperate attempt to secure The Beatles a recording deal, Brian Epstein entered this record store around 8 February 1962. He sought out the shop's manager Bob Boast, whom Epstein had met in Hamburg at a record retailers' fair, to see if he could help. With the assistance of Jim Foy the tapes Brian had were converted onto disk, and Epstein was referred to Syd Coleman from music publishers Ardmore and Beechwood in the same building. Coleman offered to put Brian in touch with the head of Parlophone Records, George Martin. Little did Coleman realise how important that introduction that would be.

The last hope for Brian eventually brought him to George Martin.

95–99 Holloway Road

As John and Yoko started to become more active in supporting causes, they befriended a Trinidadian activist who went by the name of Michael X, or Michael Abdul Malik. Michael X staged a 'ceremony' on the roof of his house where John and Yoko gave Michael their recently shaven hair in a bag. In exchange, they received a pair of Muhammad Ali's boxing shorts, which they were to auction at a later date. There was little press coverage, and Michael X was later executed for a double murder back home in Trinidad in 1975.

House of Nutter, Savile Row

The strangely named tailor, Tommy Nutter, provided the suits for Paul's wedding to Linda, and for those worn by John, Paul and Ringo for the photo-shoot for the *Abbey Road* album cover.

Hyde Park

With their new album *Beatles For Sale* due out, thoughts turned to the cover. Robert Freeman brought The Beatles to the southern end of Hyde Park on 24 October 1964 and took the cover photo. They did a further photo shoot here in May 1967 for *Time* magazine. The famous Speakers' Corner at Hyde Park has long been used for the public to speak on any matter close to their heart and on 14 December 1969 a protest was begun by a couple in a bag: John and Yoko. The label attached read, 'SILENT PROTEST by John & Yoko'. The couple were there to draw attention to their latest 'cause' – James Hanratty. Hanratty had been hanged for the notorious 'A6 Murder' in 1962, but ever since questions had been raised about the guilty verdict. By 1969 those claiming a miscarriage of justice had achieved considerable public awareness. John and

Yoko became involved in the campaign, joining a march to Downing Street after their silent protest, calling for an inquiry into the conviction. Many years later DNA evidence proved beyond a doubt that he was guilty.

Another timeless album cover

Indiacraft, 51 Oxford Street

It was in this shop that George purchased his first sitar in the summer of 1965.

Indica Gallery, 6 Mason's Yard

Over a drink in The Scotch of St James Club, Barry Miles, Peter Asher and John Dunbar decided to open a bookshop and art gallery, which they named after the cannabis *indica*. Peter Asher's housemate was Paul McCartney, who was dating Asher's sister Jane at the time, so Paul became a regular supporter and visitor of the Indica, even helping move the furniture in and designing the wrapping paper. It was here on 8 November 1966 that a Japanese avant-garde artist named Yoko Ono held an exhibition, *Unfinished Paintings and Objects*. Dunbar decided to invite his friend John Lennon to attend a preview the day before it opened (there is some debate as to the exact date Lennon attended the gallery, with some sources suggesting 9 November, but as the opening party was on 8 November, the preview was most likely the day before). As Lennon remembered, it was the *Ceiling Painting*, consisting of a stepladder and, at the top, a magnifying glass through which he viewed the word 'Yes', that caught his attention. Dunbar introduced Lennon to Yoko and so began the relationship that would last for the rest of his life.

A pivotal moment in the life of John and the future of The Beatles. Yes, or no?

Inn on the Park, Hamilton Place, Park Lane

John and Yoko stayed in this hotel during the summer of 1969, while their new Sunningdale home, Tittenhurst Park, purchased in May, underwent considerable renovations. John returned here the following year when work on the home studio at Tittenhurst interrupted his initial primal therapy sessions with Arthur Janov, which had been taking place there.

Institute of Contemporary Arts, 17–18 Dover Street

This art museum, in fashionable Mayfair, was the location for the screening of John and Yoko's films over two evenings. The first, on 10 September 1969, showed *Two Virgins, Rape, Smile, Honeymoon* and *Self-Portrait*, and the second evening showed *Apotheosis*.

International Broadcasting Company (IBC) Studios, Portland Place

On 19 April 1964, The Beatles visited this studio to record the soundtrack for their television special *Around The Beatles*. Ringo also visited here on 30 September 1964 to help his old band, Rory Storm and The Hurricanes, now managed by Brian. Another of Brian's groups, The Silkie, recorded the Lennon/McCartney song 'You've Got To Hide Your Love Away' here, produced by John. Grapefruit, the first band signed to Apple, also had their first recording session at the IBC Studios in November 1967.

InterTel (VTR Services) Limited, Wycombe Road, Stonebridge Park

On 10 and 11 December 1968, John and Yoko came here to take part in *The Rolling Stones Rock And Roll Circus* being videotaped, where John played 'Yer Blues'.

The Ivy, 1 West Street

This high-class central London restaurant was host to George's twenty-first birthday party attended by the other Beatles and a collection of George's friends.

J Lyons & Co, Coventry Street

To celebrate New Year's Eve in 1966, George and Brian brought their party of friends to this restaurant, after earlier being refused entry to Annabel's nightclub.

Kay's Restaurant, 20 Grove End Gardens

Opposite the Abbey Road studios was this restaurant where The Beatles would often go in between recording sessions.

22-24 Kensington Church Street

Photographer Philip Gotlop held a photo shoot for The Beatles here in April 1963 where they wore their famous grey, collarless suits.

King's College Hospital, Denmark Hill

Yoko Ono was admitted here on 12 October 1969, and sadly miscarried. John stayed with her. Paul and Linda had a happier time here when their daughter Stella was born on 13 September 1971.

Kingsway Recording Studio, 124-129 Kingsway

The Beatles came here to record 'It's All Too Much', and some untitled musical jams on four occasions between 25 May 1967 and 2 June 1967.

La Maisonette, 27 Tottenham Court Road

Music publisher Dick James took Brian Epstein to lunch at this restaurant on 27 November 1962, and secured the deal for publishing the Lennon/ McCartney songs that would make him a wealthy man.

Lansdowne Recording Studios, Holland Park

At this West London studio on 3 October 1969 the Plastic Ono Band recorded 'Don't Worry Kyoko'.

The London Clinic, 20 Devonshire Place

During a stressful time in their relationship, Yoko checked in to this clinic between 5 and 9 May 1970.

Leyton Swimming Baths, High Street, Leyton

On 8 April 1963 The Beatles performed in front of a few hundred people in this small swimming baths, similar to those that Ringo and George would have visited back in Liverpool. As well as being a public bathhouse, the location doubled as a dance hall when they covered the pool with a dance floor. The Beatles performed several of the tracks featured on their *Please Please Me* album and previewed their forthcoming single 'From Me To You'.

This was a particularly significant date for John, as Cynthia Lennon gave birth to their first child, John Charles Julian Lennon, at Sefton General Hospital, Smithdown Road, Liverpool on this day. John would not see his son until 11 April, the night before the group played at Liverpool's Cavern club.

Lisson Gallery, 66-68 Bell Street

This was the venue for an art exhibition by Yoko Ono called *Half-A-Wind Show (Yoko Plus Me)*, which ran from 11 October to 14 November 1964. John sponsored the exhibition anonymously, the first time they had collaborated on a venture like this.

London Arts Gallery, 22 New Bond Street

It was at this gallery that John hosted an exhibition of his etchings under the title *Bag One*. They included several of Yoko naked, which, after complaints, prompted a police raid where eight of the original etchings were removed under the Obscene Publications Act. John was eventually prosecuted under an ancient law for distributing indecent material in a 'thoroughfare'. As it was a gallery, not a thoroughfare, the case was dismissed.

London Hilton Hotel, Park Lane

John, Paul and George attended a lecture in this Mayfair hotel on Transcendental Meditation by Maharishi Mahesh Yogi, the first time they had met. After the public lecture, the three had a private meeting with the Maharishi.

London Palladium, Argyll Street

The Beatles first appeared here on 13 October 1963 for the TV show *Val Parnell's Sunday Night At The London Palladium*, watched by an estimated audience of 18 million people. Alas, the footage of that show was not kept. The fact that The Beatles were mobbed by hundreds of screaming fans made the national newspapers, leading to the famous term 'Beatlemania' being used for the first time. From then on, they were featured regularly in the press as the next great thing – a blessing and a curse at the same time.

Where would newspapers be without the term Beatlemania?

The Beatles returned to the Palladium twice more, on 12 January 1964 for a second appearance on *Sunday Night At The London Palladium* (for more details of these two *Sunday Night Palladium* appearances, see relevant entries in *TV* section) and then again on 23 July of that year for a charity revue, *The Night of the Hundred Stars*, in aid of the Combined Theatrical Charities Appeals Council.

London Pavilion, Piccadilly

This cinema, in the heart of London, was the venue for the premiere of The Beatles' films, *A Hard Day's Night, Help!, Yellow Submarine* and *Let It Be*. Fans packed the streets around the venue on each occasion, though with the *Let It Be* film not shown

until 20 May 1970, there were no Beatles to be seen as they had broken up the month before.

An important cinema that saw The Beatles on celluloid first.

Lyceum, Wellington Street

Under the name of the Plastic Ono Supergroup, John and Yoko appeared at this theatre with George, Eric Clapton, Keith Moon and Billy Preston at a UNICEF benefit concert on 15 December 1969. The performance that night was recorded and released as part of the *Some Time In New York City* album in 1972.

A prelude to Live Aid and other more recent benefit concerts.

Majestic Ballroom, Stroud Green Road, Finsbury Park

One of The Beatles' earliest performances in London was here on 24 April 1963, the third of the *Mersey Beat Showcase* concerts.

Prior to the gig, the four Beatles went to the West London flat of Georgia-born film-maker Giorgio Gomelsky to discuss his idea for a Beatles movie. At the time he was owner of The Crawdaddy Club in London, where the Rolling Stones were the resident house band. Gomelsky's plan was to produce a day-in-the-life style film about The Beatles. Peter Clayton, screenwriter and columnist for *Jazz Beat* magazine, was also present. The only stumbling block, as far as Gomelsky and everyone was concerned, was the approval of Brian Epstein, who, in the words of Clayton, 'exhibited a combination of shyness [and] profound suspicion of the ways of showbiz.' In Gomelsky's opinion, Epstein 'didn't know his ass from his elbow in those early days.'

Several months after the meetings, the US film company United Artists, desperate to buy into

Beatlemania, offered The Beatles a three-picture deal. With a budget of just $20,000 (United Artists offered twenty times that) Gomelsky, Epstein realised, couldn't compete with the big boys so The Beatles' manager simply handed the treatment from Gomelsky and Clayton to screenwriter, Alun Owens. United Artists received it shortly afterwards and in July 1964 it became *A Hard Day's Night*. A couple of years later, with Gomelsky not only involved with the management of the Stones but also The Yardbirds, Epstein wrote to him apologising for his actions.

However, there was another possible reason why the Epstein–Gomelsky collaboration failed to take place. Late one night, during a walk home, Gomelsky suddenly turned nasty and pushed Epstein up against the wall in a dark alley. With one hand grasped firmly round The Beatles' manager's neck, Giorgio screamed like a madman, and told him what a great idea the movie was. Naturally terrified, Epstein immediately cut all ties with the man.

55 Manchester Street, Marylebone

George Martin moved here in 1964, when it was occupied by his secretary (and later wife) Judy Lockhart Smith. Paul, in particular, made several visits to the address, including one in June 1965 when he brought round 'Yesterday', which George then arranged for the orchestra.

Marquee Studio, 10 Richmond Mews

Situated in Soho, this studio was visited by The Beatles at the end of October 1965, with the aim of recording their latest Christmas record for the fan clubs. Unfortunately, it was not a successful day, so they tried again at Abbey Road Studios soon after.

Marylebone Magistrates' Court, 181 Marylebone Road

On 19 October 1968, after being arrested the day before following a drugs raid by police, John

and Yoko appeared in court here for the first time. When they returned on 28 November, John pleaded guilty to possession of cannabis, so that Yoko's visa would not be affected. Little did he realise the implications of the guilty plea, which affected his application for a green card in the US during the seventies.

This event would come back to haunt John during his long fight to live in America.

Marylebone Railway Station, Melcombe Place

The opening scene of *A Hard Day's Night* features The Beatles running along the side of the railway station in Boston Place. They then enter the station through the front doors and by the ticket office. George and Ringo are also seen using the telephone boxes inside the station. They eventually run onto the platform and join a train, which was supposed to be in Liverpool, before travelling to London.

Probably one of the most recognisable scenes from the film.

Marylebone Register Office, 97-113 Marylebone Road

This register office, also known as Old Marylebone Town Hall, was where Paul married Linda on 12 March 1969 and in April 1981 where Ringo married actress Barbara Bach. Because of the attention from the press and fans, Paul and Linda had to enter through the rear of the building.

Maximum Sound Studios, 488 Old Kent Road

When Liverpool group The Escorts entered this studio, Paddy Chambers invited Paul McCartney to sit in on the session. He was soon behind the mixing desk and producing the session for their new single, 'From Head to Toe'.

MUSICIANS FOR HIRE

John Lennon and Paul McCartney
Backing vocals: 'We Love You' by the Rolling Stones
(1967)

John Lennon, least active Beatle when it came to
session work unless he was working with Yoko. Some
examples:
Guitar: 'Don't Worry Kyoko (Mummy's Only Looking For
A Hand In The Snow)' by Yoko Ono (1969)
Guitar, backing vocals: 'Lucy In The Sky With Diamonds'
by Elton John (1974)
Guitar: 'Across The Universe' and 'Fame' by David Bowie
(1975), 'Fame' co-written by Lennon and Bowie
Electric piano: 'Wind Ridge' by Elephant's Memory
(1972)
Vocal, guitar: 'I Saw Her Standing There' by Elton John
(1975)

Paul McCartney, jack-of-all-trades as a session
musician.
Tambourine: 'I Knew Right Away' by Alma Cogan
(1964)
Rhythm guitar: 'You've Got To Hide Your Love Away' by
The Silkie (1965)
Chewing vegetables: 'Vegetables' by The Beach Boys
(1967)
Drums: 'And The Sun Will Shine' by Paul Jones (1968)
Tambourine, backing vocal: 'Atlantis' by Donovan
(1968)
Bass: 'Carolina In My Mind' by James Taylor (1968)
Backing vocal, bass, drums: 'My Dark Hour' by the Steve
Miller Band (1969)
Kazoo: 'You're Sixteen' by Ringo Starr (1973)
Backing vocal, synthesizer: *I Survive* by Adam Faith
(1974)

Backing vocals: 'One Of Those Days In England' by Roy
Harper (1977)
Drums: *Holly Days* by Denny Laine (1977)

George Harrison, plenty of session work but don't say
it's him. Some examples:
Tambourine, tapping on back of guitar: 'You've Got To
Hide Your Love Away' by The Silkie (1965)
Guitar as L'Angelo Misterioso: 'Badge' by Cream (1969)
Guitar: 'Thumbin' A Ride' by Jackie Lomax (1969)
Guitar: 'Tell The Truth' by Derek and The Dominoes
(1970)
Guitar: 'Ain't That Cute' by Doris Troy (1970)
Guitar: *Leon Russell* (1970)
Guitar, piano: 'Instant Karma' by the Plastic Ono Band
(1970)
Guitar as George O'Hara: *Footprint* by Gary Wright
(1971)
Guitar in house band: *The Concert For Bangla Desh*
(1971)
Slide guitar: 'Crippled Inside' by John Lennon (1971)
Guitar: 'You're Breakin' My Heart (so fuck you)' by
Nilsson (1972)
Guitar, slide guitar, bass, backing vocals as Hari
Georgeson: 'So Sad' by Alvin Lee (1973), a Harrison
song
12-string acoustic, backing vocal: 'Photograph' by
Ringo Starr (1973), co-written
Guitar: 'Basketball Jones' by Cheech y Chong (1973)
Backing vocal, guitar: 'Far East Man' by Ron Wood
(1974), a Harrison song
Guitar: 'Make Love Not War' by Peter Skellern (1975)

Ringo Starr, mainly a drummer.
Drums: 'Cold Turkey' by the Plastic Ono Band (1969)

Drums: *John Lennon/Plastic Ono Band* (1970)

Drums: *All Things Must Pass* by George Harrison (1970)

Drums: *Leon Russell* (1970)

Drums: 'To A Flame' and 'We Are Not Helpless' by Stephen Stills (1970)

Drums as Richie: 'I Ain't Superstitious' by Howlin' Wolf (1971)

Drums: *BB King In London* (1971)

Drums in house band: *The Concert For Bangla Desh* (1971)

Drums: 'Oo Wee Baby, I Love You' by Bobby Hatfield (1972)

Drums as Richie Snare: *Son Of Schmillson* by Nilsson (1972)

Drums: 'The Lodger' and 'Alright' by Peter Frampton (1972)

Drums: 'Rock And Roller' by Billy Lawrie (1973), co-written with Billy Lawrie

Drums: *Land's End* by Jimmy Webb (1974)

Narration: *Son Of Dracula* by Nilsson (1974)

Finger clicks: 'Step Lightly' by David Hentschel (1975)

Announcer: *Two Sides Of The Moon* by Keith Moon (1975)

Drums, vocal: 'Band Of Steel' by Guthrie Thomas (1976), a Ringo song

Tambourine: 'Don't You Remember When' by Vera Lynn (1976)

Drums: 'Zindy Lou' and 'SOS' by Manhattan Transfer (1976)

As the voice of Jesus: 'Men's Room, LA' by Kinky Friedman (1976); an unbelievable appearance for a former Beatle.

May Fair Hotel, Stratton Street

When Dylan was in town, he would stay here and be visited by all of the leading groups, including The Beatles. Out of all of them, it was George who became closest to Dylan, though there were many obvious influences on John's songwriting too.

13 Monmouth Street, Seven Dials

When The Beatles moved to London in May 1963 NEMS Enterprises took offices in Service House at this address, above a sex shop. This became the home of the Official Beatles Fan Club. New PR guru Tony Barrow was also given an office, which in turn led to The Beatles sometimes spending hours here in between press conferences. Brian also used the offices for business meetings.

16 Montagu Mews West, Marylebone

Neil Aspinall and Mal Evans shared a flat here and were often joined by The Beatles.

15 Montagu Place, Marylebone

The Beatles Mr Fix-it, Alistair Taylor, lived here. Brian's assistant since his days in NEMS Liverpool, Taylor eventually became Apple General Manager. He was at the top of Allen Klein's list to be removed as the restructuring of Apple began.

34 Montagu Square, Marylebone

This address has seen some of the biggest names in the music industry associated with it, people such as Jimi Hendrix, Chas Chandler, Paul McCartney and John Lennon. Ringo Starr set up home here first in 1965 with his wife Maureen. Although he moved out soon after to Weybridge, Surrey, he kept hold of the apartment. Paul used the basement as a recording studio in 1966, which included his demo for 'Eleanor Rigby'. Cynthia's mother Lilian briefly lived here, until John's affair with Yoko saw Cynthia move out of their Kenwood home and join her mother here. However, as divorce procedures commenced, John and Yoko moved into this flat as Cynthia moved back to Kenwood. As they were working on their album *Two Virgins*, they decided to photograph themselves naked in the flat to be used on the cover of their album. Not long after, on 18 October 1968, the flat was raided by the police and a small amount of cannabis was found in their possession for which John pleaded guilty to save Yoko being convicted as she would have been deported. Although this saved Yoko the conviction came back to haunt John in his bid for citizenship in the US. This was the last straw for the landlord who forced Ringo to sell the property. Look out for the blue plaque.

Small apartment with a big history.

Morgan Studios, 169-171 High Road, Willesden

Paul came here to record what would be his first solo album, *McCartney*, at the beginning of 1970, not long before The Beatles finally split up. Probably on the advice of Paul, Ringo decided to follow and record some of the tracks for his first solo album, *Sentimental Journey*.

New Arts Theatre, Great Newport Street

Brian Epstein's love for the theatre took a new direction when he directed an Alan Plater play, *A Smashing Day*. The premiere on 17 February 1966 was attended by John with his wife Cynthia and Ringo with his wife Maureen.

71-75 New Oxford Street, Westminster

When Dick James Publishing left their first premises at Charing Cross Road, he moved here on 4 May 1964, where almost every Beatles song under their company Northern Songs was published. James also had a small recording studio in the building that The Beatles used to record their

Christmas Fan Club record on 25 November 1966. Paul also auditioned Mary Hopkin here before signing her to Apple Records.

The Beatles' songs became their most valuable commodity – little did they know that Dick James would later sell his rights and Lennon and McCartney would lose control.

Odeon Cinema, Loampit Vale, Lewisham

The Beatles played here twice in 1963, but the difference in the reaction couldn't have been greater. By the time of their first appearance on 29 March 1963, during the Chris Montez/Tommy Roe tour, they were starting to become popular. When they returned on 8 December as part of their autumn tour, it was not long after their appearance on the *Royal Variety Show* and the term 'Beatlemania' had been coined. They were now national stars and soon to be going to America. What a difference a year makes.

Odeon Theatre, 261 Kensington High Street

The charity world premiere of *The Magic Christian*, starring Ringo and Peter Sellers, was held here on 11 December 1969. Paul had also written the title theme song 'Come And Get It', performed by Badfinger. Another film that Ringo had a part in, *Candy*, had a premiere here too on 20 February 1969.

Old Vic Theatre, The Cut

This former Royal Victoria Music Hall hosted the National Theatre's one-act production of John Lennon's play *In His Own Write*, which opened on 18 June 1968. John came to the premiere with Yoko, and not his wife Cynthia.

Old Vienna Restaurant, 94 New Bond Street

Four lucky winners of a competition run in the teen magazine, *Boyfriend*, got the chance to meet

The Beatles at this restaurant on 17 October 1963. The prize also included the four girls watching a recording session.

Olympic Studios, Church Road, Barnes

One of the best studios in London. The Beatles recorded 'Baby, You're A Rich Man' in May 1967 and then returned in May 1969 to record parts of 'Something' and 'You Never Give Me Your Money'. EMI later purchased Olympic, though it has now closed as a studio and been converted into a cinema.

A little known but important recording studio.

15 Ovington Mews, Knightsbridge

In 1964, this small house was rented for Pattie Boyd by her new boyfriend, George Harrison, who lived nearby in Williams Mews.

Parkes, 4 Beauchamp Place

This restaurant was a favourite hang-out for The Beatles. According to John, one of the flower displays, with its petals turned inside out, inspired him to write 'Glass Onion'.

You know the place where nothing is real?

Pickwick Club, Great Newport Street

When The Beatles settled in London during 1963, this was one of the first clubs they frequented. After their first experience with LSD, John and George visited here.

Sounds like they enjoyed their trip.

Pigalle Club, Piccadilly

The Beatles made one appearance here on 21 April 1963, hot-foot from their earlier appearance at the *NME Poll-Winners All-Star Concert* at the Empire Pool, Wembley. The agreement for the show, between NEMS Enterprises Ltd and Clayman Entertainments Ltd, of Woodford Green, in Essex, was drawn up on 29 February 1963 and provided that the latter would 'provide and pay for microphone equipment and (a) grand piano' for The Beatles. The band received £100 for their 30-minute performance. Supporting them were The Castaways, who featured Tony Rivers, and who recalled The Beatles arriving at the Pigalle Club and discovering their famous, collarless Beatle suits, worn just a few hours earlier, had suddenly gone missing!

Playhouse Theatre, Northumberland Avenue

Used by the BBC to record several sessions with The Beatles for their radio shows.

Hotel President, 62-72 Russell Square

Having moved down to London in 1963, after a short stay at the Royal Court Hotel, The Beatles relocated to here. Photographer Dezo Hoffman took many photos of The Beatles at this hotel as he sought to show the fans a typical day in the life of the Fab Four. After giving up hotel life, they moved to an apartment at 57 Green Street in September 1963.

Prince of Wales Theatre, Coventry Street

The Beatles' performance here for the *Royal Variety Performance* has gone down in folklore. On 4 November 1963, in front of the Queen Mother and Princess Margaret, John asked the audience to 'rattle your jewellery'. (See *Royal Variety Show* entry in *TV* section for more detail.)

At the end of the show The Beatles lined up alongside the other acts to meet the Queen Mother, who asked Paul, 'Where are you playing tomorrow night?' 'Slough,' he replied. To which she responded, 'Ah, that's near us.' Slough and Windsor are just two miles apart.

Another legendary performance when the group rattled the audience and charmed both the British public and the Royal Family.

The band returned to the Prince of Wales Theatre on 31 May 1964 for the fifth in a series of concerts under the title *Pops Alive*, promoted by Brian Epstein. The concerts ran from 2 May–14 June, and were introduced by DJ Alan Freeman. Headlining the other concerts in the series were The Searchers, Billy J. Kramer and The Dakotas, Roy Orbison, Freddie and The Dreamers, Gerry and The Pacemakers and Dusty Springfield.

Prospect Studios, Seaforth Lodge, Barnes High Street

Yet another photo session for The Beatles was carried out here on 3 June 1964 by John Launois for the *Saturday Evening Post*, a US weekly maga-

zine. It was during this photo shoot that Ringo collapsed and was taken to hospital suffering from tonsillitis, resulting in him missing the start of their imminent world tour. Jimmie Nicol was brought in to replace him for the first few concerts.

Radha Krishna Temple, 7 Bury Place

In 1969 this temple, close to the British Museum in Bloomsbury, became the first headquarters of the International Society for Krishna Consciousness (ISKCON) in the UK. George Harrison was a co-signee on the lease. Before then they had been given temporary accommodation in an outbuilding at Tittenhurst Park, known as Tittenhurst Temple, in the grounds of John Lennon's mansion near Ascot. When the Bury Place temple began to outgrow the number of devotees who lived there, George offered his help again, explaining that if they found a suitable building then he would purchase it. In 1972, the devotees found Piggotts Manor, a former nursing home with

BEATLES WASH THEIR HAIR!

The British national newspapers were not always that complimentary about The Beatles, especially in the early years, but eventually did come round to them. In November 1963, after The Beatles had appeared on the *Royal Variety Show*, the *Daily Mirror* was exceedingly impressed.

'How refreshing to see these rumbustious young Beatles take a middle-aged *Royal Variety Performance* by the scruff of their necks and have them beatling like teenagers. Fact is the Beatle People are everywhere. From Wapping to Windsor. Aged seven to seventy. And it's plain to see why these four energetic, cheeky lads from Liverpool go down so big.

They're young, new. They're high-spirited, cheerful. What a change from the self-pitying moaners crooning their lovelorn tunes from the tortured shallows of lukewarm hearts.

The Beatles are whacky. They wear their hair like a mop – but it's WASHED, it's super clean. So is their fresh young act. They don't have to rely on off-colour jokes about homos for their fun.

Youngsters like The Beatles – and Cliff Richard and The Shadows – are doing a good turn for show business – and the rest of us – with their new sounds, new looks.

GOOD LUCK, BEATLES!'

17 acres of land, in the Hertfordshire countryside. The property, which became known as Bhaktive-danta Manor, was purchased for £230,000. It has gone on to become one of the most famous Krishna temples outside of India.

Regent Sound, 164–167 Tottenham Court Road

This independent studio saw The Beatles' first recording session outside of Abbey Road. They came here on just the one occasion, 9 February 1967, to record 'Fixing A Hole'.

Ristorante Alpino, Marylebone High Street

On 4 September 1962, after their first recording session as John, Paul, George and Ringo, George Martin (at EMI/Abbey Road Studios) took The Beatles for a meal in the early evening, before they returned to the studio.

The Ritz, 150 Piccadilly

One of London's finest hotels. The Beatles attended many ceremonies and award presentations here. On 12 March 1969, the evening of their wedding, Paul and Linda held a reception at the hotel.

Riverside Studios, Crisp Road

The longest-running pop show on British television was *Top of the Pops*, and The Beatles filmed two appearances for the show at these Hammersmith studios, on 16 November 1964 and 10 April 1965.

Robert Fraser Gallery, 69 Duke Street,

Fraser's gallery was host to John's first solo art exhibition, *You Are Here (To Yoko from John Lennon, with Love)*, on 1 July 1968.

John's first attempt to draw a crowd.

Ronnie Scott's, 47 Frith Street

Located in Soho, and one of the most famous jazz clubs in the world. The Beatles came here in the early hours of John's twenty-third birthday to watch Roland Kirk. Ronnie Scott, who founded the club in 1958, played tenor saxophone on 'Lady Madonna' in February 1968.

Round Hill, Compton Avenue

Having had enough of his time in the country, Ringo decided to move back into London and purchased a house in an exclusive area in Highgate beside Hampstead Heath. Ringo and his family moved in on 5 December 1969, but their stay was short-lived as the couple divorced, with the house being sold at the end of 1973.

The Roundhouse, Chalk Farm Road

This was the setting for The Beatles' return to live performance in December 1968, or so it should have been. Apple reserved four dates between December 1968 and January 1969, but unfortunately the four of them couldn't agree about taking this giant step again and the dates were scrapped. Their compromise was the eventual appearance on the roof of the Savile Row building.

Royal Academy of Dramatic Art (RADA), 62 Gower Street

To attend this famous drama school was the ultimate ambition of any budding actor. Brian Epstein, who loved the theatre, auditioned here on 19 September 1956 and was duly offered a two-year placement commencing on 1 October. He never completed the course and returned to Liverpool.

How important was Brian's decision to move back to Liverpool and not complete the course? He would soon tread the boards on the world stage.

Royal Albert Hall, Kensington Gore

When they weren't counting how many holes it took to fill it, The Beatles played twice at one of England's finest concert venues. On 18 April 1963, they appeared as part of *Swinging Sound '63* for BBC Light Programme radio. Backstage during rehearsals Paul was introduced to 17-year-old actress, Jane Asher, who was writing a piece about the group for the BBC's weekly listings magazine, the *Radio Times*. For the next five years at least, she become his regular companion.

The Beatles returned to the Royal Albert Hall for their second and last performances on 15 September of the same year, as the headline act for *The Great Pop Prom*. This afternoon show, an annual fundraising event for the Printers' Pension Corporation, was sponsored by the teen magazines *Marilyn*, *Valentine* and *Roxy*. Also performing that day were the Rolling Stones, marking this as the first time the two bands had appeared together on the same bill.

Although The Beatles never performed again at the Royal Albert Hall, they were all in attendance together at the venue on one further occasion – as audience members at *The Golden Ball* on 18 February 1965.

John returned here on 18 December 1969 with Yoko for the *Alchemical Wedding*, a Christmas party for the avant-garde members of the art community. John and Yoko appeared inside a white sack on stage, with the concept of 'Bagism' being promoted.

One of the most prestigious concert venues in England.

Royal Court Hotel, 8–10 Sloane Square

When The Beatles came to London in February 1963, they all stayed at this hotel.

Royal Courts of Justice, Strand

Paul McCartney attended these courts between 19 February and 12 March 1971 where he oversaw the legal action against John, George and Ringo that effectively ended The Beatles. As a result of his victory, an official receiver was appointed to take over control of their financial affairs from Allen Klein.

Royal Hotel, 38–52 Woburn Place

When The Beatles made the long journey down to London for their Decca audition on 1 January 1962, John, Paul, George and Pete Best stayed here the night before. It being New Year's Eve, they made the mistake of joining in the traditional celebrations in Trafalgar Square when really they should have been preparing for their important appointment in the morning.

Royal Lancaster Hotel, Lancaster Terrace

The Beatles visited this Bayswater hotel on two occasions, linked to their movies. Firstly, with the upcoming showing of *Magical Mystery Tour* on BBC television, they held a fancy dress party, which was also the Apple Christmas party. The following year, just after *Yellow Submarine* had been premiered, they returned on 17 July 1968 for another party.

Rupert Court, Soho

When photographer Dezo Hoffmann was looking for a photo shoot location for The Beatles, he decided on this narrow link between Rupert Street and Wardour Street in the heart of Soho. It became one of the most iconic photos of the early Beatles as they walk through the alley with strip clubs either side.

Russell Square Gardens

Another of the many Dezo Hoffmann photo shoots took place in this central London park on 2 July 1963.

Saddle Room, 7 Hamilton Place

When George and Ringo were living in Green Street, they would often pop into this nearby club. They could even go home in a horse and cart.

3 Savile Row

(See entry for Apple Headquarters)

Saville Theatre, 135–149 Shaftesbury Avenue

A lifelong frustrated thespian, Brian leased this theatre in 1965 so that he could put on plays, operas and dances, though it also held many rock nights too. The Beatles never performed here, but saw many of the top acts of the time, most notably when Jimi Hendrix surprised the audience by playing 'Sgt Pepper's Lonely Hearts Club Band' just a few days after it had been released.

Savoy Hotel, Strand

At a lunch hosted by the Variety Club of Great Britain on 10 September 1963, The Beatles received an award for *Best Vocal Disk of The Year* for 'From Me To You' as voted for by the readers of *Melody Maker*. Paul returned on 13 July 1965 for an Ivor Novello lunch at which he picked up awards on behalf of himself and John.

The Scotch of St James, Masons Yard

One of the many 'hip' clubs popular with The Beatles, as shown by their own nameplate on 'their' table. The club saw the debut in the UK of Jimi Hendrix and was where Paul met Stevie Wonder for the first time.

Sibylla's, 9 Swallow Street

The Mayfair nightclub was part-financed by George Harrison. All four Beatles attended the grand opening on 23 June 1966.

Simpsons, Piccadilly

The Beatles had a real taste of their new-found fame when, before going into the nearby radio station, they popped into this famous clothing store. However, when they were recognised, they had to be escorted into a private room where staff brought the clothes in to them. It was certainly successful. The Beatles spent hundreds of pounds.

5 Somers Crescent, Hyde Park

From 1966, this was the home of producer George Martin, and where Paul McCartney made several visits as he sat down with Martin to discuss the orchestral arrangements of the latest Beatles songs. Paul, of course, couldn't read or write music, so had to describe to Martin what he wanted.

30 South Street, Mayfair

When Allen Klein visited London to oversee the restructuring of Apple, they rented this house for him, in which he also held private meetings with The Beatles.

102 Southampton Row

John, Paul and George supported the 'underground' newspaper *IT*, the *International Times*, located here, giving them interviews and even financial assistance too. In 1966 the Indica gallery bookshop moved here.

Speakeasy, 48 Margaret Street

Opened in 1966, the entrance of this club, complete with a coffin to resemble an undertaker's parlour, was through a wardrobe door. The Beatles, among others, would hang out here. They soon changed the 'Prohibition' inspired theme to an Indian one in 1967.

105 St George's Square, Pimlico

The home of Apple's film producer Denis O'Dell.

St John's Wood Church, Lord's Roundabout

After getting married at Marylebone Register Office on 12 March 1969, Paul and Linda had their marriage blessed here.

St James' Church Hall, 8-12 Gloucester Terrace

BBC Television used this hall to evaluate groups. On 23 November 1962, The Beatles turned up to be auditioned by Ronnie Lane, of BBC Light Entertainment, as to their suitability to appear on television, resulting in the band having to cancel their scheduled lunchtime appearance at the Cavern.

9 Stratford Street, Mayfair

Brian rented a private office at this address in 1965, located on the fourth floor of the building. With his assistant and secretary, Brian conducted The Beatles' business from here until he died, and The Beatles continued to visit the office until NEMS relocated.

2 Strathearn Place, Flat 1, Paddington

It was at the home of dentist John Riley that John, Cynthia, George and Pattie Boyd were invited to a party in July 1965 and had their first experience with LSD. Riley laced their coffee with the drug, but instead of staying in the house they hit the town, and even let Pattie drive home, very carefully.

Sutherland House, 5-6 Argyll Street

Brian Epstein's offices. NEMS Enterprises moved into this building on 9 March 1964, right next door to the London Palladium. However, due to its location in the heart of the shopping district of London, it wasn't easy for Brian's stars to enter the building without being mobbed by fans. Two special interviews were recorded here. Firstly, after their marriage in January 1966, George and his new bride Pattie gave a press conference here. The most famous, or should we say infamous, interview was conducted here by the *London Evening*

Standard's journalist Maureen Cleave. The interview, which hardly caused a ripple in the UK, featured John's legendary comments about The Beatles being more popular than Jesus.

More popular than The Beatles.

The Talk of the Town, Leicester Square

For most of its time, this venue was known as the London Hippodrome. However, from 1958 and through the 1960s, it was The Talk of the Town. Paul and Jane Asher were regular visitors to this popular variety club. Ringo would later come here to shoot a promotional video for his new album, *Sentimental Journey*, on 15 March 1970.

Television House, 4-12 Kingsway

Ready Steady Go! was one of the most popular television programmes devoted to the latest chart songs, and The Beatles made two live appearances on the show, filmed here. The first was on 4 October 1963 and the second on 20 March 1964. In the same building, John and Yoko appeared with presenter Eamonn Andrews on his show *Today*, on 1 April 1969.

Another important studio and key programme to be seen on.

1 The Vale, Chelsea

The most controversial of all The Beatles' album covers, the 'Butcher' image for the US album *The Beatles Yesterday And Today* was shot in a small studio here by Robert Whitaker on 25 March 1966. The replacement photo, by Nigel Dickson and Robert Whitaker, was also taken here.

Probably the most controversial album cover created here.

5 The Village, North End Way

When Derek Taylor became Brian's assistant in spring 1964, he moved from Manchester to this house, which he rented during his stay in London.

Trident Studios, 17 St Anne's Court

Established in 1967 by Barry and Norman Sheffield, this Soho studio offered the leading technology at the time, a Dolby 8-track recording system. It had a similar layout to the more famous Abbey Road. The Beatles entered the studio here on 31 July 1968 to record 'Hey Jude', and later returned for the *White Album* tracks 'Honey Pie', 'Savoy Truffle', 'Dear Prudence' and 'Martha My Dear', under the watchful eye of George Martin, though engineered by Barry Sheffield. 'I Want You (She's So Heavy)' on *Abbey Road* was also recorded here. Apple artist James Taylor recorded his first album here too. Following the success of the 'Hare Krishna Mantra' single by Radna Krishna Temple, plans for a follow-up were made in early 1970. Another traditional chant, 'Govinda', was chosen, which was recorded here on 7 February 1970. George Harrison produced the session, played acoustic guitar and Klaus Voormann played bass guitar.

Doesn't get the attention of Abbey Road, but was ahead of its competition.

TVC, 36–38 Dean Street

The home of TVC (TV Cartoons), the Soho production company that created *The Beatles*, the US television series that ran from 1965–66, and *Yellow Submarine*. The Beatles made several visits here during production of the film, one of which was filmed and included as an extra on the *Yellow Submarine* DVD.

Not in the town where they were born.

UFO, 31 Tottenham Court Road

Paul McCartney was a regular visitor to this club on a Friday night, where he would recall seeing the early Pink Floyd shows. During the week it was known as the Blarney Club. Richard Porter, a professional Beatles guide in London, says that the UFO could have stood for Unidentified Flying Object, but more likely 'Unlimited Freak Out'.

University College Hospital, 25 Grafton Way

No stranger to hospitals in his youth, Ringo was admitted here after collapsing during a photo session in Barnes on 3 June 1964, just prior to The Beatles embarking on a world tour. He was diagnosed with tonsillitis and pharyngitis, and was bed-bound for a while. Instead of cancelling the upcoming tour, the band hired Jimmie Nicol as replacement drummer until Ringo could join up with them. Ringo returned here at the beginning of December 1964 to have the tonsils removed.

University of London Union, Malet Street

In early 1963 London photographer Derek Berwin arranged an unusual photo shoot for teenage magazines *Valentine* and *Fabulous*, featuring The Beatles in the basement swimming pool of this university union.

Vesuvio, Tottenham Court Road

This club, originally opened in 1961, was taken over by Mick Jagger, Keith Richards and Tony Sanchez and reopened on 26 July 1968. Paul was in attendance and played The Beatles' new single 'Hey Jude' before it was released. This was its first public performance.

Vogue House, Hanover Square

The headquarters of *Vogue* magazine. John, Paul and Brian were photographed here in January 1965 by David Bailey, one of the country's leading photographers.

29 Wardour Street, Soho

Dezo Hoffmann was one of the best photographers The Beatles worked with, and his studio was here from 1960 until his death in 1986. The Beatles visited on four occasions between April and July 1963, including the photoshoot where the pictures of the Fab Four in the famous grey, collarless suits were taken, which were originally sketched by Stuart Sutcliffe.

Warner Cinema, 1 Cranbourne Street

Paul and Jane Asher attended the world premiere of the film *The Family Way* here, for which Paul had written the score and Jane had appeared in.

Wembley TV Studios, 128 Wembley Park Drive

One of The Beatles' earliest television appearances was on a show called *Tuesday Rendezvous*, where they appeared live on 4 December 1962. They made a further appearance on this programme 9 April 1963. When they were booked to appear on a television special, *Around The Beatles*, they rehearsed on 27 April 1964 and they recorded the following day, to be shown on 6 May 1964. *Ready Steady Go!*, one of the most popular pop music shows, showed The Beatles on the show on 27 November 1964, though they had recorded their appearance four days before. John and George were interviewed on the show when it had been retitled for a short period as *Ready Steady Goes Live!*, on 16 April 1965, and another popular show, *The Frost Programme*, hosted by David Frost, had John and George on 29 September and 4 October 1967, Paul on 27 December 1967 and then, on 24 August 1968, John and Yoko appeared on the show, now called *Frost On Saturday*, as well as an appearance with Simon Dee on 7 February 1970.

One of their most visited television studios.

Flat 15 Whaddon House, Williams Mews

Brian Epstein found himself this Belgravia flat in late 1963. When he told George and Ringo that another flat had become available, they left the Green Street apartment they had shared with John and Paul and moved into this exclusive mews. Brian was the one who led the exotic lifestyle and held many lavish parties here, including one in the summer of 1964 on the roof with many show-business celebrities.

7 ½, 5 White Horse Street

Another of the nightclubs frequented by The Beatles, this Mayfair establishment opened in 1967.

95 Wigmore Street, Marylebone

The Beatles moved their newly formed company Apple here in January 1968, where the most successful of the Apple companies, Apple Records, was set up with Peter Asher as its A&R man. After a rather unhappy stay at this address, Neil Aspinall found a more suitable building at 3 Savile Row, where they moved in July 1968.

Wimbledon Common

The first programme in the series from comedy duo Peter Cook and Dudley Moore, *Not Only … But Also*, featured John Lennon, who filmed a sequence on Wimbledon Common while acting out one of his poems from *In His Own Write*, 'Deaf Ted, Danoota, (and me)'. Filming took place on 20 November 1964 and it was broadcast on 9 January 1965.

Wimbledon Palais, Merton High Street

A week after their special concert in Liverpool for members of their Northern Area Fan Club, they did the same for the members of the Southern Area, with a performance here on 14 December. The mostly female audience that afternoon totalled 3,000. Fearing damage to both the group and their famous sprung dance floor, the management of the Palais assembled a makeshift, wooden plank platform for the group to stand on, and a steel cage to hold back the surging crowds. In a reference to the structure, John joked, 'If they press any harder they'll come through as chips.' In fact, the cage did begin to buckle under the strain. A local policeman managed to save the day by holding the fans back while a brave man managed to tighten the structure with a spanner. Following the show, The Beatles stood behind the venue's bar, drank black coffee and shook hands with every one of the fans present. Unsurprisingly, a few girls fainted. The group eventually had to stop dispensing signatures when the line grew too long.

57 Wimpole Street, Marylebone

The Asher family home. Paul, who was dating Jane, was invited to live with the family, giving him his own apartment within the home. John was a frequent visitor here and he and Paul would write together in the basement, including 'I Want To Hold Your Hand'. However, it is probably the song Paul 'dreamt' that is the most important he wrote here – 'Yesterday'. When his location was discovered, many fans camped outside to see their favourite Beatle. It became almost impossible for Paul to leave through the front door, so he developed an escape route via his bedroom window, the next-door property and into Browning Mews behind the houses, to be picked up by chauffeur Alf Bicknell. Those days of climbing in and out of his Forthlin Road home in Liverpool came in very handy. Paul and Jane moved out together in 1966 and set up home in Cavendish Avenue.

Home for Paul and site of the writing of some classic Beatles songs, where all his troubles seemed so far away.

LUTON

Majestic Ballroom, Mill Street

Located just 30 miles north of London is the Bedfordshire town of Luton. The Beatles made just the one appearance at the Magestic on 17 April 1963.

'We were performing and soaking wet with the heat,' John remembered, 'when a fan grabbed hold of my tie, and the knot got so tight I could not take it off. I was so dead tired that I left it on all night. Matched my pyjamas a treat! Come the morning, the only thing I could do was cut if off.' The crowd of 250 each paid six shillings and sixpence for a ticket. At the end of the show, fans lined up to meet the group and get signatures. Fan Janet sat on John's lap and allowed him to use her back as a rest when he signed a promotional postcard of the group. The rest of the group also signed it, with Paul adding the inscription, 'To Janet, love from The Beatles.' During this, Ringo ate a bag of crisps.

Odeon Cinema, 127 Dunstable Road, Bury Park

One appearance here, on 6 September 1963. The famous, group portrait of them looking into the camera, straightening their ties, was taken backstage on this third night of their brief, four-date, John Smith-promoted mini-tour.

Ritz Cinema, 16–42 Gordon Street

After a busy morning in the Abbey Road studios where several songs were mixed, The Beatles made the 30-mile journey north to Luton for two shows here on 4 November 1964, for which they were paid £850.

LYDNEY

Town Hall, Church Road

After playing the previous day in Chester and Liverpool, The Beatles made the 165-mile journey south to Gloucestershire where they played here in the Town Hall Chambers on 31 August 1962. This was their only appearance in Lydney.

MACCLESFIELD

El Rio Club, El Rio Dance Hall, Queen Victoria Street

The exotic sounding El Rio Dance Hall was in the not-so-exotic Cheshire town of Macclesfield where, on 26 January 1963, The Beatles played before travelling 20 miles to Stoke for their second appearance of the day.

MANCHESTER

Abbotsfield Park, Chassen Road

An annual bank holiday Manchester event, which on 5 August 1963 showcased four groups in a large marquee, headlined by The Beatles and including Brian Poole and The Tremeloes in the line-up.

ABC Cinema, Stockport Road, Ardwick

The Beatles were filmed here on 20 November 1963 by Pathé News before and during their first of two shows (for more details see *Beatles Come To Town* in *TV* section) and were also filmed backstage by Granada TV.

The Beatles returned to the venue on 14 October 1964, where they played two shows and were then interviewed by the BBC's *Look North* on 14 October 1964.

They made their final appearance at the Ardwick ABC, without television cameras, on 7 December 1965, seen by 2,693 fans at each of their two performances. During their journey up from Liverpool, where they had played two shows on 5 December 1965, the group hit a wall of fog that had started in the Manchester suburbs and brought the city's traffic to an almost standstill. For over four hours The Beatles' chauffeur, Alf Bicknell, steered their Princess car through Manchester's streets at a snail's pace. The group finally arrived at the venue 12 minutes after they were due to go on stage. An extra intermission was inserted into the show while The Beatles rushed to their dressing room and quickly changed into their stage costumes. They were pictured immediately after their arrival wearing protective air masks. Movie producer Walter Shenson paid a visit to the group's dressing room to discuss their next film.

Co-operative Hall, Long Street, Middleton

Just a short drive from Liverpool took The Beatles to Middleton in Manchester where they made their only appearance here on 11 April 1963, performing before a sell-out 300 crowd. The *Middleton Guardian* reported as follows. 'The four Beatles came off the stage pouring in sweat. They were cheerful and cracking jokes with each other … They ran the inevitable gauntlet of autograph hunters as they tried to wind down and get changed in time to get back to Liverpool for a well earned rest. Out of their dramatic maroon suits, they got comfortable and passed round the cigarettes. Less than 30 minutes after facing a crowd of perspiring fans, The Beatles were still a group, but this time just another group of homeward bound travellers on the Liverpool road.' Barry Chaytow was the promoter of the show. After the performance, The Beatles drove to Sefton General Hospital where John met his newborn son Julian for the first time.

Didsbury Studio Centre

After performing at Sheffield City Hall, they made a 40-mile trip to Manchester to record an interview with David Hamilton in studio two for *ABC At Large* on 2 March 1963.

Embassy Club, Rochdale Road

The Beatles reportedly made an appearance here, although no date is known. It is thought to have been in 1961, before Brian Epstein became their manager. The club was owned by the family of the late Manchester comedian Bernard Manning.

Granada Television Centre, Studio Four, Quay Street

After spending a rare night at home in Liverpool, The Beatles made the short drive to Manchester on 14 August 1963 where they recorded two songs for Granada's *Scene at 6.30* show, the first of which – 'Twist And Shout' – went out live, with the second – 'She Loves You' – broadcast on 19 August.

Hippodrome, Ardwick

Competing in a Carroll Levis *TV Star Search* talent show, John, Paul and George performed in this theatre as Johnny and The Moondogs in the week beginning 24 November 1958, having passed the audition in Liverpool.

Oasis Club, Lloyd Street

With Brian Epstein recently appointed as Beatles manager, he wanted to look outside of Liverpool for bookings, and the first of these was here on 2 February 1962. They went on to make a further three appearances here, on 29 September 1962, 8 December 1962 and 22 February 1963.

Odeon Cinema, Oxford Street

Just one appearance here at the Odeon Cinema in Oxford Street, Manchester, on 30 May 1963 during the Roy Orbison tour.

'Roy, who had numerous hits at that stage, was top of the bill,' Beatles fan Joan Dawkins recalled. 'The Beatles closed the first half of the show [but] by the time Roy came on to perform, the theatre had virtually emptied of the hundreds of teenage girls in the audience, who had fled outside hoping to catch a glimpse of the Fab Four. My friend Anna and I saw Roy sing a couple of bars of "Only The Lonely", looked at one another and, to my

eternal shame and regret, fled the theatre too. By then, there were only a handful of people watching Roy. The theatre was almost empty.'

Derek Taylor, the theatre critic and columnist for the Northern edition of the London *Daily Express*, sitting in the front row at the venue, favourably reviewed the concert in the following morning's edition of the paper. 'The Liverpool Sound came to Manchester last night,' he wrote, 'and I thought it was magnificent ... Indecipherable, meaningless nonsense, of course, but as beneficial and invigorating as a week on a beach at the pier head overlooking the Mersey.'

With their future employee and trusted friend, Derek Taylor, among the crowd watching, this was another highly important gig in The Beatles' career.

Playhouse Theatre, Warwick Street

The Playhouse Theatre in Hulme was the venue for the radio show *Teenagers' Turn – Here We Go*, for which The Beatles recorded in 1962. In 1963, they returned for several programmes for the *Pop Go The Beatles* show, broadcast on the BBC Radio Light Programme.

The Beatles' first radio appearances, in Manchester not Liverpool.

Southern Sporting Club, Birch Street

The Beatles made two appearances on the night of 13 June 1963, the first in Stockport and the second here at the former Corona Cinema.

Three Coins Club, Fountain Street

The Beatles played twice at this club, part owned by radio DJ Jimmy Savile. Their first appearance was on 5 November 1961 and they returned on

27 January 1963. Among the audience that night was Eric Stewart, soon of Wayne Fontana and The Mindbenders and later 10cc, and a future McCartney collaborator. Stewart's forthcoming 10cc bandmate Graham Gouldman was also present.

MANSFIELD

Granada Cinema, West Gate

It was in this Nottinghamshire town that The Beatles rejoined the Helen Shapiro tour on 23 February 1963.

Before going out to perform in the first show of the evening, the not-quite-yet Fab Four crowded into the one dressing room at the venue with a television, headliner Helen Shapiro's, to watch their performance of 'Please Please Me' on the ABC/ITV show *Thank Your Lucky Stars*, taped in Teddington, Middlesex the previous Sunday. 'Helen was the star,' Ringo admitted. 'She had the telly in her dressing room and we didn't have one. We had to ask her if we could watch hers.' Shapiro recalled, 'I remember sitting with them as they watched themselves on their first national TV appearance. They could not believe what they looked like."

The Beatles returned to the venue just over a month later, on 26 March 1963, during the Chris Montez/Tommy Roe tour.

MARGATE

Winter Gardens, Margate

The Beatles left the northern seaside resort of Blackpool and made the 320-mile trip to another holiday destination, Margate in the south-east of England, where from 8–13 July 1963 they played two shows per night.

Their stay in Kent was interrupted when they had to return to London on the morning of 10 July to tape two appearances for the BBC Light Programme radio show *Pop Go The Beatles*. (For more details see relevant entry in *Radio* section.)

MIDDLESBROUGH

Astoria Ballroom, Wilson Street

The Beatles left London on 25 June 1963 and made the long trip to the North East, to make their only appearance at this venue, supported by the Johnny Taylor 5 from Billingham.

MORECAMBE

Floral Hall Ballroom, Promenade

Just up the coast from Blackpool is Morecambe in Lancashire, where The Beatles made two appearances, the first on 29 August 1962, and the second on 18 June 1963 for which Les Hurst, the road manager for Gerry and The Pacemakers, was forced to fill-in for a flu-hit Neil Aspinall.

NELSON

Imperial Ballroom, Carr Road

This small mill town in Lancashire played host to The Beatles at this venue, commonly known as 'The Imp', twice in 1963, on 11 May (for which tickets cost six shillings in advance, seven shillings on the night) and 31 July (tickets seven shillings sixpence in advance, eight shillings sixpence on the night), where they were welcomed by around two thousand fans. Paul also judged a beauty contest here on 13 September 1963.

NEWCASTLE-UPON-TYNE

City Hall, Northumberland Road

The City Hall in the north-east city of Newcastle became a popular venue for The Beatles. They made their first appearance there on 23 March

1963 during the Chris Montez/Tommy Roe tour, followed by three further concerts, on 8 June (Roy Orbison tour) and 23 November (autumn tour) of the same year, and 4 December 1965 as part of their final UK tour, seen by 3,500 for each of the two shows.

With snow falling quite heavily in the city in November 1965, chauffeur Alf Bicknell had a tough time driving through it to reach the venue. There were scenes of pandemonium outside where 120 fans had to be given first aid treatment, with seven hospitalised.

Majestic Ballroom, Westgate Road

The Beatles played here on two occasions, the first on 28 January 1963, for which the admission price on the door was three shillings and sixpence. Their second appearance was on 26 June 1963. Prior to this show, and influenced by Bobby Rydell's recent hit 'Forget Him', while they were facing each other on the twin beds in their shared room at the Royal Turks Head Hotel, John and Paul began composing 'She Loves You'. The pair completed the song the following day at Paul's family home, 20 Forthlin Road, Liverpool.

NEWTON-LE-WILLOWS
Town Hall, Market Street, Earlestown

The Beatles made one appearance in this market town near St Helens, on 30 November 1962, for an evening's entertainment billed as 'The Big Beat Show 2', promoted by the football section of the T&T Vicars Sports and Social Club.

NORTHAMPTON
ABC Cinema, Abington Square

The Beatles made two appearances here in 1963, on 27 March as part of the Chris Montez/ Tommy Roe tour, and on 6 November during their autumn tour.

NORTHWICH
Memorial Hall, Chester Way

Northwich, in North Cheshire, was only a 28-mile drive from Liverpool, and The Beatles played six times at this venue for promoter Lewis Buckley, between 23 June 1962 and 14 September 1963. That first concert was basically an audition for Buckley, an important promoter who organised beat music dances at various locations around Britain. Anxious to make a good impression, Brian Epstein urged the group to give a great performance. They obviously did as Buckley went on to book The Beatles, as well as Brian's other NEMS acts, several more times over the coming years.

Prior to their penultimate show here, on 6 July 1963, the group attended the annual Northwich Carnival at Verdin Park, Norwich, with Paul crowning the new Carnival Queen.

NORWICH
Grosvenor Rooms, Prince of Wales Road

The Beatles left London and headed for Norfolk on 17 May 1963 to perform two 20-minute sets here, their only concert at this venue. The fee for the gig was £250. The promoters of the event were Peter Holmes and Ray Aldous; the contract was signed on 19 April 1963. The poster for the shows, outside the venue and in the local press read, 'Fabulous Attraction, Great Visit – TV Stars … It's a must for those who like to twist, jive, rave. They are entertainment themselves. Please Please Me, From Me To You, who else could make such sensational recordings other than . . . The Beatles, the group with the 1963 sound.'

The 1,700 in attendance had each paid seven shillings and sixpence for a ticket, a sharp increase from the usual two shillings and sixpence Friday-night entrance fee to the venue. The Beatles arrived during the afternoon, in their blue Bedford van. With no roadies in tow, they were forced to set up their own equipment on the tiny stage. Those present were shocked by how scruffy John looked. While Paul, George and Ringo were dressed smartly in T-shirts, jumpers and jeans, Lennon's trousers were held up by a big nappy pin. The group signed their signatures for a number of waiting fans, and then, following a soundcheck, left for some food and watched a film at the next-door but one ABC cinema. John strained his eyes watching the movie so Paul had to escort him back to the Grosvenor building.

Fan Diane Rolls and a friend were given front-row places to the show, so close in fact that she was able to hold on to Paul's foot during the performance. Another worshipper, Jill Daynes, recalled, 'The atmosphere was fantastic. When they did "Roll Over Beethoven" everybody was singing. It was just magical. They looked so lovely in their Beatles suits.' When the curtains came down, the group lugged their equipment back into their van. As he watched them, promoter Peter Holmes noticed something in The Beatles' vehicle ... two young ladies. Peter naturally asked, 'Have you brought the girlfriends with you, then?' 'No,' Ringo replied, 'we've never seen them before.' Minus their drummer, who had been detained by the fans back at the Grosvenor, the other Beatles then walked down the road for some cod and chips in Valori's takeaway in Rose Lane, the so-called 'best-known catering dynasty in Norwich.' Employee Jimmy Hughes was the man who served them that night. John became annoyed when told by Hughes that his original choice of haddock was not on the menu.

NOTTINGHAM
Elizabethan Ballroom, Co-op House, Upper Parliament Street

The first of the *Mersey Beat Showcase* concerts, arranged by Brian Epstein and sponsored by promoters John Smith, took place here on 7 March 1963. Epstein's idea was to package all of his artists in one show; the other acts on the bill were Gerry and The Pacemakers, The Big Three and Billy J. Kramer and The Dakotas. To keep in line with the Liverpool theme, the Cavern DJ Bob Wooler was the compère of the event. NEMS Enterprises organised two coaches to transport 80 paying fans from Liverpool to Nottingham to watch the gig. Tickets for the show were priced at six shillings and sixpence.

Odeon Cinema, Angel Row

As the Roy Orbison tour resumed, The Beatles left Ipswich for Nottingham, a 140-mile drive, and made the first of their three appearances here, on 23 May 1963. Officer Peter Gibson of the Nottingham City Police Force, was assigned to guard The Beatles dressing room that night. 'The band walked past me every now and then,' he remembered. 'They were very talkative young guys.' At the start of the evening, as it had become the custom to do back then, fans handed in autograph books and albums at the box office hoping for signatures and at the end of the night, those same fans would crowd round the back and shout for the stars of the night to present themselves. Loud screams rang out when The Beatles did just that, suddenly appearing through a door on top of the fire escape waving. However, the fans' excitement swiftly turned to anger and sadness when John placed a huge pile of their books and albums onto the railing and sent them raining down onto the youngsters below. All their precious items were torn to pieces by the crowd. Many young girls were distraught at losing their books, some of which were already full of famous signatures. The Beatles however thought it was amusing and went back inside laughing, leaving scenes of mayhem below. Later, the group, unmoved by the unhappiness they had just caused, went for a couple of drinks in the private bar at the local police station on Shakespeare Street.

The Beatles returned to the venue on 12 December as part of their autumn tour, and for a final time on 5 November 1964.

OLDHAM

Astoria Ballroom, King Street

On Tuesday 12 February 1963, just a day after the group had recorded ten of the songs for their debut album *Please Please Me*, The Beatles were back on the concert trail playing either side of the Pennines. First came an appearance in Sheffield, Yorkshire, before the group headed over to Lancashire and the Astoria Ballroom in Oldham. Suffering from a heavy cold, and after nearly wrecking his voice singing 'Twist And Shout' in the studio the previous day, John still took to the stage. 'Every time I swallowed,' he said, 'it was like sandpaper.'

There were around 800 fans in attendance that night. It was estimated that bouncer Fred Lowe, who also ran a junk store in the market during the day, had turned away an estimated 2,000. The Beatles were late arriving at the venue, but when they did turn up, they received a telegram from Maurice Kinn, editor of the *New Musical Express*. Paul asked for quiet and then read it out to the assembled crowd of friends, fans and reporters. 'Congratulations, The Beatles' "Please Please Me" is Number One on the *NME* charts!' They were ecstatic and hugged each other. 'Fuck me!' John exclaimed. 'Anyone got a Prelly?' The white

Preludine (appetite depressant) tablets were then passed round. He took two, dropping them with a Scotch and coke.

A reporter from the *Oldham Evening Chronicle* was there to record events. 'As hundreds of fans swamped the ballroom entrance in a bid to see their idols, the steel pedestrian guards collapsed, spilling dozens into the Star Inn road junction, and holding up traffic. Only 800 were let in, many were turned away, and excited fans rushed the stage. One woman's dress was ripped in the melee, as The Beatles sang their hits "Love Me Do" and "Please Please Me". During the latter, fainting girls had to be dragged onto stage to save them from being crushed by the human avalanche. George was horrified when a girl broke through the crowd and threw herself around his neck.'

Following the performance, the group returned to their dressing room, where John disappeared with a fan into the adjoining toilet. Paul welcomed a man from Shaw, just outside Oldham, whom he introduced to everyone as 'an old mucker of me dad's.' The elderly gentleman then invited them all to his house for a cup of tea. 'What do you think, John?' Paul asked his bandmate as Lennon left the toilet. 'Why not,' he replied, before asking the man, 'Do yer 'ave any cheese sarnies?'

A notable show, due to the fact it took place when The Beatles had just secured their very first No. 1 disc.

ORMSKIRK

Scarisbrick Water Works, Southport Road

During the summer of 1959, John's art college friend Tony Carricker got him a job on the building site of the new Mill Brow water treatment centre, known as the Scarisbrick Water Works, just outside of Ormskirk, about 16 miles from

Liverpool. Carricker's father was the building supervisor on the site and managed to secure work for his son and John for the six weeks over the summer at £5 per week, a considerable sum for the time. Although the work was hard, John used the money towards buying a new guitar.

For someone like John who liked to sleep, only a guitar could have got him out of bed.

OXFORD

Carfax Assembly Rooms, Cornmarket Street

One of London's top promoters, John Smith, booked The Beatles for their appearance at the heart of the city that boasts the oldest English-speaking university in the world for one performance here on 16 February 1963, a sell-out show attended by 300 fans. It was their only concert in Oxford.

With George and Ringo arriving late for the afternoon soundcheck, Will Jarvis and Neil Robinson of the support act The Madisons happily filled in and jammed with John and Paul. Lead guitarist Jarvis took them out for a Chinese meal in Ship Street after the show. For drummer Neil it wasn't so pleasant when, at the end of the evening, he discovered his jacket had been stolen. It was found, one day later, at the side of the road in Basingstoke, with his wallet missing.

The Beatles also met Jeffrey Archer at the concert. The group accepted his invitation to visit Brasenose's senior common room briefly after the gig for a few drinks. The broadcaster Sheridan Morley, who was also present that night, recalled bumping into Ringo during a visit to the toilet. 'He asked if I knew this Jeffrey Archer bloke,' Morley recalled. 'I said everyone in Oxford was trying to work out who he was and Ringo said,

"He strikes me as a nice enough fella, but he's the kind of bloke who would bottle your piss and sell it."'

PETERBOROUGH

Embassy Cinema, Broadway

The Beatles' first appearance here on 2 December 1962 was a disaster. Brian had booked them to appear on the same bill as Frank Ifield, but they didn't go down well at all, being upstaged by the Australian-born Columbia Records singer according to the reviews. Ifield naturally performed his No. 1 smash hit 'I Remember You', which would soon become part of the Fab Four's set-list. Their rendition of it, recorded later that month during their final nightclub appearance in Hamburg, would appear on the 1977 double album *Live! At The Star-Club*.

Thankfully, their second and final appearance here, on 17 March 1963 as part of the Chris Montez/Tommy Roe tour, went much more smoothly.

PLYMOUTH

ABC Cinema, George Street

Chaos surrounded The Beatles when they arrived for their performance in this Devon town on 13 November 1963 as part of their autumn tour. The Beatles had to be smuggled out for a television interview with presenter Stuart Hutchinson for the teenager-aimed, Westward ITV television show *Move Over, Dad* and then back into the cinema through the side door. That night the group secretly managed to take up residence in Torquay's Imperial Hotel before going on to Exeter.

They returned to the ABC in Plymouth for one more appearance on 29 October 1964. On the way to the show, the very tired and weary Beatles stopped their Austin Princess car, walked into a confection-ery shop and bought two pounds of sweets. 'That meant a lot to us,' Ringo later admitted. 'The free-dom of the moment made a real impact on me. It was just like jumping school, doing something that wasn't on the schedule, and pleasing yourself as to what you do at a certain moment, instead of being hemmed in and timed to do everything at a given minute. We enjoyed those sweets more than many a big caviar or an expensive meal.'

Westward Television Studios, Derry's Cross

While they were playing in Plymouth, Westward Television arranged to interview The Beatles for their teenage programme, *Move Over, Dad*. They filmed it on 13 November 1963 in the Athenaeum Theatre.

PORTSMOUTH

Guildhall, Guildhall Square

Whereas the first appearance of The Beatles here on 30 March 1963 as part of the Chris Montez/ Tommy Roe tour went without a hitch, their second booking on 12 November 1963 had to be postponed because Paul had gastric flu, one of the only times they had to rearrange a concert. A new date of 3 December was scheduled in, before a few days' well-earned rest.

Although the November date had to be cancelled, the group still managed to give two television interviews on that day in their dress-ing room at the Guildhall, for BBC TV's *South Today* magazine programme and Southern ITV's similar show, *Day By Day*, during which reporter Jeremy James asked them, 'How did you get here tonight?' Paul humorously replied, 'A van.' Jones continued, 'You're getting so much publi-city these days, and even the egghead papers are writing about you. Have you been just a little bit

worried that you might be going over the top fairly soon?' 'No,' John replied, 'When you gotta go, you gotta go.' James pressed further. 'What are you going to do when your time comes?' 'Sail on me yacht,' George retorted.

Savoy Ballroom, South Parade, Southsea

Having played in Buxton, Derbyshire the night before, The Beatles made the 210-mile journey to the south coast of England to play here on 7 April 1963, for a fee of just £50.

They almost never made it to the gig. Their van broke down on the A3, forcing Neil Aspinall to call the venue and ask whether Ringo could borrow the kit belonging to Terry Wiseman of the support act Mike Devon and The Diplomats. While their vehicle was being towed away for repair, The Beatles climbed into a car and carried what they could. In Ringo's case it was his sticks and snare, which never left his side. The Beatles finally arrived at the venue at 5pm and had to battle for 15 minutes to make their way through the crowd. As soon as they had successfully made their way into the venue, Paul asked where the piano was. 'He had composed something in his head on the way down in the car,' Terry recalled, 'and wanted to set it down in music before it faded from his memory.' Unfortunately, what this song actually was does seem to have faded from everyone's memory.

The dressing room set-up was unusual, with the two bands sharing. As both acts changed into their suits for the concert, their regular clothes were lumped together in a pile. There was no star treatment for The Beatles on this occasion. A problem arose over the borrowed drum kit during the show. Two stages had been built, a large one for The Beatles and a smaller one for The Diplo-mats, so, once the latter had finished their first set, Terry's drum kit, drums, cymbals and stands had to be carried over to the other stage in order for Ringo to use them.

As part of their performance, The Diplomats, known locally as a Beatles tribute act, intended to sing several numbers by the Fab Four: 'Love Me Do', 'Please Please Me', 'I Saw Her Standing There', 'Do You Want To Know A Secret', 'There's A Place' and 'Twist And Shout'. Given whom they were supporting, they decided to ask permission first and Paul told them to go ahead. They then thought it best to check whether their sets were likely to be very similar. If so, would that be a problem? 'So what?' was Paul's response. 'We play them again and again, no problem.' After the successful evening had ended, the two groups met in the makeshift dressing room for a drink of Coke and a chat.

PRESTON

Public Hall, Lune Street

A 'Rock & Beat Spectacular' was how The Beatles' first appearance in Preston was billed, on 26 October 1962. They travelled the 35 miles up from Liverpool, having played at the Cavern that lunchtime. They came here for a second and final time on 13 September 1963, after which Paul headed 25 miles straight down the Ribble Valley to the mill town of Nelson where he was forced, obviously against his will, to judge the 'Imperial Miss 1963' beauty contest, part of the yearly *Young Ones Ball*, sponsored by the local paper, the *Nelson Leader*.

ROCHESTER

Rochester Cathedral

On Christmas Eve 1969, John and Yoko were driven to Rochester Cathedral as part of an anti-war demonstration due to take place in various countries, for which the couple had tape-recorded a greeting to be played. The intention was to join a fast and sit-in calling for peace and to highlight world poverty. They arrived, accompanied by comedian Dick Gregory, in a white Rolls-Royce. They were due to take part in a 24-hour sleepover with the homeless of Kent. However, a small crowd was already present when they arrived, and it was felt likely that their continued presence would have caused a commotion, so they stepped inside the cathedral, where they attended midnight mass, before returning to their home at Tittenhurst.

ROMFORD

ABC Cinema , South Street

The ABC Cinema on South Street, Romford was host to The Beatles for the first and only time on 20 March 1963 as part of the Chris Montez/Tommy Roe tour.

86 George Street

Ringo's stepfather Harry Graves was born here in 1913 and moved north to Liverpool. Harry married Ringo's mother Elsie in 1954.

Odeon Cinema, corner of South Street and Havana Close

When they appeared here on 16 June 1963, The Beatles were at number one in the charts and their support acts, Billy J. Kramer and the Dakotas plus Gerry and The Pacemakers, were at numbers two and three respectively. This appearance was the last of Brian Epstein's *Mersey Beat Showcase* concerts, promoted by John Smith. Ringo's step-grandparents, James and Louisa Graves, lived round the corner, in George Street, and following their performance, the group popped round to visit them.

RUNCORN

La Scala Ballroom, High Street

Runcorn, situated on the River Mersey south of Liverpool, was host to The Beatles on 16 October 1962, where they backed Liverpool doo-wop singers The Chants. They returned here just a few weeks later on 11 December.

SALISBURY

City Hall, Fisherton Street

The Beatles performed a concert here in front of more than 1,500 people on 15 June 1963. Promoted by Jaybee Clubs, and arranged back in April, the group's fee was £300, but as the date drew nearer Brian Epstein offered Jaybee £200 to cannel the booking, fearing for the band's safety in such a small venue. His offer was refused.

SCARBOROUGH

Futurist Theatre, Foreshore Road, South Bay

After playing in Doncaster the night before, The Beatles stayed in Yorkshire for the first of their two appearances in this seaside town venue, 11 December 1963. The band returned to the Futurist nine months later, on 9 August 1964.

SEVENOAKS

Knole Park

A Kentish deer park where, in January 1967, Swedish film director Peter Goldmann directed the promotional films for 'Penny Lane' and 'Strawberry Fields Forever'.

A preview of what would become The Beatles' *Sgt Pepper* music.

SHEFFIELD

Azena Ballroom, White Lane, Gleadless

Before travelling back to Lancashire for a performance in Oldham, The Beatles made their only appearance at the Sheffield Azena Ballroom on 12 February 1963.

The concert took place during a break in their tour with singer Helen Shapiro. The venue was so-called in honour of its owners, Arnold and Zena Fidler.

The 22-year-old entrepreneur and future night-club owner Peter Stringfellow was responsible for booking The Beatles. Brian Epstein's original fee for the concert was £50, which Stringfellow thought exorbitant. 'Excuse me,' he told Epstein, 'I only pay Screaming Lord Sutch £50, and nobody has heard of The Beatles!' Having thought it over, Stringfellow then called back to confirm, at which point Brian cheekily upped the asking price to £65. Within days, he had increased it again, this time to £100. 'The Beatles have another single coming out ["Please Please Me"],' Epstein told Stringfellow, 'and this will go to the top of the charts.' Stringfellow fought back and, after further negotiations (carried out via the public call box on the council estate where he lived), he managed to barter Epstein down to £85.

They had originally been scheduled for The Black Cat Club (aka St Aiden's Church Hall), but in between hiring them and the date of the event, ticket sales skyrocketed, thanks in part to the release of 'Please Please Me'. 'By January,' Stringfellow recalled, 'I knew I had sold in excess of 1,500 tickets. I also knew that The Black Cat could hold only 700, so I knew I had to find another venue.' He did, the larger Azena Ballroom, 'Sheffield's poshest dance hall,' on the outskirts of the city.

On the night, Stringfellow collected The Beatles from their hotel and squeezed them into the back of his Ford Anglia. 'When we arrived at the Azena,' he recalled, 'there were people crawling all over the roof [of his car] trying to get in. The Beatles went in by the fire exit and set up on the stage while I tried to contain the crowd.' Stringfellow had cannily managed to sell 2,000 tickets for the show. Reports suggested that a further 1,000 fans had turned up on the tiniest hope of getting in. A few did, paying six shillings and sixpence, one shilling over the original asking price, to an enterprising ticket tout outside the venue. The concert was a major success, despite the fact Paul's Hofner bass wasn't working, so he had to borrow one from John Bealy, a singer in the support band at the gig.

City Hall, Barker's Pool

Their first appearance here was on 2 March 1963 as part of the Helen Shapiro tour. After this gig they drove to Manchester to record an interview with David Hamilton. Their second appearance coincided with another interview, but this time it was in London. As soon as it had finished, they had to drive 160 miles north to make it in time for their appearance on the Chris Montez/ Tommy Roe tour. It was a popular venue; they made three more uneventful appearances here on 25 May (Roy Orbison tour) and 2 November 1963, plus 9 November 1964. The final appearance of a Beatle at this venue was another London to Sheffield drive, this time for George, who played back-up guitar here on 4 December 1969 with husband and wife act Delaney & Bonnie on their brief UK tour.

Gaumont Theatre, Barker's Pool

On their final UK tour The Beatles played two shows here on 8 December 1965, watched by a crowd of 2,300 at each. *The Beatles Book Monthly* photographer Leslie Bryce was on hand to shoot images of the concerts.

SHREWSBURY
Granada Cinema, Castle Gates

Although The Beatles' appearance here on 28 February 1963 during the Helen Shapiro tour may be insignificant, the journey from York saw John and Paul write their third single, 'From Me To You'. The composition had been inspired by *From You To Us*, the letters section of the *New Musical Express*.

Music Hall, The Square

A popular venue for most of the leading acts of the day. The Beatles played here on 14 December 1962 and 26 April 1963.

Backstage at the 1962 gig, the group spent time with their friend, the British beat poet Royston Ellis, who was taking a brief holiday back in the UK.

SKEGNESS
Butlin's Holiday Camp

Ringo was playing with Rory Storm and The Hurricanes at Butlin's here in the summer of 1962 when he was prised away to join The Beatles and become the final member of the group that would be known as the Fab Four.

For Ringo this could have been his future until The Beatles came along.

SLOUGH
Adelphi Cinema

The third UK tour started here on 18 May 1963 with The Beatles (initially) supporting Roy Orbison on a nationwide tour (as The Beatles' popularity soared they soon shared top billing). Gerry and The Pacemakers were also on the bill for the tour, which was promoted by Arthur Howes. Tickets ranged in price from five shillings to nine shillings and sixpence. Lennon later remarked about Orbison, 'It was pretty hard to keep up with that man. He really put on a show, well, they all did, but Orbison had that fantastic voice.'

There were two shows per night on the tour, with the first one here, at 6pm, failing to sell out (many fans were working and unable to make it to the early concert). The second one, at 8.30pm, however, broke all records for the theatre when, within five days of going on sale, every seat had been sold. The theatre's manager, Nigel Lockyer, excitedly announced he could have 'sold them three times over!'

To thunderous applause, George Martin surprised everyone by presenting on stage silver discs to both The Beatles for half-a-million sales of 'From Me To You', and to Gerry Marsden, of Gerry and The Pacemakers, for the same number of sales of 'How Do You Do It?'. After the presentation, Gerry jokingly grabbed The Beatles' disc and playfully presented it back to them with the words, 'From me to you, for "From Me To You".' Pictures of John, Paul, George and Ringo posing with some of the acts on the bill were taken in one of the venue's dressing rooms.

In between shows, Ringo told a reporter from the *Slough Express* newspaper, 'When you're successful in show business, you certainly look back on milestones, like this show in Slough. I hope we'll be back again.' They were, a little under six-months later.

Another high spot in The Beatles' career, supporting the American singing legend, Roy Orbison.

They made their second appearance here, during their autumn tour, on 5 November 1963, after filming in a London taxi for the Associated-Redifusion television programme *This Week* earlier in the day.

The group arrived at the venue at 4.25pm and were pictured by local newspaper reporters entering the stage door. A crowd of 100 fans was waiting to greet them; so too were Mr G.H. Wilkinson, Deputy Chief of Constables of Bucks, and Chief Superintendent L. Harman, in charge of operations. 'Our plan is to get you out immediately as the fans are leaving the theatre,' Harman told them. A plan was hatched, whereby a louder than usual national anthem was played at the end of the night and while hundreds of fans were still standing inside the theatre, The Beatles would dash off the stage, race out through the stage door and into the waiting car. 'They were really co-operative,' Harman declared. 'We could not have wished to deal with a nicer group of lads. They agreed to our plans and went along with it, to the letter. It had to be done that way. Once the fans were out of the theatre, anything could have happened.'

'The Beatles were playing that evening at the Adelphi Cinema in Slough,' local fan Pamela recalled. 'I took the afternoon off school and went to the cinema, but someone said the boys were down in the town, doing some shopping in Woolworths.' But this was a lie.

They were actually inside the cinema signing promotional pictures, three big boxes of autograph books and a copy of their *Please Please Me* album, which was going to be raffled for the 'Slough Freedom From Hunger' campaign, which had been launched that day by the Eton and Slough MP, Mr Fenner Brockway. 'The Beatles spent most of their time between shows on the floor of their dressing room, the theatre manager, Nigel Lockyer, confirmed, 'forming a chain to sign all the books. It took all their time to finish two of the boxes. They just could not get through the other.'

Another fan outside the venue that day was 15-year-old Jennifer Gillberry, who announced that she and her friends had told their foreman they were taking the day off to see The Beatles. 'When he said, "It's your jobs or The Beatles," we chose The Beatles,' she said.

Anticipating the mayhem that seemed to be following the group everywhere they went, 80 extra policemen had been drafted in from places as far away as High Wycombe and Chesham. There was a black market for tickets for the shows, with five-shilling tickets being offered for as much as between a pound and five pounds. But by show time, in particular for the second house, prices had fallen to between ten shillings and three pounds because there were no takers.

During the second show, excited fans hurled balls of paper and posies onto the stage and a thrown toilet roll got tangled in Paul's bass. Two fans sprinted down the gangway from the back of the stalls and tried to climb onto the stage. They were dragged back by attendants. A crew from St John Ambulance treated 11 girls who had fainted. 'There was so much noise,' one fan complained, 'I couldn't hear myself scream.'

The Beatles made their getaway shortly before 11pm, less than 30 seconds after the final curtain had fallen. They raced to their waiting Austin Princess car and, with Jaguar police cars in front and behind, sirens blazing, they made their way through the crowd. One young girl managed to break the police cordon and run straight into the path of a car. Thankfully she was pulled back in time. As they passed through Mackenzie Street, they caught sight of one solitary man who was standing on the roadside holding aloft a placard that read, 'I hate The Beatles.'

Cashing in on the group's visit, the town's local master hair-stylist, Keymilla, in the High Street, launched a new style to entice the fans. Entitled 'Beatlette', it was a roaring success.

Two years later, on 16 November 1965, driven by The Beatles' regular chauffeur, Alf Bicknell, Paul returned to the venue as the unannounced compère for the night, headlined by the American singer, Gene Pitney. He remained hidden from the audience throughout. Standing behind the theatre's huge, dark-red curtains, Paul's first introduction went as follows, 'Arthur Howe presents … the Gene Pitney Show! And to start the show in swinging style, The Mike Cotton Sound!' His then girlfriend, Jane Asher, told a *Slough Observer* reporter, 'He decided to introduce the show just for a giggle. Haven't you heard Paul's supah English accent? No one will ever recognise him.'

In between houses, when the curtain was down, and after the first audience had left, Paul, wearing an open-neck, black and white check shirt and a black cord jacket, with a big floppy collar, knocked out a quiet rhythm on the drums. 'I just came along with Peter [Jane Asher's brother] and Gordon to see the show,' he told the reporter. 'It's a long time since I've been able to watch a show, instead of taking part in one.' With fans mobbing him wherever he went, the reporter naturally asked him how he managed to get into the building. 'I drove up to the stage door,' the Beatle replied, 'in Peter and Gordon's car, and whipped straight inside. I'm beginning to know this stage door now; we've been through it at least twice before.'

SMETHWICK

Smethwick Baths Ballroom, Thimblemill Road

Monday 19 November 1962 was a crazy day on the road for The Beatles. It began with a lunchtime session at the Cavern, followed by a trip to Smethwick, around 85 miles, where they played in this ballroom, also known as Thimblemill Baths, before moving on to the Adelphi Ballroom in West Bromwich near Birmingham.

In Smethwick, Beatles fan Jane met the group at the venue. Paul, George and Ringo gave autographs, but John spelt her name wrong, signing his name to 'Jayne'. He crossed it out and re-did it correctly. George bought Jane and her cousin a glass of orange juice each.

SOUTHAMPTON

Gaumont Cinema, Commercial Road

The Beatles' first appearance here was on 20 May 1963 on the Roy Orbison tour. 'A friend of mine and I bunked off school,' a teenager at the event recalled, 'and went to wait with autograph books in sweaty hands at the stage door of the theatre. The tour bus rolled up and The Beatles got off. I approached Lennon and politely asked him for his signature, he pushed me in the chest and told me to fuck off! … My friend and I were hanging around the Gaumont car park after The Beatles had arrived, and up rolled this huge American car. Roy was behind the wheel. Compared with John Lennon, he was a gentleman. He signed autographs and chatted happily for five minutes or more, before rushing off to practise his high notes.'

The Beatles returned to the Gaumont on Friday 13 December 1963 for the final show of their autumn tour.

Their last performance at the venue was on 6 November 1964. Prior to the show, they recorded a television interview in their dressing room with Tony Bilbow for Southern ITV's nightly news magazine show *Day By Day*.

Southern Independent Television Centre, Northam

While based in Bournemouth during the summer of 1963, The Beatles made the trip along the coast to Southampton where on 22 August they were filmed for the regional show *Day by Day*.

SOUTHEND-ON-SEA

Odeon Cinema, High Street

The first of two appearances here was on 31 May 1963 during the Roy Orbison tour, with a second show the same year on 9 November as part of The Beatles' autumn tour. Prior to that show, the band recorded yet another television interview.

SOUTHPORT

Air Training Corps Club, Upper Aughton Road, Birkdale

Situated in Birkdale just outside Southport. The Beatles made one appearance here on 9 March 1961. Following this gig they then played at the Labour Club on Devonshire Road.

Cambridge Hall, Lord Street

The Beatles appeared here once on 26 July 1962, the first of two consecutive shows headlined by Joe Brown and The Bruvvers (the second was at the Tower Ballroom, New Brighton). Joe Brown was then riding high in the singles charts with 'A Picture Of You', one of Brian Epstein's favourite songs. The concerts were sponsored by Epstein's NEMS Enterprises. John, Paul, George and Pete were once again billed as 'The Sensational Beatles'. Harry Prytherch, the drummer with The Remo Four, one of the support acts, retained a hand-painted poster advertising the gig.

Floral Hall, Promenade

The Beatles played here four times, twice in 1962 on 20 February and 20 November, and twice in 1963 on 23 April and 15 October. It was a popular locale because it had a proper theatre auditorium, unlike many of the smaller clubs.

Glen Park Club, Lord Street

The Beatles appeared here once on 5 November 1961.

Kingsway Club, Promenade

The Beatles appeared here eight times in 1962, on various Monday nights from 22 January to 23 July. The club was licensed, which caused a problem because their audience was mainly teenagers who were not permitted to drink alcohol. To solve this the band played upstairs in the hall as it didn't have a bar.

Brian Epstein's parents, Harry and Malka ('Queenie'), were present in the audience for their first night here and would meet the group for the first time after the show. 'I had never been to a rock 'n' roll concert before, and I had no idea what to wear,' Queenie recalled.

The band's third date here, 5 February, is also notable because Ringo was on drums. (For more details, see Cavern club entry for this date.)

Labour Club, Devonshire Road

The Beatles played here on 9 March 1961, having the same night performed a few miles away at the ATC. Now called the 'Devonshire', it is still an active club in Southport.

The Little Theatre, Hoghton Street

The Beatles didn't perform here, but were filmed at this location for a documentary on 27 August 1963 called *The Mersey Sound*. It was shown on BBC television on 9 October 1963, John Lennon's twenty-third birthday.

Odeon Cinema, Lord Street

The Beatles performed at this cinema, now the site of a Sainsbury's supermarket, on 1 March 1963 as part of the Helen Shapiro tour. Later that same year, they took up a six-night residency here from 26–31 August, playing two houses each evening.

Queens Hotel, Promenade

This used to be a very popular hotel and dance venue. The Beatles made just one appearance here on 6 December 1962 in the Club Django, which was predominantly a jazz club.

ST HELENS
Plaza Ballroom, Duke Street

The Beatles played at the Plaza Ballroom, a popular venue, on four consecutive Mondays from 25 June 1962. It was here that Pete Best remembers having to ask Brian Epstein about his place in the band, after Liverpool promoter Joe Flannery had said to him, 'Do you want to join my band, oops?', as if Flannery knew something was going on. Flannery was a close friend of Epstein's. Epstein dismissed Pete's fears. 'Rest assured, my boy, nothing like that is going to happen to you.' It was only a few weeks later that he was called into Epstein's office to hear the news that he was sacked.

The Beatles' final appearance here was on 4 March 1963, their first £100 gig.

STOCKPORT
Palace Theatre Club, Turncroft Lane

On Thursday 13 June 1963 The Beatles played two cabaret clubs just ten miles apart. The first was at this theatre, before heading over to Hyde Road in Manchester.

STOCKTON-ON-TEES
Globe Cinema, High Street

On 22 November 1963 The Beatles were in the north-east of England, performing at the Globe for the first time. Teenagers had queued all night waiting for the box office to open to buy the tickets, which had been priced between six shillings and sixpence and ten shillings and sixpence for the seats at the front. All tickets were sold within two hours, two of which were then put up for auction by the landlady of the local Brunswick Hotel in Wilson Street, Middlesbrough in aid of Leukaemia Research. Bidding was fierce, escalating from the original thirteen shillings for the two tickets up to seven pounds, which at that time represented an average week's wage. One lucky fan, Annette, managed to secure the prizes when her Uncle John offered the pub a sink unit worth £20 for the two tickets. A group of school friends from the Darlington High School for girls organised a coach to travel to the show but the venue would only allow four tickets per person, so they had to send the appropriate number of people to purchase the number of tickets needed to fill a coach. Straws were drawn to decide which of them had to go to Stockton and queue all night. This group had to miss a day from school and the rest of them had to forge notes from their parents explaining their absence. Unfortunately their scheme backfired when those queuing were interviewed by a local TV news reporter and appeared on the six o'clock news. 'Our group enjoyed the evening,' one schoolgirl recalled, 'and we left the theatre on a high. However, we arrived home to discover that the US President John F. Kennedy had been assassinated in Dallas, Texas.'

They returned to the venue on 15 October 1964 playing two shows and, as was becoming the norm, they were interviewed in their dressing room beforehand. As it coincided with the UK general election, they were asked for their views on British politics. They were surprisingly quite subdued. Maybe the interviewers should have come back a few years later as they would have met a totally different group of opinionated musicians who weren't afraid to speak their minds.

STOKE-ON-TRENT
King's Hall, Glebe Street

Another double booking for the Fab Four on 26 January 1963 saw them move from the exotic-sounding El Rio Club in the less-than-exotic Macclesfield to Stoke-on-Trent. Before the show, John and Paul started work on 'Misery', which they hoped imminent tour-mate Helen Shapiro would record. The concert featured a unique Beatles performance of The Rooftop Singers' then current hit 'Walk Right In'

They returned once more to this venue on 19 April 1963 for the second *Mersey Beat Showcase* night, orchestrated by Brian Epstein and comprising his acts.

STOWE
Roxburgh Hall, Stowe School

One of the strangest performances the Fab Four ever played was at this public school for boys, on 4 April 1963. The group arrived at approximately 4.30pm and performed at 5.30pm. Photos of the performance, for which they were paid £100, show row after row of pupils sitting emotionless, watching the group. Not quite the same without screaming girls.

Communications about the gig, between Stowe schoolboy, Liverpool-born David Moores and Brian Epstein, had begun in January of that year. But due to Moores naturally being under 21 years of age, the contract between Epstein and the schoolboy had to be endorsed by a representative of Stowe School itself. Following the show, after meeting the staff there and being shown round the building, The Beatles took up residency at the Green Man Hotel at Brackley Hatch, Syresham. A photographic record of the event was taken by the Hungarian snapper Dezo Hoffmann.

STROUD

Subscription Rooms, George Street

After the disaster that was The Beatles' first trip down south, with Sam Leach, to Aldershot, Brian wasn't going to make the same mistake twice. Using the Cana Variety Agency, Epstein brought them to Stroud on 31 March 1962 for a better evening than their prior adventure. They quickly dashed back home to the safety of playing the Casbah the following night. It can't have been too bad as they returned on 1 September 1962, this time with a different drummer and a recording contract in hand.

SUNDERLAND

Empire Theatre, High Street West

This venue and performance on 9 February 1963 marked the end of The Beatles' participation in the first part of the Helen Shapiro tour, with the band leaving to record the required number of songs for what was to become their debut album *Please Please Me*. They were replaced the following night, in Peterborough, by Peter Jay and The Jaywalkers and rejoined the tour in Mansfield on 23 February 1963.

Ticket prices ranged between three shillings and eight shillings and sixpence. *Sunderland Echo* reporter Carol Roberton, 18, reviewed the show. Under the title 'A Mistress of Her Art' (a reference to Shapiro), Roberton's piece appeared in the 11 February 1963 edition and became one of the first provincial reviews to mention The Beatles outside of Liverpool. Shapiro's singing received approval but her banjo playing did not, nor the 'noisier efforts' of most of the supporting acts. This was an obvious reference to The Beatles, whose instrumental qualifications, in her opinion, 'did not measure up to the high standard of [support act] The Red Price Band.'

They made one further appearance at this north-east theatre on 30 November 1963, as part of their autumn tour. Anticipating a trouble-free night, the Empire's manager, Mr B. Cotton, was quoted as saying before the show the police 'could be [made] available', confidently adding, 'We've had full houses before. We're used to a lot of people.' As an added security precaution, an iron gate was installed at the venue to allow admission one at a time and tickets were going to be carefully examined so there would be no confusion about anybody going to wrong parts of the theatre. 'The only crowds expected to gather outside the theatre,' Mr Cotton said, 'would be those who wanted to see The Beatles coming and going.'

Crowds for the concerts had started gathering before noon but were informed by staff at the Empire the band wouldn't be arriving until late afternoon. Reporters of the *Sunderland Echo* cruelly related a rumour that said The Beatles had been involved in a road accident and wouldn't be appearing. This was disproved when Neil Aspinall and Mal Evans arrived to prepare for the evening's shows, all 4,200 tickets for which were sold. Fans who did not have tickets later surrounded the theatre and began singing 'She Loves You' at the dressing room windows in hope of catching The Beatles' attention.

The band's departure from the venue was covered by the American journalist, Michael Braun in his 1964 book *"Love Me Do!" – The Beatles' Progress*. He joined the band on their tour in 1963, starting here at the Sunderland Empire, witnessing the hysteria first hand and what the group had to do to survive it. 'The Beatles managed their escape from the Sunderland theatre,' he wrote, 'by rushing through the darkened auditorium to the fire station next door and sliding down a firepole. Then, while engine number one clanged out as a decoy they rode off in a police car.'

Rink Ballroom, Park Lane

The Beatles made one appearance here on 14 May 1963, having made the 200-mile journey from Birmingham the night before.

The Beatles were the only artists on the bill that night and arrived at the venue in a little red Renault Dauphine car at roughly 5.30pm. The queue of fans outside was approximately 12-deep and wound round a nearby car park and then about 200 yards into the town centre. The show became so boisterous that, in order to give the band some space and safety on the stage, benches were brought in and stacked, one on top of the other, three high around them. The walkway that ran behind the stage was blocked off during the gig so the group could use it as a dressing room and place of refuge. Fans standing close to the stage recalled John singing 'Twist And Shout' with excessive amounts of sweat pouring down his face. When the piled benches came tumbling down, the band rushed off stage and headed to their haven. As Paul exited he accidentally whacked a female fan on the head with his guitar.

Gluttons for punishment, the following day saw The Beatles drive 180 miles back to the north-west of England and the city of Chester, close to their Liverpool homes.

SUNNINGDALE

Tittenhurst Park

John Lennon, through his publishing company Maclen, bought this fine Georgian house, situated near Ascot and within a 72-acre estate, on 4 May 1969 for £145,000. John and Yoko moved in on 11 August and lived here for just over two years. The historic gardens had been open to the public until the Lennons moved in. Originally, the main house comprised many small rooms, but the walls were ripped out at John and Yoko's request to create a more open space. Much of the ground floor at the front of the house was converted to the famous single large room, decorated in white. Tittenhurst Park was the location for the final photo session showing the four Beatles together to promote the forthcoming *Abbey Road* album, a historic event that took place on Friday 22 August 1969 two days after their last recording session together. Throughout 1970 an 8-track recording studio was gradually installed here, as well as film editing equipment. But the studio, named Ascot Sound, wouldn't be ready until the following year.

John and Yoko left Tittenhurst in 1971, when Ringo moved in, making this his home until the late 1980s.

John and Yoko's home and Ringo and Maureen's home, plus The Beatles' final photo shoot.

SWINDON

McIlroy's Ballroom, Havelock Square

In the summer of 1962, as John, Paul, George and Pete were celebrating having been accepted by EMI, they made a third journey down south and played here on 17 July, another of the Jaybee clubs. They were billed as 'The Most Popular Group in the North'. Also playing that night was a band called The Whispers, the lead vocalist and guitarist of which was Justin Hayward, later of The Moody Blues. Hayward later revealed that he left the venue early and did not see The Beatles perform, much to his regret.

TAMWORTH

Assembly Rooms, Corporation Street

On 1 February 1963, a double engagement in the Midlands awaited The Beatles as they played first in Maney Hall, Sutton Coldfield, near Birmingham, before making the short trip to Tamworth.

An advert for the Tamworth show was first place in the *Tamworth Herald* on 18 January, where the group was advertised as 'Stars of T.V., Radio and Stage'. The gig however, did not go down well with some of the attendees. One week after the event, the same paper ran a story on its front page saying some of the teenagers had complained about being misled and had not received value for money. Tickets for the concert cost six shillings and sixpence and The Beatles only performed for half an hour (between 11.45pm and 12.15am), having already played in Maney earlier in the evening. Many were under the false impression the group would be on stage for most of the night. Frances Brewer, 17, of Wyndhams, Deer Park, Fazeley, was quoted as saying, 'The hall was full and I think everyone was disappointed. Certainly all my friends had gone under the impression that The Beatles would be appearing for a considerable part of the dance. That is why we went along. What we saw of The Beatles we thoroughly enjoyed but I don't think we got our money's worth for a half-an-hour appearance.' She concluded by saying, 'By the time they did appear, many youngsters had gone home.'

TAUNTON

Gaumont Cinema, Corporation Street

When the Helen Shapiro tour resumed here on 26 February 1963 after a day off, Shapiro was suffering from a cold, and had to miss this performance. Danny Williams became top of the bill.

They made one further appearance here on 5 September 1963, on the second night of their brief, four-date, John Smith-promoted mini-tour.

TEDDINGTON

Teddington TV Studios, Teddington Lock

The Beatles made several visits to this television studio on the River Thames, near Richmond in Greater London, between 1963 and 1965, where ABC made programmes with the Fab Four. *Thank Your Lucky Stars*, a prime time Saturday night show, hosted The Beatles, and they recorded here on 17 February and 14 April 1963 and 14 November 1964. British comedians the brothers Mike and Bernie Winters had a popular show called *Big Night Out* on which The Beatles appeared, having recorded their segments here on 23 February 1964. A further show, *Lucky Stars (Summer Spin)*, had a live appearance by The Beatles on 11 July 1964, where they made their approach to the studio in a boat on the River Thames. Their final television appearance here was on *The Eamonn Andrews Show* on 11 April 1965. (For more information on these shows see entries in *TV* section.)

Some of the most important television programmes for The Beatles.

TENBURY WELLS

Riverside Dancing Club, Bridge Hotel, Teme Street

In between recording at the television studios in Teddington and Granada television in Manchester, The Beatles appeared here in this rural market town in Worcestershire on 15 April 1963. Their fee was £100, with members' tickets costing three shillings and sixpence. Before the show, local hairdresser Pat Lambert, who also co-ran the club with her husband, Tony and ten other like-minded people, sat down for a buffet supper with The Beatles in the Bridge Hotel's dining room. 'I took my autograph book along and I asked them all to sign it, which they did.' In an interview for the *Shropshire Star* in 2009, she recalled George being 'nice'.

Interestingly, before their appearance, the Fab Four had decided to take a stroll around the town and soak up the sights. Pat was in her hairdressing salon in Teme Street that afternoon and recalled someone shouting, 'The Beatles are here, they've just come out of the cafe opposite!' and some of her clients running out of the shop halfway through their perms with their rollers still in. Black and white souvenir pictures were taken, of the group looking happy and relaxed and of Ringo enjoying an ice-cream cornet. John was short of money that day. Locals remembered him scrounging cigarettes off passers-by.

TORQUAY

Princess Theatre, Torbay Road

Another tour of the UK in a day saw The Beatles head off from Llandudno in Wales to the television studios in Birmingham and then to the south coast of Devon to appear here on 18 August 1963 during their Sunday evening summer seaside tour. The journey was almost 400 miles, but the two performances that night were as good as ever, with ticket prices ranging between six shillings and ten shillings and sixpence. After the concerts, the group signed an autograph book belonging to Helen, a fan. Using a black fountain pen, all four Beatles signed one page, while John humorously inscribed another, 'Benny Higgins (Juggler)'. A full set of signatures, scrawled on a folded piece of Imperial Hotel headed paper, where they stayed, later sold at auction for £2,410.

TRENTHAM

Trentham Gardens, Stone Road

After filming with Liverpool comedian Ken Dodd for his television show, The Beatles headed north

to Trentham Gardens, near Stoke, for a one-off performance in the Trentham Ballroom on 11 October 1963.

TWICKENHAM

5-11 Ailsa Avenue

One of the most iconic scenes in the movie *Help!* was when The Beatles enter what looks like four separate houses, at 5, 7, 9 and 11 Ailsa Avenue, only for them to be joined on the inside to create one large house.

Who didn't want a house like that?

Madingley Club, Willoughby Road

The penultimate photo shoot of their career as Beatles, the Fab Four were snapped by three photographers, including Bruce McBroom, posing at this music venue and then nearby at 4 Ducks Walk and also in a boat on the River Thames.

Twickenham Film Studios, St Margarets

These legendary studios, now known simply as Twickenham Studios, became a regular destination for The Beatles during their career. While shooting scenes in *A Hard Day's Night*, *Help!* and the protracted *Let It Be*, they also visited Twickenham for promotional video shoots. November 1965 was their busiest month, shooting five promotional videos for songs. One of the most memorable was for 'Hey Jude', shot on 4 September 1968, with The Beatles joined by fans to sing along to the epic single.

Probably the most important film studio in The Beatles' career.

A TRIP WITH THE BEATLES?

Many records in the sixties and seventies were banned by British and American radio stations for their alleged drug connotations. Because the terminology was often adapted from standard speech, it was easy enough for songwriters to protest. 'Of course it's not about drugs. We weren't thinking of that at all.' However, Paul has said in interviews, though not at the time, that when they came up with the line, 'I'd love to turn you on,' they gave each other 'a little look'.

It's possible that some songwriters were genuinely surprised when they were accused of writing drug songs but it is more likely that they denied the allegations because they did not want anyone to think they could only write songs with the help of stimulants, and more importantly they did not want cops knocking down their doors.

When Bob Dylan first met The Beatles he congratulated them for putting 'I get high' into 'I Want To Hold Your Hand'. They were, of course, singing, 'I can't hide'. He then introduced them to marijuana, which can be seen as a natural high as opposed to a chemically induced one.

The Beatles though were not new to drugs. They had sometimes been off their heads on Preludin in Hamburg, once causing John Lennon to throw a steak knife at an opponent (see Peter Brown's book *The Love You Make*). At the Cavern, Bob Wooler would sometimes ask, 'Is anybody travelling by tube tonight?'

The Beatles' early drug experiences did not have any effect upon their early songwriting but there *could* be an album: *The Beatles Greatest Trips* – 'Got To Get You Into My Life' ('I took a ride'), 'Ticket To Ride', 'Magical Mystery Tour', 'Dr Robert' (possibly about a drug dealer), 'She Said She Said' (definitely about Peter Fonda tripping) and 'She's A Woman' ('Turn me on when I get lonely').

The ultimate psychedelic single 'Penny Lane'/'Strawberry Fields Forever' probably has drug connotations – a happy trip one side and a tougher one for the other. The distress and the downside of drugs may well be reflected in 'Rain', 'Tomorrow Never Knows' and 'Across The Universe'. Could anyone listening to 'A Day In The Life' possibly think that taking drugs was a good idea?

Then there is the listlessness of 'I'm Only Sleeping' and 'I'm So Tired'. These are predominantly John Lennon compositions so can you see a pattern here? John admitted that he wrote 'Cold Turkey' after coming off heroin. The other Beatles thought it was too strong for one of their singles so John recorded it as the Plastic Ono Band.

The Beatles' 'I Am The Walrus' and 'Hole In My Shoe' by Traffic are both full of highly imaginative imagery. There is also the unissued (until *Anthology 3*) 'What's The New Mary Jane', an affectionate term for marijuana. John Lennon's innocence over the mnemonic LSD in 'Lucy In The Sky With Diamonds' might be true but how come Jimi Hendrix was also singing about 'Laughing Sam's Dice' at the same time? An amusing pact between the two performers?

After hearing the *Sgt Pepper* album, BBC director Frank Gillard wrote to Sir Joseph Lockwood, the chairman of EMI, about his acid test for 'A Day In The Life': 'I never thought the day would come when we would have to put a ban on an EMI record but sadly that is what has happened over this track. We have listened to it over and over again with great care, and we cannot avoid coming to the conclusion that the words "I'd love to turn you on" followed by that mounting montage of sound, could have a rather sinister meaning.'

He continued, 'The recording may have been made in innocence and good faith, but we must take account of the interpretation that young people would inevitably put upon it. "Turned on" is a phrase which can be used in many different circumstances, but it is currently much in vogue in the jargon of the drug-addicts. We do not feel that we can take the responsibility of appearing to favour or encourage these unfortunate habits, and that is why we shall not be playing the recording in any of our programmes on radio or television.'

The DJ John Peel soon found himself in trouble for violating the ban and playing 'A Day In The Life', but he did it defiantly and deliberately. The Beatles did sign the Legalise Pot petition in 1967.

In 1970 the Federal Communications Commission, the US broadcasting regulator, produced a list of songs that appeared to be 'eulogising the use of narcotics'. They included 'Happiness Is A Warm Gun', 'Everybody's Got Something To Hide Except Me And My Monkey' and 'With A Little Help From My Friends'. In a similar vein, David Elkind, a university professor in Massachussetts, commented that 'Hey Jude' referred to Judas who betrayed Christ and by the same token, heroin is a friend until you 'let her into your heart'. QED

WAKEFIELD

ABC Cinema, Kirkgate

The fourth night of the Helen Shapiro tour saw The Beatles make their only appearance here on 7 February 1963.

WALTON-ON-THAMES

Esher and Walton Magistrates' Court, Elm Grove, Hersham Road

George Harrison and his wife Pattie were called here on 18 March 1969 and again on 31 March 1969, charged with possession of cannabis. They pleaded guilty and were fined £250 each.

Keep off the grass.

WARBURTON

Kingsley Hill, Chapmans Town Road

Brian Epstein purchased this historic East Sussex building, located around 60 miles from London, for £25,000. On 25 August 1967, he drove back from Kingsley Hill to his flat in Chapel Street, where two days later he was found dead.

WARRINGTON

Bell Hall, Orford Lane

Although it is less than 20 miles east of Liverpool, The Beatles only made one appearance in this Lancashire town. After a lunchtime appearance at the Cavern, the group played here on the evening of 20 July 1962.

Sevenoaks, Appleton

In 1965, after Beatlemania became too much for the Harrisons, George bought them this house, located about 20 miles outside of Liverpool, near Warrington.

George's gift to his parents.

WEST BROMWICH

Adelphi Ballroom, New Street

After playing at the Cavern for their usual lunchtime performance, The Beatles made a near 100-mile journey to the Midlands on 19 November 1962, where they first played in Smethwick and then took a short drive to West Bromwich to play at the Adelphi Ballroom.

WESTON-SUPER-MARE

Odeon Cinema, The Centre

The Beatles played a six-night residency at this seaside resort between 22 and 27 July 1963, two shows per night.

Joining them for all six days was the photographer, Dezo Hoffman, who took photos and colour 8mm home movie footage of the band at their hotel and on Weston beach at Brean Down where they went go-karting and dressed up in striped Victorian-era bathing costumes. In the room at their hotel, The Beatles, notably John, George, and support act Gerry and The Pacemakers, spent time fooling around with Lennon's newly acquired reel-to-reel tape machine and recorded themselves reading psalms from the Bible, singing the hymns 'The Lord Is My Shepherd' and 'There's A Green Hill Far Away' and later putting on comic voices to ask bemused residents for directions to the golf course. At 5pm on 23 July both bands huddled round the radio to listen to show six of *Pop Go The Beatles* on the BBC Light Programme and at approximately 5.15pm John taped 'Love Me Do' from the show on his reel-to-reel machine.

He would hand this and four other, informal, poor-quality tapes to their chauffeur Alf Bicknell as a farewell present in 1966. After being stored in a white plastic bag in his garage for over two decades, the reels were found by biographer Gerry Marsh and put up for sale in 1989 as part of the Alf Bicknell Collection at a Sotheby's auction in London. When Marsh played them, he discovered they contained many other interesting pieces of audio, many of which post-dated the Weston residency. George's demo of 'Don't Bother Me', for instance, had been recorded between 19 and 24 August 1963 during their residency in Bournemouth, John's demos of 'If I Fell' had been taped on New Year's Eve 1963, Paul's guitar instrumen-

tals for 'Michelle' and 'Three Coins In A Fountain' came from 1965 and (strangely) an excerpt from the unreleased Apple film *Raga*, featuring the voice of the sitar legend Ravi Shankar, dated from 1968, by which time Bicknell was no longer in The Beatles' employment. Demos of other released tracks, such as 'It Won't Be Long', 'Love Me Do' and 'Please Mr Postman' (a control room playback from 30 July 1963) were also featured on the reels. However, when Apple learnt of this they came forward, insisting the tape that contained the performances was their copyright and could not be sold. Withdrawn from sale, these recordings, however, soon appeared as a 1992 bootleg CD release, aptly titled *Garage Tapes – For Sale By Auction* and then later, *Maybe You Can Drive My Car*. The non-music tapes in the collection sold for $45,000. To quote his spokesman at the time, 'Mr Bicknell has every reason to be satisfied with the result, which will enable him to publish [his] upcoming book.'

WEYBRIDGE

Kenwood, St George's Hill Estate

John purchased this house in Surrey for £20,000 on 15 July 1964, and spent another £40,000 getting Kenwood the way he wanted it, ready for him and his family. However, the improvements took 9 months to complete, so John, Cynthia and Julian were forced to live in the former staff quarters at the top of the property. When Hunter Davies was researching his Beatles biography he visited John several times and described the house and John, 'knocking rooms around, decorating and furnishing, landscaping the garden and building a swimming pool. In the garden he has a psychedelically painted caravan that was done to match the patterns of the painted Rolls-Royce. The house is on a slight hill, with grounds rolling beneath. There is a full-time gardener, a house-keeper called Dot and chauffeur called Anthony. The reception rooms might as well be corridors. Nobody ever seems to use them, although they are kept beautifully. They just walk through them to get out. All the living is done in one little rect-angular room at the back of the house. It has one wall completely made of glass and looks over the garden and trees beyond.' John felt isolated out in the stockbroker belt, possibly because he felt that he was unable to escape domestic life and continue his philandering. To further complicate family life, John's father Freddie turned up without warning. Cynthia let him into the house, which was a shock when John came home. The two managed to have an uneasy relationship, with John buying a house nearby for his father. An even greater shock visitor to Kenwood greeted Cynthia on her return from holiday in May 1968 when she found John with Yoko, and their marriage was at an end. Because of the ensuing divorce, Kenwood was sold.

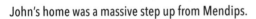

John's home was a massive step up from Mendips.

Sunny Heights, St George's Hill Estate

This house was purchased by Ringo on 24 July 1965, less than a kilometre from John's house Kenwood. Ringo and his new wife Maureen moved in soon afterwards and stayed for three years until 19 November 1968 when, now with two children, they bought Peter Sellers' house in Elstead. John and Yoko lived here for a short time when he left Kenwood after John and Cynthia's divorce and also after they had been forced to leave Ringo's central London flat in Montagu Square following their drug bust. Ringo allowed John and Yoko to stay here until they were ready to buy a property of their own. Ringo sold Sunny Heights in May 1969.

WHITCHURCH
Town Hall Ballroom, Pauls Moss, Dodington

Just the one appearance here in this Shropshire town on 19 January 1963, coinciding with their debut on the ITV pop show *Thank Your Lucky Stars*, recorded six days earlier. With Neil Aspinall still unwell, The Beatles' roadie duties once again fell to Gerry and The Pacemakers road manager Les Hurst. GPO telephone engineer, Cavern club regular-cum-bouncer and keen rock 'n' roll fan, six feet three inches Mal Evans was hired by Brian Epstein for lugging duties the following day. Mal used to sit in the front rows at the club when The Beatles performed. They would even dedicate songs to him.

WIDNES
Queen's Hall, Victoria Road

The small industrial town of Widnes, situated just 14 miles south of Liverpool, became a regular stop for The Beatles in the early years, promoted by Brian's NEMS Enterprises. They played at the Queen's Hall on 3, 10 and 17 September 1962, each time after playing at the Cavern that lunchtime. Their 22 October 1962 visit saw them share the bill with Lee Curtis and The All Stars, meaning another awkward encounter with former sticks man Pete Best. The Beatles' final appear-ance here was on 18 February 1963 when they played two shows.

WIGAN
ABC Cinema, Station Road

Having spent a day at Abbey Road on 12 Octo-ber 1964, The Beatles headed north the following day to this Lancashire town to make their only appearance here. Their fee for the two shows that evening was £850.

JOHN LENNON AND FANS

There is an image of John as being rough and rude with fans. Eyewitnesses observed him telling fans to fuck off, refusing to sign autographs if he was not in the mood, even if they were in tears having already got the other three Beatles.

And yet there are just as many stories about him being amazingly friendly, often stupidly so, allowing total strangers into his house, into his life.

On 9 August 1967, 15-year-old Frank Lawson from Newcastle, down in Surrey visiting friends during the school hols, arrived at Kenwood early in the morning, clutching a copy of *Beatles Monthly* (No. 4, August 1967). He was eventually joined by around 20 other fans – all of whom, in little parties, were eventually allowed into the garden, able to wander round on their own, even though John was clearing working, finishing a drawing. John talked to all of them and signed autographs, including Frank's *Beatles Monthly*. Alas, his camera had run out of film. He rushed into Weybridge, bought another film, rushed back – and was allowed in again while John posed for photos. 'My lasting memory of John was how good he was to his fans. He didn't have to let us into his garden and pose for photos, especially during the summer holidays. The hard, slightly sneering image that came across in the media just wasn't there that day. He was a lovely person. The memory of meeting him has remained with me as one of the highlights of my life.'

Early in 1968, a couple from Ireland, Richard Hall and his wife Maureen, along with a German girl who was travelling with them, turned up unannounced at John's house. John came to the door, with Julian standing behind. For about ten minutes John sheltered Julian, until eventually deciding the trio at the door were harmless and inviting all three in.

They stayed for 45 minutes, took photos of themselves with John and were taken round the house and garden. When they left, they asked for a keepsake. John looked around and picked up a statue The Beatles had been awarded, an Ivor Novello award (for 'She's Leaving Home'). They said no, no at first, this is too personal, but John insisted they should have it.

They sold it some years later at a London auction house, scared to keep it at home any more, having realised how valuable it was. But they still have the photo of Maureen standing with John, holding up the statue.

On 28 May 1968 a 19-year-old American art student called Michael Herring arrived at John's door. 'Well then, what's it all about?' asked John. 'John,' replied Michael, 'I wish you could be me now so that you know what it's like to meet you.' This so charmed John that the youth was invited in for breakfast with John and Yoko. She had recently moved in and possibly was not exactly thrilled by the uninvited guest. Later, John drove him in his Mini to George's house where they were working on tracks for the *White Album*. George, who was much more suspicious that John, asked who the boy was. 'This is Michael,' John explained. 'An artist I found in me garden.'

According to Michael, while he was there, a messenger arrived with a letter from Paul. George opened it and, again according to Michael, announced, 'He's not coming. Paul is quitting.' Then they carried on playing.

Could it be true that Paul was quitting? Was George just being funny? Paul at that stage was the dominant force in the group, driving them on – but perhaps in a moment of pique he got fed up with carrying the load.

Michael took several photos, in one of which George can be seen with the letter in his pocket. Michael is convinced he witnessed a dramatic moment in pop music history, but historically, that day was not the end. The Beatles performed together for at least another year and did not officially part till 1970.

John drove the young man he had never met before back to Weybridge and dropped him at the station, having allowed him the rare honour of witnessing The Beatles perform in private. In 2014 Mr Herring decided to sell his photos – which went for £10,000 at an action house in Manchester.

Was John simply being nice and kind when he allowed all these total strangers into his life, or showing off, or dicing with danger? It was being kind to Mark Chapman in 1980, another total stranger, that led to his death.

WOLVERHAMPTON

Gaumont Cinema, Snow Hill

With John once again missing, supposedly still in bed with a bad cold, Paul and George shared the vocals on their first performance here on 14 March 1963 as part of the Chris Montez/Tommy Roe tour.

On their second, and final, appearance here, they had to dash up from London after an award ceremony to make an evening appearance, this time with all of the Fab Four, on 19 November 1963.

WORCESTER

Gaumont Cinema, Foregate Street

After an 80-mile trip from South Wales to Worcester, The Beatles made the first of two appearances here on 28 May 1963 as part of the Roy Orbison tour. They returned to the venue on 4 September 1963 for the opening night of the brief, four-date, John Smith-promoted mini-tour, with support acts Ian Crawford and The Boomerangs, Mike Berry and The Innocents, Freddie Starr and The Midnighters, and Rocking Henry and The Hayseeds. The shows were compèred by DJ Ted King.

YORK

Rialto Theatre, Fishergate

On their first appearance here, 27 February 1963, The Beatles were without the headline act, Helen Shapiro, who was still missing with a bad cold. They made three further appearances here in 1963, on 13 March during the Chris Montez/Tommy Roe tour, with John once again missing from the line-up as a result of an alleged illness, on 29 May with the Roy Orbison tour and 27 November 1963 as part of their own autumn tour.

SCOTLAND

Scotland was a summer refuge for John when he visited his family, a place he would always remember. Scotland also gave John, Paul and George their first taste of a tour in 1960, even if it was just for two weeks. This preparation, backing Johnny Gentle as The Silver Beatles, would stand them in good stead for their trip to Hamburg just 3 months later.

ABERDEEN

Beach Ballroom, Esplanade, Sea Beach

The fourth and concluding night of their short Scottish jaunt saw The Beatles perform here on

6 January 1963 as part of the venue's (known locally as 'Scotland's finest social centre') weekly Sunday Night Concert. The following day they travelled to Glasgow and on the Tuesday made an appearance on the children's television programme *Roundup*, where they mimed their latest record 'Please Please Me'.

ALLOA
Town Hall, Marshill

During their audition on 10 May 1960, The Silver Beatles did not impress Larry Parnes enough to be hired by him to back Billy Fury (for more details, see Wyvern Club entry under Liverpool in this section). However, they were thought good enough to back another one of the artists, Johnny Gentle – real name John Askew – on a seven-date tour of Scotland, promoted as 'The Beat Ballad Show' throughout. And so it was here in the Highlands, in Clackmannanshire, on 20 May 1960, that the band destined to evolve into The Beatles took to the stage with only 30 minutes' rehearsal for the start of their first ever tour.

The Silver Beatles were not given their own billing, as each poster simply announced the ensemble as 'Johnny Gentle and his group'. In true show-biz style each member of The Silver Beatles adopted a stage name: Long *John* Silver, *Paul* Ramon (from which The Ramones would go on to take their name), Carl *Harrison* (in honour of his hero Carl Perkins) and *Stuart* de Stael (in honour of the Russian painter Nicholas de Stael).

The trek was the brainchild of the London-based promoter Parnes, who was affectionately known in the industry as 'Parnes, Shillings and Pence' thanks to his love of money. As Paul recalled, 'I was on the brink of going on to teacher's training college when I made a slight mistake. I should have been getting ready for the exam, but I couldn't. I was on a tour of Scotland with Johnny Gentle. It was ridiculous.'

Also playing tonight was a support act billed as 'Scotland's Own Tommy Steele', better known as Alex Harvey, who would go on to become one of the country's most sensational rock stars.

Their first stop on their tour of Scotland, and the beginning of fulfilling their dreams of being professional musicians.

BRIDGE OF ALLAN
Museum Hall, Henderson Street

From the far north of Scotland, the Fab Four headed south to Stirlingshire for their third concert in the mini tour of Scotland, with a one-off, infamous appearance here on 5 January 1963. The 'Love Me Do' boys, as they were billed, were pelted by coins and jeered off stage by around 100 drunk farmers, many of whom were supposedly annoyed by the lack of women in the room. One coin struck Paul's bass guitar.

DINGWALL
Town Hall, High Street

Having driven the 50 miles from Elgin, The Beatles played their second gig of the mini tour of Scotland here on 4 January 1963. It proved to be a low point for the group as they found themselves playing to an audience totalling, at best, between 19 and 30 (according to some reports, by 10pm there were just ten people there). Due to the poor attendance, The Beatles wrapped up their show early and headed off to the nearby Pavilion theatre. Meanwhile, just a few miles along the road, at the Spa Pavilion at Strathpeffer, a massive crowd of 1,200 had crammed in to hear a performance by local heroes The Melotones.

DUNDEE

Caird Hall, City Square

The final date on the short three-venue tour of Scotland ended here on 7 October 1963, before they returned to London.

They returned to Caird Hall on 20 October 1964 for the second night of the 3-date Scottish leg of their extensive UK tour. The tour had begun in Bradford on 9 October, and as it rolled through Scotland and then back south, each night became identical to the last. A succession of matching dressing rooms and hotel suites, it became impossible for them to tell one town from another during this period. The music and screams were just the same and following each performance, The Beatles would return to their cramped dressing room, which was invariably crowded with sweaty T-shirts, pots of tea, trays of French fries, badly cooked steaks and the inevitable TV set, which they would watch whilst sipping Scotch from paper cups. Life on the road was certainly not glamorous for the band.

Backstage at the venue The Beatles were interviewed by June Shields for local TV show *Grampian Week*, aired on 23 October 1964. The broadcast also included footage from before and during the show.

'The rooms drove them crazy,' Neil Aspinall admitted, 'and there were lots of arguments. You couldn't go anywhere and you felt like a criminal.'

DURNESS

56 Sangomore, Sango Bay

This small croft was owned by John's uncle, Robert Sutherland, who was married to his Aunt 'Mater'. John visited here during his summer holidays when he was younger and loved the open space in this wild, rural part of Scotland. One of his fondest memories was salmon fishing here. It was on a visit to see his family that John crashed the car he was driving near Loch Eriboll.

John's trips brought him respite from his troubled family back in Liverpool.

EDINBURGH

ABC Cinema, Lothian Road

The Beatles returned to Scotland for two big concerts in spring 1964, the first of which was here on 29 April (Glasgow Odeon followed the next night). The Right Honourable Lord Provost of Edinburgh, the convener of the City, courted controversy when it was revealed that he had unashamedly asked the group for a £100,000 donation towards the running costs of the city's annual summer event, the Edinburgh Festival. The request became even more embarrassing for him when it was disclosed that he had left the cinema that night without even bothering to see the group's performance.

The Beatles returned on 19 October 1964. This was the first concert in the 3-date Scottish leg of their month-long, 27-venue autumn tour of the UK. As research for his *Playboy* magazine interview with the band, the New York radio host Jean Shepherd met the group for the first time here. 'I joined The Beatles in Edinburgh in the midst of a wild, swinging personal-appearance tour they were making throughout the British Isles,' he recalled. 'The first glimpse I had of them was in a tiny, overheated, cigarette smoke filled, totally disorganised dressing room backstage between their first and second shows … All of them looked up suspiciously as I walked in, and then went back to eating, drinking, and tuning guitars as though I didn't exist.'

15 Ormidale Terrace

This was the family home of John's Aunt Elizabeth 'Mater' Sutherland and her husband Robert. John's cousin Stanley was a good friend and they enjoyed many happy days during the summers in Scotland.

ELGIN

Two Red Shoes Ballroom, South College Street

The Fab Four played a concert here on 3 January 1963, promoted by The Elgin Folk Music Club. The Beatles were billed as the 'Love Me Do' boys. The venue's unusual, L-shaped ballroom resulted in many in the audience only *hearing* the group's performance, which was the start of what was meant to be a five-night jaunt around various Scottish towns. However, the original tour opener scheduled for the previous evening, a New Year's Dance at Longmore Hall in Keith, had to be cancelled due to the poor weather and snow-blocked roads. Instead, John flew home to Liverpool for a quick visit, returning to Scotland early on the day of the Elgin concert.

FORRES

Town Hall, High Street

Another town hall, another Scottish highland town. This time Forres in Morayshire on stage five of the Johnny Gentle tour, 26 May 1960. Now desperately short of money, the group was calling tour promoter Larry Parnes daily for cash advances. As a result of their financial difficulties, they allegedly drove away from their hotel, The Royal Station, the morning after the gig without settling their bill.

FRASERBURGH

Dalrymple Hall, Seaforth Street

Driving around Scotland on the back roads was always going to be hazardous during the tour with Johnny Gentle, but when Johnny Gentle took to the wheel to drive them to Fraserburgh, he managed to crash the van into an oncoming car. Silver Beatle drummer Tommy Moore was thrown forward, suffering concussion and loosening a few teeth when the band's equipment fell on him. Laid up in hospital, Moore didn't know where he was. However, he was needed, so John Lennon went to the hospital with a representative from Dalrymple Hall and they dragged poor Tommy out of bed and took him to the venue for their third appearance on this Scottish tour, on 23 May 1960. If you have concussion, what is the instrument you don't want to play? The drums. Poor Tommy – at least he was too dazed to realise where he was. According to Tommy, John kept turning round to him and trying to make him laugh so that the stitches in his lips would burst.

GLASGOW

Concert Hall, Argyle Street

Returning to Scotland for a mini-tour, The Beatles opened in Glasgow on 5 October 1963, 12 months after 'Love Me Do' had been released in the UK. The Fab Four played just 3 times on this short tour, moving on to Kirkcaldy the next day, followed by Dundee.

Odeon Cinema, Renfield Street

The Beatles' first ever concert in Glasgow was at this city centre venue on 7 June 1963 as part of the Roy Orbison tour. They returned to the Odeon twice the following year, on 30 April and again on 21 October, the final date in the Scottish leg of their month-long, 27-venue autumn tour of the UK. From Glasgow they headed south to Leeds and then on to London.

They returned to Glasgow one last time, on 3 December 1965, appearing at the Glasgow Odeon on the opening night of their final UK tour. There were two houses, with a crowd of 2,784 at each.

The group had gathered at Mal Evans's flat on 1 December 1965 to assemble and rehearse a set for this ten-day tour, the 16-page programme of which featured a drawing from the new, animated American TV series *The Beatles* on its front page. Compèred by the new, showbiz personality Jerry Stevens, the other acts on the bill were the Liverpool singers Beryl Marsden and Steve Aldo, and the groups The Moody Blues (including future Wings member Denny Laine on guitar and vocals), The Paramounts (who later emerged as Procol Harum), The Marionettes (the pop-soul vocal group) and The Koobas (from Liverpool).

The Beatles' journey to Glasgow, on the M1 motorway, was blighted when, during the evening of 2 December 1965, the car they were travelling in hit a bump on the A1 section at Berwick-upon-Tweed, causing one of George's highly treasured guitars to reach an untimely end. 'Fourteen of our guitars were strapped to the roof of our Austin Princess and the only one lost was my Gretsch Tennessean,' Harrison lamented at the time. 'It fell onto the road and into the path of the oncoming traffic. About 13 lorries went over it before our chauffeur [Alf Bicknell] could get near it. One of the lorries stopped and the driver came up with the dangling remains of it and said, "Oy! Is this banjo anyfink to do wiv you?" Some people would say I shouldn't worry... but I kind of got attached to it.' When Alf originally found it to be missing, and had informed the others, John told him, 'Well, if you can find it, you'll get a bonus.' 'What's the bonus then?' Alf asked.

'You can have your job back!' Lennon replied. Amazingly, The Beatles' journey to Glasgow had taken them two days.

During their first press conference on the tour, the group were naturally asked why they chose this mode of transport instead of flying to reach the city. 'We don't like flying,' John replied. 'If we can go by road, we do. We've done so much flying without really having any incidents, so that the more we do, the more we worry. I suppose we think that, sooner or later, something might happen. Anyway, we weren't in a hurry, as long as we got here in time.' Another reporter quizzed them about the choice of The Moody Blues on the tour. 'We've always been friends with them,' George announced. 'We seem to get on well with them. I don't think we specifically asked for them, but I know we all agreed when their name was mentioned.' John made many laugh when he grabbed Paul's brightly coloured, paisley-styled tie and proceeded to blow his nose on it.

Later, in their dressing room at the Odeon Theatre, The Beatles taped a special welcoming message for a new pirate station, Radio Scotland. John's cousin Stanley also paid a surprise visit to the group in between their two shows. (The start of the tour coincided with the UK releases of their new album, *Rubber Soul*, and single, 'Day Tripper'/'We Can Work It Out'.)

INVERNESS

Northern Meeting Room, Church Street

After the opening night of their tour with Johnny Gentle in Alloa, The Silver Beatles journeyed 150 miles north in their little van to Inverness for a show that also featured Ronnie Watt and The Chekkers Rock Dance Band. This night, 21 May 1960, should have seen them on stage in Seaforth, at Lathom Hall following their successful appearance the week before, but instead they were 375 miles north of Liverpool in a small, upstairs ballroom, with a handful of fans in this remote Highland venue.

In their hotel after the performance, Johnny Gentle continued work on a song he was writing, entitled, 'I've Just Fallen For Someone'. John would help out on the middle eight. The track was later recorded by Gentle under another different alias, Darren Young, and released in August 1962 as the B-side of his Parlophone single 'My Tears Will Turn To Laughter'. John was not credited.

KEITH

Longmore Hall, Church Road

A triumphant return to the town of Keith that they had visited with Johnny Gentle in May 1960 ended in disaster when this concert, scheduled for 2 January 1963, was cancelled due to bad weather. Visiting Scotland at the beginning of January was always going to be a gamble, and it was therefore no surprise that icy winds and snow forced this show to be abandoned.

St Thomas' Hall, Chapel Street

After the band's disastrous journey to Fraserburgh put drummer Tommy Moore in hospital, fortunately he had the next day off to help him recover as they travelled to Keith in Banffshire for their next performance in the Johnny Gentle tour on 25 May 1960, which passed without incident. About this time, they were still experimenting with group names, and while on tour in Scotland, they signed autographs as 'The Beatals', using the stage names of Johnny Lennon, Paul Ramon, Carl Harrison and Stuart de Stael, although Tommy Moore signed his as simply Thomas Moore. In 2010 the Keith & District

Heritage Group commemorated the fiftieth anniversary of the gig by unveiling a blue plaque at the hall.

KIRKCALDY

Carlton Theatre, Park Road

The second date of a short tour of Scotland saw The Beatles arrive in Kirkcaldy on 6 October 1963 to perform twice to around 1,500 fans at each concert. 'It was mobbed!' the organiser of the show, Bert Caira, recalled. 'A huge triumph.'

LOCH ERIBOLL

On 1 July 1969, while travelling in the far north of Scotland to see his Aunt 'Mater' in Durness, John crashed his Austin Maxi, containing his wife Yoko, son Julian and Yoko's daughter Kyoko. They were taken to Lawson Memorial Hospital in Golspie, Sutherland on the east coast, where they stayed for five days. John received 17 stitches on his face, while Yoko had 19 stitches to her forehead. John later commented, 'If you're going to have a car crash, try to arrange for it to happen in the Highlands. The hospital there was just great.' Yoko saw the crash as a 'happening' so had the car shipped to their house in Ascot and mounted on a concrete plinth in the condition it was found.

John driven to distraction as usual.

NAIRN

Regal Ballroom, Leopold Street

Making the short 10-mile trip along the coast from Forres, the Johnny Gentle tour arrived in Nairn on 27 May 1960, and Gentle was beginning to notice how much better his backing band were becoming, with George Harrison's guitar playing 'greatly improved,' and 'the close harmonies of Lennon and McCartney near perfect'.

The band's dire financial predicament continued, however. During a call made by Gentle to tour promoter Larry Parnes in London, John angrily grabbed the receiver, as Gentle recalled to the *John Lennon: The Life* biographer, Philip Norman. 'He didn't hold back. It was like, "We're fuckin' skint up here. We haven't got a pot to piss in. We need money, Larry!"' It seemed to do the trick. The group's manager Allan Williams sent up a few pounds.

PETERHEAD

Rescue Hall, Prince Street

The final date of the tour of Scotland with Johnny Gentle was here on 28 May 1960, although Gentle would perform briefly with them again just five weeks later, on 2 July, at the Grosvenor Ballroom in Liscard. By this point the band were broke, tired and hungry, but they had completed their first tour. It would serve them well for the future and their next tour, in Hamburg.

WALES

In just 30 minutes, The Beatles could get from Liverpool into North Wales, and so it is no surprise that they made several trips here in the early days. Paul and George enjoyed a couple of trips into Wales when they hitchhiked to Harlech.

ABERGAVENNY

Town Hall ballroom, Cross Street

The Beatles made one appearance in this Monmouthshire town, for a fee of £250, on 22 June 1963. John only just made it in time. He had stayed behind in London to record an appearance on *Juke Box Jury* and after the taping had wrapped at 9.15pm he was rushed to Battersea Helipad, from where – for costs in excess of £100 – he took a chartered helicopter flight to Wales, landing in Abergavenny's Pen-y-Pound football stadium 35 minutes later at 9.50pm, from where he was driven straight to the Town Hall to join his fellow Beatles on stage. At the conclusion of the show, all four members signed autographs that were sold for three pence each to the 600 fans in attendance that night, proceeds going to the local branch of the Freedom From Hunger Campaign. Incidentally, while John was away at the BBC Television Studios in London, the remaining Beatles were treated to an afternoon civic reception given by the Mayor and Mayoress of Abergavenny, Councillor and Mrs J.F. Thurston.

CARDIFF

Capitol Cinema, Queen Street

Their first appearance in Cardiff was here on 27 May 1963 during the Roy Orbison tour. The budding musician Dave Edmunds, who would have a chart hit with 'I Hear You Knocking' seven years later, was then an employee in a Cardiff musical instruments store, and was sent by his manager to the venue with strict instructions to try and sell The Beatles anything they might need for their concert. Stumbling across them during their soundcheck, he ended up staying the entire day and watched them perform from the wings. Too nervous to charge for anything, he eventually handed Paul a set of bass strings.

The Beatles returned to the Capitol Cinema on 7 November 1964 for two shows during their long autumn UK tour, in front of 2,500 fans each. Tickets ranged in price between eight shillings and sixpence and fifteen shillings. The group travelled to St Mellons, Cardiff, in Brian Epstein's chauffeur-driven limousine. As a decoy, they then climbed inside a Black Maria police van, in which they were driven to the venue.

On Sunday 12 December 1965 The Beatles once again performed two shows at this cinema, with 2,800 fans in the audience for each. Little did they know that this would be the last night of their last ever British tour. The shows could have sold out several times over, with 25,000 fans applying for tickets. In between the two houses, The Beatles gave interviews to the *South Wales Argus* and *South Wales Echo* newspapers and ate a meal of sausages and mash in their dressing room. They also relaxed by watching a western on television. During their second performance, when John introduced 'Day Tripper', a male fan jumped up onstage and attempted to grab Paul and George. Security staff quickly removed him and threw him out of the building. Immediately after the show, The Beatles climbed into their limousine and headed back to London, where they attended an early, end-of-tour, Christmas party at the Scotch of St James nightclub.

Notable for being The Beatles' very last scheduled, proper gig in the UK.

HARLECH
Queens Hotel

On a hitchhiking holiday to Wales, Paul and George ended up in Harlech, and joined up with local group The Vikings. In July 1958, Paul, George and two local musicians John Brierley and Aneurin Thomas teamed up for a performance at the Queens Hotel, run by Aneurin's father.

LLANDUDNO
Odeon Cinema, Gloddaeth Street

A short trip along the North Wales coast from Liverpool saw The Beatles take up a six-night residency in the seaside resort from 12–17 August 1963, playing two houses each night.

Tickets cost four shillings and sixpence, six shillings and sixpence or eight shillings and sixpence. Joining them on the bill were Billy J. Kramer and The Dakotas, The Lana Sisters, Sons of the Piltdown Men, Tommy Wallis & Beryl, and Tommy Quickly. The compère was Billy Baxter. Among the audience one night was 13-year-old Mary Hopkin, who five years later would sign for The Beatles' record company Apple.

The Odeon Cinema later became known as the Astra and closed in 1986, being demolished and replaced with a housing complex called Ormeside Grange.

MOLD
Assembly Hall, High Street

On 24 January 1963, The Beatles made a personal appearance in Brian Epstein's record store NEMS, in Whitechapel, Liverpool, where they gave a brief acoustic performance from the staircase of both sides of their recently released 'Please Please Me/Ask Me Why' and signed copies of the single. They then headed off to the market town of Mold in the county of Flintshire, North Wales to play a concert at the Assembly Hall in front of 200 fans.

In honour of their original booking, their fee for the night was just £50. By this time, The Beatles were commanding payments of up to £700 a night. The Cavern DJ Bob Wooler travelled down to compère the night. Prior to the show, the group took part in a two-hour interview with David Sandison of the *Wrexham Leader* newspaper. (His piece was published five days later on 29 January 1963.) At the end of the performance a fan tried to grab Paul's scarf but he wouldn't let her have it. 'It's the only one I've got,' he screamed. Later, the group happily signed autographs for the fans. 'We'd like to come back to Mold,' John was heard saying to the reporter David Sandison, 'but I don't know if they will want us back.'

George rounded off the night by visiting his Aunt Jinnie in nearby Broughton, while his three bandmates drove to the Talbot Arms Hotel in Holywell, where the landlady brought them drinks and a tray of sandwiches. The pub's former landlord, Ian Brown, had been at the concert with his 17-year-old sister, Moya, a friend of Gerry and The Pacemakers' tour manager, and invited them back. John amused himself playing a tune or two on the pub's upright piano. Just as John, Paul and Ringo were about to leave, the landlady rushed over and asked them to pay for the food, so they handed her 30 shillings.

PORTMEIRION

Hotel Portmeirion

When Brian Epstein returned from The Beatles' tour in the summer of 1966, he was so ill that a doctor ordered him to take a month vacation. He chose to stay at this luxury hotel situated in the village of Portmeirion. This unique village, designed in the style of an Italian village by Sir Clough Williams-Ellis, was used as the location for the village in the sixties television series *The Prisoner*. Brian only stayed four days before the furore in the US surrounding John Lennon's comments about The Beatles being 'more popu-

lar than Jesus' erupted, forcing him to return to London and then fly to New York to try and save the upcoming American tour.

Unique surrounding for Brian to rest in - until he had to rush back.

PRESTATYN

Royal Lido Ballroom, Central Beach

Before being reduced to playing sets of 30 minutes (at Brian Epstein's insistence, so they could pack two shows into an evening, where possible), The Beatles played for two hours at this ballroom on 24 November 1962. The Royal Lido was later refurbished and renamed the Nova Centre. The dance floor was removed and replaced with carpet, but the stage remained.

Tickets for the concert cost six shillings. The Beatles' fee was just £30. Their demand before taking to the stage for this concert was a plate of jam sandwiches from the Lido's head chef, Alan Veech. Joe Flannery, a close friend of Brian Epstein, was in charge of booking bands for the venue and The Beatles were the first act he signed. A clause in the group's contract stipulated they should not perform within a ten-mile radius of the ballroom in the ten weeks prior to the concert.

RHYL

Regent Dansette, High Street

Even though it was situated only 43 miles from Liverpool, The Beatles' first live performance in Wales wasn't until 14 July 1962, when they appeared in this small ballroom set above a branch of Burton Menswear. Prior to the show the group explored the seaside resort, and paid a visit to the local funfair. Admission to the concert was just five shillings.

Ritz Ballroom, Promenade

Twelve months after making their debut above a menswear shop in Rhyl, The Beatles returned for two sold-out shows at the Ritz Ballroom on the promenade of the seaside resort of Rhyl on 19 and 20 July 1963.

NORTHERN IRELAND

The Beatles found themselves in Northern Ireland on only two occasions.

BELFAST

King's Hall, Balmoral

In the original plan, 2 November 1964 was supposed to be a rest day. However, under pressure from promoter Arthur Howes, Brian Epstein agreed for The Beatles to play in Northern Ireland for this one-off concert, sandwiched in between an appearance in Finsbury Park and a return to Studio 2 at Abbey Road.

Ritz Cinema, Fisherwick Place

After The Beatles' only appearance in the Republic of Ireland, they drove north from Dublin, stopping off near the border with Northern Ireland to record an interview with Jimmy Robinson for Ulster News, which was broadcast as part of the 6.25pm news programme on 8 November 1963. When they arrived in Belfast, The Beatles were taken to the BBC's Studio 8 at Broadcasting House, Ormeau Avenue in Belfast to record a second interview with Sally Ogle for the TV news programme *Six Ten*, transmitted at 6.10pm. They then performed at the Ritz Cinema as part of their autumn tour, before returning to London.

'On the day of the concerts,' local fan Jean recalled, 'the whole city was in an acute state of excitement. The streets near the cinema were cordoned off and only ticket holders were allowed in. I was at the later show and, while we were queuing to get in, the audience from the earlier performance came out. The girls were almost fainting, some still screaming! My friend and I were seated in the middle of the front row of the stalls, and while the other acts were performing, we were able to see John and George standing in the wings. John still had his glasses on. At that time he never wore them in public so we really felt we were sharing an intimate moment ... When The Beatles finally came on stage, the whole place erupted with everyone rushing towards the front and the security staff just managed to hold the crowd back. Because we were so close we were actually able to hear some of the music, but the noise of the screaming behind us was deafening.

'The Beatles played through their set, ignoring the uproar and pandemonium. I wasn't a screamer but during a lull, when Paul was saying something, I yelled out Ringo's name. He looked around and smiled, so I'm sure he heard me. After "Twist And Shout" [they actually finished on 'From Me To You'] the curtain came down and it was all over. The national anthem was played immediately so no one could move which gave them time to get The Beatles safely out of the cinema. Despite the fact that their actual performance had been so short and that most of the audience probably never heard any of it, no one came out disappointed.'

REPUBLIC OF IRELAND

Even though it was just a hop across the Irish Sea, and there were many Beatles familial connections with the Republic of Ireland, they played here only once, though John once said this was where he planned to retire.

Dorinish, County Mayo

John had a vision of creating a perfect 'hippy' community, so he purchased a small island, Dorinish, off the west coast of Ireland in 1967 for £1,700. A small community of 25 hippies, under the leadership of Sid Rawle, lived there for two years from 1970, but in the end headed home because of the bad weather. Although John never did retire on the island, he was actively making plans to return there in the 1980s. It was sold by Yoko in 1984 for £30,000, and the proceeds were donated to a local orphanage.

DUBLIN

Adelphi Cinema, 98–101 Middle Abbey Street

The Beatles' only appearance in the Republic of Ireland was on 7 November 1963 on their autumn tour. Frank Hall, of the RTE television news-magazine show, *In Town*, interviewed them shortly after their arrival at Dublin Airport. The piece was broadcast on the station later that evening. The *Record Mirror* reporter, Peter Jay, wrote of the Adelphi Cinema concerts: 'The fans there really do go mad. Girls who fainted in the crowds outside the theatre were carried into their seats by attendants. Outside there was the biggest riot yet. It's a fact that cars were overturned and the police had to make several arrests.' Observing the concert and subsequent hysteria was Alun Owen, the scriptwriter hired by producer Walter Shenson to pen the script for the group's first film, soon to be called *A Hard Day's Night*. Owen had flown with The Beatles from London to Dublin, and ended up spending three days with them to witness first hand their characters and riotous lifestyle.

The Beatles loved
the USA, and the
USA loved them.
Here they are,
posing in front of
the flag in 1964.

© Michael Ochs Archives / Stringer

UNITED STATES OF AMERICA

For any pop star, breaking America was the ultimate ambition. Many had tried, but none had successfully made the breakthrough. American music had been the inspiration for The Beatles, with even the skiffle music of The Quarrymen having its roots in American bluegrass and folk. To play in the country that had produced Buddy Holly, Little Richard, Chuck Berry and, of course, Elvis Presley, was a dream come true. And for anyone brought up in post-war austerity Britain, just to visit the USA was an excitement in itself.

ALTON, MISSOURI

Pigman Ranch in Alton, Missouri, was a 'dude' ranch where guests could enjoy the ranch lifestyle. This one was owned by Reed Pigman who operated the charter airline that was flying The Beatles between concert venues. The Beatles spent the weekend with Pigman, arriving on 18 September 1964, before heading off for the next leg of their tour.

ANCHORAGE, ALASKA

Anchorage Airport

The Beatles made an unscheduled stop in Alaska, on 27 June 1966. 'My only great memory of Alaska is at the airport they have a huge white bear in a glass case,' Ringo commented. The Beatles were on their way to Japan for a concert, when typhoon warnings in Tokyo forced them to make a nine-hour stop in Anchorage until it blew over. The Beatles stayed at The Westwood Hotel, got to party at the hotel club called, appropriately, the 'Top of the World', and were given a quick tour of the city by a local DJ. He also spread the word about the famous out-of-town guests, giving the girls of Anchorage the thrill of a lifetime, and

causing them to descend on the hotel in screaming numbers, which shows how far Beatlemania had spread.

ATLANTA, GEORGIA

Atlanta Stadium, Capitol Avenue South West

After appearing in Toronto, The Beatles flew south to Atlanta where they played in the new baseball stadium on 18 August 1965 in front of approximately 150 policemen and 36,000 fans, many of whom watched for free after several radio stations, supermarkets and drug stores (such as the Enloe Drug Store) ran competitions with the winners each receiving two tickets for the show.

The band's 'rider' stated: 'Food and beds for their contingent, so they will not have to venture out of their dressing room in the face of over-zealous fans, three limousines, a 40-passenger bus and a truck to handle the party and luggage.'

After being loaned monitor speakers, The Beatles were able to hear themselves playing for the first time in a large venue. Unfortunately, they were unable to keep them. The local Atlanta Transit Authority provided 'Beatles Shuttle Buses' on the night of the concert that ran from downtown to the venue. Vendors outside sold many items of memorabilia, including Beatles balloons that one barker shouted were 'Kissed by Ringo!' James L. Moseley, the Atlanta police traffic superintendent in charge of security on the night, had been to Shea Stadium three days earlier, to see how the police there handled the excitable fans.

Memorable for the fact that the group were able to hear themselves play in a large venue for the very first time.

ATLANTIC CITY, NEW JERSEY
Convention Hall, Boardwalk and Mississippi Avenue

The week after the Democratic National Convention, Atlantic City's Convention Hall played host to The Beatles on Sunday 30 August 1964 in front of 18,000 adoring fans, certainly having a better reception than President Lyndon Johnson had received a few days previously.

During their visit, the group took up residency on the eighth floor of the Lafayette Hotel. Also staying there was the BBC reporter Peter Woods, who had been covering the Convention. Woods was not pleased that his slumber had been broken by the sound of thousands of screaming Beatles fans gathered outside the building. He was so annoyed by the turn of events, he put out a heartfelt message of sympathy to this effect on his next BBC News bulletin. 'I've never seen anything like this,' he announced. 'Beatlemania is guzzling around the place. You can't sleep at night because of the screaming.' Not wishing to miss a good opportunity, Woods then confronted the band about it. 'How on earth do you put up with all this noise all the time?' 'Well, you shouldn't stay in cheap hotels, should ya?' John cheekily replied. 'You don't notice it very much,' Paul said. 'You forget about it,' Ringo added. 'Close the windows,

put the air conditioning on, and that's it, and away you go,' was George's response.

On 31 August 1964, in the group's hotel room, orchestrated by the *New Musical Express* paper, Paul placed a call through to the King of Rock 'n' Roll, Elvis Presley. The Beatle asked him about his new bass guitar. 'Yeah,' Elvis replied, 'I've got blisters on my fingers.' (McCartney remembered this remark and would get Ringo to say it at the end of the 1968 *White Album* track, 'Helter Skelter', the stereo version.) Paul responded by saying, 'Don't worry, man, it'll soon go.' The phone conversation came to a close after the group's roadie Mal Evans had spoken to Presley. During their stay at that hotel, John and Paul also penned the track, 'Every Little Thing', which would appear on the next album, *Beatles For Sale*, at the tail end of the year.

BALTIMORE, MARYLAND
Civic Center, 201 West Baltimore Street

Sandwiched in between a trip to Boston and Pittsburgh, The Beatles performed two shows here on 13 September 1964, to a combined total of 28,000 fans. The best seat in the house cost a mere $3.75.

Prior to the concerts, The Beatles took part in another press conference. 'What do you think of American television?' the group was asked. 'It's great,' Ringo replied. 'You get 18 stations, but you can't get a good picture on any of them.' 'What will you do when the Beatlebubble bursts?' 'We'll play baseball,' John retorted. Other answers included John admitting he was backing Eisenhower in the current US Presidential contest; Paul admitting he hated being asked what he would do when the group's popularity had waned and Ringo revealing he would indeed undergo a tonsillectomy that year, but it would be done in England, 'where it's free'. While the press call was going on, a group of girls attempted the ancient Trojan Horse routine to try to smuggle two of their gang into The Beatles' dressing room. The females were secreted in a cardboard box, which had been tied with a large red ribbon and labelled, 'Beatles Fan Mail'. They were caught when a guard at the Civic Center checked the box as it was being wheeled into the venue.

BENTON, ILLINOIS

113 McCann St

Before The Beatles conquered America in 1964, George had been to the US the year before visiting his sister Louise Harrison Caldwell, who had emigrated there in early 1963. George arrived on 16 September 1963, becoming the first of The Beatles to visit America. 'I'd been to America before,' he explained, 'being the experienced Beatle that I was. I went to New York and St Louis in 1963, to look around, and to the countryside in Illinois, where my sister was living at the time. I went to record stores. I bought Booker T and the MGs' first album *Green Onions*, and I bought some Bobby Bland, all kind of things.'

BIRMINGHAM, ALABAMA

WAQY radio station

On 4 March 1966 the *Evening Standard* published an interview between Maureen Cleave and John Lennon entitled 'How Does A Beatle Live?' In the course of a description of The Beatles and their everyday life in Weybridge, Cleave quoted Lennon as saying, 'Christianity will go. It will vanish and shrink. I needn't argue about that. I'm right and I will be proved right. We're more popular than Jesus now. I don't know which will go first – rock 'n' roll or Christianity.' When it was reprinted in an American magazine four months later on the

eve of a Beatles tour of the USA, it caused an outrage. KLUE radio in Longview, Texas staged a public burning of Beatle records. Station WAQY in Birmingham, Alabama encouraged its listeners to destroy Beatles discs. In all, 22 radio stations banned the group's music from the airwaves and the Ku Klux Klan arranged anti-Beatles demonstrations. The Vatican denounced Lennon and Beatles albums were banned in South Africa.

A radio station that thought they were bigger than The Beatles.

BOSTON, MASSACHUSETTS

Boston Garden, Causeway Street

After the hurricane had almost wrecked their appearance in Florida the night before, The Beatles had an easier task entertaining the 13,909 crowd in Boston on 12 September 1964. Their takings from the show was the guaranteed minimum of $60,000.

The group arrived earlier in the day, at 3.20am, on a chartered plane at Hanscom Air Force base in suburban Bedford under one of the heaviest protective guards in the City's history. More than 100 military policemen, a score of state troopers and at least 100 local police, from Bedford, Concord, Lexington and Lincoln, were in charge of the group's safety. This meant that for the first time in a long while the group were not molested by a single teenager on their arrival. The Massachusetts state police were in such a hurry to get The Beatles from the airport to their accommodation – the Hotel Madison – that they accidentally left behind press spokesman Derek Taylor.

Suffolk Downs Racetrack, Waldemar Avenue

Having experienced theatres, arenas and stadiums, The Beatles played in the middle of this famous

Massachusetts racetrack (a unique venue for them) in front of 25,000 fans on 18 August 1966.

Portions of the concert were captured on colour, 8mm home movie cameras by several enterprising members of the audience, which included 35 members of the Kennedy family who drove up from their home in Hyannis Port especially. Included in this entourage were Joe Kennedy, his sister, Kathleen, and the children of Senator Bobby Kennedy. The 200 policemen in attendance patrolled a ten-feet wide no man's land separating the fans from the track. However, some still managed to break through the barricade. One young girl injured her ankle when she leaped over a chain link fence, and a young, shaggy-haired man scaled two fences and slipped past the policemen to reach The Beatles during their final number, 'Long Tall Sally'. Dancing from Beatle to Beatle, he was caught from behind and tossed off stage by a burly bodyguard just as he was about to gyrate alongside Ringo.

CHICAGO, ILLINOIS

International Amphitheatre, 42nd Street/South Halsted Street

The Beatles made their first of two appearances here on 5 September 1964. Their second appearance opened their final US tour, on 12 August 1966; they had arrived in Chicago the day before.

The Beatles' fee for their 1964 performance was reportedly $30,000. Shortly after checking into their rooms at the Stock Yard Inn, the group tucked in to some freshly cooked steaks. The fans in Chicago were very inventive, as roadie Mal Evans recalled. 'We were coming out of our hotel, ready for the show and suddenly I spied a girl in the crowd and she was about to slam a handcuff on Paul's wrist. What she had done was attach one end of the handcuff onto her wrist and she was

going to attach the other end onto Paul's wrist. It was a great idea, but she just didn't make it.'

The press conference that afternoon, held in the Stock Yard Inn, was memorable for Ringo's prediction that Lyndon B. Johnson would be the next US President. In less memorable sound bites, Paul announced he was looking forward to seeing Chicago's gangsters with their, 'broad brimmed hats and wide ties,' while John declared that it took him longer to dry his hair because it was longer.

Since 1963, Ringo had been regularly using Ludwig drums, made by a company whose main office was in Chicago. In honour of the publicity and free advertising, before the concert William Ludwig Jr. presented Ringo with a specially made, one-of-a-kind, gold snare drum, attached to which was a plaque that read, 'Ringo Starr, the Beatles'. During the presentation Ludwig Jr. announced, 'I have never known a drummer more widely acclaimed and publicised than you, Ringo Starr. On behalf of the employees and management of the Ludwig Drum Company, I would like to thank you for choosing our instruments and for the major role you are playing in the music world today.'

Vee-Jay Records, 1449 South Michigan Avenue

Vee-Jay Records was the most successful black-owned and operated record company before Motown. Founded 1953 in Gary, Indiana, by Vivian Carter (the 'Vee') and her husband, James 'Jimmy' Bracken ('Jay') Vee-Jay contributed a tremendous catalogue of blues, R&B, doo-wop, jazz, soul, pop and rock 'n' roll music. The Beatles signed in January 1963 and released 'Please Please Me'. Vee-Jay then released 'From Me To You', followed by the album *Introducing ... The Beatles* on 10 January 1964, just ten days before Capitol issued *Meet The Beatles!* Vee-Jay's biggest success occurred between 1962–1964, with the ascendancy of The Four Seasons and the distribution of early Beatles material.

The Beatles singles they issued were: 'Please Please Me'/'Ask Me Why', 'From Me To You'/'Thank You Girl', and 'Do You Want To Know A Secret'/'Thank You Girl'. They also issued 'Twist And Shout'/'There's A Place' and 'Love Me Do'/'P.S. I Love You' via its subsidiary Tollie Records, plus re-releasing some of their licensed tracks on an EP and reissuing singles. In total, Vee-Jay brought out four LPs, six singles, four reissued singles and an EP, despite only having the rights to 14 Beatles songs.

Once Capitol, the subsidiary of EMI, had realised the popularity and potential of The Beatles, they 'capitolised' on their EMI connections and made sure they became the sole distributors of Beatles records. After expensive lawsuits involving The Four Seasons and The Beatles, management chaos at the company and the loss of the right to release any new Beatles records after 15 October 1964, Vee-Jay couldn't compete and in 1965 the label collapsed and eventually closed its doors in May 1966.

Capitol job, Vee-Jay Records.

White Sox Park/Comiskey Park, 35th and Shields

The Beatles left Houston, Texas, and made the 1,000-mile trip north to Chicago where they played twice at the stadium on 20 August 1965, to a total of over 63,000 fans.

For their two performances, the group's share of the gate receipts was $155,000. In a contract between NEMS Enterprises and promoters Triangle Theatrical Productions Inc, dated 31 April 1965, they agreed that Triangle should receive '65 per cent of the gross box-office receipts' and their share of it should 'not be less than $81,999'.

The soft-drinks company 7-Up ran a competition that offered purchasers the chance to win a pair of tickets for one of the shows.

CINCINNATI, OHIO

Cincinnati Gardens, 2250 Seymour Avenue

After leaving Colorado, The Beatles travelled to Cincinnati to make their only appearance at the Cincinnati Gardens on 27 August 1964, arriving at the venue shortly before 6pm, where they spoke to Elvis Presley on the telephone backstage. Many of the 14,000 fans at the concert passed out on actually seeing the group perform. This level of hysteria provoked local politicians to query the event itself. In a press conference carried out the following day, one Ohio State official announced to reporters, 'The question is, can you take 14,000 children and pack them in to one stadium and they know they're coming there to get hysterical and the whole show was based on producing hysteria, the preliminary acts, as well as The Beatles. And then these girls went into a coma. They ranted, they fainted, and their eyes were glassy. Some pulled their hair out. Some tore their dresses. They threw notes of a very undesirable nature onto the stage. Some girls, after the performance, kissed the stage, and some even went up and kissed the seats on which The Beatles had sat.'

Crosley Field, Findlay Street/Western Avenue

Although The Beatles were supposed to play the Cincinnati Reds baseball team on Sunday 20 August 1966, heavy rain forced the show to be rearranged for the following day at noon, after which they travelled 340 miles to St Louis, Missouri, for an 8.30pm show. 'The promoter had been trying to save himself a few cents by not putting a roof over the stage,' Nat Weiss, attorney and friend of Brian Epstein, recalled 'It started

TOPPERMOST OF THE POPPERMOST

Capitol's failure to spot the potential of The Beatles' first singles worked in the group's favour as the smaller labels that had released them saw this as an opportunity to ride on The Beatles' wave and have their own hit singles.

In the normal course of events, two singles by the same artist are not released at the same time, as a label would not want an artist to be competing with himself. This hardly mattered with The Beatles as all the fans wanted everything and the various singles raced up the charts. Things came to a head on 4 April 1964, when the Top 5 positions on the *Billboard Hot 100* were all held by The Beatles, with 'Can't Buy Me Love' (Capitol), 'Twist And Shout' (Tollie, a subsidiary of Vee-Jay), 'She Loves You' (Swan), 'I Want To Hold Your Hand' (Capitol) and 'Please Please Me' (Vee-Jay). Also in the charts were a couple of singles from Capitol of Canada, and even Tony Sheridan and The Beatles' 'My Bonnie' had been picked up by MGM and was selling well. The Beatles sold 60 per cent of all the singles that had been bought that week.

But The Beatles did even better in Australia where for three consecutive weeks in March/April 1964, they held the Top 6 positions.

to rain and The Beatles couldn't go on because they would have been in danger of electrocution. They had to turn away 35,000 screaming fans, who were all given passes for a concert the next day. The strain had obviously been too much for Paul. When I got back to the hotel, he was already there, throwing up with all his tension.'

CLEVELAND, OHIO

Cleveland Stadium, West 3rd Street

The Beatles played their only show at the home of the Cleveland Indians baseball team on Sunday 14 August 1966. As if waiting for the signal, 2,500 fans crashed through a security fence and rushed on to the field during 'Day Tripper' in a scene reminiscent of the band's 1964 appearance at the Public Auditorium, Cleveland. The concert was held up for about 30 minutes before The Beatles could return to the stage.

Public Auditorium (aka Public Hall), East 6th Street

During their only appearance at this venue on Tuesday 15 September 1964, a small group of fans managed to break through the police cordon and climb on to the stage. The Beatles were playing 'All My Loving' at the time. Fearing for the group's safety, Police Inspector Michael Blackwell and Deputy Inspector Carl Bare decided to abort the show, with DI Bare announcing over the microphone that the performance was over and instructing the crowd to sit down. The Beatles continued to play during this, until eventually downing instruments and leaving the stage. In their dressing room, John remarked to the KYW Radio DJ Art Schreiber, 'This has never happened to us before. We have never had a show stopped. These policemen are a bunch of amateurs.' Brian Epstein was having none of this, insisting that the police were right in what they did. 'The enthusiasm of the crowd was building much too early,' he offered. After ten minutes, Derek Blackwell walked on the stage and over the public address system told the crowd the show would resume if they remained in their seats. They did and The Beatles returned to finish their set shortly afterwards. It would be almost two years before the group played in Cleveland again, in a concert also marked by a crowd disturbance.

DALLAS, TEXAS

Dallas Memorial Auditorium, South Akard Street

When the group arrived at Dallas Love Field airport for their only concert in the city, on 18 September 1964, they were welcomed by hordes of fans, standing shoulder-to-shoulder behind a large chain fence. Almost immediately, The Beatles were handed ill-fitting white Stetson hats from an opera association. They were then driven to the Cabana Motor Hotel, which was then owned by actress Doris Day. The Beatles' journey from their car to the building's rear entrance proved hazardous, with both George and Ringo losing their footing as the crowd chased them in scenes reminiscent of *A Hard Day's Night*.

At the hotel, things turned even nastier when the horde of fans began to push against the plate glass window of the building, eventually breaking it and sending people through the broken shards. One fan was so badly injured that she had to be rushed to hospital.

Shortly before their performance, the group gave a television interview in their dressing room at the Dallas Memorial Auditorium, wearing another set of cowboy hats, presented to them by Yolanda Hernandez and Stephanie Pinter of the Dallas chapter of the National Beatles Fan Club. The interviewer asked John, 'What kind of girls do you prefer?' 'My wife,' he replied. 'Your wife?' the quizzer responded, 'What kind of girl is she?' 'She's a nice girl,' the Beatle replied. The interviewer then asked George the same question, 'What kind of girl do you like?' George paused before replying, 'Uh … John's wife.' During the press conference that followed, which took place at 7pm in the basement of the venue, girls from The Beatles Ltd fan club, Suzie Chapman and Dell Perry presented western belts to each of the group.

The performance was delayed after a bomb threat was telephoned in, but nothing was found.

The show eventually began at 10pm, in front of 15,000 fans, with The Beatles playing on a stage that was three times the regular height for one of their concerts.

Immediately after their performance, the group headed back to Love Field, and shortly after 11pm caught a flight to Walnut Ridge, Arkansas. There Reed Pigman, ranch owner and Texas airline magnate, picked them up in his twin-engine seven-passenger Cessna and flew them out to his ranch in Oregon County, near Alton and Riverton, Missouri. His company, American Flyers, had a contract to fly The Beatles on this, their second US visit. They arrived at his ranch at 3am on Saturday morning and played poker until dawn. Brian Epstein and Bill Black of the Bill Black Combo, a support act on the tour, joined them.

On Saturday, The Beatles spent the day playing more games of poker, riding horses and posing for pictures, some with Reed Pigman, Jr., son of their host. George also took the opportunity to drive a yellow go-cart around the barn. The 23 October 1964 edition of *Life* magazine carried several photographs of these activities. Photographer Curt Gunther was also on hand to take snaps of the day. The Beatles' chance of spending the weekend relaxing in seclusion, before heading on to New York to complete their tour, was scuppered when, by mid-morning on 19 September 1964, the media had spread the word of the group's unlikely vacation spot and fans began to converge on the place

DENVER, COLORADO

Red Rocks Amphitheatre, Lawrence Street

This famous natural amphitheatre provided the backdrop to The Beatles' only appearance here on 26 August 1964 in front of only seven thousand fans, each paying $6.60 a ticket. Even though a couple of thousand tickets remained unsold, the group still managed to set a box office record for this 30-year-old venue. One reviewer wrote, 'The Beatles appeared before a howling crowd of jelly bean throwing teenagers… and confused adults.'

Amazing setting for a concert.

DETROIT, MICHIGAN

Olympia Stadium, Grand River Avenue/McGraw Avenue

Their first trip to the home of Motown was on 6 September 1964, where they played two shows at the Olympia Stadium.

The group arrived at the Whittier Hotel at 1.17am and took up residency in Executive Suite number 1566. They checked out a little less than 12 hours later, at 2.05pm. Following their departure, the sheets they had slept on were purchased by Larry Einhorn and Ruby Victor of WBKB Television in Detroit, cut into 164,000 tiny squares, and sold on to fans. On each was a note saying which Beatle had used it. But that was a lie. As Victor later admitted, 'We had no idea which of The Beatles had slept on each sheet. We were just given bags full of sheets and we had to guess who slept on each sheet. For all we know, all four of them slept in the same bed with four girls.'

Expecting to make $164,000 from the project, they were shocked to discover they made … nothing! Just 750 were sold. 'Don't ask me why,' Victor admitted years later. 'I've never understood it. I thought it was because people thought we were phoneys. There was so much Beatle junk being sold in those days, I don't think anyone really believed that we had bought The Beatles' actual bedsheets.' He added, 'We lost money. We didn't even get back what we paid for the sheets.' There were further

troubles for the pair when they received a cease and desist order from The Beatles' New York attorney, Walter Hofer, who told them their activities were 'causing great damage to our clients.'

The Beatles returned here once more, on 13 August 1966 when again they played two shows, to a combined total of 28,000 fans, approximately 2,000 short of a sell-out. Prior to each concert the group sat quietly in their dressing room and listened to Indian music.

DISNEY WORLD, ORLANDO, FLORIDA

Polynesian Village Hotel, Disney World

After Paul, George and Ringo had signed the papers to dissolve The Beatles, John finally added his name in this hotel on 29 December 1974 and The Beatles were no more.

No happy-ever-after ending.

HOUSTON, TEXAS

Sam Houston Coliseum, Bagby Street

With two shows on 19 August 1965, The Beatles had only arrived in Houston at 2am, having made the trip from Atlanta, Georgia. They played two sell-out shows at the 12,000 capacity stadium, billed as 'The Sixth Annual Back-to-School Show'.

The concerts were taped and broadcast by sponsors KILT, the local radio station. Tickets cost $5, with The Beatles receiving a combined fee of $85,000. Soundboard and radio recordings exist of both afternoon and evening performances. John's ongoing throat problem was a downside of the shows. 'I remember both years,' George recalled in 1974. 'When we went to Dallas or Houston on The Beatles' tours, the first year we went to Dallas, we almost got killed and the second year, we went to Houston and we almost got killed, so my concept of Texas has been … I'm not going to Texas because they're all so mad!'

With no time to rest, the group headed straight off to Chicago for their concert the next day.

INDIANAPOLIS, INDIANA

Indiana State Fair Coliseum, East 38th Street

After appearing in Philadelphia, The Beatles headed 650 miles west to Indianapolis where they played two shows to a combined total of nearly 29,337 people on 3 September 1964, netting $85,232.

Prior to the shows, the group faced another obligatory press conference. Before proceedings began, and before The Beatles had even entered the room, their press officer, Derek Taylor, laid down a few ground rules; photos would be taken first, then the interviews, and finally the television cameras would be allowed to film some material. Before the questions began, the group were presented with an original cartoon, drawn by the *Indianapolis News* sketch-artist Robbie Robinson, and met two special people – current Miss Indiana State Fair Cheryl Lee Garrett, and 15-year-old Elaine May, winner of the 'I want to meet a Beatle because…' newspaper competition run by the *Indianapolis News*. Elaine was allowed to ask one question and chose to ask John if he was going to write another book. He replied, 'Yes, tomorrow.'

One journalist wondered why The Beatles weren't in the British draft. 'We all miss it,' Lennon said. 'If not, we'd be hiding in the south of Ireland.' 'What do you do all day locked in your hotel rooms?' quizzed another reporter. 'We play tennis and water polo and we hide from our security,' John quickly responded. The group were also asked about their haircuts. John's reply was the most interesting, 'We've told so many lies we've forgotten.'

JACKSONVILLE, FLORIDA

Gator Bowl Stadium, East Adams Street

This show on 11 September 1964 has become famous because The Beatles faced a political row when, having been informed that the audience was to be segregated, they made it clear they would not play under such circumstances. The show eventually went ahead, with the fans integrated, after the enactment of the Civil Rights Act made race discrimination illegal.

Another problem arose when The Beatles refused to go on stage until the newsreel and television cameramen had left. Eventually their press officer, Derek Taylor, was forced to go on stage and inform the impatient crowd, 'The Beatles are 100 feet away. They came thousands of miles to be here. The only thing preventing their appearance is the cine cameramen.' The announcement clearly worked, and almost immediately, two police captains gave orders for the filming to end.

There was also a third problem, with approximately 9,000 of the 32,000 ticket holders unable to reach the Bowl because of the damage caused by the recent Hurricane Dora, which had left much of Jacksonville without electricity for several days. The Beatles blew in and out like a hurricane themselves, with the briefest of stops in Florida before heading off for Milwaukee.

The Beatles made it clear in black and white that they would not accept segregation

KANSAS CITY, MISSOURI

Municipal Stadium, 22nd and Brooklyn

The Beatles played here on 17 September 1964, although the date was originally scheduled as a free day for them. However, local promoter

Charles O. Finley, the controversial owner of the Oakland Athletics Major League Baseball team, who at the time were based in Kansas City, having first offered $60,000 and then $100,000 finally persuaded Brian Epstein to add the venue to the tour schedule with a bid of $150,000. The sum was more than seven times what they could expect to make for a show and the largest take for a single show in show-business history.

The concert was attended by 20,280 fans, with tickets costing between $2 and $8.50. The Beatles added 'Kansas City'/'Hey-Hey-Hey-Hey' to the end of the set-list in honour of Finley.

Paul McCartney remembered the occasion well. 'Our days off were sacred. If you look at our 1964 timetable you can see why. I didn't realise until recently that we used to have a whole year of work, and then get something like 23rd November off – and then have to judge a beauty competition that day. So, by the time we got to Kansas City, we probably needed a day off. I can't actually remember falling out with Brian about him wanting us to work on a day off, we'd talk to each other rather than fall out.'

Prior to the show, The Beatles faced yet another press conference. However, this one was much more humorous. 'Who is the most exciting woman you've ever met?' the group was asked. 'Ringo's mother is pretty hot,' John replied. 'What do you think of Paul?' a reporter enquired. 'He's okay,' Lennon retorted, 'but we have to put him down sometimes.' 'What will you do when the group breaks up?' 'I'll roller-skate,' said George. 'Do you like the girls tearing up your sheets and going crazy?' 'I don't mind,' Ringo announced, 'as long as I'm not in them.' 'What do you boys do when you are confined to your hotel room?' Ringo again answered. 'Well, we sleep, watch the telly, listen to the radio, play cards and sometimes we even talk to each other.'

As with their appearance in Cleveland two days before, the concert was temporarily interrupted when fans invaded the pitch, forcing The Beatles to leave the stage until calm was restored.

'The Beatles came on, and the whole place went completely wild,' Bess Coleman, in charge of the NEMS office in America, recalled. 'All of the fans broke through all of the barriers and, within minutes, everybody that was in a seat was on the pitch.' Fearing for their safety, The Beatles and their entourage were forced to return to their trailer. 'I was sitting in a caravan with the four Beatles and Derek Taylor,' Coleman recalled, 'and suddenly it began to rock, and it rocked, and rocked, until finally we were over. It was a very funny experience to be sitting in a caravan the wrong side up. The noise was unbelievable! Police were screaming through tannoy systems, saying, "Get away, get away," but no one was going away. I don't know how the caravan was righted, but eventually it was … Derek Taylor had to get up on stage and, sort of, yell at the fans, through the speakers, saying that, if they didn't sit down again, the police were going to cancel the concert. I don't know how it happened, but the fans did sit down and the concert was finished. But at the end of that, the fans broke through again, so the police had to provide a guard to get The Beatles back to their car and out of the arena.'

This was the only time The Beatles performed in Kansas City. On 4 November 2008 a two-minute, colour, silent 8mm film of them performing at this concert was sold at an auction in Reading, Berkshire for £4,100, approximately $6,600. It was shot by fan, Drew Dimmel, who as a boy smuggled a movie camera into the concert hall, the brand new device having been loaned by his father. Dimmel's plan was to stand at the front of the stage and record parts of the show, but after being instructed by a security guard to return to his seat, he passed the camera to a journalist who offered to film the show from the press-pit. After getting the film developed, the young fan placed it at the bottom of a desk drawer, where it stayed for 44 years. He rediscovered it in 2008, during a clear-out of his parents' belongings, still in its original photo-lab box with the words 'Beatles 1964' scrawled in blue ballpoint pen across the back.

LAS VEGAS, NEVADA
Convention Center, Paradise Road

The Beatles' only visit to the bright lights of Las Vegas was on 20 August 1964, though they were warned not to visit the casinos as it would set a bad example. Their plane landed at 1.00am at McCarran International Airport, from where they were driven to the Sahara Hotel. Two thousand fans defied the city curfew to see them arrive. The Beatles gave two performances, at 4pm and 9pm, for which they received a payment of $30,000. They then headed off to Seattle.

'Till There Was You' was temporarily added to their set-list for the second show. Show-business luminaries, singer Pat Boone and flamboyant pianist Liberace, were among the 8,000 in attendance at each gig. 'The kids here weren't as unruly as kids in some cities we've been to,' John remarked.

LOS ANGELES, CALIFORNIA

Los Angeles would become a mecca for The Beatles, both before and after they split, as a group and as individuals. They would meet Elvis here, perform at the legendary Hollywood Bowl and many years later, after primal therapy, John would lose a weekend here too.

2850 Benedict Canyon Drive, Beverly Hills

The Beatles arrived in Los Angeles on 22 August 1965 and had five days of rest in this large house

they rented, owned by actress Zsa Zsa Gabor, prior to their upcoming concerts, which would bring an end to this American tour. As with most of their residences on tour, the address had been announced by radio stations, and the local police were called in to keep fans away from the property. George remembered the house, though not because of Zsa Zsa. 'We stayed in the house that Hendrix later stayed in. It was a horseshoe-shaped house on a hill off Mulholland. It had a little gatehouse, which Mal and Neil stayed in, decorated by Arabian-type things draped on the walls.' That evening, The Beatles went to a party at the Bel Air home of Capitol Records president Alan Livingstone, where they were presented with a number of awards. Also attending were some of the biggest stars of the day: Edward G. Robinson, Jack Benny, Vince Edwards, Gene Barry, Richard Chamberlain, Jane Fonda, Rock Hudson, Groucho Marx, Dean Martin, Hayley Mills and James Stewart.

On 24 August, The Beatles welcomed Peter Fonda plus David Crosby and Roger McGuinn from The Byrds, and had an experience with LSD. McGuinn recalled what happened. 'There were girls at the gates, police guards. We went in and David, John Lennon, George Harrison and I took LSD to help get to know each other better. There was a large bathroom in the house and we were all sitting on the edge of a shower passing around a guitar, taking turns to play our favourite songs. John and I agreed "Be-Bop-A-Lula" was our favourite fifties rock record. I showed George Harrison some Ravi Shankar sounds, which I'd heard because we shared the same record company, on the guitar. I told him about Ravi Shankar and he said he had never heard Indian music before. You can hear what I played him from the Byrds song "Why". I had learned to play it on the guitar from listening to records of Ravi Shankar.'

What a difference from the Indra Club in Hamburg, staying in a house where many of the stars had lived.

Capitol Records, 1750 Vine Street

The headquarters of Capitol Records. Initially the company was slow to react to the popularity of The Beatles, in spite of being owned by their UK record label EMI since 1955. In the early days, Beatles records in the US were being released on different labels such as Swan and Vee-Jay. Capitol eventually caught up and started releasing albums as often as they could to make the most of Beatlemania. Outside this building are the stars on the Hollywood 'Walk of Fame', dedicated to the individual Beatles.

Great concept building in the shape of a stack of records, though the early executives were slow to catch on to the magic of The Beatles.

Footnote: On 26 August 1966 The Beatles faced a standard press conference here at Capitol Records Tower. It was a mildly star-studded affair, with celebrities in attendance such as David Crosby from The Byrds, and Robert Vaughn from the TV series *The Man From Uncle*. It would be the last of its kind The Beatles would ever face as a collective group.

7655 Curson Terrace, Beverly Hills

As The Beatles came to the end of their final tour in August 1966, they stayed at this property and were visited by the Beach Boys Brian and Carl Wilson.

Wouldn't it be nice.

NBC Studios, Burbank

While Ringo was in Los Angeles promoting his new film, *The Magic Christian*, he made an appearance on the TV show *Rowan & Martin's Laugh-In*. The edition was first broadcast in the US on Monday 23 February 1970, from 8–9pm EST. Its first UK showing was on BBC 2 on Sunday 12 April, from 7.25–8.15pm, the difference in running time due to the absence of commercial breaks on the BBC.

841 Nimes Road, Bel Air

While attending Arthur Janov's clinic around April 1970 for their primal therapy, John and Yoko rented this property.

356 St Pierre Road, Bel-Air

With a rare day off on 24 August 1964, The Beatles rested up in this rented property before heading off to the luxury home of Alan Livingston, president of Capitol Records. Tickets for the party, held in aid of the Haemophilia Foundation of Southern California, cost $25, and the event raised $10,000.

900 Sunset Drive, Bel-Air

The clinic of Arthur Janov that John and Yoko visited as they continued their primal therapy sessions.

For John, therapy took him back to his troubled childhood.

Dodger Stadium, Elysian Park Avenue

The penultimate Beatles concert of their last ever tour was at the home of the LA Dodgers on Sunday 28 August 1966, following three days resting in the luxury of Beverly Hills.

In sharp contrast to their previous visits to the country, this and a great number of shows on this tour had failed to sell out. Following its conclusion, fans clashed with police during a rush for the main gates. Dozens were injured and 25 arrested. The Beatles' limousine was forced to turn back after fans started to climb all over it. Bottles and sticks were thrown at the police before control could be restored. Many in the audience were forced to remain in the venue for some time after The Beatles had left the stage. The group eventually had to leave in an armoured van from the opposite side of the stadium. 'The first year [1964 – Hollywood Bowl], McCartney and Harrison were really friendly,' the concert's promoter Bob Eubanks recalled. 'The second year, McCartney was real friendly. But in the third year, they were a real pain. But I forgave them … because they were really tired; they were tired of their own music, and they were tired of each other. They'd had it by the third year.'

Four Star Theatre, 5112 Wilshire Boulevard

On 29 January 1970, Ringo attended the US premiere of his new film *The Magic Christian*, with co-star Peter Sellers. Ringo's wife Maureen accompanied him, and after the premiere, they partied at the Beverly Hills Hotel.

Hollywood Bowl, North Highland Avenue

One of the most picturesque venues The Beatles ever played, first on 23 August 1964 and then again on 29 and 30 August 1965, was the Hollywood Bowl, an outdoor amphitheatre in the hills around Los Angeles.

Recalling the 1964 concert, KRLA radio presenter Bob Eubanks said, 'They wanted $25,000, [but] I didn't have $25,000, so my partner Mickey Brown and I borrowed money on a house we had as an investment and that was the beginning of my concert promotion career.' The Beatles only performed once in 1964, but a second was intended. 'We tried to get two shows at the Hollywood Bowl,' Eubanks said, 'because we sold the first one out. Bang! Just like that. No one had ever sold out a concert that rapidly.'

Tickets went on sale four months before the concert and sold out in three-and-a-half hours. They were so scarce that, apparently, even both Frank Sinatra and Dean Martin had their requests for some refused. At the concert, the screaming of the crowd was so loud, no one could hear the music. After the show, fans mobbed the backstage area and the producers were forced to use a limousine as a decoy while putting The Beatles in a Dodge Dart automobile and getting them out before the crowd had realised they were gone. Eubanks revealed the group earned $58,000 for their half an hour set, while he made $1,000 profit, just enough for him to save his home. However, playing at such a landmark venue did not impress John. 'I didn't like the Hollywood Bowl,' he blasted years later. 'It was awful! I hated it. Those places were built for fucking orchestras, not groups.'

The day after the concert things became heated in Los Angeles when, at a private party at the Whiskey-A-Go-Go nightclub, attended by Hollywood stars such as Jayne Mansfield, George angrily threw a glass of water at one overbearing reporter. 'He was a very nasty man,' Harrison recalled at the time. 'We asked him to leave because he was taking too many pictures and we couldn't see anything. And so, I just decided that he ought to be baptised.'

George Martin and engineers from Capitol Records, located nearby, recorded the 1964 performance, which lasted just under 30 minutes. Nothing was done with the original 3-track recording as it was deemed unsuitable for release, until it was dusted down, remastered by George Martin and Geoff Emerick and, using excerpts from the 1965 shows, released in May 1977 on the official album *The Beatles At The Hollywood Bowl*.

News that the first concert was being taped failed to reach the band. 'If we knew we were being recorded, it was death,' John admitted in 1971. 'We were so frightened. You could never hear yourself and you knew they were fucking it up on the tape anyway. There was no bass and they never recorded the drums. You could never hear them!'

A brief, 48-second excerpt of 'Twist And Shout' also featured on the 1964 Capitol Records, US-only documentary album, *The Beatles' Story*. The concert was also filmed by CBS. See the entry in *TV* section.

The two 1965 concerts, also recorded, were once more promoted by Bob Eubanks and the radio station KRLA; tickets were sold by mail from a newspaper advertisement placed in the *LA Times*. (Eubanks would also bring the group to Dodger Stadium one year later, on 28 August 1966.) The Beatles' share of the $156,000 gross gate receipts was $90,000. After the previous year's chaos, with fans causing pandemonium wherever the group went, the venue's management decided to hire a Brinks armoured truck to bring The Beatles to and from their hotel.

A silent, 8mm colour film of parts of the group's first performance exists. Positioned straight on and featuring some nice medium shots, it included nearly all of 'Can't Buy Me Love', while the b&w version also featured very long range clips of the first two songs, 'She's A Woman' and 'I Feel Fine'. Prior to this first show, the group attended a press conference at the Capitol Tower at Hollywood and Vine, where Alan Livingston, president of Capitol Records, presented them with gold discs for sales of the *Help!* soundtrack album.

The first night had technical problems, but on the second night, in spite of the screaming fans, Capitol Records was able to capture enough quality recording on half-inch, 3-track tape. The label's A&R man, Voyle Gilmore, was in charge. 'The Hollywood Bowl has a pretty good stereo sound system so we plugged our mikes right in there. I didn't do an awful lot. There wasn't much we could do. They just played their usual show and we recorded it.' Thinking they could be released, shortly after Gilmore took the tapes to the studio and began labouring on them. 'I worked on the applause, edited it down, made it play and EQd it quite a bit,' he recalled in 1977. 'The Beatles heard it and they all wanted copies. I had five or six copies made and sent them over. That's where the bootlegs must have come from. We had a system at Capitol and we knew where all our copies were. The Beatles said they liked the tapes, that it sounded pretty good, but they still didn't want to release them.'

The idea to try again to issue the recordings came from Bhaskar Menon, the president of Capitol Records. He mentioned them to George Martin in 1976 and asked whether he would listen to them. 'My original reaction was the original tapes had a rotten sound,' the Beatles producer recalled. 'But when I listened to the Hollywood Bowl tapes, I was amazed at the rawness and vitality of The Beatles' singing. So I told Bhaskar I'd see if I could bring the tapes into line with today's recordings. I enlisted the technical expertise of Geoff Emerick and we transferred the recordings from 8-track to 24-track tapes. The two tapes combined 22 songs and we whittled those down to 13. Some tracks had to be discarded because the music was obliterated by the screams. Once the technical work had been completed, EMI needed approval from all four Beatles before the album could be released. I had to go to New York anyway, so I rang John Lennon and told him about the recordings. I told him that I had been very sceptical at first, but now I was very enthusiastic because I thought the album would be a piece of history, which should be preserved. I said to John, "I want you to hear it after I've gone. You can be as rude as you like, but if you don't like it, give me a yell." I spoke to him the following day and he was delighted in it. The reaction of George and Ringo was, however, much cooler.' 'The thing is,' Harrison admitted later, 'it's only important historically, but as a record it's not very good.'

Paul too was uninterested in Martin's work and, once it was released officially in May 1977, had no desire whatsoever to even listen to the completed Hollywood Bowl album. Speaking then, he said, 'Geoff [Emerick] keeps telling me to, because he did it … but I'm just not bothered. I've got a lot of those tapes anyway in my private collection.' Harrison was actually angered by the release, revealing at the time, 'While each of The Beatles was on EMI/Capitol, the LP wouldn't have been released because we didn't like it. But as soon as we left, and we lost control of our material, it was released.' His resentment became obvious when he declared, 'The sound quality on the album sounds just like a bootleg, but because Capitol is bootlegging it, it's legitimate.'

On the album, 'Things We Said Today', 'Roll Over Beethoven', 'Boys,' 'All My Loving', 'She Loves You' and 'Long Tall Sally' featured from 1964; 'Twist And Shout', 'She's a Woman', 'Dizzy Miss Lizzy', 'Ticket To Ride', 'Can't Buy Me Love', 'A Hard Day's Night' and 'Help!' from 1965. ('Dizzy Miss Lizzy' was a composite edit of the two performances because of poor quality on the original recordings.)

Further excerpts from the tapes would re-appear 19 years later, in 1996, when John's spoken introduction to 'Baby's In Black' featured on the second 'new' Beatles single, 'Real Love', along with the complete version from the 30 August 1965 performance.

One of the greatest venues in the world, and recorded for posterity.

565 Perugia Way, Bel Air

On 27 August 1965, during one of their days off, The Beatles left their temporary residence at 2850 Benedict Canyon, Beverly Hills and pulled up here, the home of Elvis Presley, at around 11pm for a pre-arranged meeting between the two biggest names in the history of popular music. There are many stories regarding this meeting, and different versions of events too. John recalled: 'It was very exciting, we were all nervous as hell, and we met him in his big house in LA – probably as big as the one we were staying in, but it still felt like, "Big house, big Elvis". He had lots of guys around him, all these guys that used to live near him (like we did from Liverpool; we always had thousands of Liverpool people around us, so I guess he was the same). And he had pool tables! Maybe a lot of American houses are like that, but it seemed amazing to us; it was like a nightclub.' When Elvis called for some guitars, a brief jam session took place. For Tony Barrow, there were regrets that nobody photographed or recorded the meeting: 'I can't remember all the things that they played but I do remember one of the songs was "I Feel Fine". And I remember Ringo, who of course didn't have an instrument, tapping out the backbeat with his fingers on the nearest bits of wooden furniture. Everybody was singing. Elvis strummed a few bass guitar chords for Paul and said, "See, I'm practising." And Paul came back with some quip about, "Don't worry, between us, me and Brian Epstein will make a star of you soon." It would be wonderful to have either photographs or recordings. That recording would be invaluable, surely. It would be a multimillion-dollar piece of tape. But it wasn't to be. It was an amazing session to listen to.'

The place of the meeting of the greatest solo singer and greatest group of the twentieth century.

THE BEATLES MEET ELVIS

On Friday 3 September 1965, the *New Musical Express* described the momentous meeting, which their writer Chris Hutchins had helped to organise.

'The get-together took three days of planning and was shrouded in secrecy to avoid two armies of Beatles and Presley fans gathering in one spot. The Beatles accepted Elvis' invitation to spend last Friday evening [August 27] at his home.

Colonel Parker escorted The Beatles to Presley's Bel-Air home shortly after 10pm. Police stopped traffic to prevent fans tailing them. The Colonel's associate, Tom Diskin, and I collected Brian Epstein from Los Angeles Airport, to which he had flown specially from New York to be present, and we arrived at the house a few minutes after The Beatles.

When we entered Elvis was sitting with Paul on one side of him and his current girlfriend on the other. John sat next to Paul. George cross-legged on the floor. Ringo was at the other side of the room inspecting Elvis' collection of records. They were watching a colour television set in the centre of the room.

"Somebody bring in the guitars," said Elvis.

One of the ten pals he employs as his constant companions obliged. Three electric guitars were plugged into amplifiers scattered around the room.

"Here's how I play the bass. Not too good, but I'm practising," he told Paul, and joined in to accompany a record on the player.

Ringo, in a white jerkin and white trousers, looked at the guitarists without smiling.

"Too bad we left the drums in Memphis," Elvis consoled him.

"Zis is ze way it should be," said Lennon, in a mock Peter Sellers accent: "Ze small homely gathering wiz a few friends and a little music!" Elvis smiled.'

MEMPHIS, TENNESSEE

Mid-South Coliseum, Mid-South Fairgrounds, Early Maxwell Boulevard

Although the two performances at this arena on 19 August 1966 may not have been too significant, when somebody let off a firecracker during the performance, all eyes turned to each other and then to John as they feared he had been shot after his 'more popular than Jesus' furore. The audio of the show, recorded on a reel-to-reel audio deck by two teenage female fans, reveals that the explosion took place during 'If I Needed Someone'.

John's controversial comments consistently dogged the tour and there was much opposition to them being there. This was particularly fierce in the US Bible Belt region, which includes Tennessee, evidenced by local preacher, the Reverend Jimmy Stroad, staging a rally outside the Coliseum.

MILWAUKEE, WISCONSIN

Milwaukee Arena, West Kilbourn Avenue/West State Street

With their US tour in full swing, the Fab Four made a stop in Milwaukee for one performance on 4 September 1964, before heading off to Chicago.

Within a week of going on sale, all 12,000 tickets, costing between $3.50 and $5.50, had been sold. Prior to the show, the group faced another press conference, but this one was different; John was missing. For the only time ever in Beatles American press call history, just three members of the group were present. So, while Lennon was resting up in his hotel suite, Paul, George and Ringo were left to answer another set of futile questions from the gathered bunch of reporters. The main issue raised was why they chose not to wave to fans at the airport. (The plane they had arrived on had unexpectedly landed on the far side of the airfield and therefore out of the eyesight of the waiting fans.) 'It wasn't The Beatles' idea to snub the fans,' Paul announced, 'it was the police who said we could not wave to the fans.' The reporters weren't listening and chose to blame Brian Epstein for what happened.

MINNEAPOLIS, MINNESOTA

Metropolitan Stadium, Cedar Avenue, Bloomington

The Beatles had visited Toronto, Atlanta, Houston and Chicago on consecutive days before arriving in Minneapolis on 21 August 1965 for a show in front of around 25,000 people. Tickets ranged from $2.50 to $5.50.

The Beatles' fee for the show was $50,000. Prior to their performance, thanks to the locker room facilities of resident baseball team the Minnesota Twins, each member of the group took a sauna for the first time. Brian Epstein had arrived at the venue with several briefcases crammed full of approximately 5,000 tour programmes and quickly arranged for them to be sold to the crowd in the stands. The money raised was handed to Epstein. He gave it to The Beatles, who then gambled with it on their own roulette wheel, in their dressing room shortly before their show. Later, as a souvenir, the group signed a baseball for the backroom staff.

Due to John's ongoing throat problem, 'Twist And Shout' was dropped from tonight's performance.

NEW ORLEANS, LOUISIANA

City Park Stadium, City Park

A famous Louisiana city more renowned for its jazz than rock 'n' roll. The Beatles' only appearance here was on 16 September 1964 before a capacity audience of 12,000. The Beatles were scheduled to arrive at New Orleans Lakefront Airport in the early hours of the morning. It had been arranged for a helicopter to meet them there and transport them directly to their hotel, the Congress Inn on Chef Menteur Highway. Originally The Beatles had intended staying at the Roosevelt Hotel, but had to change their plans when the management there became spooked by reports emanating from the hotels that had already hosted the band on their tour about the trouble caused by overzealous fans.

Further changes were then required when their helicopter was grounded with a mechanical problem, and couldn't pick them up. Limousines were arranged, but were driven to the wrong airport – New Orleans International. Captain Cooper diverted to the airport, and landed at Moisant Field, a secluded spot at the west end of the airfield. The Beatles and their entourage were driven to the Congress Inn; they were initially accompanied by a police motorcade, but became separated during the journey. As their limousine neared the hotel, it was spotted by fans who quickly surrounded it. The police arrived and forced the fans aside, but as the limousine reversed it hit a Kenner Police Department escort car, causing slight damage. The Beatles ran through the hotel lobby, into the laundry room and finally into their three-room suite, room 100.

At the obligatory press conference, a reporter asked The Beatles their views on the topless bathing suit. 'We like them,' George replied. 'We've been wearing them for years.' Another enquired, 'You've experienced both, what's the big difference between poverty and riches?' John's reply was quick, 'Money!' Another reporter wondered whether the draft would break the group up. 'There is no draft in England any more,' John replied. 'We'll let you Yanks do the fighting.'

Following that afternoon's press 'grilling', and still at the hotel, The Beatles were then presented with the keys to the city and certificates of honorary citizenship by Mayor Schiro, who announced it 'Beatles Day' in New Orleans. Upon bestowing them with the proclamation, Schiro produced a duplicate copy and requested that each Beatle sign it, which they duly did.

The Beatles had one major request in New Orleans: to meet legendary R&B, rock 'n' roll pianist and singer-songwriter Fats Domino. He agreed and arrived unannounced in their trailer-house dressing room at the City Park Stadium immediately prior to their performance. Paul spoke about their hero: 'Fats Domino we admired. We met him in New Orleans. He had a very big diamond watch in the shape of a star, which was very impressive.'

The performance was taped, and broadcast by the local WNOE-AM radio station in 1974, on the tenth anniversary of the concert. Although most of the songs were inaudible, due to the screaming, the band's banter in between tracks still makes for interesting listening. After approximately 100 members of the crowd had broken through a police cordon and attempted to invade the stage, John is heard saying, 'We'd like to continue with our next number… if you would stop playing football in the middle of the field.'

NEW YORK, NEW YORK

The city that first welcomed The Beatles to America would eventually become home to John Lennon. It was the location of the theatre where, on *The Ed Sullivan Show*, The Beatles would be launched into the homes of 73 million Americans.

1700 Broadway

The offices of Allen Klein's business, ABKCO Music, formed in 1968, were opposite The Ed Sullivan Theatre, and a short walk from the offices of Eastman and Eastman, his rival for control of The Beatles.

Carnegie Hall, Seventh Avenue/West 57th Street

Carnegie Hall, at 881 Seventh Avenue, was built by Andrew Carnegie in 1891, and is one of the best concert venues for both classical and pop music. On their first visit to New York, and just a few days after their *Ed Sullivan Show* debut, The Beatles played two shows here on 12 February 1964.

The shows were promoted by New York impresario Sid Bernstein. In 1962 he had been taking a Political Science course at the News School for Social Research in Greenwich Village. The teachers urged the students, as part of the curriculum, to read English newspapers. As most of the papers were from the north of the country, Bernstein began to notice, from October onwards, the steady rise in coverage devoted to The Beatles. 'I'd been reading about them,' he recalled, 'little stories about this group from Liverpool that was causing a lot of hysteria and I said [to myself] I want to bring them here… I brought them because the language was the same, and kids in England were responding to their music.' Discovering they were managed by Brian Epstein, he decided to call him. 'Epstein was a proper Englishman, like you saw in the movies. He spoke the language beautifully, and [was] a gentleman. I was the first American to call him [in mid-October 1963] and I offered him something he couldn't resist … Carnegie Hall. He said, "I've heard about Carnegie Hall."'

Bernstein offered $6,500 for the two shows and proposed a date at least three months away. Epstein said he would not bring the group to New York before 1964, assuming they had made headway in the American market by then. Flicking through his desk calendar, Bernstein then proposed a tentative date of 12 February 1964, when he knew teenagers would be out of school as it was Abraham Lincoln's birthday and a public holiday. Epstein reluctantly agreed, and Bernstein quickly booked two shows for that night. 'We never had a contract. Our contract was done over the phone. I saw them, in person, for the very first time when I presented them, that night at Carnegie Hall,' he amazingly admitted. As Bernstein recalled, he couldn't get his agency [GAC, the General Artists Corporation] interested in the group, so he had to handle the job himself.

Beatlemania was rife before the concerts. 'We had almost 20,000 people behind wooden horses because Carnegie Hall was blockaded from 57th all the way round to 56th,' Bernstein remembered. 'The police estimated there were, at least, 20,000 people waiting to get a glimpse of them. The kids were not very violent, but exuberant. There was a lot of tears and a lot of screaming.' Top Welsh singer Shirley Bassey was among those backstage to wish The Beatles well. The group also received a gold disc there by Swan Records, acknowledging a million copies sold of their single, 'She Loves You'.

Tickets for the two 34-minute shows, before a crowd of 2,900 at each, had gone on sale on 27 January 1964, and had completely sold out within 24 hours. Such was the demand extra seats were even placed on the stage, adjacent to the group while they played. Watching the shows alongside Bassey was the band's British agent, Vic Lewis. 'When The Beatles came on to the stage,' he recalled, 'it was unbelievable!! Screams and people jumping up in their seats surrounding us; Shirley couldn't stand it and said, "I can't take any more of this, this is mad! I'll have to go back." We watched the rest of the [first] show backstage.'

As Bernstein later admitted, 'Carnegie Hall didn't have to worry about its sacred property or paintings on the wall. They shook a little bit and they asked me never to come back again!' Prior to their performances, the group spoke with the American broadcast personality and news announcer, Ed Rudy. He was the only reporter permitted to travel with the group for the entire duration of that first American visit. Segments of his interviews were aired across the country on Radio Pulsebeat News as a series of ongoing reports.

Producer George Martin had wanted to record the group's Carnegie Hall performances and, although Capitol Records had given him the green light, he was denied permission by the AFM (American Federation of Musicians), a labour union set up to represent professional musicians in both the United States and Canada.

It wasn't a great loss though, as John later admitted, 'Carnegie Hall was terrible! The acoustics were terrible and they had all these people sitting on the stage with us and it was just like Rockefeller's children backstage and it all got out of hand. It wasn't a rock show; it was just a sort of circus where we were in cages. We were being pawed and talked at and met and touched, backstage and onstage. We were just like animals.'

Following the second show, Bernstein led Epstein outside the venue and offered him $25,000, plus a $5,000 donation to the British Cancer Fund, for a follow-up concert, pencilled in for the following week at New York's equally legendary Madison Square Garden, assuring him it would be another instant sell-out. Let's leave this for next time, Epstein replied. That next time would be the truly historic Shea Stadium concert on 15 August 1965.

The Beatles' one and only performance at this legendary, world-famous venue. Impressive? Not according to John.

Eastman and Eastman, 39 West 54th Street

The offices of Eastman and Eastman, where Paul's father-in-law was a partner. Paul wanted Eastman to represent The Beatles, whereas John, George and Ringo opted for Allen Klein, whose office was just a short walk away.

The Ed Sullivan Theater, 1697 Broadway

Possibly the most famous theatre in America, it was opened in 1927 as Hammerstein's and after undergoing numerous name changes, in 1950 it was converted to a television studio. The legendary Ed Sullivan began broadcasting his variety show on 20 June 1948 and it ran until 6 June 1971. *The Ed Sullivan Show* moved into this theatre in the early 1960s and was the scene of The Beatles' debut on American television on 9 February 1964.

Ladies and Gentlemen, The Beatles.

Forest Hills Tennis Stadium, Tennis Place, Queens

The Beatles performed two shows here, one per night on 28 and 29 August, to wrap up the *1964 Forest Hills Music Festival*, which also featured singer Barbra Streisand (12 July), Trini Lopez and Count Basie (25 July), Joan Baez (8 August) and Johnny Mathis (15 August). For both nights, all 15,983 regular priced seats were sold out, with

extra ones, costing an extortionately high $6.50, soon made available.

It was the first of two performances, the second of which took place the following night, in front of 16,000 fans at the Forest Hills Stadium in Queens, New York City, on 28 August 1964.

The Beatles had landed at Kennedy Airport at 3.02am on 28 August, where 3,000 waiting fans greeted them. They were driven to the Delmonico Hotel on Park Avenue and 59th Street where more fans were waiting, even though their stay was supposed to be a secret.

During the evening of 28 August, at the Delmonico Hotel, The Beatles were introduced to the American folk singer Bob Dylan, who arrived with rock journalist, Al Aronowitz and roadie, Victor Maimudes. With only champagne to offer the party, Brian Epstein suggested sending out for some cheap wine. Dylan said there was no need. He would drink whatever was available. Aronowitz, however, said he would rather smoke some marijuana. Although The Beatles said that they had never taken any drugs before, aside from Ringo, all of them had. John had dabbled for the first time at a party in London, one year earlier, and in 1973, in the *International Times*, he admitted that beat poet Royston Ellis was the first person to turn him on to drugs in the early 1960s. Along with Stuart Sutcliffe, John, Paul and George were introduced to getting high when Ellis cracked open a Vicks inhaler and showed them the strip of Benzedrine inside, nicknamed a 'spitball'; they chewed it and the amphetamine inside managed to keep them awake all night.

Nervous about consuming pot that night with Dylan, The Beatles were curious about how it would make them feel. Aronowitz assured them it would make them 'feel good'. Once the joint had been rolled, Dylan handed it to John, who immediately passed it to Ringo. 'You try it,' he insisted.

The act instantly revealed The Beatles' pecking order. 'Ringo was the low-man on the pecking order,' Aronowitz recalled. 'When Ringo hesitated, John made some sort of wisecrack about Ringo being his royal taster.' He took a puff on it and soon got the giggles and, in no time, was laughing hysterically. Everyone in The Beatles' circle, including Brian Epstein, Mal Evans and Derek Taylor, took a turn on the joint. Brian kept saying, 'I'm so high, I'm on the ceiling.' 'We did nothing but laugh all night,' John recalled. 'He [Dylan] kept answering our phone and saying, "Hello, this is Beatlemania here."' From that point on, whenever Lennon wanted to smoke some pot, he would say to the others, 'Come on, let's have a larf.'

Manny's Music, West 48th Street

Manny's was situated between Sixth and Seventh Avenue, and as one of the most famous music stores in New York, was where Ringo, in February 1964, turned to acquire a mini drum kit to add to the snare drum, cymbals and drum head he had brought over with him. He used this kit on *The Ed Sullivan Show* and subsequently on tour.

Paramount Theatre, Broadway/43rd Street

The final date of The Beatles' first North American tour was 20 September 1964, where they performed before 3,682 people for no fee at a benefit concert in aid of the United Cerebral Palsy of New York City and Retarded Infants Services. The group took to the stage at approximately 10.05pm. There was chaos as around 200 policemen tried to contain 100,000 screaming fans outside of the venue.

The event, aptly called *An Evening With The Beatles*, was arranged by Leo Hausman, the president of the United Cerebral Palsy organisation. The people in attendance, a combination of young fans and New York's wealthy elite, had paid up to $100 each for a ticket. Ed Sullivan paid The Beatles a visit backstage. Joining the group this night, also for no fee, were Steve Lawrence, Eydie Gorme, Bobby Goldsboro, Jackie DeShannon, Nancy Ames, The Shangri-la's, The Brothers Four and Leslie Uggams and The Tokens.

Following their performance, The Beatles were honoured with a presentation of a scroll by Leonard H. Goldenson, chairman of the United Cerebral Palsy organisation. It read: 'To John Lennon, George Harrison, Paul McCartney, Ringo Starr who, as the Beatles, have brought an excitement to the entertainment capitals of the world and who, as individuals, have given their time and talent to bring help and hope to the handicapped children of America.' The group then dashed off the stage and rushed out of the building. The time was 10.45pm. It was the last US performance by The Beatles in 1964. They stayed at the Riviera Motel near Kennedy Airport before flying home.

The evening ended on a bad note when the group's publicist, Derek Taylor, had a major falling-out with Brian Epstein. After working his three months' notice, Taylor left his post with the group in December of that year and headed off to Los Angeles where he started his own public relations company.

Plaza Hotel, Fifth Avenue

When The Beatles arrived in New York on 7 February 1964, they stayed at this high-class hotel on the edge of Central Park. They were surrounded by screaming teenage girls, much to their surprise and the hotel staff's annoyance. One young fan, Judith Kristen, recorded her memories in a book, *A Date With A Beatle*, detailing how she climbed a ladder, lied to police and sneaked in to The Beatles' interview, all to meet her idol, George Harrison. How she did it captures Beatlemania in the USA, 1964.

However, on 19 December 1974, The Beatles were virtually ended when Paul and George signed the papers to dissolve the band at the Plaza Hotel, where ten years before they were celebrating one of the high points of their career. Ringo had already signed earlier in the week, but John said the stars weren't right, so he delayed, even though he lived close by. He finally signed at Disney World, Florida, on 29 December 1974.

Where The Beatles tasted American Beatlemania and ended The Beatles.

Shea Stadium (William A. Shea Municipal Stadium), 126th Street/Roosevelt Avenue, Queens

The home of the New York Mets baseball team played host to The Beatles at the start of their 1965 tour on 15 August, watched by 55,600 fans. The show set a world record for attendance figures, and for gross revenue. The group pocketed $160,000 of the $304,000 box-office takings.

'Brian Epstein wasn't too anxious to do Shea Stadium,' explained promoter Sid Bernstein. 'So [on 10 January 1965] I offered to pay him for every seat that was unsold or empty, and that turned his head around. He said, "Okay, let's do it."' Details of the gig were leaked to the press three months later, on 16 April 1965. 'I let the word out, and the phones came off the wall. I didn't have a formal contract, nor did I have the agreed $100,000 fee. I didn't even have $10,000. I was in bad shape because I had lost heavily on some other concert venues. Carnegie Hall, a year ago, had just helped pay off some old debts. I asked Brian to draw up a contract, but by the time I heard from him again, I already had $180,000 in the bank on [advance] tickets sold. Brian asked for $50,000 on signing, and another $50,000 was payable about a month before the concert in

August. When he sent me the contract, he was surprised to get the full $100,000 immediately.' By 25 April 1965, half of the tickets had been sold.

The Beatles touched down at New York's Kennedy Airport at 2.30pm on 13 August and travelled to the Warwick Hotel, 54th Street at Sixth Avenue. Later that afternoon in the hotel, in front of 250 journalists and television and radio news crews, the group gave their first press conference of this tour. A reporter began by referring to John as 'the chief Beatle' in the question, 'What is the duty of the chief Beatle?' 'Uh, nothing,' Lennon replied. 'Nothing I can think of. I was just tagged chief Beatle.' 'It's 'cos he's the oldest,' Ringo jokingly remarked. 'How does it feel to be back in the States?' another journalist asked. 'Marvellous,' John announced, before being asked another question. 'John, do you always do press conferences chewing gum?' 'Uh, no,' he retorted, 'only in America.' 'Only in America you chew gum?' the man pressed. 'Yes, 'cos people give you gum all the time over here,' Lennon offered. One reporter asked, 'Is matrimony in the immediate future for the two unmarried members of your group?' 'No, matrimony is not in the immediate future,' Paul replied. 'Paul won't have me,' George joked. To which the same reporter retorted, 'I noticed the two married men are sitting together, and the two single boys are sitting together.' 'That's 'cos we're queer!' John replied. 'But don't tell anybody, will you?' Ringo joked. 'It's a secret.'

Next day the group travelled to CBS Studio 50 for their fourth and final studio appearance on *The Ed Sullivan Show*. Rehearsing and recording through most of the day, the performance the group was finally happy with was made at 8.30pm. (See entry in *TV* section for further details.) The Beatles then returned to the Warwick Hotel. Just as they arrived, passer-by John Morgan, who was stepping out of a yellow cab at the doorway, noticed them. Since his daughter was a huge fan, especially of John, he wanted to get something signed. Thinking quickly, he rushed over to the group, pulled out a dollar bill from his wallet and handed it to Lennon. Having signed it, John passed it back to Morgan, and said with a wink, 'It's worth more now, mate!' (Coming with enough providence to rival anything owned by The Hard Rock Cafe, it's now in a frame on the lounge wall of the noted British film director, Alan G. Parker.)

On the day of the concert Paul consented to an interview with the BBC DJ Brian Matthew, in their room on the 32nd floor of the Warwick. This was for Matthew's 45-minute radio special, *The Beatles Abroad*, the taping for which ran over two consecutive days. John's contribution, portions of which were broadcast, was particularly interesting. In one exchange he revealed the legendary American composer, conductor and pianist, Leonard Bernstein, had been composing tunes to his poems. John also stated that his children, accompanied on one occasion by the Kennedy family youngsters, often played a game in which they took turns to sing a new melody to 'The Moldy Moldy Man', a poem that first appeared in John's 1964 book *In His Own Write*.

The interviews were interrupted when, with near military precision, The Beatles headed out to Shea Stadium. 'We spent weeks drawing up plans,' Sid Bernstein said, 'as if they were battle plans, trying to ensure The Beatles' safety.' 'The roads were opened right across the centre of New York, which was a sight to be seen,' Tony Barrow, the NEMS press officer, recalled. 'We drove across New York without stopping at any intersection or at any lights all the way from the hotel to the heliport. We then got into this helicopter and then flew out to Shea Stadium.'

The Beatles boarded the tandem-rotor New York Airways Boeing Vertol 107-ii helicopter at the heliport on top of the Pan Am building in Manhattan. The Beatles had originally hoped to land on the stadium field, but the New York City authorities blocked this idea. Instead they were transported to the World's Fair heliport. 'When we got on the helicopter,' George recalled, 'instead of going right to the show, the fellow [the pilot] started zooming around, going, "Look at that. Isn't that great?" We're hanging on by the skin of our teeth, thinking, "Let's get out of here!" They wouldn't allow us to drop right into the arena so we had to land on the roof of the World's Fair building and, from there, we went 100 yards into the stadium in a Wells Fargo armoured truck, which was good.' (While on board the vehicle, each Beatle was given a Wells Fargo agent badge.)

The helicopter journey was filmed by Ed Sullivan's company Sullivan Productions, in association with NEMS Enterprises and Subafilms, owned by Brian Epstein and The Beatles. The concert itself was also filmed by 12 camera operators.

'I asked Ed Sullivan, who was a good friend, to introduce them,' explained Sid Bernstein. 'I would have liked to reserve that pleasure for myself, but I felt Ed, being the good friend and showman that he was, should do it.' Having been delivered by Wells Fargo to the back door of the stadium, at 9.16pm The Beatles appeared from the dug-out, ran out onto the field, and up onto their stage, which had been positioned at second base on the stadium's baseball diamond. The mania in the crowd reached fever pitch. Brian Matthew, Meryl Streep, the future Mrs Starr, Barbara Bach and Mick Jagger and Keith Richard were among those sitting in the stands. 'It was deafening!' the latter recalled.

Brian Epstein became annoyed when the phrase 'The Rascals Are Coming!' was repeatedly flashed up on the giant scoreboard in the stadium and immediately ordered it to stop. The 'Rascals' in question were the relatively new American blue-eyed soul group, The Young Rascals, who just happened to be managed by one Sid Bernstein. Security was breached when amateur photographer Marc Weinstein used a fake press pass to stand next to the stage during the show. The only other photographer present ran out of film during the gig. (Weinstein's 61 b&w images would fetch £30,680 at an auction in America in April 2014.)

'I think it was the biggest live show that anyone has ever done,' John recalled. 'It was fantastic!' (The band had originally intended to close their set with 'Long Tall Sally' but decided to make a change 30 minutes before the start of the concert.) 'We did "I'm Down" because I did the organ part on the record. I decided to play it on stage for the first time. I didn't know what to do because I felt naked without a guitar, and George couldn't play it for laughing.' However, years after, when dust had settled on the landmark gig, his opinion towards it had somewhat changed. 'It would have better if we could have heard what we were playing,' he remarked. 'I wasn't sure what key I was in during two numbers. It was ridiculous! You couldn't hear a thing. I heard one jet taking off and I thought it was one of our amplifiers blowing up and I got quite scared. We couldn't hear ourselves sing. All we could hear were our guitars, which were turned up and going full blast!'

The Beatles are as synonymous with Shea Stadium as with the Cavern in Liverpool. A record-breaking concert that raised the bar for ever for rock concerts. A true landmark in musical history.

Footnote: In 1976 Sid Bernstein offered the four ex-Beatles a staggering $100 million to reunite for a reunion tour. They declined.

The Beatles returned to Shea Stadium the following year, on 23 August 1966.

Unlike in 1965, this second concert did not sell out, with 11,000 of the 55,600 tickets still available by show time. Incredibly, the group still made more money from this appearance than they did from their first, receiving $189,000, which was 65 per cent of the gross $292,000 box-office takings. Joining them on this leg of the tour was the Liverpudlian DJ Kenny Everett, who was covering the group's jaunt for both Radio London and *Melody Maker*. During a press conference held at New York's Warwick hotel the previous day, a reporter asked John about having his hair shortened for his role as Musketeer Private Gripweed in the new Richard Lester film *How I Won The War*, which was set to begin filming in Celle, West Germany on 6 September 1966. 'I don't have any pains about having my hair cut for the role as a solider,' John replied. 'Though I do not like the idea of a centre parting.' (Two years on, he would frequently wear his hair that way.)

Earlier that day, again at the Warwick, the group participated in a question and answer session that was very different from their usual press scrum. Going under the banner of a 'Beatles Junior Press Conference', it was attended by the winners of a radio contest who were handed the chance to talk directly to the group and ask them any question they liked. Following a suggestion by The Beatles themselves, the event had been arranged just two days earlier by Gary Stevens and 'The Good Guys' at the New York radio station, WMCA. In just 48 hours, the station received 48,000 postcards. With the 75 winners being allowed to bring along a guest, it meant The Beatles faced 150 attendees that day. When they walked into the conference room at the Warwick, the crowd went wild, many of them screaming their heads off. This was certainly a very different kind of press call for the band.

Questioning began when Paul was asked, 'Are you going to marry Jane Asher?' With the room full of youngsters yelling with excitement, he replied by saying he probably would. Another teenager asked John who his favourite American group was. 'There are a lot of them,' he replied. 'Beach Boys, Lovin' Spoonful, Byrds, Mamas And Papas,' Paul offered. One fan asked John about his upcoming movie and wondered when he would be filming it. 'When I get home from doing this.' Many other interesting questions followed, for instance, why there was speaking at the start of 'Taxman' on the group's latest album, *Revolver*. 'It's just the bit before we recorded it,' George revealed. 'It's what happened to be on the tape. That part usually gets cut off. We thought you'd like to hear it.' Another wondered whether any of them had seen the Beatles cartoon series. 'Yeah,' Ringo replied. 'What do you think of it?' the fan asked. 'It's okay,' the drummer offered. 'Do you think it's a good portrayal of your character?' the youngster continued. 'It's not really like us,' Paul announced, 'but it's fun.' Later, Gary Stevens happily admitted, 'The kids did a great job … and The Beatles got such a kick out of it. I could tell they were really digging it.' (A similar contest had been held by the official American Beatles Fan Club.)

Sheraton Hotel, Times Square

In an attempt to defuse the controversy surrounding John Lennon's comments that The Beatles were 'more popular than Jesus', the group's manager Brian Epstein held a special press conference in this Manhattan hotel on 6 August 1966.

Despite suffering from glandular fever, in the morning Brian had cut short his holiday in Portmeirion, North Wales, and flown from England to the US. He was afraid that The Beatles' imminent US tour might have to be cancelled, as by this point public outcry had grown to the extent that 30 US radio stations had banned The Beatles' records.

Epstein began by reading a statement approved by Lennon, before taking questions from the press.

'The quote which John Lennon made to a London columnist more than three months ago has been quoted and represented entirely out of context. Lennon is deeply interested in religion, and was at the time having serious talks with Maureen Cleave who is both a friend of The Beatles and a representative for the London *Evening Standard*. The talks were concerning religion. What he said and meant was that he was astonished that in the last 50 years, the church in England, and therefore Christ, had suffered a decline in interest. He did not mean to boast about The Beatles' fame, he meant to point out that The Beatles' effect appeared to be to him a more immediate one upon certainly the younger generation. The article which was in depth was highly complimentary to Lennon as a person and was understood by him and myself to be exclusive to the *Evening Standard*. It was not anticipated that it would be displayed out of context and in such a manner as it was in an American teenage magazine. And in these circumstances, John is deeply concerned and regrets that people with certain religious beliefs should have been offended in any way whatsoever.'

There followed time for questions.

Question: 'We're wondering whether you're going to change the itinerary of The Beatles to avoid areas where radio stations are now burning their records and their pictures?'

Brian: 'This is highly unlikely. I've spoken to many of the promoters this morning. When I leave here, I have a meeting with several of the promoters who are not anxious that any of the concerts should be cancelled, at all. Actually, if any of the promoters were so concerned and it was their wish that a concert should be cancelled, I wouldn't, in fact, stand in their way.'

The Warwick, 65 West 54th Street

On 22 August 1966, The Beatles flew into New York where they gave a press interview at this hotel. They were asked for their opinions on the Vietnam War.

'Would any of you care to comment on any aspect of the war in Vietnam?' 'We don't like it,' John replied.

PHILADELPHIA, PENNSYLVANIA
Convention Hall, 34th Street/Curie Avenue

The Beatles played their only concert here on 2 September 1964 in front of 12,037 fans. There had been race riots in Philadelphia the week before this concert, and the Fab Four were angry that their audience was all white.

Before the show The Beatles faced another press conference. 'When you were here last February,' one reporter asked, 'you said you found American girls too forward. What do you think of them now?' 'Forward? No, backward,' John insisted. The concert was sponsored by WIBBAGE radio. One month before the show, the station ran a contest and nine girls were chosen (nine because of the call numbers 99 of the station) to meet the group in person at the conference.

One of the support acts, The Righteous Brothers, complained to Brian Epstein that their music was being drowned out by the audience's screams for The Beatles. This was not the first time this had happened, nor the first time The Righteous Brothers had complained. They ended up leaving the tour.

John F. Kennedy Stadium, Broad Street and Pattison Avenue

'Rain' is perhaps one of the most underrated of Beatles songs, but they had more than they wanted on 16 August 1966 when a torrential rainstorm with lightning lasted until ten minutes after The Beatles' concert had ended in Pennsylvania, where they performed in front of 21,000 people, a third of the venue's capacity.

Swan Records, 1405 Locust Street

This record label released 'She Loves You' in the US, numbered 'Swan 4152', and on 21 March 1964 it reached No. 1. In the same year Swan also released a German version of the song, 'Sie Liebt Dich', which reached No. 97.

The Beatles' swansong.

PITTSBURGH, PENNSYLVANIA
Civic Arena, Auditorium Place

Pittsburgh is sandwiched in between Baltimore and Cleveland, and the Fab Four popped up here for one concert in front of 12,603 fans on 14 September 1964, before heading off for Cleveland. Tickets for the performance cost $6.60 with The Beatles taking to the stage at 9.10pm and leaving 35 minutes later. 'It was quite an awesome experience,' DJ, Chuck Brinkman, the show's emcee, recalled. 'I've never seen anything like it.' Cathy Walsh, a 13-year-old fan, was also impressed. 'It was the most exciting day in my life,' she said. However, Stephanie Rucker, also in attendance that night, was not. 'I didn't like The Beatles,' she told a UPI reporter, 'and in person, they didn't improve. They can't sing, or if they can, I never heard them … they look like girls with that long hair. And their expressions? Strictly dead. Yeah, yeah, yeah, so who cares was the feeling I got after watching their stupid show.'

PORTLAND, OREGON
Memorial Coliseum, North Wheeler Avenue

Two shows on 22 August 1965, before a combined total of 20,000 fans. Tickets were priced at $4, $5 and $6. There were also a small number of pink tickets for the venue's upper level, which were given away.

Earlier in the day, during the flight to Portland there was a fire in one of the engines of their Lockheed Electra, sufficiently frightening John for him to write a few 'farewell' messages that he placed inside a film canister for protection. The plane landed safely, upon which Lennon yelled out, 'Beatles, women and children first!'

The contract for the two concerts, between NEMS Enterprises Inc and Northwest Releasing Corporation, had been drawn up on 24 March that year and agreed that the group should be paid a guaranteed total of $50,000 ($25,000 per show) against 65 per cent of the gross box-office receipts after deduction of Federal, State and Local Admission Taxes. Clause 5 in the contract stipulated that, 'Artists [The Beatles and support acts] will not be required to perform before a segregated audience.'

Their 'rider' for the shows was, by today's standards, decidedly modest. All they required was 150 police officers for protection, a hi-fidelity sound system with adequate number of speakers, and a platform for Ringo and his drum kit. Their dressing room demands were equally humble, amounting to 'four cots, mirrors, an ice cooler, portable TV set and clean towels.'

Beat poet Allen Ginsberg was in the audience and wrote a poem about the performance entitled 'Portland Coliseum'. In between the two shows The Beatles were visited by Ginsberg and Carl Wilson and Mike Love of The Beach Boys. God only knows why they met up.

SAN DIEGO, CALIFORNIA
Balboa Stadium, Russ Boulevard

The Beatles flew in to Los Angeles on 23 August 1965 for some good rest and relaxation, before performing at Balboa Stadium on Russ Boulevard in San Diego on 28 August 1965. The previous day, they had made the trip to Beverly Hills for a meeting with the King of Rock 'n' Roll Elvis Presley at his home in Perugia Way, Beverly Hills.

The gig failed to sell out, with 10,028 of the 27,041 seats being unoccupied. At a press conference prior to the concert, local fan Susan Clark, after petitioning Mayor Frank Curran, had the opportunity to present to the group the keys to the city. In the roughly six hours The Beatles spent on San Diego soil, according to the promoter's balance sheet, the group earned $50,135.17, a mere $135.17 over their guaranteed appearance fee. During their journey back to Los Angeles after the show, the group's tour bus broke down and they needed California Highway Patrolmen to escort them on their way.

SAN FRANCISCO, CALIFORNIA
Candlestick Park, Jamestown and Harney Way

What would go down in the history books as the final scheduled concert by The Beatles was at Candlestick Park in San Francisco on 29 August 1966, exactly seven years to the day from when John, Paul, George and Ken Brown opened the Casbah Coffee Club back in 1959. After taking to the stage at approximately 9.27pm, and departing at 10pm, The Beatles returned to Los Angeles before flying home to London, the end of their last tour.

This final show of that tour was actually set to take place at the city's Cow Palace on Geneva Avenue, where The Beatles had performed twice before, on 19 August 1964 and 31 August 1965, but the promoters, Tempo Productions, opted instead for a bigger venue, Candlestick Park. It was a bad move. The event failed to sell out. Just 25,000 of the 42,500 tickets – ranging between

$4.50 and $6.50 in price – were sold and in the region of 50 were given away free. With The Beatles' fee of around $90,000 – approximately 65 per cent of the gross – and the city of San Francisco taking 15 per cent of the paid admissions, it was no wonder that the promoters made a loss on the night. Interestingly, those who did attend that night were handed flyers that read 'The Monkees Are Coming', a plug for the new, manufactured-for-TV pop group/music series, which was set for its NBC debut on 12 September 1966.

Backstage, there was minimal hospitality for The Beatles. Bits of food, and a few beers and soft drinks had been spread out across a simple white tablecloth. 'There was a sort of end-of-term spirit thing going on,' press officer Tony Barrow recalled, 'and there was this kind of feeling that among all of us around The Beatles that this might be the last concert that they will ever do. I remember Paul, casually at the very last minute, saying, "Have you got your cassette recorder with you?" And I said, "Yes, of course." Paul then said, "Tape it, will you? Tape the show." Which I did, literally just holding the microphone up in the middle of the field. As a personal souvenir of the occasion, it was a very nice thing to have.'

'There was a certain amount of relief after Candlestick Park,' George admitted. 'Before one of the last numbers, we set up this camera, I think it had a fish-eye, a wide-angle lens. We set it up on the amplifier and Ringo came off the drums and we stood with our backs to the audience and posed for a photograph because we knew it was the last one.' 'Coming out of San Francisco that night, getting aboard the charter flight, to fly back down from the West Coast to LA,' Barrow remembered, 'one of the first things that George Harrison said when he leant back in the plane and took a drink was, "Well, that's it. I'm finished. I'm not a Beatle any more."' John tended to

agree. 'After we stopped touring it always seemed embarrassing. Should we have dinner together? It always got so formal that none of us wanted to go through with it any more. When you don't see someone for a few months, you feel stilted and you have to start again.'

15-year-old Beatles fan, Barry Hood, travelled 450 miles on a Greyhound bus to watch the performance and captured on 8mm Kodachrome colour film clips of the group arriving in their bus, the preparations for the concert and excerpts of the show itself. In August 1986, the twentieth anniversary of the show, Hood released a limited edition, 50-minute, VHS documentary about the final show and his footage. Marketed through fan clubs and magazines, it was entitled *One Last Time*.

Brian Epstein missed the concert. He had stayed at his hotel in Beverly Hills, and underwent an experience that disturbed him immensely. He had gone out to dinner with his attorney and close friend Nat Weiss, and returned to find their briefcases had been stolen from their rooms. Shortly after, he received a ransom note from a man threatening to expose him because of certain letters and pills that were in the cases. The police were called and a man was arrested. The culprit was a former boyfriend of Brian's who had held him at knifepoint and taken his briefcase before. Once more, Brian failed to press charges.

McCartney returned to Candlestick Park on 14 August 2014 to play the very last concert there. With some 50,000 people in attendance, his show wrapped around midnight. As with The Beatles 48 years earlier, his final number was Little Richard's 'Long Tall Sally'. During the concert, Paul also revealed rare pictures taken by famed photographer Jim Marshall at that historic 1966 gig. Candlestick Park, where the city's beloved Giants and 49ers celebrated some of their greatest triumphs, has been demolished to make way for a housing, retail and entertainment complex.

The Beatles' very last scheduled performance.

Cow Palace, 2600 Geneva Avenue, Daly City

The Beatles made two significant appearances at Cow Palace. The first opened their 1964 26-date North American tour on 19 August. They had been in the northern British seaside resort of Blackpool only three days earlier – the contrast couldn't have been greater. All 17,130 tickets were sold. Gate receipts totalled $91,670, of which The Beatles went away with $47,600 gross.

Their second appearance closed their ten-date 1965 tour on 31 August, with two appearances seen by nearly 29,000 fans. The following day they flew home to London.

SEATTLE, WASHINGTON

Seattle Center Coliseum, Harrison Street

During 1964, The Beatles' first trip to Washington State was to the Coliseum on 21 August 1964 where they played in front of 14,000 fans. They returned at the end of their final tour in 1966, playing twice on 25 August.

During the 1964 show, a young girl, who had managed to clamber high above the stage, fell and landed just in front of Ringo's drum riser. When the time came for the group to leave the Coliseum, a screaming mob surged through the police barricades and trapped the group in their limousine for 29 minutes, forcing them to head back to their dressing room. Half an hour later, after several more attempts to flee had failed, another plan was hatched. An ambulance was backed into a dark alley, a group of sailors climbed in with The Beatles among them, and the vehicle managed to drive out of the building safely. However, a crowd of 200 fans became angry when they realised they'd been duped and began chasing after the vehicle.

In 1966 The Beatles played an afternoon and evening show. The later concert was a sell-out, but only 8,000 of the then 15,000 available tickets for the 3pm performance were snapped up by fans. Despite this, the group still picked up a wage of $73,717.81. The total gross take for the shows was $118,071, the largest in Seattle entertainment history. The stage the group performed on was just ten feet high. Pickets outside the Coliseum carried hand-drawn banners that read, 'Beware False Prophets'. Marchers said they were protesting against John's statement that The Beatles were more popular than Jesus.

Before the gigs, the group attended a press conference, held at the Edgewater Inn. One reporter asked Paul about the rumour he would be marrying Jane Asher. 'Yeah, I've heard about her,' he responded, before adding, 'It's a joke. How did it start? Does anyone know? I got in today and found out I was getting married tonight.' John's upcoming movie, *How I Won The War*, was also discussed. 'I don't know anything about it,' he offered, 'except for I'm in it, and it's about the last world war.' George had this interesting thing to say about The Beatles' next film. 'Somebody gave us a good idea, so we told him to go and write it into a script. So we won't really be able to tell if we're gonna make the film until we've read the script, and as he hasn't finished the script, we haven't read the script, so we won't know yet until about Christmas, maybe. But if it is a good one and we like it, we'll probably start it 'round about January, February, or March … or December.'

ST LOUIS, MISSOURI

Busch Memorial Stadium, Stadium Plaza

With their scheduled appearance of 20 August 1966 at Crosley Field in Cincinnati postponed until the following day, The Beatles ended up playing twice on 21 August 1966, in cities nearly 350 miles apart. In heavy rain and performing beneath inside a corrugated iron, tarpaulin-covered shelter, built around the stage to help keep them dry, The Beatles played at 8.30pm before 23,000 fans. The makeshift protection failed to do its job. Water still dripped onto their amplifiers. With no rest possible, they had to board a flight to New York where they rested up in the Warwick Hotel.

WALNUT RIDGE, ARKANSAS

Walnut Ridge Airport

When The Beatles were heading to stay on Reed Pigman's ranch in Missouri in September 1964, they caused a stir at this small airport when word got out that the Fab Four were in town. For a few minutes, they stood on the tarmac and chatted with locals before heading off to play cowboys. 'We were kids and had a big story to tell,' recalls one of the boys, Richard Thomas, now a 65-year-old financial planner. 'You never would have expected to find The Beatles in Walnut Ridge, Arkansas.'

Walnut Ridge learned the local teens weren't fibbing when a pilot staying at a motel leaked to townsfolk that he'd indeed flown the band – and that they were returning to the airport to fly out again. Word got around and by the time The Beatles returned to Arkansas to fly to a gig in New York that Sunday, several hundred excited fans were waiting for them, screaming and taking photographs. 'It was just a real fast, in and out, but the girls were beside themselves, touching the ground where they had walked.'

On 18 September 2011, the event's forty-seventh anniversary, Walnut Ridge unveiled a metal sculpture of The Beatles, modelled on the famed *Abbey Road* album cover. The locals also hold an annual Beatles festival; not bad for a place where The Beatles hardly spent any time.

Beatlemania at its best.

WASHINGTON, DC

DC Stadium, East Capitol Street

As The Beatles headed towards the end of their final tour, they stopped off in the US capital on 15 August 1966 to play a concert in front of 32,164 people at the home of the Washington Senators baseball team.

Prior to the start of the show, five members of Prince George's County Ku Klux Klan, led by the Imperial Grand Wizard of the Maryland clan, fronted a parade outside the venue in protest against John's misguided comments about The Beatles being more popular than Jesus. Backstage, each member of the group signed baseballs for the children of Fred Baster, the Washington Senator's equipment manager.

Washington Coliseum, 3rd and M Streets

Here on 11 February 1964 The Beatles played their first full-length concert on American soil.

The show began at approximately 8.30pm but was marred by fans who kept throwing jelly beans at The Beatles, the result of a New York newspaper that had resurrected the old story about John's claim that 'George had eaten all my jelly babies.' The group was naturally most annoyed by this. 'That night,' Harrison blasted, 'we were absolutely pelted by the fucking things! They don't have soft jelly babies there, they have hard jelly beans. To make matters worse, we were on a circular stage, so they hit us from all sides. Imagine waves of rock-hard little bullets raining down on you from the sky. It's a bit dangerous, you know,' 'cos if a jelly bean, travelling about 50 miles an hour, through the air, hits you in the eye, you're finished! You're blind, aren't you?'

Prior to the show, The Beatles took part in the obligatory, pre-show radio/TV/newspaper conference. Controlled by their press agent, Brian Sommerville, this one was held on the stage at the venue before the doors were opened to the public. Standing before a group of microphones, with their voices reverberating in the largely empty hall, the group faced questions from the press and once more took the opportunity to display their sense of humour. Ron Oberman, music columnist for the *Washington Star* paper, asked George if he had a girlfriend. 'Yes,' he replied. 'You, love.' Another wondered, 'Do the four of you ever fight among yourselves?' 'Only in the morning,' John quipped. 'No, we're very good friends,' Ringo said. 'Did you always have your hair this way?' 'Only in the morning,' John replied.

Venue owner and concert arranger Harry Lynn had been stationed in Liverpool during the war, and admitted he felt he had some kind of connection with the band. Once the concert was over and everybody had left, he remembered the venue smelt of pee, from all the girls who had got over-excited. Lynn took the profits he made from the concert and purchased a brand new Lincoln Continental convertible for his wife.

Utterly historic! The Beatles' very first concert appearance in America.

Footnote: If 16-year-old Luci Baines Johnson, the younger daughter of then President Lyndon B. Johnson, had had her way, The Beatles could well have played their first US concert at one of America's most famous residences. 'I asked my father if we could have The Beatles come to play at the White House,' she recalled back in 1974. 'I was very excited about it but he said quite decisively, no, without even any moment of trying to soften the blow.' As she admitted, he thought the idea would be seen as 'self-serving'. Luci however, saw it as a good thing for a grieving America, following the assassination of her father's predecessor John F. Kennedy just a couple of months earlier, and a great way to honour The Beatles' talent and strengthen ties between the US and Great Britain; not to mention a golden opportunity for her and her friends. Feeling the time was wrong, however, President Johnson was against the idea and simply did not want the group to perform there.

REST OF THE WORLD

In just a few years of touring, mainly 1963–66, The Beatles managed to visit many different countries on their world tours. Included in the Rest of The World are: Australia, Austria, Canada, Channel Islands, Denmark, France, Germany, Gibraltar, Greece, Hong Kong, India, Italy, Japan, Netherlands, New Zealand, Philippines, Spain and Sweden.

AUSTRALIA

The Beatles' trip to Australia is perhaps most memorable because of their drummer. With Ringo back home recovering, Jimmie Nicol stepped in and ably deputised for Ringo until the Fab Four were complete again when they played Melbourne.

ADELAIDE

Centennial Hall, Showgrounds, Wayville, south of Greenhill Road.

The Beatles landed briefly in Darwin Airport at 2.35am on the morning of 11 June 1964 and were met by 400 fans. They then flew to Sydney through a horrendous rainstorm, before spending the night in Sydney. They opened their Australian tour, with Jimmie Nicol deputising for Ringo, at Centennial Hall on 12 and 13 June.

Over 50,000 applications had been made for tickets to see the group's four shows at the Hall, which had a 3,000 seating capacity. The group played two sets on this day, and two more the following day.

Adelaide was not included in the group's original schedule. But after petitioning from local fans and the 5AD radio DJ Bob Francis, and once the Adelaide-based company John Martin & Co. Ltd had assented to the promotional and financial responsibilities for the tour, The Beatles arrived in

Adelaide on 12 June 1964 to the biggest welcome they would ever receive. The estimated 300,000 crowd, approximately a third of South Australia's population, lined the streets all the way from the airport to the city, and outside the Southern Australian Hotel where the band was booked to stay. 'You could hardly move on the streets,' tour co-promoter, Kym Bonython, recalled. 'Everyone was packed, standing shoulder-to-shoulder. Even at 4pm, there were hundreds of teenagers in the street, screaming, "We want The Beatles! We want The Beatles!"' They were asked about the amazing Adelaide reception at a press conference shortly afterwards. 'Oh, it was great,' John beamed. 'The best ever! We'd never done one of those "drives" as well. It was marvellous!'

Following an agreement with Brian Epstein, the self-professed 'Beatles radio station' 3UZ recorded one of the first night's concerts. It was broadcast three days later, during the evening of 15 June 1964, in a programme entitled *Beatles Show* and featured sponsorship from the washing detergent, Surf. Ringo's replacement, Jimmie Nicol, was on drums. (See entries for Melbourne Festival Hall, below, and KB Hallen, Denmark.) The Beatles' farewell to Adelaide on Sunday afternoon allegedly attracted an even bigger crowd that the one which welcomed them.

Historic. The Beatles' very first concerts in Australia.

BRISBANE

Festival Hall, Charlotte Street

The last stop on The Beatles' world tour, after six dates in New Zealand, was in Brisbane, Queensland, where they played four final shows on 29 and 30 June 1964. They left Brisbane the following day, flying back to London.

MELBOURNE

Festival Hall, Dudley Street

The Beatles' second stop on the Australasian leg of their tour was in Melbourne from 15–17 June 1964, where they welcomed back Ringo in place of his temporary replacement, Jimmie Nicol.

At 8am on that first day in Melbourne, Jimmie left the hotel, The Southern Cross on Bourke Street, and was driven by Brian Epstein to Essendon Airport where he was handed a final agreed fee of £500, as well as a present; a gold watch with the engraving: 'To Jimmy, with appreciation and gratitude – Brian Epstein and The Beatles.' Inside his bag was a two-day-old copy of the *Advertiser* newspaper. Splashed across its front page was a picture of him, with John, Paul, George and DJ, Bob Francis, standing on the Adelaide Town Hall balcony in front of thousands of adoring fans. The Beatles were not there to bid their farewells; they were back at their hotel, sleeping off their hangovers from the previous night's party, which had celebrated Ringo's return.

'John, Paul and George made me feel welcome from the start,' Nicol reflected at the time, 'but the funny thing is, I [also] felt like an intruder, as though I had wandered into the most exclusive club in the world. They have their own atmosphere and their own sense of humour. It's a little clique and outsiders just can't break in … They spend their lives in little boxes in airliners, hotel rooms and dressing rooms. They live out of suitcases. Paul is not the clean chap he wants the world to see; his love of blonde women and his general dislike of the crowds are not told. John, on the other hand, enjoyed the people but used his sense of humour to ward off any he didn't care for. He also drank in excess. In Denmark, for instance, his head was a balloon. He had drunk so much the night before. He was on stage sweating like a pig. George was not shy at all, as the press have tried to paint him. He was into sex as well as partying all night with the rest of us. On my last night with them in Australia, when Ringo came back, I just wanted to go out and walk about but I wasn't allowed to. Brian Epstein said he didn't think it was a good idea. But that night, I nearly went potty. They said there had to be a security guard with me. I said, "But I'm finished with them now." It was ridiculous but they insisted so I went to bed.' During his brief spell with the group, John and Paul often asked him how he felt he was coping being a Beatle, to which he frequently replied, 'It's getting better.' The phrase would inspire the track 'Getting Better' on the group's 1967 *Sgt Pepper* album.

On 17 June Channel 9 television cameras were present to videotape excerpts of the sixth and final show of the group's Melbourne tour. See entry for *The Beatles Sing For Shell* in *TV* section.

SYDNEY

The Stadium, New South Head Road/ Neild Avenue, Rushcutter's Bay

Before heading off to New Zealand, The Beatles played six shows in Sydney, two each day, on 18, 19 and 20 June 1964.

It was quite possibly promoter Kenn Brodziak's greatest ever coup engaging the group for an Australian tour before they had become world famous. They played for a fraction of the fee they could command elsewhere. 'I got The Beatles due to luck and instinct,' he recalled. 'Back in June 1963 I was given a list of five names by an agent in London, who said, "I've got some good groups who I'd you to take to Australia." I said, "OK, but I don't want to book five groups, I'll just take one, and if that one works, I'll book the others." "All right," the agent said, "which one would you like?" And I said, "I'll take The Beatles." I didn't know anything about them, except the name sounded familiar. I think because of them playing in Germany. For their performances in Australia, I paid them £2,500 per week. For that, they were entitled to do 12 shows a week, two shows a day, for six days. That was absolute peanuts because they were earning far more at this time.'

AUSTRIA

Although The Beatles never played in Austria, they filmed scenes on ski slopes here for their movie *Help!* John and Yoko also visited here for a Bag Event.

VIENNA

Hotel Sachur, Philharmonikerstrasse 4

After the end of John and Yoko's honeymoon in Amsterdam, the newly-weds headed for Vienna and the Hotel Sachur on 31 March 1969 to promote their new film *Rape*, which had been commissioned by Austrian television. John and Yoko appeared inside a bag again, refusing to come out, saying, 'This is a Bag Event – total communication. This isn't just about The Beatles. What's happening to this girl is happening in Vietnam, Biafra, everywhere.'

BAHAMAS

The Bahamas, officially known as the Commonwealth of The Bahamas, is an island country made up of over 700 islands, whose capital, Nassau, is on New Providence Island. In this most exotic of locations, The Beatles filmed parts of their second film, *Help!*.

New Providence Island

The Beatles arrived on 23 February 1965 and, although the first day was intended as a rest day following their trip from London, they began filming straight away. The Bahamas had been chosen after The Beatles' financial adviser, Dr Walter Strach, had established a tax shelter there, and had to spend a year living in the British colony as part of the set-up. Partly as a gesture of goodwill, the group agreed to film there, staying for two weeks at the Balmoral Club near Cable Beach. They shot scenes at various locations over the next 14 days, before returning home.

CANADA

With entry to the US proving difficult for John, he often found refuge in Canada, where he enjoyed a good relationship with the Prime Minister Pierre Trudeau.

MONTREAL

Chateau Champlain Hotel, Place du Canada

On 22 December 1969, during their time in Canada, John and Yoko gave a press conference here. 'We think this was a positive decade, not a depressing one. This is just the beginning. What we've got to do is keep hope alive, because without it we'll sink,' said Lennon. John and Yoko

"Sevenoaks"
Pewterspear Lane,
Appleton,
Warrington,
Lancs.

Dear

So many people have been asking "are the Beatles splitting up"? The truth about the Beatles is that they are definately <u>not</u> Splitting up, they have been working, solidly, since long before Christmas , recording the new L.P. and filming for T.V. shows etc. So I think that this proves that they have no plans what-so-ever of parting company.

I still receive hundreds of letters every week from all over the world and as you will understand, I find it rather difficult to answer them all so I do hope you will not mind receiving this typewritten note.

All my best wishes

George's mother, Louise Harrison, who always encouraged her son, took it upon herself to answer fan letters. In 1967, overwhelmed by all the letters about various rumours that they were splitting up, she did a round robin reply. 'Certainly not' was the answer. But she gave away her real home address, so fans could always write again.

were dressed in black and were surrounded by 'War Is Over' posters. A brief colour clip from the conference was later included in the 1988 documentary *Imagine: John Lennon*.

The Forum, St Catherine Street

The Beatles travelled to Montreal after their successful Toronto shows for two performances in front of 21,000 fans in total on 8 September 1964.

With the group having received death threats from French-Canadian separatists, police marksmen were present at the two Montreal concerts, which passed without incident. Before the start of the concerts, a fan called Joy Koyama presented the group with a telegram containing a welcome message from 40,000 local teenagers. During the press conference that afternoon, Janette Bertrand asked The Beatles if they realised that 80 per cent of the audience that night would be French-speaking. Her question was ignored and the next one was asked. When the conference ended, Janette felt a hand on her shoulder. She turned round and saw it was John. He asked her where they were, and she told them in Quebec. John and the others had no idea whatsoever where exactly in Canada they were.

After Montreal, The Beatles' flight was diverted to Key West to avoid the incoming Hurricane Dora heading for their next destination, Jacksonville. The hurricane caused so much damage that The Beatles didn't fly into Jacksonville until 11 September.

Queen Elizabeth Hotel, 900 Rene Levesque Boulevard

After the success of their Amsterdam bed-in, John and Yoko planned a second in New York. However, due to their recent drug conviction, the location had to move to the Bahamas, at the Sheraton Oceanus Hotel. They flew there on 24 May 1969,

but after spending one night in the heat, they decided to move to Montreal on 26 May, where they stayed in Rooms 1738, 1740, 1742 and 1744 at the Queen Elizabeth Hotel. During their 7-day stay, they invited Timothy Leary, Tommy Smothers, Dick Gregory, Murray the K, Al Capp, Allen Ginsberg and others, and all but Capp sang on the peace anthem 'Give Peace A Chance', recorded by André Perry in the hotel room on 1 June. The Canadian Broadcasting Corporation conducted interviews from the hotel room.

John used his Beatle status to promote world peace.

OTTAWA
Centre Block, Parliament Hill

On 23 December 1969, during their visit to Canada, John and Yoko met with Canadian Prime Minister Pierre Trudeau at his Ottawa offices. The planned interview should have been only 15 minutes but they talked for 50 minutes. John described Trudeau as a 'beautiful person' and was obviously impressed. 'We spent about 50 minutes together, which was longer than he had spent with any head of state. If all politicians were like Mr Trudeau there would be world peace.'

TORONTO
CBC Studio, Bay Street

Making his second TV appearance of the day, John went to the studios of the Canadian Broadcasting Club on 20 December 1969 to appear on the current affairs programme, *CBC Weekend*.

Maple Leaf Gardens, Carlton Street

With two shows in one evening before a combined total of over 35,000 people, Mal Evans stepped in for a poorly Neil Aspinall in supporting The Beatles in Toronto on 7 September 1964. They returned to Maple Leaf Gardens on 17 August 1965 for two performances and exactly a year later, 17 August 1966, for two shows before heading to Boston.

A television documentary about the group's 1964 visit was broadcast on CFTO-TV in the Toronto area, five days later on 12 September. Derek Taylor, as usual, was in control of the press conference that afternoon. The attendance of newsmen and newspaper reporters was, by far, the largest on this tour. Taylor began by reading two telegrams; one from a man in Chicago who wanted The Beatles' tonsils when they were removed, another from a man in Saskatchewan who wanted their bathwater. The group also posed for the obligatory pictures, with disc jockeys, fan club presidents, and the local beauty queen, in this instance, Miss Canada. The questions soon started, many of which had previously been asked on the tour. 'How much money do you make collectively?' 'A lot,' John replied. 'Will you leave show business when you have made enough to leave?' 'We've made enough to leave now,' Lennon responded, 'but we're not going to.' 'We're greedy,' added George swiftly.

In 1966 the 18,000-seat venue did not sell out, by approximately 4,000 tickets over the two shows. Prior to the performances, in a press conference at the venue's Hot Stove Lounge, a local reporter asked John if the band would ever split up. 'We obviously are not going to go around holding hands for ever,' he replied. 'We've got to split up or progress … it might happen. It's quite possible.'

Ontario Science Centre, 770 Don Mills Road

After visiting Ronnie Hawkins' ranch, John and Yoko made an appearance here on 17 December 1969 where they gave a press conference to more than 50 members of the media about their 'War Is Over' campaign and to announce the planned Peace and Music festival the following year. 'We aim to make it the biggest music festival in history,' said John, 'and we're going to be asking everybody who's anybody to play. We'll try and get everyone we know to donate their time. But people will be paid for their performance and we'll try and cream some off the top to set up a peace fund. I can just see some of the performers thinking, "He's going to come and hassle us and do something for nothing." So, we've got to give them something to get them interested and to pull them away from whatever work they're doing. We hope to take in Russia and, in fact, take it around the world.' A reporter asked, 'Will The Beatles play at this festival?' John replied, 'I'll try and hustle them. Maybe I'll get one or two of them. I got George on the other night for Unicef in London. I can't speak for The Beatles because I'm only me. But if I can get them, I'll try. I'll even try and get Elvis.' Sadly, the concert never happened.

Ronnie Hawkins' Ranch, Mississauga

On their way to Montreal in December 1969, John and Yoko stopped off at the ranch of rockabilly star Ronnie Hawkins, where they set up camp ready to address the media. Arriving on 16 December, they put in enough phone lines so that they could conduct interviews both at the ranch and by telephone. This was all part of their latest peace campaign, 'War Is Over'. During their time at the ranch, they partied with Hawkins and, among others, the Canadian Prime Minister Pierre Trudeau. An interviewer asked. 'You got stoned with Pierre Trudeau?' Hawkins replied, 'Well, I don't know whether he did or not, but I certainly did.'

University of Toronto

In the Department of Culture and Technology on 20th December 1969, John appeared on CBS-TV in conversation with author Marshall McLuhan.

Varsity Stadium, 299 Bloor Street West

It was here, on 13 September 1969, that the Plastic Ono Band made its debut as a last-minute call-up by the organisers to John to help make the concert a success.

VANCOUVER

22 August 1964, Empire Stadium, Exhibition Park

In this stadium on 22 August 1964, The Beatles made their first appearance in Canada.

The performance began at 9.25pm on a stage was situated on the north end of the stadium and was broadcast live by the local radio station CKNW. 'I Want To Hold Your Hand' was dropped from their set-list. Tickets went on sale six weeks before the show and the box office was swarmed by fans, many of whom had queued up two days in advance. Amazingly, there was no publicity for the concerts. Ed Moyer, in charge of promotions at the venue, remarked, 'We were led to believe there would be a deluge so we didn't advertise.' For their stay in Vancouver, The Beatles took up the entire twelfth floor of the Hotel Georgia.

CHANNEL ISLANDS

Situated in the English Channel, the Channel Islands are British Crown Dependencies near the Normandy coast of France. Made up of several islands, they include the Bailiwicks of Guernsey and Jersey. They have a total population of about 170,000 people.

GUERNSEY

Candie Gardens, Candie Road, St Peter Port

Their only appearance on this channel island was in the auditorium at Candie Gardens on 8 August 1963. The plane that flew between Jersey and Guernsey could only carry the passengers, and so their equipment had to be transported by ferry.

Promoted by Baron Pontin, tickets for the two *Top Pop* shows, as they were called, ranged from ten shillings to seventeen shillings and sixpence. The group travelled there in a 12-seater plane. Their musical instruments followed them on a ferry. Exceptionally loud screams greeted The Beatles when they climbed out of their craft. They then travelled to the Candie Gardens venue and spent the afternoon rehearsing with one of the support acts on the bill, The Robert Brothers, namely Ivan and Graham. At the end of the shows, The Beatles were smuggled out of the venue via another door, leaving The Robert Brothers to face a large crowd that had assembled outside the proper stage one. 'That's the only time in my life that I've been really frightened,' Graham admitted, 'as there was nobody there to control things. We were just mobbed and my brother and I thought we were goners.'

George played a MS500 Mastersound guitar throughout the two performances, after which John met up with an old friend, the British beat poet Royston Ellis, got drunk and spent the evening in bed with him and his girlfriend, Stephanie. The experience of kinky sex and black polythene, which she wore for the night, inspired the 1969 *Abbey Road* track, 'Polythene Pam'.

JERSEY

Springfield Ballroom, Janvrin Road, St Saviour

The first two nights in the Channel Islands saw The Beatles perform on 6 and 7 August 1963, then take the short trip to Guernsey before returning here for their last shows on 9 and 10 August.

The Beatles received £1,000 for their four performances, a contract for which had been drawn up on 30 March 1963 between the Jersey-based concert promoter, Les De La Mare, and The Beatles' manager Brian Epstein. On the morning of the shows, the group spent the time go-karting and relaxing by the pool. Silent, colour, 8mm home movies were taken of these events.

DENMARK

Though The Beatles only visited two venues in Copenhagen, both were with the stand-in drummer Jimmie Nicol, replacing Ringo who was left behind in hospital.

COPENHAGEN

Falkoner Theatre, Falkoner Allé 9

George appeared here on 10–12 December 1969 with Delaney & Bonnie.

KB Hallen, Peter Bangs Vej, Frederiksberg

The Beatles started their 19-date, one-and-only, world tour here on 4 June 1964; it continued in the Netherlands, through Hong Kong, Australia and New Zealand.

Ringo missed the start, remaining in London, having been hospitalised with tonsillitis and pharyngitis the previous day. He had collapsed in Barnes during a photo session for the *Saturday Evening Post* newspaper. As their friend and roadie Neil Aspinall recalled, 'I was with them when it happened. I got quite a fright when I saw Ringo sink to his knees.' His temporary replacement was Jimmie Nicol, whose first appearance was here in Copenhagen. George, in particular, wasn't happy about replacing Ringo and fought long and hard about aborting the tour altogether. 'I was dead against carrying on without Ringo,' he admitted. 'Imagine, The Beatles without Ringo!'

'He was downright truculent,' producer George Martin said. 'He said, "If Ringo's not going, then neither am I. You can find two replacements."' 'Brian argued with us for more than an hour to change our minds about abandoning the tour,' Paul recalled. 'He pleaded that thousands of Dutch and Australian fans had already bought tickets, and it would be cruel to disappoint them. It was this plea of Brian's that finally brought us around.'

Nicol was immediately thrust into the limelight and managed to witness Beatlemania first hand for the next five dates of the tour. 'I had my first experience at the airport,' he remembered. 'How we managed to get to the hotel I'll never know … I was very nervous the first time I went on stage with them, but it soon wore off … the first number we did was 'I Want To Hold Your Hand". I kept thinking, "Am I doing it right?" Although the fans were disappointed at not seeing Ringo, they made me more than welcome. John explained the situation in his announcement and gave me a great build-up.' As Paul humorously recalled, 'He [Nicol] was sitting up on his rostrum, just eyeing up all the women. We'd start "She Loves You", one, two, and nothing. One, two, still nothing.'

The order of the first two songs was switched for the night's second performance in Copenhagen, and for all subsequent dates of the tour. As the trek progressed, 'Twist And Shout' would occasionally replace 'Long Tall Sally' as the closing number.

HANHARRED, NORTH JUTLAND
Ellidsbølvej 37, Vust

On 29 December 1969, John and Yoko flew to Denmark to stay at the farmhouse where Yoko's ex-husband Tony Cox now lived, with his new wife Melinde, plus Kyoko, Yoko and Tony Cox's daughter. Their presence in the village eventually attracted interest, however, and a press conference was held on 5 January. They performed a Danish folk song called 'O Kirstelighed', and pledged to donate all their future royalties to their peace campaign. During his stay in Denmark, Lennon decided to withdraw his support for the International Peace Festival, which he had announced would be held in Canada in 1970 but which never took place. John also controversially decided to crop his hair to an inch, which he and Yoko did while in Denmark on 20 January. While staying at the farm for almost a month, John gave Cox a cassette containing 25 minutes of compositional demos for 'She Said She Said'. This was auctioned at Christie's on 30 April 2002 for £58,750. Lennon also gave him a second tape containing recordings of him and Kyoko singing and improvising stories, which later sold for £75,250. Two further tapes from this period, known as *Denmark III* and *Denmark IV*, were auctioned in 2003. The first contained 16 minutes of recordings from the Lennons' stay, including Kyoko singing with John and Yoko. *Denmark IV* lasts for 30 minutes, including 13 of Tony Cox playing a Jew's harp. The remaining 17 minutes contained Lennon and Kyoko inventing stories and songs together.

FRANCE

John and Paul had visited Paris to celebrate John's twenty-first birthday, and it was where they visited Jürgen Vollmer who gave them their moptop haircut. Paris was also the inspiration for the Cavern. For some reason, The Beatles never really conquered France, and their tour of France was one of the least successful of their career.

LYON

Palais d'Hiver de Lyon, Rue Louis Guerin, Villeurbanne

The second stop on their 1965 European tour. The Beatles played two shows to audiences of around 3,500 on 22 June, they then headed off to Milan, Italy.

NICE

Palais des Expositions, Esplanade Marechal de Lattre de Tassigny

This trip to the south coast of France on 30 June 1965 as part of the European tour was sandwiched in between performances in Italy and Spain.

PARIS

Georges V Hotel, 31 Avenue George V

While staying at this hotel during their tour of France, on 16 January 1964 The Beatles received confirmation that their single, 'I Want To Hold Your Hand' had reached No. 1 in the US *Cashbox* charts the previous day. The timing couldn't have been better as they prepared to fly to New York to appear on *The Ed Sullivan Show*.

To mark the historic news, Brian Epstein threw a party at the hotel. It got out of hand when some journalists hired prostitutes to provide a lesbian show for the group in the room next to Epstein's.

Hilton Hotel

After leaving Denmark where they had been staying with Yoko's ex-husband Tony Cox, John and Yoko stayed here on 26 January 1970 as their plane back to England had been delayed due to fog, and John gave an interview to Reuters. Sadly, Lennon appeared surly and uncommunicative, giving brief, curt answers to topics such as his peace plans and The Beatles' future releases.

Le Caveau de la Huchette, 5 Rue de la Huchette

When Alan Sytner, a Liverpool jazz fan, visited Paris, he found himself inside this legendary jazz club. The building actually dates from the sixteenth century, and became a jazz club in 1946. This moody basement club gave Sytner an idea – he should do the same back in Liverpool. With his friend Keith Hemmings, Sytner established a basement jazz club of his own, its name inspired by its French counterpart Le Caveau: they called it the Cavern, and it opened on 16 January 1957.

Vive la France.

Olympia Theatre (Paris Olympia), 28 Boulevard des Capucines

The first of 18 days of concerts (excluding 21 and 28 January) at this world-famous music hall, the oldest such venue in Paris, was on 16 January 1964. This was The Beatles' second ever concert in France. Through to 4 February they played twice, and sometimes three times, a day to what could be an ambivalent audience, and despite closing each show, The Beatles still shared top billing, at varying times, with the French singer Sylvie Vartan or American vocalist Trini Lopez

'On the first night,' Paul recalled, 'we had a bit of trouble because we suddenly found out that there was a radio programme just sort of plugging into everything. They had overloaded all the amps, and they all went "Bomf!" They like the wilder stuff over there, so we stuck in a wilder number ["Long Tall Sally"] to finish off with.'

Part of the matinee show on 19 January was broadcast live on French radio station Europe 1's weekly series *Musicorama* (see entry for the series in *Radio* section).

On 24 January, the group was interviewed for radio by Harold Kelley of the Armed Forces Network. He asked Paul, 'Can you compare the French audience with what you're familiar with back in England?' 'Well,' Paul replied, 'there's a lot of difference because in England the audiences are 75 per cent female. Here, 74 per cent male. And that's the main difference, really. Because they still appreciate it, but you don't get the full noise and the atmosphere of a place.' 'No screams,' George interjected. 'No screams and fainting.' Kelley asked, 'Why is it 75 per cent boys?' 'I don't know,' George replied, 'I think they don't let the girls out at night.'

Palais des Sports, Place de la Portes de Versailles

Host to two shows by The Beatles on 20 June 1965, their first of a short European tour incorporating 15 concerts spread over nine dates.

Both shows were recorded by the French radio station Europe 1, the first broadcast a week later, on 27 June 1965, as part of the *Musicorama* series; the second was transmitted live, in a show entitled *Les Beatles (en direct du Palais des Sports)*. (See entries in *Radio* section.) The evening performance was also filmed by the French national TV channel Channel 2, and was transmitted on 31 October 1965 (see *Les Beatles* entry in *TV* section). During the concert, in a burst of excitement, Brian Epstein rushed up to the venue's control booth to take a picture of the group performing, but unfortunately hit his head on the low concrete lintel on the doorway and was sent flying back, nearly plunging down the building's spiral staircase.

Pathé Marconi Studios, Rue de Sevres, Boulogne-sur-Seine

On 29 January 1964, in the middle of their first tour of France, The Beatles went into this studio to record two of their songs, 'She Loves You' and 'I Want To Hold Your Hand' in German, using the original rhythm tracks.

VERSAILLES

Cinéma Cyrano, 7 Rue Rameau

Warm-up show directly ahead of 18-date run at the Olympia Theatre, Paris. Sylvie Vartan and Trini Lopez joined The Beatles on the bill. When John, Paul and George arrived at Le Bourget airport on 14 January 1964, there were 60 schoolgirls waiting for them. Ringo flew out the following day and they performed for one night only in Versailles, on 15 January.

GERMANY (WEST)

The Beatles were born in Liverpool but, as John Lennon said, 'We grew up in Hamburg.' It was there they matured, both as young men and musicians, and there's an argument to say that without their hours on stage in Hamburg they would not have become the musicians they did. It was just 15 years after the end of a world war that had seen both Liverpool and Hamburg heavily bombed, yet they were made very welcome in Germany, in spite of the misgivings of their parents.

ESSEN

Grugahalle, Norbertstrasse

Having played the night before in Munich, The Beatles took a train to Essen to perform two shows on 25 June 1966.

The journey to and from Essen was special; aboard a train used by Queen Elizabeth II one year earlier, during her royal visit to the country. In the dressing room at the venue, Mal Evans handed The Beatles the very first acetate cutting of their latest album, *Revolver*. Their next trip was to a place they knew well – Hamburg.

HAMBURG

Airport Fuhlsbüttel

On 5 December 1960, Pete Best and Paul McCartney were put on a plane here for Liverpool after being deported. When The Beatles were returning to the city to open the Star-Club, they flew into Hamburg airport for the first time. John, Paul and Pete arrived on 10 April 1962 to be greeted by Astrid Kirchherr. When John enquired where Stu was, she had to tell them that Stuart had just died. Their final visit here was on 26 June 1966 when they touched down to appear at the Ernst Merck Halle before flying on to Tokyo.

Akustik Studio, Kirchenallee 57

On 15 October 1960, The Beatles' manager, Allan Williams, became the first to unite John, Paul, George and Ringo, when he decided to record the bass player of The Hurricanes, Wally Eymond, known as Lou Walters. Williams arranged for John, Paul and George, along with Ringo and Walters, to make a record at Akustik Studio on the fifth floor of the Klockmann House. No recordings survive and even a definitive list of the songs played cannot be confirmed. What is agreed is that Walters sang 'Fever', 'Summertime' and 'September Song'.

The first time John, Paul, George and Ringo recorded together.

Alsteranleger Alte Rabenstrasse

This dock for the small boats, the Alster steamers, was where Jürgen Vollmer shot his first pictures of George. Jürgen asked George if he could photograph the rest of the group too.

Bambi Kino, 33 Paul-Roosen-Strasse

When Bruno Koschmider brought The Beatles to Hamburg, they stayed at the Bambi-Filmkunsttheater during their stint at the Indra and Kaiser-keller clubs. In two windowless and barely lit rooms, John, Paul, George, Stuart and Pete spent their nights. They had to wash in the cinema toilets. The most famous incident here was when Paul and Pete returned to the Bambi for the final time, lit a condom, which they pinned to the wall, grabbed their belongings and left. Koschmider told the police that Paul and Pete had tried to burn the Bambi down, and so had them arrested. After a night in the cells, Herr McCartney and Herr Best were deported.

What a dump. And they thought Gambier Terrace was bad.

Blockhutte, Grosse Freiheit 66

Next to the Indra was the Blockhutte, a club where the musicians performing at the Star-Club would meet each other, and with fans, for a drink.

British Seaman's Mission (Britische Seemannsmission), Johannisbollwerk 20

The British Seaman's Mission was a little taste of Britain in Hamburg. It offered English food, English newspapers, and the chance for The Beatles to converse in their own language with visiting seamen. It was the ideal place for them to feel less homesick.

A home from home, a bit of England in Germany.

Chum Yuen Poon, Schmuckstrasse

A restaurant located in what was historically the location of Hamburg's Chinatown, the Chum Yuen Poon, remembered as Chum Ou by Paul McCartney and Klaus Voormann, was a great place to get a Chinese meal.

Davidwache, Spielbudenplatz 31vaga

This police station was where, having been arrested for the alleged arson of the Bambi Kino, Paul McCartney and Pete Best spent a night in a cell.

Stuck inside these four walls, sent inside for ever.

Der Lachende Vagabund, Grosse Freiheit 50

Horst Fascher, a great friend to The Beatles while in Hamburg, worked at this club after quitting his job at the Top Ten Club. The Beatles would stop by most days to see their friend.

45a Eimsbütteler Strasse

This was the home of the Kirchherr family, where Stuart went to live with Astrid and her family. Astrid's mother made a fuss of The Beatles and often cooked them an English breakfast and always made them feel welcome. Stuart had a room in the loft where he spent many hours painting, often after coming straight from playing on stage at the Kaiserkeller when he couldn't sleep. Astrid photographed Stuart here and, after he had died, John asked Astrid to photograph him in the same spot.

Ernst Merck Halle, Jungtusstrasse

The Beatles played here twice, to 5,600 people at each show, during their Bravo Blitztournee on 26 June 1966.

The group arrived in Hamburg at 6am that day, having whiled away their time on the train from Munich by playing cards. Singer Peter Asher, of Peter and Gordon, one of the support acts on the tour, and brother of Paul's then girlfriend Jane, admitted McCartney won £25 off him during one game. 'The games were often the best parts of the tour,' as Neil Aspinall admitted. 'Brian used to enjoy raising the stakes by about five times to scare his partners.'

The questions from reporters at the Ernst Merck Halle press conference left a lot to be desired. Ringo was stupidly asked what he put on his face to help with his complexion and Paul was quizzed about what he dreamt about when he slept. 'The same as everyone,' he replied. 'Standing in their underpants …' He was cut short when John, clearly agitated by the standard of questioning, angrily shouted, 'What do you think we are? *What do you dream of*? Fuckin' 'ell!' However, one question did stand out, an accusation from one journalist that Lennon had plagiarised material for one of his books. 'John, somebody said that you have stolen parts of your book. Is that true?' 'Well, I have,' he confessed. 'It's true! Why not? [It's from] some old Italian translation book, or something. I thought it was dead and buried, but they found out.'

This was The Beatles' first visit to Hamburg since 1 January 1963. During their stay, John paid a visit to old friend, artist and photographer Astrid Kirchherr, who handed him several letters written by Stuart Sutcliffe. The Beatles were also visited by the easy listening orchestra leader and songwriter, Bert Kaempfert, who had produced their 1961 recordings with Tony Sheridan, and even

Bettina Derlien, the blonde barmaid from the Star-Club nightclub. Following the two shows at Ernst Merck Hall, John and Paul made a nostalgic, midnight trip to the notorious Reeperbahn in Hamburg's St Pauli district.

Fotostudio Reinhart Wolf

Both Astrid Kirchherr and Jürgen Vollmer worked as assistants in this photo studio and, when Brian Epstein wanted some publicity shots of The Beatles, he arranged with Astrid for her to photograph them here in November 1962.

Friedrich-Ebert-Halle

When producer Bert Kaempfert decided to record Tony Sheridan for Polydor, he chose this location as the perfect place to set up his recording equipment. And so it was on 22 and 23 June 1961 that Kaempfert recorded Tony Sheridan and The Beat Brothers – John, Paul, George and Pete – performing 'My Bonnie' to be issued for the German market. In all, Kaempfert recorded eight songs over the two days, including the first original 'Beatles' song to be recorded, the Lennon–Harrison credited instrumental 'Cry For A Shadow'. When Beatles fans in

TONY SHERIDAN REMEMBERS

Anthony Esmond Sheridan McGinnity, known as Tony Sheridan, was bigger in Hamburg than The Beatles. In March 1964 he shared some of his memories with the *New Musical Express*.

'I did the singing and they backed me up. Life was one long rave from morning to night. Those haircuts? Well when they first arrived in Germany they all had ordinary short hairstyles but money was tight and no one wanted to waste money on trivialities. So it just grew. We all lived in an attic above the club. Bare floorboards, freezing draughts. Bit like Oliver Twist. There were bunk beds. John used have the top bunk and he'd crash around when he got up because he could never see a thing without his glasses on. Once he started banging around, we all had to get up. The others were a little quieter, but they were all ravers. There was never any thoughts of making the big time. We were there for the kicks and the laughs – and we got plenty of them.'

Liverpool started asking at Brian Epstein's record store NEMS for 'My Bonnie' by The Beatles, it triggered a series of events culminating in Epstein becoming their manager.

With Kaempfert and Sheridan, The Beatles were finally on a record.

Gretel und Alfons, Grosse Freiheit 29

A restaurant named after the couple who opened it in 1953. This was a favourite hangout for The Beatles and other musicians and, on a visit in 1989, Paul McCartney returned here and paid all of his outstanding debts from 1962, with lots of interest too, leaving the owners with a signed poster that is still displayed on the wall.

Hauptbahnhof

George Harrison boarded a train at this railway station on 21 November 1960 to head for the Hook of Holland after being deported. Not long after, John followed suit as he made his way back to Liverpool. Their next visit was a better one, as The Beatles disembarked from their train on 27 March 1961 to begin their engagement at the Top Ten Club.

Heiligengeistfeld

Not long after meeting The Beatles, Astrid Kirchherr asked to photograph them. She took them to this area of the city where the Dom, a fair that takes place in Hamburg three times a year, was on. 'I thought the heavy tractors and the equipment of the exhibitors excellently matched the hard rocker image of The Beatles,' recalled Astrid.

Some of the greatest ever photographs of The Beatles were taken here by Astrid.

Herbertstrasse

Located between the Reeperbahn and the River Elbe, Herbertstrasse branches off Davidstrasse. Sealed at both ends by partitions was a sex alley where prostitutes offered their services to The Beatles and other musicians. When not in Herbertstrasse, the ladies of the night were often to be found in the Indra, Kaiserkeller and Star-Club.

Hotel Germania, Detlev-Bremer-Strasse 8

Manfred Weissleder would provide accommodation for The Beatles and other artists playing at the Star-Club. The Beatles stayed here during their second engagement at the Star-Club between 1 November and 14 December 1962.

Hotel Pacific, Neuer Pferdemarkt 30

When The Beatles returned to Hamburg at the end of 1962, this is where they stayed.

Indra Club, Grosse Freiheit 64

The Indra was opened by Bruno Koschmider in 1950, and was the first club that The Beatles played on their 1960 visit to Hamburg. They made their Indra debut with their new drummer Pete Best on 17 August 1960, for 30 Marks each per day. This was the start of a 48-night residency during which they played for between four and five hours a night during the week, and six hours on Saturdays. Their final performance here was on 3 October 1960, after which they were moved to Koschmider's other club, the Kaiserkeller.

Their baptism of fire in Hamburg, where they began to Mach Schau.

Jagerpassage 1

One of the best known images from The Beatles' time in Hamburg is located at this address, where

Jürgen Vollmer photographed John Lennon in the doorway. In the photo, the blurred figures of George, Stuart and Paul are walking by. The photo was used on the cover of John's 1975 album *Rock 'N' Roll*.

Another memorable photograph of their Hamburg days.

Kaiserkeller, Grosse Freiheit 36

Opened by Bruno Koschmider on 14 October 1959, the Kaiserkeller was the bigger of Koschmider's two clubs and, after their engagement at the Indra was ended, The Beatles moved here. The first group to play here was The Jets, featuring Tony Sheridan. The first Liverpool group in Hamburg was Derry and The Seniors (who until their arrival in the German city had been billed as Howie Casey and The Seniors), who were quickly followed by Rory Storm and The Hurricanes, including their drummer, Ringo Starr. The Beatles first appeared here on 4 October 1960, sharing the bill with Rory Storm and The Hurricanes, changing places every hour. It was while playing here that they were observed by Klaus Voormann, who went to find his girlfriend Astrid Kirchherr and their mutual friend Jürgen Vollmer, to tell them about this great new group from Liverpool. When The Beatles' contract was terminated by Koschmider after 58 appearances, because they had decided to move to the Top Ten Club, Koschmider then told the authorities that George Harrison was under 18, so he was deported. He also alleged that Paul and Pete had attempted to burn down the Bambi Kino, and they were also deported.

Where John, Paul and George got to know Ringo and establish themselves in Hamburg.

Musikhaus Rotthoff, Schanzenstrasse 71

This popular music store was regularly visited by The Beatles and every other travelling musician. It later moved premises next to the Hotel Pacific.

Paul Hundertmark Jeans & Western Store, Spielbudenplatz

This store, named after the exhibitors who settled there in the eighteenth century, is where The Beatles purchased their cowboy boots.

Polydor, Harvestehuder Weg 1-4

This German record company still owns the rights to the Tony Sheridan/Beatles recordings made in 1961.

Schloss Trembüttel

In contrast to the appalling Bambi Kino accommodation they had to endure on their first visit to Hamburg in 1960, when The Beatles returned in June 1966 as the biggest pop group in the world, they stayed in this upmarket hotel, 30 miles outside of Hamburg and under the watchful eye of a number of guards.

St Joseph's Church (St Joseph-Kirche)

Did The Beatles pee from the balcony onto passing nuns in April/May 1962? John recalled it in a 1971 interview: 'There's all big exaggerated stories about us in Hamburg, about us "pissing on nuns" and things like that. What actually happened was we had a balcony in these flats and one Sunday morning we were all just pissing into the street as people were going to church. And there were some nuns over the road, going into the church. It was just a Sunday morning in the club district, with everyone walking about, and three or four people peeing into the street.'

Myths about this event are merely taking the p…

St Pauli

This area of the city is situated on the northern bank of the River Elbe and was a harbour and amusement district. The district was named after the church of St Pauli in 1933, and became part of Hamburg in 1894. The first theatres opened here in 1840, and it soon became the bohemian area of Hamburg. The main street in St Pauli is the Reeperbahn, and parallel to it were Grosse Freiheit and Kleine Freiheit. Grosse Freiheit means 'Great Freedom', which refers back to the seventeenth century where there was an unconditional freedom of trade and religion. The Grosse Freiheit was home to the Indra, the Kaiserkeller and the Star-Club where The Beatles learned their trade.

Star-Club, Grosse Freiheit 39

On 13 April 1962, Manfred Weissleder opened the doors of the Star-Club and promoted its 'Rock and Twist' parade. The Beatles were the first to play, along with Roy Young, dubbed 'Britain's Little Richard'. As well as The Beatles, the Star-Club played host to the biggest names in rock 'n' roll, such as Little Richard and Gene Vincent. The Beatles' first stint at the Star-Club ran from 13 April to 31 May for which they were paid a fee of 500 DM each per week. They returned for two more runs in 1962, from 1 November to 14 November and from 18 December to 31 December.

Following a request from Ted 'King Size' Taylor, of the Merseyside group King Size Taylor and The Dominoes, the club's stage manager, Adrian Barber, recorded in mono – at a speed of three and three-quarters – several portions of The Beatles' performances with his portable, domestic, Grundig reel-to-reel tape recorder. Four tracks at least were taped at their final night at the venue, 31 December 1962. Although not the greatest recordings, it gives a rare insight into The Beatles, slightly inebriated, performing in Hamburg.

After being handed to Taylor, the tapes remained in obscurity until June 1973 when, after a Sunday lunchtime drink, during research for his book, *The Man Who Gave The Beatles Away*, the former Beatles manager Allan Williams and a local sound engineer rediscovered the recordings languishing under a pile of rubbish in the audiophile's then derelict Hackins Hey studio in Liverpool. (In 1963, after Brian Epstein had offered only £20 for them, as he felt they had no intrinsic value, Taylor had given the tapes to the engineer and handed him the task of editing and preparing them for a hopeful release by himself. It came to nothing.)

Sensing the significance of his finding, Williams immediately began contacting the press. The *Daily Mail* newspaper ran a piece on 12 July 1973, announcing that Williams was planning on contacting Neil Aspinall, the then managing director of Apple Corps, about them. His demand for a £100,000 down payment for the tapes, and a cut of the record sales, was flatly rejected by Aspinall.

With John being stateside and Paul unwilling to speak to him, on 15 August 1973 Williams arranged a meeting with George and Ringo at Apple's offices at 54 St James Street, London. His offer of £5,000 for copies of the recordings was also rejected by the pair, but they requested four gratis duplicates be made, two for John, two for Paul. As part of an alternative deal, George suggested having copies of Williams' old Hamburg Beatles contracts for their own archive as well. Preferring a straight cash deal instead, Williams was having none of it and negotiations swiftly came to an end. As a parting gift, George gave Williams a small pouch containing 16 uncut rubies, which Allan was instructed by George and Ringo to give to his wife Beryl for a birthday present. Attached to the small package was a note that read, 'Dear Beryl, happy birthday. (Give Allan a kick.) – God bless!

George H. Ringo S.' Now severely frustrated, Williams even admitted to *Melody Maker*, 'I'll release it [the tape], even if it's a bootleg!'

Citing financial difficulties, and sensing that this might be his last real chance to make some real money out of The Beatles, Williams then approached Paul Murphy, head of BUK Records, about issuing the recordings. He agreed and, at a cost of £50,000, started preparing them for release on the Lingasong Records label, which he formed especially for the sole purpose of producing and marketing the album. His work went on for over three years. However, on 5 April 1977, just three days before the release of his painstaking re-mastering, Mr Richard Scott, QC, acting on behalf of The Beatles and their company, Apple, applied for a High Court injunction against Murphy issuing the recordings. He was resilient, robustly saying outside court, 'I [still] plan to release the records.' One day later, 6 April 1977, The Beatles lost the case. High Court vice-chancellor, Sir Robert Megarry, turned down their application after hearing Ted Taylor say, 'The Beatles had originally agreed to the tape provided I bought them a beer.' The judge ruled in favour of Paul Murphy and Lingasong due to the 'inactivity of the plaintiffs [Apple] until Friday, 1 April.'

His ruling went on. 'Until then they had given no sign of objection or protest; they had long known of the tapes [four years] and of attempts to exploit them commercially... Not until the defendants [Lingasong] were far along the road towards issuing the record, and had incurred the expense of processing the tapes to improve the quality [£50,000], and had manufactured the records, did the plaintiffs strike on the very day when they uttered their first warning. Such inactivity was inequitable enough to make the court reluctant to intervene by granting the equitable remedy of injunction. Furthermore,

it was common ground that some sort of oral contract was given to the making of the original tape and that consent might well have been wide enough to authorise all that has been done, which failed to satisfy section 1 of the 1958 Act, only because the consent was not in writing.' When told of the court's decision, from their London headquarters, EMI Records, who had a new, but official live package of their own, *The Beatles At The Hollywood Bowl* ready to roll, issued a short two-word statement. 'No comment.'

With the legal dispute resolved, the 1962 Star-Club recordings were released as planned, on 8 April 1977, in both Germany (on the Bellaphon label) and in the UK as *Live! At the Star-Club in Hamburg, Germany; 1962* (on the Lingasong label). Besides the lure of hard cash, their other intention was to pre-empt sales of the aforementioned, official EMI live package, which was set to be released just one month later, on 4 May 1977.

Lingasong immediately joined forces with several other record labels in other countries for distribution of the album, and the songs themselves were later licensed out to other record companies. Singles, featuring individual tracks, also appeared. For the album's 13 June 1977 US release, in association with Atlantic Records, four songs were removed and replaced with four different songs from the tapes. In 1979, Pickwick Records in the UK performed some additional audio filtering and equalisation of the songs on the Lingasong US version and issued it over two volumes as *First Live Recordings*; the set also included 'Hully Gully', which was mistakenly credited to The Beatles (See below). Two years later, in 1981, Audio Fidelity Enterprises in the UK released *Historic Sessions*, the first single package to feature all 30 Beatles tracks from the original Star-Club releases. Lingasong Records released the album again, but this time on CD in 1996, which unsurprisingly prompted another Apple lawsuit, reaching London's High Court on 5 May 1998. But this time, their defence was much stronger when, one day later, 6 May 1998, their star witness was George Harrison, who entered the witness box to testify on behalf of the group and their company. 'The Star-Club recording was the crummiest recording ever made in our name,' he blasted. 'There was no organised recording. It was a wild affair; we were just a whole bunch of drunken musicians grabbing guitars.'

Lingasong lost the case two years later, and, after a ruling by Mr Justice Neuberger, agreed to stop all further sales of the album, surrender the original tapes to The Beatles and pay both sides' costs. The two-decade long tradition of small record labels releasing records and CDs made from these 1962 tapes had come to an end. Insiders believe Apple only decided to take decisive action over the Star-Club recordings when the much bigger, highly reputable label Sony Music entered the fray, releasing the material across two CDS in September 1991 as *The Beatles At The Star-Club Live!*

The Star-Club suffered serious fire damage in 1983 and was demolished in 1987.

Not just The Beatles, but all the stars played here.

Footnote: Although the original master tape was indeed accounted for and returned to Apple, the 'noise-reduced', 1977 safety master version of the original tape, with a different running order of the songs than the records, replete with recordings made by two other groups at the venue, remained with the album's original US executive producer, Larry Grossberg. Housed in its hinged BASF tape box, on a chipped plastic reel, the tape is a unique item of Beatles memorabilia. The five tracks on the original tapes, which did not feature

The Beatles in any shape or form, were 'Sparkling Brown Eyes' (aka, 'Beautiful Girl' or 'Ramshackle Shake'), 'Lovesick Blues', 'First Taste Of Love', 'Dizzy Miss Lizzy', which were by King Size Taylor and The Dominoes, and 'Hully Gully' by Cliff Bennett and The Rebel Rousers.

Steinway-Haus, Colonnaden 29

Steinway is still a well-known name in the music world, especially for their pianos, but in Beatles lore it is for the sale from their shop in Hamburg of one particular guitar that it is best remembered. This is where John Lennon purchased his Rickenbacker guitar. George also purchased his Gibson amplifier here.

Studio X

Uwe Fascher, brother of The Beatles' friend Horst, ran this strip club, where he says that The Beatles performed without George Harrison who had just been deported back to Liverpool for being underage.

Top Ten Club, Reeperbahn 136

The Top Ten Club, located in the former Hippodrom, became one of the most important venues in Hamburg. Owner Peter Eckhorn hired The Beatles to play there from 1 April–1 July 1961, a total of 92 appearances. The audience from the Kaiserkeller soon flocked to the Top Ten when The Beatles started their run. It was here that The Beatles got to know one of the most influential musicians in their career, Tony Sheridan.

Their collaboration with the 'Teacher' was crucial to their evolution.

University of Fine Arts (Staatliche Hochschule Fur Bildende Kunste)

An undoubtedly talented artist, Stuart Sutcliffe was granted a scholarship to study at this prestigious art school under Eduardo Paolozzi, which he commenced in the summer of 1961.

MUNICH

Circus-Krone-Bau, Marsstrasse,

Unlike their 1960 trip to Hamburg, The Beatles flew into Germany in style, landing in Munich on 23 June 1966. This was the start of their 'Bravo Blitztournee' tour, incorporating West Germany, Japan and the Philippines. They played two shows here on 24 June.

At the beginning of this tour The Beatles were faced with a unique problem. Several months of work on their latest album, *Revolver*, had meant that, aside from the truncated *NME 1965–66 Annual Poll-Winners' All-Star Concert* appearance on 1 May 1966, they hadn't performed any of their old numbers for more then six months. The group's previous full-length concert appearance had been at the Capitol Theatre in Cardiff on 12 December 1965. Upon their arrival at the Bayerischer Hof Hotel in Munich, Paul quickly organised rehearsals for the band.

GIBRALTAR

British Consulate Office

After Paul and Linda's marriage, John and Yoko suddenly decided they should get married, though John was more keen than Yoko. John and Yoko drove down to Southampton to try and catch a ship that was sailing for the Bahamas, in the hope that the captain could marry them, but they were too late. When he couldn't then get on a ferry to France, John hired a private jet and they flew to Paris, again without success. Peter Brown, who was holidaying in Amsterdam, was enlisted to find a suitable venue in Holland, but with a requirement to be resident there for at least two weeks, Brown suggested Gibraltar, the British colony near Spain, where they wouldn't need passports or have residency problems. On 20 March 1969, John and Yoko were married at the British Consulate Office. 'We chose Gibraltar because it is quiet, British and friendly,' said John. 'We tried everywhere else first. I set out to get married on the car ferry and we would have arrived in France married, but they wouldn't do it. We were no more successful with cruise ships. We tried embassies, but three weeks' residence in Germany or two weeks' in France were required.' This memorable event was preserved in 'The Ballad Of John And Yoko'. Within an hour, the happy couple were on their way to Paris for a press conference to announce their marriage. They were then driven to the Hilton in Amsterdam for their famous honeymoon bed-in for peace.

GREECE

LESLO

The Beatles decided to buy a Greek island, often referred to as 'Leslo', though no island of that name exists. They headed off on 26 July 1967 to look around the Greek islands for some to purchase, as Derek Taylor explained in *Anthology*. 'We were all going to live together now, in a huge estate. The four Beatles and Brian would have their network at the centre of the compound: a dome of glass and iron tracery (not unlike the old Crystal Palace) above the mutual creative/play area, from which arbours and avenues would lead off like spokes from a wheel to the four vast and incredibly beautiful separate living units. In the outer grounds, the houses of the inner clique: Neil, Mal, Terry [Doran] and Derek, complete with partners, families and friends.' 'They've tried everything else,' said John. 'Wars, nationalism, fascism, communism, capitalism, nastiness, religion – none of it works. So why not this?'

They were taken around the islands to the south of Athens aboard their hired yacht, the MV Arvi. The boat had 24 berths and a crew of eight, including the captain, a chef and two stewards. George remembered it well. 'We rented a boat and sailed it up and down the coast from Athens, looking at islands. Somebody had said we should invest some money, so we thought, "Well, let's buy an island. We'll just go there and drop out." It was a great trip. John and I were on acid all the time, sitting on the front of the ship playing ukuleles. Greece was on the left; a big island on the right. The sun was shining and we sang "Hare Krishna" for hours and hours. Eventually we landed on a little beach with a village, but as soon as we stepped off the boat it started pouring with rain. There were storms and lightning, and the only building on the island was a little fisherman's cottage – so we all piled in: "'Scuse us, squire. You don't mind if we come and shelter in your cottage, do you?" The island was covered in big pebbles, but Alex [Alexis 'Magic Alex' Mardas] said, "It doesn't matter. We'll have the military come and lift them all off and carry them away." But we got back on the boat and sailed away, and never thought about the island again.'

Alistair Taylor had been instructed to purchase the island, which he did. Owning an island semed like a great idea at first but after a couple of weeks, the novelty wore off, and the island was resold. Due to an improvement in the exchange rate, they made a profit of just over £11,000.

HONG KONG

Princess Theatre, Un Chau Street, Tsim Sha Tsui, Kowloon

There were many stopovers for The Beatles on this trip to the Far East. They left Amsterdam on 7 June 1964, and flew to London, where they made a connecting flight and headed for Hong Kong. They had brief stops at Zurich, Beirut, Karachi, Calcutta and Bangkok, each time being greeted by a small group of fans. However when they arrived at Hong Kong's Kai Tak Airport they had over a thousand fans waiting for them. They played two concerts here on 9 June.

Neither show was a sell-out, possibly due to the fact the promoter had decided to charge HK $75 for a ticket, the equivalent to an average week's wage then. But those who did attend were relatively sedate. Speaking in 1964, John remarked, 'In Hong Kong, the paper said, "The Beatles fought a losing battle against the screams." Compared with other audiences, they were quiet.'

INDIA

The country that would become more than just a destination, India became central to George's life, and inspirational to all of The Beatles, both personally and spiritually.

BOMBAY

St Thomas Cathedral

John Best married Mona Shaw here on 7 March 1944.

MADRAS

Egmore District

Pete Best was born Randolph Peter Scanland to Donald Peter Scanland and Alice Mona Shaw on 24 November 1941 in Madras.

Rishikesh

The Maharishi Mahesh Yogi's ashram was situated in Rishikesh, which is known as the 'Valley of the Saints', located in the foothills of the Himalayas. Along with their wives, girlfriends, assistants and numerous reporters, The Beatles arrived in India in February 1968, and joined the group of 60 people who were training to be Transcendental Meditation teachers, including musicians Donovan, Mike Love of the Beach Boys and flautist Paul Horn. While there, John Lennon, Paul McCartney and George Harrison wrote many songs and Ringo Starr finished writing his first ('Don't Pass Me By'). Eighteen of those songs were recorded for *The Beatles* (the *White Album*), two songs appeared on *Abbey Road*, and others were used for various solo projects. Ringo and his wife Maureen left on 1 March, after a ten-day stay; Paul and girlfriend Jane Asher left after one month due to other commitments; John Lennon and George Harrison stayed about six weeks but left abruptly following financial disagreements and rumours of inappropriate behaviour by the Maharishi.

ITALY

GENOA

Palazzo dello Sport, Piazza Kennedy

After playing in Milan the previous evening, The Beatles continued their tour in Italy in Genoa on 25 June 1965 playing two concerts in this arena, which could hold 25,000 people. Unfortunately, only 5,000, still a good-sized crowd, saw their afternoon performance. The evening concert did, however, sell out.

MILAN

Velodromo Vigorelli, Via Arona

The Beatles' only trip to play in Italy opened in Milan on 24 June 1965 at the open-air arena, which could hold around 22,000 people. The evening show sold around 20,000 tickets, though the afternoon attendance was poor, with only 7,000.

ROME

Teatro Adriano, Piazza Cavour

After their shows in Genoa, The Beatles flew on to Rome, where they played four shows over two days on 27 and 28 June 1965, though none of the shows were a sell-out.

Following the second show on 27 June, Paul met the renowned playwright, Noël Coward, an attendee that night. Their meeting took place at the Parco dei Principi Hotel. Originally, the group had no interest in seeing him. Pressing his desire to encounter them in person, he instructed Wendy Hanson, Brian Epstein's assistant, to go and fetch one of them personally. She soon reappeared with only Paul. Coward passed on his messages of congratulations about their performance that evening to him and his colleagues. But it was a charade. As Coward later admitted, 'The message I would have liked to have sent them was that they were bad-mannered little shits.'

The closing night of The Beatles' eight-concert, four-date, Italian tour was on 28 June. Ticket sales were, once more, poor. The Associated Press news agency blamed the heat wave engulfing certain parts of the country for the extremely lacklustre ticket sales, with purchases barely reaching more than half the number available. Incredibly, despite the relatively poor response, this date had still been added to the schedule after the first date in Rome had been pencilled in.

And that was ciao to Italy as they headed to France.

JAPAN

Although John didn't know it, Japan would feature heavily in his future life. Tokyo was where Yoko Ono was born. In Tokyo, The Beatles also played at one of the city's most prestigious venues, the Budokan.

Having flown out from Hamburg, at some point in their journey to Japan The Beatles touched down in Thailand, at Bangkok Airport, for refuelling. At the insistence of the local authorities, who had a strong dislike of the group, they weren't allowed to get off the plane. However, the daughters of Air Force Colonel Robert Uhrig were permitted onto the craft to meet the band and get their signatures. The group landed at Haneda Airport, Tokyo, at 3.40am, 30 June 1966.

Hilton Hotel, Tokyo

During their three-night residency at the Tokyo Hilton, in room 1005, the Presidential Suite, room 1005, The Beatles collaborated on a watercolour painting. Working by the light of a table lamp, which had been placed in the centre of the table, each member focussed on a particular section of the 30 x 40-inch paper, supplied by the Japanese promoter, Tats Nagashima. John's part of the picture had a dark centre surrounded by thick oils; Paul's had a symmetrical, psychedelic feel while George's was large and colourful. Ringo's was, unsurprisingly, cartoon-like. Photographer Robert Whitaker, touring with the band,

was on hand to capture images of the four while they worked. When the piece was complete, the lamp was removed and The Beatles signed the empty space next to their contribution. The artwork became known as *Images Of A Woman* and is believed to be the only painting in existence by all four members of the group. Nagashima suggested that the painting should be auctioned for charity. After going through several auction sites, in September 2012 it was put up for sale again through Philip Weiss Auctions and reached $155,250, including the buyer's premium.

The promoter did his utmost to try and keep The Beatles happy during their stay in Tokyo, even offering them the very best Japanese prostitutes, dressed in the finest kimonos. They declined the offer. After receiving death threats before the trip, The Beatles had been advised not to leave their hotel. 'We didn't get to see much of the place,' George lamented, 'because there were riots happening at the time and there was the mania. So all I remember is the drive from the airport to the hotel.' As they were seldom able to do any shopping themselves, many Japanese items were brought in for them to buy. One such thing was a Fukusuke doll, a traditional china figurine associated with good luck in Japan. Robert Whitaker even took a photograph of it. The group would later use it on the cover of *Sgt Pepper*. It can be seen near bottom left, above the Snow White statue, and next to the tuba. By which time, a moustache, mimicking The Beatles' current facial accessory, had been added to it.

Nippon Budokan Hall, Daikan-cho, Chiyoda-ku

The Beatles played five shows at the Nippon Budokan Hall, the first rock shows to be performed here. The first show was on 30 June 1966, followed by two performances on both 1 and 2 July. Their first two shows were recorded in colour for the Japanese network, Nippon Tele-vision. Footage from the 1 July performance was broadcast in the programme *The Beatles Recital From Nippon Budokan, Tokyo* (see relevant entry in *TV* section).

Following their two performances that day, John and Neil Aspinall finally succeeded in a carefully planned break away from their hotel rooms and visited a local ivory shop where John purchased a 100-year-old antique snuffbox for just £50. Paul managed to escape too, taking a stroll with Mal Evans around the Imperial Palace.

The Beatles' record of playing for three succes-sive nights at the venue was broken in April 1977 when the US rock group Kiss performed on four straight dates, as the closing gigs of their *Rock & Roll Over Tour*.

One of the greatest venues, where many legends played and recorded.

NETHERLANDS (Holland)

The Beatles first crossed through the Neth-erlands in August 1960 on their way to Hamburg. When The Beatles returned in 1964, Jimmie Nicol was still behind the drums due to Ringo's illness.

AMSTERDAM

Amsterdam Hilton, Apollolaan 138

On 20 March 1969, John and Yoko were married and decided to spend their honeymoon making a protest for world peace. From 25–31 March, they held a bed-in at the Amsterdam Hilton in room 702. The world's media were expect-ing something outrageous to happen, but were instead just shown banners saying 'Hair Peace' and 'Bed Peace'.

ARNHEM

Arnhem Oosterbeek War Cemetery

Having left Arnhem on their way to Hamburg in August 1960, Allan Williams decided to stop the van at the war cemetery at Oosterbeek, just outside Arnhem, where one of the best-known photographs of The Beatles was taken. Pictured are Allan Williams, his wife Beryl, calypso singer Lord Woodbine, Stuart Sutcliffe, Paul McCart-ney, George Harrison and Pete Best in front of a memorial with the prophetic words, 'Their Name Liveth For Evermore'. Not in the picture are John Lennon, the photographer Barry Chang (broth-er-in-law of Allan Williams) and their German translator, Herr Steiner.

The prophetic photograph in a place of remembrance of the past.

Muziekhandel Bergmann, Koninsstraat

This little music shop in the town of Arnhem was visited by The Beatles on their first trip to Hamburg. Having browsed the instruments for sale, they left the store without making a purchase. However, John had managed to steal a harmonica, which, if he had been caught, could have finished their trip.

BLOKKER

Veilinghal Op Hoop Van Zegen, Veilingweg

In a hall situated in a field in the town of Blok-ker, 40 kilometres north of Amsterdam, on 6 June 1964 The Beatles played their only two shows on Dutch soil to a crowd of just 2,000 in the afternoon. However, a full house of 7,000 fans saw their evening performance

Excerpts of 'I Saw Her Standing There', from that second, 25-minute show, were filmed by newsreel cameras. Audio of the songs 'I Want To Hold Your Hand', 'All My Loving', 'She Loves You', 'Twist And Shout' and 'Long Tall Sally' also survive from this performance. Prior to the shows, The Beatles and Jimmie Nicol toured the canals of Amsterdam in a glass-topped tourist boat, and it was during this jaunt that John, Paul and George caught sight of a young man, in the crowds lined up on both sides of the canal, wearing a groovy-looking cape. One year later, it would inspire their look for the *Help!* album cover and film.

NEW ZEALAND

John's father Alf nearly emigrated here, and could have taken John with him. Aunt Mimi nearly moved to New Zealand, and still had family out there when The Beatles went on tour, so she accompanied them.

AUCKLAND

Town Hall, Queen Street

Even though the Fab Four played four shows over two nights on 24 and 25 June 1964, that was still only 10,000 fans in one of New Zealand's largest towns.

CHRISTCHURCH

Majestic Theatre, Manchester Street

The last concert of their week in New Zealand was on 27 June 1964 at the Majestic Theatre. The Beatles then waved goodbye and headed off to

Brisbane, Australia, where they played four shows before heading back to London.

DUNEDIN

Town Hall, Moray Place

There was anxiety on the flight from Auckland to Dunedin after a threat was made anonymously that there was a 'germ' bomb on the plane. Thankfully, it was a hoax and the journey went without a hitch. The Beatles played two shows to around 4,000 fans at each performance on 26 June 1964.

WELLINGTON

Town Hall, Cuba Street

Having left Australia, The Beatles arrived in New Zealand to play four shows, two per night, on 22 and 23 June 1964.

PHILIPPINES

The Beatles would be remembered in the Philippines for what they didn't do, more than what they did do, almost causing an international incident, and were lucky to escape unscathed.

Rizal Memorial Football Stadium, Vito Cruz Street, Manila

Performing before tens of thousands of screaming fans over two shows on 4 July 1966, The Beatles seemed to be the most popular people on the island of Manila. However, due to a mix-up involving First Lady of The Philippines, Imelda Marcos, what followed was one of the most infamous events on a Beatles tour.

The Smart Araneta Coliseum in Cubao, Quezon City, was the first choice of venue for The Beatles in Manila, but it had to be switched to the Rizal Memorial Football Stadium because the Coliseum's 17,000 capacity was not large enough for the expected audience. The decision turned out to be quite prophetic. The combined attendance of the group's two concerts that day was 80,000, with the evening performance alone registering 50,000, thus becoming The Beatles' second biggest concert ever; the first being their Shea Stadium show on 15 August 1965.

The Manila visit was beset with trouble from the start. The Beatles' suitcases, allegedly containing their stash of marijuana, went missing soon after they disembarked from their Cathay Pacific plane. The luggage was quickly located, left unattended on the MIA runway. George, fearing they would be caught and charged, exclaimed, 'This is it; we're going to get busted.' The group then inadvertently became embroiled in controversy when they were accused of snubbing the First Lady, who had invited them for an 11am luncheon at the Malacañang Palace on 4 July.

'I remember Brian didn't give a direct answer that first evening,' press officer, Tony Barrow recalled. 'He said he would reply to the invitation the next day. While we were watching TV that night, we saw a news report that surprised us. The palace dignitaries were waiting for The Beatles to show up and the next edition of Manila's newspapers carried the headline, "Beatles Snub President". There was uproar and Brian was invited to go on TV and explain what had happened, but for some reason, his speech was drowned out by terrible interference, and nobody could make out what he said. Sentiment was running so strongly against The Beatles that we actually had the feeling their lives might be in danger.'

He was correct. In confidential documents retrieved from the country's Malacañang files, it was discovered that that a plot was hatched to kill the group, during their stay in India two years later.

For a fee of 25,000 rupees, a driver was to be hired to ram, head-on, the American Cadillac in which the group or certain members were travelling.

Troubles for the group continued on 5 July 1966, the day after the show and supposed snubbing. Breakfast was not served to them, escalators in their hotel suddenly did not work, and cars scheduled to transport them to the airport did not arrive. And when they did manage to reach the airport, they were greeted with scenes of sheer pandemonium; Ringo was knocked to the floor, Brian Epstein was hit on the face, and chauffeur Alf Bicknell was punched by an angry young thug. 'I remember running across the tarmac with my hand on my back, thinking if a bullet hit me, it wouldn't hurt me so much,' Vic Lewis, the tour organiser, recalled. 'Mal Evans had his ribs kicked in … I don't think any of The Beatles got physically hurt, but wherever we were going, people were throwing things at us and it was awful.'

Once aboard their KLM 62 flight, Mal's ribs and Brian's head wound were attended to. Almost immediately, two official-looking men climbed onto the plane and quizzed them about their passports and asked about their declaration of income tax from the two shows. The Beatles' management was accused of making an incorrect income statement and charged for not paying the corresponding tax. Epstein, roadie Mal Evans and Tony Barrow were asked to disembark and Misael Vera, of the Philippine Tax Authority, insisted they would not be able to leave until they had paid what was owed. 'There was a man saying, "I'm from the department of income tax and you owe us $80,000,"' Vic Lewis recalled. 'I naturally said to him, "I beg your pardon … you're completely wrong. I am the agent of this whole affair and I set the whole deal up. I know exactly the contract from top to bottom without reading it. I'll bring out a copy." This I did, and showed him the relevant clause where it stated that all income taxes, whether domestic or internal, connected to the tour, would be borne by the promoter in each country. So I told Brian about this and he said, "We don't want to have any trouble with these people, so let's just get out of here."'

Brian immediately issued an $18,000 bond as a payment. It was common practice for him to ask concert promoters, most usually the foreign ones, to place the group's share of the undeclared income from ticket sales in a brown paper bag. Either Epstein or one of his assistants would hand-carry this bag onto the plane just prior to their departure. John would later write about this underhand tactic in his 1967, anti-Epstein song, 'Baby, You're a Rich Man', which featured the line, 'You keep all your money in a big brown bag inside the zoo.'

The brown bag from this occasion, supposedly containing $17,000, went missing and Lennon later confirmed to a journalist that, in his opinion, it had been confiscated and never accounted for. Five years later, in 1971, the group allegedly tried to retrieve the bag, but it came to nothing.

The Philippines clearly left a bad taste with the group. As George once remarked, 'If I go back [there], it will be with an H-Bomb to drop on it … I have never been so terrified in my life!'

Notable concert in The Beatles' history, but only for the wrong reasons.

SPAIN

From a 'honeymoon' for John and Brian, to the inspiration for one of The Beatles' greatest songs, Spain had a great attraction, especially for Brian who became a big fan of bullfighting.

John of course would later become a Spaniard, if only in the works.

ALMERIA

Santa Isabel

John Lennon headed for Spain in 1966 to play Private Gripweed in the Richard Lester film, *How I Won The War*. After spending some time at a seafront apartment, John and Cynthia moved to a villa, Santa Isabel near Almeria. It was while he was here that he wrote 'Strawberry Fields Forever'.

Inspirational location in his spare time.

BARCELONA

Plaza de Toros Monumental, Avenue de les Corts Catalanes

This second and last Spanish show, performed on 3 July in front of the Lord Mayor, his family, and various other dignitaries in a large bullring in Barcelona, concluded The Beatles' 1965 European tour.

They headed back to England the following morning and were asked by the press their opinions on how the tour had gone. 'The visit was a knockout,' Paul enthused. 'There were some reports that The Beatles were a flop in Milan, well, there were 10,000 at the first show, and 22,000 at the second. I don't think that was too bad, do you?' George was in agreement. 'The whole tour was great! Barcelona and Milan were fantastic! In Milan it was fantastic playing in a cycling stadium and in Spain, we played a bullring. Great!'

MADRID

Plaza de Toros de Las Ventas, Plaza Las Ventas

With bullfighting being one of Brian's favourite interests, it was no surprise that he booked The

Beatles to appear at a bullring. They made one appearance at the Plaza de Toros de Las Ventas (which means Bullring of the Sales) on 2 July 1965, their first appearance in Spain. They only played one other concert in Spain, the following day in Barcelona.

TORREMOLINOS

Just after John became a father in April 1963, he set off for a Spanish holiday with his manager, Brian Epstein. With Brian being homosexual, the rumours back in Liverpool spread like wildfire, leading to cavern DJ Bob Wooler being beaten up by John for making a reference to the holiday. John spoke about it: 'I was on holiday with Brian Epstein in Spain, where the rumours went around that he and I were having a love affair. Well, it was almost a love affair, but not quite. It was never consummated. But it was a pretty intense relationship. It was my first experience with a homosexual that I was conscious was homosexual. He had admitted it to me. We had this holiday together because Cyn was pregnant, and I went to Spain and there were lots of funny stories. We used to sit in a café in Torremolinos looking at all the boys and I'd say, "Do you like that one, do you like this one?" I was rather enjoying the experience, thinking like a writer all the time: I am experiencing this, you know. And while he was out on the tiles one night, or lying asleep with a hangover one afternoon, I remember playing him the song "Bad To Me". That was a commissioned song, done for Billy J. Kramer, who was another of Brian's singers.'

SWEDEN

Sweden was The Beatles' first foreign tour, in October 1963, after a successful year during which they had established themselves in the music press and were beginning to sell lots of records. The Beatles' fee throughout the tour was £140 a night. Swedish newspapers humorously wrote about their impending visit; *Expressen*, in particular, declared that 'a new cult was about to hit Sweden' and that the word 'Beatles' was another word for 'brutal' in Liverpool. Their piece even offered a word of advice for concerned adults. 'The first sign that there's a Beatle in the house,' explained the article, 'is that the son is letting his hair grow and spends hours in front of the mirror to get it right.'

Following this tour they would only return to the country again for a lightning visit on 28 July 1964.

BORAS

Boråshallen, Bockasjogatan

Following on from their shows in Stockholm and Gothenburg The Beatles gave one performance here on 28 October 1963. With 2,500 people in attendance, it became the group's biggest show to date in Sweden. That afternoon, they had done a couple of hours' record signing session at the Waidele Record shop in the town. According to newspaper reports, thousands of fans had made their way there.

ESKILSTUNA

Sporthallen, Hamngatan

The final performance of The Beatles' tour of Sweden was on 29 October 1963, although they did return to Stockholm the following day to record an appearance for *Drop In*, a Swedish television show, which was transmitted on 3 November. The recording was made in the small theatre of

Narren-Teatern in the Gröna Lund amusement park in Stockholm before a live audience.

With the tour over, they returned to London on 31 October, and their first taste of 'airport Beatlemania', witnessed by an American television presenter by the name of Ed Sullivan. 'Who the hell are The Beatles?' he asked.

GÖTEBORG (GOTHENBURG)

Cirkus, Lorensbergsparken

The Beatles crossed Sweden, from the east-coast Stockholm for west-coast Gothenburg for three shows on 27 October 1963. These performances prompted one local paper to write the following day: 'Never ever had so many shoes stamped the floor at Cirkus in Lorensbergsparken as this particular day.' A 15-second, silent, colour film clip of this concert survives.

KARLSTAD

Nya Aulan, Sundsta Läroverk, Sundstavagen

The Swedish tour began in Karlstad on 25 October 1963 in the freshly built hall of a secondary school. It was estimated that the 750-people venue was only three-quarters full for both shows, but the fans who were there went wild at their new pop heroes even though John's microphone packed up during the very last number of the night. The local newspaper reporter decided The Beatles were of no musical importance.

STOCKHOLM

Johanneshovs Isstadion, Sandstuvagen

The Beatles performed two concerts each day at this ice hockey arena on 28 and 29 July 1964. The first afternoon concert failed to sell out.

During the first show, as per their visit to the country nine months earlier, John and Paul both received mild electrical shocks from ungrounded microphones. A soundboard recording of this performance, captured by Swedish TV, with a running time of 17 minutes 36 seconds and featuring – bar 'All My Loving' – the first seven numbers, survives.

Shortly after The Beatles' arrival, they were interviewed by a local television crew. In the short piece, conducted at the Scandic Hotel Foresta in Lidingo, John humorously introduced his bandmates as 'George Parasol', 'Ringo Stone' and 'Paul Ma-Charmly'. After light-heartedly discussing their plans for the future, John recited 'Good Dog Nigel' from his poems book *In His Own Write*. At the conclusion of which, George tried to stop him reading and managed it by tearing out some of the pages from it. At which point, John helped him by tearing out some more.

Karlaplansstudion, Karlaplan

Having put the finishing touches to their second album in London, The Beatles headed overseas for the first time on 23 October 1963. The following day, they went to record a radio appearance at this studio, in front of some very excited fans. The performance was recorded and transmitted on 11 November 1963.

Kungliga Tennishallen, Lidingovagen,

After their opening night success in Karlstad, The Beatles remained in Stockholm, where they were based, for two shows on 26 October 1963. The group was second on the bill to the American group, Joey Dee and The Starliters. A film was apparently made of The Beatles' evening performance but it later went missing. The performance was marred by both John and Paul receiving an electric shock. 'I felt like all my teeth had dropped out,' Paul fumed.

The Beatles perform at Shea Stadium on 15 August 1964

SECTION FOUR
Beatles Broadcast and Cinema

Introduction

When The Beatles, before that wonderful incarnation The Quarrymen, first started out on the path that would eventually lead to the likes of 'I Want To Your Your Hand', 'Eleanor Rigby' and 'Strawberry Fields Forever', the idea that they would progress from smoke-filled rooms and dingy dance halls to performances on radio, television and, for goodness sake, movies, can scarcely have entered any of their minds. Except in their dreams.

But in fact The Quarrymen did make one performance in a recording studio. Some time in the middle of 1958 they entered the back room of a house in Liverpool and in a little booth cut one copy of a song called 'In Spite Of All The Danger'. That was really the height of The Quarrymen's musical career – and their end.

John, Paul and George then went on to become The Beatles, while the other original members of The Quarrymen went out into what we call the ordinary, everyday world.

During the next ten years, till 1970, not only did The Beatles pack out some of the largest, noisiest concerts ever known (and appear in pantomime sketches ...) they also dominated the airwaves and made smash hit (according to the fans at least) movies. And it is all described here, thanks to our audio/visual expert Keith Badman.

The ratings system, of which we are inordinately fond, does not of course work for all these radio and TV shows as, scandalously, many in the early days were not recorded, or were wiped or lost. Unperturbed, however, we have given it our very best shot.

Bootlegs do exist of some of their early radio and TV shows, which have been passed around among fans, sold from stalls or backstreet shops, which naturally we could not encourage you to purchase, but after all these years they have become familiar to most diehard fans and it is impossible now to tell where they originally came from.

Thanks to the wonders of technology, there is now a massive quantity of videos, DVDs and Blu-rays of The Beatles at their height, performing away, from Germany to Japan, and also scarce footage and recordings of the early days. Fans who never saw them in the flesh can now listen for ever to them singing and playing their hearts out in the radio studio, watch them perform on television, and, of course, sit back with the popcorn and savour their films. The days of the only option being to sit in a dark room listening to their records are gone. Shame really.

We kick off with their Radio performances, because that's where they first began to broadcast, on a show called *Teenagers' Turn – Here We Go*, heard by the British nation on 8 March 1962. Here we go, indeed. Turn on, tune in.

BEATLES ON THE RADIO

Introduction

The Beatles performed (live or recorded) a total of 56 times from 7 March 1962–20 June 1965 on a wide variety of radio programmes (52 times for the BBC in the UK, one for Sveriges Radio in Sweden and three for Europe 1 France). This is an alphabetical list of them, detailing the show's title, studios used, recording and broadcast dates/times and the songs played. In total 275 songs were broadcast by the BBC, 88 different ones, of which 36 were never issued officially during the group's time together. Some were recorded many times, others only once. To date, Apple has released two 'official' compilations of the tracks; *Live At The BBC* in the UK on 30 November 1994 (US on 6 December 1994) and *On Air – Live At The BBC Volume 2* on 11 November 2013 (US same date). Five tracks from the group's 24 October 1963 session for Sveriges Radio in Sweden appeared on the 21 November 1995 Apple/EMI release *The Beatles Anthology 1*.

By the early 1970s, the Corporation held just *four* of the group's BBC programmes in their archive. Most of The Beatles' original broadcast tapes had been either systematically wiped or junked. The BBC's television and radio archiving policy at the time amounted to the head of the department saying, 'This material is taking up too much room. We've got to get rid of it!' So, for the recovery of those lost/missing/scrapped shows, we are in debt to the 'illegal' home-taping enthusiasts, engineers who had worked on (and made private copies of) the programmes and the salvaged transcription discs (distributed by the BBC in the sixties for airplay on stations in the US and across the British Empire for a show called *Top Of The Pops*, hosted by DJ Brian Matthew).

The first sign that many of these recordings actually survived outside the BBC's ever-dwindling archive came on 12 June 1971 when the so-called 'British Bootleg King' Jeffrey Collins, who ran a record shop in Chancery Lane, London, announced in the music press he was releasing a Beatles double album entitled *Rock 'N' Roll*, featuring 20 tracks comprised mainly of the group's *Saturday Club* sessions. It seemed to open the floodgates. Eager to outdo each other, bootleggers moved quickly to be the next to issue their own unofficial BBC Beatles album, one of which, *Yellow Matter Custard*, was issued by the legendary Californian label TMOQ (Trade Mark of Quality) in August 1971. Deriving from shows such as *Pop Go The Beatles*, this contained 14 cuts, 13 of which had never been recorded for EMI; the other being 'Slow Down', which had been taped for the tenth episode of the programme on 16 July 1963.

With more recordings seemingly being uncovered, May 1972 saw the release of two more TMOQ albums. Bearing the titles *Out-takes 1* and *Out-takes 2*, these contained BBC versions of 21 officially released songs, along with 'Lucille' and 'Hippy Hippy Shake', from *Pop Go The Beatles* and *Saturday Club* respectively. Three recordings, broadcast by the BBC in May/June 1972, during the 13-part Radio 1 series *The Beatles Story*, also soon found their way onto new bootlegs. In August 1975, Wizardo Records in America compiled 20 of the best available tracks for the album *Words Of Love*. After a short lull, in May 1978 a new batch of recordings suddenly flooded the market, the most notable of which was the Ruthless Rhymes release *From Us To You – A Parlophone Rehearsal Session*. Issued as a ten-inch coloured vinyl disc, it featured the group running through their repertoire for show four of *From Us To You* on 17 July 1964. (It reappeared one month later, repackaged as a compilation called *Youngblood*.)

Two years on, in 1980, the class of unofficial audios of The Beatles' BBC sessions suddenly went up a notch when an excellent-quality tape, featuring four tracks and conversation from the group's 16 July 1963 *Pop Go The Beatles* recordings, was released by Hohrweite Stereophonie on a seven-inch EP entitled *Four By The Beatles*. The same company, cheekily on either a green or black 'BBC Transcription Service' label, issued these and 14 other, superb-quality tracks in July 1980 on an album called *Broadcasts*. Other equally impressive releases soon followed, such as *Silver Days (Air Time)*, containing a near perfect copy of the group's 24 October 1963 Swedish radio concert, and January 1982's *Beautiful Dreamer*, the first to contain songs from the group's very early BBC appearances, and in particular the title track, taped for their first *Saturday Club* slot on 22 January 1963.

In early 1982, following a suggestion by a Beatle fan, the BBC in London chose to produce a programme to commemorate the twentieth anniversary of the group's first session for the Corporation. With precious little in their archives, this was quite an undertaking. But after collating what they had, and pulling in some of the various unofficial releases, they managed to compile a two-hour show, aired on Radio 1 in the UK on 7 March 1982. (Various American radio networks broadcast it a little over two months later, between 29–31 May 1982.) On 27 December 1982, the BBC transmitted an expanded version of it, with more recently recovered recordings. (This three-hour show was aired in America during May 1983.)

Three years later, in October 1986, just as the BBC and collectors were beginning to think there was nothing left to uncover, a most significant series of top-quality, unofficial Beatles BBC releases suddenly started to appear. Entitled *The Beatles At The Beeb Vol. 1*, and running through to *Vol. 13*, the albums featured a huge amount of previously unreleased, long-thought-lost sessions, conversations and announcements. Lovingly preserved by a professionally minded, UK-based audiophile/Beatles collector, this archive started in 1963, unfortunately missing the group's earlier 1962 sessions. Collectors were now able to substitute poor quality recordings with much improved ones. Released intermittently, the landmark series, with superbly designed covers and highly informative sleeve notes, ended in December 1988. Eager to cash in on this treasure trove, the BBC acquired the vinyls, and on 1 October 1988 began airing a new 14-episode memorial series entitled *The Beeb's Lost Beatles Tapes*, concluding on 31 December 1988. Although it featured quite heavily on the newly found audios, the run did also include recently uncovered transcription discs, some private tapes supplied by those who had worked on the original sixties shows, and excerpts from two, newly discovered ten-inch audio reels that had been found in the BBC's archives by producer and author Kevin Howlett. (Selected US networks ran the programmes the following year.)

Six years later, on 30 November 1994 in the UK (6 December 1994 in the US), after much remixing and remastering of a selection of these tracks, Apple, in conjunction with EMI, released their first official compilation of these recordings, on a double album entitled *Live At The BBC*. Obviously not wishing to announce the fact that most of the material featured on it had actually derived from misplaced tapes, unreturned albums and illegal home recordings, the BBC press machine ridiculously declared they had miraculously found the recordings in one of their 'dust-encrusted' vaults. (The Corporation repeated the myth, to a much lesser degree, with the second release 19 years later.) Further highly definitive, unofficial releases have appeared since then, either on CD or as bundled flac and cue files on the internet. The most notable being material released by Yellow Dog, Italian label Great Dane's 1993 ten-disc set *The Complete BBC Sessions* (deemed an official release in their home country because Italian law meant that the copyright on these recordings had expired there), and Purple Chick's 2004 *The Complete BBC Sessions*, followed its 2010 updated and expanded 12-disc version (plus one of bonus artwork) called *Unsurpassed Broadcasts*, which incredibly contained even more recordings previously thought lost (*The Complete BBC Sessions* itself was separately updated in 2011).

In alphabetical order, here then are those Beatles radio sessions in full, along with details of what does and does not survive.

BEAT SHOW, THE

Playhouse Theatre, St John's Road, Hulme, Manchester, England
Recorded: 3 July 1963 (8.00–9.00pm), broadcast BBC Light Programme: 4 July 1963 (1.00–1.30pm)
From Me To You, A Taste Of Honey, Twist And Shout

Presented by Gay Byrne and produced by Geoff Lawrence, this was the only appearance by The Beatles on the midday show. Taped in front of a small studio audience, the group performed three songs. Joining them on the programme were The Trad Lads and the BBC's NDO (Northern Dance Orchestra), one of several big bands employed by the BBC to fulfil a long-held agreement with the Musicians' Union. Bands such as the NDO and the Midlands Dance Orchestra were Union members, and to offset the amount of time relinquished to the playing of records ('needle time' in radio idiom) they had to be employed to fulfil the Corporation's commitment to live music. It was because of that covenant that groups such as The Beatles, the Rolling Stones, The Kinks etc., were booked to perform. (**'From Me To You' is missing from surviving tapes of this session.**)

Another pretty standard Beatles radio appearance.

BEATLES (INVITE YOU TO TAKE A TICKET TO RIDE), THE

Studio One, Piccadilly Theatre, 201 Piccadilly, London, England
Recorded: 26 May 1965 (2.30–6.00pm), broadcast BBC Light Programme: 7 June 1965 (10.00am–12.00pm)
Ticket To Ride (excerpt), Everybody's Trying To Be My Baby, I'm A Loser, The Night Before, Honey Don't, Dizzy Miss Lizzy, She's A Woman, Ticket To Ride (complete)

Presented by Denny Piercy and produced by Keith Bateson, this was The Beatles' fifty-second and last appearance on BBC radio performing music live in the studio. By the time of this show the group no longer needed the Light Programme to promote them, and since *From Us To You* (see entries) no longer seemed like an apt title considering how much they had changed musically in the past two years, they suggested a new one: *The Beatles (Invite You To Take A Ticket To Ride)*. Seven songs were recorded for this 'Whit Monday Beat Special', as the BBC weekly listings magazine *Radio Times* billed the show, the most notable being 'Ticket To Ride', which was aired twice (faded out after 37 seconds at the start and played in full at the end, and featuring a slightly different drum rhythm track), and 'The Night Before', which became the only live rendition of the song by the group in their entire career. The Beatles also chatted with the host, musician and broadcaster Denny Piercy, but many listeners thought that they were uninterested and fairly unresponsive with their answers covering, among other things, Bob Dylan, John's second book *A Spaniard In The Works*, the upcoming film *Help!* and their forthcoming tour of America. Joining John, Paul, George and Ringo on the show were The Atlantics, The Lorne Gibson Trio, Julie Grant, The Hollies, The Ivy League, Danny Street and the in-house bank holiday regulars The Kenny Salmon Seven. The group's fee for their appearance was £100. (**The Beatles' complete 21 minutes 59 seconds appearance survives.**)

Historic final BBC radio appearance, by which time the group had moved on to bigger and better things … and it shows in the recordings.

Footnote: On 12 March 1965, during a seminar with Donald MacLean, the chief assistant of popular music sound productions at the BBC, Brian Epstein promised that the group would record more holiday music specials for the Corporation, chiefly on 30 August and 26 December that year. However, despite even an on-air announcement to this effect, it didn't happen. But the group did participate in another bank holiday show for the BBC, the 45-minute interview-only *The Beatles Abroad* special, aired on the Light Programme on 30 August 1965. (See entry for Shea Stadium 15 August 1965 in *Places* section).

THE BEATLES PUPPGRUPP FRAN LIVERPOOL PA BESOK I STOCKHOLM (BEATLES – POP GROUP FROM LIVERPOOL ON A VISIT IN STOCKHOLM, THE)

Karlaplan Studios, Karlaplan, Stockholm, Sweden
Recorded: 24 October 1963 (2.00-2.30pm), broadcast as *The Beatles Puppgrupp Fran Liverpool Pa Besok I Stockholm*, Channel One, Sveriges Radio: 11 November 1963 (10.05-10.30pm)
I Saw Her Standing There, From Me To You, Money (That's What I Want), Roll Over Beethoven, You Really Got A Hold On Me, She Loves You, Twist And Shout

Produced for his series *Pop '63* by Klas Burling, a personal friend of The Beatles, and with sound engineer Hans Westman, this is the only non-BBC appearance in the listing. The Beatles arrived at the Karlaplan Studios, a familiar location for many Swedish music programmes of the fifties and sixties, in a panic; their instruments and Vox amplifiers hadn't arrived in time. So another musician, Hasse Rosén, present in the studio that day with his band The Norsemen, was obliged to offer his instruments and Fender amps to the group. Even though only 100 tickets were available, some 250 Beatles fans had turned up to watch. In a session lasting 26 minutes 5 seconds, the band presented their seven tracks, at the end of which there was further panic. The building did not possess a stage door, forcing the group to flee the studio by pushing their way through

RIGHT: John holding a hoe, posing with his wife Cynthia, holding a mop and their son Julian. This was taken by Robert Whitaker at their home in 1964. John just loved doing any housework. Hoe hoe. © Robert Whitaker / Contributor

BOTTOM RIGHT: Derek Taylor (right, with the cigarette), with the band at a press conference. He was their great friend and, for many years, their press officer.

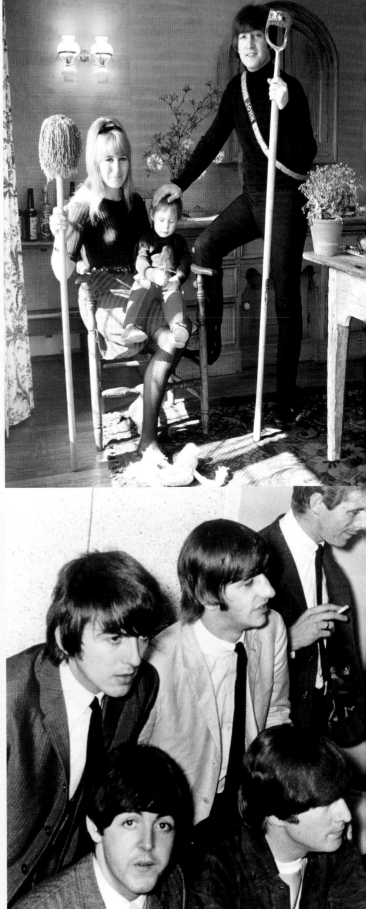

ABOVE: 11 February 1964, Washington, D.C.
The Beatles' first concert in the USA. © Fred Ward / Corbis

BELOW: The Beatles on *The Ed Sullivan Show*,
February 1964 in New York.

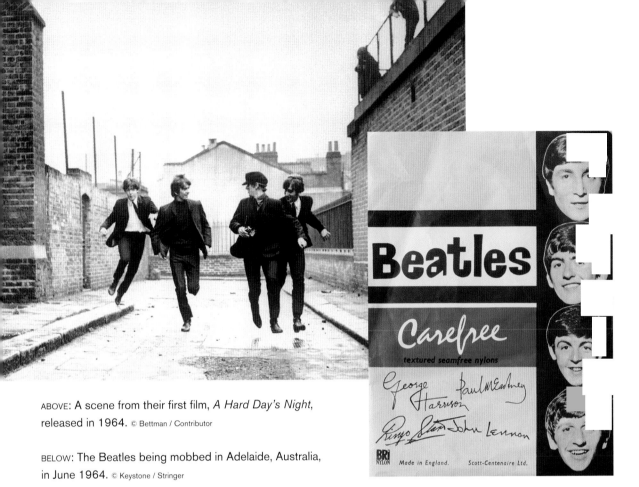

ABOVE: A scene from their first film, *A Hard Day's Night*, released in 1964. © Bettman / Contributor

BELOW: The Beatles being mobbed in Adelaide, Australia, in June 1964. © Keystone / Stringer

OPPOSITE: The Beatles playing to 14,000 fans at the Seattle Center Coliseum, August 1964. © William Lovelace / Stringer

RIGHT: Big in America – this is the cover for the US album, *The Beatles' Second Album*, 1964. Truly electrifying ...

BELOW LEFT: Concert programme for their appearance at the Blackpool Opera House, August 1964.

BELOW RIGHT: Brian Epstein, nicely signed, who became the band's manager in December 1961.

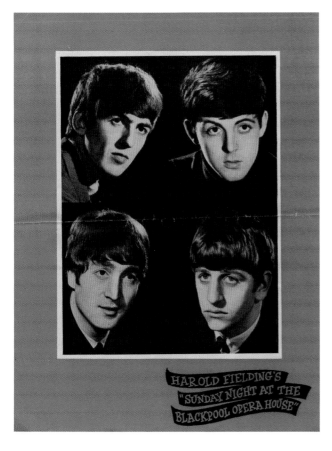

LEFT: Alf Lennon, John's father, in 1965. He was never there when John was growing up, but suddenly reappeared when he realised John had become famous. © ANL / REX / SHUTTERSTOCK

BELOW: A ticket for The Beatles at the Shea Stadium, 15 August 1965.

BOTTOM: The Beatles, trying to be heard at the Shea Stadium. © Michael Ochs Archives / Stringer

ABOVE: Scene from the band's second film, *Help!*, 1965, shot in the Bahamas. © Bettman / Contributor

LEFT: A Beatles scrapbook.

BELOW: The Mexican poster for *Help!*

LEFT: John in 1966 with his Aunt Mimi, who brought him up. © ITV / REX / Shutterstock

ABOVE: George marries Pattie Boyd in 1966. Brian Epstein is standing to the left, beside Paul. © Manchester Daily Express / Contributor

LEFT: Jane Asher in 1966, the inspiration for many of Paul's songs, to whom he became engaged the following year.

© Popperfoto / Contributor

excited fans and exiting via the doors at the front of the house.

Sveriges Radio sound engineer Hans Westman described his work on the recording as 'The worst I've ever made, totally chaotic,' citing the group's lack of rehearsal time as the main reason. John Lennon was having none of this. He loved it. Recalling the songs they recorded at Karlaplan that day, distortions et al., he described it as the best live recordings that The Beatles ever made, as well as for the sound and for the feeling. (**Five songs from the session, I Saw Her Standing There, From Me To You, Money (That's What I Want), You Really Got A Hold On Me and Roll Over Beethoven, would appear on the official November 1995 Apple/EMI release** *Anthology 1*.**)**

Great live studio appearance. Superb and exciting. No wonder Lennon loved it!

KEN DODD SHOW, THE

Paris Studio, Lower Regent Street, London, England
Recorded: 9 October 1963 (10.00–11.00pm), broadcast BBC Light Programme: 3 November 1963 (2.30–3.00pm)
She Loves You

Produced by Bill Worsley, this was the group's one and only appearance on the comic and fellow Liverpudlian's radio programme. During the 30-minute show in front of a studio audience, they performed a live rendition of the A-side of their latest Parlophone/EMI single, 'She Loves You'. 'They were guests on my radio show,' Dodd recalled several years later, 'and Paul said to me, "We've been on with you before Doddy, don't you remember that charity show in Maghull. We were shocking weren't we?"' (McCartney was

referring to the local St John Ambulance charity fundraising event, held at the Albany Cinema on 15 October 1961.) The Beatles' fee for the show was fifty-two pounds ten shillings. (**The recording of 'She Loves You' survives.**)

Nice, but pretty average, Beatles appearance.

Footnote: The group's interview on the BBC Light Programme show *The Public Ear* followed immediately on from *The Ken Dodd Show* that day, during which money-conscious George announced they had been misquoted about earning £7,000 a week. 'We probably do make quite a bit,' he added, 'but we don't actually see it, because record royalties, things like that, take months before they come in … But we've also got an accountant and a company, Beatles Limited; they see the money. The thing is, indirectly, we are and we aren't doing it for the money, really because, don't forget, we played for about three or four years, or maybe longer just earning hardly anything. Well, we wouldn't have done that, if we were doing it for the money, we wouldn't have lasted out all those years. We like it sufficiently to do it not for the money too, but the money does help, let's face it.'

EASY BEAT (1)

Playhouse Theatre, Northumberland Avenue, London, England
Recorded: 3 April 1963 (8.30–9.45pm), broadcast BBC Light Programme: 7 April 1963 (10.31–11.30am)
Please Please Me, Misery, From Me To You

Presented by Brian Matthew and produced by Ron Belchier, this was The Beatles' debut on this highly popular Sunday morning Light Programme pop show, taped in front of a studio audience. Fellow Liverpool musician Gerry Marsden of

Gerry and The Pacemakers was on hand to introduce The Beatles' rendition of 'From Me to You'. John and Paul also popped up to review records on a panel with fellow guests Laura Lee and Clare O'Rourke as part of the show's 'Going Up?' feature. They cast their judgement on new releases by Cleo Laine, Bert Weedon, The Vernons Girls and former tour partner Tommy Roe, and were paid one pound one shilling each for doing so.

First transmitted in 1960, *Easy Beat* was one of the earliest BBC programmes to feature pop tunes and, similar to the contemporary *Saturday Club* (see entries), it was initially presented by the future *Thank Your Lucky Stars* presenter Brian Matthew. (Later hosts included David Symonds and *Ready Steady Go!*'s Keith Fordyce.) When Radio 1 was launched on 30 September 1967, the show continued for several more months but under the new banner of *Happening Sunday*, with DJ Ed Stewart at the helm, before being dropped altogether later that year. **(Only 'From Me To You' from this show survives.)**

Another run-of-the-mill show, but enjoyable just the same.

EASY BEAT (2)

Playhouse Theatre, Northumberland Avenue, London, England
Recorded: 19 June 1963 (8.45-9.45pm), broadcast BBC Light Programme: 23 June 1963 (10.31-11.30am)
Some Other Guy, A Taste Of Honey, Thank You Girl, From Me To You

Presented by Brian Matthew and produced by Ron Belchier. Alongside their renditions of the Jerry Leiber, Mike Stoller and Richard Barrett composition 'Some Other Guy', Bobby Scott and Ric Marlow's 'A Taste Of Honey' and Lennon/McCartney's 'From Me To You', a most inter-esting version of 'Thank You Girl' was also performed today, notable for Paul and George singing (compared to the EMI single) a different arrangement for the background vocals. **(All tracks survive.)**

Memorable for the unique rendition of 'Thank You Girl'.

EASY BEAT (3)

Playhouse Theatre, Northumberland Avenue, London, England
Recorded: 17 July 1963 (8.45-9.45 pm), broadcast BBC Light Programme: 21 July 1963 (10.31-11.30am)
I Saw Her Standing There, A Shot Of Rhythm And Blues, There's A Place, Twist And Shout

Presented by Brian Matthew and produced by Ron Belchier. In front of a studio audience, the group performed four numbers, of which 'A Shot Of Rhythm And Blues' was recorded for the BBC for the second time (the first being for show 3 of *Pop Go The Beatles* on 1 June 1963). However this version was noticeably different, with its slightly slower arrangement and George's bluesy, albeit brief, guitar break. This was also the only time that the group performed it in front of a live audience. **(The Beatles' complete appearance survives.)**

Enjoyable, but pretty much standard appearance.

EASY BEAT (4)

Playhouse Theatre, Northumberland Avenue, London, England
Recorded: 16 October 1963 (9.00-10.00pm), broadcast BBC Light Programme: 20 October 1963 (10.31-11.30am)
I Saw Her Standing There, Love Me Do, Please Please Me, From Me To You, She Loves You

Presented by Brian Matthew and produced by Ron Belchier. Performed in front of a studio audience to celebrate, as Matthew described it, 'a year since The Beatles first hit the show-business jackpot.' The five tracks they sang were the band's most favoured and successful songs from the past 12 months, all of which were chosen by the group themselves. This was also their final appearance on *Easy Beat*. Due to their popularity and concerns for their safety from over-zealous fans, Brian Epstein told BBC executives he would no longer allow radio appearances in front of studio audiences. This decision led to the scuppering of a planned fifth *Easy Beat* show, which was set to take place on 4 December 1963. 'I Saw Her Standing There' from the show would appear on the official November 1994 EMI/Apple collection *Live At The BBC*.

During a break in rehearsals at the Playhouse Theatre that morning, The Beatles gave two interviews to BBC reporter Peter Woods (one for radio, one for TV) about the announcement that they had just been invited to perform at this year's Royal Command Performance on 4 November 1963. It seemed to solidify the notion that the group was now more than just one-hit wonders, and they were fast becoming a national phenomenon. 'George … how long do you think you're going to be successful?' Woods asked in his piece for radio. 'You've had this monumental rise. Obviously this sort of thing can't go on, but do you think you can settle down to a life in show business?' 'Well, we're hoping to,' Harrison responded. 'I mean, not necessarily a life in show business, but at least a couple more years … I mean, if we do as well as Cliff [Richard] and The Shadows have done up to now, well I mean, we won't be moaning.' Wood's reports appeared on that evening's BBC TV and Light Programme news bulletins. (**The *Easy Beat* show survives, as do both the television and radio interviews.**)

Another run-of-the-mill appearance.

FROM US TO YOU (1)

Paris Studio, Lower Regent Street, London, England
Recorded: 18 December 1963 (7.00–10.30pm), broadcast BBC Light Programme: 26 December 1963 (10.00am–12.00pm)
From Us To You, She Loves You, All My Loving, Roll Over Beethoven, Till There Was You, Boys, Money (That's What I Want), I Saw Her Standing There, Tie Me Kangaroo Down Sport, I Want To Hold Your Hand, From Us To You

Presented by Rolf Harris and produced by Bryant Marriott, this was the first of five Beatles bank holiday specials, the first four of which were called *From Us To You*. The (now disgraced) Australian host Rolf Harris had had a hit in 1960 with 'Tie Me Kangaroo Down, Sport' (which he re-recorded in 1963 with producer George Martin) and he performed it here with The Beatles. Unsurprisingly this version featured some highly amusing parody lyrics. E.g. 'I think George's guitar is on the blink, I think, George's guitar is on the blink.' 'Prop me up by the wall, Paul, prop me up by the wall' At the conclusion of the song, with reference to the fact that the rendition hadn't quite gone to plan, Harris said, 'What about messing up that ending, after all the rehearsal we did?' To which John immediately hit back, 'You forgot the words, didn't ya, Rolf?' Incidentally, the opening and closing theme of the show, performed by The Beatles, was a variation of their hit, with the words 'I' and 'Me' replaced by 'We' and 'Us'. (**The complete show survives.**)

Interesting first show, notable for the new version of their third EMI single.

FROM US TO YOU (2)

Studio One, Piccadilly Studios, 201 Piccadilly, London, England
Recorded: 28 February 1964 (6.30–9.00pm), broadcast BBC Light Programme: 30 March 1964 (10.00am–12.00pm)
From Us To You, You Can't Do That, Roll Over Beethoven, Till There Was You, I Wanna Be Your Man, Please Mister Postman, All My Loving, This Boy, Can't Buy Me Love, From Us To You

Presented by Alan Freeman and produced by Bryant Marriott, this was The Beatles' second bank holiday special for the Corporation. The audience research reports for the programme (dated 6 May 1964) revealed a third of those listening regarded it as 'noisy, boring and a waste of time.' A security guard echoed those sentiments by saying he thought The Beatles were 'vastly overrated, their performance was decidedly amateur and their entertainment value – nil.' **(The complete show survives.)**

Interesting, but pretty standard, really.

FROM US TO YOU (3)

Paris Studio, Lower Regent Street, London, England
Recorded: 1 May 1964 (6.30–9.00pm), broadcast BBC Light Programme: 18 May 1964 (10.00am–12.00pm)

From Us To You, Whit Monday To You, I Saw Her Standing There, Kansas City/Hey-Hey-Hey-Hey!, I Forgot To Remember To Forget, You Can't Do That, Sure To Fall (In Love With You), Can't Buy Me Love, Matchbox, Honey Don't (with John on lead vocal), From Us To You

Presented by Alan Freeman and produced by Bryant Marriott, this was the group's third bank holiday special for the BBC. 'The Beatles used to come in [to the studio],' Freeman recalled, 'and amazingly enough, they used to record something like eight songs in about two-and-a-half-hours. Quite often, people used to say to me, "They weren't so hot live, were they?" but if you listen to these sessions, you realise what a great live band they really were.' An interesting show due to its inclusion of four tracks that were unreleased by the band at the time: 'Kansas City/Hey-Hey-Hey-Hey!', 'I Forgot To Remember To Forget', 'Sure To Fall (In Love With You)' and 'Honey Don't', which featured John on lead vocals. When the group recorded it for their fourth EMI album, *Beatles For Sale*, at the tail end of 1964, Ringo took over. 'Kansas City' would also appear on that disc, but the group never commercially released the other. The recording of 'From Us To You' used in this broadcast was lifted from show 2, the 28 February 1964 edition of this series. This was also the last BBC programme to feature the group performing songs that would not make it on to disc. The Beatles' fee for the show was £100. (**The performance survives.**)

Interesting, but pretty standard radio spot.

FROM US TO YOU (4)

Paris Studio, Lower Regent Street, London, England
Recorded: 17 July 1964 (2.15–6.15pm), broadcast BBC Light Programme: 3 August 1964 (10.00am–12.00pm)
From Us To You, Long Tall Sally, If I Fell, I'm Happy Just To Dance With You, Things We Said Today, I Should Have Known Better, Boys, Kansas City/Hey-Hey-Hey-Hey!, A Hard Day's Night, From Us To You

Presented by Don Wardell and produced by Bryant Marriott, in this fourth consecutive bank holiday special, besides performing, The Beatles were heard chatting with the host and reading listeners' requests. John also read out the show's closing credits. The Beatles' fee for the show was £100. (**The complete show survives, as does a 27-minute tape, out-takes et al., of the group recording the session. Entitled *From Us To You – A Parlophone Rehearsal Session*, this first appeared in May 1978, as a ten-inch coloured vinyl bootleg, on the Ruthless Rhymes label. It reappeared one month later as another unofficial disc called *Youngblood*.**)

Great show, with interesting 'A Hard Day's Night' era songs.

HERE WE GO (1)

Playhouse Theatre, St John's Road, Hulme, Manchester, England
Recorded: 25 October 1962 (8.00–8.45pm), broadcast BBC Light Programme: 26 October 1962 (5.00–5.29pm)
Love Me Do, A Taste Of Honey, PS I Love You (Sheila – taped but not transmitted)

Presented by Ray Peters and produced by Peter Pilbeam. Before a studio audience, and with their new member Ringo Starr on drums, The Beatles taped four songs, but with time only for three, the final track 'Sheila', made famous by the US singer Tommy Roe, was dropped. The group's decision to feature 'A Taste Of Honey' was interesting, considering it had just been released by the American singer Lenny Welch five weeks earlier, on 17 September 1962. It meant that The Beatles had wasted no time in learning the track. *Here We Go* was originally titled *Teenagers' Turn – Here We Go*, on which the group made their radio debut on 8 March 1962 (see entry). The Beatles' fee for the show was thirty-seven pounds eighteen shillings (plus expenses). (**Only 'A Taste Of Honey' survives from this session.**)

With the performance of 'A Taste Of Honey' and new drummer Ringo on board, this was a most interesting programme.

HERE WE GO (2)

Playhouse Theatre, St John's Road, Hulme, Manchester, England
Recorded: 16 January 1963 (8.00–8.45pm), broadcast BBC Light Programme: 25 January 1963 (5.00–5.29pm)
Chains, Please Please Me, Ask Me Why (Three Cool Cats – taped but not transmitted)

During one of the coldest English winters on record, The Beatles returned to the Playhouse Theatre in Manchester to perform four songs in front in front of an enthusiastic studio audience: 'Chains', 'Please Please Me', 'Ask Me Why' and 'Three Cool Cats'. The latter was ultimately cut from the finished broadcast nine days later, while tracks two and three, respectively, were the A- and B-sides of their latest EMI single. While in the city, The Beatles also made an appearance on the regional Granada ITV show *People And Places* where they mimed to two songs, 'Ask Me Why' and 'Please Please Me'. (**The three transmitted tracks survive.**)

Interesting but standard appearance.

HERE WE GO (3)

Playhouse Theatre, St John's Road, Hulme, Manchester, England
Recorded: 6 March 1963 (8.00–8.45pm), broadcast BBC Light Programme: 12 March 1963 (5.00–5.29pm)
Misery, Do You Want To Know A Secret, Please Please Me (I Saw Her Standing There – taped but not transmitted)

Presented by Ray Peters and produced by Peter Pilbeam. Taped in front of a studio audience, this was the first time that listeners had the chance to hear 'Do You Want To Know A Secret' and 'Misery', two tracks from the group's forthcoming debut album *Please Please Me*, set for launch in the UK on 22 March 1963, the same day comedian and singer Kenny Lynch released his cover of 'Misery'. (Fellow Epstein-managed band Billy J. Kramer and The Dakotas issued their version of 'Do You Want To Know A Secret' as a Parlophone

single on 26 April 1963.) The Beatles' appearance came three days before the start of their UK tour, where they opened for singers Tommy Roe and Chris Montez. Brian Epstein later cancelled three further appearances on *Here We Go*, which had been scheduled for June and July. (**One of the other acts on the bill that day recorded on a seven-inch open-reel tape, from an FM broadcast, a 13-minute 46-seconds extract of the programme. His recording thankfully managed to capture The Beatles' entire three-track performance.**)

Another run-of-the-mill radio appearance.

LES BEATLES
(EN DIRECT DU PALAIS DES SPORTS)

Palais des Sports, Place de la Portes de Versailles, France
Recorded: 20 June 1965, broadcast live Europe 1 France: 20 June 1965
Twist And Shout (short version), She's A Woman, I'm A Loser, Can't Buy Me Love, Baby's In Black, I Wanna Be Your Man, A Hard Day's Night, Everybody's Trying To Be My Baby, Rock And Roll Music, I Feel Fine, Ticket To Ride, Long Tall Sally

This was the first engagement in The Beatles' short nine-date European tour. The Yardbirds were also

FIRST FIVE RADIO APPEARANCES (ALL ON THE BBC)

In recording date order, here are The Beatles first five radio appearances. Further info on each can be found in the relevant entries above.

1. *Teenagers' Turn – Here We Go*: recorded 7 March 1962 and broadcast BBC Light Programme 8 March 1962
2. *Teenagers' Turn – Here We Go*: recorded 11 June 1962 and broadcast BBC Light Programme 15 June 1962
3. *Here We Go*: recorded 25 October 1962 and broadcast BBC Light Programme 26 October 1962
4. *The Talent Spot*: recorded 27 November 1962 and broadcast BBC Light Programme: 4 December 1962
5. *Here We Go*: recorded 16 January 1963 and broadcast BBC Light Programme 25 January 1963

on the bill. French radio station Europe 1 recorded both shows today, with the first transmitted one week later as part of the weekly music series *Musicorama* (see entry 2). The second performance was aired live for this special programme entitled *Les Beatles (en direct du Palais des Sports)*. The same evening performance was also taped by French TV station Channel 2 and screened on 31 October in a programme entitled simply *Les Beatles* (see entry in *TV* section). **(The show survives in the French archive.)**

Cracking live performance. The Beatles really knew how to rock!

MUSICORAMA (1)

Paris Olympia, 28 Boulevard des Capucines, France
Recorded: 19 January 1964, broadcast Europe 1 France: 19 January 1964
From Me To You, This Boy, I Want To Hold Your Hand, She Loves You, Twist And Shout

Europe 1's weekly music series *Musicorama* broadcast live part of The Beatles' matinee show on this day at the Paris Olympia. This was the fourth of 18 dates The Beatles would play at this world-famous music hall, the run extending through to 4 February. **(The show survives in the French archive.)**

Historic, pleasing, charming. The Beatles were a delight in this early European tour.

MUSICORAMA (2)

Palais des Sports, Place de la Portes de Versailles, France
Recorded: 20 June 1965, broadcast Europe 1 France: 27 June 1965

Twist And Shout (short version), She's A Woman, I'm A Loser, Can't Buy Me Love, Baby's In Black, I Wanna Be Your Man, A Hard Day's Night, Everybody's Trying To Be My Baby, Rock And Roll Music, I Feel Fine, Ticket To Ride, Long Tall Sally

This was the first engagement in The Beatles' short nine-date European tour. The Yardbirds were also on the bill. French radio station Europe 1 recorded both shows today, with the first transmitted a week later as part of the station's weekly music series *Musicorama*. The Beatles' second show was broadcast live (see entry for *Les Beatles*). **(The show survives in the French archive.)**

Another superb performance. This clearly demonstrates just how good a live band they were during 1965.

ON THE SCENE

Studio One, Piccadilly Studios, 201 Piccadilly, London, England
Recorded: 21 March 1963 (1.00–2.00pm), broadcast BBC Light Programme: 28 March 1963 (5.00–5.29pm)
Misery, Do You Want To Know A Secret, Please Please Me

Presented by Brian Matthew and produced by Jimmy Grant and Bernie Andrews. The Beatles ran through a simple, trouble-free three-track set. **(No copy is thought to exist.)**

Yet another standard radio appearance and one we'll in all probability never hear again.

PARADE OF THE POPS

Playhouse Theatre, Northumberland Avenue, London, England
Recorded: 20 February 1963, broadcast live BBC Light Programme: 20 February 1963 (12.31–1.30pm)
Love Me Do, Please Please Me

Presented by Denny Piercy and produced by John Kingdon. The Beatles' first live radio broadcast for the BBC. (**No copy is thought to exist.**)

Historic first live appearance by the group for the Beeb, and another wiped by their short-sighted archivists at the time. Scandalous.

POP GO THE BEATLES (1)

Studio Two, Aeolian Hall, 135-137 New Bond Street, London, England
Recorded: 24 May 1963 (2.00-6.00pm), broadcast BBC Light Programme: 4 June 1963 (5.00-5.29pm)
Pop Go The Beatles, From Me To You, Everybody's Trying To Be My Baby, Do You Want To Know A Secret, You Really Got A Hold On Me, Misery, Hippy Hippy Shake, Pop Go The Beatles

Presented by Lee Peters and produced by Terry Henebery, with guest group The Lorne Gibson Trio. With The Beatles regularly pulling in UK audiences of around ten million for their appearances on *Saturday Club* (see entries) and a myriad of other BBC radio pop programmes, on 30 April 1963 BBC studio manager Vernon Lawrence suggested to his manager, assistant department head Donald MacLean, that the group should be given a radio series of their own. With Lawrence's reputation as a good judge of contemporary values, MacLean approved the idea and commissioned four programmes, with the option for a further 11 if successful. With a working title of *Beatle Time*, the budget for each 30-minute show was £100. Terry Henebery was handed the task of producing the shows, a strange choice considering he was a massive jazz fan and harboured a huge dislike for The Beatles' music.

Ultimately renamed *Pop Go The Beatles*, an idea conceived by Francis Line, one of the department's secretaries, the first four shows were presented by DJ Lee Peters (or 'Pee Litres' as The Beatles jokingly renamed him). Peters played the role of a rather posh straight man struggling to keep the riotous Liverpudlians under control. Introducing the songs, reading cards from fans and having fun with the announcer were regular occurrences for the group on each programme. Chosen by the BBC and normally taped in a different session, a special guest act would also feature each week. Each show started and ended with a rock 'n' roll, uptempo version of the 1853 nursery rhyme 'Pop Goes The Weasel'. The Beatles' version of this was recorded on this day. For the first programme, the group performed six songs, 'From Me To You', 'Everybody's Trying To Be My Baby', 'Do You Want To Know A Secret', 'You Really Got A Hold On Me', 'Misery' and 'Hippy Hippy Shake', of which only tracks 1, 3 and 5 had previously been recorded for EMI. Of the others, 'Everybody's Trying To Be My Baby' and 'You Really Got A Hold On Me' were still unreleased by the band at the time of broadcast, and 'Hippy Hippy Shake' failed to make it onto any EMI disc at all.

The audience research report (dated 2 August 1963) for this first episode revealed many listeners liked, 'the sound of The Beatles and their lively beat,' and felt Peters made 'a good compère ... he kept the programme going well.' However, some were not impressed, complaining the group's singing was 'noisy, harsh and untuneful,' and that they had 'nothing better to offer than many other groups of this kind.' The Beatles' fee for the show was £42 plus £10 travelling expenses. (**Of note here, just one recording is missing from the entire *Pop Go The Beatles* series: 'From Me To You' from show 1**)

Great! The very first edition of the group's own radio series. Delight to listen to. Wonderful.

POP GO THE BEATLES (2)

Paris Studio, Lower Regent Street, London, England
Recorded: 1 June 1963 (1.30-5.30pm), broadcast BBC
Light Programme: 11 June 1963 (5.00-5.29pm)
Pop Go The Beatles, Too Much Monkey Business, I Got To
Find My Baby, Young Blood, Baby It's You, Till There Was
You, Love Me Do, Pop Go The Beatles

Presented by Lee Peters and produced by Terry Henebery, with guest group The Countrymen. Peters read out a card from two fans reminding everyone that it had been Ringo's birthday the previous Friday, and John meanwhile asked Peters to do his rather impressive impersonation of actor James Mason when he introduced 'Baby It's You'. This programme was taped on the same day as *Pop Go The Beatles* show 3. The Beatles' fee was £42 plus £10 travelling expenses. 'Baby It's You' from this session would be released by Apple/EMI as an EP on 20 March 1995, accompanied by three other BBC recordings: 'I'll Follow The Sun' (from *Top Gear*, recorded on 17 November 1964), 'Devil In Her Heart' (*Pop Go The Beatles*, 16 July 1963) and 'Boys' (*Pop Go The Beatles*, 17 June 1963). **(The complete show survives.)**

Interesting appearance, with rarely performed tracks.

POP GO THE BEATLES (3)

Paris Studio, Lower Regent Street, London, England
Recorded: 1 June 1963 (9.30am-1.30pm), broadcast BBC
Light Programme: 18 June 1963 (5.00-5.29pm)
Pop Go The Beatles, A Shot Of Rhythm And Blues, Memphis,
Tennessee, A Taste Of Honey, Sure To Fall (In Love With You),
Money (That's What I Want), From Me To You, Pop Go The
Beatles

Presented by Lee Peters and produced by Terry Henebery, with guest group Carter-Lewis and The Southerners. To celebrate Paul's twenty-first birthday, a raucous version of 'Happy Birthday' was featured before 'A Taste Of Honey'. Arthur Alexander's 'A Shot Of Rhythm And Blues' was performed for the BBC for the first time today. The Beatles' fee for the show was £42 plus £10 travelling expenses. (This programme was taped prior to recording show 2 of *Pop Go The Beatles*.) **(The complete show survives.)**

Great show with more interesting performances.

POP GO THE BEATLES (4)

Studio Five, Maida Vale Studios, Delaware Road, London, England
Recorded: 17 June 1963 (10.30am-1.00pm), broadcast BBC Light Programme: 25 June 1963 (5.00-5.29pm)
Pop Go The Beatles, I Saw Her Standing There, Anna (Go To Him), Boys, Chains, PS I Love You, Twist And Shout, Pop Go The Beatles

Presented by Lee Peters and produced by Terry Henebery, with guest group the top Irish singing trio The Bachelors, this was the last show in the original commission. As a mark of its growing popularity, the BBC's weekly listings paper the *Radio Times* noted that producer Henebery had received over a hundred cards from listeners, from all over the country, expressing their delight that The Beatles had their own radio programme. Unsurprisingly, the option for a further 11 shows was taken up shortly after (see entry for first *Pop Go The Beatles*). The Beatles' fee for the show was £42 plus £10 travelling expenses. Following the taping on 17 June 1963, the group ate in the BBC canteen and then went outside for a separate photo shoot, giving Paul the birthday bumps on the Delaware Road. (He turned 21 the following day.) They were accompanied throughout by the photographer Dezo Hoffman, who also took a number of pictures during the BBC session. The Beatles returned to Liverpool that night. The version of 'Boys' from today's show was released on the official *Baby It's You* EP on 20 March 1995. **(The complete show survives.)**

Nice but pretty standard show.

POP GO THE BEATLES (5)

Studio Five, Maida Vale Studios, Delaware Road, London, England
Recorded: 2 July 1963 (6.30-9.30pm), broadcast BBC Light Programme: 16 July 1963 (5.00-5.29pm)
Pop Go The Beatles, That's All Right (Mama), There's A Place, Carol, Soldier Of Love (Lay Down Your Arms), Lend Me Your Comb, Clarabella, Pop Go The Beatles (Three Cool Cats, Sweet Little Sixteen and Ask Me Why were taped but not transmitted)

Presented by Rodney Burke and produced by Terry Henebery, with guest group Duffy Power and The Graham Bond Quartet. Returning after a three-week break, Burke's introduction at the start of the show was brilliant. 'It's five o'clock, we're ready to pop, it's the *Pop Go The Beatles* spot!' Following the success of the first four editions, this was the first of a further 11 commissioned by the Corporation, coming with a ten pounds ten shillings pay increase for the band. Their fee per show was now fifty-two pounds ten shillings plus ten pounds travelling expenses. The song 'Three Cool Cats' failed to make the finished cut of the programme, the same fate as befell the group's previous attempt at it, on 16 January 1963 during a recording of *Here We Go* (see entry). Along with show 8 in the series, because of the songs they performed this was a highly significant programme in the run, with only 'There's A Place' familiar to

the Beatle-record buyers. Of the others, 'That's All Right (Mama)', 'Carol', 'Soldier Of Love (Lay Down Your Arms)', 'Lend Me Your Comb' and 'Clarabella' would not appear on any official EMI/Parlophone release during the group's time together. **(The complete show survives.)**

Notable for the most unfamiliar tracks performed by the group today.

POP GO THE BEATLES (6)

Studio Two, Aeolian Hall, 135-137 New Bond Street, London, England
Recorded: 10 July 1963 (10.30am-1.30pm), broadcast: 23 July 1963 (5.00-5.30pm)
Pop Go The Beatles, Sweet Little Sixteen, A Taste Of Honey, Nothin' Shakin', Love Me Do, Lonesome Tears In My Eyes, So How Come (No One Loves Me), Pop Go The Beatles

Presented by Rodney Burke and produced by Terry Henebery, with guest group Carter-Lewis and The Southerners. The Beatles' fee for the show was fifty-two pounds ten shillings plus ten pounds travelling expenses. This was taped on the same day as *Pop Go The Beatles*, show 7. Interestingly, while on tour and sitting in his Weston-super-Mare hotel room, John taped a copy of 'Love Me Do' from this broadcast on his newly acquired reel-to-reel recorder. **(The complete show survives.)**

Interesting programme.

POP GO THE BEATLES (7)

Studio Two, Aeolian Hall, 135-137 New Bond Street, London, England
Recorded: 10 July 1963 (1.30-3.30pm), broadcast BBC Light Programme: 30 July 1963 (5.00-5.29pm)

Pop Go The Beatles, Memphis Tennessee, Do You Want To Know A Secret, Till There Was You, Matchbox, Please Mister Postman, Hippy Hippy Shake, Pop Go The Beatles

Presented by Rodney Burke and produced by Terry Henebery, with guest group The Searchers. Taped on the same day as *Pop Go The Beatles* show 6. At the time of broadcast 'Matchbox' and 'Please Mr Postman' were still unreleased commercially by the band, while the songs 'Memphis, Tennessee' and 'Hippy Hippy Shake' never made it onto any EMI/Parlophone disc at all. The Beatles' fee for the show was fifty-two pounds ten shillings plus ten pounds travelling expenses. The group interrupted their six-day residency at the Winter Gardens in Margate especially to record these two editions. (**The complete show survives.**)

Nice mix of common and unfamiliar Beatles tracks.

POP GO THE BEATLES (8)

Paris Studio, Lower Regent Street, London, England
Recorded: 16 July 1963 (3.00–5.30pm), broadcast BBC Light Programme: 6 August 1963 (5.00–5.29pm)
Pop Go The Beatles, I'm Gonna Sit Right Down And Cry (Over You), Crying Waiting Hoping, Kansas City/Hey-Hey-Hey-Hey!, To Know Her Is To Love Her, The Honeymoon Song, Twist And Shout, Pop Go The Beatles

Presented by Rodney Burke and produced by Terry Henebery, with guest group The Swinging Blue Jeans. In a lengthy session, lasting 3.00–10.30pm, The Beatles taped three editions of *Pop Go The Beatles* today, shows 8, 9 and 10. As with show 5, this was another highly significant programme in the series with only 'Twist And Shout' being familiar to the Beatle-record buying public. Of the others, 'Kansas City/Hey-Hey-Hey-Hey!' would not appear officially for another 16 months

when it graced their fourth album *Beatles For Sale*, while 'I'm Gonna Sit Right Down And Cry (Over You)', 'Crying, Waiting, Hoping', 'To Know Her Is To Love Her' and 'The Honeymoon Song' would never be played for the BBC again. The latter, the title track from the 1959 film *Honeymoon*, was first performed by Manuel and The Music of The Mountains, and later Paul would produce a version of it for Mary Hopkin, featured on her debut Apple album *Post Card* in 1969. The Beatles' fee for the show was fifty-two pounds ten shillings plus ten pounds travelling expenses. (**The complete show survives.**)

Notable for their renditions of some rarely performed songs.

POP GO THE BEATLES (9)

Paris Studio, Lower Regent Street, London, England
Recorded: 16 July 1963 (6.00–8.30pm), broadcast BBC Light Programme: 13 August 1963 (5.00–5.29pm)
Pop Go The Beatles, Long Tall Sally, Please Please Me, She Loves You, You Really Got A Hold On Me, I'll Get You, I Got A Woman, Pop Go The Beatles

Presented by Rodney Burke and produced by Terry Henebery, with guest group The Hollies. The Beatles unveiled both sides of their latest EMI single, 'She Loves You' and 'I'll Get You', during today's session. It would be released on August 23 1963, ten days after the recordings aired. The Beatles' fee for the show was fifty-two pounds ten shillings plus ten pounds travelling expenses. (**The complete show survives.**)

Standard show, but notable for the unveiling of their latest single, the classic 'She Loves You'.

POP GO THE BEATLES (10)

Paris Studio, Lower Regent Street, London, England
Recorded: 16 July 1963 (8.45-10.50pm), broadcast BBC
Light Programme: 20 August 1963 (5.00-5.29pm)
Pop Go The Beatles, She Loves You (repeat performance from show 9), Words Of Love, Glad All Over, I Just Don't Understand, Devil In Her Heart, Slow Down, Pop Go The Beatles

Presented by Rodney Burke and produced by Terry Henebery, with guest group Russ Sainty and The Nu-Notes. More unfamiliar songs were performed today. 'Words Of Love' and 'Devil In Her Heart' would not be released officially until November 1963's *With The Beatles* album, and 'Slow Down' would not appear on any EMI disc until 19 June 1964's *Long Tall Sally* EP. Of the others, 'Glad All Over', a 1957 song recorded by rock 'n' roll legend Carl Perkins, and 'I Just Don't Understand', a song released by the Swedish-born singer and actress Ann-Margret, would not appear in any shape or form whatsoever during the group's time together. 'Devil In Her Heart' would be released on 20 March 1995, alongside three other BBC recordings as part of the official Apple/EMI EP *Baby It's You*. The Beatles' fee for the show was fifty-two pounds ten shillings plus ten pounds travelling expenses. (**The complete show survives.**)

Some rare tracks here; great.

POP GO THE BEATLES (11)

Playhouse Theatre, St John's Road, Hulme, Manchester, England
Recorded: 1 August 1963 (1.30-4.00pm), broadcast BBC
Light Programme: 27 August 1963 (5.00-5.29pm)
Pop Go The Beatles, Ooh! My Soul, Don't Ever Change, Twist And Shout, She Loves You, Anna (Go To Him), A Shot Of Rhythm And Blues, Pop Go The Beatles

Presented by Rodney Burke and produced by Terry Henebery, with guest group The Cyril Davies Rhythm & Blues All-Stars with Long John Baldry. Rare performances today of the songs 'Ooh! My Soul' (with Paul on lead vocals) and 'Don't Ever Change' (which featured a rare harmony duet between Paul and George). The group would not perform them for the BBC again. The Beatles' fee for the show was fifty-two pounds ten shillings plus ten pounds travelling expenses. Show 12 in this series was also taped today. (**The complete show survives.**)

Nice programme.

POP GO THE BEATLES (12)

Playhouse Theatre, St John's Road, Hulme, Manchester, England
Recorded: 1 August 1963 (4.00-6.00pm), broadcast BBC
Light Programme: 3 September 1963 (5.00-5.29pm)
Pop Go The Beatles, From Me To You, I'll Get You, Money (That's What I Want), There's A Place, Honey Don't (with John on lead vocals), Roll Over Beethoven, Pop Go The Beatles (Lucille and Baby It's You were also taped but not transmitted)

Presented by Rodney Burke and produced by Terry Henebery, with guest group Brian Poole and The Tremeloes. Taped on the same day as show 11 in this series. The Beatles' fee for the show was fifty-two pounds ten shillings plus ten pounds travelling expenses. (**The complete show survives.**)

Another standard radio appearance.

POP GO THE BEATLES (13)

Studio Two, Aeolian Hall, 135–137 New Bond Street, London, England
Recorded: 3 September 1963 (2.00–4.30pm), broadcast BBC Light Programme: 10 September 1963 (5.00–5.29pm)
Pop Go The Beatles, Too Much Monkey Business, Love Me Do, She Loves You, I'll Get You, A Taste Of Honey, Hippy Hippy Shake, Pop Go The Beatles

Presented by Rodney Burke and produced by Terry Henebery, with guest group Johnny Kidd and The Pirates. In one long session, from 2.00–10.00pm, The Beatles taped 19 songs for the final three shows (13, 14 and 15) of this series. The version of 'She Loves You' from this broadcast was repeated two weeks later during the final edition. The Beatles' fee for the show was fifty-two pounds ten shillings plus ten pounds travelling expenses. (**The complete show survives.**)

Yet another run-of-the-mill radio spot.

POP GO THE BEATLES (14)

Studio Two, Aeolian Hall, 135–137 New Bond Street, London, England
Recorded: 3 September 1963 (5.00–7.30pm), broadcast BBC Light Programme: 17 September 1963 (5.00–5.29pm)
Pop Go The Beatles, Chains, You Really Got A Hold On Me, Misery, Lucille, From Me To You, Boys, Pop Go The Beatles

Presented by Rodney Burke and produced by Ian Grant, with guest group The Marauders. The Beatles began recording this edition immediately following a 30-minute break after taping show 13. Their rendition today of the Gerry Goffin and Carole King track 'Chains' is quite different from the released EMI attempt, and closely resembles the version released by Little Eva's backing singers The Cookies in November 1962. The Beatles'

fee for the show was fifty-two pounds ten shillings plus ten pounds travelling expenses. (**The complete show survives.**)

Notable for the new arrangement of 'Chains'.

POP GO THE BEATLES (15)

Studio Two, Aeolian Hall, 135–137 New Bond Street, London, England
Recorded: 3 September 1963 (8.00–10.00pm), broadcast BBC Light Programme: 24 September 1963 (5.00–5.29pm)
Pop Go The Beatles, She Loves You, Ask Me Why, Devil In My Heart, I Saw Her Standing There, Sure To Fall (In Love With You), Twist And Shout, Pop Go The Beatles

Presented by Rodney Burke and produced by Ian Grant, with guest group Tony Rivers and The Castaways. The performance of 'She Loves You' was lifted from show 13 in this series. The Beatles' fee for the show was fifty-two pounds ten shillings plus ten pounds travelling expenses. A special edition of *Pop Go The Beatles* ('show 16') was produced by the BBC in 1988 as part of their 14-episode, Radio 1 series *The Beeb's Lost Beatles Tapes*, and featured interviews with the original producer and recording engineer on the series. (**The complete show survives.**)

End of the series, and a bit of an anticlimax in truth.

SATURDAY CLUB (1)

Playhouse Theatre, Northumberland Avenue, London, England
Recorded: 22 January 1963 (4.00–5.00pm), broadcast BBC Light Programme: 26 January 1963 (10.00am–12.00pm)
Some Other Guy, Love Me Do, Please Please Me, Keep Your Hands Off My Baby, Beautiful Dreamer

Presented by Brian Matthew and produced by Jimmy Grant, this was the first of ten appearances on the show. Evolving from *Saturday Skiffle Club*, which was first broadcast in 1958, *Saturday Club* was set up to offer listeners a unique mix of pop, jazz, country and rock, and considering it was the only chance of hearing this kind of music in the UK at the time, it soon gained popularity and became an essential promotional tool for any recording artist. Driven to London by Mal Evans, The Beatles seized this opportunity to present their new EMI single 'Please Please Me', along with their first one, 'Love Me Do'.

The show also showcased two rarities by the group, 'Keep Your Hands Off My Baby' (with John on lead vocals) and 'Beautiful Dreamer' (Paul), these recordings of which are the only known surviving by the band. The Beatles also recorded an appearance for another BBC show today, *The Talent Spot* (see entry 2), as well as giving an interview for the live BBC programme *Pop Inn*. Prior to the shows, the group went on an early-morning shopping spree in Regent Street. Paul and George bought trousers, and George also purchased a shirt. Once tapings for the two shows had wrapped, at 8.15pm, The Beatles visited Brian Epstein's room in the May Fair Hotel for a *Daily Mail* interview. With Mal once again at the wheel, they left London for Liverpool at 10pm, stopping at the Forte restaurant on the M1 motorway for dinner, which The Beatles paid for. Their journey home was disrupted when they ran into a blanket of fog, and the windscreen of their van cracked. Mal came to the rescue by breaking a hole in it to see. After stopping again for tea at a transport cafe, they arrived back in Liverpool at 5am. (**A tape of the complete show survives; however only a small excerpt esists of 'Please Please Me'. Interestingly, Brian Epstein supposedly had a part of today's session cut as a 45rpm**

acetate. **Courtesy of Percy Phillips, of Philipps Sound Recording Services, 38 Kensington, Liverpool 7, the disc contained the three, non-EMI released tracks: 'Some Other Guy', 'Beautiful Dreamer' and 'Keep Your Hands Off My Baby'.**)

First appearance on the BBC's legendary Saturday Club, notable for the inclusion of two rarities by the band, 'Keep Your Hands Off My Baby' and 'Beautiful Dreamer'.

SATURDAY CLUB (2)

Studio 3A, Broadcasting House, Portland Place, London, England
Recorded: 16 March 1963, broadcast live BBC Light Programme: 16 March 1963 (10.00am–12.00pm)
I Saw Her Standing There, Misery, Too Much Monkey Business, I'm Talkin' About You, Please Please Me, Hippy Hippy Shake

Presented by Brian Matthew and produced by Jimmy Grant and Bernie Andrews. As a consequence of John's cold and their *Friday Spectacular* (Radio Luxembourg) interview commitment, the group was forced to cancel their *Saturday Club* recording on 11 March 1963. To make amends The Beatles played today's show live. With the studio at Broadcasting House used mainly for interviews, discussions and small drama productions, extra microphones had to be drafted in at short notice. With the release of their first LP just a week away, the group chose to play three songs from it, 'I Saw Her Standing There', 'Misery' and the title track 'Please Please Me'. (**The complete show survives.**)

A last-minute live appearance.

SATURDAY CLUB (3)

Playhouse Theatre, Northumberland Avenue, London, England
Recorded: 21 May 1963 (5.30–6.30pm), broadcast BBC Light Programme: 25 May 1963 (10.00am–12.00pm)
I Saw Her Standing There, Do You Want To Know A Secret, Boys, Long Tall Sally, From Me To You, Money (That's What I Want)

Presented by Brian Matthew and produced by Jimmy Grant and Bernie Andrews. The Beatles' rise to prominence was recognised today when host Matthew introduced the group as 'our bill-toppers!' Sessions for two different BBC shows were taped on this day, both at the Playhouse Theatre – this one and *Steppin' Out* (see entry). (**The complete show survives.**)

Another pretty standard Beatles appearance.

SATURDAY CLUB (4)

Playhouse Theatre, Northumberland Avenue, London, England
Recorded: 24 June 1963 (5.30–6.30pm), broadcast BBC Light Programme: 29 June 1963 (10.00am–12.00pm)
I Got To Find My Baby, Memphis Tennessee, Money (That's What I Want), Till There Was You, From Me To You, Roll Over Beethoven

Presented by Brian Matthew and produced by Jimmy Grant and Bernie Andrews. A predominantly Chuck Berry-inspired session, with three of his songs performed, 'I Got To Find My Baby', Memphis, Tennessee' and 'Roll Over Beethoven', all of which, plus 'Money', were unreleased by The Beatles at the time of broadcast. The latter two would appear five months later in November 1963, on the group's second album *With The Beatles*, while the former two

would never be cut to disc at all by the group during their time together. (**The complete show survives.**)

A landmark appearance due to its inclusion of three Chuck Berry-inspired songs.

SATURDAY CLUB (5)

Playhouse Theatre, Northumberland Avenue, London, England
Recorded: 30 July 1963 (5.30–6.30pm), broadcast BBC Light Programme: 24 August 1963 (10.00am–12.00pm)
Long Tall Sally, She Loves You, Glad All Over, Twist And Shout, You Really Got A Hold On Me, I'll Get You

Presented by Brian Matthew and produced by Jimmy Grant and Bernie Andrews. 'Interviewing The Beatles, or attempting to interview them, was like a good-humoured battle,' Matthew recalled. 'They were always out to bring me down, but not in a malicious way. But the interesting thing was, how clearly distinguished they were, all four of them, from each other... Paul was the one who attempted to try and make some sense of what was going on, to give you the news and tell you what they were really doing; John was by far the wittiest of the quartet, and would always have gentle jibes, he'd always have a little go; George was the shy one, a bit of a dark horse; and Ringo was the one who took all the insults, all the time. He used to like reading comics. They were all so very, very different, but they so melded so magnificently.' (**The complete show survives.**)

Nice but fairly straightforward appearance.

BEATLES BEWARE – REVIEWS FROM THE MUSIC PRESS

'After reading Nigel Hunter's review of *With The Beatles*, I thought it was going to be even better than their *Please Please Me* album. So you can imagine how disappointed I was when I heard it. I have never anything so deplorable in my life.' Molly Burringer, London, *Disc*, 7 December 1963

'*With The Beatles* is definitely not the album of the year. The piano is used to such an extent that The Beatles' sound is almost unrecognisable.' A. Mattlock, Tetbury, *Disc*, 14 December 1963

'Beatlemania has gone too far. Heaven knows I liked the group and I shared the enthusiasm but the novelty has worn thin.' Alan Freeman, *Disc*, 28 December 1963

'Because of the semi-savage conduct of the audience at the show given by The Beatles at the weekend, Glasgow is likely to ban all feature Beat shows from its concert hall. City treasurer Richard Buchanan said that it took 40 policemen and 50 attendants to keep the fans under control after the show.' *Disc*, 12 October 1963

As early as December 1963, there were letters suggesting The Beatles had gone off, had it, were overdone, overblown, over the top.

'The Beatles had better watch themselves or they will be shortening their own lives in the pop world. This constant plugging of their success in the national newspapers day in and day out – how long can it go on? People must realise that if The Beatles are constantly shoved down the public's throat every day of the week, they will seal their own fate. I am a Beatles fan myself, but I am worried by this constant plugging. Watch out Beatles - or you might not be around to enjoy much more success.' Letter from David Irving, Childwall, Liverpool, *Melody Maker*, 7 December 1963

'I entirely disagree with the *Melody Maker* review of The Beatles' new LP. [*With The Beatles*, released 22 November 1963] I don't know what happens to stars when they reach the top, but the quality of their records certainly has dropped. It seems they have just gone into a recording studio and said. "Come on fellas, we've got to make another LP and it might as well be now." I am an ardent Beatles fan, but I think someone should have the courage to protest.' Miss A. Philips, Hackney, London, *Melody Maker*, 7 December 1963

SATURDAY CLUB (6)

Playhouse Theatre, Northumberland Avenue, London, England
Recorded: 7 September 1963 (1.00–4.00pm), broadcast BBC Light Programme: 5 October 1963 (10.00am–12.00pm)
I Saw Her Standing There, Memphis Tennessee, Happy Birthday Dear Saturday Club, I'll Get You, She Loves You, Lucille

Presented by Brian Matthew and produced by Jimmy Grant and Bernie Andrews. Special fifth birthday edition, hence the rendition of 'Happy Birthday' with amended lyrics. Due to its stellar line-up of stars either in the studio or in pre-taped messages – The Everly Brothers, Frank Ifield, Joe Brown and The Bruvvers, Brenda Lee, Ricky Nelson, Roy Orbison, Cliff Richard, Del Shannon, to name but a few – the *Radio Times* wasted no time in (correctly) describing the programme as 'the most spectacular bill of stars ever invited to the *Club*!'. 'She Loves You' was repeated during the 21 December 1963 edition of the programme. (**The complete show survives.**)

Nice historic appearance.

SATURDAY CLUB (7)

Playhouse Theatre, Northumberland Avenue, London, England
Recorded: 17 December 1963 (3.00–6.30pm), broadcast BBC Light Programme: 21 December 1963 (10.00am–12.00pm)
All I Want For Christmas, All My Loving, This Boy, I Want To Hold Your Hand, Till There Was You, Roll Over Beethoven, She Loves You, Crimble Medley

Presented by Brian Matthew and produced by Jimmy Grant and Bernie Andrews. A special Christmas edition. Hot on the heels of Paul's genuine, heartfelt festive goodwill gesture to the listeners, 'Crimble Medley' was a short, 29-second medley comprising of John singing brief snippets of 'Love Me Do', 'Please Please Me', 'From Me To You', 'She Loves You', 'I Want To Hold Your Hand' and 'Rudolph The Red-Nosed Reindeer'. The linking riff, played on guitar and bass, was from Duane Eddy's 1960 song 'Shazam!'. (Interestingly, The Beatles would, albeit briefly, resurrect the song on 23 January 1969, during Day Twelve of the *Get Back/Let It Be* project.) The group's rendition of 'She Loves You' was extracted from the 5 October 1963 edition of the show. (**'All My Loving' from this broadcast is missing; only Paul's intro to it survives.**)

Rather nice, humorous festive appearance.

SATURDAY CLUB (8)

Playhouse Theatre, Northumberland Avenue, London, England
Recorded: 7 January 1964 (2.30–4.00pm), broadcast BBC Light Programme: 15 February 1964 (10.00am–12.00pm)
All My Loving, Money (That's What I Want), Hippy Hippy Shake, I Want To Hold Your Hand, Roll Over Beethoven, Johnny B. Goode, I Wanna Be Your Man

Presented by Brian Matthew and produced by Jimmy Grant and Bernie Andrews. The performance of 'I Want To Hold Your Hand' in this edition was a repeat of the show 7 recording of 17 December 1963. The performance of 'Johnny B. Goode' was the group's only rendition of it for the BBC. (**The performance survives.**)

Interesting for the performance of 'Johnny B. Goode' alone.

SATURDAY CLUB (9)

Playhouse Theatre, Northumberland Avenue, London, England
Recorded: 31 March 1964 (7.00–10.30pm), broadcast BBC Light Programme: 4 April 1964 (10.00am–12.00pm)
Everybody's Trying To Be My Baby, I Call Your Name, I Got A Woman, You Can't Do That, Can't Buy Me Love, Sure To Fall (In Love With You), Long Tall Sally

Presented by Brian Matthew and produced by Jimmy Grant and Bernie Andrews. An interesting show for two reasons; today's performance of 'I Call Your Name' was the only time the group sang it for the BBC, and their rendition of 'I Got A Woman', their second for the BBC (originally show 9 of *Pop Go The Beatles*, recorded 16 July 1963), was notably different from the first due to John's double-tracked vocals, an extremely rare occurrence at the Corporation during this time.

The Beatles' fee for the show was £100. (**The performance survives.**)

Another fascinating programme, due to its inclusion of 'I Call Your Name' and 'I Got A Woman'.

SATURDAY CLUB (10)

Studio One, BBC Aeolian Hall, 135–137 New Bond Street, London, England
Recorded: 25 November 1964 (7.00–10.30pm), broadcast BBC Light Programme: 26 December 1964 (10.00am–12.00pm)
Rock And Roll Music, I'm A Loser, Everybody's Trying To Be My Baby, I Feel Fine, Kansas City/Hey-Hey-Hey-Hey!, She's A Woman

Presented by Brian Matthew and produced by Jimmy Grant and Brian Willey. Two new tracks were recorded for this show – 'Rock And Roll Music' and 'Kansas City' – while the other four were repeat performances, originally recorded for an episode of *Top Gear* (first transmitted on 26 November 1964, see entry). Selections from both

NON-SEXY BEATLES
Prophetic letter published in *Record Mirror*, 1 August 1964

'How can people suggest The Beatles get to Number One because of their sex appeal? I ask you – what is sexy about a record, a round disc of plastic? The Beatles do not do, or sing, anything sexy. The Stones are more in that category. If The Beatles recorded a song with strings and playing mandolins it would still get high in the charts, if it was a good song.' Janet Clarke, Oldham, Lancs.

programmes, music and chat, were compiled for an episode of the *Top Of The Pops* radio series in America during January 1965. The Beatles' fee for the show was £100. (**The performance survives.**)

Pity so much of today's programme was made up of repeat performances.

SIDE BY SIDE (1)

Studio One, Piccadilly Studios, 201 Piccadilly, London.
Recorded: 1 April 1963 (2.30–5.30pm), broadcast BBC Light Programme: 22 April 1963 (5.00–5.29pm)
Side By Side Theme, I Saw Her Standing There, Do You Want To Know A Secret, Baby It's You, Please Please Me, From Me To You, Misery

Presented by John Dunn and produced by Bryant Marriot. Two editions were taped this day, shows 1 and 2. The Karl Denver Trio performed the title track, with John and Paul adding their vocals to Denver's. The backing track was used for all three of The Beatles' appearances. This was actually set to be the first of seven on the show. However, after the group cancelled a recording on 4 April 1963 (see entry for *Side By Side* (3)) the remaining four appearances were abandoned. (**The show survives.**)

First appearance on the show, which featured the band mixing it with different musicians.

SIDE BY SIDE (2)

Studio One, Piccadilly Studios, 201 Piccadilly, London, England
Recorded: 1 April 1963 (6.30–10.30pm), broadcast BBC Light Programme: 13 May 1963 (5.00–5.29pm)
Side By Side Theme, From Me To You, Long Tall Sally, A Taste Of Honey, Chains, Thank You Girl, Boys

Presented by John Dunn and produced by Bryant Marriot. The performance of 'Long Tall Sally' pre-dated the official EMI version by almost a year. During the show, John took the opportunity to repeat the tale, first told to journalists in 1961, on the origin of The Beatles' name involving a vision of a man on a flaming pie. (**The complete show survives, aside from 'From Me To You', for which only the spoken intro exists.**)

Pleasant, highly enjoyable appearance by the band.

SIDE BY SIDE (3)

Paris Studio, Lower Regent Street, London, England
Recorded: 4 April 1963 (11.00am–2.00pm), broadcast BBC Light Programme: 24 June 1963 (5.00–5.29pm)
Side By Side Theme, Too Much Monkey Business, Love Me Do, Boys, I'll Be On My Way, From Me To You

Presented by John Dunn and produced by Bryant Marriott. The Beatles performed the Lennon/McCartney track 'I'll Be On My Way' for the only time today. It had already been given to Billy J. Kramer, who taped it for EMI on the same day as this Beatles session. By the time this edition of *Side By Side* had been broadcast, Kramer had already reached No. 2 in the charts with the song, due to its appearance on the B-side of another Lennon/McCartney composition 'Do You Want To Know A Secret'. (The Beatles' version of 'I'll Be On My Way' was released officially in November 1994 on the *Live At The BBC* compilation. However, the first release of it, albeit in an inferior form, was on the US *Soldier Of Love* bootleg album during the summer of 1974.)

In order for the group to travel to Stowe for a concert on 4 April 1963 (see entry in the *Places* section), a fourth *Side By Side* appearance (pencilled in for taping that day between 2.00–6.00pm) was cancelled ahead of time. This clearly angered the BBC's Light Entertainment booking manager, Miss M.J. Quinault who, in a letter sent on 10 July 1963 to the show's producer, Bryant Marriott, promptly announced she was not booking the group again for this series. (The Beatles had been pencilled in to appear on the *Side By Side* shows set to be aired on 15 July 1963, 19 August 1963 and 16 September 1963.)

Following the session, Karl Denver Trio guitarist Kevin Neill shot an 8mm, silent colour film of The Beatles and Neil Aspinall, on Regent Street preparing to leave. The footage would be used in Apple's promotional film for the 20 March 1995 EP *Baby It's You*, and since then it has been officially released on the bonus disc of the Beatles' 1+ DVD/Blu-ray, released on 6 November 2015. Dezo Hoffmann and his assistant, David Magnus, were also on hand to shoot some images outside the Paris Studio, a couple of which (with some major, cosmetic alterations) later appeared on Apple's November 1994 *Live At The BBC* album cover. Following the BBC session, and prior to travelling to Stowe, the group stopped by Cecil Gee's menswear clothing store at 39 Shaftesbury Avenue, where Hoffmann snapped them scanning the wares. (**Unheard in 52 years, 'Love Me Do' from this broadcast has recently been unearthed and features the group's only cold ending performance of the song, rather than the traditional fade-out versions heard on the official EMI studio recordings.**)

Great show, notable for the extremely rare renditions of 'Love Me Do' and 'I'll Be On My Way'.

STEPPIN' OUT

Playhouse Theatre, Northumberland Avenue, London, England
Recorded: 21 May 1963 (10.00-11.15pm), broadcast BBC Light Programme: 3 June 1963 (10.31-11.30am)
Please Please Me, I Saw Her Standing There, Roll Over Beethoven, Thank You Girl, From Me To You, Twist And Shout

Presented by Diz Disley and produced by Terry Henebery. Two sessions for two different BBC radio shows were taped on this day, both at the Playhouse Theatre – this one and their third appearance on *Saturday Club*. This was The Beatles' first BBC performance of Chuck Berry's 'Roll Over Beethoven' and pre-dated its official release on the group's second album, *With The Beatles*, by roughly six months. (**Only 'Please Please Me' and 'I Saw Her Standing There' survive from this show.**)

Interesting for the early, pre-release rendition of 'Roll Over Beethoven'.

SWINGING SOUND '63

Royal Albert Hall, Kensington Gore, London, England
Recorded: 18 April 1963, broadcast live BBC Light Programme: 18 April 1963 (9.10-10.15pm)
Twist And Shout, From Me To You (Please Please Me and Misery from their first set were not recorded or transmitted)

Presented by George Melly and Rolf Harris, and produced by Terry Henebery and Ron Belchier. Separated by an interval, the *Swinging Sound '63* show took place in two parts, with The Beatles taking the stage twice, at 8.40pm and again at 10pm, introduced both times by jazz legend George Melly. The group performed two songs in their first set, 'Please Please Me' and 'Misery', neither of which were taped or broadcast by the

BBC. In the second set, transmitted live 9.10–10.15pm, they played 'Twist And Shout' and 'From Me To You'. The show's finale featured the group alongside the other acts on the bill – Del Shannon, The Springfields, Kenny Lynch and Rolf Harris – in an instrumental version of 'Mack The Knife', a song made famous by American singer Bobby Darin in 1959.

The Beatles invited the Rolling Stones to the event, but in the end only Brian Jones, Mick Jagger, Keith Richards and their manager Giorgio Gomelsky took up the offer. At the end of the evening, Brian and Giorgio helped Neil Aspinall and Mal Evans carry out The Beatles' equipment. The girls outside, seeing Brian's long hair and thinking he was one of the stars of the show, started to grab at him shouting, 'Can I have an autograph?! Can I have an autograph?!' Brian replied, 'But I'm not a Beatle!'

Radio Times reporter Tony Aspler was asked to cover the concert for the magazine, but feeling inexperienced in such events he decided to invite along someone better suited for the role – teenage actress, and occasional panellist on the popular Saturday night BBC TV pop show *Juke Box Jury*, Jane Asher. She agreed, passing on her comments to Aspler as she listened to the performances. Asher was immediately impressed by The Beatles and even posed for a couple of *Radio Times* pictures of her screaming for them. Naturally she wanted to meet the band, and during the interval she and Aspler went down into the dressing room to say hello. Ringo immediately said, 'Would you like to go to a party?' Asher said she would and asked Aspler to join her, but because he had to be up for work early the next morning he declined the offer. After the show, The Beatles, along with Asher and Shane Fenton (later to become famous in the seventies as glam-rock singer Alvin Stardust), headed to the Chelsea flat of the *Disc/New*

Musical Express music journalist Chris Hutchins, where Paul and Jane ended up in a bedroom together doing nothing but talking and getting to know each other. They began dating, and became engaged in December 1967 but separated six months later. (**Both tracks from the broadcasted *Swinging Sound '63* show survives.**)

Nice 1963 live appearance. Enjoyable.

TALENT SPOT, THE (1)

Paris Studio, Lower Regent Street, London, England
Recorded: 27 November 1962 (7.00–8.00pm), broadcast BBC Light Programme: 4 December 1962 (5.00–5.29pm)
Love Me Do, PS I Love You, Twist And Shout

Presented by Gary Marshal and produced by Brian Willey. The Beatles' first radio session in London, where they performed 'Twist And Shout' for the initial time on BBC Radio. Interestingly, the rendition today pre-dated its commercial release on the album *Please Please Me* by four months. The group's fee for the show was thirty-seven pounds eighteen shillings. (**No copy is thought to exist.**)

Early appearance, historic but missing. Cultural vandalism.

TALENT SPOT, THE (2)

Paris Studio, Lower Regent Street, London, England
Recorded: 22 January 1963 (8.45–9.30pm), broadcast BBC Light Programme: 29 January 1963 (5.00–5.29pm)
Please Please Me, Ask Me Why, Some Other Guy

Presented by Gary Marshal and produced by Brian Willey. Two BBC radio sessions in one day – this one and their debut appearance on *Saturday Club*. In order to promote their latest single 'Please Please Me', The Beatles also gave an interview today for the live BBC programme *Pop Inn*. See *Saturday Club* (1) entry for more about this day. (**Only 'Ask Me Why' survives from this session.**)

Nice but fairly average appearance.

TEENAGERS' TURN – HERE WE GO (1)

Playhouse Theatre, St John's Road, Hulme, Manchester, England
Recorded: 7 March 1962 (8.00–8.45pm), broadcast BBC Light Programme: 8 March 1962 (5.00–5.29pm)
Dream Baby (How Long Must I Dream?), Memphis Tennessee, Please Mister Postman (Hello Little Girl was taped but not transmitted)

Presented by Ray Peters and produced by Peter Pilbeam. With Pete Best on drums, this was The Beatles' historic BBC radio debut. It came as a result of the group's successful 12 February 1962 audition for producer Pilbeam requesting a try-out for the group. Their performance that day, which took place at BBC Broadcasting House, Piccadilly Gardens, Manchester, consisted of two Lennon/McCartney compositions, 'Hello Little Girl' (lead vocal, John) and 'Like Dreamers Do' (Paul), plus covers of 'Till There Was You' (Paul) and 'Memphis, Tennessee' (John). Only the latter would be played again for this first broadcast. Pilbeam voted 'no' on Paul's performance that day, but voted 'yes' on John's. His overall assessment was, 'An unusual group, not as "Rocky" as most, more C&W with a tendency to play music.' But thankfully for the band, his ultimate answer was 'yes'. A booking for The Beatles to record an appearance on the BBC Light Programme show *Teenagers' Turn – Here*

We Go on 7 March 1962 was swiftly arranged, a contract for which was issued eight days later on 20 February 1962.

In front of a live studio audience, and wearing their smart Beno Dorn suits for the first time, obtained from a tailor in Grange Road West, Birkenhead, they performed the numbers 'Dream Baby (How Long Must I Dream?)' (Paul), 'Memphis, Tennessee' (John) and 'Please Mister Postman' (John), all of which were covers of US hits. A fourth song, 'Hello, Little Girl' was also cut to tape, but it failed to make the broadcast. The Beatles were paid twenty-six pounds eighteen shillings for their appearance, and a further two pounds eighteen shillings to cover the costs of their train tickets. Also see entries for *Here We Go*. (**The three-track performance survives.**)

Beatles landmark. First BBC radio appearance, with Pete Best on drums and featuring a rare performance of 'Dream Baby'.

TEENAGERS' TURN – HERE WE GO (2)

Playhouse Theatre, St John's Road, Hulme, Manchester, England
Recorded: 11 June 1962 (8.45-9.30pm), broadcast BBC Light Programme: 15 June 1962 (5.00-5.29pm)
Ask Me Why, Bésame Mucho, A Picture Of You
Presented by Ray Peters and produced by Peter Pilbeam. Now boasting a Parlophone record contract, The Beatles performed for a second time on the show. The recording is the last-known to feature Pete Best. Also of note here, 'A Picture of You', a recent No. 2 hit by Joe Brown and The Bruvvers, was the first to feature George on lead vocals at the BBC. Equally significant, the performance of 'Ask Me Why' marked the initial time that a Lennon/McCartney compos-

ition was aired on the radio. Fans in the audience comprised mainly members of The Beatles Fan Club, who had been ferried in on a coach especially for the occasion. Photos of the session were taken by Paul's brother Mike. The Beatles' fee for the show was twenty-six pounds eighteen shillings (plus expenses). (**An inferior copy of the show survives.**)

Last radio appearance of The Beatles with Pete Best in the line-up. Historic.

TOP GEAR (1)

Studio S2, Broadcasting House, Portland Place, London, England
Recorded: 14 July 1964 (7.00-11.00pm), broadcast BBC Light Programme: 16 July 1964 (10.00-11.55pm)
Long Tall Sally, Things We Said Today, A Hard Day's Night (the Abbey Road recording was dubbed onto the middle eight of the performance), And I Love Her, I Should Have Known Better (Abbey Road recording), If I Fell, You Can't Do That

Presented by Brian Matthew and produced by Bernie Andrew. The Beatles were the headliners on this first edition of a new weekly, late-night Light Programme music show. (In honour of the host, the working title of the series was *The Brian Matthew Show*.) Of note here, this was the only occasion on which the group performed a live version of 'And I Love Her' outside the confines of EMI's Abbey Road Studios. The Lennon/McCartney composition never once made it into their stage repertoire, and despite its popularity, the group never performed it again during their other numerous radio and television appearances. Another oddity here was the inclusion of 'I Should Have Known Better'. The Beatles did not sing the song during this session, but the EMI/

Abbey Road studio recording was played as if it had been. Further dubbing was also required on another track. Due to George's difficulty in playing the guitar break in 'A Hard Day's Night', the EMI studio recording of that section was played instead. The Beatles' fee for the show was £100. Prior to the session, Paul alone taped a 13-minute interview with Michael Smee for the BBC's General Overseas Service programme *Highlight*. An extract lasting a little under six minutes was first broadcast on 18 July 1964. (**The complete show performance survives.**)

Unique performances of 'And I Love Her' and 'A Hard Day's Night', and the odd inclusion of 'I Should Have Known Better'.

TOP GEAR (2)

Playhouse Theatre, Northumberland Avenue, London, England
Recorded: 17 November 1964 (7.30–11.30pm), broadcast

BBC Light Programme: 26 November 1964 (10.00am–12.00pm)
I'm A Loser, Honey Don't, She's A Woman, Everybody's Trying To Be My Baby, I'll Follow The Sun, I Feel Fine

Presented by Brian Matthew and produced by Bernie Andrews. Essentially an appearance to promote the group's new album *Beatles For Sale*, and single 'I Feel Fine'/'She's A Woman'. Ringo was on lead vocals for 'Honey Don't' instead of John, who had sung it during the previous two occasions (*Pop Go The Beatles* (12), recorded 1 August 1963; *From Us To You* (3), recorded 1 May 1964). Note: four of the recordings today; 'I'm A Loser', 'Everybody's Trying To Be My Baby', 'I Feel Fine' and 'She's A Woman' would be repeated during the 26 December 1964 edition of *Saturday Club* (see entry). 'I'll Follow The Sun' from this session would be released on the *Baby It's You* EP on 20 March 1995. The Beatles' fee for the show was £100. (**The complete show survives.**)

Interesting late 1964 session by the band.

BEATLES ON TV

During their lifetime as a band, The Beatles were seen playing and singing on around 80 television broadcasts, featuring performances recorded between 22 August 1962 and 30 July 1968 (there were other appearances, interviews and such like, but here we are only interested in performances). In addition, they also appeared in a number of especially shot promo films and videos that were then shown on TV. Here is an alphabetical list of them, detailing the show/item's title, production company/television station, studio/location used, recording/broadcast/release dates and the songs performed. (All mimed to pre-existing recordings unless where noted.)

AROUND THE BEATLES
(ASSOCIATED REDIFFUSION FOR ITV)

Wembley Studios, 128 Wembley Park Drive, Middlesex, London, England
Recorded: 28 April 1964, broadcast UK on ITV Network: 6 May 1964
Concert sequence: Twist And Shout (short version), Roll Over Beethoven, I Wanna Be Your Man, Long Tall Sally, Love Me Do/Please Please Me/From Me To You/She Loves You/I Want To Hold Your Hand (performed as medley), Can't Buy Me Love, Shout! (Mimed to audio, which had been taped at the IBC Studios, 35 Portland Place, London, on 19 April 1964. The song Boys was also taped during the session but failed to make the final edit.)

Shot in the form of 'theatre in the round', with the 500-strong, studio audience either up on staging or on the studio floor encompassing the stage, *Around The Beatles* was a 51-minute, b&w special produced for ITV by Associated Rediffusion and the *Oh Boy!* television show maker Jack Good. Besides appearing in their own concert sequence (as listed above), The Beatles also returned to perform their own rather unique take on a scene

from William Shakespeare's *A Midsummer Night's Dream* (Act V, Scene 1). In this seven-minute spoof, where they were heckled throughout by a small section of the crowd, John was cast in the role of the fairest maiden, Thisbe; Paul the handsomest youth, Pyramus; George was Moonshine; Ringo the grisly lion. (In the play Pyramus and Thisbe were a pair of ill-fated lovers.) Joining the group on the show were the upcoming singers and performers, Millie, Long John Baldry, The Vernons Girls, P.J. Proby, Cilla Black and the group Sounds Incorporated. The visiting American DJ, Murray the K, was also on the programme, but due to his misguided claim of being the 'Fifth Beatle', The Beatles would end up despising him. Despite that, Paul and Ringo would later say this was their favourite Beatles television appearance.

The footage of 'Can't Buy Me Love' was officially released on the first disc of the *Beatles 1/Beatles 1+* DVD/Blu-ray, on 6 November 2015. **(The 16mm b&w film footage of the complete show survives. On 29 April 1985, featuring a misleading title of *The Beatles Live – Ready Steady Go Special Edition (1964)*, a re-edited version of**

Back in April 1964, the Beatles felt they had to do silly costume changes; here they are in costume for a Shakespeare sketch in the TV show *Around the Beatles.*

© Roger Jackson / Stringer

the group's performance from this show was released on VHS in the UK by Dave Clark International (DC1) under licence to EMI Records Ltd/Picture Music International (PMI).)

With the concert and a rarity of the group in a Shakespeare-spoof, this was a truly unique studio appearance by The Beatles.

Footnote: The American singer Proby became a star because of this show. His appearance led to him recording a new arrangement of the Little/Oppenheim/Schuster ballad, 'Hold Me', which P.J. turned into an uptempo rocker. Released by Decca just nine days after *Around The Beatles* was broadcast, the single would reach No. 3 in the UK charts.

BABY IT'S YOU
(PROMOTIONAL FILM CLIP/APPLE)

Lower Regent Street, London, England
Filmed: 4 April 1963

On 4 April 1963, The Beatles made their third appearance on the BBC Light Programme radio show *Side By Side* (see entry in *Radio* section), recorded at the Paris Theatre, Lower Regent Street, London. After their performance, the group, along with Neil Aspinall, were filmed by Kevin Neill (guitarist with the Karl Denver Trio) leaving the theatre, and also outside on the street. The resulting footage (8mm, silent, colour) was much later used in Apple's promotional film for the 20 March 1995 EP *Baby It's You*, and since then has been officially released on the bonus disc of the *Beatles 1+* DVD/Blu-ray, on 6 November 2015. (**The colour footage survives.**)

Great clips, fabulous compilation.

BALLAD OF JOHN AND YOKO, THE
(PROMOTIONAL FILM CLIP/APPLE FILMS)

Various locations, Amsterdam, Paris, UK, Vienna
Filmed: March 1969, broadcast: UK on BBC1 *Top Of The Pops*, 5 June 1969; West Germany on Erstes Deutsches Fernsehen/ARD *Beat Club*, 2 August 1969; America on ABC TV *Music Scene*, 22 September 1969

Serving more as a documentary of events surrounding John's marriage to Yoko in Gibraltar on 20 March 1969, and their subsequent honeymoon in Amsterdam, this 16mm colour promotional clip was interrupted periodically by a full-screen exclamation at the point when John sang the word 'Christ!' Other attempts to match images with the lyrics were made: John and Yoko pictured sitting near the river ('Honeymooning down by the Seine') and personal assistant Peter Brown picking up the phone, calling to say, 'you can make it okay', for instance. Footage shot during the pair's first 'bed-in', at the Amsterdam Hilton Hotel, between 25 and 31 March 1969, as well as unused scenes from the first day's shooting of The Beatles' *Get Back/Let It Be* project (2 January 1969 – see entry in *Movies* section), were also included. The film premiered in the UK (in monochrome) on BBC1's *Top Of The Pops* during the edition aired on 5 June 1969. The top German monthly, Erstes Deutsches Fernsehen (First German Television)/ARD pop programme *Beat Club* broadcast it (again b&w) as part of the show screened on 2 August 1969. The first US TV airing took place on 22 September 1969 during the pilot edition of ABC TV's new, weekly series *Music Scene*. The first UK TV colour screening of the film did not come until 31 March 1995, when it was aired (unlawfully) on the late-night Channel 4 music series *The White Room*. John's decision to marry Yoko was quite unexpected; coming just eight days after Paul had married Linda Eastman. The

colour version of the film was officially released on the first disc of the *Beatles 1/Beatles 1+* DVD/Blu-ray, on 6 November 2015.

(**Master film footage, as well as some out-takes still survives in Yoko Ono's archives.**)

Great film, with interesting footage of the Lennons as well as rare, alternate, albeit brief footage from The Beatles' *Get Back/Let It Be* project.

BEATLES AT SHEA STADIUM, THE
(SULLIVAN PRODUCTIONS, INC./NEMS ENTERPRISES LTD./SUBAFILMS LTD. – INCORPORATED ON 7 JANUARY 1964, THE LATTER WAS A CO-OWNED, MOTION PICTURE PRODUCTION AND DISTRIBUTION COMPANY SET UP BY BRIAN EPSTEIN AND THE BEATLES)

William A. Shea Municipal Stadium, Queens, Flushing Meadows, Corona Park, New York, USA

Recorded: 15 August 1965, broadcast: UK on BBC1 1 March 1966 (b&w); West Germany on ZDF, 2 August 1966 (b&w); America on ABC, 10 January 1967 (colour)

Twist and Shout (partial), I Feel Fine, Dizzy Miss Lizzy, Ticket To Ride, Can't Buy Me Love, Baby's In Black, Act Naturally, A Hard Day's Night, Help!, I'm Down (Live, but with many studio overdubs for the benefit of the television documentary; Note: Two songs, She's A Woman and Everybody's Trying To Be My Baby, were also filmed but failed to make the final cut of the 48-minute programme)

Shea Stadium had been the home of the New York Mets baseball team for just 16 months when The Beatles gave their historic, first performance there on 15 August 1965, which was part of their third US visit. Using new, 100-watt amplifiers, especially designed by Vox for the tour, their entire set (using 12 cameras) was filmed. However, before transmission could take place, the group was compelled to overdub musical parts onto several sections of the soundtrack. The general consensus was that, according to the group, and recording producer George Martin, the Shea soundtrack was chiefly lacking bass in various places, and evidently not as predominant as on their records. So, at a session at the CTS Studios, in Kensington Gardens Square, London, on 5 January 1966, bass was added to the tracks 'I'm Down' (as well as a new organ part), 'Dizzy Miss Lizzy', 'Can't Buy Me Love' and 'Baby's In Black'. 'I Feel Fine' and 'Help!' were re-recorded completely, as was 'Ticket To Ride', but this remained chiefly unused, with only minor parts making it on to the documentary's soundtrack. With 'Twist And Shout' and 'Act Naturally', it was another matter entirely. With time running out at this January 1966 session, for the former, the unreleased 30 August 1965, Hollywood Bowl, audio of the song, recorded by the legendary producer Bob Fine, had to be mixed into the Shea recording and, once in place, John double-tracked his live vocal. (Selected segments of that Hollywood Bowl audio were also used comprehensively during post-production on the Shea Stadium documentary, most notably the screaming fans, dubbed over the top of the two, new London recordings.) For the latter track, due to the inadequacy of the original Shea recording, specifically Ringo's lead vocal, the 17 June 1965 EMI Abbey Road recording of the song was simply dubbed over the footage.

Joining The Beatles on the bill at Shea that night were Brenda Holloway and The King Curtis Band, Cannibal and The Headhunters, Sounds Incorporated and The Young Rascals. The group would return to Shea one more time, on 23 August 1966. In 1965, they could have sold out the ballpark ten times over, but one year later, they couldn't sell it out once. So, unlike the previous year, concert posters were created to market the event and help push the flagging ticket sales.

Broadcasts of the Shea Stadium show have been few and far between since the original 1966/1967 screenings (see above). Following a repeat screening on BBC1 on 27 August 1966, its last in the UK came on 23 December 1979, during BBC2's *The Beatles At Christmas* season. A rare American TV airing took place when several PBS (Public Broadcasting Stations) screened it during the evening of 22 August 1983. A newly edited clip, featuring footage from the 1965 show and set to 'Eight Days a Week', was officially released on the first disc of the *Beatles 1/Beatles 1+* DVD/Blu-ray, on 6 November 2015. (For more on the 1965 concert itself, see listing in the *Places* section.) **(The original 35mm colour footage survives. Of note here, on 5 November 1965, Brian Epstein received an early, 54-minute print of the Shea Stadium film, which at this point contained both 'She's A Woman' and 'Everybody's Trying To Be My Baby'. However, by the time the documentary had been re-edited – down to 48 minutes – and re-dubbed, both tracks had been removed. The Beatles company, Apple Corps, supposedly does not have these out-takes.)**

Promoted by the music producer Sid Bernstein, this 1965 outdoor show was a landmark in several ways. A new world record for a pop concert was set when more than 55,000 fans attended the event, and The Beatles themselves also set a new benchmark with their $160,000 share of the $304,000 gross receipts for the show.

Footnote: On 18 July 2008, Paul joined singer Billy Joel to play the last concert at the Shea Stadium venue before it was closed and partially demolished. The show was documented in the movie *Last Play At Shea*. He returned to perform again, one year later, on 17 July 2009 when the newly renovated stadium, now called Citi Field, reopened once more for business.)

BEATLES COME TO TOWN, THE
(PATHÉ NEWS)

ABC Ardwick, Stockport Road, Manchester, Lancashire, England
Recorded 20 November 1963, released to UK cinemas for one week only: 22 December 1963; US premiere: Fargo, North Dakota, 22 April 1964
She Loves You, Twist And Shout (Live)

Produced with the prerequisite that the group received an undisclosed share in its profits, *The Beatles Come To Town* was a 35mm, Techniscope Technicolor, mini-documentary filmed by British Pathé News for their Pathé Pictorial series. Released to many UK cinemas on 22 December 1963, it was sandwiched in between some of the most popular 'A' and 'B' movies of the day. The six-minute short included scenes of highly excited fans gathered outside the venue, alongside footage of the group arriving, posing for the cameras with a giant panda toy and backstage preparing for the concert. Two live tracks from the group's first show that evening, 'She Loves You' and 'Twist And Shout', were included.

An attendee in the audience of 2,500 that night was Derek Taylor, the English journalist, writer and publicist. It was the second time he had seen the group perform. (The first being the Odeon Cinema, Manchester on 30 May earlier that year.) Once more suitably impressed, he went backstage after the concert to meet the band, but only managed to encounter George.

In April 1965, *The Beatles Come To Town* feature was added to the full-length, Pathé colour movie *Pop Gear* (aka *Go Go Mania)*, which also featured many of the acts likewise managed by Beatles manager Brian Epstein. The 70-minute special, fundamentally a collection of studio-based, lip-synched performances by some of the top British musical acts of the day, including singers Matt Monro and Billie Davis, and groups The Animals, Herman's Hermits, The Honeycombs, The Spencer Davis Group, Sounds Incorporated, The Nashville Teens, The Fourmost, Tommy Quickly, The Four Pennies, Peter and Gordon, Billy J. Kramer with The Dakotas. **(The colour footage, as well as some out-takes featuring The Beatles backstage, playing with the panda, still survives.)**

Extremely nice colour footage of The Beatles; both backstage and in performance.

BEATLES IN NEDERLAND, THE
(VARA TV HOLLAND)

Cafe-Restaurant, Treslong, Hillegom, Vosselaan 15, Netherlands
Recorded: 5 June 1964, broadcast Netherlands on Nederland 1: 8 June 1964
She Loves You, All My Loving, Twist And Shout, Roll Over Beethoven, Long Tall Sally, Can't Buy Me Love (Occasional live vocals over pre-taped tracks)

The group kicked off their 1964 world tour in Holland with session drummer Jimmie Nicol standing in for a hospitalised Ringo. The Beatles began their appearance, for Dutch public broadcaster VARA, by answering questions from the 150-strong audience. With John introducing himself as 'John Leopard', they were seen seated in the bar with show host Berend Boudewijn, who translated their answers and conveyed them to co-presenter Herman Stok, seated in the adjacent studio with the spectators. Questioning over, the group took their positions and set about miming to six tracks along to their released EMI record-

ings. However, due to the microphones being left on viewers could occasionally and inadvertently hear the group's live vocal performances as well. Another blip in the proceedings came when, from 'Long Tall Sally' onwards, members of the predominantly male audience managed to step onto the stage and gyrate alongside John, Paul and George. The numbers soon swelled and by the time of the final number, 'Can't Buy Me Love', the group was completely swarmed. The ever-reliable roadies and confidantes, Mal Evans, Neil Aspinall and Derek Taylor, tried in vain to clear the stage, but eventually, with no studio security to hand, the three Beatles conceded and were forced to flee, leaving both the music and Jimmie Nicol to carry on playing without them. ZDF in West Germany aired the programme one month later, on 3 July 1964, under the revised banner *Die Beatles – Vorsicht Ansteckend*. **(The b&w footage survives.)**

Unique television appearance with Nicol and not Starr. Worthwhile watching for that alone.

BEATLES RECITAL FROM NIPPON BUDOKAN, TOKYO, THE (2)
(BEATLES JAPAN CONCERT) (NTV – NIPPON TELEVISION NETWORK CORPORATION – JAPAN)

Nippon Budokan Hall (Martial Arts Hall), Tokyo, Japan
Recorded: 1 July 1966, broadcast Japan on NTV Channel 4: 1 July 1966
Rock And Roll Music, She's A Woman, If I Needed Someone, Day Tripper, I Wanna Be Your Man, Baby's In Black, I Feel Fine, Yesterday, Nowhere Man, Paperback Writer, I'm Down (Live)

The second show to be videotaped in Japan (again in colour by NTV) was the afternoon show on 1 July 1966 and featured the same set-list as the group's previous night's concert. Once more taking to the stage at 7.35pm, The Beatles this time wore matching, light-grey, pinstriped jackets with black trousers. It was far more satisfactory than their earlier effort (see entry for *Tokyo Concert*). NTV transmitted the show for the first time later that evening in a Channel 4 programme entitled *The Beatles Recital From Nippon Budokan, Tokyo*. Also known as *Beatles Japan Concert*, the show contained some b&w footage of the group's arrival in the country, their press conference, and miscellaneous shots of the group walking in the corridor at their hotel as well as clips of the Japanese support acts at the concerts (taped on 30 June). **(The original, colour, videotape footage survives.)**

Superb pristine colour, VT footage of The Fabs live, just seven weeks prior to their on-stage retirement.

BEATLES SING FOR SHELL, THE
(CHANNEL NINE, AUSTRALIA)

Festival Hall, Melbourne, Australia
Recorded: 17 June 1964, broadcast Australia on Channel Nine: 1 July 1964
You Can't Do That, All My Loving, She Loves You, Can't Buy Me Love, Twist And Shout, Long Tall Sally (Live)

The group performed six concerts in Melbourne during this tour, the last of which (the 8pm show) was videotaped and aired as the b&w television special *The Beatles Sing For Shell*, because of the Australian oil subsidiary that had sponsored the event. By the time of it, now fully recovered from his bout of tonsillitis, Ringo was back on his drum stool. Suitably impressed by the footage Channel Nine captured that night, Brian Epstein agreed to let 20 minutes from the show be used in the TV special, instead of the previously agreed 12. Before their last song, 'Long Tall Sally', Paul said

to the audience, 'It's very nice for all of us to have back with us now, Ringo!' At which point, Starr rose to his feet and raised his fist and drumsticks to the screaming crowd. At the conclusion of 'Long Tall Sally', a man sporting a moptop haircut rushed onto the stage to shake John's hand. While the police escorted the fan off, Lennon laughed and kept on playing. The Beatles' full set list that evening was: I Saw Her Standing There, You Can't Do That, All My Loving, She Loves You, Till There Was You, Roll Over Beethoven, Can't Buy Me Love, This Boy, Long Tall Sally. The group reappeared on stage after their closing number, but only to take a bow. **(The b&w videotape footage survives, as do very brief clips of 'Till There Was You' and 'Roll Over Beethoven'. 'This Boy' was not taped at all.)**

Excellent, exciting, crystal-clear b&w footage of the group performing to their worshippers on the other side of the globe.

BIG BEAT '64 (1)
(AKA NEW MUSICAL EXPRESS 1963–64 ANNUAL POLL-WINNERS' ALL-STAR CONCERT) (ABC FOR ITV)

The Empire Pool, Wembley, Middlesex, London, England
Recorded: 26 April 1964, broadcast UK on ITV Network in two parts as Big Beat '64: 3 and 10 May 1964 (in which The Beatles' segment was included)
She Loves You, You Can't Do That, Twist And Shout, Long Tall Sally, Can't Buy Me Love (Live)

Held in front of 10,000 screaming fans, the annual, star-studded, *New Musical Express 1963–64 Annual Poll-Winners' All-Star Concert* once more took place at the Empire Pool, Wembley and The Beatles were, naturally, top of the bill. (This live appearance was their second at the event. However, this 1964 show was the first to be filmed and broadcast.) As well as receiving an award for 'World Vocal Group' from *The Saint* TV star, Roger Moore they performed five live numbers (listed above). Due to the filming of *A Hard Day's Night*, it was their first show in two months and the first time that they had ever sung 'You Can't Do That' live, and it showed; John's scream, anticipating George's guitar solo, came a verse too early and when the instrumental break did come, with Paul seemingly forgetting how the song went, George stood *alone* at the microphone, trying to recreate the backing vocals on his own. Joining them today were fellow poll-winners, and contemporary chart rivals, the Rolling Stones, Cliff Richard, The Shadows, The Merseybeats, The Hollies, Manfred Mann, Kathy Kirby, The Swinging Blue Jeans, Freddie and The Dreamers, Brian Poole and The Tremeloes, Joe Brown and The Bruvvers, Gerry and The Pacemakers and Billy J. Kramer and The Dakotas, among others. The American DJ Murray the K introduced The Beatles. (**The b&w, 16mm footage survives.**)

A nice slice of The Fabs in live action at the height of UK Beatlemania.

BIG NIGHT OUT (1)
(ABC – ASSOCIATED BRITISH CORPORATION – FOR ITV)

Didsbury Studio Centre, Manchester, England
Recorded: 1 September 1963, broadcast UK on ITV Network: 7 September 1963
From Me To You, She Loves You, Twist And Shout, I Saw Her Standing There (incomplete)

Hosted by the English double act, the comedic brothers Mike and Bernie Winters, this was The Beatles' debut appearance on ABC TV's weekly, top-rated, fast-moving, all-star variety show. Filmed in front of a 600-strong studio audience, the group mimed four numbers in a mock-up of Liverpool's famous Cavern club. Joining them on the 25-minute show were the comedian Billy Dainty, singer/actress Patsy Ann Noble and dancer Lionel Blair, who, just seven months later, would cameo in the group's first movie, *A Hard Day's Night*. (**The original, 16mm b&w footage survives.**)

Great early TV appearance, which thankfully survives.

BIG NIGHT OUT (2)
(ABC FOR ITV)

Teddington Studio Centre, Teddington Lock, Broom Road, England Recorded: 23 February 1964, broadcast UK on ITV Network: 29 February 1964
All My Loving, I Wanna Be Your Man, Till There Was You, Please Mr Postman, I Want To Hold Your Hand (Money (That's What I Want) was also performed but was edited out prior to transmission.)

Fresh from their first, highly successful trip to the States, the group recorded their second guest spot on Mike and Bernie Winters' *Big Night Out*. They appeared in various comedy sketches with the brothers, including a scene where they arrived at customs armed with suitcases crammed full of money, and one where the kitchen they were standing in, making a cup of tea, suddenly blew up. The Beatles mimed six recent recordings in the show, one of which failed to make the final edit (as listed above). Unique colour photographs of the rehearsals that afternoon were taken by the show's sound engineer. *Big Night Out* ceased broadcasting on 10 April 1965. (**The original, 16mm b&w broadcast copy survives.**)

Great early television show, with some fine, rather corny, comedy sketches.

BLACKPOOL NIGHT OUT (1)
(ABC FOR ITV)

ABC Theatre, 130–140 Church Street, Blackpool, England
Recorded: 19 July 1964, broadcast UK on ITV Network: 19 July 1964
A Hard Day's Night, Things We Said Today, You Can't Do That, If I Fell (with false start), Long Tall Sally (Live)

The group's debut on the b&w, star-studded, live summer spin-off of Mike and Bernie Winters' ITV networked *Big Night Out* show (see entries). Besides performing five live numbers, the group also appeared in the obligatory comedy sketch with the brothers, this time in an operating theatre with Ringo as the patient. **(The original 16mm film of the show is missing from the archives; however a short, silent ITN newsreel, taken during rehearsals of the above sketch, does survive.)**

Another, pretty much standard television appearance, but one we will sadly never see again.

BLACKPOOL NIGHT OUT (2)
(ABC FOR ITV)

ABC Theatre, 130–140 Church Street, Blackpool, England
Recorded: 1 August 1965, broadcast UK on ITV Network: 1 August 1965
I Feel Fine, I'm Down, Act Naturally, Ticket To Ride, Yesterday (Paul solo), Help! (Live)

Sandwiched in between their European and American tours, The Beatles made their second (and final) appearance on ABC television's *Blackpool Night Out*, once more hosted by Mike and

Bernie Winters, they sang six songs live. Little did the viewers realise that this performance was actually a dress rehearsal for the group's next appearance on *The Ed Sullivan Show* in just 13 days' time (see entry). The group also took part in a comedy sketch at the start of the show, where they pretended to be asleep while Mike and Bernie talked about the anticipation in the town because of the show. They then counted down to the opening, at which The Beatles woke up singing, 'Oh, I do like to be beside the seaside.' Ringo was also seen in another sketch, alone this time, chatting to Mike, and making another introduction to the programme. Also noteworthy was George's intro to Paul's rendition of 'Yesterday'. 'We'd like to do something now which we've never ever done before,' he said, 'and it's a track off our new LP, and this song's called "Yesterday", and so, for Paul McCartney of Liverpool, opportunity knocks.' This was a reference to the weekly, ITV up-and-coming talent show, hosted by Canadian Hughie Green. **(The original b&w tele-recording of their performance survives, but alas their comedy sketches do not)**

Great live TV appearance, with The Fabs looking decidedly cool.

CHISWICK HOUSE
(PROMOTIONAL FILM CLIPS FOR 'PAPERBACK WRITER', 'RAIN'/NEMS)

Burlington Lane, Chiswick, west London Borough of Hounslow, England
Filmed: 20 May 1966, broadcast UK on BBC1 *Top Of The Pops*: 2, 9 and 23 June 1966 (See entries for 'Paperback Writer' and 'Rain' for more precise info.)

Shot in colour on 16mm film, and directed by Michael Lindsay-Hogg. The Beatles were seen wandering, resting, sitting, posing and singing in the verdant gardens of Chiswick House, the eighteenth-century house and gardens in west London. 'Those clips only came about because it became too difficult to go into the TV companies and just do our *Top Of The Pops* bit,' George revealed. 'It was too much mania at the time, so we thought we'd just get a camera, a cameraman, and a 16mm and we'd go off into a field and just do it. There wasn't a concept.' As NEMS employee Tony Bramwell admitted, 'We filmed them sitting in the trees, and running [sic] around the conservatory because we weren't sure if the videotapes [recorded at Abbey Road the previous day, 19 May 1966, see entries] would work.' A girl from the school opposite managed to break through the group's cordon and meet the Fab Four. 'It was so touching,' photographer Bob Whittaker remembered. 'The Beatles were so friendly towards her and behaved like perfect gentlemen.' The girl in question was 14-year-old Anne Welburn, who recalled, 'The gates [of Chiswick House] were locked but I climbed over a wall and there they were. My legs turned to jelly but they were so friendly. John asked what I was doing for my O-levels and Ringo offered me his fish and chips. I was in a daze and the other girls [at the school] didn't believe me until they saw the photo.'

The 'Paperback Writer' clip received its UK TV debut on BBC1's *Top Of The Pops* (in b&w) during the edition aired on 2 June 1966, 'Rain' one week later. Unseen footage from the session appeared for the first time during the group's 1995 *Anthology* series. (**The original colour, 16mm film, along with selected out-takes, survives in the Apple archive.**)

Truly superb colour footage of the ultra-cool, mega-trendy, Revolver-era Beatles.

DAY BY DAY
(SOUTHERN TELEVISION FOR ITV)

Southern Independent Television Centre, Northam, Southampton, England

Recorded: 22 August 1963, broadcast regionally later that evening: 22 August 1963

She Loves You

The Beatles' only performance on this regional, Southern ITV news magazine show, where they mimed the A-side of their latest single, 'She Loves You'. During the day of this broadcast, in a dark corridor of Bournemouth's Palace Court Hotel, where the group were staying, photographer Robert Freeman took the front cover photograph for the group's second Parlophone/EMI album, *With The Beatles*. Inspired by Astrid Kirchherr's famous Hamburg photos of the band, it used a chiaroscuro (light and dark) effect. The image also appeared on the cover of *Meet The Beatles!*, their first Capitol album in North America. Freeman would also go on to shoot three further album covers for the group: *Beatles For Sale*, *Help!* and *Rubber Soul*. (**Their mimed rendition of 'She Loves You' is missing from the archives.**)

Another standard TV appearance, one that sadly we'll never see again.

DAY IN THE LIFE, A
(PROMOTIONAL FILM CLIP/NEMS ENTERPRISES/ RINGO AND OTHERS HOME MOVIES)

Studio One, Abbey Road Studios, 3 Abbey Road, London, England

Filmed: 10 February 1967, first broadcast UK on BBC2 as part of the *Late Night Line-Up, Abbey Road* album special: 19 September 1969

Unseen at the time, chiefly due to the song's ban by the BBC, this was a powerful film for a powerful song, an incoherent sequence of sped up, slowed down, unfocused, and double-exposed, Flower Power-inspired imagery intercut at superfast speed. Shot by Tony Bramwell for NEMS, and Ringo with his hand-held 16mm camera, the psychedelic colour footage depicted the recording of the orchestral overdubs, as well as the bizarre recording sessions for the song itself: friend and roadie Neil Aspinall ejecting female fans from the studio; 40 highly talented musicians wearing evening dress, funny noses, hairpieces and masks; a woman, dressed in a long flowing gown, waving sparklers amidst an orchestra conducted by Paul and George Martin. (The former leader of the Royal Philharmonic Orchestra, David McCallum, even joined in on the fun by sporting a bright red false nose.)

Intertwined with miscellaneous stock footage, humour in the completed clip was allowed to shine through when a shot of London's Big Ben tower popped up at the sound of the alarm clock during McCartney's segment of the song. Stars at the session were also seen: Marianne Faithfull, Pattie Boyd (Harrison), Donovan, Rolling Stones' Mick Jagger and Keith Richards, and Simon and Marijke of the hippie, psychedelic design group The Fool. So too was Mike Nesmith of The Monkees, who was on a promotional trip to the country with fellow bandmate, drummer Micky Dolenz. Inspired by how John and Paul had formed 'A Day In The Life' from two unfinished tracks, Nesmith would use this trick for 'Writing Wrongs', a song that would grace The Monkees' 1968 RCA album *The Birds, The Bees And The Monkees*.

Directed by Tony Bramwell for a mooted but ultimately never completed *Sgt Pepper* TV special, the 'A Day In The Life' film received its first screening not in 1967 but two years later, on 19 September 1969 to be precise, in a special *Abbey Road* album edition of *Late Night Line-Up* (see separate entry). Following a repeat airing on 10 October 1969, the film was thought lost. Then in 1983 the archive library Filmfinders, run by film historian and former BBC employee Philip Jenkinson, found a copy languishing in the archives, 14 years after it had been handed to the BBC by Apple for inclusion in the aforementioned *Late Night Line-Up* show.

After much fanfare on the show, the clip received its third screening, on the Channel 4 music series *The Tube*, during the edition aired on 4 November 1983. The delightful, late-1960s pleasantries once shared between Jenkinson, The Beatles and their company were soon forgotten when Apple quickly came forward, claiming ownership of the footage, and demanding in no uncertain terms that the film be returned to them *immediately*, certainly within 24 hours or legal actions would result. Their sharp, forceful, underhanded, bully-boy tactics prompted Jenkinson to remark at the time, 'I wish now I had burnt the film.' The 'A Day In The Life' film reappeared (this time with the correct soundtrack; previously 'Come Together' had been dubbed over the 'A Day In The Life' footage – see *Late Night Line-Up* entry) over a decade later, alongside several other unseen clips from the session, in the group's official, 1995 documentary series *Anthology*. Most recently, the film was officially released on the bonus disc of the *Beatles 1+* DVD/Blu-ray, on 6 November 2015. **(Master footage, as well as Ringo's out-takes from the session, survive in the Apple archive.)**

Classic, candid footage of The Beatles, and their pop-star friends, in the studio, at work on a legendary track.

DAY TRIPPER

(See entry for InterTel (VTR Services) Promotional Videos)

DIE BEATLES
(ZDF – ZWEITES DEUTSCHES FERNSEHEN – TV, WEST GERMANY)

Circus-Krone-Bau, Marsstrasse, Munich, West Germany
Recorded: 24 June 1966, broadcast West Germany on ZDF Channel 2: 5 July 1966
Rock And Roll Music, She's A Woman (very short fragment), Baby's In Black, I Feel Fine, Yesterday, Nowhere Man, I'm Down (Live)

Utilising a five-camera set-up, the national West German broadcasting network ZDF videotaped (in b&w) the second of the group's two shows at the Circus-Krone-Bau in Munich. Seven songs were included in the finished programme, which was entitled *Die Beatles*. Also appearing were the support acts on the tour: Cliff Bennett and The Rebel Rousers, Peter and Gordon and The Rattles, who started their career in the same Hamburg scene where many Liverpool-based, beat groups were born. They encountered The Beatles for the first time in 1962 and played alongside them on three occasions in West Germany, in Essen, Hamburg and Munich. The West German part of The Beatles' brief international concert tour was dubbed the 'Bravo Blitztournee', due to its sponsorship by the country's entertainment magazine *Bravo*. (**The original videotape survives.**)

Rather nice videotape footage of the roadweary, under-rehearsed Beatles live in concert.

DISCS-A-GOGO
(TWW – TELEVISION WALES AND WEST – FOR ITV)

TWW Television Centre, Bath Road, Bristol, England
Recorded: 3 December 1962, broadcast live regionally: 3 December 1962
Love Me Do

The group journeyed to Bristol for their only appearance on this popular, weekly, 24-minute pop music programme. By 1963 this much-forgotten show, which was transmitted from the Television Wales and West studios, regularly attracted up to nine million viewers. It was set in the fictional, fifties-style coffee bar Gogos, the so-called 'gayest coffee bar in town', where acts such as The Beatles would come to play. Hosted by the future ITV wrestling commentator Kent Walton, *Discs-A-Gogo* wasn't networked, leaving only viewers in the TWW, Anglia and Tyne-Tees regions of the ITV network able to see The Beatles' mimed rendition of 'Love Me Do', the music originating from the bar's jukebox. In line with the bar's name, the regular dance troupe was The Go-Jos, who would later appear on BBC TV's rival show, *Top Of The Pops*. The show caused a bit of fuss when it was revealed in the papers that the black dancer on the show was going out with a white female performer on the programme. However, the couple, John and Muriel, known for being excellent 'jivers' and 'boppers', soon became local celebrities in Bristol during the time of the programme's run. The show's mascot was a fox called Foxy, and viewers were invited to write in to the station for their free *Discs-A-Gogo* badge featuring him. Other top names from the era, such as Tom Jones, Lulu, Dusty Springfield, Sandie Shaw, The Beach Boys, The Animals and The Dave Clark Five, to name but a few, also appeared on the programme, which ceased broadcasting in December 1965. (**Missing from archives.**)

An important early TV appearance by the band; one we'll never see again.

DON'T LET ME DOWN
(PROMOTIONAL FILM CLIP/APPLE)

Twickenham Film Studios, St Margaret's, London, England
Filmed: 6 and 30 January 1969, broadcast America on CBS
TV *The Glen Campbell Goodtime Hour*: 30 April 1969

Alternate footage from the ill-fated *Get Back/Let It Be* project was put to great use in this 16mm colour clip, which juxtaposes scenes from Twickenham Film Studios on 6 January 1969 (Day Three of the sessions) with the Apple rooftop performance on 30 January 1969 (Day Nineteen of the sessions). Directed by Michael Lindsay-Hogg, the film debuted on episode 13 of CBS TV's *The Glen Campbell Goodtime Hour*, alongside the promo for 'Get Back', on 30 April 1969. (For more, see *Let It Be* entry in *Movies* section.) **(Master footage, as well as out-takes, survives in the Apple archive.)**

Great footage of The Fabs performing a John Lennon classic, in the studio and on the roof of Apple.

DROP IN
(SVERIGES TELEVISION – SVT, SWEDISH TV)

The Narren-teatern (arena theatre), a hall in Stockholm's Gröna Lund amusement park, Stockholm, Sweden
Recorded: 30 October 1963, broadcast Sweden on SVT: 3 November 1963
She Loves You, Twist And Shout, I Saw Her Standing There, Long Tall Sally, and while the credits rolled, the group was also seen clapping along to the show's closing theme tune (Live)

Prior to the taping for Sweden's national public broadcaster, Paul McCartney and Ringo Starr went in Klas Burling's (the show's presenter and an old friend of the group) Fiat car for a bit of shopping at NK, Stockholm's largest department store, where McCartney bought perfume for his then girlfriend, the actress Jane Asher. Just before recording commenced at 7pm, The Beatles performed an acoustic version of the as yet unreleased Lennon/McCartney composition 'I Want To Hold Your Hand' for Burling, who later announced he 'knew immediately that it would be a hit'. For the *Drop In* show itself, in front of a small live audience, The Beatles had originally intended to perform just two numbers, 'She Loves You' and 'Twist And Shout', but Burling managed to persuade them to keep the onlookers happy and continue with one more. They went with 'I Saw Her Standing There', after which the programme's presenter, Kersti Adams-Ray, attempted to start up the show's theme tune. But The Beatles weren't finished. Burling asked them to play another track to round off the show. They duly obliged, delivering 'Long Tall Sally', after which they joined in with handclaps with the rest of the cast for the *Drop In* closing theme song. When taping had concluded, the show's producer, Lasse Sarri, remarked to John, 'I hope you didn't mind doing the extra numbers,' to which Lennon whimsically responded, 'No, not at all. I always talk like this.' This recording fell on the penultimate day of the group's nine-day trip to Sweden, their first real tour outside of Britain. **(The original videotape survives, and is now owned outright by Apple Corps who obtained sole rights to it during work on the *Anthology* series between 1992 and 1995. The footage of 'She Loves You' was officially released on the first disc of the *Beatles 1/Beatles 1+* DVD/Blu-ray, on 6 November 2015.)**

Truly wonderful, b&w videotape of the band performing live, early in their career, in the confines of a European television studio.

EAMONN ANDREWS SHOW, THE
(ABC FOR ITV)

Teddington Studio Centre, Teddington Lock, Broom Road, England
Recorded: 11 April 1965, broadcast UK on ITV Network: 11 April 1965
Ticket To Ride, Yes It Is

After their appearance at the *NME Poll-Winners' All-Star Concert* (see separate entry), the group gave an interview and performed for ABC TV's late-night *The Eamonn Andrews Show*, hosted by the Irish radio presenter and UK TV talk-show pioneer Eamonn Andrews. The Beatles appeared in three segments. In the first, the interview part of the show, John joined Andrews at the host's desk, while Paul sat in a swivel chair and George and Ringo shared a sofa. They were their usual irreverent selves.

Eamonn began by congratulating Ringo on the announcement that his wife Maureen was expecting their first child. 'How does it feel to be an expectant dad?' he asked. 'Not so bad, you know,' Ringo replied. 'Not so bad. I hope it's a boy or a girl.' 'It might be an eye,' John bizarrely interjected. 'Now this is your second film [*Help!*],' the host continued. 'The first one was compared to the Marx Brothers. Remember?' 'Oh, aye,' John said. 'Have you ever seen the Marx Brothers?' Eamonn asked. 'Yes,' Paul replied, 'nothing like us.' 'Nothing like you,' Eamonn responded, 'I believe that.' 'And we're nothing like them,' Paul quickly interjected. 'Well, what sort of thing – this is addressed to all of you,' the host continued, ' – what sort of thing makes you fellas laugh?' 'Uh,' Paul paused before replying, 'the Marx Brothers.'

In the second part of the programme The Beatles lip-synched both sides of their latest release, 'Ticket To Ride' and 'Yes It Is', while in the third the group participated in a discussion with the critic Wolf Mankowitz, and journalist Katherine Whitehorn. (**ABC broadcast the show live, but failed to keep their original videotape recording.**)

A great programme, if only we could see it, but sadly we can't. Notable for another in-studio performance of 'Yes It Is'.

ED SULLIVAN SHOW, THE (1)
(CBS – COLUMBIA BROADCASTING SYSTEM – BROADCASTING, INC. FOR THE CBS NETWORK IN AMERICA)

CBS Television, Studio 50, New York, New York, USA
Recorded: 9 February 1964, broadcast America on CBS: 9 February 1964
All My Loving, Till There Was You, She Loves You, I Saw Her Standing There, I Want To Hold Your Hand (Live)

The Beatles' legendary live debut on CBS TV's *The Ed Sullivan Show* attracted the biggest television audience recorded at the time, with an estimated 73 million viewers in 23 million homes tuning in. The 728 seating capacity within CBS's Studio 50 complex could even have been filled several times over. Their offices received over 50,000 requests for tickets to the show.

George missed the first *Sullivan* run-through, on 8 February 1964, due to his high temperature of 104, but returned in time for the broadcast. 'I eventually made the theatre for the *Ed Sullivan Show*,' he recalled, 'and we did a lot of rehearsals for the sound people. They kept going into the control room and checking out the sound. Finally, when they got a balance between the instruments and the vocals, they marked the boards, by the controls, and then everyone broke for lunch. Then, when we came back to tape the show, the cleaners had been round and had polished all the marks off the board.' The set designer on the show was asked what the idea was behind the arrows pointing inwards. 'To symbolise the fact that The Beatles are here,' he replied.

The group taped their 23 February 1964 appearance on the show (their third, see below) during the afternoon of 9 February 1964 before their famed, live debut on the programme had even taken place. Leading up to that broadcast, Brian Epstein walked up to Ed Sullivan and politely

said, 'I would like to know the exact wording of you introduction.' Sullivan replied, 'I would like you to get lost.'

Just minutes before the show was due to go on air, the host told the screaming audience, 'Now, you kids can holler all you want when The Beatles come on, but I want you to show proper respect for our other acts.' His plea went unheeded. They still screamed. At the beginning of the show,

LAUNCHING THE BEATLES INVASION

'The Beatles are delightful,' said Sullivan at a society luncheon shortly after their first appearance on his show. 'They are the nicest boys I've ever met. They have the greatest sense of humour and are well-mannered.' Incensed by the accolades Sullivan was receiving, TV rival Jack Paar was quick to point out to the press that *his* show was the first top, mainstream American television programme to broadcast footage of The Beatles performing. Some five weeks before their famed *Sullivan* debut, Parr's vehicle, *The Jack Paar Show*, had screened film of the group (at a cost of £225) sing-ing 'She Loves You', from the 1963 BBC TV documentary *The Mersey Sound*, during the 3 January 1964 edition of his programme. 'It is quite wrong to say Sullivan introduced them to America,' he blasted at the time.

However, despite what Jack Paar claimed, his wasn't actually the first US TV programme to air footage of the Fab Four in action. That accolade went to ABC, CBS and NBC TV news who (between 18–22 November 1963 and 10 Decem-ber 1963), in response to the so-called 'epidemic of Beatlemania' in Britain, began screening b&w film of the group performing 'She Loves You' at the Winter Gardens Theatre in Bournemouth on 16 November 1963 (or, in some cases, the BBC TV *The Mersey Sound* clip of the song). The screaming fans rendered the original audio unuseable, so the EMI recording of the song had to be dubbed on top of it.

The very first report to be aired was journalist Edwin Newman's four-minute account, during the 18 November 1963 edition of the flagship NBC evening news programme *The Huntley–Brinkley Report*. But of these, the CBS ver-sion is the most memorable, albeit for the wrong reasons. First broadcast during their morning news show on 22 November 1963, it was planned to re-air later that evening. However, with the assassination of President John F. Ken-nedy in Dallas, Texas, that afternoon, it was shelved until 10 December 1963, when the legendary news anchorman Walter Cronkite decided that such a story would raise the nation's spirits. Featuring the broadcast journalist Alexander Kendrick at the helm, his report from 'Beatle-land, formerly known as Britain,' included him dismissively describing The Beatles as symbolic of the "twentieth century non-hero', who 'make non-music, wear non-haircuts and give non-mercy.' Siting at a desk, with piles of fan letters in front of him, he even cheekily announced his surprise that the group's fans 'can write'. Footage of activities inside the Beatles fan club and of them arriving at the Bournemouth theatre in their van were also featured in the report, as was an interview with them, conducted in their dressing room by fellow CBS reporter Josh Darsa, who asked, 'Do you fear that your public will get tired of you and eventually move on to a new favourite?' 'They probably will,' John replied, 'depends how long it takes [for them] to get tired.'

Sullivan read out a congratulatory telegram from Colonel Tom Parker and The King, Elvis Presley. (Years later, The Beatles learnt Presley knew nothing about it.) Some saw this as a 'passing of the torch' moment in popular music. During the broadcast, each of the four Beatles' names was put up on the television screen to identify them to the captivated American audience. At this point in time, most Americans could not tell one Beatle from another. None of them had achieved any kind of individual identity as yet. So while Paul crooned his way through 'Till There Was You', the caption under John read, 'Sorry girls, he's married.' It was believed that, during the show, the US youth crime rate dipped to just 3 per cent, its lowest in 50 years. Even the Christian evangelist Billy Graham broke with tradition by watching television on the Sabbath.

Just as they were about to go on stage to perform their second set, at the request of *Sullivan* stagehand Jerry Gort, The Beatles signed a piece of the large, moveable, hard wall traveller backdrop used on the broadcast. With a black marking pen, used to mark the floor where the sets would stand, each Beatle signed their name (Paul called himself 'Uncle') and drew a humorous caricature of himself (George's unsurprisingly featured him smoking a cigarette). The author of the inscription, 'The Beatles Were Here 2/9/64' is unknown. Ringo made a mad rush to his drum kit immediately after finishing his inscriptions. Aside from the Fab Four, various other people signed the Bill Bohnert-designed wall, including a member of Liverpool group The Searchers, who performed on *The Ed Sullivan Show* one month later, on 5 April 1964.

When the plastic staging was dismantled on 6 September 1964, at the end of that season's run, it was put in the bin ready to be dumped, but was rescued by an alert Gort. He cut out a 16 x 48-inch section and sent it to the wheelchair-dependent Beatles fan, Lofton Sproles. In the mid-1980s, Lofton sold it to Rodney Cary, the owner of the Southdowns Lounge in Baton Rouge, Louisiana, where it was put on display for several years. In 2002, Cary sold it to a dealer who then sold it to an anonymous Los Angeles collector, who put it up for sale in October 2014. Memorabilia specialists Rockaway Records of Los Angeles auctioned it with an asking price of $550,000.

Joining the Fab Four on the *Ed Sullivan Show* that historic night was the Broadway cast of *Oliver!*, featuring Georgia Brown and Davy Jones (later one of *The Monkees*), the comedian and impressionist, and future *Batman* TV villain, Frank Gorshin, the comedy team Mitzi McCall and Charlie Brill, singer Tessie O'Shea, magician Fred Kapps and the acrobatic team Wells and the Four Fays. Following the broadcast, the American public took the group to their hearts and opened the door to the so-called British Invasion that followed. In the month after the show, The Beatles sold 2.5 million records in the States alone. The world's leading ice-cream manufacturer, Baskin-Robbins, even introduced a new flavour to celebrate the group's arrival – Beatle Nut. How wrong then was *The New York Times*, which on 3 January 1964 had confidently predicted that 'Beatlemania will never take hold in America.' **(Master tape in b&w and a 16mm tele-recording survives.)**

One of the most important nights in music and television history.

ED SULLIVAN SHOW, THE (2)
(CBS BROADCASTING, INC. FOR THE CBS NETWORK)

Deauville Hotel, Miami, Florida, USA
Recorded: 16 February 1964, broadcast America on CBS: 16 February 1964

She Loves You, This Boy, All My Loving, I Saw Her Standing There, From Me To You, I Want To Hold Your Hand (Live)

The television audience for this particular show was estimated to be 70 million. During the broadcast, Sullivan introduced the 3,500 audience in the hotel, and the vast television crowd, to two boxers, Sonny Liston, the heavyweight champion of the world, and former champ Joe Louis, who were sitting among the spectators enjoying the show. Not to be outdone, two days after the broadcast, The Beatles were the guests of boxer Cassius Clay at his training camp in Miami Beach, Florida. In just a week's time, he and Liston would fight for the WBA/WBC Heavyweight Championship belt at the Convention Hall, Miami Beach. Clay would be the victor.

On the 1 March 1964 edition of *The Ed Sullivan Show*, the host humorously declared, 'I saw the Liston–Clay fight. This was the stinker of all time. I swear The Beatles could beat the two of 'em! No kidding!' (Incidentally, the 16 February 1964 episode of *The Ed Sullivan Show* was repeated on the CBS Television network on 20 September, later that year).

Prior to the live broadcast, and still at the Deauville Hotel, The Beatles performed a quite spirited dress rehearsal of the same six numbers to be sung in the show. Lennon took more liberties than usual during the between-song banter, saying, 'Shut up while he's talkin'!' when McCartney's intro to 'I Want To Hold Your Hand' was interrupted by loud shrieks from the audience. And then, when Paul urged them to clap their hands and stamp their feet, John performed his infamous cripple imitation, forcing Paul to direct a dirty look.

'Miami was incredible,' Paul recalled. 'It was the first time that we had seen police motorbike outriders with guns. It was amazing!' On the plane over, Paul asked the National Airlines flight attendant Carol Gallagher, 'Do you think anyone will be in Miami to meet us?' At the airport 7,000 fans were waiting. Miami policeman Buddy Dresner escorted The Beatles throughout their time there. 'I took 'em to the first drive-in movie they ever went to,' he revealed, 'gave 'em their first grilled-cheese sandwich, they drank Scotch with warm Coke and Paul ate dessert before the main meal. I told him, "You can't do that in America, you gotta eat the salad first, and then hit the steak and potatoes."' **(The original b&w master tape survives, as does the videotape recording of the afternoon rehearsal.)**

Another legendary appearance on this top-rated American TV show.

ED SULLIVAN SHOW, THE (3)
(CBS BROADCASTING, INC. FOR THE CBS NETWORK)

CBS Television, Studio 50, New York, New York, USA
Recorded: 9 February 1964, broadcast America on CBS: 23 February 1964
Twist And Shout, Please Please Me, I Want To Hold Your Hand (Live)

The Beatles actually recorded this three-track live set during the afternoon of 9 February 1964, just hours before their famed, live debut on the programme had even taken place (see above). The performance of 'Please Please Me' was officially released on the bonus disc of the *Beatles 1+* DVD/Blu-ray, on 6 November 2015. **(A 16mm film print of this afternoon performance survives.)**

Once again, The Beatles were in fine form before the Sullivan cameras.

LADIES AND GENTLEMEN, THE BEATLES!

Originally running on CBS from 20 June 1948, as a show called *Toast Of The Town,* to 6 June 1971, *The Ed Sullivan Show* was a highly influential, coast-to-coast American TV variety show that was fronted by the New York entertainment columnist Ed Sullivan. Each Sunday night it would play host to every conceivable type of family entertainment. Being invited on was like a seal of approval. See entry of 'Sullivan, Ed' in Beatles People.

When Sullivan and his wife Sylvia were passing through London Airport (Heathrow since 1966), en route back to New York, they were informed their outbound flight home had been delayed because hordes of hysterical teenage girls had mobbed the airport. Many in the enormous, 1,500 crowd were holding up signs that read, 'Welcome Home Beatles'. Naturally curious, with the group still unknown in the States, he approached an airport attendant and asked, 'Who the hell are these Beatles? Is it an animal act?' He was told it was England's most popular singing group.

Once back in America, Sullivan immediately got someone in his office to check out The Beatles and soon learnt that a New York promoter, Sid Bernstein, had already booked them for two performances at Carnegie Hall on 12 February 1964. (See entry in *Places* section.) She asked him what he thought of the band. 'They're a phenomenon,' he replied. When told of this, Sullivan called Brian Epstein who flew out to New York one week later to negotiate The Beatles' appearance on his show, the first being three days prior to their Carnegie Hall concerts. Sullivan had originally considered using them as a minor, novelty item, in a show constructed around a well-known American star, but Epstein was having none of it. He wanted top billing, so a comprise was reached. Sullivan's producer, Bob Precht, agreed to pay The Beatles' airfares, but only if they agreed to make three appearances on the show; and, as they say, the rest is history. The Beatles received a fee of $10,000 for their performances.

After the June 1966 broadcast, the group would never again appear personally for (or on) *The Ed Sullivan Show*. However, on 26 November 1967 the programme did screen their new promotional film for 'Hello, Goodbye' (version one, see entry below). Prior to its airing, Sullivan read out a cablegram, sent by The Beatles from London. 'Dear ed, winter has come once again to our great britain … we sit by our fires warming our feet … stop … we send all our love to you and everyone looking in … we are happy to be on your show too … stop … have a beautiful Christmas and a sincere new year. Love the beatles … john lennon paul mccartney ringo starr george Harrison'. Two clips from their as yet unreleased movie *Let It Be* ('Two Of Us' and 'Let It Be') were also screened on the 15 February 1970 edition of the show. In 1992 Paul, now solo, appeared again at the now renamed Ed Sullivan Theatre on an MTV *Up Close* special, and Ringo played there with his All-Starr Band in 2000. The pair returned to the venue, this time together, for the star-studded *The Beatles: The Night That Changed America – A Grammy Salute,* a CBS Television special, which aired in America on 9 February 2014, precisely 50 years to the date (and time) of the group's first appearance on *The Ed Sullivan Show*. (ITV1, in England screened the programme for the first time three months later, on 2 May 2014.)

And finally, whatever happened to some of the drums Ringo played on that classic 9 February 1964 edition of *The Ed Sullivan Show*? Well, the simple answer is Paul McCartney broke one of them. According to drummer Jim Keltner, when Paul came over to visit John at his rented Santa Monica beach house in April 1974, he played Ringo's legendary set and accidentally damaged one of them. 'Oh my God,' Keltner recalled saying. 'That was the *Ed Sullivan* head!' Paul replied simply, 'Oh, I'll get him another one.'

ED SULLIVAN SHOW, THE (4)
(CBS BROADCASTING, INC. FOR THE CBS NETWORK)

Scala Theatre, London, England
Recorded: 31 March 1964, broadcast America on CBS: 24 May 1964
You Can't Do That (Live)

Basically just a promotional tool for their first film, *A Hard Day's Night*, the footage of 'You Can't Do That' was recorded at a concert in front of 350 screaming fans and had been originally intended for inclusion in the film, but ultimately failed to make the final cut. However, the clip had fortuitously been sent over to CBS before that decision was made. The broadcast on 24 May also included an interview that Ed had taped with the group in England.

Due to the saving of this priceless *A Hard Day's Night* movie out-take.

ED SULLIVAN SHOW, THE (5)
(CBS BROADCASTING, INC. FOR THE CBS NETWORK)

CBS Television, Studio 50, New York, New York, USA
Recorded: 14 August 1965, broadcast America on CBS: 12 September 1965
I Feel Fine, I'm Down, Act Naturally, Ticket To Ride, Yesterday (Paul solo), Help! (Live)

The group's fourth (and final) *Ed Sullivan* studio appearance, where they performed the exact same set as they did on *Blackpool Night Out*, just 13 days earlier. (See entry.) The group spent most of 14 August 1965 rehearsing and then watching videotape playbacks of their performance. The one deemed suitable for broadcast (four weeks from

then) was recorded at 8.30pm. Like the Blackpool show, this performance is also best remembered for Paul's classic, solo in the spotlight, acoustic version of 'Yesterday'. 'I had to sing "Yesterday" live in front of all those people,' he said. 'It was pretty nerve-wracking but it was very exciting.' 'We did six numbers on *The Ed Sullivan Show*,' John recalled. 'I played organ on 'I'm Down'. I can't really play it but I treated them to an elbow exercise with one hand and did a few chords with the others. The other songs we did were "Ticket To Ride", "I Feel Fine," "Yesterday", which Paul sang straight with three violins, "Act Naturally", Ringo's country and western number and "Help!". We didn't go out after the show, but just played around in the hotel. We thought about going to see Cilla's closing night at The Persian Rooms, but it was impossible to get out of our hotel.' Sullivan began The Beatles' slot by introducing them individually, at which point each member of the group walked on, stage right, to shake Ed's hand. Ringo confused things by entering stage left. Possibly due to nerves, John messed up the lyrics to 'I Feel Fine' and 'Help!'; Paul did the same on 'I'm Down'. First transmitted in b&w on 12 September 1965, it was the first in the new season. Just one week later, from the 19 September 1965 edition onwards, the show began broadcasting on the CBS network in full colour. Paul's performance of 'Yesterday' was officially released on the first disc of the *Beatles 1/Beatles 1+* DVD/Blu-ray, on 6 November 2015. (**Master tape in b&w survives, as does a rehearsal of the song 'Help!'**)

Looking great, but under-rehearsed, the Fab Four once more delighted the Sullivan crowds.

ED SULLIVAN SHOW, THE (6)
(CBS BROADCASTING, INC. FOR THE CBS NETWORK)

Studio One Abbey Road Studios, 3 Abbey Road, London, England
Recorded: May 19, 1966, broadcast America on CBS: 5 June 1966
Paperback Writer, Rain

The Beatles could not logistically appear in person, so they sent along two, colour videotape clips of themselves performing their latest single, 'Paperback Writer' and 'Rain' (see separate entries for both). Directed by Michael Lindsay-Hogg, who, among other things, in January 1969 would direct the group's movie *Let It Be*, the footage he shot was notable for a number of reasons: Paul's chipped front tooth, a result of a recent moped accident at his father Jim's house in Heswall, Cheshire; a photo taken during this performance would be used for the back cover of their August 1966 *Revolver* album; thirdly, it opens with the group holding transparencies – taken by photographer Robert Whittaker – of the infamous 'Butcher' album cover in front of their faces, later used on first pressings of the Capitol Records *Yesterday And Today* album. Also, in the specially recorded introduction by The Beatles themselves, for the first time Ringo acted as the spokesman for the group, explaining that they had been too busy with 'the washin' and the cookin'' to visit Ed personally. John switched sunglasses in the clips, from a larger, orange-tinted pair to smaller yellow-tinted, rectangular shaped ones, and a near replica of those made famous by Jim (Roger) McGuinn of the highly popular American pop group The Byrds. The Abbey Road 'Paperback Writer' footage, prefaced with a short introduction by Ringo, was officially released on the bonus disc of the *Beatles 1*+ DVD/Blu-ray, on 6 November 2015. (**The original NTSC 525-line colour master tape survives.**)

Absolutely stunning colour, videotape footage of The Beatles, miming two classic tracks during their coolest period.

EXPERIMENT IN TELEVISION

(See entry for Music!)

GET BACK
(PROMOTIONAL FILM CLIP/APPLE CORPS)

Apple Rooftop, 3 Savile Row, London, England
Filmed: 30 January 1969, broadcast: UK on BBC1 *Top Of The Pops*, 24 April 1969; West Germany on Erstes Deutsches Fernsehen/ARD *Beat Club*, 26 April 1969; America on CBS TV *The Glen Campbell Goodtime Hour*, 30 April 1969

Filmed for the as yet unreleased *Let It Be* movie, this colour clip, distributed by Apple in April 1969 to accompany the single of the same name, featured footage from The Beatles' 30 January 1969 lunchtime performance on the roof of their Apple HQ in Savile Row. (See relevant entries in the *Places* and *Movies* sections.) Like the other two promo films, 'Don't Let Me Down' and 'Let It Be' (see entries), this was also different to the footage that would appear in the May 1970 film. Opening with a spectacular, panoramic long-distance shot of the band up on the roof, it featured a clever mix of edits from all three renditions that day; whereas the version appearing in the full-length film was an edit of only two. BBC1's *Top Of The Pops* screened the film (b&w) on 24 April 1969; German TV's *Beat Club* aired it two days later. An alternate version of this clip, with slightly different edits and scenes, was to feature in the pilot episode of *The Dave Cash Radio Programme* for the HTV region in England, however this one-off show was never broadcast. The US TV debut for the film took place on 30 April 1969 during episode 13 of CBS

TV's *The Glen Campbell Goodtime Hour*, alongside the promo for 'Don't Let Me Down'. A new, digitally remastered version of the clip, featuring performances from the Apple rooftop synched to the record, was officially released on the first disc of the *Beatles 1/Beatles 1+* DVD/Blu-ray, on 6 November 2015. (**Master film footage survives in the Apple archive.**)

Wonderful, alternate footage of The Beatles up on the roof, performing live, for the very last time.

HELLO, GOODBYE
(PROMOTIONAL FILM CLIP/NEMS ENTERPRISES)

Saville Theatre, Shaftsbury Avenue, London, England
Filmed: 10 November 1967, version one broadcast: UK, not complete until 9 May 1986 (see below); America (colour) on CBS TV *The Ed Sullivan Show*, 6 November 1967, and ABC TV *The Hollywood Palace*, 27 November 1967; West Germany (b&w) on Erstes Deutsches Fernsehen/ARD *Beat Club*, 25 November 1967

Directed by Paul, and shot on the stage at London's Saville Theatre (then owned by the late Brian Epstein's company NEMS), the group performed and horsed around in three 35mm colour film clips. Against a psychedelic backcloth, the first version was a simple, straightforward performance film, with each member attired in their brightly coloured *Sgt Pepper* costumes playing their respective instruments: John on acoustic guitar, Paul on bass, George on electric guitar, Ringo on drums. Humorous cutaway footage of them waving to the camera in their famous, collarless, 1963 Pierre Cardin jackets was also included. During the finale, garland-wearing hula girls in grass skirts entered to dance alongside the group as the curtain fell. This version was officially

released on the first disc of the *Beatles 1/Beatles 1+* DVD/Blu-ray, on 6 November 2015.

In the second version, featuring the same instrumental line-up as before, each Beatle sported their everyday, casual garb but the clip ended the same way, with the Hawaiian dancing girls. Unlike the first clip, Ringo's bass drum was now adorned with the group's logo. The very first TV broadcast of this, anywhere in the world, would not take place until 18 September 1993 when the ITV network screened it on *The Chart Show*, as part of promotion for the launch of the compilations *The Beatles 1962–1966* and *The Beatles 1967–1970* on compact disc. The recently remastered clip, emblazoned with a huge Apple logo, was even transmitted in glorious NICAM digital stereo. Another airing came on 1 November 1993, as part of MTV Europe's designated 'Beatles Day', alongside (on an intermittent loop) new interviews with Paul and George, the 1965 InterTel promos, the 1969 'Something' clip (see entries in this section) and the 1967 *Magical Mystery Tour* film, unseen in the UK since its BBC2 screening on 21 December 1979. The clip has since been officially issued on the bonus disc of the *Beatles 1+* DVD/Bly-ray, released 6 November 2015.

The third clip, however, was very different. In front of yet another backcloth, it comprised largely out-takes from the first two versions. Of note here was John's most humorous attempt at the Charleston, while George looked decidedly unconvinced that the whole thing was a good idea. To this day, the clip has never received a complete television screening, although as with the second version, it was included on the bonus disc of the 2015 *Beatles 1+* DVD/Blu-ray.

A fourth and final clip was then filmed, featuring the group simply standing, singing directly to the camera. This is affectionately known as the 'Pantomime Version' by fans because of the way the Fab Four ham up the lyrics of the song. The clip remains officially unseen to this day.

Edited by Roy Benson, the first 'Hello, Goodbye' film debuted in the States on the 26 November 1967 edition of CBS TV's *The Ed Sullivan Show*. ABC's *The Hollywood Palace* showed it one night later. The other two versions were never screened. Due to the June 1966 Musicians' Union ban on miming, which they believed was killing music, the films were not broadcast in Britain at the time. (Much to the annoyance of Apple, who had not granted permission, the very first, complete UK screening of any of the 'Hello, Goodbye' films came on 9 May 1986 when the *Sgt Pepper* version (1) was broadcast, alongside the films for 'Penny Lane' and 'Strawberry Fields Forever', as part of BBC1's six-and-a-half-hour special *Video Jukebox*. This extravagance focused on the history and development of the rock film/video, from the musicals and promotional shorts of the thirties, to the modern-day, big-scale, expensive, MTV-inspired promotional clips of the eighties.) A b&w version of the first 'Hello, Goodbye' clip was broadcast during the 25 November 1967 edition of West Germany's Erstes Deutsches Fernsehen/ARD's top monthly pop show, *Beat Club*.

So, in a desperate attempt to get a new clip screened on the BBC's flagship pop programme *Top Of The Pops*, in particular during the 23 November 1967 edition, a fifth film for 'Hello, Goodbye' was also produced, by the BBC itself. Once more edited by Roy Benson, this one, filmed at Norman's Film Productions in London on 21 November 1967, juxtaposed shots of John, Paul, Ringo, Benson (and most fleetingly George, Mal Evans, and a couple of *Magical Mystery Tour* extras) at work in the studio preparing *Magical Mystery Tour*, alongside miscellaneous stop-animation scenes of four teenagers, two girls, two boys, who were seen out in the snow, standing,

jumping and climbing into a car, appearing and vanishing from sight in time with the respective 'hello', 'goodbye', 'stop' and 'go, go, go' lyrics of the song.

However, it failed to appear. Instead, much to the group's annoyance, at the very last minute the BBC played the song to an accompaniment of the 'Can't Buy Me Love' sequence from the three-and-a-half-year-old film *A Hard Day's Night*, supplied to the BBC by United Artists *without* The Beatles' knowledge. In a 27 November 1967 letter to NEMS, the BBC's head of Light Entertainment, Tom Sloan, defended the Corporation's actions by saying, 'Had this clip not been available, it is difficult to see how "Hello, Goodbye" could have been used in Top Of The Pops at all.' In discussions with the BBC about which clip they should use to accompany the song, Tony Barrow at NEMS had suggested an excerpt from *Help!*, as it was more recent than *A Hard Day's Night*. NEMS even dispatched to the BBC some recent, up-to-date images of the group to be set against the track, but due to their insistence that the images be returned later the *same day*, it was impossible for *Top Of The Pops* to make use of them in time for the broadcast. The Norman's Film Productions version would not air until the 7 December 1967 edition of the BBC1 show. It was later released officially in October 2012 as an extra on the official Apple *Magical Mystery Tour* Blur-ray/DVD. (**The master films for all four 'Hello, Goodbye' clips survive in the Apple archive.**)

Wonderful colour footage of the Pepper-era, studio-years Beatles … just months before the rot started to set in.

Footnote: A sixth version of 'Hello, Goodbye' was even prepared at the time. It was again edited by Benson, and featured out-takes from *Magical*

Mystery Tour, including scenes from 'I Am The Walrus' and 'Your Mother Should Know', plus the John-directed, bathing beauties sequence. This 16mm b&w compilation has, at the time of writing (2016), never officially been seen in public.

The custom-built, Jumbo Silver Sparkle drum kit seen in the Saville Theatre films was sold at an auction of Ringo's memorabilia in Beverly Hills, California, in December 2015.

HELP!

(See entry for InterTel (VTR Services) Promotional Videos)

HELP!
(PROMOTIONAL FILM CLIP/NEMS)

Stage 1, Twickenham Studios, St Margaret's, Twickenham, London, England

Recorded: 22 April 1965, broadcast: UK on BBC1 *Top Of The Pops*, 29 July 1965, 19 August 1965; ITV *Thank Your Lucky Stars – Lucky Stars Anniversary Show*, 17 July 1965 and TWW (Television Wales and the West) *Discs-A-Gogo*, 26 July 1965

Simple, straightforward, b&w performance clip by The Beatles. Produced by NEMS, it was distributed to television companies by United Artists to help promote the film of the same name. It would reappear during the movie's opening title sequence, projected onto a cinema screen at which the character Clang, played by Leo McKern, angrily threw darts. **(Master 16mm, b&w film footage survives in the Apple archive.)**

Delightful, yet simple film of the group miming an absolute John Lennon classic.

HEY BULLDOG

(See entry for Lady Madonna)

HEY JUDE
(PROMOTIONAL FILM/VIDEOTAPE CLIP/APPLE CORPS)

Stage 1, Twickenham Studios, St Margaret's, Twickenham, London, England

Recorded: 4 September 1968, broadcast: England (b&w) on ITV/London Weekend Television *Frost On Sunday*, 8 September 1968, and UK on BBC1 *Top Of The Pops*, 12 and 26 September 1968 plus *Top Of The Pops '68*, 26 December 1968; America (colour) on CBS TV *The Smothers Brothers Comedy Hour*, 13 October 1968; West Germany (b&w) on Erstes Deutsches Fernsehen/ARD *Beat Club*, 16 November 1968

Straightforward, colour performance clips. (Several takes, shot on videotape for the American market; film for the UK and European one.) Recorded the same day as 'Revolution', they were directed by Michael Lindsay-Hogg, with whom the group had previously worked on the ITV pop show *Ready Steady Go!* and the promotional clips for 'Paperback Writer' and 'Rain'. He would be reunited with them at the same location four months later, on 2 January 1969, for the *Get Back/Let It Be* project.

Beginning at 1.30pm, 'Hey Jude' was the first to be produced. With Paul seated at an upright piano, John and George nearby on a podium and Ringo up on a drum riser immediately behind them, the group played along with the official studio recording, but new live vocals, particularly by McCartney, were added as they went along. (With the ongoing Musicians' Union ban on miming still posing a problem with screenings on shows such as *Top Of The Pops*, Paul's live vocals were an attempt to conceal this.)

As the track edged towards its climax, a large multicultural group began filtering onto the stage to crowd around them and join in on the song's lengthy, fade-out chorus. (The 300-strong assortment of singing, swaying and clapping adults and teenagers had been invited by The Beatles' assistant Mal Evans, who had seen them standing, waiting for the group outside EMI's Abbey Road Studios.) The camera then zoomed out to reveal a full, 36-piece, white-tuxedo-wearing orchestra, which had been assembled just behind Ringo's kit. (At the beginning of the shoot, Paul had toyed with having the orchestra stand during the performance but decided against it.)

The Beatles made three serious attempts at the clip, all featuring the same basic storyline of band performs with audience and orchestra joining in at the end. To help promote the single, Apple distributed the first two worldwide – take 1 (on videotape) to America for inclusion in CBS TV's *The Smothers Brothers Comedy Hour* and take 2 (on 16mm colour and b&w film) to UK TV/Europe/rest of the world for inclusion in, among other places, LWT's *Frost On Sunday*, BBC1's *Top Of The Pops* and Erstes Deutsches Fernsehen/ARD's *Beat Club*. A clip of the then unreleased third version, edited with scenes from the other two, was seen for the first time in the group's official 1995 *Anthology* documentary series. (Sadly, one young man, seen in some clips standing behind Ringo, died of cancer one week after the taping. He was the son of Dennis O'Dell, the chief of Apple's film division.)

The take 2 clip received its world premiere on the 8 September 1968 edition of *Frost On Saturday*. To make it seem that the group was performing especially for his programme, the show's host, David Frost, visited Twickenham on 4 September 1968 just to record an introduction. Before singing 'Hey Jude', The Beatles jammed a brief lounge-style rendition of the show's theme tune 'By George! It's The David Frost Theme', composed by George Martin, to which Frost said, 'Beautiful, absolute poetry. Welcome back to part three, as you can see, [I'm] with the greatest tearoom orchestra in the world. Right? Beautiful, beautiful. Absolutely, beautiful. As you can see, making their first audience appearance for over a year, ladies and gentlemen, The Beatles!' The group then broke into an impromptu, off-key rendition of Elvis Presley's 1960 hit 'It's Now Or Never', although this would be edited out of the television broadcasts. (Giving rise to the rumours that more Frost introductions survive, a previously unseen intro appeared in the *Anthology* series where George was seen asking Frost if the show was in colour, to which Frost replied it was not.)

Roy Benson, with whom The Beatles had worked on *Magical Mystery Tour* and the 'Hello, Goodbye' promo films (see entry), had originally envisioned a storyboard sequence for the 'Hey Jude' clip, running to 38 pages long, and set to feature them playing in front of a prison backdrop. But the group shunned the idea when they realised it would take several days to complete. Incredibly, the first UK TV transmission of one 'Hey Jude' clip was actually scheduled to take place just a day later, on the 5 September 1968 edition of *Top Of The Pops*, and three days prior to the Frost screening. But with obviously no time at all to prepare a clip for transmission, the item was pulled at the eleventh hour and held back for the following week's show, meaning David Frost got what he had wanted all along; the television premiere of The Beatles singing their latest song. The clip was officially released on the first disc of the *Beatles 1/Beatles 1+* DVD/Blu-ray, on 6 November 2015, while an edit of take 1 and take 3, featuring the David Frost introduction from *Anthology*, also appeared on the bonus disc.

Sadly it wasn't recorded, but according to Lindsay-Hogg the group actually ran through 'Hey Jude' seven or eight times during the session, but only three properly. In between those, they entertained the crowd with off-the-cuff renditions of several Tamla Motown classics and even the African-American spiritual number, 'Michael, Row The Boat Ashore'.

Just five months after the session, Paul was critical about Hogg's direction of the 'Hey Jude' clips, pointing out that they had hired an orchestra for the session but, 'not once,' he said, 'do we get a close-up [of them] since Hogg spent far too much time focussing on the kids in the studio.' **(Master film and videotape copies of both this and the 'Revolution' performances reside in the Apple archive.)**

Superb videotape clips of the band delivering a McCartney masterpiece.

Footnote: You would think a rare British television appearance by The Beatles, their first since *Our World* over a year previously (on 25 June 1967 – see entry), performing a completely new song would be a thrill to millions of viewers, but alas no. One disgruntled watcher, H.A. Earl, of London N12, felt compelled to write, 'If The Beatles had auditioned for [the weekly talent show] *Opportunity Knocks*, I'm sure the door would have been slammed in their face.' (Letter published in the weekly ITV listings magazine the *TV Times*, edition dated 28 September – 4 October 1968.)

HOLLYWOOD BOWL
(CBS – COLUMBIA BROADCASTING SYSTEM – BROADCASTING, INC.)

Hollywood Bowl, Los Angeles, California, USA
Recorded: 23 August 1964, broadcast: not in its entirety

but Twist And Shout/She Loves You did feature in America on a future edition of CBS TV *The Ed Sullivan Show*
Twist And Shout, You Can't Do That, All My Loving, She Loves You, Things We Said Today, Roll Over Beethoven, Boys, A Hard Day's Night, Long Tall Sally (Live)

The Beatles' second visit to America and their first concert at the world-famous Hollywood Bowl. Their entire performance (as well as their 1965 ones at the venue) was audio recorded by the group's US label Capitol Records, for a proposed live album, and much of the show was shot on 16mm b&w film by a CBS newsreel team. Positioned within the audience, front left-hand side of the stage, a total of 21 minutes was captured that night, but the songs 'Can't Buy Me Love', 'If I Fell' and 'I Want To Hold Your Hand' were not. A second film was also shot, again b&w, the camera positioned onstage left for 'Twist And Shout' and 'She Loves You' only. With no audience shots at all, this was available as a mail order, Super 8 reel in the late 1960s and early 1970s. There seems to be no footage at all of 'I Want to Hold Your Hand' from the concert, which is incredible since, above all others, this was the one defining track that helped crack the group in America. **(The 16mm b&w master film survives.)**

There in all its glory, American Beatlemania caught first hand, as-it-happened, by a CBS news crew.

I FEEL FINE

(See entry overleaf for InterTel (VTR Services) Promotional Videos)

INTERTEL (VTR SERVICES) PROMOTIONAL VIDEOS (NEMS ENTERPRISES)

Stage 3, Twickenham Studios, St Margaret's, Twickenham, London, England

Taped: 23 November 1965 (into the early hours of 24 November 1965), broadcast: UK on *Top Of The Pops*, *Thank Your Lucky Stars*; America on *Hullaballoo*; West Germany on *Beat Club* (More info below.)

Brian Epstein's decision to record these clips liberated the group from having to make personal appearances on various British and foreign television shows while enabling them to be seen by audiences around the globe with minimum effort. In the all-day shoot (that stretched into the early hours of the following morning), directed by 25-year-old Glasgow-born film-maker Joe McGrath of InterTel and featuring sets designed by Nicholas Ferguson of *Ready Steady Go!*, the group recorded ten promotional videos; six for their forthcoming single 'We Can Work It Out'/'Day Tripper', and four for three of their slightly older songs, 'I Feel Fine', 'Ticket To Ride' and 'Help!' Working with a team comprising Tony Bramwell and Vyvienne Moynihan of NEMS, a lighting technician, a sound man, a runner (David Mallett, later to become a renowned director in his own right) from InterTel (the first independent video company in Europe), and four cameramen, two of whom were moonlighting from their duties at the BBC, the group recorded:

We Can Work It Out – Three versions, each a simple, straightforward performance clip, featuring Paul on bass, George on guitar, Ringo on drums and John sitting at an organ. Decidedly more humorous, the third version, with the band wearing the costumes from their historic Shea Stadium concert on 15 August 1965, began with Robert Whitaker's famous photograph of Lennon with a sunflower covering his right eye and ended with John and Paul having a fit of giggles. This was no doubt triggered by a sketch of a man with his tongue sticking out, which had been placed directly in front of McCartney on the organ.

Day Tripper – Three versions, with very minor variations. The first two were simple, straightforward performance clips with each member playing their recognised instrument. In the third, with the group once again sporting their Shea Stadium outfits, George and Ringo stood behind a railway carriage prop, while John and Paul were nearby, positioned behind a cut-out of a twenties-style aeroplane. As the clip progressed, Starr swapped his tambourine for some drumsticks and then a handsaw, with which he began to dismantle the set.

Help! – One version. Sitting astride a long plank of wood that sat on top of two workbenches, the group, with John at the front, mimed, bobbed and swayed away to the song. With no drums to play, Ringo held up a white umbrella instead. Towards the end of the clip, fake snow fell on the group; a piece of it landed in Paul's mouth.

I Feel Fine – Two versions. Ideas flowed freely during this shoot, with at one point someone even suggesting the group should be filmed leaving the lavatory; Brian Epstein was having none of it, and insisted they be serious. In the first take, with the song already underway, John, Paul and George, guitars in hand, wandered into view and mimed the track on a set strewn with various bits of gym equipment. John and Paul sang straight to camera while George lip-synched (the wrong words) into a punch ball. Ringo joined them shortly after and began pedaling away on an exercise bike. At the conclusion of the take, The Beatles sent out for fish and chips from the local fish bar, at 113 St Margarets Road. When the food duly arrived, courtesy of the InterTel soundman, the band took a break, eating and making chip butties, with Paul standing while the others crouched on the floor

BEATLES V STONES

John Lennon said in 1971, 'I would like to just list what we did and what the Stones did two months after, on every fucking album and every fucking thing we did.'

'That is the truth. Look at the history. The Beatles go to America, a year later they come too,' said Paul McCartney in 2013. 'We wrote their first single [sic] "I Wanna Be Your Man". We go psychedelic; they go psychedelic. We dress as wizards, they dress as wizards …'

Was all this true? Did the Rolling Stones copy The Beatles? The answer is yes on occasion, but the Rolling Stones weren't The Rutles. The Stones always did it their way so that it was more like a take on The Beatles than a direct pinch.

When Andrew Loog Oldham started managing the Stones in 1963, he saw how he could market them as the anti-Beatles. By not wearing suits and growing their hair even longer than The Beatles, they represented non-conformity. However…

1. The Beatles are in half-shadow on their first album, *With The Beatles*, and David Bailey's photograph for *The Rolling Stones* is in the same vein.
2. The Rolling Stones' first Top 20 hit was with 'I Wanna Be Your Man', a Lennon/McCartney song from *With The Beatles*.
3. Prompted by the success of Lennon and McCartney, Andrew Loog Oldham encouraged Jagger and Richards to become a songwriting team.
4. Following Lennon and McCartney's success with MOR ballads, Mick and Keith wrote 'As Tears Go By', a hit for Marianne Faithfull. (You could argue that this then prompted Paul to write 'Yesterday'.)
5. After The Beatles featured a sitar on 'Norwegian Wood', Brian Jones featured the instrument on 'Paint It Black'.
6. It seems unlikely that we would have had 'Ruby Tuesday' if The Beatles hadn't recorded 'Eleanor Rigby'.
7. Copying *Sgt Pepper*, the Stones went psychedelic with *Their Satanic Majesties Request*, which was totally out of character for them. Like *Pepper, Satanic Majesties* had elaborate, spaced-out packaging, full of symbolism, but in the Stones' case, nobody cared.
8. Mick Jagger attended the live recording of 'All You Need Is Love' and a few weeks later, *et voilà*, the Stones release 'We Love You'.
9. After hearing the long fade-out on 'Hey Jude', Mick Jagger said, 'We may do something like that on the next album.' Could that be the seven and a half minutes of 'You Can't Always Get What You Want'?
10. After the lavish packaging for *Sgt Pepper*, The Beatles released the *White Album* and the Stones offered the starkness of *Beggars Banquet*. Some good came from this though, as the Stones also stripped down their sound and returned to basics for this outstanding album.

But in one thing, the Stones were definitely first – in being managed by Allen Klein.

of the set, with the gym equipment. The director Joe McGrath suggested keeping the cameras rolling for an (un-numbered) second version, with the view to laying the 'I Feel Fine' track over the footage. Epstein was horrified. Watching close by, at the end of the song he walked over to McGrath and said, 'You can't show that. It makes them look like real people, like the Rolling Stones.' In the recording, when the song's playback began, you could see by the look on their faces that the Fab Four had been caught unaware, oblivious to the fact that the taping was continuing. John's brief first attempt at miming his lead vocal didn't come until 1 minute 45 seconds into the clip, cut short when he stopped momentarily to scan the newspaper in which the food had been wrapped, while George climbed aboard the bike midway through. None of this footage had been broadcast anywhere for 50 years, until the evening of 11 November 2015 when for the first time ever sections were aired on UK television during the ITV network special *The Nation's Favourite Beatles Number Ones*.

Ticket To Ride – One version, simple, straightforward performance clip. The group mimed the track in front of a backdrop comprising of supersized bus, taxi and train tickets (Kings Cross and Haringey West). While John, Paul and George sat in wooden director's chairs, Ringo stood while playing his drums.

The 'Help!' and 'Ticket To Ride' recordings, the second versions of 'We Can Work It Out' and 'Day Tripper', plus the first version of 'I Feel Fine', were all officially released on the first disc of the *Beatles 1/Beatles 1+* DVD/Blu-ray, on 6 November 2015. The first versions of 'We Can Work It Out' and 'Day Tripper' (both featuring the Shea Stadium clothing) and the second version of 'I Feel Fine' (fish and chips) were included on the bonus disc of the *Beatles 1+* DVD/Blu-ray.

'We did these in the same studios as we made *A Hard Day's Night* and *Help!*,' John recalled at the time of the Twickenham recording session, but he was left disappointed by the results. 'We had great ideas for them,' he said, 'we thought it was going to be an outdoor thing, and with more of a visual

thing. [But] I'm not really happy with the way they've turned out.'

Regardless of Lennon's feelings, BBC1 still screened some of the clips during various editions of their flagship pop music show *Top Of The Pops*: 'We Can Work It Out' and 'Day Tripper' (aired 2 December 1965); 'We Can Work It Out' (9 December 1965); 'I Feel Fine', 'Help!' and 'Ticket To Ride' (Christmas Day 1965); 'We Can Work It Out' (30 December 1965); and 'We Can Work It Out' and 'Day Tripper' (26 December 1966). A brief clip of 'I Feel Fine' reappeared in the *Ten Years Of Top Of The Pops* special on 27 December 1973. ITV naturally also picked up the videos, but screened only two, 'We Can Work It Out' and 'Day Tripper', during the 4 December 1965 edition of ABC TV's *Thank Your Lucky Stars*. US TV screenings were surprisingly sparse, with NBC acquiring only two, 'We Can Work It Out' and 'Day Tripper', for inclusion in the 3 January 1966 edition of *Hullabaloo*. In West Germany, Erstes Deutsches Fernsehen/ARD screened 'Ticket To Ride', 'We Can Work It Out' (version 3) and 'Day Tripper' (extract only) during the 12 February 1966 edition of the country's top pop show *Beat Club*. Two further clips, 'I Feel Fine' (version 1) and 'Help!' were aired during the edition broadcast six weeks later, on 26 March 1966.

A 4-page promotional folder, on grey and black textured medium card, measuring 35cm by 48cm, showing small black and white photos from each of the taped songs and boasting the title 'A Subafilms Production: THE BEATLES performing their biggest hits', was prepared by Bernard Lee of NEMS to announce their worldwide availability.

With charges of £1,750 to broadcasters for use of any of the clips, NEMS soon made a hefty profit on them. The entire production cost of the items had set them back just £750. But EMI still wasn't happy, and according to Bramwell they called and complained that the sum was far too much. In the end, only nine of the videos would be distributed as Brian Epstein refused to include the 'fish and chips' version of 'I Feel Fine' in the package. It remains un-transmitted in its complete form to this day. (**Masters of every clip from this session survive on videotape – and film transfers – in the Apple archive.**)

Superb, yet simple performance clips. We love them, but John didn't.

IT'S THE BEATLES!
(BBC TV)

Empire Theatre, Lime Street, Liverpool, England
Recorded: 7 December 1963, broadcast UK on BBC TV: 7 December 1963
From Me To You, I Saw Her Standing There, All My Loving, Roll Over Beethoven, Boys, Till There Was You, She Loves You, This Boy, I Want to Hold Your Hand, Money (That's What I Want), Twist And Shout (they finished by reprising an instrumental version of From Me To You before bursting into a short spontaneous version of The Harry Lime Theme (aka The Third Man); the latter however was not transmitted) (Live)

In front of 2,500 lucky fans, The Beatles held a special concert for their Northern Area Fan Club in their home town of Liverpool. The show was videotaped by the BBC and was broadcast as a special programme later that day, entitled *It's The Beatles!* However, the production was beset with technical problems. Possibly owing to a lack of rehearsal time, both The Beatles and senior figures at the Corporation expressed their concerns at the often embarrassing nature of the footage, particularly the inferior sound balance, most notably the absence of Ringo's lead vocals during 'Boys'

and the director, Barney Colehan, focusing on the incorrect members of the band during key moments of the show.

Clearly troubled by the results, and eager to apologise for the quality of the programme, Colehan drafted a two-page letter about it to the boss of BBC Television. 'The Fan Club audience just went crazy when The Beatles showed up,' he explained, 'and when the actual recording started it was obvious from the wild behaviour and frantic screaming of the fans, that this sadly under-rehearsed programme would not go according to plan.' He went on, 'The noise in the theatre was so deafening that The Beatles could not hear their own internal balance, and were therefore singing out of tune for some of the time. The camera crew could not hear my instructions due to the ear-splitting noise … and the prearranged shots were useless. I had to resort to bellowing down my microphone in order to convey any instructions whatsoever.'

A response to Colehan's memo, from the head of Light Entertainment, was most forgiving. 'I do not think that you should be depressed over this,' he said. 'The conditions under which you had to work were obviously most difficult…'

(**The sub-par results may possibly explain why the Corporation chose not to retain the complete programme. Today, just over nine minutes of the 30-minute show survives in the BBC's archive; experts believe the original tape was used, unfortunately, by the Corporation as part of a training exercise on how to physically edit and splice videotape together.**)

Great videotape footage of the group live, before an adoring hometown crowd … pity then only a third of the show now survives.

JUKE BOX JURY
(BBC TV)

Empire Theatre, Lime Street, Liverpool, England
Recorded: 7 December 1963, broadcast UK on BBC TV:
7 December 1963

Although The Beatles didn't actually perform on the show, it certainly still warrants a mention in this section of the book. For one time only, the group made up the 'jury' on this hugely popular BBC TV teatime panel game show, in which a team of celebrities would sit in judgement on some of the forthcoming releases and vote 'hit' or 'miss'. If the voting was tied, it would be passed on to a second panel, seated in the audience. For this recording, that second panel featured various Beatles Fan Club secretaries, including national secretary Freda Kelly. It was hosted as always by the BBC DJ David Jacobs, and members of the group's Northern Area Fan Club filled a large part of the audience. The Beatles judged 13 songs during the afternoon taping: I Could Write A Book (Liverpool group The Chants), Kiss Me Quick (Elvis Presley), The Hippy Hippy Shake (The Swinging Blue Jeans), Did You Have A Happy Birthday? (Paul Anka), The Nitty Gritty Song (Shirley Ellis), I Can't Stop Talking About You (Steve and Eydie), Do You Really Love Me? (Billy Fury), There! I've Said It Again (Bobby Vinton), Love Hit Me (The Orchids), I Think Of You (The Merseybeats), Broken Home (Shirley Jackson), Where Have You Been All My Life (Gene Vincent) and Long Time Ago (The Bachelors). Only the first ten made the broadcast on BBC TV later that evening between 6.05pm and 6.35pm, where it was watched by an estimated 23 million people.

The group rather harshly judged The Orchids a three to one 'miss'. '[It's] just a big con,' John blasted. '[It's] a pinch from The Crystals and Ronettes.' Ringo too was unflattering, remarking, 'It'll sell a few, but not many.' At this point

Jacobs introduced the singers who were sitting out in the audience; an action that John described as a 'lousy trick'. They soon apologised for their decision. 'Sorry,' George said. '[I] didn't mean it.' Switching his card around, John joked, 'I'll change it to "hit,"' before adding, 'I'll buy it! I'll buy two! I didn't know you were here!' The Beatles fee' for the show was £1,750. (**Missing from the official archives, an inferior, reel-to-reel audio recording made by a fan at the time was handed to the BBC on 20 September 2001. A complete tele-recorded copy of the show itself survives in the hands of a private collector. Keen to see the programme again, The Beatles requested a copy of the show immediately after broadcast. Ringo became the custodian of the 16mm print they received in 1964 but, as legend has it, he lost it, as well as several other pieces of prized Beatles memorabilia, on 28 November 1979 when a fire destroyed his rented house in the Hollywood Hills, Los Angeles. Following suit, George also requested a print of his 1964 appearance, which still survives.)**

An absolute classic edition of the long-running show, and one the Corporation chose not to keep, which is an absolute travesty.

Footnote: The show was based on the American programme of the almost identical same name, *Jukebox Jury*, which ran on ABC between 13 September 1953 and 28 March 1954. The BBC1 version was launched on 1 June 1959 and ran weekly until 27 December 1967, before returning to our screens in 1979. Although The Beatles wouldn't appear collectively on *Juke Box Jury* again after their December 1963 appearance, some did feature solo. John had already been on the programme, during the 22 June 1963 edition, while George would appear in the broadcast on 25 July 1964. Taped the same day as Harrison, Ringo guested on the programme one week later, 1 August 1964. Brian Epstein meanwhile popped up as a panellist during the edition broadcast on 18 July 1964. Paul never appeared on the programme again.

KNOW THE NORTH
(GRANADA TELEVISION FOR ITV)

Cavern Club, Liverpool, England
Recorded: 22 August 1962, broadcast regionally on Granada ITV: 6 November 1963
Some Other Guy (Live)

On 22 August 1962, a small film crew from the Manchester-based ITV station Granada captured a few minutes of The Beatles' lunchtime stage performance at the Cavern. Their intention was to include the material in their regional news magazine show *Know The North*. The grainy, 16mm b&w footage acquired that day would become the earliest known professionally shot footage of the band in concert. But Lennon wasn't happy about it. 'There we were, in suits,' he recalled in 1969, 'but it just wasn't us. Watching that film, I knew that was where we started to sell out.'

In charge that day was the young Granada TV researcher Leslie Woodhead, who had been asked to uncover subjects for short films, two to three minutes long, which would offer contrasts in their area between tradition and modernisation. A number were soon shot, including one that differentiated between a clog maker and a fashion designer, and it wasn't long before a music-themed addition was suggested. A session involving a rousing performance by the top-league, Yorkshire-based Brighouse and Rastrick Brass Band was soon filmed. As contrast, the contemporary raucous sound and images of rock 'n' roll was proposed. Woodhead placed

a call through to Brian Epstein and a meeting was arranged. A visit to the nearby Cavern followed that afternoon. Packed tight against the hot, damp, sweaty brick walls, among a crowd of highly excited teenagers, Woodhead watched The Beatles in performance for the very first time. 'I thought they were totally thrilling,' he recalled, 'unlike anything I had ever seen before. The music went straight to my guts.'

Woodhead returned to the Cavern a few days later, on 22 August, to shoot his legendary film. George Harrison recalled, 'I remember Granada TV cameras coming to the Cavern. It was really hot and we were asked to dress up properly. We had shirts, and ties and little black pullovers. So we looked quite smart. It was our first television appearance. It was big-time, a TV company coming to film us and even John was into it.' (The station's producer, Johnny Hamp, recalled each of the group was paid £12 for their performance.)

As Woodhead recalled, the temperature from the lights turned the club into a sauna. The crew, who had practised their talents shooting local news items with individuals such as sheep farmers, were naturally ill at ease. With the crowd packed tightly around them, two songs were filmed, 'Kansas City/Hey, Hey, Hey, Hey' and 'Some Other Guy' (twice), the soundtrack of which was recorded via a single microphone onto a magnetic stripe welded to the b&w film. During The Beatles' performance of 'Kansas City', cameraman David Woods clambered onto the edge of the stage with a hand-held clockwork camera to shoot fleeting, mute, cutaway, rear and close-up images of the band; guitars, drums, faces, and their trendy Cuban-heeled boots as well as shots of the audience dancing, scanning the latest issue of *Mersey Beat* newspaper or just listening intently. These snippets, some barely lasting more than a second, would be edited and dropped into the full-length

'Some Other Guy', in an attempt to try and seize something of the Cavern's clammy and claustrophobic atmosphere.

In less than an hour, after some miscellaneous shots of the audience milling around had also been taken, the first professional film of The Beatles had been captured on celluloid. Woodhead noted he was surprised to see the group now had a new drummer. A boy next to him in the crowd that day informed him the new chap was called Ringo, and he'd joined the band just four days earlier. 'We hate him,' the boy said, gazing angrily at the new member, and shouting, 'They dumped Pete Best.' Incredibly, the anger even turned towards Woodhead and his small team. 'I recall the kids in the crowd were yelling, "We want Pete!"' he revealed. 'We had to stay in the club for a while after the gig, as Pete Best fans were waiting to give us a tough time for filming with Ringo.'

Back at the Granada studios, Quay Street, Manchester, when presented with the results, the *Know The North* producers were reasonably happy with the visuals that had been recorded, but with the audio, they were *not*. The soundtrack was certainly less than perfect, verging below broadcast standard. So on 5 September, two weeks after the first shoot, Granada sent their audio engineer, Gordon J. Butler, back to the club to re-record the group's night-time performance with the intention of dubbing this recording onto the 22 August film. (Arrangements to do this had been made at approximately 5pm the previous day, the same time The Beatles were in London at EMI's Abbey Road Studio Two rehearsing – and later recording – 'Love Me Do' and 'How Do You Do It?'.) At the original session only one microphone was used, but this time there were three; one for the drums, one for the guitars, and, in a desperate attempt to record the vocals, one was taped to one of the Ferrograph-produced, Reslo Ribbon microphones that fed the Cavern's PA system.

(Butler's recordings took place sometime between 7.30–11.15pm. Apparently he taped one hour's worth of the group's performance, but regrettably it was later junked and no longer exists. This probably happened shortly after the recording was made, during a clean-out of the studio's Audiotape Room at the behest of Granada's founding chairman, Sydney Bernstein. However, two songs from it have survived, 'Some Other Guy' and 'Kansas City/Hey, Hey, Hey, Hey'. As prominent Beatles historian Dave Ravenscroft revealed, 'A 12-inch test acetate was first cut of "Some Other Guy", then a further five 7-inch 45rpm two-sided acetates, containing both songs, were also cut.' He went on, 'Butler returned to the Cavern during the evening of 12 September, taking along two of the 7-inch acetates to give to The Beatles and also in the hope of recording more of their performance that night. But unfortunately, when he arrived the group on stage was Freddie and The Dreamers, so no further recordings were made.')

According to one legend, at the time Granada's decision to abandon the screening of their Beatles piece in *Know The North* was down to its all-round substandard quality, a result of the Cavern's mediocre acoustics and notoriously dark and murky filming conditions. Not so. It was actually because of the exorbitant Musicians' Union fees that the station would have been liable for should the screenings have taken place, as Woodhead confirmed. 'The brass band, which was to have been the other half of the Beatles film, was discovered to be too expensive because of the Musicians' Union fees that would have been due to the 16 members of the band. The charge would have wiped out the show's entire budget for the rest of the week. So, as a consolation, we invited

The Beatles to do a couple of numbers on Granada's nightly magazine programme *People And Places* [on 17 October 1962 – see entry], live in the Manchester studios. It would be their first ever TV appearance.'

So the musical comparison angle on *Know The North* was scrapped and The Beatles (and Brass Band) film was assigned to the vaults, where it was filed under 'L' for Liverpool. However, one year later, with the group's popularity now in its ascendancy, the August 1962 performance of 'Some Other Guy' was dusted down and premiered during the Wednesday, 6 November 1963 edition of the Granada news and current affairs programme, *Scene at 6.30*.

Two interesting uses of the 'Some Other Guy' clip came in December 1969. Firstly, John and Yoko were filmed at his Tittenhurst Park mansion, viewing a 16mm copy of it during the BBC TV documentary *24 Hours (The World Of John And Yoko)* and then an excerpt of it (chosen by Lennon himself) appeared in the ATV/ITV documentary *Man Of The Decade*. This latter programme featured Lennon, as chosen by the well respected author, zoologist and anthropologist Desmond Morris, as one of three most eminent personalities of the decade. (The other two being the US President John F. Kennedy, as chosen by the broadcaster and author, Alistair Cooke; and the Vietnamese communist leader Ho Chi Minh, as chosen by the American novelist and political writer Mary McCarthy.) The 16mm 'Some Other Guy' film was screened again on 26 December 1972 when it appeared during that night's edition of *The Old Grey Whistle Test* on BBC2. Another notable airing came when several short excerpts of it appeared in the Beatles episode of the influential, 17-part television documentary series *All You Need Is Love: The Story of Popular Music*. Directed by Tony Palmer, episode 14, 'Mighty Good', was

screened across the entire ITV network during the evening of 14 May 1977.

Now digitally restored, this superb, historic, 1962 footage (once cleared for broadcast by Apple) has been a staple diet of practically every major Beatles-related documentary or film ever since. (**Footage survives. Contrary to popular belief, aside from the footage listed above, no other lengthy, unseen clips from this historic session remain in the Granada/ TN Source vaults.**)

Stunning … Historic … An absolutely legendary piece of pop film and the only known footage of the group performing live at the world-famous Cavern.

LADY MADONNA
(PROMOTIONAL FILM CLIP/APPLE FILMS – ALSO HEY BULLDOG)

Studio Three, Abbey Road Studios, 3 Abbey Road, London, England

Filmed: 11 February 1968, broadcast: West Germany (b&w) on Erstes Deutsches Fernsehen/ARD *Beat Club*, 9 March 1968; UK (b&w) on BBC1 *Top Of The Pops*, 14 March 1968, 4 April 1968, Christmas Day 1968, and *All Systems Freeman*, 15 March 1968; America (colour) on ABC TV *The Hollywood Palace*, 30 March 1968

Colour, 16mm film of the group working in the recording studio, with John (as well as Paul) at the microphone, Paul at the piano, George with his guitar and Ringo at the drums. Shot during a ten-hour, 4pm–2am session, cameras eavesdropped on The Beatles while they taped the track 'Hey Bulldog' for *Yellow Submarine*. The entire session was filmed because they wanted a promotional piece for their next single, 'Lady Madonna', to be issued in their absence while they were away meditating in India.

THE AMBITIONS OF THE BEATLES

In 1964, the *Sunday Times* had a quote from each of The Beatles, plus their ambitions.

'None of us has quite grasped what it is all about yet. It's washing over our heads like a huge tidal wave. But we're young. Youth is on our side. And it's youth that matters right now. I don't care about politics.' Ringo Starr, 23, Drummer. Ambition: 'to be happy'.

'I wouldn't do all of this if I didn't like it. I wouldn't do anything I didn't want to, would I?' George Harrison, 21, Lead Guitarist. Ambition: 'to design a guitar'.

'Security is the only thing I want. Money to do nothing with, money to have in case you wanted to do something.' Paul McCartney, 22, Bass Guitarist. Ambition: 'to be successful'.

'People say we're loaded with money, but by comparison with those who are supposed to talk the Queen's English that's ridiculous. We're only earning. They've got capital behind them and they're earning on top of that. The more people you meet the more you realise it's all a class thing.' John Lennon, 23, Rhythm Guitarist. Ambition: 'to write a musical'.

Directed by Tony Bramwell, and distributed by NEMS Enterprises, the first version of the clip debuted on BBC1's *Top Of The Pops* during the edition aired on 14 March 1968. Further screenings that year included Christmas Day, when it was screened as part of the programme's first ever year-end wrap-up, *Top Of The Pops '68*. At a cost of £100, another BBC TV pop programme, *All Systems Freeman*, hosted by the Radio1 DJ Alan Freeman, screened the film again (once more b&w) on 15 March 1968. The 'Lady Madonna' film received its US TV debut on 30 March 1968, when it was aired on the highly rated ABC variety show *The Hollywood Palace*. While in Europe, the top West German Erstes Deutsches Fernsehen/ARD pop show *Beat Club* screened it for the very first time anywhere, on 9 March 1968, the very same night that it was due to receive its UK premiere on *Good Evening*, the top Saturday night pop show hosted by DJ Jonathan King. However, ATV rejected the chance, with a spokesman for Sir Lew Grade's organisation explaining, 'It just didn't fit in with the format of the show.' In the Netherlands the film was broadcast on VARA's (Vereeniging van Arbeiders Radio Amateurs) show *Fanclub*, during the edition aired on 15 March 1968. Excerpts from the footage popped up again as part of the pretentious Tony Palmer-produced pop documentary *All My Loving*, which BBC1 screened for the first time, in b&w, on 3 November 1968. (BBC2 aired it in colour six months later, on 18 May 1969.) Two different edits of the 'Lady Madonna' footage were made, with variations including George tucking into (Heinz) beans on toast. The first version was officially released on the first disc of the *Beatles 1/ Beatles 1+* DVD/Blu-ray, on 6 November 2015.

In September 1999, to help promote the re-release of the 1968 film *Yellow Submarine*, the original 11 February 1968 studio footage was dusted down and restructured to fit the song they had recorded that day. 'It was Neil Aspinall who found out that,' Harrison recalled at the time. 'When you watched and listened to what the original thing was, we were recording "Bulldog". So what he did was, he put it all back together again and put the "Bulldog" soundtrack onto it, and there it was.' The new video was premiered in America on the 17 September 1999 edition of ABC's *20/20* news programme. Billed as 'The last video ever made of a Beatles performance', to the annoyance of legions of fans it featured a voice-over by host Barbara Walters throughout. Thankfully, a clean, unaltered copy of the film was aired on VH-1 in America three days later. A week on from there, the European premiere of the clip took place on the French/Belgium station RTBF-La Deux, on 27 September 1999, just prior to the first screening of the official Apple documentary *The Making Of Yellow Submarine*. The 'Hey Bulldog' film received its UK debut on 13 October 1999 when it was screened as part of that night's edition of the BBC2 archive music show *TOTP2*. It has since been officially issued on the bonus disc of the 2015 *Beatles 1*+ DVD/Bly-ray. **(The original 16mm colour films, as well as many out-takes, survive in the Apple archive.)**

Delightful crystal-clear, colour footage of the group at work in the recording studio.

LATE NIGHT LINE-UP
(BBC2)

Abbey Road album special, broadcast: UK on BBC2 19 September 1969

Being fans of the programme, and the film montages that often featured in it, it was The Beatles themselves who proposed the idea of premiering their new album on this late-night, colour, BBC2 arts show. Ideas for the programme were discussed over lunch one afternoon at 3 Savile Row (on or around 10 August 1969), between the group, the show's host Rowan Ayers and editor Philip Jenkinson. As Ayers recalled, Paul and

Ringo were enthusiastic about the project, John was laconic and George seemed 'lost in thought'.

The 33-minute show was aired for the first time during the evening of 19 September 1969, a full week before *Abbey Road* was set to hit the shops. Aside from 'I Want You (She's So Heavy)', 'Oh! Darling' and 'She Came In Through The Bathroom Window', the rest of the album was set to either miscellaneous movie clips (supplied by Jenkinson) or Beatles-related animated sequences, brimming with varying styles and eye-catching, visual gimmickry. 'Maxwell's Silver Hammer', for instance, was accompanied by a cartoon of the four contemporary Beatles dancing, dressed up as a barbershop quartet. In total, Apple supplied a little over four minutes of footage, but surprisingly, none of it modern. As it had never been screened, they instead shipped out a mute copy of the 1967 promo film for 'A Day In The Life' (see entry). Accompanying it was an audio-tape of an early (free from lead guitar overdubs) version of the new track, 'Come Together'. A repeat screening of the programme occurred on the station three weeks later, on 10 October 1969. **(The 'Come Together' footage resides in the Apple archive and a 2000 clip of it, produced by Melon Dezign and intended for the launch of the band's official website and the original *Beatles 1* album, was officially released on the first disc of the *Beatles 1/Beatles 1*+ DVD/ Blu-ray, on 6 November 2015. Footage of the *Late Night Line-Up* show does not exist. Once their permitted two screenings had taken place, the BBC chose to wipe their tape of it shortly after broadcast.)**

This was a ground-breaking idea for the group; pity then the BBC chose not to keep it.

LATE SCENE EXTRA/SCENE AT 6.30
(GRANADA TELEVISION FOR ITV)

Studio Four, Granada TV Centre, Quay Street, Manchester, England
Recorded 25 November 1963, broadcast regionally Granada TV: I Want To Hold Your Hand – alongside an interview with Liverpool comedian Ken Dodd – was included in an episode of *Late Scene Extra*, 27 November 1963, plus a rendition of This Boy was featured in *Scene at 6.30*, 20 December 1963

With Beatlemania now engulfing the country, the group took a break from their current autumn tour to spend the afternoon of 25 November 1963 in Studio Four at Granada, filming a performance and interview for *Late Scene Extra* and *Scene at 6.30,* two of the station's popular magazine shows. Against a backdrop of enlarged, fictitious headlines from the *Daily Echo,* and with John strumming his Gibson J-160E acoustic/electric guitar, they began by lip-synching two tracks, their forthcoming Parlophone/EMI single 'I Want To Hold Your Hand' and its B-side 'This Boy'. Joining them on the set that day was the famous Liverpudlian comedian Ken Dodd. Their collaboration took shape by way of a lengthy, humorous, off-the-cuff discussion. In charge of the proceedings was the Irish-born presenter Gay Byrne. It was during his stint at the station that on 17 October 1962 he became the first person ever to introduce The Beatles on television when they made their small-screen debut on the station's local news programme *People And Places* (see entry).

Byrne began by announcing, 'We have always thought that it might be a good question to put to Mr Kenneth Dodd and the members of The Beatles to what extent do they attribute their success to their hairstyles, and we'll start by asking that question now of Mr Ken Dodd.'

'Hairstyles,' the funny man replied, 'I think it has a great deal to do with my, with my what? Success, oh yes. I like to keep it in trim. I eat a lot of shredded wheat because it's good for the herr [hair] and I have it cut twice a year, whether it needs it or not, short-back-and-sides and a bit off the shoulders.' 'What do you think of the boys?' Byrne asked. 'Well, I think it's a wonderful style,' Dodd replied. 'Because they're different from me, with them being Martians. The Professor of Archaeology at Knotty Ash University discovered some tablets which say The Beatles are definitely Martians [and] Grundy's their leader... and as Martians I think it's a very good hairstyle, lads.'

The host then turned the tables and asked the group, 'Do you think he [Dodd] owes his success to his hairstyle?' Lennon replied humorously, 'No, I don't think it helped at all,' with Harrison chipping in, 'Well, it would have been better if he was bald.' The 15-minute exchange, with Dodd doing most of the talking, covered many different topics including the writing of a fictitious film script. 'We've cast Ringo in the part of King Charles,' he joked, 'and he goes along to Nell Gwynn and pinches her Jaffas ... John is a courtier and in this film he wears a long golden wig of beautiful curls, and a blue velvet jacket, and sort of knickerbockers with laces round the bottom and buckle shoes with diamante clips on and he's walking round on the film set and a there's a policeman standing on the side saying, "We'll pinch him when he comes off."'

Excerpts from the footage were first aired in the 27 November edition of *Late Scene Extra* and then in the 20 December edition of *Scene at 6.30*. Both songs and another clip from the interview were repeated six days later on 26 December during another edition of *Scene at 6.30*. Furthermore, both songs and the interview were repeated as part of the 26 December 1963 episode of *Scene at 6.30*. *Late Scene Extra* was, as the title suggested, a late-night version of Granada's *Scene at 6.30*. The footage of 'I Want To Hold Your Hand' was officially released on the first disc of the *Beatles 1/Beatles 1+* DVD/Blu-ray, on 6 November 2015. (**The complete, unedited interview was thought lost until it was rediscovered in the Granada vaults in the early 1980s by producer Johnny Hamp during research for the station's ITV networked January 1984 documentary** *The Early Beatles.*)

Wonderful late-1963 studio footage of the group in performance and with the legendary Dodd. A sheer delight.

LES BEATLES (AKA THE BEATLES MEET PARIS) (CHANNEL 2, FRANCE)

Palais des Sports, 1, place de la Porte de Versailles, Paris, France
Recorded: 20 June 1965, broadcast France on Channel 2: 31 October 1965
Twist And Shout (short version), She's A Woman, Ticket To Ride, Can't Buy Me Love, I'm A Loser, I Wanna Be Your Man, A Hard Day's Night, Baby's In Black, Rock And Roll Music, Everybody's Trying To Be My Baby, Long Tall Sally (Live, I Feel Fine was taped but not broadcast)

The group's last European jaunt (15 concerts over nine dates) commenced with two shows at the 4,500-seater, indoor sports arena, Palais des Sports in Paris. French national TV station Channel 2 was there to capture the second one. The group's full, 12-song repertoire was recorded that night, but 'I Feel Fine' failed to make the final cut when it was aired for the first time, as a 30-minute concert film entitled *Les Beatles* on 31 October 1965 (7.30–8.00pm). Prior to Channel 2's reshuffling of the tracks, the group's original set-list for the show was as follows: Twist And Shout (short version), She's A Woman, I'm A Loser, Can't Buy Me Love,

Baby's In Black, I Wanna Be Your Man, A Hard Day's Night, Everybody's Trying To Be My Baby, Rock and Roll Music, I Feel Fine, Ticket To Ride, Long Tall Sally. It had also boasted an alternate title of *The Beatles Meet Paris*. The producer of the show was Jean-Christophe Averty and the director of photography was Lucien Billard. Brian Epstein retained a 16mm film copy of the television programme for his own archives. Excerpts from the footage (with BBC audio recordings dubbed over the top of it) appeared in November 1994 as part of the EPK (Electronic Press Kit) for *The Beatles Live At The BBC* release. The performance footage of 'A Hard Day's Night' was officially released on the first disc of the *Beatles 1/Beatles 1+* DVD/Blu-ray, on 6 November 2015. (**The original, b&w master tele-recording survives.**)

Truly great footage. Free of any overdubbing whatsoever, this is possibly the very best example of just how good The Beatles were as a live act during this period.

LET IT BE (PROMOTIONAL FILM CLIP/APPLE CORPS)

Apple, 3 Savile Row, London, England
Filmed: 31 January 1969, broadcast: UK on BBC1 *Top Of The Pops*, 5 March 1970; West Germany on Erstes Deutsches Fernsehen/ARD's *Beat Club*, 28 March 1970

For the single's March 1970 release, Apple pulled from their vaults the group's 31 January 1969 performance for the (as yet unreleased) *Let It Be* movie. Filmed in the recording studio in the basement of their Apple HQ, the colour clip Apple distributed was actually different to the one that would appear later in the film, notably Paul's facial expressions to the camera and the close-ups of Ringo at the start of George's guitar solo. BBC1 premiered the clip during the 5 March 1970 edition of *Top Of The Pops*. In West Germany, Erstes Deutsches Fernsehen/ ARD's *Beat Club* screened it on 28 March 1970. (**Master footage, as well as out-takes, survives in the Apple archive.**)

Nice colour footage of the band, in the studio, delivering another McCartney gem.

LUCKY STARS (1)
(SUMMER SPIN) (ABC FOR ITV)

Alpha Television Studios, Aston, Birmingham, England
Recorded: 18 August 1963, broadcast UK on ITV Network: 24 August 1963
From Me To You, I Saw Her Standing There

The Beatles were the headline act on a special, all Merseyside, Merseybeat edition of *Lucky Stars (Summer Spin)*, the summer spin-off of *Thank Your Lucky Stars*. Once again, this transmission, the concluding ten minutes of it at least, clashed with another Beatles-related UK television broadcast, this time John's appearance as a juror on BBC's *Juke Box Jury*, which had been recorded the previous Saturday, 22 June. Ringo's brand-new £350 Ludwig Oyster Black Pearl drum kit received its television debut during the broadcast.

At an auction in Beverly Hills, California, organised by the Julien's Auctions website on 5 December 2015, Ringo sold his kit for $2.1 million. It was purchased by Jim Irsay, owner of the US football team Indianapolis Colts. Part of the proceeds of the sale of more than 800 of the drummer's items went to the Lotus Foundation. Founded by Starr and his wife Barbara, the organisation helps fund and promote charitable projects aimed at advancing social welfare. (**Missing from archives.**)

Another, pretty standard television appearance by the band, and one we'll sadly never see again.

LUCKY STARS (2)
(SUMMER SPIN) (ABC FOR ITV)

Teddington Studio Centre, Teddington Lock, Broom Road, England
Recorded: 11 July 1964, broadcast UK on ITV Network: 11 July 1964
A Hard Day's Night, Long Tall Sally, Things We Said Today, You Can't Do That (Live)

As a promotional tool for their latest film, album and EP, The Beatles made their second appearance on *Lucky Stars (Summer Spin)*, miming four tracks, three of which, 'A Hard Day's Night', 'Things We Said Today' and 'You Can't Do That', appeared on their latest album *A Hard Day's Night*, released in the UK one day prior to this broadcast. The fourth track, 'Long Tall Sally', had featured on the EP of the same name, which had been issued in the UK three weeks earlier. (**Missing from archives.**)

Another run-of-the-mill TV appearance and another we'll never delight in watching again.

LUCKY STARS ON MERSEYSIDE
(ABC FOR ITV)

Alpha Television Studios, Aston, Birmingham, England
Recorded: 15 December 1963, broadcast UK on ITV Network: 21 December 1963
All My Loving, Twist And Shout, She Loves You, I Want to Hold Your Hand

The Beatles were top of the bill in a special, all-Mersey edition of *Thank Your Lucky Stars*. To

The Beatles with The Searchers, Billy J Kramer with The Dakotas and Cilla Black – the performers on the all-Merseybeat edition of Thank Your Lucky Stars in 1963. © *David Redfern / Staff*

close the broadcast, the programme's host, Brian Matthew, presented The Beatles' record producer George Martin with two gold discs, in recognition of the success of the singles 'She Loves You' and 'I Want To Hold Your Hand'. **(After being thought lost for years, the original, two-inch master tape was discovered in 1991 languishing in the Australian Channel 7 archive.)**

Great programme and one we can, thankfully, watch again.

MERSEY SOUND, THE
(BBC TV)

Several locations in and around Manchester and Liverpool
Filmed: 27 August 1963–30 August 1963, broadcast: UK on BBC TV: 9 October 1963 between 10.10–10.40pm in London and northern England regions only, with first nationwide broadcast on 13 November that year, between 7.10–7.40pm

Described by the BBC's weekly listings magazine the *Radio Times* as, 'nobody quite knows what this is, but it is very loud indeed, and profitable,' *The Mersey Sound* was the first major television documentary to concern itself with The Beatles, and the so-called Mersey Sound itself. Featuring the

working title of *The Beatles* and with the BBC's Manchester-based documentary maker Don Haworth at the helm, day one of the production focused on The Beatles performing 'Twist And Shout', 'She Loves You' and 'Love Me Do' to an empty Little Theatre in Hoghton Street, Southport. Haworth knew that if he filmed an actual Beatles show, the penetrating, ear-piercing shrills from the fans would render his footage, in particular the audio, unuseable. So mute scenes of a screaming audience from the group's concert at the Odeon in Southport the previous evening, 26 August, were shot and intercut with Little Theatre performances.

On day two (28 August) interviews and miscellaneous backstage shots of the band at BBC House, Dickenson Road, were filmed. During these the group spoke about their past, future plans and their belief that the present beat music boom wouldn't last for ever. 'How long are you gonna last?' John pondered. 'Well, you can't say, you know. You can be big-headed and say, "Yeah, we're gonna last ten years," but as soon as you've said that you think, "We're lucky if we last three months," you know.' Paul also gave his view on the subject. 'Well, obviously we can't keep playing the same sort of music until we're about forty,

WHAT THE REVIEWERS AND CRITICS THOUGHT

In August 1963, *Melody Maker* asked top DJs for their opinions on 'She Loves You', their fourth single.

David Jacobs: 'I find the new Beatles record rather disappointing, probably because one expects so much. I don't feel is up to the standards of their others. Not as powerful.'

Brian Matthew: 'It is the first Beatles record that hasn't knocked me out. I know they go for simplicity of lyrics in appealing to teenagers but this time they've carried it to the idiotic. The kids will buy it and be very disappointed. I think is a nothing record – which will be a big success.'

Jimmy Savile: 'The Beatles' new record? Great, man, great. Great beat, great atmosphere all the way through. What? Have I heard it? No ...'

sort of, old men playing "From Me To You". Nobody is going to want to know at all about that sort of thing.' Footage of the band in their dressing room, applying make-up, chomping on sandwiches, wading through bags of fan mail and waiting in the wings, instruments in hand, in a sequence that was intended to precede the concert footage filmed the day before, was also captured.

Day three (29 August) included the shooting of a trip on the ferry across the Mersey, from Liverpool Pier Head to Wallasey, where they were seen meeting fans on board and signing autographs. Later the band filmed a mock airport arrival at Speke Airport (later renamed Liverpool John Lennon Airport) where they pretended they were arriving back in England by descending the steps of an aeroplane.

Day four (30 August) focused on Ringo and George outside 10 Admiral Grove, Liverpool 8, the drummer's family home. He was filmed leaving the house through the front door, being crowded by a waiting horde of local children, and departing in George's open-top sports car. John and Paul were also present at the shoot but footage of them taken this day failed to make the final edit. Following this, in the salon at the Horne Bros clothes store in Lord Street, Liverpool, to illustrate Ringo's desire to own a ladies hairdressing salon once the group had finished, Haworth supervised a scene in which he was seen walking alongside a row of women sitting underneath hairdryers. A newly edited version of the 'Love Me Do' footage was officially released on the first disc of the *Beatles 1*/*Beatles 1+* DVD/Blu-ray, on 6 November 2015. (**The master film/tape transfer survives.**)

🐞🐞🐞🐞🐞🐞🐞🐞🐞🐞

Nice, charming, innocent, but rather over-used footage of The Beatles and their Merseybeat contemporaries.

Footnote: The performance footage of 'She Loves You' was also broadcast on NBC's *The Jack Paar Program*, as part of the 3 January 1964 edition, five weeks before their historic appearance on CBS's *The Ed Sullivan Show*, where it became only the second time that footage of The Beatles performing live had been screened in America. (For further information, see panel after *The Ed Sullivan Show* entry.)

MORECAMBE AND WISE SHOW, THE (ATV FOR ITV)

ATV's Elstree Studio Centre, Borehamwood, Hertfordshire, England
Recorded: 2 December 1963, broadcast UK on ITV Network: 18 April 1964
This Boy, All My Loving, I Want To Hold Your Hand and Moonlight Bay performed with Morecambe and Wise (Live)

The group's one and only television appearance with the famous British comedy double act, Eric Morecambe and Ernie Wise. In front of a small studio audience, after performing three songs live, and following a short comedy sketch (in which Morecambe referred to the group as 'The Kaye Sisters' and called Ringo 'Bongo'), The Beatles joined the pair in a rendition of the 1912 Percy Wenrich/Edward Madden composition 'Moonlight Bay'. The scene ended with John starting to tell a joke about, 'two old men sitting in a dirty deckchair'. He failed to finish it.

The fun began before the cameras had even started to roll. 'Hello boys,' said Ernie. 'Great to have you on the show. Just great. Er, will you sign your autographs?' 'On these blank cheques please,' added Eric. 'Hi, great to meet you,' Paul said. 'We're fans. Really. We've been watching you for years.' Ernie (shaking hands with George) remarked, 'Hello, I'm Ernie Wise, the one with …'. Eric completed the sentence, '… the short fat hairy legs.' 'Hi, I'm George,' the Beatle said, 'the one with …'. This time Ringo cut in, '… the short fat hairy head!' 'Seriously,' John said, 'we *are* Morecambe and Wise fans. I once saw you, Eric walking around Liverpool when you were appearing in a pantomime there.' 'Funny,' Eric replied, 'I've never walked around Liverpool in a pantomime.' 'Must have been a strolling company,' John joked. 'At least we can still walk around Liverpool,' Eric continued. 'You can't. They'd have you. The girls, you know, scragged [roughed up], you'd be. Not us. We can wander around unmolested. Provided we stay in our cars.' 'Who wants to walk around Liverpool anyway?' asked Ernie. 'Policemen,' Paul replied.

Interestingly, during the recording the show's producer, Colin Clews, was heard to mutter to a colleague, 'The show won't be aired for a couple of months. Let's hope they're still popular then.' (**The master film/tape transfer survives.**)

Marvellous film of two of Britain's finest performing together.

MUSIC!
(NATIONAL MUSIC COUNCIL OF GREAT BRITAIN AKA EXPERIMENT IN TELEVISION)

Abbey Road Studios, Studio Two, 3 Abbey Road, London, England
Recorded: 30 July 1968, broadcast/screened: UK cinemas during October 1969; America on as *Experiment In Television*, 22 February 1970
Hey Jude (Live rehearsals of take 9)

Produced by the National Music Council of Great Britain for a documentary entitled *Music!* (which would play a significant part in The Beatles' 1969/70 movie *Let It Be*), this programme featured colour, 35mm footage of three of The Beatles rehearsing what was to be their next single. Because he was not required musically at this point, George was instead seen up in the control box, sitting alongside engineer Ken Scott and regular producer George Martin. This was a fascinating, pre-*Let It Be* insight into the Fab Four at work in the recording studio. Highlights include Paul ad-libbing and improvising snippets of 'St Louis Blues' and Little Richard's 'Tutti Frutti', John breaking a guitar string, and George informing his fellow band members there'd be 'two crates [of beer] if you sing "Twist And Shout".' John was also heard asking those in the control booth, 'How we doing, Hal?' a line in honour of the HAL 9000 computer, which featured in John's favourite movie, the just three-month-old Stanley Kubrick space epic, *2001: A Space Odyssey*. Martin responded by saying, 'There were some great moments' singing in that, Paul, but it wasn't the one.' The Beatles segment concluded with Lennon briefly singing, 'Boogie woogie, boogie woogie,' and Ringo complaining that he kept getting his trousers caught on his bass drum pedal, to which, John replied, 'Take 'em off!' Its alternate American title was *Experiment In Television* when it was screened as an NBC special on 22 February 1970. (**Master colour film survives, as do several out-takes from the session, some of which were seen in the group's official 1995 documentary series *Anthology*.**)

Precursor to the *Get Back/Let It Be* project. Although brief, this is still great colour film of the group at work in the studio.

MUSIC OF LENNON AND MCCARTNEY, THE
(GRANADA TELEVISION FOR ITV)

Studio Six, Granada TV Centre, Quay Street, Manchester, England

Recorded: 1–2 November 1965, broadcast UK on Rediffusion (ITV London only): 16 December 1965, and all other ITV regions one day later

The 50-minute, b&w, Granada television special *The Music Of Lennon And McCartney* was videotaped over the course of two days and featured a number of contemporary stars and musical artists performing a collection of well-known, well-loved Lennon/McCartney compositions. The brainchild of Johnny Hamp, Granada's head of Light Entertainment, it was his homage to the songwriting genius of the pair. The Beatles themselves even popped up to praise them, miming 'Day Tripper' and 'We Can Work It Out', both sides of their current double-A sided EMI single. The harmonium John was seen playing in the latter song was actually a prop borrowed from the nearby hall of the Church Mission, where it had been frequently played by the character Ena Sharples in the highly popular, long-running ITV soap opera *Coronation Street*. 'One of the reasons why we made this show,' Paul admitted, 'was as a favour to Johnny Hamp, who risked his job by including us on an early TV show when we were unknowns.' (See *People And Places* entry – 17 October 1962). Negotiations for The Beatles' appearance had begun two months prior to the taping.

With John and Paul on hand to deliver corny pieces of scripted dialogue, other songs played in the tribute included I Feel Fine (instrumental by the 25-piece George Martin Orchestra); World Without Love (Peter and Gordon); I Saw Him Standing There (Lulu); From Me to You (jazz organist Alan Haven, and drummer Tony Crombie); She Loves You/medley (instrumental, Fritz Spiegel's Ensemble); Day Tripper (The Beatles, mimed); part 2 of the show began with Yesterday (Paul miming the first part only, then Marianne Faithfull from then on); She Loves You (Antonio Vargas); Things We Said Today (in French by Dick Rivers); Bad To Me (Billy J. Kramer and

The Dakotas); It's For You (Cilla Black); part 3 began with Ringo's Theme [This Boy] (George Martin Orchestra); If I Fell (instrumental, Henry Mancini); And I Love Him (Esther Phillips) and A Hard Day's Night (by film star and former Goon Peter Sellers who was dressed as Shakespeare's Richard III). 'Peter Sellers did this mock Shakespearian version of "A Hard Day's Night",' NEMS employee Tony Bramwell recalled, 'and he was stoned out of his mind the whole time. But it was during this show that he and Ringo struck up a real friendship.' At the end of Cilla's performance of 'It's For You', which involved her descending a flight of steps, at the bottom of which Lennon and McCartney were sitting, John whispered something rude to her causing her to break out in a fit of giggles. For years she refused to disclose what, but eventually she came clean. 'John said, "I can see next week's washing,"' she revealed, 'meaning he could see my knickers.' In April 2016, it was announced that Dawn Swane, a former ballet dancer working as a make-up artist at Granade, had shot a 49-second silent, Super 8mm, b&w film of the band backstage, having champagne in the make-up room and mucking about. Airings of the special have been extremely scarce over the past five decades. The last one in the UK took place on Channel 4 during the evening of 30 December 1985. The Beatles' performance of 'Day Tripper' was officially released on the bonus disc of the *Beatles 1+* DVD/Blu-ray, on 6 November 2015. **(A second-generation copy of *The Music Of Lennon And McCartney* special, as well as an out-take performance by Sellers, survives in the archive.)**

Great tribute show, with two fine Beatles performances as well.

NME 1964–65 POLL-WINNERS' ALL-STAR CONCERT
(ABC FOR ITV)

Empire Pool, Wembley, Middlesex, England
Recorded: 11 April 1965, broadcast UK on ITV Network: 18 and 25 April 1965
She's A Woman, Ticket To Ride, Long Tall Sally (Live)

For a third consecutive year, in front of a hysterical 10,000 crowd, The Beatles performed live at the *New Musical Express Annual Poll-Winners' All Star Concert* at the Empire Pool, Wembley. The DJ and *Ready Steady Go!* co-host Keith Fordyce introduced them to the stage with the simple words, 'Let's just have it completely silent for one second while I say … The Beatles!' Joining them on the bill that night were the Rolling Stones, The Searchers, The Moody Blues, The Seekers, Herman's Hermits, The Ivy League, Sounds Incorporated, Cilla Black, Donovan, Them, The Animals, The Kinks, Freddie and The Dreamers, Georgie Fame and The Blue Flames and Wayne Fontana and The Mindbenders.

The American singer Tony Bennett and the *NME*'s Maurice Kinn were on hand to present trophies to The Beatles who, in Derek Johnson's (also of the *NME*) own words, had been voted 'Top British Vocal Group, indeed the Top Vocal Group in the World!' John also collected an award, after being voted 'Runner-Up as British Vocal Personality'. As he held aloft his trophy, he read in mock disgust, 'Runner-Up!' (Note: Due to a disagreement between ABC TV and NEMS, cameras were forbidden from filming The Beatles' – as well as that of the Stones – performance at the following year's event, which took place on 1 May 1966. Their sole appearance in the 15 May 1966 television broadcasts – on selected ITV regions – came in the shape of them receiving their awards from the American actor Clint Walker.) **(Videotape of the complete Beatles performance survives.**

During research on *Anthology* in 1992, Apple Corps paid for ABC's original 1965 recording to be transferred from the old 405 VHF – Very High Frequency – to the then modern UHF – Ultra High Frequency – broadcast medium. Master footage from The Beatles' brief televised appearance at the 1966 event also survives.)

Truly great footage of The Fabs, sporting their Shea Stadium outfits, performing live in the UK.

OUR FAIR BEATLES
(WISH TV, NEWS 8, INDIANAPOLIS, INDIANA – A CBS AFFILIATED STATION)

Indianapolis State Fair Coliseum, Indianapolis, Indiana, USA
Recorded: 3 September 1964, broadcast America on News 8: September 1964
She Loves You, If I Fell (Live)

Sponsored by Kinney's Shoe Center in Indianapolis, the 30-minute special featured newsreel footage of the group, among other things, arriving at Indianapolis Airport, facing another lengthy press conference, performing 'She Loves You' and 'If I Fell' (albeit part of) from one of the night's two shows at the Coliseum and meeting the local beauty queen at the Speedway Hotel. Entitled *Our Fair Beatles*, the completed, b&w, News Channel 8 documentary was shown locally only by WISH TV. It was Brian Epstein's decision to restrict the amount of live footage their cameras caught of the group in performance; in this instance, just four minutes. **(Footage survives, as does raw footage of The Beatles walking onto and exiting the stage.)**

A nice slice of The Beatles during their first proper US tour.

OUR WORLD
(BBC TV/VARIOUS STATIONS ACROSS THE WORLD)

Studio One, Abbey Road Studios, 3 Abbey Road, London, England
Recorded: 25 June 1967, broadcast: 25 June 1967
All You Need Is Love (Live vocals to pre-taped backing track, which had been recorded at the Olympic Sound Studios in Barnes, London, between 14 and 23 June 1967.)

A historic moment in television history, when this programme became the very first to air, via satellite, around the world. It was the brainchild of the BBC; 18 different countries participated in the broadcast. The two-and-a-half-hour event would, naturally, boast the largest television audience ever up to that point with an estimated 400 million people around the globe tuning in. Besides the BBC in London, the 17 other stations to participate and supply their own unique item for the event were ABC (Australia), ARD (West Germany), CBC (Canada), NET (United States), NHK (Japan), ORF (Austria), ORTF (France), RAI (Italy), SRT (Sweden), TS Mexicana (Mexico), TVE (Spain), RTT (Tunisia), along with the state networks in the Soviet Union, Poland, East Germany, Czechoslovakia and Hungary. Thirteen other countries, Belgium, Bulgaria, Denmark, Ireland, Finland, Luxembourg, Monaco, the Netherlands, Norway, Portugal, Romania, Switzerland and Yugoslavia, agreed to carry the show but declined to contribute an item. The Soviet Union and several other Eastern bloc countries pulled out a few days before the event in protest of the west's involvement in the Six-Day War.

The Beatles' invitation came from Derek Burrell-Davis, who requested a song with 'nice easy words, so that everyone can understand it.' Paul's contribution, 'Your Mother Should Know', was dismissed, but John's 'All You Need Is Love' wasn't. It fitted the mood and time of the event perfectly. The song itself had been composed just three weeks before the broadcast. In order to create a festive atmosphere and to help them on the song's chorus, seated on the floor around them were some of The Beatles' closest friends, including singer Marianne Faithfull, Cream guitarist Eric Clapton (sporting a freshly done perm), Who drummer Keith Moon, Walker Brother Gary Leeds, Paul's brother Mike McGear, as well as Mick Jagger and Keith Richards from the Rolling Stones. They had all been rounded up by Tony Bramwell, the previous evening, from trendy London hang-outs such as The Speakeasy, the Cromwellian, the Bag O'Nails and The Scotch of St James. His invitation was simple, ''Ere, you, party tomorrow, 2 o'clock, EMI.' 'I found Keith Moon in The Speakeasy,' Bramwell recalled, 'absolutely enjoying himself, throwing peanuts everywhere.' Bramwell himself made an appearance in the broadcast, albeit briefly, when he was seen walking around the studio wearing a sandwich board. Hollies singer, songwriter and guitarist Graham Nash was also present. His invitation had come by way of a 9.30 phone call from McCartney on the morning of the broadcast.

Featuring an introduction by the musician and broadcaster Steve Race, and with shots of George Martin in the control booth sitting alongside Geoff Emerick and Richard Lush, The Beatles' performance of 'All You Need Is Love' began at precisely 8.54pm GMT. 'The studio was piled high with floral displays and balloons,' Race remembered, 'and The Beatles had climbed into their psychedelic outfits.' At the conclusion of the broadcast, Brian Epstein was quoted as saying, '"All You Need Is Love" is the best thing they've done … they wrote it because they really wanted to give the world a message.' To help promote the *Our World* event, the group had attended a press call at Abbey

Road Studios one day earlier, on 24 June 1967. The Beatles' fee for the broadcast was £2,000.

(**For its usage in the official 1995 documentary series** *Anthology*, **the group's original, b&w performance was colourised, using colour photographs taken at the event as a reference. The copy they used, located during research on the series, came from the SRT Television archives in Sweden. When Harrison was shown the 'new' colourised version, he said he saw nothing different or unusual about it, admitting he thought The Beatles' historic 1967 television performance had been in colour all along. This colourised version was officially released on the first disc of the** *Beatles 1/Beatles 1+* **DVD/Blu-ray, on 6 November 2015.**)

Only one word can describe this: historic.

PAPERBACK WRITER
(PROMOTIONAL FILM CLIPS/TV APPEARANCES – 1966; A ROUND-UP)

The Beatles appeared in several especially made videos, promotional films and TV appearances for this song, as well as its B-side 'Rain' (see separate entry).

Abbey Road Studios, London, England, filmed: 19 May 1966, directed by Michael Lindsay-Hogg

Unwilling to do the round of television appearances to promote their latest release, they elected instead to take part in a two-day film/video shoot. (The second day of filming took place on 20 May 1966 at Chiswick House, see separate entry.) As Harrison himself admitted during the *Anthology* series, 'It was too much trouble to go and fight our way through all the screaming hordes of people to

mime the latest single on *Ready Steady Go!* Also, in America, they never saw the footage anyway.'

The events of the 19 May shoot were jotted down in a notebook by one of the InterTel (VTR Services) crew, with whom The Beatles worked all day in the studio. Strikingly, all the performances filmed/recorded that day – eight in total –were each done in one take. They were all mimed, but even so, with no mistakes it is clear The Beatles had their minds on the job at hand.

The two performances for their latest *Ed Sullivan* appearance were completed first (see below for details). A break was then taken for lunch. The Beatles left the studio at approximately 2.15pm, and were chauffeur-driven with Michael Lindsay-Hogg to the Genevieve restaurant, 13 Thayer Street, while the technicians at Abbey Road swapped the US NTSC equipment they had been using over to UK/European PAL. At around 3.15pm, The Beatles returned and set about taping further clips for the benefit of UK/European TV viewers. Six simple, straightforward performances were taped from 3.30–6.15pm, four for 'Paperback Writer' and two for 'Rain'.

These were recorded on 405-line (analogue television broadcasting system) colour video-tape, using Marconi cameras first used for US TV broadcasts of the 1964 Winter Olympics. InterTel was the forerunner for early colour VT recordings at the time. Just two months earlier, in March 1966, with the American market in mind they had recorded the first colour episode of the weekly, top-rated Sir Lew Grade ATV/ITV series *Sunday Night At The London Palladium*. Aside from the versions of both songs bound for *Ed Sullivan*, once the other six clips were completed, kinescope/tele-recorded copies were made of them onto 16mm colour and b&w film for broadcast in the UK and across Europe (colour transmission on British TV would not be introduced across the full network until November 1969; most Continental European stations made the transition around the same time). The colour transfers had a reddish tint to them.

So, to round up the various clips, the first take of 'Paperback Writer', featuring The Beatles sitting, was screened in colour on *Ed Sullivan*. The second version, with The Beatles again sitting, but taken from different angles, and the second of 'Rain', were shown (in b&w) for the first time on *Ready Steady Go!* during the edition aired (in certain regions of the ITV network) on 3 June 1966. The pop show had never previously broadcast footage not originating from its own studio. The same version of 'Paperback Writer' was then shown again on Granada ITV's regional show *Scene at 6.30* on 13 June 1966. The second versions of both songs also featured as part of *Goodbye Lucky Stars*, the final edition of the long-running ITV music show *Thank Your Lucky Stars*, broadcast in most regions on 25 June 1966. The fourth version of 'Paperback Writer' along with the 'Rain' version shown on *Ready Steady Go!* (version 2) were screened in West Germany on Erstes Deutsches Fernsehen/ARD's top monthly pop show *Beat Club*, during the edition aired on 18 June 1966. The third version of 'Paperback Writer' featured The Beatles standing, as did the fourth, but this was filmed from a different angle (it is thought that this is the only take from the post-lunch session to survive in colour). **(The original 405-line colour recordings made after lunch were later wiped, meaning that all the performances from that session – bar the fourth – now only survive in b&w kinescopes/tele-recordings. A colour 16mm clip of 'Paperback Writer' (version 4) also survives, it is believed, having been dispatched abroad to *Beat Club* and retained in German TV archives. Aside from one screening on the *Beat Club* John Lennon tribute** programme *They Are Not Dead*, **aired simultaneously on German stations HR, NDR, R&B, SFB and WDR in December 1980, that colour clip has not been re-broadcast since.)**

Abbey Road Studios, Studio One, London, England, videotaped in colour: 19 May 1966, broadcast exclusively on 5 June 1966 edition of *The Ed Sullivan Show* in America

For this, the group's sixth appearance on the show, straightforward studio performances of 'Paperback Writer' and its B-side 'Rain' were taped in colour on American NTSC 525-line equipment. 'Rain' was first, at 10.42am. There then followed a heated discussion on how the clips should be performed (John was against simple studio performances) followed by various camera run-throughs, before 'Paperback Writer' was shot just after 2pm. Finally, once the six clips recorded after lunch (see above) had been completed, and following two brief rehearsals, at 6.19pm The Beatles, with Ringo as surprise spokesman, recorded a short greetings message for *The Ed Sullivan Show*. This recording took ten minutes. (For further information on this particular appearance, see separate entry for *Ed Sullivan Show* 6.)

Footnote: Work on the filming/taping of the various clips and the *Ed Sullivan* greeting was completed at approximately 7pm. Their day had started on arrival at the studio at 9.42am. The Beatles, however, were not done. Instead, they relocated to Studio Three for a session that lasted until 11pm, during which they overdubbed a solo horn section by musician Alan Civil onto one of their current, works-in-progress tracks, 'For No One', later to appear on their album *Revolver*.

Chiswick House, west London, England, filmed: 20 May 1966, directed by Michael Lindsay-Hogg

Like the previous day's shoot at Abbey Road, the

group worked with a crew supplied by InterTel (VTR Services). However, unlike then, which was on primitive videotape, today's footage was captured on glorious 16mm colour film. The group was filmed miming to the song in the statue garden, and inside the conservatory; some of this was also used in the 'Rain' clip. Scenes of them walking in the grounds were edited into both films. The 'Paperback Writer' clip was first shown in b&w on BBC1's *Top Of The Pops* during the edition broadcast on 2 June 1966 (then again three weeks later, on 23 June 1966).

Lindsay-Hogg originally intended setting the 'Paperback Writer' film around a narrative, with Paul playing a writer in the room at the top of his house. However, Brian Epstein was having none of it, and told him storyline clips had no future and fans simply wanted to see the band perform. (Also see separate entry for Chiswick House.) The worldwide television premiere of the colour version of the 'Paperback Writer' Chiswick House promo film came when ITV's *The Chart Show* screened it on 7 September 1996 as part of promotions for the forthcoming *Anthology* video box-set. (A re-edited version of the colour Chiswick House 'Rain' film, complete with unseen out-takes, was screened on the programme one week later, on 14 September.) The Chiswick House film of 'Paperback Writer' was officially released on the first disc of the *Beatles 1/Beatles 1*+ DVD/Blu-ray, on 6 November 2015.

Top Of The Pops (BBC TV), Studio 2, BBC Television Centre, London, England, recorded: 16 June 1966, broadcast live: BBC1 16 June 1966

The Beatles mimed 'Rain' first and then 'Paperback Writer' for that week's live edition. They were introduced by that week's host, the DJ Pete Murray. (For more on this show, see entry for *Top Of The Pops*.)

PENNY LANE
(PROMOTIONAL FILM CLIP/SUBAFILMS)

Angel Lane, Stratford, London/Knole Park, Sevenoaks, Kent, England
Filmed: 5 and 7 February 1967, broadcast: UK on BBC1 *Juke Box Jury*, 11 February 1967, *Top Of The Pops*, 16 and 23 February 1967, and on ITV *As You Like It*, 11 March 1967; America on *The Hollywood Palace*, 25 February 1967, *Clay Cole's Diskotec*, 11 March 1967, *American Bandstand*, 11 March 1967, *Where The Action Is*, 14 March 1967; West Germany on Erstes Deutsches Fernsehen/ARD's *Beat Club*, 25 February 1967

Produced by Tony Bramwell for Subafilms and directed by Swedish, TV pop show maker Peter Goldmann, the highly memorable, colour 16mm 'Penny Lane' film made you think The Beatles were actually taking a horseback ride through their home town of Liverpool. In fact they never went there. With the group reluctant to travel north, their street scenes were actually filmed in and around Angel Lane in London's East End, during a four-hour session on 5 February 1967. It was Goldmann's idea to use horses. Thinking it was typically British, he had hatched the plan during his flight over from Sweden. 'I wanted to present their new music in an original and interesting manner on TV,' he said at the time.

Discussed during their first meeting, at Ringo's house, his original plan was for the group to ride the mares down a narrow street. Good on paper, but not during the shoot itself. The surprising sight of four horses (three white ones, one black, which George rode) being ridden by the four most famous pop stars on the planet became too much for many of the passers-by, and they started to call and yell. Their din became so loud that the horses got scared, and the group had to escape to a nearby pub for their own safety. When the situation had calmed down, a photographer was asked to take some pictures of the occasion. The pub's proprietor, wife, kids, employees, everyone lined up to have their pic taken with The Beatles, who also took time out to talk and shake hands with the locals. Unsurprisingly, the plans to shoot their scenes with the horses that day were scrapped, and alternate ones had to be made.

Two days later, on 7 February 1967, The Beatles, along with Bramwell, Goldmann, his film crew, Paul's sheepdog Martha, Ringo's small dog Tiger and the group's big catering bus, returned to Knole Park in Sevenoaks to complete the 'Penny Lane' film. (It was a familiar setting, with the band having filmed scenes for 'Strawberry Fields Forever' there the previous week, on 30 and 31 January 1967. See entry.) But there were still troubles to contend with. For some strange reason, the horses once more became scared and, out of the blue, after each Beatle had dismounted, they bolted away over the big field and stood shaking at the far end of the park, refusing to move. One even kicked out at a field gate, as though wanting to escape.

Desperate to salvage any kind of horse-related footage from the session, Goldmann quickly planned a simple sequence for the group. Still aboard the horses, and wearing red hunting jackets bought especially for the occasion, the group had to stride across the park and through the archway in a decaying wall. As he noted, Paul was the best rider of the four. Another high spot of the clip was when The Beatles, still sporting the bright-coloured coats, sat down at a banquet table. Adorned with tablecloth and candelabra, it had been positioned in the middle of the field. Their wig-wearing butlers, played by Mal Evans and Tony Bramwell, then walked into shot and 'served' John, Paul and George their instruments. With Lennon getting irritated by the filming, he orchestrated the scene where the group upturned the table on which they'd been sitting. A strange scene involving a

frogman climbing out of a nearby pond and trailing some young, female fans failed to make the finished cut of the film. To add local flavour to the clip, Goldmann (who had been recommended to The Beatles by Klaus Voormann) travelled up to Liverpool to film scenes of the city's green Liverpool buses and a brief overhead view of the 'shelter in the middle of the roundabout.'

A short excerpt of 'Penny Lane' debuted on BBC1's *Juke Box Jury* during the edition aired on 11 February 1967. The Corporation's flagship pop programme *Top Of The Pops* naturally screened it during the shows broadcast on 16 February 1967 (along with 'Strawberry Fields Forever') and 23 February 1967. Over on ITV, the film was broadcast as part of the very first edition of Mike Mansfield's new Southern pop show *As You Like It*, on 11 March 1967. In the States, 'Penny Lane' (as well as 'Strawberry Fields Forever') was aired on ABC TV's *The Hollywood Palace* (on 25 February 1967), WNTA-TV's *Clay Cole's Diskotec* (11 March 1967), ABC TV's *American Bandstand* (same day, 11 March 1967) and ABC TV's *Where The Action Is* (14 March 1967). In West Germany, the clip was screened on Erstes Deutsches Fernsehen/ARD's *Beat Club* on 25 February 1967 and in the Netherlands on VARA's (Vereeniging van Arbeiders Radio Amateurs) show *Fanclub*, during the edition broadcast on 14 March 1967. With the group out of the spotlight since they gave their last concert at Candlestick Park on 29 August 1966 (see entry in *Places* section), for many it was the first chance to see the 'new-look' Beatles, with their facial hair and outlandish, psychedelic clothes.

For many modern UK Beatles fans, the first opportunity to view the 'Penny Lane' film complete was when Channel 4's music series *The Tube* screened it (in b&w) on 3 December 1982 as part of their *Beatle Movie* special. Much to Apple's annoyance – they had not granted permission – another UK airing came on 9 May 1986 when this, as well as the films for 'Hello, Good-bye' (version 1) and 'Strawberry Fields Forever' were screened as part of BBC1's extravagant, six-and-a-half-hour *Video Jukebox* special. A 35mm print of the film was recently recovered and officially issued on the first disc of the *Beatles 1/ Beatles 1+* DVD/Blu-ray, released 6 November 2015. Both 'Penny Lane' and 'Strawberry Fields Forever' were selected by New York's MoMA (Museum of Modern Art) as some of the most influential pop music videos of the late 1960s. **(Along with the recently recovered 35mm print, a two-inch tape of** *The Hollywood Palace* **broadcast survives, as do out-takes from the shoot.)**

Wonderful film of the new-look group, out and about, and gallivanting on horses.

PEOPLE AND PLACES (1)
(GRANADA TELEVISION FOR ITV)

Studio Four, Granada TV Centre, Manchester, England
Recorded: 17 October 1962, broadcast live regionally:
17 October 1962
Some Other Guy, Love Me Do

Coming as a result of the group's ill-fated, originally un-broadcast, Cavern club film (see entry for *Know The North*, 22 August 1962), and following a recommendation by the Granada producer Johnny Hamp, this nightly TV news show was actually responsible for giving The Beatles their first genuine television debut, introduced by the Irish-born presenter Gay Byrne. They were paid £35. Hamp fought long and hard to get The Beatles on the programme and even risked losing his job over it. 'I first saw The Beatles in a club in Hamburg,' he recalled. 'They were very scruffy characters indeed, but they had a beat in their music, which I liked. I put them on one of our TV shows [*People And Places*] and I got into a lot of trouble over it. Everyone said they were too rough and too untidy. But I liked them and put them on again and again. People upstairs didn't really like the whole thing.' **(Missing from archives)** (See also entry for *The Music Of Lennon and McCartney.*)

Another historic early TV appearance, lost to the hands of television archivists of the day.

PEOPLE AND PLACES (2)
(GRANADA TELEVISION FOR ITV)

Studio Four, Granada TV Centre, Manchester, England
Recorded: 29 October 1962, broadcast regionally:
2 November 1962
Love Me Do, A Taste Of Honey

In this now lost performance, for their rendition of 'Love Me Do', John was guitar-less and seated high above the rest, in the style of a solo singer and his backing band. The Beatles would never recreate this formation again. **(Missing from archives, but thankfully images captured by a fan off a television set during the broadcast survive.)**

A wonderful, truly unique appearance with John acting as the frontman of the band … and one we'll sadly never see again. Scandalous.

PEOPLE AND PLACES (3)
(GRANADA TELEVISION FOR ITV)

Studio Four, Granada TV Centre, Manchester, England
Recorded: 17 December 1962, broadcast live regionally:
17 December 1962
Love Me Do, Twist And Shout

Third appearance on the regional Granada ITV show, which was notable for another mimed performance of 'Love Me Do'. (**Missing from archives.**)

Missing. Gone for ever.

PEOPLE AND PLACES (4)
(GRANADA TELEVISION FOR ITV)

Studio Four, Granada TV Centre, Manchester, England
Recorded: 16 January 1963, broadcast live regionally: 16 January 1963
Ask Me Why, Please Please Me

Sandwiched in between rehearsals and the broadcast of this show, the group also recorded four numbers for the BBC Radio show *Here We Go* at the city's Playhouse Theatre. This two-track television appearance curiously took place behind a prop of a large cannon, with John alone sitting on a stool. (**Missing from archives.**)

Yet another gem we'll never see again.

POPS AND LENNY
(BBC TV)

BBC Television Theatre, Shepherd's Bush Green, London, England
Recorded: 16 May 1963, broadcast UK live on BBC TV: 16 May 1963
From Me To You, Please Please Me (one-minute segment of)

The Beatles' second national TV appearance. This short-lived BBC children's show was hosted by Terry Hall and his glove puppet foil Lenny the Lion. To close this particular edition, the group was also joined by the regular cast of the show – The Raindrops, Patsy Ann Noble and musicians

The Bert Hayes Octet, for a one-minute rendition of the jazz standard 'After You've Gone'. The Beatles' departure from the venue was delayed when their van, driven by Neil Aspinall, was held up in traffic. John's wife Cynthia was with them, dressed in a cape. With fans beginning to gather around the stage door, and with him eager not to let on he was married or in a steady relationship, John pretended to everyone she was a reporter, and kept saying to her, 'Did you get that? Did you get that?' The Beatles' fee for the show was one hundred and twenty-four pounds eight shillings, which included four return rail fares from Liverpool. (**Missing from archives, but several photographs of the show, snapped off the TV by an enterprising 13-year-old fan in Liverpool at the time of broadcast, exist.**)

Another historic show missing from the BBC archive. Cultural vandalism at its worst.

RAIN
(PROMOTIONAL FILM CLIPS/TV APPEARANCES – 1966; A SUMMARY)

The Beatles appeared in several especially made videos, promotional films and TV appearances for this song, as well as its A-side 'Paperback Writer' (see separate entry). Here are the details of them, all of which, bar *Top Of The Pops*, survive in the respective archives.

Abbey Road Studios, Studio One, London, England, filmed: 19 May 1966, directed by Michael Lindsay-Hogg.

Unwilling to do the obligatory trek of television shows to promote their latest release, they elected instead to take part in a two-day film/video shoot. (The second day's shoot, 20 May 1966, took

THE BEATLES' FIRST FIVE TELEVISION APPEARANCES

In order of recording, here are The Beatles' first five appearances before the television cameras. For more details on each, see relevant entries.

1. *Know The North* (Granada TV for ITV): Cavern club, Liverpool, England, recorded: 22 August 1962, broadcast Granada ITV: 6 November 1963; Some Other Guy (live)

2. *People And Places* (Granada TV for ITV): Granada TV Centre, Manchester, England, recorded: 17 October 1962, broadcast live regionally: Wednesday 17 October 1962; Some Other Guy, Love Me Do

3. *People And Places* (Granada TV for ITV): Granada TV Centre, Manchester, England, recorded: 29 October 1962, broadcast regionally: 2 November 1962; Love Me Do, A Taste Of Honey

4. *Discs-A-Gogo* (TWW for ITV): TWW Television Centre, Bristol, England, recorded: 3 December 1962, broadcast live regionally: 3 December 1962; Love Me Do

5. *Tuesday Rendezvous* (Associated-Rediffusion for ITV): Wembley Studios, Middlesex, London, England, recorded: 4 December 1962, broadcast live ITV Network: 4 December 1962; Love Me Do, and part of P.S. I Love You

place at Chiswick House, see separate entry.) After the two performances for their *Ed Sullivan Show* appearance had been completed (see below), and following lunch, The Beatles set to work recording several clips for TV viewers, once more working with a crew supplied by InterTel (VTR Services). Six simple, straightforward performances were recorded, four for 'Paperback Writer' and two for 'Rain'. (For detailed recording information, and what footage survives, see equivalent 'Paperback Writer' entry.)

The first version of 'Rain', featuring John standing on the left, was aired in colour on *Ed Sullivan*. The second version (originally intended for *Top Of The Pops*, but not used), in which John does not smile during the opening verse, together with the second of 'Paperback Writer', were shown (in b&w) for the first time on *Ready Steady Go!* during the edition aired (in certain regions of ITV) on 3 June 1966. The pop show had never previously broadcast footage not originating from its own studio. This same clip of 'Rain' together with the fourth version of 'Paperback

Writer' was also screened in West Germany on Erstes Deutsches Fernsehen/ARD's top monthly pop show *Beat Club*, during the edition aired on 18 June 1966. In the third version of 'Rain' filmed this day, John is standing and smiling for the opening verse. A new edit of 'Rain' (from versions 2 and 3), in b&w, was officially released on the bonus disc of the *Beatles 1+* DVD/Blu-ray, on 6 November 2015.

Abbey Road Studios, Studio One, London, England, videotaped in colour: 19 May 1966, broadcast exclusively on 5 June 1966 edition of *The Ed Sullivan Show* in America

The group's sixth appearance on the show, this was a straightforward studio performance of the song (as well as its A-side 'Paperback Writer'). Both were taped on American NTSC 525-line equipment. 'Rain' was the first to be taped; 'Paperback Writer' was recorded later, just before lunch. (For further information on the recording of theses clips, see the Paperback Writer entry; for information on the show itself, see *Ed Sullivan Show* 6.)

Chiswick House, west London, England, filmed: 20 May 1966, directed by Michael Lindsay-Hogg

Like the previous day's shoot at Abbey Road, the group worked with a crew supplied by InterTel (VTR Services). However, unlike then, which was on b&w tape, today's footage was captured on glorious 16mm colour film. Beginning with a long shot of Ringo walking towards the camera, the clip showed John lip-synching the song's words whilst standing in some bushes. The Beatles were also filmed outside the gates, walking through the conservatory, relaxing in the garden and sitting on low branches of a cedar tree. While they performed, small children played among the branches. With no drums to play, Ringo was also seen sitting on a large stone plinth. The film concluded with the group walking back through the conservatory, and George and Ringo waving to the cameraman as he walked away. (Also see separate entry for Chiswick House.) The clip was first shown (in b&w) during the 9 June 1966 edition of BBC1's *Top Of The Pops*. The first chance many second-generation Beatles fans had to see the clip came in 1983 when a b&w version appeared in the *Abbey Road Studios Presents The Beatles* video presentation, held in Number Two studio at the world-famous recording studios between 18 July and 11 September. A re-edited version of the colour Chiswick House 'Rain' film, complete with unseen out-takes, was screened for the very first time on ITV's *The Chart Show* on 14 September 1996, as part of promotions for the forthcoming *Anthology* video box-set. (The worldwide television premiere of the colour version of the 'Paperback Writer' Chiswick House promo film had taken place on the show one week earlier, on 7 September 1996.) The 1996 edit of 'Rain' at Chiswick House was officially released on the bonus disc of the *Beatles 1+* DVD/Blu-ray, on 6 November 2015.

Top Of The Pops, Studio 2, BBC Television Centre, London, England, recorded: 16 June 1966, broadcast UK live on BBC1 16 June 1966

The Beatles mimed 'Rain' first and then 'Paperback Writer' for that week's live edition. They were introduced by the host, the DJ Pete Murray. (For more on this show, see entry for *Top Of The Pops*.)

READY STEADY GO! (1)
(ASSOCIATED REDIFFUSION FOR ITV)

Television House, Kingsway, London
Recorded: 4 October 1963, broadcast UK live on ITV London area only: 4 October 1963 (other regions different days and times)
Twist And Shout, I'll Get You, She Loves You

Ready Steady Go!, with its famous 'The Weekend Starts Here' slogan, was one of the first truly genuine teenage-pop television shows in Britain, although it stayed on air for just four seasons, 1963–66. It showcased some of music's biggest names of the day, including The Beach Boys, the Rolling Stones, The Hollies, The Searchers, The Dave Clark Five and The Who, to name but a few. At the time of The Beatles' first appearance the programme was still in its first season. Early episodes featured the singer, and fellow chart star, Dusty Springfield as the co-interviewer and presenter. (Others included the English DJ Keith Fordyce and the demure mod Cathy McGowan.)

Sandwiched in between The Beatles' three songs that day, Dusty interviewed the group. Topics such as whether Paul slept with his eyes open, if they minded having girls screaming all through their act and how the group obtained their name were discussed. 'I just thought of it,' John comically responded. The inane questioning continued when Dusty quizzed him about his teeth. 'Do you have false teeth,' she asked, 'as they always look so even.' 'No!' he replied, 'They're all chipped and battered.'

Other Beatles-related scenes during the broadcast included singer Helen Shapiro miming to 'Look Who It Is', with cameos by John, Ringo and George, and Paul acting as the judge in the Mime Time competition, presiding over four teenage girls while they lip-synched Brenda Lee's 'Let's Jump The Broomstick'. Four years later one of the girls, Melanie Coe, would become the real-life inspiration for one of his *Sgt Pepper* tracks, 'She's Leaving Home', after she ran away from home herself. Paul penned the song after reading a newspaper report about the incident. (**The original 16mm tele-recording survives.**)

Wonderful early-era appearance with the group in delightful form.

Footnote: Michael Lindsay-Hogg, one of the show's directors (the others being Peter Croft, Rollo Gamble and Daphne Shadwell) would go on to direct the clips for 'Paperback Writer' and 'Rain' in May 1966, the 'Hey Jude' and 'Revolution' videos in September 1968 as well as their final movie, *Let It Be*, in January 1969.

READY STEADY GO! (2)
(ASSOCIATED REDIFFUSION FOR ITV)

Television House, Kingsway, London
Recorded: 20 March 1964, broadcast UK live on ITV London area only: 20 March 1964 (other regions different days and times)
It Won't Be Long, Can't Buy Me Love, You Can't Do That

During a break in filming on their first movie, *A Hard Day's Night*, The Beatles performed on *Ready Steady Go!* for the second time. Besides perusing a selection of paintings of them, sent in by *RSG!* viewers (on which, equipped with pens, each of The Beatles begin adding various scribbles and doodles), the show's co-host Keith Fordyce presented them with an award from *Billboard* magazine in America for the unique achievement of having their singles at Nos. 1, 2 and 3 in the US charts. The programme's other presenter, Cathy McGowan, asked Ringo, 'Do you think you're a mod? Do you know what a mod is, Ringo?' To which he replied, 'No, I'm not a mod, or a rocker. I'm a mocker.' Querying his book *In His Own Write*, Keith Fordyce asked Lennon, 'Tell us what's in it, then we might feel like buying it.' To which the Beatle replied, 'Rubbish!' The Beatles' fee for the show was £1,000. (**The original 16mm tele-recording survives.**)

The Beatles clearly enjoyed doing this show. Great to watch too.

READY STEADY GO! (3)
(ASSOCIATED REDIFFUSION FOR ITV)

Studio One, Wembley Studios, 128 Wembley Park Drive, Middlesex, London, England
Recorded: 23 November 1964, broadcast UK live on ITV London area only: 27 November 1964 (other regions different days and times.
I Feel Fine, She's A Woman, Baby's In Black, Kansas City/Hey Hey Hey Hey!

On what was to become their third and final appearance on the programme, The Beatles mimed four tracks, both sides of their latest single 'I Feel Fine' and 'She's A Woman' plus two from their forthcoming LP *Beatles For Sale* ('Baby's In Black', 'Kansas City/Hey Hey Hey Hey!'). They were also interviewed by the show's hosts Cathy McGowan and Keith Fordyce, who asked Ringo if he had written any songs ('One,' he replied, 'but it was pinched off another, so we couldn't do it.') and quizzed John about the rumours of the group splitting up ('It's a lot of rubbish,' he retorted. 'It's just one of the stories that started in the States.'). John and George did make one final trip to the *RSG!* studios, during the live 16 April 1965 edition (retitled *Ready Steady Goes Live!* for a short period) where they took the opportunity to plug their current single 'Ticket To Ride', and alongside The Kinks, joined in with singers Adam Faith and Doris Troy, plus the band The Roulettes, on their rendition of the 1962 Dee Dee Ford hit 'I Need Your Lovin''.

(The original 16mm tele-recording of the 23 November 1964 show, complete with The Beatles' insert clip, survives, but alas the 16 April 1965 programme does not.)

Great 1964 appearance. Relatively simple and straightforward but still enjoyable.

REVOLUTION
(PROMOTIONAL FILM/VIDEOTAPE CLIP)

Stage 1, Twickenham Studios, St Margaret's, Twickenham, London, England
Recorded: 4 September 1968, broadcast: UK (b&w) on BBC1 *Top Of The Pops*, 19 September 1968; America (colour) on CBS TV's *The Smothers Brothers Comedy Hour*, 13 October 1968; West Germany on Erstes Deutsches Fernsehen/ARD's *Beat Club*, 16 November 1968
(Live vocals over pre-taped backing track. The Musicians' Union had a ban in place on miming, so their live vocals were an attempt to conceal this.)

Straightforward, colour performance clips. (Two takes, shot on videotape for use in America, and 16mm film for UK and Europe.) Directed by Michael Lindsay-Hogg, with whom the group had previously worked on the promotional films for 'Paperback Writer' and 'Rain' (see separate entries). For the 'Revolution' clips, The

Beatles overdubbed a new vocal track onto the hard-rocking studio version. Paul screamed during the introduction, and both he and George added live, fifties-style, 'shoo-be doo-wop' backing vocals, in the manner of 'Revolution 1', the slow *White Album* version of the song, which at that point had yet to be released. The group spent time running through many takes, sadly not recorded, so that Paul and George could try out different harmony arrangements, but only two were done properly. Untrimmed copies of the most commonly seen, first version of the song feature John briefly singing 'It's Now Or Never' as the clip fades. The rare second version received its debut in the group's 1995 *Anthology* documentary series. Unlike the 'Hey Jude' clip, shot on the same day, there was no audience present. In the footage officially released on the bonus disc of the *Beatles 1+* DVD/Blu-ray, on 6 November 2015, John's vocal is completely live, as is most of Paul and George's backing singing, while the instrumentation, including the electric piano from English session keyboard player Nicky Hopkins, is from the original studio master tape. **(Master film and videotape copies of both this and the 'Hey Jude' performances still survive in the Apple archive.)**

Stunning, visually exciting video clip. A sheer joy to watch. A masterpiece.

ROUNDUP
(STV – SCOTTISH TELEVISION – FOR ITV)

Theatre Royal, Hope Street, Glasgow, Scotland
Recorded: 8 January 1963, broadcast live STV only: 8 January 1963
Please Please Me

Presented by Paul Young and Morag Hood, this was The Beatles' only performance on this children's television show (although they did record an interview for the show on 30 April 1964). They mimed their latest single 'Please Please Me', which wasn't set for release in the UK for another three days. While they sat in the 'green room' waiting to go on, John placed a call through to the studio's control booth, asking if they could be paid some extra money because their van was having mechanical troubles. The group were worried whether they would make it back to Liverpool or not. The request was then passed on to STV's hierarchy but their response wasn't positive. Relayed via the studio's soundman Len Southam, The Beatles were told, 'Sorry. You'll get your pay, but no extra.' Times were definitely tight. The group even had to bring along the single they mimed to that day. (**Not taped, as the studio did not even possess a video recorder.**)

Gone for ever.

ROYAL VARIETY SHOW, THE
(ATV FOR ITV)

Prince of Wales Theatre, London, England
Recorded 4 November 1963, broadcast UK on ITV Network: 10 November 1963
From Me To You, She Loves You, Till There Was You, Twist And Shout (Live)

In the presence of the Queen Mother, Princess Margaret and Lord Snowdon, this was the group's legendary Royal Command Performance during which John invited both the audience and royalty to 'rattle their jewellery' rather than clap. Concocted the previous evening, during a stopover in Leeds for two performances at the Odeon Cinema, his quote in full: 'For our last number, I'd like to ask your help. Will the people in the cheaper seats clap your hands? And the rest of

you, if you'll just rattle your jewellery...' After they had left the stage, the show's host, comedian Dickie Henderson, walked on and said, 'Thank you Beatles. Aren't they fabulous? So successful, so young ... frightening,' before despairingly putting his head in his hands. Though appearing seventh on the 19-act bill, they were far and away the most anticipated performers. At the very end of the presentation, and in front of the entire cast, including The Beatles, singer and *Goon* comedy-team member Harry Secombe quickly placed a bald wig on his head and joked, 'Look, The Beatles in 50 years' time.' Later, the Queen Mother announced to the theatre and stage impresario Bernard Delfont, 'It was the most enjoyable variety show I have ever seen.'

But Harrison wasn't happy. Shortly after the appearance he moaned, 'I don't want to sound ungrateful, or anything like that, but why are The Beatles on the same stage as a mass of show-business greats? It's not like we've acted in *Hamlet*, or written an Academy Awards winning song. We haven't! We're just four normal folk who have had a couple of hit records.' Even the structuring of the event annoyed him. 'The problem with the *Royal Variety Show*,' he remarked at the time, 'is that, unfortunately, it's not thrown open to the public at prices they can afford, you know, the prices that people normally pay to see us. Frankly, that upsets us more than anything. On an occasion like this, we would have liked some of our fans in the audience to make us feel more at home. After all, it was those people who made it possible for us in the first place.'

Even with repeated attempts to lure them back, The Beatles unsurprisingly declined all subsequent invitations to reappear on the show. Speaking in 1970, John remarked, 'We did the *Royal Variety Show*, and we were asked discreetly to do it every year after that, but we always said, "Stuff it." So every year there was a story in the news-papers, "Why no Beatles for the Queen?", which was pretty funny because they didn't know we'd refused.' A digitally remastered version of the 'From Me To You' footage was officially released on the first disc of the *Beatles 1/Beatles 1+* DVD/Blu-ray, on 6 November 2015. (**Original b&w film footage survives.**)

A true legendary appearance.

SCENE AT 6.30 (1)
(GRANADA TELEVISION FOR ITV) (SEE ALSO ENTRY FOR LATE SCENE EXTRA.)

Studio Four, Granada TV Centre, Quay Street, Manchester, England
Recorded: 16 April 1963, broadcast live regionally: 16 April 1963
From Me To You

Broadcast each weekday night, January 1963–July 1966, *Scene at 6.30* was a Granada region magazine programme of local news and topical features. Interestingly, this live broadcast went out head-to-head against the group's appearance on *The 625 Show*, which had been taped for the BBC just three days earlier. (**Missing from archives.**)

Sadly missing, presumably lost for ever.

SCENE AT 6.30 (2)
(GRANADA TELEVISION FOR ITV) – TWO SEPARATE SHOWS

Studio Four, Granada TV Centre, Quay Street, Manchester, England
First show Recorded: 14 August 1963, broadcast live regionally: 14 August 1963
Twist And Shout

Second show Recorded: 14 August 1963, broadcast regionally: 19 August 1963
She Loves You

Only 'Twist And Shout' survives from this day's recording (officially released on the bonus disc of the *Beatles 1+* DVD/Blu-ray, on 6 November 2015), where the group were seen sporting black, polo-neck pullovers and jeans. (**Partial survival in archives.**)

Great b&w clip of the group in their early years.

SCENE AT 6.30 (3)
(GRANADA TELEVISION FOR ITV)

Studio Four, Granada TV Centre, Quay Street, Manchester, England
Recorded: 18 October 1963, broadcast regionally: 18 October 1963
She Loves You

Third appearance on the regional show. Filmed in the afternoon, and broadcast that evening between 6.30–7.00pm. The recording, where The Beatles mimed 'She Loves You', was later junked.

Just another regular TV appearance.

SCENE AT 6.30 (4)
(GRANADA TELEVISION FOR ITV)

Studio Four, Granada TV Centre, Quay Street, Manchester, England
Recorded: 14 October 1964, broadcast regionally: 16 October 1964
I Should Have Known Better

By late 1964, with worldwide dominance now secured, The Beatles' world had changed. No

NOËL COWARD ON THE BEATLES

In 1969, Hunter Davies interviewed Noël Coward in Switzerland for the *Sunday Times*, on the occasion of Coward's seventieth birthday.

'I happened to mention the John Lennon remark at the *Royal Variety Performance*. When he told those in the stalls to clap their hands while the ones upstairs could rattle their jewellery. Until then, Coward and his personal assistant had been constantly giggling, but the giggles suddenly stopped.

"I consider that the height of bad taste," said Coward. "It must have put the Royal Family at a terrible disadvantage. Perhaps they did laugh. That doesn't matter. They're well trained. It just isn't funny. I'm not at all amused.

"Taste can be vulgar, but it must never be embarrassing. There is no need to embarrass anyone. I deplore the bad manners of today. I did see The Beatles once in Rome. I enjoyed their concert and went backstage. I met Paul McCartney who was very charming. I said I wanted to come to the dressing room. He came back and told me the others didn't want to see me. I marched straight in and told them what I thought of them. Would I have come to their dressing room if I hadn't liked their work?

"If you're a star you should behave like one. I always have. Naturally you get asked for your autograph at awkward times. I was once saying goodbye to a dear friend and a woman interrupted to ask me for my autograph. I could have throttled her, the silly bitch, but I signed. The public are very demanding. They have a right to be. I believe in good manners. It is frightfully bad to make people like reporters wish to Christ they'd never come, which I know some stars do."'

longer desperate for any kind of television exposure, the group could afford to be choosy about whose show they would or would not do, but surprisingly, on 14 October 1964, just four dates into their latest British tour, The Beatles decided against taking a well-earned day off and elected instead to accept an invitation to record another slot (their third) for Granada Television's daily regional news show, *Scene at 6.30*.

With no new single, album or film to promote, just their aforementioned tour, their appearance on the show was most out of character, especially when they chose to lip-synch the already three-month-old *A Hard Day's Night* film song 'I Should Have Known Better' for the transmission. Sporting his dark, Roy Orbison/Bob Dylan inspired sunglasses, John mouthed the words while his three bandmates happily mimed along. A short interview about how their current tour was

progressing accompanied the performance, which was aired exclusively in the Granada region of ITV two days later on 16 October.

Regrettably, this transmission is missing from the archives, but thankfully something has survived from the group's visit to Manchester that day. On hand to capture The Beatles' return to Granada were two of the studio's cameramen, who proceeded to shoot (on 16mm b&w film) the group's arrival in a limousine at the rear of the studios and (seemingly within moments of their arrival) the first run-through of their performance before the cameras. Later, with The Beatles now suitably attired for the occasion, the hovering cameras were also present to shoot the comings and goings surrounding their first proper dress rehearsal.

Further highlights of this amazing candid footage captured the group's unscheduled, impromptu visits to the studio's two prop stores. Cameras

The Official
Beatles FAN CLUB

First Floor, Service House,
13 Monmouth Street, London, W.C.2

REF. NO 65.
CLUB MEMBERSHIP, 113468.
20/10/63.

DAVID ARNOT
CARLISLE.

Welcome to the Fan Club!

Hope our efforts continue to please you because thats all that really matters to us.

Thanks for the fab way you've treated us since the beginning of 1963.

George Harrison   *John Lennon*

Ringo Starr   *Paul McCartney*

A letter from the Beatles Fan Club in 1963, then in Monmouth Street London, to a lucky new fan in Carlisle. Supposedly in their own hand writing, complete with grammatical mistakes, which John, Paul and George would never have made, having gone to grammar school.

floated around as they ran amok, grabbing at a ticket parking meter, a bus stop sign, a set of hospital bed curtains, a steering wheel, a large picture of the about-to-become new Prime Minister, Harold Wilson, and his soon-to-be predecessor, Alec Douglas-Home. (Their visit to Granada occurred just 24 hours before the 1964 General Election. Eagle-eyed viewers of this footage noticed the Election 64 props ready for television coverage of the balloting the following day.) During The Beatles' frenzied meander through the prop room, the group even came face-to-face with large 1963 cardboard cut-outs of themselves!

Their frenzied amble through a second prop room at the studios was just as bizarre. We witnessed John climbing aboard, and attempting to ride away on, a small bicycle; Paul and Ringo taking turns at punching an inflatable kangaroo; George setting about popping some balloons; and Paul picking up and shooting a toy rifle at the camera. Ringo joined in on the fun by grabbing a broom and sweeping the floor. At one point, Paul stopped in his tracks because he noticed that John was missing, but he soon laughed when he realised that his songwriting partner wasn't far away – he was still pedaling away feverishly on the bicycle, which he rode right up and into The Beatles' cramped dressing room. Once inside the poky surroundings, John soon lost interest in the vehicle and humorously discarded it, perching it on the room's dressing table in front of the mirror.

The 17 minute 22 seconds film ended with the group, now inside their limousine, leaving at the rear of Granada's studios, chased by a small contingent of loyal fans. To date, just a few clips of this amazing footage have been screened in public, mostly for illustrative purposes in various Beatle-related reports on Granada Television over the years and most notably in the station's superb January 1984 documentary, *The Early Beatles*,

networked on ITV. (**Original transmission is missing from the archives.**)

A great pity the original 'I Should Have Known Better' performance is missing, but the survival of the other, unique material does make up for it.

SHINDIG!
(ABC TV FOR THE ABC NETWORK IN AMERICA)

Granville Studio, London, England
Recorded: 3 October 1964, broadcast America on ABC TV: 7 October 1964
Kansas City/Hey Hey Hey Hey!, I'm A Loser, Boys (Lip-synched to pre-taped live studio recording.)

The Beatles' one and only performance on this top-rated American pop music show, created by its host, DJ Jimmy O'Neill, with the help of his wife Sharon Sheeley and the production executive Art Stolnitz. It ran on the ABC network 16 September 1964–8 January 1966 and regularly featured major celebrity guests such as actors alongside the top musical acts of the day. For their appearance, videotaped in London in b&w, in front of an audience comprising mainly members from the group's Fan Club, The Beatles performed three numbers. The vocals were added live to an especially taped backing track, which interestingly featured a different harmonica solo from John in 'I'm A Loser' and an alternate guitar part from George during 'Boys'. Before their second number Jimmy O'Neill introduced it with his description of the group, calling them, 'The entertainment phenomenon of the century.' The Beatles reappeared at the end of the programme, joining the other stars of the show, Sandie Shaw, Tommy Quickly, Sounds Incorporated, and Lyn Cornell and The Carefrees in the traditional end-of-show finale. (**Master tape of the show** survives, as does an alternate, audience-less soundtrack for The Beatles' section of the programme. The complete, uncut, 25-minute videotape recording of the group's appearance, where Ringo got into a strop and The Beatles apparently performed a quick rendition of the song 'The House Of The Rising Sun', supposedly survives in private hands.)

Great, crystal-clear, videotape footage of the late-1964 Beatles, in a television studio setting.

625 SHOW, THE
(BBC TV)

Studio E, Lime Grove Studios, Shepherd's Bush, West London, England
Recorded: 13 April 1963, broadcast UK on BBC TV: 16 April 1963
From Me To You, Thank You Girl, Please Please Me

Compèred by the young singer, bit-part actor and future BBC radio DJ Jimmy Young, this was The Beatles' BBC television debut. Despite the fact that up to this point they had already made 11 appearances on various regional and independent ITV television programmes, this performance for the Corporation meant that the group were now reaching a nationwide audience for the first time. *The 625 Show*, known for showcasing the nation's 'artists of the future', was so-called due to the time it was aired. The Beatles' final mimed performance of 'Please Please Me' closed the show, during which they were joined by the show's entire cast, singer Bobbi Carrol, singer/guitarist Hank Locklin, singers/guitarists Rolf and Tino, guitarist Wout Steenhuis, orchestra leader Micky Greeve, pianist Johnny Pearson and musical conductor Edwin Braden, as well as host Jimmy Young. The Beatles' historic BBC TV debut was watched by 11 per cent of the (then) 49 million UK population. Regionally, the highest percentage was in Northern Ireland where 19 per cent of the 1,290,000 population tuned in. In London, where the programme was taped, it was estimated that just ten per cent of the capital's 13,245,000 viewers had watched. The BBC's audience Reaction Index for the show was a disappointing, slightly below average with 56 out of 100.

THE BEATLES' FIRST FIVE BBC TV APPEARANCES
For more details on each, see relevant entries.

1. *The 625 Show*. Lime Grove Studios, Shepherd's Bush, west London, England, recorded: 13 April 1963, broadcast: 16 April 1963; From Me To You, Thank You Girl, Please Please Me
2. *Pops And Lenny*. BBC Television Theatre, Shepherd's Bush Green, London, England, recorded: 16 May 1963, broadcast live: 16 May 1963; From Me To You, and short segment of Please Please Me
3. *The Mersey Sound*. locations in and around Manchester and Liverpool, filmed: 27–30 August 1963, broadcast: 9 October 1963
4. *Juke Box Jury*: Empire Theatre, Liverpool, England, recorded: 7 December 1963, broadcast: 7 December 1963
5. *It's The Beatles!*. Empire Theatre, Liverpool, England, recorded: 7 December 1963, broadcast: 7 December 1963; From Me To You, I Saw Her Standing There, All My Loving, Roll Over Beethoven, Boys, Till There Was You, She Loves You, This Boy, I Want to Hold Your Hand, Money (That's What I Want), Twist And Shout, From Me To You (reprise)

The Beatles chose to stay in London for the night and attend a party thrown at the North Harrow home of Shadows guitarist Bruce Welch. It was here that they met the British singer Cliff Richard for the first time. John, however, was more pleased that he met lead guitarist Hank Marvin. (**Missing from archives. The engineering department of the BBC, as part of their routine of wiping tapes for reuse, erased their two-inch videotape of this performance in, or around, January 1967.**)

The group's BBC TV debut. Historic, but absent from the archives. Totally unforgiveable.

SOMETHING
(PROMOTIONAL FILM CLIP/APPLE CORPS)

Brookfield, Elstead, Surrey (Ringo & Maureen); Campbeltown, Argyll, Scotland (Paul & Linda); Kinfauns, Esher, Surrey (George & Patti); Tittenhurst Park, Ascot, Berkshire (John & Yoko)
Filmed between 23 and 26 October 1969, broadcast: UK on BBC1 *Top Of The Pops*, 13 November 1969; West Germany on Erstes Deutsches Fernsehen/ARD's *Beat Club*, 29 November 1969

For the most part, the film features John and Yoko, Paul and Linda, George and Pattie, and Ringo and Maureen, their then wives and sweethearts, simply walking through fields (at their respective homes) or just staring lovingly into each other's eyes. There are, however a few moments of action; Paul with his partner frolicking with their sheepdog Martha, and Ringo and his wife (in separate sequences) riding on Tony Bramwell's £50 Honda 50cc 'Monkee-bike'. With The Beatles no longer operating as a cohesive unit, at no point in the film did you see any of the group together. In fact, Paul and Linda shot their scenes themselves

and sent the undeveloped 16mm footage down to London for processing. Edited by close friend and Apple employee Neil Aspinall, the rather touching, colour film debuted on BBC1's *Top Of The Pops* (in b&w) during the edition aired on 13 November 1969. Erstes Deutsches Fernsehen/ ARD's *Beat Club* screened the clip (also monochrome) in *Beat Club* just over two weeks later, on 29 November 1969. A rare airing came on 1 November 1993, as part of MTV Europe's designated 'Beatles Day', alongside (on an intermittent loop) new interviews with Paul and George, the second 'Hello, Goodbye' film from 1967, the InterTel promos from 1965 (see entries) and the 1967 *Magical Mystery Tour* movie, unseen in the UK since its screening on BBC2 on 21 December 1979. A digitally remastered version of the clip was officially released on the first disc of the *Beatles 1/Beatles 1+* DVD/Blu-ray, on 6 November 2015. (**Master film/footage survives.**)

Truly wonderful late-1960s footage of The Beatles, and their wives, on the cusp of breaking up.

STRAWBERRY FIELDS FOREVER
(PROMOTIONAL FILM CLIP/SUBAFILMS)

Knole Park, Sevenoaks, Kent, England
Filmed: 30 and 31 January 1967, broadcast: UK on BBC1 *Top Of The Pops*, 16 February 1967 and 2 March 1967; America on ABC TV *The Hollywood Palace*, 25 February 1967, *American Bandstand*, 11 March 1967, WNTA-TV *Clay Cole's Diskotec*, 11 March 1967, *Where The Action Is*, 14 March 1967; West Germany on Erstes Deutsches Fernsehen/ARD *Beat Club*, 1 May 1967

Directed by the Swedish, TV pop show maker, Peter Goldmann, and produced by Tony Bramwell for Subafilms, one of The Beatles' two film production companies, 'Strawberry Fields Forever' was an enjoyable, highly colourful, psychedelic promotional film clip. Captured on 16mm colour film, the group was seen moving through an odd landscape of colour-reversed and colour-filtered scenery, often in slow motion or backwards. The first scenes to be shot, during the late evening of 30 January 1967 in the National Trust park, featured the group walking around a large, dead, weird-looking oak tree piano. 'Klaus Voorman came up with the idea of a strange instrument in a tree for the Strawberry Fields promo,' Bramwell recalled. 'We found an old piano, ripped it up, and then spent ages going up and down the tree with miles and miles of glittery string you use to wrap Christmas presents.'

They returned the following day to shoot further scenes, most notably the one where Paul dropped down from the aforementioned tree and ran backwards towards the piano, which, when projected in reverse, gave the impression he was running towards the tree and leaping up onto the branch. Scenes where they overturned the old piano with strings attached to the tree were also shot this day. There were seven costume changes during the filming. Nearly all came from the group's own wardrobes. John drove to Knole Park in his especially equipped Rolls-Royce and, during the afternoon of 31 January 1967, amused himself and the others by cheekily offering, via a microphone and a loudspeaker that had been built into his vehicle, comments and advice to Goldmann on how to shoot the film. The noise was loud enough to attract truant boys from a nearby boarding school who came to see what the commotion was about. Dressed in uniforms and straw hats, they asked for autographs and souvenirs. On this bitterly cold day, The Beatles still stood and chatted to the arriving fans. John took out his Bolex spring-wound, 16mm movie camera and began filming them. He instructed them to jump. 'I want everybody to

jump,' he told them, but they were uninterested in doing so, so he had to make do with miscellaneous scenes of the trees and the piano. (Ringo also brought along his 16mm Bolex camera to the shoot; clips he shot that day would appear in the group's official 1995 *Anthology* documentary series. He would use the camera again during the shooting of the 'A Day In The Life' promo film, just ten days later. See separate entry.)

The 'Strawberry Fields Forever' film debuted in the UK (in b&w alongside 'Penny Lane') on BBC1's *Top Of The Pops* during the edition broadcast on 16 February 1967. It appeared again as part of the programme transmitted on 2 March 1967. In America it was screened alongside 'Penny Lane' on the following television programmes: ABC TV's *The Hollywood Palace* (on 25 February 1967), WNTA-TV's *Clay Cole's Diskotec* (11 March 1967), ABC TV's *American Bandstand* (same day 11 March 1967) and ABC TV's *Where The Action Is* (14 March 1967). In the Netherlands the film was broadcast on VARA's (Vereeniging van Arbeiders Radio Amateurs) show *Fanclub*, during the edition aired on 28 March 1967. For many modern UK Beatles fans, the first time they had a chance to see the film was when it was screened on BBC2's serious, late-night music show *The Old Grey Whistle Test* in December 1980 as a tribute to John. Excerpts of it reappeared two years later when the weekly Channel 4 music series *The Tube* screened it on 3 December 1982 as part of their *Beatle Movie* special. Much to Apple's annoyance, as they had not granted permission, another airing in the UK came on 9 May 1986 when this, as well as the films for 'Hello, Goodbye' (version 1) and 'Penny Lane', were screened as part of BBC1's extravagant, six-and-a-half-hour *Video Jukebox* special. A version of the film with newly restored footage was officially released on the bonus disc of the *Beatles 1+* DVD/Blu-ray, on 6 November 2015. Both 'Strawberry Fields Forever' and 'Penny Lane' were selected by New York's MoMA (Museum of Modern Art) as some of the most influential pop music videos of the late 1960s. **(Master film/footage survives.)**

Legendary piece of Beatles footage with the group in their psychedelic finery.

Footnote: During a break in filming, John and George visited a local antique shop and purchased items, George a small lamp, John a poster. Dating from 1843, the poster, advertising a circus in Rochdale, would provide the inspiration for the song 'Being For The Benefit Of Mr Kite!', which would appear on The Beatles' legendary 1967 album *Sgt Pepper's Lonely Hearts Club Band*.

SUNDAY NIGHT AT THE LONDON PALLADIUM, VAL PARNELL'S (1)
(ASSOCIATED TELEVISION – ATV FOR ITV)

London Palladium, Argyll Street, London, England
Recorded: 13 October 1963, broadcast UK live on ITV Network: 13 October 1963
From Me To You, I'll Get You, She Loves You, Twist And Shout (Live)

Watched regularly by around 15 million viewers (in approximately 9.7 million British homes), *Sunday Night At The London Palladium* was a weekly, top-rated, ITV peak-time variety show. Affectionately known as the 'Home Of The Stars', the Palladium had never witnessed so many screaming fans both inside and outside the theatre as on the night of this show. They completely blocked the streets outside, a sight that provided photographers with pictures for the front page of many of the following morning's papers and gave rise to the term 'Beatlemania', which was first coined

by Fleet Street writers that day. The term would appear regularly in the papers and on both TV and radio from this point on for many years to come.

On the night of the show itself, they appeared at the very start, performing a snippet of 'From Me To You', before the compère, the comedian/entertainer Bruce Forsyth, informed the audience, 'If you want to see them again they'll be back in 42 minutes.' And indeed they were. The Beatles were the top of the bill, and closed the 50-minute show with four numbers, 'From Me To You', 'I'll Get You', 'She Loves You' and then the finale 'Twist And Shout'. McCartney's attempt to announce it was drowned out by the screams of the frenzied audience, so Lennon instructed them to 'shut up', causing the older members in the audience to applaud. The Beatles' highly successful appearance featured on the ITN news, along with footage from the group's dressing room. Newsreel cameras, hovering about outside the venue that night, caught a glimpse of the group rushing to their car, with roadie Neil Aspinall at the wheel. 'It was the greatest experience we have had so far,' John recalled at the time. 'As soon as we were clear of the theatre, we all agreed on that. It was nerve-wracking, waiting for everything to start, but once we were on stage, everything was great. There's a marvellous atmosphere there about the whole place, and as soon as we were on, we lost our nervous feeling.'

On the back of this show, The Beatles' status as a new music and show-business phenomenon had been cemented. They received a £250 fee for this appearance, their first of three at the venue. (Of note, this appearance was also the group's first for the Ukrainian-born, British media proprietor and impresario Sir Lew Grade's channel, ATV.) The Beatles' booking for New York's famed Carnegie Hall (in February 1964) came on the back of this Palladium show. The American concert promoter Sid Bernstein, reading in the press about the group, the appearance and the scenes of pandemonium, immediately began hunting down Brian Epstein with a view to booking the band. 'If Beatlemania had touched Britain,' he said, 'it was inevitable that it would touch our shores. I did three weeks of exploratory work and found Brian Epstein's home number. I got him at home. We made a deal, $65,000 for two shows at New York's Carnegie Hall.' (**The Palladium show is missing from the archives.**)

The Beatles' debut appearance on this famous, long-running, ITV variety show. Sadly missing. How on earth could this tape be either wiped or junked?

SUNDAY NIGHT AT THE LONDON PALLADIUM, VAL PARNELL'S (1)
(ASSOCIATED TELEVISION – ATV FOR ITV)

London Palladium, Argyll Street, London, England
Recorded: 12 January 1964, broadcast UK live on ITV Network: 12 January 1964
I Want To Hold Your Hand, This Boy, All My Loving, Money (That's What I Want), Twist And Shout (Live)

The Beatles' first television appearance of 1964 was a return visit to the Palladium. Besides singing five songs live, they also performed a comedy sketch with the show's host Bruce Forsyth, where they were seen on stage holding placards that made up the saying, 'Get Off You Nit' (a line directed at Forsyth). In recognition of their increasing fame and reputation, The Beatles' fee for appearing on the show had quadrupled from £250 (for their first, 13 October 1963 appearance) to £1,000. (**Missing from archives.**)

Second appearance, equally historic, but again absent from the television libraries.

THANK YOUR LUCKY STARS (1)
(ABC FOR ITV)

Alpha Television Studios, Aston, Birmingham, England
Recorded: 13 January 1963, broadcast UK on ITV Network: 19 January 1963
Please Please Me

Running weekly for five years, 1961–1966, *Thank Your Lucky Stars* was a British television pop music show made by ABC TV, broadcast on ITV. For millions of British teenagers, with its unique mix of both British and American artists, it was truly essential viewing. Since the programme was fully networked across every ITV station, this was in truth The Beatles' first real major UK TV appearance. Interestingly, the group's famous 'dropped T' in the Beatles logo was unveiled at the last minute on this day, just in time to film the broadcast. Acting as press agent for the English singer Mark Wynter, another guest on the show, Andrew Loog Oldham was present at the recording and watched The Beatles' performance from the wings. He would describe the experience as a 'pop epiphany'. After the performance, he excitedly walked over to Lennon and asked him who their manager was. The Beatle stuck his thumb in the direction of Brian Epstein who was standing in a hallway, dressed in an expensive overcoat and a paisley scarf. 'I studied this unpop-looking hotshot for a moment,' Loog Oldham recalled, 'and quickly decided he was worth a hustle. He was definitely a man on a mission and I wanted in.' He would soon manage and produce one of The Beatles' biggest rivals, the Rolling Stones. (**Missing from archives**).

The group's historic debut on ITV's long-running pop show and one we'll never see again.

THANK YOUR LUCKY STARS (2)
(ABC FOR ITV)

Teddington Studio Centre, Teddington Lock, Broom Road, Middlesex, England
Recorded: 17 February 1963, broadcast UK on ITV Network: 23 February 1963
Please Please Me

The Beatles were at the Granada Cinema, Mansfield, when this show was broadcast. They watched it, and their performance, in Helen Shapiro's dressing room. Being the star of the tour, she was the only one with a television set. The Beatles were third in the running order, with singer Adam Faith top of the bill. A short excerpt from this show was repeated in the 2 March 1963 edition of the regional magazine show *ABC At Large*, alongside a new, live interview with the group and Brian Epstein conducted by the host of the programme, David Hamilton. 'I remember passing Brian Epstein and the boys on the steps up to my announcers booth,' he said, 'and hearing Brian getting very angry with one of them because he hadn't been to the dentist!'

A set of notebooks, one containing Beatles autographs from this February 1963 appearance, sold at auction for £3,500 in 2010. The signatures, alongside a host of other famous sixties names, including Gerry and The Pacemakers and Cliff Richard and The Shadows, were collected by John Rees, a cameraman who worked on the show. (**Missing from archives.**)

Another standard, run-of-the-mill television appearance.

THANK YOUR LUCKY STARS (3)
(ABC FOR ITV)

Teddington Studio Centre, Teddington Lock, Broom Road, Middlesex, England

Recorded: 14 April 1963, broadcast UK on ITV Network: 20 April 1963
From Me To You

After recording their mimed appearance, The Beatles drove to Richmond to see a new pop group, the Rolling Stones, who were performing at the Station Hotel's Crawdaddy Club. 'We were playing a little club in Richmond and I was doing this song,' Stones lead singer Mick Jagger recalled, 'and suddenly... there they were, right in front of me; John, Paul, George and Ringo! The four-headed monster; they never went anywhere alone at this point. And they had on these beautiful long, black leather trench coats. "I could really die for one of those," I thought. "Even if I have to learn to write songs."'(**Missing from archives.**)

Another simple, straightforward mimed TV appearance.

THANK YOUR LUCKY STARS (4)
(ABC FOR ITV)

Alpha Television Studios, Aston, Birmingham, England
Recorded 12 May 1963, broadcast UK on ITV Network: 18 May 1963
From Me To You, I Saw Her Standing There

Their first appearance on the show as the headline act, and to celebrate the fact Ringo played his newly acquired £238 Ludwig Downbeat drum kit in public for the first time. It was from Drum City, a large music store on Salisbury Street, London; he went there set on purchasing another Premier kit, but after viewing the stock on offer he immediately fell in love with the new Oyster Black Pearl drum finish and when, after some gentle persuasion from salesman Dave Martin, he discovered that it was only available on the Ludwig range, the deal was sealed.

After local sign writer Eddie Stokes had painted for a £5 fee the famous 'The Beatles' logo onto the front of the 20-inch bass drum skin, Drum City manager Gerry Evans hastily drove up to the Alpha Television Studios to deliver the kit in person. Ringo's then current Premier kit was set up on stage for rehearsals, but the switch to the new one was made just prior to taping of the broadcast. Ringo christened his new purchase with the track 'From Me To You'. Incidentally, Gerry took the Premier kit back to his Drum City shop, renovated it in their workshop, and then sold it. (**Missing from archives.**)

For Ringo's new drum kit alone, this is yet another historic UK TV show missing from the archives.

THANK YOUR LUCKY STARS (5)
(ABC FOR ITV)

Alpha Television Studios, Aston, Birmingham, England
Recorded: 20 October 1963, broadcast UK on ITV Network: 27 October 1963
All My Loving, Money (That's What I Want), She Loves You

Two of the songs, 'All My Loving' and 'Money (That's What I Want)', had not been heard in public prior to this broadcast. Producer Philip Jones had been given acetate discs of the tracks, and successfully convinced Brian Epstein to have them premiered on his show before the official UK release on 22 November 1963, on the group's new album *With The Beatles*. (**Discovered in the Australian Channel 7 television news archives, 'Money (That's What I Want)' is the only song from this appearance that survives.**)

Another simple, straightforward television appearance.

THANK YOUR LUCKY STARS (6)
(AKA LUCKY STARS SPECIAL – ABC FOR ITV)

Teddington Studio Centre, Teddington Lock, Broom Road, Middlesex, England
Recorded: 14 November 1964, broadcast UK on ITV Network: 21 November 1964
I Feel Fine, She's A Woman, I'm A Loser, Rock And Roll Music

Against a huge backdrop of the word 'Beatles' spelt out in light bulbs, the group mimed four tracks, both sides of their latest single, 'I Feel Fine', 'She's A Woman', and two from their latest album *Beatles For Sale*, 'I'm A Loser' and 'Rock And Roll Music'. When the third number was played, the lights were dimmed and the bulbs illuminated. Throughout, John strummed his Gibson J-160E acoustic guitar (adding a harmonica during 'I'm A Loser'), Paul plucked his regular Hofner violin bass, George played his Gretsch Tennessean, while Ringo, positioned on a podium behind his bandmates, pretended to play his Ludwig drum kit. They also participated in a couple of short, obligatory comedy sketches, in which the show's host Brian Matthew was unveiled and later covered up again, like a statue. In honour of their appearance, the show's title was changed from *Thank Your Lucky Stars* to *Lucky Stars Special*. (**The four-track appearance survives, but *not* in the official archives. The appearance was wiped shortly after broadcast, but thankfully a copy had been sent abroad for screening, and never returned. A clip from it was used in the 1983 *Abbey Road Studios Presents The Beatles* video presentation, held in Number Two studio between 18 July and 11 September.**)

A simple, straightforward television appearance, which thankfully survives … but not in the official archives.

THANK YOUR LUCKY STARS (7)
(ABC FOR ITV)

Alpha Television Studios, Aston, Birmingham, England
Recorded: 28 March 1965, broadcast UK on ITV Network: 3 April 1965
Eight Days A Week, Yes It Is, Ticket To Ride

The Beatles took a break from filming their latest movie, *Help!*, to record their seventh (and final) studio appearance on *Thank Your Lucky Stars*. (They would, however, appear via a promo clip of 'Paperback Writer' in the very last edition of the show, *Goodbye Lucky Stars*, which was transmitted on several ITV stations on 25 June 1966, and hosted by actor, comic and 'Georgie Girl' lyricist, Jim Dale.) 'When I first went on *Thank Your Lucky Stars* with "It's Not Unusual",' Welsh singer Tom Jones recalled, 'The Beatles were [also] on there. You had to do a camera rehearsal in the afternoon, so I'm sitting there, waiting for them to come out, just to see them close up. John Lennon came up [to me], gives me a look and sings, "It's not a unicorn, it's an elephant," you know, taking the piss. He said to me, "How are you doing, you Welsh poof?" I said, "You Scouse bastard! Come here and I'll show you." Gordon Mills [Tom's manager] said, "It's his sense of humour," and I replied, "I'll give him sense of humour."' **(Missing from archives.)**

Another great TV appearance missing from the archives, especially as it featured mega-rare studio performances of 'Eight Days A Week' and 'Yes It Is'. Unbelievable how the tape was either wiped or lost.

TICKET TO RIDE

(See entry for InterTel (VTR Services) Promotional Videos)

TOKYO CONCERT (1)
(NTV – NIPPON TELEVISION NETWORK CORPORATION – JAPAN)

Nippon Budokan Hall (Martial Arts Hall), Tokyo, Japan
Recorded: 30 June 1966, broadcast: un-transmitted at the time (see below)
Rock And Roll Music, She's A Woman, If I Needed Someone, Day Tripper, I Wanna Be Your Man, Baby's In Black, I Feel Fine, Yesterday, Nowhere Man, Paperback Writer, I'm Down

In front of 10,000 fans, The Beatles performed five shows at the Nippon Budokan Hall, Tokyo, with the first two videotaped by Nippon TV, a network commonly known as Nihon Terebi. A total of six cameras were used; three colour, three b&w. This first recording was the group's only show on 30 June, and featured their regular set-list for the tour. They took to the stage at 7.35pm, wearing dark, bottle green suits. Joining them on the bill were the singers Yuya Uchida and Isao Bitoh. There was substantial right-wing opposition, including death threats to The Beatles, for playing at the Nippon Budokan Hall. The structure was viewed by many as a national shrine to Japan's war dead, and it was therefore seen as disrespectful for a rock 'n' roll group to perform there. (Ironically, it would later become one of Tokyo's main rock venues.) Legend has it that due to unsatisfactory elements in the show (i.e. microphones that had a life of their own and kept on inadvertently moving), Brian Epstein refused permission for this recording to be aired and even carried the tape of it back to London. A recording of the following day's first show was swiftly arranged. (See entry for *Beatles Recital From Nippon Budokan*.)

Wonderful, colour videotape footage of the roadweary, under-rehearsed Beatles in action, live. Superb to see.

TOP OF THE POPS (1)
(BBC TV)

Television Theatre, Shepherd's Bush, London, England
Recorded: 19 March 1964, broadcast UK on BBC TV:
25 March 1964
Can't Buy Me Love, You Can't Do That

The Beatles' debut appearance on the nation's new, weekly pop show, where they mimed to both sides of their latest single. Both performances were aired for the first time on 25 March 1964, while 'Can't Buy Me Love' reappeared during the edition broadcast on 8 April 1964. Although the programme was being recorded each week in Manchester, The Beatles had been allowed to tape their performance in London where they had been busy filming scenes for *A Hard Day's Night* at Twickenham Studios, giving an interview for the BBC Light Programme show *Movie-Go-Round*, and attending the twelfth annual luncheon of the Variety Club of Great Britain at the Dorchester Hotel, in Park Lane. The Beatles' fee for the show was £500. **(Missing from archives. The engineering department of the BBC, as part of their routine of wiping tapes for reuse, erased their two-inch videotape of this appearance in, or around, November 1967.)**

The group's historic debut on the country's most famous pop show; and one we'll sadly never see again.

TOP OF THE POPS (2)
(BBC TV)

Studio E, Lime Grove Studios, Shepherd's Bush, West London, England
Recorded: 7 July 1964, broadcast UK on BBC1: 8 and 29 July 1964
Hard Day's Night, Long Tall Sally, Things We Said Today

The Beatles' second appearance on the show got off to a bad start when they arrived decidedly late, and in a weary state, for their 2pm rehearsal. (The previous evening's party for the London premiere of *A Hard Day's Night* had gone on until the early hours, and the group were still suffering from a hangover.) Producer Duncan Wood was so annoyed by this that he even drafted a letter of complaint to BBC executive Bill Cotton Jr., and Tom Sloan, the station's head of Light Entertainment. Once taping finally got underway, the group mimed lacklustre performances of 'A Hard Day's Night', 'Long Tall Sally' and 'Things We Said Today', the first two of which were broadcast the following evening, on 8 July 1964. ('A Hard Day's Night' received two further airings, during the 22 July 1964 edition and as part of the show's best-of-the-year special *Top Of The Pops '64*, on 24 December 1964.) 'Things We Said Today' was broadcast for the first and only time on 29 July 1964. The Beatles' fee for this recording was £1,000, upped by £500 following a complaint by Brian Epstein that rival ITV pop show *Ready Steady Go!* was paying them double what the BBC was offering for their appearances. **(Missing from archives. The engineering department of the BBC, as part of their routine of wiping tapes for reuse, erased their two-inch videotape recording of the appearance in, or around, April 1968.)**

Historic, but sadly missing.

TOP OF THE POPS (3)
(BBC TV)

Studio Two, Riverside Studios, Hammersmith, London, England
Recorded: 16 November 1964, broadcast UK on BBC1: 3 December 1964
I Feel Fine, She's A Woman

The Beatles' third appearance on this long-running show, where they mimed to the both sides of their latest EMI single. Both performances were aired for the first time two weeks later, during the edition aired on 3 December 1964. 'She's A Woman' was screened again during the show broadcast a week later, on 10 December 1964, while 'I Feel Fine' reappeared as part of the best-of-the-year special *Top Of The Pops '64*, transmitted on Christmas Eve 1964. The Beatles' fee for the taping was £1,000. (**Missing from archives. The engineering department of the BBC, as part of their routine of wiping tapes for reuse, erased their two-inch video-tape recording of the insert in, or around, August 1968.**)

Another standard television appearance.

TOP OF THE POPS (4)
(BBC TV)

Studio Two, Riverside Studios, Hammersmith, London, England
Recorded: 10 April 1965, broadcast UK on BBC1: 15 April 1965
Ticket To Ride, Yes It Is

The Beatles' fourth appearance on *Top Of The Pops*, where once again they mimed both sides of their latest single release, throughout which all four members performed on their own podium, wearing their fawn-coloured (future-famed) Shea Stadium jackets. Both clips aired for the first time on 15 April 1965. 'Yes It Is' alone was screened again a week later, on 22 April 1965, while 'Ticket To Ride' popped up during the edition broadcast on 29 April 1965. The Beatles' fee for the appearance was £1,000. Despite the complete show being wiped, a 25-second excerpt of 'Ticket To Ride' does survive, thanks to its inclusion in the 22 May 1965 edition

of the long-running BBC science-fiction series *Dr Who*. The episode is called 'The Executioners', part one of the six-part Dalek adventure *The Chase*, in which the cast, including Maureen O'Brien, the doctor's assistant, and the doctor himself, played by William Hartnell, was seen watching the group's performance on a flickering, small-screen 'time and space visualiser'. The Beatles received a fee of 125 guineas for this. (**The engineering department of the BBC, as part of their routine of wiping tapes for reuse, erased their two-inch videotape recording of The Beatles' appearance in, or around, January 1969. A partial clip of 'Ticket To Ride' currently survives in the BBC archives, through its inclusion in *Dr Who*.**)

With The Fabs sporting their Shea Stadium outfits, it's great a very small clip of the show survives.

TOP OF THE POPS (5)
(BBC TV)

Studio 2, BBC Television Centre, Wood Lane, London, England
Recorded: 16 June 1966, broadcast UK live on BBC1: 16 June 1966
Rain, Paperback Writer

The Beatles' first (and only) live appearance on *Top Of The Pops*. (Their fee for the show was £1,000.) Previously they had appeared in pre-recorded, exclusive performances for the two-year-old show, but in a letter drafted on 13 June 1966, the show's producer Johnnie Stewart approached Brian Epstein about the possibility of the group appearing in person. Eppy spoke to John, Paul, George and Ringo about it, while they were in Studio Two at Abbey Road working on a new track called 'Here, There And Everywhere', and they surprisingly agreed.

Two days later, following their vaccinations against cholera in preparation for their upcoming tour of the Far East, The Beatles faced the press at BBC Television Centre, Wood Lane, London. Surprisingly, George was the most vocal. His resentment about doing the show, and life as a Beatle in general, was evident to all. 'We've only done this *Top Of The Pops* because Brian asked us. I believe there have been loads of requests to the BBC ... I know we've had a lot of requests at the office, so here we are. We know we've been out of the public eye for a long time and there have been lots of critics, but personally I don't care what people think of us. If we do too much TV or radio, people start complaining. If we do too little, they do the same.' His interesting rant continued when he revealed that, 'The Beatles are just a small part of me, and I'd like to keep it that way. We've changed a lot in the last two years. It used to be Beatles Beatles Beatles all the time! We have got to live like everybody else, so that's what we're doing.' His anger about facing reporters was also clear. 'We always do interviews like this, provided people have something definite to ask us. We know as well as the next person that nearly everything that could be written about The Beatles has been done. We tire of being asked what we had for breakfast, or what time we got up. I don't care if they never write another word about me. As I said, The Beatles are just a small part of my life now, and I want to keep it that way.'

Now wearing ties, and with Paul, George and Ringo sporting red carnations, The Beatles mimed both sides of their latest record for that week's live edition of the show. They were introduced by that week's host, the BBC DJ Pete Murray, who could barely hide his excitement that the legendary group was in his presence. 'And a welcome to the *Top Of The Pops* studio,' he said, 'with first, the B-side, "Rain", yes, in person, the fabulous Beatles!' Viewers then marvelled at the close-up shot of Ringo pretending to strike his snare drum to launch the track. John on lead vocal was seen standing away from the others. When the performance ended, and while he and Paul swapped positions, the camera returned to Murray for his next introduction. 'Well, how about that?' he said almost breathlessly. 'It's marvellous to see the boys again, just before they leave on a trip to the Far East, and particularly in answer to all those people who've been hoping to see them on the show, with their new single ... well, here they are, with the A-side of the disc, yet another song John and Paul have written, "Paperback Writer".' The screen then cut to an oblique shot of all four Beatles. A two-bar, close-up image of George playing the guitar intro to the song immediately followed. With the circle of lights shining brightly behind them as they played, it was a classic, rather exciting moment in *Top Of The Pops* history.

An 82-second clip of 'Rain' was screened the following night, 17 June 1966, on the late-night BBC2 show *Line-Up Review*. 'Paperback Writer' meanwhile was repeated two weeks later during the *Top Of The Pops* edition aired on 30 June 1966, and again on 26 December 1966 as part of the *Top Of The Pops '66 – Part 1* year-end round-up, both on BBC1. (**The engineering department of the BBC, as part of their routine of wiping tapes for reuse, erased their two-inch videotape recording of the show in, or around, March 1970, and 'mislaid' their 16mm, three-reel tele-recording of it circa 1971. That copy now survives in a private collection.**)

A monumental two-track, studio appearance on UK TV's flagship pop show; unfortunately missing from the official archives.

Footnote: Should The Beatles have turned down Stewart's request, one of the recent Abbey Road/Chiswick House 'Paperback Writer' promotional clips would have been screened instead. John would return to the *Top Of The Pops* studio on 11 February 1970 to videotape two performances of 'Instant Karma'. They were aired during the editions broadcast on BBC1 on 12 and 19 February 1970.)

TUESDAY RENDEZVOUS (1)
(ASSOCIATED-REDIFFUSION FOR ITV)

Studio Four, Wembley Studios, 128 Wembley Park Drive, Middlesex, London, England
Recorded: 4 December 1962, broadcast UK live on ITV Network: 4 December 1962
Love Me Do, PS I Love You (part of)

Presented by Muriel Young, the famous guitarist Bert Weedon, Howard Williams (and later by Wally Whyton of the skiffle band The Vipers), and ably assisted by the show's two glove puppets, Fred Barker and Pussy Cat Willum, this was The Beatles' first of two mimed appearances on this highly popular children's television show. Of note, the programme was responsible for providing the group with their television debut in the London/South Eastern region of the country. Paul's brother Mike captured images of the appearance off his television set at home. (**Missing from archives.**)

Historic show, responsible for providing the group with their television debut in the London and South Eastern region of the country; pity then it is missing.

TUESDAY RENDEZVOUS (2)
(ASSOCIATED-REDIFFUSION FOR ITV)

Studio Four, Wembley Studios, 128 Wembley Park Drive, Middlesex, London, England
Recorded: 9 April 1963, broadcast UK live on ITV Network: Tuesday 9 April 1963
From Me To You, Please Please Me (short snippet, performed as the closing credits rolled)

Return appearance on this popular, children's teatime television show, where they mimed two tracks. (**Missing from archives.**)

A standard television performance, which is lost for ever.

WASHINGTON COLISEUM
(CBS – COLUMBIA BROADCASTING SYSTEM – BROADCASTING, INC.)

Washington Coliseum (formerly Uline Arena), 3rd and M Streets, Northeast, Washington, D.C., USA
Recorded: 11 February 1964, premiered in selected US movie theatres as a closed-circuit broadcast on 14 and 15 March 1964
Roll Over Beethoven, From Me To You, I Saw Her Standing There, This Boy, All My Loving, I Wanna Be Your Man, Please Please Me, Till There Was You, She Loves You, I Want To Hold Your Hand, Twist And Shout, Long Tall Sally (Live)

The group's first, albeit brief, US concert tour kicked off on 11 February 1964 with a sell-out show at the Coliseum in Washington DC, and CBS were there to capture it. Watching the b&w videotape footage today, anybody would be shocked by how appallingly amateur the set-up and conditions were. Here were the country's then biggest entertainment phenomenon, the new kings of American pop, less than 48 hours after their monumental appearance on *The Ed Sullivan Show*; but it was evident that The Beatles didn't even possess a proper crew of roadies of their own to help with the heavy lifting. They had to, more or less, do some of the lugging themselves. As the videotape demonstrates, so that each section of the 8,092-strong crowd had at least one chance to see them face on, they had to rotate their positions and instruments every few minutes, after one or two songs. Ringo's drum riser was turned 180 degrees after the third song by roadie Mal Evans. This was repeated after 'I Wanna Be Your Man', and following 'She Loves You', the group turned a further 45 degrees. As the venue's owner Harry Lynn admitted, he wanted to fit as many people as he could into the place and if the group had played with the stage at one end, they would've only been able to accommodate 6,000; but with the stage in the middle, they could fit in over 8,000. Tickets, ranging in price between $2 and $4, were sold through one single newspaper advert.

The equipment The Beatles were forced to use was also sub-par; George's microphone wasn't working during the opening number, 'Roll Over Beethoven'. (The decision to open with that song was last-minute by the group.) The replacement was also faulty. However, it didn't dampen the audience's appreciation. They responded with typical screams of Beatlemania, causing one of the 362 police officers on duty to block his ears with bullets. To help satisfy the demand for The Beatles, and also naturally make money in the process, the videotape of their performance (apart from the tail end of 'Twist And Shout' and 'Long Tall Sally' in its entirety) was transferred to 16mm film and shown in movie theatres by the National General Corporation, one of the country's largest theatre chains, as a closed-circuit broadcast in US cinemas on 14 and 15 March 1964 alongside separate, unrelated performance footage of the top American group The Beach Boys and singer Lesley Gore.

National General Corporation produced a trailer for it. Fearing confusion over an *Ed Sullivan* type of appearance by the group, it largely alluded to the fact that the ticket fans would be buying was to a movie and *not* an in-person performance, even telling viewers not to 'confuse this with home TV'. (For the record, the opening acts at the Coliseum that night were the group Jay and The Americans and the two-piece singing duo The Righteous Brothers. An East Coast snowstorm had prevented the original supports, the singing group The Chiffons and singer Tommy Roe, from travelling to Washington.)

The first chance viewers in the UK had to see any of the Washington footage was on 30 January 1973 when, in celebration of the tenth anniversary of The Beatles' first No.1 single, three tracks from the show – 'Please Please Me', 'From Me To You' and 'I Saw Her Standing There' – were screened on BBC2 during that evening's edition of the weekly, adult-orientated music series *The Old Grey Whistle Test*. Home movie enthusiasts were able to acquire an 8mm print of the concert when the London-based bootleg company Mountain Films released it in the seventies. The same company even issued their version of the concert on the fledgling new home video format VHS in 1980, in a title called *Beatles USA*, which also contained a below-par (quality-wise) copy of the group's 15 August 1965 performance at Shea Stadium.

Missing for 31 years, the original two-inch Scotch videotape recording of the Washington concert was located by Beatles archivist Ron Furmanek in 1995, which meant that, for the first time ever, aside from the lucky 8,000 at the show itself, we were able to see the group's final two numbers of the concert. Keen to publicise The Beatles' *Anthology* series, which was about to be premiered on ITV the following evening, Derek Taylor took a copy of the concluding number,

'Long Tall Sally', and allowed it to be screened for the first time anywhere in the world during the 25 November 1995 edition of the late-night BBC2 music series *Later…With Jools Holland*. Although promoted as a special one-off broadcast, the clip had in fact already been prepared for a simultaneous limited release to various other important music-related stations across Europe and America.

Fifteen years later, in 2010, iTunes used the Washington concert film to advertise the fact The Beatles' recording legacy was now available for digital downloading. Speculations were rife that the film would be made available to the general public in 2014 via an official DVD/Blu-ray *Beatles Live* box-set, but at the time of writing (2016) it has yet to appear.

Short, silent, colour 8mm shots of the Washington show, from close to the stage, were taken by Mal Evans and appeared in the official 1995 *Anthology* series. Film-maker Albert Maysles also shot small portions of the concert for his 1964 documentary *What's Happening! The Beatles In The USA*, footage of which made up the bulk of the official 1991 Apple documentary *The Beatles: The First U.S. Visit*. With no permission given, he had to sneak his cameras into the arena and take up position a fair distance away from where the group played. **(Missing for 31 years, the original, full-length two-inch Scotch videotape of the concert was found by Beatles archivist Ron Furmanek in 1995. It now survives in the Apple tape library.)**

Historic, wonderfully exciting, yet chaotic b&w footage of The Beatles performing their very first concert in America.

Footnote: A special, forty-seventh anniversary unveiling of the newly remastered Washington videotape took place at the Egyptian Theater in Los Angeles on 11 February 2011. For the first time ever, all three concerts (Beatles, Beach Boys and Lesley Gore) were shown in their original, uncut length.

WE CAN WORK IT OUT

(See entry for InterTel (VTR Services) Promotional Videos)

WORDS OF LOVE
(APPLE CORPS FILM)

Compiled: 2013
Broadcast: Rarely screened

A promotional film for the November 2013 release of the BBC Radio compilation album *On Air – Live At The BBC Volume 2*. The film included excerpts from the *A Hard Day's Night* film, home movies made by photographer Dezo Hoffman during 1963 – between 25 March at Allerton Golf Course, Sefton Park, Liverpool, and 4 April at the BBC Paris Studio, London, then twice on 27 July in Somerset, at the Royal Pier Hotel, Weston-super-Mare, and later that afternoon, riding go-karts and fooling around in Victorian pyjamas on Brean Down beach – *The Mersey Sound* (BBC), *Follow The Beatles* (BBC TV documentary about the making of *A Hard Day's Night*, shot and screened in 1964), the 1963 *Royal Variety Show*, various Granada TV clips, miscellaneous Pathé News/ITV newsreels and some clever, modern-day animation. The film was officially released on the bonus disc of the *Beatles 1+* DVD/Blu-ray, on 6 November 2015.

Petty nice compilation, with use of regularly seen clips.

BEATLES AT THE MOVIES

There were five Beatles films, four intended for the cinema. They appeared as themselves in three (*A Hard Day's Night, Help!* and *Let It Be*), while in the other – the animated *Yellow Submarine* – they made a brief cameo appearance at the end. Their fifth movie, *Magical Mystery Tour*, was made especially for television. Here are the details of the movies; the title, year released, production and distribution credits, shooting dates, location details, selective alphabetical cast list, when premiered, songs featured and general information about the film itself.

HARD DAY'S NIGHT, A
(1964 – PRODUCED BY PROSCENIUM FILMS/WALTER SHENSON FILMS/MALJACK PRODUCTIONS (UNCREDITED); DISTRIBUTED BY UNITED ARTISTS)

Filming dates: 2 March 1964–24 April 1964.
Locations: Twickenham Studios, St Margaret's, London, England and various other sites across London/Surrey/the West Country
Directed by Richard Lester, produced by Walter Shenson, written by Alun Owen
Also starring: Lionel Blair, John Bluthal (uncredited), Wilfrid Brambell, Deryck Guyler, Kenneth Haigh (uncredited), Susan Hampshire (uncredited), David Janson, John Junkin, Jeremy Lloyd (uncredited), Dougie Millings (The Beatles' real-life tailor, uncredited), Derek Nimmo (uncredited), Margaret Nolan (uncredited), Anna Quayle, Charlotte Rampling (uncredited), Robin Ray, Norman Rossington, Victor Spinetti and Richard Vernon
World premiere: Pavilion Theatre, London, 6 July 1964
Songs featured: A Hard Day's Night, I Should Have Known Better, I Wanna Be Your Man (clip), Don't Bother Me (clip), All My Loving (clip), If I Fell, Can't Buy Me Love, And I Love Her, I'm Happy Just To Dance With You, Tell Me Why and She Loves You (The song This Boy was played as a non-Beatle-connected instrumental during Ringo's solo sequence.)

The Beatles' first film, the title of which was apparently inspired by one of Ringo's observations, as John recalled. 'Late one night,' Lennon said, 'when we were all pretty much tired after a heavy day, somebody said, "We've had a hard day," and Ringo followed up with, "A hard day? Look at the clock. You mean a hard day's night, don't you?" We all looked at each other and said, "That's it, that's the title of the film we've been after."' Or had they, we wonder, in desperation for a name simply reworked the title of singer Eartha Kitt's latest Columbia single, 'I Had A Hard Day Last Night', released in the UK just four months earlier in November 1963?

Working with a budget of only £200,000, United Artists quickly assembled the production team for the movie. As far as the financiers were concerned, thinking The Beatles' popularity wouldn't last, they wanted to make the film as cheaply as possible and have it rushed out into the cinemas by July of 1964 to capitalise on Beatlemania while it was still hot around the country. Producer Walter Shenson and the British production head of United Artists' film division, Bud Ornstein, had agreed to offer The Beatles 25 per cent of the movie's net profits, together with a flat fee of £20,000. However they were surprised when at a meeting Epstein informed them, 'I should warn you now. I'm *not* prepared to settle for less than 7.5 per cent.' Fortunately, due to the group's continuing success, Ornstein voluntarily increased the share to 20 per cent and their flat fee to £25,000.

The Beatles began work on the picture at 8.30am on 2 March 1964, on platform five at London's Paddington Station, just minutes after joining the actors' union Equity. Their memberships were proposed and seconded by their two main co-stars on the movie; Norman Rossington and the *Steptoe and Son* BBC TV comedy star Wilfrid Brambell. 'Brambell was great,' Paul said, '[but] the only terrible thing for us was that Wilfrid kept forgetting his lines. We couldn't believe it. We expected all the actors to be very professional and word perfect and we couldn't imagine that an actor like Wilfrid could ever do a thing like forget his lines. We were very shocked and embarrassed by this.' (The Beatles knew him, having already shared the bill with the actor at the *Royal Variety Performance* on 4 November 1963; see entry in *TV* section for more detail.)

Based on an (uncredited) idea by film-maker Giorgio Gomelsky and screenwriter Peter Clayton, and a story by Alun Owens, this b&w, semi-documentary affair portrayed a couple of madcap days in the lives of the group, as they travelled down from Liverpool to London to record a television show. Along the way they were harassed by their flustered manager (played by Rossington), troubled by Paul's unconventional grandfather (Brambell), escaped hordes of screaming fans, visited a gambling casino, encountered the press and a highly agitated TV director (Victor Spin-etti), sang songs, including 'I Should Have Known Better' in a tiny, make-believe train carriage, larked around in a field to 'Can't Buy Me Love', and went in search of Ringo who went missing after Paul's grandfather, a 'villain, a real mixer,' convinced him that he should be outside, experiencing life instead of reading books. The climax of the film focused on him, with just hours to spare before the show, heeding the advice and causing havoc in a local pub, taking a leisurely stroll down by the River Thames and being arrested, along with Paul's grandfather, by the local constabulary. Unsurprisingly, it all ended well when he returned just in time for the concert.

In total, The Beatles spent 40 days working on the movie. Critics loved it, but Lennon didn't. 'We were a bit infuriated by the glibness of it,' he admitted, 'and the shittiness of the dialogue. We were trying to make it more realistic ... but they wouldn't have it ... He [Alun Owen] had come round with us to see what we were like, but he was a bit phony. He was like a professional Liverpool man, like a professional American. He stayed with us for two days, and he wrote the whole thing based on our characters then; me, witty; Ringo, dumb; George, this, Paul, that.'

A Hard Day's Night was premiered at the London Pavilion, Piccadilly, on 6 July 1964, in the presence of royalty. 'Nobody thought Princess Margaret [and husband, Lord Anthony Snowdon] would agree to come,' producer Walter Shenson admitted. 'So no one invited her. I said, "We should at least ask her." It turned out that she and Lord Snowdon had an engagement for dinner [that night] but they'd love to stop by for a drink first. Anyway, we were all in the anteroom, having drinks before going in for food when George gave me a look and whispered, "When do we eat?" I told him, "We can't, until Princess Margaret leaves." Although the Princess and Lord Snowdon had this dinner engagement, they stayed longer and longer at the party, having a drink and chatting. Finally, George went across to Princess Margaret and said, "Ma'am, we're starved and Walter says we can't eat until you leave." With that, the Princess burst out laughing and said, "Come on Tony, we're in the way."' (A charity gala screening of the movie took place four days later in Liverpool, at the Odeon Cinema, on 10 July 1964.)

Trivia

George met his wife-to-be, the model and Smiths crisps TV commercial star Patricia Boyd, on the film (2 March 1964) when she made a brief, uncredited, appearance as one of the schoolgirls. 'George hardly said hello,' she said, recalling her first meeting with the group, 'but the others came and chatted to us. When we started filming, I could feel George looking at me … Ringo seemed the nicest and easiest to talk to and so was Paul. But I was terrified of John.' She began dating Harrison once she had finished with her then long-standing boyfriend Eric Swayne. They married at Epsom Register Office, Surrey, on 21 January 1966. Her only word in the movie – 'Prisoners?'

It was George who asked Victor Spinetti to be in the film. In 1963, he and John had seen him in the West End stage musical *Oh! What A Lovely War* and went backstage afterwards to meet him. Harrison said to him, 'Oh, Vic. You've got to be in our film. If you're not in our film, me mom won't come because she fancies you.'

Filmed on 31 March 1964, at London's Scala Theatre, the concert sequence was shot in front of 350 screaming teenagers, one of whom was 13-year-old Phil Collins, future drummer and singer with the British pop/rock band Genesis. 'We had six cameras shooting continuously,' director, Richard Lester recalled, 'and I was running between them all the time. I briefed the camera-men to pan and look for anything interesting, just like as if it was for a documentary. Three of the cameramen I knew and three I didn't. Because the noise [of the screaming] was so loud, one of them lost two back teeth.'

The song 'You Can't Do That' was filmed as part of it, but before the decision had been made to excise it from the film the footage had fortuitously been shipped by United Artists to CBS's *The Ed Sullivan Show* as a teaser for the upcoming movie. The clip was aired on the 24 May 1964 edition of the programme (see entry in *TV* section), alongside a brief interview with The Beatles especially filmed by Sullivan in London. An extract of the song later appeared in the 1995 MPI Home Video/Saltair Productions documentary *You Can't Do That: The Making of A Hard Day's Night*.

Ringo was suffering from a hangover when he shot his solo sequence for the movie. Filmed just hours after he had left a nightclub drunk, he was seen taking a leisurely stroll down by the river and chancing upon a 14-year-old teenager, played by David Janson, who would later find fame in his own right in the 1975 Thames/ITV RAF comedy series *Get Some In!* The sequence was shot at the River Thames towpath in Kew, Surrey, on 9 April 1964 – the drummer later admitted he didn't (or couldn't) even see the boy. 'I was out of my brain,' Starr admitted. 'The scene was meant to be a dialogue scene but I could not speak. I had the continuity lady shout my lines and I'd go, "So why are you off school?" We tried it several ways. Richard Lester decided that he had to do something so he had me walk along and it turned out like a silent movie scene. I was really dejected. I felt ready to die. Then, when the film came out, they [the critics] all said, "Oh God! Fantastic!"'

In the movie, Ringo was invited to Le Cercle gambling club, on Hamilton Place, where two years earlier James Bond had made his first film appearance, in *Dr No*. Coincidentally, both this and *A Hard Day's Night* were released by United Artists.

The extremely short rock 'n' roll instrumental, heard when Ringo turned on his transistor radio during the train carriage sequence near the start of the movie, had been recorded in London by a group of session musicians; allegedly among them was Tornado Clem Cattini on drums and legendary Yardbird Jimmy Page on guitar.

After filming at the Scala Theatre had ended on 1 April 1964, John met his father Alfred for the first time in 17 years. Accompanied by a journalist, he had walked into the NEMS office at 5/6 Argyll Street, London, and explained to the receptionist who he was. Brian Epstein was informed and sent for a car to pick up John and the rest of The Beatles, with the exception of Paul. The meeting was unsuccessful. John's first words to his father were, 'What do you want?' and after several heated exchanges, he furiously ordered him off the premises. Their meeting had lasted no more than 20 minutes. The encounter was kept out of the newspapers by trading with the journalist exclusive stories about the other acts Epstein managed.

Lennon was missing from the tail end of the 'Can't Buy Me Love'/Thornbury Playing Fields, Isleworth, sequence (shot 23 April 1964) due to his appearance at a literary luncheon, held in his honour at the Dorchester Hotel, London. His 'I'll Cry Instead' was the original choice for that scene, until Lester decided otherwise.

John's written answer to the female reporter who asked him, during the press conference sequence, if he had any hobbies was the word 'tits'.

A Hard Day's Night took in more than £12 million at the box office, and proved so popular that more than 1,600 prints of the movie were in circulation at the same time.

A running joke in the movie was the description of Paul's grandfather as being 'a very clean old man'. This was a reference to Wilfrid Brambell's character Albert Steptoe in *Steptoe and Son*, where he was frequently called a 'dirty old man' by his on-screen son Harold, played by Harry H. Corbett. Brambell was actually only 30 years older than Paul when they shot the film.

The words 'The Beatles' were never once spoken throughout the entire movie; however they were visible on Ringo's drum kit, on the stage lighting behind the group at the end of 'She Loves You', and on the helicopter in the final sequence. In a conversation with the *NME*, Richard Lester said he thought George was the best actor in the band because 'he didn't try to do too much, but always hit it right in the middle.' His solo sequence in the picture, where he got lost, ended up in an advertising studio and was mistaken for an advertising model by the executive, played by Kenneth Haigh, led to the word 'grotty' becoming absorbed into the English language. A noted Shakespearian actor and a good friend of the movie's screenwriter, Alun Owen, Haigh didn't want his name in the film's credits. Similar to a number of established stars back then, he didn't want to be associated with The Beatles. He soon changed his mind though and began listing *A Hard Day's Night* in his role call of achievements at every opportunity. According to Norman Rossington, in the dressing room scene where John took the scissors, cut the tailor's tape and said, 'I now declare this bridge open,' John improvised several other versions where, instead of 'bridge' he would say 'synagogue' or 'fish-and-chips stand' etc. The uncredited tailor in the scene, Dougie Millings, was actually the group's real-life one.

During their time at Twickenham, the band, and in particular Paul, struck up a friendship with actor Christopher Lee who was at the studio doing post-production work on his latest movie, the

Hammer Film adventure *The Devil-Ship Pirates*. Their bond endured, and a decade later Lee would appear alongside several other celebrities on the Paul/Wings *Band On The Run* album cover.

A Hard Day's Night competed for two Academy Awards, losing in both categories: Best Adapted score (George Martin) and Best Screenplay (Alun Owen). None of The Beatles' original songs were nominated.

The movie was premiered in America at the Beacon Theatre in New York on 12 August 1964 and opened in 500 cinemas throughout the country the next day. A newly restored, fiftieth anniversary version of the movie played in more than 50 cities across the States over the 4 July 2014 weekend, while in the UK, at the same time it had an extended run at the BFI (British Film Institute) on the South Bank, London.

Variations on the *A Hard Day's Night* movie title included *Os Reis Do Iê-Iê-Iê (The Kings Of Yeah-Yeah-Yeah)* in Brazil, *Quatre Garçons Dans Le Vent (Four Boys In The Wind)* in France, *Tutti Per Uno (All For One)* in Italy and *Yeah! Yeah! Tässä tulemme! (Yeah! Yeah! Here We Come!)* in Finland.

A Hard Day's Night did not become eligible for television screenings until July 1969. Its first in the UK came when BBC1 broadcast it during the afternoon of 28 December 1970. John watched it at his then home in Ascot and felt compelled to pen the track 'I'm The Greatest', which he later donated to Ringo for his eponymous 1973 album.

Noticeably different to the ones before it, in ways of style and the way Lester shot it, this was a true landmark rock 'n'

HIT OR MISS?

Not all of America immediately took to The Beatles. These comments appeared in *Newsweek*, 24 February 1964.

'Musically, they are a near disaster; guitars slamming out a merciless beat that does away with secondary rhythms, harmony and melody. Their lyrics (punctuated by nutty shouts of "yeah, yeah, yeah!") are a catastrophe, a preposterous farrago of Valentine-card romantic sentiments.'

Noël Coward, the famous composer and playwright, noted in a diary entry that his singular experience at a Beatles concert (1965) was less than thrilling. 'The noise was deafening throughout, and I couldn't hear a word they sang or a note they played, just one long ear-splitting din.'

His impression of them afterwards, as recorded in his diary, was not very flattering. 'It is still impossible to judge from their public performance whether they have talent or not. They were professional, had a certain guileless charm, and stayed on mercifully for not too long.'

One of the most vitriolic attacks on The Beatles was by Paul Johnson in the *New Statesman* on 28 February 1964. Under headline 'The Menace of Beatlism' Johnson referred to 'this apotheosis of inanity' and described fans as 'a bottomless chasm of vacuity.' He also dismissed the pop critics who were praising them as 'barely more literate or articulate than those who buy the records in the first place'.

roll movie. And over 50 years later it still looks great. We all loved it, but John didn't.

Footnote: In 1979, after the 15-year leasing arrangement with United Artists had expired, the rights to *A Hard Day's Night* reverted back to its producer Walter Shenson.

HELP!
(1965 – PRODUCED BY WALTER SHENSON FILMS/DISTRIBUTED BY UNITED ARTISTS)

Filming dates: 23 February 1965–11 May 1965
Locations: Twickenham Studios, St Margaret's, London, England and various nearby sites, plus Strand-on-the-Green, Chiswick/Knighton Down, Larkhill, Wiltshire/Cliveden House, Cliveden, Maidenhead, Berkshire; and abroad at New Providence Island, Bahamas/Obertauern, Austrian Alps. Post-production work on the movie continued at Twickenham Studios until 16 June 1965
Directed by Richard Lester, produced by Walter Shenson, written by Marc Behm and Charles Wood
Also starring Alfie Bass, John Bluthal, Eleanor Bron, Patrick Cargill, Roy Kinnear, Leo McKern, Warren Mitchell and Victor Spinetti
World premiere: Pavilion Theatre, London, 29 July 1965
Songs featured: Help!, You're Going To Lose That Girl, You've Got To Hide Your Love Away, Ticket To Ride, I Need You, The Night Before, Another Girl, She's A Woman (heard in the background, on a tape machine, underground during the Salisbury Plain sequence) (Other songs were featured, but only as non-Beatles-connected instrumentals: 'A Hard Day's Night', mimed by a band (actually actors) during the Indian restaurant sequence, 'I'm Happy Just To Dance With You', during the bike-riding scene and 'You Can't Do That', during the Austrian Alps sequence.)

Help! was a colourful, surreal, freewheeling comedy-adventure that saw Ringo as the human sacrifice target of an Eastern cult. He inadvertently had their sacrificial ring, and cult members Clang (played by Leo McKern), Ahme (Eleanor Bron) and Bhuta (John Bluthal), along with several others, headed to London to retrieve it. After several failed attempts to steal it back, Ringo learnt that if he did not return it soon, he would become the next sacrifice. But there was a problem. The ring was stuck firmly on his finger. So it was a race against time with John, Paul and George trying their best to protect him while being chased themselves, not only by Clang and his followers, but by two mad, bumbling scientists (Victor Spinetti and Roy Kinnear) and the Superintendent of Scotland Yard (played by Patrick Cargill). Would Ringo be saved, or sacrificed, we wondered?

Filming began in the Bahamas, at New Providence Island on the 23 February 1965 after the group's financial adviser Dr Walter Strach had instituted a tax shelter there. Partly as a goodwill gesture, the group agreed to shoot at the location, staying for two weeks at the highly luxurious Balmoral Club near Cable Beach. As with the group's previous effort, Walter Shenson was in charge of production. 'The [untitled] film will have a very spectacular look about it,' he said at the time. 'We aim to make it even more exciting visually than *A Hard Day's Night*. Dick Lester is very excited about the prospect of filming in the tropics and in the Alps. The colour of the Bahamas and the snow of the Alps will provide a wonderful background for The Beatles and the action of the film ... there will be a good deal of action ... It will be plottier.'

The uncertainty over its title remained until 17 March 1965, when three weeks into filming it was announced to the press that the name of the movie would be *Eight Arms To Hold You*. (Just prior to that, its working title had been *Beatles Phase II*, or *Beatles Mark II*, an obvious reference to it being their second feature film.) Unlike *A Hard Day's Night*, there were fewer constraints this time round. As Lester admitted, 'We had more time, and lots more money.' The group used this new-found freedom, exploring their then favoured recreational activity of choice. 'During the filming,' he admitted, 'The Beatles enjoyed a lot of marijuana. There was lots of smiling.' 'Marijuana was a giggle to the boys,' John's then wife Cynthia admitted, 'and it enabled them to relax. Trouble was, they smoked it whenever they could, in the recording studio, at home. When they smoked, the merry-go-round stopped for a while; the world looked brighter.' 'We were smoking marijuana for breakfast during this period,' Lennon admitted. 'Nobody could communicate with us because it was all glazed eyes and giggling all the time in our own world.'

One sequence, where Ringo had to dive off a yacht and fall 30 feet into the sea, was particularly alarming. 'They had a bunch of people watching the area for sharks,' his co-star in the sequence, Victor Spinetti, recalled. 'So Dick Lester said, "Let's do another shot." They dried Ringo off and he was shivering because it was out of season and very cold. So we did another take, and then another, and after the third take Lester said, "Let's do another one," and Ringo said, "Do we have to?" Dick replied, "Well, I'd like another one, why?" and Ringo said, "Because I can't swim." Lester went white and said, "Why on earth didn't you tell me?" and Ringo said, "Well, I didn't like to say." The first day of filming was almost the end of the film and the end of The Beatles.'

In the Rajahama Indian restaurant sequence, the scene featured a few Indian musicians (actually actors) strumming along as a backdrop. It was The Beatles' first exposure to the country's music. 'On the set, in a scene in a restaurant,' recalled John, 'they had these sitars. It was supposed to be an Indian band playing in the background, and George kept staring and looking at them.' In

between takes, Harrison picked up one of their sitars, started to pluck it and thought, 'This is a funny sound.' *Help!* co-star Roy Kinnear remembered George being 'very interested in it all,' adding, 'before we knew it, he had someone run out and buy him a cheap sitar from one of those Indian shops near the British Museum.'

The name of legendary sitar virtuoso Ravi Shankar was coincidentally mentioned to George shortly after. Then, after talking about him with David Crosby of The Byrds, he went and bought a Ravi record and, as George himself admitted in *Billboard* magazine in Decembers 1992, the music, 'hit a certain spot in me that I can't explain, but it seemed very familiar to me. My intellect didn't know what was going on and yet this other part of me identified with it. It just called on me.' Several months later, Harrison met a man from the Asian Music Circle organisation who told him Ravi was going to visit his house for dinner and asked him to come too. George said yes.

Help! received its world premiere at the London Pavilion, Piccadilly, on 29 July 1965 with Princess Margaret once more in attendance. 'We saw her just before we went in to see the film,' George recalled. 'She said she was looking forward to seeing it because she had enjoyed *A Hard Day's Night*. In fact, she cancelled her holiday to go to the premiere.' The Beatles had arrived at the venue to be greeted by the sight of hundreds of screaming fans, standing shoulder-to-shoulder behind railings and a police cordon, while many others had escaped and were swarming hysterically across the streets. As the group's limousine pulled up, catching sight of the pandemonium in front of them, John said to the others, 'Push Paul out first, he's the prettiest.'

Loved by the fans, *Help!* was panned by the columnists. 'What did the critics expect from it?' an exasperated George remarked. '*Cleopatra* or

King of Kings?' Ringo agreed. 'Some of the critics seemed to be going out of their way to knock it, or us,' he said. 'I have come to the conclusion that it would not have had the rave reviews even if had been noticeably better than it was, or even better than *A Hard Day's Night.'* John wasn't impressed with the film either, admitting the best stuff in *Help!* was, 'on the cutting room floor, with us breaking up and falling about all over the place.' While in another interview at the time, he said, 'We were ashamed of the film … the film won't harm us, but we weren't in full control.'

Trivia

The title *Help* was already being considered by someone else for a film, but the producers were able to get round the problem by adding an exclamation mark at the end of it.

The steed Paul rode in the Austrian Alps 'Ticket To Ride' sequence was a Haflinger. Also known as the Avelignese, it's a breed developed in Austria and northern Italy during the late nineteenth century. When The Beatles are at the piano at the end of the scene, a hand suddenly appears on Ringo's right shoulder, obviously a crew member giving the signal for them to leave. The Beatles' record producer George Martin joined the group in Austria for a skiing vacation, but unfortunately broke his ankle on the very first day. The group's long-time friend and roadie Mal Evans made a cameo in the movie as a lost swimmer who popped up through a hole in the Alps' ice-covered water and asked directions for the 'White Cliffs of Dover'. He reappeared, later in the film, during the scenes shot in the Bahamas. During filming there, each of The Beatles hired a sports car, drove to a rock quarry and began having races and smashing into each other for fun. Cut from the finished film, there is surviving evidence of this; in the theatrical trailer, where they are seen for a few brief seconds driving around the quarry and Paul through a large puddle.

When work on *Help!* shifted to Twickenham Studios, on 24 March 1965, in between takes Paul frequently played the piano that sat on the soundstage where the group was working. One track in particular he tinkered with more than any other. Boasting a working title of 'Scrambled Eggs', it later famously became known as 'Yesterday'. 'He was playing "Scrambled Eggs" all the time,' Lester recalled. 'It got to the point where I said to him, "If you play that bloody song any longer, I'll have the piano taken off the stage. Either finish it or give it up."'

Near the start of the film, the book that John took from the shelf and kissed before settling down to read was his own, *A Spaniard In The Works.*

A lengthy, ten-minute scene involving the famous British comedy actor Frankie Howerd (shot at Twickenham on 28 April 1965) ended up on the cutting room floor. 'Frankie just couldn't work with The Beatles,' Lester admitted. 'He was one of the world's greatest ad-libbers, but to him The Beatles were just on another planet. It just did not work.' Set to be sandwiched between The Beatles' escape from Clang and the John/Ringo elevator sequence, the scene involved the group hiding out at the Sam Ahab School of Transcendental Elocution, an acting school run by Sam Ahab (played by Howerd). Sam Ahab spelt backwards is Bahamas, where The Beatles would end up later in the movie. His pupil, Lady Macbeth (played by a young Wendy Richard, who would later star as Miss Brahms in the popular seventies BBC sitcom, *Are You Being Served?*) performed a meditation song that caused George to block his ears with earplugs while Clang and his men, who were secreted in the fireplace, played a piece of music that sent everyone else into a deep trance. A fight followed as Clang attempted to chop Ringo's hand off with a hatchet to retrieve the ring, but the gang were fought off by the non-hypnotised Harrison. After the men fled, and the hatchet was hurled by Clang into a mirror, the others were revived and the scene ended with John handing a hatchet to Lady Macbeth and saying, 'Is this a chopper that you see before you?', which was a quirky reworking of the line, 'Is this a dagger I see before me,' from Shakespeare's *Macbeth*, Act 2, Scene 1. Another unused scene shot for the movie involved a live cow that Ringo kept in his closet for fresh milk.

The four seemingly modest terraced houses behind which The Beatles inhabit a single luxury suite are actually numbers 5, 7, 9 and 11 Ailsa Avenue, just over Twickenham Bridge in St Margaret's, conveniently adjacent to Twickenham Film Studios. In between takes of the 'Go on, wave,' 'I don't like to,' sequence, which was shot outside no. 7 and featured the actresses Gretchen Franklin and Dandy Nichols as they watched the group leave their houses and climb into their car, they were served tea by the resident of the house, Beatrice Pennington. It was during this period that Franklin had been offered the part of Else, the long-suffering Mrs Alf Garnett in the new BBC TV sitcom *Till Death Us Do Part*, starring opposite Warren Mitchell, but due to her commitment to the West End stage production of *Spring And Port Wine* she was unable to accept the role. She recommended her friend Nichols for the part instead, which she got. The pilot edition of this ultimately controversial series was broadcast on BBC1 on 22 July 1965, one week before *Help!* was premiered in London. Coincidentally Mitchell also appeared in the movie, as Abdul.

The eight-foot Beatle boot, used in the movie to make Paul look tiny after he was inadvertently injected with reducing fluid, ended up at the bottom of John's garden at his home in Weybridge.

Legend has it that the first time John appeared in public wearing his trademark round glasses was in the 1967 Richard Lester film *How I Won the War*. Not so. He can be seen wearing circular granny glasses during the scene in which the group are in disguise at an airport, waiting for a flight to the Bahamas, while in an earlier scene, at the Indian restaurant, he can be seen spooning the same pair out of his soup.

The 'ferocious man-eating tiger' that terrified Ringo in the cellar of the pub was actually only a ten-month-old cub. But for safety reasons, when he came to shoot the scene he was still positioned behind several inches of glass.

The 'Buckingham Palace' sequences were in fact shot at the stylish nineteenth-century stately home Cliveden House in Maidenhead, Berkshire, famous for being where the then British government war minister Jack Profumo began his relationship with the 19-year-old model and showgirl Christine Keeler, in July 1961. Their sexual liaisons discredited the Conservative government of Harold Macmillan and in 1963 became known as the Profumo Affair, one of Britain's greatest political scandals of the twentieth century. Shot over two days, 10 and 11 May 1965, The Beatles were filmed in the south-western corner of the house, playing cards, leaning out of a window to see the effects of poison gas, and larking around in the ground's bluebell woods for the humorous 'intermission' sequence. In between takes on the second day, the group took part in a relay race around the location's sumptuous gardens. Joined by Neil Aspinall, Mal Evans and chauffeur Alf Bicknell, they competed against three other teams, each comprising six members of the film's crew – carpenters, electricians and camera operators. In the end, The Beatles' team won. The spirited action was captured by one of the movie's technicians on an 8mm, colour home movie camera.

During that break in filming, the group also spent time chatting with a visitor to the set, Houston DJ Buddy McGregor, who began by remarking on the contest. 'Quite a race was run on the lawn here at the Astor mansion today,' he said, 'and The Beatles did win … You ran a very good race.' 'Thank you very much. Thank you,' Paul replied. 'Had you ever done this before?' McGregor asked. 'Not since school, you know,' McCartney responded. 'This was quite a long course out there,' the DJ announced. 'Well, yes,' Paul confirmed. 'Fifteen furlongs, I'd say.' This day marked The Beatles' last on the film. In total, they had spent 54 days working on the picture.

In the movie's final, 'I'm going to miss the sacrifice,' scene, where The Beatles, Ahme, Clang's men and the police are on the beach, rolling and fighting around in the sand, a strange shot of a shapely pair of very feminine, sand covered legs suddenly flash on screen for less than a second.

The Beatles reappeared during the film's end-credits sequence, embellishing Rossini's 1786 composition *The Barber Of Seville*, throughout which they and their co-stars take turns appearing as a reflection in a giant ruby. Harrison can also be heard in voice-over, proclaiming, '"I Need You" written by George Harrison!' repeating this same information twice. John's image is the last to appear in the ruby.

The film ends with a respectful dedication to 'the memory of Mr Elias Howe, who in 1846 had invented the sewing machine.' However, this wasn't quite correct. He actually invented the machine in 1845, and was awarded the patent in September of the following year (for a machine with a lock-stitch design). Furthermore, there were actually other machines of this kind in existence prior to Howe's, but he was indeed responsible for overseeing significant refinements to the earlier, substandard versions.

DON'T NEED ANYBODY

'They're all personal songs. My songs have always been like personalised diaries. I wrote those books which are personalised diaries, mostly in the first person or incomplete madness kind of talk. It's no different from that except that it just happens to be an album [*Help!*] about the same theme.' John, *Melody Maker*, 2 October 1971

The semaphore flags positions held by The Beatles on both the poster and album cover don't spell out the word *HELP*, but in fact *NUJV*. This was done deliberately because the cover's photographer, Robert Freeman, thought the correct positions didn't look right, so the flag postures were improvised. (The American album cover featured the group in different positions.)

Alternate titles for *Help!* included *Socorro!* in Brazil, *Aiuto!* in Italy and *Hi-Hi-Hilfe!* in West Germany.

The film did not become eligible for television screenings until July 1970. Its first in the UK came when BBC1 broadcast it during the evening of 6 July 1971, as part of the station's 'sixties pop movies' season.

Maybe not as ground-breaking as *A Hard Day's Night*, but it's still hugely enjoyable, and highly colourful too – despite John being displeased with the results.

LET IT BE
(1970 – PRODUCED BY APPLE FILMS; DISTRIBUTED BY UNITED ARTISTS)

Filming dates/locations: 2 January 1969–15 January 1969, Twickenham Studios, St Margaret's, London, England; 22 January 1969–31 January 1969, Apple Studios, 3 Savile Row, London, England
Directed by Michael Lindsay-Hogg, executive producers The Beatles, produced by Neil Aspinall for Apple Corps
World premiere: Pavilion Theatre, London, 20 May 1970

Enthused by their interaction with the crowd at Twickenham Studios on 4 September 1968 (see entry for 'Hey Jude' in the *TV* section), Paul saw it as a catalyst for revitalising the band into making a return to live performances. McCartney put forward his plan to the other Beatles during a round-the-table meeting at Savile Row on or around 6 October 1968. They did not share his enthusiasm. 'But why? What for?' John asked, before adding, 'Oh, I get it. You want a job!' They clearly didn't. 'They were happy to sit around [all day], languishing,' as Paul desolately admitted. Eventually he managed to win them over; in November 1968 the UK press revealed the group was planning on giving three shows, at London's Chalk Farm Roundhouse, starting 15 December 1968, with Apple artists Mary Hopkin and Jackie Lomax as support acts. As the report said, 'The shows will benefit charity and a one-hour TV spectacular may be built around the shows.' Apple employee Derek Taylor announced at the time, 'The group will be playing tracks from their album, old rock 'n' roll tunes and anything they feel like … it will be informal and flexible.'

Seeing the report, Bill Cotton Jr., head of Variety and Light Entertainment at the BBC, wasted no time in drafting a letter to McCartney at The Beatles' HQ in central London. In it, he wondered whether there was a possibility that the BBC and Apple could share creative duties in the programme. Four days later on 12 November 1968, Neil Aspinall replied on behalf of Paul, saying Apple's plans for the production were 'now complete,' revealing it would be 'produced by Apple Films Limited in American colour video.'

With the other Beatles still indifferent to the project, and with George now out of the country in Los Angeles, among other places, where he was working with Lomax on his forthcoming Apple album, the December date and charity concert idea soon passed. McCartney then devised another one, on his own: to film the group for an unparalleled, warts-and-all, half-hour 'Beatles At Work' kind of TV documentary (something along the lines of the *Music!* programme on 30 July 1968 – see entry in *TV* section), which would see them jamming, rehearsing, and recording their new album. Alistair Taylor, the one-time personal assistant to Brian Epstein and then general manager of Apple Corps, enthusiastically remarked at the time, 'It's never been done before. There's never been a film of The Beatles actually at work. It'll all be there, the works, the breaks, everything. When the shooting is finished, and the thing has been edited, it will be offered for sale to world TV companies.'

However, unlike the *Music!* programme, this one would culminate with a live show. According to some, their original idea was to perform in an ancient amphitheatre somewhere in Rome, among the ruins. John and Paul took a shine to the idea, unlike Ringo, who did not wish to leave the country. Another plan, which Lennon surprisingly liked, looked at the possibility of the group performing on a small ocean liner, filled with British Beatles fans en route to some exotic destination. Neither of these materialised, so after learning of the recent exploits by the American pop/rock group Jefferson Airplane (see Day Nineteen), they too settled for a rooftop, that of Apple headquarters at 3 Savile Row, London.

Production began on the second day of January 1969, with Soundstage Three of Twickenham Studios chosen as the venue. Having worked there several times since shooting *A Hard Day's Night* five years earlier, the venue was familiar. With the idea of capturing the sessions on videotape now scrapped, instead two 16mm film cameras were wheeled in. Since the audio needed to be good enough for use in a television production, the music The Beatles performed was preserved on two monaural, Nagra IV-L reel-to-reel, quarter-inch tape machines; one for camera A, one for camera B. Because only 16 minutes' worth of audio could be recorded on any one tape, the two machines were started at different intervals. Nagra tape recorders were the standard sound recording systems for motion picture and single-camera television productions at that time. Designed by Polish inventor Stefan Kudelski, the machines were produced by Kudelski SA at their factory based in Cheseaux-sur-Lausanne, Switzerland.

The *Get Back* sessions (as they were originally called) followed a regimented Monday to Friday schedule, with each day frequently starting late, in the region of 11am and 1pm. The director of the project was Michael Lindsay-Hogg, whom the group had worked with several times over the years, including the pop music show *Ready Steady Go!* as well as the videos and promotional film clips for 'Paperback Writer,' 'Rain', 'Hey Jude' and 'Revolution' (see entries in *TV* section). He was clearly an admirer of the group. Writing in his 2011 book *Luck And Circumstance,* recalling the start of his association with The Beatles, he said, 'I was going to work for the four most famous people in the history of the world.'

Filming day/date, venue and songs performed/ jammed, including short fragments/and where applicable the number of times the track was attempted

(Note – songs with no credit are written by Lennon/McCartney, Harrison or Starkey; less well-known compositions by the four are credited individually; '(Beatles)' indicates the band were jamming/improvising the track (some titles are presumed); other songs are credited to the composer(s) and/or artist most recognised for the track)

Day One: 2 January 1969 – Soundstage Three, Twickenham Studios:

Don't Let Me Down (fifteen takes), All Things Must Pass (two takes), Dig A Pony, Let It Down (Harrison, two takes), Brown Eyed Handsome Man (Chuck Berry), A Case Of The Blues (Lennon), Child Of Nature (Lennon), Revolution, I Shall Be Released (Bob Dylan), Sun King (five takes), Mailman, Bring Me No More Blues (Buddy Holly), Speak To Me (Jackie Lomax), I've Got A Feeling (twenty takes), The Mighty Quinn (Bob Dylan, 1968 hit for Manfred Mann), Well ... Alright (Buddy Holly), Two Of Us (nine takes), Everybody Got Song (aka Everybody Got Soul, Lennon), The Teacher Was A-Lookin' (Beatles), We're Goin' Home (Beatles), It's Good To See The Folks Back Home (McCartney)

Work officially got underway at around 9.30am when director Lindsay-Hogg filmed a white Apple van carrying The Beatles' instruments reversing into Soundstage Three. Scenes of Mal Evans and the group's equipment manager Kevin Harrington unloading it and setting the gear up in the cavernous surroundings were also captured. (Excerpts of which, where the pair was seen carrying Ringo's bass drum skin, the band's guitars and microphone stands, assembling Ringo's drum stool and podium, and pushing the piano into position, would appear at the very start of the *Let It Be* film.) Expected at 8am, The Beatles didn't start to arrive until 11am. John and George were the first, the former with his then girlfriend, the Japanese artist Yoko Ono. Ringo turned up shortly after. However, Paul was late. He arrived at 12.30pm, after being delayed on public transport.

A vast number of songs were performed (or jammed) during these sessions, some of which never saw the light of day, though many did, emerging on either the group's final two albums, *Abbey Road* and *Let It Be*, or on their early solo releases. As a warm-up, and sometimes just to ease the boredom, the band also played a diverse range of other tunes, from early, pre-'Love Me Do' compositions to improvised songs, nursery rhymes and rock 'n' roll classics. But from day one, The Beatles realised they had chosen the wrong place to shoot the movie. 'We couldn't get into it,' John recalled for *Rolling Stone's* Jann Wenner in 1970. 'It was a dreadful, dreadful feeling in Twickenham Studio, and being filmed all the time. I just wanted them to go away.' Also immediately he began voicing his opinion that they should be in a smaller environment.

George was unhappy too. Having returned from America where he'd been happily hanging out with Bob Dylan and The Band who were rehearsing at Big Pink, and producing Jackie Lomax in Los Angeles, he noticed instantly how difficult it was for him to be reunited with his old bandmates. 'I was optimistic about this thing, it was the New Year, I had this new approach,' he later recalled, 'but it became apparent, it wasn't anything new. It was going to be painful again … straight away; it was just weird vibes … I found I was starting to be able to enjoy being a musician [again] but the moment I got back with The Beatles, it was just too difficult. There were just too

many limitations based upon our being together for so long. Everyone was, sort of, pigeonholed. It was frustrating.'

The candid banter between the crew and band members was sometimes as interesting as the music itself. During a break early in the first session, John declared his approval to Ringo of the cover by Eric Burdon and The Animals of the Johnny Cash track 'Ring Of Fire', which appeared on their then recent 1968 album *Love Is*. 'It's great,' Lennon proclaimed, comparing it to their big 1964 hit 'The House Of The Rising Sun', but poured scorn on the recent reunion of the band's original members for a benefit concert at Newcastle's City Hall. 'Fuckin' terrible,' was his description. (Of note, some of the footage shot today would appear in the Apple promotional film for the group's May 1969 single 'The Ballad Of John And Yoko'.) Aside from a few Hare Krishna devotees, especially invited by Harrison, Beatles producer George Martin was one of the visitors to the soundstage today.

Day Two: 3 January 1969 – Soundstage Three, Twickenham Studios

The Long And Winding Road, Oh! Darling (two takes), Maxwell's Silver Hammer (eleven takes), Adagio For Strings (Samuel Barber, two takes), Tea For Two Cha-Cha (Tommy Dorsey, two takes), Chopsticks (Euphemia Allen), Torchy The Battery Boy (Roberta Leigh), Whole Lotta Shakin' Goin' On (Jerry Lee Lewis), Let It Be, Taking A Trip To Carolina (Starkey, two versions), Please Mrs Henry (Bob Dylan), Picasso (Starkey), Hey Jude, All Things Must Pass (thirty-seven takes), Don't Let Me Down (ten takes), Crackin' Up (Bo Diddley, two takes), All Shook Up (Otis Blackwell, Elvis Presley), Your True Love (Carl Perkins), Blue Suede Shoes (Carl Perkins), Three Cool Cats (Jerry Leiber/Mike Stoller, 1958 song by The Coasters), Blowin' In The Wind (Bob Dylan), Lucille (Little Richard), I'm So Tired, Ob-La-Di Ob-La-Da (three takes), Third Man Theme (Anton Karas), Sun King (four versions), I've Got A Feeling (six takes), Going Up The Country (based on Bull Doze Blues, recorded in 1928 by Texas bluesman Henry Thomas, a recent hit for American blues/boogie rock band Canned Heat), On The Road Again (Floyd Jones, a recent hit for Canned Heat), The One After 909 (three takes), A Pretty Girl Is Like·A Melody (Irving Berlin), Thinking Of Linking (McCartney), Bring It On Home To Me (Sam Cooke), Hitch Hike (Marvin Gaye/William 'Mickey' Stevenson/Clarence Paul, Marvin Gaye), You Can't Do That, Hippy Hippy Shake (Chan Romero), All Along The Watchtower (Bob Dylan), Short Fat Fannie (Larry Williams), Midnight Special (Lonnie Donegan), When You're Drunk You Think Of Me (traditional), What's The Use Of Getting Sober (When You're Gonna Get Drunk Again) (Louis Jordan), Two Of Us, What Do You Want To Make Those Eyes At Me For? (Joseph McCarthy/Howard Johnson/James V. Monaco, a hit for Emile Ford and The Checkmates), Money (That's What I Want), Gimme Some Truth (Lennon), The Weight (Robbie Robertson, 1968 hit for The Band), I'm A Tiger (Ronnie Scott/Marty Wilde, 1968 hit for Lulu), Back In The USSR, Every Little Thing, Piece Of My Heart (Erma Franklin, two takes), Sabre Dance (Aram Khachaturian, 1968 hit for Welsh rock band Love Sculpture), I've Been Good To You (Smokey Robinson), Ramblin' Woman (Harrison), Is It Discovered (Harrison), Your Name Is Ted (Beatles), Get On The Phone (Lennon/McCartney), My Words Are In My Heart (McCartney), Negro In Reserve (Lennon/McCartney), Because I Know You Love Me So (Lennon/McCartney), I'll Wait Till Tomorrow (Lennon/McCartney), Won't You

Please Say Goodbye (Lennon/McCartney), Over And Over Again (McCartney)

10.40am start. Paul was the first to arrive and began by amusing himself at the piano, working his way through several, in-progress compositions – 'The Long And Winding Road' and 'Oh Darling' along with 'Maxwell's Silver Hammer', replete with lyrics thrown in by both Ringo and Mal Evans once they'd arrived. He also tinkered briefly with the theme tune from Gerry Anderson's 1960–61 ITV children's puppets show *Torchy The Battery Boy*. Once John arrived, rehearsals for George's 'All Things Must Pass' became strained when, as a sign of the bitterness growing between them, George remarked to Paul during one conversation, 'You're so full of shit.' However, when times were less fraught, the group amused themselves by running through recent cuts by the groups The Band, Canned Heat and Love Sculpture and even the Scottish singer Lulu.

Two early compositions, dating back to 1957, were introduced today – Paul's 'Thinking Of Linking' (inspired by a cinema advertisement for a furniture company) and Lennon/McCartney's 'The One After 909'. Initially played straight, in the style of John's early skiffle group The Quarrymen, the latter was tried out several times during the sessions but it wasn't until 28 January (Day Seventeen), by which time keyboardist Billy Preston had become involved, that serious work on the track got underway. Yoko Ono brought her video camera along to record her own footage of today's session, excerpts of which later appeared in the 1996 American documentary *Yoko Ono Lennon (Then and Now)*.

Day Three: 6 January 1969 - Soundstage Three, Twickenham Studios

Oh! Darling, C'mon Marianne (Raymond Bloodworth/Russell L. Brown, 1967 hit for The Four

Seasons), I've Got A Feeling (three takes), High School Confidential (Jerry Lee Lewis), Hear Me Lord (Harrison, eight takes), For You Blue (two takes), All Things Must Pass (nine takes), Carry That Weight (four takes), Octopus's Garden, The Palace Of The King Of The Birds (McCartney instrumental), Across The Universe (two takes), I Want You (Bob Dylan), Don't Let Me Down (twenty-eight takes), The One After 909 (three takes), That's All Right (Arthur Crudup, Elvis Presley), Thirty Days (Chuck Berry), Leaning On A Lamp-post (Noel Gay, recorded in 1937 by the British actor, singer-songwriter and ukulele-strumming comedian George Formby), Annie (Lennon), I'm Talking About You (Chuck Berry), The Tracks Of My Tears (Smokey Robinson/ Pete Moore/Marv Tarplin, 1965 hit for Smokey Robinson and The Miracles), Dizzy Miss Lizzy (Larry Williams), Money (That's What I Want), Fools Like Me (Jerry Lee Lewis), Sure To Fall (In Love With You) (Carl Perkins), Right String Baby But The Wrong Yo-Yo (Carl Perkins), Send Me Some Lovin' (Little Richard), Two Of Us (twenty versions), Frère Jacques (the 1811 French nursery melody), It Ain't Me Babe (Bob Dylan), When The Saints Go Marching In (the American gospel hymn), Loop De Loop (Johnny Thunder), Let's Dance (Jim Lee, 1962 hit for Chris Montez), She Came In Through The Bathroom Window (seven versions), You Wear Your Women Out (McCartney), My Imagination (McCartney), I'm Gonna Pay For His Ride (McCartney), They Call Me Fuzz Face (McCartney), Maureen (Dylan/Harrison, composed for Ringo's wife)

Another 11am start. Among the musical highlights was McCartney's 'The Palace Of The King Of The Birds', an instrumental track he would re-title 'King Of The Birds' when he recorded it later in his solo career for the unreleased *Rupert The Bear* album. The group meanwhile amused themselves with brief renditions of George Formby's 'Leaning On A Lamp-post', the American gospel hymn 'When The Saints Go Marching In' as well as the French nursery rhyme 'Frère Jacques'. Ringo's future *Abbey Road* recording 'Octopus's Garden' made its first appearance at the sessions today. Serious work at 'All Things Must Pass', 'Don't Let Me Down', 'She Came In Through The Bathroom Window' and 'Two Of Us' was also attempted. However, during rehearsals for the latter, possibly the result of a clash in working styles, and John's distinct lack of participation, another curt exchange took place between McCartney and Harrison. As seen in the movie, George was heard saying to Paul, 'Yeah, okay, well, I don't mind. I'll play, you know, whatever you want me to play. Or I won't play at all if you don't want me to play, you know. Whatever it is that'll please you, I'll do it.' Concerned by the general mood of the day, director Lindsay-Hogg felt the need to remind them on their way out of the studio that night that they needed to arrive at 10.10am the following day. (Of note: scenes of the group rehearsing 'Don't Let Me Down' today would appear in the official April 1969 Apple promotional film for the song.)

Day Four: 7 January 1969 – Soundstage Three, Twickenham Studios

The Long And Winding Road (two takes), Golden Slumbers, Carry That Weight, The Palace Of The King Of The Birds (McCartney instrumental, two takes), Lady Madonna, She Came In Through The Bathroom Window (four takes), Lowdown Blues Machine (McCartney), What'd I Say (Ray Charles, two takes), Shout (1959 self-penned hit for The Isley Brothers, and a 1964 UK hit for Lulu and The Luvvers), Get Back (four takes), My Back Pages (Bob Dylan), I've Got A Feeling (fourteen takes), Stuck Inside Of Mobile

With The Memphis Blues Again (Bob Dylan), I Shall Be Released (Bob Dylan), To Kingdom Come (Robbie Robertson, a 1968 track by The Band), For You Blue (two takes), Bo Diddley (Bo Diddley), What The World Needs Now Is Love (Hal David/Burt Bacharach composition, a 1965 hit for Jackie DeShannon), First Call (traditional), Maxwell's Silver Hammer (eighteen takes), Oh! Darling (two takes), Rule Britannia (British patriotic song by James Thomson), Norwegian Wood (This Bird Has Flown), Speak To Me (Jackie Lomax track), When I'm Sixty-Four, A Shot Of Rhythm And Blues (Arthur Alexander), (You're So Square) Baby I Don't Care (Jerry Leiber/Mike Stoller; Elvis Presley), Across The Universe (twelve takes), Gimme Some Truth (Lennon, three takes), A Case Of The Blues (Lennon, two takes), Cuddle Up (McCartney), From Me To You, Rock And Roll Music, Lucille (Little Richard), Lotta Lovin' (Gene Vincent, two takes), Gone Gone Gone (Carl Perkins), Dig A Pony, The One After 909 (five takes), Don't Let Me Down (twelve takes), Devil In Her Heart (Richard Drapkin), Thirty Days (Chuck Berry), Revolution, Be-Bop-A-Lula (Gene Vincent), Somethin' Else (Eddie Cochran), FBI (Peter Gormley, 1961 instrumental hit for The Shadows), Mr Epstein Said It Was White Gold (McCartney), Woman Where You Been So Long (Beatles), Oh! Julie Julia (McCartney)

Paul, as usual, was the first to arrive (at a little after the requested time, though) and characteristically began by playing the piano while he waited for the others. Among the tunes he tinkered with again was 'The Palace Of The King Of The Birds'. Highlights from this day include the earliest known rendition of McCartney's 'Get Back'. (John later claimed that, during rehearsals of the song, Paul would look at Yoko every time he sang the words, 'Get back to where you once belonged,' in order to intimidate her. McCartney,

of course, denied this, putting John's thoughts down to 'paranoia'.) John hindered attempts at a song first recorded back in early February 1968, 'Across The Universe', because he was struggling to remember the first line and was not in possession of his lyric sheet. He was also perturbed by how the track was starting. Calling his original intro 'Crummy,' he suggested to George he should play an organ on it.

Among the noteworthy covers jammed today; 'Shout' by The Isley Brothers, 'My Back Pages' by Bob Dylan, 'To Kingdom Come' by The Band, 'What The World Needs Now Is Love' by Jackie DeShannon and 'FBI' by The Shadows.

Debate over The Beatles' proposed live show also reared its ugly head today. Lindsay-Hogg suggested doing it at various exotic locations, but Ringo was dead set against going abroad. Already fed up with the project, George was pessimistic about almost any idea offered, while John was notably absent from most of the conversations. Unsurprisingly, Paul proposed several ideas and wanted a decision from the others as soon as possible, but none was coming, which naturally prompted him to ask the others why they even 'bother showing up,' if they didn't want to do the show. Predictably, he had no response. The idea for a live concert was, for the time being anyway, effectively quashed. For The Beatles as a group, George suggested that perhaps 'a divorce' was in order.

Day Five: 8 January 1969 – Soundstage Three, Twickenham Studios

Honey Hush (Johnny Burnette Trio), Stand By Me (Ben E. King), Hare Krishna Mantra (traditional arrangement Adhikary, Hindu mantra, two takes), I Me Mine (forty-one takes), I've Got A Feeling (two takes), Two Of Us, You Got Me Going (McCartney), Twist And Shout (Bert

Berns/Phil Medley), Don't Let Me Down (two takes), St Louis Blues (W.C. Handy), The One After 909, Too Bad About Sorrows (Lennon/McCartney), Just Fun (Lennon/McCartney), She Said She Said, She Came In Through The Bathroom Window, One Way Out (James/Sehorn/Williamson, hit for Elmore James), MacArthur Park (Jimmy Webb, made famous by actor Richard Harris, Elvis Presley, and later Donna Summer), All Things Must Pass (eleven takes), Mean Mr Mustard, Fools Like Me (Jerry Lee Lewis), You Win Again (Jerry Lee Lewis), Right String Baby But Wrong Yo (Carl Perkins), Boogie Woogie (Lennon), Baa Baa Black Sheep (traditional), Mr Bass Man (Johnny Cymbal), Maxwell's Silver Hammer (thirteen takes), How Do You Think I Feel (Wayne Walker/Webb Pierce, Elvis Presley), The Ballad Of Bonnie And Clyde (Georgie Fame), Hello Mudduh Hello Fadduh (A Letter From Camp) (Sherman/Busch, 1963 novelty song by Allan Sherman), FBI (Peter Gormley, The Shadows), Oh! Darling, Let It Be (three takes), The Fool (Sanford Clark), Domino (Louis Ferrari/Jacques Plante/Don Raye, Doris Day), The Long And Winding Road (six takes), Adagio For Strings (Samuel Barber), True Love (Cole Porter, Elvis Presley), Shout (The Isley Brothers), Sweet Little Sixteen (Chuck Berry), Malagueña (traditional), Almost Grown (Chuck Berry), What Am I Living For (Chuck Willis), Rock And Roll Music, To Kingdom Come (Robbie Robertson, The Band), Get Your Rocks Off (Harrison), Well If You're Ready (McCartney), Life Is What You Make It (Beatles), I'm Going To Knock Him Down Dead (Lennon), Tell All The Folks Back Home (McCartney)

Incredibly, George and Ringo beat Paul to the studios today. Highlights included the debut of the future *Abbey Road* track 'Mean Mr Mustard'. The version the group performed differed little from the final released version, although in the lyrics 'Pam' was then known as 'Shirley'. George teaching his new composition 'I Me Mine' to his bandmates was another high spot, the first attempt occurring at the start of the day while waiting for John and Paul to arrive. With Ringo and Lindsay-Hogg listening in, George picked up a guitar, most likely John's, and ran through the song acoustically once or twice.

When Paul did arrive, George played it through again for him, explaining, It's just a very short one.' At this point there was a flamenco style guitar break in the middle, sandwiched between two verses that George sang in a high pitch. Writing in haste, George had already finalised all of the lyrics and at the conclusion asked Paul, Ringo and Michael if the second verse line, 'flowing more freely than wine,' was grammatically correct. Paul suggested he change it to 'flowing much freer'. George was unsure that 'freer' was even a proper word, but Paul assured him it was and pointed out that it's like 'queer'. With John now present, 41 versions were attempted that day, but more often than not they were incomplete. During a break in these run-throughs, while the group waited for recording equipment to be set up, George made a remark about Ringo's drumming, accusing him of 'doin' the 'MacArthur Park' thing again.' ('MacArthur Park' was a 1968 hit by the actor Richard Harris, and featured several notable sequences of elaborate drumming.)

Although discussed again, this was the only time in the sessions that 'I Me Mine' was actually played. Regrettably for George, there was little leaning to return to it. As soon as he introduced the song, John mocked it, jokingly asking for an accordion and bagpipes for it, then during the many run-throughs taking a break to waltz with Yoko. (This appeared in the *Let It Be* film.) 'John and Paul had written songs for so long that it was difficult,' Harrison admitted in 1976, '... because they had such a lot of tunes, they automatically thought that theirs should be the priority. So, for me, I'd always have to wait through ten of their songs before they would even listen to one of mine. That's why [the album] *All Things Must Pass* had so many songs, because it was like, you know, I had been constipated.'

(Worth noting here, the electric version of 'I Me Mine' heard on the 1970 *Let It Be* album was actually recorded a full year later, at Studio Two, Abbey Road, on 3 January 1970. John, who was in Aalborg, Denmark, with Yoko, did not participate in the recording. Since 'I Me Mine' was only a minute and a half long, *Let It Be* album producer Phil Spector extended the song by editing in a repeat of part of the first verse and chorus, making it nearly a minute longer. The song can be heard in its true length on *The Beatles Anthology 3* compilation. George would reuse his title for the name of his autobiographical, limited edition book that was published by Genesis Publications in 1980.)

Notable covers today included fragments of the 'Hare Krishna Mantra' (with Paul singing 'Harry Pinsker' instead of 'Hare Krishna'), Georgie Fame's 'The Ballad Of Bonnie And Clyde', Allan Sherman's Grammy-winning novelty song 'Hello Mudduh, Hello Fadduh' and Johnny Burnette's 'Honey Hush'. (Paul would return to the latter 30 years later, during recordings for his *Run Devil Run* album.) Early Lennon/McCartney compositions 'Too Bad About Sorrows' (which dates back to late-1957) and 'Just Fun' (from the same era), as well as the 1966 *Revolver* track 'She Said She Said', were also tackled today. Interestingly, after their brief rendition of 'Too Bad About Sorrows', John uttered the line, 'Queen says no to pot-smoking FBI members,' which would appear on the May 1970 *Let It Be* album, just prior to 'For You Blue'. It was the only piece of audio

recorded at Twickenham Studios to feature on the record; everything else originated from either the Apple or Abbey Road sessions.

During the afternoon, another long, intense discussion about the proposed live show took place. Despite McCartney and Harrison reaffirming Ringo's wish about not going abroad, it now seemed that that they would be travelling after all. The show idea had somehow progressed into the group taking a voyage to North Africa on a boat filled with British Beatles fans and, most unlike his earlier conversations, Lennon was actually very vocal in his approval of such an excursion. Although he did not outright refuse, Ringo still wasn't keen and tried talking them out of it. He really did not want to go. He had his heart set on a show in England. Unsurprisingly, George also hated the notion, and argued strongly against it from both a personal and a practical perspective. They were asked to sleep on it, so they could decide on their plans the following day. An excerpt of 'You Win Again' from today's session was used in Neil Aspinall's ultimately unreleased 1970 movie of the Beatles story, *The Long And Winding Road*.

Day Six: 9 January 1969 – Soundstage Three, Twickenham Studios

Another Day (McCartney), The Palace Of The King Of The Birds (McCartney), Let It Be (sixteen takes), The Long And Winding Road (five takes), Her Majesty, Golden Slumbers, Carry That Weight, Oh! Darling, For You Blue (fifteen takes), Two Of Us (eight takes), Baa Baa Black Sheep (traditional English nursery rhyme), Don't Let Me Down, Suzy's Parlour (Lennon), I've Got A Feeling (five takes), The One After 909 (four takes), Norwegian Wood (This Bird Has Flown), She Came In Through The Bathroom Window (seven takes), Be-Bop-A-Lula (Gene Vincent), Get Back (six takes), Penina (McCartney), Across

The Universe (twelve takes), Teddy Boy (McCartney), Junk (McCartney), Move It (Ian Samwell, Cliff Richard and The Shadows), Good Rockin' Tonight (Roy Brown, Elvis Presley), Tennessee (Carl Perkins), The House Of The Rising Sun (authorship uncertain, The Animals), Honey Hush (Johnny Burnette Trio), Hitch Hike (Marvin Gaye/William 'Mickey' Stevenson/Clarence Paul, Marvin Gaye), All Together Now, I Threw It All Away (Bob Dylan), Mama You Been On My Mind (Bob Dylan), That'll Be The Day (Buddy Holly), Jenny Jenny (Little Richard), Slippin' And Slidin' (Little Richard), Shakin' In The Sixties (Lennon), Commonwealth (McCartney), Enoch Powell (McCartney), Get Off (Lennon/McCartney), Quit Your Messing Around (Lennon), Ramblin' Woman (Harrison)

Along with girlfriend Linda Eastman, Paul was the first of The Beatles to arrive, and spent the time alone performing several tunes at the piano. Making their debuts today were 'Her Majesty' and 'Another Day'; the latter went on to become his first solo single in February 1971. 'The Palace Of The King Of The Birds' was also reprised. Starr arrived during this performance and was greeted by Paul with the words, 'Goodnight!', an obvious jibe at Ringo's continuing struggle with the group's early (for them) daytime schedule. Paul's jokes continued when he informed the drummer they were going to do the live show on a farm in Scotland. 'What? What?' screamed Ringo in mock anger. Paul responded reassuringly with, 'Just joking, we're doing the show on a farm in Yugoslavia.' George blamed his appetite for his late arrival. 'I was so hungry,' he announced to his bandmates. 'I had to be late just to eat my breakfast, if you want an excuse.' 'Let It Be' was afforded more attention once John had arrived. With McCartney on piano, John switched to bass. 'Get Back' had now developed into a driving rock

song, with incomplete lyrics about the characters Theresa and Joe. At one point, McCartney improvised with controversial lines about not digging, 'Pakistanis taking all the people's jobs,' and how they 'Don't need no Puerto Ricans living in the USA,' which later led to accusations of racism. In truth he was parodying the right-wing attitudes shared by many in Britain at the time, particularly the Conservative Party politician Enoch Powell, and the fact that several of that morning's newspapers carried reports about Powell's re-patriation movement, which involved the sending back to their country of origin all non-white citizens of the British Empire living on visas in the UK.

The former *Daily Express* and now *Daily Mirror* journalist George Gale had evidently written something that upset George, forcing him to cancel his newspaper deliveries altogether. 'George Gale's such an ignorant bastard,' Harrison blasted. While discussing equipment problems with sound engineer Glyn Johns, Paul improvised a ditty called 'Commonwealth', once more featuring the hotly debated topic of the repatriation of immigrants, which then segued into another called 'Enoch Powell'. With Paul clearly impersonating Elvis, the song's simple chorus had him shouting 'Commonwealth' with John hyperactively responding to him in the affirmative. As the fifties-style rock 'n' roll song ran on, the pair waxed lyrically about Britain's entry into the European Common Market, which had been denied in late 1968, making a joke out of the phrase 'common market'. (After watching Powell's 3 January 1969 interview with David Frost for his weekly ITV chat show *Frost On Friday*, the controversial MP was evidentially still on McCartney's mind.)

Paul's compositions 'Teddy Boy', 'Junk' and 'Penina' were also performed today. Singer Carlos Mendes recorded the latter for a 1969 single, while only 'Teddy Boy' was reprised during the sessions. Also attempted (albeit briefly) today was the *Rubber Soul* track 'Norwegian Wood (This Bird Has Flown)', the eighteenth-century English nursery rhyme 'Baa, Baa, Black Sheep' and The Animals' 1964 hit 'The House Of The Rising Sun', as well as the rocker 'Suzy's Parlour', which was included in the *Let It Be* film, but mistitled as 'Suzy Parker' when copyrighted by Apple in 1971. George performed solo acoustic versions of Bob Dylan's 'Mama, You Been On My Mind' and the (as yet unreleased) 'I Threw It All Away'. He also played a Dylan-esque new composition, which was never developed but was later entitled 'Ramblin' Woman' by some entrepreneurial boot-leggers. Another highlight was Ringo joining Paul for a lengthy performance of the instrumental 'The Palace Of The King Of The Birds', with the drummer desperately trying to find a beat for it.

Further evidence of the strain and complete disregard of George's material, especially from John, became evident today during run-throughs of 'For You Blue'. The first was cut short by Paul who claimed he could not hear George. Following a discussion about the tune's arrangement, the song resumed but broke down again at the start of the first verse. Paul, however, kept going. They then all morphed back into a brief jam, one that almost bordered on another track entirely, John's 'Mean Mr Mustard'. Picking up on this, Paul shouted, 'Let's pick and choose John!' Now on acoustic, George began his song again but it soon broke down.

During a lull in proceedings, discussions about the proposed live show came up again, and in particular how they would present it. 'Bass amps in the middle, do you think?' Paul eagerly suggested, 'And guitar on the side? Once we decide that and everything that we're going to actually do ... we can get into it; where the amps are going to be and where we stand. It's a bit silly rehearsing sitting, facing this way when we're actually going to play standing, facing that way. We should get into that.' To which George sarcastically responded, 'We've still got our dance steps to learn yet.' 'Oh yes,' Paul retorted, 'and the jokes in between the numbers.' Harrison then sardonically asked if they should perform other people's tunes as well as their own for the show. John replied, saying he didn't 'know any', and he could 'only just bear doing your songs, never mind strangers'.' George retaliated by saying that the 'others' songs are much better than ours,' to which Lennon came back with, 'That's why I don't learn them!' With that, George started playing 'For You Blue' again, while Paul continued to sing goofy lines over him. The strain of all this unpleasantness would come to a head for Harrison one day later.

Day Seven: 10 January 1969 - Soundstage Three, Twickenham Studios

The Long And Winding Road (three takes), Let It Be, Don't Let Me Down (two takes), Maxwell's Silver Hammer (four takes), I've Got A Feeling (four takes), Get Back (twenty-two takes), She's A Woman, Hi-Heel Sneakers (Robert Higginbotham aka Tommy Tucker, two takes), Long Tall Sally (Robert 'Bumps' Blackwell/Enotris Johnson/ Richard Penniman (aka Little Richard), Little Richard), Theme from The Beatles ABC TV Cartoon series, Catch A Falling Star (Paul Vance/Lee Pock-riss, Perry Como), Two Of Us (six takes), I'm Talking About You (Chuck Berry), A Quick One, While He's Away (Pete Townshend, The Who, four takes), Till There Was You (Meredith Willson), C'mon Everybody (Eddie Cochran), Mack The Knife (Marc Blitzstein/Turk Murphy, Bobby Darin), Don't Be Cruel (Otis Blackwell, Elvis Presley), Adagio for Strings (Samuel Barber), Martha My Dear, Sun King, Dear Prudence, Medley: On A Sunny Island (improvised)/Brazil (aka Aquarela

Do Brasil) (Barroso/Russell); The Peanut Vendor (Sunshine/Gilbert/Simons); Groovin' (Cavaliere/Brigati); I Got Stung (Schroeder/Hill, Elvis Presley); It's Only Make Believe (Twitty/Nance); Through A London Window (McCartney)

As expected, the day began with Paul working alone at the piano, running through a number of tunes that The Beatles had been working on during the previous week. These included solo versions of 'Get Back' and 'I've Got A Feeling'. The group worked on the former during the morning session with John taking over lead vocals during one run-through. Discussions about Tucson, Arizona, as a setting in the song also ensued. The music publisher and co-founder of Northern Songs, Dick James, was a visitor today. With thoughts of another batch of royalties about to fill his coffers, he had arrived early to inform them excitedly that the Forces Sweetheart Vera Lynn was to be a star guest on tomorrow evening's BBC1 Saturday night, peak-time variety programme *The Rolf Harris Show* singing her new Columbia single, the Lennon/McCartney *White Album* track 'Good Night'. (Its B-side was another by the pair, 'The Fool On The Hill'.) John however was not pleased to see him, slyly referring to him as a 'pig' and a 'fascist bum' to George.

As director Lindsay-Hogg recalled, Harrison was noticeably silent and withdrawn that morning and he felt that something was simmering inside him. After several more attempts at 'Get Back', the group moved onto 'Two Of Us'. They then broke for lunch, and went to the studio canteen where John and Yoko were keen for more macrobiotic food, while the others were up for roast and chips; George did not immediately join them.

'We'd finished the first course,' the director remembered, 'when George arrived to stand at the end of the table.' 'See you 'round the clubs,' George said before leaving. As Harrison himself

recalled during the 1995 *Anthology* series, 'I thought, "What's the point of this? I'm quite capable of being relatively happy on my own and I'm not able to be happy in this situation. I'm getting out of here."' So he did. Lindsay-Hogg managed to tape the entire exchange. His sound technician had secreted a microphone inside the flowerpot on their dinner table. (His so-called 'spy mikes' were used extensively during the filming. Among the other revelations caught by the director was John's admission that he hated having to play bass and his discussion with Neil Aspinall about how John and Paul constantly teamed up against George.) Ringo later admitted he thought that Lindsay-Hogg was a contributing factor in George's decision to leave. 'Paul was dominating him,' the drummer confirmed. 'Well he was, because Michael Lindsay-Hogg liked Paul, I would think, more than the rest of us. So it's like Paul's film, actually.' 'That period was the low of all time,' Harrison recalled. 'In normal circumstances I had not let his attitude bother me and, to get a peaceful life, I had always let him have his own way, even when this meant that songs which I had composed were not being recorded.' Recalling that day's argument, George educed, 'In front of the cameras, as we were actually being filmed, Paul started to get at me about the way I was playing.'

McCartney refused to be drawn in to the Harrison row, and after lunch the three remaining Beatles returned to the soundstage where they joined Yoko in a ferocious, free-style, violent jam, featuring John's reprise of 'Soon Be Home' from The Who's *A Quick One, While He's Away*, replete with guitars, drums, feedback from Paul's bass and Ono's howling. (Uncomfortable on a stool, she had positioned herself on George's blue cushion at the edge of the stage.) Harrison meanwhile had headed home, where that afternoon he composed a track that he would record for his first solo album, the triple disc *All Things Must Pass*, released in November 1970. 'I went home and wrote 'Wah-Wah', George recalled. 'It'd given me a wah-wah, like I had such a headache with that whole argument. It was such a headache.'

When the serious work resumed, John, Paul and Ringo played versions of 'I've Got A Feeling' and 'Don't Let Me Down', with Lennon screaming during parts of the latter. He also managed to sing parts of 'Maxwell's Silver Hammer' in an exaggerated German accent. With George's absence a natural concern, the music stopped when the group felt the need to discuss the future of the *Get Back* project with the crew. Paul chose not to participate, electing instead to return to his piano where his playing was accompanied by more of Yoko's wailing. Tapes recorded that day reveal John, in conversation with director Lindsay-Hogg, unsympathetically suggesting George should be replaced by another guitarist, and a well-known one at that. 'If George doesn't come back by Monday or Tuesday,' John said, 'we'll ask Eric Clapton to play. Eric will be pleased … he'd have enough scope to play the guitar. The point is, George leaves and do we want to carry on The Beatles? I certainly do.' Lindsay-Hogg even suggested saying George's absence from the live show was down to him being sick. In one further exchange, the concerned director asked what they intended to do next. John jokingly replied they were 'gonna split up George's equipment among them!' There were other troubles to contend with. Ringo was set to start work on his next film, *The Magic Christian*, with his comedy actor friend and former Goon Peter Sellers, once work on the *Get Back* project had completed. Sensing that the production may well be delayed due to George's sudden departure, Lindsay-Hogg even toyed with the idea of bringing in the Cream drummer Ginger Baker,

or a session musician, to replace Ringo if he was forced to leave.

Two days later, at midday on 12 January 1969, following Neil Aspinall's phone call to George, all four Beatles agreed to meet at Ringo's new home, Brookfield, in Elstead, Surrey, a recent purchase from Sellers. The original intention of the meeting was to sort out, once and for all, the direction the *Get Back* project was going to take. It was fruitless, ending with the feuds between Harrison and both John and Paul still simmering. In readiness for his trip up north to see his parents in Liverpool, Harrison left abruptly without agreeing to rejoin the band.

Day Eight: 13 January 1969 – Soundstage Three, Twickenham Studios

Ob-La-Di, Ob-La-Da (two takes), Otis Sleep On (Arthur Conley), Baby Come Back (Eddy Grant, The Equals), Build Me Up Buttercup (Mike d'Abo/Tony Macaulay, 1968 hit for The Foundations, three takes), Dig A Pony (two takes), Get Back (fifteen takes), On The Road Again (Floyd Jones, a recent hit for the American blues/boogie rock band Canned Heat)

With George still AWOL and John missing for most of the day (he didn't arrive until after 3pm), the main bulk of today's session focused on conversations rather than music, and revealing they were too. During a late-afternoon discussion, Lennon was heard wondering whether he wanted George to be a part of the group any more, and agreeing with Paul that he had drifted away from the others in recent months. McCartney, ever the envoy, freely admitted that since they were at school, there had always been a pecking order within The Beatles and that he and John had always been the band's leaders. Admitting that their music had now become formulaic, Lennon remarked that the only challenge left for them now was to go solo, although he confessed he was uncertain about stepping away from the group. Away from the sessions, Paul took out his frustrations with the project by cutting down and re-employing some of the Apple staff, in particular the ever-loyal Mal Evans. Once he'd been managing director at Apple; McCartney told him his new role in The Beatles' camp was that of office boy. On take-home pay of just £38 each week, and with just £70 to his name, he was deeply hurt by the demotion. Fearing for his and his wife Lily's financial future, three months later and seriously in the red, on 24 April 1969 he had to come clean and inform George Harrison he was broke.

Day Nine: 14 January 1969 – Soundstage Three, Twickenham Studios

Martha My Dear, San Francisco Bay Blues (Jesse Fuller), The Day I Went Back To School (McCartney), Lady Jane (Jagger/Richards, 1966 hit for the Rolling Stones, two takes), Talking Guitar Blues (traditional arrangement, Ernest Tubb), Jazz Piano Song (McCartney/Starr), Woman (McCartney, three takes), Cocaine Blues (Johnny Cash), Flushed From The Bathroom Of Your Heart (Johnny Cash), On A Clear Day (You Can See Forever) (Burton Lane/Alan Jay Lerner, Frank Sinatra, Barbra Streisand), The Back Seat Of My Car (McCartney, two takes), Hello Dolly! (Jerry Herman, Louis Armstrong), Mean Mr Mustard (two takes), Madman (Lennon, three takes), Watching Rainbows (Lennon, two takes), Take This Hammer (traditional, Lonnie Donegan), Johnny B. Goode (Chuck Berry, two takes), Get Back, You Know My Name (Look Up The Number), Oh! Darling (two takes), Ob-La-Di Ob-La-Da, Oh Baby I Love You (McCartney), Song Of Love (McCartney), As Clear As A Bell (Says La Scala, Milan) (McCartney), You Are Definitely Inclined Towards It (Lennon), Don't Start Running (Lennon)

Paul was again the first to arrive. Sitting at the piano, he ran through various versions of the Stones track 'Lady Jane' and soon began to wonder if he would be the only Beatle to show up today. When Ringo finally did arrive, they burst into 'Jazz Piano Song', a boogie duet that can be seen in the *Let It Be* film. Paul also tinkered with 'Back Seat Of My Car' (a highlight of his 1971 album *Ram*), with someone commenting on how Beach Boys-ish it sounded. He then exaggerated it to the extreme, replete with vocalisations as to how the American vocal group would have orchestrated it. His performance was cut short when he went to answer the phone.

George was still boycotting the sessions. When John eventually arrived, the three Beatles jammed a mix of improvised songs, golden oldies and original compositions. These included 'Martha My Dear', 'Woman', a song Paul had given to the British singing duo Peter and Gordon in 1966, and the Lennon compositions 'Watching Rainbows' and 'Madman', during which Ringo dropped out, prompting John to yell, 'Ringo, it's been great working with you!' The drummer, who was feeling ill that day, was leaving. Lennon responded to this with 'He's walking out, as George did.' John also played a brief snippet of 'You Know My Name (Look Up The Number)', the still unreleased song the group had begun working on in May 1967. During this they began to discuss George, with Paul announcing that Harrison would be returning from Liverpool the following day, and John enthusiastically suggested going to see him. A discussion about the future of the film project followed, with director Lindsay-Hogg asking whether they should relocate the filming to EMI's studios and abandon the idea of a live show altogether, but Lennon, in a rare showing of loyalty, explained that any decisions should be made with Harrison. The day concluded with Paul sitting alone at the piano, performing 'Oh! Darling' and a brief version of 'Ob-La-Di, Ob-La-Da', especially for engineer Glyn Johns to test his audio equipment.

Comedy actor and friend of the group, Peter Sellers, was a visitor early in the day's session. Unsurprisingly, the banter between him and the band was both candid and jovial. 'Remember when I gave you that grass in Piccadilly?' John remarked. 'It really stoned my mind,' Sellers retorted. 'Acapulco Gold, wasn't it?' The fleeting visit concluded with him leaving to visit the toilet. 'Just don't leave the needles lying around,' Lennon shouted. Then speaking in the third person, he continued to the others, 'We've got a bad reputation now, with John getting bust and all that. I know what it's like for show-business people. They're under a great strain and they need a little relaxation … It's a choice between that and exercising, you know and drugs win hands down …' 'Shooting is exercise,' Yoko interjected. 'Shooting is exercise, oh yeah,' John responded, 'especially for the birds.'

At approximately midday, soon after a short run-through of 'Hello, Dolly!', John and Yoko were interviewed by a reporter from the Canadian CBC TV station. Lasting in the region of 30 minutes, and with him clearly in withdrawal from heroin, it has since become known as the 'Two Junkies' interview. As the interview progressed, he grew increasingly paler and more restless, eventually having to apologise, saying, 'Excuse me, I feel a bit sick,' and the camera was turned off. He needed to visit the toilet. The second half of the piece was noticeably more animated, with John discussing live performances, inspiration, the recently released and controversial *Two Virgins* album, and the couple's future plans. Paul and Lindsay-Hogg referred to the interview as it happened and wondered whether they should film it for the *Get Back* movie.

This session was The Beatles' last true one at Twickenham. The final one at the studio, 15 January 1969, doesn't really count. Due to the planned meeting with George that day, no group recordings took place. Instead, Paul turned up alone and ran through a couple of tunes ('Oh! Darling' and 'Ob-La-Di, Ob-La-Da') for the benefit of the film crew. At noon, the four-man Beatles, with the recently arrived McCartney, held a five-hour meeting at Apple HQ, during which they agreed to George's demands to abandon the cold and dreary Twickenham studios and start recording in their new studio, located in the basement of the building. He consented to the idea of being filmed making an album, and did not rule out a live performance to round off the film. With everyone in high spirits and keen to continue with the *Let It Be* project, a date was set to resume the project – one week later on 20 January. However, there were unseen troubles afoot.

Day Ten: 21 January 1969 – Apple Headquarters, 3 Savile Row, Mayfair, London

Window Window (Harrison), Somethin' Else (Sharon Sheeley/Bob Cochran, Eddie Cochran), Daydream (John Sebastian, a 1966 hit for The Lovin' Spoonful), You Are My Sunshine (Jimmie Davis/Charles Mitchell), Whispering (John Schoenberge/Richard Coburn/Vincent Rose), I'm Beginning To See The Light (Duke Ellington/Don George/Johnny Hodges/Harry James, Duke Ellington), Dig A Pony (twenty-one takes), I've Got A Feeling (four takes), Every Night (McCartney), Watch Your Step (Bobby Parker), New Orleans (Gary U.S. Bonds), Madman (Lennon), The Fool (Lee Hazlewood, Sanford Clark), Run For Your Life, My Baby Left Me (Arthur Crudup, Elvis Presley), That's All Right (Arthur Crudup, Elvis Presley), Hallelujah, I Love Her So (Ray Charles), Milk Cow Blues (Kokomo

Arnold), I'm A Man (Bo Diddley), Little Quee-nie (Chuck Berry), When Irish Eyes Are Smiling (Chauncey Olcott/George Graff Jr.), Queen Of The Hop (Woody Harris, Bobby Darin), Five Feet High And Rising (Johnny Cash), In The Middle Of An Island (Nick Acquaviva/Ted Varnick, Tony Bennett), Gilly Gilly Ossenfeffer Katzenel-len Bogen By The Sea (Al Hoffman/Dick Manning, popularised by The Four Lads), Good Rockin' Tonight (Roy Brown, Elvis Presley), Forty Days (Ronnie Hawkins), Too Bad About Sorrows (Lennon/McCartney), I'm Ready (Fats Domino), Papa's Got A Brand New Bag (James Brown), Shout (The Isley Brothers), You've Got Me Thinking (Jackie Lomax), Don't Let Me Down (two takes), Let's Dance (Jim Lee, 1962 hit for Chris Montez), Get Back, For You Blue, She Came In Through The Bathroom Window (five takes), Madman (Lennon), My Rock And Roll Finger Is Bleeding (Lennon), Do The Bunny Hop (Lennon), Blossom Dearie They Call Me (Lennon, two takes), Oh How I Love The 12-Bar Blues (Lennon), All I Want Is You (Lennon), William Smith Boogie (Beatles), San Ferry Ann (McCartney), You Gotta Give Back (Beatles), Well Well Well (McCartney), Is That A Chicken Joke? (Beatles), Etcetera (McCartney)

Purchased on 22 June 1968, the five-storey, eighteenth-century property on Savile Row, known principally for its traditional bespoke tailoring for men, had cost the group £500,000 (freehold). Once the property of Lord Nelson's Lady Hamil-ton, and later home to entertainment impresario Jack Hilton, it became The Beatles' Apple HQ when they officially moved in on 15 July 1968, with a basement set to house their purpose-built 16-track recording studio. In charge of assembling it was John's great friend, the blond, Greece-born inventor and so-called electronics engineer Alex Mardas, aka 'Magic Alex'. Lennon loved him, and

enjoyed the electrical toys Alex would give to him. Mardas, placed in charge of running Apple Elec-tronics, informed the group that EMI's Studios at Abbey Road were no good and he could build them a better one. He couldn't.

The group arrived in the basement on 20 Janu-ary 1969 to discover a largely vacant room, offering neither the normal studio fixtures nor the special technical innovations promised by their alleged expert. As Harrison later admitted, 'it was chaos. He [Alex] just had 16 little speakers up around the room. He didn't finish anything, except for a toilet with a radio in it. Alex's recording studio at Apple was the biggest disaster of all time. He didn't have a clue what he was doing.' Unsurprising, since by his own admission he was actually a 'rock gardener' and then a 'chemist' by trade.

Recording engineer Dave Harries recalled the desk, 'looked like the control panel of a B-52 bomber.' The so-called mixing console had been constructed from a bit of wood and an old oscil-loscope. The Beatles attempted to record on it, but when the tape was played back it was full of hiss and hum, so Alex's desk had to be ripped out and two portable, four-track consoles rented from Abbey Road. These were to be used alongside a 3M 8-track tape recording machine, one of several purchased by EMI just eight months previously. But even this caused a problem. Transported over on 21 January 1969, as Ringo recalled, 'EMI, this huge monster company, when they brought [over] the 8-track, the first in England, they were so cheap, they didn't even buy the plug to plug it in.' The studio at Apple seemed to pose problems from the off. Sound cables had to be pulled through under the door and the building's noisy central heating system (also housed in the basement) had to be turned off while the band worked. However, the problems were soon resolved and the recordings began again. As Neil Aspinall admitted, 'The room we played in was much nicer, much cosier. We felt much more at home.'

Beginning at 1pm in Abbey Road Studio Two, and following his stab at it the day before, highlights from the session today included Paul resuming work on 'Etcetera'. An instrumental version of it, called 'Thingumybob', had already been released in the UK by Apple Records (as Apple 4) on 6 September 1968, recorded by the Yorkshire-based Black Dyke Mills Band, and appeared as the theme tune to the Yorkshire Television/ITV sitcom of the same name starring Stanley Holloway. (Freely admitting he hated the track, Paul was the producer of this version, which had been taped in Saltaire near Bradford on 30 June 1968.) In late 1968, with freshly written lyrics and a newly penned middle section, he had hoped Marianne Faithfull would record it. She didn't.

Paul brought another new track into the session. Entitled 'Every Night', it was attempted again three days later, but would be held over for his debut solo album *McCartney* in 1970. 'Too Bad About Sorrows', which has the distinction of being the very first song Lennon and McCartney co-wrote, was reprised during the day's sessions. John introduced one of today's many takes of 'Dig A Pony' with the words, 'I Dig A Pygmy by Charles Hawtrey and the Deaf Aids. Phase one, in which Doris gets her oats,' which later appeared as the opening for the *Let It Be* album. The only other recording from this day to be given an official release was a take of 'She Came In Through The Bathroom Window'. With John on Fender Rhodes electric piano, it appeared on 1996's *Anthology 3*. The guitar riff of another track tinkered with today, 'New Orleans' by Gary U.S. Bonds, was an influence on The Beatles' 1964 'I Feel Fine'.

George Martin was the producer at the session and Glyn Johns the engineer.

Day Eleven: 22 January 1969 - Apple Headquarters, 3 Savile Row, Mayfair, London

I Shall Be Released (Bob Dylan, two takes), Let It Down (Harrison), Don't Let Me Down (eighteen takes), I've Got A Feeling (twenty-nine takes), Some Other Guy (Richie Barrett), Johnny B. Goode (Chuck Berry), Dig A Pony (at this point entitled All I Want Is You, twenty-four takes), Going Up The Country (based on Bull Doze Blues, recorded in 1928 by Texas bluesman Henry Thomas, a recent hit for the American blues/boogie rock band, Canned Heat), The Long And Winding Road (three takes), A Taste Of Honey (Bobby Scott/Ric Marlow), Oh! Darling, I'm Ready (Fats Domino), Rocker (Beatles), Save The Last Dance For Me (The Drifters), Carol (Chuck Berry)

11am start and the first *Get Back/Let It Be* session to feature keyboardist Billy Preston. An old friend of the band, he had first encountered The Beatles in Hamburg in the early 1960s, and was in London playing with American musician Ray Charles. Harrison had been in the audience at one of the shows, and a day later Preston called George and accepted his request to come over to Apple. 'Billy Preston walked into the office,' George recalled. 'I grabbed him and brought him down to the studio and said, "How would you like to play piano?" It put everything more at ease, because having a fifth person there, it sort of offset the vibes. There was a 100 per cent improvement.' Ringo agreed, 'When we started to work on something good,' he recalled, 'the bullshit went out of the window and we got back to doing what we did well.' Acting as an emollient, Preston smoothed out the friction within the band at the time. (Takes of 'Dig A Pony' and 'I've Got A Feeling' from today's session were included on Apple's 1996's *Anthology 3* compilation.) Curio of the day: The Beatles' brief stab at 'A Taste Of

Honey', a track recorded for their *Please Please Me* album almost six years earlier.

George Martin was the producer at the session and Glyn Johns the engineer.

Day Twelve: 23 January 1969 – Apple Headquarters, 3 Savile Row, Mayfair, London

Octopus's Garden, Two Of Us (two takes), I've Got A Feeling (three takes), Get Back (forty-three takes), Words Of Love (Buddy Holly), Twenty Flight Rock (Eddie Cochran), Oh! Darling (three takes), Let It Be (two takes), Mean Mr Mustard, Let's Twist Again (Chubby Checker), The Long And Winding Road (two takes), Everything's Alright (Billy Preston), I Want To Thank You (Billy Preston), You've Been Acting Strange (Billy Preston), Use What You Got (Billy Preston), Happiness Runs (Donovan), Shazam! (Duane Eddy/Lee Hazlewood, Duane Eddy), Dig A Pony, I'll Get You, Help!, Please Please Me, Hey Hey Georgie (ad-lib, Harrison), If You Need Me (McCartney), Love Is The Thing To Me (Billy Preston), Together In Love (Billy Preston), It Blew Again (Lennon)

The performances of 'Help!' and 'Please Please Me' today were simply send-ups, lasting less than a minute. With Billy Preston once more in attendance, Paul's 'Get Back' had a serious workover today and practically dominated the session, while Ringo's 'Octopus's Garden' resurfaced. Footage of each Beatle arriving and entering the Apple building appeared in the *Let It Be* movie.

George Martin was the producer at the session and Glyn Johns the engineer.

Day Thirteen: 24 January 1969 – Apple Headquarters, 3 Savile Row, Mayfair, London

Get Back (twenty-one takes), (I Can't Get No) Satisfaction (Jagger/Richards, a 1965 hit for the Rolling Stones), What'd I Say (Ray Charles, two takes), Don't Let Me Down, Ob-La-Di Ob-La-Da, Soldier Of Love (Arthur Alexander, two takes), Cathy's Clown (The Everly Brothers), Where Have You Been (Arthur Alexander, two takes), Love Is A Swingin' Thing (Luther Dixon/Willie Denson/Shirley Owens, The Shirelles, two takes), She Said Yeah (Larry Williams), Child Of Nature (Lennon), Two Of Us (twenty-one takes), You're So Good To Me (Brian Wilson/Mike Love, a 1965 hit for The Beach Boys), She Came In Through The Bathroom Window, Teddy Boy (McCartney, six takes), Ach Du Lieber Augustin (traditional German children's song), Maggie Mae (two takes – in 1964 the creator of *Oliver!*, Lionel Bart, used this traditional song, credited on the album as arranged by all four Beatles, as the inspiration for a musical centred on the Liverpool docks), Fancy My Chances With You (Lennon/McCartney), Polythene Pam, The Long And Winding Road, Window Window (Harrison, two takes), Her Majesty, Every Night (McCartney), Hot As Sun (McCartney), Catswalk (McCartney), Hello Goodbye, Diggin' My Potatoes (Lonnie Donegan), Hey Liley Liley Lo (The Vipers Skiffle Group), Rock Island Line (Lonnie Donegan), Tiger Rag (Original Dixieland Jass Band), Michael Row The Boat Ashore (Lonnie Donegan), Rock-A-Bye Baby (traditional), Singing The Blues (Guy Mitchell), Knee Deep In The Blues (both Marty Robbins and Guy Mitchell), Dig It (Lennon/McCartney/Harrison/Starkey, four takes), Little Demon (Screamin' Jay Hawkins), Maybellene (Chuck Berry), You Can't Catch Me (Chuck Berry), Brown Eyed Handsome Man (Chuck Berry), Short Fat Fannie (Larry Williams), Green Onions (Booker T. Jones/Steve Cropper/Lewie Steinberg/Al Jackson Jr., Booker T. and The MGs), Bad Boy (Larry Williams), Sweet Little Sixteen (Chuck Berry), Around And Around (Chuck Berry), School Day (Chuck Berry), Stand

By Me (Ben E. King), Lady Madonna, Lovely Rita, Lonely Sea (Brian Wilson/Gary Usher, The Beach Boys), Ramrod (Duane Eddy), Balls To Your Partner (McCartney), There You Are Eddie (McCartney, three takes), Pillow For Your Head (McCartney, two takes)

Work on Paul's 'Get Back' once more dominated today's proceedings, along with another of his compositions, 'Two Of Us'. The group dropped the uptempo arrangement for the latter and finally settled on a delicate, folk-rock feel. McCartney's 'Teddy Boy' also made an appearance. Although it was discarded by The Beatles, he would re-record the track for his 1970 debut album *McCartney*.

Other Paul songs attempted today included 'There You Are, Eddie', never officially released either by him or The Beatles. Penned just a month earlier, in December 1968, he composed the track while staying at the Portugal home of Beatles official biographer Hunter Davies. 'He had written it on the lavatory,' Davies recalled. 'He rarely went there without his guitar. I don't think he ever completed it. He had discovered that my first Christian name is Edward, something I've always kept quiet. I always hoped it would have appeared on an album, so I could boast for ever. Many years later, on a *Let it Be* bootleg, I heard him playing the song to John and he had added another verse about, "You think you are part of the in crowd". Then they added lists of other names, apart from Eddie. It was a good song, I thought. Just a shame they never recorded it.'

For the only time during these *Get Back/Let It Be* get-togethers, John played his future *Abbey Road* album track, 'Polythene Pam'. The Lennon/McCartney song, 'Fancy My Chances With You', was also attempted and would later appear on the bonus *Fly On The Wall* disc that accompanied early copies of *Let It Be … Naked* in 2003.

Paul's instrumental 'Catswalk', which The Beatles had performed in concert between 1958–62, also appeared for the first and only time during the sessions today. (A tape containing two rehearsals of this song was recorded in an empty Cavern club on or around 7 October 1962. See relevant entry in the *Places* section. It was retitled 'Catcall' and on 20 July 1967 The Chris Barber Band recorded an over-the-top arrangement of it and released it as a single in the UK on Marmalade Records on 20 October 1967.) As Mal Evans noted in his diary today, '[The] Beatles [are] really playing together. Atmosphere is lovely in the studio; everyone seems so much happier than of recent times.'

George Martin was the producer at today's session and Glyn Johns the engineer.

Day Fourteen: 25 January 1969 – Apple Headquarters, 3 Savile Row, Mayfair, London

Another Day (McCartney), Two Of Us (seven takes), Act Naturally (Johnny Russell/Voni Morrison, Buck Owens and The Buckaroos), Nashville Cats (John Sebastian, a 1966 hit for The Lovin' Spoonful), I've Got A Feeling, On The Road Again (Floyd Jones, a recent hit for the American blues/boogie rock band Canned Heat), I Lost My Little Girl (McCartney), Bye Bye Love (The Everly Brothers), For You Blue (twenty-eight takes), Take This Hammer (Lonnie Donegan), Let It Be (eighteen takes), Please Please Me, Mean Mr Mustard, The Tracks Of My Tears (Smokey Robinson/Pete Moore/Marv Tarplin, 1965 hit for Smokey Robinson and The Miracles), Piece Of My Heart (Erma Franklin), Little Yellow Pills (Jackie Lomax), Early In The Morning (Buddy Holly), Window Window (Harrison), I'm Talking About You (Chuck Berry), Martha My Dear, Love Story (Randy Newman), Cannonball (Duane Eddy), Shazam! (Duane Eddy/Lee Hazlewood, Duane Eddy), Isn't It A Pity (Harrison), Sorry

When Beatlemania began, they were not only over all our ears, but in every sort of newspaper and magazine, keeping scores of cartoonists in employment. In January 1964, the magazine Film Review delighted us with a selection drawn of Beatles cartoons by 'Bry'.

I Left You Bleeding (Lennon), Crazy Feet (McCartney), Well It's Eight O'Clock (Lennon), Fast Train To San Francisco (Beatles)

With the idea of performing on Apple's rooftop now gaining momentum, Paul, director Michael Lindsay-Hogg, roadie Mal Evans and Beatles equipment manager Kevin Harrington went up there on a reconnaissance ahead of the concert. Back in the basement, three tracks featured prominently today, 'Two Of Us', 'For You Blue' and 'Let It Be'. Among the day's other musical highlights was a rendition of 'I Lost My Little Girl'. Dating back to October/November 1956, and written shortly after his mother's death, it was the first song Paul ever wrote. Today's performance was notable since it featured John on lead vocals, and lasted a little under ten minutes. In addition to 'For You Blue', two other Harrison songs were also played, 'Isn't It A Pity' (which made its debut at the sessions, but was eventually held back for his 1970 *All Things Must Pass* triple album) and 'Window, Window', which most surprisingly was chiefly led by Paul. The song was never released officially in any shape or form in George's lifetime. A version of 'For You Blue' from today's session later appeared on Apple's *Anthology 3* compilation in 1996, as did one take of 'Let It Be', featuring Paul's ad-libbed vocals and alternate lyrics. 'Act Naturally', a track recorded by the group some four years earlier, was reprised today. While The Beatles rehearsed, Yoko Ono sellotaped pieces of blank art paper onto a wall and amused herself by painting doodles onto it.

George Martin was the producer at the session and Glyn Johns the engineer. Billy Preston was missing from today's get-together.

Day Fifteen: 26 January 1969 – Apple Headquarters, 3 Savile Row, Mayfair, London

Isn't It A Pity (Harrison), Window Window (Harrison), Let It Down (Harrison, two takes), Octopus's Garden (eight takes), Little Piece Of Leather (Lennon), Two Of Us, Dig A Pony, Let It Be (twenty-eight takes), High School Confidential (Jerry Lee Lewis), Great Balls Of Fire (Jerry Lee Lewis), Don't Let The Sun Catch You Cryin' (Ray Charles), Suicide (McCartney), Do Not Forsake Me Oh My Darlin' (Tex Ritter), You Really Got A Hold On Me (Smokey Robinson, Smokey Robinson and the Miracles, two takes), Like A Rolling Stone (Bob Dylan), Twist And Shout (Bert Berns/Phil Medley), Dig It (Lennon/McCartney/Harrison/Starkey), Rip It Up/Shake, Rattle And Roll/Blue Suede Shoes (medley, Little Richard/Jesse Stone/Carl Perkins), Kansas City (Jerry Leiber/Mike Stoller), Miss Ann (Little Richard), Lawdy Miss Clawdy (Lloyd Price), The Tracks Of My Tears (Smokey Robinson/Pete Moore/Marv Tarplin, 1965 hit for Smokey Robinson and The Miracles), Agent Double-O-Soul (Edwin Starr), SOS (Edwin Starr), Rockin' Pneumonia And The Boogie Woogie Flu (Huey 'Piano' Smith), I'm Movin' On (Ray Charles), Little Yellow Pills (Jackie Lomax), The Long And Winding Road (sixteen takes), It Was So Blue (McCartney), I Left My Home In The World (McCartney), I Told You Before (Beatles)

11am start. Focusing mainly on two tracks, 'Let It Be' and 'The Long And Winding Road', this was a surprising Sunday session for The Beatles. George and Ringo were the first to arrive. The session began with Harrison performing 'Isn't It A Pity', 'Let It Down' and the unreleased 'Window, Window' alone on an acoustic guitar. He also assisted Ringo with the composition 'Octopus's Garden', a part of which can be seen in the finished *Let It Be* film. Covers of various Jerry Lee Lewis, Ray Charles, Little Richard, Bob Dylan and Smokey Robison and The Miracles hits peppered the day's session, which concluded with an almost hour-long workout of Paul's 'The

Long And Winding Road', with him on piano and John on bass, a take from which was included on *Anthology 3*. Producer Phil Spector garnished it with orchestral and choral overdubs for the 1970 *Let It Be* album. An extract of 'Dig It', also recorded today, which was part of a 12-minute take, also appeared on that LP. Cover versions of the tracks 'Rip It Up', 'Shake, Rattle And Roll' and 'Blue Suede Shoes' later appeared as a medley on *Anthology 3*. Among today's other musical high points was McCartney's Sinatra-inspired composition 'Suicide', which he wrote as a teenager, a snippet of which was later included on his 1970 debut album *McCartney*, and in the Wings 1974 MPL film *One Hand Clapping*.

During a meeting today, held round the conference table at Apple, while John and Yoko tucked into their macrobiotic food and the others chomped their way through a spread containing roast chicken, vegetables and potatoes, served with red and rosé wine, the idea of an unannounced live performance the following Thursday on the roof of their own office building was raised again. John announced he wanted to blast out around that area of central London and provide free entertainment for the nearby office and shop workers; Ringo was still unimpressed and emphatic that he would not participate; George remained only lukewarm as he simply didn't want the band to perform in public again. It was only the combined force of John and Paul that would make it happen.

George Martin was the producer at today's session and Glyn Johns the engineer. Joining them was Billy Preston and Paul's then girlfriend, the photographer Linda Eastman, and her daughter Heather.

Day Sixteen: 27 January 1969 – Apple Headquarters, 3 Savile Row, Mayfair, London

The Castle Of The King Of The Birds/Strawberry Fields Forever, Old Brown Shoe (thirteen takes), Baby Let's Play House (Arthur Gunter, Elvis Presley), Oh! Darling (four takes), Let It Be (twelve takes), The Long And Winding Road (six takes), Little Demon (Screamin' Jay Hawkins), Save The Last Dance For Me (Doc Pomus/Mort Shuman, Ben. E King and The Drifters), Hi-Heel Sneakers (Tommy Tucker), Get Back (thirty-two takes), Water Water (McCartney), Don't Let Me Down (five takes), Hava Nagilah (traditional Jewish folk song), I've Got A Feeling (nine takes), You Are My Sunshine (Jimmie Davis/Charles Mitchell), Bring It On Home To Me (Sam Cooke), Take These Chains From My Heart (Ray Charles), You Won't Get Me That Way (McCartney), The Walk (Jimmy McCracklin), I Told You Before (Harrison, two takes)

Aside from several run-throughs of 'Oh! Darling', 'Let It Be', 'The Long And Winding Road,' 'Don't Let Me Down', 'Old Brown Shoe' and 'I've Got A Feeling', most of today's session was devoted to Paul's 'Get Back', with 32 attempts. At one brief point he elected to sing the lyrics in German, but ended the take singing the final chorus in French. John's line, 'Sweet Loretta Fart, she thought she was a cleaner, but she was a frying pan,' during one of the run-throughs, later appeared on the group's May 1970 Apple album *Let It Be*. With John singing the lyrics, the track 'Water, Water' was an interesting, yet bizarre, variation of 'Get Back'. Performed in a bluesy, half-time signature, it featured Lennon strumming a grungy rhythm guitar while Harrison added Rickenbacker fills. During the sessions, John told George Martin, 'I don't want any of your production shit. We want this to be an honest album … I don't want any editing; I don't want any overdubbing; it's got to be like it is. We just record the song and that's it, okay?' Martin reluctantly agreed. 'So we would start the track,' he recalled, 'but it wasn't quite right, so we'd do it again and then we'd get to take 19 and I'd say, "Well, John, the bass wasn't as good as it was on take 17 but the voice was pretty good," so we'd start again, and we'd go on for ever, because it was never perfect and it got very tedious.' Ringo agreed. 'Everyone was getting tired of us,' he admitted. The day concluded with everyone agreeing that take 11 of 'Get Back' was the best.

An engineer also appeared today to assess the roof of Savile Row. He told the group that it would take 5lbs per square inch of weight, and they would need to erect scaffolding to make a platform on which to perform. It was easy to sort; the rooftop show was now pretty much on. Buoyed by the news, the team even enquired about a helicopter to shoot aerial shots of the performance, and with excitement engulfing the building, Alistair Taylor acted on the decision of Mal Evans and ordered a toasted sandwich machine.

It's worth noting that when the group, in particular Paul, came to choosing which version they wanted for the 'Get Back' single (released in the UK on 11 April 1969), he chose one from today but edited on to it a coda taped the following day. Other high points today included McCartney's future *Abbey Road* track 'Oh! Darling', with John on the Fender VI, six-string bass, the same instrument that George had played on the "Hey Jude" performance at Twickenham the previous year (see 'Hey Jude' entry in *TV* section). One take lasted nearly seven minutes; an abridged version was included on the official 1996 *Anthology 3* release, replete with John's declaration that Yoko's divorce from the American film-maker Tony Cox had been finalised. (He was actually mistaken. It didn't come through for another week, on 2 February 1969.)

George's 'Old Brown Shoe', inspired by an unforeseen incident with some dog poo that his shiny footwear had come into contact with,

was performed for the first time today. Opening versions featured him singing the track alone at the piano, while John listened intently, but later ones were with the rest of the band. The track (re-recorded at Abbey Road in February and April 1969) would appear as the flip side to the group's single 'The Ballad Of John And Yoko'. Interestingly, Paul also chose today's session to sing a rendition of 'Strawberry Fields Forever', which seamlessly followed another run-through of 'The Castle Of The King Of The Birds', this time featuring Lennon's occasional guitar fills. Further dialogue about hiring a helicopter for the filming of their upcoming rooftop concert was also caught on tape.

As usual, George Martin was the producer today and Glyn Johns (who'd had a run-in with a police vehicle on his way to the studio that day) the engineer. Linda Eastman and Billy Preston (who was still waiting for delivery of his especially ordered Hammond organ) were also present.

Day Seventeen: 28 January 1969 – Apple Headquarters, 3 Savile Row, Mayfair, London

The Long And Winding Road, I've Got A Feeling (seventeen takes), The Inner Light, Blue Yodel No. 1 ('T' For Texas) (Jimmie Rodgers), Tea For Two Cha-Cha (Tommy Dorsey), Dig It (Lennon/McCartney/Harrison/Starkey), Child Of Nature (Lennon, two takes), Dig A Pony (twelve takes), Get Back (seven takes), Love Me Do, Teddy Boy (McCartney, two takes), Don't Let Me Down (four takes), The One After 909 (four takes), Old Brown Shoe (eight takes), Sticks And Stones (Ray Charles), Something (five takes), Bo Diddley (Bo Diddley), Two Of Us (five takes), All Things Must Pass (four takes), Positively 4th Street (Bob Dylan, two takes), The River Rhine (McCartney), Shazam! (Duane Eddy/Lee Hazlewood, Duane Eddy), I Will Always Look For You (McCartney),

Unless He Has A Song (Billy Preston), How Do You Tell Someone? (Harrison), Greasepaint On Your Face (McCartney), Rainy Day Women #12 & 35 (Bob Dylan), I Want You (She's So Heavy) (four takes)

In what could be described as a day of fine-tuning, The Beatles spent a great deal of today working on tracks earmarked for their *Get Back* album – 'Dig A Pony', 'Two Of Us', 'The One After 909', 'Get Back' (the coda from one particular take today was tagged onto the end of one of the previous day's recordings and released as a single in April 1969), 'I've Got A Feeling' (with one take lasting a full 15 minutes, others featuring John on lead vocals) and 'Don't Let Me Down' (the version appearing as the B-side to 'Get Back' was recorded today, with additional backing vocals added at EMI).

In addition, the group spent time working on tracks that wouldn't appear on the album. George resumed work on 'Old Brown Shoe', and after one particular take The Beatles, along with Billy Preston, began experimenting with a stylophone, an instrument made famous by the (now shamed) Australian television and radio personality Rolf Harris. This was the group's only known use of the hand-held gadget.

Harrison also turned his attention to another new track today, 'Something'. Five attempts were made at it. Recordings reveal that at this point the song was still in need of lyrics, with George asking the others for help in finishing it off. 'Just say what comes into your head each time,' John told him, suggesting, 'Attracts me like a cauliflower.'

Lennon too introduced a new track, 'I Want You (She's So Heavy)', which would later appear on the group's September 1969 album *Abbey Road*. The first takes of this today were simply instrumentals. Two versions of Paul's 'Teddy Boy' were also performed, one of which was later

edited with a take from Day Thirteen's recordings (24 January) and issued on 1996's *Anthology 3* compilation. Same too for John's 'Child Of Nature', which at this point was still known as 'On The Road To Marrakesh'. (John had taped a demo of 'Child Of Nature' at Kinfauns, George's bungalow in Esher, Surrey, during a Beatles *White Album* demos session at the tail end of May 1968. The tune would eventually appear as 'Jealous Guy', complete with altered lyrics, on John's 1971 solo album *Imagine*.) 'Love Me Do', replete with a slow arrangement, as well as a brief stab at George's 1968 composition 'The Inner Light', released as the B-side to 'Lady Madonna', were also jammed today. The former failed to impress the group, but another oldie, 'The One After 909', recorded at EMI almost six years earlier, and last jammed at these sessions on 9 January, certainly did.

George Martin was the producer at the session and Glyn Johns the engineer.

At the conclusion of today's get-together, at a little before 9pm The Beatles put down their instruments and climbed the stairs to one of the boardrooms at Savile Row. They had arranged an appointment with Allen Klein, the record label executive and, most notably, Rolling Stones manager. Following a recommendation by Linda Eastman's father, John, Klein began by announcing he would make enquiries into Lennon's financial position, whereupon George and Ringo asked him to do the same for them. At this point Paul stormed out of the meeting. The remaining Beatles then had a general discussion about the proposed purchase of NEMS, their former manager Brian Epstein's musical act management company, and Klein informed them that he could not recommend John to proceed with the purchase while the relevant information about the position of The Beatles themselves remained to be ascertained. With both McCartney and Eastman absent from the meeting, Klein felt there was no point in debating the matter further so another meeting was arranged, for 1 February, when Eastman and Paul would hopefully be present. (Klein spent the remainder of that week in the offices of The Beatles' personal accountants Bryce Hanmer, Isherwood & Company, in particular with Harry Pinsker, a partner in the firm, obtaining the required information for Lennon, Harrison and Starkey. By the end of the week, Klein had collected a reasonable amount of information about the group's personal financial situations, but did not have enough time to make a full investigation into the affairs of their companies, so was not in a position to assess their true overall fiscal position.)

Day Eighteen: 29 January 1969 – Apple Headquarters, 3 Savile Row, Mayfair, London

Singing The Blues (Guy Mitchell, five versions), Rule Britannia (British patriotic song by James Thomson), I Walk The Line (Johnny Cash), Dig A Pony, I've Got A Feeling, Don't Let Me Down, Get Back, The One After 909 (three takes), She Came In Through The Bathroom Window (three takes), Two Of Us (three takes), Let It Be, The Long And Winding Road (two takes), For You Blue (three takes), Something (two takes), All Things Must Pass (four takes), Let It Down (Harrison, four takes), I Want You (She's So Heavy) (two takes), Sexy Sadie, Old Brown Shoe, Dig It (Lennon/McCartney/Harrison/Starkey), Bésame Mucho (Consuelo Velázquez), Three Cool Cats (Jerry Leiber/Mike Stoller, 1958 song by The Coasters), I Got To Find My Baby (Chuck Berry), Some Other Guy (Richie Barrett), Honky Tonk (Bill Doggett), Vacation Time (Chuck Berry), Cannonball (Duane Eddy), Not Fade Away (Buddy Holly), Hey Little Girl (In The High School Sweater) (Dee Clark), Bo Diddley (Bo Diddley), Maybe Baby (Buddy Holly), Peggy Sue Got Married (Buddy Holly), Thinking Of Linking (McCartney), Crying Waiting Hoping (Buddy Holly), Mailman Bring Me No More Blues (Buddy Holly), Teddy Boy (McCartney), Bring Your Own Band (McCartney), Lotta Lovin' (Gene Vincent), Sorry Miss Molly (McCartney), Also (McCartney), She Gets Heavy (Lennon)

On the eve of the group's rooftop concert, about which Harrison was still reluctant, today the group barely touched the songs they would perform, choosing instead to work on the other tracks earmarked for the *Get Back* album.

George Martin was the producer at today's session and Glyn Johns the engineer.

Day Nineteen: 30 January 1969 – Apple Headquarters (rooftop), 3 Savile Row, Mayfair, London

Set-list in order: Get Back (take 1), Get Back (take 2), I Want You (She's So Heavy) (brief guitar burst), Get Back (take 3), Don't Let Me Down (take 1), I've Got A Feeling (take 1), The One After 909 (take 1, false start), The One After 909 (take 2), Danny Boy (John, brief quote), Dig A Pony (take 1, false start), Dig A Pony (take 2), God Save The Queen (ad-lib instrumental), I've Got A Feeling (take 2), A Pretty Girl Is Like A Melody (quote), Get Back (take 4, false start), Don't Let Me Down (take 2), Get Back (take 5)

At midday, while a bitterly cold wind blew across the rooftops of central London, The Beatles gave their very last live performance. In order for them to be heard down in the streets, technicians had to bring over, at approximately 4am, some exceptionally large speakers from EMI. To cope with the extreme, seasonal weather, John borrowed Yoko's fur coat and Ringo wore his wife Maureen's red mac. While the movie cameras were being set up, The Beatles began their unannounced show with a rehearsal of 'Get Back'.

Then, following some fairly polite applause from spectators on a nearby roof, which reminded Paul of a cricket match, he stepped back to the microphone and muttered some words about the Sussex and England cricketer Ted Dexter. John trumped him by announcing, 'We've had a request from Martin Luther.' Another version of 'Get Back' followed. (An edit of these two takes was included in the *Let It Be* film.)

Following a short burst of John's 'I Want You (She's So Heavy)', 'Don't Let Me Down' was performed next. (This too featured in the released movie.) The group then launched straight into further versions of 'Get Back' and 'Don't Let Me Down'. 'I've Got A Feeling' followed (by which time it was estimated that the police had received 30 complaints) and then 'The One After 909', both tracks featuring in/on the *Let It Be* film and album. At the end of the latter, John broke into a brief, impromptu rendition of 'Danny Boy', the 1913 standard and a 1959 hit for Conway Twitty. 'Dig A Pony' was up next. A short rehearsal was played first, with Lennon asking for the words. A proper performance of the song followed with the redheaded Kevin Harrington, assistant to Mal Evans, kneeling in front of him holding aloft a clipboard bearing the lyrics. (Harrington had been an office junior at NEMS since 1966, and was originally Brian Epstein's personal office boy.) The track began with a false start. Ringo wasn't ready. In the film he could be seen putting his cigarette down and crying out, 'Hold it!' This, and the full version that followed, were both included in the album and film, although on the LP, the, 'All I want is …' refrain, which opened and closed the song, was cut by producer Phil Spector.

Time for a tape change. While operator Alan Parsons organised this in Apple's basement studio, the group, along with Billy Preston, performed a short off-the-cuff version of the British national anthem, 'God Save The Queen'. This was never used, nor were the second attempts at 'I've Got A Feeling' and 'Don't Let Me Down'. The last full song attempted was 'Get Back', although The Beatles were almost prevented from performing it when two policemen, one of whom, Ken Wharfe, on duty in Piccadilly Circus and acting on complaints from nearby businesses, arrived with orders for the group to either turn the music down or stop altogether. When they knocked on the door, Apple staff originally refused entry until they said, 'Well, if you don't let us in we're going to arrest everyone in the building.'

'The Beatles show stopped the traffic,' Apple general manager Alistair Taylor recalled, 'and it sent the police hurtling round … We knew the police would be there saying, "You can't do this! This isn't on!" because the Savile Row police station is only about three hundred yards away, at No. 27, down at the bottom of Savile Row and we were virtually at the top end … They [the group] were doing this in the middle of the highly respected tailoring industry and we knew that the other residents would complain.'

Now up on the roof, the other officer (policeman No. 503 of the Greater Westminster Council) demanded that Mal Evans turn off the group's Fender Twin amplifiers. He complied, but George did not and immediately turned his back on. Realising his mistake, Evans immediately turned John's back on too. The amplifiers took several seconds to work again, and when they did the group managed to play long enough to complete the song. The track reached a tremendous climax when Paul brilliantly ad-libbed the lines, 'You've been playing on the roofs again, and that's no good, and you know your Mummy doesn't like that … she gets angry … she's gonna have you arrested! Get back!' The show was over, and in recognition of Ringo's wife's enthusiastic cheering, McCartney marked it with a simple, 'Thanks Mo.' This was shadowed by John's closing line, 'I'd like to say thank you on behalf of the group and ourselves, and I hope we passed the audition.' (Both these comments were featured at the end of 'Get Back' on the *Let It Be* album, although the version of the song that had preceded it was not from the rooftop performance.) The Beatles were apparently disappointed that the police only asked them to stop. They were hoping that they would be arrested and dragged off to jail for disturbing the peace! Paul said that it would have been a 'great ending for the movie'.

Immediately following the show, The Beatles, along with Lindsay-Hogg, George Martin and Linda Eastman, excitedly gathered in the basement studio to listen to a playback of the performance. (The concert had been recorded by George Martin, engineer Glyn Johns and tape operator Alan Parsons on the two 8-track machines housed in Apple's basement.) 'It's come off actually much better than I thought it would,' Martin declared. John liked it too, announcing he thought it was 'fantastic' but was annoyed he missed a line on 'Don't Let Me Down'. Paul comforted him by insisting, 'We'll edit it.' Buoyed by what had just happened, Harrison joked, 'I think for taking over London,' with John suggesting, 'the Hilton tomorrow'. Humour aside, Harrison wanted reassurance that there wouldn't be any more concerts like this. 'No more rooftops,' Paul assured him, 'that was the rooftop. That's it …' He then suggested that they should 'record the other stuff we didn't do up there, the acoustic stuff,' down in the Apple basement studio. (The tracks he was referring to, 'Two Of Us', 'Let It Be' and 'The Long And Winding Road', would be taped there the following day.)

Later that night, at Olympic Studios in Barnes, certain (unspecified) tracks were mixed into stereo by Glyn Johns. He then had acetate discs

cut from his mixes and presented them to each of The Beatles. On 5 February 1969, this time at the group's Apple Studios, another stereo mix of the rooftop performance, along with a compilation, was prepared. Tracks included 'I've Got A Feeling' (two versions), 'Don't Let Me Down', 'Get Back' (two versions), 'The One After 909' and 'Dig A Pony'.

For the record, about half of the group's 42-minute rooftop performance was used in the *Let It Be* film and edits of 'I've Got A Feeling', 'The One After 909' and 'Dig A Pony' were featured on the movie's album. The final take of 'Get Back' was included in the *Let It Be* film, and later appeared on the 1996 Apple/EMI compilation *Anthology 3*. Furthermore, an edit of the two 'Don't Let Me Down' takes was included on 2003's *Let It Be … Naked*, which also featured an edit of the rooftop performance of 'I've Got A Feeling', along with another version taped on a previous date. Brief, incomplete attempts at 'I Want You (She's So Heavy)', 'God Save The Queen', 'A Pretty Girl Is Like A Melody' and 'Danny Boy' were fooled around with in between the group's proper songs, but only the latter was included in the film and on the album. Their rendition of 'God Save The Queen' had coincided with Alan Parsons changing the tapes.

Vicki Wickham, the producer of the ITV pop show *Ready Steady Go!*, was one of many onlookers on adjacent rooftops, which served as precarious perches for fans. The Beatles staff at Savile Row were as surprised as everyone by the unannounced show. Employee Jean Nisbet was one of them. 'When they started playing right above me, my office ceiling began to vibrate. I thought it was time to move so I rushed out of the front door and into the street to find the other office girls hanging out of windows screaming and hundreds of passers-by gazing up to the roof … the traffic was at a standstill. Everyone was in good humour, except for a few of our neighbours.' One of these was Stanley Davis, a director of the cloth wholesalers Wain, Shiel & Son, based next door to Apple. 'It's disgraceful,' he blasted that day. 'I want this bloody noise stopped! All hell has let loose. We are not amused. Work came to a standstill and our switchboard operators couldn't hear anyone.'

The Beatles' rooftop performance was not an original one. The American band Jefferson Airplane had played atop the Schuyler Hotel in Midtown Manhattan, for a proposed Jean-Luc Goddard film, *One A.M.*, on 7 December 1968. Just like the Fab Four's version, it too was cut short by the local police. With pans up of the building, and pans down to people staring up at the concert they could not see, intercut with shots of passers-by milling around and bemused people viewing from adjacent windows and rooftops, The Beatles' version was practically an unintentional, scene-by-scene carbon-copy of that shot by the legendary film director, Jean-Luc Godard, just nine weeks earlier.

However, Jefferson Airplane themselves were not the first pop/rock group to perform on a roof. The first to do this was another legendary line-up, The Grateful Dead, who played on top of the Chelsea Hotel, New York City for the Andy Warhol crowd, over a year earlier on 10 August 1967. Or was it done even before that? Were they all really inspired by Dick Van Dyke and his chimney sweep pals, and their rooftop performance in the 1964 Walt Disney film *Mary Poppins*?

Trivia: Harrison didn't want any of his new songs to be played on the roof, since he didn't think any of them had been rehearsed well enough. 'Old Brown Shoe' was the only track he thought of possibly playing.

The Beatles' long-time friend, roadie and confidante Neil Aspinall missed the show due to a pre-arranged dentist's appointment.

A film crew from ITN (Independent Television News) was present that lunchtime eagerly capturing the scenes in and around Savile Row. Soon after it was screened on that evening's ITN bulletin, on the ITV network, the truly exclusive b&w film report went missing from their archives. The good old BBC chose not to send any news crew along at all.

Day Twenty: 31 January 1969 – Apple Headquarters, 3 Savile Row, Mayfair, London

Two Of Us (seven takes), Hey Good Lookin' (Hank Williams), Take This Hammer (Lonnie Donegan), Long Lost John (Lonnie Donegan), Five Feet High And Rising (Johnny Cash), Bear Cat Mama (Jimmie Davis), Black Dog Blues (Blind Blake), Right String Baby But The Wrong Yo-Yo (Carl Perkins), Run For Your Life, Step Inside Love (two takes), Friendship (Cole Porter), Turkey In The Straw (traditional nineteenth-century American folk song), Tales Of Frankie Rabbit (Lennon/McCartney), 'Deed I Do (Fred Rose/Walter Hirsch), I Got Stung (Elvis Presley), Let It Be (twenty-two takes), The Long And Winding Road (nineteen takes), All Along the Watchtower (riff – Bob Dylan), Lady Madonna, I Want You (She's So Heavy), Build Me Up Buttercup (Mike d'Abo/Tony Macaulay,1968 hit for The Foundations), Let's Have A Party (Elvis Presley), Twelfth Street Rag (Euday L. Bowman), Oh! Darling (two takes)

The twentieth and final filming day of the *Get Back/Let It Be* project. With their rooftop show now done and dusted, the main purpose of today's session was to allow the crew to film and tape satisfactory versions of 'Two Of Us', 'Let It Be' and 'The Long And Winding Road'. (A performance of 'Two Of Us' recorded today was included in the film and as the opening song on the 1970 *Let It Be* album.) Following their lunchtime break, work focused mainly on McCartney's 'The Long

And Winding Road'; one take in particular would later appear on the 2003 Apple album *Let It Be ... Naked*. The group also worked tirelessly on another of his compositions, 'Let It Be', which proved slightly more problematic, mainly due to John's increasing boredom with it, which became evident when he cheekily reworded some of its lyrics. 'And in my hour of darkness, she is standing left in front of me, squeaking turds of whisky over me.' Paul did some altering of his own, most notably a reference to 'Brother Malcolm' (in all likelihood the group's long-standing friend Mal Evans), and substituting, 'times of trouble,' for 'times of heartache'. In the end, 22 attempts were made at it. The early ones, which featured John on lead vocals, boasted a skiffle-style arrangement and a different melody.

With The Beatles' work on the important songs rounding off early, this allowed plenty of time for them to lark around with various golden oldies, among them hits by Hank Williams, Johnny Cash, Lonnie Donegan, Carl Perkins and Elvis Presley. Others attempted included the recent chart hit 'Build Me Up Buttercup' by British soul band The Foundations, as well as more of their own, 'Run For Your Life', 'Lady Madonna' and 'Step Inside Love', which Paul had composed for British singer Cilla Black the year before. John's future *Abbey Road* album track 'I Want You (She's So Heavy)' was also reprised, interestingly with Paul on lead vocals. Recordings concluded in the early evening, and with that the group's *Get Back/Let It Be* project came to an end. By Derek Taylor, Apple's press officer's estimation, 'The Beatles ended up recording 160 hours [worth] of film and sound,' and in his opinion, the music they had written was 'even better than their last double LP [the *White Album*].'

Post-production on both the movie and soundtrack album rumbled on for several months. Then on 20 July 1969, the day Neil Armstrong walked on the moon, in a screening room at Twickenham Studios, London, the first rough-cut of the film was presented to The Beatles, as well as their wives, girlfriends and associates, including Terry Doran, a former car salesman and a long-time friend of Brian Epstein's. George's parents, Harold and Louise, were also there, as was Yoko Ono who elected to take colour pictures at the event. With a running time of approximately 140 minutes, it featured controversial discussions, several scenes of boredom, and many involving just John and Yoko. This naturally didn't please the other Beatles, who complained and insisted it should be a much nicer movie. Allen Klein was unhappy too, and said he only wanted to see the four Beatles in it and no one else. As producer, Glyn Johns, once remarked, 'It wasn't directed well, and there was no continuity on a lot of it ... so a lot of it obviously was unusable.' So Lindsay-Hogg worked on it again, reducing the running time to 90 minutes.

Another year passed, by which time, with 'Get Back' already released as a single in April 1969, the film's title had switched from *The Beatles Get Back* to simply *Let It Be*. The ownership of it also changed. On 6 April 1970, Allen Klein arrived back in London to conclude a deal whereby all rights to the movie, without any authorisation whatsoever from McCartney, were transferred from his company ABKCO to United Artists. Trouble ensued when the company then decided the *Let It Be* material should instead be used for a theatrical release, requiring the original 16mm, TV friendly (4:3 aspect ratio) footage to be blown up to 35mm (with a 16:9 ratio) to accommodate the equipment (and screens) used in many big cinemas. By doing this, some images, on the top and bottom of certain frames, were either repositioned or totally obscured. (The 1981 US MPI home video of the movie – released by United Artists on VHS and Betamax tape, and on Laserdisc via a license to Magnetic Video – was in fact a 'pan-and-scan' of this version, which cropped both sides of the image, resulting in the viewer quite frequently only seeing the very centre of the frame.)

The decision to release it as a big-screen, world-wide, so-called 'Bioscopic experience' feature film was largely a contractual and financial one; United Artists were still demanding another movie from The Beatles and Apple's accountants were assuring the group that, with so much money having been lavished on the project, they simply could not afford to bury it, however much they wanted to. John firmly believed Lindsay-Hogg had edited out shots of him and Yoko in favour of ones featuring Paul. Lennon also argued that the cameras were set up to show McCartney and not anybody else. Ringo complained that most of the clowning he performed, at the director's request, was never used. And George, after all the tantrums and arguments with both John and Paul, simply hated the project anyway. 'There are scenes in it like the rooftop concert that was good,' Harrison remarked, 'but most of it makes me so aggravated. I can't watch it because it was a particularly bad experience that we were having at that time and it's bad enough having it, let alone having it filmed and recorded so you've got to watch it for the rest of your life. I don't like it!'

Releasing it to the cinemas, as their moneymen informed them, would recoup their costs more efficiently than a TV special. So *Let It Be* became just that (to begin with at least), a released-to-the-cinemas-only feature film. It would become The Beatles' final one. Following an 18 May 1970 screening at the London Pavilion, for the benefit of the press and close friends, *Let It Be* was premiered at the theatre two days later, on 20 May 1970, with none of the group in attendance. Noted

celebrities who did show, however, included director Richard Lester, comedian and former *Goon* Spike Milligan, singers Lulu, Julie Felix and Mary Hopkin, as well as various members of Fleetwood Mac, the Rolling Stones and the Hare Krishna movement. Cynthia Lennon and Jane Asher, two women no longer involved with John and Paul respectively, were the surprise attendees. A simultaneous, invite-only screening of the movie also took place at the Gaumont, London Road, Liverpool. (The movie was released in America on 28 May 1970 as well as in 100 major cities across the globe shortly after.)

Critics were once again quick to pan the movie. Tom Hutchinson, of Liverpool's *Daily Post* newspaper, spoke for many when he described it as 'an occasion for sadness,' adding, 'Watching this 81-minute long, U-certificated account of The Beatles making their latest LP, I felt I was sitting at the deathbed of one of the greatest group talents ever to escape from the trivial treadmill of so much pop music.' He concluded by saying, 'So I regret the passing of an institution, as I regret that this film should be judged as the most suitable hearse for that institution.'

The release of the movie on VHS and DVD

Following the aforementioned short-lived 1981 home video release of the film, and later Laserdisc version, the movie was set to make its official European debut on VHS in Germany in 1984. Issued by Warner Home Video, the cassette was available at first as a rental-only release, at a pricey 100 DM, but just months after its appearance the VHS was pulled from the market; legal problems between Warner/UA Home Video and Apple were cited as the reasons. The film's official UK debut, in 1985, courtesy once more of Warner Home Video, also failed to materialise; we suspect largely due to the ongoing legal problems and the fact its cover was set to feature just John! Several advance copies of a Dutch VHS release that same year, with an alternate sleeve, also crept out, but they were soon withdrawn.

In 1991, in readiness for the official documentary series, the Beatles film archivist Ron Furmanek set about remixing and remastering both audio and visuals of the film. (The original 16mm film negatives were used, with audio work carried out at Abbey Road.) His 81-minute version of the movie was completed on 31 March 1992. (One year earlier, he had digitally remastered the *Shea Stadium* documentary as well, for a future release.)

Five years later, in 1997, the UK-based company VCI announced they were planning to issue that version in Britain, but it too was withdrawn at the eleventh hour. A release of this restored, digitally remastered version of the film, with additional unseen material from the movie, was slated for DVD release by Apple in 2003, to accompany the official *Let It Be ... Naked* album. However, when Apple Corps, the two remaining Beatles, wives, families and estates of both Lennon and Harrison, came to re-examine the contents of the release they discovered that the additional unreleased footage contained too many delicate and controversial issues that still needed to be resolved. The project was shelved and the album came out alone.

A glimmer of hope about the movie's release came in October 2011, when director Michael Lindsay-Hogg, during promotions for his autobiography *Luck And Circumstance: A Coming of Age in Hollywood, New York, and Points Beyond,* announced the film may be released as a two-disc DVD/Blu-ray set sometime around May of 2013. In an interview with the radio station WNYC-FM he said work on *Let It Be* had pretty much been going on every year for the last couple of years and the plan was to fill the second disc with film

out-takes. 'When we first put *Let It Be* out,' he said, 'I had to cut out a lot of stuff that I really liked and wanted to stay in there. The stuff in the new DVD has a lot of the stuff that had to be cut out. So for me, it's like the egg is now complete.' However, that version also bit the dust.

In a press statement made around that time, both Paul and Ringo decided that the movie, and its additional material, would not be released on DVD during their lifetimes, over concerns that it could hurt the Beatles brand. Thereafter, rumours again began to circulate that there would be an official release on a forthcoming DVD/Blu-ray. So far, that has not transpired. We shall see. However, a newly built promo film of 'Let It Be', constructed from the original footage and different to that featured in the movie, together with the clip of 'The Long And Winding Road' lifted directly from the *Let It Be* film, was officially released on the first disc of the *Beatles 1/Beatles 1+* DVD/Blu-ray, on 6 November 2015. (Samples of the amazing, remastered footage can, however, be seen in the official 1995 Beatles *Anthology* series and in the EPKs (Electronic Press Kits) and promo films distributed at the time *Let It Be ... Naked* was released.)

Trivia: During the afternoon of 8 June 1970, in an otherwise empty San Francisco cinema, as part of his primal therapy treatment with psychologist and psychotherapist Dr Arthur Janov, John sat and watched *Let It Be* alongside Yoko, Janov and the *Rolling Stone* editor Jann Wenner.

With legal wrangling over the picture gaining momentum, in particular between Apple and Allen Klein's ABKCO, television broadcasts of *Let It Be* became scarcer as the years rolled by. Following its UK TV premiere on BBC1 during the morning of 26 December 1975, and further screenings on 24 August 1976 (again on BBC1) and 26 December 1979 (this time on BBC2, in a rare widescreen

INSTRUMENTALLY SPEAKING

Beatle instrumentals:

The Bill Justis hit 'Raunchy' was George's audition piece for The Quarrymen.

The Quarrymen had a fondness for Duane Eddy's 1957 instrumental 'Movin 'n' Groovin'' and they did put their version on tape in August 1960.

Another Duane Eddy instrumental taped by The Quarrymen was 'Ramrod', and John once played this with The Big Three.

'Winston's Walk' was played by The Quarrymen, but did John write it?

'Catswalk' was written as an instrumental by Paul around 1959 and they probably performed in Hamburg. They recorded it privately in 1962 and it was offered to EMI producer Wally Ridley for Bert Weedon. Bert didn't record it but The Chris Barber Band released it as a single, 'Cat Call', in 1967, produced by Paul and with him adding catcalls.

When in Hamburg, Rory Storm told The Beatles of a new Shadows track, 'The Frightened City'. John and George pretended they had heard it and played their own composition for Rory. The Beatles recorded it as 'Cry For A Shadow' in Hamburg in 1961.

The Beatles' first instrumental for EMI was '12-Bar Original', featuring The Beatles in their standard line-up, with George Martin on harmonium. The full version lasts nearly seven minutes and a shortened version was released on *Anthology 2*.

Originally called 'Aerial Tour Instrumental', 'Flying' was an instrumental written for the *Magical Mystery Tour* soundtrack and credited to all four Beatles. It included a wordless vocal chant.

'Shirley's Wild Accordion' was played by Shirley Evans in *Magical Mystery Tour* with Reg Wale, Paul and Ringo helping out.

Throughout their career The Quarrymen/Beatles had played 'The Harry Lime Theme' from *The Third Man* to amuse themselves and they recorded it for the *Let It Be* sessions. There are several uncredited instrumental pieces recorded during the *Let It Be* sessions, a bit of a piano boogie or a bit of guitar riffing here and there.

35mm theatrical print), its very last on British television was on BBC2 during the afternoon of 8 May 1982. Its final one in Europe was believed to be in West Germany on 26 December 1983, when it was simultaneously screened by the stations ARD, SWF/SR 3 (south-west Germany), Bayern 3 (Bavarian TV – Munich) and WDR (western area TV in Cologne).

Exciting and interesting to some; boring and dour to others. This was the group, warts and all nearing the end of their time together. George hated it.

MAGICAL MYSTERY TOUR
(1967 – PRODUCED BY DENNIS O'DELL FOR APPLE FILMS)

Filming dates: 11 September 1967–3 November 1967; Paul alone 30–31 October 1967

Locations: various in Hampshire, Devonshire, Cornwall and Somerset, plus, West Malling Air Station and High Street, West Malling, Maidstone, Kent/Sunny Heights, Weybridge; in London Acanthus Road, Lavender Hill/Raymond Revue-bar, Walkers' Court, Soho; and Nice, South of France.

Director: 'Director? What fuckin' director?' John Lennon 1970

Also starring: The Bonzo Dog Doo-Dah Band, Jan Carson, George Claydon, Ivor Cutler, Mal Evans, Shirley Evans, Nat Jackley, Nicola Hale, Freda Kelly, Mike McGear (McCartney), Peggy Spencer's Dance Group, Jessie Robins, Derek Royle, Victor Spinetti, Wendy Winters, Maggie Wright

World TV premiere: BBC1 (UK), 26 December 1967

Songs featured: Magical Mystery Tour, The Fool On The Hill, Flying (instrumental), I Am The Walrus, Blue Jay Way, Your Mother Should Know, Hello, Goodbye (clip in closing credits) (The unreleased instrumental 'Jessie's Dream' (copyrighted to McCartney/Starkey/Harrison/Lennon) also featured as part of the soundtrack, as did 'She Loves You' and 'All My Loving', which appeared as orchestrated, background music, but neither featured The Beatles; The Bonzo Dog Doo-Dah Band performed 'Death Cab For Cutie'.)

Magical Mystery Tour was influenced by the exploits of Ken Kesey and The Merry Pranksters, who on 17 June 1964, to celebrate American author Kesey's second novel *Sometimes A Great Notion*, set off from California and headed eastward across the United States to visit the 1964 World's Fair in New York City. The idea was to see what would happen when hallucinogenic-inspired spontaneity confronted what he saw as the triteness and conventionality of American society. Enthusiastic users of amphetamines, marijuana and the mind-bending drug LSD,

The Pranksters embarked on their lengthy road trip in a psychedelically painted school bus they called Furthur.

The Beatles' mode of transport was somewhat less grand. Acquired from the coach company Fox of Hayes, theirs was a new, Plaxton-bodied, Bedford VAL Panorama I coach, licence number URO 913E. 'Paul said to me, "What we need is a really bright, garish, coloured coach. Can you find one?"' Alistair Taylor, the one-time personal assistant to Brian Epstein, and the group's so-called 'Mr Fix-it', recalled. 'I said yes and shortly after, I was in Eastbourne with my wife and we were sitting having lunch in the Queen's Hotel … I was looking out of the window when this hideous yellow and blue coach pulled off from the car park outside the window. I dropped my knife and fork and shouted, "I've found it. I've found it!" I leapt up and ran out into the pouring rain. I ran round the back of the coach and saw it was from Fox of Hayes. I jumped up onto the coach and I asked the driver, who was looking at me as though I had gone out of my head, if they hired these coaches out. He told me they did so I got a card from him and I came back and told Paul I had found the coach. I got the prices and, of course, it was the birth of *Magical Mystery Tour*.'

Filming began on 11 September 1967, just two weeks after Epstein's death. Intended for worldwide television screening, to keep happy all the fans who said the group should show themselves for a change, it was an extravagant, spontaneous, un-scripted, psychedelically colourful film, crammed to the rafters with unusual happenings and exciting new Beatles music. As Taylor admitted, '*Magical Mystery Tour* was McCartney's brainchild … The idea was Paul's baby, right from the word go. He put everything into it.' As the group's press officer Tony Barrow remembered, the movie also had a hidden agenda for Paul; to launch himself as a film producer, and kick start the beginning of a new phase in The Beatles' career.

Paul had mapped the outline of the film during his flight back from America on 11 April 1967 and constructed it, upon his return to Britain, by way of a hand-drawn, circular diagram, which was divided up into eight segments. He then explained to the others, 'We can have a song here, a dream sequence there.' In Paul's original plan, the Victor Spinetti 'recruiting' sequence was to fill section 2 of the circle, the 'marathon' was 3, John's dream was 5 and the 'stripper and band' sequence was to be 7 etc. Lennon invited Spinetti to appear by way of a phone call, during which he cryptically told Victor he was going to send him something. Within days a *Sgt Pepper* record cover arrived, on the back of which John had scribbled the words, 'Dear Vic, we're gonna do own our film, we've got no script, so do that thing you did in *Oh What A Lovely War*. PS, have you got any uppers?' (Spinetti had been in the cast of the WWI musical satire *Oh, What A Lovely War!* which had highly successful runs both in London and on Broadway between March 1963–January 1965.)

'Basically the idea [of *Magical Mystery Tour*] was that it took a coach load of people,' Taylor recalled, 'off around the country and instead of saying, "On your left was such and such a castle," the courier would say this but instead there'd be a freak-out or something else would happen.' And in the words of the five magicians in the movie (played by the four Beatles and Mal Evans), strange things began to happen, and they certainly weren't wrong. Along with their motley crew of assorted friends, fan club secretaries and oddball performers hired from the casting book *Spotlight*, The Beatles found themselves chancing upon a British Army drill sergeant (Spinetti) who shouted incomprehensibly at the assembled onlookers and instructed them on how to attack a stuffed cow,

and a waiter (Lennon, based on a dream he had) who shovelled cooked spaghetti onto the table at which Ringo's recently widowed, rather stout, Aunt Jessie (played by Jessie Robbins) was seated.

Even The Beatles' close friend, Apple employee and former long-time roadie Neil Aspinall was forced to concede at the time, 'We went out to make a film but nobody had the vaguest idea of what it was all about.' John agreed, later calling it 'Fucking rubbish and cock-eyed,' before adding, 'We didn't even have a director.' 'I kind of directed it,' Paul later confessed. 'Although we said The Beatles directed it at the end, I was there most of the time, having late-night chats with the cameramen about what we were going to do tomorrow. It tended to be me, rather than the others.'

'Talk about the blind leading the blind,' Tony Barrow recalled. 'No one knew enough about the film business. The Beatles didn't want to hire anybody professional. They wanted to handle it all themselves.' There wasn't even a proper script. On 15 September 1967, when the bus stopped at Smedley's fish and chip shop, at 108 Roman Road in Taunton, Somerset, the cast and crew were unsure whether they were stopping for a lunch break or it was the location for the next scene to be shot. (As it was, footage was indeed taken during this stopover, 44 seconds of which appeared in the finished film, appearing in a circle, in the top-left of the picture, at the tail end of the 'I Am The Walrus' sequence. Further excerpts of the footage were seen for the first time during promotions for the release of the newly remastered official Apple DVD/Blu-ray release of *Magical Mystery Tour* in October 2012.)

As you'd expect, there was no end of chaos during the filming. Before shooting had even begun, on 11 September 1967, when the coach picked up John, George and Ringo in a quiet country lane at Virginia Waters, Surrey, Paul leapt off the bus, rushed over to Ringo and said, 'Listen, I've got to tell you one thing about your auntie … she stinks! Do you want to go on with this?' He did. The three rather amateurish cameramen hired for it were completely unaware they'd be expected to film hand-held on a moving bus, without any tripods or lighting.

The mystical signs, stars and lettering that decorated the vehicle also caused trouble when they began to fall off early in the production. John helped them on their way when, back at their Plymouth hotel, in a fit of temper, he yanked off the tattered remnants. There was further chaos when the 62-seater vehicle got stuck on a little stone bridge en route to the tiny village of Wide-combe-in-the-Moor, Devon, causing a traffic jam. (The driver had driven past – and completely ignored – a notice that read: 'Narrow Bridge – Unsuitable for heavy traffic – maximum width 7ft 10ins'; The Beatles' coach was four inches wider.) As Neil Aspinall later admitted, 'That's what we should have filmed, the chaos we caused. The bus trying to get over that narrow bridge, with the traffic building up behind us, then having to reverse past all the drivers who had been cursing us and John getting in a fury and ripping all the posters off the sides [of the coach].'

Oblivious to the fact that Twickenham Studios in Shepperton, or any other film studio in London, or anywhere for that matter, had to be booked months if not years in advance, NEMS and The Beatles were forced into hiring West Malling's USAF Airbase in Maidstone, Kent, in particular Hangar 3. They had filmed the 'Strawberry Fields Forever' promo film near there, at Knole Park (see entry in *TV* section), just eight months earlier so they knew it would be easy to get to. (The 'Magicians Laboratory' scene, as well as John's 'Jessie's Dream', was shot in the hangar, as were the ones for 'Blue Jay Way' and 'Your Mother Should Know,' filmed on 21 and 24 September 1967 respectively. Exteriors scenes for the aforementioned marathon and tug-of-war scenes, in addition to the classic 'I Am The Walrus' sequence, were also shot at West Malling.)

Following a recommendation by Paul's brother Mike, whose group Scaffold had toured with them, The Bonzo Dog Doo-Dah Band were the group hired to perform alongside the 24-year-old stripper Jan Carson near the end of the movie. (This was shot at the Raymond Revuebar, Soho, on 18 September 1967; McCartney had origin-ally wanted The New Vaudeville Band to appear. Similar in style to the Bonzos with their thirties, Rudy Vallée-inspired, megaphone style of croon-ing, they had topped the US charts in December 1966, and had actually beaten The Beatles – with 'Eleanor Rigby' – to that year's Grammy for 'Best Contemporary (R&R) Recording' with the song 'Winchester Cathedral'.) The Bonzos' manage-ment sent McCartney a copy of the group's latest album *Gorilla*, and he chose a track off it, the Elvis Presley parody, 'Death Cab For Cutie', for the film. Its title had been inspired by the title of a story featured in the American *True Crimes* magazine. An admirer of the group's harpsichord piece, 'Head Ballet', McCartney was already aware of the band prior to his brother's suggestion and most probably had seen the group's performance of 'Death Cab For Cutie' in a recent episode of the popular children's ITV series *Do Not Adjust Your Set*, on which the band appeared regularly.

Shot at the ungodly hour of 6.30am on a Monday morning, Carson and the Bonzos could not begin their performance until some musical instruments had been delivered to the club; their own ones had been stolen following a show in Dulwich, south London, the previous evening. While Carson stripped away, John and Ringo took their own private copies of her performance, on their clockwork, Bolex spring-wound, 16mm movie cameras. When Bonzo Neill Innes asked them what they were doing, John replied, 'Oh, we're doing the Weybridge version.' In other words, for private screenings at their homes. Paul coaxed Bonzo lead singer Vivian Stanshall into wearing a pink chiffon scarf for the performance, to make him look trendier.

Scenes involving John, Paul, George and Ringo each looking through a telescope, Happy Nat The Rubber Man (Nat Jackley) chasing bikini-clad women around the Atlantic Hotel's outdoor swimming pool (which John directed) and the hip, English pop/rock band Traffic performing their hit 1967 song 'Here We Go Round The Mulberry Bush' were also shot, but ended up on the cutting room floor. (The latter, however was saved and released, alongside many other out-takes, as part of the bonus features on the official *Magical Mystery Tour* DVD/Blu-ray release in October 2012.)

Once edited, and with their mentor Brian Epstein no longer around to advise, The Beatles were lost as to what to do with the movie. 'We didn't know who to give it to,' Neil Aspinall recalled, 'so we gave it to NEMS ... screening it for NBC, ABC and CBS (in America), all simultaneously, and hearing them all say, "We don't like it." Where do we go after that?' Thankfully, there was a place, the good ol' BBC in London, England, who (subject to content approval) agreed to purchase it for £10,000 and transmit it, in b&w, as part of their BBC1 Christmas schedule on Boxing Day evening 1967. An estimated 20 million people tuned in to watch The Beatles' latest movie effort, while others put the figure at a rather less impressive 3,930,000.

Ranked the twenty-fifth most popular television programme transmitted during the concluding week of the year, it was loved and loathed in equal measures. The Corporation's weekly listings magazine, the *Radio Times*, reflected this when, in the letters section of the edition dated 13–19 January 1968, viewer Mrs Margaret Grubb, of London N22, wrote, 'I should like the opportunity to thank BBC1 for televising The Beatles' *Magical Mystery Tour*. My family and I sat enthralled by 50 minutes of fantasy and piquant humour. The marathon race was hilarious and many of the other scenes were very beautiful. How I wish we had colour television...' While in another, J. Maddison of Ilford, Essex, put pen to paper to blast, 'May I award an Oscar for the biggest load of pure unadulterated tripe to The Beatles for their *Magical Mystery Tour*. It was such utter rubbish that it took great control on my part not to ring the BBC. I could not even fathom what it was all about.'

However, many did call. The Corporation's switchboards were flooded with complaints during and after the screening. With pressure growing, BBC chiefs almost at once announced they would be holding an inquest on the show at their next programme review meeting, set for the following Wednesday. They also moved quickly to defend themselves saying, 'The Beatles made the film, *not* the BBC!' The knives were certainly out for the group at this point. It had been a long time since they had taken this amount of hammering, especially in print. 'The bigger they are, the harder they fall,' wrote James Thomas of the *Daily Express*. 'And what a fall it was ... The whole boring saga confirmed a long-held suspicion of mine that The Beatles are four rather pleasant young men who have made so much money that they can apparently afford to be contemptuous of the public.' James Green, TV critic for the *Evening News*, wrote, 'Appalling! I watched it. There was precious little magic and the only mystery was how the BBC came to buy it.'

The noted film and television critic and *Radio Times* previewer Robert Ottaway was another to pour scorn on the flick, writing, 'This witless home movie scotches the myth of their genius for good and all.' While the *Daily Mirror* summed it up succinctly with the words, 'Rubbish … Piffle … Nonsense!' The last words, however, should be left to a man, a viewer, a shipbuilder by trade, who described it in a 9 February 1968 BBC viewer survey as, 'Just about the worst entertainment in a long time.' He went on, 'It seems that success has gone to the heads of The Beatles. They believe they can offer the public any old tripe and expect them to accept it. I watched it expecting some redeeming feature. It never came. Maybe I was the fool?'

With the outcry over the movie gaining momentum, and the BBC keen to distance themselves from it, Paul made the unprecedented decision of defending *Magical Mystery Tour* on Rediffusion's top-rated, late-evening chat show *The Frost Programme*. Hosted by the well-known journalist, comedian, writer and media personality David Frost, the show was taped and aired on 27 December 1967, one day after the BBC screening, ironically on the Corporation's rival station ITV. 'Why don't you think the critics like this film?' Frost asked. 'I don't know,' Paul remarked. 'They just didn't seem to like it … I think one or two people were looking for a plot, but there wasn't one.' He ended by saying, 'I quite liked it myself.'

However, in an interview published in the following day's *Daily Mail*, Paul was forced into admitting they had gaffed with *Magical Mystery Tour*. 'It was a mistake because we thought people would understand that it was "magical" and a "mystery tour",' he said. 'We thought the title was explanation enough. We could put on a moptop show, but we don't really like that sort of entertainment anymore … But was the film really so bad compared with the rest of the Christmas TV? Frankie and Bruce's show with Frankie Howerd and Bruce Forsyth on ITV on Saturday

just wasn't funny. And you could hardly call the Queen's speech a gasser!'

After successfully selling a copy of *Magical Mystery Tour* to the Dutch public broadcasting station, VARA – Vereeniging van Arbeiders Radio Amateurs – who broadcast it for the first time in Europe on 10 February 1968, the BBC re-screened the film on BBC2, on 5 January 1968, but this time in colour, despite the fact many millions of viewers in the UK still only had, or could afford, b&w sets. For many, the first real opportunity they had to view it in colour, and indeed see the movie itself, came on 21 December 1979 when it was re-broadcast, this time complete (see Trivia information below), on the opening night of BBC2's *The Beatles At Christmas* season. A rare fourth UK TV screening came 14 years later, on 1 November 1993, when it was aired as part of MTV Europe's designated 'Beatles Day', alongside (on an intermittent loop) new interviews with Paul and George, the 1969 clip for 'Something' and the 1965 InterTel promos (see entries in the *TV* section). The UK TV premiere of the newly remastered, high-definition version of the film came when BBC 2 HD aired it on 6 October 2012, immediately after the *Arena* documentary *Magical Mystery Tour Revisited*, which focused on the making of the movie.

The original 52-minute edit of *Magical Mystery Tour* did not receive a proper American release until New Line Cinema acquired the limited theatrical and non-theatrical distribution rights to it in 1974. Due to its extremely poor reviews in Britain, its only US showings prior to that came in May 1968, when to coincide with John and Paul's visit to New York to launch Apple, the film was screened at selected cinemas and 'after midnight' theatres across the country. On 11 August 1968 it was showcased at the Fillmore East venue in New York City as part of a fundraiser for the Liberation

News Service (the counter-culture equivalent of Associated Press), receiving much acclaim from the usually harsh and hard to please American film critics. 'I can't imagine how or why it was not cheered or applauded in England,' wrote one, 'and as for it being pointless, don't you people have underground cinema over there?'

Trivia: As revealed in the BBC's official audience research report of Boxing Day 1967, *Magical Mystery Tour* was watched by 25.7 per cent of the UK population and unsurprisingly received a very low score of 23 in the Reaction Index of viewers.

Although not officially 'banned' by the Corporation, following a discussion between BBC head Paul Fox and Anna Instone, head of Gramophone Programmes at the Corporation, 'I Am The Walrus' was pulled from several BBC radio and television shows due to its, as the Corporation called it, 'very offensive passage'. ('Boy you been a naughty girl, you let your knickers down.') The song had tentatively been set to feature on *Top Of The Pops, Juke Box Jury* and even in the 24 November 1967 edition of the late-night BBC1 comedy sketch series *Twice A Fortnight*.

The 'egg man' lyric featured in the song was inspired by Ted O'Dell, who ran a daily egg delivery round in the Newquay area. He first encountered the group when he walked into the Sailor's Arms public house and the barman greeted him with the words, 'Ah, the egg man's here,' and told him The Beatles were there having a drink during a break in the filming of their movie. Ted immediately grabbed his lager, walked over to the group and said hello. One day later, during a delivery to the Atlantic Hotel, the group were seen taking photographs of his 'egg man' van.

Aunt Jessie's daydream on the beach, about falling in love with fellow traveller Buster Bloodvessel (Ivor Cutler), was cut by Paul Fox prior to its first transmission, on the grounds that the scene was 'insulting to old people'.

For the surrealistic scenes in 'Flying', Denis O'Dell, a close friend of The Beatles from the early days and one of the directors for the group's new organisation, Apple Corps, managed to obtain aerial out-takes from the 1964 Stanley Kubrick film *Dr Strangelove*.

The young, white-gloved police constable seen among the large crowd on the record sleeve and in the movie's opening sequence was called Alan Russell. Aware of the masses The Beatles regularly attracted, he had been drafted in on crowd control, and during the set-up for a group photograph that The Beatles, cast, family, friends and various others were about to have taken, Russell noticed a young boy in the horde had fallen over. He rushed over to see if the lad was all right, and as he did so his helmet fell off. He bent down to pick it up, and as he rose he smiled and waved embarrassingly to the cheering crowd. Shortly after the double EP's release, he was summoned to a meeting with his chief inspector, who had the seen the image on the window of a local record shop, and was told he had committed a disciplinary offence by appearing in the picture and was even cautioned for it.

The penultimate scene to be filmed took place on 30 and 31 October 1967. On an impulse and without any luggage, Paul took a 16mm camera and a couple of friends (Mal Evans and cameraman Aubrey Dewar) to Nice, in the South of France, to film the sequences for 'The Fool On The Hill'. Accidentally leaving home in the early hours without his passport, he had to persuade the immigration authorities they knew who he was before he was allowed to board the plane. Filmed up in the mountains, and using his little Philips cassette player to mime to, Paul ad-libbed the entire time, which, as he later admitted, was against union rules. In Paul's 1997 book *Many Years From Now,* by Barry Miles, he said, 'We shouldn't have really had just one cameraman, it was anti-union. That was another reason to go to France. The unions wouldn't have allowed it in Britain, nor probably in France, but they didn't know we were doing it … there was none of this grips, best boy, gaffer, none of that.'

There were further troubles when on the night of 30 October 1967, Paul, Mal and Aubrey were refused entry to a hotel's restaurant because, in the words of the management, they 'didn't look the part'. They headed off to a local nightclub instead, but with money in short supply they soon returned to their hotel and were forced to eat dinner in their room. With what little cash they had already being spent on food and clothes, after the first round of drinks had been consumed they arranged credit with the manager. The next day, Mal and Paul returned to the club and, since the money from The Beatles' office in London still hadn't arrived, they were forced once again to ask for credit. With news about the Beatle's visit to the club now spreading, the place was packed. He began ordering drinks for everyone and a huge bar bill was soon racked up. Hearing this, the club's manager arrived demanding that they settled up immediately. On explaining who Paul was and what had happened, he replied, 'You either pay the bill, or I call the police.' Eventually the hotel manager agreed to cover the money.

In late 1974, with Harrison using 'The Lumberjack Song' as the opener for his US concert tour, the Monty Python comedy team considered screening *Magical Mystery Tour* as a curtain-raiser to their upcoming film *Monty Python And The Holy Grail.* So, on 10 January 1975, after receiving permission from all four Beatles, *Python* members Graham Chapman, Terry Jones and Michel Palin gathered to watch it in Apple's

ALL IN THE STARS

'We saw eye to eye musically a lot in the old days. Geminis and Libras are supposed to get on well together, according to the astrologers' theories. We worked well because we both like the same people and the same music. Even in the early days we used to write things separately because Paul was always more advanced than I was. He was always a couple of chords ahead and his songs had more chords in them. His dad played the piano.'

John talking to *Record Mirror*, 2 October 1971

offices at 54 St James's Street, London (Apple HQ having moved from Savile Row in 1972). Representing The Beatles were Neil Aspinall and press officer Derek Taylor. Ringo even appeared at the get-together. But according to Palin in his *Diaries* book, he thought 'The Fool On The Hill' section in particular was 'tacky and dated' and the *Python* plan to use the movie was shelved shortly afterwards. (Incidentally, one day before that meeting, The Beatles' partnership was officially dissolved.)

You either truly love this, or deeply hate it. This was The Beatles without Epstein and with Paul in charge. 'It wasn't the greatest thing we'd ever done,' he admitted, '[but] I defend it on the lines that, nowhere else do you see a performance of "I Am The Walrus". That's the only performance ever, so things like that are enough to make it an interesting film.' Once classed as rubbish, it's now seen as a classic early pop video.

YELLOW SUBMARINE
(1968 – APPLE FILMS/KING FEATURES PRODUCTION/TVC LONDON, COPYRIGHTED THE HEARST CORPORATION (KING FEATURES SYNDICATE DIVISION) AND SUBAFILMS LTD.; DISTRIBUTED BY UNITED ARTISTS)

Filming dates: July 1967–June 1968

Locations: Studios of TVC London, Soho Square, London, England, and Twickenham Studios, St Margaret's, London, England for The Beatles' section only

Directed by George Dunning, produced by Al Brodax, written by Lee Minoff, Al Brodax, Jack Mendelsohn, Erich Segal and Roger McGough (uncredited) of the pop/vocal/comedy group, Scaffold. Director of art, Heinz Edelmann and featuring the voices of: Paul Angelis (as Ringo/Chief Blue Meanie/George), Peter Batten (uncredited as George), John Clive (John), Dick Emery (Jeremy/Lord Mayor/Max), Geoff Hughes (Paul), Lance Percival ('Young/Old' Fred)

World premiere: Pavilion Theatre, London, 17 July 1968

Songs featured: Yellow Submarine (the May/June 1966 recording on opening titles), Eleanor Rigby, Love You To (clip, played during George's entrance), A Day In The Life (clip, starting as the submarine takes off), All Together Now, When I'm Sixty-Four, Only A Northern Song, Nowhere Man, Lucy In The Sky With Diamonds, Sea Of Green (short vocal clip from Yellow Submarine recording, used when Ringo discovers the green hole that leads to Pepperland), Think For Yourself (out-take, short excerpt, a line is sung a cappella style when they revive the Lord Mayor), Sgt Pepper's Lonely Hearts Club Band, With A Little Help From My Friends (short clip, directly following Sgt Pepper's Lonely Hearts Club Band, without a break, as it appeared on the group's 1967 album of the same name), All You Need Is Love, Baby, You're A Rich Man (clip, played as Sgt Pepper's Lonely Hearts Club Band are released from the anti-music bubble), Hey Bulldog, It's All Too Much, All Together Now (reprise, closing sequence, footage of the real Beatles singing, intercut with numbers and letters, and the words, 'all together now' translated into various languages)

Yellow Submarine was a colourful, music-filled, animated fantasy based on the group's attempts to save the peaceful, undersea, music-loving, unearthly paradise of Pepperland from being taken over by the nasty, music-hating 'Blue Meanies'. (Heinz Edelmann, the German-speaking, Czech graphic designer, in charge of every character and scene in the movie, had actually envisioned them to be purple in colour.)

Following the negative response to *Magical Mystery Tour*, The Beatles were not enthusiastic about acting in another picture. However, the main reason for their dislike of *Yellow Submarine* was the involvement of Al Brodax as producer. As head of the motion picture/television department at King Features Syndicate, he was the brains behind *The Beatles* cartoon series. Premiering on ABC TV in America in September 1965, it ran for 39 episodes and grossed $3 million in its first year alone. But, despite its immense popularity, the group thought it was a travesty. Fearing *Yellow Submarine* would become the same type of parody, they effectively turned their back on the movie as soon as they became aware of his and his company's involvement in it. However, after seeing it as an easy way out of fulfilling their three-film, Brian Epstein-arranged commitment to United Artists, and to meet their legal obligation of actually appearing in it, The Beatles agreed to film a live-action cameo appearance for it.

Shot at Twickenham Studios, St Margaret's, on 25 January 1968, just three weeks prior to their trip to India, the group were seen at the end of the movie kicking off a reprise of the song 'All Together Now'. Unfortunately, because of their relatively small roles, and the fact it was animated, United Artists felt The Beatles contractually still owed them another one. (In truth, aside from this cameo, their only other real contribution to *Yellow Submarine* was four new songs – 'All Together

Now', 'Only A Northern Song', 'Hey Bulldog' and 'It's All Too Much'. John, however, was riled, feeling he had actually contributed much more, later claiming some of the ideas in the film were his. 'Brodax got half of *Yellow Submarine* out of my mouth,' Lennon later revealed. '… the idea for the hoover? The machine that sucks people up? All those were my ideas. They used to come to the studio and sort of chat, "Hi John, got any ideas for the film?" And I'd just spout out all this stuff and they went off and did it.')

With the young and inexperienced animation company TVC (TV Cartoons) at the helm, production on *Yellow Submarine* began in Swinging London in July 1967. Peter Batten provided George's voice for the first half of the film, but when it was discovered he was a deserter from the British Army in Germany (the British Army of the Rhine), he was arrested and his lines had to be finished by Paul Angelis, who was providing Ringo's voice in the film. Lance Percival was a natural choice for the movie as he had provided the voices of both Paul and Ringo for the aforementioned cartoon series. Liverpool poet Roger McGough, of the group Scaffold, was drafted in to add a slice of Liverpudlian flavour to proceedings. He was paid £500 for his services, but did not receive an on-screen credit.

At the start, contrary to what we believe now, all four Beatles were actually keen on the film. 'They have been calling us at all times with ideas,' Brodax revealed at the time, 'and eager to voice their characters in the movie.' However their desires proved to be transient. 'We kept asking them [along to the studio],' John Coates, the line producer on the film recalled, 'and pursuing them, and inviting them, but we could never tie them down. In the end, we were left with no alternative but to hire actors and fake the voices, and they did a pretty good job.' However, on 6 November 1967, the group

did make one solitary trip to the TVC studios, to see how the production was going and to pose with cut-out figures and a submarine as advance publicity for the film. Al Brodax was unflattering about them. 'I felt Paul was a wise-ass kind of guy and Ringo was a klutz, who turned up one day at the studio stoned, and spent the entire time walking round and round until he eventually prostrated himself by tripping over a glockenspiel. The resounding "clang" was kept on the soundtrack.'

Three months prior to that, in August 1967, one month into the production, the team of 40 animators and 140 technical artists were informed that the movie had to be finished in time for a July 1968 premiere in London, which meant many late nights and the running of two shifts in the ink and paint department. Thankfully, they reached the deadline on time. Coates recalled, 'When we finally got The Beatles along to a screening of the completed version [at the Bowater House Cinema in Knightsbridge, London, on 8 July 1968], they all seemed very pleased until they got outside. Paul was the first one to come up to Brodax and say, "Listen, I think you did a great job on the other three, but my voice sounds awful! Can't you do anything about it?" Then, one by one, they all came up and said the same thing. "They sound great, but I'm all wrong."'

Naive when it came to contract negotiations, Coates and director George Dunning were completely oblivious to the fact they could, in fact, own a percentage of a film's gross or profits. They simply produced the movie for a pre-set sum of money. Regrettably, with *Yellow Submarine* going over budget, they actually ended up losing money on it. Their association ended the day they previewed the film for King Features, gained their approval and were handed the final payment for their work. With their task completed, King Features had no need to contact them ever again.

The movie premiered in London at the Pavilion in Piccadilly on 17 July 1968. A crowd of approximately 10,000 was there to see John, Yoko, Paul, George, Pattie, Ringo and Maureen arrive. '*Yellow Submarine* bombed,' Lennon later admitted. 'It was ripped to shreds but it was a great movie. All the kids loved it [but] it was attacked because everyone expected The Beatles to be in the movie, but we had nothing to do with it and we sort of resented them. It was the third film we owed United Artists. Brian set it up and we had nothing to do with it.' McCartney agreed. Speaking at the time, he said, 'It's not our film … It's not us. I won't take the credit, even if it's a big smash. It's like saying *Bambi* made Walt Disney.'

Besides a seven-and-a-half-minute Tarot Associates Inc. making-of documentary called *The Beatles Mod Odyssey,* United Artists issued two versions of the completed *Yellow Submarine* film, one featuring 'Hey Bulldog', and one without, which was distributed in the United States. (The British print ran for 89 minutes, the American one for 85 minutes.) The company felt American audiences would become tired at the duration of the film, so they excised the entire song and sequence. The decision to axe that scene in particular was largely down to the fact the animation that accompanied it, by animation director Jack Stokes, was considered to be of a different style to the rest of the film. (In 1999, the segment was reinstated into every version of the movie when United Artists and Apple began the task of digitally remixing the film's soundtrack for a highly successful theatrical and home video re-release. Though the visuals were not digitally enhanced, a new transfer was done after cleaning the original film negative and refreshing the colour. A soundtrack album to accompany this new version was also issued – *Yellow Submarine Songtrack*, in September 1999 – which featured the first extensive, 5.1 surround-sound, digital stereo remixes of original Beatles material.) A newly created montage from original *Yellow Submarine* footage, together with the 'Eleanor Rigby' clip from the original movie, was officially released on the first disc of the *Beatles 1/Beatles 1+* DVD/Blu-ray, on 6 November 2015.

Trivia

John's second son Sean knew nothing about his father's fame as a Beatle until he saw *Yellow Submarine* on TV at his babysitter's house. When asked about it, Lennon explained he had renounced that life to spend more time with him and Yoko.

At the movie's conclusion, the title 'All Together Now' was shown 27 times in 16 languages: in order, English, French, German, Spanish, Chinese, Italian, Hebrew, Greek, Swedish, Russian, Japanese, English, Greek, Italian, Dutch, Arabic, Spanish, Farsi, Swahili, Sanskrit, French, Hebrew, Swedish, Chinese, German, Japanese and English.

Paul Angelis created the sound of Chief Blue Meanie's teeth chattering by clanking two saucer plates together.

Selected episodes of the DePatie-Freleng Enterprises cartoon series *The Pink Panther* were run as the support feature at the 1968 London premiere.

Yellow Submarine did not become eligible for television screenings until July 1973. Its first airing on UK TV came when BBC1 broadcast it on Easter Monday evening, 15 April 1974.

In August 2009, it was reported that Disney and Oscar-winning director Robert Zemeckis were negotiating with Apple to produce a 3D computer-animated remake of *Yellow Submarine*. As with his previous animated films, *The Polar Express, Beowulf* and *A Christmas Carol,* motion capture techniques would be employed. As CEO of Apple Corps Jeff Jones said at the time, the deal with Disney brought together 'two of the best-loved creative entities in the world'. Disney announced they planned to release the film in time for the 2012 Summer Olympics in London. Disney and Apple Corps officially announced the remake on 11 September 2009 at the inaugural D23 Expo, the ultimate Disney fan convention, held in Anaheim, California. But in May 2010, after the successful, yet unsatisfactory box office performance of *A Christmas Carol*, and the highly negative criticism towards the motion capture technology, Disney decided to close the Zemeckis digital film studio ImageMovers Digital, and on 14 March 2011,

after lavishing several millions of dollars on it, they abandoned the *Yellow Submarine* remake project altogether, citing the disastrous opening takings of the Zemeckis movie *Mars Needs Moms* at the box office. Budgeted at roughly $150 million, the flick took just $6.9 million in its inaugural weekend.

A marvellous animated epic. Hugely entertaining, it is crammed full of fabulous music and superb psychedelic imagery. Fans and critics alike loved it, as John himself did.

APPENDIX A
Beatles Places to Visit

LIVERPOOL

For all tourists, information on Liverpool, and up-to-date details on all Beatles related excitements, events and locations, contact: visitliverpool.com

Or try a free website specifically to help Beatles fans plan their visit: triptoliverpool.com

The Beatles Story

Albert Dock, Liverpool: beatlesstory.com
Beatle exhibition and museum centre, which recreates The Beatles' lives. Lots of displays, but not much original memorabilia. Loads of stuff to buy.

Very commercial.

Cavern City Tours

10 Mathew Street, Liverpool, L2 6RE: cavernclub.org

Always fun.

Annual Beatles Week

Held every August. Organised by Cavern City Tours.

Fab, monster event, worth going to at least once.

Mendips and 20 Forthlin Road

nationaltrust.org.uk/beatles-childhood-homes
John's and Paul's old homes. Now owned by the National Trust and open to visitors.

A must for any Lennon and McCartney fans.

Cavern Club

Mathew Street: cavernclub.org
Not quite the original, as that was knocked down, but almost on the same site. Interesting wall of performers who have appeared at the Cavern. There are tribute acts in the daytime, which you can see for free, and the club also encourages new music.

Once is enough, unless there is something interesting on.

Hard Days Night Hotel

harddaysnighthotel.com
Themed hotel, for visitors who can't get enough – but non-Beatles fans can still enjoy it. The John Lennon suite has a white piano. (Not the original.)

Worth it for the hotel notepaper.

Penny Lane Hotel

thepennylanehotel.com
Beatles themed hotel on the Penny Lane Roundabout.

Also worth it for the hotel notepaper.

Casbah Club

8 Hayman's Green: petebest.com/casbah-coffee-club.aspx
Where The Beatles used to play in their early days. Opening hours irregular, so check in advance.

Very atmospheric, as not a lot has changed.

Shops: Beatles Shop, Mathew Street

LONDON

Richard Porter's tours, London Beatles walks: beatlesinlondon.com

Abbey Road Recording Studios

3 Abbey Road, NW8
First place in London for all Beatle people to gape at, though not open to the public. This was where the Fab Four recorded almost all their records, from 'Love Me Do' in 1962 to *Abbey Road* in 1969. The famous zebra crossing, if you want to be photographed walking over it, is at the corner of Abbey Road and Grove End Road.

Crossing the crossing is free, unlike many Beatles sites, but do take care.

British Library, Euston Road

In the Treasures Gallery, next to Magna Carta, Da Vinci, Shakespeare, Handel et al. you will find The Beatles' case, with around ten original handwrit-ten manuscript versions of their songs, plus some John letters – the biggest exhibition of original-manuscript Beatles material open to the public, anywhere.

A window into how on earth they did it. And admission is free.

7 Cavendish Avenue, St John's Wood, NW8

Just a few streets away. Paul's London home, which he bought in 1965. Still owns it, though he lives elsewhere, on the south coast, at an address we dare not reveal. Hundreds of fans used to sleep outside here, hoping for a glimpse.

Mostly an outside wall, so you have to imagine.

34 Montagu Square, Marylebone

The lower ground and basement flat was once lived in by Ringo – later by John and Yoko who were living there in 1968 when the police raided them looking for drugs. On the wall is a Blue Plaque, put up by English Heritage, which reads: 'John Lennon 1940–1980, Musician and Songwriter lived here in 1968'.

Not open to the public, but breathe in the history.

3 Savile Row, W1

HQ of the utterly incredible, utterly daft, Apple Corps, though nothing to do with them now. The Beatles' last performance in front of an audience was recorded on its roof on 30 January 1969.

Could be a clothes shop by now, but the front should remain, so worth a snap.

94 Baker Street, W1

Home of the ill-fated Apple Boutique from 1967–1968, when The Beatles decided to give away all the clothes. Oh, those were the days.

Little to see now.

3 Soho Square, W1

Your best chance of spotting Paul today. This is the HQ of MPL, Paul's business organisation.

But still a very slim chance. He's not daft.

Shops

London Beatles Store, 231 Baker Street, NW1
Souvenirs and information on Beatles events nationally.
Beatles Coffee Shop on Abbey Road: beatlescoffeeshop.com

FAN CLUBS

British Beatles fan club

www.britishbeatlesfanclub.co.uk
Good magazine

German

beatlesmuseum.net
Also has a good magazine.

APPENDIX B
UK Discography

Discography of Beatles original records released in the UK. All compositions by Lennon/McCartney unless otherwise stated.

Note: As the backing group for singer Tony Sheridan they recorded eight numbers in Germany in 1961. Only one was an original composition, an instrumental number called 'Cry For A Shadow', written by Lennon and Harrison. On one other, 'Ain't She Sweet', John Lennon was the lead singer. On the other six they were simply the backing group: 'My Bonnie', 'The Saints', 'Sweet Georgia Brown', 'Take Out Some Insurance On Me, Baby', 'Why', 'Nobody's Child'.

SINGLE RECORDS BY THE BEATLES ISSUED BY PARLOPHONE RECORDS

1962	Oct	Love Me Do/P.S. I Love You
1963	Jan	Please Please Me/Ask Me Why
	Apr	From Me To You/Thank You Girl
	Aug	She Loves You/I'll Get You
	Nov	I Want To Hold Your Hand/ This Boy
1964	Mar	Can't Buy Me Love/You Can't Do That
	Jul	A Hard Day's Night/Things We Said Today
	Nov	I Feel Fine/She's A Woman
1965	Apr	Ticket To Ride/Yes It Is
	Jul	Help!/I'm Down
	Dec	Day Tripper/We Can Work It Out

1966	Jun	Paperback Writer/Rain
	Aug	Yellow Submarine/Eleanor Rigby
1967	Jan	Penny Lane/Strawberry Fields Forever
	Jul	All You Need Is Love/Baby, You're a Rich Man
	Nov	Hello, Goodbye/I Am The Walrus
1968	Mar	Lady Madonna/The Inner Light (Harrison)

SINGLE RECORDS ISSUED BY APPLE RECORDS

1968	Aug	Hey Jude/Revolution
1969	Apr	Get Back/Don't Let Me Down
	May	The Ballad Of John And Yoko/Old Brown Shoe (Harrison)
	Oct	Something (Harrison)/Come Together
1970	Mar	Let It Be/You Know My Name

LONG PLAYING RECORDS ISSUED BY PARLOPHONE

1963 Mar *PLEASE PLEASE ME*

I Saw Her Standing There, Misery, Ask Me Why, Please Please Me, Love Me Do, P.S. I Love You, Do You Want To Know A Secret, There's A Place
Songs not composed by The Beatles:
Anna, Chains, Boys, Baby It's You, A Taste Of Honey, Twist And Shout

Nov *WITH THE BEATLES*

It Won't Be Long, All I've Got To Do, All My Loving, Don't Bother Me (Harrison), Little Child, Hold Me Tight, I Wanna Be Your Man, Not A Second Time
Songs not composed by The Beatles:
Till There Was You, Please Mr Postman, Roll Over Beethoven, You Really Got A Hold On Me, Devil In Her Heart, Money

1964 Jul *A HARD DAY'S NIGHT*

A Hard Day's Night, I Should Have Known Better, If I Fell, I'm Happy Just To Dance With You, And I Love Her, Tell Me Why, Can't Buy Me Love, Any Time At All, I'll Cry Instead, Things We Said Today, When I Get Home, You Can't Do That, I'll Be Back

Dec *BEATLES FOR SALE*

No Reply, I'm A Loser, Baby's In Black, I'll Follow The Sun, Eight Days A Week, Every Little Thing, I Don't Want To Spoil The Party, What You're Doing
Songs not composed by The Beatles:
Rock And Roll Music, Mr Moonlight, Kansas City, Words Of Love, Honey Don't, Everybody's Trying To Be My Baby

1965 Aug *HELP!*

Help!, The Night Before, You've Got To Hide Your Love Away, I Need You (Harrison), Another Girl, You're Going To Lose That Girl, Ticket To Ride, It's Only Love, You Like Me Too Much (Harrison), Tell Me What You See, I've Just Seen A Face, Yesterday
Songs not composed by The Beatles:
Act Naturally, Dizzy Miss Lizzy

Dec *RUBBER SOUL*

Drive My Car, Norwegian Wood, You Won't See Me, Nowhere Man, Think For Yourself (Harrison), The Word, Michelle, What Goes On (Lennon, McCartney and Starkey), Girl, I'm Looking Through You, In My Life, Wait, If I Needed Someone (Harrison), Run For Your Life

1966 Aug *REVOLVER*

Taxman (Harrison), Eleanor Rigby, I'm Only Sleeping, Love You To (Harrison), Here There And Everywhere, Yellow Submarine, She Said She Said, Good Day Sunshine, And Your Bird Can Sing, For No One, Doctor Robert, I Want To Tell You (Harrison), Got To Get You Into My Life, Tomorrow Never Knows

1967 Jun *SGT PEPPER'S LONELY HEARTS CLUB BAND*

Sgt Pepper's Lonely Hearts Club Band, With A Little Help From My Friends, Lucy In The Sky With Diamonds, Getting Better, Fixing A Hole, She's Leaving Home, Being For The Benefit Of Mr Kite!, Within You Without You (Harrison), When I'm Sixty-Four, Lovely Rita, Good Morning Good Morning, A Day In The Life

LONG PLAYING RECORDS ISSUED BY APPLE RECORDS

1968 Nov *THE BEATLES* (double album)

Back In The USSR, Dear Prudence, Glass Onion, Ob-La-Di Ob-La-Da, Wild Honey Pie, The Continuing Story Of Bungalow Bill, While My Guitar Gently Weeps (Harrison), Happiness Is A Warm Gun, Martha My Dear, I'm So Tired, Blackbird, Piggies, Rocky Raccoon, Don't Pass Me By, Why Don't We Do It In The Road, I Will, Julia; Birthday, Yer Blues, Mother Nature's Son, Everybody's Got Something To Hide

Except Me And My Monkey, Sexy Sadie, Helter Skelter, Long Long Long, Revolution 1, Honey Pie, Savoy Truffle, Cry Baby Cry, Revolution 9, Good Night

1969 Jan *YELLOW SUBMARINE*

Yellow Submarine, Only A Northern Song, All Together Now, Hey Bulldog, It's All Too Much, All You Need Is Love. Plus orchestrated pieces not by the Beatles – Pepperland, Sea Of Time; Sea Of Holes, Sea Of Monsters, March Of The Meanies, Pepperland Laid Waste, Yellow Submarine In Pepperland

Sep *ABBEY ROAD*

Come Together, Something (Harrison), Maxwell's Silver Hammer, Oh! Darling, Octopus's Garden, I Want You, Here Comes the Sun (Harrison), Because, You Never Give Me Your Money, Sun King, Mean Mr Mustard, Polythene Pam, She Came In Through The Bathroom Window; Golden Slumbers, Carry That Weight, The End

1970 May *LET IT BE*

Two Of Us, Dig A Pony, Across The Universe, I Me Mine (Harrison), Dig It (Lennon, McCartney, Harrison, Starkey), Let It Be (version two), Maggie Mae (arr. Lennon, McCartney, Harrison, Starkey), I've Got A Feeling, One After 909, The Long And Winding Road, For You Blue (Harrison), Get Back (version two)

1967 Dec *MAGICAL MYSTERY TOUR* (double EP)

Magical Mystery Tour, Your Mother Should Know, I Am The Walrus, The Fool On The Hill, Flying (Lennon, McCartney, Harrison, Starkey), Blue Jay Way (Harrison)

NOTE: There were 12 other extended players, but only one contains a song ('I Call Your Name' on the EP *Long Tall Sally*) not already on an LP or single.

APPENDIX C
Chronology

1934 **19 Sept:** Brian Samuel Epstein born
1940 **7 July:** Richard Starkey born
9 Dec: John Lennon born
1942 **18 June:** James Paul McCartney born
1943 **25 Feb:** George Harrison born
1945 **19 June:** Julia Lennon gives birth to John Lennon's half-sister Victoria
1947 **6 July:** Richard Starkey (Ringo) is rushed to hospital with appendicitis
1956 **July:** The Quarrymen are formed
31 Dec: Paul McCartney's mother Mary dies
11 Nov: Lonnie Donegan performs in Liverpool
1957 **16 Jan:** Cavern Club opens in Mathew Street, Liverpool
9 June: The Quarrymen appear at the Liverpool Empire Theatre
22 June: The Quarrymen perform in Rosebery St, Liverpool
6 July: John Lennon meets Paul McCartney at St Peter's Church summer fete, Woolton
7 Aug: The Quarrymen first play the Cavern Club
Sept: John enrols at Liverpool Art College
18 Oct: Paul McCartney's first paid gig with The Quarrymen, New Clubmoor Hall, Liverpool
7 Nov: Wilson Hall, Liverpool
16 Nov: Stanley Abattoir Social Club, Liverpool
23 Nov: New Clubmoor Hall, Liverpool
7 Dec: Wilson Hall, Liverpool, George Harrison auditions for The Quarrymen
1958 **10 Jan:** New Clubmoor Hall, Liverpool
24 Jan: Cavern Club, Liverpool
6 Feb: Wilson Hall, Liverpool
8 Mar: Ian Harris's wedding – first colour photo of The Quarrymen
13 Mar: Morgue Skiffle Cellar, Liverpool
12 July: The Quarrymen record at Percy Phillips' Studio, Liverpool

15 July: Julia Lennon is knocked down and killed by a car
24 Nov: Johnny and The Moondogs play at Carroll Levis TV Star Search competition, Ardwick
20 Dec: Wedding reception for Harry Harrison, 25 Upton Green, Speke
1959 **1 Jan:** Wilson Hall, Liverpool
24 Jan: The Quarrymen play Woolton Village Club, Liverpool, and soon after disband
Feb: George Harrison joins the Les Stewart Quartet
2 Mar: La Scala Ballroom, Runcorn, the only known appearance of John, Paul and George as Japage 3
July: The Les Stewart Quartet turn down the Casbah residency
29 Aug: Reformed Quarrymen open the Casbah Coffee Club, Liverpool
5, 12, 19, 26 Sept: Casbah Coffee Club, Liverpool
10 Dec: Ken Brown leaves The Quarrymen
3, 10 Dec: Casbah Coffee Club, Liverpool
1960 **23–24 Apr:** The Nerk Twins (John and Paul), Fox And Hounds, Caversham
1 May: Tommy Moore joins The Silver Beatles
5 May: Allan Williams becomes The Silver Beatles manager
10 May: Wyvern Club audition for Larry Parnes
14 May: Lathom Hall, Liverpool, performing for the only time as The Silver Beats
15 May: Iron Door, Liverpool
20 May: Town Hall, Alloa, start of seven-date tour of Scotland as backing band for Johnny Gentle
21 May: Northern Meeting Ballroom, Inverness, Johnny Gentle tour
23 May: Dalrymple Hall, Fraserburgh, Johnny Gentle tour

25 May: St Thomas's Hall, Keith, Johnny Gentle tour

26 May: Town Hall, Forres, Johnny Gentle tour

27 May: Regal Ballroom, Nairn, Johnny Gentle tour

28 May: Rescue Hall, Peterhead, final date of tour with Johnny Gentle

30 May: Jacaranda Club, Liverpool

2, 9, 16, 23, 30 June: The Institute, Neston, consecutive Thursdays evening here

4, 6, 11, 18, 25 June: Grosvenor Ballroom, Wallasey

11 June: Not only did they play this night at the Grosvenor Ballroom, Wallasey, with a drummer called Ronnie 'The Ted', but also, according to beat poet Royston Ellis, this is the date when the band changed their name to The Beatles

13 June: Jacaranda Club, Liverpool

June: Norman Chapman joins The Silver Beatles

7 July: The Institute, Neston, final Thursday evening at venue

2, 9, 16, 23, 30 July: Grosvenor Ballroom, Wallasey

12 Aug: Paul McCartney offers audition to mystery drummer

12 Aug: Pete Best auditions for The Beatles

16 Aug: The Beatles travel from Liverpool to Hamburg

17 Aug: The Beatles first performance in Hamburg at the Indra Club

3 Oct: The Beatles final performance at the Indra Club, Hamburg after 48 appearances

4 Oct: The Beatles first performance at the Kaiserkeller, Hamburg

15 Oct: Recording: Lu Walters records with John, Paul, George and Ringo

30 Oct: The Beatles agree with Peter Eckhorn to move to the Top Ten Club

1 Nov: Bruno Koschmider terminates The Beatles contract but they continue to play at Kaiserkeller

21 Nov: George Harrison is deported from Germany

28 Nov: Last appearance at the Kaiserkeller, Hamburg, after 58 appearances

29 Nov: Paul McCartney and Pete Best are arrested in Hamburg for arson

5 Dec: Paul McCartney and Pete Best deported from Hamburg

10 Dec: John Lennon returns to Liverpool

17 Dec: The Beatles, with Chas Newby on bass, Casbah Coffee Club, Liverpool

24 Dec: Grosvenor Ballroom, Wallasey

27 Dec: Litherland Town Hall, Liverpool

31 Dec: Casbah Coffee Club, Liverpool

1961 5 Jan: Litherland Town Hall, Liverpool

6 Jan: St John's Hall, Bootle

7 Jan: Aintree Institute and Lathom Hall, Seaforth, Liverpool

13–14, 18, 27 Jan: Aintree Institute, Liverpool

15, 29 Jan: Casbah Coffee Club, Liverpool

19 Jan: Alexandra Hall, Crosby

20, 30 Jan: Lathom Hall, Seaforth, Liverpool

21 Jan: Lathom Hall, Seaforth, and Aintree Institute, Liverpool

25 Jan: Hambleton Hall, Huyton, Liverpool

26 Jan: Litherland Town Hall, Liverpool

28 Jan: Lathom Hall, Seaforth, and Aintree Institute, Liverpool

1 Feb: Hambleton Hall, Huyton, Liverpool

2 Feb: Litherland Town Hall, Liverpool

3 Feb: St John's Hall, Bootle

4 Feb: Lathom Hall, Seaforth, Liverpool

5 Feb: Blair Hall, Walton, Liverpool

6 Feb: Lathom Hall, Seaforth, Liverpool

7 Feb: Merseyside Civil Service Club, Liverpool

8 Feb: Aintree Institute, Liverpool, and Hambleton Hall, Huyton

9 Feb: The Beatles first Cavern Club show, at lunchtime

10 Feb: Aintree Institute and Lathom Hall, Seaforth, Liverpool

11 Feb: Lathom Hall, Seaforth and first appearance at Cassanova Club, Liverpool

12 Feb: Casbah Coffee Club, Liverpool

14 Feb: Cassanova Club, London Road, and Litherland Town Hall, Liverpool

15 Feb: Aintree Institute, Liverpool, and Hambleton Hall, Huyton

16 Feb: Cassanova Club, London Road, and Litherland Town Hall, Liverpool

17 Feb: St John's Hall, Tuebrook, Liverpool

18 Feb: Aintree Institute, Liverpool

19, 26 Feb: Casbah Coffee Club, Liverpool

1961 **21 Feb:** Cavern Club, Cassanova Club and
(cont.) Litherland Town Hall, Liverpool
22 Feb: Aintree Institute, Liverpool, and
Hambleton Hall, Huyton
24 Feb: Grosvenor Ballroom, Wallasey
25 Feb: Aintree Institute and Lathom Hall,
Seaforth, Liverpool
28 Feb: Cavern Club, Cassanova Club and
Litherland Town Hall, Liverpool
1, 4 Mar: Aintree Institute, Liverpool
2 Mar: Litherland Town Hall, Liverpool
3 Mar: St John's Hall, Bootle
5 Mar: Casbah Coffee Club, Liverpool
6 Mar: Cavern Club and Liverpool Jazz Society,
Liverpool
7 Mar: Cassanova Club, London Road, Liverpool
8 Mar: Cavern Club, Aintree Institute, Liverpool,
and Hambleton Hall, Huyton
9 Mar: Air Training Corp Club, Birkdale, and
Labour Club, High Park
10 Mar: Cavern Club, Liverpool, Grosvenor
Ballroom, Wallasey, and St John's Hall, Tuebrook,
Liverpool
11 Mar: Aintree Institute and Liverpool Jazz
Society, Liverpool
12 Mar: Casbah Coffee Club and Cassanova Club,
Liverpool, final appearance at this venue
13 Mar: Cavern Club and Liverpool Jazz Society,
Liverpool
14, 16, 22, 24 Mar: Cavern Club, Liverpool
15 Mar: Cavern Club and Liverpool Jazz Society,
Liverpool
15 Mar: Stuart returns to Hamburg
17 Mar: Mossway Hall, Croxteth and Liverpool
Jazz Society, Liverpool
19, 26 Mar: Casbah Coffee Club, Liverpool
20 Mar: Cavern Club and Hambleton Hall,
Huyton, Liverpool
21 Mar: The Beatles first evening gig at the Cavern
1 Apr: Top Ten Club, Hamburg, West Germany
until 1 July, making a total of 92 appearances
22–23 June: Recording: 'My Bonnie' with Tony
Sheridan
1 July: Last performance at Top Ten Club,
Hamburg
2 July: The Beatles travel back from Hamburg,
arrriving home the following day

6 July: Bill Harry launches *Mersey Beat*
7 July: Ringo Starr's 21st birthday
13 July: St John's Hall, Tuebrook, Liverpool
14 July: Cavern Club, Liverpool, lunchtime and
evening
15 July: Holyoake Hall, Wavertree, Liverpool
16 July: Blair Hall, Walton, Liverpool
17 July: Cavern Club and Litherland Town Hall,
Liverpool
19 July: Cavern Club, Liverpool, lunchtime and
evening
20 July: St John's Hall, Tuebrook, Liverpool
21 July: Cavern Club and Aintree Institute,
Liverpool
22 July: Holyoake Hall, Wavertree, Liverpool
23 July: Blair Hall, Walton, Liverpool
24 July: Litherland Town Hall, Liverpool
25–26 July: Cavern Club, Liverpool (lunchtime
and evening on 26 July)
27 July: Cavern Club where the Beatles back Cilla
Black and St John's Hall, Tuebrook, Liverpool
28 July: Aintree Institute, Liverpool
29 July: Blair Hall, Walton, Liverpool
30 July: Blair Hall, Walton, Liverpool, final
appearance at this venue
31 July: Cavern Club and Litherland Town Hall,
Liverpool
1 Aug: Performed at private party, Iron Door/
Storyville Jazz Club
2 Aug: Cavern Club, Liverpool, lunchtime and
evening
3 Aug: St John's Hall, Tuebrook, Liverpool
4 Aug: Cavern Club and Aintree Institute,
Liverpool
5, 8–9, 11, 14, 16 Aug: Cavern Club, Liverpool
(all-night session on 5 Aug)
6, 13 Aug: Casbah Coffee Club, Liverpool
7 Aug: Litherland Town Hall, Liverpool
10 Aug: Cavern Club and St John's Hall,
Tuebrook, Liverpool
12, 19 Aug: Aintree Institute, Liverpool
17 Aug: St John's Hall, Tuebrook, Liverpool
18 Aug: Cavern Club and Aintree Institute,
Liverpool
20 Aug: Hambleton Hall, Huyton
21, 23, 28–30 Aug: Cavern Club, Liverpool
24 Aug: St John's Hall, Tuebrook, Liverpool

25 Aug: Cavern Club lunchtime and MV Royal Iris, River Mersey

26 Aug: Aintree Institute, Liverpool

27 Aug: Casbah Coffee Club, Liverpool

28–30 Aug: Cavern Club, Liverpool

31 Aug: St John's Hall, Tuebrook, Liverpool

1, 5–6, 11, 13, 19–20, 25, 27 Sept: Cavern Club, Liverpool (lunchtime and evening on 1, 13 and 27 Sept)

2, 16, 23 Sept: Aintree Institute, Liverpool

3 Sept: Hambleton Hall, Huyton, Liverpool

7 Sept: Cavern Club and Litherland Town Hall, Liverpool

8 Sept: St John's Hall, Tuebrook, Liverpool

10, 24 Sept: Casbah Coffee Club, Liverpool

14 Sept: Litherland Town Hall, Liverpool

15 Sept: Cavern Club lunchtime, Grosvenor Ballroom, Wallasey, final appearance, and Knotty Ash Village Hall, Liverpool

17 Sept: Hambleton Hall, Huyton, Liverpool

21 Sept: Cavern Club and Litherland Town Hall, Liverpool

22 Sept: Knotty Ash Village Hall, Liverpool

28 Sept: Litherland Town Hall, Liverpool

29 Sept: Cavern Club and Knotty Ash Village Hall, Liverpool

30 Sept: John Lennon and Paul McCartney travel to Paris

9 Oct: John Lennon celebrates his 21st birthday with Paul McCartney in Paris

15 Oct: Albany Cinema, Maghull and Hambleton Hall, Huyton, Liverpool

16, 24–26, 30 Oct: Cavern Club, Liverpool

17 Oct: David Lewis Theatre, Liverpool

18 Oct: Cavern Club, Liverpool, lunchtime and evening

19 Oct: Litherland Town Hall, Liverpool

20 Oct: Cavern Club and Knotty Ash Village Hall, Liverpool

21 Oct: Cavern Club, Liverpool, all-night session, two performances either side of midnight

22 Oct: Casbah Coffee Club, Liverpool

27 Oct: Knotty Ash Village Hall, Liverpool

28 Oct: Aintree Institute, Liverpool

28 Oct: Raymond Jones orders 'My Bonnie' from Brian Epstein

29 Oct: Hambleton Hall, Huyton, Liverpool

31 Oct: Litherland Town Hall, Liverpool

1, 3–4, 8, 13, 15 Nov: Cavern Club, Liverpool (lunchtime and evening on 1 and 15 Nov)

5 Nov: Glen Park Club, Southport and late-night session at Three Coins Club, Manchester

7 Nov: Cavern Club lunchtime, Merseyside Civil Service Club and Cavern Club, Liverpool

9 Nov: Brian Epstein visits Cavern to see The Beatles, lunchtime performance

9 Nov: Cavern Club and Litherland Town Hall, Liverpool

10 Nov: Tower Ballroom, New Brighton, Wallasey, first *Operation Big Beat*, and Knotty Ash Village Hall, Liverpool

11 Nov: Aintree Institute, Liverpool

12 Nov: Hambleton Hall, Huyton, Liverpool

14 Nov: Merseyside Civil Service Club and Cavern Club, Liverpool

17 Nov: Cavern Club and Knotty Ash Village Hall, Liverpool

18, 22–23, 27, 29 Nov: Cavern Club, Liverpool (lunchtime and evening on 29 Nov)

19 Nov: Casbah Coffee Club, Liverpool

21 Nov: Cavern Club and Merseyside Civil Service Club, Liverpool

24 Nov: Casbah Coffee Club, Liverpool, and Tower Ballroom, New Brighton, Wallasey, second *Operation Big Beat*, where they backed US singer Davy Jones for two numbers

26 Nov: Hambleton Hall, Huyton, Liverpool, their first show after returning from their first-ever performances in the south

28 Nov: Merseyside Civil Service Club, Liverpool

1 Dec: Cavern Club, Liverpool and Tower Ballroom, New Brighton, Wallasey

2, 5–6 Dec: Cavern Club, Liverpool

3, 17 Dec: Casbah Coffee Club, Liverpool

6 Dec: Brian Epstein offers to manage The Beatles

8 Dec: Cavern Club, Liverpool and Tower Ballroom, New Brighton, Wallasey

9 Dec: Palais Ballroom, Aldershot, and late night/ early morning at Blue Gardenia Club, Soho, London

10 Dec: Hambleton Hall, Huyton, Liverpool

10 Dec: The Beatles sign the contract with Brian at the Casbah

11, 13, 16 Dec: Cavern Club, Liverpool (lunchtime and evening on 13 Dec, with Mike

1961 Smith from Decca Records watching the 2nd
(cont.) performance)

15 Dec: Cavern Club, Liverpool and Tower
Ballroom, New Brighton, Wallasey

18–21, 23, 27, 29–30 Dec: Cavern Club,
Liverpool (all-night session on 23 December, 'The
Beatles Christmas Party' on the 27 Dec)

26 Dec: Tower Ballroom, New Brighton, Wallasey

1962 1 Jan: The Beatles audition for Decca Records

3, 5–6, 9–11, 15, 17, 20, 24, 30–31 Jan:
Cavern Club, Liverpool (lunchtime and evening
on 3 and 24 Jan)

7, 14, 21–28 Jan: Casbah Coffee Club, Liverpool

12 Jan: Cavern Club, Liverpool and Tower
Ballroom, New Brighton, Wallasey

13 Jan: Hambleton Hall, Huyton, Liverpool, final
appearance at this venue

19 Jan: Cavern Club, Liverpool and Tower
Ballroom, New Brighton, Wallasey

22 Jan: Cavern Club, Liverpool and Kingsway
Club, Southport, first of eight Monday night
concerts here

24 Jan: The Beatles sign a second amended
contract at NEMS

26 Jan: Cavern Club, Liverpool, lunchtime and
evening, and Tower Ballroom, New Brighton,
Wallasey

27 Jan: Aintree Institute, Liverpool, final
appearance at this venue

29 Jan: Kingsway Club, Southport, second
Monday night here

1 Feb: Cavern Club, Liverpool, the first
appearance under Brian's management at the
Thistle Cafe, West Kirby.

2 Feb: Oasis Club, Manchester

3 Feb: Cavern Club, Liverpool

4, 11 Feb: Casbah Coffee Club, Liverpool

5 Feb: Cavern Club, Liverpool, and Kingsway
Club, Southport, third Monday night here, Ringo
on drums as Pete Best unwell

7 Feb: Cavern Club, Liverpool, lunchtime and
evening, Pete Best back on drums

9 Feb: Cavern Club, Liverpool, lunchtime and
evening, and Technical College Hall, Birkenhead

10 Feb: St Paul's Presbyterian Church Hall,
Birkenhead

12 Feb: Audition for *Teenagers' Turn* radio show
in Manchester

12 Feb: Decca turn The Beatles down

13–14, 17, 19 Feb: Cavern Club, Liverpool

15 Feb: Cavern Club, Liverpool and Tower
Ballroom, New Brighton, Wallasey

16 Feb: Technical College Hall, Birkenhead

18 Feb: Casbah Coffee Club, Liverpool

20 Feb: Floral Hall, Southport

21, 27–28 Feb: Cavern Club, Liverpool
(lunchtime and evening on 21 Feb)

23 Feb: Cavern Club, Liverpool, lunchtime,
Tower Ballroom, New Brighton, Wallasey, two
shows, and in between those performances
Technical College Hall, Birkenhead

24 Feb: YMCA, Hoylake, and Cavern Club,
Liverpool, all-night session

25 Feb: Casbah Coffee Club, Liverpool

26 Feb: Kingsway Club, Southport, fourth
Monday night here

27–28 Feb: Cavern Club, Liverpool

1 Mar: Cavern Club, and Storyville Jazz Club,
Liverpool

2 Mar: St John's Hall, Bootle

3–6 Mar: Cavern Club, Liverpool

4 Mar: Casbah Coffee Club, Liverpool

5 Mar: Cavern Club, Liverpool, and Kingsway
Club, Southport, fifth Monday night here

7 Mar: Radio recording: The Beatles BBC
radio debut, for *Teenager's Turn – Here We Go*,
Playhouse Theatre, Manchester

8 Mar: Storyville Jazz Club, Liverpool

9 Mar: Cavern Club, Liverpool, lunchtime and
evening

10 Mar: St Paul's Presbyterian Church Hall,
Birkenhead

12 Mar: Kingsway Club, Southport, sixth Monday
night here

13–14, 16 Mar: Cavern Club, Liverpool

15 Mar: Cavern Club, and Storyville Jazz Club,
Liverpool

17 Mar: Knotty Ash Village Hall, Liverpool

18 Mar: Casbah Coffee Club, Liverpool

19 Mar: Kingsway Club, Southport, seventh
Monday night here

20–22, 23 Mar: Cavern Club, Liverpool
(lunchtime and evening on 23 Mar)

ABOVE: The Beatles in an early BBC TV show, miming away.

BELOW LEFT: The Beatles miming again on Top of The Pops, 1966. © REX/Shutterstock

BELOW RIGHT: The first of two appearances John and George made on *The Frost Programme*, discussing transcendental meditation in September 1967. © Mark and Colleen Hayward / Contributor

LEFT: Paul with his father Jim in 1967.
© Mirrorpix

BELOW: Ringo with his wife Maureen and baby Zak, in 1967.
© Keystone-France / Contributor

THE FABULOUS BEATLES JEWELLERY BROOCH

COPYRIGHT — REGD. DESIGN
By arrangement with The "BEATLES"
INVICTA PLASTICS LTD., LEICESTER, ENG.

ABOVE: Maharishi (at the back), with The Beatles and their wives, girlfriends and other chums, in India in 1967.
© Hulton Archive / Stringe

BELOW: Filming for the *Magical Mystery Tour* in Devon, 1967. Paul is prominent in his stripy pully. Extra points for spotting George, John and Ringo. © Tracks Ltd

ABOVE: Some 1960s foreign record sleeves – from Yugoslavia, Japan and Israel.

BELOW: The artist Peter Blake, posing with the cover of the
Sgt Pepper album, which he created in 1967. © Matt Cardy / Stringer

LEFT: Lucy in the Sky – well, at least in the garden. John's son Julian with his little friend from nursery school, Lucy Voddon, who inspired John's song in 1967. © Tracks Ltd

BELOW: The one and only Martha, Paul's German shepherd dog, inspiration for Paul's song 'Martha My Dear'. © Tracks Ltd

BOTTOM: The Beatles perform 'All You Need Is Love' for the mega, global TV show *Our World* in 1967.

© David Magnus/REX/Shutterstock

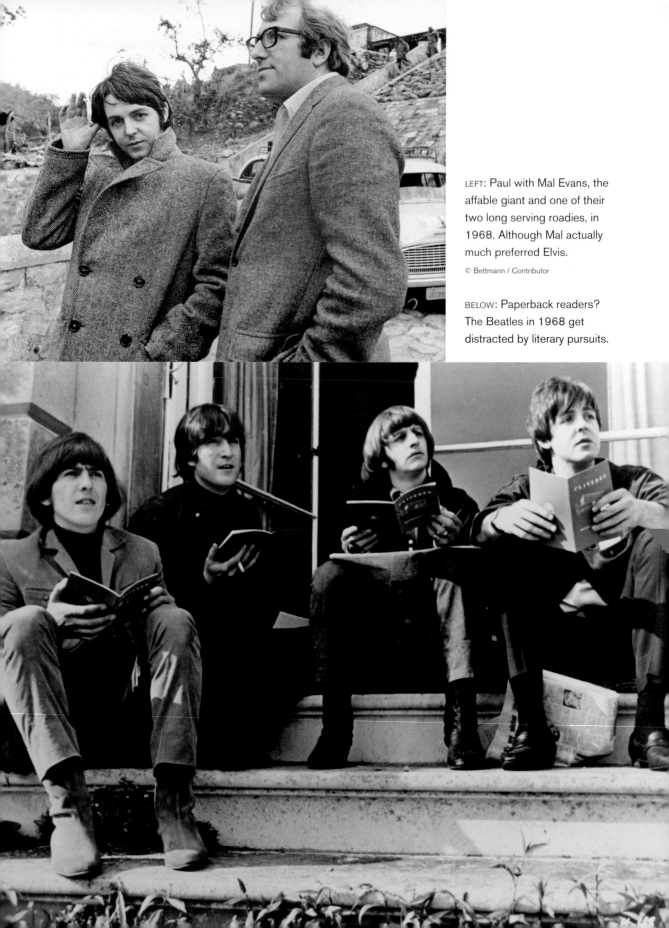

LEFT: Paul with Mal Evans, the affable giant and one of their two long serving roadies, in 1968. Although Mal actually much preferred Elvis.

© Bettmann / Contributor

BELOW: Paperback readers? The Beatles in 1968 get distracted by literary pursuits.

RIGHT: Linda Eastman and Paul at their wedding in 1969.

© C. Maher / Stringer

BELOW: Yoko and John in 1970. Note his old school tie, which ex-pupils of Quarry Bank High School will of course spot at once.

© Moviestore/REX/Shutterstock

30 January 1969. The Beatles on the Apple roof in Savile Row, performing publicly for the last time. © Express / Stringer

24 Mar: Heswall Jazz Club, Barnston
25 Mar: Casbah Coffee Club, Liverpool
26 Mar: Cavern Club, Liverpool, and Apollo Roller Rink, Moreton
28, 30 Mar: Cavern Club, Liverpool (lunchtime and evening on both days)
29 Mar: Odd Spot Club, Liverpool
31 Mar: Subscription Rooms, Stroud
1 Apr: Casbah Coffee Club, Liverpool
2 Apr: Cavern Club, and Pavilion Theatre, Liverpool
4–5 Apr: Cavern Club, Liverpool (lunchtime and evening on 4 Apr)
6 Apr: Cavern Club, Liverpool, and Tower Ballroom, New Brighton, Wallasey
7 Apr: Casbah Coffee Club and Cavern Club, Liverpool, both without unwell George
8 Apr: Casbah Coffee Club, Liverpool, without unwell George
10 Apr: Stuart Sutcliffe dies
11 Apr: John Lennon, Paul McCartney and Pete Best fly to Hamburg
12 Apr: George Harrison, Brian Epstein and Millie Sutcliffe fly to Hamburg
13 Apr: The Beatles make their debut at the Star-Club, Hamburg, West Germany in a run of 48 performances through to 31 May
23 Apr: Bert Kaempfert records The Beatles with Tony Sheridan
9 May: Brian secures a contract with Parlophone
31 May: Final appearance of this tour at the Star-Club, Hamburg
2 June: The Beatles fly home to Liverpool via London
3–4 June: The Beatles rehearse at the Cavern
5 June: The Beatles drive to London
6 June: Recording: Besame Mucho, Love Me Do, P.S. I Love You, Ask Me Why, Studio Two EMI, London, The Beatles first session with George Martin at Abbey Road
7 June: The Beatles return to Liverpool
9 June: Cavern Club, Liverpool, 'The Beatles Welcome Home Show'
11 June: Radio recording: *Teenager's Turn – Here We Go*, Playhouse Theatre, Manchester
12–13, 15–16, 19–20 June: Cavern Club, Liverpool (lunchtime and evening on 12,13,15,19 and 20 June)

21 June: Tower Ballroom, New Brighton, Wallasey
22 June: Cavern Club, Liverpool, lunchtime and evening
23 June: Memorial Hall, Northwich
24 June: The Beatles play at the last night of Casbah Coffee Club, Liverpool
25 June: Cavern Club, Liverpool, and Plaza Ballroom, St Helens
27 June: Cavern Club, Liverpool, lunchtime and evening
28 June: Majestic Ballroom, Birkenhead
29 June: Cavern Club, Liverpool, and Tower Ballroom, New Brighton, Wallasey
30 June: Heswall Jazz Club, Barnston
1, 3–4 July: Cavern Club, Liverpool
2 July: Plaza Ballroom, St Helens
5 July: Majestic Ballroom, Birkenhead
6 July: MV Royal Iris, River Mersey
7 July: Hulme Hall, Port Sunlight
8 July: Cavern Club, Liverpool
9 July: Plaza Ballroom, St Helens
10–11, 15 July: Cavern Club, Liverpool
12 July: Cavern Club, Liverpool, and Majestic Ballroom, Birkenhead
13 July: Tower Ballroom, New Brighton, Wallasey
14 July: Regent Dansette, Rhyl
16 July: Cavern Club, Liverpool, and Plaza Ballroom, St Helens
17 July: McIlroys Ballroom, Swindon
18 July: Cavern Club, Liverpool, lunchtime and evening
19 July: Majestic Ballroom, Birkenhead
20 July: Cavern Club, Liverpool, and Bell Hall, Warrington
21 July: Tower Ballroom, New Brighton, Wallasey
22, 24 July: Cavern Club, Liverpool
23 July: Kingsway Club, Southport, eighth and final Monday night here
25 July: Cavern Club, lunchtime and evening, and Cabaret Club, Duke Street, Liverpool
26 July: Cambridge Hall, Southport
27 July: Tower Ballroom, New Brighton, Wallasey
28 July: Cavern Club, Liverpool, and Majestic Ballroom, Birkenhead
30 July: Cavern Club, Liverpool, and St John's Hall, Bootle

1962 **1, 5, 7, 9, 12 Aug:** Cavern Club, Liverpool
(cont.) (lunchtime and evening on 1 and 7 Aug)
    3 Aug: Grafton Rooms, Liverpool
    4 Aug: Victoria Hall, Higher Bebington
    8 Aug: Co-op Ballroom, Doncaster
    10 Aug: MV Royal Iris, River Mersey
    11 Aug: Odd Spot Club, Liverpool
    13 Aug: Cavern Club, Liverpool, and Majestic Ballroom, Crewe
    15 Aug: Cavern Club, Liverpool, lunchtime and evening, Pete Best's final Beatles performance
    16 Aug: Pete Best is sacked from The Beatles
    16 Aug: Riverpark Ballroom, Chester, first of four Thursdays at venue
    17 Aug: Majestic Ballroom, Birkenhead, and Tower Ballroom, New Brighton, Wallasey
    18 Aug: Hulme Hall, Port Sunlight, Ringo makes his official debut with The Beatles
    19 Aug: Cavern Club, Liverpool, Ringo's first performance here as an official Beatle
    20 Aug: Majestic Ballroom, Crewe
    22 Aug: Cavern Club, Liverpool, lunchtime and evening, Granada TV films The Beatles at lunchtime session for *Know The North*
    23 Aug: John Lennon marries Cynthia Powell
    23 Aug: Riverpark Ballroom, Chester, second Thursday of four at venue
    24 Aug: Cavern Club, Liverpool, and Majestic Ballroom, Birkenhead
    25 Aug: Marine Hall Ballroom, Fleetwood
    26, 28 Aug: Cavern Club, Liverpool
    29 Aug: Floral Hall Ballroom, Morecambe
    30 Aug: Cavern Club, Liverpool, and Riverpark Ballroom, Chester, third Thursday of four at venue
    31 Aug: Town Hall, Lydney, Forest of Dean
    1 Sept: Subscription Rooms, Stroud
    2, 5, 9 Sept: Cavern Club, Liverpool
    3 Sept: Cavern Club, Liverpool, and Queen's Hall, Widnes, first of three Monday nights here
    4 Sept: Recording, mixing: How Do You Do It, Love Me Do, Studio Two EMI, London, The Beatles first session as John, Paul, George and Ringo, Abbey Road
    6 Sept: Cavern Club and Rialto Ballroom, Toxteth, Liverpool
    7 Sept: Village Hall (Mary Newton School of Dance), Irby

8 Sept: YMCA and Majestic Ballroom, Birkenhead
10 Sept: Cavern Club, Liverpool, and Queen's Hall, Widnes, second of three Monday nights here
11 Sept: Recording, mixing: P.S. I Love You, Love Me Do, Please Please Me, Studio Two EMI, London, with Andy White on drums
12 Sept: Cavern Club, Liverpool, where the Beatles back Simone Jackson
13 Sept: Cavern Club, Liverpool, and Riverpark Ballroom, Chester, final Thursday of four at venue
14 Sept: Tower Ballroom, New Brighton, Wallasey
15 Sept: Memorial Hall, Northwich
16, 19–20, 23, 26 Sept: Cavern Club, Liverpool (lunchtime and evening on 26 Sept)
17 Sept: Cavern Club, Liverpool and Queens Hall, Widnes, last of three Monday nights here
21 Sept: Tower Ballroom, New Brighton, Wallasey
22 Sept: Majestic Ballroom, Birkenhead
25 Sept: Heswall Jazz Club, Barnston
28 Sept: Cavern Club, Liverpool, MV Royal Iris, River Mersey
29 Sept: Oasis Club, Manchester
30 Sept: Cavern Club, Liverpool
2–4, 7 Oct: Cavern Club, Liverpool
5 Oct: UK single release: 'Love Me Do'
6 Oct: Hulme Hall, Port Sunlight
8 Oct: Radio recording: interview for Radio Luxembourg *The Friday Spectacular*, EMI House, London
9 Oct: Interview with *Dance News* music paper, London
10, 13 Oct: Cavern Club, Liverpool (lunchtime and evening on 13 Oct)
11 Oct: Rialto Ballroom, Toxteth, Liverpool
12 Oct: Cavern Club, Liverpool, and Tower Ballroom, New Brighton, Wallasey, headlined by Little Richard
15 Oct: Majestic Ballroom, Birkenhead
16 Oct: La Scala Ballroom, Runcorn
17 Oct: Cavern Club, Liverpool, lunchtime and evening; in between shows recording and broadcasting of TV debut: *People And Places* – Studio Four Granada TV Centre, Manchester
19, 21 Oct: Cavern Club, Liverpool
20 Oct: Majestic Ballroom, Witham, Hull
22 Oct: Queens Hall, Widnes

25 Oct: Radio recording: *Here We Go* at Playhouse Theatre, Manchester

26 Oct: Cavern Club, Liverpool, and Public Hall, Preston

27 Oct: Radio: The Beatle first radio interview, with Monty Lister for hospital Radio Clatterbridge, Port Sunlight

27 Oct: Hulme Hall, Port Sunlight

28 Oct: Empire Theatre, Liverpool, first appearance at venue, two shows, headlined by Little Richard, and in which The Beatles also backed Craig Douglas

29 Oct: Television recording: ITV *People And Places*, Granada TV Centre, Manchester

1–14 Nov: Star-Club, Hamburg

16 Nov: Return from Hamburg and interview with *Disc* music paper, London

16 Nov: Radio recording: interview for Radio Luxembourg *The Friday Spectacular*, EMI House, London

17 Nov: Matrix Hall, Fletchamstead Highway, Coventry

18 Nov: Cavern Club, Liverpool

19 Nov: Cavern Club, Liverpool, Smethwick Baths Ballroom, Smethwick and Adelphi Ballroom, West Bromwich

20 Nov: Floral Hall, Southport

21 Nov: Cavern Club lunchtime and evening, with The Beatles backing The Chants at the lunchtime session

22 Nov: Majestic Ballroom, Birkenhead

23 Nov: BBC audition at St James's Church Hall, Gloucester Terrace, London, and Tower Ballroom, New Brighton, Wallasey

24 Nov: Royal Lido Ballroom, Prestatyn

25 Nov: Cavern Club, Liverpool

26 Nov: Recording: Please Please Me, Studio Two EMI, London

27 Nov: Radio recording: BBC *The Talent Spot*, Paris Studio, London

28 Nov: Cavern Club and 527 Club in Lewis's Department Store, Ranelagh Street, Liverpool

29 Nov: Majestic Ballroom, Birkenhead

30 Nov: Cavern Club, Liverpool, and Town Hall, Newton-le-Willows

1 Dec: Memorial Hall, Northwich

2 Dec: Embassy Cinema, Peterborough, two shows, headlined by Frank Ifield

3 Dec: Television live: ITV *Discs-A-Gogo*, TWW TV Centre, Bristol

4 Dec: Television live: ITV *Tuesday Rendezvous*, Wembley Studios, London

5 Dec: Cavern Club lunchtime and evening

6 Dec: Club Django, Queens Hotel, Southport

7 Dec: Cavern Club, Liverpool, and Tower Ballroom, New Brighton, Wallasey

8 Dec: Oasis Club, Manchester

9 Dec: Cavern Club, Liverpool, with George Martin in audience

10 Dec: Cavern Club, Liverpool

11 Dec: La Scala Ballroom, Runcorn

12 Dec: Cavern Club, Liverpool, lunchtime and evening

13 Dec: Corn Exchange, Bedford, stepping in for original headline act Joe Brown

14 Dec: Music Hall, Shrewsbury

15 Dec: Majestic Ballroom, Birkenhead, followed post-midnight by *Mersey Beat* poll awards show

16 Dec: Cavern Club, Liverpool

17 Dec: Television live: ITV *People And Places*, Granada TV Centre, Manchester

18–31 Dec: The Beatles final trip to Star-Club, Hamburg

31 Dec: The Beatles are recorded at request of Kingsize Taylor, during final night at Star-Club

1963 **2 Jan:** Longmore Hall, Keith, Banffshire (cancelled)

3 Jan: Two Red Shoes Ballroom, Elgin, first actual date of five-night tour of Scotland

4 Jan: Town Hall, Dingwall

5 Jan: Museum Hall, Bridge of Allan

6 Jan: Beach Ballroom, Aberdeen, concluding night of mini Scottish tour

8 Jan: Television live: ITV *Roundup*, Theatre Royal, Glasgow

10 Jan: Grafton Rooms, Liverpool

11 Jan: UK single release: 'Please Please Me'

11 Jan: Cavern Club, Liverpool, and Plaza Ballroom, Old Hill, Dudley

11 Jan: Ritz Ballroom, Kings Heath, Birmingham (postponed)

12 Jan: Invicta Ballroom, Chatham

13 Jan: Television recording: *Thank Your Lucky Stars*, Alpha TV, Birmingham

1963 **14 Jan:** Civic Hall, Ellesmere Port
(cont.) **16 Jan:** Radio recording: *Here We Go*, Playhouse
Theatre, Manchester
16 Jan: Television live: ITV *People And Places*,
Granada TV Centre, Manchester
17 Jan: Cavern Club, Liverpool, and Majestic
Ballroom, Birkenhead
18 Jan: Floral Hall Ballroom, Morecambe
19 Jan: Town Hall Ballroom, Whitchurch
20 Jan: Cavern Club, Liverpool, Mal Evans first
night as roadie
21 Jan: Radio live: interview Radio Luxembourg
The Friday Spectacular, EMI House, London
22 Jan: Radio live: interview BBC *Pop Inn*, Paris
Studio, London
22 Jan: Radio recording: *Saturday Club*,
Playhouse Theatre, London
22 Jan: Radio recording: *The Talent Spot*, Paris
Studio, London
23 Jan: Cavern Club, Liverpool
24 Jan: NEMS, Liverpool, then Assembly Hall
25 Jan: Co-operative Hall, Darwen
26 Jan: El Rio Club, Macclesfield and King's Hall,
Stoke-on-Trent
27 Jan: Three Coins Club, Manchester
28 Jan: Majestic Ballroom, Newcastle
30 Jan: Cavern Club, Liverpool
31 Jan: Cavern Club, Liverpool, and Majestic
Ballroom, Birkenhead
1 Feb: Maney Hall, Sutton Coldfield and
Assembly Rooms, Tamworth
2 Feb: Gaumont Cinema, Bradford, opening night
of Helen Shapiro tour, two shows at each venue
3 Feb: Cavern Club, Liverpool, with The Beatles
headlining an eight-hour 'Rhythm & Blues'
marathon with Earl Preston and The TTs, The
Fourmost, The Hollies, Kingsize Taylor and The
Dominoes (with guest vocalist Cilla Black), The
Merseybeats, The Swinging Blue Jeans, and The
Roadrunners
4 Feb: Cavern Club, Liverpool, final lunchtime
performance
5 Feb: Gaumont Cinema, Doncaster, Helen
Shapiro tour
6 Feb: Granada Cinema, Bedford, Helen Shapiro
tour

7 Feb: ABC Cinema, Kirkgate, Wakefield, Helen
Shapiro tour
8 Feb: ABC Cinema, Carlisle, Helen Shapiro tour
9 Feb: Empire Theatre, Sunderland, Helen
Shapiro tour
11 Feb: Recording: *Please Please Me* album, Studio
Two EMI, London
12 Feb: Azena Ballroom, Sheffield
12 Feb: Astoria Ballroom, Oldham
13 Feb: Majestic Ballroom, Hull
14 Feb: Locarno, Liverpool
15 Feb: Ritz Ballroom, King's Heath,
Birmingham
16 Feb: Carfax Assembly Rooms, Oxford
17 Feb: Television recording: ITV *Thank Your
Lucky Stars*, Teddington Studios
18 Feb: Queen's Hall, Widnes, two shows
19 Feb: Cavern Club, Liverpool
20 Feb: Radio live: *Parade Of The Pops*, Playhouse
Theatre, London
20 Feb: Recording: Misery, Baby It's You, Studio
One EMI, London
20 Feb: St James' Street Baths, Doncaster
21 Feb: Majestic Ballroom, Birkenhead, two
shows
22 Feb: Northern Songs is set up to look after
John and Paul's songs
22 Feb: Oasis Club, Manchester
23 Feb: Granada Cinema, Mansfield, Helen
Shapiro tour
24 Feb: Coventry Theatre, Coventry, Helen
Shapiro tour
25 Feb: Casino Ballroom, Leigh
25 Feb: US single release: 'Please Please Me'
26 Feb: Gaumont Cinema, Taunton, Helen
Shapiro tour
27 Feb: Rialto Theatre, York, Helen Shapiro tour
28 Feb: Granada Cinema, Shrewsbury, Helen
Shapiro tour
1 Mar: Odeon Cinema, Southport, Helen Shapiro
tour
2 Mar: City Hall, Sheffield, Helen Shapiro tour
2 Mar: Television live: interview for *ABC At
Large*, Didsbury Studio Centre, Manchester
3 Mar: Gaumont Cinema, Hanley, Stoke-on-
Trent, final night of Helen Shapiro tour
4 Mar: Plaza Ballroom, St Helens

5 Mar: Photo session in London

5 Mar: Recording: From Me To You, Thank You Girl, One After 909, Studio Two EMI, London

6 Mar: Radio recording: *Here We Go*, Playhouse Theatre, Manchester

7 Mar: Elizabethan Ballroom, Nottingham, first *Mersey Beat Showcase* concert

8 Mar: Royal Hall, Harrogate

9 Mar: Granada Cinema, East Ham, London, opening night of the Chris Montez/Tommy Roe tour, two shows at each venue on tour

10 Mar: Hippodrome Theatre, Birmingham, Chris Montez/Tommy Roe tour

11 Mar: Radio recording: interview for Radio Luxembourg *The Friday Spectacular*, EMI House, London

12 Mar: Granada Cinema, Bedford, Chris Montez/Tommy Roe tour

13 Mar: Recording, mixing: Thank You Girl, Studio Two EMI, London

13 Mar: Rialto Theatre, York, Chris Montez/Tommy Roe tour

14 Mar: Gaumont Cinema, Wolverhampton, Chris Montez/Tommy Roe tour

15 Mar: Colston Hall, Bristol, Chris Montez/Tommy Roe tour

16 Mar: City Hall, Sheffield, Chris Montez/Tommy Roe tour

16 Mar: Radio live: *Saturday Club*, Broadcasting House, London

17 Mar: Embassy Cinema, Peterborough, Chris Montez/Tommy Roe tour

18 Mar: Regal Cinema, Gloucester, Chris Montez/Tommy Roe tour

19 Mar: Regal Cinema, Cambridge, Chris Montez/Tommy Roe tour

20 Mar: ABC Cinema, Romford, Chris Montez/Tommy Roe tour

21 Mar: ABC Cinema, Croydon, Chris Montez/Tommy Roe tour

21 Mar: Radio recording: *On The Scene*, Piccadilly Studios, London

22 Mar: Gaumont Cinema, Doncaster, Chris Montez/Tommy Roe tour

22 Mar: UK Album release: *Please Please Me*

23 Mar: City Hall, Newcastle, Chris Montez/Tommy Roe tour

24 Mar: Empire Theatre, Liverpool, Chris Montez/Tommy Roe tour

26 Mar: Granada Cinema, Mansfield, Chris Montez/Tommy Roe tour

27 Mar: ABC Cinema, Northampton, Chris Montez/Tommy Roe tour

28 Mar: ABC Cinema, Exeter, Chris Montez/Tommy Roe tour

29 Mar: Odeon Cinema, Lewisham, Chris Montez/Tommy Roe tour

30 Mar: Guildhall, Portsmouth, Chris Montez/Tommy Roe tour

31 Mar: De Montfort Hall, Leicester, final date of Chris Montez/Tommy Roe tour

1 Apr: Radio recording: *Side By Side*, Piccadilly Studios, London

3 Apr: Radio recording: *Easy Beat*, Playhouse Theatre, London

4 Apr: Radio recording: *Side By Side*, Paris Studio, London

4 Apr: Stowe School

5 Apr: The Beatles receive their first silver disc ('Please Please Me' single) at EMI House, London, and perform a short set

6 Apr: Pavilion Gardens Ballroom, Buxton

7 Apr: Savoy Ballroom, Southsea, Portsmouth

8 Apr: Julian Charles Lennon born

8 Apr: Leyton Swimming Baths, London

9 Apr: Gaumont State Cinema, Kilburn, London

9 Apr: Radio live: interview BBC *Pop Inn*, Paris Studio, London

9 Apr: Television live: ITV *Tuesday Rendezvous*, Wembley Studios, London

10 Apr: Majestic Ballroom, Birkenhead, last appearance at venue

11 Apr: Co-operative Hall, Middleton

11 Apr: John Lennon meets son Julian for first time, Sefton General Hospital, Liverpool

11 Apr: UK single release: 'From Me To You'

12 Apr: Cavern Club, Liverpool, headlining another 'Rhythm & Blues' marathon

13 Apr: Television recording: BBC *The 625 Show*, Lime Grove Studios, London, BBC TV debut

14 Apr: Television recording: ITV *Thank Your Lucky Stars*, Teddington Studios

14 Apr: The Beatles see Rolling Stones perform for the first time, Crawdaddy Club, Richmond

1963 **15 Apr:** Riverside Dancing Club, Bridge Hotel,
(cont.) Tenbury Wells

16 Apr: Television live: ITV *Scene at 6.30*,
Granada TV, Manchester; and broadcast of first
BBC TV appearance, *The 625 Show*

17 Apr: Majestic Ballroom, Luton

18 Apr: Paul McCartney meets Jane Asher at
Swinging Sound '63 concert, Royal Albert Hall,
London

19 Apr: King's Hall, Stoke, second *Mersey Beat
Showcase* concert

20 Apr: Mersey View Pleasure Grounds, Frodsham.

21 Apr: *NME Poll-Winners' All-Star Concert*,
Empire Pool, Wembley

21 Apr: Pigalle Club, London

23 Apr: Floral Hall, Southport

24 Apr: Majestic Ballroom, Finsbury Park,
London, third *Mersey Beat Showcase* concert

25 Apr: Fairfield Hall, Croydon, fourth *Mersey
Beat Showcase* concert, two shows

26 Apr: Music Hall, Shrewsbury

27 Apr: Memorial Hall, Northwich

28 Apr: John Lennon and Brian Epstein leave for
12-day holiday in Barcelona, Spain

11 May: Imperial Ballroom, Nelson

12 May: Television recording: ITV *Thank Your
Lucky Stars*, Alpha TV, Birmingham

14 May: Rink Ballroom, Sunderland

15 May: Royalty Theatre, Chester

16 May: Television live: BBC *Pops And Lenny*,
Television Theatre, London

17 May: Grosvenor Rooms, Norwich, two
20-minute sets

18 May: Adelphi Cinema, Slough; Opening night
of Roy Orbison tour, two shows at each venue

19 May: Gaumont Cinema, Hanley, Stoke-on-
Trent, Roy Orbison tour

20 May: Gaumont Cinema, Southampton, Roy
Orbison tour

21 May: Radio recording: *Steppin' Out* and
Saturday Club, Playhouse Theatre, London

22 May: Gaumont Cinema, Ipswich, Roy Orbison
tour

23 May: Odeon Cinema, Nottingham, Roy
Orbison tour

24 May: Granada Cinema, Walthamstow, London,
Roy Orbison tour

24 May: Radio recording: *Pop Go The Beatles*,
Aeolian Hall, London

25 May: City Hall, Sheffield, Roy Orbison tour

26 May: Empire Theatre, Liverpool, Roy Orbison
tour

27 May: US single release: 'From Me To You'

27 May: Capitol Cinema, Cardiff, Roy Orbison
tour

28 May: Gaumont Cinema, Worcester, Roy
Orbison tour

29 May: Rialto Theatre, York, Roy Orbison tour

30 May: Odeon Cinema, Manchester, Roy
Orbison tour

31 May: Odeon Cinema, Southend-on-Sea, Roy
Orbison tour

1 June: Granada Cinema, Tooting, London, Roy
Orbison tour

1 June: Radio recording: *Pop Go The Beatles*, Paris
Studio, London

2 June: Hippodrome, Brighton, Roy Orbison tour

3 June: Granada Cinema, Woolwich, London, Roy
Orbison tour

4 June: Town Hall, Birmingham, Roy Orbison
tour

5 June: Odeon Cinema, Leeds, Roy Orbison tour

7 June: Odeon Cinema, Glasgow, Roy Orbison
tour

8 June: City Hall, Newcastle, Roy Orbison tour

9 June: King George's Hall, Blackburn, final date
of Roy Orbison tour

10 June: Pavilion, Bath

12 June: Grafton Rooms, Liverpool, NSPCC
charity concert

13 June: Palace Theatre Club, Stockport and
Southern Sporting Club, Manchester

14 June: Tower Ballroom, New Brighton,
Wallasey, fifth *Mersey Beat Showcase* concert

15 June: City Hall, Salisbury

16 June: Odeon Cinema, Romford, final night of
the *Mersey Beat Showcase* concert series

17 June: Radio recording: *Pop Go The Beatles*,
Maida Vale Studios, London

18 June: Paul McCartney's 21st birthday party
at which John Lennon assaults Cavern DJ Bob
Wooler, Huyton, Liverpool

19 June: Radio recording: *Easy Beat*, Playhouse
Theatre, London

20 June: John Lennon apologises to Bob Wooler for assault

20 June: The Beatles Ltd is formed

21 June: John Lennon's assault of Bob Wooler reported in *Daily Mirror*

21 June: Odeon Cinema, Guildford, two shows

22 June: Television recording: John Lennon on BBC *Juke Box Jury*, Television Theatre, London, then concert at Town Hall, Abergavenny.

24 June: Radio recording: *Saturday Club*, Playhouse Theatre, London

25 June: Astoria Ballroom, Middlesbrough

26 June: Majestic Ballroom, Newcastle

27 June: Lennon and McCartney finish writing 'She Loves You' at Paul's family home, Forthlin Road; they had started writing the previous day in the Royal Turks Head Hotel, Newcastle

28 June: Queens Hall, Leeds, concert with Acker Bilk, two shows

30 June: ABC Cinema, Great Yarmouth, start of ten-week run of Sunday evening seaside resort concerts, two shows per night during this tour

1 July: Recording: She Loves You, I'll Get You, Studio Two EMI, London

2 July: Radio recording: *Pop Go The Beatles*, Maida Vale, London

3 July: Radio recording: *The Beat Show*, Playhouse Theatre, Manchester

4 July: Editing, mixing: She Loves You, I'll Get You, Studio Two EMI, London

5 July: Plaza Ballroom, Old Hill, Dudley

6 July: Memorial Hall, Northwich.

7 July: ABC Theatre, Blackpool, second in seaside resorts tour

8–13 July: Winter Gardens, Margate, six-night residency, two shows per night

10 July: Radio recording: two episodes *Pop Go The Beatles*, Aeolian Hall, London

12 July: UK EP release: 'Twist And Shout'

14 July: ABC Theatre, Blackpool, third in seaside resorts tour

16 July: Radio recording: three episodes *Pop Go The Beatles* Paris Studio, London

17 July: Radio recording: *Easy Beat*, Playhouse Theatre, London

18 July: Recording: You Really Got A Hold On Me, Money, Devil In Her Heart, Till There Was You, Studio Two EMI, London

19–20 July: Ritz Ballroom, Rhyl, two shows each night.

21 July: Queen's Theatre, Blackpool, fourth in seaside resorts tour

28 July: ABC Cinema, Great Yarmouth, fifth in seaside resorts tour

30 July: Radio recording: interview for *Non Stop Pop* and *Saturday Club*, Playhouse Theatre, London

30 July: Recording: Please Mr Postman, It Won't Be Long, Money, Till There Was You, Roll Over Beethoven, All My Loving, Studio Two EMI, London

31 July: Imperial Ballroom, Nelson.

22–27 July: Odeon Cinema, Weston-super-Mare, six-night residency, two shows per night

1 Aug: Radio recording: two episodes *Pop Go The Beatles*, Playhouse Theatre, London

2 Aug: Grafton Rooms, Liverpool

3 Aug: Cavern Club, Liverpool, The Beatles final show at the venue.

4 Aug: Queen's Theatre, Blackpool, sixth in seaside resorts tour

5 Aug: Abbotsfield Park, Urmston.

6–7, 9–10 Aug: Springfield Ballroom, Jersey, four nights

8 Aug: Candie Gardens, Guernsey, two shows

11 Aug: ABC Theatre, Blackpool, seventh in seaside resorts tour

12–17 Aug: Odeon Cinema, Llandudno, six-night residency, two shows per night

14 Aug: Television live broadcast and recording: ITV *Scene at 6.30*, Granada TV Centre, Manchester

18 Aug: Television recording: ITV *Lucky Stars (Summer Spin)*, Alpha TV, Birmingham

18 Aug: Princess Theatre, Torquay, eighth in seaside resorts tour

19–24 Aug: Gaumont Cinema, Bournemouth, six-night residency, two shows per night

21 Aug: Editing, mixing: *With The Beatles*, Studio Three EMI, London

22 Aug: Television recording broadcast same day: ITV *Day By Day*, Southern Independent TV Centre, Southampton

1963 **23 Aug:** UK single release: 'She Loves You'
(cont.) **25 Aug:** ABC Theatre, Blackpool, ninth in seaside resorts tour
26 Aug: Paul McCartney receives one-year driving ban
26–31 Aug: Odeon Cinema, Southport, six-night residency, two shows per night
27–30 Aug: Television recording: filming around Stockport, Manchester and Liverpool for BBC documentary *The Mersey Sound*
1 Sept: Television recording: ITV *Big Night Out*, Didsbury Studio Centre, Manchester
3 Sept: Radio recording: final three episodes *Pop Go The Beatles*, Aeolian Hall, London
4 Sept: Gaumont Cinema, Worcester, opening night of John Smith promoted mini-tour, two shows each night
5 Sept: Gaumont Cinema, Taunton, second night of John Smith promoted mini-tour
6 Sept: Odeon Cinema, Luton, third night of John Smith promoted mini-tour
6 Sept: UK EP release: *The Beatles' Hits*
7 Sept: Fairfield Hall, Croydon, fourth and final night of John Smith promoted mini-tour
7 Sept: Radio recording: *Saturday Club*, Playhouse Theatre, London
8 Sept: ABC Theatre, Blackpool, final concert in seaside resorts tour
10 Sept: Lennon and McCartney given Variety Club award, Savoy Theatre, London
11 Sept: Recording: I Wanna Be Your Man, Little Child, All I've Got To Do, Not A Second Time, Don't Bother Me, Studio Two EMI, London
12 Sept: Recording: Messages To Australia, Hold Me Tight, Don't Bother Me, Little Child, I Wanna Be Your Man, Studio Two EMI, London
13 Sept: Public Hall, Preston, two shows
14 Sept: Memorial Hall, Northwich
15 Sept: Royal Albert Hall, London, *The Great Pop Prom*
16 Sept: George Harrison holidays with his sister Louise in Benton, Illinois
16 Sept: John and Cynthia Lennon holiday in Paris
16 Sept: Paul McCartney and Ringo Starr holiday in Greece
16 Sept: US single release: 'She Loves You'

30 Sept: Recording, editing, mixing: Little Child, Hold Me Tight, Money, I Wanna Be Your Man, All I've Got To Do, Don't Bother Me, Not A Second Time, Studio Two EMI, London
3 Oct: Radio recording: interviews for *The Public Ear*, NEMS Enterprises, London
3 Oct: Recording: I Wanna Be Your Man, Little Child, Studio Two EMI, London
4 Oct: Television live: ITV *Ready Steady Go!*, Television House, London, debut on show
5 Oct: Concert Hall, Glasgow, first of three-date Scottish tour, two shows
6 Oct: Carlton Theatre, Kirkcaldy, second date on Scottish tour, two shows
7 Oct: Caird Hall, Dundee, final date of Scottish tour
9 Oct: Radio recording: *The Ken Dodd Show*, Paris Studio, London, and regional broadcast of BBC documentary The Mersey Sound
11 Oct: Trentham Gardens Ballroom, Trentham
13 Oct: Television live: ITV *Sunday Night At The London Palladium*, Beatlemania begins
15 Oct: Floral Hall, Southport
16 Oct: Radio recording: *Easy Beat*, Playhouse Theatre, London
17 Oct: Recording: The Beatles' Christmas Record, You Really Got A Hold On Me, I Want To Hold Your Hand, This Boy, Studio Two EMI, London
18 Oct: Television recording broadcast same day: ITV *Scene at 6.30*, Granada TV Centre, Manchester
19 Oct: Pavilion Gardens Ballroom, Buxton
20 Oct: Television recording: *Thank Your Lucky Stars*, Alpha Television, Birmingham
23 Oct: Recording, mixing: I Wanna Be Your Man, Little Child, Hold Me Tight, Studio Two EMI, London
23 Oct: The Beatles fly to Sweden from London
24 Oct: Radio recording: Karlaplansstudion, Stockholm, Sweden
25 Oct: Sundsta Läroverk, Karlstad, opening night of tour of Sweden
26 Oct: Kungliga Tennishallen, Stockholm, Sweden, two shows
27 Oct: Cirkus, Gothenburg, Sweden, three shows
28 Oct: Boråshallen, Borås, Sweden

29 Oct: Sporthallen, Eskilstuna, Sweden
30 Oct: Television recording: *Drop In*, Stockholm, Sweden
31 Oct: The Beatles fly back to UK from Stockholm; at London Airport Ed Sullivan witnessed screaming fans
1 Nov: Odeon Cinema, Cheltenham, opening night of 34-date autumn tour, two shows at each venue on tour
1 Nov: UK EP release: *The Beatles (No. 1)*
2 Nov: City Hall, Sheffield, autumn tour
3 Nov: Odeon Cinema, Leeds, autumn tour
4 Nov: Royal Variety Performance, Prince of Wales Theatre, London
5 Nov: Adelphi Cinema, Slough, autumn tour
6 Nov: ABC Cinema, Northampton, autumn tour
7 Nov: Adelphi Cinema, Dublin, Ireland, autumn tour
7 Nov: Television interview: RTE *In Town*, Dublin Airport
8 Nov: Television interviews: Ulster News and BBC *Six Ten*, Broadcasting House, Belfast
8 Nov: Ritz Cinema, Belfast, autumn tour
9 Nov: Granada Cinema, East Ham, London, autumn tour
10 Nov: Hippodrome, Birmingham, autumn tour
12 Nov: Guildhall, Portsmouth (postponed)
12 Nov: Television recording broadcast same day: interviews for ITV *Day By Day*, Portsmouth, and BBC *South Today*, Southsea
13 Nov: Television recording: ITV *Move Over, Dad*, Westward TV Studios, Plymouth, and national broadcast of BBC documentary *The Mersey Sound*
13 Nov: ABC Cinema, Plymouth, autumn tour
14 Nov: ABC Cinema, Exeter, autumn tour
15 Nov: Colston Hall, Bristol, autumn tour
16 Nov: Winter Gardens Theatre, Bournemouth, autumn tour
17 Nov: Coventry Theatre, Coventry, autumn tour
18 Nov: EMI presents The Beatles with silver discs, EMI House, London
18 Nov: First coverage of The Beatles aired in USA on NBC's *The Huntley-Brinkley Report*
19 Nov: Gaumont Cinema, Wolverhampton, autumn tour

20 Nov: ABC Cinema, Ardwick, Manchester, autumn tour
21 Nov: ABC Cinema, Carlisle, autumn tour
22 Nov: Globe Cinema, Stockton-on-Tees, autumn tour
22 Nov: UK LP release: *With The Beatles*
23 Nov: City Hall, Newcastle, autumn tour
24 Nov: ABC Cinema, Hull, autumn tour
25 Nov: Television recording: ITV *Late Scene Extra, Scene at 6.30*, Granada TV Centre, Manchester
26 Nov: Regal Cinema, Cambridge, autumn tour
27 Nov: Rialto Theatre, York, autumn tour
28 Nov: ABC Cinema, Lincoln, autumn tour
29 Nov: ABC Cinema, Huddersfield, autumn tour
29 Nov: UK single release: 'I Want To Hold Your Hand'
30 Nov: Empire Theatre, Sunderland, autumn tour
1 Dec: De Montfort Hall, Leicester, autumn tour
2 Dec: Grosvenor House Hotel, London, concert in aid of cerebral palsy sufferers
2 Dec: Television recording: ITV *The Morecambe And Wise Show*, Elstree Studios, Borehamwood
3 Dec: Guildhall, Portsmouth, autumn tour
7 Dec: Television live: BBC *It's The Beatles!*, Empire Theatre, Liverpool
7 Dec: Empire Theatre, Liverpool, recording of *Juke Box Jury* followed by Northern Fan Club concert, recorded by BBC and broadcast in evening as *It's The Beatles!*
7 Dec: Odeon Cinema, Liverpool, autumn tour
8 Dec: Odeon Cinema, Lewisham, autumn tour
9 Dec: Odeon Cinema, Southend-on-Sea, autumn tour
10 Dec: Gaumont Cinema, Doncaster, autumn tour
11 Dec: Futurist Theatre, Scarborough, autumn tour
12 Dec: Odeon Cinema, Nottingham, autumn tour
13 Dec: Gaumont Cinema, Southampton, final date of autumn tour
14 Dec: Wimbledon Palais, London. Southern Fan Club concert
15 Dec: Television recording: ITV *Lucky Stars on Merseyside*, Alpha TV, Birmingham

1963 **17 Dec:** Radio recording: *Saturday Club*,
(cont.) Playhouse Theatre, London
18 Dec: Radio recording: *From Us To You*, Paris
Studio, London
21 Dec: Gaumont Cinema, Bradford, Christmas
Show preview, two shows
22 Dec: Empire Theatre, Liverpool, Christmas
Show preview, two shows
26 Dec: US single release: 'I Want To Hold Your
Hand'
27 Dec: *The Times* article: What Songs The Beatles
Sang by William Mann

1963 **24, 26–28, 30–2, 4, 6–11 Dec/Jan:** Astoria
/64 Cinema, Finsbury Park, London, *Beatles Christmas
Show,* two shows each night, except 24 and 31
December when only one, 30 shows in total

1964 **4 Jan:** Radio recording: various interviews, EMI
House, London
5 Jan: Radio recording: George and Ringo
interviews for *The Public Ear*, London
7 Jan: Radio recording: *Saturday Club*, Playhouse
Theatre, London
10 Jan: US LP release: *Introducing … The Beatles*
12 Jan: Television live: ITV *Sunday Night At The
London Palladium*
14 Jan: John, Paul and George fly to Paris and
stay at George V Hotel
15 Jan: Cinéma Cyrano, Versailles, France
15 Jan: The Beatles reach No. 1 in American
Cashbox charts with 'I Want To Hold Your Hand'
16–20, 22–27, 29–4 Jan/Feb: Olympia Theatre,
Paris, numerous shows over 18 days
19 Jan: Radio: part of matinee show at Olympia
Theatre broadcast live on *Musicorama*, Europe 1
20 Jan: US LP release: *Meet The Beatles!*
24 Jan: Radio recording: interview for *American
Forces Network*, Paris Studio, London
27 Jan: The Beatles were due to record at a local
Paris studio but didn't turn up; George Martin was
not happy
27 Jan: US single release: 'My Bonnie'/'The
Saints' by The Beatles With Tony Sheridan
28 Jan: Travel: Lennon and Harrison fly from
Paris to London and return the following day
29 Jan: Recording: Komm Gib Mir Deine Hand
(I Want to Hold Your Hand), Sie Liebt Dich (She
Loves You), Can't Buy Me Love in English, Pathé
Marconi Studios, Paris

30 Jan: US single re-release: 'Please Please Me'
5 Feb: The Beatles return to UK from Paris and
give press conference at London Airport
6 Feb: Interview: John Lennon and George
Harrison with June Harris, *Disc*
7 Feb: The Beatles American invasion begins
7 Feb: UK EP release: *All My Loving*
8 Feb: Radio broadcast: interviews from New York
on previous evening, for *Saturday Club*
8 Feb: Rehearsal for *The Ed Sullivan Show*, Studio
50, New York
9 Feb: Television recording: The Beatles record
third *Ed Sullivan Show* appearance broadcast 23
February, Studio 50, New York
9 Feb: Television live: The Beatles first *Ed Sullivan
Show*, Studio 50, New York
10 Feb: The Beatles give series of interviews to
US media outlets and are awarded a gold disc by
Alan Livingstone, President Capitol Records, for 'I
Want To Hold Your Hand' and *Meet The Beatles*,
Plaza Hotel, New York
11 Feb: Washington Coliseum, Washington, DC,
The Beatles first full-length concert in the US
12 Feb: Carnegie Hall, New York City, two shows
13 Feb: The Beatles fly to Miami from New York
14–15 Feb: Rehearsal for *The Ed Sullivan Show*,
Deauville Hotel, Florida
16 Feb: Television live: The Beatles second *Ed
Sullivan Show*, Deauville Hotel, Florida
17 Feb: Day off in Miami
18 Feb: The Beatles meet Cassius Clay at his
training camp in Miami Beach
21 Feb: The Beatles return to UK from Miami, via
New York, arriving the following day when they
give a press conference and various interviews at
Kingsford-Smith suite, London Airport
23 Feb: Television recording: ITV *Big Night Out,*
Teddington Studios
23 Feb: Broadcast of The Beatles third *Ed
Sullivan Show*, Studio 50, New York
25 Feb: George Harrison's 21st birthday
25 Feb: Recording: Can't Buy Me Love, You
Can't Do That, And I Love Her, I Should Have
Known Better, Studio Two EMI, London
26 Feb: Recording, mixing: You Can't Do That,
Can't Buy Me Love, I Should Have Known Better,
And I Love Her, Studio Two EMI, London

27 Feb: Recording: And I Love Her, Tell Me Why, If I Fell, Studio Two EMI, London

28 Feb: Radio recording: *From Us To You*, Piccadilly Studios, London

1 Mar: Recording: I'm Happy Just To Dance With You, Long Tall Sally, I Call Your Name, Studio Two EMI, London

2–6, 9–13, 16–20, 23–26, 31 Mar: Filming: *A Hard Day's Night*, various locations across London, Surrey, West Country

2 Mar: US single release: 'Twist And Shout'

9 Mar: NEMS enterprises move into Sutherland House, London

10 Mar: Recording, mixing: Can't Buy Me Love, Long Tall Sally, I Call Your Name, You Can't Do That, Komm Gib Mir Deine Hand, Sie Liebt Dich, Studio Two EMI, London

16 Mar: US single release: 'Can't Buy Me Love'

18 Mar: Radio recording: interviews for *The Public Ear*, Twickenham Studio

19 Mar: The Beatles are given Variety Club awards

19 Mar: Television recording: BBC *Top Of The Pops*, Television Theatre, London, debut appearance

20 Mar: Television live: ITV *Ready Steady Go!*, Television House, London

20 Mar: UK single release: 'Can't Buy Me Love'

23 Mar: Television live: John Lennon interview at Lime Grove Studios, London, for BBC *Tonight*, promoting that day's publication of *In His Own Write*

23 Mar: Television live: BBC *The Carl Alan Awards*, Duke of Edimburgh present The Beatles with two awards, Empire Ballroom, London

23 Mar: US EP release: *The Beatles*

23 Mar: US single release: 'Do You Want To Know A Secret'

31 Mar: Radio recording: *Saturday Club*, Playhouse Theatre, London

1–3, 5–7, 9–10, 12–18, 22–24 Apr: Filming: *A Hard Day's Night*, various locations in and around London

1 Apr: John Lennon reunited with father Alf, NEMS Enterprises, London

4 Apr: The Beatles occupy the Billboard Hot 100 Top 5

10 Apr: US LP release: *The Beatles' Second Album*

15 Apr: Television recording: Paul McCartney interview on BBC *A Degree Of Frost*, Television Centre, London

16 Apr: Recording: *A Hard Day's Night*, Studio Two EMI, London

17 Apr: Interview with Ed Sullivan recorded in garden of Les Ambassadeurs club, London

18 Apr: Rehearsal: *Around The Beatles*, Chelsea Manor Buildings Hall of Remembrance, London

19 Apr: Recording: *Around The Beatles*, IBC Studios, London

20–21 Apr: Filming: Paul McCartney's unused scene in *A Hard Day's Night*, Shepherd's Bush, London

25 Apr: Rehearsal: *Around The Beatles*, Chelsea Manor Buildings Hall of Remembrance, London

26 Apr: *NME Poll-Winners' All-Star Concert*, Empire Pool, Wembley

27 Apr: Rehearsal: *Around The Beatles*, Wembley Studios, London

27 Apr: US single release: 'Love Me Do'

28 Apr: Television recording: ITV *Around The Beatles*, Wembley Studios, London

29 Apr: ABC Cinema, Edinburgh, two shows

30 Apr: Television recording broadcast same day: interview for BBC *Six Ten* news programme, Callendar, Perthshire, and afternoon recording of interview for STV show *Roundup*, Theatre Royal Studios

30 Apr: Odeon Cinema, Glasgow, two shows

1 May: Radio recording: *From Us To You*, Paris Studio, London

6 May: Television: broadcast ITV *Around The Beatles*

11 May: US EP release: *Four By The Beatles*

21 May: US single release: 'Sie Liebt Dich'

22 May: Recording: You Can't Do That, Studio Two EMI, London

31 May: Prince Of Wales Theatre, London, *Pops Alive* concert, two shows

1 June: Recording: Matchbox, I'll Cry Instead, Slow Down, I'll Be Back, Studio Two EMI, London

2 June: Recording: Any Time At All, Things We Said Today, When I Get Home, Studio Two EMI, London

1964 **3 June:** Recording: You Know What To Do,
(cont.) You're My World, No Reply, Any Time At All,
Things We Said Today, Studio Two EMI, London
3 June: Ringo Starr is taken ill before The Beatles
world tour, collapsing at photo shoot in Barnes,
London
4 June: Recording, mixing, editing: Long Tall
Sally, Matchbox, I Call Your Name, Slow Down,
When I Get Home, Any Time At All, I'll Cry
Instead, Studio Two EMI, London
4 June: The Beatles world tour begins in KB
Hallen, Copenhagen, Denmark, two shows
5 June: Recording TV show *The Beatles in
Nederland*, Treslong, Hillegom, Netherlands
6 June: Blokker, the Netherlands, world tour, two
shows
7 June: The Beatles fly to Hong Kong from
Amsterdam, arriving the following day
9 June: Princess Theatre, Kowloon, Hong Kong,
world tour, two shows
10 June: The Beatles fly to Sydney from Hong
Kong, arriving the following day, and give
interview to DJ Bob Rogers before the flight
12–13 June: Centennial Hall, Adelaide, first dates
of Australasian leg of world tour, two shows both
dates, with Jimmie Nicol on drums
14 June: Ringo re-joins The Beatles in Australia
and holds press conference at Sydney airport
15–17 June: Festival Hall, Melbourne, world
tour, two shows each date, with Ringo back on
drums
18–20 June: The Stadium, Sydney, world tour,
two shows each date
19 June: UK EP release: *Long Tall Sally*
21 June: The Beatles fly to Auckland from Sydney
22–23 June: Town Hall, Wellington, New
Zealand, world tour, two shows each night
24–25 June: Town Hall, Auckland, New Zealand,
world tour, two shows both dates
26 June: Town Hall, Dunedin, New Zealand,
world tour, two shows
26 June: US LP release: *A Hard Day's Night*
27 June: Majestic Theatre, Christchurch, New
Zealand, world tour
29–30 June: Festival Hall, Brisbane, Australia,
final dates of world tour, two shows each night
1 July: The Beatles return to UK from Australia

2 July: John and Paul join George Martin for Cilla
Black's recording of their song 'It's For You', EMI
Studio, London
6 July: World premiere of *A Hard Day's Night*,
Pavilion Theatre, London
7 July: Television recording: BBC *Top Of The Pops*,
Lime Grove Studios, London; interview broadcast
same day ITV *Scene at 6.30,* Television House,
London
7 July: Radio recording: John Lennon interview
The Teen Scene, Television House, London
10 July: Civic Reception at Liverpool Town Hall
10 July: Liverpool premiere at Odeon Cinema of
A Hard Day's Night
10 July: UK single and LP release: *A Hard Day's
Night*
11 July: Television live: ITV *Lucky Stars (Summer
Spin)*, Teddington Studios
12 July: Hippodrome, Brighton, two shows
13 July: US single release: 'A Hard Day's Night'
14 July: Radio recording: *Top Gear*, Broadcasting
House, London
15 July: John Lennon buys Kenwood, Weybridge
17 July: Radio recording: *From Us To You*, Paris
Studio, London
19 July: Television live: ITV *Blackpool Night Out*,
ABC Theatre, Blackpool
20 July: US LP release: *Something New*
20 July: US singles release: 'And I Love Her' and
'I'll Cry Instead'
23 July: London Palladium, charity revue, *The
Night of the Hundred Stars*
25 July: Television live: George on *Juke Box Jury*,
Television Theatre, London
25 July: Television recording: Ringo on *Juke Box
Jury*, Television House, London
26 July: Opera House, Blackpool, two shows
28, 29 July: Johanneshovs Isstadion, Stockholm,
Sweden, two shows on each date
30 July: The Beatles return to UK from
Stockholm
2 Aug: Gaumont Cinema, Bournemouth, two
shows
9 Aug: Futurist Theatre, Scarborough, two shows
11 Aug: Recording: Baby's In Black, Studio Two
EMI, London
12 Aug: Radio recording: Ringo interview for *The*

Teen Scene, Williams Mews, London, while at Brian Epstein's party

14 Aug: Recording, mixing: I'm A Loser, Mr Moonlight, Baby's In Black, Leave My Kitten Alone, Studio Two EMI, London

16 Aug: Opera House, Blackpool, two shows

19 Aug: Cow Palace, San Francisco, opening night of 26-date North American tour

20 Aug: Convention Center, Las Vegas, two shows

21 Aug: Seattle Center Coliseum, Seattle

22 Aug: Empire Stadium, Vancouver, The Beatles first appearance in Canada

23 Aug: Hollywood Bowl, Los Angeles

24 Aug: Day off in Bel-Air, Los Angeles, during which The Beatles meet Burt Lancaster at his home and then Jayne Mansfield at Whiskey a Go Go nightclub

24 Aug: US single release: 'Matchbox'

26 Aug: Red Rocks Amphitheatre, Denver

27 Aug: Cincinnati Gardens, Cincinnati

28 Aug: The Beatles are introduced to Bob Dylan and smoke cannabis with him, Delmonico Hotel, New York

28–29 Aug: Forest Hills Tennis Stadium, New York

30 Aug: Convention Hall, Atlantic City

31 Aug: Day off in Cape May, New Jersey

2 Sept: Convention Hall, Philadelphia

3 Sept: Indiana State Fair Coliseum, Indianapolis, two shows

4 Sept: Milwaukee Arena, Milwaukee

5 Sept: International Amphitheatre, Chicago

6 Sept: Olympia Stadium, Detroit

7 Sept: Maple Leaf Gardens, Toronto, two shows

8 Sept: The Forum, Montreal, two shows

10 Sept: Day off in Key West, Florida

11 Sept: Gator Bowl Stadium, Jacksonville

12 Sept: Boston Garden, Boston

13 Sept: Civic Center, Baltimore, two shows

14 Sept: Civic Arena, Pittsburgh

15 Sept: Public Auditorium, Cleveland

16 Sept: City Park Stadium, New Orleans

17 Sept: Municipal Stadium, Kansas City

18 Sept: Dallas Memorial Auditorium, Dallas

19 Sept: Day off in Alton, Missouri

20 Sept: Paramount Theatre, New York, final date of first North American tour

21 Sept: The Beatles return to UK from New York

27 Sept: Ringo Starr judges the *National Beat Group Competition*, Prince of Wales Theatre, London

29 Sept: Recording: Every Little Thing, I Don't Want To Spoil The Party, What You're Doing, Studio Two EMI, London

30 Sept: Recording: Every Little Thing, What You're Doing, No Reply, Studio Two EMI, London

2 Oct: Rehearsal: *Shindig!*, Granville Studio, London

3 Oct: Television recording: US show *Shindig!*, Granville Studio, London

6 Oct: Recording: Eight Days A Week, Studio Two EMI, London

8 Oct: Recording: She's A Woman, Studio Two EMI, London

9 Oct: Gaumont Cinema, Bradford, opening night of 27-date autumn UK tour, two shows per night at each venue

10 Oct: De Montfort Hall, Leicester, autumn UK tour

11 Oct: Odeon Cinema, Birmingham, autumn UK tour

13 Oct: ABC Cinema, Wigan, autumn UK tour

14 Oct: ABC Cinema, Ardwick, Manchester, autumn UK tour

14 Oct: Television recording: ITV *Scene at 6.30*, Granada TV, Manchester

15 Oct: Globe Cinema, Stockton-on-Tees, autumn UK tour

16 Oct: ABC Cinema, Hull, autumn UK tour

18 Oct: Recording: Eight Days A Week, Kansas City/Hey-Hey-Hey-Hey!, Mr Moonlight, I Feel Fine, I'll Follow The Sun, Everybody's Trying To Be My Baby, Rock And Roll Music, Words Of Love, Studio Two EMI, London

19 Oct: ABC Cinema, Edinburgh, autumn UK tour

20 Oct: Caird Hall, Dundee, autumn UK tour

21 Oct: Odeon Cinema, Glasgow, autumn UK tour

22 Oct: Odeon Cinema, Leeds, autumn UK tour

23 Oct: Gaumont State Cinema, Kilburn, London, autumn UK tour

1964 **24 Oct:** Photo shoot in Hyde Park for *Beatles For*
(cont.) *Sale* album cover

24 Oct: Granada Cinema, Walthamstow, London,
autumn UK tour

25 Oct: Hippodrome, Brighton, autumn UK tour

26 Oct: Recording, mixing: I Don't Want To
Spoil The Party, Rock And Roll Music, Words Of
Love, Baby's In Black, I'm A Loser, Kansas City/
Hey-Hey-Hey-Hey!, Honey Don't, What You're
Doing, Another Beatles Christmas Record, Studio
Two EMI, London

27 Oct: Recording, mixing: What You're Doing,
Honey Don't, Mr Moonlight, Every Little Thing,
Eight Days A Week, Studio Two EMI, London

28 Oct: ABC Cinema, Exeter, autumn UK tour

28 Oct: Interview with Jean Shepherd for *Playboy*,
Torquay

29 Oct: ABC Cinema, Plymouth, autumn UK
tour

30 Oct: Gaumont Cinema, Bournemouth,
autumn UK tour

31 Oct: Gaumont Cinema, Ipswich, autumn UK
tour

1 Nov: Astoria Cinema, Finsbury Park, London,
autumn UK tour

2 Nov: King's Hall, Belfast, autumn UK tour

4 Nov: Ritz Cinema, Luton, autumn UK tour

4 Nov: UK EP release: *Extracts From The Film A
Hard Day's Night*

5 Nov: Odeon Cinema, Nottingham, autumn UK
tour

6 Nov: Gaumont Cinema, Southampton, autumn
UK tour

6 Nov: UK EP release: *Extracts From The Album
A Hard Day's Night*

7 Nov: Capitol Cinema, Cardiff, autumn UK tour

8 Nov: Empire Theatre, Liverpool, autumn UK
tour

9 Nov: City Hall, Sheffield, autumn UK tour

10 Nov: Colston Hall, Bristol, final night of
autumn UK tour

14 Nov: Television recording: ITV *Thank Your
Lucky Stars,* Teddington Studios

16 Nov: Television recording: BBC *Top Of The
Pops,* Riverside Studios, Hammersmith, London

17 Nov: Radio recording: *Top Gear,* Playhouse
Theatre, London

20 Nov: Television recording: John Lennon
films sequence with Dudley Moore and Norman
Rossington for BBC *Not Only... But Also,*
Wimbledon Common, London

23 Nov: Television live: ITV *Ready Steady Go!,*
Wembley Studios, London, final appearance

23 Nov: US LP release: *The Beatles' Story*

23 Nov: US single release: 'I Feel Fine'

25 Nov: Radio recording: *Saturday Club,* Aeolian
Hall, London

27 Nov: UK single release: 'I Feel Fine'

28 Nov: John Lennon is interviewed for *New
Musical Express* and BBC radio *The Teen Scene*,
Kenwood, Weybridge

29 Nov: Television recording: John Lennon with
Dudley Moore and Norman Rossington on BBC
Not Only... But Also, Television Centre, London

30 Nov: Brian Epstein appears on the radio show
Desert Island Discs

30 Nov: Ringo Starr give interview for *Melody
Maker*

1 Dec: Ringo Starr goes into University College
Hospital, London, and has tonsils removed the
following day

4 Dec: UK LP release: *Beatles For Sale*

8 Dec: George Harrison visits Ringo Starr in
hospital

9 Dec: Paul McCartney visits Ringo Starr in
hospital

10 Dec: Ringo Starr leaves hospital

15 Dec: US LP release: *Beatles '65*

21–23 Dec: Rehearsals for *Another Beatles
Christmas Show*, Hammersmith Odeon, London

1964 **24, 26, 28–2, 4–9, 11–16 Dec/Jan:**
/65 Hammersmith Odeon, London, *Another Beatles
Christmas Show*, two shows each night, except 24
and 29 December when only one, 38 shows in
total

1965 **1 Feb:** US EP release: *4 By The Beatles*

11 Feb: Ringo Starr marries Maureen Cox

15 Feb: Recording: Ticket To Ride, Another Girl,
I Need You, Studio Two EMI, London

15 Feb: US single release: 'Eight Days A Week'

16 Feb: Recording: I Need You, Another Girl, Yes
It Is, Studio Two EMI, London

17 Feb: Recording: The Night Before, You Like
Me Too Much, Studio Two EMI, London

18 Feb: Northern Songs is floated on stock exchange

18 Feb: Recording, mixing: Ticket To Ride, Another Girl, I Need You, Yes It Is, You've Got To Hide Your Love Away, The Night Before, You Like Me Too Much, If You've Got Trouble, Tell Me What You See, Studio Two EMI, London

19 Feb: Recording: You're Going To Lose That Girl, Studio Two EMI, London, and party at Connaught Hotel, Mayfair, hosted by EMI chairman

20 Feb: Recording, mixing: If You've Got Trouble, Tell Me What You See, You're Going To Lose That Girl, That Means A Lot, You've Got To Hide Your Love Away, Studio Two EMI, London

22 Feb: The Beatles fly to the Bahamas to film *Help!*

23–9 Feb/Mar: The Beatles begin filming *Help!* in the Bahamas

10 Mar: The Beatles fly back to UK from Bahamas

14–20 Mar: Filming: *Help!*, Austria

22 Mar: The Beatles fly back to UK from Austria

22 Mar: US LP release: *The Early Beatles*

24–26, 29–31 Mar: Filming: *Help!* Twickenham Studios

28 Mar: Television recording: The Beatles final ITV *Thank Your Lucky Stars,* Alpha TV, Birmingham

30 Mar: Recording: That Means A Lot, Studio Two EMI, London

1–2, 5–9, 12–14, 20–23, 27–30 Apr: Filming: *Help!*, Twickenham Studios

1 Apr: Brian Epstein leases Saville Theatre, London

6 Apr: UK EP release: *Beatles For Sale*

9 Apr: UK single release: 'Ticket To Ride'

10 Apr: Television recording: BBC *Top Of The Pops*, Riverside Studios, Hammersmith, London

11 Apr: *NME Poll-Winners' All-Star Concert*, Empire Pool, Wembley

11 Apr: Television live: ITV *The Eamonn Andrews Show,* Teddington Studios

13 Apr: Paul McCartney buys 7 Cavendish Avenue, London

13 Apr: Radio live: interview for *Pop Inn*, Twickenham Studios

13 Apr: Recording: Help!, Studio Two EMI, London

16 Apr: Television live: George and John interviewed on ITV *Ready Steady Goes Live!*, Wembley Studios, London

19 Apr: US single release: 'Ticket To Ride'

24 Apr: Filming: *Help!*, Chiswick, London

2 May: The Beatles arrive in Amesbury, Wiltshire

3–5 May: Filming *Help!*, Salisbury Plain, Wiltshire

7 May: Filming: *Help!*, Twickenham Studios

9 May: Filming: *Help!*, London

9 May: The Beatles attend Bob Dylan concert at Royal Albert Hall, and meet singer afterwards at Savoy Hotel, London

10–11 May: Filming: *Help!*, Cliveden House, Maidenhead, final two days shooting

10 May: Recording, mixing: Dizzy Miss Lizzy, Bad Boy, Studio Two EMI, London

18 May: Recording: post-sync work for *Help!* film, Twickenham Studios

25 May: Television recording: John Lennon interviewed for US show *The Merv Griffin Show*, Cannes film festival

26 May: The Beatles final BBC radio session, Studio One BBC Piccadilly Studios, London

2 June: John, George and Ringo attend premiere of *The Knack (And How To Get It)* directed by Richard Lester, Pavilion Theatre, London

3 June: John, George, Cynthia and Pattie attend Allen Ginsberg's 39th birthday party, London

4 June: UK EP release: *Beatles For Sale No. 2*

11 June: The Beatles to be awarded MBEs

12 June: Press conference on MBEs, Twickenham Studios

14 June: Recording: I've Just Seen A Face, I'm Down, Yesterday, Studio Two EMI, London

14 June: US LP release: *Beatles VI*

15 June: Recording: It's Only Love, Studio Two EMI, London

16 June: Radio Appearance: *The World Of Books*, NEMS Enterprises, London

16 June: Recording: post-sync work for *Help!* film, Twickenham Studios

17 June: Recording, mixing: Act Naturally, Wait, Yesterday, Studio Two EMI, London

18 June: Radio Appearance: *BBC European Service*, Lime Grove Studios, London

1965 **18 June:** Television recording broadcast same day:
(cont.) John Lennon interview for BBC *Tonight*, Lime
Grove Studios, London

20 June: Palais des Sport, Paris, European tour
consisting of 15 concerts over nine dates begins
here with two shows

21 June: Day off in Paris

22 June: Palais d'Hiver, Lyon, France, two shows

23 June: The Beatles travel to Milan by train

24 June: *A Spaniard In The Works* is published

24 June: Velodromo Vigorelli, Milan, Italy, two
shows

25 June: Palazzo dello Sport, Genoa, Italy, two
shows

27–28 June: Teatro Adriano, Rome, Italy, two
shows each date

29 June: The Beatles fly to Nice from Rome

30 June: Palais des Expositions, Nice, France

1 July: The Beatles fly to Madrid from Nice

2 July: Plaza de Toros de Las Ventas, Madrid,
Spain

3 July: Plaza de Toros Monumental, Barcelona,
Spain

4 July: The Beatles fly back to UK from Spain

13 July: Lennon and McCartney receive five Ivor
Novello awards Savoy Hotel, London

19 July: US single release: 'Help!'

23 July: UK single release: 'Help!'

24 July: Ringo Starr buys Sunny Heights,
Weybridge

29 July: World premiere of *Help!*, Pavilion
Theatre, London

30 July: The Beatles rehearse for up-coming
North America tour, Saville Theatre, London

1 Aug: Television live: ITV *Blackpool Night Out*,
ABC Theatre, Blackpool

6 Aug: UK LP release: *Help!*

13 Aug: The Beatles fly to New York from London

13 Aug: US LP release: *Help!*

14 Aug: Television recording: The Beatles fourth
and final studio appearance on *Ed Sullivan Show*,
Studio 50, New York

15 Aug: Shea Stadium, New York, opening night
of 1965 North American tour

16 Aug: Day off in New York

16 Aug: John Lennon's mellotron delivered to his
house Kenwood, Weybridge

17 Aug: Maple Leaf Gardens, Toronto, 1965
North American tour, two shows, I Wanna Be
Your Man replaced Act Naturally

18 Aug: Atlanta Stadium, Atlanta, 1965 North
American tour, I Wanna Be Your Man replaced Act
Naturally

19 Aug: Sam Houston Coliseum, Houston, 1965
North American tour, two shows, I Wanna Be
Your Man replaced Act Naturally

20 Aug: White Sox/Comiskey Park, Chicago,
1965 North American tour, two shows

21 Aug: Metropolitan Stadium, Minneapolis,
1965 North American tour, Twist And Shout
dropped because of John's throat, I Wanna Be
Your Man replaced Act Naturally

22 Aug: Memorial Coliseum, Portland, 1965
North American tour, two shows, I Wanna Be
Your Man replaced Act Naturally

23 Aug: Day off in Los Angeles

24 Aug: The Beatles experience LSD with The
Byrds and Peter Fonda, Beverly Hills, Los Angeles

25 Aug: Day off in Los Angeles

27 Aug: The Beatles meet Elvis Presley at his
home, Bel-Air, Los Angeles

28 Aug: Balboa Stadium, San Diego, 1965 North
American tour, I Wanna Be Your Man replaced Act
Naturally

29–30 Aug: Hollywood Bowl, Los Angeles, 1965
North American tour, I Wanna Be Your Man
replaced Act Naturally

31 Aug: Cow Palace, San Francisco, final night of
1965 North American tour, two shows, I Wanna
Be Your Man replaced Act Naturally

1 Sept: The Beatles fly back to UK from San
Francisco

13 Sept: US single release: 'Yesterday'

13 Sept: Zak Starkey born

25 Sept: *The Beatles* cartoon series premieres on
ABC TV in US

9 Oct: The Beatles celebrate John Lennon's 25th
birthday, London

12 Oct: Recording: Run For Your Life,
Norwegian Wood (This Bird Has Flown), Studio
Two EMI, London

13 Oct: Recording: Drive My Car, Studio Two
EMI, London

16 Oct: Recording: Day Tripper, If I Needed Someone, Studio Two EMI, London

18 Oct: Recording: If I Needed Someone, In My Life, Studio Two EMI, London

19 Oct: Recording: unused Christmas fan club messages, Marquee Studios, London

20 Oct: Recording: We Can Work It Out, Studio Two EMI, London

21 Oct: Recording: Norwegian Wood (This Bird Has Flown), Nowhere Man, Studio Two EMI, London

22 Oct: Recording: In My Life, Nowhere Man, Studio Two EMI, London

24 Oct: Recording: I'm Looking Through You, Studio Two EMI, London

26 Oct: The Beatles collect their MBEs

29 Oct: Recording, mixing: We Can Work It Out, Day Tripper, Studio Two EMI, London

1–2 Nov: Television recording: ITV *The Music Of Lennon And McCartney*, Granada TV Centre, Manchester

3 Nov: Recording: Michelle, Studio Two EMI, London

4 Nov: Recording: What Goes On, 12-Bar Original, Studio Two EMI, London

6 Nov: Recording: I'm Looking Through You, Studio Two EMI, London

8 Nov: Recording: Beatle Speech, Think For Yourself, The Beatles' Third Christmas Record, Studio Two EMI, London

10 Nov: Recording, mixing: Run For Your Life, We Can Work It Out, The Word, I'm Looking Through You, Room 65/Studio Two EMI, London

11 Nov: Recording, mixing: The Word, You Won't See Me, Girl, Wait, I'm Looking Through You, Room 65/Studio Two EMI, London

16 Nov: *Rubber Soul* running order settled by George Martin

16 Nov: Paul McCartney acts as compere for Gene Pitney show, hidden behind curtain, Adelphi Cinema, Slough

23 Nov: Promotional films for 'We Can Work It Out', 'Day Tripper', 'Help!', 'I Feel Fine', 'Ticket To Ride', Twickenham Studios

25 Nov: Harrods in London opens up in evening for The Beatles Christmas shopping

29 Nov: Radio recording: interview for *Saturday Club*, Aeolian Hall, London

30 Nov: Radio recording: interviews for *Pop Profile*, NEMS Enterprises, London

2 Dec: George Harrison's Gretsch guitar smashed and ruined when dislodged from car on way to Glasgow, at Berwick-upon-Tweed

3 Dec: Odeon Cinema, Glasgow, opening night of nine-date final UK tour, two shows per night at each venue

3 Dec: UK LP release: *Rubber Soul*

3 Dec: UK single release: 'We Can Work It Out'/'Day Tripper'

4 Dec: City Hall, Newcastle, final UK tour

5 Dec: Empire Theatre, Liverpool, final UK tour and last ever Liverpool concerts

6 Dec: UK EP release: *The Beatles' Million Sellers*

6 Dec: US LP release: *Rubber Soul*

6 Dec: US single release: 'We Can Work It Out'/'Day Tripper'

7 Dec: ABC Cinema, Ardwick, Manchester, final UK tour

8 Dec: Gaumont Cinema, Sheffield, final UK tour

9 Dec: Odeon Cinema, Birmingham, final UK tour

10 Dec: Hammersmith Odeon, London, final UK tour

11 Dec: Astoria Cinema, Finsbury Park, London, final UK tour

12 Dec: Capitol Cinema, Cardiff, concluding night of final UK tour

13 Dec: The Beatles meet to discuss next film, NEMS Enterprises, London

16 Dec: Television: broadcast ITV *The Music Of Lennon And McCartney*

26 Dec: George Harrison surprise visit to family, Appleton, Warrington

26 Dec: Paul McCartney moped accident, Liverpool

1966 **5 Jan:** Recording: overdubs for *The Beatles At Shea Stadium*, CTS Studios, London

12 Jan: John Lennon and Ringo Starr holiday in Trinidad

13 Jan: George Harrison and Mick Jagger visit Dolly's nightclub, London

21 Jan: George Harrison marries Pattie Boyd

22 Jan: George and Pattie Harrison press conference, London

1966
(cont.)

3 Feb: Paul attends Stevie Wonder gig and meets the singer backstage, Scotch of St James, London

8 Feb: George and Pattie Harrison honeymoon in Barbados

12 Feb: John Lennon and Ringo Starr visit Scotch Of St James nightclub, London

13 Feb: The Beatles receive ten Grammy Awards nominations

21 Feb: US single release: 'Nowhere Man'

1 Mar: Television: *The Beatles At Shea Stadium* premiered on BBC1

4 Mar: John Lennon: 'We're more popular than Jesus' comment published in London *Evening Standard*

4 Mar: UK EP release: *Yesterday*

6 Mar: Paul McCartney and Jane Asher holiday in Switzerland

15 Mar: The Beatles fail to win any Grammy Awards

20 Mar: Paul McCartney and Jane Asher return to UK from Switzerland

24 Mar: The Beatles attend premiere of *Alfie*, Plaza Theatre, London

25 Mar: The Beatles 'Butcher' album cover photo session, The Vale, London

28 Mar: George and Ringo meet Roy Orbison at his Granada Cinema concert, Walthamstow, London

1 Apr: John Lennon buys Timothy Leary book *The Psychedelic Experience*, Indica gallery bookshop, London

6 Apr: Recording: Tomorrow Never Knows, Studio Three EMI, London

7 Apr: Recording: Tomorrow Never Knows, Got To Get You Into My Life, Studio Three EMI, London

8 Apr: Recording: Got To Get You Into My Life, Studio Three EMI, London

11 Apr: Recording, mixing: Got To Get You Into My Life, Love You To, Studio Two EMI, London

13 Apr: Recording, mixing: Love You To, Paperback Writer, Studio Three EMI, London

14 Apr: Recording, mixing: Paperback Writer, Rain, Studio Three EMI, London

16 Apr: Recording, mixing: Rain, Studio Two EMI, London

17 Apr: Recording: Doctor Robert, Studio Two EMI, London

18 Apr: John and George attend Lovin' Spoonful concert, Marquee Club, London

19 Apr: Recording, mixing: Doctor Robert, Studio Two EMI, London

20 Apr: Recording, mixing: And Your Bird Can Sing, Taxman, Studio Two EMI, London

21 Apr: Recording: Taxman, Studio Two EMI, London

22 Apr: Recording: Taxman, Tomorrow Never Knows, Studio Two EMI, London

26 Apr: Recording: And Your Bird Can Sing, Studio Two EMI, London

27 Apr: Recording, mixing: Taxman, And Your Bird Can Sing, Tomorrow Never Knows, I'm Only Sleeping, Studio Three EMI, London

28 Apr: Recording: Eleanor Rigby, Studio Two EMI, London

29 Apr: Recording, mixing: Eleanor Rigby, I'm Only Sleeping, Studio Three EMI, London

1 May: *NME Poll-Winners' All-Star Concert*, Empire Pool, Wembley, The Beatles final UK scheduled concert

2 May: Paul McCartney, Bob Dylan and Rolling Stones visit Dolly's nightclub, London

2 May: Radio recording: interviews for *Saturday Club* and *Pop Profile*, Playhouse Theatre, London

5 May: Recording: I'm Only Sleeping, Studio Three EMI, London

6 May: Recording: I'm Only Sleeping, Studio Two EMI, London

9 May: Recording: For No One, Studio Two EMI, London

16 May: Recording, mixing: Taxman, For No One, Studio Two EMI, London

18 May: Recording, mixing: Got To Get You Into My Life, Studio Two EMI, London

19 May: Filming: 'Paperback Writer', 'Rain' Studio One EMI, London

19 May: Recording: For No One, Studio Three EMI, London

20 May: Filming: 'Paperback Writer', 'Rain', Chiswick, London

26 May: Recording: Yellow Submarine, Studio Three EMI, London

27 May: John Lennon and Bob Dylan filmed in car from Kenwood, Weybridge, to May Fair Hotel, London

30 May: US single release: 'Paperback Writer'

31 May: Ringo Starr photo shoot for *The Beatles Book Monthly*, Sunny Heights, Weybridge

1 June: Recording: Yellow Submarine, Studio Two EMI, London

2–3 June: Recording, mixing: I Want To Tell You, Yellow Submarine, Studio Two EMI, London

6 June: Recording, mixing: And Your Bird Can Sing, For No One, I'm Only Sleeping, Tomorrow Never Knows, Eleanor Rigby, Studio Three EMI, London

8 June: Recording: Good Day Sunshine, Studio Two EMI, London

9 June: Recording, mixing: Good Day Sunshine, Studio Two EMI, London

10 June: UK single release: 'Paperback Writer'

14 June: Recording: Here There And Everywhere, Studio Two EMI, London

16 June: Recording: Here There And Everywhere, Studio Two EMI, London

16 June: Television live: The Beatles only live BBC *Top Of The Pops*, Television Centre, London

17 June: Paul McCartney buys High Park Farm, Campbeltown, Scotland

17 June: Recording, mixing: Here There And Everywhere, Got To Get You Into My Life, Studio Two EMI, London

20 June: US LP release: *Yesterday And Today*

21 June: Recording, mixing: She Said She Said, Studio Two EMI, London

24 June: Circus-Krone-Bau Munich, West Germany, two shows, opening night of tour including Japan and the Philippines

25 June: Grugahalle, Essen, West Germany, two shows

26 June: Ernst Merck Halle, Hamburg, West Germany, two shows

27 June: The Beatles aim to fly from Hamburg to Japan, via London, but bad weather diverts flight to Alaska

28 June: The Beatles fly to Tokyo from Alaska

30–2 June/July: Nippon Budokan Hall, Tokyo, Japan, one show on first day, two each on following days

3 July: The Beatles arrive in Manila, Philippines

4 July: Rizal Memorial Football Stadium, Manila, Philippines, two shows

5 July: The Beatles leave the Philippines

6 July: The Beatles first trip to India

7 July: The Beatles go sightseeing in India

8 July: The Beatles fly back to UK from India

8 July: UK EP release: *Nowhere Man*

12 July: The Beatles receive three Ivor Novello awards

29 July: US magazine *Datebook* republishes John's 'more popular than Jesus' comments

1 Aug: Radio recording: Paul McCartney interviewed for *David Frost At The Phonography*, Broadcasting House, London

2 Aug: George and Pattie Harrison holiday in Devon

5 Aug: UK LP release: *Revolver*

5 Aug: UK single release: 'Eleanor Rigby'/'Yellow Submarine'

6 Aug: Brian Epstein holds a press conference, Sheraton Hotel, New York

6 Aug: Radio recording: *The Lennon And McCartney Songbook*, Cavendish Avenue, London

8 Aug: The South African Broadcasting Corporation bans The Beatles music

8 Aug: US LP release: *Revolver*

8 Aug: US single release: 'Eleanor Rigby'/'Yellow Submarine'

11 Aug: The Beatles fly to Chicago from London

12 Aug: International Amphitheatre, Chicago, opening date of final North American tour, two shows

12 Aug: Press conference at Astor Tower Hotel, Chicago

13 Aug: *KLUE* radio in Texas organises a public Beatles bonfire

13 Aug: Olympia Stadium, Detroit, final North American tour, two shows

14 Aug: Cleveland Stadium, Cleveland, Ohio, final North American tour

14 Aug: *KLUE* radio, Texas, is struck by lightning

15 Aug: DC Stadium, Washington, DC, final North American tour

16 Aug: John F. Kennedy Stadium, Philadelphia, final North American tour, Long Tall Sally replaced I'm Down

17 Aug: Maple Leaf Gardens, Toronto, final North American tour, two shows, Long Tall Sally replaced I'm Down

1966
(cont.)

18 Aug: Suffolk Downs Racetrack, Boston, final North American tour, Long Tall Sally replaced I'm Down

19 Aug: Mid-South Coliseum, Memphis, final North American tour, two shows, Long Tall Sally replaced I'm Down

20 Aug: Cincinnati concert is postponed due to rain

21 Aug: Crosley Field, Cincinnati and Busch Memorial Stadium, St Louis, final North American tour

22 Aug: Junior press conference followed by regular press conference, Warwick hotel, New York City

23 Aug: Shea Stadium, New York, final North American tour

24 Aug: Day off in Los Angeles

25 Aug: Seattle Center Coliseum, Seattle, final North American tour, two shows

26 Aug: Press conference at Capitol Records Tower, LA, the last they would ever face as a collective group

27 Aug: Day off in Los Angeles

28 Aug: Dodger Stadium, Los Angeles, final North American tour, Long Tall Sally replaced I'm Down

29 Aug: Candlestick Park, San Francisco, concluding night of final North American tour and last ever scheduled Beatles concert, Long Tall Sally replaced I'm Down

30 Aug: The Beatles fly back to UK from Los Angeles

5 Sept: John Lennon flies to Hanover, Germany

6 Sept: John Lennon begins wearing round-shaped NHS 'granny' glasses for filming *How I Won The War*

7–14 Sept: John films *How I Won The War* in various locations in Celle, West Germany

14 Sept: George and Pattie Harrison fly to India, using the pseudonyms Mr and Mrs Sam Wells

15 Sept: Paul McCartney attends experimental music concert, Royal College of Art, London

16 Sept: John, Paul, Neil Aspinall and Brian Epstein meet in Paris for weekend holiday

18 Sept: John Lennon travels to Carboneras, Spain

19–25, 27–31 Sept: John Lennon films *How I Won The War* in various locations in Carboneras, Spain

19 Sept: George and Pattie Harrison hold press conference, Taj Mahal Hotel, Bombay, India

20 Sept: Radio recording: George gives BBC interview, Bombay

26 Sept: Brian Epstein admitted to a clinic in London

3 Oct: Brian Epstein denies rumours The Beatles are splitting up

4 Oct: Ringo Starr joins John Lennon in Spain

9 Oct: John Lennon celebrates his 26th birthday in Spain

22 Oct: George and Pattie Harrison leave India

31 Oct: EMI decide to release a 'greatest hits' LP in the UK for the Christmas market under the title *A Collection of Beatles Oldies*, several tracks need remixing into stereo, Studio One EMI, London

1–31 Oct: John Lennon films *How I Won The War* in various locations in Carboneras, Spain

1–6 Nov: John Lennon films *How I Won The War* in various locations in Carboneras, Spain

4 Nov: NEMS leaves 13 Monmouth Street, London, permanently, with entire business located now in Argyll Street

6 Nov: Paul McCartney flies to France

6 Nov: The Beatles turn down TV charity concert request for victims of the Aberfan disaster

6 Nov: John Lennon flies back to UK from Spain

7 Nov: John Lennon meets Yoko Ono at Indica Gallery (possibly 9 November)

12 Nov: Paul McCartney meets Mal Evans in Bordeaux for sightseeing in France and few days later fly to Kenya

19 Nov: Paul has the idea for *Sgt Pepper* on flight back from Kenya

20 Nov: Brian Epstein hosts party at home for The Four Tops, Chapel Street, London

24 Nov: Recording: Strawberry Fields Forever, Studio Two EMI, London

25 Nov: Recording: Pantomime – Everywhere It's Christmas, Dick James House, London

27 Nov: John Lennon films a sequence for *Not Only... But Also,* Broadwick Street, London

28–29 Nov: Recording, mixing: Strawberry Fields Forever, Studio Two EMI, London

6 Dec: Recording: Christmas radio messages, When I'm Sixty-Four, Studio Two EMI, London

8 Dec: Recording, editing: When I'm Sixty-Four, Strawberry Fields Forever, Studio One/Two EMI, London

9 Dec: Recording, mixing: Strawberry Fields Forever, Studio Two EMI, London

9 Dec: UK LP release: *A Collection Of Beatles Oldies*

15 Dec: Recording, mixing: Strawberry Fields Forever, Studio Two EMI, London

16 Dec: UK single release to fan club: 'The Beatles' Fourth Christmas Record – Pantomime: Everywhere It's Christmas'

18 Dec: Paul McCartney and Jane Asher attend *The Family Way* premiere, Warner Cinema, London

18 Dec: Tara Browne dies

20 Dec: Recording: When I'm Sixty-Four, Studio Two EMI, London

20 Dec: Television recording: interviews for ITV *Reporting ' 66*, EMI Studios, London

21 Dec: Recording, mixing: When I'm Sixty-Four, Strawberry Fields Forever, Studio Two EMI, London

29 Dec: Recording, mixing, editing: When I'm Sixty-Four, Strawberry Fields Forever, Penny Lane, Studio Three/Two EMI, London

30 Dec: Recording, mixing: When I'm Sixty-Four, Penny Lane, Studio Two EMI, London

31 Dec: George Harrison is refused entry to Annabel's nightclub in London

1967 4 Jan: Recording: Penny Lane, Studio Two EMI, London

5 Jan: Recording: Penny Lane, Carnival Of Light, Studio Two EMI, London

6 Jan: Recording: Penny Lane, Studio Two EMI, London

6 Jan: UK LP release: McCartney soundtrack for *The Family Way*

9 Jan: Recording, mixing: Penny Lane, Studio Two EMI, London

10 Jan: Recording: Penny Lane, Studio Three EMI, London

11 Jan: Paul and Ringo attend Jimi Hendrix Experience concert, Bag O'Nails club, London

12 Jan: Recording, mixing: Penny Lane, Studio Three EMI, London

15 Jan: Paul and George attend Donovan sell-out concert, Royal Albert Hall, London

17 Jan: John Lennon begins writing 'A Day In The Life'

17 Jan: Recording, mixing: Penny Lane, Studio Two EMI, London

18 Jan: Television recording: Paul McCartney interviewed for ITV *Scene Special*, Granada TV, London

19–20 Jan: Recording: A Day In The Life, Studio Two EMI, London

30–31 Jan: Filming: 'Strawberry Fields Forever', Knole Park, Sevenoaks

1 Feb: Recording: Sgt Pepper's Lonely Hearts Club Band, Studio Two EMI, London

2 Feb: Recording, mixing: Sgt Pepper's Lonely Hearts Club Band, Studio Two EMI, London

3 Feb: Recording: A Day In The Life, Studio Two EMI, London

5 Feb: Filming: 'Penny Lane', Angel Lane, Stratford, London

7 Feb: Filming: 'Penny Lane', Knole Park, Sevenoaks

8 Feb: Recording: Good Morning Good Morning, Studio Two EMI, London

9 Feb: Recording: Fixing A Hole, Regent Sound Studio, London

10 Feb: Recording: A Day In The Life, Studio One EMI, London

13 Feb: Recording, mixing: A Day In The Life, Only A Northern Song, Studio Two EMI, London

13 Feb: US single release: 'Penny Lane'/'Strawberry Fields Forever'

14 Feb: Recording, mixing: Only A Northern Song, Studio Two EMI, London

16 Feb: Recording, mixing: 'Good Morning Good Morning, Studio Three EMI, London

17 Feb: Recording, mixing: Being For The Benefit Of Mr Kite!, Studio Two EMI, London

17 Feb: UK single release: 'Penny Lane'/'Strawberry Fields Forever'

20 Feb: Recording, mixing: Being For The Benefit Of Mr Kite!, Good Morning Good Morning, Studio Three EMI, London

21 Feb: Recording, mixing: Fixing A Hole, Studio Two EMI, London

22 Feb: Recording, mixing: A Day In The Life, Studio Two EMI, London

1967 23 Feb: Recording, mixing, editing: A Day In The
(cont.) Life, Lovely Rita, Studio Two EMI, London

24 Feb: Recording: Lovely Rita, Studio Two EMI,
London

28 Feb: Recording: Lucy In The Sky With
Diamonds, Studio Two EMI, London

1 Mar: Recording: A Day In The Life, Lucy
In The Sky With Diamonds, Studio Two EMI,
London

2 Mar: Recording, mixing: Lucy In The Sky With
Diamonds, Studio Two EMI, London

3 Mar: Recording, mixing: Sgt Pepper's Lonely
Hearts Club Band, Lucy In The Sky With
Diamonds, Studio Two EMI, London

6 Mar: Recording, mixing: Sgt Pepper's Lonely
Hearts Club Band, Studio Two EMI, London

7 Mar: Recording: Lovely Rita, Studio Two EMI,
London

9–10 Mar: Recording: Getting Better, Studio Two
EMI, London

13 Mar: Recording: Good Morning Good
Morning, Studio Two EMI, London

15 Mar: Recording: Within You Without You,
Studio Two EMI, London

17 Mar: Recording: She's Leaving Home, Studio
Two EMI, London

20 Mar: Recording, mixing: Beatle Talk, She's
Leaving Home, Studio Two EMI, London

21 Mar: Recording, mixing, editing: Getting
Better, Lovely Rita, Studio Two EMI, London

22 Mar: Recording, mixing: Within You Without
You, Studio Two EMI, London

23 Mar: Recording, mixing: Getting Better,
Studio Two EMI, London

28 Mar: Recording: Good Morning Good
Morning, Being For The Benefit Of Mr Kite!,
Studio Two EMI, London

29 Mar: Recording: Good Morning Good
Morning, Being For The Benefit Of Mr Kite!,
With A Little Help From My Friends, Studio Two
EMI, London

30 Mar: Cover shoot for *Sgt Pepper*, Chelsea
Manor Studios, London

30 Mar: Recording: With A Little Help From My
Friends, Studio Two EMI, London

31 Mar: Recording, mixing: With A Little Help

From My Friends, Being For The Benefit Of Mr
Kite!, Studio Two EMI, London

1 Apr: Recording, mixing: Sgt Pepper's Lonely
Hearts Club Band (Reprise), Studio One EMI,
London

3 Apr: Paul McCartney flies to Los Angeles

3 Apr: Recording, mixing: Within You Without
You, Studio One EMI, London

4 Apr: Paul McCartney flies to San Francisco

5 Apr: Paul McCartney flies to Denver for Jane
Asher's 21st birthday

7 Apr: Paul McCartney films Jane Asher in Denver

8 Apr: Paul McCartney and Mal Evans sightseeing
around Denver while Jane Asher appears in
Shakespeare play

9 Apr: Paul McCartney flies from Denver to Los
Angeles

10 Apr: Paul McCartney performs on The Beach
Boys 'Vegetables'

11 Apr: Paul McCartney performs with Brian
Wilson and John and Michelle Phillips in early
hours of the morning

11 Apr: Paul McCartney returns to UK from
America

19 Apr: The Beatles & Co is formed

20 Apr: Recording, mixing: Sgt Pepper's Lonely
Hearts Club Band (Reprise), Only A Northern
Song, Studio Three/Two EMI, London

21 Apr: Recording, mixing: Only A Northern
Song, Sgt Pepper run-out groove, Studio Two
EMI, London

24 Apr: The Beatles attend Donovan concert,
Saville Theatre, London

25–26 Apr: Recording: Magical Mystery Tour,
Studio Three EMI, London

27 Apr: Recording, mixing: Magical Mystery
Tour, Studio Three EMI, London

29 Apr: John Lennon attends the *14-Hour
Technicolour Dream* Alexandra Palace, London

3 May: Recording: Magical Mystery Tour, Studio
Three EMI, London

9 May: Recording: untitled instrumentals, Studio
Two EMI, London

11 May: Recording, mixing: Baby You're A Rich
Man, Olympic Sounds Studios, London

12 May: Recording, mixing: All Together Now,
Studio Two EMI, London

15 May: Paul McCartney meets Linda Eastman at Bag O'Nails club, London

17 May: Recording: You Know My Name (Look Up The Number), Studio Two EMI, London

19 May: Press launch for *Sgt Pepper* at Brian Epstein's house, Chapel Street, London

20 May: The BBC bans 'A Day In The Life'

24 May: The Beatles attend Procol Harum concert, Speakeasy club, London

25 May: Recording: It's All Too Much, De Lane Lea Recording Studios, London

28 May: The Beatles and wives attend a party at Kingsley Hill, Brian Epstein's East Sussex house

31 May: Recording, mixing: It's All Too Much, De Lane Lea Recording Studios, London

1 June: Recording: untitled instrumentals, De Lane Lea Recording Studios, London

1 June: UK LP release: *Sgt Pepper*

2 June: Recording, mixing: It's All Too Much, De Lane Lea Recording Studios, London

2 June: US LP release: *Sgt Pepper*

4 June: Paul, George, Jane and Pattie attend Jimi Hendrix Experience concert, Saville Theatre, London

7–8 June: Recording: You Know My Name (Look Up The Number), Studio Two EMI, London

9 June: Editing, mixing: You Know My Name (Look Up The Number), Studio Two EMI, London

12 June: Lennon and McCartney sing on Rolling Stones 'We Love You'

12 June: US LP release: McCartney soundtrack for *The Family Way*

14 June: Recording: All You Need Is Love, Olympic Sound Studios, London

19 June: Paul McCartney admits taking LSD

19 June: Recording: All You Need Is Love, Studio Three EMI, London

23–24 June: Recording: All You Need Is Love, Studio One EMI, London

25 June: Recording: All You Need Is Love, Studio One EMI, London, for BBC *Our World*

26 June: Recording, mixing: All You Need Is Love, Studio Two EMI, London

28 June: George Harrison is fined for speeding

3 July: Lennon, McCartney and Harrison attend a party for The Monkees, Speakeasy Club, London

4 July: George Harrison visits his parents with Pattie, Appleton, Warrington

7 July: UK single release: 'All You Need Is Love'

17 July: US single release: 'All You Need Is Love'

20 July: George Harrison and Ringo Starr travel to Greece

22 July: John Lennon and Paul McCartney travel to Greece

24 July: The Beatles and Brian Epstein put names to advertisement in *The Times* for legalisation of marijuana

25 July: John Lennon and Ringo Starr go shopping in Athens

26 July: Ringo Starr returns to UK from Greece

26 July: John, Paul and George visit a Greek island they intended to purchase

29 July: George Harrison returns to UK from Greece

31 July: John Lennon and Paul McCartney return to UK from Greece

31 July: Radio recording: Ringo's farewell message for Radio London, Curzon Street, London

1 Aug: George and Pattie Harrison fly to Los Angeles

2 Aug: George Harrison meets Ravi Shankar in Los Angeles

3 Aug: George Harrison and Ravi Shankar press conference, Los Angeles

3 Aug: Pattie Harrison reads about Maharishi Mahesh Yogi

4 Aug: George Harrison attends Ravi Shankar concert, Hollywood Bowl, Los Angeles

5 Aug: George Harrison attends tabla player Alla Rakha recording session, Los Angeles

6 Aug: George Harrison dines at Ravi Shankar's house, Los Angeles

7 Aug: George Harrison visits Haight-Ashbury in San Francisco

9 Aug: George and Pattie Harrison return from America

11 Aug: Photo shoot at Thomson House, London, taken by US photographer Richard Avedon

19 Aug: Jason Starkey born

22–23 Aug: Recording: Your Mother Should Know, Chappell Recording Studio, London

1967 **24 Aug:** The Beatles meet Maharishi Mahesh
(cont.) Yogi, Hilton Hotel, London
25 Aug: The Beatles travel to Bangor, Wales
26 Aug: The Beatles hold press conference with
Maharishi Yogi in Bangor at which they announce
they have given up taking drugs
27 Aug: Brian Epstein found dead
27 Aug: On learning of Brian Epstein's death,
John, George and Ringo give brief interviews in
Bangor as Paul returns to London
31 Aug: The Beatles issue statement on future of
Brian Epstein's NEMS Enterprises
1 Sept: The Beatles meet at Paul's house in St
John's Wood following Brian Epstein death, to talk
over the band's future
5 Sept: Recording: I Am The Walrus, Studio One
EMI, London
6 Sept: Recording, mixing: I Am The Walrus, The
Fool On The Hill, Blue Jay Way, Studio Two EMI,
London
7 Sept: Recording: Blue Jay Way, Studio Two
EMI, London
8 Sept: Recording, mixing: Flying, Studio Three
EMI, London
11–15, 18–24 Sept: Filming: *Magical Mystery
Tour*, various location in London, south west of
England, Kent
16 Sept: Recording, mixing: Your Mother Should
Know, Blue Jay Way, Studio Three EMI, London
25 Sept: Editing of Magical Mystery Tour film
begins, Norman's Film Productions, London
25 Sept: Recording, mixing: The Fool On The
Hill, Studio Two EMI, London
26 Sept: Recording: The Fool On The Hill,
Studio Two EMI, London
27 Sept: Recording, mixing: I Am The Walrus,
Studio One/Two EMI, London
28 Sept: Recording, mixing, editing: I Am The
Walrus, Flying, Studio Two EMI, London
29 Sept: Recording, mixing, editing: I Am The
Walrus, Your Mother Should Know, Studio Two
EMI, London
29 Sept: Television recording broadcast same
day: John and George ITV *The Frost Programme*,
Wembley Studios, London
1, 29–31 Oct: Filming: *Magical Mystery Tour*,
locations in London, Kent, Nice in south of France

2 Oct: Recording, mixing: Your Mother Should
Know, Hello Goodbye, Studio Two EMI, London
4 Oct: Television recording broadcast same day:
John and George ITV *The Frost Programme*,
Wembley Studios, London
6 Oct: Recording: Blue Jay Way, Studio Two
EMI, London
9 Oct: John Lennon's 27th birthday
12 Oct: Recording, mixing, editing: Blue Jay
Way, Shirley's Wild Accordion, Studio Three EMI,
London
17 Oct: Memorial service for Brian Epstein at
New London Synagogue
18 Oct: Premiere of *How I Won The War*, London
Pavilion
19 Oct: Recording: Hello Goodbye, Studio One
EMI, London
20 Oct: Recording: The Fool On The Hill, Hello
Goodbye, Studio Three EMI, London
25 Oct: Recording, mixing, editing: The Fool
On The Hill, Hello Goodbye, Studio Two EMI,
London
1 Nov: Recording, mixing, editing: Untitled
Sound Effects, Hello Goodbye, The Fool On The
Hill, Studio Three EMI, London
2 Nov: Recording, mixing: Hello Goodbye,
Studio Three EMI, London
3 Nov: Filming: final day of *Magical Mystery Tour*,
Sunny Heights, Weybridge
7 Nov: Recording, mixing, editing: Blue Jay Way,
Flying, Magical Mystery Tour, Studio Two/One
EMI, London
10 Nov: Filming: 'Hello, Goodbye', Saville
Theatre, London
24 Nov: UK single release: 'Hello, Goodbye'
27 Nov: US LP release: *Magical Mystery Tour*
27 Nov: US single release: 'Hello, Goodbye'
28 Nov: Recording, mixing: Christmas Time (Is
Here Again), Studio Three EMI, London
29 Nov: Editing: Christmas Time (Is Here Again),
Studio One EMI, London
3 Dec: Ringo flies to Rome to film *Candy*
5 Dec: Launch party at the Apple Boutique, Baker
Street, London
7–16 Dec: Ringo in Italy filming *Candy*
7 Dec: The Apple Boutique opens, Baker Street,
London

8 Dec: UK EP release: *Magical Mystery Tour*

17 Dec: Ringo returns to London from Italy

17 Dec: John and George host party for secretaries and friends of Fan Club, Hanover Banqueting Rooms, London

25 Dec: Paul McCartney and Jane Asher announce their engagement

26 Dec: *Magical Mystery Tour* is premiered on BBC1

27 Dec: Television recording broadcast same day: Paul on ITV *The Frost Programme* justifying *Magical Mystery Tour*, Wembley Studios, London

1968 **5 Jan:** George produces session for *Wonderwall*, Studio Two EMI, London

7 Jan: George Harrison flies to EMI's studio in Bombay, India to record the soundtrack to *Wonderwall*

9–11 Jan: Recording: *Wonderwall* music by George Harrison, EMI Recording Studio, Bombay, India

12 Jan: Recording: The Inner Light, *Wonderwall* music, EMI Recording Studio, Bombay, India

13 Jan: Recording: *Wonderwall* music by George Harrison, EMI Recording Studio, Bombay, India

22 Jan: Apple opens offices at 95 Wigmore Street, London

25 Jan: Pattie Harrison models at fashion show for Ossie Clark, Revolution discotheque, Mayfair, London

25 Jan: The Beatles film *Yellow Submarine* appearance, Twickenham Studios

27 Jan: Radio recording: John Lennon interview for BBC Radio 1 *Kenny Everett Show*, Kenwood, Weybridge

1 Feb: Ringo Starr rehearses for Cilla Black's television show *Cilla*, TV Rehearsal Rooms, North Acton, London

2 Feb: Ringo Starr rehearses for Cilla Black's television show *Cilla*, TV Rehearsal Rooms, North Acton, London

3 Feb: Recording: Lady Madonna, Across The Universe, Studio Three EMI, London

4 Feb: Recording: Across The Universe, Studio Three EMI, London

5 Feb: Ringo Starr rehearses for Cilla Black's television show *Cilla*, BBC Television Theatre, London

6 Feb: Recording, mixing: The Inner Light, Lady Madonna, Studio One EMI, London

6 Feb: Television live: Ringo Starr on Cilla Black's BBC *Cilla*, Television Theatre, London

8 Feb: Recording, mixing: The Inner Light, Across The Universe, Studio Two EMI, London

11 Feb: Recording, mixing: Hey Bulldog, Studio Three EMI, London

14 Feb: Mal Evans flies to India

15 Feb: John, George and wives fly to India, arriving in Rishikesh the following day

19 Feb: Paul, Jane, Ringo and Maureen fly to India, arriving in Rishikesh the following day

29 Feb: Yoko Ono and Ornette Coleman perform at Royal Albert Hall, London

1 Mar: Ringo and Maureen leave India and return to UK, arriving back on 3 March

15 Mar: UK single release: 'Lady Madonna'

18 Mar: US single release: 'Lady Madonna'

26 Mar: Paul and Jane leave India and return to UK, arriving back the following day

12 Apr: John, George and wives leave Rishikesh

19 Apr: Apple Corps places press adverts, requesting tapes from talented singers and musicians

11 May: John and Paul begin four-day visit to New York, promote Apple and meet with Ron Kass, head of Apple US the folllowing day

13 May: John and Paul give various interviews to US media, St Regis Hotel, New York

14 May: John and Paul press conference, Americana Hotel, New York, followed by live television appearance on NBC *The Tonight Show*

19 May: John Lennon and Yoko Ono record *Two Virgins*, Kenwood, Weybridge

22 May: John and Yoko and George and Pattie attend press launch of Apple Tailoring, Chelsea, London; first public appearance for John and Yoko

23 May: Apple Tailoring opens, King's Road, London

23 May: Television recording: Paul and Ringo interviewed for BBC *Omnibus* special, *All My Loving*, EMI Studios, London

24 May: Approximate date for demo recordings for the *White Album*, Kinfauns, Esher

30 May: Recording: Revolution 1 (and 9), Studio Two EMI, London

1968 **31 May:** Recording: Revolution 1, Studio Three
(cont.) EMI, London

4 June: Recording, mixing: Revolution 1, Studio
Three EMI, London

5 June: Recording: Don't Pass Me By, Studio
Three EMI, London

6 June: BBC interview with John Lennon and
Victor Spinetti, EMI Studios, London

6 June: Radio recording: interviews for BBC
Radio 1 *Kenny Everett Show*, EMI Studios, London

6 June: Recording, mixing: Don't Pass Me By,
Revolution 9, Studio Two EMI, London

7 June: George and Pattie Harrison and Ringo
Starr and Maureen fly to California

8 June: George Harrison and Ringo Starr visit
Joan Baez in California

8 June: Paul McCartney best man at brother
Mike's wedding, Carrog village, Wales

10–11 June: George Harrison films scenes for
Ravi Shankar film *Raga*, Big Sur, San Francisco

10 June: Recording: Revolution 9, Studio Three
EMI, London

11 June: Paul McCartney and Mary Hopkin film
promotional clip for Apple Records, EMI Studios,
London

11 June: Recording, mixing: Blackbird,
Revolution 9, Studio Two/Three EMI, London

15 June: John and Yoko plant acorns for peace at
Coventry Cathedral

16 June: Television recording: Paul McCartney
and Mary Hopkin on US show *David Frost
Presents ... Frankie Howerd*, Stonebridge House,
Wembley, London

18 June: George, Ringo and wives return to UK
from US

18 June: Paul McCartney celebrates his 26th
birthday at Apple

18 June: Premiere of the *In His Own Write* stage
play, Old Vic, London

20 June: Paul McCartney flies from New York to
Los Angeles

20 June: Recording: Revolution 9, Studio One/
Two/Three EMI, London

21 June: Recording, mixing: Revolution 1,
Revolution 9, Studio Two EMI, London

22 June: Paul McCartney addresses Capitol
Records conference, Beverly Hills, Los Angeles

22 June: The Beatles purchase Apple HQ, 3 Savile
Row, London

23 June: Paul McCartney and Linda Eastman
spend time together in Los Angeles

24–26 June: George Harrison produces Jackie
Lomax's 'Sour Milk Sea', Studio Three EMI,
London

24 June: Paul and Linda sail to Santa Catalina
Island, California

25 June: Paul McCartney flies back to UK from
New York

26–27 June: Recording: Everybody's Got
Something To Hide Except Me And My Monkey,
Studio Two EMI, London

28 June: Recording: Good Night, Studio Two
EMI, London

30 June: Paul McCartney produces
'Thingumybob' by Black Dyke Mills Band,
Saltaire, Yorkshire

1 July: John Lennon and Yoko Ono launch art
exhibition *You Are Here*, Robert Fraser Gallery,
London

1 July: Recording: Everybody's Got Something
To Hide Except Me And My Monkey, Studio Two
EMI, London

2 July: Recording: Good Night, Studio Two EMI,
London

3–5 July: Recording: Ob-La-Di Ob-La-Da, Studio
Two EMI, London

8 July: The Beatles attend press screening of
Yellow Submarine, Bowater House Cinema,
Knightsbridge, London

8 July: Recording, mixing: Ob-La-Di Ob-La-Da,
Studio Two EMI, London

9 July: Recording: Ob-La-Di Ob-La-Da,
Revolution, Studio Three EMI, London

9 July: Ringo Starr clapping on Solomon King's
'A Hundred Years Or More', Studio Two EMI,
London

10 July: Recording: Revolution, Studio Three
EMI, London

11 July: John Lennon is best man at wedding of
Alexis Mardas, Bayswater, London

11 July: Recording, mixing: Revolution, Ob-La-
Di Ob-La-Da, Studio Three EMI, London

12 July: Recording, mixing: Don't Pass Me By,

Ob-La-Di Ob-La-Da, Revolution, Studio Two
EMI, London

13 July: John Lennon visits Aunt Mimi in Poole,
Dorset and introduces Yoko

15 July: Recording, mixing: Revolution, Ob-
La-D, Ob-La-Da, Cry Baby Cry, Studio Two EMI,
London

15 July: The Beatles move into the Apple HQ, 3
Savile Row, London

16 July: Recording: Cry Baby Cry, Studio Two
EMI, London

17 July: World premiere of *Yellow Submarine*,
Pavilion Theatre, London

18 July: Recording: Cry Baby Cry, Helter Skelter,
Studio Two EMI, London

19 July: Recording: Sexy Sadie, Studio Two EMI,
London

20 July: Jane Asher announces split from Paul
McCartney on TV show *Dee Time*

22 July: Recording: Don't Pass Me By (A
Beginning), Good Night, Studio Two EMI,
London

23 July: Recording, mixing: Everybody's Got
Something To Hide Except Me And My Monkey,
Good Night, Studio Two EMI, London

24 July: Recording: Sexy Sadie, Studio Two EMI,
London

25 July: Recording: While My Guitar Gently
Weeps, Studio Two EMI, London

28 July: *The Mad Day Out* photo shoot

29 July: Recording: Hey Jude, Studio Two EMI,
London

30 July: Recording, mixing: Hey Jude, Studio
Two EMI, London

31 July: Recording: Hey Jude, Trident Studios,
London

31 July: The Apple Boutique closes down

1 Aug: Recording: Hey Jude, Trident Studios
London

7 Aug: Recording: Not Guilty, Studio Two EMI,
London

8 Aug: Recording, mixing: Hey Jude, Not Guilty,
Studio Two EMI, London

9 Aug: Recording: Not Guilty, Mother Nature's
Son, Studio Two EMI, London

10 Aug: Paul McCartney interviewed for *New
Musical Express*

12 Aug: John Lennon and Yoko Ono attend an
Ossie Clark fashion show, Revolution discotheque,
Mayfair, London

12 Aug: Recording, mixing: Not Guilty, Studio
Two EMI, London

13 Aug: Recording, editing: Sexy Sadie, Yer Blues,
Studio Two/annexe EMI, London

14 Aug: Recording, mixing: Yer Blues, What's
The New Mary Jane, Studio Two EMI, London

15 Aug: Recording, mixing: Rocky Raccoon,
Studio Two EMI, London

16 Aug: Recording: While My Guitar Gently
Weeps, Studio Two EMI, London

17 Aug: George and Pattie fly to Greece for a few
days of holiday

20 Aug: Recording, mixing, editing: Yer Blues,
Mother Nature's Son, Etcetera, Wild Honey Pie,
Studio Three/Two EMI, London

21 Aug: George and Pattie Harrison return to UK
from Greece

21 Aug: Recording, mixing: Sexy Sadie, Studio
Two EMI, London

22 Aug: Cynthia Lennon sues John for divorce

22 Aug: Recording: Back In The USSR, Studio
Two EMI, London

22 Aug: Ringo Starr quits The Beatles

23 Aug: Recording, mixing: Back In The USSR

24 Aug: Television live: John Lennon and Yoko
Ono on ITV *Frost On Saturday*, Wembley Studios,
London

26 Aug: US single release: 'Hey Jude'

28 Aug: Recording: Dear Prudence, Trident
Studios, London

29 Aug: Recording: Dear Prudence, Trident
Studios, London

30 Aug: Recording, mixing: Dear Prudence,
Trident Studios, London

30 Aug: UK single release: 'Hey Jude'

3 Sept: Recording: While My Guitar Gently
Weeps, Studio Two EMI, London

3 Sept: Ringo Starr re-joins The Beatles

4 Sept: Filming: 'Hey Jude', 'Revolution',
Twickenham Studios

5 Sept: Recording: While My Guitar Gently
Weeps, Studio Two EMI, London

6 Sept: Recording: While My Guitar Gently
Weeps, Studio Two EMI, London

1968 **6 Sept:** Television recording: Paul McCartney
(cont.) and Mary Hopkin filmed for ITV *Magpie*, EMI
Studios, London

9 Sept: Recording: Helter Skelter, Studio Two
EMI, London

10 Sept: Recording: Helter Skelter, Studio Two
EMI, London

11 Sept: Recording: Glass Onion, Studio Two
EMI, London

12 Sept: Recording: Glass Onion, Studio Two
EMI, London

13 Sept: Recording: Glass Onion, Studio Two
EMI, London

16 Sept: Recording: I Will, Glass Onion, Studio
Two EMI, London

17 Sept: Recording, mixing: Helter Skelter, I
Will, Studio Two EMI, London

18 Sept: George Harrison is interviewed for *New
Musical Express*, also recorded for BBC *Scene And
Heard*, EMI Studios, London

18 Sept: Recording, mixing: Birthday, Studio
Two EMI, London

19 Sept: Recording: Piggies, Studio One/Two
EMI, London

20 Sept: Recording: Piggies, Studio Two EMI,
London

23–24 Sept: Recording: Happiness Is A Warm
Gun, Studio Two EMI, London

25 Sept: Editing, recording, mixing: Happiness
Is A Warm Gun, Studio Two EMI, London

30 Sept: *The Beatles* biography by Hunter Davies
is published

1 Oct: Recording, mixing: Honey Pie, Trident
Studios, London

2 Oct: Recording: Honey Pie, Trident Studios,
London

3 Oct: Recording: Savoy Truffle, Trident Studios,
London

4 Oct: Recording: Martha My Dear, Honey Pie,
Trident Studios, London

5 Oct: Recording, mixing: Savoy Truffle, Martha
My Dear, Honey Pie, Dear Prudence, Trident
Studios, London

7 Oct: Mixing, recording: While My Guitar
Gently Weeps, Long Long Long, Studio Two
EMI, London

8 Oct: Recording: Long Long Long, I'm So
Tired, The Continuing Story Of Bungalow Bill,
Studio Two EMI, London

9 Oct: Recording, mixing: The Continuing Story
Of Bungalow Bill, Long Long Long, Why Don't
We Do It In The Road, Studio Two/One EMI,
London

10 Oct: Recording, mixing: Piggies, Glass
Onion, Rocky Raccoon, Long Long Long, Why
Don't We Do It In The Road, Studio Two/
Three EMI, London

11 Oct: Recording, mixing: Savoy Truffle,
Piggies, Don't Pass Me By, Good Night, Studio
Two EMI, London

13 Oct: Recording, mixing: Julia, Dear
Prudence, Wild Honey Pie, Back In The USSR,
Blackbird, Studio Two EMI, London

14 Oct: Recording, mixing: I Will, Birthday,
Savoy Truffle, While My Guitar Gently Weeps,
Long Long Long, Yer Blues, Sexy Sadie, What's
The New Mary Jane, Studio Two EMI, London

16 Oct: George Harrison flies to Los Angeles

18 Oct: John Lennon and Yoko Ono are arrested
for drugs possession, Montagu Square, London

19 Oct: John and Yoko appear in court on drugs
charges, Marylebone Magistrates' Court, London

20 Oct: Paul and Linda begin holiday in New
York

22, 24–25, 31 Oct: George Harrison produces
Is This What You Want? by Jackie Lomax, Sound
Recorders Studio, Los Angeles

25 Oct: John Lennon and Yoko Ono announce
pregnancy

1, 8–11 Nov: George Harrison produces *Is
This What You Want?* by Jackie Lomax, Sound
Recorders Studio, Los Angeles

1 Nov: UK LP release: *Wonderwall*, music by
George Harrison

4 Nov: Yoko Ono admitted to Queen Charlotte's
Hospital, London

7 Nov: John Lennon writes *A Short Essay On
Macrobiotics*

8 Nov: John and Cynthia Lennon are divorced

11 Nov: US LP release: *Two Virgins* by John
Lennon and Yoko Ono

12 Nov: Recording: side two of *Electronic Sound*
by George Harrison, Sound Recorders Studio,
Los Angeles

15 Nov: Television recording: George Harrison on US show *The Smothers Brothers Comedy Hour*, CBS Studios, Los Angeles

20 Nov: Radio recording: Paul McCartney interviewed for Radio Luxembourg, Cavendish Avenue, London

21 Nov: George Harrison performs on 'Badge' by Cream, Wally Heider Studios, Los Angeles

21 Nov: Yoko Ono suffers a miscarriage

22 Nov: UK LP release: *The Beatles* (*White Album*)

25 Nov: US LP release: *The Beatles* (*White Album*)

28 Nov: John Lennon pleads guilty to cannabis possession and fined £150 plus costs, Yoko Ono discharged, Marylebone Magistrates' Court, London

29 Nov: UK LP release: *Two Virgins* by John Lennon and Yoko Ono

2 Dec: US LP release: *Wonderwall* music by George Harrison

4 Dec: George Harrison invites Hell's Angels to Apple

10 Dec: John Lennon rehearses for Rolling Stones *Rock And Roll Circus*, InterTel, Stonebridge Park, London

11 Dec: John Lennon appears in Rolling Stones *Rock And Roll Circus,* InterTel, Stonebridge Park, London

12 Dec: John Lennon and Yoko Ono are interviewed for BBC radio's *Night Ride*, BBC Broadcasting House, London

12 Dec: John Lennon and Yoko Ono are interviewed for Dutch television, Knightsbridge, London

18 Dec: John Lennon and Yoko Ono appear in a white bag at Royal Albert Hall, London

10–12 Dec: Paul and Linda holiday with Hunter Davies in Praia da Luz, Algarve, Portugal

1969 2–31 Jan: Filming, recording *Get Back/Let It Be* sessions, 20 days, Twickenham Studios and Apple HQ, 3 Savile Row, London

10 Jan: *Get Back/Let It Be* sessions: Day Seven – George Harrison quits The Beatles, Twickenham Studios

12 Jan: The Beatles meet at Ringo Starr's Brookfield house, Elstead

13 Jan: US LP release: *Yellow Submarine*

15 Jan: George Harrison re-joins The Beatles

17 Jan: UK LP release: *Yellow Submarine*

20 Jan: The Beatles meet at Apple's basement studio, Apple HQ, London

21 Jan: Radio recording: Ringo Starr interviewed for the BBC *Scene And Heard*, Elstead

28 Jan: Allen Klein meets The Beatles, Apple HQ, London

30 Jan: *Get Back/Let It Be* sessions: Day Nineteen – Apple rooftop concert, 3 Savile Row, London

1 Feb: Allen Klein discusses The Beatles purchase of NEMS

3 Feb: Allen Klein is appointed The Beatles manager

3 Feb: Zapple Records launched: *Electronic Music* by George Harrison, and *Unfinished Music No. 2: Life With The Lions* by John and Yoko are the only two albums released before it is closed by Allen Klein

22 Feb: Recording: I Want You (She's So Heavy), Trident Studios, London

25 Feb: Recording: Old Brown Shoe, All Things Must Pass, Something, EMI Studios, London

1 Mar: Paul McCartney produces Mary Hopkin's 'Goodbye', Morgan Studios London

2 Mar: John Lennon and Yoko Ono perform in Lady Mitchell Hall, Cambridge

2 Mar: Paul McCartney produces Mary Hopkin's 'Goodbye', Morgan Studios, London

4 Mar: Radio recording: George Harrison interviewed for the BBC *Scene And Heard*, Apple HQ, London

11 Mar: Paul McCartney and George Harrison produce a Jackie Lomax session, Apple HQ, London

12 Mar: George and Pattie Harrison's home is raided by the Drugs Squad

12 Mar: Paul McCartney marries Linda Eastman, Marylebone Register Office, London

13 Mar: Ringo films for *The Magic Christian*

16 Mar: John Lennon and Yoko Ono fly to Paris

16 Mar: Paul and Linda McCartney begin honeymoon in US

18 Mar: George and Pattie Harrison appear in court on drugs charges, Esher and Walton Magistrate's Court

1969 **18 Mar:** Ringo films for *The Magic Christian*
(cont.) **20 Mar:** John Lennon marries Yoko Ono in
Gibraltar
24 Mar: John Lennon and Yoko Ono meet
Salvador Dalí, Paris
31 Mar: George and Pattie Harrison are fined for
drugs possession, Esher and Walton Magistrate's
Court
31 Mar: John and Yoko's 'lightning trip to
Vienna'
25–31 Mar: John and Yoko's first bed-in for
peace, Hilton Hotel, Amsterdam
1 Apr: Ringo films for *The Magic Christian*
1 Apr: Television live: John Lennon and Yoko
Ono interviewed on ITV *Today*, Television
House, London
3 Apr: Television live: John Lennon and Yoko
Ono on ITV *The Eamonn Andrews Show*, Cafe
Royal, London
3 Apr: Radio appearance: George Harrison
interviewed for *The World At One*, Broadcasting
House, London
9 Apr: Ringo films for *The Magic Christian*
11 Apr: UK single release: 'Get Back'
14 Apr: Recording, mixing: The Ballad Of John
And Yoko, Studio Three EMI, London
16 Apr: Recording, mixing: Old Brown Shoe,
Something, Studio Three EMI, London
18 Apr: Recording, mixing: Old Brown Shoe, I
Want You (She's So Heavy), Studio Three/Two
EMI, London
20 Apr: Recording, mixing: I Want You (She's
So Heavy), Oh! Darling, Studio Three EMI,
London
22 Apr: John Lennon changes his middle name
to Ono
22 Apr: Recording, mixing: John And Yoko,
Studio Two EMI, London
26 Apr: Recording: Oh! Darling, Octopus's
Garden, Studio Two EMI, London
27 Apr: Recording: John And Yoko, Studio Two
EMI, London
29 Apr: Recording, mixing: Octopus's Garden,
Studio Three EMI, London
30 Apr: Recording, mixing: Let It Be, You Know
My Name (Look Up The Number), Studio Three
EMI, London

2 May: Recording: Something, Studio Three
EMI, London
2 May: Television recording broadcast same day:
John Lennon and Yoko Ono interviewed for BBC
How Late It Is, Lime Grove Studios, London
4 May: John Lennon and Yoko Ono buy
Tittenhurst Park, Sunningdale
4 May: Wrap party for *The Magic Christian*
attended by Ringo, John and Paul, Les
Ambassadeurs, London
5 May: Recording: Something, Olympic Sound
Studios, London
5 May: US single release: 'Get Back'
6 May: Recording, mixing: You Never Give Me
Your Money, Olympic Sound Studios, London
8 May: Radio recording: John Lennon and Yoko
Ono interviewed for BBC *Scene And Heard*,
Apple HQ, London
9 May: Paul McCartney performs under the
pseudonym Paul Ramon on Steve Miller's 'My
Dark Hour', Olympic Sound Studios, London
11 May: George Harrison performs on a Jack
Bruce session, Morgan Studios, London
15 May: Radio recording: Paul McCartney is
interviewed for BBC Radio Merseyside *Light And
Local*, Rembrandt, Heswall
16 May: Paul and Linda McCartney travel to
Corfu for holiday
16 May: Ringo Starr and Maureen set sail on
QE2 from Southampton to New York
22 May: Ringo Starr and Maureen to Bahamas
from New York
24 May: John Lennon and Yoko Ono fly to
Barbados
25 May: John Lennon and Yoko Ono fly from
Barbados to Toronto, Canada
26 May: Zapple Records launched in the US
26–31 May: John and Yoko's second bed-in
for peace: Room 1742 Hotel Raine Elizabeth,
Montreal
28 May: Mixing, master compilation: Let It Be,
Get Back LP, Olympic Sound Studios, London
30 May: UK single release: 'The Ballad Of John
And Yoko'
1–2 June: John and Yoko's second bed-in for
peace: Room 1742 Hotel Raine Elizabeth,
Montreal

1 June: George and Pattie Harrison fly to Sardinia for three-week holiday

1 June: John Lennon and Yoko Ono record 'Give Peace A Chance'

1 June: John Lennon argues with Al Capp in Montreal

4 June: US single release: 'The Ballad Of John And Yoko'

14 June: Television recording: John Lennon and Yoko Ono on US show *The David Frost Show*, InterTel Studios, Stonebridge Park, London

23 June: John and Ono travel to Cardigan Bay, Wales, for short break

29 June: John and Yoko drive to Scotland for a holiday

1 July: John Lennon crashes Austin Maxi car near Loch Eriboll in Scotland

1 July: Recording: You Never Give Me Your Money, Studio Two EMI, London

2 July: Recording: Her Majesty, Golden Slumbers, Carry That Weight, Studio Two EMI, London

3 July: Recording, editing: Golden Slumbers, Carry That Weight, Studio Two EMI, London

4 July: Recording: Golden Slumbers, Carry That Weight, Studio Two EMI, London

7 July: Recording: Here Comes The Sun, Studio Two EMI, London

8 July: Recording, mixing: Here Comes The Sun, Studio Two EMI, London

9 July: Recording: Maxwell's Silver Hammer, Studio Two EMI, London

10 July: Recording, mixing: Maxwell's Silver Hammer, Studio Two EMI, London

11 July: Recording, mixing: Maxwell's Silver Hammer, Something, You Never Give Me Your Money, Studio Two EMI, London

15 July: Recording, mixing: You Never Give Me Your Money, Studio Three/Two EMI, London

16 July: Recording: Here Comes The Sun, Something, Studio Three/Two EMI, London

17 July: Recording: Oh! Darling, Octopus's Garden, Studio Three/Two EMI, London

18 July: Recording, mixing: Oh! Darling, Octopus's Garden, Studio Three/Two EMI, London

21 July: Recording: Come Together, Studio Three/Two EMI, London

22 July: Recording: Oh! Darling, Come Together, Studio Three EMI, London

23 July: Recording: Oh! Darling, Come Together, The End, Studio Three/Two EMI, London

24 July: Recording, mixing: Come And Get It, Sun King, Mean Mr Mustard, Studio Two EMI, London

25 July: Recording: Sun King, Mean Mr Mustard, Come Together, Polythene Pam, She Came In Through The Bathroom Window, Studio Two EMI, London

28 July: Recording: Polythene Pam, She Came In Through The Bathroom Window, Studio Three/Two EMI, London

29 July: Recording: Come Together, Sun King, Mean Mr Mustard, Studio Three EMI, London

30 July: Recording, mixing: You Never Give Me Your Money, Come Together, Polythene Pam, She Came In Through The Bathroom Window, Golden Slumbers, Carry That Weight, Sun King, Mean Mr Mustard, Her Majesty, The End, Studio Two/Three EMI, London

31 July: Recording: You Never Give Me Your Money, Golden Slumbers, Carry That Weight, Studio Two EMI, London

1 Aug: Recording: Because, Studio Two EMI, London

2 Aug: Paul McCartney produces 'Come And Get It' by The Iveys, Studio Two EMI, London

4 Aug: Recording, mixing: Because, Something, Here Comes The Sun, Studio Two/Three EMI, London

5 Aug: Recording: You Never Give Me Your Money, Because, The End, Studio Three/Room 43/Studio Two EMI, London

6 Aug: Recording, mixing: Here Comes The Sun, Maxwell's Silver Hammer, Studio Three/Room 43/Studio Two EMI, London

7 Aug: Recording, mixing: Come Together, The End, Studio Two/Three EMI, London

8 Aug: Recording: The End, I Want You (She's So Heavy), Oh! Darling, Studio Two/Three EMI, London

8 Aug: The *Abbey Road* cover photography session

1969 **11 Aug:** John and Yoko move into Tittenhurst
(cont.) Park, Sunningdale
11 Aug: Recording, editing: I Want You (She's
So Heavy), Oh! Darling, Here Comes The Sun,
Studio Two EMI, London
14 Aug: Radio Appearance: *Everett Is Here*,
control room Studio Two EMI, London
15 Aug: Recording: Golden Slumbers, Carry
That Weight, The End, Something, Here Comes
The Sun, Studio One/Two EMI, London
17 Aug: Paul McCartney produces Mary
Hopkin's 'Que Sera, Sera', EMI Studios, London
18 Aug: Recording, mixing: Golden Slumbers,
Carry That Weight, The End, Studio Two EMI,
London
19 Aug: Recording, mixing: The End, Golden
Slumbers, Carry That Weight, Something, Here
Comes The Sun, Studio Two EMI, London
20 Aug: Mixing: I Want You (She's So Heavy),
Studio Three EMI, and compiling final running
order for *Abbey Road*, Studio Two EMI, London,
the final time all four Beatles together in Abbey
Road Studios
22 Aug: The Beatles final photo session, at
Tittenhurst Park
25 Aug: Recording, editing: Maxwell's Silver
Hammer, The End, Studio Two EMI, London
26 Aug: George Harrison meets Bob Dylan in
Portsmouth
28 Aug: Apple launch party for the Radha
Krishna Temple(London) single, Sydenham Hill,
London
28 Aug: George and Pattie Harrison travel to the
Isle of Wight to see Bob Dylan
28 Aug: Mary McCartney born
30 Aug: John Lennon and Ringo Starr travel to
the Isle of Wight to see Bob Dylan
31 Aug: Lennon, Harrison and Starr watch Bob
Dylan perform at the Isle of Wight Festival
1 Sept: Bob Dylan and George Harrison visit
John Lennon at Tittenhurst Park
10 Sept: *Self-Portrait* and *Mr & Mrs Lennon's
Honeymoon* by John Lennon and Yoko Ono are
premiered in London
12 Sept: John Lennon and Yoko Ono are
interviewed for various publications, Apple HQ,
London

12 Sept: John Lennon makes decision to leave
The Beatles
13 Sept: The Plastic Ono Band performs at the
Toronto Rock and Roll Revival festival Varsity
Stadium, University of Toronto, Canada
16 Sept: Maclen (Music) Limited begins legal
proceedings against Northern Songs
19 Sept: Radio recording: Paul gives interview
for BBC *Scene And Heard*, Apple HQ, London
20 Sept: John Lennon tells the group he is
leaving The Beatles
25 Sept: Recording: Cold Turkey by Plastic Ono
Band, Studio Three EMI, London
26 Sept: UK LP release: *Abbey Road*
28 Sept: Plastic Ono Band remake: Cold Turkey,
Trident Studios, London
1 Oct: US LP release: *Abbey Road*
3 Oct: Plastic Ono Band recording: Don't Worry
Kyoko, Studio A Lansdowne Studios, London
5 Oct: Plastic Ono Band recording, mixing: Cold
Turkey, Don't Worry Kyoko, Studio Two EMI,
London
6 Oct: US single release: 'Something'/'Come
Together'
8 Oct: Interview George Harrison BBC *Scene
And Heard*, Apple HQ, London
9 Oct: Yoko Ono in hospital in London, where
she later suffers a miscarriage
20 Oct: Plastic Ono Band mixing: Don't Worry
Kyoko, Studio Three EMI, London
24 Oct: Radio recording: Paul McCartney BBC
interview with Chris Drake to stop rumours of his
death, Campbeltown, Scotland
27 Oct: Ringo Starr begins recording first solo
album *Sentimental Journey*, Studio Three EMI,
London
31 Oct: UK single release: 'Something'/'Come
Together'
25 Nov: John Lennon returns his MBE to the
queen
26 Nov: Recording, mixing, editing: You Know
My Name (Look Up The Number), What's The
New Mary Jane, Studio Two EMI, London
1 Dec: The final *Beatles Book Monthly* magazine is
published
2 Dec: Television recording: John Lennon

filmed for ATV documentary *Man of the Decade*, Tittenhurst Park, Sunningdale

2 Dec: George appears with Delaney & Bonnie, Colston Hall, Bristol

3 Dec: George appears with Delaney & Bonnie, Town Hall, Birmingham

4 Dec: George appears with Delaney & Bonnie, City Hall, Sheffield

5 Dec: John and Yoko filmed for experimental film *Apotheosis 2* in Suffolk

6 Dec: George appears with Delaney & Bonnie, Empire Theatre, Liverpool

6 Dec: John and Yoko film for *24 Hours (The World of John and Yoko)* in Suffolk

6 Dec: Television recording broadcast same day: Ringo appears on ITV *Frost On Sunday* with Peter Sellers and Spike Milligan promoting *The Magic Christian*, Wembley Studios, London

7 Dec: George appears with Delaney & Bonnie, Fairfiled Hall, Croydon

7 Dec: Television live: John and Yoko appear on BBC1 religious programme *The Question Why*, Lime Grove Studios, London

8 Dec: Recording: Octopus's Garden, Studio Two EMI, London

11 Dec: World premier of *The Magic Christian*, starring Ringo, Odeon Theatre, London

14 Dec: Television recording: Ringo appears on ITV spectacular *With A Little Help From My Friends* with George Martin, Television Centre, Leeds

15 Dec: Glyn Johns starts work editing the *Get Back* tapes, Olympic Sound Studios, London

15 Dec: Ringo records a piece on behalf of the British Wireless for the Blind Fund, Apple HQ, London

15 Dec: The Plastic Ono Supergroup at the Lyceum Ballroom, London, as part of the UNICEF *Peace For Christmas* concert

20 Dec: Television recording: John and Yoko filmed for CBS-TV at the University of Toronto with Marshall McLuhan; Television live: John and Yoko interview for CBC Weekend, CBC Studios, Toronto

22 Dec: John and Yoko press conference, Chateau Champlain Hotel, Montreal

23 Dec: John and Yoko met with Canadian Prime Minister Pierre Trudeau, Parliament Building, Ottawa

10–12 Dec: George appears with Delaney & Bonnie for final time at the Falkoner Theatre, Copenhagen

1970 3 Jan: Recording: I Me Mine, Studio Two EMI, London

4 Jan: Recording, mixing: Let It Be, Studio Two EMI, London, the final Beatles recording session as a group

5 Jan: Glyn Johns compiles the second *Get Back* LP, Olympic Sound Studios, London

8 Jan: Recording, mixing: Let It Be, For You Blue, Olympic Sound Studios, London, George Harrison's final Beatles recording session

14 Jan: Ringo records 'Love Is A Many Splendoured Thing' and 'Sentimental Journey' for his *Sentimental Journey* album, Olympic Sound Studios, London

3 Feb: Ringo records 'Love Is A Many Splendoured Thing' for *Sentimental Journey*, Studio Two EMI, London

5 Feb: Ringo records 'Love Is A Many Splendoured Thing' for *Sentimental Journey*, *Studio Two EMI, London*

6 Feb: Radio recording: John and Yoko record interview for *Scene And Heard*, Apple HQ, London

7 Feb: John and Yoko record an appearance on *The Simon Dee Show*, Studio One, Wembley Studios, London

9 Feb: Ringo records 'Whispering Grass' and 'Have I Told You Lately That I Love You' for *Sentimental Journey*, Studio Two EMI, London

10 Feb: George Martin records orchestra for *Sentimental Journey*, Studio Two EMI, London

11 Feb: Plastic Ono Band appears on *Top Of The Pops* performing 'Instant Karma'

11 Feb: Ringo records 'I'm A Fool To Care' for *Sentimental Journey*, Studio Two EMI, London

12 Feb: Ringo records 'Let The Rest of the World Go By' for *Sentimental Journey*, Studio Two EMI, London

17 Feb: Recording orchestra for *Sentimental Journey*, Studio Two, London

18 Feb: Ringo records 'Have I Told You Lately That I Love You' and 'Let The Rest of the World

Go By' for Sentimental Journey and 'It Don't Come Easy' under the title 'You Gotta Pay Your Dues', assisted by George Harrison, Studio Two, EMI, London

19 Feb: Ringo records 'It Don't Come Easy', Studio Two EMI, London

21 Feb: Up until today Paul McCartney had been recording tracks for his solo album at home and at Morgan Studios (under the pseudonym Billy Martin), this was his first session at EMI Studios, London

22 Feb: Paul records 'Every Night' and 'Maybe I'm Amazed' for his solo album, Studio Two EMI, London

24 Feb: Ringo records vocal for 'Blue Turning Grey Over You' for *Sentimental Journey*, Studio One EMI, London

25 Feb: Paul records 'Man We Was Lonely' for his solo album, Studio Two EMI, London

25 Feb: Ringo oversees the orchestra recording 'You Always Hurt The One You Love', De Lane Lea Recording Studios, London

26 Feb: US LP release: *Hey Jude*

5 Mar: Ringo records 'Whispering Grass' and 'Bye Bye Blackbird' for *Sentimental Journey*, Morgan Studios, London

6 Mar: Final recording session for Ringo's *Sentimental Journey*, Morgan Studios, and mixing at EMI Studios, London

6 Mar: UK single release: 'Let It Be'

8 Mar: Ringo remakes 'It Don't Come Easy' with George, possibly at Trident Studios, London

11 Mar: George is interviewed for BBC radio show *The Beatles Today*, Aeolian Hall, London

11 Mar: Recording of Ringo's 'It Don't Come Easy' with George producing, at Trident Studios, London

11 Mar: US single release: 'Let It Be'

15 Mar: Ringo films a promotional film for *Sentimental Journey* at the Talk of the Town in London

23 Mar: Phil Spector is brought in to work on the *Get Back* tapes, which will now be called *Let It Be*

25 Mar: Radio recording: Ringo gives interview for BBC *Scene And Heard*, Apple HQ, London

29 Mar: Television live: Ringo on ITV *Frost*

On Sunday promoting *The Magic Christian* and *Sentimental Journey*, Wembley Studios, London

31 Mar: Radio live: Ringo appears on *Open House* on BBC Radio 2, Broadcasting House, London

1 Apr: Recording: Across The Universe, The Long And Winding Road, I Me Mine, Studio One EMI, London, the final Beatles recording session, with only Ringo in attendance

10 Apr: Paul McCartney announces The Beatles split

10 Apr: Television recording: George interview for the BBC theological series *Fact Or Fantasy* at Apple HQ, London

10 Apr: The Beatles final press release, Apple Corps, London

8 May: UK LP release: *Let It Be*

11 May: US single release: 'The Long And Winding Road'

18 May: US LP release: *Let It Be*

20 May: UK premiere of *Let It Be*, Pavilion Theatre, London

28 May: US release of *Let It Be* film

31 Dec: Paul McCartney files a lawsuit to dissolve The Beatles partnership

1974 19 Dec: Paul and George sign the papers for the dissolution of The Beatles at Plaza Hotel, New York – Ringo had signed earlier in the week; John said, 'the stars weren't right,' so didn't attend

29 Dec: John signs the dissolution papers at the Polynesian Village Hotel, Disney World, Florida, and The Beatles are officially over

APPENDIX D
Bibliography

Aldridge, Alan, *The Beatles Illustrated Lyrics*. London: Omnibus Press, 2014

Beatles, The: *The Beatles Anthology*. London: Cassell & Co, 2000

Best, Roag, *The Beatles: True Beginnings*. London: ScreenPress Books, 2002

Betts, Graham, *Complete British Hit Albums*. London: Collins, 2004

Betts, Graham, *Complete UK Hit Singles 1952-2005*. London: Collins, 2005

Braun, Michael, *Love Me Do: The Beatles' Progress*. London: Penguin Books, 1964

Davies, Hunter, *The Beatles: The Only Ever Authorised Biography*, updated edition. London: Ebury Press, 2009

Davies, Hunter, *The Beatles Lyrics: The Unseen Story Behind Their Music*. London: Weidenfeld & Nicolson, 2014

Davies, Hunter (ed), *The John Lennon Letters*. London: Weidenfeld & Nicolson, 2012

Epstein, Brian, *A Cellarful of Noise*. New York: Byron Preiss Visual Publications, 1964

Harry, Bill, *The John Lennon Encyclopedia*. London: Virgin Books, 2000

Howlett, Kevin, *The Beatles At The Beeb: The Story of Their Radio Career*. London: BBC Books, 1982

Kristen, Judit, *A Date with a Beatle*. Pennsauken: Aquinas and Krone Publishing, 2011

Larkin, Colin (ed), *Virgin Encyclopedia of Popular Music*, 3rd Edition. London: Virgin, 1999

Lennon, Cynthia, *A Twist of Lennon*. London: Avon, 1978

Lewisohn, Mark, *All These Years: Volume One: Tune In*. London: Little Brown, 2013

Lewisohn, Mark, *The Beatles: Recording Sessions*. New York: Harmony, 1988

Lewisohn, Mark, *The Complete Beatles Chronicle*. London: Pyramid, 1982

MacDonald, Ian, *Revolution in the Head*. London: Vintage, 2008

McCartney, Paul and Barry Miles, *Many Years From Now*. London: Secker and Warburg, 1997

Miles, Barry, *The Beatles: A Diary*. London: Omnibus Press, 2007

Norman, Philip, *John Lennon: The Life*. London: HarperCollins, 2008

Norman, Philip, *Shout! The True Story Of The Beatles*. London: Elm Tree Books, 1981

Peel, Ian, *The Unknown Paul McCartney*. London: Reynolds Hearn Ltd, 2002

Schultess, Tom, *A Day in the Life*. London: Pedigree Books, 1981

Shepherd, Billy, *The True Story of the Beatles*. West Sussex: Beat Books, 1964

Sounes, Howard, *Fab: An Intimate Life of Paul McCartney*. London: HarperCollins, 2010

Spitz, Bob, *The Beatles: The Biography*. London: Aurum, 2005

Turner, Steve, *A Hard Day's Write*. London: Index, 1999

Walker, John, *Halliwell's Film, Video & DVD Guide 2006*. London: HarperCollins, 2005

Williams, Allan and William Marshall, *The Man Who Gave the Beatles Away*. London: Macmillan, 1975

beatlesbible.com
beatlebilia.co.uk
beatlesinterviews.org
fincharie.com

Index

Page references in *italics* indicate photographs.